Econometric Theory and Methods

Econometric Theory and Methods

Russell Davidson
James G. MacKinnon

New York Oxford
OXFORD UNIVERSITY PRESS
2004

To our students

Oxford University Press

Oxford New York
Auckland Bangkok Buenos Aires Cape Town Chennai
Dar es Salaam Delhi Hong Kong Istanbul Karachi Kolkata
Kuala Lumpur Madrid Melbourne Mexico City Mumbai
Nairobi São Paulo Shanghai Taipei Tokyo Toronto

Published by Oxford University Press, Inc.
198 Madison Avenue, New York, New York 10016
www.oup.com

Library of Congress Cataloging-in-Publication Data

Davidson, Russell.
Econometric theory and methods / Russell Davidson, James G. MacKinnon.
p. cm.
Includes bibliographical references and index.
ISBN 0-19-512372-7 (cloth)
1. Econometrics. I. MacKinnon, James G. II. Title.
HB139.D3678 2004
330′.01′5195–dc21 2003056468

Printing number: 9 8 7 6 5 4 3 2 1

Printed in the United States of America
on acid-free paper

Contents

Preface

This book is the second graduate-level econometrics textbook that we have written. Our first one, *Estimation and Inference in Econometrics*, appeared eleven years ago and has been quite successful. Why then did we choose to write this book instead of a second edition of the first one? Although it would have been quicker and easier to write a second edition, there were several compelling reasons that drove us to write an entirely new book.

It seems unavoidable that the second edition of a book is longer than its predecessor. *Estimation and Inference in Econometrics* is by no means short. Indeed, it contains too much material even for most two-course sequences. This book is significantly shorter. The entire book can be taught in a two-course sequence, as we explain below in detail, and a substantial fraction of it can be taught in a single course, possibly at a somewhat lower level.

The subject of econometrics has evolved as rapidly in the last ten years as it did in the ten years prior to that. This means not only that there are many new things that students of econometrics should learn, but also that there are new and perhaps better ways of understanding older material. Although many parts of *Estimation and Inference in Econometrics* have held up well, we would have had to reorganize and rewrite it radically if we were to produce a second edition that we could be truly happy with.

Another reason for preferring to write a new book is that the level of our earlier one, especially in several key chapters in the first half, is too high for the first graduate courses at many institutions. With hindsight, this was a mistake. One of our goals in writing this book has been to start at a more modest level and work up from there gradually as the book proceeds. Some of the earlier chapters do contain some fairly advanced material, but much of it is confined to exercises, and the rest is in sections and subsections that can be skipped without serious loss of continuity.

Features of This Book

Cheap personal computers were already a fact of life around 1990. Since then, computers have become vastly more powerful and even less expensive. It is no surprise that econometrics, always a computer-intensive discipline, should have been profoundly affected by the development of computers. Ten years ago, one could have predicted that they would make the practice of econometrics a lot easier, and of course that is what has happened. What was less predictable is that the ability to perform simulations easily and quickly would change many of the directions of econometric theory as well as econometric practice. The use of the computer in econometrics, especially for simulation, has blossomed so quickly that no textbook like this one can reasonably avoid a serious discussion of simulation.

Simulation-based methods greatly enhance the asymptotic theory that has been at the heart of econometrics for many decades. Problems that are intractable analytically are often simple to handle by simulation, and a wide variety of new techniques that exploit this fact has been proposed during the last ten years. Of these techniques, the one that seems most general in its application is the bootstrap, and we make a point of introducing this important topic early on. Other methods can do things that the bootstrap cannot, and we discuss some of these more briefly in later chapters. We are happy to confess that we have ourselves learned a great deal by exploring new simulation-based methods while preparing this book, and we are now enthusiastic in our use of these methods.

We have for many years been advocates of the use of artificial regressions for many purposes in econometrics. They are useful not only for simplifying many numerical procedures but also for providing better theoretical understanding. The best-known, and no doubt the most widely used, artificial regression is the Gauss-Newton regression. We use it as a model for a host of other artificial regressions, some of which were developed expressly for this book.

Estimating functions and estimating equations are topics that are not terribly familiar to most econometricians. We ourselves became aware of them only in the mid-1990s, when V. P. Godambe, of the University of Waterloo, prodded us to look more closely at a theme that he had himself pioneered back in the 1960s. In this book, these concepts are not introduced until Chapter 9, but they are present implicitly in the earlier chapters, usually in the guise of the method of moments. Once introduced, estimating equations make it much easier to explore the theory of the generalized method of moments than the methods conventionally used in econometrics. Some of the more advanced topics that we treat in the last third of the book are also greatly simplified by an approach based on estimating equations.

Every chapter has a substantial number of exercises. We put a great deal of effort into posing and solving these, and we made numerous changes to the text itself as a result of doing so. There are several types of exercises, intended for different purposes. Some of the exercises are empirical, designed to give students the opportunity to become familiar with a variety of practical econometric methods. Others involve simulation, including some that ask students to conduct small Monte Carlo experiments. Many are fairly straightforward theoretical exercises that good students should find illuminating and, we hope, not too difficult. Some exercises have several parts, and instructors may want to assign only some of them. For obvious reasons, we urge instructors to look at the solution to an exercise before assigning all or part of it.

We have tried hard to present material in a logical way, introducing new ideas as they are needed and building on the material developed earlier. This applies also to mathematical and statistical techniques that, in many cases, students may already be somewhat familiar with. Instead of treating these in appendices, we discuss them when they are first used, in the context of their applications to econometrics. We have found that this approach generally works very well in the classroom. The sections on mathematics or statistics are never too long, and we make every effort to motivate them by indicating their relevance to econometrics. This probably means that the book is not appropriate for students with a really weak mathematical or statistical background. It also means that readers will need to use the Subject Index rather than the Table of Contents when they want to look up basic mathematical and statistical concepts. Although this book is intended more as a text than as a reference, we have put a great deal of effort into making the Subject Index as complete and comprehensive as possible.

While it is generally not hard to develop a consistent and appropriate notation for an individual topic, it is exceedingly hard to maintain notation consistent across all the chapters of a book of this length. We do not claim to have done so, but we have made strenuous efforts in that direction. We have been influenced by the suggestions of Karim Abadir, of the University of York, and Jan Magnus, of Tilburg University, on many vexed points of notation. Although we have not followed their counsel in all cases, we wholeheartedly support their efforts to develop a useful and consistent notation for modern econometrics, and we hope that this book will complement their efforts.

How to Use This Book

This book can be used for either a one-term course or a two-term sequence of courses at either the Master's level (in a serious graduate program) or the Ph.D. level. It could also be used in upper-level undergraduate courses for specialists if the students have sufficient background, motivation, and ability.

A two-term course sequence at the (North American) Master's level should be able to cover every chapter in the book, although instructors will undoubtedly wish to omit a few topics that are particularly advanced or specialized. A one-term course should be able to cover approximately the first ten chapters, although a certain amount of material will have to be omitted, depending on the background of the students and the interests of the instructor. See the chapter-by-chapter discussion below.

A two-term course sequence at the Ph.D. level should be able to cover the entire book with no difficulty. Some relatively elementary material in the first few chapters should probably be dealt with rather quickly, and instructors may wish to go into more depth on some topics than we have done in the text. A number of the exercises provide opportunities to do so. A wide variety of one-term courses at the Ph.D. level could be based on various combinations of chapters and sections.

Our earlier book has been used in many European countries, and it is still in use in a number of universities on that continent. We hope that this book will be at least as attractive to European readers. One of the authors (Davidson) teaches in France, and he has successfully used preliminary versions of the book in courses ranging from the senior undergraduate to the doctoral level. It would, however, be rash to make any specific suggestions as to how best to use the book in the European context. The efforts of the European Union to harmonize university education across countries with widely different traditions have, temporarily one hopes, thrown many educational structures into disarray.

Some of the exercises are really quite challenging, as we discovered while preparing solutions to them. These exercises are starred, as are a number of other exercises for which we think that the solutions are particularly illuminating, even if they are not particularly difficult. In some cases, these starred exercises allow us to present important results without proving them in the text. In other cases, they are designed to allow instructors to cover advanced material that is not in the text itself. Because the solutions to the starred exercises should be of considerable value to students, they are available from the website for the book. All the data needed for the exercises are also available from the website, as are corrections made since the book was printed.

An instructor's manual provides solutions to all the exercises. It is available, on CD-ROM, to instructors only. The URL of our website and instructions for obtaining the CD-ROM may be found in the section entitled "Data, Solutions, and Corrections" which immediately follows the Preface.

Organization of This Book

This book has fifteen chapters, which fall naturally into three groups of five. The first five chapters deal with a number of fundamental concepts of estimation and statistical inference, almost always in the context of ordinary least squares. The next five chapters deal with alternative estimation methods, namely, nonlinear least squares (NLS), generalized least squares (GLS), instrumental variables (IV), the generalized method of moments (GMM), and maximum likelihood (ML), in that order. The final five chapters deal with a variety of more specialized topics, including discrete and limited dependent variables, systems of equations, time series, and specification testing.

Most of Chapter 1 is fairly elementary, and much of the material in it should already be familiar to students who have a good background in statistics, econometrics, and matrix algebra at the undergraduate level. Such students will probably be able to read and understand the chapter without any detailed guidance. For other students, with different backgrounds, instructors will have to decide how much of the material to discuss in detail. The discussion of how to simulate a regression model in Section 1.3 introduces some concepts that are not often taught in undergraduate econometrics courses but are crucial to understanding bootstrap methods. Section 1.5 is even more important, because it treats linear regression in a way that is probably quite new to most students. The treatment, based on the method of moments, leads naturally to the use of estimating equations later in the book. Thus it is important to spend some time on this section in courses at all levels.

Chapter 2, a fundamental chapter, deals with the geometry of least squares in some detail. Just how much time should be devoted to this chapter may depend on the level of the course and the inclinations of the instructor. Not all instructors find the geometrical approach quite as intuitive as we do. However, our experience is that many students do find it extremely helpful. The chapter introduces a number of fundamental concepts that reappear many times in various places. These include the application of Pythagoras' Theorem to ordinary least squares, the subspace spanned by the columns of a matrix of regressors and its orthogonal complement, orthogonal projection matrices, and the Frisch-Waugh-Lovell Theorem. The material on leverage and influential observations in Section 2.6 could, perhaps, be dealt with a little later in the course, but we feel strongly that the topic is important and, as presented here, no harder to understand than the rest of the contents of this chapter.

Chapter 3 is also a fundamental chapter. It deals with the statistical properties of the ordinary least squares (OLS) estimator and introduces such important concepts as unbiasedness, probability limits, consistency, covariance matrices, efficiency, the Gauss-Markov Theorem, the properties of residuals, and the consequences of model misspecification. Students with a strong background in statistics should be at least somewhat familiar with much of this material.

Chapter 4 provides a detailed introduction to hypothesis testing in the linear regression model. An unusual feature of the chapter is that three types of hypothesis tests are discussed: exact tests, asymptotic tests, and simulation-based tests. Some of the material in this chapter should probably be omitted, or at least watered down, in less advanced courses. For example, the explanation in Section 4.3 of why linear combinations of normal random variables are normally distributed could be omitted, as could some of the detailed discussion of t and F tests in Section 4.4. Sections 4.5, 4.6, and 4.7 are a little more advanced than the earlier sections, and it would be natural in less advanced courses to treat some of this material a bit more superficially than we have done. However, since Section 4.5 introduces several fundamental concepts of asymptotic theory and Section 4.6 introduces the basic ideas of simulation-based testing and the bootstrap, these sections cannot simply be skipped.

The first four sections of Chapter 5 deal with confidence intervals, a topic that, in our experience, is often grossly misunderstood even by advanced students. Here, confidence intervals are explicitly constructed by inverting test statistics. In less advanced courses, it may be tempting to omit the section on bootstrap confidence intervals and the section on confidence regions. However, we recommend that Figure 5.3 at least should be discussed in some detail. If students truly understand this figure, then they understand the meaning of confidence intervals and confidence regions, even if they do not necessarily know how to construct them in practice. Section 5.5 introduces the well-known heteroskedasticity-consistent covariance matrix estimator (HCCME). This is the first, but by no means the last, sandwich covariance matrix that appears in this book. Finally, Section 5.6 discusses the delta method and some related topics. Much of this material could be omitted in a one-term course at the Master's level.

Chapter 6, the first of five chapters on widely-used estimation methods, deals with nonlinear least squares. We do not attempt to provide a detailed treatment of the asymptotic theory of NLS estimation. Instead, we discuss a class of method-of-moments estimators and show that the results can be extended, heuristically, to the NLS case. This approach simplifies the asymptotic theory and provides a useful introduction to the treatment of IV and GMM estimation in later chapters. Nevertheless, instructors will probably want to treat Sections 6.2 and 6.3 fairly superficially in lower-level courses. The remainder of the chapter deals with methods for computing NLS estimates, the Gauss-Newton regression, one-step estimation, and hypothesis testing. The section on one-step estimation could be omitted in applied courses, and the section on heteroskedasticity-robust tests could be treated very superficially.

Chapter 7 deals with a number of related topics, including GLS, feasible GLS, heteroskedasticity, serial correlation, and panel data. It is no accident that this chapter immediately follows Chapter 6. The linear regression model with AR(1) errors, which was introduced in Chapter 6 as a simple model to which NLS can be applied, is discussed extensively. Moreover, both the tests for heteroskedasticity that we discuss and the tests for serial correlation that we recommend are based on the Gauss-Newton regression. The discussion of autoregressive and moving-average processes in Section 7.6 is deliberately very superficial; a somewhat more detailed discussion is found in Section 13.2. The last two parts of Section 7.8, which compare GLS and NLS methods for estimating models with autoregressive errors, are relatively advanced. On the other hand, Section 7.9, which deals with common factor restrictions, and Section 7.10, which deals with panel data, are much less so. The material in these two sections is particularly relevant for applied work.

Chapter 8 introduces instrumental variables estimation. Because method-of-moments estimators have been discussed extensively in earlier chapters, the basic ideas should already be familiar. Section 8.2 discusses errors in variables and simultaneous equations, primarily to motivate the use of IV estimation. Section 8.3 introduces both the simple and the generalized IV estimators; the latter is equivalent to two-stage least squares. Although this section is moderately long, several theoretical results are dealt with only in exercises, and instructors of advanced courses may wish to discuss some of these. The following section, which deals with the finite-sample properties of IV estimators, is quite advanced. The practical implications of these properties are summarized at the end of the section and should be discussed in applied courses. The next three sections deal with hypothesis testing, including Durbin-Wu-Hausman (DWH) tests and Sargan tests of overidentifying restrictions. Sections 8.8 and 8.9 cover bootstrap testing, which is fairly complicated in simultaneous equations models, and IV estimation of nonlinear models, respectively. Both of these sections could be omitted in a less advanced course.

Chapter 9 deals with the generalized method of moments. The first four sections, which are suitable for use in most courses, deal only with univariate linear regression models in which some of the regressors may be correlated with the error terms. Section 9.5 is a good deal more advanced. It provides a reasonably complete, although by no means fully rigorous, treatment of nonlinear GMM estimation. Our approach, based on the theory of estimating functions, is somewhat novel in the econometric literature. The overview at the end of Section 9.5 summarizes the key practical results of the section and could be used in an applied course. Section 9.6, which is even more advanced, introduces the method of simulated moments (MSM) as an application of GMM. In order to show how MSM works in the context of a very simple model, part of this section is devoted to a detailed discussion of MSM estimation of the parameters of the lognormal distribution. This subsection could be omitted or replaced by discussion of another application.

Chapter 10 provides a comprehensive introduction to the theory of maximum likelihood estimation. Since ML estimation is widely used in applied work, and in the remaining chapters of this book, this is a very important chapter. Some parts of it deal with rather advanced theory, and they should be treated lightly, or skipped entirely, in lower-level courses. These parts include much of Section 10.3, which deals with the asymptotic properties of the ML estimator, and most of Section 10.6, which deals with the relationship among the three classical tests. An exception is the subsection that includes Figure 10.3, which is intended to provide an intuitive and geometrical understanding of the relationship among the classical tests. However, other parts of the chapter, including Sections 10.2, 10.7, and 10.8, are reasonably accessible and suitable for an applied course.

The last five chapters deal with a variety of topics and are, on average, somewhat more advanced and specialized than the first ten chapters. These chapters are intended for two-term courses and for courses beyond the introductory graduate level, since students would have difficulty getting much beyond Chapter 10 in a one-term course at the senior undergraduate or Master's level. In addition, it would be difficult to teach any of the last five chapters to students who were not reasonably familiar with the material in the first two-thirds of the book. Chapter 11 could be skipped without serious consequences for the following chapters, and most of Chapter 15 could be taught right after Chapter 10. However, Chapter 14 depends on Chapter 13, and an important part of that chapter depends in turn on Chapter 12.

Chapter 11 deals with a variety of models that are primarily of interest in the context of cross-sectional data. These include binary response models, models for more than two discrete responses, models for count data, models for censored and truncated data, sample selectivity, and duration models. Most parts of the chapter make no use of advanced theory. The part that gives rise to the most complicated, if not the most advanced, theory is Section 11.4, which deals with multinomial and nested logit models, the artificial regression associated with them, and the multinomial probit model. This chapter provides numerous examples of ML estimation.

Chapter 12 is the first to deal with multivariate models and the estimation of two or more equations at once. It begins with a fairly detailed discussion of the multivariate linear regression (SUR) model, and then moves on to systems of nonlinear regressions and linear simultaneous equations models. All the standard estimation methods for the latter (2SLS, 3SLS, LIML, and FIML) are discussed, and the relationships among them are explained, usually by a comparison of estimating equations. This is the first chapter to have an appendix; it deals with some material that is more than usually advanced. The exercises are particularly numerous, and some of them are quite challenging.

Chapter 13 is intended to be reasonably accessible while containing a good deal of material about several important topics. It deals with methods for stationary time-series data. Section 13.2 provides a more detailed discussion of autoregressive and moving-average processes than did Section 7.6; some instructors may wish to teach the material from both these sections at the same time. The next section discusses methods of estimating autoregressive (AR), moving-average (MA), and autoregressive moving-average (ARMA) models and briefly introduces a new method of estimation, namely, indirect inference. Section 13.4 discusses several types of single-equation dynamic models, including the partial adjustment model, autoregressive distributed lag (ADL) models, and error-correction models. Section 13.5 discusses seasonality and seasonal adjustment. Section 13.6 provides a moderately detailed introduction to the currently very popular models of autoregressive conditional heteroskedasticity (ARCH). Finally, Section 13.7 provides a brief introduction to vector autoregressions and Granger causality. This is the only part of the chapter that depends on Chapter 12. Thus almost all of Chapter 13 could be taught directly after Chapter 10, if desired.

Chapter 14, which is fairly advanced, is the second chapter on time series. It deals with methods for nonstationary time-series data. Most of the basic ideas are introduced in Section 14.2, where we also present the same-order (or big O) notation. Instructors in relatively advanced courses may wish to discuss this topic in conjunction with some of the material on asymptotic theory in earlier chapters. Sections 14.3 and 14.4 deal with unit root tests, and Sections 14.5 and 14.6 deal with cointegration. The chapter can be taught at more than one level, depending on the extent to which the distinctly challenging theoretical exercises are exploited.

The final chapter deals with specification testing. Much of this chapter could be taught immediately after Chapter 10, although some use is made of the big O notation. Section 15.2 discusses some general results for model specification tests based on artificial regressions and then uses them to derive conditional moment tests and information matrix tests. The first part of this section is quite advanced, although the most difficult parts are relegated to an appendix. Section 15.3 provides a fairly detailed introduction to nonnested hypothesis testing. Section 15.4 introduces the AIC and BIC criteria for model selection. Finally, Section 15.5 provides an introduction to kernel estimation, of both distribution and density functions, and then to kernel regression.

More detailed discussions of each chapter may be found in the instructor's manual, which we discussed earlier.

Acknowledgments

It has taken us nearly six years to write this book, and during that time we have received assistance and encouragement from a large number of people. Bruce McCullough, of Drexel University, read every chapter, generally at an early stage, and made a great many valuable comments and suggestions. Thanasis Stengos, of the University of Guelph, also read the entire book and made several suggestions that have materially improved the final version. Richard Parks, of the University of Washington, taught out of the unfinished manuscript and found an alarming number of errors that have since been corrected. Others who read at least part of the book with care and provided us with useful feedback include John Galbraith (McGill University), Ramazan Gencay (University of Windsor), Sílvia Gonçalves (Université de Montréal), Manfred Jäger (Martin Luther University), Richard Startz (University of Washington), Arthur Sweetman (Queen's University), and Tony Wirjanto (University of Waterloo). There are numerous other colleagues who also deserve our thanks, but the list is much too long to include here.

We made use of draft chapters of this book in courses at both the Master's and Ph.D. levels at Queen's University, McGill University, and the University of Toronto in Canada, as well as at the Université de la Méditerranée and GREQAM in France. A great many students found errors or pointed out aspects of the exposition that were unclear. The book has been improved enormously by addressing their comments, and we are very grateful to all of them. We are also grateful to the many students at the above institutions, and also at the University of Washington, who expressed enthusiasm for the book when it was still a long way from being finished and thereby encouraged us to finish a task that, at times, seemed almost incapable of completion.

We also owe a debt of gratitude to the thousands of talented programmers who have contributed to the development of free, open-source, software, without which it would have been much more difficult to write this book. The book was typeset entirely by us using the teTeX distribution of TeX running on the Debian distribution of the Linux operating system. We also made extensive use of the gcc and g77 compilers, and of many other excellent free programs that run on Linux.

Finally, we must give thanks to our wives, Pamela Davidson and Susan Gentleman, and also to James's son, Andrew, for putting up with the two of us during the seemingly endless period during which the book was being written.

Data, Solutions, and Corrections

The website for this book is located at

http://www.econ.queensu.ca/ETM/ .

This website provides all the data needed for the exercises, solutions to the starred exercises, and corrections made since the book was printed. The solutions and corrections are provided as PDF files, which almost all modern computers should have the software to view and print.

The website provides solutions only to the starred exercises. In addition, there is an instructor's manual, available to instructors only, which comes on a CD-ROM and contains solutions to all the exercises. For information about how to obtain it, please contact your local Oxford University Press sales representative or visit the Oxford higher education website at

http://www.oup-usa.org/highered .

The authors are happy to hear from readers who have found errors that should be corrected. Their affiliations are given below:

Russell Davidson
<russell.davidson@mcgill.ca>

GREQAM
Centre de la Vieille Charité
2 rue de la Charité
13002 Marseille
France

Department of Economics
McGill University
855 Sherbrooke St. West
Montreal, Quebec, H3A 2T7
Canada

James G. MacKinnon
<jgm@qed.econ.queensu.ca>

Department of Economics
Queen's University
Kingston, Ontario, K7L 3N6
Canada

Chapter 1

Regression Models

1.1 Introduction

Regression models form the core of the discipline of econometrics. Although econometricians routinely estimate a wide variety of statistical models, using many different types of data, the vast majority of these are either regression models or close relatives of them. In this chapter, we introduce the concept of a regression model, discuss several varieties of them, and introduce the estimation method that is most commonly used with regression models, namely, **least squares**. This estimation method is derived by using the **method of moments**, which is a very general principle of estimation that has many applications in econometrics.

The most elementary type of regression model is the **simple linear regression model**, which can be expressed by the following equation:

$$y_t = \beta_1 + \beta_2 x_t + u_t. \tag{1.01}$$

The subscript t is used to index the **observations** of a **sample**. The total number of observations, also called the **sample size**, will be denoted by n. Thus, for a sample of size n, the subscript t runs from 1 to n. Each observation comprises an observation on a **dependent variable**, written as y_t for observation t, and an observation on a single **explanatory variable**, or **independent variable**, written as x_t.

The relation (1.01) links the observations on the dependent and the explanatory variables for each observation in terms of two unknown **parameters**, β_1 and β_2, and an unobserved **error term**, u_t. Thus, of the five quantities that appear in (1.01), two, y_t and x_t, are observed, and three, β_1, β_2, and u_t, are not. Three of them, y_t, x_t, and u_t, are specific to observation t, while the other two, the parameters, are common to all n observations.

Here is a simple example of how a regression model like (1.01) could arise in economics. Suppose that the index t is a time index, as the notation suggests. Each value of t could represent a year, for instance. Then y_t could be household consumption as measured in year t, and x_t could be measured disposable income of households in the same year. In that case, (1.01) would represent what in elementary macroeconomics is called a **consumption function**.

If for the moment we ignore the presence of the error terms, β_2 is the **marginal propensity to consume** out of disposable income, and β_1 is what is sometimes called **autonomous consumption**. As is true of a great many econometric models, the parameters in this example can be seen to have a direct interpretation in terms of economic theory. The variables, income and consumption, do indeed vary in value from year to year, as the term "variables" suggests. In contrast, the parameters reflect aspects of the economy that do not vary, but take on the same values each year.

The purpose of formulating the model (1.01) is to try to explain the observed values of the dependent variable in terms of those of the explanatory variable. According to equation (1.01), for each t, the value of y_t is given by a linear function of x_t, plus what we have called the error term, u_t. The linear (strictly speaking, affine[1]) function, which in this case is $\beta_1 + \beta_2 x_t$, is called the **regression function**. At this stage we should note that, as long as we say nothing about the unobserved quantity u_t, equation (1.01) does not tell us anything. In fact, we can allow the parameters β_1 and β_2 to be quite arbitrary, since, for any given β_1 and β_2, the model (1.01) can always be made to be true by defining u_t suitably.

If we wish to make sense of the regression model (1.01), then, we must make some assumptions about the properties of the error term u_t. Precisely what those assumptions are will vary from case to case. In all cases, though, it is assumed that u_t is a **random variable**. Most commonly, it is assumed that, whatever the value of x_t, the expectation of the random variable u_t is zero. This assumption usually serves to **identify** the unknown parameters β_1 and β_2, in the sense that, under the assumption, equation (1.01) can be true only for specific values of those parameters.

The presence of error terms in regression models means that the explanations these models provide are at best partial. This would not be so if the error terms could be directly observed as economic variables, for then u_t could be treated as a further explanatory variable. In that case, (1.01) would be a relation linking y_t to x_t and u_t in a completely unambiguous fashion. Given x_t and u_t, y_t would be completely explained without error.

Of course, error terms are not observed in the real world. They are included in regression models because we are not able to specify all of the real-world factors that determine the value of y_t. When we set up a model like (1.01) with u_t as a random variable, what we are really doing is using the mathematical concept of randomness to model our *ignorance* of the details of economic mechanisms. When we suppose that the mean of an error term is zero, we are implicitly assuming that the factors determining y_t that we ignore are just as likely to make y_t bigger than it would have been if those factors were absent as they are to make y_t smaller. Thus we are assuming that, on average, the

[1] A function $g(x)$ is said to be **affine** if it takes the form $g(x) = a + bx$ for two real numbers a and b.

effects of the neglected determining factors tend to cancel out. This does not mean that those effects are necessarily small. The proportion of the variation in y_t that is accounted for by the error term will depend on the nature of the data and the extent of our ignorance. Even if this proportion is large, and it can be very large indeed in some cases, regression models like (1.01) can be useful if they allow us to see how y_t is related to the variables, like x_t, that we can actually observe.

Much of the literature in econometrics, and therefore much of this book, is concerned with how to estimate, and test hypotheses about, the parameters of regression models. In the case of (1.01), these parameters are the **constant term**, or **intercept**, β_1, and the **slope coefficient**, β_2. Although we will begin our discussion of estimation in this chapter, most of it will be postponed until later chapters. In this chapter, we are primarily concerned with understanding regression models as statistical models, rather than with estimating them or testing hypotheses about them.

In the next section, we review some elementary concepts from probability theory, including random variables and their expectations. Many readers will already be familiar with these concepts. They will be useful in Section 1.3, where we discuss the meaning of regression models and some of the forms that such models can take. In Section 1.4, we review some topics from matrix algebra and show how multiple regression models can be written using matrix notation. Finally, in Section 1.5, we introduce the method of moments and show how it leads to ordinary least squares as a way of estimating regression models.

1.2 Distributions, Densities, and Moments

The variables that appear in an econometric model are treated as what statisticians call **random variables**. In order to characterize a random variable, we must first specify the set of all the possible values that the random variable can take on. The simplest case is a **scalar random variable**, or **scalar r.v.** The set of possible values for a scalar r.v. may be the real line or a subset of the real line, such as the set of nonnegative real numbers. It may also be the set of integers or a subset of the set of integers, such as the numbers 1, 2, and 3.

Since a random variable is a collection of possibilities, random variables cannot be observed as such. What we do observe are **realizations** of random variables, a realization being one value out of the set of possible values. For a scalar random variable, each realization is therefore a single real value.

If X is any random variable, **probabilities** can be assigned to subsets of the full set of possibilities of values for X, in some cases to each point in that set. Such subsets are called **events**, and their probabilities are assigned by a **probability distribution**, according to a few general rules.

Discrete and Continuous Random Variables

The easiest sort of probability distribution to consider arises when X is a **discrete random variable**, which can take on a finite, or perhaps a countably infinite number of values, which we may denote as $x_1, x_2, \ldots$. The probability distribution simply assigns probabilities, that is, numbers between 0 and 1, to each of these values, in such a way that the probabilities sum to 1:

$$\sum_{i=1}^{\infty} p(x_i) = 1,$$

where $p(x_i)$ is the probability assigned to x_i. Any assignment of nonnegative probabilities that sum to one automatically respects all the general rules alluded to above.

In the context of econometrics, the most commonly encountered discrete random variables occur in the context of **binary data**, which can take on the values 0 and 1, and in the context of **count data**, which can take on the values 0, 1, 2, ...; see Chapter 11.

Another possibility is that X may be a **continuous random variable**, which, for the case of a scalar r.v., can take on any value in some continuous subset of the real line, or possibly the whole real line. The dependent variable in a regression model is normally a continuous r.v. For a continuous r.v., the probability distribution can be represented by a **cumulative distribution function**, or **CDF**. This function, which is often denoted $F(x)$, is defined on the real line. Its value is $\Pr(X \leq x)$, the probability of the event that X is equal to or less than some value x. In general, the notation $\Pr(A)$ signifies the probability assigned to the event A, a subset of the full set of possibilities. Since X is continuous, it does not really matter whether we define the CDF as $\Pr(X \leq x)$ or as $\Pr(X < x)$ here, but it is conventional to use the former definition.

Notice that, in the preceding paragraph, we used X to denote a random variable and x to denote a realization of X, that is, a particular value that the random variable X may take on. This distinction is important when discussing the meaning of a probability distribution, but it will rarely be necessary in most of this book.

Probability Distributions

We may now make explicit the general rules that must be obeyed by probability distributions in assigning probabilities to events. There are just three of these rules:

(i) All probabilities lie between 0 and 1;

(ii) The null set is assigned probability 0, and the full set of possibilities is assigned probability 1;

(iii) The probability assigned to an event that is the union of two disjoint events is the sum of the probabilities assigned to those disjoint events.

We will not often need to make explicit use of these rules, but we can use them now in order to derive some properties of any well-defined CDF for a scalar r.v. First, a CDF $F(x)$ tends to 0 as $x \to -\infty$. This follows because the event $(X \leq x)$ tends to the null set as $x \to -\infty$, and the null set has probability 0. By similar reasoning, $F(x)$ tends to 1 when $x \to +\infty$, because then the event $(X \leq x)$ tends to the entire real line. Further, $F(x)$ must be a weakly increasing function of x. This is true because, if $x_1 < x_2$, we have

$$(X \leq x_2) = (X \leq x_1) \cup (x_1 < X \leq x_2), \tag{1.02}$$

where $\cup$ is the symbol for set union. The two subsets on the right-hand side of (1.02) are clearly disjoint, and so

$$\Pr(X \leq x_2) = \Pr(X \leq x_1) + \Pr(x_1 < X \leq x_2).$$

Since all probabilities are nonnegative, it follows that the probability that $(X \leq x_2)$ must be no smaller than the probability that $(X \leq x_1)$.

For a continuous r.v., the CDF assigns probabilities to every interval on the real line. However, if we try to assign a probability to a single point, the result is always just zero. Suppose that X is a scalar r.v. with CDF $F(x)$. For any interval $[a, b]$ of the real line, the fact that $F(x)$ is weakly increasing allows us to compute the probability that $X \in [a, b]$. If $a < b$,

$$\Pr(X \leq b) = \Pr(X \leq a) + \Pr(a < X \leq b),$$

whence it follows directly from the definition of a CDF that

$$\Pr(a \leq X \leq b) = F(b) - F(a), \tag{1.03}$$

since, for a continuous r.v., we make no distinction between $\Pr(a < X \leq b)$ and $\Pr(a \leq X \leq b)$. If we set $b = a$, in the hope of obtaining the probability that $X = a$, then we get $F(a) - F(a) = 0$.

Probability Density Functions

For continuous random variables, the concept of a **probability density function**, or **PDF**, is very closely related to that of a CDF. Whereas a distribution function exists for any well-defined random variable, a PDF exists only when the random variable is continuous, and when its CDF is differentiable. For a scalar r.v., the density function, often denoted by f, is just the derivative of the CDF:

$$f(x) \equiv F'(x).$$

Because $F(-\infty) = 0$ and $F(\infty) = 1$, every PDF must be **normalized** to integrate to unity. By the Fundamental Theorem of Calculus,

$$\int_{-\infty}^{\infty} f(x)\,dx = \int_{-\infty}^{\infty} F'(x)\,dx = F(\infty) - F(-\infty) = 1. \tag{1.04}$$

It is obvious that a PDF is nonnegative, since it is the derivative of a weakly increasing function.

Standard Normal CDF:

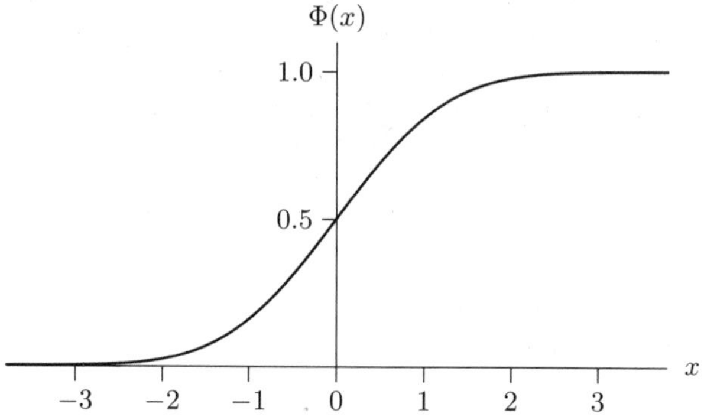

Standard Normal PDF:

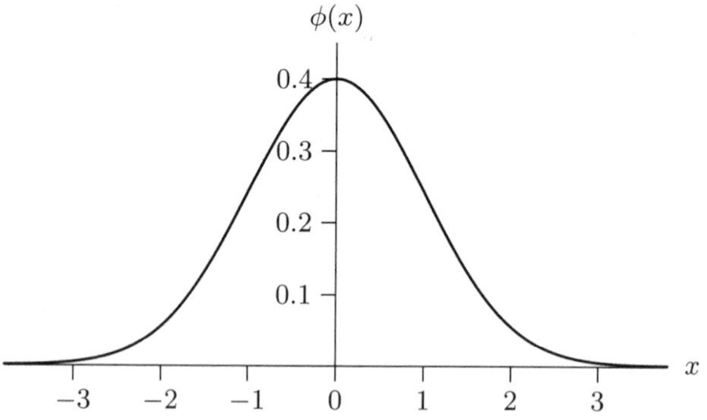

Figure 1.1 The CDF and PDF of the standard normal distribution

Probabilities can be computed in terms of the PDF as well as the CDF. Note that, by (1.03) and the Fundamental Theorem of Calculus once more,

$$\Pr(a \le X \le b) = F(b) - F(a) = \int_a^b f(x)\,dx. \tag{1.05}$$

Since (1.05) must hold for arbitrary a and b, it is clear why $f(x)$ must always be nonnegative. However, it is important to remember that $f(x)$ is not bounded above by unity, because the value of a PDF at a point x is not a probability. Only when a PDF is integrated over some interval, as in (1.05), does it yield a probability.

The most common example of a continuous distribution is provided by the **normal distribution**. This is the distribution that generates the famous or infamous "bell curve" sometimes thought to influence students' grade distributions. The fundamental member of the normal family of distributions is the **standard normal distribution**. It is a continuous scalar distribution, defined

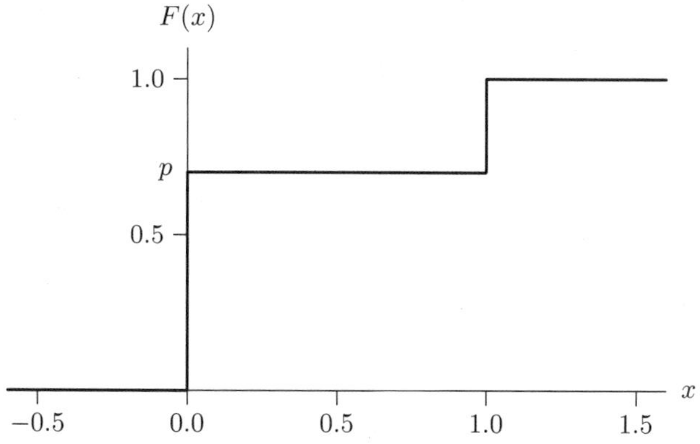

Figure 1.2 The CDF of a binary random variable

on the entire real line. The PDF of the standard normal distribution is often denoted $\phi(\cdot)$. Its explicit expression, which we will need later in the book, is

$$\phi(x) = (2\pi)^{-1/2} \exp\big(-\tfrac{1}{2}x^2\big). \tag{1.06}$$

Unlike $\phi(\cdot)$, the CDF, usually denoted $\Phi(\cdot)$, has no elementary closed-form expression. However, by (1.05) with $a = -\infty$ and $b = x$, we have

$$\Phi(x) = \int_{-\infty}^{x} \phi(y)\, dy.$$

The functions $\Phi(\cdot)$ and $\phi(\cdot)$ are graphed in Figure 1.1. Since the PDF is the derivative of the CDF, it achieves a maximum at $x = 0$, where the CDF is rising most steeply. As the CDF approaches both 0 and 1, and consequently, becomes very flat, the PDF approaches 0.

Although it may not be obvious at once, discrete random variables can be characterized by a CDF just as well as continuous ones can be. Consider a binary r.v. X that can take on only two values, 0 and 1, and let the probability that $X = 0$ be p. It follows that the probability that $X = 1$ is $1 - p$. Then the CDF of X, according to the definition of $F(x)$ as $\Pr(X \le x)$, is the following discontinuous, "staircase" function:

$$F(x) = \begin{cases} 0 & \text{for } x < 0 \\ p & \text{for } 0 \le x < 1 \\ 1 & \text{for } x \ge 1. \end{cases}$$

This CDF is graphed in Figure 1.2. Obviously, we cannot graph a corresponding PDF, for it does not exist. For general discrete random variables, the discontinuities of the CDF occur at the discrete permitted values of X, and the jump at each discontinuity is equal to the probability of the corresponding value. Since the sum of the jumps is therefore equal to 1, the limiting value of F, to the right of all permitted values, is also 1.

Using a CDF is a reasonable way to deal with random variables that are neither completely discrete nor completely continuous. Such hybrid variables can be produced by the phenomenon of **censoring**. A random variable is said to be censored if not all of its potential values can actually be observed. For instance, in some data sets, a household's measured income is set equal to 0 if it is actually negative. It might be negative if, for instance, the household lost more on the stock market than it earned from other sources in a given year. Even if the true income variable is continuously distributed over the positive and negative real line, the observed, censored, variable has an **atom**, or bump, at 0, since the single value of 0 now has a nonzero probability attached to it, namely, the probability that an individual's income is nonpositive. As with a purely discrete random variable, the CDF has a discontinuity at 0, with a jump equal to the probability of a negative or zero income.

Moments of Random Variables

A fundamental property of a random variable is its **expectation**. For a discrete r.v. that can take on m possible finite values $x_1, x_2, \ldots, x_m$, the expectation is simply

$$\mathrm{E}(X) \equiv \sum_{i=1}^{m} p(x_i)x_i. \tag{1.07}$$

Thus each possible value x_i is multiplied by the probability associated with it. If m is infinite, the sum above has an infinite number of terms.

For a continuous r.v., the expectation is defined analogously using the PDF:

$$\mathrm{E}(X) \equiv \int_{-\infty}^{\infty} x f(x)\, dx. \tag{1.08}$$

Not every r.v. has an expectation, however. The integral of a density function always exists and equals 1. But since X can range from $-\infty$ to ∞, the integral (1.08) may well diverge at either limit of integration, or both, if the density f does not tend to zero fast enough. Similarly, if m in (1.07) is infinite, the sum may diverge. The expectation of a random variable is sometimes called the **mean** or, to prevent confusion with the usual meaning of the word as the mean of a sample, the **population mean**. A common notation for it is μ.

The expectation of a random variable is often referred to as its **first moment**. The so-called **higher moments**, if they exist, are the expectations of the r.v. raised to a power. Thus the **second moment** of a random variable X is the expectation of X^2, the **third moment** is the expectation of X^3, and so on. In general, the kth moment of a continuous random variable X is

$$m_k(X) \equiv \int_{-\infty}^{\infty} x^k f(x)\, dx.$$

Observe that the value of any moment depends only on the probability distribution of the r.v. in question. For this reason, we often speak of the moments of the distribution rather than the moments of a specific random variable. If a distribution possesses a kth moment, it also possesses all moments of order less than k.

The higher moments just defined are called the **uncentered moments** of a distribution, because, in general, X does not have mean zero. It is often more useful to work with the **central moments**, which are defined as the ordinary moments of the difference between the random variable and its expectation. Thus the kth central moment of the distribution of a continuous r.v. X is

$$\mu_k \equiv \mathrm{E}\big(X - \mathrm{E}(X)\big)^k = \int_{-\infty}^{\infty} (x-\mu)^k f(x)\,dx,$$

where $\mu \equiv \mathrm{E}(X)$. For a discrete X, the kth central moment is

$$\mu_k \equiv \mathrm{E}\big(X - \mathrm{E}(X)\big)^k = \sum_{i=1}^{m} p(x_i)(x_i - \mu)^k.$$

By far the most important central moment is the second. It is called the **variance** of the random variable and is frequently written as $\mathrm{Var}(X)$. Another common notation for a variance is σ^2. This notation underlines the important fact that a variance cannot be negative. The square root of the variance, σ, is called the **standard deviation** of the distribution. Estimates of standard deviations are often referred to as **standard errors**, especially when the random variable in question is an estimated parameter.

Multivariate Distributions

A **vector-valued random variable** takes on values that are vectors. It can be thought of as several scalar random variables that have a single, joint distribution. For simplicity, we will focus on the case of **bivariate random variables**, where the vector is of length 2. A continuous, bivariate r.v. (X_1, X_2) has a distribution function

$$F(x_1, x_2) = \Pr\big((X_1 \le x_1) \cap (X_2 \le x_2)\big),$$

where $\cap$ is the symbol for set intersection. Thus $F(x_1, x_2)$ is the joint probability that both $X_1 \le x_1$ and $X_2 \le x_2$. For continuous variables, the PDF, if it exists, is the **joint density function**[2]

$$f(x_1, x_2) = \frac{\partial^2 F(x_1, x_2)}{\partial x_1 \partial x_2}. \tag{1.09}$$

[2] Here we are using what computer scientists would call "overloaded function" notation. This means that $F(\cdot)$ and $f(\cdot)$ denote respectively the CDF and the PDF of whatever their argument(s) happen to be. This practice is harmless provided there is no ambiguity.

This function has exactly the same properties as an ordinary PDF. In particular, as in (1.04),

$$\int_{-\infty}^{\infty}\int_{-\infty}^{\infty} f(x_1, x_2)\, dx_1 dx_2 = 1.$$

More generally, the probability that X_1 and X_2 jointly lie in any region is the integral of $f(x_1, x_2)$ over that region. A case of particular interest is

$$\begin{aligned} F(x_1, x_2) &= \Pr\big((X_1 \leq x_1) \cap (X_2 \leq x_2)\big) \\ &= \int_{-\infty}^{x_1}\int_{-\infty}^{x_2} f(y_1, y_2)\, dy_1 dy_2, \end{aligned} \tag{1.10}$$

which shows how to compute the CDF given the PDF.

The concept of joint probability distributions leads naturally to the important notion of **statistical independence**. Let (X_1, X_2) be a bivariate random variable. Then X_1 and X_2 are said to be **statistically independent**, or often just **independent**, if the joint CDF of (X_1, X_2) is the product of the CDFs of X_1 and X_2. In straightforward notation, this means that

$$F(x_1, x_2) = F(x_1, \infty)F(\infty, x_2). \tag{1.11}$$

The first factor here is the joint probability that $X_1 \leq x_1$ and $X_2 \leq \infty$. Since the second inequality imposes no constraint, this factor is just the probability that $X_1 \leq x_1$. The function $F(x_1, \infty)$, which is called the **marginal CDF** of X_1, is thus just the CDF of X_1 considered by itself. Similarly, the second factor on the right-hand side of (1.11) is the marginal CDF of X_2.

It is also possible to express statistical independence in terms of the **marginal density** of X_1 and the marginal density of X_2. The marginal density of X_1 is, as one would expect, the derivative of the marginal CDF of X_1,

$$f(x_1) \equiv F_1(x_1, \infty),$$

where $F_1(\cdot)$ denotes the partial derivative of $F(\cdot)$ with respect to its first argument. It can be shown from (1.10) that the marginal density can also be expressed in terms of the joint density, as follows:

$$f(x_1) = \int_{-\infty}^{\infty} f(x_1, x_2)\, dx_2. \tag{1.12}$$

Thus $f(x_1)$ is obtained by integrating X_2 out of the joint density. Similarly, the marginal density of X_2 is obtained by integrating X_1 out of the joint density. From (1.09), it can be shown that, if X_1 and X_2 are independent, so that (1.11) holds, then

$$f(x_1, x_2) = f(x_1)f(x_2). \tag{1.13}$$

Thus, when densities exist, statistical independence means that the joint density factorizes as the product of the marginal densities, just as the joint CDF factorizes as the product of the marginal CDFs.

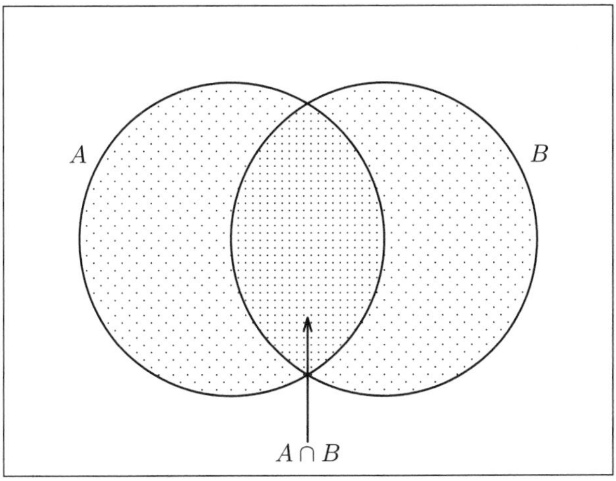

Figure 1.3 Conditional probability

Conditional Probabilities

Suppose that A and B are any two events. Then the probability of event A **conditional** on B, or given B, is denoted as $\Pr(A \mid B)$ and is defined implicitly by the equation

$$\Pr(A \cap B) = \Pr(B)\Pr(A \mid B). \tag{1.14}$$

For this equation to make sense as a definition of $\Pr(A \mid B)$, it is necessary that $\Pr(B) \neq 0$. The idea underlying the definition is that, if we know somehow that the event B has been realized, this knowledge can provide information about whether event A has also been realized. For instance, if A and B are disjoint, and B is realized, then it is certain that A has not been. As we would wish, this does indeed follow from the definition (1.14), since $A \cap B$ is the null set, of zero probability, if A and B are disjoint. Similarly, if B is a subset of A, knowing that B has been realized means that A must have been realized as well. Since in this case $\Pr(A \cap B) = \Pr(B)$, (1.14) tells us that $\Pr(A \mid B) = 1$, as required.

To gain a better understanding of (1.14), consider Figure 1.3. The bounding rectangle represents the full set of possibilities, and events A and B are subsets of the rectangle that overlap as shown. Suppose that the figure has been drawn in such a way that probabilities of subsets are proportional to their areas. Thus the probabilities of A and B are the ratios of the areas of the corresponding circles to the area of the bounding rectangle, and the probability of the intersection $A \cap B$ is the ratio of its area to that of the rectangle.

Suppose now that it is known that B has been realized. This fact leads us to redefine the probabilities so that everything outside B now has zero probability, while, inside B, probabilities remain proportional to areas. Event B now

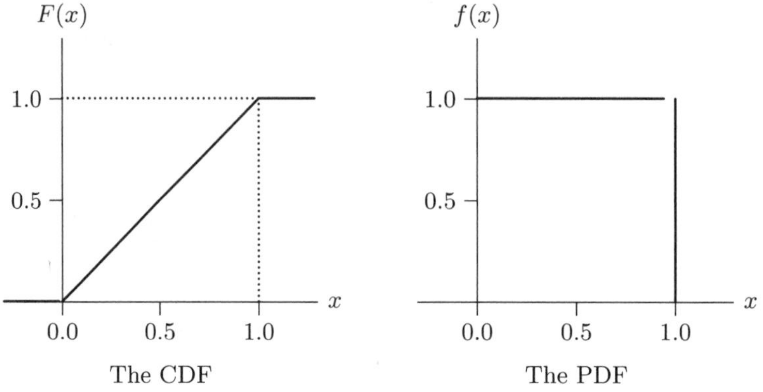

Figure 1.4 The CDF and PDF of the uniform distribution on $[0, 1]$

has probability 1, in order to keep the total probability equal to 1. Event A can be realized only if the realized point is in the intersection $A \cap B$, since the set of all points of A outside this intersection has zero probability. The probability of A, conditional on knowing that B has been realized, is thus the ratio of the area of $A \cap B$ to that of B. This construction leads directly to equation (1.14).

There are many ways to associate a random variable X with the rectangle shown in Figure 1.3. Such a random variable could be any function of the two coordinates that define a point in the rectangle. For example, it could be the horizontal coordinate of the point measured from the origin at the lower left-hand corner of the rectangle, or its vertical coordinate, or the Euclidean distance of the point from the origin. The realization of X is the value of the function it corresponds to at the realized point in the rectangle.

For concreteness, let us assume that the function is simply the horizontal coordinate, and let the width of the rectangle be equal to 1. Then, since all values of the horizontal coordinate between 0 and 1 are equally probable, the random variable X has what is called the **uniform distribution** on the interval $[0, 1]$. The CDF of this distribution is

$$F(x) = \begin{cases} 0 & \text{for } x < 0 \\ x & \text{for } 0 \leq x \leq 1 \\ 1 & \text{for } x > 1. \end{cases}$$

Because $F(x)$ is not differentiable at $x = 0$ and $x = 1$, the PDF of the uniform distribution does not exist at those points. Elsewhere, the derivative of $F(x)$ is 0 outside $[0, 1]$ and 1 inside. The CDF and PDF are illustrated in Figure 1.4. This special case of the uniform distribution is often denoted the $\mathrm{U}(0, 1)$ distribution.

If the information were available that B had been realized, then the distribution of X conditional on this information would be very different from the

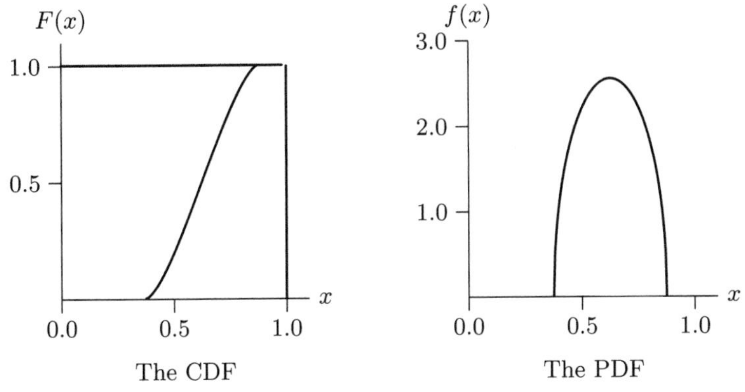

Figure 1.5 The CDF and PDF conditional on event B

U(0, 1) distribution. Now only values between the extreme horizontal limits of the circle of B are allowed. If one computes the area of the part of the circle to the left of a given vertical line, then for each event $a \equiv (X \leq x)$ the probability of this event conditional on B can be worked out. The result is just the CDF of X conditional on the event B. Its derivative is the PDF of X conditional on B. These are shown in Figure 1.5.

The concept of conditional probability can be extended beyond probability conditional on an event to probability conditional on a random variable. Suppose that X_1 is a r.v. and X_2 is a discrete r.v. with permitted values $z_1, \ldots, z_m$. For each $i = 1, \ldots, m$, the CDF of X_1, and, if X_1 is continuous, its PDF, can be computed conditional on the event $(X_2 = z_i)$. If X_2 is also a continuous r.v., then things are a little more complicated, because events like $(X_2 = x_2)$ for some real x_2 have zero probability, and so cannot be conditioned on in the manner of (1.14).

On the other hand, it makes perfect intuitive sense to think of the distribution of X_1 conditional on some specific realized value of X_2. This conditional distribution gives us the probabilities of events concerning X_1 when we know that the realization of X_2 was actually x_2. We therefore make use of the **conditional density** of X_1 for a given value x_2 of X_2. This conditional density, or **conditional PDF**, is defined as

$$f(x_1 \,|\, x_2) = \frac{f(x_1, x_2)}{f(x_2)}. \tag{1.15}$$

Thus, for a given value x_2 of X_2, the conditional density is proportional to the joint density of X_1 and X_2. Of course, (1.15) is well defined only if $f(x_2) > 0$. In some cases, more sophisticated definitions can be found that would allow $f(x_1 \,|\, x_2)$ to be defined for all x_2 even if $f(x_2) = 0$, but we will not need these in this book. See, among others, Billingsley (1979).

Conditional Expectations

Whenever we can describe the distribution of a random variable, X_1, conditional on another, X_2, either by a conditional CDF or a conditional PDF, we can consider the **conditional expectation** or **conditional mean** of X_1. If it exists, this conditional expectation is just the ordinary expectation computed using the conditional distribution. If x_2 is a possible value for X_2, then this conditional expectation is written as $\mathrm{E}(X_1 \,|\, x_2)$.

For a given value x_2, the conditional expectation $\mathrm{E}(X_1 \,|\, x_2)$ is, like any other ordinary expectation, a deterministic, that is, nonrandom, quantity. But we can consider the expectation of X_1 conditional on *every* possible realization of X_2. In this way, we can construct a new random variable, which we denote by $\mathrm{E}(X_1 \,|\, X_2)$, the realization of which is $\mathrm{E}(X_1 \,|\, x_2)$ when the realization of X_2 is x_2. We can call $\mathrm{E}(X_1 \,|\, X_2)$ a deterministic function of the random variable X_2, because the realization of $\mathrm{E}(X_1 \,|\, X_2)$ is unambiguously determined by the realization of X_2.

Conditional expectations defined as random variables in this way have a number of interesting and useful properties. The first, called the **Law of Iterated Expectations**, can be expressed as follows:

$$\mathrm{E}\big(\mathrm{E}(X_1 \,|\, X_2)\big) = \mathrm{E}(X_1). \tag{1.16}$$

If a conditional expectation of X_1 can be treated as a random variable, then the conditional expectation itself may have an expectation. According to (1.16), this expectation is just the ordinary expectation of X_1.

Another property of conditional expectations is that any deterministic function of a conditioning variable X_2 is its own conditional expectation. Thus, for example, $\mathrm{E}(X_2 \,|\, X_2) = X_2$, and $\mathrm{E}(X_2^2 \,|\, X_2) = X_2^2$. Similarly, conditional on X_2, the expectation of a product of another random variable X_1 and a deterministic function of X_2 is the product of that deterministic function and the expectation of X_1 conditional on X_2:

$$\mathrm{E}\big(X_1 h(X_2) \,|\, X_2\big) = h(X_2)\mathrm{E}(X_1 \,|\, X_2), \tag{1.17}$$

for any deterministic function $h(\cdot)$. An important special case of this, which we will make use of in Section 1.5, arises when $\mathrm{E}(X_1 \,|\, X_2) = 0$. In that case, for any function $h(\cdot)$, $\mathrm{E}(X_1 h(X_2)) = 0$, because

$$\begin{aligned} E\big(X_1 h(X_2)\big) &= \mathrm{E}\big(\mathrm{E}(X_1 h(X_2) \,|\, X_2)\big) \\ &= \mathrm{E}\big(h(X_2)\mathrm{E}(X_1 \,|\, X_2)\big) \\ &= \mathrm{E}(0) = 0. \end{aligned}$$

The first equality here follows from the Law of Iterated Expectations, (1.16). The second follows from (1.17). Since $\mathrm{E}(X_1 \,|\, X_2) = 0$, the third line then follows immediately. We will present other properties of conditional expectations as the need arises.

1.3 The Specification of Regression Models

We now return our attention to the regression model (1.01) and revert to the notation of Section 1.1 in which y_t and x_t, respectively, denote the dependent and independent variables. The model (1.01) can be interpreted as a model for the mean of y_t conditional on x_t. Let us assume that the error term u_t has mean 0 conditional on x_t. Then, taking conditional expectations of both sides of (1.01), we see that

$$\mathrm{E}(y_t \,|\, x_t) = \beta_1 + \beta_2 x_t + \mathrm{E}(u_t \,|\, x_t) = \beta_1 + \beta_2 x_t.$$

Without the key assumption that $\mathrm{E}(u_t \,|\, x_t) = 0$, the second equality here would not hold. As we pointed out in Section 1.1, it is impossible to make any sense of a regression model unless we make strong assumptions about the error terms. Of course, we could define u_t as the difference between y_t and $\mathrm{E}(y_t \,|\, x_t)$, which would give $\mathrm{E}(u_t \,|\, x_t) = 0$ by definition. But if we require that $\mathrm{E}(u_t \,|\, x_t) = 0$ and also specify (1.01), we must necessarily have $\mathrm{E}(y_t \,|\, x_t) = \beta_1 + \beta_2 x_t$.

As an example, suppose that we estimate the model (1.01) when in fact

$$y_t = \beta_1 + \beta_2 x_t + \beta_3 x_t^2 + v_t \tag{1.18}$$

with $\beta_3 \neq 0$ and an error term v_t such that $\mathrm{E}(v_t \,|\, x_t) = 0$. If the data were generated by (1.18), the error term u_t in (1.01) would be equal to $\beta_3 x_t^2 + v_t$. By the results on conditional expectations in the last section, we see that

$$\mathrm{E}(u_t \,|\, x_t) = \mathrm{E}\big(\beta_3 x_t^2 + v_t \,|\, x_t\big) = \beta_3 x_t^2,$$

which we have assumed to be nonzero. This example shows the force of the assumption that the error term has mean zero conditional on x_t. Unless the mean of y_t conditional on x_t really is a linear function of x_t, the regression function in (1.01) is not **correctly specified**, in the precise sense that (1.01) cannot hold with an error term that has mean zero conditional on x_t. It will become clear in later chapters that estimating incorrectly specified models usually leads to results that are meaningless or, at best, seriously misleading.

Information Sets

In a more general setting, what we are interested in is usually not the mean of y_t conditional on a single explanatory variable x_t but the mean of y_t conditional on a set of potential explanatory variables. This set is often called an **information set**, and it is denoted Ω_t. Typically, the information set contains more variables than would actually be used in a regression model. For example, it might consist of all the variables observed by the economic agents whose actions determine y_t at the time they make the decisions that cause them to perform those actions. Such an information set could be very large.

As a consequence, much of the art of constructing, or specifying, a regression model is deciding which of the variables that belong to Ω_t should be included in the model and which of the variables should be excluded.

In some cases, economic theory makes it fairly clear what the information set Ω_t should consist of, and sometimes also which variables in Ω_t should make their way into a regression model. In many others, however, it may not be at all clear how to specify Ω_t. In general, we want to condition on **exogenous** variables but not on **endogenous** ones. These terms refer to the *origin* or *genesis* of the variables: An exogenous variable has its origins *outside* the model under consideration, while the mechanism generating an endogenous variable is *inside* the model. When we write a single equation like (1.01), the only endogenous variable allowed is the dependent variable, y_t.

Recall the example of the consumption function that we looked at in Section 1.1. That model seeks to explain household consumption in terms of disposable income, but it makes no claim to explain disposable income, which is simply taken as given. The consumption function model can be correctly specified only if two conditions hold:

(i) The mean of consumption conditional on disposable income is a linear function of the latter.

(ii) Consumption is *not* a variable that contributes to the determination of disposable income.

The second condition means that the origin of disposable income, that is, the mechanism by which disposable income is generated, lies outside the model for consumption. In other words, disposable income is exogenous in that model. If the simple consumption model we have presented is correctly specified, the two conditions above must be satisfied. Needless to say, we do not claim that this model is in fact correctly specified.

It is not always easy to decide just what information set to condition on. As the above example shows, it is often not clear whether or not a variable is exogenous. This sort of question will be discussed in Chapter 8. Moreover, even if a variable clearly is exogenous, we may not want to include it in Ω_t. For example, if the ultimate purpose of estimating a regression model is to use it for forecasting, there may be no point in conditioning on information that will not be available at the time the forecast is to be made.

Error Terms

Whenever we specify a regression model, it is essential to make assumptions about the properties of the error terms. The simplest assumption is that all of the error terms have mean 0, come from the same distribution, and are independent of each other. Although this is a rather strong assumption, it is very commonly made in practice.

Mutual independence of the error terms, when coupled with the assumption that $\mathrm{E}(u_t) = 0$, implies that the mean of u_t is 0 conditional on all of the other error terms u_s, $s \neq t$. However, the implication does not work in the other direction, because the assumption of mutual independence is stronger than the assumption about the conditional means. A very strong assumption which is often made is that the error terms are **independently and identically distributed**, or **IID**. According to this assumption, the error terms are mutually independent, and they are in addition realizations from the same, identical, probability distribution.

When the successive observations are ordered by time, it often seems plausible that an error term is correlated with neighboring error terms. Thus u_t might well be correlated with u_s when the value of $|t-s|$ is small. This could occur, for example, if there is correlation across time periods of random factors that influence the dependent variable but are not explicitly accounted for in the regression function. This phenomenon is called **serial correlation**, and it often appears to be observed in practice. When there is serial correlation, the error terms cannot be IID because they are not independent.

Another possibility is that the variance of the error terms may be systematically larger for some observations than for others. This happens if the conditional variance of y_t depends on some of the same variables as the conditional mean. This phenomenon is called **heteroskedasticity**, and it also often appears to be observed in practice. For example, in the case of the consumption function, the variance of consumption may well be higher for households with high incomes than for households with low incomes. When there is heteroskedasticity, the error terms cannot be IID, because they are not identically distributed. It is perfectly possible to take explicit account of both serial correlation and heteroskedasticity, but doing so would take us outside the context of regression models like (1.01).

It may sometimes be desirable to write a regression model like the one we have been studying as

$$\mathrm{E}(y_t \,|\, \Omega_t) = \beta_1 + \beta_2 x_t, \tag{1.19}$$

in order to stress the fact that this is a model for the mean of y_t conditional on a certain information set. However, by itself, (1.19) is just as incomplete a specification as (1.01). In order to see this point, we must now state what we mean by a **complete specification** of a regression model. Probably the best way to do this is to say that a complete specification of any econometric model is one that provides an unambiguous recipe for simulating the model on a computer. After all, if we can use the model to generate simulated data, it must be completely specified.

Simulating Econometric Models

Consider equation (1.01). When we say that we **simulate** this model, we mean that we generate numbers for the dependent variable, y_t, according to equation (1.01). Obviously, one of the first things we must fix for the simulation is the sample size, n. That done, we can generate each of the y_t, $t = 1, \ldots, n$, by evaluating the right-hand side of the equation n times. For this to be possible, we need to know the value of each variable or parameter that appears on the right-hand side.

If we suppose that the explanatory variable x_t is exogenous, then we simply take it as given. So if, in the context of the consumption function example, we had data on the disposable income of households in some country every year for a period of n years, we could just use those data. Our simulation would then be specific to the country in question and to the time period of the data. Alternatively, it could be that we or some other econometricians had previously specified another model, for the explanatory variable this time, and we could then use simulated data provided by that model.

Besides the explanatory variable, the other elements of the right-hand side of (1.01) are the parameters, β_1 and β_2, and the error term u_t. The key feature of the parameters is that we do not know their true values. We will have more to say about this point in Chapter 3, when we define the twin concepts of models and data-generating processes. However, for purposes of simulation, we could use either values suggested by economic theory or values obtained by estimating the model. Evidently, the simulation results will depend on precisely what values we use.

Unlike the parameters, the error terms cannot be taken as given; instead, we wish to treat them as random. Luckily, it is easy to use a computer to generate "random" numbers by using a program called a **random number generator**; we will discuss these programs in Chapter 4. The "random" numbers generated by computers are not random according to some meanings of the word. For instance, a computer can be made to spit out exactly the same sequence of supposedly random numbers more than once. In addition, a digital computer is a perfectly deterministic device. Therefore, if random means the opposite of deterministic, only computers that are not functioning properly would be capable of generating truly random numbers. Because of this, some people prefer to speak of computer-generated random numbers as **pseudo-random**. However, for the purposes of simulations, the numbers computers provide have all the properties of random numbers that we need, and so we will call them simply random rather than pseudo-random.

Computer-generated random numbers are mutually independent **drawings**, or realizations, from specific probability distributions, usually the uniform $U(0, 1)$ distribution or the standard normal distribution, both of which were defined in Section 1.2. Of course, techniques exist for generating drawings from many other distributions as well, as do techniques for generating drawings that are not independent. For the moment, the essential point is that we must always specify the probability distribution of the random numbers we use in a simulation. It is important to note that specifying the expectation of a distribution, or even the expectation conditional on some other variables, is not enough to specify the distribution in full.

Let us now summarize the various steps in performing a simulation by giving a sort of generic recipe for simulations of regression models. In the model specification, it is convenient to distinguish between the **deterministic specification** and the **stochastic specification**. In model (1.01), the deterministic specification consists of the regression function, of which the ingredients are the explanatory variable and the parameters. The stochastic specification ("stochastic" is another word for "random") consists of the probability distribution of the error terms, and the requirement that the error terms should be IID drawings from this distribution. Then, in order to simulate the dependent variable y_t in (1.01), we do as follows:

- Fix the sample size, n;
- Choose the parameters (here β_1 and β_2) of the deterministic specification;
- Obtain the n successive values x_t, $t = 1, \ldots, n$, of the explanatory variable. As explained above, these values may be real-world data or the output of another simulation;
- Evaluate the n successive values of the regression function $\beta_1 + \beta_2 x_t$, for $t = 1, \ldots, n$;
- Choose the probability distribution of the error terms, if necessary specifying parameters such as its mean and variance;
- Use a random-number generator to generate the n successive and mutually independent values u_t of the error terms;
- Form the n successive values y_t of the dependent variable by adding the error terms to the values of the regression function.

The n values y_t, $t = 1, \ldots, n$, thus generated are the output of the simulation; they are the **simulated values** of the dependent variable.

The chief interest of such a simulation is that, if the model we simulate is correctly specified and thus reflects the real-world generating process for the dependent variable, our simulation mimics the real world accurately, because it makes use of the same data-generating mechanism as that in operation in the real world.

A complete specification, then, is anything that leads unambiguously to a recipe like the one given above. We will define a **fully specified parametric model** as a model for which it is possible to simulate the dependent variable once the values of the parameters are known. A **partially specified parametric model** is one for which more information, over and above the parameter values, must be supplied before simulation is possible. Both sorts of models are frequently encountered in econometrics.

To conclude this discussion of simulations, let us return to the specifications (1.01) and (1.19). Both are obviously incomplete as they stand. In order to complete either one, it is necessary to specify the information set Ω_t and the distribution of u_t conditional on Ω_t. In particular, it is necessary to know whether the error terms u_s with $s \neq t$ belong to Ω_t. In (1.19), one aspect of the conditional distribution is given, namely, the conditional mean. Unfortunately, because (1.19) contains no explicit error term, it is easy to forget that it is there. Perhaps as a result, it is more common to write regression models in the form of (1.01) than in the form of (1.19). However, writing a model in the form of (1.01) does have the disadvantage that it obscures both the dependence of the model on the choice of an information set and the fact that the distribution of the error term must be specified conditional on that information set.

Linear and Nonlinear Regression Models

The simple linear regression model (1.01) is by no means the only reasonable model for the mean of y_t conditional on x_t. Consider, for example, the models

$$y_t = \beta_1 + \beta_2 x_t + \beta_3 x_t^2 + u_t \tag{1.20}$$

$$y_t = \gamma_1 + \gamma_2 \log x_t + u_t, \quad \text{and} \tag{1.21}$$

$$y_t = \delta_1 + \delta_2 \frac{1}{x_t} + u_t. \tag{1.22}$$

These are all models that might be plausible in some circumstances.[3] In equation (1.20), there is an extra parameter, β_3, which allows $\mathrm{E}(y_t \mid x_t)$ to vary quadratically with x_t whenever β_3 is nonzero. In effect, x_t and x_t^2 are being treated as separate explanatory variables. Thus (1.20) is the first example we have seen of a **multiple linear regression model**. It reduces to the simple linear regression model (1.01) when $\beta_3 = 0$.

In the models (1.21) and (1.22), on the other hand, there are no extra parameters. Instead, a nonlinear transformation of x_t is used in place of x_t itself. As a consequence, the relationship between x_t and $\mathrm{E}(y_t \mid x_t)$ in these two models is necessarily nonlinear. Nevertheless, (1.20), (1.21), and (1.22) are all said to be linear regression models, because, even though the mean of y_t may depend nonlinearly on x_t, it always depends linearly on the unknown parameters of the regression function. As we will see in Section 1.5, it is quite easy to estimate a linear regression model. In contrast, genuinely nonlinear models, in which the regression function depends nonlinearly on the parameters, are somewhat harder to estimate; see Chapter 6.

Because it is very easy to estimate linear regression models, a great deal of applied work in econometrics makes use of them. It may seem that the linearity assumption is very restrictive. However, as the examples (1.20), (1.21), and (1.22) illustrate, this assumption need not be unduly restrictive in practice, at least not if the econometrician is at all creative. If we are

[3] In this book, all logarithms are natural logarithms. Thus $a = \log x$ implies that $x = e^a$. Some authors use "ln" to denote natural logarithms and "log" to denote base 10 logarithms. Since econometricians should never have any use for base 10 logarithms, we avoid this aesthetically displeasing notation.

willing to transform the dependent variable as well as the independent ones, the linearity assumption can be made even less restrictive. As an example, consider the nonlinear regression model

$$y_t = e^{\beta_1} x_{t2}^{\beta_2} x_{t3}^{\beta_3} + u_t, \tag{1.23}$$

in which there are two explanatory variables, x_{t2} and x_{t3}, and the regression function is multiplicative. If the notation seems odd, suppose that there is implicitly a third explanatory variable, x_{t1}, which is constant and always equal to e. Notice that the regression function in (1.23) can be evaluated only when x_{t2} and x_{t3} are positive for all t.[4] It is a genuinely nonlinear regression function, because it is clearly linear neither in parameters nor in variables. For reasons that will shortly become apparent, a nonlinear model like (1.23) is very rarely estimated in practice.

A model like (1.23) is not as outlandish as may appear at first glance. It could arise, for instance, if we wanted to estimate a Cobb-Douglas production function. In that case, y_t would be output for observation t, and x_{t2} and x_{t3} would be inputs, say labor and capital. Since e^{β_1} is just a positive constant, it plays the role of the scale factor that is present in every Cobb-Douglas production function.

As (1.23) is written, everything enters multiplicatively except the error term. But it is easy to modify (1.23) so that the error term also enters multiplicatively. One way to do this is to write

$$y_t = e^{\beta_1} x_{t2}^{\beta_2} x_{t3}^{\beta_3} + u_t \equiv \big(e^{\beta_1} x_{t2}^{\beta_2} x_{t3}^{\beta_3}\big)(1 + v_t), \tag{1.24}$$

where the error factor $1 + v_t$ multiplies the regression function. If we now assume that the underlying errors v_t are IID, it follows that the additive errors u_t are proportional to the regression function. This may well be a more plausible specification than that in which the u_t are supposed to be IID, as was implicitly assumed in (1.23). To see this, notice first that the additive error u_t has the same units of measurement as y_t. If (1.23) is interpreted as a production function, then u_t is measured in units of output. However, the multiplicative error v_t is dimensionless. In other words, it is a pure number, like 0.02, which could be expressed as 2 percent. If the u_t are assumed to be IID, then we are assuming that the error in output is of the same order of magnitude regardless of the scale of production. If, on the other hand, the v_t are assumed to be IID, then the error is proportional to total output. This second assumption is almost always more reasonable than the first.

If the model (1.24) is a good one, the v_t should be quite small, usually less than about 0.05. For small values of the argument w, a standard approximation to

[4] If x and a are real numbers, x^a is not usually a real number unless $a > 0$. Think of the square root of -1.

the exponential function gives us that $e^w \cong 1 + w$. As a consequence, (1.24) is very similar to the model

$$y_t = e^{\beta_1} x_{t2}^{\beta_2} x_{t3}^{\beta_3} e^{v_t}, \tag{1.25}$$

whenever the error terms are reasonably small.

Now suppose we take logarithms of both sides of (1.25). The result is

$$\log y_t = \beta_1 + \beta_2 \log x_{t2} + \beta_3 \log x_{t3} + v_t, \tag{1.26}$$

which is a **loglinear regression model**. This model is linear in the parameters and in the logarithms of all the variables, and so it is very much easier to estimate than the nonlinear model (1.23). Since (1.25) is at least as plausible as (1.23), it is not surprising that loglinear regression models, like (1.26), are estimated very frequently in practice, while multiplicative models with additive error terms, like (1.23), are very rarely estimated. Of course, it is important to remember that (1.26) is not a model for the mean of y_t conditional on x_{t2} and x_{t3}. Instead, it is a model for the mean of $\log y_t$ conditional on those variables. If it is really the conditional mean of y_t that we are interested in, we will not want to estimate a loglinear model like (1.26).

1.4 Matrix Algebra

It is impossible to study econometrics beyond the most elementary level without using matrix algebra. Most readers are probably already quite familiar with matrix algebra. This section reviews some basic results that will be used throughout the book. It also shows how regression models can be written very compactly using matrix notation. More advanced material will be discussed in later chapters, as it is needed.

An $n \times m$ **matrix** $\boldsymbol{A}$ is a rectangular array that consists of nm elements arranged in n rows and m columns. The name of the matrix is conventionally shown in boldface. A typical element of $\boldsymbol{A}$ might be denoted by either A_{ij} or a_{ij}, where $i = 1, \ldots, n$ and $j = 1, \ldots, m$. The first subscript always indicates the row, and the second always indicates the column. It is sometimes necessary to show the elements of a matrix explicitly, in which case they are arrayed in rows and columns and surrounded by large brackets, as in

$$\boldsymbol{B} = \begin{bmatrix} 2 & 3 & 6 \\ 4 & 5 & 8 \end{bmatrix}.$$

Here $\boldsymbol{B}$ is a 2×3 matrix.

If a matrix has only one column or only one row, it is called a **vector**. There are two types of vectors, **column vectors** and **row vectors**. Since column vectors are more common than row vectors, a vector that is not specified to be a row vector is normally treated as a column vector. If a column vector has n elements, it may be referred to as an n–vector. Boldface is used to denote vectors as well as matrices. It is conventional to use uppercase letters for matrices and lowercase letters for column vectors. However, it is sometimes necessary to ignore this convention.

If a matrix has the same number of columns and rows, it is said to be **square**. A square matrix $\boldsymbol{A}$ is **symmetric** if $A_{ij} = A_{ji}$ for all i and j. Symmetric matrices occur very frequently in econometrics. A square matrix is said to be **diagonal** if $A_{ij} = 0$ for all $i \neq j$; in this case, the only nonzero entries are those on what is called the **principal diagonal**. Sometimes a square matrix has all zeros above or below the principal diagonal. Such a matrix is said to be **triangular**. If the nonzero elements are all above the diagonal, it is said to be **upper-triangular**; if the nonzero elements are all below the diagonal, it is said to be **lower-triangular**. Here are some examples:

$$\boldsymbol{A} = \begin{bmatrix} 1 & 2 & 4 \\ 2 & 3 & 6 \\ 4 & 6 & 5 \end{bmatrix} \qquad \boldsymbol{B} = \begin{bmatrix} 1 & 0 & 0 \\ 0 & 4 & 0 \\ 0 & 0 & 2 \end{bmatrix} \qquad \boldsymbol{C} = \begin{bmatrix} 1 & 0 & 0 \\ 3 & 2 & 0 \\ 5 & 2 & 6 \end{bmatrix}.$$

In this case, $\boldsymbol{A}$ is symmetric, $\boldsymbol{B}$ is diagonal, and $\boldsymbol{C}$ is lower-triangular.

The **transpose** of a matrix is obtained by interchanging its row and column subscripts. Thus the ij^{th} element of $\boldsymbol{A}$ becomes the ji^{th} element of its transpose, which is denoted $\boldsymbol{A}^{\top}$. Note that many authors use $\boldsymbol{A}'$ rather than $\boldsymbol{A}^{\top}$ to denote the transpose of $\boldsymbol{A}$. The transpose of a symmetric matrix is equal to the matrix itself. The transpose of a column vector is a row vector, and vice versa. Here are some examples:

$$\boldsymbol{A} = \begin{bmatrix} 2 & 5 & 7 \\ 3 & 8 & 4 \end{bmatrix} \qquad \boldsymbol{A}^{\top} = \begin{bmatrix} 2 & 3 \\ 5 & 8 \\ 7 & 4 \end{bmatrix} \qquad \boldsymbol{b} = \begin{bmatrix} 2 \\ 4 \\ 6 \end{bmatrix} \qquad \boldsymbol{b}^{\top} = [2 \quad 4 \quad 6].$$

Note that a matrix $\boldsymbol{A}$ is symmetric if and only if $\boldsymbol{A} = \boldsymbol{A}^{\top}$.

Arithmetic Operations on Matrices

Addition and **subtraction** of matrices works exactly the way it does for scalars, with the proviso that matrices can be added or subtracted only if they are **conformable**. In the case of addition and subtraction, this just means that they must have the same dimensions, that is, the same number of rows and the same number of columns. If $\boldsymbol{A}$ and $\boldsymbol{B}$ are conformable, then a typical element of $\boldsymbol{A} + \boldsymbol{B}$ is simply $A_{ij} + B_{ij}$, and a typical element of $\boldsymbol{A} - \boldsymbol{B}$ is $A_{ij} - B_{ij}$.

Matrix multiplication actually involves both additions and multiplications. It is based on what is called the **inner product**, or **scalar product**, of two vectors.

Suppose that $\boldsymbol{a}$ and $\boldsymbol{b}$ are n–vectors. Then their inner product is

$$\boldsymbol{a}^\top\boldsymbol{b} = \boldsymbol{b}^\top\boldsymbol{a} = \sum_{i=1}^{n} a_i b_i.$$

As the name suggests, this is just a scalar.

When two matrices are multiplied together, the ij^{th} element of the result is equal to the inner product of the ith row of the first matrix with the jth column of the second matrix. Thus, if $\boldsymbol{C} = \boldsymbol{AB}$,

$$C_{ij} = \sum_{k=1}^{m} A_{ik} B_{kj}. \tag{1.27}$$

For (1.27) to make sense, we must assume that $\boldsymbol{A}$ has m columns and that $\boldsymbol{B}$ has m rows. In general, if two matrices are to be conformable for multiplication, the first matrix must have as many columns as the second has rows. Further, as is clear from (1.27), the result has as many rows as the first matrix and as many columns as the second. One way to make this explicit is to write something like

$$\underset{n\times m}{\boldsymbol{A}}\;\underset{m\times l}{\boldsymbol{B}} = \underset{n\times l}{\boldsymbol{C}}.$$

One rarely sees this type of notation in a book or journal article. However, it is often useful to employ it when doing calculations, in order to verify that the matrices being multiplied are indeed conformable and to derive the dimensions of their product.

The rules for multiplying matrices and vectors together are the same as the rules for multiplying matrices with each other; vectors are simply treated as matrices that have only one column or only one row. For instance, if we multiply an n–vector $\boldsymbol{a}$ by the transpose of an n–vector $\boldsymbol{b}$, we obtain what is called the **outer product** of the two vectors. The result, written as $\boldsymbol{ab}^\top$, is an $n \times n$ matrix with typical element $a_i b_j$.

Matrix multiplication is, in general, not commutative. The fact that it is possible to **premultiply** $\boldsymbol{B}$ by $\boldsymbol{A}$ does not imply that it is possible to **postmultiply** $\boldsymbol{B}$ by $\boldsymbol{A}$. In fact, it is easy to see that both operations are possible if and only if one of the matrix products is square, in which case the other matrix product is square also, although generally with different dimensions. Even when both operations are possible, $\boldsymbol{AB} \neq \boldsymbol{BA}$ except in special cases.

A special matrix that econometricians frequently make use of is $\mathbf{I}$, which denotes the **identity matrix**. It is a diagonal matrix with every diagonal element equal to 1. A subscript is sometimes used to indicate the number of rows and columns. Thus

$$\mathbf{I}_3 = \begin{bmatrix} 1 & 0 & 0 \\ 0 & 1 & 0 \\ 0 & 0 & 1 \end{bmatrix}.$$

The identity matrix is so called because when it is either premultiplied or postmultiplied by any matrix, it leaves the latter unchanged. Thus, for any matrix $\boldsymbol{A}$, $\boldsymbol{A}\mathbf{I} = \mathbf{I}\boldsymbol{A} = \boldsymbol{A}$, provided, of course, that the matrices are conformable for multiplication. It is easy to see why the identity matrix has this property. Recall that the only nonzero elements of $\mathbf{I}$ are equal to 1 and are on the principal diagonal. This fact can be expressed simply with the help of the symbol known as the **Kronecker delta**, written as δ_{ij}. The definition is

$$\delta_{ij} = \begin{cases} 1 & \text{if } i = j, \\ 0 & \text{if } i \neq j. \end{cases} \tag{1.28}$$

The ij^{th} element of $\mathbf{I}$ is just δ_{ij}. By (1.27), the ij^{th} element of $\boldsymbol{A}\mathbf{I}$ is

$$\sum_{k=1}^{m} A_{ik}\mathrm{I}_{kj} = \sum_{k=1}^{m} A_{ik}\delta_{kj} = A_{ij},$$

since all the terms in the sum over k vanish except that for which $k = j$.

A special vector that we frequently use in this book is $\boldsymbol{\iota}$. It denotes a column vector every element of which is 1. This special vector comes in handy whenever one wishes to sum the elements of another vector, because, for any n–vector $\boldsymbol{b}$,

$$\boldsymbol{\iota}^{\top}\boldsymbol{b} = \sum_{i=1}^{n} b_i. \tag{1.29}$$

Matrix multiplication and matrix addition interact in an intuitive way. It is easy to check from the definitions of the respective operations that the **distributive** properties hold. That is, assuming that the dimensions of the matrices are conformable for the various operations,

$$\begin{aligned} \boldsymbol{A}(\boldsymbol{B}+\boldsymbol{C}) &= \boldsymbol{AB}+\boldsymbol{AC}, \quad \text{and} \\ (\boldsymbol{B}+\boldsymbol{C})\boldsymbol{A} &= \boldsymbol{BA}+\boldsymbol{CA}. \end{aligned}$$

In addition, both operations are **associative**, which means that

$$\begin{aligned} (\boldsymbol{A}+\boldsymbol{B})+\boldsymbol{C} &= \boldsymbol{A}+(\boldsymbol{B}+\boldsymbol{C}), \quad \text{and} \\ (\boldsymbol{AB})\boldsymbol{C} &= \boldsymbol{A}(\boldsymbol{BC}). \end{aligned}$$

The transpose of the product of two matrices is the product of the transposes of the matrices with the order reversed. Thus

$$(\boldsymbol{AB})^{\top} = \boldsymbol{B}^{\top}\boldsymbol{A}^{\top}. \tag{1.30}$$

The reversal of the order is necessary if the transposed matrices are to be conformable for multiplication. The result (1.30) can be proved immediately by writing out the typical entries of both sides and checking that

$$(\boldsymbol{AB})^{\top}_{ij} = (\boldsymbol{AB})_{ji} = \sum_{k=1}^{m} A_{jk} B_{ki} = \sum_{k=1}^{m} (\boldsymbol{B}^{\top})_{ik} (\boldsymbol{A}^{\top})_{kj} = (\boldsymbol{B}^{\top}\boldsymbol{A}^{\top})_{ij},$$

where m is the number of columns of $\boldsymbol{A}$ and the number of rows of $\boldsymbol{B}$. It is always possible to multiply a matrix by its own transpose: If $\boldsymbol{A}$ is $n \times m$, then $\boldsymbol{A}^{\top}$ is $m \times n$, $\boldsymbol{A}^{\top}\boldsymbol{A}$ is $m \times m$, and $\boldsymbol{A}\boldsymbol{A}^{\top}$ is $n \times n$. It follows directly from (1.30) that both of these matrix products are symmetric:

$$\boldsymbol{A}^{\top}\boldsymbol{A} = (\boldsymbol{A}^{\top}\boldsymbol{A})^{\top} \quad \text{and} \quad \boldsymbol{A}\boldsymbol{A}^{\top} = (\boldsymbol{A}\boldsymbol{A}^{\top})^{\top}.$$

It is frequently necessary to multiply a matrix, say $\boldsymbol{B}$, by a scalar, say α. **Multiplication by a scalar** works exactly the way one would expect: Every element of $\boldsymbol{B}$ is multiplied by α. Since multiplication by a scalar is commutative, we can write this either as $\alpha\boldsymbol{B}$ or as $\boldsymbol{B}\alpha$, but $\alpha\boldsymbol{B}$ is the more common notation.

Occasionally, it is necessary to multiply two matrices together element by element. The result is called the **direct product** of the two matrices. The direct product of $\boldsymbol{A}$ and $\boldsymbol{B}$ is denoted $\boldsymbol{A} * \boldsymbol{B}$, and a typical element of it is equal to $A_{ij}B_{ij}$.

A square matrix may or may not be **invertible**. If $\boldsymbol{A}$ is invertible, then it has an **inverse matrix** $\boldsymbol{A}^{-1}$ with the property that

$$\boldsymbol{A}\boldsymbol{A}^{-1} = \boldsymbol{A}^{-1}\boldsymbol{A} = \mathbf{I}.$$

If $\boldsymbol{A}$ is symmetric, then so is $\boldsymbol{A}^{-1}$. If $\boldsymbol{A}$ is triangular, then so is $\boldsymbol{A}^{-1}$. Except in certain special cases, it is not easy to calculate the inverse of a matrix by hand. One such special case is that of a diagonal matrix, say $\boldsymbol{D}$, with typical diagonal element D_{ii}. It is easy to verify that $\boldsymbol{D}^{-1}$ is also a diagonal matrix, with typical diagonal element D_{ii}^{-1}.

If an $n \times n$ square matrix $\boldsymbol{A}$ is invertible, then its **rank** is n. Such a matrix is said to have **full rank**. If a square matrix does not have full rank, and therefore is not invertible, it is said to be **singular**. If a square matrix is singular, its rank must be less than its dimension. If, by omitting j rows and j columns of $\boldsymbol{A}$, we can obtain a matrix $\boldsymbol{A}'$ that is invertible, and if j is the smallest number for which this is true, the rank of $\boldsymbol{A}$ is $n - j$. More generally, for matrices that are not necessarily square, the rank is the largest number m for which an $m \times m$ nonsingular matrix can be constructed by omitting some rows and some columns from the original matrix. The rank of a matrix is closely related to the geometry of vector spaces, which will be discussed in the next chapter.

Regression Models and Matrix Notation

The simple linear regression model (1.01) can easily be written in matrix notation. If we stack the model for all the observations, we obtain

$$\begin{aligned} y_1 &= \beta_1 + \beta_2 x_1 + u_1 \\ y_2 &= \beta_1 + \beta_2 x_2 + u_2 \\ \vdots \quad & \quad \vdots \qquad \vdots \qquad \vdots \\ y_n &= \beta_1 + \beta_2 x_n + u_n. \end{aligned} \tag{1.31}$$

Let $\boldsymbol{y}$ denote an n–vector with typical element y_t, $\boldsymbol{u}$ an n–vector with typical element u_t, $\boldsymbol{X}$ an $n \times 2$ matrix that consists of a column of 1s and a column with typical element x_t, and $\boldsymbol{\beta}$ a 2–vector with typical element β_i, $i = 1, 2$. Thus we have

$$\boldsymbol{y} = \begin{bmatrix} y_1 \\ y_2 \\ \vdots \\ y_n \end{bmatrix}, \quad \boldsymbol{u} = \begin{bmatrix} u_1 \\ u_2 \\ \vdots \\ u_n \end{bmatrix}, \quad \boldsymbol{X} = \begin{bmatrix} 1 & x_1 \\ 1 & x_2 \\ \vdots & \vdots \\ 1 & x_n \end{bmatrix}, \quad \text{and} \quad \boldsymbol{\beta} = \begin{bmatrix} \beta_1 \\ \beta_2 \end{bmatrix}.$$

Equations (1.31) can now be rewritten as

$$\boldsymbol{y} = \boldsymbol{X\beta} + \boldsymbol{u}. \tag{1.32}$$

It is easy to verify from the rules of matrix multiplication that a typical row of (1.32) is a typical row of (1.31). When we postmultiply the matrix $\boldsymbol{X}$ by the vector $\boldsymbol{\beta}$, we obtain a vector $\boldsymbol{X\beta}$ with typical element $\beta_1 + \beta_2 x_t$.

When a regression model is written in the form (1.32), the separate columns of the matrix $\boldsymbol{X}$ are called **regressors**, and the column vector $\boldsymbol{y}$ is called the **regressand**. In (1.31), there are just two regressors, corresponding to the constant and one explanatory variable. One advantage of writing the regression model in the form (1.32) is that we are not restricted to just one or two regressors. Suppose that we have k regressors, one of which may or may not correspond to a constant, and the others to a number of explanatory variables. Then the matrix $\boldsymbol{X}$ becomes

$$\boldsymbol{X} = \begin{bmatrix} x_{11} & x_{12} & \cdots & x_{1k} \\ x_{21} & x_{22} & \cdots & x_{2k} \\ \vdots & \vdots & & \vdots \\ x_{n1} & x_{n2} & \cdots & x_{nk} \end{bmatrix}, \tag{1.33}$$

where x_{ti} denotes the tth observation on the ith regressor, and the vector $\boldsymbol{\beta}$ now has k elements, β_1 through β_k. Equation (1.32) remains perfectly valid when $\boldsymbol{X}$ and $\boldsymbol{\beta}$ are redefined in this way. A typical row of this equation is

$$y_t = \boldsymbol{X}_t\boldsymbol{\beta} + u_t = \sum_{i=1}^{k} \beta_i x_{ti} + u_t, \tag{1.34}$$

where we have used $\boldsymbol{X}_t$ to denote the tth row of $\boldsymbol{X}$.

In equation (1.32), we used the rules of matrix multiplication to write the regression function, for the entire sample, in a very simple form. These rules make it possible to find equally convenient expressions for other aspects of regression models. The key fact is that every element of the product of two matrices is a summation. Thus it is often very convenient to use matrix algebra when dealing with summations. Consider, for example, the matrix of sums of squares and cross-products of the $\boldsymbol{X}$ matrix. This is a $k \times k$ symmetric matrix, of which a typical element is either

$$\sum_{t=1}^{n} x_{ti}^2 \quad \text{or} \quad \sum_{t=1}^{n} x_{ti}x_{tj},$$

the former being a typical diagonal element and the latter a typical off-diagonal one. This entire matrix can be written very compactly as $\boldsymbol{X}^\top\boldsymbol{X}$. Similarly, the vector with typical element

$$\sum_{t=1}^{n} x_{ti}\, y_t$$

can be written as $\boldsymbol{X}^\top\boldsymbol{y}$. As we will see in the next section, the least-squares estimates of $\boldsymbol{\beta}$ depend only on the matrix $\boldsymbol{X}^\top\boldsymbol{X}$ and the vector $\boldsymbol{X}^\top\boldsymbol{y}$.

Partitioned Matrices

There are many ways of writing an $n \times k$ matrix $\boldsymbol{X}$ that are intermediate between the straightforward notation $\boldsymbol{X}$ and the full element-by-element decomposition of $\boldsymbol{X}$ given in (1.33). We might wish to separate the columns while grouping the rows, as

$$\underset{n\times k}{\boldsymbol{X}} = \big[\, \underset{n\times 1}{\boldsymbol{x}_1} \quad \underset{n\times 1}{\boldsymbol{x}_2} \quad \underset{\ldots}{\cdots} \quad \underset{n\times 1}{\boldsymbol{x}_k} \,\big],$$

or we might wish to separate the rows but not the columns, as

$$\boldsymbol{X} = \underset{n\times k}{\begin{bmatrix} \boldsymbol{X}_1 \\ \boldsymbol{X}_2 \\ \vdots \\ \boldsymbol{X}_n \end{bmatrix}} \begin{matrix} 1\times k \\ 1\times k \\ \\ 1\times k \end{matrix} .$$

To save space, we can also write this as $\boldsymbol{X} = \left[\boldsymbol{X}_1 \vdots \boldsymbol{X}_2 \vdots \ldots \vdots \boldsymbol{X}_n\right]$. There is no restriction on how a matrix can be partitioned, so long as all the **submatrices** or **blocks** fit together correctly. Thus we might have

$$\boldsymbol{X} = \begin{array}{c} \\ \end{array}\begin{matrix} k_1 & k_2 \\ \left[\begin{matrix} \boldsymbol{X}_{11} \\ \boldsymbol{X}_{21} \end{matrix}\right. & \left.\begin{matrix} \boldsymbol{X}_{12} \\ \boldsymbol{X}_{22} \end{matrix}\right] \end{matrix}\begin{matrix} \\ n_1 \\ n_2 \end{matrix}$$

with the submatrix $\boldsymbol{X}_{11}$ of dimensions $n_1 \times k_1$, $\boldsymbol{X}_{12}$ of dimensions $n_1 \times k_2$, $\boldsymbol{X}_{21}$ of dimensions $n_2 \times k_1$, and $\boldsymbol{X}_{22}$ of dimensions $n_2 \times k_2$, with $n_1 + n_2 = n$ and $k_1 + k_2 = k$. Thus $\boldsymbol{X}_{11}$ and $\boldsymbol{X}_{12}$ have the same number of rows, and also $\boldsymbol{X}_{21}$ and $\boldsymbol{X}_{22}$, as required for the submatrices to fit together horizontally. Similarly, $\boldsymbol{X}_{11}$ and $\boldsymbol{X}_{21}$ have the same number of columns, and also $\boldsymbol{X}_{12}$ and $\boldsymbol{X}_{22}$, as required for the submatrices to fit together vertically as well.

If two matrices $\boldsymbol{A}$ and $\boldsymbol{B}$ of the same dimensions are partitioned in exactly the same way, they can be added or subtracted block by block. A simple example is

$$\boldsymbol{A} + \boldsymbol{B} = [\,\boldsymbol{A}_1 \quad \boldsymbol{A}_2\,] + [\,\boldsymbol{B}_1 \quad \boldsymbol{B}_2\,] = [\,\boldsymbol{A}_1 + \boldsymbol{B}_1 \quad \boldsymbol{A}_2 + \boldsymbol{B}_2\,],$$

where $\boldsymbol{A}_1$ and $\boldsymbol{B}_1$ have the same dimensions, as do $\boldsymbol{A}_2$ and $\boldsymbol{B}_2$.

More interestingly, as we now explain, matrix multiplication can sometimes be performed block by block on partitioned matrices. If the product $\boldsymbol{AB}$ exists, then $\boldsymbol{A}$ has as many columns as $\boldsymbol{B}$ has rows. Now suppose that the columns of $\boldsymbol{A}$ are partitioned in the same way as the rows of $\boldsymbol{B}$. Then

$$\boldsymbol{AB} = [\,\boldsymbol{A}_1 \quad \boldsymbol{A}_2 \quad \cdots \quad \boldsymbol{A}_p\,]\begin{bmatrix} \boldsymbol{B}_1 \\ \boldsymbol{B}_2 \\ \vdots \\ \boldsymbol{B}_p \end{bmatrix}.$$

Here each $\boldsymbol{A}_i$, $i = 1, \ldots, p$, has as many columns as the corresponding $\boldsymbol{B}_i$ has rows. The product can be computed following the usual rules for matrix multiplication just as though the blocks were scalars, yielding the result

$$\boldsymbol{AB} = \sum_{i=1}^{p} \boldsymbol{A}_i \boldsymbol{B}_i. \tag{1.35}$$

To see this, it is enough to compute the typical element of each side of equation (1.35) directly and observe that they are the same. Matrix multiplication can also be performed block by block on matrices that are partitioned both horizontally and vertically, provided all the submatrices are conformable; see Exercise 1.19.

These results on multiplying partitioned matrices lead to a useful corollary. Suppose that we are interested only in the first m rows of a product $\boldsymbol{AB}$, where $\boldsymbol{A}$ has more than m rows. Then we can partition the rows of $\boldsymbol{A}$ into two blocks, the first with m rows, the second with all the rest. We need not partition $\boldsymbol{B}$ at all. Then

$$\boldsymbol{AB} = \begin{bmatrix} \boldsymbol{A}_1 \\ \boldsymbol{A}_2 \end{bmatrix} \boldsymbol{B} = \begin{bmatrix} \boldsymbol{A}_1\boldsymbol{B} \\ \boldsymbol{A}_2\boldsymbol{B} \end{bmatrix}. \tag{1.36}$$

This works because $\boldsymbol{A}_1$ and $\boldsymbol{A}_2$ both have the full number of columns of $\boldsymbol{A}$, which must be the same as the number of rows of $\boldsymbol{B}$, since $\boldsymbol{AB}$ exists. It is clear from the rightmost expression in (1.36) that the first m rows of $\boldsymbol{AB}$ are given by $\boldsymbol{A}_1\boldsymbol{B}$. In order to obtain any subset of the rows of a matrix product of arbitrarily many factors, the rule is that we take the submatrix of the leftmost factor that contains just the rows we want, and then multiply it by all the other factors unchanged. Similarly, if we want to select a subset of columns of a matrix product, we can just select them from the rightmost factor, leaving all the factors to the left unchanged.

1.5 Method-of-Moments Estimation

Almost all econometric models contain unknown parameters. For most of the uses to which such models can be put, it is necessary to have **estimates** of these parameters. To compute parameter estimates, we need both a model containing the parameters and a sample made up of observed data. If the model is correctly specified, it describes the real-world mechanism which generated the data in our sample.

It is common in statistics to speak of the "population" from which a sample is drawn. Recall the use of the term "population mean" as a synonym for the mathematical term "expectation"; see Section 1.2. The expression is a holdover from the time when statistics was biostatistics, and the object of study was the human population, usually that of a specific town or country, from which random samples were drawn by statisticians for study. The average weight of all members of the population, for instance, would then be estimated by the mean of the weights of the individuals in the sample, that is, by the **sample mean** of individuals' weights. The sample mean was thus an estimate of the **population mean**. The underlying idea is just that the sample *represents* the population from which it has been drawn.

In econometrics, the use of the term population is simply a metaphor. A better concept is that of a **data-generating process**, or **DGP**. By this term, we mean whatever mechanism is at work in the real world of economic activity giving rise to the numbers in our samples, that is, precisely the mechanism that our econometric model is supposed to describe. A data-generating process is thus the analog in econometrics of a population in biostatistics. Samples may be drawn from a DGP just as they may be drawn from a population. In both cases, the samples are assumed to be representative of the DGP or population from which they are drawn.

A very natural way to estimate parameters is to replace population means by sample means. This technique is called the **method of moments**, and it is one of the most widely-used estimation methods in statistics. As the name implies, it can be used with moments other than the mean. In general, the method of moments, sometimes called **MM** for short, estimates population moments by the corresponding sample moments. In order to apply this method to regression models, we must use the facts that population moments are expectations, and that regression models are specified in terms of the conditional expectations of the error terms.

Estimating the Simple Linear Regression Model

Let us now see how the principle of replacing population means by sample means works for the simple linear regression model (1.01). The error term for observation t is

$$u_t = y_t - \beta_1 - \beta_2 x_t,$$

and, according to our model, the expectation of this error term is zero. Since we have n error terms for a sample of size n, we can consider the sample mean of the error terms:

$$\frac{1}{n}\sum_{t=1}^{n} u_t = \frac{1}{n}\sum_{t=1}^{n}(y_t - \beta_1 - \beta_2 x_t). \tag{1.37}$$

We would like to set this sample mean equal to zero.

Suppose to begin with that $\beta_2 = 0$. This reduces the number of parameters in the model to just one. In that case, there is just one value of β_1 which allows the right-hand side of equation (1.37) to equal zero. The equation defining this value is

$$\frac{1}{n}\sum_{t=1}^{n}(y_t - \beta_1) = 0. \tag{1.38}$$

Since β_1 is common to all the observations and thus does not depend on the index t, (1.38) can be written as

$$\frac{1}{n}\sum_{t=1}^{n} y_t - \beta_1 = 0.$$

We can easily solve this equation to obtain an estimate $\hat{\beta}_1$. This estimate is just the mean of the observed values of the dependent variable,

$$\hat{\beta}_1 = \frac{1}{n}\sum_{t=1}^{n} y_t. \tag{1.39}$$

Thus, if we wish to estimate the population mean of the y_t, which is what β_1 is in our model when $\beta_2 = 0$, the method of moments tells us to use the sample mean as our estimate.

It is not obvious at first glance how to use the method of moments if we put the second parameter β_2 back into the model. Equation (1.38) would become

$$\frac{1}{n}\sum_{t=1}^{n}(y_t - \beta_1 - \beta_2 x_t) = 0, \tag{1.40}$$

but this is just one equation, and there are two unknowns. In order to obtain another equation, we can use the fact that our model specifies that the mean of u_t is 0 *conditional* on the explanatory variable x_t. Actually, it may well specify that the mean of u_t is 0 conditional on many other things as well, depending on our choice of the information set Ω_t, but we will ignore this for now. The conditional mean assumption implies that not only is $\mathrm{E}(u_t) = 0$, but that $\mathrm{E}(x_t u_t) = 0$ as well, since, by (1.16) and (1.17),

$$\mathrm{E}(x_t u_t) = \mathrm{E}\big(\mathrm{E}(x_t u_t \,|\, x_t)\big) = \mathrm{E}\big(x_t \mathrm{E}(u_t \,|\, x_t)\big) = 0. \tag{1.41}$$

Thus we can supplement (1.40) by the following equation, which replaces the population mean in (1.41) by the corresponding sample mean,

$$\frac{1}{n}\sum_{t=1}^{n} x_t(y_t - \beta_1 - \beta_2 x_t) = 0. \tag{1.42}$$

The equations (1.40) and (1.42) are two linear equations in two unknowns, β_1 and β_2. Except in rare conditions, which can easily be ruled out, they have a unique solution that is not difficult to calculate. Solving these equations yields the MM estimates.

We could just solve (1.40) and (1.42) directly, but it is far more illuminating to rewrite them in matrix form. Since β_1 and β_2 do not depend on t, these two equations can be written as

$$\begin{aligned} \beta_1 + \Big(\frac{1}{n}\sum_{t=1}^{n} x_t\Big)\beta_2 &= \frac{1}{n}\sum_{t=1}^{n} y_t \\ \Big(\frac{1}{n}\sum_{t=1}^{n} x_t\Big)\beta_1 + \Big(\frac{1}{n}\sum_{t=1}^{n} x_t^2\Big)\beta_2 &= \frac{1}{n}\sum_{t=1}^{n} x_t y_t. \end{aligned}$$

Multiplying both equations by n and using the rules of matrix multiplication that were discussed in the last section, we can also write them as

$$\begin{bmatrix} n & \sum_{t=1}^{n} x_t \\ \sum_{t=1}^{n} x_t & \sum_{t=1}^{n} x_t^2 \end{bmatrix} \begin{bmatrix} \beta_1 \\ \beta_2 \end{bmatrix} = \begin{bmatrix} \sum_{t=1}^{n} y_t \\ \sum_{t=1}^{n} x_t y_t \end{bmatrix}. \tag{1.43}$$

Equations (1.43) can be rewritten much more compactly. As we saw in the last section, the model (1.01) is simply a special case of the **multiple linear regression model**

$$\boldsymbol{y} = \boldsymbol{X\beta} + \boldsymbol{u}, \tag{1.44}$$

where the n–vector $\boldsymbol{y}$ has typical element y_t, the k–vector $\boldsymbol{\beta}$ has typical element β_i, and, in general, the matrix $\boldsymbol{X}$ is $n \times k$. In this case, $\boldsymbol{X}$ is $n \times 2$; it can be written as $\boldsymbol{X} = [\boldsymbol{\iota} \;\; \boldsymbol{x}]$, where $\boldsymbol{\iota}$ denotes a column of 1s, and $\boldsymbol{x}$ denotes a column with typical element x_t. Thus, recalling (1.29), we see that

$$\boldsymbol{X}^{\top}\boldsymbol{y} = \begin{bmatrix} \sum_{t=1}^{n} y_t \\ \sum_{t=1}^{n} x_t y_t \end{bmatrix}$$

and

$$\boldsymbol{X}^{\top}\boldsymbol{X} = \begin{bmatrix} n & \sum_{t=1}^{n} x_t \\ \sum_{t=1}^{n} x_t & \sum_{t=1}^{n} x_t^2 \end{bmatrix}.$$

These are the principal quantities that appear in the equations (1.43). Thus it is clear that we can rewrite those equations as

$$\boldsymbol{X}^{\top}\boldsymbol{X\beta} = \boldsymbol{X}^{\top}\boldsymbol{y}. \tag{1.45}$$

To find the estimator $\hat{\boldsymbol{\beta}}$ that solves (1.45), we simply multiply it by the inverse of the matrix $\boldsymbol{X}^{\top}\boldsymbol{X}$, assuming that this inverse exists. This yields the famous formula

$$\hat{\boldsymbol{\beta}} = (\boldsymbol{X}^{\top}\boldsymbol{X})^{-1}\boldsymbol{X}^{\top}\boldsymbol{y}. \tag{1.46}$$

The estimator $\hat{\boldsymbol{\beta}}$ given by this formula is generally called the **ordinary least squares**, or **OLS**, estimator for the linear regression model.[5] Why it is called this, rather than the MM estimator, will be explained shortly.

Estimating the Multiple Linear Regression Model

The formula (1.46) gives us the OLS, and MM, estimator for the simple linear regression model (1.01), but in fact it does far more than that. As we now show, it also gives us the MM estimator for the multiple linear regression model (1.44). Since each of the explanatory variables is required to be in the information set Ω_t, we have, for $i = 1, \ldots, k$,

$$\mathrm{E}(x_{ti}\,u_t) = 0.$$

[5] Econometricians generally make a distinction between an **estimate**, which is simply a number used to estimate some parameter, normally based on a particular data set, and an **estimator**, which is a rule, such as (1.46), for obtaining estimates from any set of data.

In the corresponding sample mean form, this yields

$$\frac{1}{n}\sum_{t=1}^{n} x_{ti}(y_t - \boldsymbol{X}_t\boldsymbol{\beta}) = 0; \tag{1.47}$$

recall from equation (1.34) that $\boldsymbol{X}_t$ denotes the tth row of $\boldsymbol{X}$. As i varies from 1 to k, equation (1.47) yields k equations for the k unknown components of $\boldsymbol{\beta}$. In most cases, there is a constant, which we may take to be the first regressor. If so, $x_{t1} = 1$, and the first of these equations simply says that the sample mean of the error terms is 0.

In matrix form, after multiplying them by n, the k equations of (1.47) can be written as

$$\boldsymbol{X}^\top(\boldsymbol{y} - \boldsymbol{X}\boldsymbol{\beta}) = \mathbf{0}. \tag{1.48}$$

The notation $\mathbf{0}$ is used to signify a **zero vector**, here a k–vector, each element of which is zero. Equations (1.48) are clearly equivalent to equations (1.45). Thus solving them yields the estimator (1.46), which applies no matter what the number of regressors.

It is easy to see that the OLS estimator (1.46) depends on $\boldsymbol{y}$ and $\boldsymbol{X}$ exclusively through a number of scalar products. Each column $\boldsymbol{x}_i$ of the matrix $\boldsymbol{X}$ corresponds to one of the regressors, as does each row $\boldsymbol{x}_i^\top$ of the transposed matrix $\boldsymbol{X}^\top$. Thus we can write $\boldsymbol{X}^\top\boldsymbol{y}$ as

$$\boldsymbol{X}^\top\boldsymbol{y} = \begin{bmatrix} \boldsymbol{x}_1^\top \\ \boldsymbol{x}_2^\top \\ \vdots \\ \boldsymbol{x}_k^\top \end{bmatrix} \boldsymbol{y} = \begin{bmatrix} \boldsymbol{x}_1^\top\boldsymbol{y} \\ \boldsymbol{x}_2^\top\boldsymbol{y} \\ \vdots \\ \boldsymbol{x}_k^\top\boldsymbol{y} \end{bmatrix}.$$

The elements of the rightmost expression here are just the scalar products of the regressors $\boldsymbol{x}_i$ with the regressand $\boldsymbol{y}$. Similarly, we can write $\boldsymbol{X}^\top\boldsymbol{X}$ as

$$\boldsymbol{X}^\top\boldsymbol{X} = \begin{bmatrix} \boldsymbol{x}_1^\top \\ \boldsymbol{x}_2^\top \\ \vdots \\ \boldsymbol{x}_k^\top \end{bmatrix} \begin{bmatrix} \boldsymbol{x}_1 & \boldsymbol{x}_2 & \cdots & \boldsymbol{x}_k \end{bmatrix} = \begin{bmatrix} \boldsymbol{x}_1^\top\boldsymbol{x}_1 & \boldsymbol{x}_1^\top\boldsymbol{x}_2 & \cdots & \boldsymbol{x}_1^\top\boldsymbol{x}_k \\ \boldsymbol{x}_2^\top\boldsymbol{x}_1 & \boldsymbol{x}_2^\top\boldsymbol{x}_2 & \cdots & \boldsymbol{x}_2^\top\boldsymbol{x}_k \\ \vdots & \vdots & \ddots & \vdots \\ \boldsymbol{x}_k^\top\boldsymbol{x}_1 & \boldsymbol{x}_k^\top\boldsymbol{x}_2 & \cdots & \boldsymbol{x}_k^\top\boldsymbol{x}_k \end{bmatrix}.$$

Once more, all the elements of the rightmost expression are scalar products of pairs of regressors. Since $\boldsymbol{X}^\top\boldsymbol{X}$ can be expressed exclusively in terms of scalar products of the variables of the regression, the same is true of its inverse, the elements of which are in general complicated functions of those scalar products. Thus $\hat{\boldsymbol{\beta}}$ is a function solely of scalar products of pairs of variables.

Least-Squares Estimation

We have derived the OLS estimator (1.46) by using the method of moments. Deriving it in this way has at least two major advantages. Firstly, the method of moments is a very general and very powerful principle of estimation, one that we will encounter again and again throughout this book. Secondly, by using the method of moments, we were able to obtain (1.46) without making any use of calculus. However, as we have already remarked, (1.46) is generally referred to as the OLS estimator, not the MM estimator. It is interesting to see why this is so.

For the multiple linear regression model (1.44), the expression $y_t - \boldsymbol{X}_t\boldsymbol{\beta}$ is equal to the error term for the tth observation, but only if the correct value of the parameter vector $\boldsymbol{\beta}$ is used. If the same expression is thought of as a function of $\boldsymbol{\beta}$, with $\boldsymbol{\beta}$ allowed to vary arbitrarily, then it is called a **residual**, more specifically, the residual associated with the tth observation. Similarly, the n–vector $\boldsymbol{y} - \boldsymbol{X}\boldsymbol{\beta}$ is called the vector of residuals. The sum of the squares of the components of the vector of residuals is called the **sum of squared residuals**, or **SSR**. Since this sum is a scalar, the sum of squared residuals is a scalar-valued function of the k–vector $\boldsymbol{\beta}$:

$$\mathrm{SSR}(\boldsymbol{\beta}) = \sum_{t=1}^{n} (y_t - \boldsymbol{X}_t\boldsymbol{\beta})^2. \tag{1.49}$$

The notation here emphasizes the fact that this function can be computed for arbitrary values of the argument $\boldsymbol{\beta}$ purely in terms of the observed data $\boldsymbol{y}$ and $\boldsymbol{X}$.

The idea of **least-squares** estimation is to minimize the sum of squared residuals associated with a regression model. At this point, it may not be at all clear why we would wish to do such a thing. However, it can be shown that the parameter vector $\hat{\boldsymbol{\beta}}$ which minimizes (1.49) is the same as the MM estimator (1.46). This being so, we will regularly use the traditional terminology associated with linear regressions, based on least squares. Thus, the parameter estimates which are the components of the vector $\hat{\boldsymbol{\beta}}$ that minimizes the SSR (1.49) are called the **least-squares estimates**, and the corresponding vector of residuals is called the vector of **least-squares residuals**. When least squares is used to estimate a linear regression model like (1.01), it is called **ordinary least squares**, or **OLS**, to distinguish it from other varieties of least squares that we will encounter later, such as nonlinear least squares (Chapter 6) and generalized least squares (Chapter 7).

Consider briefly the simplest case of (1.01), in which $\beta_2 = 0$ and the model contains only a constant term. Expression (1.49) becomes

$$\mathrm{SSR}(\beta_1) = \sum_{t=1}^{n} (y_t - \beta_1)^2 = \sum_{t=1}^{n} y_t^2 + n\beta_1^2 - 2\beta_1 \sum_{t=1}^{n} y_t. \tag{1.50}$$

Differentiating the rightmost expression in equations (1.50) with respect to β_1 and setting the derivative equal to zero gives the following first-order condition for a minimum of the sum of squared residuals:

$$\frac{\partial \text{SSR}}{\partial \beta_1} = 2\beta_1 n - 2\sum_{t=1}^{n} y_t = 0. \tag{1.51}$$

For this simple model, the matrix $\boldsymbol{X}$ consists solely of the constant vector, $\boldsymbol{\iota}$. Therefore, by (1.29), $\boldsymbol{X}^\top\boldsymbol{X} = \boldsymbol{\iota}^\top\boldsymbol{\iota} = n$, and $\boldsymbol{X}^\top\boldsymbol{y} = \boldsymbol{\iota}^\top\boldsymbol{y} = \sum_{t=1}^{n} y_t$. Thus, if the first-order condition (1.51) is multiplied by one-half, it can be rewritten as $\boldsymbol{\iota}^\top\boldsymbol{\iota}\beta_1 = \boldsymbol{\iota}^\top\boldsymbol{y}$, which is clearly just a special case of (1.45). Solving (1.51) for β_1 yields the sample mean of the y_t,

$$\hat{\beta}_1 = \frac{1}{n}\sum_{t=1}^{n} y_t = (\boldsymbol{\iota}^\top\boldsymbol{\iota})^{-1}\boldsymbol{\iota}^\top\boldsymbol{y}. \tag{1.52}$$

We already saw, in equation (1.39), that this is the MM estimator for the model with $\beta_2 = 0$. The rightmost expression in (1.52) makes it clear that the sample mean is just a special case of the famous formula (1.46).

Not surprisingly, the OLS and MM estimators are also equivalent in the multiple linear regression model. For this model,

$$\text{SSR}(\boldsymbol{\beta}) = (\boldsymbol{y} - \boldsymbol{X}\boldsymbol{\beta})^\top(\boldsymbol{y} - \boldsymbol{X}\boldsymbol{\beta}). \tag{1.53}$$

If this inner product is written out in terms of the scalar components of $\boldsymbol{y}$, $\boldsymbol{X}$, and $\boldsymbol{\beta}$, it is easy enough to show that the first-order conditions for minimizing the SSR (1.53) can be written as (1.45); see Exercise 1.22. Thus we conclude that (1.46) provides a general formula for the OLS estimator $\hat{\boldsymbol{\beta}}$ in the multiple linear regression model.

Final Remarks

We have seen that it is perfectly easy to obtain an algebraic expression, (1.46), for the OLS estimator $\hat{\boldsymbol{\beta}}$. With modern computers and appropriate software, it is also easy to obtain OLS estimates numerically, even for regressions with millions of observations and dozens of explanatory variables; the time-honored term for doing so is "running a regression." What is not so easy, and will occupy us for most of the next four chapters, is to understand the properties of these estimates.

We will be concerned with two types of properties. The first type, **numerical properties**, arise as a consequence of the way that OLS estimates are obtained. These properties hold for every set of OLS estimates, no matter how the data were generated. That they hold for any data set can easily be verified by direct calculation. The numerical properties of OLS will be discussed in Chapter 2. The second type, **statistical properties**, depend on the way in which the data were generated. They can be verified theoretically, under certain assumptions, and they can be illustrated by simulation, but we can never prove that they are true for any given data set. The statistical properties of OLS will be discussed in detail in Chapters 3, 4, and 5.

Readers who seek a deeper treatment of the topics dealt with in the first two sections may wish to consult Gallant (1997), Mittelhammer (1996), or some other text on mathematical statistics.

1.6 Notes on the Exercises

Each chapter of this book is followed by a set of exercises. These exercises are of various sorts, and they have various intended functions. Some are, quite simply, just for practice. Others have a tidying-up function. Details left out of the discussions in the main text are taken up, and conscientious readers can check that unproved claims made in the text are in fact justified. Some of these exercises are particularly challenging. They are starred, and solutions to them are available on the book's website.

A number of exercises serve chiefly to extend the material presented in the chapter. In many cases, the new material in such exercises recurs later in the book, and it is hoped that readers who have worked through them will follow later discussions more easily. A case in point concerns the **bootstrap**. Some of the exercises in this chapter and the next two are designed to familiarize readers with the tools that are used to implement the bootstrap, so that, when it is introduced formally in Chapter 4, the bootstrap will appear as a natural development.

Many of the exercises require the reader to make use of a computer, sometimes to compute estimates and test statistics using real or simulated data, and sometimes for the purpose of doing simulations. There are a great many computer packages that are capable of doing the things we ask for in the exercises, and it seems unnecessary to make any specific recommendations as to what software would be best. Besides, we expect that many readers will already have developed their own personal preferences for software packages, and we know better than to try to upset such preferences.

Some exercises require, not only a computer, but also actual (or simulated) economic data. It cannot be stressed enough that econometrics is an empirical discipline, and that the analysis of economic data is its *raison d'être*. All of the data files needed for the exercises are available from the website for this book. The address is

http://www.econ.queensu.ca/ETM/ .

This website will ultimately contain corrections and updates to the book as well as the data and the solutions to the starred exercises.

1.7 Exercises

1.1 Consider a sample of n observations, $y_1, y_2, \ldots, y_n$, on some random variable Y. The **empirical distribution function**, or **EDF**, of this sample is a discrete distribution with n possible points. These points are just the n observed points, $y_1, y_2, \ldots, y_n$. Each point is assigned the same probability, which is just $1/n$, in order to ensure that all the probabilities sum to 1.

Compute the expectation of the discrete distribution characterized by the EDF, and show that it is equal to the **sample mean**, that is, the unweighted average of the n sample points, $y_1, y_2, \ldots, y_n$.

1.2 A random variable computed as the ratio of two independent standard normal variables follows what is called the **Cauchy distribution**. It can be shown that the density of this distribution is

$$f(x) = \frac{1}{\pi(1+x^2)}.$$

Show that the Cauchy distribution has no first moment, which means that its expectation does not exist.

Use your favorite random number generator to generate samples of 10, 100, 1,000, and 10,000 drawings from the Cauchy distribution, and as many intermediate values of n as you have patience or computer time for. For each sample, compute the sample mean. Do these sample means seem to converge to zero as the sample size increases? Repeat the exercise with drawings from the standard normal density. Do these sample means tend to converge to zero as the sample size increases?

1.3 Consider two events A and B such that $A \subset B$. Compute $\Pr(A \mid B)$ in terms of $\Pr(A)$ and $\Pr(B)$. Interpret the result.

1.4 Prove **Bayes' Theorem**. This famous theorem states that, for any two events A and B with nonzero probabilities,

$$\Pr(A \mid B) = \frac{\Pr(B \mid A)\Pr(A)}{\Pr(B)}.$$

Another form of the theorem deals with two continuous random variables X_1 and X_2, which have a joint density $f(x_1, x_2)$. Show that, for any values x_1 and x_2 that are permissible for X_1 and X_2, respectively,

$$f(x_1 \mid x_2) = \frac{f(x_2 \mid x_1)f(x_1)}{f(x_2)}.$$

1.5 Suppose that X and Y are two binary random variables. Their joint distribution is given in the following table.

	$Y=0$	$Y=1$
$X=0$	.16	.37
$X=1$	.29	.18

What is the marginal distribution of Y? What is the distribution of Y conditional on $X = 0$? What is the distribution of Y conditional on $X = 1$?

Demonstrate the Law of Iterated Expectations explicitly by showing that $\mathrm{E}(\mathrm{E}(X \mid Y)) = \mathrm{E}(X)$. Let $h(Y) = Y^3$. Show explicitly that $\mathrm{E}(Xh(Y) \mid Y) = h(Y)\mathrm{E}(X \mid Y)$ in this case.

1.6 Using expression (1.06) for the density $\phi(x)$ of the standard normal distribution, show that the derivative of $\phi(x)$ is the function $-x\phi(x)$, and that the second derivative is $(x^2 - 1)\phi(x)$. Use these facts to show that the expectation of a standard normal random variable is 0, and that its variance is 1. These two properties account for the use of the term "standard."

1.7 A normally distributed random variable can have any mean μ and any positive variance σ^2. Such a random variable is said to follow the $\mathrm{N}(\mu, \sigma^2)$ distribution. A standard normal variable therefore has the $\mathrm{N}(0, 1)$ distribution. Suppose that X has the standard normal distribution. Show that the random variable $Z \equiv \mu + \sigma X$ has mean μ and variance σ^2.

1.8 Find the CDF of the $\mathrm{N}(\mu, \sigma^2)$ distribution in terms of $\Phi(\cdot)$, the CDF of the standard normal distribution. Differentiate your answer so as to obtain the PDF of $\mathrm{N}(\mu, \sigma^2)$.

1.9 If two random variables X_1 and X_2 are statistically independent, show that $\mathrm{E}(X_1 \mid X_2) = \mathrm{E}(X_1)$.

1.10 The **covariance** of two random variables X_1 and X_2, which is often written as $\mathrm{Cov}(X_1, X_2)$, is defined as the expectation of the product of $X_1 - \mathrm{E}(X_1)$ and $X_2 - \mathrm{E}(X_2)$. Consider a random variable X_1 with mean zero. Show that the covariance of X_1 and any other random variable X_2, whether it has mean zero or not, is just the expectation of the product of X_1 and X_2.

⋆1.11 Show that the covariance of the random variable $\mathrm{E}(X_1 \mid X_2)$ and the random variable $X_1 - \mathrm{E}(X_1 \mid X_2)$ is zero. It is easiest to show this result by first showing that it is true when the covariance is computed conditional on X_2.

⋆1.12 Show that the variance of the random variable $X_1 - \mathrm{E}(X_1 \mid X_2)$ cannot be greater than the variance of X_1, and that the two variances are equal if X_1 and X_2 are independent. This result shows how one random variable can be informative about another: Conditioning on it reduces variance unless the two variables are independent.

1.13 Prove that, if X_1 and X_2 are statistically independent, $\mathrm{Cov}(X_1, X_2) = 0$.

⋆1.14 Let a random variable X_1 be distributed as $\mathrm{N}(0, 1)$. Now suppose that a second random variable, X_2, is constructed as the product of X_1 and an independent random variable Z, which equals 1 with probability $1/2$ and -1 with probability $1/2$.

What is the (marginal) distribution of X_2? What is the covariance between X_1 and X_2? What is the distribution of X_1 conditional on X_2?

1.15 Consider the linear regression models

$$\begin{aligned} H_1: \quad & y_t = \beta_1 + \beta_2 x_t + u_t \quad \text{and} \\ H_2: \quad & \log y_t = \gamma_1 + \gamma_2 \log x_t + u_t. \end{aligned}$$

Suppose that the data are actually generated by H_2, with $\gamma_1 = 1.5$ and $\gamma_2 = 0.5$, and that the value of x_t varies from 10 to 110 with an average value of 60. Ignore the error terms and consider the deterministic relations between y_t and x_t implied by the two models. Find the values of β_1 and β_2 that make the relation given by H_1 have the same level and the same value of dy_t/dx_t as the level and value of dy_t/dx_t implied by the relation given by H_2 when it is evaluated at the average value of the regressor.

Using the deterministic relations, plot y_t as a function of x_t for both models for $10 \leq x_t \leq 110$. Also plot $\log y_t$ as a function of $\log x_t$ for both models for the same range of x_t. How well do the two models approximate each other in each of the plots?

1.16 Consider two matrices $\boldsymbol{A}$ and $\boldsymbol{B}$ of dimensions such that the product $\boldsymbol{AB}$ exists. Show that the ith row of $\boldsymbol{AB}$ is the matrix product of the ith row of $\boldsymbol{A}$ with the entire matrix $\boldsymbol{B}$. Show that this result implies that the ith row of a product $\boldsymbol{ABC}\ldots$, with arbitrarily many factors, is the product of the ith row of $\boldsymbol{A}$ with $\boldsymbol{BC}\ldots$.

What is the corresponding result for the columns of $\boldsymbol{AB}$? What is the corresponding result for the columns of $\boldsymbol{ABC}\ldots$?

1.17 Consider two invertible square matrices $\boldsymbol{A}$ and $\boldsymbol{B}$, of the same dimensions. Show that the inverse of the product $\boldsymbol{AB}$ exists and is given by the formula

$$(\boldsymbol{AB})^{-1} = \boldsymbol{B}^{-1}\boldsymbol{A}^{-1}.$$

This shows that there is a **reversal rule** for inverses as well as for transposes; see (1.30).

1.18 Show that the transpose of the product of an arbitrary number of factors is the product of the transposes of the individual factors in completely reversed order:

$$(\boldsymbol{ABC}\cdots)^{\top} = \cdots \boldsymbol{C}^{\top}\boldsymbol{B}^{\top}\boldsymbol{A}^{\top}.$$

Show also that an analogous result holds for the inverse of the product of an arbitrary number of factors.

1.19 Consider the following example of multiplying partitioned matrices:

$$\begin{bmatrix} \boldsymbol{A}_{11} & \boldsymbol{A}_{12} \\ \boldsymbol{A}_{21} & \boldsymbol{A}_{22} \end{bmatrix} \begin{bmatrix} \boldsymbol{B}_{11} & \boldsymbol{B}_{12} \\ \boldsymbol{B}_{21} & \boldsymbol{B}_{22} \end{bmatrix} = \begin{bmatrix} \boldsymbol{A}_{11}\boldsymbol{B}_{11} + \boldsymbol{A}_{12}\boldsymbol{B}_{21} & \boldsymbol{A}_{11}\boldsymbol{B}_{12} + \boldsymbol{A}_{12}\boldsymbol{B}_{22} \\ \boldsymbol{A}_{21}\boldsymbol{B}_{11} + \boldsymbol{A}_{22}\boldsymbol{B}_{21} & \boldsymbol{A}_{21}\boldsymbol{B}_{12} + \boldsymbol{A}_{22}\boldsymbol{B}_{22} \end{bmatrix}.$$

Check all the expressions on the right-hand side, verifying that all products are well defined and that all sums are of matrices of the same dimensions.

1.20 Suppose that $\boldsymbol{X} = [\boldsymbol{\iota}\ \boldsymbol{X}_1\ \boldsymbol{X}_2]$, where $\boldsymbol{X}$ is $n \times k$, $\boldsymbol{\iota}$ is an n–vector of 1s, $\boldsymbol{X}_1$ is $n \times k_1$, and $\boldsymbol{X}_2$ is $n \times k_2$. What is the matrix $\boldsymbol{X}^{\top}\boldsymbol{X}$ in terms of the components of $\boldsymbol{X}$? What are the dimensions of its component matrices? What is the element in the upper left-hand corner of $\boldsymbol{X}^{\top}\boldsymbol{X}$ equal to?

1.21 Fix a sample size of $n = 100$, and simulate the very simplest regression model, namely, $y_t = \beta + u_t$. Set $\beta = 1$, and let the error terms u_t be drawings from the standard normal distribution. Compute the sample mean of the y_t,

$$\bar{y} \equiv \frac{1}{n}\sum_{t=1}^{n} y_t.$$

Use your favorite econometrics software package to run a regression with $\boldsymbol{y}$, the 100×1 vector with typical element y_t, as the dependent variable, and a constant as the sole explanatory variable. Show that the OLS estimate of the constant is equal to the sample mean. Why is this a necessary consequence of the formula (1.46)?

1.22 For the multiple linear regression model (1.44), the sum of squared residuals can be written as

$$\mathrm{SSR}(\boldsymbol{\beta}) = \sum_{t=1}^{n} (y_t - \boldsymbol{X}_t\boldsymbol{\beta})^2 = (\boldsymbol{y} - \boldsymbol{X\beta})^\top(\boldsymbol{y} - \boldsymbol{X\beta}).$$

Show that, if we minimize $\mathrm{SSR}(\boldsymbol{\beta})$ with respect to $\boldsymbol{\beta}$, the minimizing value of $\boldsymbol{\beta}$ is $\hat{\boldsymbol{\beta}}$, the OLS estimator given by (1.46). The easiest way is to show that the first-order conditions for a minimum are exactly the equations (1.47), or (1.48), that arise from MM estimation. This can be done without using matrix calculus.

1.23 The file **consumption.data** contains data on real personal disposable income and consumption expenditures in Canada, seasonally adjusted in 1986 dollars, from the first quarter of 1947 until the last quarter of 1996. The simplest imaginable model of the Canadian consumption function would have consumption expenditures as the dependent variable, and a constant and personal disposable income as explanatory variables. Run this regression for the period 1953:1 to 1996:4. What is your estimate of the marginal propensity to consume out of disposable income?

Plot a graph of the OLS residuals for the consumption function regression against time. All modern regression packages will generate these residuals for you on request. Does the appearance of the residuals suggest that this model of the consumption function is well specified?

1.24 Simulate the consumption function model you have just estimated in exercise 1.23 for the same sample period, using the actual data on disposable income. For the parameters, use the OLS estimates obtained in exercise 1.23. For the error terms, use drawings from the $\mathrm{N}(0, s^2)$ distribution, where s^2 is the estimate of the error variance produced by the regression package.

Next, run a regression using the simulated consumption data as the dependent variable and the constant and disposable income as explanatory variables. Are the parameter estimates the same as those obtained using the real data? Why or why not?

Plot the residuals from the regression with simulated data. Does the plot look substantially different from the one obtained using the real data? It should!

Chapter 2

The Geometry of Linear Regression

2.1 Introduction

In Chapter 1, we introduced regression models, both linear and nonlinear, and discussed how to estimate linear regression models by using the method of moments. We saw that all n observations of a linear regression model with k regressors can be written as

$$\boldsymbol{y} = \boldsymbol{X\beta} + \boldsymbol{u}, \tag{2.01}$$

where $\boldsymbol{y}$ and $\boldsymbol{u}$ are n–vectors, $\boldsymbol{X}$ is an $n \times k$ matrix, one column of which may be a constant term, and $\boldsymbol{\beta}$ is a k–vector. We also saw that the MM estimates of the vector $\boldsymbol{\beta}$, which are usually called the ordinary least-squares or OLS estimates, are

$$\hat{\boldsymbol{\beta}} = (\boldsymbol{X}^\top\boldsymbol{X})^{-1}\boldsymbol{X}^\top\boldsymbol{y}. \tag{2.02}$$

In this chapter, we will be concerned with the **numerical properties** of these OLS estimates. We refer to certain properties of estimates as "numerical" if they have nothing to do with how the data were actually generated. Such properties hold for every set of data by virtue of the way in which $\hat{\boldsymbol{\beta}}$ is computed, and the fact that they hold can always be verified by direct calculation. In contrast, the **statistical properties** of OLS estimates, which will be discussed in Chapter 3, necessarily depend on unverifiable assumptions about how the data were generated, and they can never be verified for any actual data set.

In order to understand the numerical properties of OLS estimates, it is useful to look at them from the perspective of Euclidean geometry. This geometrical interpretation is remarkably simple. Essentially, it involves using Pythagoras' Theorem and a little bit of high-school trigonometry in the context of finite-dimensional vector spaces. Although this approach is simple, it is very powerful. Once one has a thorough grasp of the geometry involved in ordinary least squares, one can often save oneself many tedious lines of algebra by a simple geometrical argument. We will encounter many examples of this throughout the book.

In the next section, we review some relatively elementary material on the geometry of vector spaces and Pythagoras' Theorem. In Section 2.3, we then discuss the most important numerical properties of OLS estimation from a geometrical perspective. In Section 2.4, we introduce an extremely useful result called the FWL Theorem, and in Section 2.5 we present a number of applications of this theorem. Finally, in Section 2.6, we discuss how and to what extent individual observations influence parameter estimates.

2.2 The Geometry of Vector Spaces

In Section 1.4, an n-vector was defined as a column vector with n elements, that is, an $n \times 1$ matrix. The elements of such a vector are real numbers. The usual notation for the **real line** is $\mathbb{R}$, and it is therefore natural to denote the set of n-vectors as $\mathbb{R}^n$. However, in order to use the insights of Euclidean geometry to enhance our understanding of the algebra of vectors and matrices, it is desirable to introduce the notion of a **Euclidean space** in n dimensions, which we will denote as E^n. The difference between $\mathbb{R}^n$ and E^n is not that they consist of different sorts of vectors, but rather that a wider set of operations is defined on E^n. A shorthand way of saying that a vector $\boldsymbol{x}$ belongs to an n-dimensional Euclidean space is to write $\boldsymbol{x} \in E^n$.

Addition and subtraction of vectors in E^n is no different from the addition and subtraction of $n \times 1$ matrices discussed in Section 1.4. The same thing is true of multiplication by a scalar in E^n. The final operation essential to E^n is that of the scalar or inner product. For any two vectors $\boldsymbol{x}, \boldsymbol{y} \in E^n$, their scalar product is

$$\langle \boldsymbol{x}, \boldsymbol{y} \rangle \equiv \boldsymbol{x}^\top \boldsymbol{y}.$$

The notation on the left is generally used in the context of the geometry of vectors, while the notation on the right is generally used in the context of matrix algebra. Note that $\langle \boldsymbol{x}, \boldsymbol{y} \rangle = \langle \boldsymbol{y}, \boldsymbol{x} \rangle$, since $\boldsymbol{x}^\top \boldsymbol{y} = \boldsymbol{y}^\top \boldsymbol{x}$. Thus the scalar product is **commutative**.

The scalar product is what allows us to make a close connection between n-vectors considered as matrices and considered as geometrical objects. It allows us to define the **length** of any vector in E^n. The length, or **norm**, of a vector $\boldsymbol{x}$ is simply

$$\|\boldsymbol{x}\| \equiv (\boldsymbol{x}^\top \boldsymbol{x})^{1/2}.$$

This is just the square root of the inner product of $\boldsymbol{x}$ with itself. In scalar terms, it is

$$\|\boldsymbol{x}\| \equiv \Big(\sum_{i=1}^{n} x_i^2\Big)^{1/2}. \qquad (2.03)$$

Pythagoras' Theorem

The definition (2.03) is inspired by the celebrated theorem of Pythagoras, which says that the square on the longest side of a right-angled triangle is

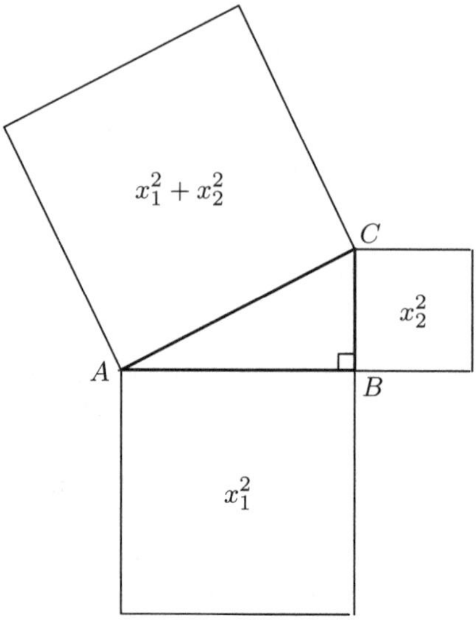

Figure 2.1 Pythagoras' Theorem

equal to the sum of the squares on the other two sides. This longest side is called the **hypotenuse**. Pythagoras' Theorem is illustrated in Figure 2.1. The figure shows a right-angled triangle, ABC, with hypotenuse AC and two other sides, AB and BC, of lengths x_1 and x_2, respectively. The squares on each of the three sides of the triangle are drawn, and the area of the square on the hypotenuse is shown as $x_1^2 + x_2^2$, in accordance with the theorem.

A beautiful proof of Pythagoras' Theorem, not often found in geometry texts, is shown in Figure 2.2. Two squares of equal area are drawn. Each square contains four copies of the same right-angled triangle. The square on the left also contains the squares on the two shorter sides of the triangle, while the

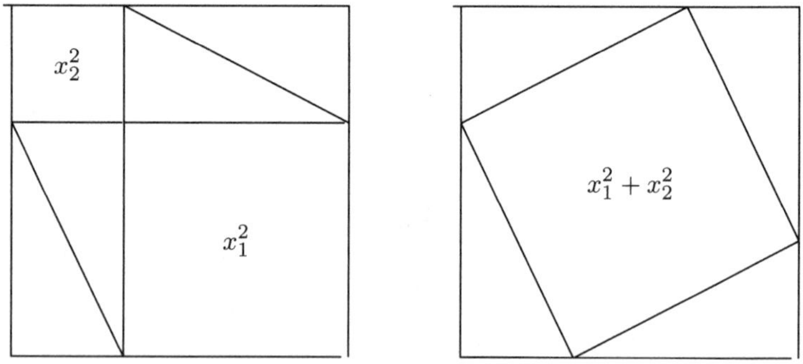

Figure 2.2 Proof of Pythagoras' Theorem

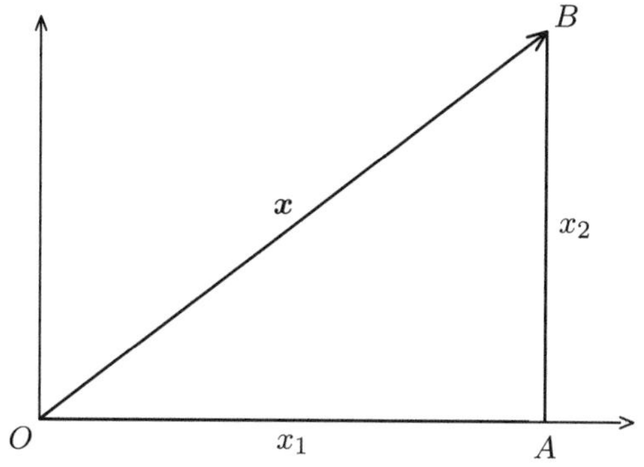

Figure 2.3 A vector $\boldsymbol{x}$ in E^2

square on the right contains the square on the hypotenuse. The theorem follows at once.

Any vector $\boldsymbol{x} \in E^2$ has two components, usually denoted as x_1 and x_2. These two components can be interpreted as the **Cartesian coordinates** of the vector in the plane. The situation is illustrated in Figure 2.3. With O as the origin of the coordinates, a right-angled triangle is formed by the lines OA, AB, and OB. The length of the horizontal side of the triangle, OA, is the horizontal coordinate x_1. The length of the vertical side, AB, is the vertical coordinate x_2. Thus the point B has Cartesian coordinates (x_1, x_2). The vector $\boldsymbol{x}$ itself is usually represented as the hypotenuse of the triangle, OB, that is, the directed line (depicted as an arrow) joining the origin to the point B, with coordinates (x_1, x_2). Pythagoras' Theorem tells us that the length of the vector $\boldsymbol{x}$, which is the hypotenuse of the triangle, is $(x_1^2 + x_2^2)^{1/2}$. By (2.03), this is what $\|\boldsymbol{x}\|$ is equal to when $n = 2$.

Vector Geometry in Two Dimensions

Let $\boldsymbol{x}$ and $\boldsymbol{y}$ be two vectors in E^2, with components (x_1, x_2) and (y_1, y_2), respectively. Then, by the rules of matrix addition, the components of $\boldsymbol{x} + \boldsymbol{y}$ are $(x_1 + y_1, x_2 + y_2)$. Figure 2.4 shows how the addition of $\boldsymbol{x}$ and $\boldsymbol{y}$ can be performed geometrically in two different ways. The vector $\boldsymbol{x}$ is drawn as the directed line segment, or arrow, from the origin O to the point A with coordinates (x_1, x_2). The vector $\boldsymbol{y}$ can be drawn similarly and represented by the arrow OB. However, we could also draw $\boldsymbol{y}$ starting, not at O, but at the point reached after drawing $\boldsymbol{x}$, namely A. The arrow AC has the same length and direction as OB, and we will see in general that arrows with the same length and direction can be taken to represent the same vector. It is clear by construction that the coordinates of C are $(x_1 + y_1, x_2 + y_2)$, that is, the coordinates of $\boldsymbol{x} + \boldsymbol{y}$. Thus the sum $\boldsymbol{x} + \boldsymbol{y}$ is represented geometrically by the arrow OC.

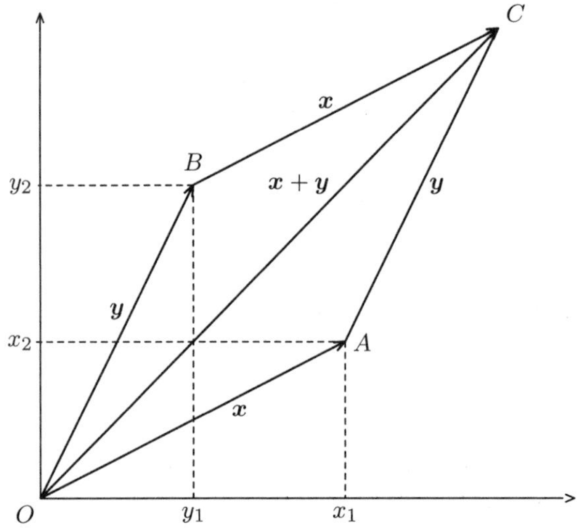

Figure 2.4 Addition of vectors

The classical way of adding vectors geometrically is to form a parallelogram using the line segments OA and OB that represent the two vectors as adjacent sides of the parallelogram. The sum of the two vectors is then the diagonal through O of the resulting parallelogram. It is easy to see that this classical method also gives the result that the sum of the two vectors is represented by the arrow OC, since the figure $OACB$ is just the parallelogram required by the construction, and OC is its diagonal through O. The parallelogram construction also shows clearly that vector addition is commutative, since $\boldsymbol{y} + \boldsymbol{x}$ is represented by OB, for $\boldsymbol{y}$, followed by BC, for $\boldsymbol{x}$. The end result is once more OC.

Multiplying a vector by a scalar is also very easy to represent geometrically. If a vector $\boldsymbol{x}$ with components (x_1, x_2) is multiplied by a scalar α, then $\alpha\boldsymbol{x}$ has components $(\alpha x_1, \alpha x_2)$. This is depicted in Figure 2.5, where $\alpha = 2$. The line segments OA and OB represent $\boldsymbol{x}$ and $\alpha\boldsymbol{x}$, respectively. It is clear that even if we move $\alpha\boldsymbol{x}$ so that it starts somewhere other than O, as with CD in the figure, the vectors $\boldsymbol{x}$ and $\alpha\boldsymbol{x}$ are always **parallel**. If α were negative, then $\alpha\boldsymbol{x}$ would simply point in the opposite direction. Thus, for $\alpha = -2$, $\alpha\boldsymbol{x}$ would be represented by DC, rather than CD.

Another property of multiplication by a scalar is clear from Figure 2.5. By direct calculation,

$$\|\alpha\boldsymbol{x}\| = \langle\alpha\boldsymbol{x}, \alpha\boldsymbol{x}\rangle^{1/2} = |\alpha|\,(\boldsymbol{x}^{\top}\boldsymbol{x})^{1/2} = |\alpha|\,\|\boldsymbol{x}\|. \tag{2.04}$$

Since $\alpha = 2$, OB and CD in the figure are twice as long as OA.

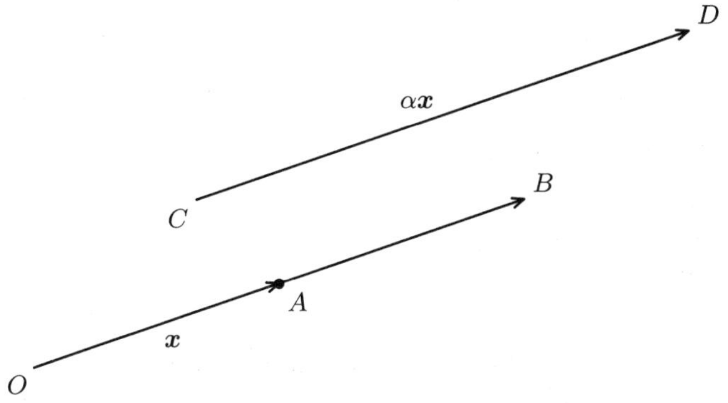

Figure 2.5 Multiplication by a scalar

The Geometry of Scalar Products

The scalar product of two vectors $\boldsymbol{x}$ and $\boldsymbol{y}$, whether in E^2 or E^n, can be expressed geometrically in terms of the lengths of the two vectors and the **angle** between them, and this result will turn out to be very useful. In the case of E^2, it is natural to think of the angle between two vectors as the angle between the two line segments that represent them. As we will now show, it is also quite easy to define the angle between two vectors in E^n.

If the angle between two vectors is 0, they must be **parallel**. The vector $\boldsymbol{y}$ is parallel to the vector $\boldsymbol{x}$ if $\boldsymbol{y} = \alpha\boldsymbol{x}$ for some suitable α. In that event,

$$\langle \boldsymbol{x}, \boldsymbol{y} \rangle = \langle \boldsymbol{x}, \alpha\boldsymbol{x} \rangle = \alpha\boldsymbol{x}^\top\boldsymbol{x} = \alpha\|\boldsymbol{x}\|^2.$$

From (2.04), we know that $\|\boldsymbol{y}\| = |\alpha|\,\|\boldsymbol{x}\|$, and so, if $\alpha > 0$, it follows that

$$\langle \boldsymbol{x}, \boldsymbol{y} \rangle = \|\boldsymbol{x}\|\,\|\boldsymbol{y}\|. \tag{2.05}$$

Of course, this result is true only if $\boldsymbol{x}$ and $\boldsymbol{y}$ are parallel and point in the same direction (rather than in opposite directions).

For simplicity, consider initially two vectors, $\boldsymbol{w}$ and $\boldsymbol{z}$, both of length 1, and let θ denote the angle between them. This is illustrated in Figure 2.6. Suppose that the first vector, $\boldsymbol{w}$, has coordinates $(1, 0)$. It is therefore represented by a horizontal line of length 1 in the figure. Suppose that the second vector, $\boldsymbol{z}$, is also of length 1, that is, $\|\boldsymbol{z}\| = 1$. Then, by elementary trigonometry, the coordinates of $\boldsymbol{z}$ must be $(\cos\theta, \sin\theta)$. To show this, note first that, if so,

$$\|\boldsymbol{z}\|^2 = \cos^2\theta + \sin^2\theta = 1, \tag{2.06}$$

as required. Next, consider the right-angled triangle OAB, in which the hypotenuse OB represents $\boldsymbol{z}$ and is of length 1, by (2.06). The length of the side AB opposite O is $\sin\theta$, the vertical coordinate of $\boldsymbol{z}$. Then the sine of

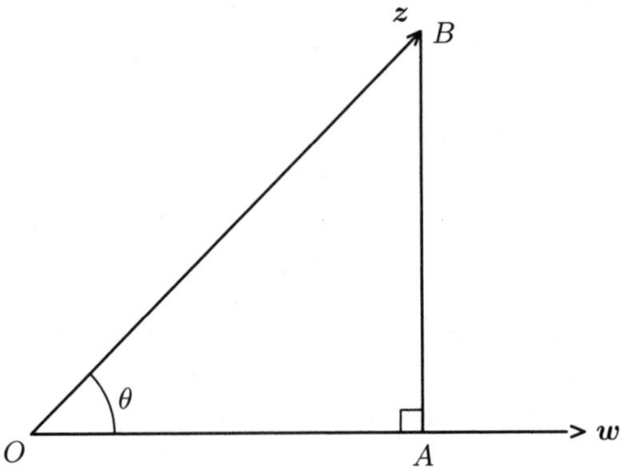

Figure 2.6 The angle between two vectors

the angle BOA is given, by the usual trigonometric rule, by the ratio of the length of the opposite side AB to that of the hypotenuse OB. This ratio is $\sin\theta/1 = \sin\theta$, and so the angle BOA is indeed equal to θ.

Now let us compute the scalar product of $\boldsymbol{w}$ and $\boldsymbol{z}$. It is

$$\langle \boldsymbol{w}, \boldsymbol{z} \rangle = \boldsymbol{w}^\top \boldsymbol{z} = w_1 z_1 + w_2 z_2 = z_1 = \cos\theta,$$

because $w_1 = 1$ and $w_2 = 0$. This result holds for vectors $\boldsymbol{w}$ and $\boldsymbol{z}$ of length 1. More generally, let $\boldsymbol{x} = \alpha\boldsymbol{w}$ and $\boldsymbol{y} = \gamma\boldsymbol{z}$, for positive scalars α and γ. Then $\|\boldsymbol{x}\| = \alpha$ and $\|\boldsymbol{y}\| = \gamma$. Thus we have

$$\langle \boldsymbol{x}, \boldsymbol{y} \rangle = \boldsymbol{x}^\top \boldsymbol{y} = \alpha\gamma \boldsymbol{w}^\top \boldsymbol{z} = \alpha\gamma \langle \boldsymbol{w}, \boldsymbol{z} \rangle.$$

Because $\boldsymbol{x}$ is parallel to $\boldsymbol{w}$, and $\boldsymbol{y}$ is parallel to $\boldsymbol{z}$, the angle between $\boldsymbol{x}$ and $\boldsymbol{y}$ is the same as that between $\boldsymbol{w}$ and $\boldsymbol{z}$, namely θ. Therefore,

$$\langle \boldsymbol{x}, \boldsymbol{y} \rangle = \|\boldsymbol{x}\|\,\|\boldsymbol{y}\| \cos\theta. \tag{2.07}$$

This is the general expression, in geometrical terms, for the scalar product of two vectors. It is true in E^n just as it is in E^2, although we have not proved this. In fact, we have not quite proved (2.07) even for the two-dimensional case, because we made the simplifying assumption that the direction of $\boldsymbol{x}$ and $\boldsymbol{w}$ is horizontal. In Exercise 2.1, we ask the reader to provide a more complete proof.

The cosine of the angle between two vectors provides a natural way to measure how close two vectors are in terms of their directions. Recall that $\cos\theta$ varies between -1 and 1; if we measure angles in radians, $\cos 0 = 1$, $\cos\pi/2 = 0$, and $\cos\pi = -1$. Thus $\cos\theta$ is 1 for vectors that are parallel, 0 for vectors that are at right angles to each other, and -1 for vectors that point in directly opposite directions. If the angle θ between the vectors $\boldsymbol{x}$ and $\boldsymbol{y}$ is a right angle, its cosine is 0, and so, from (2.07), the scalar product $\langle \boldsymbol{x}, \boldsymbol{y} \rangle$ is 0. Conversely, if $\langle \boldsymbol{x}, \boldsymbol{y} \rangle = 0$, then $\cos\theta = 0$ unless $\boldsymbol{x}$ or $\boldsymbol{y}$ is a zero vector. If $\cos\theta = 0$, it follows that $\theta = \pi/2$. Thus, if two nonzero vectors have a zero scalar product, they are at right angles. Such vectors are often said to be **orthogonal**, or, less commonly, **perpendicular**. This definition implies that the zero vector is orthogonal to everything.

Since the cosine function can take on values only between -1 and 1, a consequence of (2.07) is that

$$|\boldsymbol{x}^\top \boldsymbol{y}| \leq \|\boldsymbol{x}\|\,\|\boldsymbol{y}\|. \tag{2.08}$$

This result, which is called the **Cauchy-Schwartz inequality**, says that the inner product of $\boldsymbol{x}$ and $\boldsymbol{y}$ can never be greater than the length of the vector $\boldsymbol{x}$ times the length of the vector $\boldsymbol{y}$. Only if $\boldsymbol{x}$ and $\boldsymbol{y}$ are parallel does the inequality in (2.08) become the equality (2.05). Readers are asked to prove this result in Exercise 2.2.

Subspaces of Euclidean Space

For arbitrary positive integers n, the elements of an n–vector can be thought of as the coordinates of a point in E^n. In particular, in the regression model (2.01), the regressand $\boldsymbol{y}$ and each column of the matrix of regressors $\boldsymbol{X}$ can be thought of as vectors in E^n. This makes it possible to represent a relationship like (2.01) geometrically.

It is obviously impossible to represent all n dimensions of E^n physically when $n > 3$. For the pages of a book, even three dimensions can be too many, although a proper use of perspective drawings can allow three dimensions to be shown. Fortunately, we can represent (2.01) without needing to draw in n dimensions. The key to this is that there are only three vectors in (2.01): $\boldsymbol{y}$, $\boldsymbol{X\beta}$, and $\boldsymbol{u}$. Since only two vectors, $\boldsymbol{X\beta}$ and $\boldsymbol{u}$, appear on the right-hand side of (2.01), only two dimensions are needed to represent it. Because $\boldsymbol{y}$ is equal to $\boldsymbol{X\beta} + \boldsymbol{u}$, these two dimensions suffice for $\boldsymbol{y}$ as well.

To see how this works, we need the concept of a **subspace** of a Euclidean space E^n. Normally, such a subspace has a dimension lower than n. The easiest way to define a subspace of E^n is in terms of a set of **basis vectors**. A subspace that is of particular interest to us is the one for which the columns of $\boldsymbol{X}$ provide the basis vectors. We may denote the k columns of $\boldsymbol{X}$ as $\boldsymbol{x}_1$, $\boldsymbol{x}_2, \ldots \boldsymbol{x}_k$. Then the subspace associated with these k basis vectors is denoted by $\mathcal{S}(\boldsymbol{X})$ or $\mathcal{S}(\boldsymbol{x}_1, \ldots, \boldsymbol{x}_k)$. The basis vectors are said to **span** this subspace, which in general is a k–dimensional subspace.

The subspace $\mathcal{S}(\boldsymbol{x}_1, \ldots, \boldsymbol{x}_k)$ consists of every vector that can be formed as a **linear combination** of the $\boldsymbol{x}_i$, $i = 1, \ldots, k$. Formally, it is defined as

$$\mathcal{S}(\boldsymbol{x}_1, \ldots, \boldsymbol{x}_k) \equiv \Big\{ \boldsymbol{z} \in E^n \;\Big|\; \boldsymbol{z} = \sum_{i=1}^{k} b_i \boldsymbol{x}_i, \quad b_i \in \mathbb{R} \Big\}. \tag{2.09}$$

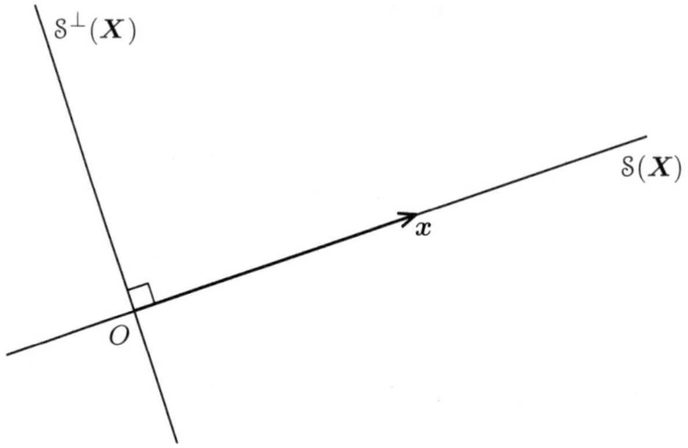

Figure 2.7 The spaces $\mathcal{S}(\boldsymbol{X})$ and $\mathcal{S}^\perp(\boldsymbol{X})$

The subspace defined in (2.09) is called the subspace spanned by the $\boldsymbol{x}_i$, $i = 1, \ldots, k$, or the **column space** of $\boldsymbol{X}$; less formally, it may simply be referred to as the **span** of $\boldsymbol{X}$, or the span of the $\boldsymbol{x}_i$.

The **orthogonal complement** of $\mathcal{S}(\boldsymbol{X})$ in E^n, which is denoted $\mathcal{S}^\perp(\boldsymbol{X})$, is the set of all vectors $\boldsymbol{w}$ in E^n that are orthogonal to everything in $\mathcal{S}(\boldsymbol{X})$. This means that, for every $\boldsymbol{z}$ in $\mathcal{S}(\boldsymbol{X})$, $\langle \boldsymbol{w}, \boldsymbol{z} \rangle = \boldsymbol{w}^\top \boldsymbol{z} = 0$. Formally,

$$\mathcal{S}^\perp(\boldsymbol{X}) \equiv \big\{ \boldsymbol{w} \in E^n \mid \boldsymbol{w}^\top \boldsymbol{z} = 0 \text{ for all } \boldsymbol{z} \in \mathcal{S}(\boldsymbol{X}) \big\}.$$

If the dimension of $\mathcal{S}(\boldsymbol{X})$ is k, then the dimension of $\mathcal{S}^\perp(\boldsymbol{X})$ is $n - k$.

Figure 2.7 illustrates the concepts of a subspace and its orthogonal complement for the simplest case, in which $n = 2$ and $k = 1$. The matrix $\boldsymbol{X}$ has only one column in this case, and it is therefore represented in the figure by a single vector, denoted $\boldsymbol{x}$. As a consequence, $\mathcal{S}(\boldsymbol{X})$ is 1–dimensional, and, since $n = 2$, $\mathcal{S}^\perp(\boldsymbol{X})$ is also 1–dimensional. Notice that $\mathcal{S}(\boldsymbol{X})$ and $\mathcal{S}^\perp(\boldsymbol{X})$ would be the same if $\boldsymbol{x}$ were *any* vector, except for the origin, parallel to the straight line that represents $\mathcal{S}(\boldsymbol{X})$.

Now let us return to E^n. Suppose, to begin with, that $k = 2$. We have two vectors, $\boldsymbol{x}_1$ and $\boldsymbol{x}_2$, which span a subspace of, at most, two dimensions. It is always possible to represent vectors in a 2–dimensional space on a piece of paper, whether that space is E^2 itself or, as in this case, the 2–dimensional subspace of E^n spanned by the vectors $\boldsymbol{x}_1$ and $\boldsymbol{x}_2$. To represent the first vector, $\boldsymbol{x}_1$, we choose an origin and a direction, both of which are entirely arbitrary, and draw an arrow of length $\|\boldsymbol{x}_1\|$ in that direction. Suppose that the origin is the point O in Figure 2.8, and that the direction is the horizontal direction in the plane of the page. Then an arrow to represent $\boldsymbol{x}_1$ can be drawn as shown in the figure. For $\boldsymbol{x}_2$, we compute its length, $\|\boldsymbol{x}_2\|$, and the angle, θ, that it makes with $\boldsymbol{x}_1$. Suppose for now that $\theta \neq 0$. Then we choose

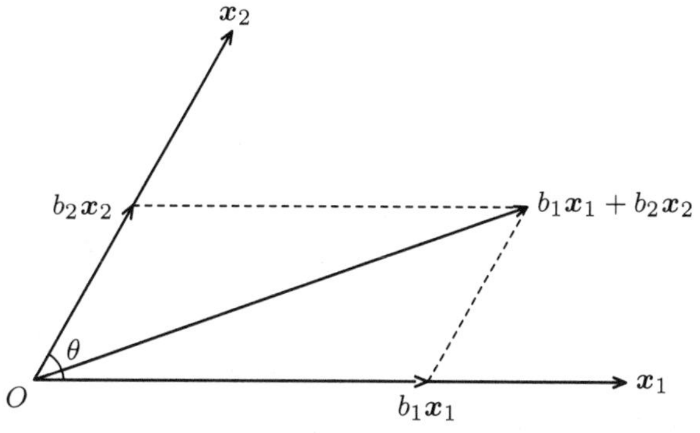

Figure 2.8 A 2-dimensional subspace

as our second dimension the vertical direction in the plane of the page, with the result that we can draw an arrow for $\boldsymbol{x}_2$, as shown.

Any vector in $\mathcal{S}(\boldsymbol{x}_1, \boldsymbol{x}_2)$ can be drawn in the plane of Figure 2.8. Consider, for instance, the linear combination of $\boldsymbol{x}_1$ and $\boldsymbol{x}_2$ given by the expression $\boldsymbol{z} \equiv b_1\boldsymbol{x}_1 + b_2\boldsymbol{x}_2$. We could draw the vector $\boldsymbol{z}$ by computing its length and the angle that it makes with $\boldsymbol{x}_1$. Alternatively, we could apply the rules for adding vectors geometrically that were illustrated in Figure 2.4 to the vectors $b_1\boldsymbol{x}_1$ and $b_2\boldsymbol{x}_2$. This is illustrated in the figure for the case in which $b_1 = {}^2/_3$ and $b_2 = {}^1/_2$.

In precisely the same way, we can represent any three vectors by arrows in 3-dimensional space, but we leave this task to the reader. It will be easier to appreciate the renderings of vectors in three dimensions in perspective that appear later on if one has already tried to draw 3-dimensional pictures, or even to model relationships in three dimensions with the help of a computer.

We can finally represent the regression model (2.01) geometrically. This is done in Figure 2.9. The horizontal direction is chosen for the vector $\boldsymbol{X\beta}$, and then the other two vectors $\boldsymbol{y}$ and $\boldsymbol{u}$ are shown in the plane of the page. It is clear that, by construction, $\boldsymbol{y} = \boldsymbol{X\beta} + \boldsymbol{u}$. Notice that $\boldsymbol{u}$, the error vector, is not orthogonal to $\boldsymbol{X\beta}$. The figure contains no reference to any system of axes, because there would be n of them, and we would not be able to avoid needing n dimensions to treat them all.

Linear Independence

In order to define the OLS estimator by the formula (1.46), it is necessary to assume that the $k \times k$ square matrix $\boldsymbol{X}^\top\boldsymbol{X}$ is invertible, or nonsingular. Equivalently, as we saw in Section 1.4, we may say that $\boldsymbol{X}^\top\boldsymbol{X}$ has full rank. This condition is equivalent to the condition that the columns of $\boldsymbol{X}$ should be **linearly independent**. This is a very important concept for econometrics. Note that the meaning of linear independence is quite different from the meaning

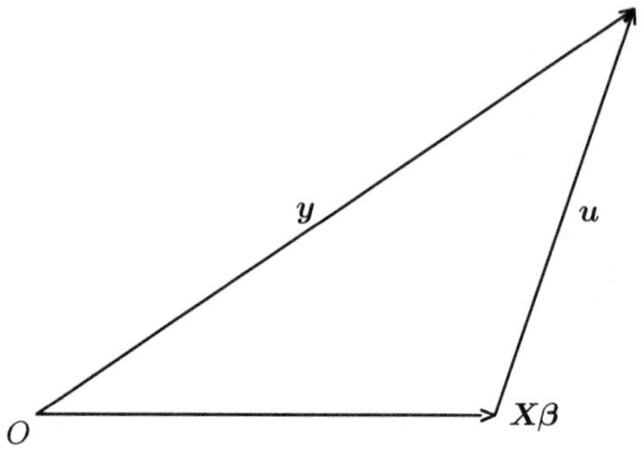

Figure 2.9 The geometry of the linear regression model

of statistical independence, which we discussed in Section 1.2. It is important not to confuse these two concepts.

The vectors $\boldsymbol{x}_1$ through $\boldsymbol{x}_k$ are said to be **linearly dependent** if we can write one of them as a linear combination of the others. In other words, there is a vector $\boldsymbol{x}_j$, $1 \leq j \leq k$, and coefficients c_i such that

$$\boldsymbol{x}_j = \sum_{i \neq j} c_i \boldsymbol{x}_i. \tag{2.10}$$

Another, equivalent, definition is that there exist coefficients b_i, at least one of which is nonzero, such that

$$\sum_{i=1}^{k} b_i \boldsymbol{x}_i = \mathbf{0}. \tag{2.11}$$

Recall that $\mathbf{0}$ denotes the **zero vector**, every component of which is 0. It is clear from the definition (2.11) that, if any of the $\boldsymbol{x}_i$ is itself equal to the zero vector, then the $\boldsymbol{x}_i$ are linearly dependent. If $\boldsymbol{x}_j = \mathbf{0}$, for example, then equation (2.11) is satisfied if we make b_j nonzero and set $b_i = 0$ for all $i \neq j$.

If the vectors $\boldsymbol{x}_i$, $i = 1, \ldots, k$, are the columns of an $n \times k$ matrix $\boldsymbol{X}$, then another way of writing (2.11) is

$$\boldsymbol{X}\boldsymbol{b} = \mathbf{0}, \tag{2.12}$$

where $\boldsymbol{b}$ is a k-vector with typical element b_i. In order to see that (2.11) and (2.12) are equivalent, it is enough to check that the typical elements of the two left-hand sides are the same; see Exercise 2.5. The set of vectors $\boldsymbol{x}_i$, $i = 1, \ldots, k$, is linearly independent if it is not linearly dependent, that is, if there are no coefficients c_i such that (2.10) is true, or (equivalently) no coefficients b_i such that (2.11) is true, or (equivalently, once more) no vector $\boldsymbol{b}$ such that (2.12) is true.

It is easy to show that, if the columns of $\boldsymbol{X}$ are linearly dependent, the matrix $\boldsymbol{X}^\top\boldsymbol{X}$ is not invertible. As we have seen, if they are linearly dependent, there must exist a nonzero vector $\boldsymbol{b}$ such that $\boldsymbol{X}\boldsymbol{b} = \mathbf{0}$. Premultiplying this equation, which is (2.12), by $\boldsymbol{X}^\top$ yields

$$\boldsymbol{X}^\top\boldsymbol{X}\boldsymbol{b} = \mathbf{0}. \tag{2.13}$$

Now suppose that the matrix $\boldsymbol{X}^\top\boldsymbol{X}$ is invertible. If so, there exists a matrix $(\boldsymbol{X}^\top\boldsymbol{X})^{-1}$ such that $(\boldsymbol{X}^\top\boldsymbol{X})^{-1}(\boldsymbol{X}^\top\boldsymbol{X}) = \mathbf{I}$. Thus equation (2.13) implies that

$$\boldsymbol{b} = \mathbf{I}\boldsymbol{b} = (\boldsymbol{X}^\top\boldsymbol{X})^{-1}\boldsymbol{X}^\top\boldsymbol{X}\boldsymbol{b} = \mathbf{0}.$$

But this is a contradiction, since we have assumed that $\boldsymbol{b} \neq \mathbf{0}$. Therefore, we conclude that the matrix $(\boldsymbol{X}^\top\boldsymbol{X})^{-1}$ cannot exist when the columns of $\boldsymbol{X}$ are linearly dependent. Thus a necessary condition for the existence of $(\boldsymbol{X}^\top\boldsymbol{X})^{-1}$ is that the columns of $\boldsymbol{X}$ should be linearly independent. With a little more work, it can be shown that this condition is also sufficient, and so, if the regressors $\boldsymbol{x}_1, \ldots, \boldsymbol{x}_k$ are linearly independent, $\boldsymbol{X}^\top\boldsymbol{X}$ is invertible.

If the k columns of $\boldsymbol{X}$ are not linearly independent, then they span a subspace of dimension less than k, say k', where k' is the largest number of columns of $\boldsymbol{X}$ that are linearly independent of each other. The number k' is called the **rank** of $\boldsymbol{X}$. Look again at Figure 2.8, and imagine that the angle θ between $\boldsymbol{x}_1$ and $\boldsymbol{x}_2$ tends to zero. If $\theta = 0$, then $\boldsymbol{x}_1$ and $\boldsymbol{x}_2$ are parallel, and we can write $\boldsymbol{x}_1 = \alpha\boldsymbol{x}_2$, for some scalar α. But this means that $\boldsymbol{x}_1 - \alpha\boldsymbol{x}_2 = \mathbf{0}$, and so a relation of the form (2.11) holds between $\boldsymbol{x}_1$ and $\boldsymbol{x}_2$, which are therefore linearly dependent. In the figure, if $\boldsymbol{x}_1$ and $\boldsymbol{x}_2$ are parallel, then only one dimension is used, and there is no need for the second dimension in the plane of the page. Thus, in this case, $k = 2$ and $k' = 1$.

When the dimension of $\mathcal{S}(\boldsymbol{X})$ is $k' < k$, $\mathcal{S}(\boldsymbol{X})$ must be identical to $\mathcal{S}(\boldsymbol{X}')$, where $\boldsymbol{X}'$ is an $n \times k'$ matrix consisting of any k' linearly independent columns of $\boldsymbol{X}$. For example, consider the following $\boldsymbol{X}$ matrix, which is 5×3:

$$\begin{bmatrix} 1 & 0 & 1 \\ 1 & 4 & 0 \\ 1 & 0 & 1 \\ 1 & 4 & 0 \\ 1 & 0 & 1 \end{bmatrix}. \tag{2.14}$$

The columns of this matrix are not linearly independent, since

$$\boldsymbol{x}_1 = \frac{1}{4}\boldsymbol{x}_2 + \boldsymbol{x}_3.$$

However, any two of the columns are linearly independent, and so

$$\mathcal{S}(\boldsymbol{X}) = \mathcal{S}(\boldsymbol{x}_1, \boldsymbol{x}_2) = \mathcal{S}(\boldsymbol{x}_1, \boldsymbol{x}_3) = \mathcal{S}(\boldsymbol{x}_2, \boldsymbol{x}_3);$$

see Exercise 2.8. For the remainder of this chapter, unless the contrary is explicitly assumed, we will assume that the columns of any regressor matrix $\boldsymbol{X}$ are linearly independent.

2.3 The Geometry of OLS Estimation

We studied the geometry of vector spaces in the last section because the numerical properties of OLS estimates are easily understood in terms of that geometry. The geometrical interpretation of OLS estimation, that is, MM estimation of linear regression models, is simple and intuitive. In many cases, it entirely does away with the need for algebraic proofs.

As we saw in the last section, any point in a subspace $\mathcal{S}(\boldsymbol{X})$, where $\boldsymbol{X}$ is an $n \times k$ matrix, can be represented as a linear combination of the columns of $\boldsymbol{X}$. We can partition $\boldsymbol{X}$ in terms of its columns explicitly, as follows:

$$\boldsymbol{X} = [\,\boldsymbol{x}_1 \quad \boldsymbol{x}_2 \quad \cdots \quad \boldsymbol{x}_k\,].$$

In order to compute the matrix product $\boldsymbol{X\beta}$ in terms of this partitioning, we need to partition the vector $\boldsymbol{\beta}$ by its rows. Since $\boldsymbol{\beta}$ has only one column, the elements of the partitioned vector are just the individual elements of $\boldsymbol{\beta}$. Thus we find that

$$\boldsymbol{X\beta} = [\,\boldsymbol{x}_1 \quad \boldsymbol{x}_2 \quad \cdots \quad \boldsymbol{x}_k\,]\begin{bmatrix}\beta_1\\ \beta_2\\ \vdots\\ \beta_k\end{bmatrix} = \boldsymbol{x}_1\beta_1 + \boldsymbol{x}_2\beta_2 + \ldots + \boldsymbol{x}_k\beta_k = \sum_{i=1}^{k}\beta_i\boldsymbol{x}_i,$$

which is just a linear combination of the columns of $\boldsymbol{X}$. In fact, it is clear from the definition (2.09) that any linear combination of the columns of $\boldsymbol{X}$, and thus any element of the subspace $\mathcal{S}(\boldsymbol{X}) = \mathcal{S}(\boldsymbol{x}_1, \ldots, \boldsymbol{x}_k)$, can be written as $\boldsymbol{X\beta}$ for some $\boldsymbol{\beta}$. The specific linear combination (2.09) is constructed by using $\boldsymbol{\beta} = [b_1 \vdots \ldots \vdots b_k]$. Thus every n–vector $\boldsymbol{X\beta}$ belongs to $\mathcal{S}(\boldsymbol{X})$, which is, in general, a k–dimensional subspace of E^n. In particular, the vector $\boldsymbol{X}\hat{\boldsymbol{\beta}}$ constructed using the OLS estimator $\hat{\boldsymbol{\beta}}$ belongs to this subspace.

The estimator $\hat{\boldsymbol{\beta}}$ satisfies equations (1.48), and so we have

$$\boldsymbol{X}^\top(\boldsymbol{y} - \boldsymbol{X}\hat{\boldsymbol{\beta}}) = \boldsymbol{0}. \tag{2.15}$$

These equations have a simple geometrical interpretation. Note first that each element of the left-hand side of (2.15) is a scalar product. By the rule for selecting a single row of a matrix product (see Section 1.4), the ith element is

$$\boldsymbol{x}_i^\top(\boldsymbol{y} - \boldsymbol{X}\hat{\boldsymbol{\beta}}) = \langle \boldsymbol{x}_i, \boldsymbol{y} - \boldsymbol{X}\hat{\boldsymbol{\beta}} \rangle, \tag{2.16}$$

since $\boldsymbol{x}_i$, the ith column of $\boldsymbol{X}$, is the transpose of the ith row of $\boldsymbol{X}^\top$. By (2.15), the scalar product in (2.16) is zero, and so the vector $\boldsymbol{y} - \boldsymbol{X}\hat{\boldsymbol{\beta}}$ is orthogonal to

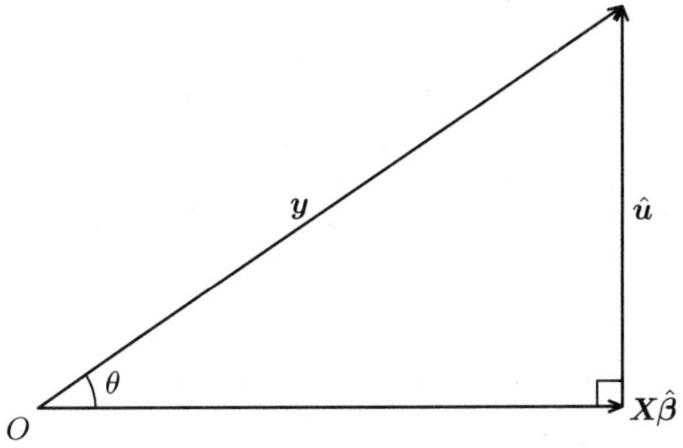

Figure 2.10 Residuals and fitted values

all of the regressors, that is, all of the vectors $\boldsymbol{x}_i$ that represent the explanatory variables in the regression. For this reason, equations like (2.15) are often referred to as **orthogonality conditions**.

Recall from Section 1.5 that the vector $\boldsymbol{y} - \boldsymbol{X\beta}$, treated as a function of $\boldsymbol{\beta}$, is called the vector of residuals. This vector may be written as $\boldsymbol{u}(\boldsymbol{\beta})$. We are interested in $\boldsymbol{u}(\hat{\boldsymbol{\beta}})$, the vector of residuals evaluated at $\hat{\boldsymbol{\beta}}$, which is often called the vector of **least-squares residuals** and is usually written simply as $\hat{\boldsymbol{u}}$. We have just seen, in (2.16), that $\hat{\boldsymbol{u}}$ is orthogonal to all the regressors. This implies that $\hat{\boldsymbol{u}}$ is in fact orthogonal to *every* vector in $\mathcal{S}(\boldsymbol{X})$, the span of the regressors. To see this, remember that any element of $\mathcal{S}(\boldsymbol{X})$ can be written as $\boldsymbol{X\beta}$ for some $\boldsymbol{\beta}$, with the result that, by (2.15),

$$\langle \boldsymbol{X\beta}, \hat{\boldsymbol{u}} \rangle = (\boldsymbol{X\beta})^{\top}\hat{\boldsymbol{u}} = \boldsymbol{\beta}^{\top}\boldsymbol{X}^{\top}\hat{\boldsymbol{u}} = \boldsymbol{0}.$$

The vector $\boldsymbol{X}\hat{\boldsymbol{\beta}}$ is referred to as the vector of **fitted values**. Clearly, it lies in $\mathcal{S}(\boldsymbol{X})$, and, consequently, it must be orthogonal to $\hat{\boldsymbol{u}}$. Figure 2.10 is similar to Figure 2.9, but it shows the vector of least-squares residuals $\hat{\boldsymbol{u}}$ and the vector of fitted values $\boldsymbol{X}\hat{\boldsymbol{\beta}}$ instead of $\boldsymbol{u}$ and $\boldsymbol{X\beta}$. The key feature of this figure, which is a consequence of the orthogonality conditions (2.15), is that the vector $\hat{\boldsymbol{u}}$ makes a right angle with the vector $\boldsymbol{X}\hat{\boldsymbol{\beta}}$.

Some things about the orthogonality conditions (2.15) are clearer if we add a third dimension to the picture. Accordingly, in panel (a) of Figure 2.11, we consider the case of two regressors, $\boldsymbol{x}_1$ and $\boldsymbol{x}_2$, which together span the horizontal plane labelled $\mathcal{S}(\boldsymbol{x}_1, \boldsymbol{x}_2)$, seen in perspective from slightly above the plane. Although the perspective rendering of the figure does not make it clear, both the lengths of $\boldsymbol{x}_1$ and $\boldsymbol{x}_2$ and the angle between them are totally arbitrary, since they do not affect $\mathcal{S}(\boldsymbol{x}_1, \boldsymbol{x}_2)$ at all. The vector $\boldsymbol{y}$ is intended to be viewed as rising up out of the plane spanned by $\boldsymbol{x}_1$ and $\boldsymbol{x}_2$.

In the 3–dimensional setup, it is clear that, if $\hat{\boldsymbol{u}}$ is to be orthogonal to the horizontal plane, it must itself be vertical. Thus it is obtained by "dropping

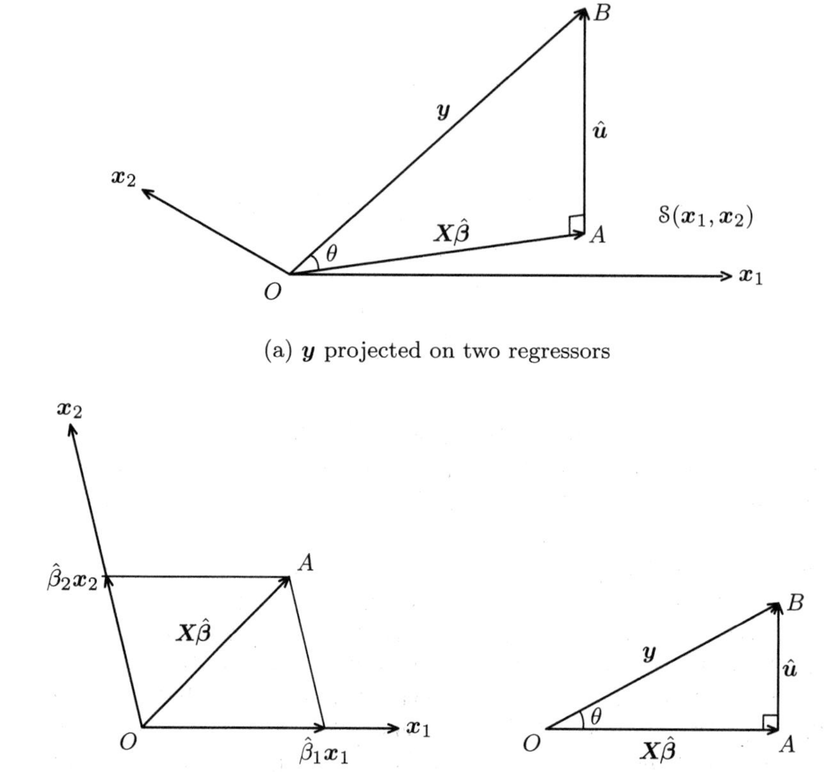

(a) $\boldsymbol{y}$ projected on two regressors

(b) The span $\mathcal{S}(\boldsymbol{x}_1, \boldsymbol{x}_2)$ of the regressors

(c) The vertical plane through $\boldsymbol{y}$

Figure 2.11 Linear regression in three dimensions

a perpendicular" from $\boldsymbol{y}$ to the horizontal plane. The least-squares interpretation of the MM estimator $\hat{\boldsymbol{\beta}}$ can now be seen to be a consequence of simple geometry. The shortest distance from $\boldsymbol{y}$ to the horizontal plane is obtained by descending vertically on to it, and the point in the horizontal plane vertically below $\boldsymbol{y}$, labeled A in the figure, is the closest point in the plane to $\boldsymbol{y}$. Thus $\|\hat{\boldsymbol{u}}\|$ minimizes $\|\boldsymbol{u}(\boldsymbol{\beta})\|$, the norm of $\boldsymbol{u}(\boldsymbol{\beta})$, with respect to $\boldsymbol{\beta}$. The squared norm, $\|\boldsymbol{u}(\boldsymbol{\beta})\|^2$, is just the sum of squared residuals, $\text{SSR}(\boldsymbol{\beta})$; see (1.49). Since minimizing the norm of $\boldsymbol{u}(\boldsymbol{\beta})$ is the same thing as minimizing the squared norm, it follows that $\hat{\boldsymbol{\beta}}$ is the OLS estimator.

Panel (b) of the figure shows the horizontal plane $\mathcal{S}(\boldsymbol{x}_1, \boldsymbol{x}_2)$ as a straightforward 2–dimensional picture, seen from directly above. The point A is the point directly underneath $\boldsymbol{y}$, and so, since $\boldsymbol{y} = \boldsymbol{X}\hat{\boldsymbol{\beta}} + \hat{\boldsymbol{u}}$ by definition, the vector represented by the line segment OA is the vector of fitted values, $\boldsymbol{X}\hat{\boldsymbol{\beta}}$. Geometrically, it is much simpler to represent $\boldsymbol{X}\hat{\boldsymbol{\beta}}$ than to represent just the vector $\hat{\boldsymbol{\beta}}$, because the latter lies in $\mathbb{R}^k$, a different space from the space E^n that contains the variables and all linear combinations of them. However, it is easy to see that the information in panel (b) does indeed determine $\hat{\boldsymbol{\beta}}$. Plainly, $\boldsymbol{X}\hat{\boldsymbol{\beta}}$ can be decomposed in just one way as a linear combination of $\boldsymbol{x}_1$ and $\boldsymbol{x}_2$, as shown. The numerical value of $\hat{\beta}_1$ can be computed as the ratio of the length of the vector $\hat{\beta}_1\boldsymbol{x}_1$ to that of $\boldsymbol{x}_1$, and similarly for $\hat{\beta}_2$.

In panel (c) of Figure 2.11, we show the right-angled triangle that corresponds to dropping a perpendicular from $\boldsymbol{y}$, labelled in the same way as in panel (a). This triangle lies in the vertical plane that contains the vector $\boldsymbol{y}$. We can see that $\boldsymbol{y}$ is the hypotenuse of the triangle, the other two sides being $\boldsymbol{X}\hat{\boldsymbol{\beta}}$ and $\hat{\boldsymbol{u}}$. Thus this panel corresponds to what we saw already in Figure 2.10. Since we have a right-angled triangle, we can apply Pythagoras' Theorem. It gives

$$\|\boldsymbol{y}\|^2 = \|\boldsymbol{X}\hat{\boldsymbol{\beta}}\|^2 + \|\hat{\boldsymbol{u}}\|^2. \tag{2.17}$$

If we write out the squared norms as scalar products, this becomes

$$\boldsymbol{y}^\top\boldsymbol{y} = \hat{\boldsymbol{\beta}}^\top\boldsymbol{X}^\top\boldsymbol{X}\hat{\boldsymbol{\beta}} + (\boldsymbol{y} - \boldsymbol{X}\hat{\boldsymbol{\beta}})^\top(\boldsymbol{y} - \boldsymbol{X}\hat{\boldsymbol{\beta}}). \tag{2.18}$$

In words, the **total sum of squares**, or **TSS**, is equal to the **explained sum of squares**, or **ESS**, plus the **sum of squared residuals**, or **SSR**. This is a fundamental property of OLS estimates, and it will prove to be very useful in many contexts. Intuitively, it lets us break down the total variation (TSS) of the dependent variable into the explained variation (ESS) and the unexplained variation (SSR), unexplained because the residuals represent the aspects of $\boldsymbol{y}$ about which we remain in ignorance.

Orthogonal Projections

When we estimate a linear regression model, we implicitly map the regressand $\boldsymbol{y}$ into a vector of fitted values $\boldsymbol{X}\hat{\boldsymbol{\beta}}$ and a vector of residuals $\hat{\boldsymbol{u}} = \boldsymbol{y} - \boldsymbol{X}\hat{\boldsymbol{\beta}}$. Geometrically, these mappings are examples of orthogonal projections. A **projection** is a mapping that takes each point of E^n into a point in a subspace of E^n, while leaving all points in that subspace unchanged. Because of this, the subspace is called the **invariant subspace** of the projection. An **orthogonal projection** maps any point into the point of the subspace that is closest to it. If a point is already in the invariant subspace, it is mapped into itself.

The concept of an orthogonal projection formalizes the notion of "dropping a perpendicular" that we used in the last subsection when discussing least squares. Algebraically, an orthogonal projection on to a given subspace can be performed by premultiplying the vector to be projected by a suitable **projection matrix**. In the case of OLS, the two projection matrices that yield the vector of fitted values and the vector of residuals, respectively, are

$$\begin{aligned} \boldsymbol{P_X} &= \boldsymbol{X}(\boldsymbol{X}^\top\boldsymbol{X})^{-1}\boldsymbol{X}^\top, \quad \text{and} \\ \boldsymbol{M_X} &= \mathbf{I} - \boldsymbol{P_X} = \mathbf{I} - \boldsymbol{X}(\boldsymbol{X}^\top\boldsymbol{X})^{-1}\boldsymbol{X}^\top, \end{aligned} \tag{2.19}$$

where $\mathbf{I}$ is the $n \times n$ identity matrix. To see this, recall (2.02), the formula for the OLS estimates of $\boldsymbol{\beta}$:

$$\hat{\boldsymbol{\beta}} = (\boldsymbol{X}^\top\boldsymbol{X})^{-1}\boldsymbol{X}^\top\boldsymbol{y}.$$

From this, we see that

$$\boldsymbol{X}\hat{\boldsymbol{\beta}} = \boldsymbol{X}(\boldsymbol{X}^\top\boldsymbol{X})^{-1}\boldsymbol{X}^\top\boldsymbol{y} = \boldsymbol{P}_{\boldsymbol{X}}\boldsymbol{y}. \tag{2.20}$$

Therefore, the first projection matrix in (2.19), $\boldsymbol{P}_{\boldsymbol{X}}$, projects on to $\mathcal{S}(\boldsymbol{X})$. For any n–vector $\boldsymbol{y}$, $\boldsymbol{P}_{\boldsymbol{X}}\boldsymbol{y}$ always lies in $\mathcal{S}(\boldsymbol{X})$, because

$$\boldsymbol{P}_{\boldsymbol{X}}\boldsymbol{y} = \boldsymbol{X}\big((\boldsymbol{X}^\top\boldsymbol{X})^{-1}\boldsymbol{X}^\top\boldsymbol{y}\big).$$

Since this takes the form $\boldsymbol{X}\boldsymbol{b}$ for $\boldsymbol{b} = \hat{\boldsymbol{\beta}}$, it is a linear combination of the columns of $\boldsymbol{X}$, and hence it belongs to $\mathcal{S}(\boldsymbol{X})$.

From (2.19), it is easy to show that $\boldsymbol{P}_{\boldsymbol{X}}\boldsymbol{X} = \boldsymbol{X}$. Since any vector in $\mathcal{S}(\boldsymbol{X})$ can be written as $\boldsymbol{X}\boldsymbol{b}$ for some $\boldsymbol{b} \in \mathbb{R}^k$, we see that

$$\boldsymbol{P}_{\boldsymbol{X}}\boldsymbol{X}\boldsymbol{b} = \boldsymbol{X}\boldsymbol{b}. \tag{2.21}$$

We saw from (2.20) that the result of acting on any vector $\boldsymbol{y} \in E^n$ with $\boldsymbol{P}_{\boldsymbol{X}}$ is a vector in $\mathcal{S}(\boldsymbol{X})$. Thus the invariant subspace of the projection $\boldsymbol{P}_{\boldsymbol{X}}$ must be contained in $\mathcal{S}(\boldsymbol{X})$. But, by (2.21), *every* vector in $\mathcal{S}(\boldsymbol{X})$ is mapped into itself by $\boldsymbol{P}_{\boldsymbol{X}}$. Therefore, the **image** of $\boldsymbol{P}_{\boldsymbol{X}}$, which is a shorter name for its invariant subspace, is precisely $\mathcal{S}(\boldsymbol{X})$.

It is clear from (2.20) that, when $\boldsymbol{P}_{\boldsymbol{X}}$ is applied to $\boldsymbol{y}$, it yields the vector of fitted values. Similarly, when $\boldsymbol{M}_{\boldsymbol{X}}$, the second of the two projection matrices in (2.19), is applied to $\boldsymbol{y}$, it yields the vector of residuals:

$$\boldsymbol{M}_{\boldsymbol{X}}\boldsymbol{y} = \big(\mathbf{I} - \boldsymbol{X}(\boldsymbol{X}^\top\boldsymbol{X})^{-1}\boldsymbol{X}^\top\big)\boldsymbol{y} = \boldsymbol{y} - \boldsymbol{P}_{\boldsymbol{X}}\boldsymbol{y} = \boldsymbol{y} - \boldsymbol{X}\hat{\boldsymbol{\beta}} = \hat{\boldsymbol{u}}.$$

The image of $\boldsymbol{M}_{\boldsymbol{X}}$ is $\mathcal{S}^\perp(\boldsymbol{X})$, the orthogonal complement of the image of $\boldsymbol{P}_{\boldsymbol{X}}$. To see this, consider any vector $\boldsymbol{w} \in \mathcal{S}^\perp(\boldsymbol{X})$. It must satisfy the defining condition $\boldsymbol{X}^\top\boldsymbol{w} = \mathbf{0}$. From the definition (2.19) of $\boldsymbol{P}_{\boldsymbol{X}}$, this implies that $\boldsymbol{P}_{\boldsymbol{X}}\boldsymbol{w} = \mathbf{0}$, the zero vector. Since $\boldsymbol{M}_{\boldsymbol{X}} = \mathbf{I} - \boldsymbol{P}_{\boldsymbol{X}}$, we find that $\boldsymbol{M}_{\boldsymbol{X}}\boldsymbol{w} = \boldsymbol{w}$. Thus $\mathcal{S}^\perp(\boldsymbol{X})$ must be contained in the image of $\boldsymbol{M}_{\boldsymbol{X}}$. Next, consider any vector in the image of $\boldsymbol{M}_{\boldsymbol{X}}$. It must take the form $\boldsymbol{M}_{\boldsymbol{X}}\boldsymbol{y}$, where $\boldsymbol{y}$ is some vector in E^n. From this, it follows that $\boldsymbol{M}_{\boldsymbol{X}}\boldsymbol{y}$ belongs to $\mathcal{S}^\perp(\boldsymbol{X})$. Observe that

$$(\boldsymbol{M}_{\boldsymbol{X}}\boldsymbol{y})^\top\boldsymbol{X} = \boldsymbol{y}^\top\boldsymbol{M}_{\boldsymbol{X}}\boldsymbol{X}, \tag{2.22}$$

an equality that relies on the symmetry of $\boldsymbol{M}_{\boldsymbol{X}}$. Then, from (2.19), we have

$$\boldsymbol{M}_{\boldsymbol{X}}\boldsymbol{X} = (\mathbf{I} - \boldsymbol{P}_{\boldsymbol{X}})\boldsymbol{X} = \boldsymbol{X} - \boldsymbol{X} = \mathbf{O}, \tag{2.23}$$

where $\mathbf{O}$ denotes a **zero matrix**, which in this case is $n \times k$. The result (2.22) says that any vector $\boldsymbol{M_X y}$ in the image of $\boldsymbol{M_X}$ is orthogonal to $\boldsymbol{X}$, and thus belongs to $\mathcal{S}^\perp(\boldsymbol{X})$. We saw above that $\mathcal{S}^\perp(\boldsymbol{X})$ was contained in the image of $\boldsymbol{M_X}$, and so this image must coincide with $\mathcal{S}^\perp(\boldsymbol{X})$. For obvious reasons, the projection $\boldsymbol{M_X}$ is sometimes called the projection **off** $\mathcal{S}(\boldsymbol{X})$.

For any matrix to represent a projection, it must be **idempotent**. An idempotent matrix is one that, when multiplied by itself, yields itself again. Thus,

$$\boldsymbol{P_X P_X} = \boldsymbol{P_X} \quad \text{and} \quad \boldsymbol{M_X M_X} = \boldsymbol{M_X}.$$

These results are easily proved by a little algebra directly from (2.19), but the geometry of the situation makes them obvious. If we take any point, project it on to $\mathcal{S}(\boldsymbol{X})$, and then project it on to $\mathcal{S}(\boldsymbol{X})$ *again*, the second projection can have no effect at all, because the point is *already* in $\mathcal{S}(\boldsymbol{X})$, and so it is left unchanged. Since this implies that $\boldsymbol{P_X P_X y} = \boldsymbol{P_X y}$ for any vector $\boldsymbol{y}$, it must be the case that $\boldsymbol{P_X P_X} = \boldsymbol{P_X}$, and similarly for $\boldsymbol{M_X}$.

Since, from (2.19),

$$\boldsymbol{P_X} + \boldsymbol{M_X} = \mathbf{I}, \tag{2.24}$$

any vector $\boldsymbol{y} \in E^n$ is equal to $\boldsymbol{P_X y} + \boldsymbol{M_X y}$. The pair of projections $\boldsymbol{P_X}$ and $\boldsymbol{M_X}$ are said to be **complementary projections**, since the sum of $\boldsymbol{P_X y}$ and $\boldsymbol{M_X y}$ restores the original vector $\boldsymbol{y}$.

The fact that $\mathcal{S}(\boldsymbol{X})$ and $\mathcal{S}^\perp(\boldsymbol{X})$ are orthogonal subspaces leads us to say that the two projection matrices $\boldsymbol{P_X}$ and $\boldsymbol{M_X}$ define what is called an **orthogonal decomposition** of E^n, because the two vectors $\boldsymbol{M_X y}$ and $\boldsymbol{P_X y}$ lie in the two orthogonal subspaces. Algebraically, the orthogonality depends on the fact that $\boldsymbol{P_X}$ and $\boldsymbol{M_X}$ are symmetric matrices. To see this, we start from a further important property of $\boldsymbol{P_X}$ and $\boldsymbol{M_X}$, which is that

$$\boldsymbol{P_X M_X} = \mathbf{O}. \tag{2.25}$$

This equation is true for any complementary pair of projections satisfying (2.24), whether or not they are symmetric; see Exercise 2.9. We may say that $\boldsymbol{P_X}$ and $\boldsymbol{M_X}$ **annihilate** each other. Now consider any vector $\boldsymbol{z} \in \mathcal{S}(\boldsymbol{X})$ and any other vector $\boldsymbol{w} \in \mathcal{S}^\perp(\boldsymbol{X})$. We have $\boldsymbol{z} = \boldsymbol{P_X z}$ and $\boldsymbol{w} = \boldsymbol{M_X w}$. Thus the scalar product of the two vectors is

$$\langle \boldsymbol{P_X z}, \boldsymbol{M_X w} \rangle = \boldsymbol{z}^\top \boldsymbol{P_X}^\top \boldsymbol{M_X w}.$$

Since $\boldsymbol{P_X}$ is symmetric, $\boldsymbol{P_X}^\top = \boldsymbol{P_X}$, and so the above scalar product is zero by (2.25). In general, however, if two complementary projection matrices are not symmetric, the spaces they project on to are not orthogonal; see Exercise 2.10.

The projection matrix $\boldsymbol{M_X}$ annihilates all points that lie in $\mathcal{S}(\boldsymbol{X})$, and $\boldsymbol{P_X}$ likewise annihilates all points that lie in $\mathcal{S}^\perp(\boldsymbol{X})$. These properties can be proved by straightforward algebra (see Exercise 2.12), but the geometry of the situation is very simple. Consider Figure 2.7. It is evident that, if we project any point in $\mathcal{S}^\perp(\boldsymbol{X})$ orthogonally on to $\mathcal{S}(\boldsymbol{X})$, we end up at the origin, as we do if we project any point in $\mathcal{S}(\boldsymbol{X})$ orthogonally on to $\mathcal{S}^\perp(\boldsymbol{X})$.

Provided that $\boldsymbol{X}$ has full rank, the subspace $\mathcal{S}(\boldsymbol{X})$ is k–dimensional, and so the first term in the decomposition $\boldsymbol{y} = \boldsymbol{P_X y} + \boldsymbol{M_X y}$ belongs to a k–dimensional space. Since $\boldsymbol{y}$ itself belongs to E^n, which has n dimensions, it follows that the complementary space $\mathcal{S}^\perp(\boldsymbol{X})$ must have $n-k$ dimensions. The number $n-k$ is called the **codimension** of $\boldsymbol{X}$ in E^n.

Geometrically, an orthogonal decomposition $\boldsymbol{y} = \boldsymbol{P_X y} + \boldsymbol{M_X y}$ can be represented by a right-angled triangle, with $\boldsymbol{y}$ as the hypotenuse and $\boldsymbol{P_X y}$ and $\boldsymbol{M_X y}$ as the other two sides. In terms of projections, equation (2.17), which is really just Pythagoras' Theorem, can be rewritten as

$$\|\boldsymbol{y}\|^2 = \|\boldsymbol{P_X y}\|^2 + \|\boldsymbol{M_X y}\|^2. \tag{2.26}$$

In Exercise 2.11, readers are asked to provide an algebraic proof of this equation. Since every term in (2.26) is nonnegative, we obtain the useful result that, for any orthogonal projection matrix $\boldsymbol{P_X}$ and any vector $\boldsymbol{y} \in E^n$,

$$\|\boldsymbol{P_X y}\| \leq \|\boldsymbol{y}\|. \tag{2.27}$$

In effect, this just says that the hypotenuse is longer than either of the other sides of a right-angled triangle.

In general, we will use $\boldsymbol{P}$ and $\boldsymbol{M}$ subscripted by matrix expressions to denote the matrices that, respectively, project on to and off the subspaces spanned by the columns of those matrix expressions. Thus $\boldsymbol{P_Z}$ would be the matrix that projects on to $\mathcal{S}(\boldsymbol{Z})$, $\boldsymbol{M}_{\boldsymbol{X},\boldsymbol{W}}$ would be the matrix that projects off $\mathcal{S}(\boldsymbol{X}, \boldsymbol{W})$, or, equivalently, on to $\mathcal{S}^\perp(\boldsymbol{X}, \boldsymbol{W})$, and so on. It is frequently very convenient to express the quantities that arise in econometrics using these matrices, partly because the resulting expressions are relatively compact, and partly because the properties of projection matrices often make it easy to understand what those expressions mean. However, projection matrices are of little use for computation because they are of dimension $n \times n$. It is never efficient to calculate residuals or fitted values by explicitly using projection matrices, and it can be extremely inefficient if n is large.

Linear Transformations of Regressors

The span $\mathcal{S}(\boldsymbol{X})$ of the regressors of a linear regression can be defined in many equivalent ways. All that is needed is a set of k vectors that encompass all the k directions of the k–dimensional subspace. Consider what happens when we postmultiply $\boldsymbol{X}$ by any nonsingular $k \times k$ matrix $\boldsymbol{A}$. This is called a **nonsingular linear transformation**. Let $\boldsymbol{A}$ be partitioned by its columns, which may be denoted $\boldsymbol{a}_i$, $i = 1, \ldots, k$:

$$\boldsymbol{XA} = \boldsymbol{X}\,[\,\boldsymbol{a}_1 \quad \boldsymbol{a}_2 \quad \cdots \quad \boldsymbol{a}_k\,] = [\,\boldsymbol{Xa}_1 \quad \boldsymbol{Xa}_2 \quad \cdots \quad \boldsymbol{Xa}_k\,].$$

Each block in the product takes the form $\boldsymbol{X}\boldsymbol{a}_i$, which is an n–vector that is a linear combination of the columns of $\boldsymbol{X}$. Thus any element of $\mathcal{S}(\boldsymbol{XA})$ must also be an element of $\mathcal{S}(\boldsymbol{X})$. But any element of $\mathcal{S}(\boldsymbol{X})$ is also an element of $\mathcal{S}(\boldsymbol{XA})$. To see this, note that any element of $\mathcal{S}(\boldsymbol{X})$ can be written as $\boldsymbol{X\beta}$ for some $\boldsymbol{\beta} \in \mathbb{R}^k$. Since $\boldsymbol{A}$ is nonsingular, and thus invertible,

$$\boldsymbol{X\beta} = \boldsymbol{XAA}^{-1}\boldsymbol{\beta} = (\boldsymbol{XA})(\boldsymbol{A}^{-1}\boldsymbol{\beta}).$$

Because $\boldsymbol{A}^{-1}\boldsymbol{\beta}$ is just a k–vector, this expression is a linear combination of the columns of $\boldsymbol{XA}$, that is, an element of $\mathcal{S}(\boldsymbol{XA})$. Since every element of $\mathcal{S}(\boldsymbol{XA})$ belongs to $\mathcal{S}(\boldsymbol{X})$, and every element of $\mathcal{S}(\boldsymbol{X})$ belongs to $\mathcal{S}(\boldsymbol{XA})$, these two subspaces must be identical.

Given the identity of $\mathcal{S}(\boldsymbol{X})$ and $\mathcal{S}(\boldsymbol{XA})$, it seems intuitively compelling to suppose that the orthogonal projections $\boldsymbol{P_X}$ and $\boldsymbol{P_{XA}}$ should be the same. This is in fact the case, as can be verified directly:

$$\begin{aligned}\boldsymbol{P_{XA}} &= \boldsymbol{XA}(\boldsymbol{A}^\top\boldsymbol{X}^\top\boldsymbol{XA})^{-1}\boldsymbol{A}^\top\boldsymbol{X}^\top \\ &= \boldsymbol{XAA}^{-1}(\boldsymbol{X}^\top\boldsymbol{X})^{-1}(\boldsymbol{A}^\top)^{-1}\boldsymbol{A}^\top\boldsymbol{X}^\top \\ &= \boldsymbol{X}(\boldsymbol{X}^\top\boldsymbol{X})^{-1}\boldsymbol{X}^\top = \boldsymbol{P_X}.\end{aligned}$$

When expanding the inverse of the matrix $\boldsymbol{A}^\top\boldsymbol{X}^\top\boldsymbol{XA}$, we used the reversal rule for inverses; see Exercise 1.17.

We have already seen that the vectors of fitted values and residuals depend on $\boldsymbol{X}$ only through $\boldsymbol{P_X}$ and $\boldsymbol{M_X}$. Therefore, they too must be invariant to any nonsingular linear transformation of the columns of $\boldsymbol{X}$. Thus if, in the regression $\boldsymbol{y} = \boldsymbol{X\beta} + \boldsymbol{u}$, we replace $\boldsymbol{X}$ by $\boldsymbol{XA}$ for some nonsingular matrix $\boldsymbol{A}$, the residuals and fitted values do not change, even though $\hat{\boldsymbol{\beta}}$ changes. We will discuss an example of this important result shortly.

When the set of regressors contains a constant, it is necessary to express it as a vector, just like any other regressor. The coefficient of this **constant vector** is then the parameter that we usually call the constant term. The constant vector is just $\boldsymbol{\iota}$, the vector of which each element equals 1. Consider the n–vector $\beta_1\boldsymbol{\iota} + \beta_2\boldsymbol{x}$, where $\boldsymbol{x}$ is any nonconstant regressor, and β_1 and β_2 are scalar parameters. The tth element of this vector is $\beta_1 + \beta_2 x_t$. Thus adding the vector $\beta_1\boldsymbol{\iota}$ to $\beta_2\boldsymbol{x}$ simply adds the scalar β_1 to each component of $\beta_2\boldsymbol{x}$. For any regression which includes a constant term, then, the fact that we can perform arbitrary nonsingular transformations of the regressors without affecting residuals or fitted values implies that these vectors are unchanged if we add any constant amount to any one or more of the regressors.

Another implication of the invariance of residuals and fitted values under nonsingular transformations of the regressors is that these vectors are unchanged if we change the **units of measurement** of the regressors. Suppose, for instance, that the temperature is one of the explanatory variables in a regression with a constant term. A practical example in which the temperature could have good explanatory power is the modeling of electricity demand: More electrical power is consumed if the weather is very cold, or, in societies where air conditioners are common, very hot. In a few countries, notably the United States, temperatures are still measured in Fahrenheit degrees, while in most countries they are measured in Celsius (centigrade) degrees. It would be disturbing if our conclusions about the effect of temperature on electricity demand depended on whether we measured it using the Fahrenheit scale or the Celsius scale.

Let the n–vector of observations on the temperature variable be denoted as $\boldsymbol{T}$ in Celsius and as $\boldsymbol{F}$ in Fahrenheit, the constant vector being denoted, as usual, by $\boldsymbol{\iota}$. Then we have the relation

$$\boldsymbol{F} = 32\boldsymbol{\iota} + \frac{9}{5}\boldsymbol{T}.$$

If the constant is included in the transformation,

$$[\,\boldsymbol{\iota} \quad \boldsymbol{F}\,] = [\,\boldsymbol{\iota} \quad \boldsymbol{T}\,]\begin{bmatrix} 1 & 32 \\ 0 & 9/5 \end{bmatrix}. \tag{2.28}$$

Thus the constant and the two different temperature measures are related by a linear transformation that is easily seen to be nonsingular, since Fahrenheit degrees can be converted back into Celsius. This implies that the residuals and fitted values are unaffected by our choice of temperature scale.

Let us denote the constant term and the slope coefficient as β_1 and β_2 if we use the Celsius scale, and as α_1 and α_2 if we use the Fahrenheit scale. Then it is easy to see that these parameters are related by the equations

$$\beta_1 = \alpha_1 + 32\alpha_2 \quad \text{and} \quad \beta_2 = 9/5\,\alpha_2. \tag{2.29}$$

To see that this makes sense, suppose that the temperature is at freezing point, which is 0° Celsius and 32° Fahrenheit. Then the combined effect of the constant and the temperature on electricity demand is $\beta_1 + 0\beta_2 = \beta_1$ using the Celsius scale, and $\alpha_1 + 32\alpha_2$ using the Fahrenheit scale. These should be the same, and, according to (2.29), they are. Similarly, the effect of a 1-degree increase in the Celsius temperature is given by β_2. Now 1 Celsius degree equals 9/5 Fahrenheit degrees, and the effect of a temperature increase of 9/5 Fahrenheit degrees is given by $9/5\,\alpha_2$. We are assured by (2.29) that the two effects are the same.

2.4 The Frisch-Waugh-Lovell Theorem

In this section, we discuss an extremely useful property of least-squares estimates, which we will refer to as the **Frisch-Waugh-Lovell Theorem**, or **FWL Theorem** for short. It was introduced to econometricians by Frisch and Waugh (1933), and then reintroduced by Lovell (1963).

Deviations from the Mean

We begin by considering a particular nonsingular transformation of variables in a regression with a constant term. We saw at the end of the last section that residuals and fitted values are invariant under such transformations of the regressors. For simplicity, consider a model with a constant and just one explanatory variable:

$$\boldsymbol{y} = \beta_1 \boldsymbol{\iota} + \beta_2 \boldsymbol{x} + \boldsymbol{u}. \tag{2.30}$$

In general, $\boldsymbol{x}$ is not orthogonal to $\boldsymbol{\iota}$, but there is a very simple transformation which makes it so. This transformation replaces the observations in $\boldsymbol{x}$ by **deviations from the mean**. In order to perform the transformation, one first calculates the mean of the n observations of the vector $\boldsymbol{x}$,

$$\bar{x} \equiv \frac{1}{n} \sum_{t=1}^{n} x_t,$$

and then subtracts the constant $\bar{x}$ from each element of $\boldsymbol{x}$. This yields the vector of deviations from the mean, $\boldsymbol{z} \equiv \boldsymbol{x} - \bar{x}\boldsymbol{\iota}$. The vector $\boldsymbol{z}$ is easily seen to be orthogonal to $\boldsymbol{\iota}$, because

$$\boldsymbol{\iota}^\top \boldsymbol{z} = \boldsymbol{\iota}^\top (\boldsymbol{x} - \bar{x}\boldsymbol{\iota}) = n\bar{x} - \bar{x}\boldsymbol{\iota}^\top \boldsymbol{\iota} = n\bar{x} - n\bar{x} = 0.$$

The operation of expressing a variable in terms of the deviations from its mean is called **centering** the variable. In this case, the vector $\boldsymbol{z}$ is the **centered** version of the vector $\boldsymbol{x}$.

Since centering leads to a variable that is orthogonal to $\boldsymbol{\iota}$, it can be performed algebraically by the orthogonal projection matrix $\boldsymbol{M}_\iota$. This can be verified by observing that

$$\boldsymbol{M}_\iota \boldsymbol{x} = (\mathbf{I} - \boldsymbol{P}_\iota)\boldsymbol{x} = \boldsymbol{x} - \boldsymbol{\iota}(\boldsymbol{\iota}^\top \boldsymbol{\iota})^{-1} \boldsymbol{\iota}^\top \boldsymbol{x} = \boldsymbol{x} - \bar{x}\boldsymbol{\iota} = \boldsymbol{z}, \tag{2.31}$$

as claimed. Here, we once again used the facts that $\boldsymbol{\iota}^\top \boldsymbol{\iota} = n$ and $\boldsymbol{\iota}^\top \boldsymbol{x} = n\bar{x}$.

The idea behind the use of deviations from the mean is that it makes sense to separate the overall level of a dependent variable from its dependence on explanatory variables. Specifically, if we rewrite equation (2.30) in terms of $\boldsymbol{z}$, it becomes

$$\boldsymbol{y} = (\beta_1 + \beta_2 \bar{x})\boldsymbol{\iota} + \beta_2 \boldsymbol{z} + \boldsymbol{u} = \alpha_1 \boldsymbol{\iota} + \alpha_2 \boldsymbol{z} + \boldsymbol{u},$$

from which it is evident that

$$\alpha_1 = \beta_1 + \beta_2 \bar{x}, \text{ and } \alpha_2 = \beta_2.$$

If, for some observation t, the value of x_t were exactly equal to the mean value, $\bar{x}$, then $z_t = 0$. Thus we find that $y_t = \alpha_1 + u_t$. We interpret this as saying that the expected value of y_t, when the explanatory variable takes on its average value, is the constant α_1.

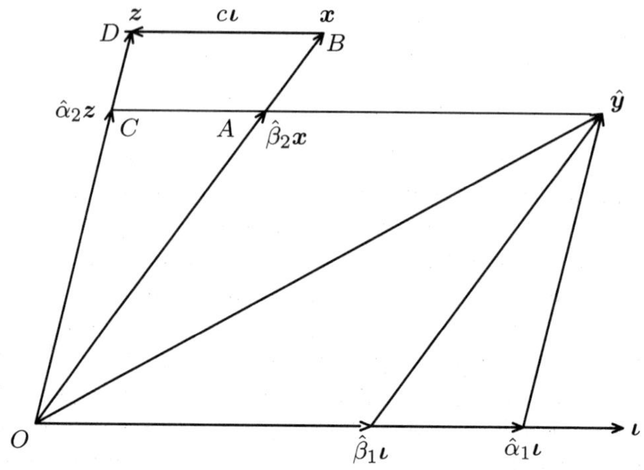

Figure 2.12 Adding a constant does not affect the slope coefficient

The effect on y_t of a change of one unit in x_t is measured by the slope coefficient β_2. If we hold $\bar{x}$ at its value before x_t is changed, then the unit change in x_t induces a unit change in z_t. Thus a unit change in z_t, which is measured by the slope coefficient α_2, should have the same effect as a unit change in x_t. Accordingly, $\alpha_2 = \beta_2$, just as we found above.

The slope coefficients α_2 and β_2 would be the same with any constant in the place of $\bar{x}$. The reason for this can be seen geometrically, as illustrated in Figure 2.12. This figure, which is constructed in the same way as panel (b) of Figure 2.11, depicts the span of $\boldsymbol{\iota}$ and $\boldsymbol{x}$, with $\boldsymbol{\iota}$ in the horizontal direction. As before, the vector $\boldsymbol{y}$ is not shown, because a third dimension would be required; the vector would extend from the origin to a point off the plane of the page and directly above (or below) the point labelled $\hat{\boldsymbol{y}}$.

The figure shows the vector of fitted values $\hat{\boldsymbol{y}}$ as the vector sum $\hat{\beta}_1\boldsymbol{\iota} + \hat{\beta}_2\boldsymbol{x}$. The slope coefficient $\hat{\beta}_2$ is the ratio of the length of the vector $\hat{\beta}_2\boldsymbol{x}$ to that of $\boldsymbol{x}$; geometrically, it is given by the ratio OA/OB. Then a new regressor $\boldsymbol{z}$ is defined by adding the constant value c, which is negative in the figure, to each component of $\boldsymbol{x}$, giving $\boldsymbol{z} = \boldsymbol{x} + c\boldsymbol{\iota}$. In terms of this new regressor, the vector $\hat{\boldsymbol{y}}$ is given by $\hat{\alpha}_1\boldsymbol{\iota} + \hat{\alpha}_2\boldsymbol{z}$, and $\hat{\alpha}_2$ is given by the ratio OC/OD. Since the ratios OA/OB and OC/OD are clearly the same, we see that $\hat{\alpha}_2 = \hat{\beta}_2$. A formal argument would use the fact that OAC and OBD are similar triangles.

When the constant c is chosen as $\bar{x}$, the vector $\boldsymbol{z}$ is said to be centered, and, as we saw above, it is orthogonal to $\boldsymbol{\iota}$. In this case, the estimate $\hat{\alpha}_2$ is the same whether it is obtained by regressing $\boldsymbol{y}$ on both $\boldsymbol{\iota}$ and $\boldsymbol{z}$, or just on $\boldsymbol{z}$ alone. This is illustrated in Figure 2.13, which shows what Figure 2.12 would look like when $\boldsymbol{z}$ is orthogonal to $\boldsymbol{\iota}$. Once again, the vector of fitted values $\hat{\boldsymbol{y}}$ is decomposed as $\hat{\alpha}_1\boldsymbol{\iota} + \hat{\alpha}_2\boldsymbol{z}$, with $\boldsymbol{z}$ now at right angles to $\boldsymbol{\iota}$.

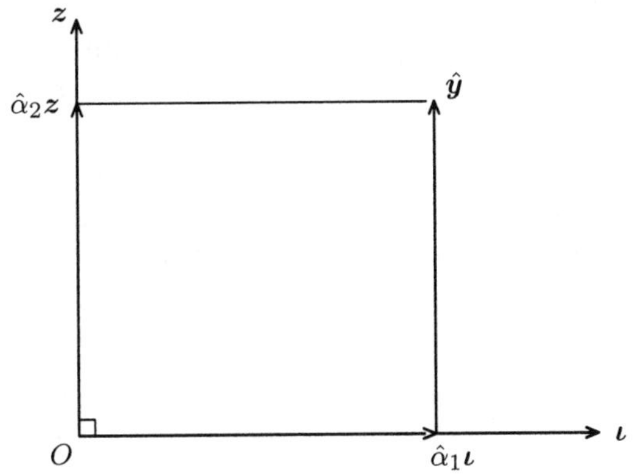

Figure 2.13 Orthogonal regressors may be omitted

Now suppose that $\boldsymbol{y}$ is regressed on $\boldsymbol{z}$ alone. This means that $\boldsymbol{y}$ is projected orthogonally on to $\mathcal{S}(\boldsymbol{z})$, which in the figure is the vertical line through $\boldsymbol{z}$. By definition,

$$\boldsymbol{y} = \hat{\alpha}_1 \boldsymbol{\iota} + \hat{\alpha}_2 \boldsymbol{z} + \hat{\boldsymbol{u}}, \tag{2.32}$$

where $\hat{\boldsymbol{u}}$ is orthogonal to both $\boldsymbol{\iota}$ and $\boldsymbol{z}$. But $\boldsymbol{\iota}$ is also orthogonal to $\boldsymbol{z}$, and so the only term on the right-hand side of (2.32) not to be annihilated by the projection on to $\mathcal{S}(\boldsymbol{z})$ is the middle term, which is left unchanged by it. Thus the fitted value vector from regressing $\boldsymbol{y}$ on $\boldsymbol{z}$ alone is just $\hat{\alpha}_2 \boldsymbol{z}$, and so the OLS estimate is the same $\hat{\alpha}_2$ as given by the regression on both $\boldsymbol{\iota}$ and $\boldsymbol{z}$. Geometrically, we obtain this result because the projection of $\boldsymbol{y}$ on to $\mathcal{S}(\boldsymbol{z})$ is the same as the projection of $\hat{\boldsymbol{y}}$ on to $\mathcal{S}(\boldsymbol{z})$.

Incidentally, the fact that OLS residuals are orthogonal to all the regressors, including $\boldsymbol{\iota}$, leads to the important result that the residuals in any regression with a constant term sum to zero. In fact,

$$\boldsymbol{\iota}^\top \hat{\boldsymbol{u}} = \sum_{t=1}^{n} \hat{u}_t = 0;$$

recall equation (1.29). The residuals also sum to zero in any regression for which $\boldsymbol{\iota} \in \mathcal{S}(\boldsymbol{X})$, even if $\boldsymbol{\iota}$ does not explicitly appear in the list of regressors. This can happen if the regressors include certain sets of **dummy variables**, as we will see in Section 2.5.

Two Groups of Regressors

The results proved in the previous subsection are actually special cases of more general results that apply to any regression in which the regressors can logically be broken up into two groups. Such a regression can be written as

$$\boldsymbol{y} = \boldsymbol{X}_1 \boldsymbol{\beta}_1 + \boldsymbol{X}_2 \boldsymbol{\beta}_2 + \boldsymbol{u}, \tag{2.33}$$

where $\boldsymbol{X}_1$ is $n \times k_1$, $\boldsymbol{X}_2$ is $n \times k_2$, and $\boldsymbol{X}$ may be written as the partitioned matrix $[\boldsymbol{X}_1 \quad \boldsymbol{X}_2]$, with $k = k_1 + k_2$. In the case dealt with in the previous subsection, $\boldsymbol{X}_1$ is the constant vector $\boldsymbol{\iota}$ and $\boldsymbol{X}_2$ is either $\boldsymbol{x}$ or $\boldsymbol{z}$. Several other examples of partitioning $\boldsymbol{X}$ in this way will be considered in Section 2.5.

We begin by assuming that all the regressors in $\boldsymbol{X}_1$ are orthogonal to all the regressors in $\boldsymbol{X}_2$, so that $\boldsymbol{X}_2^\top \boldsymbol{X}_1 = \mathbf{O}$. Under this assumption, the vector of least-squares estimates $\hat{\boldsymbol{\beta}}_1$ from (2.33) is the same as the one obtained from the regression

$$\boldsymbol{y} = \boldsymbol{X}_1\boldsymbol{\beta}_1 + \boldsymbol{u}_1, \tag{2.34}$$

and $\hat{\boldsymbol{\beta}}_2$ from (2.33) is likewise the same as the vector of estimates obtained from the regression $\boldsymbol{y} = \boldsymbol{X}_2\boldsymbol{\beta}_2 + \boldsymbol{u}_2$. In other words, when $\boldsymbol{X}_1$ and $\boldsymbol{X}_2$ are orthogonal, we can drop either set of regressors from (2.33) without affecting the coefficients of the other set.

The vector of fitted values from (2.33) is $\boldsymbol{P_X y}$, while that from (2.34) is $\boldsymbol{P}_1\boldsymbol{y}$, where we have used the abbreviated notation

$$\boldsymbol{P}_1 \equiv \boldsymbol{P}_{\boldsymbol{X}_1} = \boldsymbol{X}_1(\boldsymbol{X}_1^\top\boldsymbol{X}_1)^{-1}\boldsymbol{X}_1^\top.$$

As we will show directly,

$$\boldsymbol{P}_1\boldsymbol{P_X} = \boldsymbol{P_X}\boldsymbol{P}_1 = \boldsymbol{P}_1; \tag{2.35}$$

this is true whether or not $\boldsymbol{X}_1$ and $\boldsymbol{X}_2$ are orthogonal. Thus

$$\boldsymbol{P}_1\boldsymbol{y} = \boldsymbol{P}_1\boldsymbol{P_X}\boldsymbol{y} = \boldsymbol{P}_1(\boldsymbol{X}_1\hat{\boldsymbol{\beta}}_1 + \boldsymbol{X}_2\hat{\boldsymbol{\beta}}_2) = \boldsymbol{P}_1\boldsymbol{X}_1\hat{\boldsymbol{\beta}}_1 = \boldsymbol{X}_1\hat{\boldsymbol{\beta}}_1. \tag{2.36}$$

The first equality above, which follows from (2.35), says that the projection of $\boldsymbol{y}$ on to $\mathcal{S}(\boldsymbol{X}_1)$ is the same as the projection of $\hat{\boldsymbol{y}} \equiv \boldsymbol{P_X y}$ on to $\mathcal{S}(\boldsymbol{X}_1)$. The second equality follows from the definition of the fitted value vector from (2.33) as $\boldsymbol{P_X y}$; the third from the orthogonality of $\boldsymbol{X}_1$ and $\boldsymbol{X}_2$, which implies that $\boldsymbol{P}_1\boldsymbol{X}_2 = \mathbf{O}$; and the last from the fact that $\boldsymbol{X}_1$ is invariant under the action of $\boldsymbol{P}_1$. Since $\boldsymbol{P}_1\boldsymbol{y}$ is equal to $\boldsymbol{X}_1$ postmultiplied by the OLS estimates from (2.34), the equality of the leftmost and rightmost expressions in (2.36) gives us the result that the same $\hat{\boldsymbol{\beta}}_1$ can be obtained either from (2.33) or from (2.34). The analogous result for $\hat{\boldsymbol{\beta}}_2$ is proved in just the same way.

We now drop the assumption that $\boldsymbol{X}_1$ and $\boldsymbol{X}_2$ are orthogonal and prove (2.35), a very useful result that is true in general. In order to show that $\boldsymbol{P_X}\boldsymbol{P}_1 = \boldsymbol{P}_1$, we proceed as follows:

$$\boldsymbol{P_X}\boldsymbol{P}_1 = \boldsymbol{P_X}\boldsymbol{X}_1(\boldsymbol{X}_1^\top\boldsymbol{X}_1)^{-1}\boldsymbol{X}_1^\top = \boldsymbol{X}_1(\boldsymbol{X}_1^\top\boldsymbol{X}_1)^{-1}\boldsymbol{X}_1^\top = \boldsymbol{P}_1.$$

The middle equality follows by noting that $\boldsymbol{P_X}\boldsymbol{X}_1 = \boldsymbol{X}_1$, because all the columns of $\boldsymbol{X}_1$ are in $\mathcal{S}(\boldsymbol{X})$, and so are left unchanged by $\boldsymbol{P_X}$. The other equality in (2.35), namely $\boldsymbol{P}_1\boldsymbol{P_X} = \boldsymbol{P}_1$, is obtained directly by transposing

$\boldsymbol{P_X P_1} = \boldsymbol{P_1}$ and using the symmetry of $\boldsymbol{P_X}$ and $\boldsymbol{P_1}$. The two results in (2.35) tell us that the product of two orthogonal projections, where one projects on to a subspace of the image of the other, is the projection on to that subspace. See also Exercise 2.15, for the application of this result to the complementary projections $\boldsymbol{M_X}$ and $\boldsymbol{M_1}$.

The general result corresponding to the one shown in Figure 2.12 can be stated as follows. If we transform the regressor matrix in (2.33) by adding $\boldsymbol{X}_1\boldsymbol{A}$ to $\boldsymbol{X}_2$, where $\boldsymbol{A}$ is a $k_1 \times k_2$ matrix, and leaving $\boldsymbol{X}_1$ as it is, we have the regression

$$\boldsymbol{y} = \boldsymbol{X}_1\boldsymbol{\alpha}_1 + (\boldsymbol{X}_2 + \boldsymbol{X}_1\boldsymbol{A})\boldsymbol{\alpha}_2 + \boldsymbol{u}. \tag{2.37}$$

Then $\hat{\boldsymbol{\alpha}}_2$ from (2.37) is the same as $\hat{\boldsymbol{\beta}}_2$ from (2.33). This can be seen immediately by expressing the right-hand side of (2.37) as a linear combination of the columns of $\boldsymbol{X}_1$ and of $\boldsymbol{X}_2$.

In the present general context, there is an operation analogous to that of centering. The result of centering a variable $\boldsymbol{x}$ is a variable $\boldsymbol{z}$ that is orthogonal to $\boldsymbol{\iota}$, the constant. We can create from $\boldsymbol{X}_2$ a set of variables orthogonal to $\boldsymbol{X}_1$ by acting on $\boldsymbol{X}_2$ with the orthogonal projection $\boldsymbol{M}_1 \equiv \mathbf{I} - \boldsymbol{P}_1$, so as to obtain $\boldsymbol{M}_1\boldsymbol{X}_2$. This allows us to run the regression

$$\begin{aligned}\boldsymbol{y} &= \boldsymbol{X}_1\boldsymbol{\alpha}_1 + \boldsymbol{M}_1\boldsymbol{X}_2\boldsymbol{\alpha}_2 + \boldsymbol{u} \\ &= \boldsymbol{X}_1\boldsymbol{\alpha}_1 + \big(\boldsymbol{X}_2 - \boldsymbol{X}_1(\boldsymbol{X}_1^\top\boldsymbol{X}_1)^{-1}\boldsymbol{X}_1^\top\boldsymbol{X}_2\big)\boldsymbol{\alpha}_2 + \boldsymbol{u}.\end{aligned}$$

The first line above is a regression model with two groups of regressors, $\boldsymbol{X}_1$ and $\boldsymbol{M}_1\boldsymbol{X}_2$, which are mutually orthogonal. Therefore, $\hat{\boldsymbol{\alpha}}_2$ is unchanged if we omit $\boldsymbol{X}_1$. The second line makes it clear that this regression is a special case of (2.37), which implies that $\hat{\boldsymbol{\alpha}}_2$ is equal to $\hat{\boldsymbol{\beta}}_2$ from (2.33). Consequently, we see that the two regressions

$$\boldsymbol{y} = \boldsymbol{X}_1\boldsymbol{\alpha}_1 + \boldsymbol{M}_1\boldsymbol{X}_2\boldsymbol{\beta}_2 + \boldsymbol{u} \quad \text{and} \tag{2.38}$$

$$\boldsymbol{y} = \boldsymbol{M}_1\boldsymbol{X}_2\boldsymbol{\beta}_2 + \boldsymbol{v} \tag{2.39}$$

must yield the same estimates of $\boldsymbol{\beta}_2$.

Although regressions (2.33) and (2.39) give the same estimates of $\boldsymbol{\beta}_2$, they do not give the same residuals, as we have indicated by writing $\boldsymbol{u}$ for one regression and $\boldsymbol{v}$ for the other. We can see why the residuals are not the same by looking again at Figure 2.13, in which the constant $\boldsymbol{\iota}$ plays the role of $\boldsymbol{X}_1$, and the centered variable $\boldsymbol{z}$ plays the role of $\boldsymbol{M}_1\boldsymbol{X}_2$. The point corresponding to $\boldsymbol{y}$ can be thought of as lying somewhere on a line through the point $\hat{\boldsymbol{y}}$ and sticking perpendicularly out from the page. The residual vector from regressing $\boldsymbol{y}$ on both $\boldsymbol{\iota}$ and $\boldsymbol{z}$ is thus represented by the line segment from $\hat{\boldsymbol{y}}$, in the page, to $\boldsymbol{y}$, vertically above the page. However, if $\boldsymbol{y}$ is regressed on $\boldsymbol{z}$ alone, the residual vector is the sum of this line segment and the segment from $\hat{\alpha}_2\boldsymbol{z}$ and $\hat{\boldsymbol{y}}$, that is, the top side of the rectangle in the figure. If we want the same residuals in regression (2.33) and a regression like (2.39), we need to purge the dependent variable of the second segment, which can be seen from the figure to be equal to $\hat{\alpha}_1 \boldsymbol{\iota}$.

This suggests replacing $\boldsymbol{y}$ by what we get by projecting $\boldsymbol{y}$ off $\boldsymbol{\iota}$. This projection would be the line segment perpendicular to the page, translated in the horizontal direction so that it intersected the page at the point $\hat{\alpha}_2 \boldsymbol{z}$ rather than $\hat{\boldsymbol{y}}$. In the general context, the analogous operation replaces $\boldsymbol{y}$ by $\boldsymbol{M}_1\boldsymbol{y}$, the projection off $\boldsymbol{X}_1$ rather than off $\boldsymbol{\iota}$. When we perform this projection, (2.39) is replaced by the regression

$$\boldsymbol{M}_1\boldsymbol{y} = \boldsymbol{M}_1\boldsymbol{X}_2\boldsymbol{\beta}_2 + \text{residuals}, \tag{2.40}$$

which yields the same vector of OLS estimates $\hat{\boldsymbol{\beta}}_2$ as regression (2.33), and also the same vector of residuals. This regression is sometimes called the **FWL regression**. We used the notation "+ residuals" instead of "+ $\boldsymbol{u}$" in (2.40) because, in general, the difference between $\boldsymbol{M}_1\boldsymbol{y}$ and $\boldsymbol{M}_1\boldsymbol{X}_2\boldsymbol{\beta}_2$ is not the same thing as the vector $\boldsymbol{u}$ in (2.33). If $\boldsymbol{u}$ is interpreted as an error vector, then (2.40) would not be true if "residuals" were replaced by $\boldsymbol{u}$.

We can now formally state the FWL Theorem. Although the conclusions of the theorem have been established gradually in this section, we also provide a short formal proof.

Theorem 2.1. (Frisch-Waugh-Lovell Theorem)

1. The OLS estimates of $\boldsymbol{\beta}_2$ from regressions (2.33) and (2.40) are numerically identical.
2. The residuals from regressions (2.33) and (2.40) are numerically identical.

Proof: By the standard formula (1.46), the estimate of $\boldsymbol{\beta}_2$ from (2.40) is

$$(\boldsymbol{X}_2^\top\boldsymbol{M}_1\boldsymbol{X}_2)^{-1}\boldsymbol{X}_2^\top\boldsymbol{M}_1\boldsymbol{y}. \tag{2.41}$$

Let $\hat{\boldsymbol{\beta}}_1$ and $\hat{\boldsymbol{\beta}}_2$ denote the two vectors of OLS estimates from (2.33). Then

$$\boldsymbol{y} = \boldsymbol{P_X}\boldsymbol{y} + \boldsymbol{M_X}\boldsymbol{y} = \boldsymbol{X}_1\hat{\boldsymbol{\beta}}_1 + \boldsymbol{X}_2\hat{\boldsymbol{\beta}}_2 + \boldsymbol{M_X}\boldsymbol{y}. \tag{2.42}$$

Premultiplying the leftmost and rightmost expressions in (2.42) by $\boldsymbol{X}_2^\top\boldsymbol{M}_1$, we obtain

$$\boldsymbol{X}_2^\top\boldsymbol{M}_1\boldsymbol{y} = \boldsymbol{X}_2^\top\boldsymbol{M}_1\boldsymbol{X}_2\hat{\boldsymbol{\beta}}_2. \tag{2.43}$$

The first term on the right-hand side of (2.42) has dropped out because $\boldsymbol{M}_1$ annihilates $\boldsymbol{X}_1$. To see that the last term also drops out, observe that

$$\boldsymbol{M_X}\boldsymbol{M}_1\boldsymbol{X}_2 = \boldsymbol{M_X}\boldsymbol{X}_2 = \mathbf{O}. \tag{2.44}$$

The first equality follows from (2.35) (see also Exercise 2.15), and the second from (2.23), which shows that $\boldsymbol{M_X}$ annihilates all the columns of $\boldsymbol{X}$, in particular those of $\boldsymbol{X}_2$. Premultiplying $\boldsymbol{y}$ by the transpose of (2.44) shows that $\boldsymbol{X}_2^{\top}\boldsymbol{M}_1\boldsymbol{M_X}\boldsymbol{y} = \boldsymbol{0}$. We can now solve (2.43) for $\hat{\boldsymbol{\beta}}_2$ to obtain

$$\hat{\boldsymbol{\beta}}_2 = (\boldsymbol{X}_2^{\top}\boldsymbol{M}_1\boldsymbol{X}_2)^{-1}\boldsymbol{X}_2^{\top}\boldsymbol{M}_1\boldsymbol{y},$$

which is expression (2.41). This proves the first part of the theorem.

If we had premultiplied (2.42) by $\boldsymbol{M}_1$ instead of by $\boldsymbol{X}_2^{\top}\boldsymbol{M}_1$, we would have obtained

$$\boldsymbol{M}_1\boldsymbol{y} = \boldsymbol{M}_1\boldsymbol{X}_2\hat{\boldsymbol{\beta}}_2 + \boldsymbol{M_X}\boldsymbol{y}, \tag{2.45}$$

where the last term is unchanged from (2.42) because $\boldsymbol{M}_1\boldsymbol{M_X} = \boldsymbol{M_X}$. The regressand in (2.45) is the regressand from regression (2.40). Because $\hat{\boldsymbol{\beta}}_2$ is the estimate of $\boldsymbol{\beta}_2$ from (2.40), by the first part of the theorem, the first term on the right-hand side of (2.45) is the vector of fitted values from that regression. Thus the second term must be the vector of residuals from regression (2.40). But $\boldsymbol{M_X}\boldsymbol{y}$ is also the vector of residuals from regression (2.33), and this therefore proves the second part of the theorem. ∎

2.5 Applications of the FWL Theorem

A regression like (2.33), in which the regressors are broken up into two groups, can arise in many situations. In this section, we will study three of these. The first two, seasonal dummy variables and time trends, are obvious applications of the FWL Theorem. The third, measures of goodness of fit that take the constant term into account, is somewhat less obvious. In all cases, the FWL Theorem allows us to obtain explicit expressions based on (2.41) for subsets of the parameter estimates of a linear regression.

Seasonal Dummy Variables

For a variety of reasons, it is sometimes desirable to include among the explanatory variables of a regression model variables that can take on only two possible values, which are usually 0 and 1. Such variables are called **indicator variables**, because they indicate a subset of the observations, namely, those for which the value of the variable is 1. Indicator variables are a special case of **dummy variables**, which can take on more than two possible values.

Seasonal variation provides a good reason to employ dummy variables. It is common for economic data that are indexed by time to take the form of **quarterly data**, where each year in the sample period is represented by four observations, one for each quarter, or season, of the year. Many economic activities are strongly affected by the season, for obvious reasons like Christmas shopping, or summer holidays, or the difficulty of doing outdoor work during very cold weather. This seasonal variation, or **seasonality**, in economic activity is likely to be reflected in the economic **time series** that are used in regression models. The term "time series" is used to refer to any variable the observations of which are indexed by the time. Of course, time-series data are sometimes annual, in which case there is no seasonal variation to worry about, and sometimes monthly, in which case there are twelve "seasons" instead of four. For simplicity, we consider only the case of quarterly data.

Since there are four seasons, there may be four **seasonal dummy variables**, each taking the value 1 for just one of the four seasons. Let us denote these variables as $\boldsymbol{s}_1$, $\boldsymbol{s}_2$, $\boldsymbol{s}_3$, and $\boldsymbol{s}_4$. If we consider a sample the first observation of which corresponds to the first quarter of some year, these variables look like

$$\boldsymbol{s}_1 = \begin{bmatrix} 1\\0\\0\\0\\1\\0\\0\\0\\\vdots \end{bmatrix}, \quad \boldsymbol{s}_2 = \begin{bmatrix} 0\\1\\0\\0\\0\\1\\0\\0\\\vdots \end{bmatrix}, \quad \boldsymbol{s}_3 = \begin{bmatrix} 0\\0\\1\\0\\0\\0\\1\\0\\\vdots \end{bmatrix}, \quad \boldsymbol{s}_4 = \begin{bmatrix} 0\\0\\0\\1\\0\\0\\0\\1\\\vdots \end{bmatrix}. \tag{2.46}$$

An important property of these variables is that, since every observation must correspond to some season, the sum of the seasonal dummies must indicate every season. This means that this sum is a vector every component of which equals 1. Algebraically,

$$\boldsymbol{s}_1 + \boldsymbol{s}_2 + \boldsymbol{s}_3 + \boldsymbol{s}_4 = \boldsymbol{\iota}, \tag{2.47}$$

as is clear from (2.46). Since $\boldsymbol{\iota}$ represents the constant in a regression, (2.47) means that the five-variable set consisting of all four seasonal dummies plus the constant is linearly dependent. Consequently, one of the five variables must be dropped if all the regressors are to be linearly independent.

Just which one of the five is dropped makes no difference to the fitted values and residuals of a regression, because it is easy to check that

$$\mathcal{S}(\boldsymbol{s}_1, \boldsymbol{s}_2, \boldsymbol{s}_3, \boldsymbol{s}_4) = \mathcal{S}(\boldsymbol{\iota}, \boldsymbol{s}_2, \boldsymbol{s}_3, \boldsymbol{s}_4) = \mathcal{S}(\boldsymbol{\iota}, \boldsymbol{s}_1, \boldsymbol{s}_3, \boldsymbol{s}_4),$$

and so on. However the parameter estimates associated with the set of four variables that we choose to keep have different interpretations depending on that choice. Suppose first that we drop the constant and run the regression

$$\boldsymbol{y} = \alpha_1\boldsymbol{s}_1 + \alpha_2\boldsymbol{s}_2 + \alpha_3\boldsymbol{s}_3 + \alpha_4\boldsymbol{s}_4 + \boldsymbol{X\beta} + \boldsymbol{u}, \tag{2.48}$$

where the $n \times k$ matrix $\boldsymbol{X}$ contains other explanatory variables. Consider a single observation, indexed by t, that corresponds to the first season. The

t^{th} observations of $\boldsymbol{s}_2$, $\boldsymbol{s}_3$, and $\boldsymbol{s}_4$ are all 0, and that of $\boldsymbol{s}_1$ is 1. Thus, if we write out the tth observation of (2.48), we get

$$y_t = \alpha_1 + \boldsymbol{X}_t\boldsymbol{\beta} + u_t.$$

From this it is clear that, for all t belonging to the first season, the constant term in the regression is α_1. If we repeat this exercise for t in the second, third, or fourth season, we see at once that α_i is the constant for season i. Thus the introduction of the seasonal dummies gives us a different constant for every season.

An alternative is to retain the constant and drop $\boldsymbol{s}_1$. This yields

$$\boldsymbol{y} = \alpha_0\boldsymbol{\iota} + \gamma_2\boldsymbol{s}_2 + \gamma_3\boldsymbol{s}_3 + \gamma_4\boldsymbol{s}_4 + \boldsymbol{X\beta} + \boldsymbol{u}.$$

It is clear that, in this specification, the overall constant α_0 is really the constant for season 1. For an observation belonging to season 2, the constant is $\alpha_0 + \gamma_2$, for an observation belonging to season 3, it is $\alpha_0 + \gamma_3$, and so on. The easiest way to interpret this is to think of season 1 as the reference season. The coefficients γ_i, $i = 2, 3, 4$, measure the difference between α_0, the constant for the reference season, and the constant for season i. Since we could have dropped any of the seasonal dummies, the reference season is, of course, entirely arbitrary.

Another alternative is to retain the constant and use the three dummy variables defined by

$$\boldsymbol{s}_1' = \boldsymbol{s}_1 - \boldsymbol{s}_4, \quad \boldsymbol{s}_2' = \boldsymbol{s}_2 - \boldsymbol{s}_4, \quad \boldsymbol{s}_3' = \boldsymbol{s}_3 - \boldsymbol{s}_4. \tag{2.49}$$

These new dummy variables are not actually indicator variables, because their components for season 4 are equal to -1, but they have the advantage that, for each complete year, the sum of their components for that year is 0. Thus, for any sample whose size is a multiple of 4, each of the $\boldsymbol{s}_i'$, $i = 1, 2, 3$, is orthogonal to the constant. We can write the regression as

$$\boldsymbol{y} = \delta_0\boldsymbol{\iota} + \delta_1\boldsymbol{s}_1' + \delta_2\boldsymbol{s}_2' + \delta_3\boldsymbol{s}_3' + \boldsymbol{X\beta} + \boldsymbol{u}. \tag{2.50}$$

It is easy to see that, for t in season i, $i = 1, 2, 3$, the constant term is $\delta_0 + \delta_i$. For t belonging to season 4, it is $\delta_0 - \delta_1 - \delta_2 - \delta_3$. Thus the average of the constants for all four seasons is just δ_0, the coefficient of the constant, $\boldsymbol{\iota}$. Accordingly, the δ_i, $i = 1, 2, 3$, measure the difference between the average constant δ_0 and the constant specific to season i. Season 4 is a bit of a mess, because of the arithmetic needed to ensure that the average does indeed work out to δ_0.

Let $\boldsymbol{S}$ denote whatever $n \times 4$ matrix we choose to use in order to span the constant and the four seasonal variables $\boldsymbol{s}_i$. Then any of the regressions we have considered so far can be written as

$$\boldsymbol{y} = \boldsymbol{S\delta} + \boldsymbol{X\beta} + \boldsymbol{u}. \tag{2.51}$$

This regression has two groups of regressors, as required for the application of the FWL Theorem. That theorem implies that the estimates $\hat{\boldsymbol{\beta}}$ and the residuals $\hat{\boldsymbol{u}}$ can also be obtained by running the FWL regression

$$\boldsymbol{M_S y} = \boldsymbol{M_S X\beta} + \text{residuals}, \tag{2.52}$$

where, as the notation suggests, $\boldsymbol{M_S} \equiv \mathbf{I} - \boldsymbol{S}(\boldsymbol{S}^\top\boldsymbol{S})^{-1}\boldsymbol{S}^\top$.

The effect of the projection $\boldsymbol{M_S}$ on $\boldsymbol{y}$ and on the explanatory variables in the matrix $\boldsymbol{X}$ can be considered as a form of **seasonal adjustment**. By making $\boldsymbol{M_S y}$ orthogonal to all the seasonal variables, we are, in effect, purging it of its seasonal variation. Consequently, $\boldsymbol{M_S y}$ can be called a **seasonally adjusted**, or **deseasonalized**, version of $\boldsymbol{y}$, and similarly for the explanatory variables. In practice, such seasonally adjusted variables can be conveniently obtained as the residuals from regressing $\boldsymbol{y}$ and each of the columns of $\boldsymbol{X}$ on the variables in $\boldsymbol{S}$. The FWL Theorem tells us that we get the same results in terms of estimates of $\boldsymbol{\beta}$ and residuals whether we run (2.51), in which the variables are unadjusted and seasonality is explicitly accounted for, or run (2.52), in which all the variables are seasonally adjusted by regression. This was, in fact, the subject of the famous paper by Lovell (1963).

The equivalence of (2.51) and (2.52) is sometimes used to claim that, in estimating a regression model with time-series data, it does not matter whether one uses "raw" data, along with seasonal dummies, or seasonally adjusted data. Such a conclusion is completely unwarranted. Official seasonal adjustment procedures are almost never based on regression; using official seasonally adjusted data is therefore *not* equivalent to using residuals from regression on a set of seasonal variables. Moreover, if (2.51) is not a sensible model (and it would not be if, for example, the seasonal pattern were more complicated than that given by $\boldsymbol{S\alpha}$), then (2.52) is not a sensible specification either. Seasonality is actually an important practical problem in applied work with time-series data. We will discuss it further in Chapter 13. For more detailed treatments, see Hylleberg (1986, 1992) and Ghysels and Osborn (2001).

The deseasonalization performed by the projection $\boldsymbol{M_S}$ makes all variables orthogonal to the constant as well as to the seasonal dummies. Thus the effect of $\boldsymbol{M_S}$ is not only to deseasonalize, but also to center, the variables on which it acts. Sometimes this is undesirable; if so, we may use the three variables $\boldsymbol{s}_i'$ given in (2.49). Since they are themselves orthogonal to the constant, no centering takes place if only these three variables are used for seasonal adjustment. An explicit constant should normally be included in any regression that uses variables seasonally adjusted in this way.

Time Trends

Another sort of constructed, or artificial, variable that is often encountered in models of time-series data is a **time trend**. The simplest sort of time trend is the **linear time trend**, represented by the vector $\boldsymbol{T}$, with typical element

$T_t \equiv t$. Thus $\boldsymbol{T} = [1 \vdots 2 \vdots 3 \vdots 4 \vdots \ldots]$. Imagine that we have a regression with a constant and a linear time trend:

$$\boldsymbol{y} = \gamma_1 \boldsymbol{\iota} + \gamma_2 \boldsymbol{T} + \boldsymbol{X\beta} + \boldsymbol{u}.$$

For observation t, y_t is equal to $\gamma_1 + \gamma_2 t + \boldsymbol{X}_t \boldsymbol{\beta} + u_t$. Thus the overall level of y_t increases or decreases steadily as t increases. Instead of just a constant, we now have the linear (strictly speaking, affine) function of time, $\gamma_1 + \gamma_2 t$. An increasing time trend might be appropriate, for instance, in a model of a production function where technical progress is taking place. An explicit model of technical progress might well be difficult to construct, in which case a linear time trend could serve as a simple way to take account of the phenomenon.

It is often desirable to make the time trend orthogonal to the constant by centering it, that is, operating on it with $\boldsymbol{M}_\iota$. If we do this with a sample with an odd number of elements, the result is a variable that looks like

$$[\cdots \vdots -3 \vdots -2 \vdots -1 \vdots 0 \vdots 1 \vdots 2 \vdots 3 \vdots \cdots].$$

If the sample size is even, the variable is made up of the half integers $\pm 1/2$, $\pm 3/2$, $\pm 5/2, \ldots$. In both cases, the coefficient of $\boldsymbol{\iota}$ is the average value of the linear function of time over the whole sample.

Sometimes it is appropriate to use constructed variables that are more complicated than a linear time trend. A simple case would be a quadratic time trend, with typical element t^2. In fact, any deterministic function of the time index t can be used, including the trigonometric functions $\sin t$ and $\cos t$, which could be used to account for oscillatory behavior. With such variables, it is again usually preferable to make them orthogonal to the constant by centering them.

The FWL Theorem applies just as well with time trends of various sorts as it does with seasonal dummy variables. It is possible to project all the other variables in a regression model off the time trend variables, thereby obtaining **detrended** variables. The parameter estimates and residuals are the same as if the trend variables were explicitly included in the regression. This was in fact the type of situation dealt with by Frisch and Waugh (1933).

Goodness of Fit of a Regression

In equations (2.17) and (2.18), we showed that the total sum of squares (TSS) in the regression model $\boldsymbol{y} = \boldsymbol{X\beta} + \boldsymbol{u}$ can be expressed as the sum of the explained sum of squares (ESS) and the sum of squared residuals (SSR). This was really just an application of Pythagoras' Theorem. In terms of the orthogonal projection matrices $\boldsymbol{P_X}$ and $\boldsymbol{M_X}$, the relation between TSS, ESS, and SSR can be written as

$$\text{TSS} = \|\boldsymbol{y}\|^2 = \|\boldsymbol{P_X y}\|^2 + \|\boldsymbol{M_X y}\|^2 = \text{ESS} + \text{SSR}.$$

This allows us to introduce a measure of **goodness of fit** for a regression model. This measure is formally called the **coefficient of determination**, but it is universally referred to as the $\boldsymbol{R^2}$. The R^2 is simply the ratio of ESS to TSS. It can be written as

$$R^2 = \frac{\text{ESS}}{\text{TSS}} = \frac{\|\boldsymbol{P_X y}\|^2}{\|\boldsymbol{y}\|^2} = 1 - \frac{\|\boldsymbol{M_X y}\|^2}{\|\boldsymbol{y}\|^2} = 1 - \frac{\text{SSR}}{\text{TSS}} = \cos^2\theta, \tag{2.53}$$

where θ is the angle between $\boldsymbol{y}$ and $\boldsymbol{P_X y}$; see Figure 2.10. For any angle θ, we know that $-1 \leq \cos\theta \leq 1$. Consequently, $0 \leq R^2 \leq 1$. If the angle θ were zero, $\boldsymbol{y}$ and $\boldsymbol{X\hat{\beta}}$ would coincide, the residual vector $\boldsymbol{\hat{u}}$ would vanish, and we would have what is called a **perfect fit**, with $R^2 = 1$. At the other extreme, if $R^2 = 0$, the fitted value vector would vanish, and $\boldsymbol{y}$ would coincide with the residual vector $\boldsymbol{\hat{u}}$.

As we will see shortly, (2.53) is not the only measure of goodness of fit. It is known as the **uncentered** R^2, and, to distinguish it from other versions of R^2, it is sometimes denoted as R_u^2. Because R_u^2 depends on the data only through the residuals and fitted values, it is invariant under nonsingular linear transformations of the regressors. In addition, because it is defined as a ratio, the value of R_u^2 is invariant to changes in the scale of $\boldsymbol{y}$. For example, we could change the units in which the regressand is measured from dollars to thousands of dollars without affecting the value of R_u^2.

However, R_u^2 is not invariant to changes of units that change the angle θ. An example of such a change is given by the conversion between the Celsius and Fahrenheit scales of temperature, where a constant is involved; see (2.28). To see this, let us consider a very simple change of measuring units, whereby a constant α, analogous to the constant 32 used in converting from Celsius to Fahrenheit, is added to each element of $\boldsymbol{y}$. In terms of these new units, the regression of $\boldsymbol{y}$ on a regressor matrix $\boldsymbol{X}$ becomes

$$\boldsymbol{y} + \alpha\boldsymbol{\iota} = \boldsymbol{X\beta} + \boldsymbol{u}. \tag{2.54}$$

If we assume that the matrix $\boldsymbol{X}$ includes a constant, it follows that $\boldsymbol{P_X\iota} = \boldsymbol{\iota}$ and $\boldsymbol{M_X\iota} = \boldsymbol{0}$, and so we find that

$$\boldsymbol{y} + \alpha\boldsymbol{\iota} = \boldsymbol{P_X}(\boldsymbol{y} + \alpha\boldsymbol{\iota}) + \boldsymbol{M_X}(\boldsymbol{y} + \alpha\boldsymbol{\iota}) = \boldsymbol{P_X y} + \alpha\boldsymbol{\iota} + \boldsymbol{M_X y}.$$

This allows us to compute R_u^2 as

$$R_u^2 = \frac{\|\boldsymbol{P_X y} + \alpha\boldsymbol{\iota}\|^2}{\|\boldsymbol{y} + \alpha\boldsymbol{\iota}\|^2},$$

which is clearly different from (2.53). By choosing α sufficiently large, we can in fact make R_u^2 as close as we wish to 1, because, for very large α, the term $\alpha\boldsymbol{\iota}$ completely dominates the terms $\boldsymbol{P_X y}$ and $\boldsymbol{y}$ in the numerator and denominator, respectively. But a large R_u^2 in such a case would be entirely misleading, since the "good fit" would be accounted for almost exclusively by the constant.

It is easy to see how to get around this problem, at least for regressions that include a constant term. An elementary consequence of the FWL Theorem is that we can express all variables as deviations from their means, by the operation of the projection $\boldsymbol{M_\iota}$, without changing parameter estimates or residuals. The ordinary R^2 from the regression that uses centered variables is called the **centered** R^2. It is defined as

$$R_c^2 \equiv \frac{\|\boldsymbol{P_X M_\iota y}\|^2}{\|\boldsymbol{M_\iota y}\|^2} = 1 - \frac{\|\boldsymbol{M_X y}\|^2}{\|\boldsymbol{M_\iota y}\|^2}, \tag{2.55}$$

and it is clearly unaffected by the addition of a constant to the regressand, as in equation (2.54).

The centered R^2 is much more widely used than the uncentered R^2. When $\boldsymbol{\iota}$ is contained in the span $\mathcal{S}(\boldsymbol{X})$ of the regressors, R_c^2 certainly makes far more sense than R_u^2. However, R_c^2 does not make sense for regressions without a constant term or its equivalent in terms of dummy variables. If a statistical package reports a value for R^2 in such a regression, one needs to be very careful. Different ways of computing R_c^2, all of which would yield the same, correct, answer for regressions that include a constant, may yield quite different answers for regressions that do not. It is even possible to obtain values of R_c^2 that are less than 0 or greater than 1, depending on how the calculations are carried out.

Either version of R^2 is a valid measure of goodness of fit only when the least-squares estimates $\hat{\boldsymbol{\beta}}$ are used. If we used some other estimates of $\boldsymbol{\beta}$, say $\tilde{\boldsymbol{\beta}}$, the triangle in Figure 2.10 would no longer be a right-angled triangle, and Pythagoras' Theorem would no longer apply. As a consequence, the third equality in (2.53) would no longer hold, and the different definitions of R^2 would no longer be the same:

$$1 - \frac{\|\boldsymbol{y} - \boldsymbol{X}\tilde{\boldsymbol{\beta}}\|^2}{\|\boldsymbol{y}\|^2} \neq \frac{\|\boldsymbol{X}\tilde{\boldsymbol{\beta}}\|^2}{\|\boldsymbol{y}\|^2}.$$

If we chose to define R^2 in terms of the residuals, using the first of these expressions, we could not guarantee that it would be positive, and if we chose to define it in terms of the fitted values, using the second, we could not guarantee that it would be less than 1. Thus, when anything other than least squares is used to estimate a regression, one should be very cautious about interpreting a reported R^2. It is not a sensible measure of fit in such a case, and, depending on how it is actually computed, it may be seriously misleading.

2.6 Influential Observations and Leverage

One important feature of OLS estimation, which we have not stressed up to this point, is that each element of the vector of parameter estimates $\hat{\boldsymbol{\beta}}$ is simply a weighted average of the elements of the vector $\boldsymbol{y}$. To see this, define $\boldsymbol{c}_i$ as the ith row of the matrix $(\boldsymbol{X}^\top\boldsymbol{X})^{-1}\boldsymbol{X}^\top$ and observe from (2.02) that $\hat{\beta}_i = \boldsymbol{c}_i\boldsymbol{y}$. This fact will prove to be of great importance when we discuss the statistical properties of least-squares estimation in the next chapter.

Because each element of $\hat{\boldsymbol{\beta}}$ is a weighted average, some observations may affect the value of $\hat{\boldsymbol{\beta}}$ much more than others do. Consider Figure 2.14. This figure is an example of a **scatter diagram**, a long-established way of graphing the relation between two variables. Each point in the figure has Cartesian coordinates (x_t, y_t), where x_t is a typical element of a vector $\boldsymbol{x}$, and y_t of a vector $\boldsymbol{y}$. One point, drawn with a larger dot than the rest, is indicated, for reasons to be explained, as a high leverage point.Suppose that we run the regression

$$\boldsymbol{y} = \beta_1\boldsymbol{\iota} + \beta_2\boldsymbol{x} + \boldsymbol{u}$$

twice, once with, and once without, the high leverage observation. For each regression, the fitted values all lie on the so-called **regression line**, which is the straight line with equation

$$y = \hat{\beta}_1 + \hat{\beta}_2 x.$$

The slope of this line is just $\hat{\beta}_2$, which is why β_2 is sometimes called the **slope coefficient**; see Section 1.1. Similarly, because $\hat{\beta}_1$ is the intercept that the

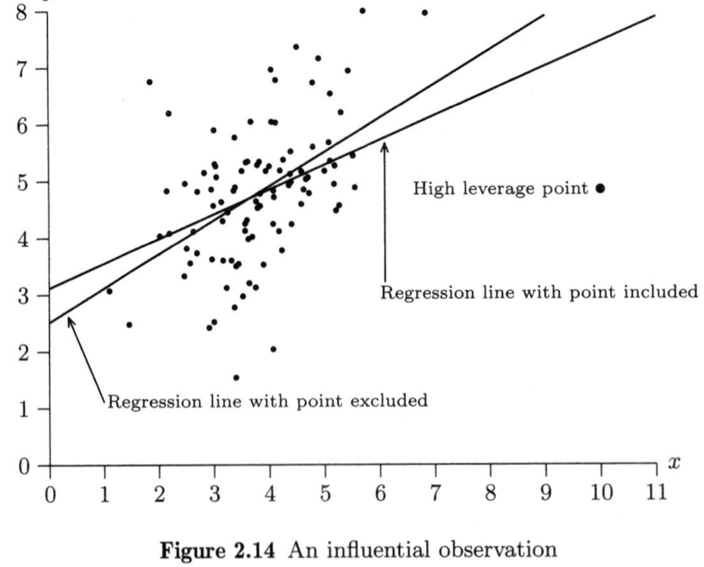

Figure 2.14 An influential observation

regression line makes with the y axis, the constant term β_1 is sometimes called the **intercept**. The regression line is entirely determined by the estimated coefficients, $\hat{\beta}_1$ and $\hat{\beta}_2$.

The regression lines for the two regressions in Figure 2.14 are substantially different. The high leverage point is quite distant from the regression line obtained when it is excluded. When that point is included, it is able, by virtue of its position well to the right of the other observations, to exert a good deal of **leverage** on the regression line, pulling it down toward itself. If the y coordinate of this point were greater, making the point closer to the regression line excluding it, then it would have a smaller **influence** on the regression line including it. If the x coordinate were smaller, putting the point back into the main cloud of points, again there would be a much smaller influence. Thus it is the x coordinate that gives the point its position of high leverage, but it is the y coordinate that determines whether the high leverage position is actually exploited, resulting in substantial influence on the regression line. In a moment, we will generalize these conclusions to regressions with any number of regressors.

If one or a few observations in a regression are highly **influential**, in the sense that deleting them from the sample would change some elements of $\hat{\boldsymbol{\beta}}$ substantially, the prudent econometrician will normally want to scrutinize the data carefully. It may be that these **influential observations** are erroneous, or at least untypical of the rest of the sample. Since a single erroneous observation can have an enormous effect on $\hat{\boldsymbol{\beta}}$, it is important to ensure that any influential observations are not in error. Even if the data are all correct, the interpretation of the regression results may change if it is known that a few observations are primarily responsible for them, especially if those observations differ systematically in some way from the rest of the data.

Leverage

The effect of a single observation on $\hat{\boldsymbol{\beta}}$ can be seen by comparing $\hat{\boldsymbol{\beta}}$ with $\hat{\boldsymbol{\beta}}^{(t)}$, the estimate of $\boldsymbol{\beta}$ that would be obtained if the tth observation were omitted from the sample. Rather than actually omit the tth observation, it is easier to remove its effect by using a dummy variable. The appropriate dummy variable is $\boldsymbol{e}_t$, an n–vector which has t^{th} element 1 and all other elements 0. The vector $\boldsymbol{e}_t$ is called a **unit basis vector**, unit because its norm is 1, basis because the set of all the $\boldsymbol{e}_t$, for $t = 1, \ldots, n$, span, or constitute a **basis** for, the full space E^n; see Exercise 2.22. Considered as an indicator variable, $\boldsymbol{e}_t$ indexes the singleton subsample that contains only observation t.

Including $\boldsymbol{e}_t$ as a regressor leads to a regression of the form

$$\boldsymbol{y} = \boldsymbol{X\beta} + \alpha \boldsymbol{e}_t + \boldsymbol{u}, \tag{2.56}$$

and, by the FWL Theorem, this gives the same parameter estimates and residuals as the FWL regression

$$\boldsymbol{M}_t \boldsymbol{y} = \boldsymbol{M}_t \boldsymbol{X\beta} + \text{residuals}, \tag{2.57}$$

where $\boldsymbol{M}_t \equiv \boldsymbol{M}_{\boldsymbol{e}_t} = \mathbf{I} - \boldsymbol{e}_t(\boldsymbol{e}_t^\top \boldsymbol{e}_t)^{-1}\boldsymbol{e}_t^\top$ is the orthogonal projection off the vector $\boldsymbol{e}_t$. It is easy to see that $\boldsymbol{M}_t\boldsymbol{y}$ is just $\boldsymbol{y}$ with its tth component replaced by 0. Since $\boldsymbol{e}_t^\top \boldsymbol{e}_t = 1$, and since $\boldsymbol{e}_t^\top \boldsymbol{y}$ can easily be seen to be the tth component of $\boldsymbol{y}$,

$$\boldsymbol{M}_t\boldsymbol{y} = \boldsymbol{y} - \boldsymbol{e}_t\boldsymbol{e}_t^\top \boldsymbol{y} = \boldsymbol{y} - y_t\boldsymbol{e}_t.$$

Thus y_t is subtracted from $\boldsymbol{y}$ for the tth observation only. Similarly, $\boldsymbol{M}_t\boldsymbol{X}$ is just $\boldsymbol{X}$ with its tth row replaced by zeros. Running regression (2.57) gives the same parameter estimates as those that would be obtained if we deleted observation t from the sample. Since the vector $\hat{\boldsymbol{\beta}}$ is defined exclusively in terms of scalar products of the variables, replacing the tth elements of these variables by 0 is tantamount to simply leaving observation t out when computing those scalar products.

Let us denote by $\boldsymbol{P}_{\boldsymbol{Z}}$ and $\boldsymbol{M}_{\boldsymbol{Z}}$, respectively, the orthogonal projections on to and off $\mathcal{S}(\boldsymbol{X}, \boldsymbol{e}_t)$. The fitted values and residuals from regression (2.56) are then given by

$$\boldsymbol{y} = \boldsymbol{P}_{\boldsymbol{Z}}\boldsymbol{y} + \boldsymbol{M}_{\boldsymbol{Z}}\boldsymbol{y} = \boldsymbol{X}\hat{\boldsymbol{\beta}}^{(t)} + \hat{\alpha}\boldsymbol{e}_t + \boldsymbol{M}_{\boldsymbol{Z}}\boldsymbol{y}. \tag{2.58}$$

Now premultiply (2.58) by $\boldsymbol{P}_{\boldsymbol{X}}$ to obtain

$$\boldsymbol{P}_{\boldsymbol{X}}\boldsymbol{y} = \boldsymbol{X}\hat{\boldsymbol{\beta}}^{(t)} + \hat{\alpha}\boldsymbol{P}_{\boldsymbol{X}}\boldsymbol{e}_t, \tag{2.59}$$

where we have used the fact that $\boldsymbol{M}_{\boldsymbol{Z}}\boldsymbol{P}_{\boldsymbol{X}} = \mathbf{O}$, because $\boldsymbol{M}_{\boldsymbol{Z}}$ annihilates both $\boldsymbol{X}$ and $\boldsymbol{e}_t$. But $\boldsymbol{P}_{\boldsymbol{X}}\boldsymbol{y} = \boldsymbol{X}\hat{\boldsymbol{\beta}}$, and so (2.59) gives

$$\boldsymbol{X}(\hat{\boldsymbol{\beta}}^{(t)} - \hat{\boldsymbol{\beta}}) = -\hat{\alpha}\boldsymbol{P}_{\boldsymbol{X}}\boldsymbol{e}_t. \tag{2.60}$$

We can compute the difference between $\hat{\boldsymbol{\beta}}^{(t)}$ and $\hat{\boldsymbol{\beta}}$ from this if we can compute the value of $\hat{\alpha}$.

In order to calculate $\hat{\alpha}$, we once again use the FWL Theorem, which tells us that the estimate of α from (2.56) is the same as the estimate from the FWL regression

$$\boldsymbol{M}_{\boldsymbol{X}}\boldsymbol{y} = \hat{\alpha}\boldsymbol{M}_{\boldsymbol{X}}\boldsymbol{e}_t + \text{residuals}.$$

Therefore, using (2.02) and the idempotency of $\boldsymbol{M}_{\boldsymbol{X}}$,

$$\hat{\alpha} = \frac{\boldsymbol{e}_t^\top \boldsymbol{M}_{\boldsymbol{X}}\boldsymbol{y}}{\boldsymbol{e}_t^\top \boldsymbol{M}_{\boldsymbol{X}}\boldsymbol{e}_t}. \tag{2.61}$$

Now $\boldsymbol{e}_t^\top \boldsymbol{M}_{\boldsymbol{X}}\boldsymbol{y}$ is the tth element of $\boldsymbol{M}_{\boldsymbol{X}}\boldsymbol{y}$, the vector of residuals from the regression including all observations. We may denote this element as $\hat{u}_t$. In like manner, $\boldsymbol{e}_t^\top \boldsymbol{M}_{\boldsymbol{X}}\boldsymbol{e}_t$, which is just a scalar, is the tth diagonal element of $\boldsymbol{M}_{\boldsymbol{X}}$. Substituting these into (2.61), we obtain

$$\hat{\alpha} = \frac{\hat{u}_t}{1 - h_t}, \tag{2.62}$$

where h_t denotes the tth diagonal element of $\boldsymbol{P_X}$, which is equal to 1 minus the tth diagonal element of $\boldsymbol{M_X}$. The rather odd notation h_t comes from the fact that $\boldsymbol{P_X}$ is sometimes referred to as the **hat matrix**, because the vector of fitted values $\boldsymbol{X}\hat{\boldsymbol{\beta}} = \boldsymbol{P_X y}$ is sometimes written as $\hat{\boldsymbol{y}}$, and $\boldsymbol{P_X}$ is therefore said to "put a hat on" $\boldsymbol{y}$.

Finally, if we premultiply (2.60) by $(\boldsymbol{X}^\top\boldsymbol{X})^{-1}\boldsymbol{X}^\top$ and use (2.62), we find that

$$\hat{\boldsymbol{\beta}}^{(t)} - \hat{\boldsymbol{\beta}} = -\hat{\alpha}(\boldsymbol{X}^\top\boldsymbol{X})^{-1}\boldsymbol{X}^\top\boldsymbol{P_X}\boldsymbol{e}_t = \frac{-1}{1-h_t}(\boldsymbol{X}^\top\boldsymbol{X})^{-1}\boldsymbol{X}_t^\top\hat{u}_t. \tag{2.63}$$

The second equality uses the facts that $\boldsymbol{X}^\top\boldsymbol{P_X} = \boldsymbol{X}^\top$ and that the final factor of $\boldsymbol{e}_t$ selects the tth column of $\boldsymbol{X}^\top$, which is the transpose of the tth row, $\boldsymbol{X}_t$. Expression (2.63) makes it clear that, when either $\hat{u}_t$ is large or h_t is large, or both, the effect of the tth observation on at least some elements of $\hat{\boldsymbol{\beta}}$ is likely to be substantial. Such an observation is said to be influential.

From (2.63), it is evident that the influence of an observation depends on both $\hat{u}_t$ and h_t. It is greater if the observation has a large residual, which, as we saw in Figure 2.14, is related to its y coordinate. On the other hand, h_t is related to the x coordinate of a point, which, as we also saw in the figure, determines the leverage, or potential influence, of the corresponding observation. We say that observations for which h_t is large have **high leverage** or are **leverage points**. A leverage point is not necessarily influential, but it has the potential to be influential.

The Diagonal Elements of the Hat Matrix

Since the leverage of the tth observation depends on h_t, the tth diagonal element of the hat matrix, it is worth studying the properties of these diagonal elements in a little more detail. We can express h_t as

$$h_t = \boldsymbol{e}_t^\top\boldsymbol{P_X}\boldsymbol{e}_t = \|\boldsymbol{P_X}\boldsymbol{e}_t\|^2. \tag{2.64}$$

Since the rightmost expression here is a square, $h_t \geq 0$. Moreover, since $\|\boldsymbol{e}_t\| = 1$, we obtain from (2.27) applied to $\boldsymbol{e}_t$ that $h_t = \|\boldsymbol{P_X}\boldsymbol{e}_t\|^2 \leq 1$. Thus

$$0 \leq h_t \leq 1. \tag{2.65}$$

The geometrical reason for these bounds on the value of h_t can be found in Exercise 2.28.

The lower bound in (2.65) can be strengthened when there is a constant term. In that case, none of the h_t can be less than $1/n$. This follows from (2.64), because if $\boldsymbol{X}$ consisted only of a constant vector $\boldsymbol{\iota}$, $\boldsymbol{e}_t^\top\boldsymbol{P}_{\boldsymbol{\iota}}\boldsymbol{e}_t$ would equal $1/n$. If other regressors are present, then we have

$$1/n = \|\boldsymbol{P}_{\boldsymbol{\iota}}\boldsymbol{e}_t\|^2 = \|\boldsymbol{P}_{\boldsymbol{\iota}}\boldsymbol{P_X}\boldsymbol{e}_t\|^2 \leq \|\boldsymbol{P_X}\boldsymbol{e}_t\|^2 = h_t.$$

Here we have used the fact that $\boldsymbol{P}_\iota \boldsymbol{P}_{\boldsymbol{X}} = \boldsymbol{P}_\iota$ since $\boldsymbol{\iota}$ is in $\mathcal{S}(\boldsymbol{X})$ by assumption, and, for the inequality, we have used (2.27). Although h_t cannot be 0 in normal circumstances, there is a special case in which it equals 1. If one column of $\boldsymbol{X}$ is the dummy variable $\boldsymbol{e}_t$, $h_t = \boldsymbol{e}_t^\top \boldsymbol{P}_X \boldsymbol{e}_t = \boldsymbol{e}_t^\top \boldsymbol{e}_t = 1$.

In a regression with n observations and k regressors, the average of the h_t is equal to k/n. In order to demonstrate this, we need to use some properties of the **trace** of a square matrix. If $\boldsymbol{A}$ is an $n \times n$ matrix, its trace, denoted $\mathrm{Tr}(\boldsymbol{A})$, is the sum of the elements on its principal diagonal. Thus

$$\mathrm{Tr}(\boldsymbol{A}) \equiv \sum_{i=1}^{n} A_{ii}.$$

A convenient property is that the trace of a product of two not necessarily square matrices $\boldsymbol{A}$ and $\boldsymbol{B}$ is unaffected by the order in which the two matrices are multiplied together. If the dimensions of $\boldsymbol{A}$ are $n \times m$, then, in order for the product $\boldsymbol{AB}$ to be square, those of $\boldsymbol{B}$ must be $m \times n$. This implies further that the product $\boldsymbol{BA}$ exists and is $m \times m$. We have

$$\mathrm{Tr}(\boldsymbol{AB}) = \sum_{i=1}^{n} (\boldsymbol{AB})_{ii} = \sum_{i=1}^{n} \sum_{j=1}^{m} A_{ij} B_{ji} = \sum_{j=1}^{m} (\boldsymbol{BA})_{jj} = \mathrm{Tr}(\boldsymbol{BA}). \qquad (2.66)$$

The result (2.66) can be extended. If we consider a (square) product of several matrices, the trace is invariant under what is called a **cyclic permutation** of the factors. Thus, as can be seen by successive applications of (2.66),

$$\mathrm{Tr}(\boldsymbol{ABC}) = \mathrm{Tr}(\boldsymbol{CAB}) = \mathrm{Tr}(\boldsymbol{BCA}). \qquad (2.67)$$

We now return to the h_t. Their sum is

$$\begin{aligned} \sum_{t=1}^{n} h_t &= \mathrm{Tr}(\boldsymbol{P}_{\boldsymbol{X}}) = \mathrm{Tr}\big(\boldsymbol{X}(\boldsymbol{X}^\top\boldsymbol{X})^{-1}\boldsymbol{X}^\top\big) \\ &= \mathrm{Tr}\big((\boldsymbol{X}^\top\boldsymbol{X})^{-1}\boldsymbol{X}^\top\boldsymbol{X}\big) = \mathrm{Tr}(\mathbf{I}_k) = k. \end{aligned} \qquad (2.68)$$

The first equality in the second line makes use of (2.67). Then, because we are multiplying a $k \times k$ matrix by its inverse, we get a $k \times k$ identity matrix, the trace of which is obviously just k. It follows from (2.68) that the average of the h_t equals k/n. When, for a given regressor matrix $\boldsymbol{X}$, the diagonal elements of $\boldsymbol{P}_{\boldsymbol{X}}$ are all close to their average value, no observation has very much leverage. Such an $\boldsymbol{X}$ matrix is sometimes said to have a **balanced design**. On the other hand, if some of the h_t are much larger than k/n, and others consequently smaller, the $\boldsymbol{X}$ matrix is said to have an **unbalanced design**.

The h_t tend to be larger for values of the regressors that are farther away from their average over the sample. As an example, Figure 2.15 plots them

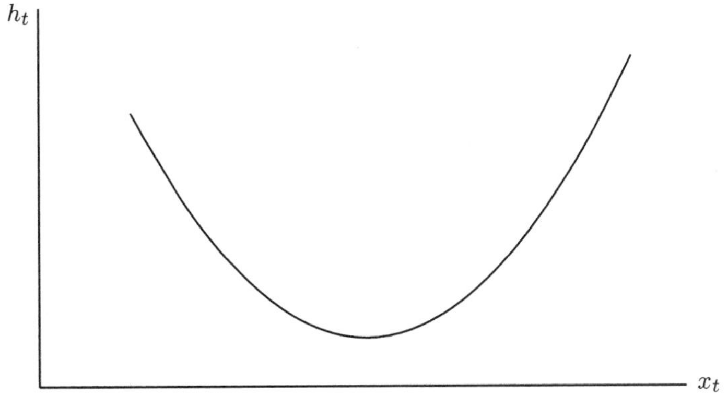

Figure 2.15 A graph of h_t as a function of x_t

as a function of x_t for a particular sample of 100 observations for the model

$$y_t = \beta_1 + \beta_2 x_t + u_t.$$

The elements x_t of the regressor are perfectly well behaved, being drawings from the standard normal distribution. Although the average value of the h_t is $2/100 = 0.02$, h_t varies from 0.0100 for values of x_t near the sample mean to 0.0695 for the largest value of x_t, which is about 2.4 standard deviations above the sample mean. Thus, even in this very typical case, some observations have a great deal more leverage than others. Those observations with the greatest amount of leverage are those for which x_t is farthest from the sample mean, in accordance with the intuition of Figure 2.14.

2.7 Final Remarks

In this chapter, we have discussed the numerical properties of OLS estimation of linear regression models from a geometrical point of view. This perspective often provides a much simpler way to understand such models than does a purely algebraic approach. For example, the fact that certain matrices are idempotent becomes quite clear as soon as one understands the notion of an orthogonal projection. Most of the results discussed in this chapter are thoroughly fundamental, and many of them will be used again and again throughout the book. In particular, the FWL Theorem will turn out to be extremely useful in many contexts.

The use of geometry as an aid to the understanding of linear regression has a long history; see Herr (1980). One valuable reference on linear models that takes the geometric approach is Seber (1980). A good expository paper that is reasonably accessible is Bryant (1984), and a detailed treatment is provided by Ruud (2000).

It is strongly recommended that readers attempt the exercises which follow this chapter before starting Chapter 3, in which we turn our attention to the statistical properties of OLS estimation. Many of the results of this chapter will be useful in establishing these properties, and the exercises are designed to enhance understanding of these results.

2.8 Exercises

2.1 Consider two vectors $\boldsymbol{x}$ and $\boldsymbol{y}$ in E^2. Let $\boldsymbol{x} = [x_1 \vdots x_2]$ and $\boldsymbol{y} = [y_1 \vdots y_2]$. Show trigonometrically that $\boldsymbol{x}^\top \boldsymbol{y} \equiv x_1 y_1 + x_2 y_2$ is equal to $\|\boldsymbol{x}\| \, \|\boldsymbol{y}\| \cos\theta$, where θ is the angle between $\boldsymbol{x}$ and $\boldsymbol{y}$.

2.2 A vector in E^n can be **normalized** by multiplying it by the reciprocal of its norm. Show that, for any $\boldsymbol{x} \in E^n$ with $\boldsymbol{x} \neq \boldsymbol{0}$, the norm of $\boldsymbol{x}/\|\boldsymbol{x}\|$ is 1.

Now consider two vectors $\boldsymbol{x}, \boldsymbol{y} \in E^n$. Compute the norm of the sum and of the difference of $\boldsymbol{x}$ normalized and $\boldsymbol{y}$ normalized, that is, of

$$\frac{\boldsymbol{x}}{\|\boldsymbol{x}\|} + \frac{\boldsymbol{y}}{\|\boldsymbol{y}\|} \quad \text{and} \quad \frac{\boldsymbol{x}}{\|\boldsymbol{x}\|} - \frac{\boldsymbol{y}}{\|\boldsymbol{y}\|}.$$

By using the fact that the norm of any nonzero vector is positive, prove the Cauchy-Schwartz inequality (2.08):

$$|\boldsymbol{x}^\top \boldsymbol{y}| \leq \|\boldsymbol{x}\| \, \|\boldsymbol{y}\|. \tag{2.08}$$

Show that this inequality becomes an equality when $\boldsymbol{x}$ and $\boldsymbol{y}$ are parallel. **Hint:** Show first that $\boldsymbol{x}$ and $\boldsymbol{y}$ are parallel if and only if $\boldsymbol{x}/\|\boldsymbol{x}\| = \pm\, \boldsymbol{y}/\|\boldsymbol{y}\|$.

2.3 The **triangle inequality** states that, for $\boldsymbol{x}, \boldsymbol{y} \in E^n$,

$$\|\boldsymbol{x} + \boldsymbol{y}\| \leq \|\boldsymbol{x}\| + \|\boldsymbol{y}\|. \tag{2.69}$$

Draw a 2–dimensional picture to illustrate this result. Prove the result algebraically by computing the squares of both sides of the above inequality, and then using (2.08). In what circumstances does (2.69) hold with equality?

2.4 Suppose that $\boldsymbol{x} = [1.0 \vdots 1.5 \vdots 1.2 \vdots 0.7]$ and $\boldsymbol{y} = [3.2 \vdots 4.4 \vdots 2.5 \vdots 2.0]$. What are $\|\boldsymbol{x}\|$, $\|\boldsymbol{y}\|$, and $\boldsymbol{x}^\top \boldsymbol{y}$? Use these quantities to calculate θ, the angle θ between $\boldsymbol{x}$ and $\boldsymbol{y}$, and $\cos\theta$.

2.5 Show explicitly that the left-hand sides of (2.11) and (2.12) are the same. This can be done either by comparing typical elements or by using the results in Section 2.3 on partitioned matrices.

2.6 Prove that, if the k columns of $\boldsymbol{X}$ are linearly independent, each vector $\boldsymbol{z}$ in $\mathcal{S}(\boldsymbol{X})$ can be expressed as $\boldsymbol{X}\boldsymbol{b}$ for one and only one k–vector $\boldsymbol{b}$. **Hint:** Suppose that there are two different vectors, $\boldsymbol{b}_1$ and $\boldsymbol{b}_2$, such that $\boldsymbol{z} = \boldsymbol{X}\boldsymbol{b}_i$, $i = 1, 2$, and show that this implies that the columns of $\boldsymbol{X}$ are linearly dependent.

2.7 Consider the vectors $\boldsymbol{x}_1 = [1 \vdots 2 \vdots 4]$, $\boldsymbol{x}_2 = [2 \vdots 3 \vdots 5]$, and $\boldsymbol{x}_3 = [3 \vdots 6 \vdots 12]$. What is the dimension of the subspace that these vectors span?

2.8 Consider the example of the three vectors $\boldsymbol{x}_1$, $\boldsymbol{x}_2$, and $\boldsymbol{x}_3$ defined in (2.14). Show that any vector $\boldsymbol{z} \equiv b_1\boldsymbol{x}_1 + b_2\boldsymbol{x}_2$ in $\mathcal{S}(\boldsymbol{x}_1, \boldsymbol{x}_2)$ also belongs to $\mathcal{S}(\boldsymbol{x}_1, \boldsymbol{x}_3)$

and $\mathcal{S}(\boldsymbol{x}_2, \boldsymbol{x}_3)$. Give explicit formulas for $\boldsymbol{z}$ as a linear combination of $\boldsymbol{x}_1$ and $\boldsymbol{x}_3$, and of $\boldsymbol{x}_2$ and $\boldsymbol{x}_3$.

2.9 Prove algebraically that $\boldsymbol{P_X M_X} = \mathbf{O}$. This is equation (2.25). Use only the requirement (2.24) that $\boldsymbol{P_X}$ and $\boldsymbol{M_X}$ be complementary projections, and the idempotency of $\boldsymbol{P_X}$.

2.10 Let $\boldsymbol{X}$ and $\boldsymbol{W}$ be two $n \times k$ matrices such that $\mathcal{S}(\boldsymbol{X}) \neq \mathcal{S}(\boldsymbol{W})$. Show that the $n \times n$ matrix $\boldsymbol{P} \equiv \boldsymbol{X}(\boldsymbol{W}^\top\boldsymbol{X})^{-1}\boldsymbol{W}^\top$ is idempotent but not symmetric. Characterize the spaces that $\boldsymbol{P}$ and $\mathbf{I} - \boldsymbol{P}$ project on to, and show that they are not orthogonal. Projections like $\boldsymbol{P}$ are called **oblique projections**.

2.11 Prove algebraically that equation (2.26), which is really Pythagoras' Theorem for linear regression, holds. Use the facts that $\boldsymbol{P_X}$ and $\boldsymbol{M_X}$ are symmetric, idempotent, and orthogonal to each other.

2.12 Show algebraically that, if $\boldsymbol{P_X}$ and $\boldsymbol{M_X}$ are complementary orthogonal projections, then $\boldsymbol{M_X}$ annihilates all vectors in $\mathcal{S}(\boldsymbol{X})$, and $\boldsymbol{P_X}$ annihilates all vectors in $\mathcal{S}^\perp(\boldsymbol{X})$.

2.13 Consider the two regressions

$$\begin{aligned}\boldsymbol{y} &= \beta_1\boldsymbol{x}_1 + \beta_2\boldsymbol{x}_2 + \beta_3\boldsymbol{x}_3 + \boldsymbol{u}, \text{ and}\\ \boldsymbol{y} &= \alpha_1\boldsymbol{z}_1 + \alpha_2\boldsymbol{z}_2 + \alpha_3\boldsymbol{z}_3 + \boldsymbol{u},\end{aligned}$$

where $\boldsymbol{z}_1 = \boldsymbol{x}_1 - 2\boldsymbol{x}_2$, $\boldsymbol{z}_2 = \boldsymbol{x}_2 + 4\boldsymbol{x}_3$, and $\boldsymbol{z}_3 = 2\boldsymbol{x}_1 - 3\boldsymbol{x}_2 + 5\boldsymbol{x}_3$. Let $\boldsymbol{X} = [\boldsymbol{x}_1 \;\; \boldsymbol{x}_2 \;\; \boldsymbol{x}_3]$ and $\boldsymbol{Z} = [\boldsymbol{z}_1 \;\; \boldsymbol{z}_2 \;\; \boldsymbol{z}_3]$. Show that the columns of $\boldsymbol{Z}$ can be expressed as linear combinations of the columns of $\boldsymbol{X}$, that is, that $\boldsymbol{Z} = \boldsymbol{XA}$, for some 3×3 matrix $\boldsymbol{A}$. Find the elements of this matrix $\boldsymbol{A}$.

Show that the matrix $\boldsymbol{A}$ is invertible, by showing that the columns of $\boldsymbol{X}$ are linear combinations of the columns of $\boldsymbol{Z}$. Give the elements of $\boldsymbol{A}^{-1}$. Show that the two regressions give the same fitted values and residuals.

Precisely how is the OLS estimate $\hat{\beta}_1$ related to the OLS estimates $\hat{\alpha}_i$, for $i = 1, \ldots, 3$? Precisely how is $\hat{\alpha}_1$ related to the $\hat{\beta}_i$, for $i = 1, \ldots, 3$?

2.14 Let $\boldsymbol{X}$ be an $n \times k$ matrix of full rank. Consider the $n \times k$ matrix $\boldsymbol{XA}$, where $\boldsymbol{A}$ is a *singular* $k \times k$ matrix. Show that the columns of $\boldsymbol{XA}$ are linearly dependent, and that $\mathcal{S}(\boldsymbol{XA}) \subset \mathcal{S}(\boldsymbol{X})$.

2.15 Use the result (2.35) to show that $\boldsymbol{M_X M}_1 = \boldsymbol{M}_1\boldsymbol{M_X} = \boldsymbol{M_X}$, where $\boldsymbol{X} = [\boldsymbol{X}_1 \;\; \boldsymbol{X}_2]$.

2.16 Consider the following linear regression:

$$\boldsymbol{y} = \boldsymbol{X}_1\boldsymbol{\beta}_1 + \boldsymbol{X}_2\boldsymbol{\beta}_2 + \boldsymbol{u},$$

where $\boldsymbol{y}$ is $n \times 1$, $\boldsymbol{X}_1$ is $n \times k_1$, and $\boldsymbol{X}_2$ is $n \times k_2$. Let $\hat{\boldsymbol{\beta}}_1$ and $\hat{\boldsymbol{\beta}}_2$ be the OLS parameter estimates from running this regression.

Now consider the following regressions, all to be estimated by OLS:

(a) $\boldsymbol{y} = \boldsymbol{X}_2\boldsymbol{\beta}_2 + \boldsymbol{u}$;

(b) $\boldsymbol{P}_1\boldsymbol{y} = \boldsymbol{X}_2\boldsymbol{\beta}_2 + \boldsymbol{u}$;

(c) $\boldsymbol{P}_1\boldsymbol{y} = \boldsymbol{P}_1\boldsymbol{X}_2\boldsymbol{\beta}_2 + \boldsymbol{u}$;

(d) $\boldsymbol{P_X y} = \boldsymbol{X}_1\boldsymbol{\beta}_1 + \boldsymbol{X}_2\boldsymbol{\beta}_2 + \boldsymbol{u}$;

(e) $\boldsymbol{P_X y} = \boldsymbol{X}_2\boldsymbol{\beta}_2 + \boldsymbol{u}$;

(f) $\boldsymbol{M}_1\boldsymbol{y} = \boldsymbol{X}_2\boldsymbol{\beta}_2 + \boldsymbol{u}$;

(g) $\boldsymbol{M}_1\boldsymbol{y} = \boldsymbol{M}_1\boldsymbol{X}_2\boldsymbol{\beta}_2 + \boldsymbol{u}$;

(h) $\boldsymbol{M}_1\boldsymbol{y} = \boldsymbol{X}_1\boldsymbol{\beta}_1 + \boldsymbol{M}_1\boldsymbol{X}_2\boldsymbol{\beta}_2 + \boldsymbol{u}$;

(i) $\boldsymbol{M}_1\boldsymbol{y} = \boldsymbol{M}_1\boldsymbol{X}_1\boldsymbol{\beta}_1 + \boldsymbol{M}_1\boldsymbol{X}_2\boldsymbol{\beta}_2 + \boldsymbol{u}$;

(j) $\boldsymbol{P_X y} = \boldsymbol{M}_1\boldsymbol{X}_2\boldsymbol{\beta}_2 + \boldsymbol{u}$.

Here $\boldsymbol{P}_1$ projects orthogonally on to the span of $\boldsymbol{X}_1$, and $\boldsymbol{M}_1 = \mathbf{I} - \boldsymbol{P}_1$. For which of the above regressions are the estimates of $\boldsymbol{\beta}_2$ the same as for the original regression? Why? For which are the residuals the same? Why?

2.17 Consider the linear regression

$$\boldsymbol{y} = \beta_1\boldsymbol{\iota} + \boldsymbol{X}_2\boldsymbol{\beta}_2 + \boldsymbol{u},$$

where $\boldsymbol{\iota}$ is an n–vector of 1s, and $\boldsymbol{X}_2$ is an $n \times (k-1)$ matrix of observations on the remaining regressors. Show, using the FWL Theorem, that the OLS estimators of β_1 and $\boldsymbol{\beta}_2$ can be written as

$$\begin{bmatrix} \hat\beta_1 \\ \hat{\boldsymbol{\beta}}_2 \end{bmatrix} = \begin{bmatrix} n & \boldsymbol{\iota}^\top\boldsymbol{X}_2 \\ 0 & \boldsymbol{X}_2^\top\boldsymbol{M}_\iota\boldsymbol{X}_2 \end{bmatrix}^{-1} \begin{bmatrix} \boldsymbol{\iota}^\top\boldsymbol{y} \\ \boldsymbol{X}_2^\top\boldsymbol{M}_\iota\boldsymbol{y} \end{bmatrix},$$

where, as usual, $\boldsymbol{M}_\iota$ is the matrix that takes deviations from the sample mean.

2.18 Using equations (2.35), show that $\boldsymbol{P_X} - \boldsymbol{P}_1$ is an orthogonal projection matrix. That is, show that $\boldsymbol{P_X} - \boldsymbol{P}_1$ is symmetric and idempotent.

★2.19 Show that $\boldsymbol{P_X} - \boldsymbol{P}_1 = \boldsymbol{P}_{\boldsymbol{M}_1\boldsymbol{X}_2}$, where $\boldsymbol{P}_{\boldsymbol{M}_1\boldsymbol{X}_2}$ is the projection on to the span of $\boldsymbol{M}_1\boldsymbol{X}_2$. This can be done most easily by showing that any vector in $\mathcal{S}(\boldsymbol{M}_1\boldsymbol{X}_2)$ is invariant under the action of $\boldsymbol{P_X} - \boldsymbol{P}_1$, and that any vector orthogonal to this span is annihilated by $\boldsymbol{P_X} - \boldsymbol{P}_1$.

2.20 Let $\boldsymbol{\iota}$ be a vector of 1s, and let $\boldsymbol{X}$ be an $n \times 3$ matrix, with full rank, of which the first column is $\boldsymbol{\iota}$. What can you say about the matrix $\boldsymbol{M}_\iota\boldsymbol{X}$? What can you say about the matrix $\boldsymbol{P}_\iota\boldsymbol{X}$? What is $\boldsymbol{M}_\iota\boldsymbol{M_X}$ equal to? What is $\boldsymbol{P}_\iota\boldsymbol{M_X}$ equal to?

2.21 Express the four seasonal variables, $\boldsymbol{s}_i$, $i = 1,2,3,4$, defined in (2.46), as functions of the constant $\boldsymbol{\iota}$ and the three variables $\boldsymbol{s}'_i$, $i = 1,2,3$, defined in (2.49).

2.22 Show that the full n–dimensional space E^n is the span of the set of **unit basis vectors** $\boldsymbol{e}_t$, $t = 1,\ldots,n$, where all the components of $\boldsymbol{e}_t$ are zero except for the tth, which is equal to 1.

2.23 The file **tbrate.data** contains data for 1950:1 to 1996:4 for three series: r_t, the interest rate on 90-day treasury bills, π_t, the rate of inflation, and y_t, the logarithm of real GDP. For the period 1950:4 to 1996:4, run the regression

$$\Delta r_t = \beta_1 + \beta_2\pi_{t-1} + \beta_3\Delta y_{t-1} + \beta_4\Delta r_{t-1} + \beta_5\Delta r_{t-2} + u_t, \tag{2.70}$$

where Δ is the **first-difference operator**, defined so that $\Delta r_t = r_t - r_{t-1}$. Plot the residuals and fitted values against time. Then regress the residuals on the fitted values and on a constant. What do you learn from this second regression? Now regress the fitted values on the residuals and on a constant. What do you learn from this third regression?

2.24 For the same sample period, regress Δr_t on a constant, Δy_{t-1}, Δr_{t-1}, and Δr_{t-2}. Save the residuals from this regression, and call them $\hat{e}_t$. Then regress π_{t-1} on a constant, Δy_{t-1}, Δr_{t-1}, and Δr_{t-2}. Save the residuals from this regression, and call them $\hat{v}_t$. Now regress $\hat{e}_t$ on $\hat{v}_t$. How are the estimated coefficient and the residuals from this last regression related to anything that you obtained when you estimated regression (2.70)?

2.25 Calculate the diagonal elements of the hat matrix for regression (2.70) and use them to calculate a measure of leverage. Plot this measure against time. On the basis of this plot, which observations seem to have unusually high leverage?

2.26 Show that the tth residual from running regression (2.56) is 0. Use this fact to demonstrate that, as a result of omitting observation t, the tth residual from the regression $\boldsymbol{y} = \boldsymbol{X\beta} + \boldsymbol{u}$ changes by an amount

$$\hat{u}_t \frac{h_t}{1 - h_t}.$$

2.27 Calculate a vector of "omit 1" residuals $\hat{\boldsymbol{u}}^{(\cdot)}$ for regression (2.70). The tth element of $\hat{\boldsymbol{u}}^{(\cdot)}$ is the residual for the tth observation calculated from a regression that uses data for every observation except the tth. Try to avoid running 185 regressions in order to do this! Regress $\hat{\boldsymbol{u}}^{(\cdot)}$ on the ordinary residuals $\hat{\boldsymbol{u}}$. Is the estimated coefficient roughly the size you expected it to be? Would it be larger or smaller if you were to omit some of the high-leverage observations?

2.28 Show that the leverage measure h_t is the square of the cosine of the angle between the unit basis vector $\boldsymbol{e}_t$ and its projection on to the span $\mathcal{S}(\boldsymbol{X})$ of the regressors.

2.29 Suppose the matrix $\boldsymbol{X}$ is 150×5 and has full rank. Let $\boldsymbol{P_X}$ be the matrix that projects on to $\mathcal{S}(\boldsymbol{X})$ and let $\boldsymbol{M_X} = \mathbf{I} - \boldsymbol{P_X}$. What is $\text{Tr}(\boldsymbol{P_X})$? What is $\text{Tr}(\boldsymbol{M_X})$? What would these be if $\boldsymbol{X}$ did not have full rank but instead had rank 3?

2.30 Generate a figure like Figure 2.15 for yourself. Begin by drawing 100 observations of a regressor x_t from the $\text{N}(0, 1)$ distribution. Then compute and save the h_t for a regression of any regressand on a constant and x_t. Plot the points (x_t, h_t), and you should obtain a graph similar to the one in Figure 2.15.

Now add one more observation, x_{101}. Start with $x_{101} = \bar{x}$, the average value of the x_t, and then increase x_{101} progressively until $x_{101} = \bar{x} + 20$. For each value of x_{101}, compute the leverage measure h_{101}. How does h_{101} change as x_{101} gets larger? Why is this in accord with the result that $h_t = 1$ if the regressors include the dummy variable $\boldsymbol{e}_t$?

Chapter 3

The Statistical Properties of Ordinary Least Squares

3.1 Introduction

In the previous chapter, we studied the numerical properties of ordinary least squares estimation, properties that hold no matter how the data may have been generated. In this chapter, we turn our attention to the **statistical** properties of OLS, ones that depend on how the data were actually generated. These properties can never be shown to hold numerically for any actual data set, but they can be proven to hold if we are willing to make certain assumptions. Most of the properties that we will focus on concern the first two moments of the least-squares estimator.

In Section 1.5, we introduced the concept of a **data-generating process**, or **DGP**. For any data set that we are trying to analyze, the DGP is simply the mechanism that actually generated the data. Most real DGPs for economic data are probably very complicated, and economists do not pretend to understand every detail of them. However, for the purpose of studying the statistical properties of estimators, it is almost always necessary to assume that the DGP is quite simple. For instance, when we are studying the (multiple) linear regression model

$$y_t = \boldsymbol{X}_t\boldsymbol{\beta} + u_t, \quad u_t \sim \text{IID}(0, \sigma^2), \tag{3.01}$$

we may wish to assume that the data were actually generated by the DGP

$$y_t = \boldsymbol{X}_t\boldsymbol{\beta}_0 + u_t, \quad u_t \sim \text{NID}(0, \sigma_0^2). \tag{3.02}$$

The symbol "$\sim$" in (3.01) and (3.02) means "is distributed as." We introduced the abbreviation IID, which means "independently and identically distributed," in Section 1.3. In the model (3.01), the notation $\text{IID}(0, \sigma^2)$ means that the u_t are statistically independent and all follow the same distribution, with mean 0 and variance σ^2. Similarly, in the DGP (3.02), the notation $\text{NID}(0, \sigma_0^2)$ means that the u_t are *normally*, independently, and identically distributed, with mean 0 and variance σ_0^2. In both cases, it is implicitly being assumed that the distribution of u_t is in no way dependent on $\boldsymbol{X}_t$.

The differences between the regression model (3.01) and the DGP (3.02) may seem subtle, but they are important. A key feature of a DGP is that it constitutes a **complete specification**, where that expression means, as in Section 1.3, that enough information is provided for the DGP to be simulated on a computer. For that reason, in (3.02) we must provide specific values for the parameters $\boldsymbol{\beta}$ and σ^2 (the zero subscripts on these parameters are intended to remind us of this), and we must specify from what distribution the error terms are to be drawn (here, the normal distribution).

A **model** is defined as a set of data-generating processes. Since a model is a set, we will sometimes use the notation $\mathbb{M}$ to denote it. In the case of the **linear regression model** (3.01), this set consists of all DGPs of the form (3.01) in which the coefficient vector $\boldsymbol{\beta}$ takes some value in $\mathbb{R}^k$, the variance σ^2 is some positive real number, and the distribution of u_t varies over all possible distributions that have mean 0 and variance σ^2. Although the DGP (3.02) evidently belongs to this set, it is considerably more restrictive.

The set of DGPs of the form (3.02) defines what is called the **classical normal linear model**, where the name indicates that the error terms are normally distributed. The model (3.01) is larger than the classical normal linear model, because, although the former specifies the first two moments of the error terms, and requires the error terms to be mutually independent, it says no more about them, and in particular it does not require them to be normal. All of the results we prove in this chapter, and many of those in the next, apply to the linear regression model (3.01), with no normality assumption. However, in order to obtain some of the results in the next two chapters, it will be necessary to limit attention to the classical normal linear model.

For most of this chapter, we assume that whatever model we are studying, the linear regression model or the classical normal linear model, is **correctly specified**. By this, we mean that the DGP that actually generated our data belongs to the model under study. A model is **misspecified** if that is not the case. It is crucially important, when studying the properties of an estimation procedure, to distinguish between properties which hold only when the model is correctly specified, and properties, like those treated in the previous chapter, which hold no matter what the DGP. We can talk about statistical properties only if we specify the DGP.

In the remainder of this chapter, we study a number of the most important statistical properties of ordinary least-squares estimation, by which we mean least-squares estimation of linear regression models. In the next section, we discuss the concept of bias and prove that, under certain conditions, $\hat{\boldsymbol{\beta}}$, the OLS estimator of $\boldsymbol{\beta}$, is unbiased. Then, in Section 3.3, we discuss the concept of consistency and prove that, under considerably weaker conditions, $\hat{\boldsymbol{\beta}}$ is consistent. In Section 3.4, we turn our attention to the covariance matrix of $\hat{\boldsymbol{\beta}}$, and we discuss the concept of collinearity. This leads naturally to a discussion of the efficiency of least-squares estimation in Section 3.5, in which we prove the famous Gauss-Markov Theorem. In Section 3.6, we discuss the estimation of σ^2 and the relationship between error terms and least-squares residuals. Up to this point, we will assume that the DGP belongs to the model being estimated. In Section 3.7, we relax this assumption and consider the consequences of estimating a model that is misspecified in certain ways. Finally, in Section 3.8, we discuss the adjusted R^2 and other ways of measuring how well a regression fits.

3.2 Are OLS Parameter Estimators Unbiased?

One of the statistical properties that we would like any estimator to have is that it should be **unbiased**. Suppose that $\hat{\theta}$ is an estimator of some parameter θ, the true value of which is θ_0. Then the **bias** of $\hat{\theta}$ is defined as $\mathrm{E}(\hat{\theta})-\theta_0$, the expectation of $\hat{\theta}$ minus the true value of θ. If the bias of an estimator is zero for every admissible value of θ_0, then the estimator is said to be unbiased. Otherwise, it is said to be **biased**. Intuitively, if we were to use an unbiased estimator to calculate estimates for a very large number of samples, then the average value of those estimates would tend to the quantity being estimated. If their other statistical properties were the same, we would always prefer an unbiased estimator to a biased one.

As we have seen, the linear regression model (3.01) can also be written, using matrix notation, as

$$\boldsymbol{y} = \boldsymbol{X\beta} + \boldsymbol{u}, \quad \boldsymbol{u} \sim \mathrm{IID}(\boldsymbol{0}, \sigma^2\mathbf{I}), \tag{3.03}$$

where $\boldsymbol{y}$ and $\boldsymbol{u}$ are n–vectors, $\boldsymbol{X}$ is an $n \times k$ matrix, and $\boldsymbol{\beta}$ is a k–vector. In (3.03), the notation $\mathrm{IID}(\boldsymbol{0}, \sigma^2\mathbf{I})$ is just another way of saying that each element of the vector $\boldsymbol{u}$ is independently and identically distributed with mean 0 and variance σ^2. This notation, which may seem a little strange at this point, is convenient to use when the model is written in matrix notation. Its meaning should become clear in Section 3.4. As we first saw in Section 1.5, the OLS estimator of $\boldsymbol{\beta}$ can be written as

$$\hat{\boldsymbol{\beta}} = (\boldsymbol{X}^\top\boldsymbol{X})^{-1}\boldsymbol{X}^\top\boldsymbol{y}. \tag{3.04}$$

In order to see whether this estimator is biased, we need to replace $\boldsymbol{y}$ by whatever it is equal to under the DGP that is assumed to have generated the data. Since we wish to assume that the model (3.03) is correctly specified, we suppose that the DGP is given by (3.03) with $\boldsymbol{\beta} = \boldsymbol{\beta}_0$. Substituting this into (3.04) yields

$$\begin{aligned} \hat{\boldsymbol{\beta}} &= (\boldsymbol{X}^\top\boldsymbol{X})^{-1}\boldsymbol{X}^\top(\boldsymbol{X\beta}_0 + \boldsymbol{u}) \\ &= \boldsymbol{\beta}_0 + (\boldsymbol{X}^\top\boldsymbol{X})^{-1}\boldsymbol{X}^\top\boldsymbol{u}. \end{aligned} \tag{3.05}$$

The expectation of the second line here is

$$\mathrm{E}(\hat{\boldsymbol{\beta}}) = \boldsymbol{\beta}_0 + \mathrm{E}\big((\boldsymbol{X}^\top\boldsymbol{X})^{-1}\boldsymbol{X}^\top\boldsymbol{u}\big). \tag{3.06}$$

It is obvious that $\hat{\boldsymbol{\beta}}$ is unbiased if and only if the second term on the right-hand side of equation (3.06) is equal to a zero vector. What is not entirely obvious is just what assumptions are needed to ensure that this condition holds.

Assumptions About Error Terms and Regressors

In certain cases, it may be reasonable to treat the matrix $\boldsymbol{X}$ as **nonstochastic**, or **fixed**. For example, this would certainly be a reasonable assumption to make if the data pertained to an experiment, and the experimenter had chosen the values of all the variables that enter into $\boldsymbol{X}$ before $\boldsymbol{y}$ was determined. In this case, the matrix $(\boldsymbol{X}^\top\boldsymbol{X})^{-1}\boldsymbol{X}^\top$ is not random, and the second term in (3.06) becomes

$$\mathrm{E}\big((\boldsymbol{X}^\top\boldsymbol{X})^{-1}\boldsymbol{X}^\top\boldsymbol{u}\big) = (\boldsymbol{X}^\top\boldsymbol{X})^{-1}\boldsymbol{X}^\top\mathrm{E}(\boldsymbol{u}). \tag{3.07}$$

If $\boldsymbol{X}$ really is fixed, it is perfectly valid to move the expectations operator through the factor that depends on $\boldsymbol{X}$, as we have done in (3.07). Then, if we are willing to assume that $\mathrm{E}(\boldsymbol{u}) = \boldsymbol{0}$, we obtain the result that the vector on the right-hand side of equation (3.07) is a zero vector.

Unfortunately, the assumption that $\boldsymbol{X}$ is fixed, convenient though it may be for showing that $\hat{\boldsymbol{\beta}}$ is unbiased, is frequently not a reasonable assumption to make in applied econometric work. More commonly, at least some of the columns of $\boldsymbol{X}$ correspond to variables that are no less random than $\boldsymbol{y}$ itself, and it would often stretch credulity to treat them as fixed. Luckily, we can still show that $\hat{\boldsymbol{\beta}}$ is unbiased in some quite reasonable circumstances without making such a strong assumption.

A weaker assumption is that the explanatory variables which form the columns of $\boldsymbol{X}$ are **exogenous**. The concept of **exogeneity** was introduced in Section 1.3. When applied to the matrix $\boldsymbol{X}$, it implies that any randomness in the DGP that generated $\boldsymbol{X}$ is independent of the error terms $\boldsymbol{u}$ in the DGP for $\boldsymbol{y}$. This independence in turn implies that

$$\mathrm{E}(\boldsymbol{u}\,|\,\boldsymbol{X}) = \boldsymbol{0}. \tag{3.08}$$

In words, this says that the mean of the entire vector $\boldsymbol{u}$, that is, of every one of the u_t, is zero conditional on the entire matrix $\boldsymbol{X}$. See Section 1.2 for a discussion of conditional expectations. Although condition (3.08) is weaker than the condition of independence of $\boldsymbol{X}$ and $\boldsymbol{u}$, it is convenient to refer to (3.08) as an **exogeneity** assumption.

Given the exogeneity assumption (3.08), it is easy to show that $\hat{\boldsymbol{\beta}}$ is unbiased. Because the expectation of $(\boldsymbol{X}^\top\boldsymbol{X})^{-1}\boldsymbol{X}^\top$ conditional on $\boldsymbol{X}$ is just itself, and the expectation of $\boldsymbol{u}$ conditional on $\boldsymbol{X}$ is assumed to be $\boldsymbol{0}$, it is clear that

$$\mathrm{E}\big((\boldsymbol{X}^\top\boldsymbol{X})^{-1}\boldsymbol{X}^\top\boldsymbol{u}\,|\,\boldsymbol{X}\big) = \boldsymbol{0}; \tag{3.09}$$

see equation (1.17). Then, applying the Law of Iterated Expectations, we see that the unconditional expectation of the left-hand side of (3.09) must be equal to the expectation of the right-hand side, which is just $\mathbf{0}$.

Assumption (3.08) is perfectly reasonable in the context of some types of data. In particular, suppose that a sample consists of **cross-section data**, in which each observation might correspond to an individual firm, household, person, or city. For many cross-section data sets, there may be no reason to believe that u_t is in any way related to the values of the regressors for any of the observations. On the other hand, suppose that a sample consists of **time-series data**, in which each observation might correspond to a year, quarter, month, or day, as would be the case, for instance, if we wished to estimate a consumption function, as in Chapter 1. Even if we are willing to assume that u_t is in no way related to current and past values of the regressors, it must be related to future values if current values of the dependent variable affect future values of some of the regressors. Thus, in the context of time-series data, the exogeneity assumption (3.08) is a very strong one that we may often not feel comfortable in making.

The assumption that we made in Section 1.3 about the error terms and the explanatory variables, namely, that

$$\mathrm{E}(u_t \mid \boldsymbol{X}_t) = 0, \tag{3.10}$$

is substantially weaker than assumption (3.08), because (3.08) rules out the possibility that the mean of u_t may depend on the values of the regressors for any observation, while (3.10) merely rules out the possibility that it may depend on their values for the current observation. For reasons that will become apparent in the next subsection, we refer to (3.10) as a **predeterminedness** condition. Equivalently, we say that the regressors are **predetermined** with respect to the error terms.

The OLS Estimator Can Be Biased

We have just seen that the OLS estimator $\hat{\boldsymbol{\beta}}$ is unbiased if we make assumption (3.08) that the explanatory variables $\boldsymbol{X}$ are exogenous, but we remarked that this assumption can sometimes be uncomfortably strong. If we are not prepared to go beyond the predeterminedness assumption (3.10), which it is rarely sensible to do if we are using time-series data, then we find that $\hat{\boldsymbol{\beta}}$ is, in general, biased.

Many regression models for time-series data include one or more **lagged variables** among the regressors. The first lag of a time-series variable that takes on the value z_t at time t has value z_{t-1} at time t. Similarly, the second lag of z_t has value z_{t-2}, and the pth lag has value z_{t-p}. In some models, lags of the dependent variable itself are used as regressors. Indeed, in some cases, the only regressors, except perhaps for a constant term and time trend or dummy variables, are **lagged dependent variables**. Such models are said to be **autoregressive**, because the conditional mean of the dependent variable depends on lagged values of the dependent variable itself. A simple example of an autoregressive model is

$$\boldsymbol{y} = \beta_1 \boldsymbol{\iota} + \beta_2 \boldsymbol{y}_1 + \boldsymbol{u}, \quad \boldsymbol{u} \sim \text{IID}(\boldsymbol{0}, \sigma^2 \mathbf{I}). \tag{3.11}$$

Here, as usual, $\boldsymbol{\iota}$ is a vector of 1s, the vector $\boldsymbol{y}$ has typical element y_t, the dependent variable, and the vector $\boldsymbol{y}_1$ has typical element y_{t-1}, the lagged dependent variable. This model can also be written, in terms of a typical observation, as

$$y_t = \beta_1 + \beta_2 y_{t-1} + u_t, \quad u_t \sim \text{IID}(0, \sigma^2).$$

It is perfectly reasonable to assume that the predeterminedness condition (3.10) holds for the model (3.11), because this condition amounts to saying that $\text{E}(u_t) = 0$ for every possible value of y_{t-1}. The lagged dependent variable y_{t-1} is then said to be predetermined with respect to the error term u_t. Not only is y_{t-1} realized before u_t, but its realized value has no impact on the expectation of u_t. However, it is clear that the exogeneity assumption (3.08), which would here require that $\text{E}(\boldsymbol{u} \,|\, \boldsymbol{y}_1) = \boldsymbol{0}$, cannot possibly hold, because y_{t-1} depends on u_{t-1}, u_{t-2}, and so on. Assumption (3.08) evidently fails to hold for any model in which the regression function includes a lagged dependent variable.

To see the consequences of assumption (3.08) not holding, we use the FWL Theorem to write out $\hat{\beta}_2$ explicitly as

$$\hat{\beta}_2 = (\boldsymbol{y}_1^{\top} \boldsymbol{M}_{\iota} \boldsymbol{y}_1)^{-1} \boldsymbol{y}_1^{\top} \boldsymbol{M}_{\iota} \boldsymbol{y}.$$

Here $\boldsymbol{M}_{\iota}$ denotes the projection matrix $\mathbf{I} - \boldsymbol{\iota}(\boldsymbol{\iota}^{\top}\boldsymbol{\iota})^{-1}\boldsymbol{\iota}^{\top}$, which centers any vector it multiplies; recall (2.31). If we replace $\boldsymbol{y}$ by $\beta_{10}\boldsymbol{\iota} + \beta_{20}\boldsymbol{y}_1 + \boldsymbol{u}$, where β_{10} and β_{20} are specific values of the parameters, and use the fact that $\boldsymbol{M}_{\iota}$ annihilates the constant vector, we find that

$$\begin{aligned} \hat{\beta}_2 &= (\boldsymbol{y}_1^{\top} \boldsymbol{M}_{\iota} \boldsymbol{y}_1)^{-1} \boldsymbol{y}_1^{\top} \boldsymbol{M}_{\iota} (\boldsymbol{y}_1 \beta_{20} + \boldsymbol{u}) \\ &= \beta_{20} + (\boldsymbol{y}_1^{\top} \boldsymbol{M}_{\iota} \boldsymbol{y}_1)^{-1} \boldsymbol{y}_1^{\top} \boldsymbol{M}_{\iota} \boldsymbol{u}. \end{aligned} \tag{3.12}$$

This is evidently just a special case of (3.05).

It is clear that $\hat{\beta}_2$ is unbiased if and only if the second term in the second line of (3.12) has expectation zero. But this term does *not* have expectation zero. Because $\boldsymbol{y}_1$ is stochastic, we cannot simply move the expectations operator, as we did in (3.07), and then take the unconditional expectation of $\boldsymbol{u}$. Because $\text{E}(\boldsymbol{u} \,|\, \boldsymbol{y}_1) \neq \boldsymbol{0}$, we also cannot take expectations conditional on $\boldsymbol{y}_1$, in the way that we took expectations conditional on $\boldsymbol{X}$ in (3.09), and then rely on the Law of Iterated Expectations. In fact, as readers are asked to demonstrate in Exercise 3.1, the estimator $\hat{\beta}_2$ is biased.

It seems reasonable that, if $\hat{\beta}_2$ is biased, so must be $\hat{\beta}_1$. The equivalent of the second line of (3.12) is

$$\hat{\beta}_1 = \beta_{10} + (\boldsymbol{\iota}^\top \boldsymbol{M}_{\boldsymbol{y}_1} \boldsymbol{\iota})^{-1} \boldsymbol{\iota}^\top \boldsymbol{M}_{\boldsymbol{y}_1} \boldsymbol{u}, \tag{3.13}$$

where the notation should be self-explanatory. Once again, because $\boldsymbol{y}_1$ depends on $\boldsymbol{u}$, we cannot employ the methods that we used in (3.07) or (3.09) to prove that the second term on the right-hand side of (3.13) has mean zero. In fact, it does not have mean zero, and $\hat{\beta}_1$ is consequently biased, as readers are also asked to demonstrate in Exercise 3.1.

The problems we have just encountered when dealing with the autoregressive model (3.11) evidently affect every regression model with random regressors for which the exogeneity assumption (3.08) does not hold. Thus, for all such models, the least-squares estimator of the parameters of the regression function is biased. Assumption (3.08) cannot possibly hold when the regressor matrix $\boldsymbol{X}$ contains lagged dependent variables, and it probably fails to hold for most other models that involve time-series data.

3.3 Are OLS Parameter Estimators Consistent?

Unbiasedness is by no means the only desirable property that we would like an estimator to possess. Another very important property is **consistency**. A **consistent** estimator is one for which the estimate tends to the quantity being estimated as the size of the sample tends to infinity. Thus, if the sample size is large enough, we can be confident that the estimate is close to the true value. Happily, the least-squares estimator $\hat{\boldsymbol{\beta}}$ is often consistent even when it is biased.

In order to define consistency, we have to specify what it means for the sample size n to tend to infinity or, in more compact notation, $n \to \infty$. At first sight, this may seem like a very odd notion. After all, any given data set contains a fixed number of observations. Nevertheless, we can certainly imagine simulating data and letting n become arbitrarily large. In the case of a pure time-series model like (3.11), we can easily generate any sample size we want, just by letting the simulations run on for long enough. In the case of a model with cross-section data, we can pretend that the original sample is taken from a population of infinite size, and we can imagine drawing more and more observations from that population. Even in the case of a model with fixed regressors, we can think of ways to make n tend to infinity. Suppose that the original $\boldsymbol{X}$ matrix is of dimension $m \times k$. Then we can create $\boldsymbol{X}$ matrices of dimensions $2m \times k$, $3m \times k$, $4m \times k$, and so on, simply by stacking as many copies of the original $\boldsymbol{X}$ matrix as we like. By simulating error vectors of the appropriate length, we can then generate $\boldsymbol{y}$ vectors of any length n that is an integer multiple of m. Thus, in all these cases, we can reasonably think of letting n tend to infinity.

Probability Limits

In order to say what happens to a stochastic quantity that depends on n as $n \to \infty$, we need to introduce the concept of a **probability limit**. The probability limit, or **plim** for short, generalizes the ordinary concept of a limit to quantities that are stochastic. If $\boldsymbol{a}(\boldsymbol{y}^n)$ is some vector function of the random vector $\boldsymbol{y}^n$, and the plim of $\boldsymbol{a}(\boldsymbol{y}^n)$ as $n \to \infty$ is $\boldsymbol{a}_0$, we may write

$$\operatorname*{plim}_{n\to\infty} \boldsymbol{a}(\boldsymbol{y}^n) = \boldsymbol{a}_0. \tag{3.14}$$

We have written $\boldsymbol{y}^n$ here, instead of just $\boldsymbol{y}$, to emphasize the fact that $\boldsymbol{y}^n$ is a vector of length n, and that n is not fixed. The superscript is often omitted in practice. In econometrics, we are almost always interested in taking probability limits as $n \to \infty$. Thus, when there can be no ambiguity, we will often simply use notation like $\operatorname{plim} \boldsymbol{a}(\boldsymbol{y})$ rather than more precise notation like that of (3.14).

Formally, the random vector $\boldsymbol{a}(\boldsymbol{y}^n)$ tends in probability to the limiting random vector $\boldsymbol{a}_0$ if, for all $\varepsilon > 0$,

$$\lim_{n\to\infty} \Pr\big(\|\boldsymbol{a}(\boldsymbol{y}^n) - \boldsymbol{a}_0\| < \varepsilon\big) = 1. \tag{3.15}$$

Here $\|\cdot\|$ denotes the Euclidean norm of a vector (see Section 2.2), which simplifies to the absolute value when its argument is a scalar. Condition (3.15) says that, for any specified tolerance level ε, no matter how small, the probability that the norm of the discrepancy between $\boldsymbol{a}(\boldsymbol{y}^n)$ and $\boldsymbol{a}_0$ is less than ε goes to unity as $n \to \infty$.

Although the probability limit $\boldsymbol{a}_0$ was defined above to be a random variable (actually, a vector of random variables), it may in fact be an ordinary nonrandom vector or scalar, in which case it is said to be nonstochastic. Many of the plims that we will encounter in this book are in fact nonstochastic. A simple example of a **nonstochastic plim** is the limit of the proportion of heads in a series of independent tosses of an unbiased coin. Suppose that y_t is a random variable equal to 1 if the coin comes up heads, and equal to 0 if it comes up tails. After n tosses, the proportion of heads is just

$$p(\boldsymbol{y}^n) \equiv \frac{1}{n}\sum_{t=1}^{n} y_t.$$

If the coin really is unbiased, $\mathrm{E}(y_t) = 1/2$. Thus it should come as no surprise to learn that $\operatorname{plim} p(\boldsymbol{y}^n) = 1/2$. Proving this requires a certain amount of effort, however, and we will therefore not attempt a proof here. For a detailed discussion and proof, see Davidson and MacKinnon (1993, Section 4.2).

The coin-tossing example is really a special case of an extremely powerful result in probability theory, which is called a **law of large numbers**, or **LLN**.

Suppose that $\bar{x}$ is the sample mean of x_t, $t = 1, \ldots, n$, a sequence of random variables, each with expectation μ. Then, provided the x_t are independent (or at least, not too dependent), a law of large numbers would state that

$$\operatorname*{plim}_{n\to\infty} \bar{x} = \operatorname*{plim}_{n\to\infty} \frac{1}{n}\sum_{t=1}^{n} x_t = \mu. \tag{3.16}$$

In words, $\bar{x}$ has a nonstochastic plim which is equal to the common expectation of each of the x_t.

It is not hard to see intuitively why (3.16) is true under certain conditions. Suppose, for example, that the x_t are IID, with variance σ^2. Then we see at once that

$$\mathrm{E}(\bar{x}) = \frac{1}{n}\sum_{t=1}^{n}\mathrm{E}(x_t) = \frac{1}{n}\sum_{t=1}^{n}\mu = \mu, \quad \text{and}$$

$$\mathrm{Var}(\bar{x}) = \left(\frac{1}{n}\right)^2\sum_{t=1}^{n}\sigma^2 = \frac{1}{n}\sigma^2.$$

Thus $\bar{x}$ has mean μ and a variance which tends to zero as $n \to \infty$. In the limit, we expect that, on account of the shrinking variance, $\bar{x}$ will become a nonstochastic quantity equal to its expectation μ. The law of large numbers assures us that this is the case.

Another useful way to think about laws of large numbers is to note that, as $n \to \infty$, we are collecting more and more information about the mean of the x_t, with each individual observation providing a smaller and smaller fraction of that information. Thus, eventually, the randomness in the individual x_t cancels out, and the sample mean $\bar{x}$ converges to the population mean μ. For this to happen, we need to make some assumption in order to prevent any one of the x_t from having too much impact on $\bar{x}$. The assumption that they are IID is sufficient for this. Alternatively, if they are not IID, we could assume that the variance of each x_t is greater than some finite nonzero lower bound, but smaller than some finite upper bound. We also need to assume that there is not too much dependence among the x_t in order to ensure that the random components of the individual x_t really do cancel out.

There are actually many laws of large numbers, which differ principally in the conditions that they impose on the random variables which are being averaged. We will not attempt to prove any of these LLNs. Section 4.5 of Davidson and MacKinnon (1993) provides a simple proof of a relatively elementary law of large numbers. More advanced LLNs are discussed in Section 4.7 of that book, and, in more detail, in Davidson (1994).

Probability limits have some very convenient properties. For example, suppose that $\{x^n\}$, $n = 1, \ldots, \infty$, is a sequence of random variables which has a nonstochastic plim x_0 as $n \to \infty$, and $\eta(x^n)$ is a smooth function of x^n. Then $\operatorname{plim} \eta(x^n) = \eta(x_0)$. This feature of plims is one that is emphatically not shared by expectations. When $\eta(\cdot)$ is a nonlinear function,

$\text{E}(\eta(x)) \neq \eta(\text{E}(x))$. Thus, it is often very easy to calculate plims in circumstances where it would be difficult or impossible to calculate expectations.

However, working with plims can be a little bit tricky. The problem is that many of the stochastic quantities we encounter in econometrics do not have probability limits unless we divide them by n or, perhaps, by some power of n. For example, consider the matrix $\boldsymbol{X}^\top\boldsymbol{X}$, which appears in the formula (3.04) for $\hat{\boldsymbol{\beta}}$. Each element of this matrix is a scalar product of two of the columns of $\boldsymbol{X}$, that is, two n–vectors. Thus it is a sum of n numbers. As $n \to \infty$, we would expect that, in most circumstances, such a sum would tend to infinity as well. Therefore, the matrix $\boldsymbol{X}^\top\boldsymbol{X}$ does not generally have a plim. However, it is not at all unreasonable to assume that

$$\operatorname*{plim}_{n\to\infty} \frac{1}{n}\boldsymbol{X}^\top\boldsymbol{X} = \boldsymbol{S}_{\boldsymbol{X}^\top\boldsymbol{X}}, \tag{3.17}$$

where $\boldsymbol{S}_{\boldsymbol{X}^\top\boldsymbol{X}}$ is a nonstochastic matrix with full rank k, since each element of the matrix on the left-hand side of (3.17) is now an average of n numbers:

$$\Big(\frac{1}{n}\boldsymbol{X}^\top\boldsymbol{X}\Big)_{ij} = \frac{1}{n}\sum_{t=1}^{n} x_{ti}\,x_{tj}.$$

In effect, when we write (3.17), we are implicitly making some assumption sufficient for a LLN to hold for the sequences generated by the squares of the regressors and their cross-products. Thus there should not be too much dependence between $x_{ti}x_{tj}$ and $x_{si}x_{sj}$ for $s \neq t$, and the variances of these quantities should not differ too much as t and s vary.

The OLS Estimator Is Consistent

We can now show that, under plausible assumptions, the least-squares estimator $\hat{\boldsymbol{\beta}}$ is consistent. When the DGP is a special case of the regression model (3.03) that is being estimated, we saw in (3.05) that

$$\hat{\boldsymbol{\beta}} = \boldsymbol{\beta}_0 + (\boldsymbol{X}^\top\boldsymbol{X})^{-1}\boldsymbol{X}^\top\boldsymbol{u}. \tag{3.18}$$

To demonstrate that $\hat{\boldsymbol{\beta}}$ is consistent, we need to show that the second term on the right-hand side here has a plim of zero. This term is the product of two matrix expressions, $(\boldsymbol{X}^\top\boldsymbol{X})^{-1}$ and $\boldsymbol{X}^\top\boldsymbol{u}$. Neither $\boldsymbol{X}^\top\boldsymbol{X}$ nor $\boldsymbol{X}^\top\boldsymbol{u}$ has a probability limit. However, we can divide both of these expressions by n without changing the value of this term, since $n \cdot n^{-1} = 1$. By doing so, we convert them into quantities that, under reasonable assumptions, have nonstochastic plims. Thus the plim of the second term in (3.18) becomes

$$\Big(\operatorname*{plim}_{n\to\infty} \frac{1}{n}\boldsymbol{X}^\top\boldsymbol{X}\Big)^{-1} \operatorname*{plim}_{n\to\infty} \frac{1}{n}\boldsymbol{X}^\top\boldsymbol{u} = \big(\boldsymbol{S}_{\boldsymbol{X}^\top\boldsymbol{X}}\big)^{-1} \operatorname*{plim}_{n\to\infty} \frac{1}{n}\boldsymbol{X}^\top\boldsymbol{u} = \boldsymbol{0}. \tag{3.19}$$

In writing the first equality here, we have assumed that (3.17) holds. To obtain the second equality, we start with assumption (3.10), which can reasonably be made even when there are lagged dependent variables among the regressors. This assumption tells us that $\mathrm{E}(\boldsymbol{X}_t^\top u_t \,|\, \boldsymbol{X}_t) = \mathbf{0}$, and the Law of Iterated Expectations then tells us that $\mathrm{E}(\boldsymbol{X}_t^\top u_t) = \mathbf{0}$. Thus, assuming that we can apply a law of large numbers,

$$\operatorname*{plim}_{n\to\infty} \frac{1}{n}\boldsymbol{X}^\top\boldsymbol{u} = \operatorname*{plim}_{n\to\infty} \frac{1}{n}\sum_{t=1}^{n} \boldsymbol{X}_t^\top u_t = \mathbf{0}.$$

Together with (3.18), (3.19) gives us the result that $\hat{\boldsymbol{\beta}}$ is consistent.

We have just seen that the OLS estimator $\hat{\boldsymbol{\beta}}$ is consistent under considerably weaker assumptions about the relationship between the error terms and the regressors than were needed to prove that it is unbiased; compare (3.10) and (3.08). This may wrongly suggest that consistency is a weaker condition than unbiasedness. Actually, it is neither weaker nor stronger. Consistency and unbiasedness are simply different concepts. Sometimes, least-squares estimators may be biased but consistent, for example, in models where $\boldsymbol{X}$ includes lagged dependent variables. In other circumstances, however, these estimators may be unbiased but not consistent. For example, consider the model

$$y_t = \beta_1 + \beta_2 \frac{1}{t} + u_t, \quad u_t \sim \mathrm{IID}(0, \sigma^2). \tag{3.20}$$

Since both regressors here are nonstochastic, the least-squares estimates $\hat{\beta}_1$ and $\hat{\beta}_2$ are clearly unbiased. However, it is easy to see that $\hat{\beta}_2$ is not consistent. The problem is that, as $n \to \infty$, each observation provides less and less information about β_2. This happens because the regressor $1/t$ tends to zero, and hence varies less and less across observations as t becomes larger. As a consequence, the matrix $\boldsymbol{S}_{\boldsymbol{X}^\top\boldsymbol{X}}$ can be shown to be singular. Therefore, equation (3.19) does not hold, and the second term on the right-hand side of equation (3.18) does not have a probability limit of zero.

The model (3.20) is actually rather a curious one, since $\hat{\beta}_1$ is consistent even though $\hat{\beta}_2$ is not. The reason $\hat{\beta}_1$ is consistent is that, as the sample size n gets larger, we obtain an amount of information about β_1 that is roughly proportional to n. In contrast, because each successive observation gives us less and less information about β_2, $\hat{\beta}_2$ is not consistent.

An estimator that is not consistent is said to be **inconsistent**. There are two types of inconsistency, which are actually quite different. If an unbiased estimator, like $\hat{\beta}_2$ in the previous example, is inconsistent, it is so because it does not tend to any nonstochastic probability limit. In contrast, many inconsistent estimators do tend to nonstochastic probability limits, but they tend to the wrong ones.

To illustrate the various types of inconsistency, and the relationship between bias and inconsistency, imagine that we are trying to estimate the population mean, μ, from a sample of data $y_t, t = 1, \ldots, n$. A sensible estimator would be the sample mean, $\bar{y}$. Under reasonable assumptions about the way the y_t are generated, $\bar{y}$ is unbiased and consistent. Three not very sensible estimators are the following:

$$\hat{\mu}_1 = \frac{1}{n+1}\sum_{t=1}^{n} y_t,$$

$$\hat{\mu}_2 = \frac{1.01}{n}\sum_{t=1}^{n} y_t, \text{ and}$$

$$\hat{\mu}_3 = 0.01 y_1 + \frac{0.99}{n-1}\sum_{t=2}^{n} y_t.$$

The first of these estimators, $\hat{\mu}_1$, is biased but consistent. It is evidently equal to $n/(n+1)$ times $\bar{y}$. Thus its mean is $\big(n/(n+1)\big)\mu$, which tends to μ as $n \to \infty$, and it is consistent whenever $\bar{y}$ is. The second estimator, $\hat{\mu}_2$, is clearly biased and inconsistent. Its mean is 1.01μ, since it is equal to $1.01\bar{y}$, and it actually tends to a plim of 1.01μ as $n \to \infty$. The third estimator, $\hat{\mu}_3$, is perhaps the most interesting. It is clearly unbiased, since it is a weighted average of two estimators, y_1 and the average of y_2 through y_n, each of which is unbiased. The second of these two estimators is also consistent. However, $\hat{\mu}_3$ itself is not consistent, because it does not converge to a nonstochastic plim. Instead, it converges to the random quantity $0.99\mu + 0.01y_1$.

3.4 The Covariance Matrix of the OLS Parameter Estimates

Although it is valuable to know that the least-squares estimator $\hat{\boldsymbol{\beta}}$ is either unbiased or, under weaker conditions, consistent, this information by itself is not very useful. If we are to interpret any given set of OLS parameter estimates, we need to know, at least approximately, how $\hat{\boldsymbol{\beta}}$ is actually distributed. For purposes of inference, the most important feature of the distribution of any vector of parameter estimates is the matrix of its central second moments. This matrix is the analog, for vector random variables, of the variance of a scalar random variable. If $\boldsymbol{b}$ is any random vector, we will denote its matrix of central second moments by $\text{Var}(\boldsymbol{b})$, using the same notation that we would use for a variance in the scalar case. Usage, perhaps somewhat illogically, dictates that this matrix should be called the **covariance matrix**, although the terms **variance matrix** and **variance-covariance matrix** are also sometimes used. Whatever it is called, the covariance matrix is an extremely important concept which comes up over and over again in econometrics.

The covariance matrix $\text{Var}(\boldsymbol{b})$ of a random k–vector $\boldsymbol{b}$, with typical element b_i, organizes all the central second moments of the b_i into a $k \times k$ symmetric matrix. The ith diagonal element of $\text{Var}(\boldsymbol{b})$ is $\text{Var}(b_i)$, the variance of b_i. The ij^{th} off-diagonal element of $\text{Var}(\boldsymbol{b})$ is $\text{Cov}(b_i, b_j)$, the **covariance** of b_i and b_j.

The concept of covariance was introduced in Exercise 1.10. In terms of the random variables b_i and b_j, the definition is

$$\operatorname{Cov}(b_i, b_j) \equiv \operatorname{E}\Big(\big(b_i - \operatorname{E}(b_i)\big)\big(b_j - \operatorname{E}(b_j)\big)\Big). \tag{3.21}$$

Many of the properties of covariance matrices follow immediately from (3.21). For example, it is easy to see that, if $i = j$, $\operatorname{Cov}(b_i, b_j) = \operatorname{Var}(b_i)$. Moreover, since from (3.21) it is obvious that $\operatorname{Cov}(b_i, b_j) = \operatorname{Cov}(b_j, b_i)$, $\operatorname{Var}(\boldsymbol{b})$ must be a symmetric matrix. The full covariance matrix $\operatorname{Var}(\boldsymbol{b})$ can be expressed readily using matrix notation. It is just

$$\operatorname{Var}(\boldsymbol{b}) = \operatorname{E}\Big(\big(\boldsymbol{b} - \operatorname{E}(\boldsymbol{b})\big)\big(\boldsymbol{b} - \operatorname{E}(\boldsymbol{b})\big)^{\top}\Big), \tag{3.22}$$

as is obvious from (3.21). An important special case of (3.22) arises when $\operatorname{E}(\boldsymbol{b}) = \mathbf{0}$. In this case, $\operatorname{Var}(\boldsymbol{b}) = \operatorname{E}(\boldsymbol{b}\boldsymbol{b}^{\top})$.

The special case in which $\operatorname{Var}(\boldsymbol{b})$ is diagonal, so that all the covariances are zero, is of particular interest. If b_i and b_j are statistically independent, $\operatorname{Cov}(b_i, b_j) = 0$; see Exercise 1.13. The converse is not true, however. It is perfectly possible for two random variables that are not statistically independent to have covariance 0; for an extreme example of this, see Exercise 1.14.

The **correlation** between b_i and b_j is

$$\rho(b_i, b_j) \equiv \frac{\operatorname{Cov}(b_i, b_j)}{\big(\operatorname{Var}(b_i)\operatorname{Var}(b_j)\big)^{1/2}}. \tag{3.23}$$

It is often useful to think in terms of correlations rather than covariances, because, according to the result of Exercise 3.6, the former always lie between -1 and 1. We can arrange the correlations between all the elements of $\boldsymbol{b}$ into a symmetric matrix called the **correlation matrix**. It is clear from (3.23) that all the elements on the principal diagonal of this matrix must be 1. This demonstrates that the correlation of any random variable with itself equals 1.

In addition to being symmetric, $\operatorname{Var}(\boldsymbol{b})$ must be a **positive semidefinite** matrix; see Exercise 3.5. In most cases, covariance matrices and correlation matrices are **positive definite** rather than positive semidefinite, and their properties depend crucially on this fact.

Positive Definite Matrices

A $k \times k$ symmetric matrix $\boldsymbol{A}$ is said to be positive definite if, for all nonzero k--vectors $\boldsymbol{x}$, the matrix product $\boldsymbol{x}^{\top}\boldsymbol{A}\boldsymbol{x}$, which is just a scalar, is positive. The quantity $\boldsymbol{x}^{\top}\boldsymbol{A}\boldsymbol{x}$ is called a **quadratic form**. A quadratic form always involves a k--vector, in this case $\boldsymbol{x}$, and a $k \times k$ matrix, in this case $\boldsymbol{A}$. By the rules of matrix multiplication,

$$\boldsymbol{x}^{\top}\boldsymbol{A}\boldsymbol{x} = \sum_{i=1}^{k}\sum_{j=1}^{k} x_i x_j A_{ij}. \tag{3.24}$$

If this quadratic form can take on zero values but not negative values, the matrix $\boldsymbol{A}$ is said to be positive semidefinite.

Any matrix of the form $\boldsymbol{B}^\top\boldsymbol{B}$ is positive semidefinite. To see this, observe that $\boldsymbol{B}^\top\boldsymbol{B}$ is symmetric and that, for any nonzero $\boldsymbol{x}$,

$$\boldsymbol{x}^\top\boldsymbol{B}^\top\boldsymbol{B}\boldsymbol{x} = (\boldsymbol{B}\boldsymbol{x})^\top(\boldsymbol{B}\boldsymbol{x}) = \|\boldsymbol{B}\boldsymbol{x}\|^2 \geq 0. \tag{3.25}$$

This result can hold with equality only if $\boldsymbol{B}\boldsymbol{x} = \boldsymbol{0}$. But, in that case, since $\boldsymbol{x} \neq \boldsymbol{0}$, the columns of $\boldsymbol{B}$ are linearly dependent. We express this circumstance by saying that $\boldsymbol{B}$ does not have **full column rank**. Note that $\boldsymbol{B}$ can have full rank but not full column rank if $\boldsymbol{B}$ has fewer rows than columns, in which case the maximum possible rank equals the number of rows. However, a matrix with full column rank necessarily also has full rank. When $\boldsymbol{B}$ does have full column rank, it follows from (3.25) that $\boldsymbol{B}^\top\boldsymbol{B}$ is positive definite. Similarly, if $\boldsymbol{A}$ is positive definite, then any matrix of the form $\boldsymbol{B}^\top\boldsymbol{A}\boldsymbol{B}$ is positive definite if $\boldsymbol{B}$ has full column rank and positive semidefinite otherwise.

It is easy to see that the diagonal elements of a positive definite matrix must all be positive. Suppose this were not the case and that, say, A_{22} were negative. Then, if we chose $\boldsymbol{x}$ to be the vector $\boldsymbol{e}_2$, that is, a vector with 1 as its second element and all other elements equal to 0 (see Section 2.6), we could make $\boldsymbol{x}^\top\boldsymbol{A}\boldsymbol{x} < 0$. From (3.24), the quadratic form would just be $\boldsymbol{e}_2^\top\boldsymbol{A}\boldsymbol{e}_2 = A_{22} < 0$. For a positive semidefinite matrix, the diagonal elements may be 0. Unlike the diagonal elements, the off-diagonal elements of $\boldsymbol{A}$ may be of either sign.

A particularly simple example of a positive definite matrix is the identity matrix, $\mathbf{I}$. Because all the off-diagonal elements are zero, (3.24) tells us that a quadratic form in $\mathbf{I}$ is

$$\boldsymbol{x}^\top\mathbf{I}\boldsymbol{x} = \sum_{i=1}^{k} x_i^2,$$

which is certainly positive for all nonzero vectors $\boldsymbol{x}$. The identity matrix was used in (3.03) in a notation that may not have been clear at the time. There we specified that $\boldsymbol{u} \sim \text{IID}(\boldsymbol{0}, \sigma^2\mathbf{I})$. This is just a compact way of saying that the vector of error terms $\boldsymbol{u}$ is assumed to have mean vector $\boldsymbol{0}$ and covariance matrix $\sigma^2\mathbf{I}$.

A positive definite matrix cannot be singular, because, if $\boldsymbol{A}$ is singular, there must exist a nonzero $\boldsymbol{x}$ such that $\boldsymbol{A}\boldsymbol{x} = \boldsymbol{0}$. But then $\boldsymbol{x}^\top\boldsymbol{A}\boldsymbol{x} = 0$ as well, which means that $\boldsymbol{A}$ is not positive definite. Thus the inverse of a positive definite matrix always exists. It too is a positive definite matrix, as readers are asked to show in Exercise 3.7.

There is a sort of converse of the result that any matrix of the form $\boldsymbol{B}^\top\boldsymbol{B}$, where $\boldsymbol{B}$ has full column rank, is positive definite. It is that, if the $k \times k$ matrix $\boldsymbol{A}$ is symmetric and positive definite, then there always exists a full-rank $k \times k$ matrix $\boldsymbol{B}$ such that $\boldsymbol{A} = \boldsymbol{B}^\top\boldsymbol{B}$. For any given matrix $\boldsymbol{A}$, the corresponding matrix $\boldsymbol{B}$ is not unique. In particular, $\boldsymbol{B}$ can be chosen to be symmetric, but it can also be chosen to be upper or lower triangular. Details of a simple algorithm (Crout's algorithm) for finding a triangular matrix $\boldsymbol{B}$ can be found in Press, Teukolsky, Vetterling, and Flannery (1992a, 1992b).

The OLS Covariance Matrix

The notation we used in the specification (3.03) of the linear regression model can now be understood in terms of the covariance matrix of the error terms, or the **error covariance matrix**. If the error terms are IID, they all have the same variance σ^2, and the covariance of any pair of them is zero. Thus the covariance matrix of the vector $\boldsymbol{u}$ is $\sigma^2\mathbf{I}$, and we have

$$\operatorname{Var}(\boldsymbol{u}) = \operatorname{E}(\boldsymbol{u}\boldsymbol{u}^\top) = \sigma^2\mathbf{I}. \tag{3.26}$$

Notice that this result does not require the error terms to be independent. It is required only that they all have the same variance and that the covariance of each pair of error terms is zero.

If we assume that $\boldsymbol{X}$ is exogenous, we can now calculate the covariance matrix of $\hat{\boldsymbol{\beta}}$ in terms of the error covariance matrix (3.26). To do this, we need to multiply the vector $\hat{\boldsymbol{\beta}} - \boldsymbol{\beta}_0$ by itself transposed. From (3.05), we know that

$$\hat{\boldsymbol{\beta}} - \boldsymbol{\beta}_0 = (\boldsymbol{X}^\top\boldsymbol{X})^{-1}\boldsymbol{X}^\top\boldsymbol{u}.$$

By (3.22), under the assumption that $\hat{\boldsymbol{\beta}}$ is unbiased, $\operatorname{Var}(\hat{\boldsymbol{\beta}})$ is the expectation of the $k \times k$ matrix

$$(\hat{\boldsymbol{\beta}} - \boldsymbol{\beta}_0)(\hat{\boldsymbol{\beta}} - \boldsymbol{\beta}_0)^\top = (\boldsymbol{X}^\top\boldsymbol{X})^{-1}\boldsymbol{X}^\top\boldsymbol{u}\boldsymbol{u}^\top\boldsymbol{X}(\boldsymbol{X}^\top\boldsymbol{X})^{-1}. \tag{3.27}$$

Taking this expectation, conditional on $\boldsymbol{X}$, and using (3.26) with the specific value σ_0^2 for the covariance matrix of the error terms, yields

$$\begin{aligned}(\boldsymbol{X}^\top\boldsymbol{X})^{-1}\boldsymbol{X}^\top\operatorname{E}(\boldsymbol{u}\boldsymbol{u}^\top)\boldsymbol{X}(\boldsymbol{X}^\top\boldsymbol{X})^{-1} &= (\boldsymbol{X}^\top\boldsymbol{X})^{-1}\boldsymbol{X}^\top\sigma_0^2\mathbf{I}\boldsymbol{X}(\boldsymbol{X}^\top\boldsymbol{X})^{-1}\\ &= \sigma_0^2(\boldsymbol{X}^\top\boldsymbol{X})^{-1}\boldsymbol{X}^\top\boldsymbol{X}(\boldsymbol{X}^\top\boldsymbol{X})^{-1}\\ &= \sigma_0^2(\boldsymbol{X}^\top\boldsymbol{X})^{-1}.\end{aligned}$$

Thus we conclude that

$$\operatorname{Var}(\hat{\boldsymbol{\beta}}) = \sigma_0^2(\boldsymbol{X}^\top\boldsymbol{X})^{-1}. \tag{3.28}$$

This is the standard result for the covariance matrix of $\hat{\boldsymbol{\beta}}$ under the assumption that the data are generated by (3.01) and that $\hat{\boldsymbol{\beta}}$ is an unbiased estimator.

Precision of the Least-Squares Estimates

For a scalar parameter, the accuracy of an estimator is often taken to be proportional to the inverse of its variance, and this is sometimes called the **precision** of the estimator. For an estimate of a parameter vector, the **precision matrix** is defined as the inverse of the covariance matrix of the estimator. Now that we have an expression for $\text{Var}(\hat{\boldsymbol{\beta}})$, we can investigate what determines the precision of the least-squares coefficient estimates $\hat{\boldsymbol{\beta}}$. There are really only three things that matter. The first of these is σ_0^2, the true variance of the error terms. Not surprisingly, $\text{Var}(\hat{\boldsymbol{\beta}})$ is proportional to σ_0^2. The more random variation there is in the error terms, the more random variation there is in the parameter estimates.

The second thing that affects the precision of $\hat{\boldsymbol{\beta}}$ is the sample size, n. It is illuminating to rewrite (3.28) as

$$\text{Var}(\hat{\boldsymbol{\beta}}) = \left(\frac{1}{n}\sigma_0^2\right)\left(\frac{1}{n}\boldsymbol{X}^\top\boldsymbol{X}\right)^{-1}. \tag{3.29}$$

If we make the assumption (3.17), the second factor on the right-hand side of (3.29) does not vary much with the sample size n, at least not if n is reasonably large. In that case, the right-hand side of (3.29) is roughly proportional to $1/n$, because the first factor is precisely proportional to $1/n$. Thus, if we were to double the sample size, we would expect the variance of $\hat{\boldsymbol{\beta}}$ to be roughly halved and the standard errors of the individual $\hat{\boldsymbol{\beta}}_i$ to be divided by $\sqrt{2}$.

As an example, suppose that we are estimating a regression model with just a constant term. We can write the model as $\boldsymbol{y} = \boldsymbol{\iota}\beta_1 + \boldsymbol{u}$, where $\boldsymbol{\iota}$ is an n–vector of ones. Plugging in $\boldsymbol{\iota}$ for $\boldsymbol{X}$ in (3.04) and (3.28), we find that

$$\hat{\beta}_1 = (\boldsymbol{\iota}^\top\boldsymbol{\iota})^{-1}\boldsymbol{\iota}^\top\boldsymbol{y} = \frac{1}{n}\sum_{t=1}^{n} y_t, \text{ and}$$
$$\text{Var}(\hat{\beta}_1) = \sigma_0^2(\boldsymbol{\iota}^\top\boldsymbol{\iota})^{-1} = \frac{1}{n}\sigma_0^2.$$

Thus, in this particularly simple case, the variance of the least-squares estimator is exactly proportional to $1/n$.

The third thing that affects the precision of $\hat{\boldsymbol{\beta}}$ is the matrix $\boldsymbol{X}$. Suppose that we are interested in a particular coefficient which, without loss of generality, we may call β_1. Then, if $\boldsymbol{\beta}_2$ denotes the $(k-1)$–vector of the remaining coefficients, we can rewrite the regression model (3.03) as

$$\boldsymbol{y} = \boldsymbol{x}_1\beta_1 + \boldsymbol{X}_2\boldsymbol{\beta}_2 + \boldsymbol{u}, \tag{3.30}$$

where $\boldsymbol{X}$ has been partitioned into $\boldsymbol{x}_1$ and $\boldsymbol{X}_2$ to conform with the partition of $\boldsymbol{\beta}$. By the FWL Theorem, regression (3.30) yields the same estimate of β_1 as the FWL regression

$$\boldsymbol{M}_2\boldsymbol{y} = \boldsymbol{M}_2\boldsymbol{x}_1\beta_1 + \text{residuals},$$

where, as in Section 2.4, $\boldsymbol{M}_2 \equiv \mathbf{I} - \boldsymbol{X}_2(\boldsymbol{X}_2^\top \boldsymbol{X}_2)^{-1}\boldsymbol{X}_2^\top$. This estimate is

$$\hat{\beta}_1 = \frac{\boldsymbol{x}_1^\top \boldsymbol{M}_2 \boldsymbol{y}}{\boldsymbol{x}_1^\top \boldsymbol{M}_2 \boldsymbol{x}_1},$$

and, by a calculation similar to that leading to (3.28), its variance is

$$\sigma_0^2 \big(\boldsymbol{x}_1^\top \boldsymbol{M}_2 \boldsymbol{x}_1\big)^{-1} = \frac{\sigma_0^2}{\boldsymbol{x}_1^\top \boldsymbol{M}_2 \boldsymbol{x}_1}. \tag{3.31}$$

Thus $\mathrm{Var}(\hat{\beta}_1)$ is equal to the variance of the error terms divided by the squared length of the vector $\boldsymbol{M}_2 \boldsymbol{x}_1$.

The intuition behind equation (3.31) is simple. How much information the sample gives us about β_1 is proportional to the squared Euclidean length of the vector $\boldsymbol{M}_2 \boldsymbol{x}_1$, which is the denominator of the right-hand side of (3.31). When $\|\boldsymbol{M}_2 \boldsymbol{x}_1\|$ is big, either because n is large or because at least some elements of $\boldsymbol{M}_2 \boldsymbol{x}_1$ are large, $\hat{\beta}_1$ is relatively precise. When $\|\boldsymbol{M}_2 \boldsymbol{x}_1\|$ is small, either because n is small or because all the elements of $\boldsymbol{M}_2 \boldsymbol{x}_1$ are small, $\hat{\beta}_1$ is relatively imprecise.

The squared Euclidean length of the vector $\boldsymbol{M}_2 \boldsymbol{x}_1$ is just the sum of squared residuals from the regression

$$\boldsymbol{x}_1 = \boldsymbol{X}_2 \boldsymbol{c} + \text{residuals}. \tag{3.32}$$

Thus the variance of $\hat{\beta}_1$, expression (3.31), is proportional to the inverse of the sum of squared residuals from regression (3.32). When $\boldsymbol{x}_1$ is well explained by the other columns of $\boldsymbol{X}$, this SSR is small, and the variance of $\hat{\beta}_1$ is consequently large. When $\boldsymbol{x}_1$ is not well explained by the other columns of $\boldsymbol{X}$, this SSR is large, and the variance of $\hat{\beta}_1$ is consequently small.

As the above discussion makes clear, the precision with which β_1 is estimated depends on $\boldsymbol{X}_2$ just as much as it depends on $\boldsymbol{x}_1$. Sometimes, if we just regress $\boldsymbol{y}$ on a constant and $\boldsymbol{x}_1$, we may obtain what seems to be a very precise estimate of β_1, but if we then include some additional regressors, the estimate becomes much less precise. The reason for this is that the additional regressors do a much better job of explaining $\boldsymbol{x}_1$ in regression (3.32) than does a constant alone. As a consequence, the length of $\boldsymbol{M}_2 \boldsymbol{x}_1$ is much less than the length of $\boldsymbol{M}_\iota \boldsymbol{x}_1$. This type of situation is sometimes referred to as **collinearity**, or **multicollinearity**, and the regressor $\boldsymbol{x}_1$ is said to be **collinear** with some of the other regressors. This terminology is not very satisfactory, since, if a regressor were collinear with other regressors in the usual mathematical sense of the term, the regressors would be linearly dependent. It would be better to speak of **approximate collinearity**, although econometricians seldom bother with this nicety. Collinearity can cause difficulties for applied econometric work, but these difficulties are essentially the same as the ones caused by having a sample size that is too small. In either case, the data simply do not contain enough information to allow us to obtain precise estimates of all the coefficients.

The covariance matrix of $\hat{\boldsymbol{\beta}}$, expression (3.28), tells us all that we can possibly know about the second moments of $\hat{\boldsymbol{\beta}}$. In practice, of course, we rarely know this expression, but we can estimate it by using an estimate of σ_0^2. How to obtain such an estimate will be discussed in Section 3.6. Using this estimated covariance matrix, we can then, if we are willing to make some more or less strong assumptions, make exact or approximate inferences about the true parameter vector $\boldsymbol{\beta}_0$. Just how we can do this will be discussed at length in Chapters 4 and 5.

Linear Functions of Parameter Estimates

The covariance matrix of $\hat{\boldsymbol{\beta}}$ can be used to calculate the variance of any linear (strictly speaking, affine) function of $\hat{\boldsymbol{\beta}}$. Suppose that we are interested in the variance of $\hat{\gamma}$, where $\gamma = \boldsymbol{w}^\top\boldsymbol{\beta}$, $\hat{\gamma} = \boldsymbol{w}^\top\hat{\boldsymbol{\beta}}$, and $\boldsymbol{w}$ is a k-vector of known coefficients. By choosing $\boldsymbol{w}$ appropriately, we can make γ equal to any one of the β_i, or to the sum of the β_i, or to any linear combination of the β_i in which we might be interested. For example, if $\gamma = 3\beta_1 - \beta_4$, $\boldsymbol{w}$ would be a vector with 3 as the first element, -1 as the fourth element, and 0 for all the other elements.

It is easy to show that

$$\mathrm{Var}(\hat{\gamma}) = \boldsymbol{w}^\top \mathrm{Var}(\hat{\boldsymbol{\beta}})\boldsymbol{w} = \sigma_0^2\boldsymbol{w}^\top(\boldsymbol{X}^\top\boldsymbol{X})^{-1}\boldsymbol{w}. \tag{3.33}$$

This result can be obtained as follows. By (3.22),

$$\begin{aligned}\mathrm{Var}(\boldsymbol{w}^\top\hat{\boldsymbol{\beta}}) &= \mathrm{E}\big(\boldsymbol{w}^\top(\hat{\boldsymbol{\beta}}-\boldsymbol{\beta}_0)(\hat{\boldsymbol{\beta}}-\boldsymbol{\beta}_0)^\top\boldsymbol{w}\big)\\ &= \boldsymbol{w}^\top\mathrm{E}\big((\hat{\boldsymbol{\beta}}-\boldsymbol{\beta}_0)(\hat{\boldsymbol{\beta}}-\boldsymbol{\beta}_0)^\top\big)\boldsymbol{w}\\ &= \boldsymbol{w}^\top\big(\sigma_0^2(\boldsymbol{X}^\top\boldsymbol{X})^{-1}\big)\boldsymbol{w},\end{aligned}$$

from which equations (3.33) follow immediately. Notice that, in general, the variance of $\hat{\gamma}$ depends on every element of the covariance matrix of $\hat{\boldsymbol{\beta}}$; this is made explicit in expression (3.68), which readers are asked to derive in Exercise 3.10. Of course, if some elements of the vector $\boldsymbol{w}$ are equal to 0, $\mathrm{Var}(\hat{\gamma})$ does not depend on the corresponding rows and columns of the covariance matrix $\sigma_0^2(\boldsymbol{X}^\top\boldsymbol{X})^{-1}$.

It may be illuminating to consider the special case used as an example above, in which $\gamma = 3\beta_1 - \beta_4$. In this case, the result (3.33) implies that

$$\begin{aligned}\mathrm{Var}(\hat{\gamma}) &= w_1^2\,\mathrm{Var}(\hat{\beta}_1) + w_4^2\,\mathrm{Var}(\hat{\beta}_4) + 2w_1w_4\mathrm{Cov}(\hat{\beta}_1,\hat{\beta}_4)\\ &= 9\mathrm{Var}(\hat{\beta}_1) + \mathrm{Var}(\hat{\beta}_4) - 6\mathrm{Cov}(\hat{\beta}_1,\hat{\beta}_4).\end{aligned}$$

Notice that the variance of $\hat{\gamma}$ depends on the covariance of $\hat{\beta}_1$ and $\hat{\beta}_4$ as well as on their variances. If this covariance is large and positive, $\text{Var}(\hat{\gamma})$ may be small, even if $\text{Var}(\hat{\beta}_1)$ and $\text{Var}(\hat{\beta}_4)$ are both large.

The Variance of Forecast Errors

The variance of the error associated with a regression-based forecast can be obtained by using the result (3.33). Suppose we have computed a vector of OLS estimates $\hat{\boldsymbol{\beta}}$ and wish to use them to forecast y_s, for s not in $1, \ldots, n$, using an observed vector of regressors $\boldsymbol{X}_s$. Then the forecast of y_s is simply $\boldsymbol{X}_s\hat{\boldsymbol{\beta}}$. For simplicity, let us assume that $\hat{\boldsymbol{\beta}}$ is unbiased, which implies that the forecast itself is unbiased. Therefore, the forecast error has mean zero, and its variance is

$$\begin{aligned} \text{E}(y_s - \boldsymbol{X}_s\hat{\boldsymbol{\beta}})^2 &= \text{E}(\boldsymbol{X}_s\boldsymbol{\beta}_0 + u_s - \boldsymbol{X}_s\hat{\boldsymbol{\beta}})^2 \\ &= \text{E}(u_s^2) + \text{E}(\boldsymbol{X}_s\boldsymbol{\beta}_0 - \boldsymbol{X}_s\hat{\boldsymbol{\beta}})^2 \\ &= \sigma_0^2 + \text{Var}(\boldsymbol{X}_s\hat{\boldsymbol{\beta}}). \end{aligned} \tag{3.34}$$

The first equality here depends on the assumption that the regression model is correctly specified, the second depends on the assumption that the error terms are serially uncorrelated, which ensures that $\text{E}(u_s\boldsymbol{X}_s\hat{\boldsymbol{\beta}}) = 0$, and the third uses the fact that $\hat{\boldsymbol{\beta}}$ is assumed to be unbiased.

Using the result (3.33), and recalling that $\boldsymbol{X}_s$ is a row vector, we see that the last line of (3.34) is equal to

$$\sigma_0^2 + \boldsymbol{X}_s\text{Var}(\hat{\boldsymbol{\beta}})\boldsymbol{X}_s^{\top} = \sigma_0^2 + \sigma_0^2\boldsymbol{X}_s(\boldsymbol{X}^{\top}\boldsymbol{X})^{-1}\boldsymbol{X}_s^{\top}. \tag{3.35}$$

Thus we find that the variance of the forecast error is the sum of two terms. The first term is simply the variance of the error term u_s. If we knew the true value of $\boldsymbol{\beta}$, this would be the variance of the forecast error. The second term, which makes the forecast error larger than σ_0^2, arises because we are using the estimate $\hat{\boldsymbol{\beta}}$ instead of the true parameter vector $\boldsymbol{\beta}_0$. It can be thought of as the penalty we pay for our ignorance of $\boldsymbol{\beta}$. Of course, the result (3.35) can easily be generalized to the case in which we are forecasting a vector of values of the dependent variable; see Exercise 3.16.

3.5 Efficiency of the OLS Estimator

One of the reasons for the popularity of ordinary least squares is that, under certain conditions, the OLS estimator can be shown to be more **efficient** than many competing estimators. One estimator is said to be more efficient than another if, on average, the former yields more accurate estimates than the latter. The reason for the terminology is that an estimator which yields more accurate estimates can be thought of as utilizing the information available in the sample more efficiently.

For scalar parameters, one estimator of a parameter is more efficient than another if the precision of the former is larger than that of the latter. For parameter vectors, there is a natural way to generalize this idea. Suppose that $\hat{\boldsymbol{\beta}}$ and $\tilde{\boldsymbol{\beta}}$ are two unbiased estimators of a k-vector of parameters $\boldsymbol{\beta}$, with covariance matrices $\text{Var}(\hat{\boldsymbol{\beta}})$ and $\text{Var}(\tilde{\boldsymbol{\beta}})$, respectively. Then, if efficiency is measured in terms of precision, $\hat{\boldsymbol{\beta}}$ is said to be more efficient than $\tilde{\boldsymbol{\beta}}$ if and only if the difference between their precision matrices, $\text{Var}(\hat{\boldsymbol{\beta}})^{-1} - \text{Var}(\tilde{\boldsymbol{\beta}})^{-1}$, is a nonzero positive semidefinite matrix.

Since it is more usual to work in terms of variance than precision, it is convenient to express the efficiency condition directly in terms of covariance matrices. As readers are asked to show in Exercise 3.8, if $\boldsymbol{A}$ and $\boldsymbol{B}$ are positive definite matrices of the same dimensions, then the matrix $\boldsymbol{A} - \boldsymbol{B}$ is positive semidefinite if and only if $\boldsymbol{B}^{-1} - \boldsymbol{A}^{-1}$ is positive semidefinite. Thus the efficiency condition expressed above in terms of precision matrices is equivalent to saying that $\hat{\boldsymbol{\beta}}$ is more efficient than $\tilde{\boldsymbol{\beta}}$ if and only if $\text{Var}(\tilde{\boldsymbol{\beta}}) - \text{Var}(\hat{\boldsymbol{\beta}})$ is a nonzero positive semidefinite matrix.

If $\hat{\boldsymbol{\beta}}$ is more efficient than $\tilde{\boldsymbol{\beta}}$ in this sense, then every individual parameter in the vector $\boldsymbol{\beta}$, and every linear combination of those parameters, is estimated at least as efficiently by using $\hat{\boldsymbol{\beta}}$ as by using $\tilde{\boldsymbol{\beta}}$. Consider an arbitrary linear combination of the parameters in $\boldsymbol{\beta}$, say $\gamma = \boldsymbol{w}^\top\boldsymbol{\beta}$, for any k-vector $\boldsymbol{w}$ that we choose. As we saw in the preceding section, $\text{Var}(\hat{\gamma}) = \boldsymbol{w}^\top\text{Var}(\hat{\boldsymbol{\beta}})\boldsymbol{w}$, and similarly for $\text{Var}(\tilde{\gamma})$. Therefore, the difference between $\text{Var}(\tilde{\gamma})$ and $\text{Var}(\hat{\gamma})$ is

$$\boldsymbol{w}^\top\text{Var}(\tilde{\boldsymbol{\beta}})\boldsymbol{w} - \boldsymbol{w}^\top\text{Var}(\hat{\boldsymbol{\beta}})\boldsymbol{w} = \boldsymbol{w}^\top\big(\text{Var}(\tilde{\boldsymbol{\beta}}) - \text{Var}(\hat{\boldsymbol{\beta}})\big)\boldsymbol{w}. \tag{3.36}$$

The right-hand side of equation (3.36) must be either positive or zero whenever the matrix $\text{Var}(\tilde{\boldsymbol{\beta}}) - \text{Var}(\hat{\boldsymbol{\beta}})$ is positive semidefinite. Thus, if $\hat{\boldsymbol{\beta}}$ is a more efficient estimator than $\tilde{\boldsymbol{\beta}}$, we can be sure that $\hat{\gamma}$ is estimated with less variance than $\tilde{\gamma}$. In practice, when one estimator is more efficient than another, the difference between the covariance matrices is very often positive definite. When that is the case, every parameter or linear combination of parameters is estimated more efficiently using $\hat{\boldsymbol{\beta}}$ than using $\tilde{\boldsymbol{\beta}}$.

We now let $\hat{\boldsymbol{\beta}}$, as usual, denote the vector of OLS parameter estimates (3.04). As we are about to show, this estimator is more efficient than any other **linear unbiased estimator**. In section 3.3, we discussed what it means for an estimator to be unbiased, but we have not yet discussed what it means for an estimator to be linear. It simply means that we can write the estimator as a linear (affine) function of $\boldsymbol{y}$, the vector of observations on the dependent variable. It is clear that $\hat{\boldsymbol{\beta}}$ itself is a linear estimator, because it is equal to the matrix $(\boldsymbol{X}^\top\boldsymbol{X})^{-1}\boldsymbol{X}^\top$ times the vector $\boldsymbol{y}$.

If $\tilde{\boldsymbol{\beta}}$ now denotes any linear estimator that is not the OLS estimator, we can always write

$$\tilde{\boldsymbol{\beta}} = \boldsymbol{A}\boldsymbol{y} = (\boldsymbol{X}^\top\boldsymbol{X})^{-1}\boldsymbol{X}^\top\boldsymbol{y} + \boldsymbol{C}\boldsymbol{y}, \tag{3.37}$$

where $\boldsymbol{A}$ and $\boldsymbol{C}$ are $k \times n$ matrices that depend on $\boldsymbol{X}$. The first equality here just says that $\tilde{\boldsymbol{\beta}}$ is a linear estimator. To obtain the second equality, we make the definition

$$\boldsymbol{C} \equiv \boldsymbol{A} - (\boldsymbol{X}^\top\boldsymbol{X})^{-1}\boldsymbol{X}^\top. \tag{3.38}$$

So far, least squares is the only estimator for linear regression models that we have encountered. Thus it may be difficult to imagine what kind of estimator $\tilde{\boldsymbol{\beta}}$ might be. In fact, there are many estimators of this type, including **generalized least-squares** estimators (Chapter 7) and **instrumental variables** estimators (Chapter 8) An alternative way of writing the class of linear unbiased estimators is explored in Exercise 3.17.

The principal theoretical result on the efficiency of the OLS estimator is called the **Gauss-Markov Theorem**. An informal way of stating this theorem is to say that $\hat{\boldsymbol{\beta}}$ is the **best linear unbiased estimator**, or **BLUE** for short. In other words, the OLS estimator is more efficient than any other linear unbiased estimator.

Theorem 3.1. (Gauss-Markov Theorem)

If it is assumed that $\mathrm{E}(\boldsymbol{u}\,|\,\boldsymbol{X}) = \mathbf{0}$ and $\mathrm{E}(\boldsymbol{u}\boldsymbol{u}^\top|\,\boldsymbol{X}) = \sigma^2\mathbf{I}$ in the linear regression model (3.03), then the OLS estimator $\hat{\boldsymbol{\beta}}$ is more efficient than any other linear unbiased estimator $\tilde{\boldsymbol{\beta}}$, in the sense that $\mathrm{Var}(\tilde{\boldsymbol{\beta}}) - \mathrm{Var}(\hat{\boldsymbol{\beta}})$ is a positive semidefinite matrix.

Proof: We assume that the DGP is a special case of (3.03), with parameters $\boldsymbol{\beta}_0$ and σ_0^2. Substituting for $\boldsymbol{y}$ in (3.37), we find that

$$\tilde{\boldsymbol{\beta}} = \boldsymbol{A}(\boldsymbol{X}\boldsymbol{\beta}_0 + \boldsymbol{u}) = \boldsymbol{A}\boldsymbol{X}\boldsymbol{\beta}_0 + \boldsymbol{A}\boldsymbol{u}. \tag{3.39}$$

Since we want $\tilde{\boldsymbol{\beta}}$ to be unbiased, we require that the expectation of the rightmost expression in (3.39), conditional on $\boldsymbol{X}$, should be $\boldsymbol{\beta}_0$. The second term in that expression has conditional mean $\mathbf{0}$, and so the first term must have conditional mean $\boldsymbol{\beta}_0$. This is the case for all $\boldsymbol{\beta}_0$ if and only if $\boldsymbol{A}\boldsymbol{X} = \mathbf{I}$, the $k \times k$ identity matrix. From (3.38), this condition is equivalent to $\boldsymbol{C}\boldsymbol{X} = \mathbf{O}$. Thus requiring $\tilde{\boldsymbol{\beta}}$ to be unbiased imposes a strong condition on the matrix $\boldsymbol{C}$.

The unbiasedness condition that $\boldsymbol{C}\boldsymbol{X} = \mathbf{O}$ implies that $\boldsymbol{C}\boldsymbol{y} = \boldsymbol{C}\boldsymbol{u}$. Since, from (3.37), $\boldsymbol{C}\boldsymbol{y} = \tilde{\boldsymbol{\beta}} - \hat{\boldsymbol{\beta}}$, this makes it clear that $\tilde{\boldsymbol{\beta}} - \hat{\boldsymbol{\beta}}$ has conditional mean zero. The unbiasedness condition also implies that the covariance matrix of $\tilde{\boldsymbol{\beta}} - \hat{\boldsymbol{\beta}}$ and $\hat{\boldsymbol{\beta}}$ is a zero matrix. To see this, observe that

$$\begin{aligned}
\mathrm{E}\big((\hat{\boldsymbol{\beta}} - \boldsymbol{\beta}_0)(\tilde{\boldsymbol{\beta}} - \hat{\boldsymbol{\beta}})^\top\big) &= \mathrm{E}\big((\boldsymbol{X}^\top\boldsymbol{X})^{-1}\boldsymbol{X}^\top\boldsymbol{u}\boldsymbol{u}^\top\boldsymbol{C}^\top\big) \\
&= (\boldsymbol{X}^\top\boldsymbol{X})^{-1}\boldsymbol{X}^\top\sigma_0^2\mathbf{I}\boldsymbol{C}^\top \\
&= \sigma_0^2(\boldsymbol{X}^\top\boldsymbol{X})^{-1}\boldsymbol{X}^\top\boldsymbol{C}^\top = \mathbf{O}.
\end{aligned} \tag{3.40}$$

Consequently, equation (3.37) says that the unbiased linear estimator $\tilde{\boldsymbol{\beta}}$ is equal to the least-squares estimator $\hat{\boldsymbol{\beta}}$ plus a random component $\boldsymbol{C}\boldsymbol{y}$ which has mean zero and is uncorrelated with $\hat{\boldsymbol{\beta}}$. The random component simply adds noise to the efficient estimator $\hat{\boldsymbol{\beta}}$. This makes it clear that $\hat{\boldsymbol{\beta}}$ is more efficient than $\tilde{\boldsymbol{\beta}}$. To complete the proof, we note that

$$\begin{aligned}\operatorname{Var}(\tilde{\boldsymbol{\beta}}) &= \operatorname{Var}\big(\hat{\boldsymbol{\beta}} + (\tilde{\boldsymbol{\beta}} - \hat{\boldsymbol{\beta}})\big)\\ &= \operatorname{Var}\big(\hat{\boldsymbol{\beta}} + \boldsymbol{C}\boldsymbol{y}\big)\\ &= \operatorname{Var}(\hat{\boldsymbol{\beta}}) + \operatorname{Var}(\boldsymbol{C}\boldsymbol{y}),\end{aligned} \tag{3.41}$$

because, from (3.40), the covariance of $\hat{\boldsymbol{\beta}}$ and $\boldsymbol{C}\boldsymbol{y}$ is zero. Thus the difference between $\operatorname{Var}(\tilde{\boldsymbol{\beta}})$ and $\operatorname{Var}(\hat{\boldsymbol{\beta}})$ is $\operatorname{Var}(\boldsymbol{C}\boldsymbol{y})$. Since it is a covariance matrix, this difference is necessarily positive semidefinite. ∎

We will encounter many cases in which an inefficient estimator is equal to an efficient estimator plus a random variable that has mean zero and is uncorrelated with the efficient estimator. The zero correlation ensures that the covariance matrix of the inefficient estimator is equal to the covariance matrix of the efficient estimator plus another matrix that is positive semidefinite, as in the last line of (3.41). If the correlation were not zero, this sort of proof would not work. Observe that, because everything is done in terms of second moments, the Gauss-Markov Theorem does not require any assumption about the normality of the error terms.

The Gauss-Markov Theorem that the OLS estimator is BLUE is one of the most famous results in statistics. However, it is important to keep in mind the limitations of this theorem. The theorem applies only to a correctly specified model with error terms that are homoskedastic and serially uncorrelated. Moreover, it does *not* say that the OLS estimator $\hat{\boldsymbol{\beta}}$ is more efficient than every imaginable estimator. Estimators which are nonlinear and/or biased may well perform better than ordinary least squares.

3.6 Residuals and Error Terms

The vector of least-squares residuals, $\hat{\boldsymbol{u}} \equiv \boldsymbol{y} - \boldsymbol{X}\hat{\boldsymbol{\beta}}$, is easily calculated once we have obtained $\hat{\boldsymbol{\beta}}$. The numerical properties of $\hat{\boldsymbol{u}}$ were discussed in Section 2.3. These properties include the fact that $\hat{\boldsymbol{u}}$ is orthogonal to $\boldsymbol{X}\hat{\boldsymbol{\beta}}$ and to every vector that lies in $\mathcal{S}(\boldsymbol{X})$. In this section, we turn our attention to the statistical properties of $\hat{\boldsymbol{u}}$ as an estimator of $\boldsymbol{u}$. These properties are very important, because we will want to use $\hat{\boldsymbol{u}}$ for a number of purposes. In particular, we will want to use it to estimate σ^2, the variance of the error terms. We need an estimate of σ^2 if we are to obtain an estimate of the covariance matrix of $\hat{\boldsymbol{\beta}}$. As we will see in later chapters, the residuals can also be used to test some of the strong assumptions that are often made about the distribution of the error terms and to implement more sophisticated estimation methods that require weaker assumptions.

The consistency of $\hat{\boldsymbol{\beta}}$ implies that $\hat{\boldsymbol{u}} \to \boldsymbol{u}$ as $n \to \infty$, but the finite-sample properties of $\hat{\boldsymbol{u}}$ differ from those of $\boldsymbol{u}$. As we saw in Section 2.3, the vector of residuals $\hat{\boldsymbol{u}}$ is what remains after we project the regressand $\boldsymbol{y}$ off $\mathcal{S}(\boldsymbol{X})$. If we assume that the DGP belongs to the model we are estimating, as the DGP (3.02) belongs to the model (3.01), then

$$\boldsymbol{M_X y} = \boldsymbol{M_X X}\boldsymbol{\beta}_0 + \boldsymbol{M_X u} = \boldsymbol{M_X u}.$$

The first term in the middle expression here vanishes because $\boldsymbol{M_X}$ annihilates everything that lies in $\mathcal{S}(\boldsymbol{X})$. The statistical properties of $\hat{\boldsymbol{u}}$ as an estimator of $\boldsymbol{u}$ follow directly from the fact that $\hat{\boldsymbol{u}} = \boldsymbol{M_X u}$ when the model (3.01) is correctly specified.

Each of the residuals is equal to a linear combination of every one of the error terms. Consider a single row of the matrix product $\hat{\boldsymbol{u}} = \boldsymbol{M_X u}$. Since the product has dimensions $n \times 1$, this row has just one element, and this element is one of the residuals. Recalling the result on partitioned matrices in Exercise 1.16, which allows us to select rows of a matrix product by selecting that row of the leftmost factor, we can write the tth residual as

$$\begin{aligned} \hat{u}_t &= u_t - \boldsymbol{X}_t(\boldsymbol{X}^\top\boldsymbol{X})^{-1}\boldsymbol{X}^\top\boldsymbol{u} \\ &= u_t - \sum_{s=1}^{n} \boldsymbol{X}_t(\boldsymbol{X}^\top\boldsymbol{X})^{-1}\boldsymbol{X}_s^\top u_s. \end{aligned} \tag{3.42}$$

Thus, even if each of the error terms u_t is independent of all the other error terms, as we have been assuming, each of the $\hat{u}_t$ is not independent of all the other residuals. In general, there is some dependence between every pair of residuals. However, this dependence generally diminishes as the sample size n increases.

Let us now assume that $\mathrm{E}(\boldsymbol{u} \,|\, \boldsymbol{X}) = \boldsymbol{0}$. This is assumption (3.08), which we made in Section 3.2 in order to prove that $\hat{\boldsymbol{\beta}}$ is unbiased. According to this assumption, $\mathrm{E}(u_t \,|\, \boldsymbol{X}) = 0$ for all t. All the expectations we will take in the remainder of this section will be conditional on $\boldsymbol{X}$. Since, by (3.42), $\hat{u}_t$ is just a linear combination of all the u_t, the expectation of $\hat{u}_t$ conditional on $\boldsymbol{X}$ must be zero. Thus, in this respect, the residuals $\hat{u}_t$ behave just like the error terms u_t.

In other respects, however, the residuals do not have the same properties as the error terms. Consider $\mathrm{Var}(\hat{u}_t)$, the variance of $\hat{u}_t$. Since $\mathrm{E}(\hat{u}_t) = 0$, this variance is just $\mathrm{E}(\hat{u}_t^2)$. As we saw in Section 2.3, the Euclidean length of the vector of least-squares residuals, $\hat{\boldsymbol{u}}$, is always smaller than that of the vector of residuals evaluated at any other value, $\boldsymbol{u}(\boldsymbol{\beta})$. In particular, $\hat{\boldsymbol{u}}$ must be shorter than the vector of error terms $\boldsymbol{u} = \boldsymbol{u}(\boldsymbol{\beta}_0)$. Thus we know that $\|\hat{\boldsymbol{u}}\|^2 \leq \|\boldsymbol{u}\|^2$. This implies that $\mathrm{E}\big(\|\hat{\boldsymbol{u}}\|^2\big) \leq \mathrm{E}\big(\|\boldsymbol{u}\|^2\big)$. If, as usual, we assume that the error variance is σ_0^2 under the true DGP, we see that

$$\begin{aligned}\sum_{t=1}^{n}\mathrm{Var}(\hat{u}_t) &= \sum_{t=1}^{n}\mathrm{E}(\hat{u}_t^2) = \mathrm{E}\Big(\sum_{t=1}^{n}\hat{u}_t^2\Big) = \mathrm{E}(\|\hat{\boldsymbol{u}}\|^2)\\ &\le \mathrm{E}(\|\boldsymbol{u}\|^2) = \mathrm{E}\Big(\sum_{t=1}^{n}u_t^2\Big) = \sum_{t=1}^{n}\mathrm{E}(u_t^2) = n\sigma_0^2.\end{aligned}$$

This suggests that, at least for most observations, the variance of $\hat{u}_t$ must be less than σ_0^2. In fact, we will see that $\mathrm{Var}(\hat{u}_t)$ is less than σ_0^2 for every observation.

The easiest way to calculate the variance of $\hat{u}_t$ is to calculate the covariance matrix of the entire vector $\hat{\boldsymbol{u}}$:

$$\begin{aligned}\mathrm{Var}(\hat{\boldsymbol{u}}) &= \mathrm{Var}(\boldsymbol{M_X u}) = \mathrm{E}(\boldsymbol{M_X u u}^\top \boldsymbol{M_X})\\ &= \boldsymbol{M_X}\mathrm{E}(\boldsymbol{uu}^\top)\boldsymbol{M_X} = \boldsymbol{M_X}\mathrm{Var}(\boldsymbol{u})\boldsymbol{M_X}\\ &= \boldsymbol{M_X}(\sigma_0^2\mathbf{I})\boldsymbol{M_X} = \sigma_0^2\boldsymbol{M_X M_X} = \sigma_0^2\boldsymbol{M_X}.\end{aligned} \tag{3.43}$$

The second equality in the first line here uses the fact that $\boldsymbol{M_X u}$ has mean $\mathbf{0}$. The third equality in the last line uses the fact that $\boldsymbol{M_X}$ is idempotent. From the result (3.43), we see immediately that, in general, $\mathrm{E}(\hat{u}_t\hat{u}_s) \neq 0$ for $t \neq s$. Thus, even though the original error terms are assumed to be uncorrelated, the residuals are not uncorrelated.

From equations (3.43), it can also be seen that the residuals do not have a constant variance, and that the variance of every residual must always be smaller than σ_0^2. Recall from Section 2.6 that h_t denotes the tth diagonal element of the projection matrix $\boldsymbol{P_X}$. Thus a typical diagonal element of $\boldsymbol{M_X}$ is $1 - h_t$. Therefore, it follows from (3.43) that

$$\mathrm{Var}(\hat{u}_t) = \mathrm{E}(\hat{u}_t^2) = (1 - h_t)\sigma_0^2. \tag{3.44}$$

Since $0 \le 1 - h_t < 1$, this equation implies that $\mathrm{E}(\hat{u}_t^2)$ is always smaller than σ_0^2. Just how much smaller depends on h_t. It is clear that high-leverage observations, for which h_t is relatively large, must have residuals with smaller variance than low-leverage observations, for which h_t is relatively small. This makes sense, since high-leverage observations have more effect on the parameter values. As a consequence, the residuals for high-leverage observations tend to be shrunk more, relative to the error terms, than the residuals for low-leverage observations.

Estimating the Variance of the Error Terms

The method of least squares provides estimates of the regression coefficients, but it does not directly provide an estimate of σ^2, the variance of the error terms. The method of moments suggests that we can estimate σ^2 by using the corresponding sample moment. If we actually observed the u_t, this sample moment would be

$$\frac{1}{n}\sum_{t=1}^{n} u_t^2. \tag{3.45}$$

We do not observe the u_t, but we do observe the $\hat{u}_t$. Thus the simplest possible MM estimator is

$$\hat{\sigma}^2 \equiv \frac{1}{n}\sum_{t=1}^{n} \hat{u}_t^2. \tag{3.46}$$

This estimator is just the average of n squared residuals. It can be shown to be consistent; see Exercise 3.13. However, because each squared residual has expectation less than σ_0^2, by (3.44), $\hat{\sigma}^2$ must be biased downward.

It is easy to calculate the bias of $\hat{\sigma}^2$. We saw in Section 2.6 that $\sum_{t=1}^{n} h_t = k$. Therefore, from (3.44) and (3.46),

$$\mathrm{E}(\hat{\sigma}^2) = \frac{1}{n}\sum_{t=1}^{n} \mathrm{E}(\hat{u}_t^2) = \frac{1}{n}\sum_{t=1}^{n}(1 - h_t)\sigma_0^2 = \frac{n-k}{n}\sigma_0^2. \tag{3.47}$$

Since $\hat{\boldsymbol{u}} = \boldsymbol{M_X u}$ and $\boldsymbol{M_X}$ is idempotent, the sum of squared residuals is just $\boldsymbol{u}^\top\boldsymbol{M_X u}$. The result (3.47) implies that

$$\mathrm{E}\big(\boldsymbol{u}^\top\boldsymbol{M_X u}\big) = \mathrm{E}\big(\mathrm{SSR}(\hat{\boldsymbol{\beta}})\big) = \mathrm{E}\bigg(\sum_{t=1}^{n} \hat{u}_t^2\bigg) = (n-k)\sigma_0^2. \tag{3.48}$$

Readers are asked to show this in a different way in Exercise 3.14. Notice, from (3.48), that adding one more regressor has exactly the same effect on the expectation of the SSR as taking away one observation.

The result (3.47) suggests another MM estimator which is unbiased:

$$s^2 \equiv \frac{1}{n-k}\sum_{t=1}^{n} \hat{u}_t^2. \tag{3.49}$$

The only difference between $\hat{\sigma}^2$ and s^2 is that the former divides the SSR by n and the latter divides it by $n - k$. As a result, s^2 is unbiased whenever $\hat{\boldsymbol{\beta}}$ is. Ideally, if we were able to observe the error terms, our MM estimator would be (3.45), which would be unbiased. When we replace the error terms u_t by the residuals $\hat{u}_t$, we introduce a downward bias. Dividing by $n - k$ instead of by n eliminates this bias.

Virtually all OLS regression programs report s^2 as the estimated variance of the error terms. The square root of this estimate, s, is called the **standard error of regression**. It is important to remember that, even though s^2 provides an unbiased estimate of σ^2, s itself does not provide an unbiased estimate of σ, because taking the square root of s^2 is a nonlinear operation. If we replace σ_0^2 by s^2 in expression (3.28), we can obtain an unbiased estimate of $\mathrm{Var}(\hat{\boldsymbol{\beta}})$,

$$\widehat{\mathrm{Var}}(\hat{\boldsymbol{\beta}}) = s^2(\boldsymbol{X}^\top\boldsymbol{X})^{-1}. \tag{3.50}$$

This is the usual estimate of the covariance matrix of the OLS parameter estimates under the assumption of IID errors.

3.7 Misspecification of Linear Regression Models

Up to this point, we have assumed that the DGP belongs to the model that is being estimated, or, in other words, that the model is correctly specified. This is obviously a very strong assumption indeed. It is therefore important to know something about the statistical properties of $\hat{\boldsymbol{\beta}}$ when the model is not correctly specified. In this section, we consider a simple case of misspecification, namely, **underspecification**. In order to understand underspecification better, we begin by discussing its opposite, **overspecification**.

Overspecification

A model is said to be **overspecified** if some variables that rightly belong to the information set Ω_t, but do not appear in the DGP, are mistakenly included in the model. Overspecification is *not* a form of misspecification. Including irrelevant explanatory variables in a model makes the model larger than it need have been, but, since the DGP remains a special case of the model, there is no misspecification. Consider the case of an overspecified linear regression model. Suppose that we estimate the model

$$\boldsymbol{y} = \boldsymbol{X\beta} + \boldsymbol{Z\gamma} + \boldsymbol{u}, \quad \boldsymbol{u} \sim \mathrm{IID}(\mathbf{0}, \sigma^2\mathbf{I}), \tag{3.51}$$

when the data are actually generated by

$$\boldsymbol{y} = \boldsymbol{X\beta}_0 + \boldsymbol{u}, \quad \boldsymbol{u} \sim \mathrm{IID}(\mathbf{0}, \sigma_0^2\mathbf{I}). \tag{3.52}$$

It is assumed that $\boldsymbol{X}_t$ and $\boldsymbol{Z}_t$, the tth rows of $\boldsymbol{X}$ and $\boldsymbol{Z}$, respectively, belong to Ω_t. Recall the discussion of information sets in Section 1.3. The overspecified model (3.51) is not misspecified, since the DGP (3.52) is a special case of it, with $\boldsymbol{\beta} = \boldsymbol{\beta}_0$, $\boldsymbol{\gamma} = \mathbf{0}$, and $\sigma^2 = \sigma_0^2$.

Suppose now that we run the linear regression (3.51). By the FWL Theorem, the estimates $\tilde{\boldsymbol{\beta}}$ from (3.51) are the same as those from the regression

$$\boldsymbol{M_Z y} = \boldsymbol{M_Z X\beta} + \text{residuals},$$

where, as usual, $\boldsymbol{M_Z} = \mathbf{I} - \boldsymbol{Z}(\boldsymbol{Z}^\top\boldsymbol{Z})^{-1}\boldsymbol{Z}^\top$. Thus we see that

$$\tilde{\boldsymbol{\beta}} = (\boldsymbol{X}^\top\boldsymbol{M_Z X})^{-1}\boldsymbol{X}^\top\boldsymbol{M_Z y}. \tag{3.53}$$

Since $\tilde{\boldsymbol{\beta}}$ is part of the OLS estimator of a correctly specified model, it should be unbiased. Indeed, if we replace $\boldsymbol{y}$ by $\boldsymbol{X\beta}_0 + \boldsymbol{u}$, we find from (3.53) that

$$\tilde{\boldsymbol{\beta}} = \boldsymbol{\beta}_0 + (\boldsymbol{X}^\top \boldsymbol{M_Z X})^{-1}\boldsymbol{X}^\top \boldsymbol{M_Z u}. \tag{3.54}$$

The conditional expectation of the second term on the right-hand side of (3.54) is $\mathbf{0}$, provided we take expectations conditional on $\boldsymbol{Z}$ as well as on $\boldsymbol{X}$; see Section 3.2. Since $\boldsymbol{Z}_t$ is assumed to belong to Ω_t, it is perfectly legitimate to do this.

If we had estimated (3.51) subject to the valid restriction that $\boldsymbol{\gamma} = \mathbf{0}$, we would have obtained the OLS estimate $\hat{\boldsymbol{\beta}}$, expression (3.04), which is unbiased and has covariance matrix (3.28). We see that both $\tilde{\boldsymbol{\beta}}$ and $\hat{\boldsymbol{\beta}}$ are unbiased estimators, linear in $\boldsymbol{y}$. Both are OLS estimators, and so it seems that we should be able to apply the Gauss-Markov Theorem to both of them. This is in fact correct, but we must be careful to apply the theorem in the context of the appropriate model for each of the estimators.

For $\hat{\boldsymbol{\beta}}$, the appropriate model is the **restricted model**,

$$\boldsymbol{y} = \boldsymbol{X\beta} + \boldsymbol{u}, \quad \boldsymbol{u} \sim \mathrm{IID}(\mathbf{0}, \sigma^2\mathbf{I}), \tag{3.55}$$

in which the restriction $\boldsymbol{\gamma} = \mathbf{0}$ is explicitly imposed. Provided this restriction is correct, as it is if the true DGP takes the form (3.52), $\hat{\boldsymbol{\beta}}$ must be more efficient than any other linear unbiased estimator of $\boldsymbol{\beta}$. Thus we should find that the matrix $\mathrm{Var}(\tilde{\boldsymbol{\beta}}) - \mathrm{Var}(\hat{\boldsymbol{\beta}})$ is positive semidefinite.

For $\tilde{\boldsymbol{\beta}}$, the appropriate model is the **unrestricted model** (3.51). In this context, the Gauss-Markov Theorem says that, when we do not know the true value of $\boldsymbol{\gamma}$, $\tilde{\boldsymbol{\beta}}$ is the best linear unbiased estimator of $\boldsymbol{\beta}$. It is important to note here that $\hat{\boldsymbol{\beta}}$ is *not* an unbiased estimator of $\boldsymbol{\beta}$ for the unrestricted model, and so it cannot be included in the class of estimators covered by the Gauss-Markov Theorem for that model. We will make this point more fully in the next subsection, when we discuss underspecification.

It is illuminating to check these consequences of the Gauss-Markov Theorem explicitly. From equation (3.54), it follows that

$$\begin{aligned}
\mathrm{Var}(\tilde{\boldsymbol{\beta}}) &= \mathrm{E}\big((\tilde{\boldsymbol{\beta}} - \boldsymbol{\beta}_0)(\tilde{\boldsymbol{\beta}} - \boldsymbol{\beta}_0)^\top\big) \\
&= (\boldsymbol{X}^\top \boldsymbol{M_Z X})^{-1}\boldsymbol{X}^\top \boldsymbol{M_Z}\mathrm{E}(\boldsymbol{uu}^\top)\boldsymbol{M_Z X}(\boldsymbol{X}^\top \boldsymbol{M_Z X})^{-1} \\
&= \sigma_0^2(\boldsymbol{X}^\top \boldsymbol{M_Z X})^{-1}\boldsymbol{X}^\top \boldsymbol{M_Z}\mathbf{I}\boldsymbol{M_Z X}(\boldsymbol{X}^\top \boldsymbol{M_Z X})^{-1} \\
&= \sigma_0^2(\boldsymbol{X}^\top \boldsymbol{M_Z X})^{-1}.
\end{aligned} \tag{3.56}$$

The situation is clear in the case in which there is only one parameter, β, corresponding to a single regressor, $\boldsymbol{x}$. Since $\boldsymbol{M_Z}$ is a projection matrix, the

Euclidean length of $\boldsymbol{M_Z x}$ must be smaller (or at least, no larger) than the Euclidean length of $\boldsymbol{x}$; recall (2.27). Thus $\boldsymbol{x}^\top \boldsymbol{M_Z x} \leq \boldsymbol{x}^\top \boldsymbol{x}$, which implies that

$$\sigma_0^2(\boldsymbol{x}^\top \boldsymbol{M_Z x})^{-1} \geq \sigma_0^2(\boldsymbol{x}^\top \boldsymbol{x})^{-1}. \tag{3.57}$$

The inequality in (3.57) almost always holds strictly. The only exception is the special case in which $\boldsymbol{x}$ lies in $\mathcal{S}^\perp(\boldsymbol{Z})$, which implies that the regression of $\boldsymbol{x}$ on $\boldsymbol{Z}$ has no explanatory power at all.

In general, we wish to show that $\mathrm{Var}(\tilde{\boldsymbol{\beta}}) - \mathrm{Var}(\hat{\boldsymbol{\beta}})$ is a positive semidefinite matrix. As we saw in Section 3.5, this is equivalent to showing that the matrix $\mathrm{Var}(\hat{\boldsymbol{\beta}})^{-1} - \mathrm{Var}(\tilde{\boldsymbol{\beta}})^{-1}$ is positive semidefinite. A little algebra shows that

$$\begin{aligned} \boldsymbol{X}^\top \boldsymbol{X} - \boldsymbol{X}^\top \boldsymbol{M_Z X} &= \boldsymbol{X}^\top (\mathbf{I} - \boldsymbol{M_Z}) \boldsymbol{X} \\ &= \boldsymbol{X}^\top \boldsymbol{P_Z X} \\ &= (\boldsymbol{P_Z X})^\top \boldsymbol{P_Z X}. \end{aligned} \tag{3.58}$$

Since $\boldsymbol{X}^\top \boldsymbol{X} - \boldsymbol{X}^\top \boldsymbol{M_Z X}$ can be written as the transpose of a matrix times itself, it must be positive semidefinite. Dividing by σ_0^2 gives the desired result.

We have established that the OLS estimator of $\boldsymbol{\beta}$ in the overspecified regression model (3.51) is at most as efficient as the OLS estimator in the restricted model (3.55), provided the restrictions are true. Therefore, adding additional variables that do not really belong in a model normally leads to less accurate estimates. Only in certain very special cases is there no loss of efficiency. In such cases, the covariance matrices of $\tilde{\boldsymbol{\beta}}$ and $\hat{\boldsymbol{\beta}}$ must be the same, which implies that the matrix difference computed in (3.58) must be zero.

The last expression in (3.58) must be a zero matrix whenever $\boldsymbol{P_Z X} = \mathbf{O}$. This condition holds whenever the two sets of regressors $\boldsymbol{X}$ and $\boldsymbol{Z}$ are mutually orthogonal, so that $\boldsymbol{Z}^\top \boldsymbol{X} = \mathbf{O}$. In this special case, $\tilde{\boldsymbol{\beta}}$ is just as efficient as $\hat{\boldsymbol{\beta}}$. In general, however, including regressors that do not belong in a model increases the variance of the estimates of the coefficients on the regressors that do belong, and the increase can be very great in many cases. As can be seen from the left-hand side of (3.57), the variance of the estimated coefficient $\tilde{\beta}$ associated with any regressor $\boldsymbol{x}$ is proportional to the inverse of the SSR from a regression of $\boldsymbol{x}$ on all the other regressors. The more other regressors there are, whether they truly belong in the model or not, the smaller is this SSR, and, in consequence, the larger the variance of $\tilde{\beta}$.

Underspecification

The opposite of overspecification is underspecification, in which we omit some variables that actually do appear in the DGP. To avoid any new notation, let us suppose that the model we estimate is (3.55), which yields the estimator $\hat{\boldsymbol{\beta}}$, but that the DGP is really

$$\boldsymbol{y} = \boldsymbol{X\beta}_0 + \boldsymbol{Z\gamma}_0 + \boldsymbol{u}, \quad \boldsymbol{u} \sim \mathrm{IID}(\mathbf{0}, \sigma_0^2 \mathbf{I}). \tag{3.59}$$

Thus the situation is precisely the opposite of the one considered above. The estimator $\tilde{\boldsymbol{\beta}}$, based on regression (3.51), is now the "correct" one to use, while the estimator $\hat{\boldsymbol{\beta}}$ is based on an underspecified model. It is clear that underspecification, unlike overspecification, *is* a form of misspecification, because the DGP (3.59) does not belong to the model (3.55).

The first point to recognize about $\hat{\boldsymbol{\beta}}$ is that it is now, in general, biased. Substituting the right-hand side of (3.59) for $\boldsymbol{y}$ in (3.04), and taking expectations conditional on $\boldsymbol{X}$ and $\boldsymbol{Z}$, we find that

$$\begin{aligned} \mathrm{E}(\hat{\boldsymbol{\beta}}) &= \mathrm{E}\big((\boldsymbol{X}^{\top}\boldsymbol{X})^{-1}\boldsymbol{X}^{\top}(\boldsymbol{X}\boldsymbol{\beta}_0 + \boldsymbol{Z}\boldsymbol{\gamma}_0 + \boldsymbol{u})\big) \\ &= \boldsymbol{\beta}_0 + (\boldsymbol{X}^{\top}\boldsymbol{X})^{-1}\boldsymbol{X}^{\top}\boldsymbol{Z}\boldsymbol{\gamma}_0 + \mathrm{E}\big((\boldsymbol{X}^{\top}\boldsymbol{X})^{-1}\boldsymbol{X}^{\top}\boldsymbol{u}\big) \\ &= \boldsymbol{\beta}_0 + (\boldsymbol{X}^{\top}\boldsymbol{X})^{-1}\boldsymbol{X}^{\top}\boldsymbol{Z}\boldsymbol{\gamma}_0. \end{aligned} \tag{3.60}$$

The second term in the last line of (3.60) is equal to zero only when $\boldsymbol{X}^{\top}\boldsymbol{Z} = \mathbf{O}$ or $\boldsymbol{\gamma}_0 = \mathbf{0}$. The first possibility arises when the two sets of regressors are mutually orthogonal, the second when (3.55) is not in fact underspecified. Except in these very special cases, $\hat{\boldsymbol{\beta}}$ is generally biased. The magnitude of the bias depends on the parameter vector $\boldsymbol{\gamma}_0$ and on the $\boldsymbol{X}$ and $\boldsymbol{Z}$ matrices. Because this bias does not vanish as $n \to \infty$, $\hat{\boldsymbol{\beta}}$ is also generally inconsistent.

Since $\hat{\boldsymbol{\beta}}$ is biased, we cannot reasonably use its covariance matrix to evaluate its accuracy. Instead, we can use the **mean squared error matrix**, or **MSE matrix**, of $\hat{\boldsymbol{\beta}}$. This matrix is defined as

$$\mathrm{MSE}(\hat{\boldsymbol{\beta}}) \equiv \mathrm{E}\big((\hat{\boldsymbol{\beta}} - \boldsymbol{\beta}_0)(\hat{\boldsymbol{\beta}} - \boldsymbol{\beta}_0)^{\top}\big). \tag{3.61}$$

The MSE matrix is equal to $\mathrm{Var}(\hat{\boldsymbol{\beta}})$ if $\hat{\boldsymbol{\beta}}$ is unbiased, but not otherwise. For a scalar parameter $\hat{\beta}$, the MSE is equal to the square of the bias plus the variance:

$$\mathrm{MSE}(\hat{\beta}) = \big(\mathrm{E}(\hat{\beta}) - \beta_0\big)^2 + \mathrm{Var}(\hat{\beta}).$$

Thus, when we use MSE to evaluate the accuracy of an estimator, we are choosing to give equal weight to random errors and to systematic errors that arise from bias.[1]

From equations (3.60), we can see that

$$\hat{\boldsymbol{\beta}} - \boldsymbol{\beta}_0 = (\boldsymbol{X}^{\top}\boldsymbol{X})^{-1}\boldsymbol{X}^{\top}\boldsymbol{Z}\boldsymbol{\gamma}_0 + (\boldsymbol{X}^{\top}\boldsymbol{X})^{-1}\boldsymbol{X}^{\top}\boldsymbol{u}.$$

Therefore, $\hat{\boldsymbol{\beta}} - \boldsymbol{\beta}_0$ times itself transposed is equal to

$$\begin{aligned} &(\boldsymbol{X}^{\top}\boldsymbol{X})^{-1}\boldsymbol{X}^{\top}\boldsymbol{Z}\boldsymbol{\gamma}_0\boldsymbol{\gamma}_0^{\top}\boldsymbol{Z}^{\top}\boldsymbol{X}(\boldsymbol{X}^{\top}\boldsymbol{X})^{-1} + (\boldsymbol{X}^{\top}\boldsymbol{X})^{-1}\boldsymbol{X}^{\top}\boldsymbol{u}\boldsymbol{u}^{\top}\boldsymbol{X}(\boldsymbol{X}^{\top}\boldsymbol{X})^{-1} \\ &+ (\boldsymbol{X}^{\top}\boldsymbol{X})^{-1}\boldsymbol{X}^{\top}\boldsymbol{Z}\boldsymbol{\gamma}_0\boldsymbol{u}^{\top}\boldsymbol{X}(\boldsymbol{X}^{\top}\boldsymbol{X})^{-1} + (\boldsymbol{X}^{\top}\boldsymbol{X})^{-1}\boldsymbol{X}^{\top}\boldsymbol{u}\boldsymbol{\gamma}_0^{\top}\boldsymbol{Z}^{\top}\boldsymbol{X}(\boldsymbol{X}^{\top}\boldsymbol{X})^{-1}. \end{aligned}$$

[1] For a scalar parameter, it is common to report the square root of the MSE, called the **root mean squared error**, or **RMSE**, instead of the MSE itself.

The second term here has expectation $\sigma_0^2(\boldsymbol{X}^\top\boldsymbol{X})^{-1}$, and the third and fourth terms, one of which is the transpose of the other, have expectation zero. Thus we conclude that

$$\mathrm{MSE}(\hat{\boldsymbol{\beta}}) = \sigma_0^2(\boldsymbol{X}^\top\boldsymbol{X})^{-1} + (\boldsymbol{X}^\top\boldsymbol{X})^{-1}\boldsymbol{X}^\top\boldsymbol{Z}\boldsymbol{\gamma}_0\boldsymbol{\gamma}_0^\top\boldsymbol{Z}^\top\boldsymbol{X}(\boldsymbol{X}^\top\boldsymbol{X})^{-1}. \tag{3.62}$$

The first term is what the covariance matrix would be if we were estimating a correctly specified model, and the second term arises because the restricted estimator $\hat{\boldsymbol{\beta}}$ is biased.

We would like to compare $\mathrm{MSE}(\hat{\boldsymbol{\beta}})$, expression (3.62), with $\mathrm{MSE}(\tilde{\boldsymbol{\beta}}) = \mathrm{Var}(\tilde{\boldsymbol{\beta}})$, which is given by expression (3.56). However, no unambiguous comparison is possible. The first term in (3.62) cannot be larger, in the matrix sense, than (3.56). If the bias is small, the second term must be small, and it may well be that $\hat{\boldsymbol{\beta}}$ is more efficient than $\tilde{\boldsymbol{\beta}}$. However, if the bias is large, the second term is necessarily large, and $\hat{\boldsymbol{\beta}}$ must be less efficient than $\tilde{\boldsymbol{\beta}}$. Of course, it is quite possible that some parameters may be estimated more efficiently by $\hat{\boldsymbol{\beta}}$ and others more efficiently by $\tilde{\boldsymbol{\beta}}$.

Whether or not the restricted estimator $\hat{\boldsymbol{\beta}}$ happens to be more efficient than the unrestricted estimator $\tilde{\boldsymbol{\beta}}$, the covariance matrix for $\hat{\boldsymbol{\beta}}$ that is calculated by a least-squares regression program is incorrect. The program attempts to estimate the first term in (3.62), but it ignores the second. However, s^2 is typically larger than σ_0^2 if some regressors have been incorrectly omitted. Thus, the program yields a biased estimate of the first term.

It is tempting to conclude from this discussion that underspecification is a much more severe problem than overspecification. After all, the former constitutes misspecification, but the latter does not. In consequence, as we have seen, underspecification leads to biased estimates and an estimated covariance matrix that may be severely misleading, while overspecification merely leads to inefficiency. Therefore, it would seem that we should always err on the side of overspecification. If all samples were extremely large, this might be a reasonable conclusion. The bias caused by underspecification does not go away as the sample size increases, but the variances of all consistent estimators tend to zero. Therefore, in sufficiently large samples, it makes sense to avoid underspecification at all costs. However, in samples of modest size, the gain in efficiency from omitting some variables, even if their coefficients are not actually zero, may be very large relative to the bias that is caused by their omission.

3.8 Measures of Goodness of Fit

A natural question to ask about any regression is: How well does it fit? There is more than one way to answer this question, and none of the answers may be entirely satisfactory in every case.

One possibility might be to use s, the estimated standard error of the regression. But s can be rather hard to interpret, since it depends on the scale of the y_t. When the regressand is in logarithms, however, s is meaningful and easy to interpret. Consider the loglinear model

$$\log y_t = \beta_1 + \beta_2 \log x_{t2} + \beta_3 \log x_{t3} + u_t. \tag{3.63}$$

As we saw in Section 1.3, this model can be obtained by taking logarithms of both sides of the model

$$y_t = e^{\beta_1} x_{t2}^{\beta_2} x_{t3}^{\beta_3} e^{u_t}. \tag{3.64}$$

The error factor e^{u_t} is, for u_t small, approximately equal to $1 + u_t$. Thus the standard deviation of u_t in (3.63) is, approximately, the standard deviation of the proportional error in the regression (3.64). Therefore, for any regression where the dependent variable is in logs, we can simply interpret $100s$, provided it is small, as an estimate of the percentage error in the regression.

When the regressand is not in logarithms, we could divide s by $\bar{y}$, the average of the y_t, or perhaps by the average absolute value of y_t if they were not all of the same sign. This would provide a measure of how large are the errors in the regression relative to the magnitude of the dependent variable. In many cases, $s/\bar{y}$ (for a model in levels) or s (for a model in logarithms) provides a useful measure of how well a regression fits. However, these measures are not entirely satisfactory. They are bounded from below, since they cannot be negative, but they are not bounded from above. Moreover, $s/\bar{y}$ is very hard to interpret if y_t can be either positive or negative.

A much more commonly used (and misused) measure of goodness of fit is the coefficient of determination, or R^2, which we introduced in Section 2.5. In that section, we discussed two versions of R^2: the centered version, R_c^2, and the uncentered version, R_u^2. As we saw there, both versions are based on Pythagoras' Theorem, which allows the total sum of squares (TSS) to be broken into two parts, the explained sum of squares (ESS) and the sum of squared residuals (SSR). Both versions of R^2 can be written as

$$R^2 = \frac{\text{ESS}}{\text{TSS}} = 1 - \frac{\text{SSR}}{\text{TSS}},$$

where ESS and TSS are calculated around zero for R_u^2 and around the mean of the regressand for R_c^2. The centered version is much more commonly encountered than the uncentered version, because it is invariant to changes in the mean of the regressand. By adding a large enough constant to all the y_t, we could always make R_u^2 become arbitrarily close to 1, at least if the regression included a constant, since the SSR would stay the same and the TSS would increase without limit. We discussed an example of this in Section 2.5.

One important limitation of both versions of R^2 is that they are valid only if a regression model is estimated by least squares, since otherwise it would not be true that TSS = ESS + SSR. Moreover, as we saw in Section 2.5, the centered version is not valid if the regressors do not include a constant term or the equivalent, that is, if $\boldsymbol{\iota}$, the vector of 1s, does not belong to $\mathcal{S}(\boldsymbol{X})$.

Another, possibly undesirable, feature of both R_u^2 and R_c^2 as measures of goodness of fit is that both increase whenever more regressors are added. To demonstrate this, we argue in terms of R_u^2, but the FWL Theorem can be used to show that the same results hold for R_c^2. Consider once more the restricted and unrestricted models, (3.55) and (3.51), respectively. Since both regressions have the same dependent variable, they have the same TSS. Thus the regression with the larger ESS must also have the larger R^2. The ESS from (3.51) is $\|\boldsymbol{P}_{\boldsymbol{X},\boldsymbol{Z}}\boldsymbol{y}\|^2$ and that from (3.55) is $\|\boldsymbol{P}_{\boldsymbol{X}}\boldsymbol{y}\|^2$, and so the difference between them is

$$\boldsymbol{y}^\top(\boldsymbol{P}_{\boldsymbol{X},\boldsymbol{Z}} - \boldsymbol{P}_{\boldsymbol{X}})\boldsymbol{y}. \tag{3.65}$$

Clearly, $\mathcal{S}(\boldsymbol{X}) \subset \mathcal{S}(\boldsymbol{X}, \boldsymbol{Z})$. Thus $\boldsymbol{P}_{\boldsymbol{X}}$ projects on to a subspace of the image of $\boldsymbol{P}_{\boldsymbol{X},\boldsymbol{Z}}$. This implies that the matrix in the middle of (3.65), say $\boldsymbol{Q}$, is an orthogonal projection matrix; see Exercise 2.18. Consequently, (3.65) takes the form $\boldsymbol{y}^\top\boldsymbol{Q}\boldsymbol{y} = \|\boldsymbol{Q}\boldsymbol{y}\|^2 \geq 0$. The ESS from (3.51) is therefore no less than that from (3.55), and so the R^2 from (3.51) is no less than that from (3.55).

The R^2 can be modified so that adding additional regressors does not necessarily increase its value. If $\boldsymbol{\iota} \in \mathcal{S}(\boldsymbol{X})$, the centered R^2 can be written as

$$R_c^2 = 1 - \frac{\sum_{t=1}^n \hat{u}_t^2}{\sum_{t=1}^n (y_t - \bar{y})^2}. \tag{3.66}$$

The numerator of the second term is just the SSR. As we saw in Section 3.6, it has expectation $(n-k)\sigma_0^2$ under standard assumptions. The denominator is $n-1$ times an unbiased estimator of the variance of y_t about its true mean. As such, it has expectation $(n-1)\mathrm{Var}(y)$. Thus the second term of (3.66) can be thought of as the ratio of two biased estimators. If we replace these biased estimators by unbiased estimators, we obtain the **adjusted $\boldsymbol{R^2}$**,

$$\bar{R}^2 \equiv 1 - \frac{\frac{1}{n-k}\sum_{t=1}^n \hat{u}_t^2}{\frac{1}{n-1}\sum_{t=1}^n (y_t - \bar{y})^2} = 1 - \frac{(n-1)\boldsymbol{y}^\top\boldsymbol{M}_{\boldsymbol{X}}\boldsymbol{y}}{(n-k)\boldsymbol{y}^\top\boldsymbol{M}_{\boldsymbol{\iota}}\boldsymbol{y}}. \tag{3.67}$$

The adjusted R^2 is reported by virtually all regression packages, often in preference to R_c^2. However, $\bar{R}^2$ is really no more informative than R_c^2. The two are generally very similar, except when $(n-k)/(n-1)$ is noticeably less than 1.

One nice feature of R_u^2 and R_c^2 is that they are constrained to lie between 0 and 1. In contrast, $\bar{R}^2$ can actually be negative. If a model has very little explanatory power, it is conceivable that $(n-1)/(n-k)$ may be greater than TSS/SSR. When that happens, $\bar{R}^2 < 0$.

The widespread use of $\bar{R}^2$ dates from the early days of econometrics, when sample sizes were often small, and investigators were easily impressed by models that yielded large values of R_c^2. We saw above that adding an extra regressor to a linear regression always increases R_c^2. This increase can be quite noticeable when the sample size is small, even if the added regressor does not really belong in the regression. In contrast, adding an extra regressor increases $\bar{R}^2$ only if the proportional reduction in the SSR is greater than the proportional reduction in $n - k$. Therefore, a naive investigator who tries to maximize $\bar{R}^2$ is less likely to end up choosing a severely overspecified model than one who tries to maximize R_c^2.

It can be extremely misleading to compare any form of R^2 for models estimated using different data sets. Suppose, for example, that we estimate Model 1 using a set of data for which the regressors, and consequently the regressand, vary a lot, and we estimate Model 2 using a second set of data for which both the regressors and the regressand vary much less. Then, even if both models fit equally well, in the sense that their residuals have just about the same variance, Model 1 has a much larger R^2 than Model 2. This can most easily be seen from (3.66). Increasing the denominator of the second term while holding the numerator constant evidently increases the R^2.

3.9 Final Remarks

In this chapter, we have dealt with many of the most fundamental, and best-known, statistical properties of ordinary least squares. In particular, we have discussed the properties of $\hat{\boldsymbol{\beta}}$ as an estimator of $\boldsymbol{\beta}$ and of s^2 as an estimator of σ_0^2. We have also derived $\mathrm{Var}(\hat{\boldsymbol{\beta}})$, the covariance matrix of $\hat{\boldsymbol{\beta}}$, and shown how to estimate it. However, we have not said anything about how to use $\hat{\boldsymbol{\beta}}$ and the estimate of $\mathrm{Var}(\hat{\boldsymbol{\beta}})$ to make inferences about $\boldsymbol{\beta}$. This important topic will be taken up in the next chapter.

3.10 Exercises

3.1 Generate a sample of size 25 from the model (3.11), with $\beta_1 = 1$ and $\beta_2 = 0.8$. For simplicity, assume that $y_0 = 0$ and that the u_t are NID(0, 1). Use this sample to compute the OLS estimates $\hat{\beta}_1$ and $\hat{\beta}_2$. Repeat at least 100 times, and find the averages of the $\hat{\beta}_1$ and the $\hat{\beta}_2$. Use these averages to estimate the bias of the OLS estimators of β_1 and β_2.

Repeat this exercise for sample sizes of 50, 100, and 200. What happens to the bias of $\hat{\beta}_1$ and $\hat{\beta}_2$ as the sample size is increased?

3.2 Consider a sequence of random variables x_t, $t = 1, \ldots, \infty$, which are such that $\mathrm{E}(x_t) = \mu_t$. By considering the centered variables $x_t - \mu_t$, show that the law of large numbers can be formulated as

$$\operatorname*{plim}_{n\to\infty} \frac{1}{n}\sum_{t=1}^{n} x_t = \lim_{n\to\infty} \frac{1}{n}\sum_{t=1}^{n} \mu_t.$$

3.3 Using the data on consumption and personal disposable income in Canada for the period 1947:1 to 1996:4 in the file **consumption.data**, estimate the model

$$c_t = \beta_1 + \beta_2 y_t + u_t, \quad u_t \sim \mathrm{NID}(0, \sigma^2),$$

where $c_t = \log C_t$ is the log of consumption and $y_t = \log Y_t$ is the log of disposable income, for the entire sample period. Then use the estimates of β_1, β_2, and σ to obtain 200 simulated observations on c_t.

Begin by regressing your simulated log consumption variable on the log of income and a constant using just the first 3 observations. Save the estimates of β_1, β_2, and σ. Repeat this exercise for sample sizes of $4, 5, \ldots, 200$. Plot your estimates of β_2 and σ as a function of the sample size. What happens to these estimates as the sample size grows?

Repeat the complete exercise with a different set of simulated consumption data. Which features of the paths of the parameter estimates are common to the two experiments, and which are different?

3.4 Plot the EDF (empirical distribution function) of the residuals from OLS estimation using one of the sets of simulated data, for the entire sample period, that you obtained in the last exercise; see Exercise 1.1 for a definition of the EDF. On the same graph, plot the CDF of the $\mathrm{N}(0, \sigma^2)$ distribution, where σ^2 now denotes the variance you used to simulate the log of consumption.

Show that the distributions characterized by the EDF and the normal CDF have the same mean but different variances. How could you modify the residuals so that the EDF of the modified residuals would have the same variance, σ^2, as the normal CDF?

3.5 In Section 3.4, it is stated that the covariance matrix $\mathrm{Var}(\boldsymbol{b})$ of any random k–vector $\boldsymbol{b}$ is positive semidefinite. Prove this fact by considering arbitrary linear combinations $\boldsymbol{w}^\top\boldsymbol{b}$ of the components of $\boldsymbol{b}$ with nonrandom $\boldsymbol{w}$. If $\mathrm{Var}(\boldsymbol{b})$ is positive semidefinite without being positive definite, what can you say about $\boldsymbol{b}$?

3.6 For any pair of random variables, b_1 and b_2, show, by using the fact that the covariance matrix of $\boldsymbol{b} \equiv [b_1 \;\vdots\; b_2]$ is positive semidefinite, that

$$\big(\mathrm{Cov}(b_1, b_2)\big)^2 \leq \mathrm{Var}(b_1)\mathrm{Var}(b_2).$$

Use this result to show that the correlation of b_1 and b_2 lies between -1 and 1.

3.7 If $\boldsymbol{A}$ is a positive definite matrix, show that $\boldsymbol{A}^{-1}$ is also positive definite.

3.8 If $\boldsymbol{A}$ is a symmetric positive definite $k \times k$ matrix, then $\mathbf{I} - \boldsymbol{A}$ is positive definite if and only if $\boldsymbol{A}^{-1} - \mathbf{I}$ is positive definite, where $\mathbf{I}$ is the $k \times k$ identity matrix. Prove this result by considering the quadratic form $\boldsymbol{x}^\top(\mathbf{I} - \boldsymbol{A})\boldsymbol{x}$ and expressing $\boldsymbol{x}$ as $\boldsymbol{R}^{-1}\boldsymbol{z}$, where $\boldsymbol{R}$ is a symmetric matrix such that $\boldsymbol{A} = \boldsymbol{R}^2$.

Extend the above result to show that, if $\boldsymbol{A}$ and $\boldsymbol{B}$ are symmetric positive definite matrices of the same dimensions, then $\boldsymbol{A} - \boldsymbol{B}$ is positive definite if and only if $\boldsymbol{B}^{-1} - \boldsymbol{A}^{-1}$ is positive definite.

3.9 Show that the variance of a sum of random variables z_t, $t = 1, \ldots, n$, with $\mathrm{Cov}(z_t, z_s) = 0$ for $t \neq s$, equals the sum of their individual variances, whatever their expectations may be.

3.10 If $\gamma \equiv \boldsymbol{w}^\top \boldsymbol{\beta} = \sum_{i=1}^{k} w_i \beta_i$, show that $\operatorname{Var}(\hat{\gamma})$, which is given by (3.33), can also be written as

$$\sum_{i=1}^{k} w_i^2 \operatorname{Var}(\hat{\beta}_i) + 2\sum_{i=2}^{k}\sum_{j=1}^{i-1} w_i w_j \operatorname{Cov}(\hat{\beta}_i, \hat{\beta}_j). \tag{3.68}$$

3.11 Using the data in the file **consumption.data**, construct the variables c_t, the logarithm of consumption, and y_t, the logarithm of income, and their first differences $\Delta c_t = c_t - c_{t-1}$ and $\Delta y_t = y_t - y_{t-1}$. Use these data to estimate the following model for the period 1953:1 to 1996:4:

$$\Delta c_t = \beta_1 + \beta_2 \Delta y_t + \beta_3 \Delta y_{t-1} + \beta_4 \Delta y_{t-2} + \beta_5 \Delta y_{t-3} + \beta_6 \Delta y_{t-4}. \tag{3.69}$$

Let $\gamma = \sum_{i=2}^{6} \beta_i$. Calculate $\hat{\gamma}$ and its standard error in two different ways. One method should explicitly use the result (3.33), and the other should use a transformation of regression (3.69) which allows $\hat{\gamma}$ and its standard error to be read off directly from the regression output.

★3.12 Starting from equation (3.42) and using the result proved in Exercise 3.9, but without using (3.43), prove that, if $\operatorname{E}(u_t^2) = \sigma_0^2$ and $\operatorname{E}(u_s u_t) = 0$ for all $s \neq t$, then $\operatorname{Var}(\hat{u}_t) = (1 - h_t)\sigma_0^2$. This is the result (3.44).

3.13 Use the result (3.44) to show that the MM estimator $\hat{\sigma}^2$ of (3.46) is consistent. You may assume that a LLN applies to the average in that equation.

3.14 Prove that $\operatorname{E}(\hat{\boldsymbol{u}}^\top \hat{\boldsymbol{u}}) = (n - k)\sigma_0^2$. This is the result (3.48). The proof should make use of the fact that the trace of a product of matrices is invariant to cyclic permutations; see Section 2.6.

3.15 Consider two linear regressions, one restricted and the other unrestricted:

$$\boldsymbol{y} = \boldsymbol{X\beta} + \boldsymbol{u}, \text{ and}$$
$$\boldsymbol{y} = \boldsymbol{X\beta} + \boldsymbol{Z\gamma} + \boldsymbol{u}.$$

Show that, in the case of mutually orthogonal regressors, with $\boldsymbol{X}^\top \boldsymbol{Z} = \mathbf{O}$, the estimates of $\boldsymbol{\beta}$ from the two regressions are identical.

3.16 Suppose that you use the OLS estimates $\hat{\boldsymbol{\beta}}$, obtained by regressing the $n \times 1$ vector $\boldsymbol{y}$ on the $n \times k$ matrix $\boldsymbol{X}$, to forecast the $n_* \times 1$ vector $\boldsymbol{y}_*$ using the $n_* \times k$ matrix $\boldsymbol{X}_*$. Assuming that the error terms, both within the sample used to estimate the parameters $\boldsymbol{\beta}$ and outside the sample in the forecast period, are $\operatorname{IID}(0, \sigma^2)$, and that the model is correctly specified, what is the covariance matrix of the vector of forecast errors?

3.17 The class of estimators considered by the Gauss-Markov Theorem can be written as $\tilde{\boldsymbol{\beta}} = \boldsymbol{Ay}$, with $\boldsymbol{AX} = \mathbf{I}$. Show that this class of estimators is in fact identical to the class of MM estimators of the form

$$\tilde{\boldsymbol{\beta}} = (\boldsymbol{W}^\top \boldsymbol{X})^{-1} \boldsymbol{W}^\top \boldsymbol{y}, \tag{3.70}$$

where $\boldsymbol{W}$ is a matrix of exogenous variables such that $\boldsymbol{W}^\top \boldsymbol{X}$ is nonsingular.

3.18 Show that the estimator (3.70) is unchanged if $\boldsymbol{W}$ is replaced by any other matrix $\boldsymbol{W}'$ of the same dimensions such that $\boldsymbol{P_W} = \boldsymbol{P_{W'}}$, or, equivalently, such that $\mathcal{S}(\boldsymbol{W}) = \mathcal{S}(\boldsymbol{W}')$. In particular, show that the estimator (3.70) is the OLS estimator if $\boldsymbol{P_X} = \boldsymbol{P_W}$.

3.19 Show that the difference between the unrestricted estimator $\tilde{\boldsymbol{\beta}}$ of model (3.51) and the restricted estimator $\hat{\boldsymbol{\beta}}$ of model (3.55) is given by

$$\tilde{\boldsymbol{\beta}} - \hat{\boldsymbol{\beta}} = (\boldsymbol{X}^\top \boldsymbol{M_Z X})^{-1} \boldsymbol{X}^\top \boldsymbol{M_Z M_X y}.$$

Hint: In order to prove this result, it is easiest to premultiply the difference by $\boldsymbol{X}^\top \boldsymbol{M_Z X}$.

3.20 Consider the linear regression model

$$y_t = \beta_1 + \beta_2 x_{t2} + \beta_3 x_{t3} + u_t.$$

Explain how you could estimate this model subject to the restriction that $\beta_2 + \beta_3 = 1$ by running a regression that imposes the restriction. Also, explain how you could estimate the unrestricted model in such a way that the value of one of the coefficients would be zero if the restriction held exactly for your data.

3.21 Prove that, for a linear regression model with a constant term, the uncentered R_u^2 is always greater than the centered R_c^2.

3.22 Consider a linear regression model for a dependent variable y_t that has a sample mean of 17.21. Suppose that we create a new variable $y_t' = y_t + 10$ and run the same linear regression using y_t' instead of y_t as the regressand. How are R_c^2, R_u^2, and the estimate of the constant term related in the two regressions? What if instead $y_t' = y_t - 10$?

3.23 Using the data in the file **consumption.data**, construct the variables c_t, the logarithm of consumption, and y_t, the logarithm of income. Use them to estimate, for the period 1953:1 to 1996:4, the following **autoregressive distributed lag**, or **ADL**, model:

$$c_t = \alpha + \beta c_{t-1} + \gamma_0 y_t + \gamma_1 y_{t-1} + u_t. \tag{3.71}$$

Such models are often expressed in first-difference form, that is, as

$$\Delta c_t = \delta + \phi c_{t-1} + \theta \Delta y_t + \psi y_{t-1} + u_t, \tag{3.72}$$

where the first-difference operator Δ is defined so that $\Delta c_t = c_t - c_{t-1}$. Estimate the first-difference model (3.72), and then, without using the results of (3.71), rederive the estimates of α, β, γ_0, and γ_1 solely on the basis of your results from (3.72).

3.24 Simulate model (3.71) of the previous question, using your estimates of α, β, γ_0, γ_1, and the error variance σ^2. Perform the simulation conditional on the income series and the first observation c_1 of consumption. Plot the residuals from running (3.71) on the simulated data, and compare the plot with that of the residuals from the real data. Comments?

Chapter 4

Hypothesis Testing in Linear Regression Models

4.1 Introduction

As we saw in Chapter 3, the vector of OLS parameter estimates $\hat{\boldsymbol{\beta}}$ is a random vector. Since it would be an astonishing coincidence if $\hat{\boldsymbol{\beta}}$ were equal to the true parameter vector $\boldsymbol{\beta}_0$ in any finite sample, we must take the randomness of $\hat{\boldsymbol{\beta}}$ into account if we are to make inferences about $\boldsymbol{\beta}$. In classical econometrics, the two principal ways of doing this are performing **hypothesis tests** and constructing **confidence intervals** or, more generally, **confidence regions**. We will discuss the first of these topics in this chapter, as the title implies, and the second in the next chapter. Hypothesis testing is easier to understand than the construction of confidence intervals, and it plays a larger role in applied econometrics.

In the next section, we develop the fundamental ideas of hypothesis testing in the context of a very simple special case. Then, in Section 4.3, we review some of the properties of several distributions which are related to the normal distribution and are commonly encountered in the context of hypothesis testing. We will need this material for Section 4.4, in which we develop a number of results about hypothesis tests in the classical normal linear model. In Section 4.5, we relax some of the assumptions of that model and introduce large-sample tests. An alternative approach to testing under relatively weak assumptions is bootstrap testing, which we introduce in Section 4.6. Finally, in Section 4.7, we discuss what determines the ability of a test to reject a hypothesis that is false.

4.2 Basic Ideas

The very simplest sort of hypothesis test concerns the (population) mean from which a random sample has been drawn. To test such a hypothesis, we may assume that the data are generated by the regression model

$$y_t = \beta + u_t, \quad u_t \sim \text{IID}(0, \sigma^2), \tag{4.01}$$

where y_t is an observation on the dependent variable, β is the population mean, which is the only parameter of the regression function, and σ^2 is the variance of the error term u_t. The least-squares estimator of β and its variance, for a sample of size n, are given by

$$\hat{\beta} = \frac{1}{n}\sum_{t=1}^{n} y_t \qquad \text{and} \qquad \operatorname{Var}(\hat{\beta}) = \frac{1}{n}\sigma^2. \tag{4.02}$$

These formulas can either be obtained from first principles or as special cases of the general results for OLS estimation. In this case, $\boldsymbol{X}$ is just an n-vector of 1s. Thus, for the model (4.01), the standard formulas $\hat{\boldsymbol{\beta}} = (\boldsymbol{X}^\top\boldsymbol{X})^{-1}\boldsymbol{X}^\top\boldsymbol{y}$ and $\operatorname{Var}(\hat{\boldsymbol{\beta}}) = \sigma^2(\boldsymbol{X}^\top\boldsymbol{X})^{-1}$ yield the two formulas given in (4.02).

Now suppose that we wish to test the hypothesis that $\beta = \beta_0$, where β_0 is some specified value of β.[1] The hypothesis that we are testing is called the **null hypothesis**. It is often given the label H_0 for short. In order to test H_0, we must calculate a **test statistic**, which is a random variable that has a known distribution when the null hypothesis is true and some other distribution when the null hypothesis is false. If the value of this test statistic is one that might frequently be encountered by chance under the null hypothesis, then the test provides no evidence against the null. On the other hand, if the value of the test statistic is an extreme one that would rarely be encountered by chance under the null, then the test does provide evidence against the null. If this evidence is sufficiently convincing, we may decide to **reject** the null hypothesis that $\beta = \beta_0$.

For the moment, we will restrict the model (4.01) by making two very strong assumptions. The first is that u_t is normally distributed, and the second is that σ is known. Under these assumptions, a test of the hypothesis that $\beta = \beta_0$ can be based on the test statistic

$$z = \frac{\hat{\beta} - \beta_0}{\big(\operatorname{Var}(\hat{\beta})\big)^{1/2}} = \frac{n^{1/2}}{\sigma}(\hat{\beta} - \beta_0). \tag{4.03}$$

It turns out that, under the null hypothesis, z must be distributed as $\mathrm{N}(0, 1)$. It must have mean 0 because $\hat{\beta}$ is an unbiased estimator of β, and $\beta = \beta_0$ under the null. It must have variance unity because, by (4.02),

$$\mathrm{E}(z^2) = \frac{n}{\sigma^2}\,\mathrm{E}\big((\hat{\beta} - \beta_0)^2\big) = \frac{n}{\sigma^2}\,\frac{\sigma^2}{n} = 1.$$

[1] It may be slightly confusing that a 0 subscript is used here to denote the value of a parameter under the null hypothesis as well as its true value. So long as it is assumed that the null hypothesis is true, however, there should be no possible confusion.

Finally, to see that z must be normally distributed, note that $\hat{\beta}$ is just the average of the y_t, each of which must be normally distributed if the corresponding u_t is; see Exercise 1.7. As we will see in the next section, this implies that z is also normally distributed. Thus z has the first property that we would like a test statistic to possess: It has a known distribution under the null hypothesis.

For every null hypothesis there is, at least implicitly, an **alternative hypothesis**, which is often given the label H_1. The alternative hypothesis is what we are testing the null against, in this case the model (4.01) with $\beta \neq \beta_0$. Just as important as the fact that z follows the $\text{N}(0, 1)$ distribution under the null is the fact that z does *not* follow this distribution under the alternative. Suppose that β takes on some other value, say β_1. Then it is clear that $\hat{\beta} = \beta_1 + \hat{\gamma}$, where $\hat{\gamma}$ has mean 0 and variance σ^2/n; recall equation (3.05). In fact, $\hat{\gamma}$ is normal under our assumption that the u_t are normal, just like $\hat{\beta}$, and so $\hat{\gamma} \sim \text{N}(0, \sigma^2/n)$. It follows that z is also normal (see Exercise 1.7 again), and we find from (4.03) that

$$z \sim \text{N}(\lambda, 1), \quad \text{with} \quad \lambda = \frac{n^{1/2}}{\sigma}(\beta_1 - \beta_0). \tag{4.04}$$

Therefore, provided n is sufficiently large, we would expect the mean of z to be large and positive if $\beta_1 > \beta_0$ and large and negative if $\beta_1 < \beta_0$. Thus we reject the null hypothesis whenever z is sufficiently far from 0. Just how we can decide what "sufficiently far" means will be discussed shortly.

Since we want to test the null that $\beta = \beta_0$ against the alternative that $\beta \neq \beta_0$, we must perform a **two-tailed test** and reject the null whenever the absolute value of z is sufficiently large. If instead we were interested in testing the null hypothesis that $\beta \leq \beta_0$ against the alternative that $\beta > \beta_0$, we would perform a **one-tailed test** and reject the null whenever z was sufficiently large and positive. In general, tests of equality restrictions are two-tailed tests, and tests of inequality restrictions are one-tailed tests.

Since z is a random variable that can, in principle, take on any value on the real line, no value of z is absolutely incompatible with the null hypothesis, and so we can never be absolutely certain that the null hypothesis is false. One way to deal with this situation is to decide in advance on a **rejection rule**, according to which we choose to reject the null hypothesis if and only if the value of z falls into the **rejection region** of the rule. For two-tailed tests, the appropriate rejection region is the union of two sets, one containing all values of z greater than some positive value, the other all values of z less than some negative value. For a one-tailed test, the rejection region would consist of just one set, containing either sufficiently positive or sufficiently negative values of z, according to the sign of the inequality we wish to test.

A test statistic combined with a rejection rule is sometimes called simply a **test**. If the test incorrectly leads us to reject a null hypothesis that is true, we are said to make a **Type I error**. The probability of making such an error is, by construction, the probability, *under the null hypothesis*, that z falls into the rejection region. This probability is sometimes called the **level of significance**, or just the **level**, of the test. A common notation for this is α. Like all probabilities, α is a number between 0 and 1, although, in practice, it is generally much closer to 0 than 1. Popular values of α include .05 and .01. If the observed value of z, say $\hat{z}$, lies in a rejection region associated with a probability under the null of α, then we reject the null hypothesis at level α. Otherwise, we do not reject the null hypothesis. In this way, we ensure that the probability of making a Type I error is precisely α.

In the previous paragraph, we implicitly assumed that the distribution of the test statistic under the null hypothesis is known exactly, so that we have what is called an **exact test**. In econometrics, however, the distribution of a test statistic is often known only approximately. In this case, we need to draw a distinction between the **nominal level** of the test, that is, the probability of making a Type I error according to whatever approximate distribution we are using to determine the rejection region, and the actual **rejection probability**, which may differ greatly from the nominal level. The rejection probability is generally unknowable in practice, because it typically depends on unknown features of the DGP.[2]

The probability that a test rejects the null is called the **power** of the test. If the data are generated by a DGP that satisfies the null hypothesis, the power of an exact test is equal to its level. In general, power depends on precisely how the data were generated and on the sample size. We can see from (4.04) that the distribution of z is entirely determined by the value of λ, with $\lambda = 0$ under the null, and that the value of λ depends on the parameters of the DGP. In this example, λ is proportional to $\beta_1 - \beta_0$ and to the square root of the sample size, and it is inversely proportional to σ.

Values of λ different from 0 move the probability mass of the $N(\lambda, 1)$ distribution away from the center of the $N(0, 1)$ distribution and into its tails. This can be seen in Figure 4.1, which graphs the $N(0, 1)$ density and the $N(\lambda, 1)$ density for $\lambda = 2$. The second density places much more probability than the first on values of z greater than 2. Thus, if the rejection region for our test was the interval from 2 to $+\infty$, there would be a much higher probability in that region for $\lambda = 2$ than for $\lambda = 0$. Therefore, we would reject the null hypothesis more often when the null hypothesis is false, with $\lambda = 2$, than when it is true, with $\lambda = 0$.

[2] Another term that often arises in the discussion of hypothesis testing is the **size** of a test. Technically, this is the supremum of the rejection probability over all DGPs that satisfy the null hypothesis. For an exact test, the size equals the level. For an approximate test, the size is typically difficult or impossible to calculate. It is often, but by no means always, greater than the nominal level of the test.

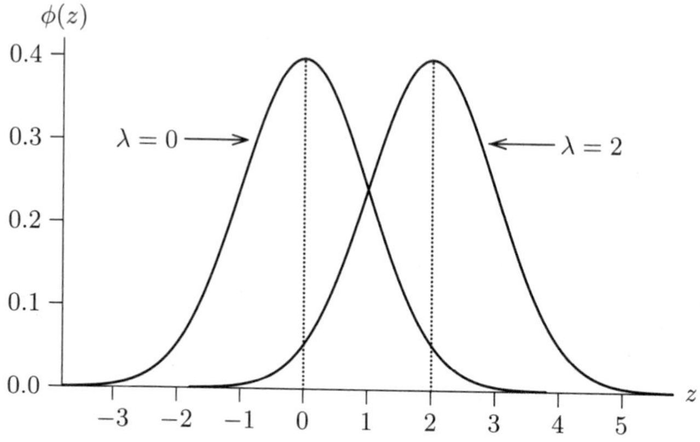

Figure 4.1 The normal distribution centered and uncentered

Mistakenly failing to reject a false null hypothesis is called making a **Type II error**. The probability of making such a mistake is equal to 1 minus the power of the test. It is not hard to see that, quite generally, the probability of rejecting the null with a two-tailed test based on z increases with the absolute value of λ. Consequently, the power of such a test increases as $\beta_1 - \beta_0$ increases, as σ decreases, and as the sample size increases. We will discuss what determines the power of a test in more detail in Section 4.7.

In order to construct the rejection region for a test at level α, the first step is to calculate the **critical value** associated with the level α. For a two-tailed test based on any test statistic that is distributed as $N(0, 1)$, including the statistic z defined in (4.04), the critical value c_α is defined implicitly by

$$\Phi(c_\alpha) = 1 - \alpha/2. \tag{4.05}$$

Recall that Φ denotes the CDF of the standard normal distribution. In terms of the inverse function Φ^{-1}, c_α can be defined explicitly by the formula

$$c_\alpha = \Phi^{-1}(1 - \alpha/2). \tag{4.06}$$

According to (4.05), the probability that $z > c_\alpha$ is $1 - (1 - \alpha/2) = \alpha/2$, and the probability that $z < -c_\alpha$ is also $\alpha/2$, by symmetry. Thus the probability that $|z| > c_\alpha$ is α, and so an appropriate rejection region for a test at level α is the set defined by $|z| > c_\alpha$. Clearly, c_α increases as α approaches 0. As an example, when $\alpha = .05$, we see from (4.06) that the critical value for a two-tailed test is $\Phi^{-1}(.975) = 1.96$. We would reject the null at the .05 level whenever the observed absolute value of the test statistic exceeds 1.96.

P Values

As we have defined it, the result of a test is yes or no: Reject or do not reject. A more sophisticated approach to deciding whether or not to reject the null hypothesis is to calculate the ***P* value**, or **marginal significance level**, associated with the observed test statistic $\hat{z}$. The P value for $\hat{z}$ is defined as the greatest level for which a test based on $\hat{z}$ fails to reject the null. Equivalently, at least if the statistic z has a continuous distribution, it is the smallest level for which the test rejects. Thus, the test rejects for all levels greater than the P value, and it fails to reject for all levels smaller than the P value. Therefore, if the P value associated with $\hat{z}$ is denoted $p(\hat{z})$, we must be prepared to accept a probability $p(\hat{z})$ of Type I error if we choose to reject the null.

For a two-tailed test, in the special case we have been discussing,

$$p(\hat{z}) = 2\big(1 - \Phi(|\hat{z}|)\big). \tag{4.07}$$

To see this, note that the test based on $\hat{z}$ rejects at level α if and only if $|\hat{z}| > c_\alpha$. This inequality is equivalent to $\Phi(|\hat{z}|) > \Phi(c_\alpha)$, because $\Phi(\cdot)$ is a strictly increasing function. Further, $\Phi(c_\alpha) = 1 - \alpha/2$, by (4.05). The smallest value of α for which the inequality holds is thus obtained by solving the equation

$$\Phi(|\hat{z}|) = 1 - \alpha/2,$$

and the solution is easily seen to be the right-hand side of (4.07).

One advantage of using P values is that they preserve all the information conveyed by a test statistic, while presenting it in a way that is directly interpretable. For example, the test statistics 2.02 and 5.77 would both lead us to reject the null at the .05 level using a two-tailed test. The second of these obviously provides more evidence against the null than does the first, but it is only after they are converted to P values that the magnitude of the difference becomes apparent. The P value for the first test statistic is .0434, while the P value for the second is 7.93×10^{-9}, an extremely small number.

Computing a P value transforms z from a random variable with the $\mathrm{N}(0,1)$ distribution into a new random variable $p(z)$ with the uniform $\mathrm{U}(0,1)$ distribution. In Exercise 4.1, readers are invited to prove this fact. It is quite possible to think of $p(z)$ as a test statistic, of which the observed realization is $p(\hat{z})$. A test at level α rejects whenever $p(\hat{z}) < \alpha$. Note that the sign of this inequality is the opposite of that in the condition $|\hat{z}| > c_\alpha$. Generally, one rejects for *large* values of test statistics, but for *small* P values.

Figure 4.2 illustrates how the test statistic $\hat{z}$ is related to its P value $p(\hat{z})$. Suppose that the value of the test statistic is 1.51. Then

$$\Pr(z > 1.51) = \Pr(z < -1.51) = .0655. \tag{4.08}$$

This implies, by equation (4.07), that the P value for a two-tailed test based on $\hat{z}$ is .1310. The top panel of the figure illustrates (4.08) in terms of the PDF of the standard normal distribution, and the bottom panel illustrates it in terms of the CDF. To avoid clutter, no critical values are shown on the

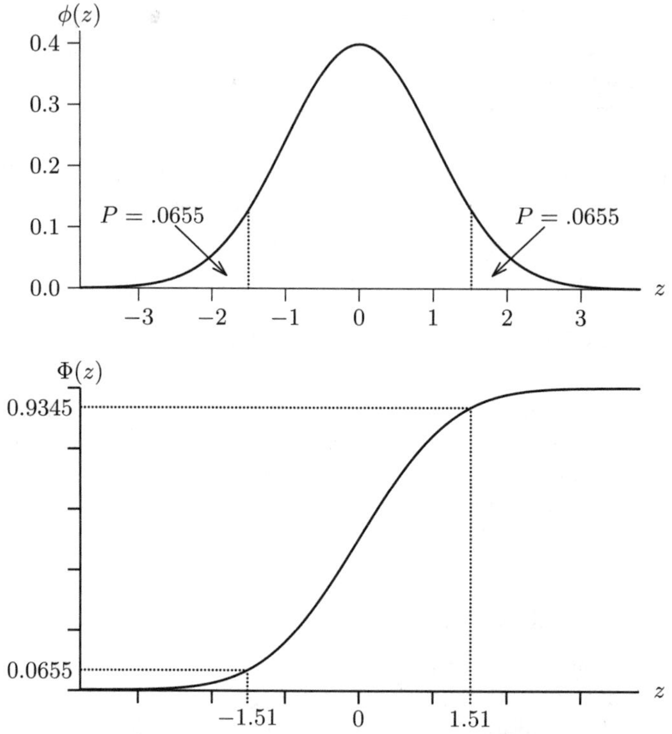

Figure 4.2 P values for a two-tailed test

figure, but it is clear that a test based on $\hat{z}$ does not reject at any level smaller than .131. From the figure, it is also easy to see that the P value for a one-tailed test of the hypothesis that $\beta \le \beta_0$ is .0655. This is just $\Pr(z > 1.51)$. Similarly, the P value for a one-tailed test of the hypothesis that $\beta \ge \beta_0$ is $\Pr(z < 1.51) = .9345$.

The P values discussed above, whether for one-tailed or two-tailed tests, are based on the symmetric $N(0, 1)$ distribution. In Exercise 4.15, readers are asked to show how to compute P values for two-tailed tests based on an asymmetric distribution.

In this section, we have introduced the basic ideas of hypothesis testing. However, we had to make two very restrictive assumptions. The first is that the error terms are normally distributed, and the second, which is grossly unrealistic, is that the variance of the error terms is known. In addition, we limited our attention to a single restriction on a single parameter. In Section 4.4, we will discuss the more general case of linear restrictions on the parameters of a linear regression model with unknown error variance. Before we can do so, however, we need to review the properties of the normal distribution and of several distributions that are closely related to it.

4.3 Some Common Distributions

Most test statistics in econometrics follow one of four well-known distributions, at least approximately. These are the standard normal distribution, the chi-squared (or χ^2) distribution, the Student's t distribution, and the F distribution. The most basic of these is the normal distribution, since the other three distributions can be derived from it. In this section, we discuss the standard, or **central**, versions of these distributions. Later, in Section 4.7, we will have occasion to introduce **noncentral** versions of all these distributions.

The Normal Distribution

The **normal distribution**, which is sometimes called the **Gaussian distribution** in honor of the celebrated German mathematician and astronomer Carl Friedrich Gauss (1777–1855), even though he did not invent it, is certainly the most famous distribution in statistics. As we saw in Section 1.2, there is a whole family of normal distributions, all based on the **standard normal distribution**, so called because it has mean 0 and variance 1. The PDF of the standard normal distribution, which is usually denoted by $\phi(\cdot)$, was defined in (1.06). No elementary closed-form expression exists for its CDF, which is usually denoted by $\Phi(\cdot)$. Although there is no closed form, it is perfectly easy to evaluate Φ numerically, and virtually every program for doing econometrics and statistics can do this. Thus it is straightforward to compute the P value for any test statistic that is distributed as standard normal. The graphs of the functions ϕ and Φ were first shown in Figure 1.1 and have just reappeared in Figure 4.2. In both tails, the PDF rapidly approaches 0. Thus, although a standard normal r.v. can, in principle, take on any value on the real line, values greater than about 4 in absolute value occur extremely rarely.

In Exercise 1.7, readers were asked to show that the full normal family can be generated by varying exactly two parameters, the mean and the variance. A random variable X that is normally distributed with mean μ and variance σ^2 can be generated by the formula

$$X = \mu + \sigma Z, \tag{4.09}$$

where Z is standard normal. The distribution of X, that is, the normal distribution with mean μ and variance σ^2, is denoted $\mathrm{N}(\mu, \sigma^2)$. Thus the standard normal distribution is the $\mathrm{N}(0, 1)$ distribution. As readers were asked to show in Exercise 1.8, the PDF of the $\mathrm{N}(\mu, \sigma^2)$ distribution, evaluated at x, is

$$\frac{1}{\sigma}\phi\Big(\frac{x-\mu}{\sigma}\Big) = \frac{1}{\sigma\sqrt{2\pi}}\exp\Big(-\frac{(x-\mu)^2}{2\sigma^2}\Big), \tag{4.10}$$

In expression (4.10), as in Section 1.2, we have distinguished between the random variable X and a value x that it can take on. However, for the following discussion, this distinction is more confusing than illuminating. For the rest of this section, we therefore use lower-case letters to denote both random variables and the arguments of their PDFs or CDFs, depending on context. No confusion should result. Adopting this convention, then, we see that, if x is distributed as $N(\mu, \sigma^2)$, we can invert equation (4.09) and obtain $z = (x - \mu)/\sigma$, where z is standard normal. Note also that z is the argument of ϕ in the expression (4.10) of the PDF of x. In general, the PDF of a normal variable x with mean μ and variance σ^2 is $1/\sigma$ times ϕ evaluated at the corresponding standard normal variable, which is $z = (x - \mu)/\sigma$.

Although the normal distribution is fully characterized by its first two moments, the higher moments are also important. Because the distribution is symmetric around its mean, the third central moment, which measures the **skewness** of the distribution, is always zero.[3] This is true for all of the odd central moments. The fourth moment of a symmetric distribution provides a way to measure its **kurtosis**, which essentially means how thick the tails are. In the case of the $N(\mu, \sigma^2)$ distribution, the fourth central moment is $3\sigma^4$; see Exercise 4.2.

Linear Combinations of Normal Variables

An important property of the normal distribution, used in our discussion in the preceding section, is that any linear combination of independent normally distributed random variables is itself normally distributed. To see this, it is enough to show it for independent standard normal variables, because, by (4.09), all normal variables can be generated as linear combinations of standard normal ones plus constants. We will tackle the proof in several steps, each of which is important in its own right.

To begin with, let z_1 and z_2 be standard normal and mutually independent, and consider $w \equiv b_1 z_1 + b_2 z_2$. If we reason conditionally on z_1, we find that

$$\mathrm{E}(w \,|\, z_1) = b_1 z_1 + b_2 \mathrm{E}(z_2 \,|\, z_1) = b_1 z_1 + b_2 \mathrm{E}(z_2) = b_1 z_1.$$

The first equality follows because $b_1 z_1$ is a deterministic function of the conditioning variable z_1, and so can be taken outside the conditional expectation. The second, in which the conditional expectation of z_2 is replaced by its unconditional expectation, follows because of the independence of z_1 and z_2 (see Exercise 1.9). Finally, $\mathrm{E}(z_2) = 0$ because z_2 is $N(0, 1)$.

The conditional variance of w is given by

$$\mathrm{E}\Big(\big(w - \mathrm{E}(w \,|\, z_1)\big)^2 \;\big|\; z_1\Big) = \mathrm{E}\big((b_2 z_2)^2 \,|\, z_1\big) = \mathrm{E}\big((b_2 z_2)^2\big) = b_2^2,$$

where the last equality again follows because $z_2 \sim N(0, 1)$. Conditionally on z_1, w is the sum of the constant $b_1 z_1$ and b_2 times a standard normal

[3] A distribution is said to be skewed to the right if the third central moment is positive, and to the left if the third central moment is negative.

variable z_2, and so the *conditional* distribution of w is normal. Given the conditional mean and variance we have just computed, we see that the conditional distribution must be $\mathrm{N}(b_1 z_1, b_2^2)$. The PDF of this distribution is the density of w conditional on z_1, and, by (4.10), it is

$$f(w \,|\, z_1) = \frac{1}{b_2}\,\phi\Big(\frac{w - b_1 z_1}{b_2}\Big). \tag{4.11}$$

In accord with what we noted above, the argument of ϕ here is equal to z_2, which is the standard normal variable corresponding to w conditional on z_1.

The next step is to find the joint density of w and z_1. By (1.15), the density of w conditional on z_1 is the ratio of the joint density of w and z_1 to the marginal density of z_1. This marginal density is just $\phi(z_1)$, since $z_1 \sim \mathrm{N}(0,1)$, and so we see that the joint density is

$$f(w, z_1) = f(z_1)\, f(w \,|\, z_1) = \phi(z_1)\frac{1}{b_2}\,\phi\Big(\frac{w - b_1 z_1}{b_2}\Big). \tag{4.12}$$

For the moment, let us suppose that $b_1^2 + b_2^2 = 1$, although we will remove this restriction shortly. Then, if we use (1.06) to get an explicit expression for this joint density, we obtain

$$\begin{aligned} &\frac{1}{2\pi b_2}\exp\Big(-\frac{1}{2b_2^2}\big(b_2^2 z_1^2 + w^2 - 2b_1 z_1 w + b_1^2 z_1^2\big)\Big) \\ &\quad = \frac{1}{2\pi b_2}\exp\Big(-\frac{1}{2b_2^2}\big(z_1^2 - 2b_1 z_1 w + w^2\big)\Big), \end{aligned} \tag{4.13}$$

The right-hand side of equation (4.13) is symmetric with respect to z_1 and w. Thus the joint density can also be expressed as in (4.12), but with z_1 and w interchanged, as follows:

$$f(w, z_1) = \frac{1}{b_2}\,\phi(w)\,\phi\Big(\frac{z_1 - b_1 w}{b_2}\Big). \tag{4.14}$$

We are now ready to compute the unconditional, or marginal, density of w. To do so, we integrate the joint density (4.14) with respect to z_1; see (1.12). Note that z_1 occurs only in the last factor on the right-hand side of (4.14). Further, the expression $(1/b_2)\phi\big((z_1 - b_1 w)/b_2\big)$, like expression (4.11), is a probability density, and so it integrates to 1. Thus we conclude that the marginal density of w is $f(w) = \phi(w)$, and so it follows that w is standard normal, unconditionally, as we wished to show.

It is now simple to extend this argument to the case for which $b_1^2 + b_2^2 \neq 1$. We define $r^2 = b_1^2 + b_2^2$, and consider w/r. The argument above shows that w/r is standard normal, and so $w \sim \mathrm{N}(0, r^2)$. It is equally simple to extend the result to a linear combination of any number of mutually independent standard normal variables. If we now let w be defined as $b_1 z_1 + b_2 z_2 + b_3 z_3$, where z_1, z_2, and z_3 are mutually independent standard normal variables, then $b_1 z_1 + b_2 z_2$ is normal by the result for two variables, and it is independent of z_3. Thus, by applying the result for two variables again, this time to $b_1 z_1 + b_2 z_2$ and z_3, we see that w is normal. This reasoning can obviously be extended by induction to a linear combination of any number of independent standard normal variables. Finally, if we consider a linear combination of independent normal variables with nonzero means, the mean of the resulting variable is just the same linear combination of the means of the individual variables.

The Multivariate Normal Distribution

The results of the previous subsection can be extended to linear combinations of normal random variables that are not necessarily independent. In order to do so, we introduce the **multivariate normal distribution**. As the name suggests, this is a family of distributions for random *vectors*, with the scalar normal distributions being special cases of it. The pair of random variables z_1 and w considered above follow the **bivariate normal distribution**, another special case of the multivariate normal distribution. As we will see in a moment, all these distributions, like the scalar normal distribution, are completely characterized by their first two moments.

In order to construct the multivariate normal distribution, we begin with a set of m mutually independent standard normal variables, z_i, $i = 1, \ldots, m$, which we can assemble into a random m–vector $\boldsymbol{z}$. Then any m–vector $\boldsymbol{x}$ of linearly independent linear combinations of the components of $\boldsymbol{z}$ follows a multivariate normal distribution. Such a vector $\boldsymbol{x}$ can always be written as $\boldsymbol{Az}$, for some nonsingular $m \times m$ matrix $\boldsymbol{A}$. As we will see in a moment, the matrix $\boldsymbol{A}$ can always be chosen to be lower-triangular.

We denote the components of $\boldsymbol{x}$ as x_i, $i = 1, \ldots, m$. From what we have seen above, it is clear that each x_i is normally distributed, with (unconditional) mean zero. Therefore, from results proved in Section 3.4, it follows that the covariance matrix of $\boldsymbol{x}$ is

$$\operatorname{Var}(\boldsymbol{x}) = \operatorname{E}(\boldsymbol{x}\boldsymbol{x}^\top) = \boldsymbol{A}\operatorname{E}(\boldsymbol{z}\boldsymbol{z}^\top)\boldsymbol{A}^\top = \boldsymbol{A}\mathbf{I}\boldsymbol{A}^\top = \boldsymbol{A}\boldsymbol{A}^\top.$$

Here we have used the fact that the covariance matrix of $\boldsymbol{z}$ is the identity matrix $\mathbf{I}$. This is true because the variance of each component of $\boldsymbol{z}$ is 1, and, since the z_i are mutually independent, all the covariances are 0; see Exercise 1.13.

Let us denote the covariance matrix of $\boldsymbol{x}$ by $\boldsymbol{\Omega}$. Recall that, according to a result mentioned in Section 3.4 in connection with Crout's algorithm, for any positive definite matrix $\boldsymbol{\Omega}$, we can always find a lower-triangular $\boldsymbol{A}$ such that $\boldsymbol{A}\boldsymbol{A}^\top = \boldsymbol{\Omega}$. Thus the matrix $\boldsymbol{A}$ may always be chosen to be lower-triangular. The distribution of $\boldsymbol{x}$ is multivariate normal with mean vector $\mathbf{0}$ and covariance matrix $\boldsymbol{\Omega}$. We write this as $\boldsymbol{x} \sim \operatorname{N}(\mathbf{0}, \boldsymbol{\Omega})$. If we add an m–vector $\boldsymbol{\mu}$ of constants to $\boldsymbol{x}$, the resulting vector must follow the $\operatorname{N}(\boldsymbol{\mu}, \boldsymbol{\Omega})$ distribution.

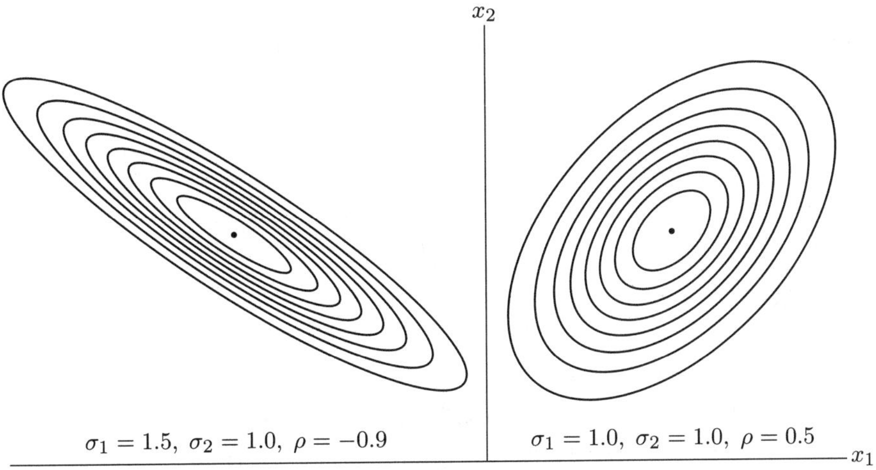

Figure 4.3 Contours of two bivariate normal densities

It is clear from this argument that any linear combination of random variables that are jointly multivariate normal is itself normally distributed. Thus, if $\boldsymbol{x} \sim \mathrm{N}(\boldsymbol{\mu}, \boldsymbol{\Omega})$, any scalar $\boldsymbol{a}^\top\boldsymbol{x}$, where $\boldsymbol{a}$ is an m–vector of fixed coefficients, is normally distributed with mean $\boldsymbol{a}^\top\boldsymbol{\mu}$ and variance $\boldsymbol{a}^\top\boldsymbol{\Omega}\boldsymbol{a}$.

We saw a moment ago that $\boldsymbol{z} \sim \mathrm{N}(\mathbf{0}, \mathbf{I})$ whenever the components of the vector $\boldsymbol{z}$ are independent. Another crucial property of the multivariate normal distribution is that the converse of this result is also true: If $\boldsymbol{x}$ is any multivariate normal vector with zero covariances, the components of $\boldsymbol{x}$ are mutually independent. This is a very special property of the multivariate normal distribution, and readers are asked to prove it, for the bivariate case, in Exercise 4.5. In general, a zero covariance between two random variables does *not* imply that they are independent.

It is important to note that the results of the last two paragraphs do not hold unless the vector $\boldsymbol{x}$ is multivariate normal, that is, constructed as a set of linear combinations of *independent* normal variables. In most cases, when we have to deal with linear combinations of two or more normal random variables, it is reasonable to assume that they are jointly distributed as multivariate normal. However, as Exercise 1.14 illustrates, it is possible for two or more random variables not to be multivariate normal even though each one individually follows a normal distribution.

Figure 4.3 illustrates the bivariate normal distribution, of which the PDF is given in Exercise 4.5 in terms of the variances σ_1^2 and σ_2^2 of the two variables, and their correlation ρ. Contours of the density are plotted, on the right for $\sigma_1 = \sigma_2 = 1.0$ and $\rho = 0.5$, on the left for $\sigma_1 = 1.5$, $\sigma_2 = 1.0$, and $\rho = -0.9$. The contours of the bivariate normal density can be seen to be elliptical. The ellipses slope upward when $\rho > 0$ and downward when $\rho < 0$. They do so more steeply the larger is the ratio σ_2/σ_1. The closer $|\rho|$ is to 1, for given values of σ_1 and σ_2, the more elongated are the elliptical contours.

The Chi-Squared Distribution

Suppose, as in our discussion of the multivariate normal distribution, that the random vector $\boldsymbol{z}$ is such that its components $z_1, \ldots, z_m$ are mutually independent standard normal random variables. An easy way to express this is to write $\boldsymbol{z} \sim \mathrm{N}(\mathbf{0}, \mathbf{I})$. Then the random variable

$$y \equiv \|\boldsymbol{z}\|^2 = \boldsymbol{z}^\top \boldsymbol{z} = \sum_{i=1}^{m} z_i^2 \tag{4.15}$$

is said to follow the **chi-squared distribution** with m **degrees of freedom.** A compact way of writing this is: $y \sim \chi^2(m)$. From (4.15), it is clear that m must be a positive integer. In the case of a test statistic, it will turn out to be equal to the number of restrictions being tested.

The mean and variance of the $\chi^2(m)$ distribution can easily be obtained from the definition (4.15). The mean is

$$\mathrm{E}(y) = \sum_{i=1}^{m} \mathrm{E}(z_i^2) = \sum_{i=1}^{m} 1 = m. \tag{4.16}$$

Since the z_i are independent, the variance of the sum of the z_i^2 is just the sum of the (identical) variances:

$$\begin{aligned} \mathrm{Var}(y) &= \sum_{i=1}^{m} \mathrm{Var}(z_i^2) = m\mathrm{E}\big((z_i^2 - 1)^2\big) \\ &= m\mathrm{E}(z_i^4 - 2z_i^2 + 1) = m(3 - 2 + 1) = 2m. \end{aligned} \tag{4.17}$$

The third equality here uses the fact that $\mathrm{E}(z_i^4) = 3$; see Exercise 4.2.

Another important property of the chi-squared distribution, which follows immediately from (4.15), is that, if $y_1 \sim \chi^2(m_1)$ and $y_2 \sim \chi^2(m_2)$, and y_1 and y_2 are independent, then $y_1 + y_2 \sim \chi^2(m_1 + m_2)$. To see this, rewrite (4.15) as

$$y = y_1 + y_2 = \sum_{i=1}^{m_1} z_i^2 + \sum_{i=m_1+1}^{m_1+m_2} z_i^2 = \sum_{i=1}^{m_1+m_2} z_i^2,$$

from which the result follows.

Figure 4.4 shows the PDF of the $\chi^2(m)$ distribution for $m = 1$, $m = 3$, $m = 5$, and $m = 7$. The changes in the location and height of the density function as m increases are what we should expect from the results (4.16) and (4.17) about its mean and variance. In addition, the PDF, which is extremely

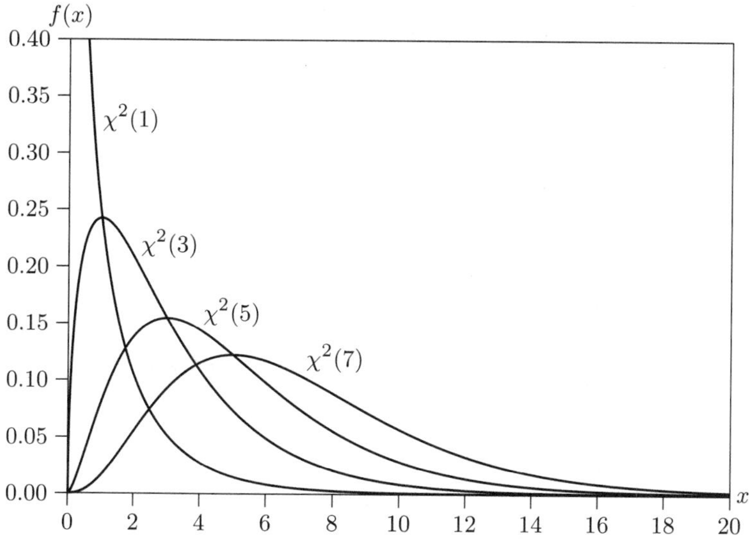

Figure 4.4 Various chi-squared PDFs

skewed to the right for $m = 1$, becomes less skewed as m increases. In fact, as we will see in Section 4.5, the $\chi^2(m)$ distribution approaches the $\mathrm{N}(m, 2m)$ distribution as m becomes large.

In Section 3.4, we introduced quadratic forms. As we will see, many test statistics can be written as quadratic forms in normal vectors, or as functions of such quadratic forms. The following theorem states two results about quadratic forms in normal vectors that will prove to be extremely useful.

Theorem 4.1.

1. If the m-vector $\boldsymbol{x}$ is distributed as $\mathrm{N}(\mathbf{0}, \boldsymbol{\Omega})$, then the quadratic form $\boldsymbol{x}^\top\boldsymbol{\Omega}^{-1}\boldsymbol{x}$ is distributed as $\chi^2(m)$;
2. If $\boldsymbol{P}$ is a projection matrix with rank r and $\boldsymbol{z}$ is an n-vector that is distributed as $\mathrm{N}(\mathbf{0}, \mathbf{I})$, then the quadratic form $\boldsymbol{z}^\top\boldsymbol{P}\boldsymbol{z}$ is distributed as $\chi^2(r)$.

Proof: Since the vector $\boldsymbol{x}$ is multivariate normal with mean vector $\mathbf{0}$, so is the vector $\boldsymbol{A}^{-1}\boldsymbol{x}$, where, as before, $\boldsymbol{A}\boldsymbol{A}^\top = \boldsymbol{\Omega}$. Moreover, the covariance matrix of $\boldsymbol{A}^{-1}\boldsymbol{x}$ is

$$\mathrm{E}\big(\boldsymbol{A}^{-1}\boldsymbol{x}\boldsymbol{x}^\top(\boldsymbol{A}^\top)^{-1}\big) = \boldsymbol{A}^{-1}\boldsymbol{\Omega}(\boldsymbol{A}^\top)^{-1} = \boldsymbol{A}^{-1}\boldsymbol{A}\boldsymbol{A}^\top(\boldsymbol{A}^\top)^{-1} = \mathbf{I}_m.$$

Thus we have shown that the vector $\boldsymbol{z} \equiv \boldsymbol{A}^{-1}\boldsymbol{x}$ is distributed as $\mathrm{N}(\mathbf{0}, \mathbf{I})$.

The quadratic form $\boldsymbol{x}^\top\boldsymbol{\Omega}^{-1}\boldsymbol{x}$ is equal to $\boldsymbol{x}^\top(\boldsymbol{A}^\top)^{-1}\boldsymbol{A}^{-1}\boldsymbol{x} = \boldsymbol{z}^\top\boldsymbol{z}$. As we have just shown, this is equal to the sum of m independent, squared, standard normal random variables. From the definition of the chi-squared distribution, we know that such a sum is distributed as $\chi^2(m)$. This proves the first part of the theorem.

Since $\boldsymbol{P}$ is a projection matrix, it must project orthogonally on to some subspace of E^n. Suppose, then, that $\boldsymbol{P}$ projects on to the span of the columns of an $n \times r$ matrix $\boldsymbol{Z}$. This allows us to write

$$\boldsymbol{z}^\top \boldsymbol{P} \boldsymbol{z} = \boldsymbol{z}^\top \boldsymbol{Z}(\boldsymbol{Z}^\top \boldsymbol{Z})^{-1} \boldsymbol{Z}^\top \boldsymbol{z}.$$

The r–vector $\boldsymbol{x} \equiv \boldsymbol{Z}^\top \boldsymbol{z}$ evidently follows the $\mathrm{N}(\boldsymbol{0}, \boldsymbol{Z}^\top \boldsymbol{Z})$ distribution. Therefore, $\boldsymbol{z}^\top \boldsymbol{P} \boldsymbol{z}$ is seen to be a quadratic form in the multivariate normal r–vector $\boldsymbol{x}$ and $(\boldsymbol{Z}^\top \boldsymbol{Z})^{-1}$, which is the inverse of its covariance matrix. That this quadratic form is distributed as $\chi^2(r)$ follows immediately from the the first part of the theorem. ■

The Student's t Distribution

If $z \sim \mathrm{N}(0, 1)$ and $y \sim \chi^2(m)$, and z and y are independent, then the random variable

$$t \equiv \frac{z}{(y/m)^{1/2}} \tag{4.18}$$

is said to follow the **Student's t distribution** with m degrees of freedom. A compact way of writing this is: $t \sim t(m)$. The Student's t distribution looks very much like the standard normal distribution, since both are bell-shaped and symmetric around 0.

The moments of the t distribution depend on m, and only the first $m - 1$ moments exist. Thus the $t(1)$ distribution, which is also called the **Cauchy distribution**, has no moments at all, and the $t(2)$ distribution has no variance. From (4.18), we see that, for the Cauchy distribution, the denominator of t is just the absolute value of a standard normal random variable. Whenever this denominator happens to be close to zero, the ratio is likely to be a very big number, even if the numerator is not particularly large. Thus the Cauchy distribution has very thick tails. As m increases, the chance that the denominator of (4.18) is close to zero diminishes (see Figure 4.4), and so the tails become thinner.

In general, if t is distributed as $t(m)$ with $m > 2$, then $\mathrm{Var}(t) = m/(m-2)$. Thus, as $m \to \infty$, the variance tends to 1, the variance of the standard normal distribution. In fact, the entire $t(m)$ distribution tends to the standard normal distribution as $m \to \infty$. By (4.15), the chi-squared variable y can be expressed as $\sum_{i=1}^{m} z_i^2$, where the z_i are independent standard normal variables. Therefore, by a law of large numbers, such as (3.16), y/m, which is the average of the z_i^2, tends to its expectation as $m \to \infty$. By (4.16), this expectation is just $m/m = 1$. It follows that the denominator of (4.18), $(y/m)^{1/2}$, also tends to 1, and hence that $t \to z \sim \mathrm{N}(0, 1)$ as $m \to \infty$.

Figure 4.5 shows the PDFs of the standard normal, $t(1)$, $t(2)$, and $t(5)$ distributions. In order to make the differences among the various densities in the

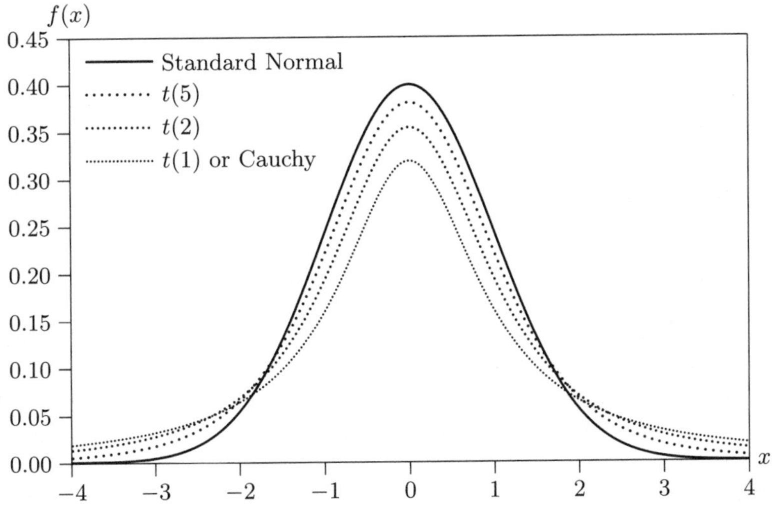

Figure 4.5 PDFs of the Student's t distribution

figure apparent, all the values of m are chosen to be very small. However, it is clear from the figure that, for larger values of m, the PDF of $t(m)$ is very similar to the PDF of the standard normal distribution.

The F Distribution

If y_1 and y_2 are independent random variables distributed as $\chi^2(m_1)$ and $\chi^2(m_2)$, respectively, then the random variable

$$F \equiv \frac{y_1/m_1}{y_2/m_2} \tag{4.19}$$

is said to follow the ***F* distribution** with m_1 and m_2 degrees of freedom. A compact way of writing this is: $F \sim F(m_1, m_2)$.[4] The $F(m_1, m_2)$ distribution looks a lot like a rescaled version of the $\chi^2(m_1)$ distribution. As for the t distribution, the denominator of (4.19) tends to unity as $m_2 \to \infty$, and so $m_1 F \to y_1 \sim \chi^2(m_1)$ as $m_2 \to \infty$. Therefore, for large values of m_2, a random variable that is distributed as $F(m_1, m_2)$ behaves very much like $1/m_1$ times a random variable that is distributed as $\chi^2(m_1)$.

The F distribution is very closely related to the Student's t distribution. It is evident from (4.19) and (4.18) that the square of a random variable which is distributed as $t(m_2)$ is distributed as $F(1, m_2)$. In the next section, we will see how these two distributions arise in the context of hypothesis testing in linear regression models.

[4] The F distribution was introduced by Snedecor (1934). The notation F is used in honor of the well-known statistician R. A. Fisher.

4.4 Exact Tests in the Classical Normal Linear Model

In the example of Section 4.2, we were able to obtain a test statistic z that was distributed as N(0, 1). Tests based on this statistic are exact. Unfortunately, it is possible to perform exact tests only in certain special cases. One very important special case of this type arises when we test linear restrictions on the parameters of the classical normal linear model, which was introduced in Section 3.1. This model may be written as

$$\boldsymbol{y} = \boldsymbol{X}\boldsymbol{\beta} + \boldsymbol{u}, \quad \boldsymbol{u} \sim \mathrm{N}(\mathbf{0}, \sigma^2\mathbf{I}), \tag{4.20}$$

where $\boldsymbol{X}$ is an $n \times k$ matrix of regressors, so that there are n observations and k regressors, and it is assumed that the error vector $\boldsymbol{u}$ is statistically independent of the matrix $\boldsymbol{X}$. Notice that in (4.20) the assumption which in Section 3.1 was written as $u_t \sim \mathrm{NID}(0, \sigma^2)$ is now expressed in matrix notation using the multivariate normal distribution. In addition, since the assumption that $\boldsymbol{u}$ and $\boldsymbol{X}$ are independent means that the generating process for $\boldsymbol{X}$ is independent of that for $\boldsymbol{y}$, we can express this independence assumption by saying that the regressors $\boldsymbol{X}$ are **exogenous** in the model (4.20); the concept of exogeneity[5] was introduced in Section 1.3 and discussed in Section 3.2.

Tests of a Single Restriction

We begin by considering a single, linear restriction on $\boldsymbol{\beta}$. This could, in principle, be any sort of linear restriction, for example, that $\beta_1 = 5$ or $\beta_3 = \beta_4$. However, it simplifies the analysis, and involves no loss of generality, if we confine our attention to a restriction that one of the coefficients should equal 0. If a restriction does not naturally have the form of a zero restriction, we can always apply suitable linear transformations to $\boldsymbol{y}$ and $\boldsymbol{X}$, of the sort considered in Sections 2.3 and 2.4, in order to rewrite the model so that it does; see Exercises 4.7 and 4.8.

Let us partition $\boldsymbol{\beta}$ as $[\boldsymbol{\beta}_1 \;\vdots\; \beta_2]$, where $\boldsymbol{\beta}_1$ is a $(k-1)$–vector and β_2 is a scalar, and consider a restriction of the form $\beta_2 = 0$. When $\boldsymbol{X}$ is partitioned conformably with $\boldsymbol{\beta}$, the model (4.20) can be rewritten as

$$\boldsymbol{y} = \boldsymbol{X}_1\boldsymbol{\beta}_1 + \beta_2\boldsymbol{x}_2 + \boldsymbol{u}, \quad \boldsymbol{u} \sim \mathrm{N}(\mathbf{0}, \sigma^2\mathbf{I}), \tag{4.21}$$

where $\boldsymbol{X}_1$ denotes an $n \times (k-1)$ matrix and $\boldsymbol{x}_2$ denotes an n–vector, with $\boldsymbol{X} = [\boldsymbol{X}_1 \;\; \boldsymbol{x}_2]$.

By the FWL Theorem, the least-squares estimate of β_2 from (4.21) is the same as the least-squares estimate from the FWL regression

$$\boldsymbol{M}_1\boldsymbol{y} = \beta_2\boldsymbol{M}_1\boldsymbol{x}_2 + \text{residuals}, \tag{4.22}$$

[5] This assumption is usually called **strict exogeneity** in the literature, but, since we will not discuss any other sort of exogeneity in this book, it is convenient to drop the word "strict."

where $\boldsymbol{M}_1 \equiv \mathbf{I} - \boldsymbol{X}_1(\boldsymbol{X}_1^\top\boldsymbol{X}_1)^{-1}\boldsymbol{X}_1^\top$ is the matrix that projects on to $\mathcal{S}^\perp(\boldsymbol{X}_1)$. By applying the standard formulas for the OLS estimator and covariance matrix to regression (4.22), under the assumption that the model (4.21) is correctly specified, we find that

$$\hat{\beta}_2 = \frac{\boldsymbol{x}_2^\top\boldsymbol{M}_1\boldsymbol{y}}{\boldsymbol{x}_2^\top\boldsymbol{M}_1\boldsymbol{x}_2} \quad \text{and} \quad \text{Var}(\hat{\beta}_2) = \sigma^2(\boldsymbol{x}_2^\top\boldsymbol{M}_1\boldsymbol{x}_2)^{-1}.$$

In order to test the hypothesis that β_2 equals any specified value, say β_2^0, we have to subtract β_2^0 from $\hat{\beta}_2$ and divide by the square root of the variance. For the null hypothesis that $\beta_2 = 0$, this yields a test statistic analogous to (4.03),

$$z_{\beta_2} \equiv \frac{\boldsymbol{x}_2^\top\boldsymbol{M}_1\boldsymbol{y}}{\sigma(\boldsymbol{x}_2^\top\boldsymbol{M}_1\boldsymbol{x}_2)^{1/2}}, \tag{4.23}$$

which can be computed only under the unrealistic assumption that σ is known. If the data are actually generated by the model (4.21) with $\beta_2 = 0$, then

$$\boldsymbol{M}_1\boldsymbol{y} = \boldsymbol{M}_1(\boldsymbol{X}_1\boldsymbol{\beta}_1 + \boldsymbol{u}) = \boldsymbol{M}_1\boldsymbol{u}.$$

Therefore, the right-hand side of (4.23) becomes

$$\frac{\boldsymbol{x}_2^\top\boldsymbol{M}_1\boldsymbol{u}}{\sigma(\boldsymbol{x}_2^\top\boldsymbol{M}_1\boldsymbol{x}_2)^{1/2}}. \tag{4.24}$$

It is now easy to see that z_{β_2} is distributed as $\text{N}(0, 1)$. Because we can condition on $\boldsymbol{X}$, the only thing left in (4.24) that is stochastic is $\boldsymbol{u}$. Since the numerator is just a linear combination of the components of $\boldsymbol{u}$, which is multivariate normal, the entire test statistic must be normally distributed. The variance of the numerator is

$$\begin{aligned} \text{E}(\boldsymbol{x}_2^\top\boldsymbol{M}_1\boldsymbol{u}\boldsymbol{u}^\top\boldsymbol{M}_1\boldsymbol{x}_2) &= \boldsymbol{x}_2^\top\boldsymbol{M}_1\text{E}(\boldsymbol{u}\boldsymbol{u}^\top)\boldsymbol{M}_1\boldsymbol{x}_2 \\ &= \boldsymbol{x}_2^\top\boldsymbol{M}_1\sigma^2\mathbf{I}\boldsymbol{M}_1\boldsymbol{x}_2 = \sigma^2\boldsymbol{x}_2^\top\boldsymbol{M}_1\boldsymbol{x}_2. \end{aligned}$$

Since the denominator of (4.24) is just the square root of the variance of the numerator, we conclude that z_{β_2} is distributed as $\text{N}(0, 1)$ under the null hypothesis.

The test statistic z_{β_2} defined in (4.23) has exactly the same distribution under the null hypothesis as the test statistic z defined in (4.03). The analysis of Section 4.2 therefore applies to it without any change. Thus we now know how to test the hypothesis that any coefficient in the classical normal linear model is equal to 0, or to any specified value, but only if we know the variance of the error terms.

In order to handle the more realistic case in which the variance of the error terms is unknown, we need to replace σ in equation (4.23) by s, the standard error of the regression (4.21), which was implicitly defined in equation (3.49). If, as usual, $\boldsymbol{M_X}$ is the orthogonal projection on to $\mathcal{S}^\perp(\boldsymbol{X})$, then we have $s^2 = \boldsymbol{y}^\top\boldsymbol{M_X}\boldsymbol{y}/(n-k)$, and so we obtain the test statistic

$$t_{\beta_2} \equiv \frac{\boldsymbol{x}_2^\top\boldsymbol{M}_1\boldsymbol{y}}{s(\boldsymbol{x}_2^\top\boldsymbol{M}_1\boldsymbol{x}_2)^{1/2}} = \left(\frac{\boldsymbol{y}^\top\boldsymbol{M_X}\boldsymbol{y}}{n-k}\right)^{-1/2}\frac{\boldsymbol{x}_2^\top\boldsymbol{M}_1\boldsymbol{y}}{(\boldsymbol{x}_2^\top\boldsymbol{M}_1\boldsymbol{x}_2)^{1/2}}. \tag{4.25}$$

As we will now demonstrate, this test statistic is distributed as $t(n-k)$ under the null hypothesis. Not surprisingly, it is called a ***t* statistic**.

As we discussed in the last section, for a test statistic to have the $t(n-k)$ distribution, it must be possible to write it as the ratio of a standard normal variable z to the square root of $y/(n-k)$, where y is independent of z and distributed as $\chi^2(n-k)$. The t statistic defined in (4.25) can be rewritten as

$$t_{\beta_2} = \frac{z_{\beta_2}}{\left(\boldsymbol{y}^\top\boldsymbol{M_X}\boldsymbol{y}/((n-k)\sigma^2)\right)^{1/2}}, \tag{4.26}$$

which has the form of such a ratio. We have already shown that $z_{\beta_2} \sim \mathrm{N}(0,1)$. Thus it only remains to show that $\boldsymbol{y}^\top\boldsymbol{M_X}\boldsymbol{y}/\sigma^2 \sim \chi^2(n-k)$ and that the random variables in the numerator and denominator of (4.26) are independent.

Under any DGP that belongs to (4.21),

$$\frac{\boldsymbol{y}^\top\boldsymbol{M_X}\boldsymbol{y}}{\sigma^2} = \frac{\boldsymbol{u}^\top\boldsymbol{M_X}\boldsymbol{u}}{\sigma^2} = \boldsymbol{\varepsilon}^\top\boldsymbol{M_X}\boldsymbol{\varepsilon}, \tag{4.27}$$

where $\boldsymbol{\varepsilon} \equiv \boldsymbol{u}/\sigma$ is distributed as $\mathrm{N}(\mathbf{0},\mathbf{I})$. Since $\boldsymbol{M_X}$ is a projection matrix with rank $n-k$, the second part of Theorem 4.1 shows that the rightmost expression in (4.27) is distributed as $\chi^2(n-k)$.

To see that the random variables z_{β_2} and $\boldsymbol{\varepsilon}^\top\boldsymbol{M_X}\boldsymbol{\varepsilon}$ are independent, we note first that $\boldsymbol{\varepsilon}^\top\boldsymbol{M_X}\boldsymbol{\varepsilon}$ depends on $\boldsymbol{y}$ only through $\boldsymbol{M_X}\boldsymbol{y}$. Second, from (4.23), it is not hard to see that z_{β_2} depends on $\boldsymbol{y}$ only through $\boldsymbol{P_X}\boldsymbol{y}$, since

$$\boldsymbol{x}_2^\top\boldsymbol{M}_1\boldsymbol{y} = \boldsymbol{x}_2^\top\boldsymbol{P_X}\boldsymbol{M}_1\boldsymbol{y} = \boldsymbol{x}_2^\top(\boldsymbol{P_X} - \boldsymbol{P_X}\boldsymbol{P}_1)\boldsymbol{y} = \boldsymbol{x}_2^\top\boldsymbol{M}_1\boldsymbol{P_X}\boldsymbol{y};$$

the first equality here simply uses the fact that $\boldsymbol{x}_2 \in \mathcal{S}(\boldsymbol{X})$, and the third equality uses the result (2.35) that $\boldsymbol{P_X}\boldsymbol{P}_1 = \boldsymbol{P}_1\boldsymbol{P_X}$. Independence now follows because, as we will see directly, $\boldsymbol{P_X}\boldsymbol{y}$ and $\boldsymbol{M_X}\boldsymbol{y}$ are independent.

We saw above that $\boldsymbol{M_X}\boldsymbol{y} = \boldsymbol{M_X}\boldsymbol{u}$. Further, from (4.20), $\boldsymbol{P_X}\boldsymbol{y} = \boldsymbol{X\beta} + \boldsymbol{P_X}\boldsymbol{u}$, from which it follows that the centered version of $\boldsymbol{P_X}\boldsymbol{y}$ is $\boldsymbol{P_X}\boldsymbol{u}$. The $n \times n$ matrix of covariances of components of $\boldsymbol{P_X}\boldsymbol{u}$ and $\boldsymbol{M_X}\boldsymbol{u}$ is thus

$$\mathrm{E}(\boldsymbol{P_X}\boldsymbol{u}\boldsymbol{u}^\top\boldsymbol{M_X}) = \sigma^2\boldsymbol{P_X}\boldsymbol{M_X} = \mathbf{O},$$

by (2.25), because $\boldsymbol{P_X}$ and $\boldsymbol{M_X}$ are complementary projections. These zero covariances imply that the vectors $\boldsymbol{P_X}\boldsymbol{u}$ and $\boldsymbol{M_X}\boldsymbol{u}$ are independent, since both are multivariate normal. Geometrically, these vectors have zero covariance because they lie in *orthogonal* subspaces, namely, the images of $\boldsymbol{P_X}$ and $\boldsymbol{M_X}$. Thus, even though the numerator and denominator of (4.26) both depend on $\boldsymbol{y}$, this orthogonality implies that they are independent.

We therefore conclude that the t statistic (4.26) for $\beta_2 = 0$ in the model (4.21) has the $t(n-k)$ distribution. Performing one-tailed and two-tailed tests based on t_{β_2} is almost the same as performing them based on z_{β_2}. We just have to use the $t(n-k)$ distribution instead of the $\mathrm{N}(0,1)$ distribution to compute P values or critical values. An interesting property of t statistics is explored in Exercise 4.9.

Tests of Several Restrictions

Economists frequently want to test more than one linear restriction. Let us suppose that there are r restrictions, with $r \leq k$, since there cannot be more equality restrictions than there are parameters in the unrestricted model. As before, there is no loss of generality if we assume that the restrictions take the form $\boldsymbol{\beta}_2 = \mathbf{0}$. The alternative hypothesis is the model (4.20), which has been rewritten as

$$H_1\colon\;\; \boldsymbol{y} = \boldsymbol{X}_1\boldsymbol{\beta}_1 + \boldsymbol{X}_2\boldsymbol{\beta}_2 + \boldsymbol{u}, \quad \boldsymbol{u} \sim \mathrm{N}(\mathbf{0}, \sigma^2\mathbf{I}). \tag{4.28}$$

Here $\boldsymbol{X}_1$ is an $n \times k_1$ matrix, $\boldsymbol{X}_2$ is an $n \times k_2$ matrix, $\boldsymbol{\beta}_1$ is a k_1–vector, $\boldsymbol{\beta}_2$ is a k_2–vector, $k = k_1 + k_2$, and the number of restrictions $r = k_2$. Unless $r = 1$, it is no longer possible to use a t test, because there is one t statistic for each element of $\boldsymbol{\beta}_2$, and we want to compute a single test statistic for all the restrictions at once.

It is natural to base a test on a comparison of how well the model fits when the restrictions are imposed with how well it fits when they are not imposed. The null hypothesis is the regression model

$$H_0\colon\;\; \boldsymbol{y} = \boldsymbol{X}_1\boldsymbol{\beta}_1 + \boldsymbol{u}, \quad \boldsymbol{u} \sim \mathrm{N}(\mathbf{0}, \sigma^2\mathbf{I}), \tag{4.29}$$

in which we impose the restriction that $\boldsymbol{\beta}_2 = \mathbf{0}$. As we saw in Section 3.8, the restricted model (4.29) must always fit worse than the unrestricted model (4.28), in the sense that the SSR from (4.29) cannot be smaller, and is almost always larger, than the SSR from (4.28). However, if the restrictions are true, the reduction in SSR from adding $\boldsymbol{X}_2$ to the regression should be relatively small. Therefore, it seems natural to base a test statistic on the difference between these two SSRs. If USSR denotes the **unrestricted sum of squared residuals**, from (4.28), and RSSR denotes the **restricted sum of squared residuals**, from (4.29), the appropriate test statistic is

$$F_{\beta_2} \equiv \frac{(\mathrm{RSSR} - \mathrm{USSR})/r}{\mathrm{USSR}/(n-k)}. \tag{4.30}$$

Under the null hypothesis, as we will now demonstrate, this test statistic follows the F distribution with r and $n-k$ degrees of freedom. Not surprisingly, it is called an ***F* statistic**.

The restricted SSR is $\boldsymbol{y}^{\top}\boldsymbol{M}_1\boldsymbol{y}$, and the unrestricted one is $\boldsymbol{y}^{\top}\boldsymbol{M_X}\boldsymbol{y}$. One way to obtain a convenient expression for the difference between these two expressions is to use the FWL Theorem. By this theorem, the USSR is the SSR from the FWL regression

$$\boldsymbol{M}_1\boldsymbol{y} = \boldsymbol{M}_1\boldsymbol{X}_2\boldsymbol{\beta}_2 + \text{residuals}. \tag{4.31}$$

The total sum of squares from (4.31) is $\boldsymbol{y}^{\top}\boldsymbol{M}_1\boldsymbol{y}$. The explained sum of squares can be expressed in terms of the orthogonal projection on to the r–dimensional subspace $\mathcal{S}(\boldsymbol{M}_1\boldsymbol{X}_2)$, and so the difference is

$$\text{USSR} = \boldsymbol{y}^{\top}\boldsymbol{M}_1\boldsymbol{y} - \boldsymbol{y}^{\top}\boldsymbol{M}_1\boldsymbol{X}_2(\boldsymbol{X}_2^{\top}\boldsymbol{M}_1\boldsymbol{X}_2)^{-1}\boldsymbol{X}_2^{\top}\boldsymbol{M}_1\boldsymbol{y}. \tag{4.32}$$

Therefore,

$$\text{RSSR} - \text{USSR} = \boldsymbol{y}^{\top}\boldsymbol{M}_1\boldsymbol{X}_2(\boldsymbol{X}_2^{\top}\boldsymbol{M}_1\boldsymbol{X}_2)^{-1}\boldsymbol{X}_2^{\top}\boldsymbol{M}_1\boldsymbol{y},$$

and the F statistic (4.30) can be written as

$$F_{\boldsymbol{\beta}_2} = \frac{\boldsymbol{y}^{\top}\boldsymbol{M}_1\boldsymbol{X}_2(\boldsymbol{X}_2^{\top}\boldsymbol{M}_1\boldsymbol{X}_2)^{-1}\boldsymbol{X}_2^{\top}\boldsymbol{M}_1\boldsymbol{y}/r}{\boldsymbol{y}^{\top}\boldsymbol{M_X}\boldsymbol{y}/(n-k)}. \tag{4.33}$$

Under the null hypothesis, $\boldsymbol{M_X}\boldsymbol{y} = \boldsymbol{M_X}\boldsymbol{u}$ and $\boldsymbol{M}_1\boldsymbol{y} = \boldsymbol{M}_1\boldsymbol{u}$. Thus, under this hypothesis, the F statistic (4.33) reduces to

$$\frac{\boldsymbol{\varepsilon}^{\top}\boldsymbol{M}_1\boldsymbol{X}_2(\boldsymbol{X}_2^{\top}\boldsymbol{M}_1\boldsymbol{X}_2)^{-1}\boldsymbol{X}_2^{\top}\boldsymbol{M}_1\boldsymbol{\varepsilon}/r}{\boldsymbol{\varepsilon}^{\top}\boldsymbol{M_X}\boldsymbol{\varepsilon}/(n-k)}, \tag{4.34}$$

where, as before, $\boldsymbol{\varepsilon} \equiv \boldsymbol{u}/\sigma$. We saw in the last subsection that the quadratic form in the denominator of (4.34) is distributed as $\chi^2(n-k)$. Since the quadratic form in the numerator can be written as $\boldsymbol{\varepsilon}^{\top}\boldsymbol{P}_{\boldsymbol{M}_1\boldsymbol{X}_2}\boldsymbol{\varepsilon}$, it is distributed as $\chi^2(r)$. Moreover, the random variables in the numerator and denominator are independent, because $\boldsymbol{M_X}$ and $\boldsymbol{P}_{\boldsymbol{M}_1\boldsymbol{X}_2}$ project on to mutually orthogonal subspaces: $\boldsymbol{M_X}\boldsymbol{M}_1\boldsymbol{X}_2 = \boldsymbol{M_X}(\boldsymbol{X}_2 - \boldsymbol{P}_1\boldsymbol{X}_2) = \mathbf{O}$. Thus it is apparent that the statistic (4.34) follows the $F(r, n-k)$ distribution under the null hypothesis.

A Threefold Orthogonal Decomposition

Each of the restricted and unrestricted models generates an orthogonal decomposition of the dependent variable $\boldsymbol{y}$. It is illuminating to see how these two decompositions interact to produce a threefold orthogonal decomposition. It turns out that all three components of this decomposition have useful interpretations. From the two models, we find that

$$\boldsymbol{y} = \boldsymbol{P}_1\boldsymbol{y} + \boldsymbol{M}_1\boldsymbol{y} \quad \text{and} \quad \boldsymbol{y} = \boldsymbol{P_X}\boldsymbol{y} + \boldsymbol{M_X}\boldsymbol{y}. \tag{4.35}$$

In Exercises 2.18 and 2.19, $\boldsymbol{P_X} - \boldsymbol{P}_1$ was seen to be an orthogonal projection matrix, equal to $\boldsymbol{P}_{\boldsymbol{M}_1\boldsymbol{X}_2}$. It follows that

$$\boldsymbol{P_X} = \boldsymbol{P}_1 + \boldsymbol{P}_{\boldsymbol{M}_1\boldsymbol{X}_2}, \tag{4.36}$$

where the two projections on the right-hand side of this equation are obviously mutually orthogonal, since $\boldsymbol{P}_1$ annihilates $\boldsymbol{M}_1\boldsymbol{X}_2$. From (4.35) and (4.36), we obtain the threefold orthogonal decomposition

$$\boldsymbol{y} = \boldsymbol{P}_1\boldsymbol{y} + \boldsymbol{P}_{\boldsymbol{M}_1\boldsymbol{X}_2}\boldsymbol{y} + \boldsymbol{M_X}\boldsymbol{y}. \tag{4.37}$$

The first term is the vector of fitted values from the restricted model, $\boldsymbol{X}_1\tilde{\boldsymbol{\beta}}_1$. In this and what follows, we use a tilde (˜) to denote the **restricted estimates**, and a hat (ˆ) to denote the **unrestricted estimates**. The second term is the vector of fitted values from the FWL regression (4.31). It equals $\boldsymbol{M}_1\boldsymbol{X}_2\hat{\boldsymbol{\beta}}_2$, where, by the FWL Theorem, $\hat{\boldsymbol{\beta}}_2$ is a subvector of estimates from the unrestricted model. Finally, $\boldsymbol{M_X}\boldsymbol{y}$ is the vector of residuals from the unrestricted model. Since $\boldsymbol{P_X}\boldsymbol{y} = \boldsymbol{X}_1\hat{\boldsymbol{\beta}}_1 + \boldsymbol{X}_2\hat{\boldsymbol{\beta}}_2$, the vector of fitted values from the unrestricted model, we see that

$$\boldsymbol{X}_1\hat{\boldsymbol{\beta}}_1 + \boldsymbol{X}_2\hat{\boldsymbol{\beta}}_2 = \boldsymbol{X}_1\tilde{\boldsymbol{\beta}}_1 + \boldsymbol{M}_1\boldsymbol{X}_2\hat{\boldsymbol{\beta}}_2. \tag{4.38}$$

In Exercise 4.10, this result is exploited to show how to obtain the restricted estimates in terms of the unrestricted estimates.

The F statistic (4.33) can be written as the ratio of the squared norm of the second component in (4.37) to the squared norm of the third, each normalized by the appropriate number of degrees of freedom. Under both hypotheses, the third component $\boldsymbol{M_X}\boldsymbol{y}$ equals $\boldsymbol{M_X}\boldsymbol{u}$, and so it consists of random noise. Its squared norm is a $\chi^2(n-k)$ variable times σ^2, which serves as the (unrestricted) estimate of σ^2 and can be thought of as a measure of the scale of the random noise. Since $\boldsymbol{u} \sim \mathrm{N}(\boldsymbol{0}, \sigma^2\mathbf{I})$, every element of $\boldsymbol{u}$ has the same variance, and so every component of (4.37), if centered so as to leave only the random part, should have the same scale.

Under the null hypothesis, the second component is $\boldsymbol{P}_{\boldsymbol{M}_1\boldsymbol{X}_2}\boldsymbol{y} = \boldsymbol{P}_{\boldsymbol{M}_1\boldsymbol{X}_2}\boldsymbol{u}$, which just consists of random noise. But, under the alternative, $\boldsymbol{P}_{\boldsymbol{M}_1\boldsymbol{X}_2}\boldsymbol{y} = \boldsymbol{M}_1\boldsymbol{X}_2\boldsymbol{\beta}_2 + \boldsymbol{P}_{\boldsymbol{M}_1\boldsymbol{X}_2}\boldsymbol{u}$, and it thus contains a systematic part related to $\boldsymbol{X}_2$. The length of the second component must be greater, on average, under the alternative than under the null, since the random part is there in all cases, but the systematic part is present only under the alternative. The F test compares the squared length of the second component with the squared length of the third. It thus serves to detect the possible presence of systematic variation, related to $\boldsymbol{X}_2$, in the second component of (4.37).

All this means that we want to reject the null whenever the numerator of the F statistic, RSSR − USSR, is relatively large. Consequently, the P value corresponding to a realized F statistic $\hat{F}$ is computed as $1 - F_{r,n-k}(\hat{F})$, where $F_{r,n-k}(\cdot)$ denotes the CDF of the F distribution with the appropriate numbers of degrees of freedom. Thus we compute the P value as if for a one-tailed test. However, F tests are really two-tailed tests, because they test equality restrictions, not inequality restrictions. An F test for $\boldsymbol{\beta}_2 = \mathbf{0}$ rejects the null hypothesis whenever $\hat{\boldsymbol{\beta}}_2$ is sufficiently far from $\mathbf{0}$, whether the individual elements of $\hat{\boldsymbol{\beta}}_2$ are positive or negative.

There is a very close relationship between F tests and t tests. In the previous section, we saw that the square of a random variable with the $t(n-k)$ distribution must have the $F(1, n-k)$ distribution. The square of the t statistic t_{β_2}, defined in (4.25), is

$$t_{\beta_2}^2 = \frac{\boldsymbol{y}^\top \boldsymbol{M}_1 \boldsymbol{x}_2 (\boldsymbol{x}_2^\top \boldsymbol{M}_1 \boldsymbol{x}_2)^{-1} \boldsymbol{x}_2^\top \boldsymbol{M}_1 \boldsymbol{y}}{\boldsymbol{y}^\top \boldsymbol{M}_{\boldsymbol{X}} \boldsymbol{y}/(n-k)}.$$

This test statistic is evidently a special case of (4.33), with the vector $\boldsymbol{x}_2$ replacing the matrix $\boldsymbol{X}_2$. Thus, when there is only one restriction, it makes no difference whether we use a two-tailed t test or an F test.

An Example of the F Test

The most familiar application of the F test is testing the hypothesis that all the coefficients in a classical normal linear model, except the constant term, are zero. The null hypothesis is that $\boldsymbol{\beta}_2 = \mathbf{0}$ in the model

$$\boldsymbol{y} = \beta_1 \boldsymbol{\iota} + \boldsymbol{X}_2 \boldsymbol{\beta}_2 + \boldsymbol{u}, \quad \boldsymbol{u} \sim \mathrm{N}(\mathbf{0}, \sigma^2 \mathbf{I}), \tag{4.39}$$

where $\boldsymbol{\iota}$ is an n-vector of 1s and $\boldsymbol{X}_2$ is $n \times (k-1)$. In this case, using (4.32), the test statistic (4.33) can be written as

$$F_{\beta_2} = \frac{\boldsymbol{y}^\top \boldsymbol{M}_\iota \boldsymbol{X}_2 (\boldsymbol{X}_2^\top \boldsymbol{M}_\iota \boldsymbol{X}_2)^{-1} \boldsymbol{X}_2^\top \boldsymbol{M}_\iota \boldsymbol{y}/(k-1)}{\big(\boldsymbol{y}^\top \boldsymbol{M}_\iota \boldsymbol{y} - \boldsymbol{y}^\top \boldsymbol{M}_\iota \boldsymbol{X}_2 (\boldsymbol{X}_2^\top \boldsymbol{M}_\iota \boldsymbol{X}_2)^{-1} \boldsymbol{X}_2^\top \boldsymbol{M}_\iota \boldsymbol{y}\big)/(n-k)}, \tag{4.40}$$

where $\boldsymbol{M}_\iota$ is the projection matrix that takes deviations from the mean, which was defined in (2.31). Thus the matrix expression in the numerator of (4.40) is just the explained sum of squares, or ESS, from the FWL regression

$$\boldsymbol{M}_\iota \boldsymbol{y} = \boldsymbol{M}_\iota \boldsymbol{X}_2 \boldsymbol{\beta}_2 + \text{residuals}.$$

Similarly, the matrix expression in the denominator is the total sum of squares, or TSS, from this regression, minus the ESS. Since the centered R^2 from (4.39) is just the ratio of this ESS to this TSS, it requires only a little algebra to show that

$$F_{\beta_2} = \frac{n-k}{k-1} \times \frac{R_c^2}{1 - R_c^2}.$$

Therefore, the F statistic (4.40) depends on the data only through the centered R^2, of which it is a monotonically increasing function.

Testing the Equality of Two Parameter Vectors

It is often natural to divide a sample into two, or possibly more than two, subsamples. These might correspond to periods of fixed exchange rates and floating exchange rates, large firms and small firms, rich countries and poor countries, or men and women, to name just a few examples. We may then ask whether a linear regression model has the same coefficients for both the subsamples. It is natural to use an F test for this purpose. Because the classic treatment of this problem is found in Chow (1960), the test is often called a **Chow test**; later treatments include Fisher (1970) and Dufour (1982).

Let us suppose, for simplicity, that there are only two subsamples, of lengths n_1 and n_2, with $n = n_1 + n_2$. We will assume that both n_1 and n_2 are greater than k, the number of regressors. If we separate the subsamples by partitioning the variables, we can write

$$\boldsymbol{y} \equiv \begin{bmatrix} \boldsymbol{y}_1 \\ \boldsymbol{y}_2 \end{bmatrix}, \quad \text{and} \quad \boldsymbol{X} \equiv \begin{bmatrix} \boldsymbol{X}_1 \\ \boldsymbol{X}_2 \end{bmatrix},$$

where $\boldsymbol{y}_1$ and $\boldsymbol{y}_2$ are, respectively, an n_1–vector and an n_2–vector, while $\boldsymbol{X}_1$ and $\boldsymbol{X}_2$ are $n_1 \times k$ and $n_2 \times k$ matrices. Even if we need different parameter vectors, $\boldsymbol{\beta}_1$ and $\boldsymbol{\beta}_2$, for the two subsamples, we can nonetheless put the subsamples together in the following regression model:

$$\begin{bmatrix} \boldsymbol{y}_1 \\ \boldsymbol{y}_2 \end{bmatrix} = \begin{bmatrix} \boldsymbol{X}_1 \\ \boldsymbol{X}_2 \end{bmatrix} \boldsymbol{\beta}_1 + \begin{bmatrix} \mathbf{O} \\ \boldsymbol{X}_2 \end{bmatrix} \boldsymbol{\gamma} + \boldsymbol{u}, \quad \boldsymbol{u} \sim \mathrm{N}(\mathbf{0}, \sigma^2 \mathbf{I}). \tag{4.41}$$

It can readily be seen that, in the first subsample, the regression functions are the components of $\boldsymbol{X}_1\boldsymbol{\beta}_1$, while, in the second, they are the components of $\boldsymbol{X}_2(\boldsymbol{\beta}_1 + \boldsymbol{\gamma})$. Thus $\boldsymbol{\gamma}$ is to be defined as $\boldsymbol{\beta}_2 - \boldsymbol{\beta}_1$. If we define $\boldsymbol{Z}$ as an $n \times k$ matrix with $\mathbf{O}$ in its first n_1 rows and $\boldsymbol{X}_2$ in the remaining n_2 rows, then (4.41) can be rewritten as

$$\boldsymbol{y} = \boldsymbol{X}\boldsymbol{\beta}_1 + \boldsymbol{Z}\boldsymbol{\gamma} + \boldsymbol{u}, \quad \boldsymbol{u} \sim \mathrm{N}(\mathbf{0}, \sigma^2 \mathbf{I}). \tag{4.42}$$

This is a regression model with n observations and $2k$ regressors. It has been constructed in such a way that $\boldsymbol{\beta}_1$ is estimated directly, while $\boldsymbol{\beta}_2$ is estimated using the relation $\boldsymbol{\beta}_2 = \boldsymbol{\gamma} + \boldsymbol{\beta}_1$. Since the restriction that $\boldsymbol{\beta}_1 = \boldsymbol{\beta}_2$ is equivalent to the restriction that $\boldsymbol{\gamma} = \mathbf{0}$ in (4.42), the null hypothesis has been expressed as a set of k zero restrictions. Since (4.42) is just a classical normal linear model with k linear restrictions to be tested, the F test provides the appropriate way to test those restrictions.

The F statistic can perfectly well be computed as usual, by running (4.42) to get the USSR and then running the restricted model, which is just the regression of $\boldsymbol{y}$ on $\boldsymbol{X}$, to get the RSSR. However, there is another way to compute the USSR. In Exercise 4.11, readers are invited to show that it is simply the sum of the two SSRs obtained by running two independent regressions on the two subsamples. If SSR_1 and SSR_2 denote the sums of squared residuals from these two regressions, and RSSR denotes the sum of squared residuals from regressing $\boldsymbol{y}$ on $\boldsymbol{X}$, the F statistic becomes

$$F_\gamma = \frac{(\text{RSSR} - \text{SSR}_1 - \text{SSR}_2)/k}{(\text{SSR}_1 + \text{SSR}_2)/(n-2k)}. \tag{4.43}$$

This **Chow statistic**, as it is often called, is distributed as $F(k, n-2k)$ under the null hypothesis that $\boldsymbol{\beta}_1 = \boldsymbol{\beta}_2$.

4.5 Large-Sample Tests in Linear Regression Models

The t and F tests that we developed in the previous section are exact only under the strong assumptions of the classical normal linear model. If the error vector were not normally distributed or not independent of the matrix of regressors, we could still compute t and F statistics, but they would not actually follow their namesake distributions in finite samples. However, like a great many test statistics in econometrics which do not follow any known distribution exactly, they would in many cases approximately follow known distributions in large samples. In such cases, we can perform what are called **large-sample tests** or **asymptotic tests**, using the approximate distributions to compute P values or critical values.

Asymptotic theory is concerned with the distributions of estimators and test statistics as the sample size n tends to infinity. It often allows us to obtain simple results which provide useful approximations even when the sample size is far from infinite. In this book, we do not intend to discuss asymptotic theory at the advanced level of Davidson (1994) or White (2000). A rigorous introduction to the fundamental ideas may be found in Gallant (1997), and a less formal treatment is provided in Davidson and MacKinnon (1993). However, it is impossible to understand large parts of econometrics without having some idea of how asymptotic theory works and what we can learn from it. In this section, we will show that asymptotic theory gives us results about the distributions of t and F statistics under much weaker assumptions than those of the classical normal linear model.

Laws of Large Numbers

There are two types of fundamental results on which asymptotic theory is based. The first type, which we briefly discussed in Section 3.3, is called a **law of large numbers**, or **LLN**. A law of large numbers may apply to any quantity which can be written as an average of n random variables, that is, $1/n$ times their sum. Suppose, for example, that

$$\bar{x} \equiv \frac{1}{n}\sum_{t=1}^{n} x_t,$$

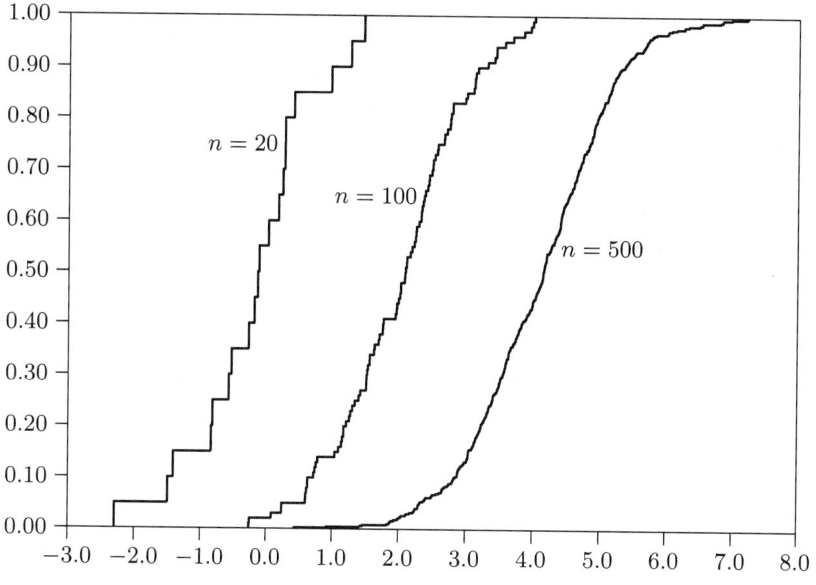

Figure 4.6 EDFs for several sample sizes

where the x_t are independent random variables, each with its own bounded finite variance σ_t^2 and with a common mean μ. Then a fairly simple LLN assures us that, as $n \to \infty$, $\bar{x}$ tends to μ.

An example of how useful a law of large numbers can be is the **Fundamental Theorem of Statistics**, which concerns the **empirical distribution function**, or **EDF**, of a random sample. The EDF was introduced in Exercises 1.1 and 3.4. Suppose that X is a random variable with CDF $F(X)$ and that we obtain a random sample of size n with typical element x_t, where each x_t is an independent realization of X. The **empirical distribution** defined by this sample is the discrete distribution that puts a weight of $1/n$ at each of the x_t, $t = 1, \ldots, n$. The EDF is the distribution function of the empirical distribution, and it can be expressed algebraically as

$$\hat{F}(x) \equiv \frac{1}{n}\sum_{t=1}^{n} I(x_t \leq x), \tag{4.44}$$

where $I(\cdot)$ is the **indicator function**, which takes the value 1 when its argument is true and takes the value 0 otherwise. Thus, for a given argument x, the sum on the right-hand side of (4.44) counts the number of realizations x_t that are smaller than or equal to x. The EDF has the form of a step function: The height of each step is $1/n$, and the width is equal to the difference between two successive values of x_t. According to the Fundamental Theorem of Statistics, the EDF consistently estimates the CDF of the random variable X.

Figure 4.6 shows the EDFs for three samples of sizes 20, 100, and 500 drawn from three normal distributions, each with variance 1 and with means 0, 2, and 4, respectively. These may be compared with the CDF of the standard normal distribution in the lower panel of Figure 4.2. There is not much resemblance between the EDF based on $n = 20$ and the normal CDF from which the sample was drawn, but the resemblance is somewhat stronger for $n = 100$ and very much stronger for $n = 500$. It is a simple matter to simulate data from an EDF, as we will see in the next section, and this type of simulation can be very useful.

It is very easy to prove the Fundamental Theorem of Statistics. For any real value of x, each term in the sum on the right-hand side of (4.44) depends only on x_t. The expectation of $I(x_t \leq x)$ can be found by using the fact that it can take on only two values, 1 and 0. The expectation is

$$\begin{aligned} \mathrm{E}\big(I(x_t \leq x)\big) &= 0 \cdot \Pr\big(I(x_t \leq x) = 0\big) + 1 \cdot \Pr\big(I(x_t \leq x) = 1\big) \\ &= \Pr\big(I(x_t \leq x) = 1\big) = \Pr(x_t \leq x) = F(x). \end{aligned}$$

Since the x_t are mutually independent, so too are the terms $I(x_t \leq x)$. Since the x_t all follow the same distribution, so too must these terms. Thus (4.44) is the mean of n IID random terms, each with finite expectation. The simplest of all LLNs (due to Khinchin) applies to such a mean, and we conclude that, for every x, $\hat{F}(x)$ is a consistent estimator of $F(x)$.

There are many different LLNs, some of which do not require that the individual random variables have a common mean or be independent, although the amount of dependence must be limited. If we can apply a LLN to any random average, we can treat it as a nonrandom quantity for the purpose of asymptotic analysis. In many cases, this means that we must divide the quantity of interest by n. For example, the matrix $\boldsymbol{X}^\top\boldsymbol{X}$ that appears in the OLS estimator generally does not converge to anything as $n \to \infty$. In contrast, the matrix $n^{-1}\boldsymbol{X}^\top\boldsymbol{X}$, under many plausible assumptions about how $\boldsymbol{X}$ is generated, tends to a nonstochastic limiting matrix $\boldsymbol{S}_{\boldsymbol{X}^\top\boldsymbol{X}}$ as $n \to \infty$.

Central Limit Theorems

The second type of fundamental result on which asymptotic theory is based is called a **central limit theorem**, or **CLT**. Central limit theorems are crucial in establishing the asymptotic distributions of estimators and test statistics. They tell us that, in many circumstances, $1/\sqrt{n}$ times the sum of n centered random variables approximately follows a normal distribution when n is sufficiently large.

Suppose that the random variables x_t, $t = 1, \ldots, n$, are independently and identically distributed with mean μ and variance σ^2. Then, according to the Lindeberg-Lévy central limit theorem, the quantity

$$z \equiv \frac{1}{\sqrt{n}} \sum_{t=1}^{n} \frac{x_t - \mu}{\sigma} \tag{4.45}$$

is **asymptotically distributed** as N(0, 1). This means that, as $n \to \infty$, the random variable z tends to a random variable which follows the N(0, 1) distribution. It may seem curious that we divide by $\sqrt{n}$ instead of by n in (4.45), but this is an essential feature of every CLT. To see why, we calculate the variance of z. Since the terms in the sum in (4.45) are independent, the variance of z is just the sum of the variances of the n terms:

$$\operatorname{Var}(z) = n\operatorname{Var}\Big(\frac{1}{\sqrt{n}}\frac{x_t - \mu}{\sigma}\Big) = \frac{n}{n} = 1.$$

If we had divided by n, we would, by a law of large numbers, have obtained a random variable with a plim of 0 instead of a random variable with a limiting standard normal distribution. Thus, whenever we want to use a CLT, we must ensure that a factor of $n^{-1/2} = 1/\sqrt{n}$ is present.

Just as there are many different LLNs, so too are there many different CLTs, almost all of which impose weaker conditions on the x_t than those imposed by the Lindeberg-Lévy CLT. The assumption that the x_t are identically distributed is easily relaxed, as is the assumption that they are independent. However, if there is either too much dependence or too much heterogeneity, a CLT may not apply. Several CLTs are discussed in Section 4.7 of Davidson and MacKinnon (1993), and Davidson (1994) provides a more advanced treatment. In all cases of interest to us, the CLT says that, for a sequence of random variables x_t, $t = 1, \ldots, \infty$, with $\mathrm{E}(x_t) = 0$,

$$\operatorname*{plim}_{n\to\infty} n^{-1/2}\sum_{t=1}^{n} x_t = x_0 \sim \mathrm{N}\Big(0, \lim_{n\to\infty}\frac{1}{n}\sum_{t=1}^{n}\operatorname{Var}(x_t)\Big).$$

We sometimes need vector, or **multivariate**, versions of CLTs. Suppose that we have a sequence of random m–vectors $\boldsymbol{x}_t$, for some fixed m, with $\mathrm{E}(\boldsymbol{x}_t) = \mathbf{0}$. Then the appropriate multivariate version of a CLT tells us that

$$\operatorname*{plim}_{n\to\infty} n^{-1/2}\sum_{t=1}^{n} \boldsymbol{x}_t = \boldsymbol{x}_0 \sim \mathrm{N}\Big(\mathbf{0}, \lim_{n\to\infty}\frac{1}{n}\sum_{t=1}^{n}\operatorname{Var}(\boldsymbol{x}_t)\Big), \tag{4.46}$$

where $\boldsymbol{x}_0$ is multivariate normal, and each $\operatorname{Var}(\boldsymbol{x}_t)$ is an $m \times m$ matrix.

Figure 4.7 illustrates the fact that CLTs often provide good approximations even when n is not very large. Both panels of the figure show the densities of various random variables z defined as in (4.45). In the top panel, the x_t are uniformly distributed, and we see that z is remarkably close to being distributed as standard normal even when n is as small as 8. This panel does not show results for larger values of n because they would have made it too hard to read. In the bottom panel, the x_t follow the $\chi^2(1)$ distribution, which exhibits extreme right skewness. The mode[6] of the distribution is 0, there

[6] A **mode** of a distribution is a point at which the density achieves a local maximum. If there is just one such point, a density is said to be **unimodal**.

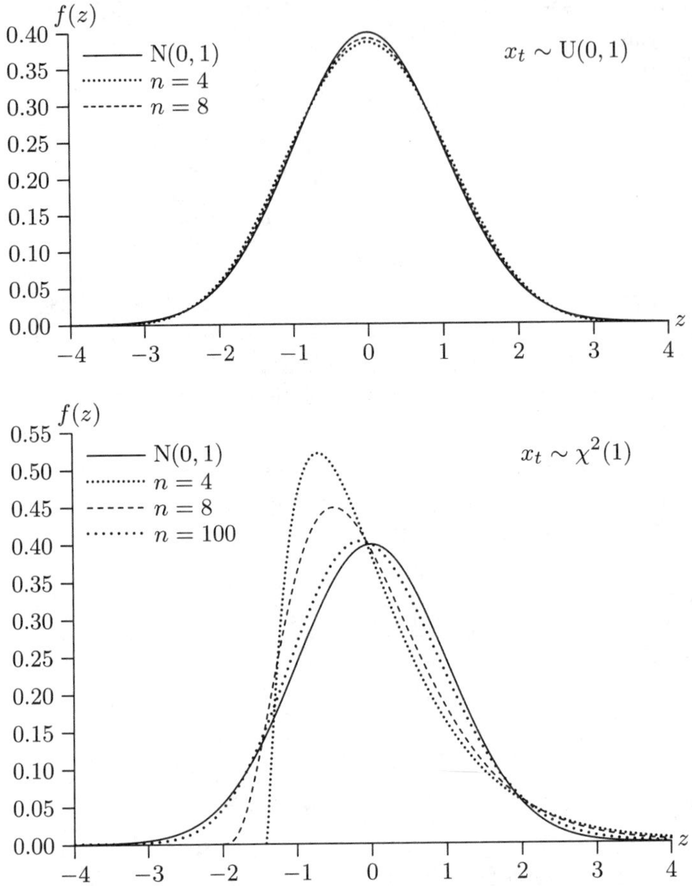

Figure 4.7 The normal approximation for different values of n

are no values less than 0, and there is a very long right-hand tail. For $n = 4$ and $n = 8$, the standard normal provides a poor approximation to the actual distribution of z. For $n = 100$, on the other hand, the approximation is not bad at all, although it is still noticeably skewed to the right.

Asymptotic Tests

The t and F tests that we discussed in the previous section are asymptotically valid under much weaker conditions than those needed to prove that they actually have their namesake distributions in finite samples. Suppose that the DGP is

$$\boldsymbol{y} = \boldsymbol{X\beta}_0 + \boldsymbol{u}, \quad \boldsymbol{u} \sim \mathrm{IID}(\mathbf{0}, \sigma_0^2\mathbf{I}), \tag{4.47}$$

where $\boldsymbol{\beta}_0$ satisfies whatever hypothesis is being tested, and the error terms are drawn from some specific but unknown distribution with mean 0 and variance σ_0^2. We allow $\boldsymbol{X}_t$ to contain lagged dependent variables, and so we abandon the assumption of exogenous regressors and replace it with assumption (3.10) from Section 3.2, plus an analogous assumption about the variance. These two assumptions can be written as

$$\mathrm{E}(u_t \,|\, \boldsymbol{X}_t) = 0 \quad \text{and} \quad \mathrm{E}(u_t^2 \,|\, \boldsymbol{X}_t) = \sigma_0^2. \tag{4.48}$$

The first of these assumptions, which is assumption (3.10), can be referred to in two ways. From the point of view of the error terms, it says that they are **innovations**. An innovation is a random variable of which the mean is 0 conditional on the information in the explanatory variables, and so knowledge of the values taken by the latter is of no use in predicting the mean of the innovation. From the point of view of the explanatory variables $\boldsymbol{X}_t$, assumption (3.10) says that they are **predetermined** with respect to the error terms. We thus have two different ways of saying the same thing. Both can be useful, depending on the circumstances.

Although we have greatly weakened the assumptions of the classical normal linear model, we now need to make an additional assumption in order to be able to use asymptotic results. We therefore assume that the data-generating process for the explanatory variables is such that

$$\operatorname*{plim}_{n\to\infty} \frac{1}{n} \boldsymbol{X}^{\top}\boldsymbol{X} = \boldsymbol{S}_{\boldsymbol{X}^{\top}\boldsymbol{X}}, \tag{4.49}$$

where $\boldsymbol{S}_{\boldsymbol{X}^{\top}\boldsymbol{X}}$ is a finite, deterministic, positive definite matrix. We made this assumption previously, in Section 3.3, when we proved that the OLS estimator is consistent. Although it is often reasonable, condition (4.49) is violated in many cases. For example, it cannot hold if one of the columns of the $\boldsymbol{X}$ matrix is a linear time trend, because $\sum_{t=1}^{n} t^2$ grows at a rate faster than n.

Now consider the t statistic (4.25) for testing the hypothesis that $\beta_2 = 0$ in the model (4.21). The key to proving that (4.25), or any test statistic, has a certain **asymptotic distribution** is to write it as a function of quantities to which we can apply either a LLN or a CLT. Therefore, we rewrite (4.25) as

$$t_{\beta_2} = \left(\frac{\boldsymbol{y}^{\top}\boldsymbol{M}_{\boldsymbol{X}}\boldsymbol{y}}{n-k}\right)^{-1/2} \frac{n^{-1/2}\boldsymbol{x}_2^{\top}\boldsymbol{M}_1\boldsymbol{y}}{(n^{-1}\boldsymbol{x}_2^{\top}\boldsymbol{M}_1\boldsymbol{x}_2)^{1/2}}, \tag{4.50}$$

where the numerator and denominator of the second factor have both been multiplied by $n^{-1/2}$. Under the DGP (4.47), $s^2 \equiv \boldsymbol{y}^{\top}\boldsymbol{M}_{\boldsymbol{X}}\boldsymbol{y}/(n-k)$ tends to σ_0^2 as $n \to \infty$. This statement, which is equivalent to saying that the OLS error variance estimator s^2 is consistent under our weaker assumptions, follows from a LLN, because s^2 has the form of an average, and the calculations leading to (3.49) showed that the mean of s^2 is σ_0^2. It follows from the consistency of s^2 that the first factor in (4.50) tends to $1/\sigma_0$ as $n \to \infty$. When the data are generated by (4.47) with $\beta_2 = 0$, we have that $\boldsymbol{M}_1\boldsymbol{y} = \boldsymbol{M}_1\boldsymbol{u}$, and so (4.50) is asymptotically equivalent to

$$\frac{n^{-1/2}\boldsymbol{x}_2^{\top}\boldsymbol{M}_1\boldsymbol{u}}{\sigma_0(n^{-1}\boldsymbol{x}_2^{\top}\boldsymbol{M}_1\boldsymbol{x}_2)^{1/2}}. \tag{4.51}$$

It is now easy to derive the asymptotic distribution of t_{β_2} if for a moment we reinstate the assumption that the regressors are exogenous. In that case, we can work conditionally on $\boldsymbol{X}$, which means that the only part of (4.51) that is treated as random is $\boldsymbol{u}$. The numerator of (4.51) is $n^{-1/2}$ times a weighted sum of the u_t, each of which has mean 0, and the conditional variance of this weighted sum is

$$\mathrm{E}(\boldsymbol{x}_2^{\top}\boldsymbol{M}_1\boldsymbol{u}\boldsymbol{u}^{\top}\boldsymbol{M}_1\boldsymbol{x}_2 \,|\, \boldsymbol{X}) = \sigma_0^2\boldsymbol{x}_2^{\top}\boldsymbol{M}_1\boldsymbol{x}_2.$$

Thus (4.51) evidently has mean 0 and variance 1, conditional on $\boldsymbol{X}$. But since 0 and 1 do not depend on $\boldsymbol{X}$, these are also the unconditional mean and variance of (4.51). Provided that we can apply a CLT to the numerator of (4.51), the numerator of t_{β_2} must be asymptotically normally distributed, and we conclude that, under the null hypothesis, with exogenous regressors,

$$t_{\beta_2} \overset{a}{\sim} \mathrm{N}(0, 1). \tag{4.52}$$

The notation "$\overset{a}{\sim}$" means that t_{β_2} is **asymptotically distributed** as $\mathrm{N}(0, 1)$. Since the DGP is assumed to be (4.47), this result does *not* require that the error terms be normally distributed.

The *t* Test with Predetermined Regressors

If we relax the assumption of exogenous regressors, the analysis becomes more complicated. Readers not interested in the algebraic details may well wish to skip to next section, since what follows is not essential for understanding the rest of this chapter. However, this subsection provides an excellent example of how asymptotic theory works, and it illustrates clearly just why we can relax some assumptions but not others.

We begin by applying a CLT to the k-vector

$$\boldsymbol{v} \equiv n^{-1/2}\boldsymbol{X}^{\top}\boldsymbol{u} = n^{-1/2}\sum_{t=1}^{n} u_t\boldsymbol{X}_t^{\top}. \tag{4.53}$$

By assumption (3.10), $\mathrm{E}(u_t \,|\, \boldsymbol{X}_t) = 0$. This implies that $\mathrm{E}(u_t\boldsymbol{X}_t^{\top}) = \boldsymbol{0}$, as required for the CLT, which then tells us that

$$\boldsymbol{v} \overset{a}{\sim} \mathrm{N}\Big(\boldsymbol{0}, \lim_{n\to\infty}\frac{1}{n}\sum_{t=1}^{n}\mathrm{Var}(u_t\boldsymbol{X}_t^{\top})\Big) = \mathrm{N}\Big(\boldsymbol{0}, \lim_{n\to\infty}\frac{1}{n}\sum_{t=1}^{n}\mathrm{E}(u_t^2\boldsymbol{X}_t^{\top}\boldsymbol{X}_t)\Big);$$

recall (4.46). Notice that, because $\boldsymbol{X}_t$ is a $1 \times k$ row vector, the covariance matrix here is $k \times k$, as it must be. The second assumption in (4.48) allows us to simplify the limiting covariance matrix:

$$\begin{aligned}\lim_{n\to\infty} \frac{1}{n}\sum_{t=1}^{n} \mathrm{E}(u_t^2 \boldsymbol{X}_t^\top \boldsymbol{X}_t) &= \lim_{n\to\infty} \sigma_0^2 \frac{1}{n}\sum_{t=1}^{n} \mathrm{E}(\boldsymbol{X}_t^\top \boldsymbol{X}_t) \\ &= \sigma_0^2 \operatorname*{plim}_{n\to\infty} \frac{1}{n}\sum_{t=1}^{n} \boldsymbol{X}_t^\top \boldsymbol{X}_t \\ &= \sigma_0^2 \operatorname*{plim}_{n\to\infty} \frac{1}{n} \boldsymbol{X}^\top \boldsymbol{X} = \sigma_0^2 \boldsymbol{S}_{\boldsymbol{X}^\top\boldsymbol{X}}.\end{aligned} \tag{4.54}$$

We applied a LLN in reverse to go from the first line to the second, and the last equality follows from (4.49).

Now consider the numerator of (4.51). It can be written as

$$n^{-1/2}\boldsymbol{x}_2^\top \boldsymbol{u} - n^{-1/2}\boldsymbol{x}_2^\top \boldsymbol{P}_1 \boldsymbol{u}. \tag{4.55}$$

The first term of this expression is just the last, or k^{th}, component of $\boldsymbol{v}$, which we can denote by v_2. By writing out the projection matrix $\boldsymbol{P}_1$ explicitly, and dividing various expressions by n in a way that cancels out, the second term can be rewritten as

$$n^{-1}\boldsymbol{x}_2^\top \boldsymbol{X}_1 (n^{-1}\boldsymbol{X}_1^\top \boldsymbol{X}_1)^{-1} n^{-1/2}\boldsymbol{X}_1^\top \boldsymbol{u}. \tag{4.56}$$

By assumption (4.49), the first and second factors of (4.56) tend to deterministic limits. In obvious notation, the first tends to $\boldsymbol{S}_{21}$, which is a submatrix of $\boldsymbol{S}_{\boldsymbol{X}^\top\boldsymbol{X}}$, and the second tends to $\boldsymbol{S}_{11}^{-1}$, which is the inverse of a submatrix of $\boldsymbol{S}_{\boldsymbol{X}^\top\boldsymbol{X}}$. Thus only the last factor remains random when $n \to \infty$. It is just the subvector of $\boldsymbol{v}$ consisting of the first $k-1$ components, which we denote by $\boldsymbol{v}_1$. Asymptotically, in partitioned matrix notation, (4.55) becomes

$$v_2 - \boldsymbol{S}_{21}\boldsymbol{S}_{11}^{-1}\boldsymbol{v}_1 = [\,-\boldsymbol{S}_{21}\boldsymbol{S}_{11}^{-1} \quad 1\,]\begin{bmatrix}\boldsymbol{v}_1 \\ v_2\end{bmatrix}.$$

Since $\boldsymbol{v}$ is asymptotically multivariate normal, this scalar expression is asymptotically normal, with mean zero and variance

$$\sigma_0^2\,[\,-\boldsymbol{S}_{21}\boldsymbol{S}_{11}^{-1} \quad 1\,]\,\boldsymbol{S}_{\boldsymbol{X}^\top\boldsymbol{X}}\begin{bmatrix}-\boldsymbol{S}_{11}^{-1}\boldsymbol{S}_{12} \\ 1\end{bmatrix},$$

where, since $\boldsymbol{S}_{\boldsymbol{X}^\top\boldsymbol{X}}$ is symmetric, $\boldsymbol{S}_{12}$ is just the transpose of $\boldsymbol{S}_{21}$. If we now express $\boldsymbol{S}_{\boldsymbol{X}^\top\boldsymbol{X}}$ as a partitioned matrix, the variance of (4.55) is seen to be

$$\sigma_0^2\,[\,-\boldsymbol{S}_{21}\boldsymbol{S}_{11}^{-1} \quad 1\,]\begin{bmatrix}\boldsymbol{S}_{11} & \boldsymbol{S}_{12} \\ \boldsymbol{S}_{21} & \boldsymbol{S}_{22}\end{bmatrix}\begin{bmatrix}-\boldsymbol{S}_{11}^{-1}\boldsymbol{S}_{12} \\ 1\end{bmatrix} = \sigma_0^2\bigl(\boldsymbol{S}_{22} - \boldsymbol{S}_{21}\boldsymbol{S}_{11}^{-1}\boldsymbol{S}_{12}\bigr). \tag{4.57}$$

The denominator of (4.51) is, thankfully, easier to analyze. The square of the second factor is

$$\begin{aligned} n^{-1}\boldsymbol{x}_2^{\top}\boldsymbol{M}_1\boldsymbol{x}_2 &= n^{-1}\boldsymbol{x}_2^{\top}\boldsymbol{x}_2 - n^{-1}\boldsymbol{x}_2^{\top}\boldsymbol{P}_1\boldsymbol{x}_2 \\ &= n^{-1}\boldsymbol{x}_2^{\top}\boldsymbol{x}_2 - n^{-1}\boldsymbol{x}_2^{\top}\boldsymbol{X}_1\big(n^{-1}\boldsymbol{X}_1^{\top}\boldsymbol{X}_1\big)^{-1}n^{-1}\boldsymbol{X}_1^{\top}\boldsymbol{x}_2. \end{aligned}$$

In the limit, all the pieces of this expression become submatrices of $\boldsymbol{S}_{\boldsymbol{X}^{\top}\boldsymbol{X}}$, and so we find that

$$n^{-1}\boldsymbol{x}_2^{\top}\boldsymbol{M}_1\boldsymbol{x}_2 \rightarrow \boldsymbol{S}_{22} - \boldsymbol{S}_{21}\boldsymbol{S}_{11}^{-1}\boldsymbol{S}_{12}.$$

When it is multiplied by σ_0^2, this is just (4.57), the variance of the numerator of expression (4.51). Thus, asymptotically, we have shown that t_{β_2} is the ratio of a normal random variable with mean zero to the standard deviation of that random variable. Consequently, we have established that, under the null hypothesis, with regressors that are not necessarily exogenous but merely predetermined, $t_{\beta_2} \overset{a}{\sim} \mathrm{N}(0,1)$. This result is what we previously obtained as (4.52) when we assumed that the regressors were exogenous.

Asymptotic *F* Tests

A similar analysis can be performed for the F statistic (4.33) for the null hypothesis that $\boldsymbol{\beta}_2 = \boldsymbol{0}$ in the model (4.28). Under the null, F_{β_2} is equal to expression (4.34), which can be rewritten as

$$\frac{n^{-1/2}\boldsymbol{\varepsilon}^{\top}\boldsymbol{M}_1\boldsymbol{X}_2(n^{-1}\boldsymbol{X}_2^{\top}\boldsymbol{M}_1\boldsymbol{X}_2)^{-1}n^{-1/2}\boldsymbol{X}_2^{\top}\boldsymbol{M}_1\boldsymbol{\varepsilon}/r}{\boldsymbol{\varepsilon}^{\top}\boldsymbol{M}_{\boldsymbol{X}}\boldsymbol{\varepsilon}/(n-k)}, \tag{4.58}$$

where $\boldsymbol{\varepsilon} \equiv \boldsymbol{u}/\sigma_0$. It is not hard to use the results we obtained for the t statistic to show that, as $n \rightarrow \infty$,

$$rF_{\beta_2} \overset{a}{\sim} \chi^2(r) \tag{4.59}$$

under the null hypothesis; see Exercise 4.13. Since $1/r$ times a random variable that follows the $\chi^2(r)$ distribution is distributed as $F(r,\infty)$, we can also conclude that $F_{\beta_2} \overset{a}{\sim} F(r, n-k)$.

The results (4.52) and (4.59) justify the use of t and F tests outside the confines of the classical normal linear model. We can compute P values using either the standard normal or t distributions in the case of t statistics, and either the χ^2 or F distributions in the case of F statistics. Of course, if we use the χ^2 distribution, we have to multiply the F statistic by r.

Whatever distribution we use, these P values are approximate, and tests based on them are not exact in finite samples. In addition, our theoretical results do not tell us just how accurate they are. If we decide to use a nominal level of α for a test, we reject if the approximate P value is less than α. In many cases, but certainly not all, such tests are probably quite accurate, committing Type I errors with probability reasonably close to α. They may either **overreject**, that is, reject the null hypothesis more than $100\alpha\%$ of the time when it is true, or **underreject**, that is, reject the null hypothesis less than $100\alpha\%$ of the time. Whether they overreject or underreject, and how severely, depends on many things, including the sample size, the distribution of the error terms, the number of regressors and their properties, and the relationship between the error terms and the regressors.

4.6 Simulation-Based Tests

When we introduced the concept of a test statistic in Section 4.2, we specified that it should have a known distribution under the null hypothesis. In the previous section, we relaxed this requirement and developed large-sample test statistics for which the distribution is known only approximately. In all the cases we have studied, the distribution of the statistic under the null hypothesis was not only (approximately) known, but also the *same* for all DGPs contained in the null hypothesis. This is a very important property, and it is useful to introduce some terminology that will allow us to formalize it.

We begin with a simple remark. A hypothesis, null or alternative, can always be represented by a *model*, that is, a set of DGPs. For instance, the null and alternative hypotheses (4.29) and (4.28) associated with an F test of several restrictions are both classical normal linear models. The most fundamental sort of null hypothesis that we can test is a **simple hypothesis**. Such a hypothesis is represented by a model that contains one and only one DGP. Simple hypotheses are very rare in econometrics. The usual case is that of a **compound hypothesis**, which is represented by a model that contains more than one DGP. This can cause serious problems. Except in certain special cases, such as the exact tests in the classical normal linear model that we investigated in Section 4.4, a test statistic has different distributions under the different DGPs contained in the model. In such a case, if we do not know just which DGP in the model generated our data, then we cannot know the distribution of the test statistic.

If a test statistic is to have a known distribution under some given null hypothesis, then it must have the same distribution for each and every DGP contained in that null hypothesis. A random variable with the property that its distribution is the same for all DGPs in a model $\mathbb{M}$ is said to be **pivotal**, or to be a **pivot**, for the model $\mathbb{M}$. The distribution is allowed to depend on the sample size, and perhaps on the observed values of exogenous variables. However, for any given sample size and set of exogenous variables, it must be invariant across all DGPs in $\mathbb{M}$. Note that *all* test statistics are pivotal for a simple null hypothesis.

The large sample tests considered in the last section allow for null hypotheses that do not respect the rigid constraints of the classical normal linear model.

The price they pay for this added generality is that t and F statistics now have distributions that depend on things like the error distribution: They are therefore not pivotal statistics. However, their *asymptotic* distributions are independent of such things, and are thus invariant across all the DGPs of the model that represents the null hypothesis. Such statistics are said to be **asymptotically pivotal**, or **asymptotic pivots**, for that model.

Simulated P Values

The distributions of the test statistics studied in Section 4.3 are all thoroughly known, and their CDFs can easily be evaluated by computer programs. The computation of P values is therefore straightforward. Even if it were not, we could always estimate them by simulation. For any pivotal test statistic, the P value can be estimated by simulation to any desired level of accuracy. Since a pivotal statistic has the same distribution for all DGPs in the model under test, we can arbitrarily choose any such DGP for generating simulated samples and simulated test statistics.

The theoretical justification for using simulation to estimate P values is the Fundamental Theorem of Statistics, which we discussed in Section 4.5. It tells us that the empirical distribution of a set of independent drawings of a random variable generated by some DGP converges to the true CDF of the random variable under that DGP. This is just as true of simulated drawings generated by the computer as for random variables generated by a natural random mechanism. Thus, if we knew that a certain test statistic was pivotal but did not know how it was distributed, we could select any DGP in the null model and generate simulated samples from it. For each of these, we could then compute the test statistic. If the simulated samples are mutually independent, the set of simulated test statistics thus generated constitutes a set of independent drawings from the distribution of the test statistic, and their EDF is a consistent estimate of the CDF of that distribution.

Suppose that we have computed a test statistic $\hat{\tau}$, which could be a t statistic, an F statistic, or some other type of test statistic, using some data set with n observations. We can think of $\hat{\tau}$ as being a realization of a random variable τ. We wish to test a null hypothesis represented by a model $\mathbb{M}$ for which τ is pivotal, and we want to reject the null whenever $\hat{\tau}$ is sufficiently large, as in the cases of an F statistic, a t statistic when the rejection region is in the upper tail, or a squared t statistic. If we denote by F the CDF of the distribution of τ under the null hypothesis, the P value for a test based on $\hat{\tau}$ is

$$p(\hat{\tau}) \equiv 1 - F(\hat{\tau}). \tag{4.60}$$

Since $\hat{\tau}$ is computed directly from our original data, this P value can be estimated if we can estimate the CDF F evaluated at $\hat{\tau}$.

The procedure we are about to describe is very general in its application, and so we describe it in detail. In order to estimate a P value by simulation, we choose any DGP in $\mathbb{M}$, and draw B samples of size n from it. How to choose B will be discussed shortly; it is typically rather large, and $B = 999$ may often be a reasonable choice. We denote the simulated samples as $\boldsymbol{y}_j^*$, $j = 1, \ldots, B$. The star (*) notation will be used systematically to denote quantities generated by simulation. B is used to denote the number of simulations in order to emphasize the connection with the bootstrap, which we will discuss below.

Using the simulated sample, for each j we compute a simulated test statistic, say τ_j^*, in exactly the same way that $\hat{\tau}$ was computed from the original data $\boldsymbol{y}$. We can then construct the EDF of the τ_j^* analogously to (4.44):

$$\hat{F}^*(x) = \frac{1}{B}\sum_{j=1}^{B} I(\tau_j^* \leq x). \tag{4.61}$$

Our estimate of the true P value (4.60) is therefore

$$\hat{p}^*(\hat{\tau}) = 1 - \hat{F}^*(\hat{\tau}) = 1 - \frac{1}{B}\sum_{j=1}^{B} I(\tau_j^* \leq \hat{\tau}) = \frac{1}{B}\sum_{j=1}^{B} I(\tau_j^* > \hat{\tau}). \tag{4.62}$$

The third equality in (4.62) can be understood by noting that the rightmost expression is the proportion of simulations for which τ_j^* is greater than $\hat{\tau}$, while the second expression from the right is 1 minus the proportion for which τ_j^* is less than or equal to $\hat{\tau}$. These proportions are obviously the same.

We can see that $\hat{p}^*(\hat{\tau})$ must lie between 0 and 1, as any P value must. For example, if $B = 999$, and 36 of the τ_j^* were greater than $\hat{\tau}$, we would have $\hat{p}^*(\hat{\tau}) = 36/999 = .036$. In this case, since $\hat{p}^*(\hat{\tau})$ is less than .05, we would reject the null hypothesis at the .05 level. Since the EDF converges to the true CDF, it follows that, if B were infinitely large, this procedure would yield an exact test, and the outcome of the test would be the same as if we computed the P value analytically using the CDF of τ. In fact, as we will see shortly, this procedure yields an exact test even for certain finite values of B.

The sort of test we have just described, based on simulating a pivotal statistic, is called a **Monte Carlo test**; Dufour and Khalaf (2001) provides a more detailed introduction and references. Simulation experiments in general are often referred to as **Monte Carlo experiments**, because they involve generating random numbers, as do the games played in casinos. Around the time that computer simulations first became possible, the most famous casino was the one in Monte Carlo. If computers had been developed just a little later, we would probably be talking now of Las Vegas tests and Las Vegas experiments.

Random Number Generators

Drawing a simulated sample of size n requires us to generate at least n random, or pseudo-random, numbers. As we mentioned in Section 1.3, a **random number generator**, or **RNG**, is a program for generating random numbers.

Most such programs generate numbers that appear to be drawings from the uniform U(0, 1) distribution, which can then be transformed into drawings from other distributions. There is a large literature on RNGs, to which Press, Teukolsky, Vetterling, and Flannery (1992a; 1992b, Chapter 7) provides an accessible introduction. See also Knuth (1998, Chapter 3) and Gentle (1998).

Although there are many types of RNG, the most common are variants of the **linear congruential generator**,

$$z_i = \lambda z_{i-1} + c \;[\text{mod } m], \quad \eta_i = \frac{z_i}{m}, \quad i = 1, 2, \ldots, \tag{4.63}$$

where η_i is the ith random number generated, and m, λ, c, and so also the z_i, are positive integers. The notation [mod m] means that we divide what precedes it by m and retain the remainder. This generator starts with a (generally large) positive integer z_0 called the **seed**, multiplies it by λ, and then adds c to obtain an integer that may well be bigger than m. It then obtains z_1 as the remainder from division by m. To generate the next random number, the process is repeated with z_1 replacing z_0, and so on. At each stage, the actual random number output by the generator is z_i/m, which, since $0 \leq z_i \leq m$, lies in the interval $[0, 1]$. For a given generator defined by λ, m, and c, the sequence of random numbers depends entirely on the seed. If we provide the generator with the same seed, we get the same sequence of numbers.

How well or badly this procedure works depends on how λ, m, and c are chosen. On 32-bit computers, many commonly used generators set $c = 0$ and use for m a prime number that is either a little less than 2^{32} or a little less than 2^{31}. When $c = 0$, the generator is said to be **multiplicative congruential**. The parameter λ, which should be large but substantially smaller than m, must be chosen so as to satisfy some technical conditions. When λ and m are chosen properly with $c = 0$, the RNG has a **period** of $m - 1$. This means that it generates every rational number with denominator m between $1/m$ and $(m - 1)/m$ precisely once until, after $m - 1$ steps, z_0 comes up again. After that, the generator repeats itself, producing the same $m - 1$ numbers in the same order each time.

Unfortunately, many random number generators, whether or not they are of the linear congruential variety, perform poorly. The random numbers they generate may fail to be independent in all sorts of ways, and the period may be relatively short. In the case of multiplicative congruential generators, this means that λ and m have not been chosen properly. See Gentle (1998) and the other references cited above for discussion of bad random number generators. Toy examples of multiplicative congruential generators are examined in Exercise 4.19, where the choice of λ and m is seen to matter.

There are several ways to generate drawings from a normal distribution if we can generate random numbers from the U(0, 1) distribution. The simplest, but not the fastest, is to use the fact that, if η_i is distributed as U(0, 1), then $\Phi^{-1}(\eta_i)$ is distributed as N(0, 1); this follows from the result of Exercise 4.20.

Most of the random number generators available in econometrics software packages use faster algorithms to generate drawings from the standard normal distribution, usually in a way entirely transparent to the user, who merely has to ask for so many independent drawings from $N(0, 1)$. Drawings from $N(\mu, \sigma^2)$ can then be obtained by use of the formula (4.09).

Bootstrap Tests

Although pivotal test statistics do arise from time to time, most test statistics in econometrics are not pivotal. The vast majority of them are, however, asymptotically pivotal. If a test statistic has a known asymptotic distribution that does not depend on anything unobservable, as do t and F statistics under the relatively weak assumptions of Section 4.5, then it is certainly asymptotically pivotal. Even if it does not follow a known asymptotic distribution, a test statistic may be asymptotically pivotal.

A statistic that is not an exact pivot cannot be used for a Monte Carlo test. However, approximate P values for statistics that are only asymptotically pivotal, or even nonpivotal, can be obtained by a simulation method called the **bootstrap**. This method can be a valuable alternative to the large sample tests based on asymptotic theory that we discussed in the previous section. The term **bootstrap**, which was introduced to statistics by Efron (1979), is taken from the phrase "to pull oneself up by one's own bootstraps." Although the link between this improbable activity and simulated P values is tenuous at best, the term is by now firmly established. We will speak of **bootstrapping** in order to obtain **bootstrap samples**, from which we compute **bootstrap test statistics** that have **bootstrap distributions** given by (4.61), which can be used to perform **bootstrap tests** on the basis of **bootstrap *P* values**, and so on.

The difference between a Monte Carlo test and a bootstrap test is that for the former, the DGP is assumed to be known, whereas, for the latter, it is necessary to estimate a **bootstrap DGP** from which to draw the simulated samples. Unless the null hypothesis under test is a simple hypothesis, the DGP that generated the original data is unknown, and so it cannot be used to generate simulated data. The bootstrap DGP is an estimate of the unknown true DGP. The hope is that, if the bootstrap DGP is close, in some sense, to the true one, then data generated by the bootstrap DGP will be similar to data that would have been generated by the true DGP, if it were known. If so, then a simulated P value obtained by use of the bootstrap DGP is close enough to the true P value to allow accurate inference.

Even for models as simple as the linear regression model, there are many ways to specify the bootstrap DGP. The key requirement is that it should satisfy the restrictions of the null hypothesis. If this is assured, then how well a bootstrap test performs in finite samples depends on how good an estimate the bootstrap DGP is of the process that would have generated the test statistic if the null hypothesis were true. In the next subsection, we discuss bootstrap DGPs for regression models.

Bootstrap DGPs for Regression Models

If the null and alternative hypotheses are regression models, the simplest approach is to estimate the model that corresponds to the null hypothesis and then use the estimates to generate the bootstrap samples, under the assumption that the error terms are normally distributed. We considered examples of such procedures in Section 1.3 and in Exercise 1.24.

Since bootstrapping is quite unnecessary in the context of the classical normal linear model, we will take for our example a linear regression model with normal errors, but with a lagged dependent variable among the regressors:

$$y_t = \boldsymbol{X}_t\boldsymbol{\beta} + \boldsymbol{Z}_t\boldsymbol{\gamma} + \delta y_{t-1} + u_t, \quad u_t \sim \text{NID}(0, \sigma^2), \tag{4.64}$$

where $\boldsymbol{X}_t$ and $\boldsymbol{\beta}$ each have $k_1 - 1$ elements, $\boldsymbol{Z}_t$ and $\boldsymbol{\gamma}$ each have k_2 elements, and the null hypothesis is that $\boldsymbol{\gamma} = \mathbf{0}$. Thus the model that represents the null is

$$y_t = \boldsymbol{X}_t\boldsymbol{\beta} + \delta y_{t-1} + u_t, \quad u_t \sim \text{NID}(0, \sigma^2). \tag{4.65}$$

The observations are assumed to be indexed in such a way that y_0 is observed, along with n observations on y_t, $\boldsymbol{X}_t$, and $\boldsymbol{Z}_t$ for $t = 1, \ldots, n$. By estimating the models (4.64) and (4.65) by OLS, we can compute the F statistic for $\boldsymbol{\gamma} = \mathbf{0}$, which we will call $\hat{\tau}$. Because the regression function contains a lagged dependent variable, however, the F test based on $\hat{\tau}$ is not exact.

The model (4.65) is a fully specified parametric model, which means that each set of parameter values for $\boldsymbol{\beta}$, δ, and σ^2 defines just one DGP. The simplest type of bootstrap DGP for fully specified models is given by the **parametric bootstrap**. The first step in constructing a parametric bootstrap DGP is to estimate (4.65) by OLS, yielding the restricted estimates $\tilde{\boldsymbol{\beta}}$, $\tilde{\delta}$, and $\tilde{s}^2 \equiv \text{SSR}(\tilde{\boldsymbol{\beta}}, \tilde{\delta})/(n - k_1)$. Then the bootstrap DGP is given by

$$y_t^* = \boldsymbol{X}_t\tilde{\boldsymbol{\beta}} + \tilde{\delta} y_{t-1}^* + u_t^*, \quad u_t^* \sim \text{NID}(0, \tilde{s}^2), \tag{4.66}$$

which is just the element of the model (4.65) characterized by the parameter estimates under the null, with stars to indicate that the data are simulated.

In order to draw a bootstrap sample from the bootstrap DGP (4.66), we first draw an n-vector $\boldsymbol{u}^*$ from the $\text{N}(\mathbf{0}, \tilde{s}^2\mathbf{I})$ distribution. The presence of a lagged dependent variable implies that the bootstrap samples must be constructed **recursively**. This is necessary because y_t^*, the tth element of the bootstrap sample, must depend on y_{t-1}^* and not on y_{t-1} from the original data. The recursive rule for generating a bootstrap sample is

$$\begin{aligned}
y_1^* &= \boldsymbol{X}_1\tilde{\boldsymbol{\beta}} + \tilde{\delta} y_0 + u_1^* \\
y_2^* &= \boldsymbol{X}_2\tilde{\boldsymbol{\beta}} + \tilde{\delta} y_1^* + u_2^* \\
\vdots \;\; & \;\;\; \vdots \qquad\; \vdots \qquad \vdots \\
y_n^* &= \boldsymbol{X}_n\tilde{\boldsymbol{\beta}} + \tilde{\delta} y_{n-1}^* + u_n^*.
\end{aligned} \tag{4.67}$$

Notice that every bootstrap sample is conditional on the observed value of y_0. There are other ways of dealing with pre-sample values of the dependent variable, but this is certainly the most convenient, and it may, in many circumstances, be the only method that is feasible.

The rest of the procedure for computing a bootstrap P value is identical to the one for computing a simulated P value for a Monte Carlo test. For each of the B bootstrap samples, $\boldsymbol{y}_j^*$, a bootstrap test statistic τ_j^* is computed from $\boldsymbol{y}_j^*$ in just the same way as $\hat{\tau}$ was computed from the original data, $\boldsymbol{y}$. The bootstrap P value $\hat{p}^*(\hat{\tau})$ is then computed by formula (4.62).

A Nonparametric Bootstrap DGP

The parametric bootstrap procedure that we have just described, based on the DGP (4.66), does not allow us to relax the strong assumption that the error terms are normally distributed. How can we construct a satisfactory bootstrap DGP if we extend the models (4.64) and (4.65) to admit nonnormal errors? If we knew the true error distribution, whether or not it was normal, we could always generate the $\boldsymbol{u}^*$ from it. Since we do not know it, we will have to find some way to estimate this distribution.

Under the null hypothesis, the OLS residual vector $\tilde{\boldsymbol{u}}$ for the restricted model is a consistent estimator of the error vector $\boldsymbol{u}$. This is an immediate consequence of the consistency of the OLS estimator itself. In the particular case of model (4.65), we have for each t that

$$\operatorname*{plim}_{n\to\infty} \tilde{u}_t = \operatorname*{plim}_{n\to\infty} \big(y_t - \boldsymbol{X}_t\tilde{\boldsymbol{\beta}} - \tilde{\delta} y_{t-1}\big) = y_t - \boldsymbol{X}_t\boldsymbol{\beta}_0 - \delta_0 y_{t-1} = u_t,$$

where $\boldsymbol{\beta}_0$ and δ_0 are the parameter values for the true DGP. This means that, if the u_t are mutually independent drawings from the error distribution, then so are the residuals $\tilde{u}_t$, asymptotically.

From the Fundamental Theorem of Statistics, we know that the empirical distribution function of the error terms is a consistent estimator of the unknown CDF of the error distribution. Because the residuals consistently estimate the errors, it follows that the EDF of the residuals is also a consistent estimator of the CDF of the error distribution. Thus, if we draw bootstrap error terms from the empirical distribution of the residuals, we are drawing them from a distribution that tends to the true error distribution as $n \to \infty$. This is completely analogous to using estimated parameters in the bootstrap DGP that tend to the true parameters as $n \to \infty$.

Drawing simulated error terms from the empirical distribution of the residuals is called **resampling**. In order to **resample the residuals**, all the residuals are, metaphorically speaking, thrown into a hat and then randomly pulled out one at a time, with replacement. Thus each bootstrap sample contains some of the residuals exactly once, some of them more than once, and some of them not at all. Therefore, the value of each drawing must be the value of one of the residuals, with equal probability for each residual. This is precisely what we mean by the empirical distribution of the residuals.

To resample concretely rather than metaphorically, we can proceed as follows. First, we draw a random number η from the U(0, 1) distribution. Then we divide the interval $[0, 1]$ into n subintervals of length $1/n$ and associate each of these subintervals with one of the integers between 1 and n. When η falls into the lth subinterval, we choose the index l, and our random drawing is the lth residual. Repeating this procedure n times yields a single set of bootstrap error terms drawn from the empirical distribution of the residuals.

As an example of how resampling works, suppose that $n = 10$, and the ten residuals are

$$6.45,\ 1.28,\ -3.48,\ 2.44,\ -5.17,\ -1.67,\ -2.03,\ 3.58,\ 0.74,\ -2.14.$$

Notice that these numbers sum to zero. Now suppose that, when forming one of the bootstrap samples, the ten drawings from the U(0, 1) distribution happen to be

$$0.631,\ 0.277,\ 0.745,\ 0.202,\ 0.914,\ 0.136,\ 0.851,\ 0.878,\ 0.120,\ 0.259.$$

This implies that the ten index values are

$$7,\ 3,\ 8,\ 3,\ 10,\ 2,\ 9,\ 9,\ 2,\ 3.$$

Therefore, the error terms for this bootstrap sample are

$$-2.03,\ -3.48,\ 3.58,\ -3.48,\ -2.14,\ 1.28,\ 0.74,\ 0.74,\ 1.28,\ -3.48.$$

Some of the residuals appear just once in this particular sample, some of them (numbers 2, 3, and 9) appear more than once, and some of them (numbers 1, 4, 5, and 6) do not appear at all. On average, however, each of the residuals appears once in each of the bootstrap samples.

If we adopt this resampling procedure, we can write the bootstrap DGP as

$$y_t^* = \boldsymbol{X}_t\tilde{\boldsymbol{\beta}} + \tilde{\delta}y_{t-1}^* + u_t^*, \quad u_t^* \sim \text{EDF}(\tilde{\boldsymbol{u}}), \tag{4.68}$$

where $\text{EDF}(\tilde{\boldsymbol{u}})$ denotes the distribution that assigns probability $1/n$ to each of the elements of the residual vector $\tilde{\boldsymbol{u}}$. The DGP (4.68) is one form of what is usually called a **nonparametric bootstrap**, although, since it still uses the parameter estimates $\tilde{\boldsymbol{\beta}}$ and $\tilde{\delta}$, it should really be called **semiparametric** rather than nonparametric. Once bootstrap error terms have been drawn by resampling, bootstrap samples can be created by the recursive procedure (4.67).

The empirical distribution of the residuals may fail to satisfy some of the properties that the null hypothesis imposes on the true error distribution, and so the DGP (4.68) may fail to belong to the null hypothesis. One case in which this failure has grave consequences arises when the regression (4.65) does not contain a constant term, because then the sample mean of the residuals is not, in general, equal to 0. The expectation of the EDF of the residuals is simply their sample mean; recall Exercise 1.1. Thus, if the bootstrap error terms are drawn from a distribution with nonzero mean, the bootstrap DGP lies outside the null hypothesis. It is, of course, simple to correct this problem. We just need to *center* the residuals before throwing them into the hat, by subtracting their mean $\bar{u}$. When we do this, the bootstrap errors are drawn from $\text{EDF}(\tilde{\boldsymbol{u}} - \bar{u}\boldsymbol{\iota})$, a distribution that does indeed have mean 0.

A somewhat similar argument gives rise to an improved bootstrap DGP. If the sample mean of the restricted residuals is 0, then the variance of their empirical distribution is the second moment $n^{-1}\sum_{t=1}^{n}\tilde{u}_t^2$. Thus, by using the definition (3.49) of $\tilde{s}^2$ in Section 3.6, we see that the variance of the empirical distribution of the residuals is $\tilde{s}^2(n-k_1)/n$. Since we do not know the value of σ_0^2, we cannot draw from a distribution with exactly that variance. However, as with the parametric bootstrap (4.66), we can at least draw from a distribution with variance $\tilde{s}^2$. This is easy to do by drawing from the EDF of the **rescaled residuals**, which are obtained by multiplying the OLS residuals by $(n/(n-k_1))^{1/2}$. If we resample these rescaled residuals, the bootstrap error distribution is

$$\text{EDF}\left(\left(\frac{n}{n-k_1}\right)^{1/2}\tilde{\boldsymbol{u}}\right), \tag{4.69}$$

which has variance $\tilde{s}^2$. A somewhat more complicated approach, based on the result (3.44), is explored in Exercise 4.21.

Although they may seem strange, these resampling procedures often work astonishingly well, except perhaps when the sample size is very small or the distribution of the error terms is very unusual; see Exercise 4.24. If the distribution of the error terms displays substantial skewness (that is, a nonzero third moment) or excess kurtosis (that is, a fourth moment greater than $3\sigma_0^4$), then there is a good chance that the EDF of the recentered and rescaled residuals does so as well.

Other methods for bootstrapping regression models nonparametrically and semiparametrically are discussed by Efron and Tibshirani (1993), Davison and Hinkley (1997), and Horowitz (2001), which also discuss many other aspects of the bootstrap. A more advanced book, which deals primarily with the relationship between asymptotic theory and the bootstrap, is Hall (1992).

How Many Bootstraps?

Suppose that we wish to perform a bootstrap test at level α. Then B should be chosen to satisfy the condition that $\alpha(B+1)$ is an integer. If $\alpha = .05$, the values of B that satisfy this condition are 19, 39, 59, and so on. If $\alpha = .01$, they are 99, 199, 299, and so on. It is illuminating to see why B should be chosen in this way.

Imagine that we sort the original test statistic $\hat{\tau}$ and the B bootstrap statistics τ_j^*, $j = 1, \ldots, B$, in decreasing order. If τ is pivotal, then, under the null hypothesis, these are all independent drawings from the same distribution. Thus the rank r of $\hat{\tau}$ in the sorted set can have $B+1$ possible values, $r = 0, 1, \ldots, B$, all of them equally likely under the null hypothesis if τ is pivotal. Here, r is defined in such a way that there are exactly r simulations for which $\tau_j^* > \hat{\tau}$. Thus, if $r = 0$, $\hat{\tau}$ is the largest value in the set, and if $r = B$, it is the smallest. The estimated P value $\hat{p}^*(\hat{\tau})$ is just r/B.

The bootstrap test rejects if $r/B < \alpha$, that is, if $r < \alpha B$. Under the null, the probability that this inequality is satisfied is the proportion of the $B+1$ possible values of r that satisfy it. If we denote by $[\alpha B]$ the largest integer that is smaller than αB, it is easy to see that there are exactly $[\alpha B] + 1$ such values of r, namely, $0, 1, \ldots, [\alpha B]$. Thus the probability of rejection is $([\alpha B] + 1)/(B + 1)$. If we equate this probability to α, we find that

$$\alpha(B + 1) = [\alpha B] + 1.$$

Since the right-hand side of this equality is the sum of two integers, this equality can hold only if $\alpha(B+1)$ is an integer. Moreover, it holds whenever $\alpha(B+1)$ is an integer. Therefore, the Type I error is precisely α if and only if $\alpha(B+1)$ is an integer. Although this reasoning is rigorous only if τ is an exact pivot, experience shows that bootstrap P values based on nonpivotal statistics are less misleading if $\alpha(B+1)$ is an integer.

As a concrete example, suppose that $\alpha = .05$ and $B = 99$. Then there are 5 out of 100 values of r, namely, $r = 0, 1, \ldots, 4$, that would lead us to reject the null hypothesis. Since these are equally likely if the test statistic is pivotal, we make a Type I error precisely 5% of the time, and the test is exact. But suppose instead that $B = 89$. Since the same 5 values of r would still lead us to reject the null, we would now do so with probability $5/90 = .0556$.

It is important that B be sufficiently large, since two problems can arise if it is not. The first problem is that the outcome of the test depends on the sequence of random numbers used to generate the bootstrap samples. Different investigators may therefore obtain different results, even though they are using the same data and testing the same hypothesis. The second problem, which we will discuss in the next section, is that the ability of a bootstrap test to reject a false null hypothesis declines as B becomes smaller. As a rule of thumb, we suggest choosing $B = 999$. If calculating the τ_j^* is inexpensive and the outcome of the test is at all ambiguous, it may be desirable to use a larger value, like 9,999. On the other hand, if calculating the τ_j^* is very expensive and the outcome of the test is unambiguous, because $\hat{p}^*$ is far from α, it may be safe to use a value as small as 99.

It is not actually necessary to choose B in advance. An alternative approach, which is a bit more complicated but can save a lot of computer time, has been proposed by Davidson and MacKinnon (2000). The idea is to calculate a sequence of estimated P values, based on increasing values of B, and to stop as soon as the estimate $\hat{p}^*$ allows us to be very confident that p^* is either greater or less than α. For example, we might start with $B = 99$, then perform an additional 100 simulations if we cannot be sure whether or not to reject the null hypothesis, then perform an additional 200 simulations if we still cannot be sure, and so on. Eventually, we either stop when we are confident that the null hypothesis should or should not be rejected, or when B has become so large that we cannot afford to continue.

Bootstrap Versus Asymptotic Tests

Although bootstrap tests based on test statistics that are merely asymptotically pivotal are not exact, there are strong theoretical reasons to believe that they generally perform better than tests based on approximate asymptotic distributions. The errors committed by both asymptotic and bootstrap tests diminish as n increases, but those committed by bootstrap tests diminish more rapidly. The fundamental theoretical result on this point is due to Beran (1988). The results of a number of Monte Carlo experiments have provided strong support for this proposition. References include Horowitz (1994), Godfrey (1998), and Davidson and MacKinnon (1999a, 1999b, 2002a).

We can illustrate this by means of an example. Consider the following simple special case of the linear regression model (4.64)

$$y_t = \beta_1 + \beta_2 x_t + \beta_3 y_{t-1} + u_t, \quad u_t \sim \mathrm{N}(0, \sigma^2), \tag{4.70}$$

where the null hypothesis is that $\beta_3 = 0.9$. A Monte Carlo experiment to investigate the properties of tests of this hypothesis would work as follows. First, we fix a DGP in the model (4.70) by choosing values for the parameters. Here $\beta_3 = 0.9$, and so we investigate only what happens under the null hypothesis. For each **replication**, we generate an artificial data set from our chosen DGP and compute the ordinary t statistic for $\beta_3 = 0.9$. We then compute three P values. The first of these, for the asymptotic test, is computed using the Student's t distribution with $n - 3$ degrees of freedom, and the other two are bootstrap P values from the parametric and semiparametric bootstraps, with residuals rescaled using (4.69), for $B = 199$.[7] We perform many replications and record the frequencies with which tests based on the three P values reject at the .05 level. Figure 4.8 shows the rejection frequencies based on 500,000 replications for each of 31 sample sizes: $n = 10, 12, 14, \ldots, 60$.

The results of this experiment are striking. The asymptotic test overrejects quite noticeably, although it gradually improves as n increases. In contrast,

[7] We used $B = 199$, a smaller value than we would ever recommend using in practice, in order to reduce the costs of doing the Monte Carlo experiments. Because experimental errors tend to cancel out across replications, this does not materially affect the results of the experiments.

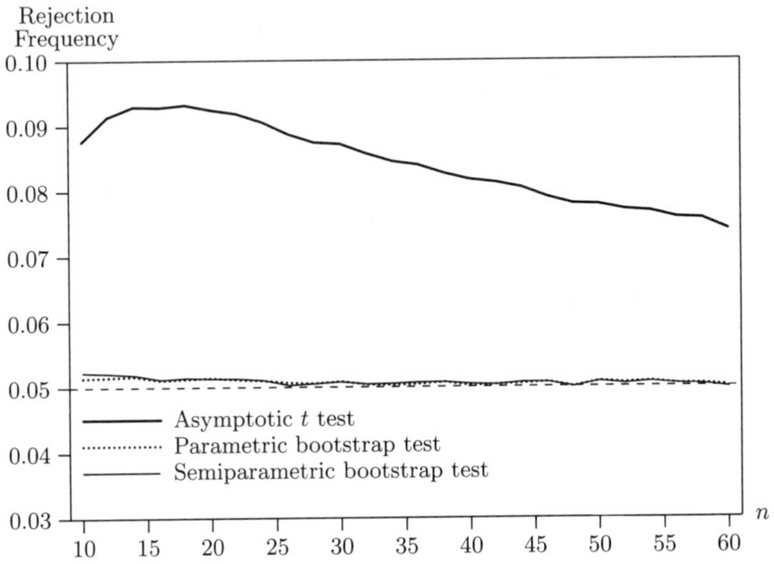

Figure 4.8 Rejection frequencies for bootstrap and asymptotic tests

the two bootstrap tests overreject only very slightly. Their rejection frequencies are always very close to the nominal level of .05, and they approach that level quite quickly as n increases. For the very smallest sample sizes, the parametric bootstrap seems to outperform the semiparametric one, but, for most sample sizes, there is nothing to choose between them.

This example is, perhaps, misleading in one respect. For linear regression models, asymptotic t and F tests generally do not perform as badly as the asymptotic t test does here. For example, the t test for $\beta_3 = 0$ in (4.70) performs much better than the t test for $\beta_3 = 0.9$; it actually underrejects moderately in small samples. However, the example is not at all misleading in suggesting that bootstrap tests often perform extraordinarily well, even when the corresponding asymptotic test does not perform well at all.

4.7 The Power of Hypothesis Tests

To be useful, hypothesis tests must be able to discriminate between the null hypothesis and the alternative. Thus, as we saw in Section 4.2, the distribution of a useful test statistic under the null is different from its distribution when the DGP does not belong to the null. Whenever a DGP places most of the probability mass of the test statistic in the rejection region of a test, the test has high **power**, that is, a high probability of rejecting the null.

For a variety of reasons, it is important to know something about the power of the tests we employ. If a test with high power fails to reject the null, this tells us more than if a test with lower power fails to do so. In practice, more than one test of a given null hypothesis is usually available. Of two equally reliable tests, if one has more power than the other against the alternatives in which we are interested, then we would surely prefer to employ the more powerful one.

The Power of Exact Tests

In Section 4.4, we saw that an F statistic is a ratio of the squared norms of two vectors, each divided by its appropriate number of degrees of freedom. In the notation of that section, these vectors are, for the numerator, $\boldsymbol{P}_{\boldsymbol{M}_1\boldsymbol{X}_2}\boldsymbol{y}$, and, for the denominator, $\boldsymbol{M}_{\boldsymbol{X}}\boldsymbol{y}$. If the null and alternative hypotheses are classical normal linear models, as we assume throughout this subsection, then, under the null, both the numerator and the denominator of this ratio are independent χ^2 variables, divided by their respective degrees of freedom; recall (4.34). Under the alternative hypothesis, the distribution of the denominator is unchanged, because, under either hypothesis, $\boldsymbol{M}_{\boldsymbol{X}}\boldsymbol{y} = \boldsymbol{M}_{\boldsymbol{X}}\boldsymbol{u}$. Consequently, the difference in distribution under the null and the alternative that gives the test its power must come from the numerator alone.

From (4.33), r/σ^2 times the numerator of the F statistic $F_{\boldsymbol{\beta}_2}$ is

$$\frac{1}{\sigma^2}\boldsymbol{y}^{\top}\boldsymbol{M}_1\boldsymbol{X}_2(\boldsymbol{X}_2^{\top}\boldsymbol{M}_1\boldsymbol{X}_2)^{-1}\boldsymbol{X}_2^{\top}\boldsymbol{M}_1\boldsymbol{y}. \tag{4.71}$$

The vector $\boldsymbol{X}_2^{\top}\boldsymbol{M}_1\boldsymbol{y}$ is normal under both the null and the alternative. Its mean is $\boldsymbol{X}_2^{\top}\boldsymbol{M}_1\boldsymbol{X}_2\boldsymbol{\beta}_2$, which vanishes under the null when $\boldsymbol{\beta}_2 = \mathbf{0}$, and its covariance matrix is $\sigma^2\boldsymbol{X}_2^{\top}\boldsymbol{M}_1\boldsymbol{X}_2$. We can use these facts to determine the distribution of the quadratic form (4.71). To do so, we must introduce the **noncentral chi-squared distribution**, which is a generalization of the ordinary, or **central**, chi-squared distribution.

We saw in Section 4.3 that, if the m–vector $\boldsymbol{z}$ is distributed as $\mathrm{N}(\mathbf{0}, \mathbf{I})$, then $\|\boldsymbol{z}\|^2 = \boldsymbol{z}^{\top}\boldsymbol{z}$ is distributed as (central) chi-squared with m degrees of freedom. Similarly, if $\boldsymbol{x} \sim \mathrm{N}(\mathbf{0}, \boldsymbol{\Omega})$, then $\boldsymbol{x}^{\top}\boldsymbol{\Omega}^{-1}\boldsymbol{x} \sim \chi^2(m)$. If instead $\boldsymbol{z} \sim \mathrm{N}(\boldsymbol{\mu}, \mathbf{I})$, then $\boldsymbol{z}^{\top}\boldsymbol{z}$ follows the noncentral chi-squared distribution with m degrees of freedom and **noncentrality parameter**, or **NCP**, $\Lambda \equiv \boldsymbol{\mu}^{\top}\boldsymbol{\mu}$. This distribution is written as $\chi^2(m, \Lambda)$. It is easy to see that its expectation is $m + \Lambda$; see Exercise 4.23. Likewise, if $\boldsymbol{x} \sim \mathrm{N}(\boldsymbol{\mu}, \boldsymbol{\Omega})$, then $\boldsymbol{x}^{\top}\boldsymbol{\Omega}^{-1}\boldsymbol{x} \sim \chi^2(m, \boldsymbol{\mu}^{\top}\boldsymbol{\Omega}^{-1}\boldsymbol{\mu})$. Although we will not prove it, the distribution depends on $\boldsymbol{\mu}$ and $\boldsymbol{\Omega}$ only through the quadratic form $\boldsymbol{\mu}^{\top}\boldsymbol{\Omega}^{-1}\boldsymbol{\mu}$. If we set $\boldsymbol{\mu} = \mathbf{0}$, we see that the $\chi^2(m, 0)$ distribution is just the central $\chi^2(m)$ distribution.

Under either the null or the alternative hypothesis, therefore, the distribution of expression (4.71) is noncentral chi-squared, with r degrees of freedom, and with noncentrality parameter given by

$$\Lambda \equiv \frac{1}{\sigma^2}\boldsymbol{\beta}_2^{\top}\boldsymbol{X}_2^{\top}\boldsymbol{M}_1\boldsymbol{X}_2(\boldsymbol{X}_2^{\top}\boldsymbol{M}_1\boldsymbol{X}_2)^{-1}\boldsymbol{X}_2^{\top}\boldsymbol{M}_1\boldsymbol{X}_2\boldsymbol{\beta}_2 = \frac{1}{\sigma^2}\boldsymbol{\beta}_2^{\top}\boldsymbol{X}_2^{\top}\boldsymbol{M}_1\boldsymbol{X}_2\boldsymbol{\beta}_2.$$

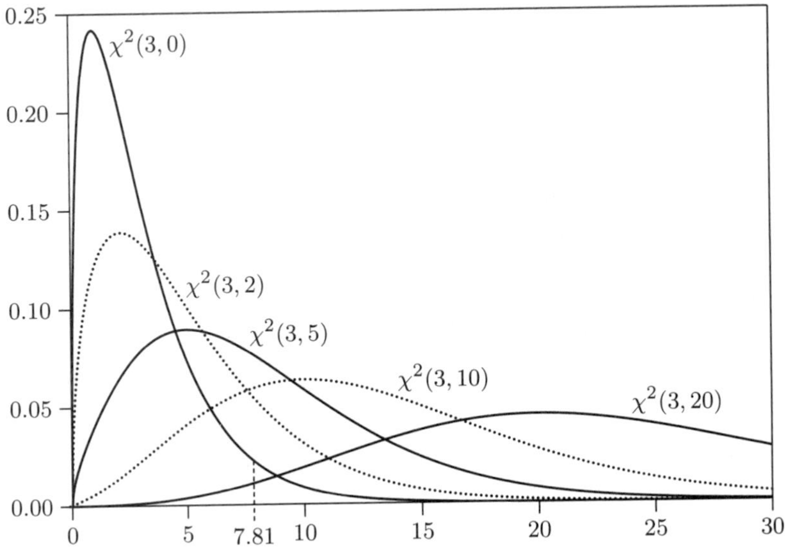

Figure 4.9 Densities of noncentral χ^2 distributions

Under the null, $\Lambda = 0$. Under either hypothesis, the distribution of the denominator of the F statistic, divided by σ^2, is central chi-squared with $n-k$ degrees of freedom, and it is independent of the numerator. The F statistic therefore has a distribution that we can write as

$$\frac{\chi^2(r, \Lambda)/r}{\chi^2(n-k)/(n-k)},$$

with numerator and denominator mutually independent. This distribution is called the **noncentral *F* distribution**, with r and $n-k$ degrees of freedom and noncentrality parameter Λ. In any given testing situation, r and $n-k$ are given, and so the difference between the distributions of the F statistic under the null and under the alternative depends only on the NCP Λ.

To illustrate this, we limit our attention to the expression (4.71), which is distributed as $\chi^2(r, \Lambda)$. As Λ increases, the distribution moves to the right and becomes more spread out. This is illustrated in Figure 4.9, which shows the density of the noncentral χ^2 distribution with 3 degrees of freedom for noncentrality parameters of 0, 2, 5, 10, and 20. The .05 critical value for the central $\chi^2(3)$ distribution, which is 7.81, is also shown. If a test statistic has the noncentral $\chi^2(3)$ distribution, the probability that the null hypothesis is rejected at the .05 level is the probability mass to the right of 7.81. It is evident from the figure that this probability is small for small values of the NCP and large for large ones.

In Figure 4.9, the number of degrees of freedom r is held constant as Λ is increased. If, instead, we held Λ constant, the density functions would move to the right as r was increased, as they do in Figure 4.4 for the special case with $\Lambda = 0$. Thus, at any given level, the critical value of a χ^2 or F test increases as r increases. It has been shown by Das Gupta and Perlman (1974) that this rightward shift of the critical value has a greater effect than the rightward shift of the density for any positive Λ. Specifically, Das Gupta and Perlman show that, for a given NCP, the power of a χ^2 or F test at any given level is strictly decreasing in r, as well as being strictly increasing in Λ, as we indicated in the previous paragraph.

The square of a t statistic for a single restriction is just the F test for that restriction, and so the above analysis applies equally well to t tests. Things can be made a little simpler, however. From equation (4.25), the t statistic t_{β_2} is $1/s$ times

$$\frac{\boldsymbol{x}_2^{\top}\boldsymbol{M}_1\boldsymbol{y}}{(\boldsymbol{x}_2^{\top}\boldsymbol{M}_1\boldsymbol{x}_2)^{1/2}}. \tag{4.72}$$

The numerator of this expression, $\boldsymbol{x}_2^{\top}\boldsymbol{M}_1\boldsymbol{y}$, is normally distributed under both the null and the alternative, with variance $\sigma^2\boldsymbol{x}_2^{\top}\boldsymbol{M}_1\boldsymbol{x}_2$ and mean $\boldsymbol{x}_2^{\top}\boldsymbol{M}_1\boldsymbol{x}_2\beta_2$. Thus $1/\sigma$ times expression (4.72) is normal with variance 1 and mean

$$\lambda \equiv \frac{1}{\sigma}(\boldsymbol{x}_2^{\top}\boldsymbol{M}_1\boldsymbol{x}_2)^{1/2}\beta_2. \tag{4.73}$$

It follows that t_{β_2} has a distribution which can be written as

$$\frac{\mathrm{N}(\lambda, 1)}{\big(\chi^2(n-k)/(n-k)\big)^{1/2}},$$

with independent numerator and denominator. This distribution is known as the **noncentral *t* distribution**, with $n-k$ degrees of freedom and noncentrality parameter λ; it is written as $t(n-k, \lambda)$. Note that $\lambda^2 = \Lambda$, where Λ is the NCP of the corresponding F test. Except for very small sample sizes, the $t(n-k, \lambda)$ distribution is quite similar to the $\mathrm{N}(\lambda, 1)$ distribution. It is also very much like an ordinary, or **central**, t distribution with its mean shifted from the origin to (4.73), but it has a bit more variance, because of the stochastic denominator.

When we know the distribution of a test statistic under the alternative hypothesis, we can determine the power of a test of given level as a function of the parameters of that hypothesis. This function is called the **power function** of the test. The distribution of t_{β_2} under the alternative depends only on the NCP λ. For a given regressor matrix $\boldsymbol{X}$ and sample size n, λ in turn depends on the parameters only through the ratio β_2/σ; see (4.73). Therefore, the power of the t test depends only on this ratio. According to assumption (4.49), as $n \to \infty$, $n^{-1}\boldsymbol{X}^{\top}\boldsymbol{X}$ tends to a nonstochastic limiting matrix $\boldsymbol{S}_{\boldsymbol{X}^{\top}\boldsymbol{X}}$. Thus, as n increases, the factor $(\boldsymbol{x}_2^{\top}\boldsymbol{M}_1\boldsymbol{x}_2)^{1/2}$ is roughly proportional to $n^{1/2}$, and so λ tends to infinity with n at a rate similar to that of $n^{1/2}$.

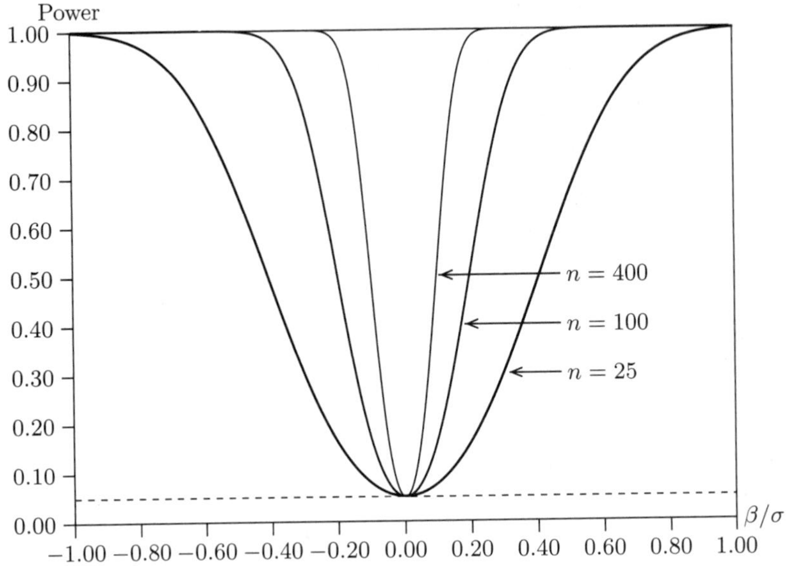

Figure 4.10 Power functions for t tests at the .05 level

Figure 4.10 shows power functions for a very simple model, in which $\boldsymbol{x}_2$, the only regressor, is a constant. Power is plotted as a function of β_2/σ for three sample sizes: $n = 25$, $n = 100$, and $n = 400$. Since the test is exact, all the power functions are equal to .05 when $\beta = 0$. Power then increases as β moves away from 0. As we would expect, the power when $n = 400$ exceeds the power when $n = 100$, which in turn exceeds the power when $n = 25$, for every value of $\beta \neq 0$. It is clear that, as $n \to \infty$, the power function converges to the shape of a T, with the foot of the vertical segment at .05 and the horizontal segment at 1.0. Thus, asymptotically, the test rejects the null with probability 1 whenever it is false. In finite samples, however, we can see from the figure that a false hypothesis is very unlikely to be rejected if $n^{1/2}\beta/\sigma$ is sufficiently small.

The Power of Bootstrap Tests

As we remarked in Section 4.6, the power of a bootstrap test depends on B, the number of bootstrap samples. The reason why it does so is illuminating. If, to any test statistic, we add random noise independent of the statistic, we inevitably reduce the power of tests based on that statistic. The bootstrap P value $\hat{p}^*(\hat{\tau})$ defined in (4.62) is simply an estimate of the **ideal bootstrap *P* value**

$$p^*(\hat{\tau}) \equiv \Pr(\tau > \hat{\tau}) = \operatorname*{plim}_{B\to\infty} \hat{p}^*(\hat{\tau}),$$

where $\Pr(\tau > \hat{\tau})$ is evaluated under the bootstrap DGP. When B is finite, $\hat{p}^*$ differs from p^* because of random variation in the bootstrap samples. This

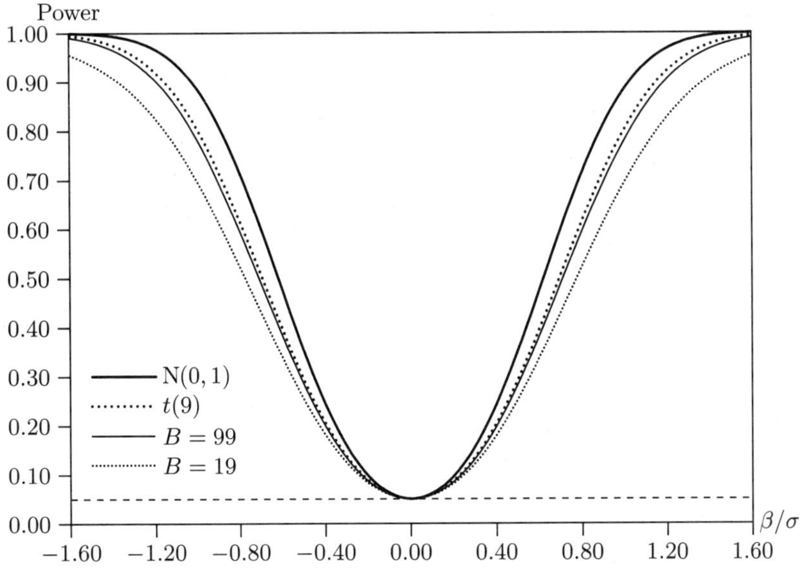

Figure 4.11 Power functions for tests at the .05 level

random variation is generated in the computer, and is therefore completely independent of the random variable τ. The bootstrap testing procedure discussed in Section 4.6 incorporates this random variation, and in so doing it reduces the power of the test.

Another example of how randomness affects test power is provided by the tests z_{β_2} and t_{β_2}, which were discussed in Section 4.4. Recall that z_{β_2} follows the N(0, 1) distribution, because σ is known, and t_{β_2} follows the $t(n-k)$ distribution, because σ has to be estimated. As equation (4.26) shows, t_{β_2} is equal to z_{β_2} times the random variable σ/s, which has the same distribution under the null and alternative hypotheses, and is independent of z_{β_2}. Therefore, multiplying z_{β_2} by σ/s simply adds independent random noise to the test statistic. This additional randomness requires us to use a larger critical value, and that in turn causes the test based on t_{β_2} to be less powerful than the test based on z_{β_2}.

Both types of power loss are illustrated in Figure 4.11. It shows power functions for four tests at the .05 level of the null hypothesis that $\beta = 0$ in the model (4.01) with normally distributed error terms and 10 observations. All four tests are exact, as can be seen from the fact that, in all cases, power equals .05 when $\beta = 0$. For all values of $\beta \neq 0$, there is a clear ordering of the four curves in Figure 4.11. The highest curve is for the test based on z_{β_2}, which uses the N(0, 1) distribution and is available only when σ is known. The next three curves are for tests based on t_{β_2}. The loss of power from using t_{β_2} with the $t(9)$ distribution, instead of z_{β_2} with the N(0, 1) distribution, is quite noticeable. Of course, 10 is a very small sample size; the loss of power from not knowing σ would be very much less for more reasonable sample sizes. There is a further loss of power from using a bootstrap test with finite B. This further loss is quite modest when $B = 99$, but it is substantial when $B = 19$.

Figure 4.11 suggests that the loss of power from using bootstrap tests is generally modest, except when B is very small. However, readers should be warned that the loss can be more substantial in other cases. A reasonable rule of thumb is that power loss is very rarely a problem when $B = 999$, and that it is never a problem when $B = 9{,}999$.

4.8 Final Remarks

This chapter has introduced a number of important concepts, which we will encounter again and again throughout this book. In particular, we will encounter many types of hypothesis test, sometimes exact but more commonly asymptotic. Some of the asymptotic tests work well in finite samples, but others do not. Many of them can easily be bootstrapped, and they perform much better when bootstrapped, but others are difficult to bootstrap or do not perform particularly well.

Although hypothesis testing plays a central role in classical econometrics, it is not the only method by which econometricians attempt to make inferences from parameter estimates about the true values of parameters. In the next chapter, we turn our attention to the other principal method, namely, the construction of confidence intervals and confidence regions.

4.9 Exercises

4.1 Suppose that the random variable z follows the $\text{N}(0, 1)$ density. If z is a test statistic used in a two-tailed test, the corresponding P value, according to (4.07), is $p(z) \equiv 2(1 - \Phi(|z|))$. Show that $F_p(\cdot)$, the CDF of $p(z)$, is the CDF of the uniform distribution on $[0, 1]$. In other words, show that

$$F_p(x) = x \quad \text{for all } x \in [0, 1].$$

4.2 Extend Exercise 1.6 to show that the third and fourth moments of the standard normal distribution are 0 and 3, respectively. Use these results in order to calculate the centered and uncentered third and fourth moments of the $\text{N}(\mu, \sigma^2)$ distribution.

4.3 Let the density of the random variable x be $f(x)$. Show that the density of the random variable $w \equiv tx$, where $t > 0$, is $(1/t)f(w/t)$. Next let the joint density of the set of random variables x_i, $i = 1, \ldots, m$, be $f(x_1, \ldots, x_m)$. For $i = 1, \ldots, m$, let $w_i = t_i x_i$, $t_i > 0$. Show that the joint density of the w_i is

$$f(w_1, \ldots, w_m) = \frac{1}{\prod_{i=1}^m t_i} f\Big(\frac{w_1}{t_1}, \ldots, \frac{w_m}{t_m}\Big).$$

⋆4.4 Consider the random variables x_1 and x_2, which are bivariate normal with $x_1 \sim \mathrm{N}(0, \sigma_1^2)$, $x_2 \sim \mathrm{N}(0, \sigma_2^2)$, and correlation ρ. Show that the expectation of x_1 conditional on x_2 is $\rho(\sigma_1/\sigma_2)x_2$ and that the variance of x_1 conditional on x_2 is $\sigma_1^2(1-\rho^2)$. How are these results modified if the means of x_1 and x_2 are μ_1 and μ_2, respectively?

4.5 Suppose that, as in the previous question, the random variables x_1 and x_2 are bivariate normal, with means 0, variances σ_1^2 and σ_2^2, and correlation ρ. Starting from (4.13), show that $f(x_1, x_2)$, the joint density of x_1 and x_2, is given by

$$\frac{1}{2\pi}\frac{1}{(1-\rho^2)^{1/2}\sigma_1\sigma_2}\exp\left(\frac{-1}{2(1-\rho^2)}\left(\frac{x_1^2}{\sigma_1^2} - 2\rho\frac{x_1x_2}{\sigma_1\sigma_2} + \frac{x_2^2}{\sigma_2^2}\right)\right). \tag{4.74}$$

Then use this result to show that x_1 and x_2 are statistically independent if $\rho = 0$.

⋆4.6 Let the random variables x_1 and x_2 be distributed as bivariate normal, with means μ_1 and μ_2, variances σ_1^2 and σ_2^2, and covariance σ_{12}. Using the result of Exercise 4.5, write down the joint density of x_1 and x_2 in terms of the parameters just specified. Then find the marginal density of x_1.

What is the density of x_2 conditional on x_1? Show that the mean of x_2 conditional on x_1 can be written as $\mathrm{E}(x_2 \,|\, x_1) = \beta_1 + \beta_2 x_1$, and solve for the parameters β_1 and β_2 as functions of the parameters of the bivariate distribution. How are these parameters related to the least-squares estimates that would be obtained if we regressed realizations of x_2 on a constant and realizations of x_1?

4.7 Consider the linear regression model

$$y_t = \beta_1 + \beta_2 x_{t1} + \beta_3 x_{t2} + u_t.$$

Rewrite this model so that the restriction $\beta_2 - \beta_3 = 1$ becomes a single zero restriction.

⋆4.8 Consider the linear regression model $\boldsymbol{y} = \boldsymbol{X\beta} + \boldsymbol{u}$, where there are n observations and k regressors. Suppose that this model is potentially subject to r restrictions which can be written as $\boldsymbol{R\beta} = \boldsymbol{r}$, where $\boldsymbol{R}$ is an $r \times k$ matrix and $\boldsymbol{r}$ is an r–vector. Rewrite the model so that the restrictions become r zero restrictions.

⋆4.9 Show that the t statistic (4.25) is $(n-k)^{1/2}$ times the cotangent of the angle between the n–vectors $\boldsymbol{M}_1\boldsymbol{y}$ and $\boldsymbol{M}_1\boldsymbol{x}_2$.

Now consider the regressions

$$\begin{aligned} \boldsymbol{y} &= \boldsymbol{X}_1\boldsymbol{\beta}_1 + \beta_2\boldsymbol{x}_2 + \boldsymbol{u}, \text{ and} \\ \boldsymbol{x}_2 &= \boldsymbol{X}_1\boldsymbol{\gamma}_1 + \gamma_2\boldsymbol{y} + \boldsymbol{v}. \end{aligned} \tag{4.75}$$

What is the relationship between the t statistic for $\beta_2 = 0$ in the first of these regressions and the t statistic for $\gamma_2 = 0$ in the second?

4.10 Show that the OLS estimates $\tilde{\beta}_1$ from the restricted model (4.29) can be obtained from those of the unrestricted model (4.28) by the formula

$$\tilde{\beta}_1 = \hat{\beta}_1 + (\boldsymbol{X}_1^\top \boldsymbol{X}_1)^{-1} \boldsymbol{X}_1^\top \boldsymbol{X}_2 \hat{\beta}_2.$$

Hint: Equation (4.38) is useful for this exercise.

4.11 Show that the SSR from regression (4.42), or equivalently, regression (4.41), is equal to the sum of the SSRs from the two subsample regressions:

$$\begin{aligned} \boldsymbol{y}_1 &= \boldsymbol{X}_1 \boldsymbol{\beta}_1 + \boldsymbol{u}_1, \quad \boldsymbol{u}_1 \sim \mathrm{N}(\mathbf{0}, \sigma^2 \mathbf{I}), \text{ and} \\ \boldsymbol{y}_2 &= \boldsymbol{X}_2 \boldsymbol{\beta}_2 + \boldsymbol{u}_2, \quad \boldsymbol{u}_2 \sim \mathrm{N}(\mathbf{0}, \sigma^2 \mathbf{I}). \end{aligned}$$

4.12 When performing a Chow test, one may find that one of the subsamples is smaller than k, the number of regressors. Without loss of generality, assume that $n_2 < k$. Show that, in this case, the F statistic becomes

$$\frac{(\mathrm{RSSR} - \mathrm{SSR}_1)/n_2}{\mathrm{SSR}_1/(n_1 - k)},$$

and that the numerator and denominator really have the degrees of freedom used in this formula.

4.13 Show, using the results of Section 4.5, that r times the F statistic (4.58) is asymptotically distributed as $\chi^2(r)$.

4.14 Consider the linear regression model

$$\boldsymbol{y} = \boldsymbol{X}\boldsymbol{\beta} + \boldsymbol{u}, \quad \boldsymbol{u} \sim \mathrm{N}(\mathbf{0}, \sigma^2 \mathbf{I}), \quad \mathrm{E}(\boldsymbol{u} \,|\, \boldsymbol{X}) = \mathbf{0},$$

where $\boldsymbol{X}$ is an $n \times k$ matrix. If σ_0 denotes the true value of σ, how is the quantity $\boldsymbol{y}^\top \boldsymbol{M}_{\boldsymbol{X}} \boldsymbol{y}/\sigma_0^2$ distributed? Use this result to derive a test of the null hypothesis that $\sigma = \sigma_0$. Is this a one-tailed test or a two-tailed test?

⋆4.15 P values for two-tailed tests based on statistics that have asymmetric distributions are not calculated as in Section 4.2. Let the CDF of the statistic τ be denoted as F, where $F(-x) \neq 1 - F(x)$ for general x. Suppose that, for any level α, the critical values c_α^- and c_α^+ are defined, analogously to (4.05), by the equations

$$F(c_\alpha^-) = \alpha/2 \quad \text{and} \quad F(c_\alpha^+) = 1 - \alpha/2.$$

Show that the marginal significance level associated with a realized statistic $\hat{\tau}$ is $2\min\bigl(F(\hat{\tau}), 1 - F(\hat{\tau})\bigr)$.

⋆4.16 The rightmost expression in equation (4.62) provides a way to compute the P value for a one-tailed bootstrap test that rejects in the upper tail. Derive comparable expressions for a one-tailed bootstrap test that rejects in the lower tail, for a two-tailed bootstrap test based on a distribution that is symmetric around the origin, and for a two-tailed bootstrap test based on a possibly asymmetric distribution. **Hint:** See Exercise 4.15.

4.17 Suppose the asymptotic distribution of a pivotal test statistic τ is $\mathrm{N}(0,1)$. In a sample of size n, the actual distribution is $\mathrm{N}(10/n,1)$. What is the asymptotic P value for a two-tailed test based on the statistic $\hat{\tau} = -1.60$ when $n = 20$? Suppose you could perform an infinite number of bootstrap simulations. Then what would be the bootstrap P value based on the (incorrect) assumption that the distribution is symmetric around the origin? What would be the bootstrap P value without making any assumptions about the shape of the distribution? Based on these results, would you reject the null hypothesis at the .05 level? **Hint:** See Exercise 4.16.

4.18 The file **classical.data** contains 50 observations on three artificial variables, namely, $\boldsymbol{y}$, $\boldsymbol{x}_2$, and $\boldsymbol{x}_3$. The data on $\boldsymbol{y}$ are generated by the classical linear regression model

$$\boldsymbol{y} = \beta_1\boldsymbol{\iota} + \beta_2\boldsymbol{x}_2 + \beta_3\boldsymbol{x}_3 + \boldsymbol{u}, \quad \boldsymbol{u} \sim \mathrm{N}(\boldsymbol{0}, \sigma^2\mathbf{I}).$$

Test the hypothesis that $\sigma = 1.2$ at the .05 level. Also compute a P value for the test. **Hint:** See Exercise 4.15.

4.19 Consider a multiplicative congruential generator with modulus $m = 7$, and with all reasonable possible values of λ, that is, $\lambda = 2, 3, 4, 5, 6$. Show that, for any integer seed between 1 and 6, the generator generates each number of the form $i/7$, $i = 1, \ldots, 6$, exactly once before cycling for $\lambda = 3$ and $\lambda = 5$, but that it repeats itself more quickly for the other choices of λ. Repeat the exercise for $m = 11$, and determine which choices of λ yield generators that return to their starting point before covering the full range of possibilities.

4.20 If F is a strictly increasing CDF defined on an interval $[a, b]$ of the real line, where either or both of a and b may be infinite, then the inverse function F^{-1} is a well-defined mapping from $[0, 1]$ on to $[a, b]$. Show that, if the random variable X is a drawing from the $\mathrm{U}(0, 1)$ distribution, then $F^{-1}(X)$ is a drawing from the distribution of which F is the CDF.

4.21 In Section 3.6, we saw that $\mathrm{Var}(\hat{u}_t) = (1 - h_t)\sigma_0^2$, where $\hat{u}_t$ is the tth residual from the linear regression model $\boldsymbol{y} = \boldsymbol{X\beta} + \boldsymbol{u}$, and h_t is the tth diagonal element of the "hat matrix" $\boldsymbol{P_X}$; this was the result (3.44). Use this result to derive an alternative to (4.69) as a method of rescaling the residuals prior to resampling. Remember that the rescaled residuals must have mean 0.

4.22 Suppose that z is a test statistic distributed as $\mathrm{N}(0, 1)$ under the null hypothesis, and as $\mathrm{N}(\lambda, 1)$ under the alternative, where λ depends on the DGP that generates the data. If c_α is defined by (4.06), show that the power of the two-tailed test at level α based on z is equal to

$$\Phi(\lambda - c_\alpha) + \Phi(-c_\alpha - \lambda).$$

Plot this power function for λ in the interval $[-5, 5]$ for $\alpha = .05$ and $\alpha = .01$.

4.23 Show that, if the m-vector $\boldsymbol{z} \sim \mathrm{N}(\boldsymbol{\mu}, \mathbf{I})$, the expectation of the noncentral chi-squared variable $\boldsymbol{z}^\top\boldsymbol{z}$ is $m + \boldsymbol{\mu}^\top\boldsymbol{\mu}$.

4.24 Using the data from the file **classical.data**, which contains 50 observations on three artificial variables, estimate the regression model

$$\boldsymbol{y} = \beta_1\boldsymbol{\iota} + \beta_2\boldsymbol{x}_2 + \beta_3\boldsymbol{x}_3 + \boldsymbol{u}, \quad \boldsymbol{u} \sim \mathrm{N}(\boldsymbol{0}, \sigma^2\mathbf{I}).$$

Compute a t statistic for the null hypothesis that $\beta_3 = 0$. On the basis of this test statistic, perform an exact test. Then perform parametric and semiparametric bootstrap tests using 99, 999, and 9,999 simulations. How do the two types of bootstrap P values correspond with the exact P value? How does this correspondence change as B increases?

4.25 Consider again the data in the file **consumption.data** and the ADL model studied in Exercise 3.23, which is reproduced here for convenience:

$$c_t = \alpha + \beta c_{t-1} + \gamma_0 y_t + \gamma_1 y_{t-1} + u_t. \tag{3.71}$$

Compute a t statistic for the hypothesis that $\gamma_0 + \gamma_1 = 0$. On the basis of this test statistic, perform an asymptotic test, a parametric bootstrap test, and a semiparametric bootstrap test using residuals rescaled according to (4.69).

Chapter 5
Confidence Intervals

5.1 Introduction

Hypothesis testing, which we discussed in the previous chapter, is the foundation for all inference in classical econometrics. It can be used to find out whether restrictions imposed by economic theory are compatible with the data, and whether various aspects of the specification of a model appear to be correct. However, once we are confident that a model is correctly specified and incorporates whatever restrictions are appropriate, we often want to make inferences about the values of some of the parameters that appear in the model. Although this can be done by performing a battery of hypothesis tests, it is usually more convenient to construct **confidence intervals** for the individual parameters of specific interest. A less frequently used, but sometimes more informative, approach is to construct **confidence regions** for two or more parameters jointly.

In order to construct a confidence interval, we need a suitable **family of tests** for a set of point null hypotheses. A different test statistic must be calculated for each different null hypothesis that we consider, but usually there is just one *type* of statistic that can be used to test all the different null hypotheses. For instance, if we wish to test the hypothesis that a scalar parameter θ in a regression model equals 0, we can use a t test. But we can also use a t test for the hypothesis that $\theta = \theta_0$ for any specified real number θ_0. Thus, in this case, we have a family of t statistics indexed by θ_0.

Given a family of tests capable of testing a set of hypotheses about a (scalar) parameter θ of a model, all with the same level α, we can use them to construct a confidence interval for the parameter. By definition, a confidence interval is an interval of the real line that contains all values θ_0 for which the hypothesis that $\theta = \theta_0$ is not rejected by the appropriate test in the family. For level α, a confidence interval so obtained is said to be a $1 - \alpha$ confidence interval, or to be at **confidence level** $1 - \alpha$. In applied work, .95 confidence intervals are particularly popular, followed by .99 and .90 ones.

Unlike the parameters we are trying to make inferences about, confidence intervals are random. Every different sample that we draw from the same DGP yields a different confidence interval. The probability that the random interval includes, or covers, the true value of the parameter is called the **coverage probability**, or just the **coverage**, of the interval. Suppose that all the tests in the family have exactly level α, that is, they reject their corresponding null hypotheses with probability exactly equal to α when the hypothesis is true. Then the coverage of the interval constructed from this family of tests must be precisely $1 - \alpha$.

Confidence intervals may be either **exact** or **approximate**. When the exact distribution of the test statistics used to construct a confidence interval is known, the coverage is equal to the confidence level, and the interval is exact. Otherwise, we have to be content with approximate confidence intervals, which may be based either on asymptotic theory or on the bootstrap. In the next section, we discuss both exact confidence intervals and approximate ones based on asymptotic theory. Then, in Section 5.3, we discuss bootstrap confidence intervals.

Like a confidence interval, a $1-\alpha$ **confidence region** for a set of k model parameters, such as the components of a k–vector $\boldsymbol{\theta}$, is a region in a k–dimensional space (often, the region is the k–dimensional analog of an ellipse) constructed in such a way that, for every point represented by the k–vector $\boldsymbol{\theta}_0$ in the confidence region, the joint hypothesis that $\boldsymbol{\theta} = \boldsymbol{\theta}_0$ is not rejected by the appropriate member of a family of tests at level α. Thus confidence regions constructed in this way cover the true values of the parameter vector $100(1-\alpha)\%$ of the time, either exactly or approximately. In Section 5.4, we show how to construct confidence regions and explain the relationship between confidence regions and confidence intervals.

In previous chapters, we assumed that the error terms in regression models are independently and identically distributed. This assumption yielded a simple form for the covariance matrix of a vector of OLS parameter estimates, expression (3.28), and a simple way of estimating this matrix. In Section 5.5, we show that it is possible to estimate the covariance matrix of a vector of OLS estimates even when we abandon the assumption that the error terms are identically distributed. Finally, in Section 5.6, we discuss a simple and widely-used method for obtaining standard errors, covariance matrix estimates, and confidence intervals for nonlinear functions of estimated parameters.

5.2 Exact and Asymptotic Confidence Intervals

A confidence interval for some scalar parameter θ consists of all values θ_0 for which the hypothesis $\theta = \theta_0$ cannot be rejected at some specified level α. Thus, as we will see in a moment, we can construct a confidence interval by "inverting" a test statistic. If the finite-sample distribution of the test statistic is known, we obtain an **exact confidence interval**. If, as is more commonly the case, only the asymptotic distribution of the test statistic is known, we obtain an **asymptotic confidence interval**, which may or may not be reasonably accurate in finite samples. Whenever a test statistic based on asymptotic theory has poor finite-sample properties, a confidence interval based on that statistic has poor coverage: In other words, the interval does not cover the true parameter value with the specified probability. In such cases, it may well be worthwhile to seek other test statistics that yield different confidence intervals with better coverage.

To begin with, suppose that we wish to base a confidence interval for the parameter θ on a family of test statistics that have a distribution or asymptotic distribution like the χ^2 or the F distribution under their respective nulls. Statistics of this type are always positive, and tests based on them reject their null hypotheses when the statistics are sufficiently large. Such tests are often equivalent to two-tailed tests based on statistics distributed as standard normal or Student's t. Let us denote the test statistic for the hypothesis that $\theta = \theta_0$ by the random variable $\tau(\boldsymbol{y}, \theta_0)$. Here $\boldsymbol{y}$ denotes the sample used to compute the particular realization of the statistic. It is the random element in the statistic, since $\tau(\cdot)$ is just a deterministic function of its arguments.

For each θ_0, the test consists of comparing the realized $\tau(\boldsymbol{y}, \theta_0)$ with the level α critical value of the distribution of the statistic under the null. If we write the critical value as c_α, then, for any θ_0, we have by the definition of c_α that

$$\Pr_{\theta_0}\big(\tau(\boldsymbol{y}, \theta_0) \le c_\alpha\big) = 1 - \alpha. \tag{5.01}$$

Here the subscript θ_0 indicates that the probability is calculated under the hypothesis that $\theta = \theta_0$. If c_α is a critical value for the asymptotic distribution of $\tau(\boldsymbol{y}, \theta_0)$, rather than for the exact distribution, then (5.01) is only approximately true. For θ_0 to belong to the confidence interval obtained by inverting the family of test statistics $\tau(\boldsymbol{y}, \theta_0)$, it is necessary and sufficient that

$$\tau(\boldsymbol{y}, \theta_0) \le c_\alpha. \tag{5.02}$$

Thus the limits of the confidence interval can be found by solving the equation

$$\tau(\boldsymbol{y}, \theta) = c_\alpha \tag{5.03}$$

for θ. This equation normally has two solutions. One of these solutions is the upper limit, θ_u, and the other is the lower limit, θ_l, of the confidence interval that we are trying to construct.

If c_α is an exact critical value for the test statistic $\tau(\boldsymbol{y}, \theta)$ at level α, then the confidence interval $[\theta_l,\ \theta_u]$ constructed in this way has coverage $1 - \alpha$, as desired. To see this, observe first that, if we can find an exact critical value c_α, the random function $\tau(\boldsymbol{y}, \theta_0)$ must be pivotal for the model $\mathbb{M}$ under consideration. In saying this, we are implicitly generalizing the definition of a pivotal quantity (see Section 4.6) to include random variables that may depend on the model parameters. A random function $\tau(\boldsymbol{y}, \theta)$ is said to be pivotal for $\mathbb{M}$ if, when it is evaluated at the true value θ_0 corresponding to some DGP in $\mathbb{M}$, the result is a random variable whose distribution does not depend on what that DGP is. Pivotal functions of more than one model parameter are defined in exactly the same way. The function is merely asymptotically pivotal if only the asymptotic distribution is invariant to the choice of DGP.

Suppose that $\tau(\boldsymbol{y}, \theta_0)$ is an exact pivot. Then, for every DGP in the model $\mathbb{M}$, (5.01) holds exactly. Since θ_0 belongs to the confidence interval if and only if (5.02) holds, this means that the confidence interval contains the true parameter value θ_0 with probability exactly equal to $1 - \alpha$, whatever the true parameter value may be.

Even if it is not an exact pivot, the function $\tau(\boldsymbol{y}, \theta_0)$ must be asymptotically pivotal, since otherwise the critical value c_α would depend asymptotically on the unknown DGP in $\mathbb{M}$, and we could not construct a confidence interval with the correct coverage, even asymptotically. Of course, if c_α is only approximate, then the coverage of the interval differs from $1-\alpha$ to a greater or lesser extent, in a manner that, in general, depends on the unknown true DGP.

Quantiles

When we speak of critical values, we are implicitly making use of the concept of a **quantile** of the distribution that the test statistic follows under the null hypothesis. If $F(x)$ denotes the CDF of a random variable X, and if the PDF $f(x) \equiv F'(x)$ exists and is strictly positive on the entire range of possible values for X, then q_α, the **α quantile** of F, for $0 \le \alpha \le 1$, satisfies the equation $F(q_\alpha) = \alpha$. The assumption of a strictly positive PDF means that F is strictly increasing over its range. Therefore, the inverse function F^{-1} exists, and $q_\alpha = F^{-1}(\alpha)$. For this reason, F^{-1} is sometimes called the **quantile function**. If F is not strictly increasing, or if the PDF does not exist, which, as we saw in Section 1.2, is the case for a discrete distribution, the α quantile does not necessarily exist, and is not necessarily uniquely defined, for all values of α.

The .5 quantile of a distribution is often called the **median**. For $\alpha = .25$, .5, and .75, the corresponding quantiles are called **quartiles**; for $\alpha = .2$, .4, .6, and .8, they are called **quintiles**; for $\alpha = i/10$ with i an integer between 1 and 9, they are called **deciles**; for $\alpha = i/20$ with $1 \le i \le 19$, they are called **vigintiles**; and, for $\alpha = i/100$ with $1 \le i \le 99$, they are called **centiles**. The quantile function of the standard normal distribution is shown in Figure 5.1. All three quartiles, the first and ninth deciles, and the .025 and .975 quantiles are shown in the figure.

Asymptotic Confidence Intervals

The discussion up to this point has deliberately been rather abstract, because $\tau(\boldsymbol{y}, \theta_0)$ can, in principle, be any sort of test statistic. To obtain more concrete results, let us suppose that

$$\tau(\boldsymbol{y}, \theta_0) \equiv \left(\frac{\hat{\theta} - \theta_0}{s_\theta}\right)^2, \tag{5.04}$$

where $\hat{\theta}$ is an estimate of θ, and s_θ is the corresponding standard error, that is, an estimate of the standard deviation of $\hat{\theta}$. Thus $\tau(\boldsymbol{y}, \theta_0)$ is the square

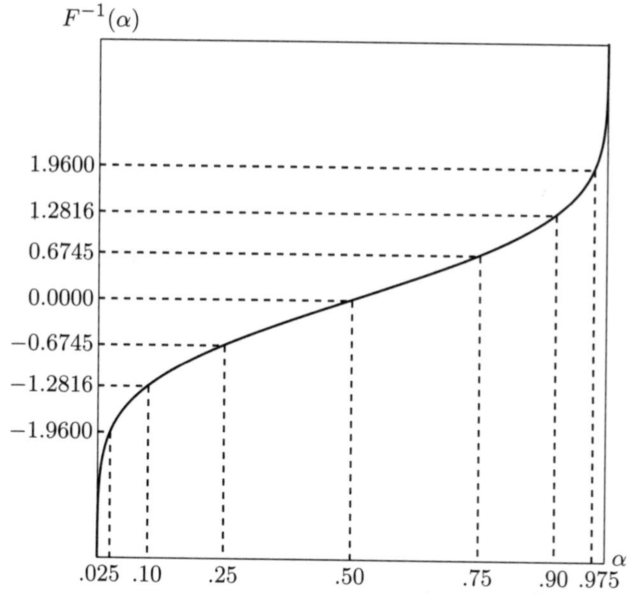

Figure 5.1 The quantile function of the standard normal distribution

of the t statistic for the null hypothesis that $\theta = \theta_0$. If $\hat{\theta}$ were an OLS estimate of a regression coefficient, then, under conditions that were discussed in Section 4.5, the test statistic defined in (5.04) would be asymptotically distributed as $\chi^2(1)$ under the null hypothesis. Therefore, the asymptotic critical value c_α would be the $1 - \alpha$ quantile of the $\chi^2(1)$ distribution.

For the test statistic (5.04), equation (5.03) becomes

$$\left(\frac{\hat{\theta} - \theta}{s_\theta}\right)^2 = c_\alpha.$$

Taking the square root of both sides and multiplying by s_θ then gives

$$|\hat{\theta} - \theta| = s_\theta\, c_\alpha^{1/2}. \tag{5.05}$$

As expected, there are two solutions to equation (5.05). These are

$$\theta_l = \hat{\theta} - s_\theta\, c_\alpha^{1/2} \quad \text{and} \quad \theta_u = \hat{\theta} + s_\theta\, c_\alpha^{1/2},$$

and so the asymptotic $1 - \alpha$ confidence interval for θ is

$$\big[\hat{\theta} - s_\theta\, c_\alpha^{1/2},\ \hat{\theta} + s_\theta\, c_\alpha^{1/2}\big]. \tag{5.06}$$

This means that the interval consists of all values of θ between the lower limit $\hat{\theta} - s_\theta\, c_\alpha^{1/2}$ and the upper limit $\hat{\theta} + s_\theta\, c_\alpha^{1/2}$. For $\alpha = .05$, the $1 - \alpha$ quantile of

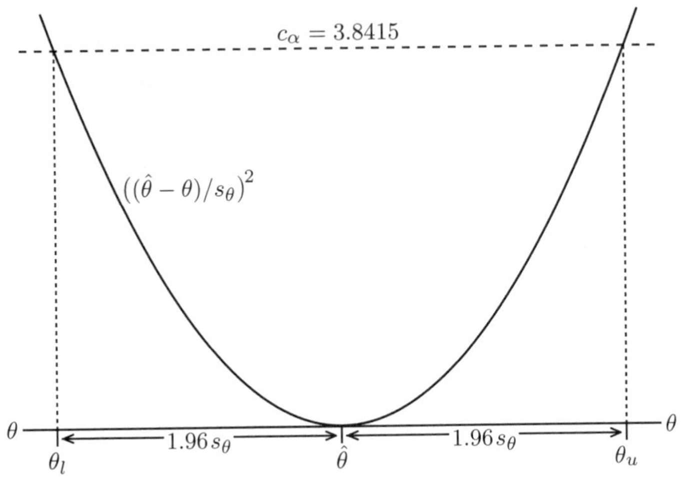

Figure 5.2 A symmetric confidence interval

the $\chi^2(1)$ distribution is 3.8415, the square root of which is 1.9600. Thus the confidence interval given by (5.06) becomes

$$\big[\hat\theta - 1.96s_\theta,\ \ \hat\theta + 1.96s_\theta\big]. \tag{5.07}$$

This interval is shown in Figure 5.2, which illustrates the manner in which it is constructed. The value of the test statistic is on the vertical axis of the figure. The upper and lower limits of the interval occur at the values of θ where the test statistic (5.04) is equal to c_α, which in this case is 3.8415.

We would have obtained the same confidence interval as (5.06) if we had started with the asymptotic t statistic $(\hat\theta - \theta_0)/s_\theta$ and used the $N(0,1)$ distribution to perform a two-tailed test. For such a test, there are two critical values, one the negative of the other, because the $N(0,1)$ distribution is symmetric about the origin. These critical values are defined in terms of the quantiles of that distribution. The relevant ones are now the $\alpha/2$ and the $1-(\alpha/2)$ quantiles, since we wish to have the same probability mass in each tail of the distribution. It is conventional to denote these quantiles of the standard normal distribution by $z_{\alpha/2}$ and $z_{1-(\alpha/2)}$, respectively. Note that $z_{\alpha/2}$ is negative, since $\alpha/2 < 1/2$, and the median of the $N(0,1)$ distribution is 0. By symmetry, it is the negative of $z_{1-(\alpha/2)}$. Equation (5.03), which has two solutions for a χ^2 test, is replaced by two equations, each with just one solution, as follows:

$$\tau(\boldsymbol{y},\theta) = \pm c.$$

Here $\tau(\boldsymbol{y},\theta)$ denotes the (signed) t statistic rather than the $\chi^2(1)$ statistic used in (5.03), and the positive number c can be defined either as $z_{1-(\alpha/2)}$ or as $-z_{\alpha/2}$. The resulting confidence interval $[\theta_l,\ \theta_u]$ can thus be written in two different ways:

$$\left[\hat{\theta} + s_\theta\, z_{\alpha/2},\ \hat{\theta} - s_\theta\, z_{\alpha/2}\right] \quad \text{and} \quad \left[\hat{\theta} - s_\theta\, z_{1-(\alpha/2)},\ \hat{\theta} + s_\theta\, z_{1-(\alpha/2)}\right]. \qquad (5.08)$$

When $\alpha = .05$, we once again obtain the interval (5.07), since $z_{.025} = -1.96$ and $z_{.975} = 1.96$.

Asymmetric Confidence Intervals

The confidence interval (5.06), which is the same as the interval (5.08), is a **symmetric** one, because θ_l is as far below $\hat{\theta}$ as θ_u is above it. Although many confidence intervals are symmetric, not all of them share this property. The symmetry of (5.06) is a consequence of the symmetry of the standard normal distribution and of the form of the test statistic (5.04).

It is possible to construct confidence intervals based on two-tailed tests even when the distribution of the test statistic is not symmetric. For a chosen level α, we wish to reject whenever the statistic is too far into either the right-hand or the left-hand tail of the distribution. Unfortunately, there are many ways to interpret "too far" in this context. The simplest is probably to define the rejection region in such a way that there is a probability mass of $\alpha/2$ in each tail. This is called an **equal-tailed confidence interval**. Two critical values are needed for each level, a lower one, c_α^-, which is the $\alpha/2$ quantile of the distribution, and an upper one, c_α^+, which is the $1 - (\alpha/2)$ quantile. A realized statistic $\hat{\tau}$ leads to rejection at level α if either $\hat{\tau} < c_\alpha^-$ or $\hat{\tau} > c_\alpha^+$. This leads to an **asymmetric confidence interval**. We will discuss such intervals, where the critical values are obtained by bootstrapping, in the next section.

It is also possible to construct confidence intervals based on one-tailed tests. Such an interval is open all the way out to infinity in one direction. Suppose that, for each θ_0, the null $\theta \le \theta_0$ is tested against the alternative $\theta > \theta_0$. If the true parameter value is finite, we never want to reject the null for any θ_0 that substantially exceeds the true value. Consequently, the confidence interval is open out to plus infinity. Formally, the null is rejected only if the signed t statistic is algebraically greater than the appropriate critical value. For the $\mathrm{N}(0,1)$ distribution, this is $z_{1-\alpha}$ for level α. The null $\theta \le \theta_0$ is not rejected if $\tau(\boldsymbol{y}, \theta_0) \le z_{1-\alpha}$, that is, if $\hat{\theta} - \theta_0 \le s_\theta z_{1-\alpha}$. The interval over which θ_0 satisfies this inequality is just

$$\left[\hat{\theta} - s_\theta z_{1-\alpha},\ +\infty\right]. \qquad (5.09)$$

P Values and Asymmetric Distributions

The above discussion of asymmetric confidence intervals raises the question of how to calculate P values for two-tailed tests based on statistics with asymmetric distributions. This rather tricky matter, which was treated briefly in Exercise 4.15, will turn out to be important when we discuss bootstrap confidence intervals in the next section.

If we denote by F the CDF used to calculate critical values or P values, the P value associated with a statistic τ should be $2F(\tau)$ if τ is in the lower tail, and $2\big(1-F(\tau)\big)$ if it is in the upper tail, as seen in Exercise 4.15. In complete generality, we have that the P value is

$$p(\tau) = 2\min\big(F(\tau), 1-F(\tau)\big). \tag{5.10}$$

A slight problem arises as to the point of separation between the left and the right sides of the distribution. This point is in fact the median, $q_{.50}$, for which $F(q_{.50}) = .50$ by definition, so that, if $\tau < q_{.50}$, the P value is $2F(\tau)$, and τ is consequently in the left-hand tail, while if $\tau > q_{.50}$, it is in the right-hand tail.

Exact Confidence Intervals for Regression Coefficients

In Section 4.4, we saw that, for the classical normal linear model, exact tests of linear restrictions on the parameters of the regression function are available, based on the t and F distributions. This implies that we can construct exact confidence intervals. Consider the classical normal linear model (4.21), in which the parameter vector $\boldsymbol{\beta}$ has been partitioned as $[\boldsymbol{\beta}_1 \vdots \beta_2]$, where $\boldsymbol{\beta}_1$ is a $(k-1)$–vector and β_2 is a scalar. The t statistic for the hypothesis that $\beta_2 = \beta_{20}$ for any particular value β_{20} can be written as

$$\frac{\hat{\beta}_2 - \beta_{20}}{s_2}, \tag{5.11}$$

where s_2 is the usual OLS standard error for $\hat{\beta}_2$.

Any DGP in the model (4.21) satisfies $\beta_2 = \beta_{20}$ for some β_{20}. With the correct value of β_{20}, the t statistic (5.11) has the $t(n-k)$ distribution, and so

$$\Pr\left(t_{\alpha/2} \le \frac{\hat{\beta}_2 - \beta_{20}}{s_2} \le t_{1-(\alpha/2)}\right) = 1-\alpha, \tag{5.12}$$

where $t_{\alpha/2}$ and $t_{1-(\alpha/2)}$ denote the $\alpha/2$ and $1-(\alpha/2)$ quantiles of the $t(n-k)$ distribution. We can use equation (5.12) to find a $1-\alpha$ confidence interval for β_2. The left-hand side of the equation is equal to

$$\begin{aligned}
&\Pr\big(s_2 t_{\alpha/2} \le \hat{\beta}_2 - \beta_{20} \le s_2 t_{1-(\alpha/2)}\big)\\
&= \Pr\big(-s_2 t_{\alpha/2} \ge \beta_{20} - \hat{\beta}_2 \ge -s_2 t_{1-(\alpha/2)}\big)\\
&= \Pr\big(\hat{\beta}_2 - s_2 t_{\alpha/2} \ge \beta_{20} \ge \hat{\beta}_2 - s_2 t_{1-(\alpha/2)}\big).
\end{aligned}$$

Therefore, the confidence interval we are seeking is

$$\big[\hat{\beta}_2 - s_2 t_{1-(\alpha/2)},\ \hat{\beta}_2 - s_2 t_{\alpha/2}\big]. \tag{5.13}$$

At first glance, this interval may look a bit odd, because the upper limit is obtained by subtracting something from $\hat{\beta}_2$. What is subtracted is negative, however, because $t_{\alpha/2} < 0$, since it is in the lower tail of the t distribution. Thus the interval does in fact contain the point estimate $\hat{\beta}_2$.

It may still seem strange that the lower and upper limits of (5.13) depend, respectively, on the upper-tail and lower-tail quantiles of the $t(n-k)$ distribution. This actually makes perfect sense, however, as can be seen by looking at the infinite confidence interval (5.09) based on a one-tailed test. There, since the null is that $\theta \le \theta_0$, the confidence interval must be open out to $+\infty$, and so only the lower limit of the confidence interval is finite. But the null is rejected when the test statistic is in the upper tail of its distribution, and so it must be the upper-tail quantile that determines the only finite limit of the confidence interval, namely, the lower limit. Readers are strongly advised to take some time to think this point through, since most people find it strongly counter-intuitive when they first encounter it, and they can accept it only after a period of reflection.

In the case of (5.13), it is easy to rewrite the confidence interval so that it depends only on the positive, upper-tail, quantile, $t_{1-(\alpha/2)}$. Because the Student's t distribution is symmetric, the interval (5.13) is the same as the interval

$$\big[\hat{\beta}_2 - s_2 t_{1-(\alpha/2)},\ \hat{\beta}_2 + s_2 t_{1-(\alpha/2)}\big]; \tag{5.14}$$

compare the two ways of writing the confidence interval (5.08). For concreteness, suppose that $\alpha = .05$ and $n - k = 32$. In this special case, $t_{1-(\alpha/2)} = t_{.975} = 2.037$. Thus the .95 confidence interval based on (5.14) extends from 2.037 standard errors below $\hat{\beta}_2$ to 2.037 standard errors above it. This interval is slightly wider than the interval (5.07), which is based on asymptotic theory.

We obtained the interval (5.14) by starting from the t statistic (5.11) and using the Student's t distribution. As readers are asked to demonstrate in Exercise 5.2, we would have obtained precisely the same interval if we had started instead from the square of (5.11) and used the F distribution.

5.3 Bootstrap Confidence Intervals

When exact confidence intervals are not available, and they generally are not, asymptotic ones are normally used. However, just as asymptotic tests do not always perform well in finite samples, neither do asymptotic confidence intervals. Since bootstrap P values and tests based on them often outperform their asymptotic counterparts, it seems natural to base confidence intervals on bootstrap tests when asymptotic intervals give poor coverage. There are a great many varieties of **bootstrap confidence intervals**; for a comprehensive discussion, see Davison and Hinkley (1997).

When we construct a bootstrap confidence interval, we wish to treat a family of tests, each corresponding to its own null hypothesis. Since, when we perform a bootstrap test, we must use a bootstrap DGP that satisfies the null hypothesis, it appears that we must use an infinite number of bootstrap DGPs if we are to consider the full family of tests, each with a different null. Fortunately, there is a clever trick that lets us avoid this difficulty completely.

It is, of course, essential for a bootstrap test that the bootstrap DGP should satisfy the null hypothesis under test. However, when the distribution of the test statistic does not depend on precisely which null is being tested, the same bootstrap distribution can be used for a whole family of tests with different nulls. If a family of test statistics is defined in terms of a pivotal random function $\tau(\boldsymbol{y}, \theta_0)$, then, by definition, the distribution of this function is independent of θ_0. Thus we could choose any value of θ_0 that the model allows for the bootstrap DGP, and the distribution of the test statistic, evaluated at θ_0, would always be the same. The important thing is to make sure that $\tau(\cdot)$ is evaluated at the *same* value of θ_0 as the one used to generate the bootstrap samples. Even if $\tau(\cdot)$ is only asymptotically pivotal, the effect of the choice of θ_0 on the distribution of the statistic should be slight if the sample size is reasonably large.

Suppose that we wish to construct a bootstrap confidence interval based on the t statistic $\hat{t}(\theta_0) \equiv \tau(\boldsymbol{y}, \theta_0) = (\hat{\theta} - \theta_0)/s_\theta$. The first step is to compute $\hat{\theta}$ and s_θ using the original data $\boldsymbol{y}$. Then we generate bootstrap samples using a DGP, which may be either parametric or semiparametric, characterized by $\hat{\theta}$ and by any other relevant estimates, such as the error variance, that may be needed. The resulting bootstrap DGP is thus quite independent of θ_0, but it does depend on the estimate $\hat{\theta}$.

We can now generate B bootstrap samples, $\boldsymbol{y}_j^*$, $j = 1, \ldots, B$. For each of these, we compute an estimate θ_j^* and its standard error s_j^* in exactly the same way that we computed $\hat{\theta}$ and s_θ from the original data, and we then compute the bootstrap "t statistic"

$$t_j^* \equiv \tau(\boldsymbol{y}_j^*, \hat{\theta}) = \frac{\theta_j^* - \hat{\theta}}{s_j^*}. \tag{5.15}$$

This is the statistic that tests the null hypothesis that $\theta = \hat{\theta}$, because $\hat{\theta}$ is the true value of θ for the bootstrap DGP. If $\tau(\cdot)$ is an exact pivot, the change of null from θ_0 to $\hat{\theta}$ makes no difference. If $\tau(\cdot)$ is an asymptotic pivot, there should usually be only a slight difference for values of θ_0 close to $\hat{\theta}$.

The limits of the bootstrap confidence interval depend on the quantiles of the EDF of the t_j^*. We can choose to construct either a symmetric confidence interval, by estimating a single critical value that applies to both tails, or an asymmetric one, by estimating two different critical values. When the distribution of the underlying test statistic $\tau(\boldsymbol{y}, \theta_0)$ is not symmetric, the latter interval should be more accurate. For this reason, and because we did not discuss asymmetric intervals based on asymptotic tests, we now discuss asymmetric bootstrap confidence intervals in some detail.

Asymmetric Bootstrap Confidence Intervals

Let us denote by $\hat{F}^*$ the EDF of the B bootstrap statistics t_j^*. For given θ_0, the bootstrap P value is, from (5.10),

$$\hat{p}(\hat{t}(\theta_0)) = 2\min\Big(\hat{F}^*(\hat{t}(\theta_0)),\ 1 - \hat{F}^*(\hat{t}(\theta_0))\Big). \tag{5.16}$$

If this P value is greater than or equal to α, then θ_0 belongs to the $1-\alpha$ confidence interval. If $\hat{F}^*$ were the CDF of a continuous distribution, we could express the confidence interval in terms of the quantiles of this distribution, just as in (5.13). In the limit as $B \to \infty$, the limiting distribution of the t_j^*, which we call the **ideal bootstrap distribution**, is usually continuous, and its quantiles define the ideal bootstrap confidence interval. However, since the distribution of the t_j^* is always discrete in practice, we must be a little more careful in our reasoning.

Suppose, to begin with, that $\hat{t}(\theta_0)$ is on the left side of the distribution. Then the bootstrap P value (5.16) is

$$2\hat{F}^*(\hat{t}(\theta_0)) = \frac{2}{B}\sum_{j=1}^{B} I\big(t_j^* \le \hat{t}(\theta_0)\big) = \frac{2r(\theta_0)}{B},$$

where $r(\theta_0)$ is the number of bootstrap t statistics that are less than or equal to $\hat{t}(\theta_0)$. Thus θ_0 belongs to the $1-\alpha$ confidence interval if and only if $2r(\theta_0)/B \ge \alpha$, that is, if $r(\theta_0) \ge \alpha B/2$. Since $r(\theta_0)$ is an integer, while $\alpha B/2$ is not an integer, in general, this inequality is equivalent to $r(\theta_0) \ge r_{\alpha/2}$, where $r_{\alpha/2}$ is the smallest integer not less than $\alpha B/2$.

First, observe that $r(\theta_0)$ cannot exceed $r_{\alpha/2}$ for θ_0 sufficiently large. Since $\hat{t}(\theta_0) = (\hat{\theta} - \theta_0)/s_\theta$, it follows that $\hat{t}(\theta_0) \to -\infty$ as $\theta_0 \to \infty$. Accordingly, $r(\theta_0) \to 0$ as $\theta_0 \to \infty$. Therefore, there exists a greatest value of θ_0 for which $r(\theta_0) \ge r_{\alpha/2}$. This value must be the upper limit of the $1-\alpha$ bootstrap confidence interval.

Suppose we sort the t_j^* from smallest to largest and denote by $c_{\alpha/2}^*$ the entry in the sorted list indexed by $r_{\alpha/2}$. Then, if $\hat{t}(\theta_0) = c_{\alpha/2}^*$, the number of the t_j^* less than or equal to $\hat{t}(\theta_0)$ is precisely $r_{\alpha/2}$. But if $\hat{t}(\theta_0)$ is smaller than $c_{\alpha/2}^*$ by however small an amount, this number is strictly less than $r_{\alpha/2}$. Thus θ_u, the upper limit of the confidence interval, is defined implicitly by $\hat{t}(\theta_u) = c_{\alpha/2}^*$. Explicitly, we have

$$\theta_u = \hat{\theta} - s_\theta c_{\alpha/2}^*.$$

As in the previous section, we see that the *upper* limit of the confidence interval is determined by the *lower* tail of the bootstrap distribution.

If the statistic is an exact pivot, then the probability that the true value of θ is greater than θ_u is exactly equal to $\alpha/2$ only if $\alpha(B+1)/2$ is an integer. This follows by exactly the same argument as the one given in Section 4.6

for bootstrap P values. As an example, if $\alpha = .05$ and $B = 999$, we see that $\alpha(B+1)/2 = 25$. In addition, since $\alpha B/2 = 24.975$, we see that $r_{\alpha/2} = 25$. The value of $c^*_{\alpha/2}$ is therefore the value of the 25th bootstrap t statistic when they are sorted in ascending order.

In order to obtain the upper limit of the confidence interval, we began above with the assumption that $\hat{t}(\theta_0)$ is on the left side of the distribution. If we had begun by assuming that $\hat{t}(\theta_0)$ is on the right side of the distribution, we would have found that the lower limit of the confidence interval is

$$\theta_l = \hat{\theta} - s_\theta c^*_{1-(\alpha/2)},$$

where $c^*_{1-(\alpha/2)}$ is the entry indexed by $r_{1-(\alpha/2)}$ when the t^*_j are sorted in ascending order. For the example with $\alpha = .05$ and $B = 999$, this is the 975th entry in the sorted list, since there are precisely 25 integers in the range $975-999$, just as there are in the range $1-25$.

The asymmetric equal-tail bootstrap confidence interval can be written as

$$\left[\theta_l,\ \theta_u\right] = \left[\hat{\theta} - s_\theta c^*_{1-(\alpha/2)},\ \hat{\theta} - s_\theta c^*_{\alpha/2}\right]. \tag{5.17}$$

This interval bears a striking resemblance to the exact confidence interval (5.13). Clearly, $c^*_{1-(\alpha/2)}$ and $c^*_{\alpha/2}$, which are approximately the $1-(\alpha/2)$ and $\alpha/2$ quantiles of the EDF of the bootstrap tests, play the same roles as the $1-(\alpha/2)$ and $\alpha/2$ quantiles of the exact Student's t distribution.

Because the Student's t distribution is symmetric, the confidence interval (5.13) is necessarily symmetric. In contrast, the interval (5.17) is almost never symmetric. Even if the distribution of the underlying test statistic happened to be symmetric, the bootstrap distribution based on finite B would almost never be. It is, of course, possible to construct a symmetric bootstrap confidence interval. We just need to invert a test for which the P value is not (5.10), but rather something like (4.07), which is based on the absolute value, or, equivalently, the square, of the t statistic. See Exercise 5.7.

The bootstrap confidence interval (5.17) is called a **studentized bootstrap** confidence interval. The name comes from the fact that a statistic is said to be **studentized** when it is the ratio of a random variable to its standard error, as is the ordinary t statistic. This type of confidence interval is also sometimes called a **percentile-*t*** or **bootstrap-*t*** confidence interval. Studentized bootstrap confidence intervals have good theoretical properties, and, as we have seen, they are quite easy to construct. If the assumptions of the classical normal linear model are violated and the empirical distribution of the t^*_j provides a better approximation to the actual distribution of the t statistic than does the Student's t distribution, then the studentized bootstrap confidence interval should be more accurate than the usual interval based on asymptotic theory.

As we remarked above, there are a great many ways to compute bootstrap confidence intervals, and there is a good deal of controversy about the relative merits of different approaches. For an introduction to the voluminous literature, see DiCiccio and Efron (1996) and the associated discussion. Some of the approaches in the literature appear to be obsolete, mere relics of the way in which ideas about the bootstrap were developed, and others are too complicated to explain here. Even if we limit our attention to studentized bootstrap intervals, there are often several ways to proceed. Different ways of estimating standard errors inevitably lead to different confidence intervals, as do different ways of parametrizing a model. Thus, in practice, there are often quite a number of reasonable ways to construct studentized bootstrap confidence intervals.

Note that specifying the bootstrap DGP is not at all trivial if the error terms are not assumed to be IID. In fact, this topic is quite advanced and has been the subject of much research: See Li and Maddala (1996) and Davison and Hinkley (1997), among others. Later in the book, we will discuss a few techniques that can be used with particular models.

Theoretical results discussed in Hall (1992) and Davison and Hinkley (1997) suggest that studentized bootstrap confidence intervals generally work better than intervals based on asymptotic theory. However, their coverage can be quite unsatisfactory in finite samples if the quantity $(\hat{\theta} - \theta)/s_\theta$ is far from being pivotal, as can happen if the distributions of either $\hat{\theta}$ or s_θ depend strongly on the true unknown value of θ or on any other parameters of the model. When this is the case, the standard errors often fluctuate wildly among the bootstrap samples. Of course, the coverage of asymptotic confidence intervals is generally also unsatisfactory in such cases.

5.4 Confidence Regions

When we are interested in making inferences about the values of two or more parameters, it can be quite misleading to look at the confidence intervals for each of the parameters individually. By using confidence intervals, we are implicitly basing our inferences on the *marginal* distributions of the parameter estimates. However, if the estimates are not independent, the product of the marginal distributions may be very different from the joint distribution. In such cases, it makes sense to construct a confidence region.

The confidence intervals we have discussed are all obtained by inverting t tests, whether exact, asymptotic, or bootstrap, based on families of statistics of the form $(\hat{\theta} - \theta_0)/s_\theta$. If we wish instead to construct a confidence region, we must invert joint tests for several parameters. These are usually tests based on statistics that follow the F or χ^2 distributions, at least asymptotically.

A t statistic depends explicitly on a parameter estimate and its standard error. Similarly, many tests for several parameters depend on a vector of parameter estimates and an estimate of their covariance matrix. Even many statistics that appear not to do so, such as F statistics, actually do so implicitly, as we will see shortly. Suppose that we have a k-vector of parameter estimates $\hat{\boldsymbol{\theta}}$, of which the covariance matrix $\mathrm{Var}(\hat{\boldsymbol{\theta}})$ can be estimated by $\widehat{\mathrm{Var}}(\hat{\boldsymbol{\theta}})$. Then, in many circumstances, the **Wald statistic**

$$(\hat{\boldsymbol{\theta}} - \boldsymbol{\theta}_0)^\top \big(\widehat{\mathrm{Var}}(\hat{\boldsymbol{\theta}})\big)^{-1} (\hat{\boldsymbol{\theta}} - \boldsymbol{\theta}_0) \tag{5.18}$$

can be used to test the joint null hypothesis that $\boldsymbol{\theta} = \boldsymbol{\theta}_0$.

The asymptotic distribution of the Wald statistic (5.18) can be found by using Theorem 4.1. It tells us that, if a k–vector $\boldsymbol{x}$ is distributed as $\mathrm{N}(\mathbf{0}, \boldsymbol{\Omega})$, then the quadratic form $\boldsymbol{x}^\top \boldsymbol{\Omega}^{-1} \boldsymbol{x}$ is distributed as $\chi^2(k)$. In order to use this result to show that the statistic (5.18) is asymptotically distributed as $\chi^2(k)$ under the null hypothesis, we must study a little more asymptotic theory.

Asymptotic Normality and Root-n Consistency

Although the notion of **asymptotic normality** is very general, for now we will introduce it for linear regression models only. Suppose, as in Section 4.5, that the data were generated by the DGP

$$\boldsymbol{y} = \boldsymbol{X}\boldsymbol{\beta}_0 + \boldsymbol{u}, \quad \boldsymbol{u} \sim \mathrm{IID}(\mathbf{0}, \sigma_0^2 \mathbf{I}), \tag{5.19}$$

given in (4.47). We have seen that the random vector $\boldsymbol{v} = n^{-1/2}\boldsymbol{X}^\top \boldsymbol{u}$ defined in (4.53) follows the normal distribution asymptotically, with mean vector $\mathbf{0}$ and covariance matrix $\sigma_0^2 \boldsymbol{S}_{\boldsymbol{X}^\top\boldsymbol{X}}$, where $\boldsymbol{S}_{\boldsymbol{X}^\top\boldsymbol{X}}$ is the plim of $n^{-1}\boldsymbol{X}^\top\boldsymbol{X}$ as the sample size n tends to infinity.

Consider now the estimation error of the vector of OLS estimates. For the DGP (5.19), it is

$$\hat{\boldsymbol{\beta}} - \boldsymbol{\beta}_0 = (\boldsymbol{X}^\top\boldsymbol{X})^{-1}\boldsymbol{X}^\top\boldsymbol{u}. \tag{5.20}$$

As we saw in Section 3.3, $\hat{\boldsymbol{\beta}}$ is consistent under fairly weak conditions. If it is, expression (5.20) tends to a limit of $\mathbf{0}$ as the sample size $n \to \infty$. Therefore, its limiting covariance matrix is a zero matrix. Thus it would appear that asymptotic theory has nothing to say about limiting variances for consistent estimators. However, this is easily corrected by the usual device of introducing a few well-chosen powers of n. If we rewrite (5.20) as

$$n^{1/2}(\hat{\boldsymbol{\beta}} - \boldsymbol{\beta}_0) = (n^{-1}\boldsymbol{X}^\top\boldsymbol{X})^{-1} n^{-1/2}\boldsymbol{X}^\top\boldsymbol{u},$$

then the first factor on the right-hand side tends to $\boldsymbol{S}_{\boldsymbol{X}^\top\boldsymbol{X}}^{-1}$ as $n \to \infty$, and the second factor, which is just $\boldsymbol{v}$, tends to a random vector distributed as $\mathrm{N}(\mathbf{0}, \sigma_0^2 \boldsymbol{S}_{\boldsymbol{X}^\top\boldsymbol{X}})$. Because $\boldsymbol{S}_{\boldsymbol{X}^\top\boldsymbol{X}}$ is deterministic, we find that, asymptotically,

$$\mathrm{Var}\big(n^{1/2}(\hat{\boldsymbol{\beta}} - \boldsymbol{\beta}_0)\big) = \sigma_0^2 \boldsymbol{S}_{\boldsymbol{X}^\top\boldsymbol{X}}^{-1} \boldsymbol{S}_{\boldsymbol{X}^\top\boldsymbol{X}} \boldsymbol{S}_{\boldsymbol{X}^\top\boldsymbol{X}}^{-1} = \sigma_0^2 \boldsymbol{S}_{\boldsymbol{X}^\top\boldsymbol{X}}^{-1}.$$

Moreover, since $n^{1/2}(\hat{\boldsymbol{\beta}} - \boldsymbol{\beta}_0)$ is, asymptotically, just a deterministic linear combination of the components of the multivariate normal random vector $\boldsymbol{v}$, we may conclude that

$$n^{1/2}(\hat{\boldsymbol{\beta}} - \boldsymbol{\beta}_0) \overset{a}{\sim} \mathrm{N}(\mathbf{0}, \sigma_0^2 \boldsymbol{S}_{\boldsymbol{X}^\top\boldsymbol{X}}^{-1}). \tag{5.21}$$

Thus, under the fairly weak conditions we used in Section 4.5, we see that the vector $\hat{\boldsymbol{\beta}}$ is **asymptotically normal**, or exhibits **asymptotic normality**.

The result (5.21) tells us that the **asymptotic covariance matrix** of the vector $n^{1/2}(\hat{\boldsymbol{\beta}} - \boldsymbol{\beta}_0)$ is the limit of $\sigma_0^2(n^{-1}\boldsymbol{X}^\top\boldsymbol{X})^{-1}$ as $n \to \infty$. In practice, we divide this matrix by n and use $s^2(\boldsymbol{X}^\top\boldsymbol{X})^{-1}$ to estimate $\mathrm{Var}(\hat{\boldsymbol{\beta}})$, where s^2 is the usual OLS estimate of the error variance; recall (3.49). However, it is important to remember that, whenever $n^{-1}\boldsymbol{X}^\top\boldsymbol{X}$ tends to $\boldsymbol{S}_{\boldsymbol{X}^\top\boldsymbol{X}}$ as $n \to \infty$, the matrix $(\boldsymbol{X}^\top\boldsymbol{X})^{-1}$, without the factor of n, simply tends to a zero matrix. As we saw a moment ago, this is just a consequence of the fact that $\hat{\boldsymbol{\beta}}$ is consistent. Thus, although it would be convenient if we could dispense with powers of n when working out asymptotic approximations to covariance matrices, it would be mathematically incorrect and very risky to do so.

The result (5.21) also gives us the **rate of convergence** of $\hat{\boldsymbol{\beta}}$ to its probability limit of $\boldsymbol{\beta}_0$. Since multiplying the estimation error by $n^{1/2}$ gives rise to an expression of zero mean and finite covariance matrix, it follows that the estimation error itself tends to zero at the same rate as $n^{-1/2}$. This property is expressed by saying that the estimator $\hat{\boldsymbol{\beta}}$ is **root-n consistent**.

Quite generally, let $\hat{\boldsymbol{\theta}}$ be a root-n consistent, asymptotically normal, estimator of a parameter vector $\boldsymbol{\theta}$. Any estimator of the covariance matrix of $\hat{\boldsymbol{\theta}}$ must tend to zero as $n \to \infty$. Let $\boldsymbol{\theta}_0$ denote the true value of $\boldsymbol{\theta}$, and let $\boldsymbol{V}$ denote the limiting covariance matrix of $n^{1/2}(\hat{\boldsymbol{\theta}} - \boldsymbol{\theta}_0)$. Then an estimator $\widehat{\mathrm{Var}}(\hat{\boldsymbol{\theta}})$ is said to be a consistent estimator of the covariance matrix of $\hat{\boldsymbol{\theta}}$ if

$$\operatorname*{plim}_{n\to\infty}\bigl(n\,\widehat{\mathrm{Var}}(\hat{\boldsymbol{\theta}})\bigr) = \boldsymbol{V}. \tag{5.22}$$

We are finally in a position to justify treating the Wald statistic (5.18) as being approximately distributed as $\chi^2(k)$ under the null hypothesis. If $\hat{\boldsymbol{\theta}}$ is root-n consistent and asymptotically normal, and if $\widehat{\mathrm{Var}}(\hat{\boldsymbol{\theta}})$ is a consistent estimator of the variance of $\hat{\boldsymbol{\theta}}$, then we can write (5.18) as

$$n^{1/2}(\hat{\boldsymbol{\theta}} - \boldsymbol{\theta}_0)^\top\bigl(n\,\widehat{\mathrm{Var}}(\hat{\boldsymbol{\theta}})\bigr)^{-1} n^{1/2}(\hat{\boldsymbol{\theta}} - \boldsymbol{\theta}_0). \tag{5.23}$$

Since $n^{1/2}(\hat{\boldsymbol{\theta}} - \boldsymbol{\theta}_0)$ is asymptotically normal under the null, with mean zero, and since the middle factor above tends to the inverse of its limiting covariance matrix, expression (5.23) is precisely in the form $\boldsymbol{x}^\top\boldsymbol{\Omega}^{-1}\boldsymbol{x}$ of Theorem 4.1. It follows that the statistic (5.18) is asymptotically distributed as $\chi^2(k)$ under the null hypothesis.

Exact Confidence Regions for Regression Parameters

Suppose that we want to construct a confidence region for the elements of the vector β_2 in the classical normal linear model (4.28), which we rewrite here for ease of exposition:

$$y = X_1\beta_1 + X_2\beta_2 + u, \quad u \sim \mathrm{N}(\mathbf{0}, \sigma^2\mathbf{I}), \tag{5.24}$$

where β_1 and β_2 are a k_1–vector and a k_2–vector, respectively. The F statistic that can be used to test the hypothesis that $\beta_2 = \mathbf{0}$ is given in (4.33). If we wish instead to test $\beta_2 = \beta_{20}$, then we can write (5.24) as

$$y - X_2\beta_{20} = X_1\gamma_1 + X_2\gamma_2 + u, \quad u \sim \mathrm{N}(\mathbf{0}, \sigma^2\mathbf{I}), \tag{5.25}$$

and test $\gamma_2 = \mathbf{0}$. It is not hard to show that the F statistic for this hypothesis takes the form

$$\frac{(\hat\beta_2 - \beta_{20})^{\top} X_2^{\top} M_1 X_2 (\hat\beta_2 - \beta_{20})/k_2}{y^{\top} M_X y/(n-k)}, \tag{5.26}$$

where $k = k_1 + k_2$; see Exercise 5.10. When multiplied by k_2, this F statistic is in the form of the Wald statistic (5.18). For the purposes of inference on β_2, regression (5.24) is, by the FWL Theorem, equivalent to the regression

$$M_1 y = M_1 X_2 \beta_2 + M_1 u.$$

Thus $\mathrm{Var}(\hat\beta_2)$ is equal to $\sigma^2(X_2^{\top} M_1 X_2)^{-1}$. Since the denominator of (5.26) is just s^2, the OLS estimate of the error variance from running regression (5.24), k_2 times the F statistic (5.26) can be written in the form of (5.18), with

$$\widehat{\mathrm{Var}}(\hat\beta_2) = s^2\big(X_2^{\top} M_1 X_2\big)^{-1}$$

providing a consistent estimator of the variance of $\hat\beta_2$; compare (3.50).

Under the assumptions of the classical normal linear model, the F statistic (5.26) follows the $F(k_2, n-k)$ distribution when the null hypothesis is true. Therefore, we can use it to construct an **exact confidence region**. If c_α denotes the $1-\alpha$ quantile of the $F(k_2, n-k)$ distribution, then the $1-\alpha$ confidence region is the set of all β_{20} for which

$$(\hat\beta_2 - \beta_{20})^{\top} X_2^{\top} M_1 X_2 (\hat\beta_2 - \beta_{20}) \le c_\alpha k_2 s^2. \tag{5.27}$$

Since the left-hand side of this inequality is quadratic in β_{20}, the confidence region is, for $k_2 = 2$, the interior of an ellipse and, for $k_2 > 2$, the interior of a k_2–dimensional ellipsoid.

Confidence Ellipses and Confidence Intervals

Figure 5.3 illustrates what a **confidence ellipse** can look like when there are just two components in the vector $\boldsymbol{\beta}_2$, which we denote by β_1 and β_2, and the parameter estimates are negatively correlated. The ellipse, which defines a .95 confidence region, is centered at the parameter estimates $(\hat{\beta}_1, \hat{\beta}_2)$, with its major axis oriented from upper left to lower right. Confidence intervals for β_1 and β_2 are also shown. The .95 confidence interval for β_1 is the line segment AB, and the .95 confidence interval for β_2 is the line segment EF. We would make quite different inferences if we considered AB and EF, and the rectangle they define, demarcated in Figure 5.3 by the lines drawn with long dashes, rather than the confidence ellipse. There are many points, such as (β_1'', β_2''), that lie outside the confidence ellipse but inside the two confidence intervals. At the same time, there are some points, like (β_1', β_2'), that are contained in the ellipse but lie outside one or both of the confidence intervals.

In the framework of the classical normal linear model, the estimates $\hat{\beta}_1$ and $\hat{\beta}_2$ are bivariate normal. The t statistics used to test hypotheses about just one of β_1 or β_2 are based on the *marginal* univariate normal distributions of $\hat{\beta}_1$ and $\hat{\beta}_2$, respectively, but the F statistics used to test hypotheses about both parameters at once are based on the *joint* bivariate normal distribution of the two estimators. If $\hat{\beta}_1$ and $\hat{\beta}_2$ are not independent, as is the case in Figure 5.3, then information about one of the parameters also provides information about

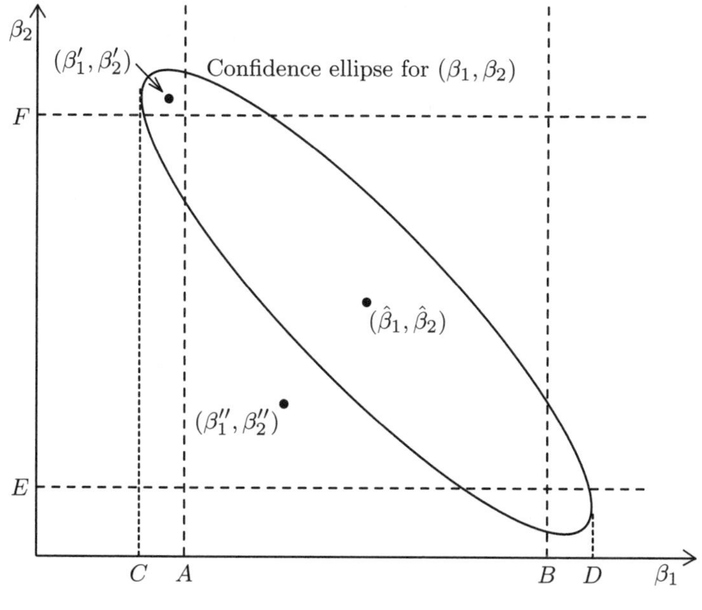

Figure 5.3 Confidence ellipses and confidence intervals

the other. Only the confidence region, based on the joint distribution, allows this to be taken into account.

An example may be helpful at this point. Suppose that we are trying to model daily electricity demand during the summer months in an area where air conditioning is prevalent. Since the use of air conditioners, and hence electricity demand, is related to both temperature and humidity, we might want to use measures of both of them as explanatory variables. In many parts of the world, summer temperatures and humidity are strongly positively correlated. Therefore, if we include both variables in a regression, they may be approximately collinear. If so, as we saw in Section 3.4, the OLS estimates must be relatively imprecise. This lack of precision implies that confidence intervals for the coefficients of both temperature and humidity are relatively long, and that confidence regions for both parameters jointly are long and narrow. However, it does not necessarily imply that the area of a confidence region is particularly large. This is precisely the situation that is illustrated in Figure 5.3. Think of β_1 as the coefficient of the temperature and β_2 as the coefficient of the humidity.

In Exercise 5.11, readers are asked to show that, when there are two explanatory variables in a linear regression model, the correlation between the OLS estimates of the parameters associated with these variables is the negative of the correlation between the variables themselves. Thus, in the example we have been discussing, a positive correlation between temperature and humidity leads to a negative correlation between the estimates of the temperature and humidity parameters, as shown in Figure 5.3. A point like (β_1'', β_2'') is excluded from the confidence region because the variation in electricity demand cannot be accounted for if *both* coefficients are small. But β_1'' cannot be excluded from the confidence interval for β_1 alone, because β_1'', which assigns a small effect to the temperature, is perfectly compatible with the data if a large effect is assigned to the humidity, that is, if β_2 is substantially greater than β_2''. At the same time, even though β_1' is outside the confidence interval for β_1, the point (β_1', β_2') is inside the confidence region, because the very high value of β_2' is enough to compensate for the very low value of β_1'.

The relation between a confidence region for two parameters and confidence intervals for each of the parameters individually is a subtle one. It is tempting to think that the ends of the intervals should be given by the extreme points of the confidence ellipse. This would imply, for example, that the confidence interval for β_1 in the figure is given by the line segment CD. Even without the insight afforded by the temperature-humidity example, however, we can see that this must be incorrect. The inequality (5.27) defines the confidence region, for given parameter estimates $\hat{\beta}_1$ and $\hat{\beta}_2$, as a set of values in the space of the vector $\boldsymbol{\beta}_{20}$. If instead we think of (5.27) as defining a region in the space of $\hat{\boldsymbol{\beta}}_2$ with $\boldsymbol{\beta}_{20}$ the true parameter vector, then we obtain a region of exactly the same size and shape as the confidence region, because (5.27) is symmetric in $\boldsymbol{\beta}_{20}$ and $\hat{\boldsymbol{\beta}}_2$. We can assign a probability of $1-\alpha$ to the event that $\hat{\beta}_2$ belongs to the new region, because the inequality (5.27) states that the F statistic is less than its $1-\alpha$ quantile, an event of which the probability is $1-\alpha$, by definition.

An exactly similar argument can be made for the confidence interval for β_1. In the two-dimensional framework of Figure 5.3, the entire infinitely high rectangle bounded by the vertical lines through the points A and B has the same size and shape as an area with probability $1-\alpha$, since we are willing to allow β_2 to take on any real value. Because the infinite rectangle and the confidence ellipse must contain the *same* probability mass, neither can contain the other. Therefore, the ellipse must protrude outside the region defined by the one-dimensional confidence interval.

It can be seen from the inequality (5.27) that the orientation of a confidence ellipse and the relative lengths of its axes are determined by $\widehat{\mathrm{Var}}(\hat{\boldsymbol{\beta}}_2)$. When the two parameter estimates are positively correlated, the ellipse is oriented from lower left to upper right. When they are negatively correlated, it is oriented from upper left to lower right, as in Figure 5.3. When the correlation is zero, the axes of the ellipse are parallel to the coordinate axes. The variances of the two parameter estimates determine the height and width of the ellipse. If the variances are equal and the correlation is zero, then the confidence ellipse is a circle.

Asymptotic and Bootstrap Confidence Regions

When test statistics like (5.26), with known finite-sample distributions, are not available, the easiest way to construct an approximate confidence region is to base it on the statistic (5.18), which can be used with any k-vector of parameter estimates $\hat{\boldsymbol{\theta}}$ that is root-n consistent and asymptotically normal and has a covariance matrix that can be consistently estimated by $\widehat{\mathrm{Var}}(\hat{\boldsymbol{\theta}})$. If c_α denotes the $1-\alpha$ quantile of the $\chi^2(k)$ distribution, then an approximate $1-\alpha$ confidence region is the set of all $\boldsymbol{\theta}_0$ such that

$$(\hat{\boldsymbol{\theta}}-\boldsymbol{\theta}_0)^{\top}\big(\widehat{\mathrm{Var}}(\hat{\boldsymbol{\theta}})\big)^{-1}(\hat{\boldsymbol{\theta}}-\boldsymbol{\theta}_0) \le c_\alpha. \tag{5.28}$$

Like the exact confidence region defined by (5.27), this **asymptotic confidence region** is elliptical or ellipsoidal.

We can also use the statistic (5.18) to construct bootstrap confidence regions, making the same assumptions as were made above about $\hat{\boldsymbol{\theta}}$ and $\widehat{\mathrm{Var}}(\hat{\boldsymbol{\theta}})$. As we did for bootstrap confidence intervals, we use just one bootstrap DGP, either parametric or semiparametric, characterized by the parameter vector $\hat{\boldsymbol{\theta}}$. For each of B bootstrap samples, indexed by j, we obtain a vector of parameter estimates $\boldsymbol{\theta}_j^*$ and an estimated covariance matrix $\mathrm{Var}^*(\boldsymbol{\theta}_j^*)$, in just the same way as $\hat{\boldsymbol{\theta}}$ and $\widehat{\mathrm{Var}}(\hat{\boldsymbol{\theta}})$ were obtained from the original data. For each j, we compute the bootstrap "test statistic"

$$\tau_j^* \equiv (\boldsymbol{\theta}_j^*-\hat{\boldsymbol{\theta}})^{\top}\big(\mathrm{Var}^*(\boldsymbol{\theta}_j^*)\big)^{-1}(\boldsymbol{\theta}_j^*-\hat{\boldsymbol{\theta}}), \tag{5.29}$$

which is the multivariate analog of (5.15). We then find the bootstrap critical value c^*_α, which is the $1-\alpha$ quantile of the EDF of the τ^*_j. This is done by sorting the τ^*_j from smallest to largest and then taking the entry numbered $(B+1)(1-\alpha)$, assuming of course that $\alpha(B+1)$ is an integer. For example, if $B = 999$ and $\alpha = .05$, then c^*_α is the 950th entry in the sorted list. The bootstrap confidence region is defined as the set of all $\boldsymbol{\theta}_0$ such that

$$(\hat{\boldsymbol{\theta}} - \boldsymbol{\theta}_0)^\top \big(\widehat{\mathrm{Var}}(\hat{\boldsymbol{\theta}})\big)^{-1}(\hat{\boldsymbol{\theta}} - \boldsymbol{\theta}_0) \le c^*_\alpha. \tag{5.30}$$

It is no accident that the bootstrap confidence region defined by (5.30) looks very much like the asymptotic confidence region defined by (5.28). The only difference is that the critical value c_α, which appears on the right-hand side of (5.28), comes from the asymptotic distribution of the test statistic, while the critical value c^*_α, which appears on the right-hand side of (5.30), comes from the empirical distribution of the bootstrap samples. Both confidence regions have the same elliptical shape. When $c^*_\alpha > c_\alpha$, the region defined by (5.30) is larger than the region defined by (5.28), and the opposite is true when $c^*_\alpha < c_\alpha$.

Although this procedure is similar to the studentized bootstrap procedure discussed in Section 5.3, its true analog is the procedure for obtaining a *symmetric* bootstrap confidence interval that is the subject of Exercise 5.7. That procedure yields a symmetric interval because it is based on the square of the t statistic. Similarly, because this procedure is based on the quadratic form (5.18), the bootstrap confidence region defined by (5.30) is forced to have the same elliptical shape (but not the same size) as the asymptotic confidence region defined by (5.28). Of course, such a confidence region cannot be expected to work very well if the finite-sample distribution of $\hat{\boldsymbol{\theta}}$ does not in fact have contours that are approximately elliptical.

In view of the many ways in which bootstrap confidence intervals can be constructed, it should come as no surprise to learn that there are also many other ways to construct bootstrap confidence regions. See Davison and Hinkley (1997) for references and a discussion of some of these.

5.5 Heteroskedasticity-Consistent Covariance Matrices

All the testing procedures we have used in this chapter and the preceding one make use, implicitly if not explicitly, of standard errors or estimated covariance matrices. If we are to make reliable inferences about the values of parameters, these estimates should be reliable. In our discussion of how to estimate the covariance matrix of the OLS parameter vector $\hat{\boldsymbol{\beta}}$ in Sections 3.4 and 3.6, we made the rather strong assumption that the error terms of the regression model are IID. This assumption is needed to show that $s^2(\boldsymbol{X}^\top\boldsymbol{X})^{-1}$, the usual estimator of the covariance matrix of $\hat{\boldsymbol{\beta}}$, is consistent in the sense of (5.22). However, even without the IID assumption, it is possible to obtain a consistent estimator of the covariance matrix of $\hat{\boldsymbol{\beta}}$.

In this section, we treat the case in which the error terms are independent but not identically distributed. We focus on the linear regression model with exogenous regressors,

$$\boldsymbol{y} = \boldsymbol{X\beta} + \boldsymbol{u}, \quad \mathrm{E}(\boldsymbol{u}) = \boldsymbol{0}, \;\; \mathrm{E}(\boldsymbol{u}\boldsymbol{u}^\top) = \boldsymbol{\Omega}, \tag{5.31}$$

where $\boldsymbol{\Omega}$, the error covariance matrix, is an $n \times n$ matrix with t^{th} diagonal element equal to ω_t^2 and all the off-diagonal elements equal to 0. Since $\boldsymbol{X}$ is assumed to be exogenous, the expectations in (5.31) can be treated as conditional on $\boldsymbol{X}$. Conditional on $\boldsymbol{X}$, then, the error terms in (5.31) are uncorrelated and have mean 0, but they do not have the same variance for all observations. These error terms are said to be **heteroskedastic**, or to exhibit **heteroskedasticity**, a subject of which we spoke briefly in Section 1.3. If, instead, all the error terms do have the same variance, then, as one might expect, they are said to be **homoskedastic**, or to exhibit **homoskedasticity**. Here we assume that the investigator knows nothing about the ω_t^2. In other words, the form of the heteroskedasticity is completely unknown.

The assumption in (5.31) that $\boldsymbol{X}$ is exogenous is fairly strong, but it is often reasonable for cross-section data, as we discussed in Section 3.2. We make it largely for simplicity, since we would obtain essentially the same asymptotic results if we replaced it with the weaker assumption (3.10) that $\boldsymbol{X}$ is predetermined, that is, the assumption that $\mathrm{E}(u_t \,|\, \boldsymbol{X}_t) = 0$. When the data are generated by a DGP that belongs to (5.31) with $\boldsymbol{\beta} = \boldsymbol{\beta}_0$, the exogeneity assumption implies that $\hat{\boldsymbol{\beta}}$ is unbiased; recall (3.09), which in no way depends on assumptions about the covariance matrix of the error terms.

Whatever the form of the error covariance matrix $\boldsymbol{\Omega}$, the covariance matrix of the OLS estimator $\hat{\boldsymbol{\beta}}$ is equal to

$$\begin{aligned}\mathrm{E}\big((\hat{\boldsymbol{\beta}} - \boldsymbol{\beta}_0)(\hat{\boldsymbol{\beta}} - \boldsymbol{\beta}_0)^\top\big) &= (\boldsymbol{X}^\top\boldsymbol{X})^{-1}\boldsymbol{X}^\top\mathrm{E}(\boldsymbol{u}\boldsymbol{u}^\top)\boldsymbol{X}(\boldsymbol{X}^\top\boldsymbol{X})^{-1} \\ &= (\boldsymbol{X}^\top\boldsymbol{X})^{-1}\boldsymbol{X}^\top\boldsymbol{\Omega}\boldsymbol{X}(\boldsymbol{X}^\top\boldsymbol{X})^{-1}.\end{aligned} \tag{5.32}$$

This form of covariance matrix is often called a **sandwich covariance matrix**, for the obvious reason that the matrix $\boldsymbol{X}^\top\boldsymbol{\Omega}\boldsymbol{X}$ is sandwiched between the two instances of the matrix $(\boldsymbol{X}^\top\boldsymbol{X})^{-1}$. The covariance matrix of an inefficient estimator very often takes this sandwich form. We can see intuitively why the OLS estimator is inefficient when there is heteroskedasticity by noting that observations with low variance presumably convey more information about the parameters than observations with high variance, and so the former should be given greater weight in an efficient estimator.

If we knew the ω_t^2, we could easily evaluate the sandwich covariance matrix (5.32). In fact, as we will see in Chapter 7, we could do even better and actually obtain efficient estimates of $\boldsymbol{\beta}$. But it is assumed that we do not know the ω_t^2. Moreover, since there are n of them, one for each observation, we cannot hope to estimate the ω_t^2 consistently without making additional assumptions. Thus, at first glance, the situation appears hopeless. However, even though we cannot evaluate (5.32), we can *estimate* it without having to attempt the impossible task of estimating $\boldsymbol{\Omega}$ consistently.

For the purposes of asymptotic theory, we wish to consider the covariance matrix, not of $\hat{\boldsymbol{\beta}}$, but rather of $n^{1/2}(\hat{\boldsymbol{\beta}} - \boldsymbol{\beta}_0)$. This is just the limit of n times the matrix (5.32). By distributing factors of n in such a way that we can take limits of each of the factors in (5.32), we find that the asymptotic covariance matrix of $n^{1/2}(\hat{\boldsymbol{\beta}} - \boldsymbol{\beta}_0)$ is

$$\Big(\lim_{n\to\infty}\frac{1}{n}\boldsymbol{X}^\top\boldsymbol{X}\Big)^{-1}\Big(\lim_{n\to\infty}\frac{1}{n}\boldsymbol{X}^\top\boldsymbol{\Omega}\boldsymbol{X}\Big)\Big(\lim_{n\to\infty}\frac{1}{n}\boldsymbol{X}^\top\boldsymbol{X}\Big)^{-1}. \tag{5.33}$$

Under assumption (4.49), the factor $(\lim n^{-1}\boldsymbol{X}^\top\boldsymbol{X})^{-1}$, which appears twice in (5.33) as the bread in the sandwich,[1] tends to a finite, deterministic, positive definite matrix $(\boldsymbol{S}_{\boldsymbol{X}^\top\boldsymbol{X}})^{-1}$. To estimate the limit, we can simply use the matrix $(n^{-1}\boldsymbol{X}^\top\boldsymbol{X})^{-1}$ itself. What is not so trivial is to estimate the middle factor, $\lim(n^{-1}\boldsymbol{X}^\top\boldsymbol{\Omega}\boldsymbol{X})$, which is the filling in the sandwich. In a very famous paper, White (1980) showed that, under certain conditions, including the existence of the limit, this matrix can be estimated consistently by

$$\frac{1}{n}\boldsymbol{X}^\top\hat{\boldsymbol{\Omega}}\boldsymbol{X}, \tag{5.34}$$

where $\hat{\boldsymbol{\Omega}}$ is an *inconsistent* estimator of $\boldsymbol{\Omega}$. As we will see, there are several admissible versions of $\hat{\boldsymbol{\Omega}}$. The simplest version, and the one suggested in White (1980), is a diagonal matrix with t^{th} diagonal element equal to $\hat{u}_t^2$, the tth squared OLS residual.

The matrix $\lim(n^{-1}\boldsymbol{X}^\top\boldsymbol{\Omega}\boldsymbol{X})$, which is the middle factor of (5.33), is a $k \times k$ symmetric matrix. Therefore, it has exactly $\frac{1}{2}(k^2+k)$ distinct elements. Since this number is independent of the sample size, the matrix can be estimated consistently. Its ij^{th} element is

$$\lim_{n\to\infty}\Big(\frac{1}{n}\sum_{t=1}^{n}\omega_t^2 x_{ti}x_{tj}\Big). \tag{5.35}$$

This is to be estimated by the ij^{th} element of (5.34), which, for the simplest version of $\hat{\boldsymbol{\Omega}}$, is

$$\frac{1}{n}\sum_{t=1}^{n}\hat{u}_t^2 x_{ti}x_{tj}. \tag{5.36}$$

[1] It is a moot point whether to call this limit an ordinary limit, as we do here, or a probability limit, as we do in Section 4.5. The difference reflects the fact that, there, $\boldsymbol{X}$ is generated by some sort of DGP, usually stochastic, while here, we do everything conditional on $\boldsymbol{X}$. We would, of course, need probability limits if $\boldsymbol{X}$ were merely predetermined rather than exogenous.

Because $\hat{\boldsymbol{\beta}}$ is consistent for $\boldsymbol{\beta}_0$, $\hat{u}_t$ is consistent for u_t, and $\hat{u}_t^2$ is therefore consistent for u_t^2. Thus, asymptotically, expression (5.36) is equal to

$$\begin{aligned}\frac{1}{n}\sum_{t=1}^{n} u_t^2 x_{ti} x_{tj} &= \frac{1}{n}\sum_{t=1}^{n}(\omega_t^2 + v_t) x_{ti} x_{tj} \\ &= \frac{1}{n}\sum_{t=1}^{n} \omega_t^2 x_{ti} x_{tj} + \frac{1}{n}\sum_{t=1}^{n} v_t x_{ti} x_{tj},\end{aligned} \tag{5.37}$$

where v_t is defined to equal u_t^2 minus its mean of ω_t^2. Under suitable assumptions about the x_{ti} and the ω_t^2, we can apply a law of large numbers to the second term in the second line of (5.37); see White (1980, 2000) for details. Since v_t has mean 0 by construction, this term converges to 0, while the first term converges to (5.35).

The above argument shows that the left-hand side of equation (5.37) tends in probability to expression (5.35). Because the former is asymptotically equivalent to expression (5.36), that expression also tends in probability to (5.35). Consequently, we can use the matrix (5.34), of which a typical element is (5.36), to estimate $\lim(n^{-1}\boldsymbol{X}^\top\boldsymbol{\Omega}\boldsymbol{X})$ consistently, and the matrix

$$(n^{-1}\boldsymbol{X}^\top\boldsymbol{X})^{-1} n^{-1}\boldsymbol{X}^\top\hat{\boldsymbol{\Omega}}\boldsymbol{X}(n^{-1}\boldsymbol{X}^\top\boldsymbol{X})^{-1} \tag{5.38}$$

to estimate expression (5.33) consistently. Of course, in practice, we ignore the factors of n^{-1} and use the matrix

$$\widehat{\mathrm{Var}}_{\mathrm{h}}(\hat{\boldsymbol{\beta}}) \equiv (\boldsymbol{X}^\top\boldsymbol{X})^{-1}\boldsymbol{X}^\top\hat{\boldsymbol{\Omega}}\boldsymbol{X}(\boldsymbol{X}^\top\boldsymbol{X})^{-1} \tag{5.39}$$

directly to estimate the covariance matrix of $\hat{\boldsymbol{\beta}}$.[2] It is not difficult to modify the arguments on asymptotic normality of the previous section so that they apply to the model (5.31). Therefore, we conclude that the OLS estimator is root-n consistent and asymptotically normal, with (5.39) being a consistent estimator of its covariance matrix.

The sandwich estimator (5.39) that we have just derived is an example of a **heteroskedasticity-consistent covariance matrix estimator**, or **HCCME** for short. It was introduced to econometrics by White (1980), although there were some precursors in the statistics literature, notably Eicker (1963, 1967) and Hinkley (1977). By taking square roots of the diagonal elements of (5.39), we can obtain standard errors that are asymptotically valid in the presence of heteroskedasticity of unknown form. These heteroskedasticity-consistent standard errors, which may also be referred to as **heteroskedasticity-robust**, are often enormously useful.

[2] The HCCME (5.39) depends on $\hat{\boldsymbol{\Omega}}$ only through $\boldsymbol{X}^\top\hat{\boldsymbol{\Omega}}\boldsymbol{X}$, which is a symmetric $k \times k$ matrix. Notice that we can compute the latter directly by calculating $k(k+1)/2$ quantities like (5.36) without the factor of n^{-1}.

Alternative Forms of HCCME

The original HCCME (5.39), which is often called HC_0, simply uses squared residuals to estimate the diagonal elements of the matrix $\boldsymbol{\Omega}$. However, it is not the best possible covariance matrix estimator. The reason is that, as we saw in Section 3.6, least-squares residuals tend to be too small. There are several better estimators that inflate the squared residuals slightly so as to offset this tendency. Three popular methods for obtaining better estimates of the ω_t^2 are the following:

- Use $\hat{u}_t^2\big(n/(n-k)\big)$, thus incorporating a degrees-of-freedom correction. In practice, this means multiplying the entire matrix (5.39) by $n/(n-k)$. The resulting HCCME is often called HC_1.
- Use $\hat{u}_t^2/(1-h_t)$, where $h_t \equiv \boldsymbol{X}_t(\boldsymbol{X}^\top\boldsymbol{X})^{-1}\boldsymbol{X}_t^\top$ is the tth diagonal element of the "hat" matrix $\boldsymbol{P_X}$ that projects orthogonally on to the space spanned by the columns of $\boldsymbol{X}$. Recall the result (3.44) that, when the variance of all the u_t is σ^2, the expectation of $\hat{u}_t^2$ is $\sigma^2(1-h_t)$. Therefore, the ratio of $\hat{u}_t^2$ to $1-h_t$ would have expectation σ^2 if the error terms were homoskedastic. The resulting HCCME is often called HC_2.
- Use $\hat{u}_t^2/(1-h_t)^2$. This is a slightly simplified version of what one gets by employing a statistical technique called the **jackknife**. Dividing by $(1-h_t)^2$ may seem to be overcorrecting the residuals. However, when the error terms are heteroskedastic, observations with large variances tend to influence the estimates a lot, and they therefore tend to have residuals that are very much too small. Thus, this estimator, which yields an HCCME that is often called HC_3, may be attractive if large variances are associated with large values of h_t.

The argument used in the preceding subsection for HC_0 shows that all of these procedures give the correct answer asymptotically, but none of them can be expected to do so in finite samples. In fact, inferences based on any HCCME, especially HC_0, may be seriously inaccurate even when the sample size is moderately large.

It is not clear which of the more sophisticated procedures works best in any particular case, although they can all be expected to work better than simply using the squared residuals without any adjustment. When some observations have much higher leverage than others, the methods that use the h_t might be expected to work better than simply using a degrees-of-freedom correction. These methods were first discussed by MacKinnon and White (1985), who found some evidence that the jackknife seemed to work best. Later simulations by Long and Ervin (2000) also support the use of HC_3. However, theoretical work by Chesher (1989) and Chesher and Austin (1991) gave more ambiguous results and suggested that HC_2 might sometimes outperform HC_3. It appears that the best procedure to use depends on the $\boldsymbol{X}$ matrix and on the form of the heteroskedasticity.

When Does Heteroskedasticity Matter?

Even when the error terms are heteroskedastic, there are cases in which we do not necessarily have to use an HCCME. Consider the ij^{th} element of $n^{-1}\boldsymbol{X}^{\top}\boldsymbol{\Omega}\boldsymbol{X}$, which is

$$\frac{1}{n}\sum_{t=1}^{n}\omega_t^2 x_{ti}x_{tj}. \tag{5.40}$$

If the limit as $n \to \infty$ of the average of the ω_t^2, $t = 1, \ldots, n$, exists and is denoted σ^2, then (5.40) can be written as

$$\sigma^2\frac{1}{n}\sum_{t=1}^{n}x_{ti}x_{tj} + \frac{1}{n}\sum_{t=1}^{n}(\omega_t^2 - \sigma^2)x_{ti}x_{tj}.$$

The first term here is just the ij^{th} element of $\sigma^2 n^{-1}\boldsymbol{X}^{\top}\boldsymbol{X}$. Should it be the case that

$$\lim_{n\to\infty}\frac{1}{n}\sum_{t=1}^{n}(\omega_t^2 - \sigma^2)x_{ti}x_{tj} = 0 \tag{5.41}$$

for $i, j = 1, \ldots, k$, then we find that

$$\lim_{n\to\infty}\frac{1}{n}\boldsymbol{X}^{\top}\boldsymbol{\Omega}\boldsymbol{X} = \sigma^2\lim_{n\to\infty}\frac{1}{n}\boldsymbol{X}^{\top}\boldsymbol{X}. \tag{5.42}$$

In this special case, we can replace the middle term of (5.33) by the right-hand side of (5.42), and we find that the asymptotic covariance matrix of $n^{1/2}(\hat{\boldsymbol{\beta}} - \boldsymbol{\beta}_0)$ is just

$$\Big(\lim_{n\to\infty}\frac{1}{n}\boldsymbol{X}^{\top}\boldsymbol{X}\Big)^{-1}\sigma^2\Big(\lim_{n\to\infty}\frac{1}{n}\boldsymbol{X}^{\top}\boldsymbol{X}\Big)\Big(\lim_{n\to\infty}\frac{1}{n}\boldsymbol{X}^{\top}\boldsymbol{X}\Big)^{-1} = \sigma^2\Big(\lim_{n\to\infty}\frac{1}{n}\boldsymbol{X}^{\top}\boldsymbol{X}\Big)^{-1}.$$

The usual OLS estimate of the error variance is

$$s^2 = \frac{1}{n-k}\sum_{t=1}^{n}\hat{u}_t^2,$$

and, if we assume that we can apply a law of large numbers, the probability limit of this is

$$\lim_{n\to\infty}\frac{1}{n}\sum_{t=1}^{n}\omega_t^2 = \sigma^2, \tag{5.43}$$

by definition. Thus we see that, in this special case, the usual OLS covariance matrix estimator (3.50) is valid asymptotically. This important result was originally shown by White (1980).

Equation (5.41) always holds when we are estimating only a sample mean. In that case, $\boldsymbol{X} = \boldsymbol{\iota}$, a vector with typical element $\iota_t = 1$, and

$$\frac{1}{n}\sum_{t=1}^{n}\omega_t^2 x_{ti}x_{tj} = \frac{1}{n}\sum_{t=1}^{n}\omega_t^2\iota_t^2 = \frac{1}{n}\sum_{t=1}^{n}\omega_t^2 \to \sigma^2 \text{ as } n \to \infty.$$

This shows that we do not have to worry about heteroskedasticity when calculating the standard error of a sample mean. Of course, equation (5.41) also holds when the error terms are homoskedastic. In that case, the σ^2 given by (5.43) is just the variance of each of the error terms.

Although equation (5.41) holds only in certain special cases, it does make one thing clear. Any form of heteroskedasticity affects the efficiency of the OLS parameter estimator, but only heteroskedasticity that is related to the squares and cross-products of the x_{ti} affects the validity of the usual OLS covariance matrix estimator.

HAC Covariance Matrix Estimators

All HCCMEs depend on the assumption that $\boldsymbol{\Omega}$ is diagonal. We are able to compute them because we can consistently estimate the matrix $n^{-1}\boldsymbol{X}^\top\boldsymbol{\Omega}\boldsymbol{X}$, even though we cannot consistently estimate the matrix $\boldsymbol{\Omega}$ itself. For essentially the same reason, we can obtain valid covariance matrix estimators even when $\boldsymbol{\Omega}$ is not a diagonal matrix. However, in order for us to be able to estimate $n^{-1}\boldsymbol{X}^\top\boldsymbol{\Omega}\boldsymbol{X}$ consistently when $\boldsymbol{\Omega}$ is unknown and is not diagonal, all the off-diagonal elements which are not close to the principal diagonal must be sufficiently small.

When the error terms of a regression model are correlated among themselves, then, as we mentioned in Section 1.3, they are said to display **serial correlation** or **autocorrelation**. Serial correlation is frequently encountered in models estimated using time series data. Often, observations that are close to each other are strongly correlated, but observations that are far apart are uncorrelated or nearly so. In this situation, only the elements of $\boldsymbol{\Omega}$ that are on or close to the principal diagonal are large. When this is the case, we may be able to obtain an estimate of the covariance matrix of the parameter estimates that is **heteroskedasticity and autocorrelation consistent**, or **HAC**. Computing a HAC covariance matrix estimator is essentially similar to computing an HCCME, but a good deal more complicated. HAC estimators will be discussed in Chapter 9.

5.6 The Delta Method

Econometricians often want to perform inference on nonlinear functions of model parameters. This requires them to estimate the standard error of a nonlinear function of parameter estimates or, more generally, the covariance matrix of a vector of such functions. One popular way to do so is called the **delta method**. It is based on an asymptotic approximation.

For simplicity, let us start with the case of a single parameter. Suppose that we have estimated a scalar parameter θ, which might be one of the coefficients of a linear regression model, and that we are interested in the parameter $\gamma = g(\theta)$, where $g(\cdot)$ is a monotonic function that is continuously differentiable. In this

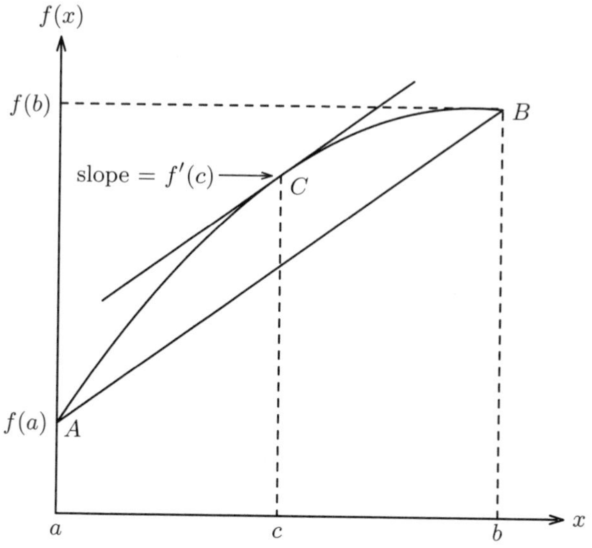

Figure 5.4 Taylor's Theorem

situation, the obvious way to estimate γ is to use $\hat{\gamma} = g(\hat{\theta})$. Since $\hat{\theta}$ is a random variable, so is $\hat{\gamma}$. The problem is to estimate the variance of $\hat{\gamma}$.

Since $\hat{\gamma}$ is a function of $\hat{\theta}$, it seems logical that $\text{Var}(\hat{\gamma})$ should be a function of $\text{Var}(\hat{\theta})$. If $g(\theta)$ is a linear or affine function, then we already know how to calculate $\text{Var}(\hat{\gamma})$; recall the result (3.33). The idea of the delta method is to find a linear approximation to $g(\theta)$ and then apply (3.33) to this approximation.

Taylor's Theorem

It is frequently necessary in econometrics to obtain linear approximations to nonlinear functions. The mathematical tool most commonly used for this purpose is **Taylor's Theorem**. In its simplest form, Taylor's Theorem applies to functions of a scalar argument that are differentiable at least once on some real interval $[a, b]$, with the derivative a continuous function on $[a, b]$. Figure 5.4 shows the graph of such a function, $f(x)$, for $x \in [a, b]$.

The coordinates of A are $(a, f(a))$, and those of B are $(b, f(b))$. Thus the slope of the line AB is $\big(f(b) - f(a)\big)/(b - a)$. What drives the theorem is the observation that there must always be a value between a and b, like c in the figure, at which the derivative $f'(c)$ is equal to the slope of AB. This is a consequence of the continuity of the derivative. If it were not continuous, and the graph of $f(x)$ had a corner, the slope might always be greater than $f'(c)$ on one side of the corner, and always be smaller on the other. But if $f'(x)$ is continuous on $[a, b]$, then there must exist c such that

$$f'(c) = \frac{f(b) - f(a)}{b - a}.$$

This can be rewritten as $f(b) = f(a) + (b-a)f'(c)$. If we let $h = b - a$, then, since c lies between a and b, it must be the case that $c = a + \lambda h$, for some λ between 0 and 1. Thus we obtain

$$f(a+h) = f(a) + hf'(a+\lambda h). \tag{5.44}$$

Equation (5.44), which is the simplest expression of Taylor's Theorem, is also known as the **Mean Value Theorem**.

Although (5.44) is an exact relationship, it involves the quantity λ, which is unknown. It is more usual just to set $\lambda = 0$, so as to obtain a linear approximation to the function $f(x)$ for x in the neighborhood of a. This approximation, called a **first-order Taylor expansion** around a, is

$$f(a+h) \cong f(a) + hf'(a), \tag{5.45}$$

where the symbol "$\cong$" means "is approximately equal to." The right-hand side of this equation is an affine function of h.

Taylor's Theorem can be extended in order to provide approximations that are quadratic or cubic functions, or polynomials of any desired order. The exact statement of the theorem, with terms proportional to powers of h up to h^p, is

$$f(a+h) = f(a) + \sum_{i=1}^{p-1} \frac{h^i}{i!} f^{(i)}(a) + \frac{h^p}{p!} f^{(p)}(a+\lambda h).$$

Here $f^{(i)}$ is the ith derivative of f, and once more $0 < \lambda < 1$. The approximate version of the theorem sets $\lambda = 0$ and gives rise to a $\boldsymbol{p}^{\textbf{th}}$**-order Taylor expansion** around a. A commonly-encountered example of the latter is the **second-order Taylor expansion**

$$f(a+h) \cong f(a) + hf'(a) + \tfrac{1}{2}h^2 f''(a).$$

Both versions of Taylor's Theorem require as a regularity condition that $f(x)$ should have a pth derivative that is continuous on $[a, a+h]$.

There are also multivariate versions of Taylor's Theorem, and we will need them from time to time. If $f(\boldsymbol{x})$ is now a scalar-valued function of the m–vector $\boldsymbol{x}$, then, for $p = 1$, Taylor's Theorem states that, if $\boldsymbol{h}$ is also an m–vector,

$$f(\boldsymbol{x}+\boldsymbol{h}) = f(\boldsymbol{x}) + \sum_{j=1}^{m} h_j f_j(\boldsymbol{x}+\lambda \boldsymbol{h}), \tag{5.46}$$

where h_j is the jth component of $\boldsymbol{h}$, f_j is the partial derivative of f with respect to its jth argument, and, as before, $0 < \lambda < 1$.

The Delta Method for a Scalar Parameter

If we assume that the estimator $\hat{\theta}$ is root-n consistent and asymptotically normal, then

$$n^{1/2}(\hat{\theta} - \theta_0) \overset{a}{\sim} \mathrm{N}\big(0, V^\infty(\hat{\theta})\big), \tag{5.47}$$

where θ_0 denotes the true value of θ. We will use $V^\infty(\hat{\theta})$ as a shorthand way of writing the asymptotic variance of $n^{1/2}(\hat{\theta} - \theta_0)$.

In order to find the asymptotic distribution of $\hat{\gamma} = g(\hat{\theta})$, we perform a first-order Taylor expansion of $g(\hat{\theta})$ around θ_0. Using (5.45), we obtain

$$\hat{\gamma} \cong g(\theta_0) + g'(\theta_0)(\hat{\theta} - \theta_0), \tag{5.48}$$

where $g'(\theta_0)$ is the first derivative of $g(\theta)$, evaluated at θ_0. Given the root-n consistency of $\hat{\theta}$, (5.48) can be rearranged into an **asymptotic equality**. Two deterministic quantities are said to be **asymptotically equal** if they tend to the same limits as $n \to \infty$. Similarly, two random quantities are said to be asymptotically equal if they tend to the same limits in probability. As usual, we need a power of n to make things work correctly. Here, we multiply both sides of (5.48) by $n^{1/2}$. If we denote $g(\theta_0)$, which is the true value of γ, by γ_0, then (5.48) becomes

$$n^{1/2}(\hat{\gamma} - \gamma_0) \overset{a}{=} g_0' n^{1/2}(\hat{\theta} - \theta_0), \tag{5.49}$$

where the symbol $\overset{a}{=}$ is used for asymptotic equality, and $g_0' \equiv g'(\theta_0)$. In Exercise 5.17, readers are asked to check that, if we perform a second-order Taylor expansion, the last term of the expansion vanishes asymptotically. This justifies (5.49) as an asymptotic equality.

Equation (5.49) shows that $n^{1/2}(\hat{\gamma} - \gamma_0)$ is asymptotically normal with mean 0, since the right-hand side of (5.49) is just g_0' times a quantity that is asymptotically normal with mean 0; recall (5.47). The variance of $n^{1/2}(\hat{\gamma} - \gamma_0)$ is clearly $(g_0')^2 V^\infty(\hat{\theta})$, and so we conclude that

$$n^{1/2}(\hat{\gamma} - \gamma_0) \overset{a}{\sim} \mathrm{N}\big(0, (g_0')^2 V^\infty(\hat{\theta})\big). \tag{5.50}$$

This shows that $\hat{\gamma}$ is root-n consistent and asymptotically normal when $\hat{\theta}$ is.

The result (5.50) leads immediately to a practical procedure for estimating the standard error of $\hat{\gamma}$. If the standard error of $\hat{\theta}$ is s_θ, then the standard error of $\hat{\gamma}$ is

$$s_\gamma \equiv \big|g'(\hat{\theta})\big|\, s_\theta. \tag{5.51}$$

This procedure can be based on any asymptotically valid estimator of the standard deviation of $\hat{\theta}$. For example, if θ were one of the coefficients of a linear regression model, then s_θ could be the square root of the corresponding diagonal element of the usual estimated OLS covariance matrix, or it could be the square root of the corresponding diagonal element of an estimated heteroskedasticity-consistent covariance matrix.

In practice, the delta method is usually very easy to use. For example, consider the case in which $\gamma = \theta^2$. Then $g'(\theta) = 2\theta$, and the formula (5.51) tells us that $s_\gamma = 2|\hat{\theta}|s_\theta$. Notice that s_γ depends on $\hat{\theta}$, something that is not true for either the usual OLS standard error or the heteroskedasticity-consistent one discussed in the preceding section.

Confidence Intervals and the Delta Method

Although the result (5.51) is simple and practical, it reveals some of the limitations of asymptotic theory. Whenever the relationship between $\hat{\theta}$ and $\hat{\gamma}$ is nonlinear, it is impossible that both of them should be normally distributed in finite samples. Suppose that $\hat{\theta}$ really did happen to be normally distributed. Then, unless $g(\cdot)$ were linear, $\hat{\gamma}$ could not possibly be normally, or even symmetrically, distributed. Similarly, if $\hat{\gamma}$ were normally distributed, $\hat{\theta}$ could not be. Moreover, as the example at the end of the last subsection showed, s_γ generally depends on $\hat{\theta}$. This implies that the numerator of a t statistic for γ is not independent of the denominator. However, independence was essential to the result, in Section 4.4, that the t statistic actually follows the Student's t distribution.

The preceding arguments suggest that confidence intervals and test statistics based on asymptotic theory are often not reliable in finite samples. Asymptotic normality of the parameter estimates is an essential underpinning of all asymptotic tests and confidence intervals or regions. When the finite-sample distributions of estimates are far from the limiting normal distribution, one cannot expect any asymptotic procedure to perform well.

Despite these caveats, we may still wish to construct an asymptotic confidence interval for γ based on (5.08). The result is

$$\left[\hat{\gamma} - s_\gamma z_{1-(\alpha/2)},\ \hat{\gamma} + s_\gamma z_{1-(\alpha/2)}\right], \tag{5.52}$$

where s_γ is the delta method estimate (5.51), and $z_{1-(\alpha/2)}$ is the $1 - (\alpha/2)$ quantile of the standard normal distribution. This confidence interval can be expected to work well whenever the finite-sample distribution of $\hat{\gamma}$ is well approximated by the normal distribution and s_γ is a reliable estimator of its standard deviation.

Using (5.08) is not the only way to obtain an asymptotic confidence interval for γ, however. Another approach, which usually leads to an asymmetric interval, is to transform the asymptotic confidence interval for the underlying parameter θ. The latter interval, which is similar to (5.08), is

$$\left[\hat{\theta} - s_\theta z_{1-(\alpha/2)},\ \hat{\theta} + s_\theta z_{1-(\alpha/2)}\right].$$

Transforming the endpoints of this interval by the function g gives the following interval for γ:

$$\big[g(\hat{\theta} - s_\theta z_{1-(\alpha/2)}),\ \ g(\hat{\theta} + s_\theta z_{1-(\alpha/2)})\big]. \tag{5.53}$$

This assumes that $g'(\theta) > 0$. If $g'(\theta) < 0$, the two ends of the interval would have to be interchanged. Whenever $g(\theta)$ is a nonlinear function, the confidence interval (5.53) is asymmetric. It can be expected to work well if the finite-sample distribution of $\hat{\theta}$ is well approximated by the normal distribution and s_θ is a reliable estimator of the standard deviation of $\hat{\theta}$.

The bootstrap confidence interval for θ, (5.17), can also be transformed by g in order to obtain a bootstrap confidence interval for γ. The result is

$$\big[g(\hat{\theta} - s_\theta c^*_{1-(\alpha/2)}),\ \ g(\hat{\theta} - s_\theta c^*_{\alpha/2})\big], \tag{5.54}$$

where $c^*_{\alpha/2}$ and $c^*_{1-(\alpha/2)}$ are, as in (5.17), the entries indexed by $(\alpha/2)(B+1)$ and $(1-(\alpha/2))(B+1)$ in the sorted list of bootstrap t statistics t^*_j.

Yet another way to construct a bootstrap confidence interval is to bootstrap the t statistic for γ directly. Using the original data, we compute $\hat{\theta}$ and s_θ, and then $\hat{\gamma}$ and s_γ in terms of them. The bootstrap DGP is the same as the one used to obtain a bootstrap confidence interval for θ, but this time, for each bootstrap sample j, $j = 1, \ldots, B$, we compute γ^*_j and $(s_\gamma)^*_j$. The bootstrap "t statistics" $(\gamma^*_j - \hat{\gamma})/(s_\gamma)^*_j$ are then sorted. If $(c_\gamma)^*_{\alpha/2}$ and $(c_\gamma)^*_{1-(\alpha/2)}$ denote the entries indexed by $(\alpha/2)(B+1)$ and $(1-(\alpha/2))(B+1)$ in the sorted list, then the (asymmetric) bootstrap confidence interval is

$$\big[\hat{\gamma} - s_\gamma (c_\gamma)^*_{1-(\alpha/2)},\ \ \hat{\gamma} - s_\gamma (c_\gamma)^*_{\alpha/2}\big]. \tag{5.55}$$

As readers are asked to check in Exercise 5.20, the intervals (5.54) and (5.55) are not the same.

The Vector Case

The result (5.50) can easily be extended to the case in which both $\boldsymbol{\theta}$ and $\boldsymbol{\gamma}$ are vectors. Suppose that the former is a k–vector and the latter is an l–vector, with $l \le k$. The relation between $\boldsymbol{\theta}$ and $\boldsymbol{\gamma}$ is $\boldsymbol{\gamma} = \boldsymbol{g}(\boldsymbol{\theta})$, where $\boldsymbol{g}(\boldsymbol{\theta})$ is an l–vector of monotonic functions that are continuously differentiable. The vector version of (5.47) is

$$n^{1/2}(\hat{\boldsymbol{\theta}} - \boldsymbol{\theta}_0) \overset{a}{\sim} \mathrm{N}\big(\mathbf{0}, \boldsymbol{V}^\infty(\hat{\boldsymbol{\theta}})\big), \tag{5.56}$$

where $\boldsymbol{V}^\infty(\hat{\boldsymbol{\theta}})$ is the asymptotic covariance matrix of the vector $n^{1/2}(\hat{\boldsymbol{\theta}} - \boldsymbol{\theta}_0)$. Using the result (5.56) and a first-order Taylor expansion of $\boldsymbol{g}(\boldsymbol{\theta})$ around $\boldsymbol{\theta}_0$, it can be shown that the vector analog of (5.50) is

$$n^{1/2}(\hat{\boldsymbol{\gamma}} - \boldsymbol{\gamma}_0) \overset{a}{\sim} \mathrm{N}\big(\mathbf{0}, \boldsymbol{G}_0 \boldsymbol{V}^\infty(\hat{\boldsymbol{\theta}}) \boldsymbol{G}_0^\top\big), \tag{5.57}$$

where $\boldsymbol{G}_0$ is an $l \times k$ matrix with typical element $\partial g_i(\theta)/\partial\theta_j$, evaluated at $\boldsymbol{\theta}_0$; see Exercise 5.18. The asymptotic covariance matrix that appears in (5.57) is an $l \times l$ matrix. It has full rank l if $\boldsymbol{V}^\infty(\hat{\boldsymbol{\theta}})$ is nonsingular and the matrix of derivatives $\boldsymbol{G}_0$ has full rank l.

In practice, the covariance matrix of $\hat{\gamma}$ may be estimated by the matrix

$$\widehat{\mathrm{Var}}(\hat{\gamma}) \equiv \hat{\boldsymbol{G}}\,\widehat{\mathrm{Var}}(\hat{\boldsymbol{\theta}})\hat{\boldsymbol{G}}^\top, \tag{5.58}$$

where $\widehat{\mathrm{Var}}(\hat{\boldsymbol{\theta}})$ is the estimated covariance matrix of $\hat{\boldsymbol{\theta}}$, and $\hat{\boldsymbol{G}} \equiv \boldsymbol{G}(\hat{\boldsymbol{\theta}})$. This result, which is similar to (3.33), can be very useful. However, like all results based on asymptotic theory, it should be used with caution. As in the scalar case discussed above, $\hat{\gamma}$ cannot possibly be normally distributed if $\hat{\boldsymbol{\theta}}$ is.

Bootstrap Standard Errors

The delta method is not the only way to obtain standard errors and covariance matrices for functions of parameter estimates. The bootstrap can also be used for this purpose. Indeed, much of the early work on the bootstrap, such as Efron (1979), was largely concerned with bootstrap standard errors.

Suppose that, as in the previous subsection, we wish to calculate the covariance matrix of the vector $\hat{\gamma} = \boldsymbol{g}(\hat{\boldsymbol{\theta}})$. A bootstrap procedure for doing this involves three steps:

1. Specify a bootstrap DGP, which may be parametric or semiparametric, and use it to generate B bootstrap samples, $\boldsymbol{y}_j^*$.
2. For each bootstrap sample, use $\boldsymbol{y}_j^*$ to compute the parameter vector $\boldsymbol{\theta}_j^*$, and then use $\boldsymbol{\theta}_j^*$ to compute γ_j^*.
3. Calculate $\bar{\gamma}^*$, the mean of the γ_j^*. Then calculate the estimated bootstrap covariance matrix,

   $$\widehat{\mathrm{Var}}^*(\hat{\gamma}) = \frac{1}{B-1}\sum_{j=1}^{B}(\gamma_j^* - \bar{\gamma}^*)(\gamma_j^* - \bar{\gamma}^*)^\top.$$

   If desired, bootstrap standard errors may be calculated as the square roots of the diagonal elements of this matrix.

Bootstrap standard errors, which may or may not be more accurate than ones based on asymptotic theory, can certainly be useful as descriptive statistics. However, using them for inference generally cannot be recommended. In many cases, calculating bootstrap standard errors is almost as much work as calculating studentized bootstrap confidence intervals. As we noted at the end of Section 5.3, there are theoretical reasons to believe that the latter yield more accurate inferences than confidence intervals based on asymptotic theory, including asymptotic confidence intervals that use bootstrap standard errors. Thus, if we are going to go to the trouble of calculating a large number of bootstrap estimates anyway, we can do better than just using them to compute bootstrap standard errors.

5.7 Final Remarks

In this chapter, we have discussed a number of methods for constructing confidence intervals. They are all based on the idea of inverting a test statistic, and most of them are in no way restricted to OLS estimation. The idea is first to construct a family of test statistics for the null hypotheses that the parameter of interest is equal to a particular value. The limits of the confidence interval are then obtained by solving the equation that sets the statistic equal to the critical values given by some appropriate distribution. The critical values may be quantiles of a finite-sample distribution, such as the Student's t distribution, quantiles of an asymptotic distribution, such as the standard normal distribution, or quantiles of a bootstrap EDF. We also briefly discussed some procedures for constructing confidence regions, which are very similar to those for constructing confidence intervals.

All of the methods for constructing confidence intervals and regions that we have discussed require standard errors or, more generally, estimated covariance matrices. The chapter therefore includes a good deal of material on how to estimate these under weaker assumptions than were made in Chapter 3. Much of this material is widely applicable. Methods for estimation of covariance matrices in the presence of heteroskedasticity of unknown form, similar to those discussed in Section 5.5, are useful in the context of many different methods of estimation. The delta method, which was discussed in Section 5.6, is even more general, since it can be used whenever one parameter, or vector of parameters, is a nonlinear function of another.

5.8 Exercises

5.1 Find the .025, .05, .10, and .20 quantiles of the standard normal distribution using a statistics package or some other computer program. Use these to obtain whatever quantiles of the $\chi^2(1)$ distribution you can.

5.2 Starting from the square of the t statistic (5.11), and using the $F(1, n-k)$ distribution, obtain a .99 confidence interval for the parameter β_2 in the classical normal linear model (4.21).

5.3 The file **earnings.data** contains sorted data on four variables for 4,266 individuals. One of the variables is income, y, and the other three are dummy variables, d_1, d_2, and d_3, which correspond to different age ranges. Regress y on all three dummy variables. Then use the regression output to construct a .95 asymptotic confidence interval for the mean income of individuals who belong to age group 3.

5.4 Using the same data as Exercise 5.3, regress y on a constant for individuals in age group 3 only. Use the regression output to construct a .95 asymptotic confidence interval for the mean income of group 3 individuals. Explain why this confidence interval is not the same as the one you constructed previously.

5.5 Generate 999 realizations of a random variable that follows the $\chi^2(2)$ distribution, and find the .95 and .99 "quantiles" of the EDF, that is the 950th and 990th entries in the sorted list of the realizations. Compare these with the .95 and .99 quantiles of the $\chi^2(2)$ distribution.

5.6 Using the data in the file **earnings.data**, construct a .95 studentized bootstrap confidence interval for the mean income of group 3 individuals. Explain why this confidence interval differs from the one you constructed in Exercise 5.4.

5.7 Explain in detail how to construct a symmetric bootstrap confidence interval based on the possibly asymptotic t statistic $(\hat{\theta} - \theta_0)/s_\theta$. Express your answer in terms of entries in a sorted list of bootstrap t statistics.

5.8 Suppose the SSR from OLS estimation of a linear regression model with 100 observations and 6 regressors is 106.44. Under the assumptions of the classical normal linear model, construct a .95 equal-tailed confidence interval for σ^2. Is this interval symmetric around the OLS variance estimate s^2?

Find the .95 confidence interval for σ that is implied by the confidence interval you just constructed. Another way to form a confidence interval for σ is to make use of the fact that, under normality, the variance of s is approximately equal to $s^2/2n$; see Section 10.4. Form a second confidence interval for σ based on this result. How are the two intervals related numerically?

5.9 You estimate a parameter θ by least squares. The parameter estimate is $\hat{\theta} = 2.5762$, and its standard error is 0.4654. You then generate 999 bootstrap samples and from each of them calculate t_j^*, the t statistic for the hypothesis that $\theta = \hat{\theta}$. When the t_j^* are sorted from smallest to largest, number 25 is equal to -2.2214, and number 975 is equal to 1.7628. Find a .95 studentized bootstrap confidence interval for θ, and compare it with the usual asymptotic confidence interval.

5.10 Show that the F statistic for the null hypothesis that $\boldsymbol{\beta}_2 = \boldsymbol{\beta}_{20}$ in the model (5.24), or, equivalently, for the null hypothesis that $\boldsymbol{\gamma}_2 = \mathbf{0}$ in (5.25), can be written as (5.26). Interpret the numerator of expression (5.26) as a random variable constructed from the multivariate normal vector $\hat{\boldsymbol{\beta}}_2$.

⋆5.11 Consider a regression model with just two explanatory variables, $\boldsymbol{x}_1$ and $\boldsymbol{x}_2$, both of which are centered:

$$\boldsymbol{y} = \beta_1 \boldsymbol{x}_1 + \beta_2 \boldsymbol{x}_2 + \boldsymbol{u}. \tag{5.59}$$

Let $\hat{\rho}$ denote the **sample correlation** of $\boldsymbol{x}_1$ and $\boldsymbol{x}_2$. Since both regressors are centered, the sample correlation is

$$\hat{\rho} \equiv \frac{\sum_{t=1}^{n} x_{t1} x_{t2}}{\left((\sum_{t=1}^{n} x_{t1}^2)(\sum_{t=1}^{n} x_{t2}^2) \right)^{1/2}},$$

where x_{t1} and x_{t2} are typical elements of $\boldsymbol{x}_1$ and $\boldsymbol{x}_2$, respectively. This can be interpreted as the correlation of the joint EDF of $\boldsymbol{x}_1$ and $\boldsymbol{x}_2$.

Show that, under the assumptions of the classical normal linear model, the correlation between the OLS estimates $\hat{\beta}_1$ and $\hat{\beta}_2$ is equal to $-\hat{\rho}$. Which, if any, of the assumptions of this model can be relaxed without changing this result?

5.12 Consider the .05 level confidence region for the parameters β_1 and β_2 of the regression model (5.59). In the two-dimensional space $\mathcal{S}(\boldsymbol{x}_1, \boldsymbol{x}_2)$ generated by the two regressors, consider the set of points of the form $\beta_{10}\boldsymbol{x}_1 + \beta_{20}\boldsymbol{x}_2$, where (β_{10}, β_{20}) belongs to the confidence region. Show that this set is a circular disk with center at the OLS estimates $(\boldsymbol{x}_1\hat{\beta}_1 + \boldsymbol{x}_2\hat{\beta}_2)$. What is the radius of the disk?

5.13 Using the data in the file **earnings.data**, regress y on all three dummy variables, and compute a heteroskedasticity-consistent standard error for the coefficient of d_3. Using these results, construct a .95 asymptotic confidence interval for the mean income of individuals that belong to age group 3. Compare this interval with the ones you constructed in Exercises 5.3, 5.4, and 5.6.

5.14 Consider the linear regression model

$$\boldsymbol{y} = \boldsymbol{X\beta} + \boldsymbol{u}, \quad \mathrm{E}(\boldsymbol{uu}^\top) = \boldsymbol{\Omega},$$

where the number of observations, n, is equal to $3m$. The first three rows of the matrix $\boldsymbol{X}$ are

$$\begin{bmatrix} 1 & 4 \\ 1 & 8 \\ 1 & 15 \end{bmatrix},$$

and every subsequent group of three rows is identical to this first group. The covariance matrix $\boldsymbol{\Omega}$ is diagonal, with typical diagonal element equal to $\omega^2 x_{t2}^2$, where $\omega > 0$, and x_{t2} is the tth element of the second column of $\boldsymbol{X}$.

What is the variance of $\hat{\beta}_2$, the OLS estimate of β_2? What is the probability limit, as $n \to \infty$, of the ratio of the conventional estimate of this variance, which incorrectly assumes homoskedasticity, to a heteroskedasticity-consistent estimate based on (5.39)?

5.15 Generate N simulated data sets, where N is between 1000 and 1,000,000, depending on the capacity of your computer, from each of the following two data generating processes:

$$\begin{aligned} &\text{DGP 1:} \quad y_t = \beta_1 + \beta_2 x_{t2} + \beta_3 x_{t3} + u_t, \quad u_t \sim \mathrm{N}(0,1) \\ &\text{DGP 2:} \quad y_t = \beta_1 + \beta_2 x_{t2} + \beta_3 x_{t3} + u_t, \quad u_t \sim \mathrm{N}(0,\sigma_t^2), \ \sigma_t^2 = (\mathrm{E}(y_t))^2. \end{aligned}$$

There are 50 observations, $\boldsymbol{\beta} = [1 \,\vdots\, 1 \,\vdots\, 1]$, and the data on the exogenous variables are to be found in the file **mw.data**. These data were originally used by MacKinnon and White (1985).

For each of the two DGPs and each of the N simulated data sets, construct .95 confidence intervals for β_1 and β_2 using the usual OLS covariance matrix and the HCCMEs HC_0, HC_1, HC_2, and HC_3. The OLS interval should be based on the Student's t distribution with 47 degrees of freedom, and the others should be based on the $\mathrm{N}(0, 1)$ distribution. Report the proportion of the time that each of these confidence intervals included the true values of the parameters.

On the basis of these results, which covariance matrix estimator would you recommend using in practice?

5.16 Using the data in the file **classical.data**, estimate the model

$$\boldsymbol{y} = \beta_1 \boldsymbol{\iota} + \beta_2 \boldsymbol{x}_2 + \beta_3 \boldsymbol{x}_3 + \boldsymbol{u}, \quad \boldsymbol{u} \sim \mathrm{N}(\mathbf{0}, \sigma^2 \mathbf{I}),$$

and obtain .95 confidence intervals for σ and σ^2. Which of these intervals is closer to being symmetric? **Hint:** See Exercise 4.14.

5.17 Write down a second-order Taylor expansion of the nonlinear function $g(\hat{\theta})$ around θ_0, where $\hat{\theta}$ is an OLS estimator and θ_0 is the true value of the parameter θ. Explain why the last term is asymptotically negligible relative to the second term.

5.18 Using a multivariate first-order Taylor expansion, show that, if $\boldsymbol{\gamma} = \boldsymbol{g}(\boldsymbol{\theta})$, the asymptotic covariance matrix of the l–vector $n^{1/2}(\hat{\boldsymbol{\gamma}} - \boldsymbol{\gamma}_0)$ is given by the $l \times l$ matrix $\boldsymbol{G}_0 \boldsymbol{V}^{\infty}(\hat{\boldsymbol{\theta}}) \boldsymbol{G}_0^{\top}$. Here $\boldsymbol{\theta}$ is a k–vector with $k \geq l$, $\boldsymbol{G}_0$ is an $l \times k$ matrix with typical element $\partial g_i(\theta)/\partial \theta_j$, evaluated at $\boldsymbol{\theta}_0$, and $\boldsymbol{V}^{\infty}(\hat{\boldsymbol{\theta}})$ is the $k \times k$ asymptotic covariance matrix of $n^{1/2}(\hat{\boldsymbol{\theta}} - \boldsymbol{\theta}_0)$.

5.19 Suppose that $\gamma = \exp(\beta)$ and $\hat{\beta} = 1.324$, with a standard error of 0.2432. Calculate $\hat{\gamma} = \exp(\hat{\beta})$ and its standard error.

Construct two different .99 confidence intervals for γ. One should be based on (5.52), and the other should be based on (5.53).

5.20 Construct two .95 bootstrap confidence intervals for the log of the mean income (*not* the mean of the log of income) of group 3 individuals from the data in **earnings.data**. These intervals should be based on (5.54) and (5.55). Verify that these two intervals are different.

5.21 Generate y_0 as a pseudo-random variable from the $\mathrm{N}(0, .36^{-1/2})$ distribution. Then use the DGP

$$y_t = 0.8 y_{t-1} + u_t, \quad u_t \sim \mathrm{NID}(0, 1)$$

to generate a sample of 30 observations conditional on y_0. (Why y_0 should be distributed in this way will be explained in Chapter 7.)

Using these simulated data, obtain estimates of ρ and σ^2 for the model

$$y_t = \rho y_{t-1} + u_t, \quad \mathrm{E}(u_t) = 0, \quad E(u_t u_s) = \sigma^2 \delta_{ts},$$

where δ_{ts} is the Kronecker delta introduced in Section 1.4. By use of the parametric bootstrap with the assumption of normal errors, obtain two .95 confidence intervals for ρ, one symmetric, the other asymmetric.

Chapter 6

Nonlinear Regression

6.1 Introduction

Up to this point, we have discussed only linear regression models. For each observation t of any regression model, there is an information set Ω_t and a suitably chosen vector $\boldsymbol{X}_t$ of explanatory variables that belong to Ω_t. A linear regression model consists of all DGPs for which the expectation of the dependent variable y_t conditional on Ω_t can be expressed as a *linear* combination $\boldsymbol{X}_t\boldsymbol{\beta}$ of the components of $\boldsymbol{X}_t$, and for which the error terms satisfy suitable requirements, such as being IID. Since, as we saw in Section 1.3, the elements of $\boldsymbol{X}_t$ may be nonlinear functions of the variables originally used to define Ω_t, many types of nonlinearity can be handled within the framework of the linear regression model. However, many other types of nonlinearity cannot be handled within this framework. In order to deal with them, we often need to estimate **nonlinear regression models**. These are models for which $\mathrm{E}(y_t \mid \Omega_t)$ is a nonlinear function of the parameters.

A typical nonlinear regression model can be written as

$$y_t = x_t(\boldsymbol{\beta}) + u_t, \quad u_t \sim \mathrm{IID}(0, \sigma^2), \quad t = 1, \ldots, n, \tag{6.01}$$

where, just as for the linear regression model, y_t is the tth observation on the dependent variable, and $\boldsymbol{\beta}$ is a k–vector of parameters to be estimated. The scalar function $x_t(\boldsymbol{\beta})$ is a **nonlinear regression function**. It determines the mean value of y_t conditional on Ω_t, which is made up of some set of explanatory variables. These explanatory variables, which may include lagged values of y_t as well as exogenous variables, are not shown explicitly in (6.01). However, the t subscript of $x_t(\boldsymbol{\beta})$ indicates that the regression function varies from observation to observation. This variation usually occurs because $x_t(\boldsymbol{\beta})$ depends on explanatory variables, but it can also occur because the functional form of the regression function actually changes over time. The number of explanatory variables, all of which must belong to Ω_t, need not be equal to k.

The error terms in (6.01) are specified to be IID. By this, we mean something very similar to, but not precisely the same as, the two conditions in (4.48). In order for the error terms to be identically distributed, the distribution of each error term u_t, conditional on the corresponding information set Ω_t, must be the same for all t. In order for them to be independent, the distribution of u_t, conditional not only on Ω_t but also on all the other error terms, should be the same as its distribution conditional on Ω_t alone, without any dependence on the other error terms.

Another way to write the nonlinear regression model (6.01) is

$$\boldsymbol{y} = \boldsymbol{x}(\boldsymbol{\beta}) + \boldsymbol{u}, \quad \boldsymbol{u} \sim \text{IID}(\mathbf{0}, \sigma^2\mathbf{I}), \tag{6.02}$$

where $\boldsymbol{y}$ and $\boldsymbol{u}$ are n–vectors with typical elements y_t and u_t, respectively, and $\boldsymbol{x}(\boldsymbol{\beta})$ is an n–vector of which the tth element is $x_t(\boldsymbol{\beta})$. Thus $\boldsymbol{x}(\boldsymbol{\beta})$ is the nonlinear analog of the vector $\boldsymbol{X\beta}$ in the linear case.

As a very simple example of a nonlinear regression model, consider the model

$$y_t = \beta_1 + \beta_2 z_{t1} + \frac{1}{\beta_2} z_{t2} + u_t, \quad u_t \sim \text{IID}(0, \sigma^2), \tag{6.03}$$

where z_{t1} and z_{t2} are explanatory variables. For this model,

$$x_t(\boldsymbol{\beta}) = \beta_1 + \beta_2 z_{t1} + \frac{1}{\beta_2} z_{t2}.$$

Although the regression function $x_t(\boldsymbol{\beta})$ is linear in the explanatory variables, it is nonlinear in the parameters, because the coefficient of z_{t2} is constrained to equal the inverse of the coefficient of z_{t1}. In practice, many nonlinear regression models, like (6.03), can be expressed as linear regression models in which the parameters must satisfy one or more nonlinear restrictions.

The Linear Regression Model with AR(1) Errors

We now consider a particularly important example of a nonlinear regression model that is also a linear regression model subject to nonlinear restrictions on the parameters. In Section 5.5, we briefly mentioned the phenomenon of **serial correlation**, in which nearby error terms in a regression model are (or appear to be) correlated. Serial correlation is very commonly encountered in applied work using time-series data, and many techniques for dealing with it have been proposed. One of the simplest and most popular ways of dealing with serial correlation is to assume that the error terms follow the **first-order autoregressive**, or **AR(1)**, process

$$u_t = \rho u_{t-1} + \varepsilon_t, \quad \varepsilon_t \sim \text{IID}(0, \sigma_\varepsilon^2), \quad |\rho| < 1. \tag{6.04}$$

According to this model, the error at time t is equal to ρ times the error at time $t-1$, plus a new error term ε_t. The vector $\boldsymbol{\varepsilon}$ with typical component ε_t satisfies the IID condition we discussed above. This condition is enough for ε_t to be an innovation in the sense of Section 4.5. Thus the ε_t are homoskedastic and independent of all past and future innovations. We see from (6.04) that, in each period, part of the error term u_t is the previous period's error term, shrunk somewhat toward zero and possibly changed in sign, and part is the innovation ε_t. We will discuss serial correlation, including the AR(1) process and other autoregressive processes, in Chapter 7. At present, we are concerned solely with the nonlinear regression model that results when the errors of a linear regression model are assumed to follow an AR(1) process.

If we combine (6.04) with the linear regression model

$$y_t = \boldsymbol{X}_t\boldsymbol{\beta} + u_t \tag{6.05}$$

by substituting $\rho u_{t-1} + \varepsilon_t$ for u_t and then replacing u_{t-1} by $y_{t-1} - \boldsymbol{X}_{t-1}\boldsymbol{\beta}$, we obtain the nonlinear regression model

$$y_t = \rho y_{t-1} + \boldsymbol{X}_t\boldsymbol{\beta} - \rho\boldsymbol{X}_{t-1}\boldsymbol{\beta} + \varepsilon_t, \quad \varepsilon_t \sim \text{IID}(0, \sigma_\varepsilon^2). \tag{6.06}$$

Since the lagged dependent variable y_{t-1} appears among the regressors, this is a **dynamic** model. As with the other dynamic models that are treated in the exercises, we have to drop the first observation, because y_0 and $\boldsymbol{X}_0$ are assumed not to be available. The model is linear in the regressors but nonlinear in the parameters $\boldsymbol{\beta}$ and ρ, and it therefore needs to be estimated by nonlinear least squares or some other nonlinear estimation method.

In the next section, we study estimators for nonlinear regression models generated by the method of moments, and we establish conditions for asymptotic identification, asymptotic normality, and asymptotic efficiency. Then, in Section 6.3, we show that, under the assumption that the error terms are IID, the most efficient MM estimator is **nonlinear least squares**, or **NLS**. In Section 6.4, we discuss various methods by which NLS estimates may be computed. The method of choice in most circumstances is some variant of Newton's Method. One commonly-used variant is based on an artificial linear regression called the Gauss-Newton regression. We introduce this artificial regression in Section 6.5 and show how to use it to compute NLS estimates and estimates of their covariance matrix. In Section 6.6, we introduce the important concept of one-step estimation. Then, in Section 6.7, we show how to use the Gauss-Newton regression to compute hypothesis tests. Finally, in Section 6.8, we introduce a modified Gauss-Newton regression suitable for use in the presence of heteroskedasticity of unknown form.

6.2 Method-of-Moments Estimators for Nonlinear Models

In Section 1.5, we derived the OLS estimator for linear models from the method of moments by using the fact that, for each observation, the mean of the error term in the regression model is zero conditional on the vector of explanatory variables. This implied that

$$\text{E}(\boldsymbol{X}_t u_t) = \text{E}\big(\boldsymbol{X}_t(y_t - \boldsymbol{X}_t\boldsymbol{\beta})\big) = \boldsymbol{0}. \tag{6.07}$$

The sample analog of the middle expression here is $n^{-1}\boldsymbol{X}^\top(\boldsymbol{y}-\boldsymbol{X\beta})$. Setting this to zero and ignoring the factor of n^{-1}, we obtained the vector of **moment conditions**

$$\boldsymbol{X}^\top(\boldsymbol{y}-\boldsymbol{X\beta}) = \boldsymbol{0}, \tag{6.08}$$

and these conditions were easily solved to yield the OLS estimator $\hat{\boldsymbol{\beta}}$. We now want to employ the same type of argument for nonlinear models.

An information set Ω_t is typically characterized by a set of variables that belong to it. But, since the realization of any deterministic function of these variables is known as soon as the variables themselves are realized, Ω_t must contain not only the variables that characterize it but also all deterministic functions of them. As a result, an information set Ω_t contains precisely those variables which are equal to their expectations conditional on Ω_t. In Exercise 6.1, readers are asked to show that the conditional expectation of a random variable is also its expectation conditional on the set of all deterministic functions of the conditioning variables.

For the nonlinear regression model (6.01), the error term u_t has mean 0 conditional on all variables in Ω_t. Thus, if $\boldsymbol{W}_t$ denotes any $1 \times k$ vector of which all the components belong to Ω_t,

$$\mathrm{E}(\boldsymbol{W}_t u_t) = \mathrm{E}\Big(\boldsymbol{W}_t\big(y_t - x_t(\boldsymbol{\beta})\big)\Big) = \boldsymbol{0}. \tag{6.09}$$

Just as the moment conditions that correspond to (6.07) are (6.08), the moment conditions that correspond to (6.09) are

$$\boldsymbol{W}^\top\big(\boldsymbol{y}-\boldsymbol{x}(\boldsymbol{\beta})\big) = \boldsymbol{0}, \tag{6.10}$$

where $\boldsymbol{W}$ is an $n \times k$ matrix with typical row $\boldsymbol{W}_t$. There are k nonlinear equations in (6.10). These equations can, in principle, be solved to yield an estimator of the k-vector $\boldsymbol{\beta}$. Geometrically, the moment conditions (6.10) require that the vector of residuals should be orthogonal to all the columns of the matrix $\boldsymbol{W}$.

How should we choose $\boldsymbol{W}$? There are infinitely many possibilities. Using almost any matrix $\boldsymbol{W}$, of which the tth row depends only on variables that belong to Ω_t, and which has full column rank k asymptotically, yields a consistent estimator of $\boldsymbol{\beta}$. However, these estimators in general have different asymptotic covariance matrices, and it is therefore of interest to see if any particular choice of $\boldsymbol{W}$ leads to an estimator with smaller asymptotic variance than the others. Such a choice would then lead to an efficient estimator, judged by the criterion of the asymptotic variance.

Identification and Asymptotic Identification

Let us denote by $\hat{\boldsymbol{\beta}}$ the MM estimator defined implicitly by (6.10). In order to show that $\hat{\boldsymbol{\beta}}$ is consistent, we must assume that the parameter vector $\boldsymbol{\beta}$ in the model (6.01) is **asymptotically identified**. In general, a vector of parameters is said to be **identified** by a given data set and a given estimation method if, for that data set, the estimation method provides a unique way to determine the parameter estimates. In the present case, $\boldsymbol{\beta}$ is identified by a given data set if equations (6.10) have a unique solution.

For the parameters of a model to be asymptotically identified by a given estimation method, we require that the estimation method provide a unique way to determine the parameter estimates in the limit as the sample size n tends to infinity. In the present case, asymptotic identification can be formulated in terms of the probability limit of the vector $n^{-1}\boldsymbol{W}^{\top}\big(\boldsymbol{y}-\boldsymbol{x}(\boldsymbol{\beta})\big)$ as $n \to \infty$. Suppose that the true DGP is a special case of the model (6.02) with parameter vector $\boldsymbol{\beta}_0$. Then we have

$$\frac{1}{n}\boldsymbol{W}^{\top}\big(\boldsymbol{y}-\boldsymbol{x}(\boldsymbol{\beta}_0)\big) = \frac{1}{n}\sum_{t=1}^{n}\boldsymbol{W}_t^{\top}u_t. \tag{6.11}$$

By (6.09), every term in the sum above has mean 0, and the IID assumption in (6.02) is enough to allow us to apply a law of large numbers to that sum. It follows that the right-hand side, and therefore also the left-hand side, of (6.11) tends to zero in probability as $n \to \infty$.

Let us now define the k–vector of deterministic functions $\boldsymbol{\alpha}(\boldsymbol{\beta})$ as

$$\boldsymbol{\alpha}(\boldsymbol{\beta}) = \operatorname*{plim}_{n\to\infty}\frac{1}{n}\boldsymbol{W}^{\top}\big(\boldsymbol{y}-\boldsymbol{x}(\boldsymbol{\beta})\big), \tag{6.12}$$

where we continue to assume that $\boldsymbol{y}$ is generated by the model (6.02) with $\boldsymbol{\beta} = \boldsymbol{\beta}_0$. Since a law of large numbers can be applied to the right-hand side of equation (6.12) whatever the value of $\boldsymbol{\beta}$, the components of $\boldsymbol{\alpha}$ are deterministic. In the preceding paragraph, we explained why $\boldsymbol{\alpha}(\boldsymbol{\beta}_0) = \mathbf{0}$. The parameter vector $\boldsymbol{\beta}$ is asymptotically identified if $\boldsymbol{\beta}_0$ is the *unique* solution to the equations $\boldsymbol{\alpha}(\boldsymbol{\beta}) = \mathbf{0}$, that is, if $\boldsymbol{\alpha}(\boldsymbol{\beta}) \neq \mathbf{0}$ for all $\boldsymbol{\beta} \neq \boldsymbol{\beta}_0$.

Although most parameter vectors that are identified by data sets of reasonable size are also asymptotically identified, neither of these concepts implies the other. It is possible for an estimator to be asymptotically identified without being identified by many data sets, and it is possible for an estimator to be identified by every data set of finite size without being asymptotically identified. To see this, consider the following two examples.

As an example of the first possibility, suppose that $y_t = \beta_1 + \beta_2 z_t$, where z_t is a random variable which follows the **Bernoulli distribution**. Such a random variable is often called a **binary variable**, because there are only two possible values it can take on, 0 and 1. The probability that $z_t = 1$ is p, and so the probability that $z_t = 0$ is $1 - p$. If p is small, there could easily be samples of size n for which every z_t was equal to 0. For such samples, the parameter β_2 cannot be identified, because changing β_2 can have no effect on $y_t - \beta_1 - \beta_2 z_t$. However, provided that $p > 0$, both parameters are identified asymptotically.

As $n \to \infty$, a law of large numbers guarantees that the proportion of the z_t that are equal to 1 tends to p.

As an example of the second possibility, consider the model (3.20), discussed in Section 3.3, for which $y_t = \beta_1 + \beta_2 1/t + u_t$, where t is a time trend. The OLS estimators of β_1 and β_2 can, of course, be computed for any finite sample of size at least 2, and so the parameters are identified by any data set with at least 2 observations. But β_2 is not identified asymptotically. Suppose that the true parameter values are β_1^0 and β_2^0. Let us use the two regressors for the variables in the information set Ω_t, so that $\boldsymbol{W}_t = [1 \;\; 1/t]$ and the MM estimator is the same as the OLS estimator. Then, using the definition (6.12), we obtain

$$\boldsymbol{\alpha}(\beta_1, \beta_2) = \operatorname*{plim}_{n\to\infty} \begin{bmatrix} n^{-1}\sum_{t=1}^{n}\big((\beta_1^0 - \beta_1) + 1/t(\beta_2^0 - \beta_2) + u_t\big) \\ n^{-1}\sum_{t=1}^{n}\big(1/t(\beta_1^0 - \beta_1) + 1/t^2(\beta_2^0 - \beta_2) + 1/t\, u_t\big) \end{bmatrix}. \tag{6.13}$$

It is known that the deterministic sums $n^{-1}\sum_{t=1}^{n}(1/t)$ and $n^{-1}\sum_{t=1}^{n}(1/t^2)$ both tend to 0 as $n \to \infty$. Further, the law of large numbers tells us that the limits in probability of $n^{-1}\sum_{t=1}^{n} u_t$ and $n^{-1}\sum_{t=1}^{n}(u_t/t)$ are both 0. Thus the right-hand side of (6.13) simplifies to

$$\boldsymbol{\alpha}(\beta_1, \beta_2) = \begin{bmatrix} \beta_1^0 - \beta_1 \\ 0 \end{bmatrix}.$$

Since $\boldsymbol{\alpha}(\beta_1, \beta_2)$ vanishes for $\beta_1 = \beta_1^0$ and for any value of β_2 whatsoever, we see that β_2 is not asymptotically identified. In Section 3.3, we showed that, although the OLS estimator of β_2 is unbiased, it is not consistent. The simultaneous failure of consistency and asymptotic identification in this example is not a coincidence: It will turn out that asymptotic identification is a necessary and sufficient condition for consistency.

Consistency

Suppose that the DGP is a special case of the model (6.02) with true parameter vector $\boldsymbol{\beta}_0$. Under the assumption of asymptotic identification, the equations $\boldsymbol{\alpha}(\boldsymbol{\beta}) = \mathbf{0}$ have a unique solution, namely, $\boldsymbol{\beta} = \boldsymbol{\beta}_0$. This can be shown to imply that, as $n \to \infty$, the probability limit of the estimator $\hat{\boldsymbol{\beta}}$ defined by (6.10) is precisely $\boldsymbol{\beta}_0$. We will not attempt a formal proof of this result, since it would have to deal with a number of technical issues that are beyond the scope of this book. See Amemiya (1985, Section 4.3) or Davidson and MacKinnon (1993, Section 5.3) for more detailed treatments.

However, an intuitive, heuristic, proof is not at all hard to provide. If we make the assumption that $\hat{\boldsymbol{\beta}}$ has a deterministic probability limit, say $\boldsymbol{\beta}_\infty$, the result follows easily. What makes a formal proof more difficult is showing that $\boldsymbol{\beta}_\infty$ exists. Let us suppose that $\boldsymbol{\beta}_\infty \neq \boldsymbol{\beta}_0$. We will derive a contradiction from this assumption, and we will thus be able to conclude that $\boldsymbol{\beta}_\infty = \boldsymbol{\beta}_0$, in other words, that $\hat{\boldsymbol{\beta}}$ is consistent.

For all finite samples large enough for $\boldsymbol{\beta}$ to be identified by the data, we have, by the definition (6.10) of $\hat{\boldsymbol{\beta}}$, that

$$\frac{1}{n}\boldsymbol{W}^{\top}\big(\boldsymbol{y}-\boldsymbol{x}(\hat{\boldsymbol{\beta}})\big)=\mathbf{0}. \tag{6.14}$$

If we take the limit of this as $n \to \infty$, we have $\mathbf{0}$ on the right-hand side. On the left-hand side, because we assume that $\operatorname{plim}\hat{\boldsymbol{\beta}} = \boldsymbol{\beta}_\infty$, the limit is the same as the limit of

$$\frac{1}{n}\boldsymbol{W}^{\top}\big(\boldsymbol{y}-\boldsymbol{x}(\boldsymbol{\beta}_\infty)\big).$$

By (6.12), the limit of this expression is $\boldsymbol{\alpha}(\boldsymbol{\beta}_\infty)$. We assumed that $\boldsymbol{\beta}_\infty \neq \boldsymbol{\beta}_0$, and so, by the asymptotic identification condition, $\boldsymbol{\alpha}(\boldsymbol{\beta}_\infty) \neq \mathbf{0}$. But this contradicts the fact that the limits of both sides of (6.14) are equal, since the limit of the right-hand side is $\mathbf{0}$.

We have shown that, if we assume that a deterministic $\boldsymbol{\beta}_\infty$ exists, then asymptotic identification is sufficient for consistency. Although we will not attempt to prove it, asymptotic identification is also necessary for consistency. The key to a proof is showing that, if the parameters of a model are not asymptotically identified by a given estimation method, then no deterministic limit like $\boldsymbol{\beta}_\infty$ exists in general. An example of this is provided by the model (3.20); see also Exercise 6.2.

The identifiability of a parameter vector, whether asymptotic or by a data set, depends on the estimation method used. In the present context, this means that certain choices of the variables in $\boldsymbol{W}_t$ may identify the parameters of a model like (6.01), while others do not. We can gain some intuition about this matter by looking a little more closely at the limiting functions $\boldsymbol{\alpha}(\boldsymbol{\beta})$ defined by (6.12). We have

$$\begin{aligned}
\boldsymbol{\alpha}(\boldsymbol{\beta}) &= \operatorname*{plim}_{n\to\infty}\frac{1}{n}\boldsymbol{W}^{\top}\big(\boldsymbol{y}-\boldsymbol{x}(\boldsymbol{\beta})\big)\\
&= \operatorname*{plim}_{n\to\infty}\frac{1}{n}\boldsymbol{W}^{\top}\big(\boldsymbol{x}(\boldsymbol{\beta}_0)-\boldsymbol{x}(\boldsymbol{\beta})+\boldsymbol{u}\big)\\
&= \boldsymbol{\alpha}(\boldsymbol{\beta}_0)+\operatorname*{plim}_{n\to\infty}\frac{1}{n}\boldsymbol{W}^{\top}\big(\boldsymbol{x}(\boldsymbol{\beta}_0)-\boldsymbol{x}(\boldsymbol{\beta})\big)\\
&= \operatorname*{plim}_{n\to\infty}\frac{1}{n}\boldsymbol{W}^{\top}\big(\boldsymbol{x}(\boldsymbol{\beta}_0)-\boldsymbol{x}(\boldsymbol{\beta})\big).
\end{aligned} \tag{6.15}$$

Therefore, for asymptotic identification, and so also for consistency, the last expression in (6.15) must be nonzero for all $\boldsymbol{\beta} \neq \boldsymbol{\beta}_0$.

Evidently, a necessary condition for asymptotic identification is that there be no $\boldsymbol{\beta}_1 \neq \boldsymbol{\beta}_0$ such that $\boldsymbol{x}(\boldsymbol{\beta}_1) = \boldsymbol{x}(\boldsymbol{\beta}_0)$. This condition is the nonlinear analog of the requirement of linearly independent regressors for linear regression models. We can now see that this requirement is in fact a condition necessary for the identification of the model parameters, both by a data set and asymptotically. Suppose that, for a linear regression model, the columns of the regressor matrix $\boldsymbol{X}$ are linearly dependent. This implies that there is a nonzero vector $\boldsymbol{b}$ such that $\boldsymbol{Xb} = \boldsymbol{0}$; recall the discussion in Section 2.2. Then it follows that $\boldsymbol{X\beta}_0 = \boldsymbol{X}(\boldsymbol{\beta}_0 + \boldsymbol{b})$. For a linear regression model, $\boldsymbol{x}(\boldsymbol{\beta}) = \boldsymbol{X\beta}$. Therefore, if we set $\boldsymbol{\beta}_1 = \boldsymbol{\beta}_0 + \boldsymbol{b}$, the linear dependence means that $\boldsymbol{x}(\boldsymbol{\beta}_1) = \boldsymbol{x}(\boldsymbol{\beta}_0)$, in violation of the necessary condition stated at the beginning of this paragraph.

For a linear regression model, linear independence of the regressors is both necessary and sufficient for identification by any data set. We saw above that it is necessary, and sufficiency follows from the fact, discussed in Section 2.2, that $\boldsymbol{X}^\top\boldsymbol{X}$ is nonsingular if the columns of $\boldsymbol{X}$ are linearly independent. If $\boldsymbol{X}^\top\boldsymbol{X}$ is nonsingular, the OLS estimator $(\boldsymbol{X}^\top\boldsymbol{X})^{-1}\boldsymbol{X}^\top\boldsymbol{y}$ exists and is unique for any $\boldsymbol{y}$, and this is precisely what is meant by identification by any data set.

For nonlinear models, however, things are more complicated. In general, more is needed for identification than the condition that no $\boldsymbol{\beta}_1 \neq \boldsymbol{\beta}_0$ exist such that $\boldsymbol{x}(\boldsymbol{\beta}_1) = \boldsymbol{x}(\boldsymbol{\beta}_0)$. The relevant issues will be easier to understand after we have derived the asymptotic covariance matrix of the estimator defined by (6.10), and so we postpone study of them until later.

The MM estimator $\hat{\boldsymbol{\beta}}$ defined by (6.10) is actually consistent under considerably weaker assumptions about the error terms than those we have made. The key to the consistency proof is the requirement that the error terms satisfy the condition

$$\operatorname*{plim}_{n\to\infty} \frac{1}{n}\boldsymbol{W}^\top\boldsymbol{u} = \boldsymbol{0}. \tag{6.16}$$

Under reasonable assumptions, it is not difficult to show that this condition holds even when the u_t are heteroskedastic, and it may also hold even when they are serially correlated. However, difficulties can arise when the u_t are serially correlated and $x_t(\boldsymbol{\beta})$ depends on lagged dependent variables. In this case, it will be seen later that the expectation of u_t conditional on the lagged dependent variable is nonzero in general. Therefore, in this circumstance, condition (6.16) does not hold whenever $\boldsymbol{W}$ includes lagged dependent variables, and such MM estimators are generally not consistent.

Asymptotic Normality

The MM estimator $\hat{\boldsymbol{\beta}}$ defined by (6.10) for different possible choices of $\boldsymbol{W}$ is asymptotically normal under appropriate conditions. As we discussed in Section 5.4, this means that the vector $n^{1/2}(\hat{\boldsymbol{\beta}} - \boldsymbol{\beta}_0)$ follows the multivariate normal distribution with mean vector $\boldsymbol{0}$ and a covariance matrix that will be determined shortly.

Before we start our analysis, we need some notation, which will be used extensively in the remainder of this chapter. In formulating the generic nonlinear regression model (6.01), we deliberately used $x_t(\cdot)$ to denote the regression function, rather than $f_t(\cdot)$ or some other notation, because this notation makes it easy to see the close connection between the nonlinear and linear regression models. It is natural to let the derivative of $x_t(\boldsymbol{\beta})$ with respect to β_i be denoted $X_{ti}(\boldsymbol{\beta})$. Then we can let $\boldsymbol{X}_t(\boldsymbol{\beta})$ denote a $1 \times k$ vector, and $\boldsymbol{X}(\boldsymbol{\beta})$ denote an $n \times k$ matrix, each having typical element $X_{ti}(\boldsymbol{\beta})$. These are the analogs of the vector $\boldsymbol{X}_t$ and the matrix $\boldsymbol{X}$ for the linear regression model. In the linear case, when the regression function is $\boldsymbol{X\beta}$, it is easy to see that $\boldsymbol{X}_t(\boldsymbol{\beta}) = \boldsymbol{X}_t$ and $\boldsymbol{X}(\boldsymbol{\beta}) = \boldsymbol{X}$. The big difference between the linear and nonlinear cases is that, in the latter case, $\boldsymbol{X}_t(\boldsymbol{\beta})$ and $\boldsymbol{X}(\boldsymbol{\beta})$ depend on $\boldsymbol{\beta}$.

If we multiply equation (6.10) by $n^{-1/2}$, replace $\boldsymbol{y}$ by what it is equal to under the DGP (6.01) with parameter vector $\boldsymbol{\beta}_0$, and replace $\boldsymbol{\beta}$ by $\hat{\boldsymbol{\beta}}$, we obtain

$$n^{-1/2}\boldsymbol{W}^\top\big(\boldsymbol{u} + \boldsymbol{x}(\boldsymbol{\beta}_0) - \boldsymbol{x}(\hat{\boldsymbol{\beta}})\big) = \boldsymbol{0}. \tag{6.17}$$

The next step is to apply Taylor's Theorem at the point $\boldsymbol{\beta} = \boldsymbol{\beta}_0$ to the components of the vector $\boldsymbol{x}(\hat{\boldsymbol{\beta}})$; see the discussion of this theorem in Section 5.6. We apply the formula (5.46) with $m = k$, replacing $f(\boldsymbol{x})$ by $x_t(\boldsymbol{\beta}_0)$ and $\boldsymbol{h}$ by the vector $\hat{\boldsymbol{\beta}} - \boldsymbol{\beta}_0$. We thus obtain, for $t = 1, \ldots, n$,

$$x_t(\hat{\boldsymbol{\beta}}) = x_t(\boldsymbol{\beta}_0) + \sum_{i=1}^{k} X_{ti}(\bar{\boldsymbol{\beta}}_t)(\hat{\beta}_i - \beta_{0i}), \tag{6.18}$$

where β_{0i} is the ith element of $\boldsymbol{\beta}_0$, and the $\bar{\boldsymbol{\beta}}_t$, which play the role of $\boldsymbol{x} + \lambda\boldsymbol{h}$ in equation (5.46), satisfy the condition

$$\big\|\bar{\boldsymbol{\beta}}_t - \boldsymbol{\beta}_0\big\| \le \big\|\hat{\boldsymbol{\beta}} - \boldsymbol{\beta}_0\big\|. \tag{6.19}$$

Substituting the Taylor expansion (6.18) into (6.17) yields

$$n^{-1/2}\boldsymbol{W}^\top\boldsymbol{u} - n^{-1/2}\boldsymbol{W}^\top\boldsymbol{X}(\bar{\boldsymbol{\beta}})(\hat{\boldsymbol{\beta}} - \boldsymbol{\beta}_0) = \boldsymbol{0}. \tag{6.20}$$

The notation $\boldsymbol{X}(\bar{\boldsymbol{\beta}})$ is convenient, but slightly inaccurate. According to (6.18), we need different parameter vectors $\bar{\boldsymbol{\beta}}_t$ for each row of that matrix. But, since all of these vectors satisfy (6.19), it is not necessary to make this fact explicit in the notation. Thus here, and in subsequent chapters, we will refer to a vector $\bar{\boldsymbol{\beta}}$ that satisfies (6.19), without implying that it must be the *same* vector for every row of the matrix $\boldsymbol{X}(\bar{\boldsymbol{\beta}})$. This is a legitimate notational convenience, because, since $\hat{\boldsymbol{\beta}}$ is consistent, as we have seen that it is under the requirement of asymptotic identification, then so too are all of the $\bar{\boldsymbol{\beta}}_t$. Consequently, (6.20) remains true asymptotically if we replace $\bar{\boldsymbol{\beta}}$ by $\boldsymbol{\beta}_0$. Doing this, and rearranging factors of powers of n so as to work only with quantities which have suitable probability limits, yields the result that

$$n^{-1/2}\boldsymbol{W}^\top\boldsymbol{u} - n^{-1}\boldsymbol{W}^\top\boldsymbol{X}(\boldsymbol{\beta}_0)\, n^{1/2}(\hat{\boldsymbol{\beta}} - \boldsymbol{\beta}_0) \overset{a}{=} \boldsymbol{0}, \tag{6.21}$$

This result is the starting point for all our subsequent analysis.

We need to apply a law of large numbers to the first factor of the second term of (6.21), namely, $n^{-1}\boldsymbol{W}^\top\boldsymbol{X}_0$, where for notational ease we write $\boldsymbol{X}_0 \equiv \boldsymbol{X}(\boldsymbol{\beta}_0)$.

Under reasonable regularity conditions, not unlike those needed for (3.17) to hold, we have

$$\operatorname*{plim}_{n\to\infty} \frac{1}{n} \boldsymbol{W}^\top \boldsymbol{X}_0 = \lim_{n\to\infty} \frac{1}{n} \boldsymbol{W}^\top \mathrm{E}\big(\boldsymbol{X}(\boldsymbol{\beta}_0)\big) \equiv \boldsymbol{S}_{\boldsymbol{W}^\top\boldsymbol{X}},$$

where $\boldsymbol{S}_{\boldsymbol{W}^\top\boldsymbol{X}}$ is a deterministic $k \times k$ matrix. It turns out that a sufficient condition for the parameter vector $\boldsymbol{\beta}$ to be asymptotically identified by the estimator $\hat{\boldsymbol{\beta}}$ defined by the moment conditions (6.10) is that $\boldsymbol{S}_{\boldsymbol{W}^\top\boldsymbol{X}}$ should have full rank. To see this, observe that (6.21) implies that

$$\boldsymbol{S}_{\boldsymbol{W}^\top\boldsymbol{X}}\, n^{1/2}(\hat{\boldsymbol{\beta}} - \boldsymbol{\beta}_0) \overset{a}{=} n^{-1/2}\boldsymbol{W}^\top\boldsymbol{u}. \tag{6.22}$$

Because $\boldsymbol{S}_{\boldsymbol{W}^\top\boldsymbol{X}}$ is assumed to have full rank, its inverse exists. Thus we can multiply both sides of (6.22) by this inverse to obtain a well-defined expression for the limit of $n^{1/2}(\hat{\boldsymbol{\beta}} - \boldsymbol{\beta}_0)$:

$$n^{1/2}(\hat{\boldsymbol{\beta}} - \boldsymbol{\beta}_0) \overset{a}{=} (\boldsymbol{S}_{\boldsymbol{W}^\top\boldsymbol{X}})^{-1} n^{-1/2}\boldsymbol{W}^\top\boldsymbol{u}. \tag{6.23}$$

From this, we conclude that $\boldsymbol{\beta}$ is asymptotically identified by $\hat{\boldsymbol{\beta}}$. The condition that $\boldsymbol{S}_{\boldsymbol{W}^\top\boldsymbol{X}}$ be nonsingular is called **strong asymptotic identification**. It is a sufficient but not necessary condition for ordinary asymptotic identification.

The second factor on the right-hand side of (6.23) is a vector to which we should, under appropriate regularity conditions, be able to apply a central limit theorem. Since, by (6.09), $\mathrm{E}(\boldsymbol{W}_t u_t) = \boldsymbol{0}$, we can show that $n^{-1/2}\boldsymbol{W}^\top\boldsymbol{u}$ is asymptotically multivariate normal, with mean vector $\boldsymbol{0}$ and a finite covariance matrix. To do this, we can use exactly the same reasoning as was used in Section 4.5 to show that the vector $\boldsymbol{v}$ of (4.53) is asymptotically multivariate normal. Because the components of $n^{1/2}(\hat{\boldsymbol{\beta}} - \boldsymbol{\beta}_0)$ are, asymptotically, linear combinations of the components of a vector that follows the multivariate normal distribution, we conclude that $n^{1/2}(\hat{\boldsymbol{\beta}} - \boldsymbol{\beta}_0)$ itself must be asymptotically normally distributed with mean vector zero and a finite covariance matrix. This implies that $\hat{\boldsymbol{\beta}}$ is root-n consistent in the sense defined in Section 5.4.

Asymptotic Efficiency

The asymptotic covariance matrix of $n^{-1/2}\boldsymbol{W}^\top\boldsymbol{u}$, the second factor on the right-hand side of (6.23), is, by arguments exactly like those in (4.54),

$$\sigma_0^2 \operatorname*{plim}_{n\to\infty} \frac{1}{n} \boldsymbol{W}^\top\boldsymbol{W} = \sigma_0^2 \boldsymbol{S}_{\boldsymbol{W}^\top\boldsymbol{W}}, \tag{6.24}$$

where σ_0^2 is the error variance for the true DGP, and where we make the definition $\boldsymbol{S}_{\boldsymbol{W}^\top\boldsymbol{W}} \equiv \operatorname{plim} n^{-1}\boldsymbol{W}^\top\boldsymbol{W}$. From (6.23) and (6.24), it follows immediately that the asymptotic covariance matrix of the vector $n^{1/2}(\hat{\boldsymbol{\beta}} - \boldsymbol{\beta}_0)$ is

$$\sigma_0^2 (\boldsymbol{S}_{\boldsymbol{W}^\top\boldsymbol{X}})^{-1} \boldsymbol{S}_{\boldsymbol{W}^\top\boldsymbol{W}} (\boldsymbol{S}_{\boldsymbol{W}^\top\boldsymbol{X}}^\top)^{-1}, \tag{6.25}$$

which has the form of a sandwich. By the definitions of $\boldsymbol{S}_{\boldsymbol{W}^\top\boldsymbol{W}}$ and $\boldsymbol{S}_{\boldsymbol{W}^\top\boldsymbol{X}}$, expression (6.25) can be rewritten as

$$\begin{aligned}
&\sigma_0^2 \operatorname*{plim}_{n\to\infty}\big((n^{-1}\boldsymbol{W}^\top\boldsymbol{X}_0)^{-1}n^{-1}\boldsymbol{W}^\top\boldsymbol{W}(n^{-1}\boldsymbol{X}_0^\top\boldsymbol{W})^{-1}\big)\\
&= \sigma_0^2 \operatorname*{plim}_{n\to\infty}\big(n^{-1}\boldsymbol{X}_0^\top\boldsymbol{W}(\boldsymbol{W}^\top\boldsymbol{W})^{-1}\boldsymbol{W}^\top\boldsymbol{X}_0\big)^{-1}\\
&= \sigma_0^2 \operatorname*{plim}_{n\to\infty}(n^{-1}\boldsymbol{X}_0^\top\boldsymbol{P}_{\boldsymbol{W}}\boldsymbol{X}_0)^{-1}, \qquad (6.26)
\end{aligned}$$

where $\boldsymbol{P}_{\boldsymbol{W}}$ is the orthogonal projection on to $\mathcal{S}(\boldsymbol{W})$, the subspace spanned by the columns of $\boldsymbol{W}$. Expression (6.26) is the asymptotic covariance matrix of the vector $n^{1/2}(\hat{\boldsymbol{\beta}} - \boldsymbol{\beta}_0)$. However, it is common to refer to it as the asymptotic covariance matrix of $\hat{\boldsymbol{\beta}}$, and we will allow ourselves this slight abuse of terminology when no confusion can result.

It is clear from the result (6.26) that the asymptotic covariance matrix of the estimator $\hat{\boldsymbol{\beta}}$ depends on the variables $\boldsymbol{W}$ used to obtain it. Most choices of $\boldsymbol{W}$ lead to an inefficient estimator by the criterion of the asymptotic covariance matrix, as we would be led to suspect by the fact that (6.25) has the form of a sandwich; see Section 5.5. It is not hard to show that an estimator which is **asymptotically efficient** is given by the choice $\boldsymbol{W} = \boldsymbol{X}_0$. To demonstrate this, we need to show that this choice of $\boldsymbol{W}$ minimizes the asymptotic covariance matrix, in the sense used in the Gauss-Markov theorem. Recall that one covariance matrix is said to be "greater" than another if the difference between it and the other is a positive semidefinite matrix.

If we set $\boldsymbol{W} = \boldsymbol{X}_0$ to define the MM estimator, the asymptotic covariance matrix (6.26) becomes $\sigma_0^2 \operatorname{plim}(n^{-1}\boldsymbol{X}_0^\top\boldsymbol{X}_0)^{-1}$. As we saw in Section 3.5, it is often easier to establish efficiency by reasoning in terms of the precision matrix, that is, the inverse of the covariance matrix, rather than in terms of the (asymptotic) covariance matrix itself. Since

$$\boldsymbol{X}_0^\top\boldsymbol{X}_0 - \boldsymbol{X}_0^\top\boldsymbol{P}_{\boldsymbol{W}}\boldsymbol{X}_0 = \boldsymbol{X}_0^\top\boldsymbol{M}_{\boldsymbol{W}}\boldsymbol{X}_0,$$

which is a positive semidefinite matrix, it follows at once that the precision of the estimator obtained by setting $\boldsymbol{W} = \boldsymbol{X}_0$ is greater than or equal to that of the estimator obtained by using any other choice of $\boldsymbol{W}$. The same precision can be obtained only if $\boldsymbol{M}_{\boldsymbol{W}}\boldsymbol{X}_0 = \mathbf{O}$, that is, if every column of the matrix $\boldsymbol{X}_0$ is in the subspace $\mathcal{S}(\boldsymbol{W})$; recall the result of Exercise 3.18. In other words, the MM estimator is asymptotically efficient whenever $\boldsymbol{X}_0$ belongs to $\mathcal{S}(\boldsymbol{W})$.

Of course, we cannot actually use $\boldsymbol{X}_0$ for $\boldsymbol{W}$ in practice, because $\boldsymbol{X}_0 \equiv \boldsymbol{X}(\boldsymbol{\beta}_0)$ depends on the unknown true parameter vector $\boldsymbol{\beta}_0$. The MM estimator that uses $\boldsymbol{X}_0$ for $\boldsymbol{W}$ is therefore said to be **infeasible**. In the next section, we will see how to overcome this difficulty. The nonlinear least-squares estimator that we will obtain turns out to have exactly the same asymptotic properties as the infeasible MM estimator.

6.3 Nonlinear Least Squares

There are at least two ways in which we can approximate the asymptotically efficient, but infeasible, MM estimator that uses $\boldsymbol{X}_0$ for $\boldsymbol{W}$. The first, and perhaps the simpler of the two, is to begin by choosing any $\boldsymbol{W}$ for which $\boldsymbol{W}_t$ belongs to the information set Ω_t and using this $\boldsymbol{W}$ to obtain a preliminary consistent estimate, say $\acute{\boldsymbol{\beta}}$, of the model parameters. We can then estimate $\boldsymbol{\beta}$ once more, setting $\boldsymbol{W} = \acute{\boldsymbol{X}} \equiv \boldsymbol{X}(\acute{\boldsymbol{\beta}})$. The consistency of $\acute{\boldsymbol{\beta}}$ ensures that $\acute{\boldsymbol{X}}$ tends to the efficient choice $\boldsymbol{X}_0$ as $n \to \infty$.

A more subtle approach is to recognize that the above procedure estimates the same parameter vector twice, and to compress the two estimation procedures into one. Consider the moment conditions

$$\boldsymbol{X}^{\top}(\boldsymbol{\beta})\big(\boldsymbol{y} - \boldsymbol{x}(\boldsymbol{\beta})\big) = \mathbf{0}. \tag{6.27}$$

If the estimator $\hat{\boldsymbol{\beta}}$ obtained by solving the k equations (6.27) is consistent, then $\hat{\boldsymbol{X}} \equiv \boldsymbol{X}(\hat{\boldsymbol{\beta}})$ tends to $\boldsymbol{X}_0$ as $n \to \infty$. Therefore, it must be the case that, for sufficiently large samples, $\hat{\boldsymbol{\beta}}$ is very close to the infeasible, efficient MM estimator.

The estimator $\hat{\boldsymbol{\beta}}$ based on (6.27) is known as the **nonlinear least-squares**, or **NLS**, estimator. The name comes from the fact that the moment conditions (6.27) are just the first-order conditions for the minimization with respect to $\boldsymbol{\beta}$ of the sum-of-squared-residuals (or SSR) function. The SSR function is defined just as in (1.49), but for a nonlinear regression function:

$$\mathrm{SSR}(\boldsymbol{\beta}) = \sum_{t=1}^{n} \big(y_t - x_t(\boldsymbol{\beta})\big)^2 = \big(\boldsymbol{y} - \boldsymbol{x}(\boldsymbol{\beta})\big)^{\top}\big(\boldsymbol{y} - \boldsymbol{x}(\boldsymbol{\beta})\big). \tag{6.28}$$

It is easy to check (see Exercise 6.4) that the moment conditions (6.27) are equivalent to the first-order conditions for minimizing (6.28).

Equations (6.27), which define the NLS estimator, closely resemble equations (6.08), which define the OLS estimator. Like the latter, the former can be interpreted as orthogonality conditions: They require that the columns of the matrix of derivatives of $\boldsymbol{x}(\boldsymbol{\beta})$ with respect to $\boldsymbol{\beta}$ should be orthogonal to the vector of residuals. There are, however, two major differences between (6.27) and (6.08). The first difference is that, in the nonlinear case, $\boldsymbol{X}(\boldsymbol{\beta})$ is a matrix of functions that depend on the explanatory variables and on $\boldsymbol{\beta}$, instead of simply a matrix of explanatory variables. The second difference is that equations (6.27) are nonlinear in $\boldsymbol{\beta}$, because both $\boldsymbol{x}(\boldsymbol{\beta})$ and $\boldsymbol{X}(\boldsymbol{\beta})$ are, in general, nonlinear functions of $\boldsymbol{\beta}$. Thus there is no closed-form expression for $\hat{\boldsymbol{\beta}}$ comparable to the famous formula (1.46). As we will see in Section 6.4, this means that it is substantially more difficult to compute NLS estimates than it is to compute OLS ones.

Consistency of the NLS Estimator

Since it has been assumed that every variable on which $x_t(\boldsymbol{\beta})$ depends belongs to Ω_t, it must be the case that $x_t(\boldsymbol{\beta})$ itself belongs to Ω_t for any choice of $\boldsymbol{\beta}$. Therefore, the partial derivatives of $x_t(\boldsymbol{\beta})$, that is, the elements of the row vector $\boldsymbol{X}_t(\boldsymbol{\beta})$, must belong to Ω_t as well, and so

$$\mathrm{E}\big(\boldsymbol{X}_t(\boldsymbol{\beta})u_t\big) = \mathbf{0}. \tag{6.29}$$

If we define the limiting functions $\boldsymbol{\alpha}(\boldsymbol{\beta})$ for the estimator based on (6.27) analogously to (6.12), we have

$$\boldsymbol{\alpha}(\boldsymbol{\beta}) = \operatorname*{plim}_{n\to\infty} \frac{1}{n}\boldsymbol{X}^{\top}(\boldsymbol{\beta})\big(\boldsymbol{y} - \boldsymbol{x}(\boldsymbol{\beta})\big).$$

It follows from (6.29) and the law of large numbers that $\boldsymbol{\alpha}(\boldsymbol{\beta}_0) = \mathbf{0}$ if the true parameter vector is $\boldsymbol{\beta}_0$. Thus the NLS estimator is consistent provided that it is asymptotically identified. We will have more to say in the next section about identification and the NLS estimator.

Asymptotic Normality of the NLS Estimator

The discussion of asymptotic normality in the previous section needs to be modified slightly for the NLS estimator. Equation (6.20), which resulted from applying Taylor's Theorem to $\boldsymbol{x}(\hat{\boldsymbol{\beta}})$, is no longer true, because the matrix $\boldsymbol{W}$ is replaced by $\boldsymbol{X}(\boldsymbol{\beta})$, which, unlike $\boldsymbol{W}$, depends on the parameter vector $\boldsymbol{\beta}$. When we take account of this fact, we obtain a rather messy additional term in (6.20) that depends on the second derivatives of $\boldsymbol{x}(\boldsymbol{\beta})$. However, it can be shown that this extra term vanishes asymptotically. Therefore, equation (6.21) remains true, but with $\boldsymbol{X}_0 \equiv \boldsymbol{X}(\boldsymbol{\beta}_0)$ replacing $\boldsymbol{W}$. This implies that, for NLS, the analog of equation (6.23) is

$$n^{1/2}(\hat{\boldsymbol{\beta}} - \boldsymbol{\beta}_0) \overset{a}{=} \Big(\operatorname*{plim}_{n\to\infty} \frac{1}{n}\boldsymbol{X}_0^{\top}\boldsymbol{X}_0\Big)^{-1} n^{-1/2}\boldsymbol{X}_0^{\top}\boldsymbol{u}, \tag{6.30}$$

from which the asymptotic normality of the NLS estimator follows by essentially the same arguments as before.

Slightly modified versions of the arguments for MM estimators of the previous section also yield expressions for the asymptotic covariance matrix of the NLS estimator $\hat{\boldsymbol{\beta}}$. The consistency of $\hat{\boldsymbol{\beta}}$ means that

$$\operatorname*{plim}_{n\to\infty} \frac{1}{n}\hat{\boldsymbol{X}}^{\top}\hat{\boldsymbol{X}} = \operatorname*{plim}_{n\to\infty} \frac{1}{n}\boldsymbol{X}_0^{\top}\boldsymbol{X}_0 \quad \text{and} \quad \operatorname*{plim}_{n\to\infty} \frac{1}{n}\hat{\boldsymbol{X}}^{\top}\boldsymbol{X}_0 = \operatorname*{plim}_{n\to\infty} \frac{1}{n}\boldsymbol{X}_0^{\top}\boldsymbol{X}_0.$$

Thus, on setting $\boldsymbol{W} = \hat{\boldsymbol{X}}$, (6.26) gives for the asymptotic covariance matrix of $n^{1/2}(\hat{\boldsymbol{\beta}} - \boldsymbol{\beta}_0)$ the matrix

$$\sigma_0^2 \operatorname*{plim}_{n\to\infty} \Big(\frac{1}{n}\boldsymbol{X}_0^{\top}\boldsymbol{P}_{\hat{\boldsymbol{X}}}\boldsymbol{X}_0\Big)^{-1} = \sigma_0^2 \operatorname*{plim}_{n\to\infty} \Big(\frac{1}{n}\boldsymbol{X}_0^{\top}\boldsymbol{X}_0\Big)^{-1}, \tag{6.31}$$

from which we see that the NLS estimator $\hat{\boldsymbol{\beta}}$ is asymptotically efficient. Moreover, it follows that a consistent estimator of the covariance matrix of $\hat{\boldsymbol{\beta}}$, in the sense of (5.22), is

$$\widehat{\operatorname{Var}}(\hat{\boldsymbol{\beta}}) = s^2(\hat{\boldsymbol{X}}^\top\hat{\boldsymbol{X}})^{-1}, \tag{6.32}$$

where, by analogy with (3.49),

$$s^2 \equiv \frac{1}{n-k}\sum_{t=1}^{n}\hat{u}_t^2 = \frac{1}{n-k}\sum_{t=1}^{n}\big(y_t - x_t(\hat{\boldsymbol{\beta}})\big)^2. \tag{6.33}$$

Of course, s^2 is not the only consistent estimator of σ^2 that we might reasonably use. Another possibility is to use

$$\hat{\sigma}^2 \equiv \frac{1}{n}\sum_{t=1}^{n}\hat{u}_t^2. \tag{6.34}$$

However, we will see shortly that (6.33) has particularly attractive properties.

NLS Residuals and the Variance of the Error Terms

Not very much can be said about the finite-sample properties of nonlinear least squares. The techniques that we used in Chapter 3 to obtain the finite-sample properties of the OLS estimator simply cannot be used for the NLS one. However, it is easy to show that, if the DGP is

$$\boldsymbol{y} = \boldsymbol{x}(\boldsymbol{\beta}_0) + \boldsymbol{u}, \quad \boldsymbol{u} \sim \operatorname{IID}(\mathbf{0}, \sigma_0^2\mathbf{I}), \tag{6.35}$$

which means that it is a special case of the model (6.02) that is being estimated, then

$$\operatorname{E}\big(\operatorname{SSR}(\hat{\boldsymbol{\beta}})\big) \le n\sigma_0^2. \tag{6.36}$$

The argument is just this. From (6.35), $\boldsymbol{y} - \boldsymbol{x}(\boldsymbol{\beta}_0) = \boldsymbol{u}$. Therefore,

$$\operatorname{E}\big(\operatorname{SSR}(\boldsymbol{\beta}_0)\big) = \operatorname{E}(\boldsymbol{u}^\top\boldsymbol{u}) = n\sigma_0^2.$$

Since $\hat{\boldsymbol{\beta}}$ minimizes the sum of squared residuals and $\boldsymbol{\beta}_0$ in general does not, it must be the case that $\operatorname{SSR}(\hat{\boldsymbol{\beta}}) \le \operatorname{SSR}(\boldsymbol{\beta}_0)$. The inequality (6.36) follows immediately. Thus, just like OLS residuals, NLS residuals have variance less than the variance of the error terms.

The consistency of $\hat{\boldsymbol{\beta}}$ implies that the NLS residuals $\hat{u}_t$ converge to the error terms u_t as $n \to \infty$. This means that it is valid asymptotically to use either s^2 from (6.33) or $\hat{\sigma}^2$ from (6.34) to estimate σ^2. However, we see from (6.36) that the NLS residuals are too small on average. Therefore, by analogy with the exact results for the OLS case that were discussed in Section 3.6, it seems plausible to divide by $n - k$ instead of by n when we estimate σ^2. In fact, as we now show, there is an even stronger justification for doing this.

Now let us apply Taylor's Theorem to a typical residual, $\hat{u}_t = y_t - x_t(\hat{\boldsymbol{\beta}})$. If we expand this quantity around the true value $\boldsymbol{\beta}_0$ and substitute $u_t + x_t(\boldsymbol{\beta}_0)$ for y_t, we obtain

$$\begin{aligned}\hat{u}_t &= y_t - x_t(\boldsymbol{\beta}_0) - \bar{\boldsymbol{X}}_t(\hat{\boldsymbol{\beta}} - \boldsymbol{\beta}_0)\\ &= u_t + x_t(\boldsymbol{\beta}_0) - x_t(\boldsymbol{\beta}_0) - \bar{\boldsymbol{X}}_t(\hat{\boldsymbol{\beta}} - \boldsymbol{\beta}_0)\\ &= u_t - \bar{\boldsymbol{X}}_t(\hat{\boldsymbol{\beta}} - \boldsymbol{\beta}_0),\end{aligned}$$

where $\bar{\boldsymbol{X}}_t$ denotes the tth row of the matrix $\boldsymbol{X}(\bar{\boldsymbol{\beta}})$, for some $\bar{\boldsymbol{\beta}}$ that satisfies condition (6.19); recall the discussion of that condition. This implies that, for the entire vector of residuals, we have

$$\hat{\boldsymbol{u}} = \boldsymbol{u} - \bar{\boldsymbol{X}}(\hat{\boldsymbol{\beta}} - \boldsymbol{\beta}_0). \tag{6.37}$$

For the NLS estimator $\hat{\boldsymbol{\beta}}$, the asymptotic result (6.23) becomes

$$n^{1/2}(\hat{\boldsymbol{\beta}} - \boldsymbol{\beta}_0) \overset{a}{=} (\boldsymbol{S}_{\boldsymbol{X}^\top\boldsymbol{X}})^{-1} n^{-1/2} \boldsymbol{X}_0^\top \boldsymbol{u}, \tag{6.38}$$

where

$$\boldsymbol{S}_{\boldsymbol{X}^\top\boldsymbol{X}} \equiv \underset{n\to\infty}{\text{plim}} \frac{1}{n} \boldsymbol{X}_0^\top \boldsymbol{X}_0. \tag{6.39}$$

We have redefined $\boldsymbol{S}_{\boldsymbol{X}^\top\boldsymbol{X}}$ here. The old definition, (3.17), applies only to linear regression models. The new definition, (6.39), applies to both linear and nonlinear regression models, since it reduces to the old one when the regression function is linear.

When we substitute $n^{-1/2}$ times the right-hand side of equation (6.38) into equation (6.37) and replace $\bar{\boldsymbol{X}}$ with $\boldsymbol{X}_0$ because $\bar{\boldsymbol{\beta}}$ tends asymptotically to $\boldsymbol{\beta}_0$, we find that

$$\begin{aligned}\hat{\boldsymbol{u}} &\overset{a}{=} \boldsymbol{u} - n^{-1/2}\boldsymbol{X}_0(\boldsymbol{S}_{\boldsymbol{X}^\top\boldsymbol{X}})^{-1} n^{-1/2}\boldsymbol{X}_0^\top\boldsymbol{u}\\ &\overset{a}{=} \boldsymbol{u} - n^{-1}\boldsymbol{X}_0(n^{-1}\boldsymbol{X}_0^\top\boldsymbol{X}_0)^{-1}\boldsymbol{X}_0^\top\boldsymbol{u}\\ &= \boldsymbol{u} - \boldsymbol{X}_0(\boldsymbol{X}_0^\top\boldsymbol{X}_0)^{-1}\boldsymbol{X}_0^\top\boldsymbol{u}\\ &= \boldsymbol{u} - \boldsymbol{P}_{\boldsymbol{X}_0}\boldsymbol{u} = \boldsymbol{M}_{\boldsymbol{X}_0}\boldsymbol{u},\end{aligned} \tag{6.40}$$

where $\boldsymbol{P}_{\boldsymbol{X}_0}$ and $\boldsymbol{M}_{\boldsymbol{X}_0}$ project orthogonally on to $\mathcal{S}(\boldsymbol{X}_0)$ and $\mathcal{S}^\perp(\boldsymbol{X}_0)$, respectively. This asymptotic result for NLS looks very much like the exact result that $\hat{\boldsymbol{u}} = \boldsymbol{M}_{\boldsymbol{X}}\boldsymbol{u}$ for OLS. A somewhat more intricate argument can be used to show that the difference between $\hat{\boldsymbol{u}}^\top\hat{\boldsymbol{u}}$ and $\boldsymbol{u}^\top\boldsymbol{M}_{\boldsymbol{X}_0}\boldsymbol{u}$ tends to zero as $n \to \infty$; see Exercise 6.8. Since $\boldsymbol{X}_0$ is an $n \times k$ matrix, precisely the same argument that was used for the linear case in (3.48) shows that $\text{E}(\hat{\boldsymbol{u}}^\top\hat{\boldsymbol{u}}) \overset{a}{=} \sigma_0^2(n-k)$. Thus we see that, in the case of nonlinear least squares, s^2 provides an approximately unbiased estimator of σ^2.

6.4 Computing NLS Estimates

We have not yet said anything about how to compute nonlinear least-squares estimates. This is by no means a trivial undertaking. Computing NLS estimates is always much more expensive than computing OLS ones for a model with the same number of observations and parameters. Moreover, there is a risk that the program may fail to converge or may converge to values that do not minimize the SSR. However, with modern computers and well-written software, NLS estimation is usually not excessively difficult.

In order to find NLS estimates, we need to minimize the sum-of-squared-residuals function $\text{SSR}(\boldsymbol{\beta})$ with respect to $\boldsymbol{\beta}$. Since $\text{SSR}(\boldsymbol{\beta})$ is not a quadratic function of $\boldsymbol{\beta}$, there is no analytic solution like the classic formula (1.46) for the linear regression case. What we need is a general algorithm for minimizing a sum of squares with respect to a vector of parameters. In this section, we discuss methods for unconstrained minimization of a smooth function $Q(\boldsymbol{\beta})$. It is easiest to think of $Q(\boldsymbol{\beta})$ as being equal to $\text{SSR}(\boldsymbol{\beta})$, but much of the discussion is applicable to minimizing any sort of **criterion function**. Since minimizing $Q(\boldsymbol{\beta})$ is equivalent to maximizing $-Q(\boldsymbol{\beta})$, it is also applicable to maximizing any sort of criterion function, such as the loglikelihood functions that we will encounter in Chapter 10.

We will give an overview of how numerical minimization algorithms work, but we will not discuss many of the important implementation issues that can substantially affect the performance of these algorithms when they are incorporated into computer programs. References on the art and science of numerical optimization, especially as it applies to nonlinear regression, include Bard (1974), Gill, Murray, and Wright (1981), Quandt (1983), Bates and Watts (1988), Seber and Wild (1989, Chapter 14), Press, Flannery, Teukolsky, and Vetterling (1992a; 1992b, Chapter 10), McCullough (2003), and McCullough and Vinod (2003).

There are many algorithms for minimizing a smooth function $Q(\boldsymbol{\beta})$. Most of these operate in essentially the same way. The algorithm goes through a series of iterations, or steps, at each of which it starts with a particular value of $\boldsymbol{\beta}$ and tries to find a better one. It first chooses a direction in which to search and then decides how far to move in that direction. After completing the move, it checks to see whether the current value of $\boldsymbol{\beta}$ is sufficiently close to a local minimum of $Q(\boldsymbol{\beta})$. If it is, the algorithm stops. Otherwise, it chooses another direction in which to search, and so on. There are three principal differences among minimization algorithms: the way in which the direction to search is chosen, the way in which the size of the step in that direction is determined, and the stopping rule that is employed. Numerous choices for each of these are available.

Newton's Method

All of the techniques that we will discuss are based on **Newton's Method**. Suppose that we wish to minimize a function $Q(\boldsymbol{\beta})$, where $\boldsymbol{\beta}$ is a k-vector and

$Q(\boldsymbol{\beta})$ is assumed to be twice continuously differentiable. Given any initial value of $\boldsymbol{\beta}$, say $\boldsymbol{\beta}_{(0)}$, we can perform a second-order Taylor expansion of $Q(\boldsymbol{\beta})$ around $\boldsymbol{\beta}_{(0)}$ in order to obtain an approximation $Q^*(\boldsymbol{\beta})$ to $Q(\boldsymbol{\beta})$:

$$Q^*(\boldsymbol{\beta}) = Q(\boldsymbol{\beta}_{(0)}) + \boldsymbol{g}_{(0)}^{\top}(\boldsymbol{\beta} - \boldsymbol{\beta}_{(0)}) + \tfrac{1}{2}(\boldsymbol{\beta} - \boldsymbol{\beta}_{(0)})^{\top}\boldsymbol{H}_{(0)}(\boldsymbol{\beta} - \boldsymbol{\beta}_{(0)}), \quad (6.41)$$

where $\boldsymbol{g}(\boldsymbol{\beta})$, the **gradient** of $Q(\boldsymbol{\beta})$, is a column vector of length k with typical element $\partial Q(\boldsymbol{\beta})/\partial \beta_i$, and $\boldsymbol{H}(\boldsymbol{\beta})$, the **Hessian** of $Q(\boldsymbol{\beta})$, is a $k \times k$ matrix with typical element $\partial^2 Q(\boldsymbol{\beta})/\partial \beta_i \partial \beta_l$. For notational simplicity, $\boldsymbol{g}_{(0)}$ and $\boldsymbol{H}_{(0)}$ denote $\boldsymbol{g}(\boldsymbol{\beta}_{(0)})$ and $\boldsymbol{H}(\boldsymbol{\beta}_{(0)})$, respectively.

It is easy to see that the first-order conditions for a minimum of $Q^*(\boldsymbol{\beta})$ with respect to $\boldsymbol{\beta}$ can be written as

$$\boldsymbol{g}_{(0)} + \boldsymbol{H}_{(0)}(\boldsymbol{\beta} - \boldsymbol{\beta}_{(0)}) = \mathbf{0}.$$

Solving these yields a new value of $\boldsymbol{\beta}$, which we will call $\boldsymbol{\beta}_{(1)}$:

$$\boldsymbol{\beta}_{(1)} = \boldsymbol{\beta}_{(0)} - \boldsymbol{H}_{(0)}^{-1}\boldsymbol{g}_{(0)}. \quad (6.42)$$

Equation (6.42) is the heart of Newton's Method. If the quadratic approximation $Q^*(\boldsymbol{\beta})$ is a strictly convex function, which it is if and only if the Hessian $\boldsymbol{H}_{(0)}$ is positive definite, then $\boldsymbol{\beta}_{(1)}$ is the global minimum of $Q^*(\boldsymbol{\beta})$. If, in addition, $Q^*(\boldsymbol{\beta})$ is a good approximation to $Q(\boldsymbol{\beta})$, $\boldsymbol{\beta}_{(1)}$ should be close to $\hat{\boldsymbol{\beta}}$, the minimum of $Q(\boldsymbol{\beta})$. Newton's Method involves using equation (6.42) repeatedly to find a succession of values $\boldsymbol{\beta}_{(1)}$, $\boldsymbol{\beta}_{(2)}, \ldots$. When the original function $Q(\boldsymbol{\beta})$ is quadratic and has a global minimum at $\hat{\boldsymbol{\beta}}$, Newton's Method evidently finds $\hat{\boldsymbol{\beta}}$ in a single step, since the quadratic approximation is then exact. When $Q(\boldsymbol{\beta})$ is approximately quadratic, as all sum-of-squares functions are when sufficiently close to their minima, Newton's Method generally converges very quickly.

Figure 6.1 illustrates how Newton's Method works. It shows the contours of the function $Q(\boldsymbol{\beta}) = \mathrm{SSR}(\beta_1, \beta_2)$ for a regression model with two parameters. Notice that these contours are not precisely elliptical, as they would be if the function were quadratic. The algorithm starts at the point marked "0" and then jumps to the point marked "1." On the next step, it goes in almost exactly the right direction, but it goes too far, moving to "2." It then retraces its own steps to "3," which is essentially the minimum of $\mathrm{SSR}(\beta_1, \beta_2)$. After one more step, which is too small to be shown in the figure, it has essentially converged.

Although Newton's Method works very well in this example, there are many cases in which it fails to work at all, especially if $Q(\boldsymbol{\beta})$ is not convex in the neighborhood of $\boldsymbol{\beta}_{(j)}$ for some j in the sequence. Some of the possibilities are illustrated in Figure 6.2. The one-dimensional function shown there has

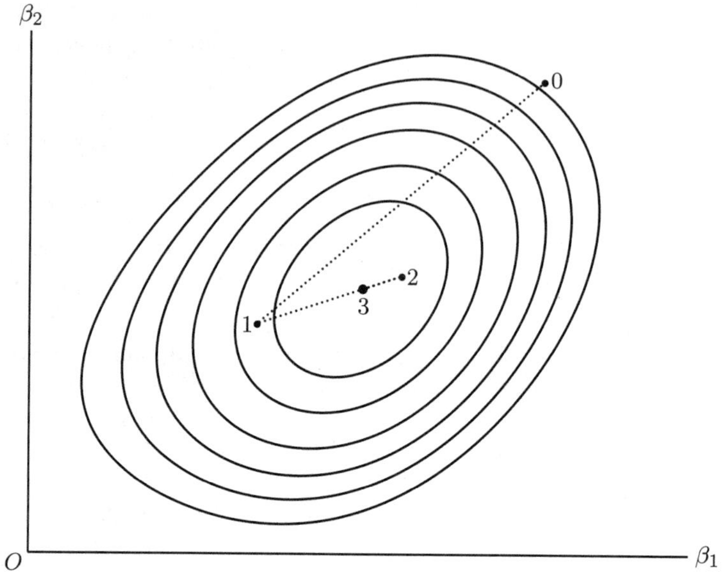

Figure 6.1 Newton's Method in two dimensions

a global minimum at $\hat{\beta}$, but when Newton's Method is started at points such as β' or β'', it may never find $\hat{\beta}$. In the former case, $Q(\beta)$ is concave at β' instead of convex, and this causes Newton's Method to head off in the wrong direction. In the latter case, the quadratic approximation at β'', $Q^*(\beta)$, which is shown by the dashed curve, is extremely poor for values away from β'', because $Q(\beta)$ is very flat near β''. It is evident that $Q^*(\beta)$ must have a minimum far to the left of $\hat{\beta}$. Thus, after the first step, the algorithm is very much further away from $\hat{\beta}$ than it was at its starting point.

One important feature of Newton's Method and algorithms based on it is that they must start with an initial value of $\boldsymbol{\beta}$. It is impossible to perform a Taylor expansion around $\boldsymbol{\beta}_{(0)}$ without specifying $\boldsymbol{\beta}_{(0)}$. As Figure 6.2 illustrates, where the algorithm starts may determine how well it performs, or whether it converges at all. In most cases, it is up to the econometrician to specify the starting values.

Quasi-Newton Methods

Most effective nonlinear optimization techniques for minimizing smooth criterion functions are variants of Newton's Method. These **quasi-Newton methods** attempt to retain the good qualities of Newton's Method while surmounting problems like those illustrated in Figure 6.2. They replace (6.42) by the slightly more complicated formula

$$\boldsymbol{\beta}_{(j+1)} = \boldsymbol{\beta}_{(j)} - \alpha_{(j)}\boldsymbol{D}_{(j)}^{-1}\boldsymbol{g}_{(j)}, \tag{6.43}$$

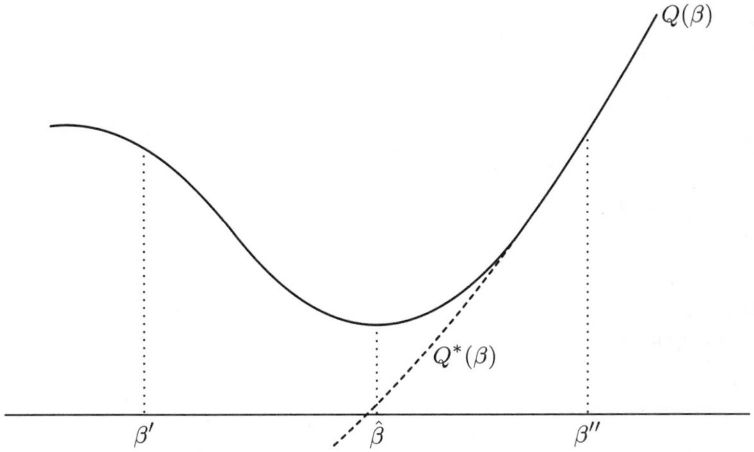

Figure 6.2 Cases for which Newton's Method will not work

which determines $\boldsymbol{\beta}_{(j+1)}$, the value of $\boldsymbol{\beta}$ at step $j + 1$, as a function of $\boldsymbol{\beta}_{(j)}$. Here $\alpha_{(j)}$ is a scalar which is determined at each step, and $\boldsymbol{D}_{(j)} \equiv \boldsymbol{D}(\boldsymbol{\beta}_{(j)})$ is a matrix which approximates $\boldsymbol{H}_{(j)}$ near the minimum but is constructed so that it is always positive definite. In contrast to quasi-Newton methods, **modified Newton methods** set $\boldsymbol{D}_{(j)} = \boldsymbol{H}_{(j)}$, and Newton's Method itself sets $\boldsymbol{D}_{(j)} = \boldsymbol{H}_{(j)}$ and $\alpha_{(j)} = 1$.

Quasi-Newton algorithms involve three operations at each step. Let us denote the current value of $\boldsymbol{\beta}$ by $\boldsymbol{\beta}_{(j)}$. If $j = 0$, this is the starting value, $\boldsymbol{\beta}_{(0)}$; otherwise, it is the value reached at iteration j. The three operations are

1. Compute $\boldsymbol{g}_{(j)}$ and $\boldsymbol{D}_{(j)}$ and use them to determine the direction $\boldsymbol{D}_{(j)}^{-1}\boldsymbol{g}_{(j)}$.
2. Find $\alpha_{(j)}$. Often, this is done by solving a one-dimensional minimization problem. Then use (6.43) to determine $\boldsymbol{\beta}_{(j+1)}$.
3. Decide whether $\boldsymbol{\beta}_{(j+1)}$ provides a sufficiently accurate approximation to $\hat{\boldsymbol{\beta}}$. If so, stop. Otherwise, return to 1.

Because they construct $\boldsymbol{D}(\boldsymbol{\beta})$ in such a way that it is always positive definite, quasi-Newton algorithms can handle problems where the function to be minimized is not globally convex. The various algorithms choose $\boldsymbol{D}(\boldsymbol{\beta})$ in a number of ways, some of which are quite ingenious and may be tricky to implement on a digital computer. As we will shortly see, however, for sum-of-squares functions there is a very easy and natural way to choose $\boldsymbol{D}(\boldsymbol{\beta})$.

The scalar $\alpha_{(j)}$ is often chosen so as to minimize the function

$$Q^\dagger(\alpha) \equiv Q\big(\boldsymbol{\beta}_{(j)} - \alpha \boldsymbol{D}_{(j)}^{-1}\boldsymbol{g}_{(j)}\big),$$

regarded as a one-dimensional function of α. It is fairly clear that, for the example in Figure 6.1, choosing α in this way would produce even faster convergence than setting $\alpha = 1$. Some algorithms do not actually minimize $Q^\dagger(\alpha)$ with respect to α, but merely choose $\alpha_{(j)}$ so as to ensure that $Q(\boldsymbol{\beta}_{(j+1)})$ is less than $Q(\boldsymbol{\beta}_{(j)})$. It is essential that this be the case if we are to be sure that the algorithm always makes progress at each step. The best algorithms, which are designed to economize on computing time, may choose α quite crudely when they are far from $\hat{\boldsymbol{\beta}}$, but they almost always perform an accurate one-dimensional minimization when they are close to $\hat{\boldsymbol{\beta}}$.

Stopping Rules

No minimization algorithm running on a digital computer ever finds $\hat{\boldsymbol{\beta}}$ exactly. Without a rule telling it when to stop, the algorithm would just keep on going forever. There are many possible **stopping rules**. We could, for example, stop when $Q(\boldsymbol{\beta}_{(j-1)}) - Q(\boldsymbol{\beta}_{(j)})$ is very small, when every element of $\boldsymbol{g}_{(j)}$ is very small, or when every element of the vector $\boldsymbol{\beta}_{(j)} - \boldsymbol{\beta}_{(j-1)}$ is very small. However, none of these rules is entirely satisfactory, in part because they depend on the magnitude of the parameters. This means that they yield different results if the units of measurement of any variable are changed or if the model is reparametrized in some other way. A more logical rule is to stop when

$$\boldsymbol{g}_{(j)}^\top \boldsymbol{D}_{(j)}^{-1} \boldsymbol{g}_{(j)} < \varepsilon, \tag{6.44}$$

where ε, the **convergence tolerance**, is a small positive number that is chosen by the user. Sensible values of ε might range from 10^{-12} to 10^{-4}. The advantage of (6.44) is that it weights the various components of the gradient in a manner inversely proportional to the precision with which the corresponding parameters are estimated. We will see why this is so in the next section.

Of course, any stopping rule may work badly if ε is chosen incorrectly. If ε is too large, the algorithm may stop too soon, when $\boldsymbol{\beta}_{(j)}$ is still far away from $\hat{\boldsymbol{\beta}}$. On the other hand, if ε is too small, the algorithm may keep going long after $\boldsymbol{\beta}_{(j)}$ is so close to $\hat{\boldsymbol{\beta}}$ that any differences are due solely to round-off error. It may therefore be a good idea to experiment with the value of ε to see how sensitive to it the results are. If the reported $\hat{\boldsymbol{\beta}}$ changes noticeably when ε is reduced, then either the first value of ε was too large, or the algorithm is having trouble finding an accurate minimum.

Local and Global Minima

Numerical optimization methods based on Newton's Method generally work well when $Q(\boldsymbol{\beta})$ is globally convex. For such a function, there can be at most one local minimum, which is also the global minimum. When $Q(\boldsymbol{\beta})$ is not globally convex but has only a single local minimum, these methods also work reasonably well in many cases. However, if there is more than one local minimum, optimization methods of this type often run into trouble. They generally converge to a local minimum, but there is no guarantee that it is the global one. In such cases, the choice of the **starting values**, that is, the vector $\boldsymbol{\beta}_{(0)}$, can be extremely important.

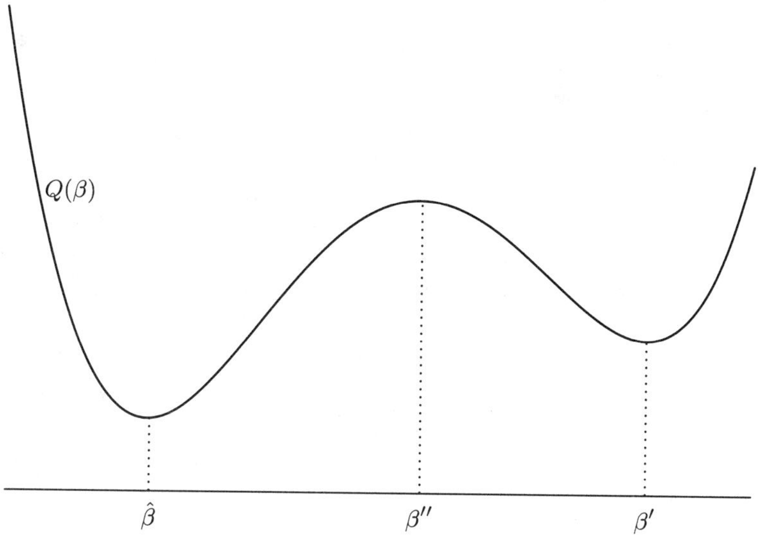

Figure 6.3 A criterion function with multiple minima

This problem is illustrated in Figure 6.3. The one-dimensional criterion function $Q(\beta)$ shown in the figure has two local minima. One of these, at $\hat{\beta}$, is also the global minimum. However, if a Newton or quasi-Newton algorithm is started to the right of the local maximum at β'', it is likely to converge to the local minimum at β' instead of to the global one at $\hat{\beta}$.

In practice, the usual way to guard against finding the wrong local minimum when the criterion function is known, or suspected, not to be globally convex is to minimize $Q(\boldsymbol{\beta})$ several times, starting at a number of different starting values. Ideally, these should be quite dispersed over the interesting regions of the parameter space. This is easy to achieve in a one-dimensional case like the one shown in Figure 6.3. However, it is not feasible when $\boldsymbol{\beta}$ has more than a few elements: If we want to try just 10 starting values for each of k parameters, the total number of starting values is 10^k. Thus, in practice, the starting values generally cover only a very small fraction of the parameter space. Nevertheless, if several different starting values all lead to the same local minimum $\hat{\boldsymbol{\beta}}$, with $Q(\hat{\boldsymbol{\beta}})$ less than the value of $Q(\boldsymbol{\beta})$ observed at any other local minimum, then it is plausible, but by no means certain, that $\hat{\boldsymbol{\beta}}$ is actually the global minimum.

Numerous more formal methods of dealing with multiple minima have been proposed. See, among others, Veall (1990), Goffe, Ferrier, and Rogers (1994), Dorsey and Mayer (1995), and Andrews (1997). In difficult cases, one or more of these methods should work better than simply using a number of starting values. However, they tend to be computationally expensive, and none of them works well in every case.

Many of the difficulties of computing NLS estimates are related to the identification of the model parameters by different data sets. The identification condition for NLS is rather different from the identification condition for the MM estimators discussed in Section 6.2. For NLS, it is simply the requirement that the function $\text{SSR}(\boldsymbol{\beta})$ should have a unique minimum with respect to $\boldsymbol{\beta}$. This is not at all the same requirement as the condition that the moment conditions (6.27) should have a unique solution. In the example of Figure 6.3, the moment conditions, which for NLS are first-order conditions, are satisfied not only at the local minima $\hat{\beta}$ and β', but also at the local maximum β''. However, $\hat{\beta}$ is the unique global minimum of $\text{SSR}(\beta)$, and so β is identified by the NLS estimator.

The analog for NLS of the strong asymptotic identification condition that $S_{\boldsymbol{W}^\top \boldsymbol{X}}$ should be nonsingular is the condition that $S_{\boldsymbol{X}^\top \boldsymbol{X}}$ should be nonsingular, since the variables $\boldsymbol{W}$ of the MM estimator are replaced by $\boldsymbol{X}_0$ for NLS. The strong condition for identification by a given data set is simply that the matrix $\hat{\boldsymbol{X}}^\top \hat{\boldsymbol{X}}$ should be nonsingular, and therefore positive definite. It is easy to see that this condition is just the sufficient second-order condition for a minimum of the sum-of-squares function at $\hat{\boldsymbol{\beta}}$.

The Geometry of Nonlinear Regression

For nonlinear regression models, it is not possible, in general, to draw faithful geometrical representations of the estimation procedure in just two or three dimensions, as we can for linear models. Nevertheless, it is often useful to illustrate the concepts involved in nonlinear estimation geometrically, as we do in Figure 6.4. Although the vector $\boldsymbol{x}(\boldsymbol{\beta})$ lies in E^n, we have supposed for the purposes of the figure that, as the scalar parameter β varies, $\boldsymbol{x}(\beta)$ traces out a curve that we can visualize in the plane of the page. If the model were linear, $\boldsymbol{x}(\beta)$ would trace out a straight line rather than a curve. In the same way, the dependent variable $\boldsymbol{y}$ is represented by a point in the plane of the page, or, more accurately, by the vector in that plane joining the origin to that point.

For NLS, we seek the point on the curve generated by $\boldsymbol{x}(\beta)$ that is closest in Euclidean distance to $\boldsymbol{y}$. We see from the figure that, although the moment, or first-order conditions, are satisfied at three points, only one of them yields the NLS estimator. Geometrically, the sum-of-squares function is just the square of the Euclidean distance from $\boldsymbol{y}$ to $\boldsymbol{x}(\beta)$. Its global minimum is achieved at $\boldsymbol{x}(\hat{\beta})$, not at either $\boldsymbol{x}(\beta')$ or $\boldsymbol{x}(\beta'')$.

We can also use Figure 6.4 to see how MM estimation with a fixed matrix $\boldsymbol{W}$ works. Since there is just one parameter, we need a single variable $\boldsymbol{w}$ that does not depend on the model parameters, and such a variable is shown in the figure. The moment condition defining the MM estimator is that the residuals should be orthogonal to $\boldsymbol{w}$. It can be seen that this condition is satisfied only by the residual vector $\boldsymbol{y}-\boldsymbol{x}(\tilde{\beta})$. In the figure, a dotted line is drawn continuing this residual vector so as to show that it is indeed orthogonal to $\boldsymbol{w}$. There are

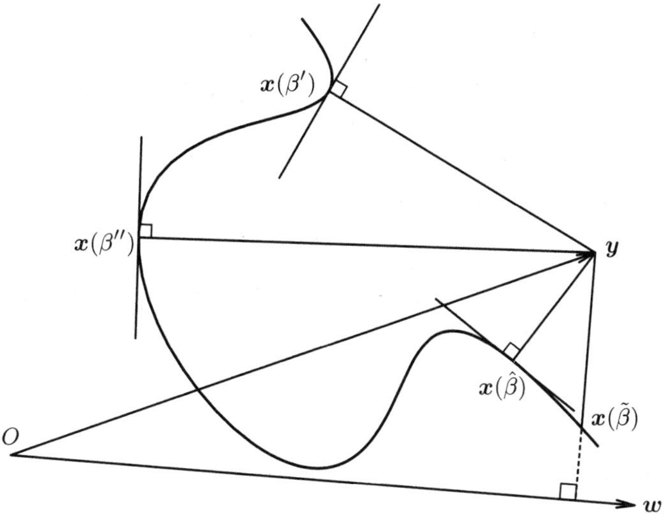

Figure 6.4 NLS and MM estimation of a nonlinear model

cases, like the one in the figure, in which the NLS first-order conditions can be satisfied for more than one value of $\boldsymbol{\beta}$ while the conditions for MM estimation are satisfied for just one value, and there are cases in which the reverse is true. Readers are invited to use their geometrical imaginations.

6.5 The Gauss-Newton Regression

When the function we are trying to minimize is a sum-of-squares function, we can obtain explicit expressions for the gradient and the Hessian used in Newton's Method. It is convenient to write the criterion function itself as $\mathrm{SSR}(\boldsymbol{\beta})$ divided by the sample size n:

$$Q(\boldsymbol{\beta}) = n^{-1}\mathrm{SSR}(\boldsymbol{\beta}) = \frac{1}{n}\sum_{t=1}^{n}\big(y_t - x_t(\boldsymbol{\beta})\big)^2.$$

Therefore, using the fact that the partial derivative of $x_t(\boldsymbol{\beta})$ with respect to β_i is $X_{ti}(\boldsymbol{\beta})$, we find that the ith element of the gradient is

$$g_i(\boldsymbol{\beta}) = -\frac{2}{n}\sum_{t=1}^{n} X_{ti}(\boldsymbol{\beta})\big(y_t - x_t(\boldsymbol{\beta})\big).$$

The gradient can be written more compactly in vector-matrix notation as

$$\boldsymbol{g}(\boldsymbol{\beta}) = -2n^{-1}\boldsymbol{X}^{\top}(\boldsymbol{\beta})\big(\boldsymbol{y} - \boldsymbol{x}(\boldsymbol{\beta})\big). \tag{6.45}$$

Similarly, it can be shown that the Hessian $\boldsymbol{H}(\boldsymbol{\beta})$ has typical element

$$H_{ij}(\boldsymbol{\beta}) = -\frac{2}{n}\sum_{t=1}^{n}\Big(\big(y_t - x_t(\boldsymbol{\beta})\big)\frac{\partial X_{ti}(\boldsymbol{\beta})}{\partial \beta_j} - X_{ti}(\boldsymbol{\beta})X_{tj}(\boldsymbol{\beta})\Big). \tag{6.46}$$

When this expression is evaluated at $\boldsymbol{\beta}_0$, it is asymptotically equivalent to

$$\frac{2}{n}\sum_{t=1}^{n} X_{ti}(\boldsymbol{\beta}_0)X_{tj}(\boldsymbol{\beta}_0). \tag{6.47}$$

The reason for this asymptotic equivalence is that, since $y_t = x_t(\boldsymbol{\beta}_0) + u_t$, the first term inside the large parentheses in (6.46) becomes

$$-\frac{2}{n}\sum_{t=1}^{n}\frac{\partial X_{ti}(\boldsymbol{\beta})}{\partial \beta_j}u_t. \tag{6.48}$$

Because $x_t(\boldsymbol{\beta})$ and all its first- and second-order derivatives belong to Ω_t, the expectation of each term in (6.48) is 0. Therefore, by a law of large numbers, expression (6.48) tends to 0 as $n \to \infty$.

Gauss-Newton Methods

The above results make it clear that a natural choice for $\boldsymbol{D}(\boldsymbol{\beta})$ in a quasi-Newton minimization algorithm based on (6.43) is

$$\boldsymbol{D}(\boldsymbol{\beta}) = 2n^{-1}\boldsymbol{X}^{\top}(\boldsymbol{\beta})\boldsymbol{X}(\boldsymbol{\beta}). \tag{6.49}$$

By construction, this $\boldsymbol{D}(\boldsymbol{\beta})$ is positive definite whenever $\boldsymbol{X}(\boldsymbol{\beta})$ has full rank. Substituting equations (6.49) and (6.45) into equation (6.43) yields

$$\begin{aligned}\boldsymbol{\beta}_{(j+1)} &= \boldsymbol{\beta}_{(j)} + \alpha_{(j)}\big(2n^{-1}\boldsymbol{X}_{(j)}^{\top}\boldsymbol{X}_{(j)}\big)^{-1}\big(2n^{-1}\boldsymbol{X}_{(j)}^{\top}(\boldsymbol{y} - \boldsymbol{x}_{(j)})\big)\\ &= \boldsymbol{\beta}_{(j)} + \alpha_{(j)}\big(\boldsymbol{X}_{(j)}^{\top}\boldsymbol{X}_{(j)}\big)^{-1}\boldsymbol{X}_{(j)}^{\top}(\boldsymbol{y} - \boldsymbol{x}_{(j)})\end{aligned} \tag{6.50}$$

The classic **Gauss-Newton method** would set $\alpha_{(j)} = 1$, so that

$$\boldsymbol{\beta}_{(j+1)} = \boldsymbol{\beta}_{(j)} + \big(\boldsymbol{X}_{(j)}^{\top}\boldsymbol{X}_{(j)}\big)^{-1}\boldsymbol{X}_{(j)}^{\top}(\boldsymbol{y} - \boldsymbol{x}_{(j)}), \tag{6.51}$$

but it is generally better to use a good one-dimensional search routine to choose α optimally at each iteration. This modified type of Gauss-Newton procedure often works quite well in practice.

The second term on the right-hand side of (6.51) can most easily be computed by means of an **artificial regression** called the **Gauss-Newton regression**, or **GNR**. This artificial regression can be expressed as follows:

$$\boldsymbol{y} - \boldsymbol{x}(\boldsymbol{\beta}) = \boldsymbol{X}(\boldsymbol{\beta})\boldsymbol{b} + \text{residuals}. \tag{6.52}$$

This is the simplest version of the Gauss-Newton regression. It is called "artificial" because the variables that appear in it are not the dependent and explanatory variables of the nonlinear regression (6.02). Instead, they are functions of these variables and of the model parameters. Before (6.52) can be run as a regression, it is necessary to choose the parameter vector $\boldsymbol{\beta}$ at which the regressand and regressors are to be evaluated.

The regressand in (6.52) is the difference between the actual values of the dependent variable and the values predicted by the regression function $\boldsymbol{x}(\boldsymbol{\beta})$ evaluated at the chosen $\boldsymbol{\beta}$. There are k regressors, each of which is a vector of derivatives of $\boldsymbol{x}(\boldsymbol{\beta})$ with respect to one of the elements of $\boldsymbol{\beta}$. It therefore makes sense to think of the ith regressor as being associated with β_i. The vector $\boldsymbol{b}$ is a vector of artificial parameters, and we write "+ residuals" rather than the usual "$+\,\boldsymbol{u}$" to emphasize the fact that (6.52) is not a statistical model in the usual sense.

The connection between the Gauss-Newton method of numerical optimization and the Gauss-Newton regression should now be clear. If the variables in (6.52) are evaluated at $\boldsymbol{\beta}_{(j)}$, the OLS parameter estimates of the artificial parameters are

$$\boldsymbol{b}_{(j)} = \big(\boldsymbol{X}_{(j)}^{\top}\boldsymbol{X}_{(j)}\big)^{-1}\boldsymbol{X}_{(j)}^{\top}(\boldsymbol{y} - \boldsymbol{x}_{(j)}),$$

from which it follows using (6.50) that the Gauss-Newton method gives

$$\boldsymbol{\beta}_{(j+1)} = \boldsymbol{\beta}_{(j)} + \alpha_{(j)}\boldsymbol{b}_{(j)}.$$

Thus the GNR conveniently and cheaply performs two of the operations necessary for a step of the Gauss-Newton method. It yields a matrix which approximates the Hessian of $\text{SSR}(\boldsymbol{\beta})$ and is always positive semidefinite. In addition, it computes a vector of artificial parameter estimates which is equal to $-\boldsymbol{D}_{(j)}^{-1}\boldsymbol{g}_{(j)}$, the direction in which the algorithm looks at iteration j.

One potential difficulty with the Gauss-Newton method is that the matrix $\boldsymbol{X}^{\top}(\boldsymbol{\beta})\boldsymbol{X}(\boldsymbol{\beta})$ may sometimes be very close to singular, even though the model is reasonably well identified by the data. If the strong identification condition is satisfied by a given data set, then $\hat{\boldsymbol{X}}^{\top}\hat{\boldsymbol{X}}$ is positive definite. However, when $\boldsymbol{X}^{\top}(\boldsymbol{\beta})\boldsymbol{X}(\boldsymbol{\beta})$ is evaluated far away from $\hat{\boldsymbol{\beta}}$, it may well be close to singular. When that happens, the algorithm gets into trouble, because $\boldsymbol{b}$ no longer lies in the same k–dimensional space as $\boldsymbol{\beta}$, but rather in a subspace of dimension equal to the effective rank of $\boldsymbol{X}^{\top}(\boldsymbol{\beta})\boldsymbol{X}(\boldsymbol{\beta})$. In this event, a Gauss-Newton algorithm can cycle indefinitely without making any progress. The best algorithms for nonlinear least squares check whether this is happening and replace $\boldsymbol{X}^{\top}(\boldsymbol{\beta})\boldsymbol{X}(\boldsymbol{\beta})$ with another estimate of $\boldsymbol{H}(\boldsymbol{\beta})$ whenever it does. See the references cited at the beginning of Section 6.4.

Properties of the GNR

As we have seen, when $\boldsymbol{x}(\boldsymbol{\beta})$ is a linear regression model with $\boldsymbol{X}$ being the matrix of independent variables, $\boldsymbol{X}(\boldsymbol{\beta})$ is simply equal to $\boldsymbol{X}$. Thus, in the case of a linear regression model, the GNR is simply a regression of the vector $\boldsymbol{y} - \boldsymbol{X\beta}$ on $\boldsymbol{X}$. A special feature of the GNR for linear models is that the classic Gauss-Newton method converges in one step from an arbitrary starting point. To see this, let $\boldsymbol{\beta}_{(0)}$ be the starting point. The GNR is

$$\boldsymbol{y} - \boldsymbol{X\beta}_{(0)} = \boldsymbol{Xb} + \text{residuals},$$

and the artificial parameter estimates are

$$\hat{\boldsymbol{b}} = (\boldsymbol{X}^\top\boldsymbol{X})^{-1}\boldsymbol{X}^\top(\boldsymbol{y} - \boldsymbol{X\beta}_{(0)}) = \hat{\boldsymbol{\beta}} - \boldsymbol{\beta}_{(0)},$$

where $\hat{\boldsymbol{\beta}}$ is the OLS estimator. It follows at once that

$$\boldsymbol{\beta}_{(1)} = \boldsymbol{\beta}_{(0)} + \hat{\boldsymbol{b}} = \hat{\boldsymbol{\beta}}. \tag{6.53}$$

This property has a very useful analog for nonlinear models that we will explore in the next section.

The properties of the GNR (6.52) depend on the choice of $\boldsymbol{\beta}$. One interesting choice is $\hat{\boldsymbol{\beta}}$, the vector of NLS parameter estimates. With this choice, regression (6.52) becomes

$$\boldsymbol{y} - \hat{\boldsymbol{x}} = \hat{\boldsymbol{X}}\boldsymbol{b} + \text{residuals}, \tag{6.54}$$

where $\hat{\boldsymbol{x}} \equiv \boldsymbol{x}(\hat{\boldsymbol{\beta}})$ and $\hat{\boldsymbol{X}} \equiv \boldsymbol{X}(\hat{\boldsymbol{\beta}})$. The OLS estimate of $\boldsymbol{b}$ from (6.54) is

$$\hat{\boldsymbol{b}} = (\hat{\boldsymbol{X}}^\top\hat{\boldsymbol{X}})^{-1}\hat{\boldsymbol{X}}^\top(\boldsymbol{y} - \hat{\boldsymbol{x}}). \tag{6.55}$$

Because $\hat{\boldsymbol{\beta}}$ must satisfy the first-order conditions (6.27), the factor $\hat{\boldsymbol{X}}^\top(\boldsymbol{y} - \hat{\boldsymbol{x}})$ must be a zero vector. Therefore, $\hat{\boldsymbol{b}} = \boldsymbol{0}$, and the GNR (6.54) can have no explanatory power whatsoever.

This may seem an uninteresting result. After all, why would anyone want to run an artificial regression all the coefficients of which are known in advance to be zero? There are in fact two very good reasons for doing so.

The first reason is to check that the vector $\hat{\boldsymbol{\beta}}$ reported by a program for NLS estimation really does satisfy the first-order conditions (6.27). Computer programs use many different techniques for calculating NLS estimates, and many programs do not yield reliable answers in every case; see McCullough (1999). By running the GNR (6.54), we can see whether the first-order conditions are satisfied reasonably accurately. If all the t statistics are less than about 10^{-4}, and the R^2 is less than about 10^{-8}, then the value of $\hat{\boldsymbol{\beta}}$ reported by the program should be reasonably accurate. If not, there may be a problem. Possibly the estimation should be performed again using a tighter convergence criterion, possibly we should switch to a more accurate program, or possibly the model in question simply cannot be estimated reliably with the data set we are using. Of course, some programs run the GNR (6.54) and perform the requisite checks automatically. Once we have verified that they do so, we need not bother doing it ourselves.

Computing Covariance Matrices

The second reason to run the GNR (6.54) is to calculate an estimate of $\mathrm{Var}(\hat{\boldsymbol{\beta}})$. The usual OLS covariance matrix from this regression is, by (3.50),

$$\widehat{\mathrm{Var}}(\hat{\boldsymbol{b}}) = s^2(\hat{\boldsymbol{X}}^\top\hat{\boldsymbol{X}})^{-1}, \tag{6.56}$$

where, since the regressors have no explanatory power, s^2 is the same as the one defined in equation (6.33). It is equal to the SSR from the original nonlinear regression, divided by $n-k$. Evidently, the right-hand side of equation (6.56) is identical to the right-hand side of equation (6.32), which is the standard estimator of $\mathrm{Var}(\hat{\boldsymbol{\beta}})$. Thus running the GNR (6.54) provides an easy way to calculate $\widehat{\mathrm{Var}}(\hat{\boldsymbol{\beta}})$.

Good programs for NLS estimation normally use the right-hand side of equation (6.56) to estimate the covariance matrix of $\hat{\boldsymbol{\beta}}$. Not all programs can be relied upon to do this, however, and running the GNR (6.54) is a simple way to check whether they do so and get better estimates if they do not. Sometimes, $\hat{\boldsymbol{\beta}}$ may be obtained by a method other than fully nonlinear estimation. For example, the regression function may be linear conditional on one parameter, and NLS estimates may be obtained by searching over that parameter and performing OLS estimation conditional on it. In such a case, it will be necessary to calculate the matrix (6.56) explicitly, and running the GNR (6.54) is an easy way to do so.

The GNR (6.54) can also be used to compute a heteroskedasticity-consistent covariance matrix estimate. Any HCCME for the parameters $\hat{\boldsymbol{b}}$ of the GNR is also perfectly valid for $\hat{\boldsymbol{\beta}}$. To see this, we start from the result (6.38). If $\mathrm{E}(\boldsymbol{u}\boldsymbol{u}^\top) = \boldsymbol{\Omega}$, this result implies that

$$\mathrm{Var}\big(\operatorname*{plim}_{n\to\infty} n^{1/2}(\hat{\boldsymbol{\beta}}-\boldsymbol{\beta}_0)\big) = (\boldsymbol{S}_{\boldsymbol{X}^\top\boldsymbol{X}})^{-1} n^{-1}\boldsymbol{X}^\top\boldsymbol{\Omega}\boldsymbol{X}(\boldsymbol{S}_{\boldsymbol{X}^\top\boldsymbol{X}})^{-1}.$$

Therefore, from the results of Section 5.5, a reasonable way to estimate $\mathrm{Var}(\hat{\boldsymbol{\beta}})$ is to use the sandwich covariance matrix

$$\widehat{\mathrm{Var}}_{\mathrm{h}}(\hat{\boldsymbol{\beta}}) \equiv (\hat{\boldsymbol{X}}^\top\hat{\boldsymbol{X}})^{-1}\hat{\boldsymbol{X}}^\top\hat{\boldsymbol{\Omega}}\hat{\boldsymbol{X}}(\hat{\boldsymbol{X}}^\top\hat{\boldsymbol{X}})^{-1}, \tag{6.57}$$

where $\hat{\boldsymbol{\Omega}}$ is an $n\times n$ diagonal matrix with the squared residual $\hat{u}_t^2$ as the tth diagonal element. This is precisely the HCCME (5.39) for the GNR (6.54). Of course, as in Section 5.5, $\hat{\boldsymbol{\Omega}}$ can, and probably should, be replaced by a modified version with better finite-sample properties.

6.6 One-Step Estimation

The result (6.53) for linear regression models has a counterpart for nonlinear models: If we start with estimates that are root-n consistent but inefficient, a single Newton, or quasi-Newton, step is all that is needed to obtain estimates that are asymptotically equivalent to NLS estimates. This important result may initially seem astonishing, but the intuition behind it is not difficult.

Let $\acute{\boldsymbol{\beta}}$ denote the initial root-n consistent estimates; see Section 5.4. The GNR (6.52) evaluated at these estimates is

$$\boldsymbol{y} - \acute{\boldsymbol{x}} = \acute{\boldsymbol{X}}\boldsymbol{b} + \text{residuals},$$

where $\acute{\boldsymbol{x}} \equiv \boldsymbol{x}(\acute{\boldsymbol{\beta}})$ and $\acute{\boldsymbol{X}} \equiv \boldsymbol{X}(\acute{\boldsymbol{\beta}})$. The estimate of $\boldsymbol{b}$ from this regression is

$$\acute{\boldsymbol{b}} = (\acute{\boldsymbol{X}}^\top\acute{\boldsymbol{X}})^{-1}\acute{\boldsymbol{X}}^\top(\boldsymbol{y} - \acute{\boldsymbol{x}}). \tag{6.58}$$

Then a **one-step estimator** is defined by the equation

$$\grave{\boldsymbol{\beta}} = \acute{\boldsymbol{\beta}} + \acute{\boldsymbol{b}}. \tag{6.59}$$

This one-step estimator turns out to be asymptotically equivalent to the NLS estimator $\hat{\boldsymbol{\beta}}$, by which we mean that the difference between $n^{1/2}(\grave{\boldsymbol{\beta}} - \boldsymbol{\beta}_0)$ and $n^{1/2}(\hat{\boldsymbol{\beta}} - \boldsymbol{\beta}_0)$ tends to zero as $n \to \infty$. In other words, after both are centered and multiplied by $n^{1/2}$, the one-step estimator $\grave{\boldsymbol{\beta}}$ and the NLS estimator $\hat{\boldsymbol{\beta}}$ tend to the same random variable asymptotically. In particular, this means that the asymptotic covariance matrix of $\grave{\boldsymbol{\beta}}$ is the same as that of $\hat{\boldsymbol{\beta}}$. Thus $\grave{\boldsymbol{\beta}}$ shares with $\hat{\boldsymbol{\beta}}$ the property of asymptotic efficiency. For this reason, $\grave{\boldsymbol{\beta}}$ is sometimes called a **one-step efficient estimator**.

In order to demonstrate the asymptotic equivalence of $\grave{\boldsymbol{\beta}}$ and $\hat{\boldsymbol{\beta}}$, we begin by Taylor expanding the expression $n^{-1/2}\acute{\boldsymbol{X}}^\top(\boldsymbol{y} - \acute{\boldsymbol{x}})$ around $\boldsymbol{\beta} = \boldsymbol{\beta}_0$. This yields

$$n^{-1/2}\acute{\boldsymbol{X}}^\top(\boldsymbol{y} - \acute{\boldsymbol{x}}) = n^{-1/2}\boldsymbol{X}_0^\top(\boldsymbol{y} - \boldsymbol{x}_0) + \boldsymbol{\Delta}(\bar{\boldsymbol{\beta}})\, n^{1/2}(\acute{\boldsymbol{\beta}} - \boldsymbol{\beta}_0), \tag{6.60}$$

where $\boldsymbol{x}_0 \equiv \boldsymbol{x}(\boldsymbol{\beta}_0)$, $\bar{\boldsymbol{\beta}}$ is a parameter vector that satisfies (6.19), in the sense explained just after that equation, with $\acute{\boldsymbol{\beta}}$ in place of $\hat{\boldsymbol{\beta}}$, and $\boldsymbol{\Delta}(\boldsymbol{\beta})$ is the $k \times k$ matrix with typical element

$$\begin{aligned} \Delta_{ij}(\boldsymbol{\beta}) &\equiv \frac{\partial}{\partial \beta_j}\left(\frac{1}{n}\sum_{t=1}^{n} X_{ti}(\boldsymbol{\beta})\big(y_t - x_t(\boldsymbol{\beta})\big)\right) \\ &= -\frac{1}{n}\sum_{t=1}^{n} X_{ti}(\boldsymbol{\beta})X_{tj}(\boldsymbol{\beta}) + \frac{1}{n}\sum_{t=1}^{n}\frac{\partial X_{ti}(\boldsymbol{\beta})}{\partial \beta_j}\big(y_t - x_t(\boldsymbol{\beta})\big). \end{aligned} \tag{6.61}$$

It can be shown that, when (6.61) is evaluated at $\bar{\boldsymbol{\beta}}$, or at any root-n consistent estimator of $\boldsymbol{\beta}_0$, the second term tends to zero but the first term does not. We have seen why this is so if we evaluate (6.61) at $\boldsymbol{\beta}_0$. In that case, the second term, like expression (6.48), becomes an average of quantities each of which has mean zero, while the first term is an average of quantities each of which has a nonzero mean. Essentially the same result holds when we evaluate (6.61) at any root-n consistent estimator. Thus we conclude that

$$\boldsymbol{\Delta}(\bar{\boldsymbol{\beta}}) \stackrel{a}{=} -n^{-1}\bar{\boldsymbol{X}}^{\top}\bar{\boldsymbol{X}} \stackrel{a}{=} -n^{-1}\boldsymbol{X}_0^{\top}\boldsymbol{X}_0, \tag{6.62}$$

where the second equality is also a consequence of the consistency of $\bar{\boldsymbol{\beta}}$. Using the result (6.62) in (6.60) shows that

$$n^{-1/2}\acute{\boldsymbol{X}}^{\top}(\boldsymbol{y}-\acute{\boldsymbol{x}}) \stackrel{a}{=} n^{-1/2}\boldsymbol{X}_0^{\top}\boldsymbol{u} - n^{-1}\boldsymbol{X}_0^{\top}\boldsymbol{X}_0\, n^{1/2}(\acute{\boldsymbol{\beta}}-\boldsymbol{\beta}_0),$$

which can be solved to yield

$$\begin{aligned} n^{1/2}(\acute{\boldsymbol{\beta}}-\boldsymbol{\beta}_0) &\stackrel{a}{=} (n^{-1}\boldsymbol{X}_0^{\top}\boldsymbol{X}_0)^{-1}\big(n^{-1/2}\boldsymbol{X}_0^{\top}\boldsymbol{u} - n^{-1/2}\acute{\boldsymbol{X}}^{\top}(\boldsymbol{y}-\acute{\boldsymbol{x}})\big) \\ &\stackrel{a}{=} (\boldsymbol{S}_{\boldsymbol{X}^{\top}\boldsymbol{X}})^{-1}n^{-1/2}\boldsymbol{X}_0^{\top}\boldsymbol{u} - (\boldsymbol{S}_{\boldsymbol{X}^{\top}\boldsymbol{X}})^{-1}n^{-1/2}\acute{\boldsymbol{X}}^{\top}(\boldsymbol{y}-\acute{\boldsymbol{x}}). \end{aligned} \tag{6.63}$$

By (6.38), the first term in the second line here is equal to $n^{1/2}(\hat{\boldsymbol{\beta}}-\boldsymbol{\beta}_0)$. By (6.58), the second term is asymptotically equivalent to $-n^{1/2}\acute{\boldsymbol{b}}$. Thus (6.63) implies that

$$n^{1/2}(\acute{\boldsymbol{\beta}}-\boldsymbol{\beta}_0) \stackrel{a}{=} n^{1/2}(\hat{\boldsymbol{\beta}}-\boldsymbol{\beta}_0) - n^{1/2}\acute{\boldsymbol{b}}.$$

Rearranging this and using the definition (6.59), we see that

$$n^{1/2}(\grave{\boldsymbol{\beta}}-\boldsymbol{\beta}_0) = n^{1/2}(\acute{\boldsymbol{\beta}}+\acute{\boldsymbol{b}}-\boldsymbol{\beta}_0) \stackrel{a}{=} n^{1/2}(\hat{\boldsymbol{\beta}}-\boldsymbol{\beta}_0), \tag{6.64}$$

which is the result that we wished to show.

Despite the rather complicated asymptotic theory needed to prove (6.64), the fundamental reason that makes a one-step efficient estimator based on the GNR asymptotically equivalent to the NLS estimator is really quite simple. The GNR minimizes a quadratic approximation to $\mathrm{SSR}(\boldsymbol{\beta})$ around $\acute{\boldsymbol{\beta}}$. Asymptotically, the function $\mathrm{SSR}(\boldsymbol{\beta})$ is quadratic in the neighborhood of $\boldsymbol{\beta}_0$. If the sample size is large enough, the consistency of $\acute{\boldsymbol{\beta}}$ implies that we must be taking the quadratic approximation at a point very near $\boldsymbol{\beta}_0$. Therefore, the approximation coincides with $\mathrm{SSR}(\boldsymbol{\beta})$ itself asymptotically.

Although this result is of great theoretical interest, it is typically of limited practical utility with modern computing equipment. Once the GNR, or some other method for taking Newton or quasi-Newton steps, has been programmed for a particular model, we might as well let it iterate to convergence, because the savings in computer time from stopping after a single step are rarely substantial. Moreover, a one-step estimator is consistent if and only if we start from an initial estimator that is consistent, while NLS is consistent no matter where we start from, provided we converge to a global minimum of $\mathrm{SSR}(\boldsymbol{\beta})$. Therefore, it may well require more effort on the part of the investigator to obtain one-step estimates than to obtain NLS ones.

One-step estimators may be useful when the sample size is very large and each step in the minimization process is, perhaps in consequence, very expensive. The large sample size often ensures that the initial, consistent estimates are reasonably close to the NLS ones. If they are, then the one-step estimates should be very close to the latter. One-step estimators can also be useful when the estimation needs to be repeated many times, as is often required by the bootstrap and other simulation-based methods. Bootstrap methods that use one-step estimators are discussed by Davidson and MacKinnon (1999a).

The Linear Regression Model with AR(1) Errors

An excellent example of one-step efficient estimation is provided by the model (6.06), which is a linear regression model with AR(1) errors. The GNR that corresponds to (6.06) is

$$\begin{aligned} y_t - \rho y_{t-1} &- \boldsymbol{X}_t\boldsymbol{\beta} + \rho\boldsymbol{X}_{t-1}\boldsymbol{\beta} \\ &= (\boldsymbol{X}_t - \rho\boldsymbol{X}_{t-1})\boldsymbol{b} + b_\rho(y_{t-1} - \boldsymbol{X}_{t-1}\boldsymbol{\beta}) + \text{residual}, \end{aligned} \tag{6.65}$$

where $\boldsymbol{b}$ corresponds to $\boldsymbol{\beta}$ and b_ρ corresponds to ρ. As with every GNR, the regressand is y_t minus the regression function for (6.06). The last regressor, which is the derivative of the regression function with respect to ρ, looks very much like a lagged residual from the original linear regression model (6.05). The remaining k regressors are the derivatives of the regression function with respect to the elements of $\boldsymbol{\beta}$.

It is easy to obtain root-n consistent estimates of the parameters ρ and $\boldsymbol{\beta}$ of the model (6.06), because it can be written as a linear regression subject to nonlinear restrictions on its parameters. The linear regression is

$$y_t = \rho y_{t-1} + \boldsymbol{X}_t\boldsymbol{\beta} + \boldsymbol{X}_{t-1}\boldsymbol{\gamma} + \varepsilon_t. \tag{6.66}$$

If we impose the nonlinear restrictions that $\boldsymbol{\gamma} + \rho\boldsymbol{\beta} = \boldsymbol{0}$, this regression is just (6.06). Thus the model (6.06) is a special case of the model (6.66). Therefore, if (6.06) is a correctly specified model, that is, if the true DGP is a special case of (6.06), then (6.66) must be a correctly specified model as well, because every DGP in (6.06) automatically belongs to (6.66). Since (6.66) is correctly specified, the standard theory of the linear regression with predetermined regressors applies to it, with the consequence that the OLS estimates $\acute{\rho}$ and $\acute{\boldsymbol{\beta}}$ obtained from (6.66) are root-n consistent.

If we evaluate the variables of the GNR (6.65) at $\acute{\rho}$ and $\acute{\boldsymbol{\beta}}$, we obtain

$$\begin{aligned} y_t - \acute{\rho} y_{t-1} &- \boldsymbol{X}_t\acute{\boldsymbol{\beta}} + \acute{\rho}\boldsymbol{X}_{t-1}\acute{\boldsymbol{\beta}} \\ &= (\boldsymbol{X}_t - \acute{\rho}\boldsymbol{X}_{t-1})\boldsymbol{b} + b_\rho(y_{t-1} - \boldsymbol{X}_{t-1}\acute{\boldsymbol{\beta}}) + \text{residual}. \end{aligned} \tag{6.67}$$

We can run this regression to obtain the artificial parameter estimates $\acute{\boldsymbol{b}}$ and $\acute{b}_\rho$, and the one-step efficient estimates are just $\acute{\boldsymbol{\beta}} + \acute{\boldsymbol{b}}$ and $\acute{\rho} + \acute{b}_\rho$.

6.7 Hypothesis Testing

Hypotheses about the parameters of nonlinear regression models can be formulated in much the same way as hypotheses about the parameters of linear regression models. Let us partition the parameter vector $\boldsymbol{\beta}$ as $\boldsymbol{\beta} = [\boldsymbol{\beta}_1 \vdots \boldsymbol{\beta}_2]$, where $\boldsymbol{\beta}_1$ is $k_1 \times 1$, $\boldsymbol{\beta}_2$ is $k_2 \times 1$, and $\boldsymbol{\beta}$ is $k \times 1$, with $k = k_1 + k_2$. Then the generic nonlinear regression model (6.02) can be written as

$$\boldsymbol{y} = \boldsymbol{x}(\boldsymbol{\beta}_1, \boldsymbol{\beta}_2) + \boldsymbol{u}, \quad \boldsymbol{u} \sim \text{IID}(\mathbf{0}, \sigma^2\mathbf{I}).$$

If we wish to test the hypothesis that $\boldsymbol{\beta}_2 = \mathbf{0}$, we can set up the models that correspond to the null and alternative hypotheses as follows:

$$H_0: \quad \boldsymbol{y} = \boldsymbol{x}(\boldsymbol{\beta}_1, \mathbf{0}) + \boldsymbol{u}; \tag{6.68}$$

$$H_1: \quad \boldsymbol{y} = \boldsymbol{x}(\boldsymbol{\beta}_1, \boldsymbol{\beta}_2) + \boldsymbol{u}. \tag{6.69}$$

Here, using notation introduced in Section 4.2, H_0 denotes the null hypothesis, and H_1 denotes the alternative.

If the regression models (6.68) and (6.69) were linear, we could test the null hypothesis by means of the F statistic (4.30). In fact, we can do this even though they are nonlinear. The test statistic

$$F_{\boldsymbol{\beta}_2} \equiv \frac{(\text{RSSR} - \text{USSR})/r}{\text{USSR}/(n-k)} \tag{6.70}$$

is computed in exactly the same way as (4.30), but with RSSR and USSR the sums of squared residuals from NLS estimation of (6.68) and (6.69), respectively. Here $r = k_2$, since the hypothesis that $\boldsymbol{\beta}_2 = \mathbf{0}$ imposes k_2 restrictions. It is not difficult to show that (6.70) is asymptotically valid: Under the null hypothesis, it follows the $F(r, \infty)$ distribution asymptotically.

First, we establish some notation. Let $\boldsymbol{X}(\boldsymbol{\beta})$ denote the $n \times k$ matrix of partial derivatives of the vector of regression functions $\boldsymbol{x}(\boldsymbol{\beta}) = \boldsymbol{x}(\boldsymbol{\beta}_1, \boldsymbol{\beta}_2)$ of (6.69). Similarly, let $\boldsymbol{X}_1(\boldsymbol{\beta})$ and $\boldsymbol{X}_2(\boldsymbol{\beta})$ denote the $n \times k_1$ and $n \times k_2$ submatrices of partial derivatives with respect to the components of $\boldsymbol{\beta}_1$ and $\boldsymbol{\beta}_2$, respectively. Finally, let $\boldsymbol{M}_1$ denote the orthogonal projection on to $\mathcal{S}^\perp(\boldsymbol{X}(\boldsymbol{\beta}_0))$, which we previously called $\boldsymbol{M}_{\boldsymbol{X}_0}$, and let $\boldsymbol{M}_0$ denote the orthogonal projection on to $\mathcal{S}^\perp(\boldsymbol{X}_1(\boldsymbol{\beta}_0))$. The projection $\boldsymbol{M}_0$ corresponds to the null hypothesis H_0, and the projection $\boldsymbol{M}_1$ corresponds to the alternative hypothesis H_1.

By the result (6.40), under both the null and alternative hypotheses, the vector of residuals $\hat{\boldsymbol{u}}$ from NLS estimation of H_1 is asymptotically equal to $\boldsymbol{M}_1\boldsymbol{u}$. By essentially the same argument, under the null hypothesis, the vector of residuals $\tilde{\boldsymbol{u}}$ from NLS estimation of H_0 is asymptotically equal to $\boldsymbol{M}_0\boldsymbol{u}$. This implies (see Exercise 6.8) that $\hat{\boldsymbol{u}}^\top\hat{\boldsymbol{u}} \overset{a}{=} \boldsymbol{u}^\top\boldsymbol{M}_1\boldsymbol{u}$ and $\tilde{\boldsymbol{u}}^\top\tilde{\boldsymbol{u}} \overset{a}{=} \boldsymbol{u}^\top\boldsymbol{M}_0\boldsymbol{u}$. Therefore, under H_0, r times the numerator of (6.70) is asymptotically equal to

$$\boldsymbol{u}^\top\boldsymbol{M}_0\boldsymbol{u} - \boldsymbol{u}^\top\boldsymbol{M}_1\boldsymbol{u} = \boldsymbol{u}^\top(\boldsymbol{M}_0 - \boldsymbol{M}_1)\boldsymbol{u} = \boldsymbol{u}^\top(\boldsymbol{P}_1 - \boldsymbol{P}_0)\boldsymbol{u},$$

where P_0 and P_1 are the projections complementary to M_0 and M_1. By the result of Exercise 2.18, $P_1 - P_0$ is an orthogonal projection matrix, which projects on to a space of dimension $k - k_1 = k_2$. Thus the numerator of (6.70) is asymptotically σ_0^2 times a χ^2 variable with k_2 degrees of freedom, divided by $r = k_2$; recall Exercise 4.13. The denominator of (6.70) is just a consistent estimate of σ_0^2, and so, under H_0, the statistic (6.70) itself is asymptotically distributed as $F(k_2, \infty) = \chi^2(k_2)/k_2$.

For linear models, we saw in Section 5.4 that the F statistic could be written as (5.26), which is a special case of the more general form (5.23). Not surprisingly, it is also possible to calculate test statistics of the form (5.23) to test the hypothesis that $\boldsymbol{\beta}_2 = \mathbf{0}$ in the nonlinear model (6.69). This type of test statistic is often called a **Wald statistic**, because the approach was suggested by Wald (1943). It can be written as

$$W_{\boldsymbol{\beta}_2} \equiv \hat{\boldsymbol{\beta}}_2^{\top}\big(\widehat{\mathrm{Var}}(\hat{\boldsymbol{\beta}}_2)\big)^{-1}\hat{\boldsymbol{\beta}}_2, \tag{6.71}$$

where $\hat{\boldsymbol{\beta}}_2$ is a vector of NLS estimates from the unrestricted model (6.69), and $\widehat{\mathrm{Var}}(\hat{\boldsymbol{\beta}}_2)$ is the NLS estimate of its covariance matrix. This is just a quadratic form in the vector $\hat{\boldsymbol{\beta}}_2$ and the inverse of an estimate of its covariance matrix. When $k_2 = 1$, the signed square root of (6.71) is equivalent to a t statistic. We will see below that the Wald statistic (6.71) is asymptotically equivalent to the F statistic (6.70), except for the factor of $1/k_2$.

Tests Based on the Gauss-Newton Regression

Since the GNR provides a one-step estimator asymptotically equivalent to the NLS estimator, and it also provides the NLS estimate of the covariance matrix of $\hat{\boldsymbol{\beta}}_2$, a statistic asymptotically equivalent to (6.71) can be computed by means of a GNR. This statistic also turns out to be asymptotically equivalent to the F statistic (6.70), except for the factor of $1/k_2$.

The Gauss-Newton regression corresponding to the model (6.69) is

$$\boldsymbol{y} - \boldsymbol{x}(\boldsymbol{\beta}_1, \boldsymbol{\beta}_2) = \boldsymbol{X}_1(\boldsymbol{\beta}_1, \boldsymbol{\beta}_2)\boldsymbol{b}_1 + \boldsymbol{X}_2(\boldsymbol{\beta}_1, \boldsymbol{\beta}_2)\boldsymbol{b}_2 + \text{residuals}, \tag{6.72}$$

where the vector of artificial parameters $\boldsymbol{b}$ has been partitioned as $[\boldsymbol{b}_1 \,\vdots\, \boldsymbol{b}_2]$, conformably with the partition of $\boldsymbol{X}(\boldsymbol{\beta})$. If the GNR is to be used to test the null hypothesis that $\boldsymbol{\beta}_2 = \mathbf{0}$, the regressand and regressors must be evaluated at parameter estimates which satisfy the null. We will suppose that they are evaluated at the point $\acute{\boldsymbol{\beta}} \equiv [\acute{\boldsymbol{\beta}}_1, \mathbf{0}]$, where $\acute{\boldsymbol{\beta}}_1$ may be any root-n consistent estimator of $\boldsymbol{\beta}_1$. Then the one-step estimator of $\boldsymbol{\beta}$ can be written as

$$\acute{\boldsymbol{\beta}} + \acute{\boldsymbol{b}} = \begin{bmatrix} \acute{\boldsymbol{\beta}}_1 + \acute{\boldsymbol{b}}_1 \\ \acute{\boldsymbol{b}}_2 \end{bmatrix}. \tag{6.73}$$

By the results of Section 6.6, $n^{1/2}\acute{\boldsymbol{b}}_2$ is asymptotically equivalent to $n^{1/2}\hat{\boldsymbol{\beta}}_2$, where $\hat{\boldsymbol{\beta}}_2$ is the NLS estimator of $\boldsymbol{\beta}_2$ from (6.69).

In practice, the two estimators that are most likely to be used for $\acute{\boldsymbol{\beta}}_1$ are $\tilde{\boldsymbol{\beta}}_1$, the restricted NLS estimator, and $\hat{\boldsymbol{\beta}}_1$, a subvector of the unrestricted NLS estimator. Here we are once more adopting the convention, previously used in Chapter 4, whereby a tilde denotes restricted estimates and a hat denotes unrestricted ones. Both these estimators are root-n consistent under the null hypothesis, but $\tilde{\boldsymbol{\beta}}_1$ is generally more efficient than $\hat{\boldsymbol{\beta}}_1$. Whether we want to use $\tilde{\boldsymbol{\beta}}_1$, $\hat{\boldsymbol{\beta}}_1$, or some other root-$n$ consistent estimator when performing GNR-based tests depends on how difficult the various estimators are to compute and on the finite-sample properties of the test statistics that result from the various choices.

Now consider the vector of residuals $\acute{\boldsymbol{u}}$ from OLS estimation of the GNR (6.72) evaluated at $\acute{\boldsymbol{\beta}}$, when the true DGP is characterized by the parameter vector $\boldsymbol{\beta}_0 \equiv [\boldsymbol{\beta}_1^0 \;\vdots\; \mathbf{0}]$. We have

$$\begin{aligned}
\acute{\boldsymbol{u}} &= \boldsymbol{y} - \boldsymbol{x}(\acute{\boldsymbol{\beta}}_1, \mathbf{0}) - \acute{\boldsymbol{X}}_1\acute{\boldsymbol{b}}_1 - \acute{\boldsymbol{X}}_2\acute{\boldsymbol{b}}_2 \\
&= \boldsymbol{y} - \boldsymbol{x}(\boldsymbol{\beta}_1^0, \mathbf{0}) - \boldsymbol{X}_1(\bar{\boldsymbol{\beta}})(\acute{\boldsymbol{\beta}}_1 - \boldsymbol{\beta}_1^0) - \acute{\boldsymbol{X}}_1\acute{\boldsymbol{b}}_1 - \acute{\boldsymbol{X}}_2\acute{\boldsymbol{b}}_2 \\
&\overset{a}{=} \boldsymbol{u} - \acute{\boldsymbol{X}}_1(\acute{\boldsymbol{\beta}}_1 + \acute{\boldsymbol{b}}_1 - \boldsymbol{\beta}_1^0) - \acute{\boldsymbol{X}}_2\acute{\boldsymbol{b}}_2.
\end{aligned} \tag{6.74}$$

Here, $\bar{\boldsymbol{\beta}}$ is a parameter vector between $\boldsymbol{\beta}_0$ and $\acute{\boldsymbol{\beta}}$. To obtain the asymptotic equality in the last line, we have used the fact that $\boldsymbol{X}_1(\bar{\boldsymbol{\beta}}) \overset{a}{=} \acute{\boldsymbol{X}}_1$. The one-step estimator (6.73) is consistent, and so the last two terms in (6.74) tend to zero as $n \to \infty$. Thus the residuals $\acute{u}_t$ are asymptotically equal to the error terms u_t, and so $n^{-1}\acute{\boldsymbol{u}}^\top\acute{\boldsymbol{u}}$ is asymptotically equal to σ_0^2, the true error variance. In fact, because of the asymptotic equivalence of the one-step estimator $\grave{\boldsymbol{\beta}}$ and the NLS estimator $\hat{\boldsymbol{\beta}}$, (6.74) tells us that $\acute{\boldsymbol{u}} \overset{a}{=} \boldsymbol{u} - \acute{\boldsymbol{X}}(\hat{\boldsymbol{\beta}} - \boldsymbol{\beta}_0)$. An argument like that of (6.40) then shows that $\acute{\boldsymbol{u}}$ is asymptotically equivalent to $\boldsymbol{M}_{\boldsymbol{X}_0}\boldsymbol{u}$. For the moment, however, we do not need this more refined result.

The GNR (6.72) evaluated at $\acute{\boldsymbol{\beta}}$ is

$$\boldsymbol{y} - \acute{\boldsymbol{x}} = \acute{\boldsymbol{X}}_1\boldsymbol{b}_1 + \acute{\boldsymbol{X}}_2\boldsymbol{b}_2 + \text{residuals}. \tag{6.75}$$

Since this is a linear regression, we can apply the FWL Theorem to it. Writing $\boldsymbol{M}_{\acute{\boldsymbol{X}}_1}$ for the projection on to $\mathcal{S}^\perp(\acute{\boldsymbol{X}}_1)$, we see that the FWL regression can be written as

$$\boldsymbol{M}_{\acute{\boldsymbol{X}}_1}(\boldsymbol{y} - \acute{\boldsymbol{x}}) = \boldsymbol{M}_{\acute{\boldsymbol{X}}_1}\acute{\boldsymbol{X}}_2\boldsymbol{b}_2 + \text{residuals}.$$

This FWL regression yields the same estimates $\acute{\boldsymbol{b}}_2$ as does (6.75). Thus, inserting the factors of powers of n that are needed for asymptotic analysis, we find that

$$n^{1/2}\acute{\boldsymbol{b}}_2 = (n^{-1}\acute{\boldsymbol{X}}_2^\top\boldsymbol{M}_{\acute{\boldsymbol{X}}_1}\acute{\boldsymbol{X}}_2)^{-1}n^{-1/2}\acute{\boldsymbol{X}}_2^\top\boldsymbol{M}_{\acute{\boldsymbol{X}}_1}(\boldsymbol{y} - \acute{\boldsymbol{x}}). \tag{6.76}$$

In addition to yielding the same parameter estimates $\acute{\boldsymbol{b}}_2$, the FWL regression has the same residuals as regression (6.75) and the same estimated covariance matrix for $\acute{\boldsymbol{b}}_2$. The latter is $\acute{\sigma}^2(\acute{\boldsymbol{X}}_2^\top \boldsymbol{M}_{\acute{\boldsymbol{X}}_1}\acute{\boldsymbol{X}}_2)^{-1}$, where $\acute{\sigma}^2$ is the error variance estimator from (6.75), which, as we just saw, is asymptotically equal to σ_0^2. If $\boldsymbol{X}_1$ and $\boldsymbol{X}_2$ denote $\boldsymbol{X}_1(\boldsymbol{\beta}_0)$ and $\boldsymbol{X}_2(\boldsymbol{\beta}_0)$, respectively, we see that

$$\begin{aligned}
n^{-1}\acute{\boldsymbol{X}}_2^\top \boldsymbol{M}_{\acute{\boldsymbol{X}}_1}\acute{\boldsymbol{X}}_2 &= n^{-1}\acute{\boldsymbol{X}}_2^\top\acute{\boldsymbol{X}}_2 - n^{-1}\acute{\boldsymbol{X}}_2^\top\acute{\boldsymbol{X}}_1(n^{-1}\acute{\boldsymbol{X}}_1^\top\acute{\boldsymbol{X}}_1)^{-1}n^{-1}\acute{\boldsymbol{X}}_1^\top\acute{\boldsymbol{X}}_2 \\
&\overset{a}{=} n^{-1}\boldsymbol{X}_2^\top\boldsymbol{X}_2 - n^{-1}\boldsymbol{X}_2^\top\boldsymbol{X}_1(n^{-1}\boldsymbol{X}_1^\top\boldsymbol{X}_1)^{-1}n^{-1}\boldsymbol{X}_1^\top\boldsymbol{X}_2 \\
&= n^{-1}\boldsymbol{X}_2^\top\boldsymbol{M}_{\boldsymbol{X}_1}\boldsymbol{X}_2,
\end{aligned}$$

where the asymptotic equality follows, as usual, from the consistency of $\acute{\boldsymbol{\beta}}$. Thus n times the covariance matrix estimator for $\acute{\boldsymbol{b}}_2$ given by the GNR (6.75) provides a consistent estimate of the asymptotic covariance matrix of the vector $n^{1/2}(\hat{\boldsymbol{\beta}}_2 - \boldsymbol{\beta}_2^0)$, as would be given by the lower right block of (6.31) if that matrix were partitioned appropriately.

The Wald test statistic (6.71) can be rewritten as

$$n^{1/2}\hat{\boldsymbol{\beta}}_2^\top\big(n\widehat{\mathrm{Var}}(\hat{\boldsymbol{\beta}}_2)\big)^{-1}n^{1/2}\hat{\boldsymbol{\beta}}_2. \tag{6.77}$$

This is asymptotically equivalent to the statistic

$$\frac{1}{\acute{\sigma}^2}n^{1/2}\acute{\boldsymbol{b}}_2^\top(n^{-1}\acute{\boldsymbol{X}}_2^\top\boldsymbol{M}_{\acute{\boldsymbol{X}}_1}\acute{\boldsymbol{X}}_2)n^{1/2}\acute{\boldsymbol{b}}_2, \tag{6.78}$$

which is based entirely on quantities from the GNR (6.75). That (6.77) and (6.78) are asymptotically equal relies on (6.76) and the fact, which we have just shown, that the covariance matrix estimator for $\acute{\boldsymbol{b}}_2$ is also valid for $\hat{\boldsymbol{\beta}}_2$.

By equation (6.76), the GNR-based statistic (6.78) can also be expressed as

$$\frac{1}{\acute{\sigma}^2}n^{-1/2}(\boldsymbol{y}-\acute{\boldsymbol{x}})^\top\boldsymbol{M}_{\acute{\boldsymbol{X}}_1}\acute{\boldsymbol{X}}_2(n^{-1}\acute{\boldsymbol{X}}_2^\top\boldsymbol{M}_{\acute{\boldsymbol{X}}_1}\acute{\boldsymbol{X}}_2)^{-1}n^{-1/2}\acute{\boldsymbol{X}}_2^\top\boldsymbol{M}_{\acute{\boldsymbol{X}}_1}(\boldsymbol{y}-\acute{\boldsymbol{x}}). \tag{6.79}$$

When this statistic is divided by $r = k_2$, we can see by comparison with (4.33) that it is precisely the F statistic for a test of the artificial hypothesis that $\boldsymbol{b}_2 = \boldsymbol{0}$ in the GNR (6.75). In particular, $\acute{\sigma}^2$ is just the sum of squared residuals from equation (6.75), divided by $n - k$. Thus a valid test statistic can be computed as an ordinary F statistic using the sums of squared residuals from the "restricted" and "unrestricted" GNRs,

$$\mathrm{GNR}_0\colon\ \boldsymbol{y}-\acute{\boldsymbol{x}} = \acute{\boldsymbol{X}}_1\boldsymbol{b}_1 + \text{residuals, and} \tag{6.80}$$

$$\mathrm{GNR}_1\colon\ \boldsymbol{y}-\acute{\boldsymbol{x}} = \acute{\boldsymbol{X}}_1\boldsymbol{b}_1 + \acute{\boldsymbol{X}}_2\boldsymbol{b}_2 + \text{residuals.} \tag{6.81}$$

In Exercise 6.9, readers are invited to show that such an F statistic is asymptotically equivalent to the F statistic computed from the sums of squared residuals from the two nonlinear regressions (6.68) and (6.69).

In the quite common event that $\acute{\beta}_1 = \tilde{\beta}_1$, the first-order conditions for $\tilde{\beta}_1$ imply that regression (6.80) can have no explanatory power. There is no need to run regression (6.80) in this case, because its SSR is always identical to the SSR from NLS estimation of the restricted model. We will see an example of this in the next subsection.

The principal advantage of tests based on the GNR is that they can be calculated without computing two nonlinear regressions, one for each of the null and alternative hypotheses. The principal disadvantage is that a number of derivatives must be calculated, one for each parameter of the unrestricted model. In many cases, it is necessary to run one nonlinear regression, so as to obtain root-n consistent estimates of the parameters under the null. However, it may sometimes happen that either the null or the alternative hypothesis corresponds to a linear model. In such cases, no nonlinear estimation at all is necessary to carry out a GNR-based test.

GNR-Based Tests for Autoregressive Errors

An example of a model which is linear under the null hypothesis is furnished by the linear regression model with autoregressive errors. With time-series data, serial correlation of the error terms is a frequent occurrence, and so one of the most frequently performed tests in all of econometrics is a test in which the null hypothesis is a linear regression model with serially uncorrelated errors and the alternative is the same model with AR(1) errors. In this case, we may think of H_1 as being the model (6.06) and H_0 as being the model

$$y_t = \boldsymbol{X}_t\boldsymbol{\beta} + u_t, \quad u_t \sim \text{IID}(0, \sigma^2). \tag{6.82}$$

When GNRs like (6.80) and (6.81) are used for testing, all the variables in them must be evaluated at a parameter vector $\acute{\boldsymbol{\beta}}$ which satisfies the null hypothesis. In this case, the null hypothesis corresponds to the restriction that $\rho = 0$. Therefore, we must set $\acute{\rho} = 0$ in the GNRs corresponding to the restricted model (6.82) and the unrestricted model (6.06). The natural choice for $\acute{\boldsymbol{\beta}}$ is then $\tilde{\boldsymbol{\beta}}$, the vector of OLS parameter estimates for (6.82).

The GNR for (6.06) was given in (6.65). If this artificial regression is evaluated at $\boldsymbol{\beta} = \tilde{\boldsymbol{\beta}}$ and $\rho = 0$, it becomes

$$y_t - \boldsymbol{X}_t\tilde{\boldsymbol{\beta}} = \boldsymbol{X}_t\boldsymbol{b} + b_\rho(y_{t-1} - \boldsymbol{X}_{t-1}\tilde{\boldsymbol{\beta}}) + \text{residual}, \tag{6.83}$$

where $\boldsymbol{b}$ corresponds to $\boldsymbol{\beta}$ and b_ρ corresponds to ρ. If we denote the OLS residuals from (6.82) by $\tilde{u}_t$, the GNR (6.83) takes on the very simple form

$$\tilde{u}_t = \boldsymbol{X}_t\boldsymbol{b} + b_\rho\tilde{u}_{t-1} + \text{residual}. \tag{6.84}$$

This is just a linear regression of the residuals from (6.82) on the regressors of (6.82) and one more regressor, namely, the residuals lagged once. Since only one restriction is to be tested, a suitable test statistic is the t statistic for the artificial parameter b_ρ in (6.84) to equal 0. This is the square root of the F statistic, which we have seen to be asymptotically valid.

Almost as simple as the above test is a test of the null hypothesis (6.82) against an alternative in which the error terms follow the **AR(2) process**

$$u_t = \rho_1 u_{t-1} + \rho_2 u_{t-2} + \varepsilon_t, \quad \varepsilon_t \sim \text{IID}(0, \sigma^2).$$

It is not hard to show that an appropriate artificial regression for testing (6.82) against the AR(2) alternative that is analogous to (6.06) is

$$\tilde{u}_t = \boldsymbol{X}_t \boldsymbol{b} + b_{\rho_1} \tilde{u}_{t-1} + b_{\rho_2} \tilde{u}_{t-2} + \text{residual}; \tag{6.85}$$

see Exercise 6.10. Since, in this case, we have a test with two degrees of freedom, we cannot use a t test. However, it is still not necessary to run two regressions in order to compute an F statistic. Consider the form taken by GNR_0 in this case:

$$\tilde{u}_t = \boldsymbol{X}_t \boldsymbol{b} + \text{residual}. \tag{6.86}$$

This is just the GNR corresponding to the linear regression (6.82). Since the regressand is the vector of residuals from estimating (6.82), it is orthogonal to the explanatory variables. Therefore, by (6.55), the artificial parameter estimates $\tilde{\boldsymbol{b}}$ are zero, and (6.86) has no explanatory power. As a result, the SSR from (6.86) is equal to the total sum of squares (TSS). But this is also the TSS from the GNR (6.85) corresponding to the alternative. Thus the difference between the SSRs from (6.86) and (6.85) is the difference between the TSS and the SSR from (6.85), or, more conveniently, the explained sum of squares (ESS) from (6.85). The GNR-based F statistic can therefore be computed by running (6.85) alone. In fact, since the denominator is just the estimate $\tilde{s}^2$ of the error variance from (6.85), the F statistic is simply[1]

$$F = \frac{\text{ESS}}{r\tilde{s}^2} = \frac{n-k}{r} \times \frac{\text{ESS}}{\text{SSR}}, \tag{6.87}$$

with $r = 2$ in this particular case.

Asymptotically, we can obtain a valid test statistic by using any consistent estimate of the true error variance σ_0^2 as the denominator. If we were to use the estimate under the null rather than the estimate under the alternative, the denominator of the test statistic would be $(n-k_1)^{-1}\sum_{t=1}^{n}\tilde{u}_t^2$. Asymptotically, it makes no difference whether we divide by $n - k_1$ or n when we estimate σ^2.

[1] We are assuming here that regression (6.85) is run over all n observations. This requires either that data for observations 0 and -1 are available, or that the unobserved residuals $\tilde{u}_0$ and $\tilde{u}_{-1}$ are replaced by zeros.

Therefore, if R^2 is the uncentered R squared from (6.85), another perfectly valid test statistic is

$$nR^2 = \frac{n\text{ESS}}{\text{TSS}} = \frac{\text{ESS}}{n^{-1}\sum_{t=1}^{n}\tilde{u}_t^2}, \tag{6.88}$$

which follows the $\chi^2(2)$ distribution asymptotically. If the regressors include a constant, the residuals $\tilde{u}_t$ must have mean zero, and the uncentered R^2 (6.88) is identical to the centered R^2 that is printed by most regression packages.

Whether we use the F statistic (6.87) or the nR^2 statistic (6.88), the GNR provides a very easy way to test the null hypothesis that the error terms are serially uncorrelated against all sorts of autoregressive alternatives. Of course, neither statistic follows its asymptotic distribution exactly in finite samples. However, there is some evidence—for example, Kiviet (1986)—that the former tends to have better finite-sample properties than the latter. This evidence accords with theory, because, as (6.40) shows, the relationship between NLS residuals and error terms is approximately the same as the relationship between OLS residuals and error terms. Therefore, it makes sense to use the F form of the statistic, which treats the estimate $\tilde{s}^2$ based on the GNR as if it were based on an ordinary OLS regression.

The above example generalizes to all cases in which $\acute{\boldsymbol{\beta}}$ is taken to be $\tilde{\boldsymbol{\beta}}$ from estimating the null hypothesis, whether or not the restricted model is linear. In such cases, because GNR_0 has no explanatory power, its SSR is equal to its TSS, which in turn is equal to the TSS of GNR_1. In consequence, we only need to run GNR_1, which in this case is

$$\boldsymbol{y} - \tilde{\boldsymbol{x}} = \tilde{\boldsymbol{X}}_1\boldsymbol{b}_1 + \tilde{\boldsymbol{X}}_2\boldsymbol{b}_2 + \text{residuals}.$$

Under the null hypothesis, nR^2 from this test regression is asymptotically distributed as $\chi^2(r)$. This is not the case for GNR_1 when $\acute{\boldsymbol{\beta}} \neq \tilde{\boldsymbol{\beta}}$. However, the F test of (6.80) against (6.81) is asymptotically valid even when $\acute{\boldsymbol{\beta}} \neq \tilde{\boldsymbol{\beta}}$. It is merely required that $\acute{\boldsymbol{\beta}}$ should satisfy the null hypothesis and be root-n consistent.

Most GNR-based tests are like the ones for serial correlation that we have just discussed, in which the GNR is evaluated at least-squares estimates under the null hypothesis. However, it is also possible to evaluate the GNR at estimates obtained under the alternative hypothesis. We will encounter tests of this type when we discuss common factor restrictions in Chapter 7.

Bootstrap Tests

Because none of the tests discussed in this section is exact in finite samples, it is often desirable to compute bootstrap P values, which, in most cases, are more accurate than ones based on asymptotic theory. The procedures for computing bootstrap P values for nonlinear regression models are essentially the same as the ones for linear models that were described in Section 4.6. We use estimates under the null to generate B bootstrap samples, usually either generating the error terms from the $\mathrm{N}(0, \tilde{s}^2)$ distribution or resampling the rescaled residuals, and we then compute a bootstrap test statistic τ_j^* using each of the bootstrap samples. For a test that rejects when the test statistic $\hat{\tau}$ is large, the bootstrap P value is then $1 - \hat{F}^*(\hat{\tau})$, where $\hat{F}^*(\hat{\tau})$ denotes the EDF of the τ_j^* evaluated at $\hat{\tau}$. Of course, this procedure can sometimes be computationally expensive; see Davidson and MacKinnon (1999a) for a way of making it somewhat less so.

6.8 Heteroskedasticity-Robust Tests

All of the tests dealt with in the preceding section are valid only under the assumption that the error terms are IID. This assumption, which may be uncomfortably strong in some cases, can be relaxed for GNR-based tests by using a modified version of the GNR.

As in Section 5.5, let us suppose that the covariance matrix of the error terms is $\boldsymbol{\Omega}$, an $n \times n$ diagonal matrix with t^{th} diagonal element ω_t^2. Then the matrix (6.57) provides a heteroskedasticity-consistent estimate of $\mathrm{Var}(\hat{\boldsymbol{\beta}})$, which can be used in place of the usual estimate. The result is a **heteroskedasticity-robust** test statistic, the asymptotic distribution of which is the same no matter what the ω_t^2 happen to be, provided the regularity conditions needed for the HCCME to be valid are satisfied.

For H_0 and H_1 as in (6.68) and (6.69), but with heteroskedastic errors, we wish to construct a Wald test statistic, similar to (6.71), that uses an HCCME to estimate the covariance matrix. Let $\acute{\boldsymbol{\beta}}$ denote a vector of parameter estimates that is root-n consistent and satisfies the null hypothesis. Often, $\acute{\boldsymbol{\beta}}$ is just $\tilde{\boldsymbol{\beta}}$, the vector of NLS estimates under the null. By arguments similar to those that led to (6.79), an appropriate Wald statistic can be written as

$$(\boldsymbol{y} - \acute{\boldsymbol{x}})^{\top} \boldsymbol{M}_{\acute{\boldsymbol{X}}_1} \acute{\boldsymbol{X}}_2 (\acute{\boldsymbol{X}}_2^{\top} \boldsymbol{M}_{\acute{\boldsymbol{X}}_1} \acute{\boldsymbol{\Omega}} \boldsymbol{M}_{\acute{\boldsymbol{X}}_1} \acute{\boldsymbol{X}}_2)^{-1} \acute{\boldsymbol{X}}_2^{\top} \boldsymbol{M}_{\acute{\boldsymbol{X}}_1} (\boldsymbol{y} - \acute{\boldsymbol{x}}), \tag{6.89}$$

where $\acute{\boldsymbol{\Omega}}$ is an $n \times n$ diagonal matrix with t^{th} diagonal element equal to $\acute{u}_t^2$. Here $\acute{u}_t$ denotes the residual $y_t - x_t(\acute{\boldsymbol{\beta}})$, and all quantities with an acute accent are evaluated at $\acute{\boldsymbol{\beta}}$. The test statistic (6.89) is a quadratic form in the vector $\acute{\boldsymbol{X}}_2^{\top} \boldsymbol{M}_{\acute{\boldsymbol{X}}_1} (\boldsymbol{y} - \acute{\boldsymbol{x}})$ and a matrix that estimates the inverse of its covariance matrix. It is easy to see that, given appropriate regularity conditions, it is asymptotically distributed as $\chi^2(r)$ under the null hypothesis.

It is possible to compute (6.89) by means of a modified GNR. Let $\acute{\boldsymbol{U}}$ be the $n \times n$ diagonal matrix with t^{th} diagonal element equal to $\acute{u}_t$. This implies that $\acute{\boldsymbol{U}} \acute{\boldsymbol{U}} = \acute{\boldsymbol{U}}^{\top} \acute{\boldsymbol{U}} = \acute{\boldsymbol{\Omega}}$. Then, for the alternative hypothesis (6.69), consider the artificial regression

$$\boldsymbol{\iota} = \boldsymbol{P}_{\acute{\boldsymbol{U}} \acute{\boldsymbol{X}}} \acute{\boldsymbol{U}}^{-1} \acute{\boldsymbol{X}} \boldsymbol{b} + \text{residuals}, \tag{6.90}$$

where, as usual, $\boldsymbol{\iota}$ is an n-vector each component of which equals 1, and $\acute{\boldsymbol{X}} = [\acute{\boldsymbol{X}}_1 \;\; \acute{\boldsymbol{X}}_2]$. The matrix $\boldsymbol{P}_{\acute{U}\acute{X}}$ is the orthogonal projection on to the k-dimensional space $\mathcal{S}(\acute{\boldsymbol{U}}\acute{\boldsymbol{X}})$. The matrix $\acute{\boldsymbol{U}}^{-1}$ is a diagonal matrix with t^{th} diagonal element equal to $\acute{u}_t^{-1}$. This is undefined if $\acute{u}_t = 0$. Therefore, in that event, it is necessary to replace $\acute{u}_t$ by a very small, positive number when constructing $\acute{\boldsymbol{U}}$.

The artificial regression (6.90) is called the **heteroskedasticity-robust Gauss-Newton regression**, or **HRGNR**. It has essentially the same properties as the ordinary GNR, except that it is valid when there is heteroskedasticity of unknown form. If we set $\acute{\boldsymbol{\beta}}$ equal to $\hat{\boldsymbol{\beta}}$, the vector of unrestricted estimates, the regressand $\boldsymbol{\iota}$ in (6.90) is seen to be orthogonal to all of the regressors. The transpose of the regressand times the matrix of regressors is

$$
\begin{aligned}
\boldsymbol{\iota}^{\top}\boldsymbol{P}_{\hat{U}\hat{X}}\hat{\boldsymbol{U}}^{-1}\hat{\boldsymbol{X}} &= \boldsymbol{\iota}^{\top}\hat{\boldsymbol{U}}\hat{\boldsymbol{X}}(\hat{\boldsymbol{X}}^{\top}\hat{\boldsymbol{U}}\hat{\boldsymbol{U}}\hat{\boldsymbol{X}})^{-1}\hat{\boldsymbol{X}}^{\top}\hat{\boldsymbol{U}}\hat{\boldsymbol{U}}^{-1}\hat{\boldsymbol{X}} \\
&= \hat{\boldsymbol{u}}^{\top}\hat{\boldsymbol{X}}(\hat{\boldsymbol{X}}^{\top}\hat{\boldsymbol{\Omega}}\hat{\boldsymbol{X}})^{-1}\hat{\boldsymbol{X}}^{\top}\hat{\boldsymbol{X}} \\
&= \mathbf{0}.
\end{aligned}
$$

The equality in the second line uses the facts that $\hat{\boldsymbol{U}}\boldsymbol{\iota} = \hat{\boldsymbol{u}}$, $\hat{\boldsymbol{U}}\hat{\boldsymbol{U}} = \hat{\boldsymbol{\Omega}}$, and $\hat{\boldsymbol{U}}\hat{\boldsymbol{U}}^{-1} = \mathbf{I}$. The one in the third line holds because the first-order conditions for NLS estimation are just $\hat{\boldsymbol{X}}^{\top}\hat{\boldsymbol{u}} = \mathbf{0}$. Thus, like the ordinary GNR, the HRGNR can be used to verify that parameter estimates satisfy the first-order conditions for NLS estimation.

When it is evaluated at any $\acute{\boldsymbol{\beta}}$ that is root-n consistent, the ordinary OLS covariance matrix from the HRGNR is an asymptotically valid HCCME. The TSS from regression (6.90) is $\boldsymbol{\iota}^{\top}\boldsymbol{\iota} = n$. Therefore, when $\acute{\boldsymbol{\beta}} = \hat{\boldsymbol{\beta}}$, the SSR is also n, and the OLS estimate of the error variance is $n/(n-k)$, which is asymptotically equal to 1. Even when $\acute{\boldsymbol{\beta}} \neq \hat{\boldsymbol{\beta}}$, the usual sort of calculation shows that the OLS estimate of the error variance from (6.90) is asymptotically equal to 1. Thus, except for the asymptotically negligible difference between $\acute{\sigma}^2$ and 1, the covariance matrix estimator from (6.90) is

$$
\begin{aligned}
(\acute{\boldsymbol{X}}^{\top}\acute{\boldsymbol{U}}^{-1}\boldsymbol{P}_{\acute{U}\acute{X}}\acute{\boldsymbol{U}}^{-1}\acute{\boldsymbol{X}})^{-1} &= \big(\acute{\boldsymbol{X}}^{\top}\acute{\boldsymbol{U}}^{-1}\acute{\boldsymbol{U}}\acute{\boldsymbol{X}}(\acute{\boldsymbol{X}}^{\top}\acute{\boldsymbol{U}}^{2}\acute{\boldsymbol{X}})^{-1}\acute{\boldsymbol{X}}^{\top}\acute{\boldsymbol{U}}\acute{\boldsymbol{U}}^{-1}\acute{\boldsymbol{X}}\big)^{-1} \\
&= \big(\acute{\boldsymbol{X}}^{\top}\acute{\boldsymbol{X}}(\acute{\boldsymbol{X}}^{\top}\acute{\boldsymbol{\Omega}}\acute{\boldsymbol{X}})^{-1}\acute{\boldsymbol{X}}^{\top}\acute{\boldsymbol{X}}\big)^{-1} \\
&= (\acute{\boldsymbol{X}}^{\top}\acute{\boldsymbol{X}})^{-1}\acute{\boldsymbol{X}}^{\top}\acute{\boldsymbol{\Omega}}\acute{\boldsymbol{X}}(\acute{\boldsymbol{X}}^{\top}\acute{\boldsymbol{X}})^{-1}.
\end{aligned}
$$

This sandwich covariance matrix estimator is just the HCCME (6.57) evaluated at $\acute{\boldsymbol{\beta}}$ instead of at $\hat{\boldsymbol{\beta}}$.

The HRGNR (6.90) also allows one-step estimation. Although this is of no practical interest, since it is easier to do one-step estimation with the ordinary GNR, it is essential that (6.90) should allow one-step estimation for tests based on it to be valid. Recall that the one-step property was necessary for our proof that statistics based on the ordinary GNR are valid. To avoid tedious asymptotic arguments, we will limit ourselves to showing that (6.90) allows one-step estimation for linear models. Extending the argument to nonlinear models is not difficult, but it would involve greater complication, chiefly notational. If we consider the linear regression model $\boldsymbol{y} = \boldsymbol{X\beta} + \boldsymbol{u}$, and evaluate the HRGNR (6.90) at an arbitrary $\acute{\boldsymbol{\beta}}$, we have

$$\acute{\boldsymbol{b}} = (\boldsymbol{X}^\top\acute{\boldsymbol{U}}^{-1}\boldsymbol{P}_{\acute{\boldsymbol{U}}\boldsymbol{X}}\acute{\boldsymbol{U}}^{-1}\boldsymbol{X})^{-1}\boldsymbol{X}^\top\acute{\boldsymbol{U}}^{-1}\boldsymbol{P}_{\acute{\boldsymbol{U}}\boldsymbol{X}}\boldsymbol{\iota}.$$

This can readily be seen to reduce to

$$\acute{\boldsymbol{b}} = (\boldsymbol{X}^\top\boldsymbol{X})^{-1}\boldsymbol{X}^\top\acute{\boldsymbol{u}} = (\boldsymbol{X}^\top\boldsymbol{X})^{-1}\boldsymbol{X}^\top(\boldsymbol{y} - \boldsymbol{X}\acute{\boldsymbol{\beta}}) = \hat{\boldsymbol{\beta}} - \acute{\boldsymbol{\beta}},$$

where $\hat{\boldsymbol{\beta}}$ is the OLS estimator. It follows that the one-step estimator $\acute{\boldsymbol{\beta}} + \acute{\boldsymbol{b}}$ is equal to $\hat{\boldsymbol{\beta}}$, as we wished to show.

In order to use the HRGNR to test the null hypothesis (6.68) against the alternative (6.69), allowing for heteroskedastic errors, we need to run two versions of it and compute the difference between the two SSRs, which is asymptotically distributed as $\chi^2(k_2)$. The two HRGNRs are

$$\text{HRGNR}_0\colon\ \boldsymbol{\iota} = \boldsymbol{P}_{\acute{\boldsymbol{U}}\acute{\boldsymbol{X}}}\acute{\boldsymbol{U}}^{-1}\acute{\boldsymbol{X}}_1\boldsymbol{b}_1 + \text{residuals, and} \tag{6.91}$$

$$\text{HRGNR}_1\colon\ \boldsymbol{\iota} = \boldsymbol{P}_{\acute{\boldsymbol{U}}\acute{\boldsymbol{X}}}\acute{\boldsymbol{U}}^{-1}\acute{\boldsymbol{X}}_1\boldsymbol{b}_1 + \boldsymbol{P}_{\acute{\boldsymbol{U}}\acute{\boldsymbol{X}}}\acute{\boldsymbol{U}}^{-1}\acute{\boldsymbol{X}}_2\boldsymbol{b}_2 + \text{residuals,} \tag{6.92}$$

where $\acute{\boldsymbol{\beta}}$ may be any root-n consistent estimator that satisfies the restrictions being tested. In many cases, it is convenient to set $\acute{\boldsymbol{\beta}} = \tilde{\boldsymbol{\beta}}$, the OLS estimates from (6.68). These equations are not hard to set up. The tth row of $\acute{\boldsymbol{U}}\acute{\boldsymbol{X}}$ is just the corresponding row of $\acute{\boldsymbol{X}}$ multiplied by $\acute{u}_t$, and the tth row of $\acute{\boldsymbol{U}}^{-1}\acute{\boldsymbol{X}}$ is just the corresponding row of $\acute{\boldsymbol{X}}$ divided by $\acute{u}_t$. It is never necessary to construct the $n \times n$ matrix $\acute{\boldsymbol{U}}$ at all.

The second of the two artificial regressions, (6.92), is simply regression (6.90) with the matrix $\acute{\boldsymbol{X}}$ explicitly partitioned. The first one, however, is *not* the HRGNR for the restricted model, because it uses the matrix $\boldsymbol{P}_{\acute{\boldsymbol{U}}\acute{\boldsymbol{X}}}$ rather than the matrix $\boldsymbol{P}_{\acute{\boldsymbol{U}}\acute{\boldsymbol{X}}_1}$. In consequence, even if we set $\acute{\boldsymbol{\beta}} = \tilde{\boldsymbol{\beta}}$, the regressand in (6.91) cannot be orthogonal to the regressors. This is why we need to run two artificial regressions. We could compute an ordinary F statistic instead of the difference between the SSRs from (6.91) and (6.92), but there would be no advantage to doing so, since the F form of the test merely divides by a stochastic quantity that tends to 1 asymptotically.

A different and more limited form of the HRGNR, which is applicable only to hypothesis testing, was first proposed by Davidson and MacKinnon (1985a); see Exercise 6.21. It was later rediscovered by Wooldridge (1990, 1991) and extended to handle other cases, including regression models with error terms that have autocorrelation of unknown form as well as heteroskedasticity of unknown form.

6.9 Final Remarks

In this chapter, we have dealt only with the estimation of nonlinear regression models by the method of moments and by nonlinear least squares. However, many of the results will reappear, in slightly different forms, when we consider estimation methods for other sorts of models. The NLS estimator is an **extremum estimator**, that is, an estimator obtained by minimizing or maximizing a criterion function. In the next few chapters, we will encounter several other extremum estimators: generalized least squares (Chapter 7), generalized instrumental variables (Chapter 8), the generalized method of moments (Chapter 9), and maximum likelihood (Chapter 10). Most of these estimators, like the NLS estimator, can be derived from the method of moments. All extremum estimators share a number of common features. Similar asymptotic results, and similar methods of proof, apply to all of them.

6.10 Exercises

6.1 Let the expectation of a random variable Y conditional on a set of other random variables $X_1, \ldots, X_k$ be the deterministic function $h(X_1, \ldots, X_k)$ of the conditioning variables. Let Ω be the information set consisting of all deterministic functions of the X_i, $i = 1, \ldots, k$. Show that $\mathrm{E}(Y \mid \Omega) = h(X_1, \ldots, X_k)$. **Hint:** Use the Law of Iterated Expectations for Ω and the information set defined by the X_i.

★6.2 Consider a model similar to (3.20), but with error terms that are normally distributed:

$$y_t = \beta_1 + \beta_2 1/t + u_t, \quad u_t \sim \mathrm{NID}(0, \sigma^2),$$

where $t = 1, 2, \ldots, n$. If the true value of β_2 is β_2^0 and $\hat{\beta}_2$ is the OLS estimator, show that the limit in probability of $\hat{\beta}_2 - \beta_2^0$ is a normal random variable with mean 0 and variance $6\sigma^2/\pi^2$. In order to obtain this result, you will need to use the results that

$$\sum_{t=1}^{\infty} (1/t)^2 = \pi^2/6,$$

and that, if $s(n) = \sum_{t=1}^{n} (1/t)$, then $\lim n^{-1} s(n) = 0$ and $\lim n^{-1} s^2(n) = 0$.

6.3 Show that the MM estimator defined by (6.10) depends on $\boldsymbol{W}$ only through the span $\mathcal{S}(\boldsymbol{W})$ of its columns. This is equivalent to showing that the estimator depends on $\boldsymbol{W}$ only through the orthogonal projection matrix $\boldsymbol{P_W}$.

6.4 Show algebraically that the first-order conditions for minimizing the SSR function (6.28) have the same solutions as the moment conditions (6.27).

6.5 Apply Taylor's Theorem to n^{-1} times the left-hand side of the moment conditions (6.27), expanding around the true parameter vector $\boldsymbol{\beta}_0$. Show that the extra term which appears here, but was absent in (6.20), tends to zero as $n \to \infty$. Make clear where and how you use a law of large numbers in your demonstration.

6.6 For the nonlinear regression model

$$y_t = \beta_1 z_t^{\beta_2} + u_t, \quad u_t \sim \text{IID}(0, \sigma^2),$$

write down the sum of squared residuals as a function of β_1, β_2, y_t, and z_t. Then differentiate it to obtain two first-order conditions. Show that these equations are equivalent to special cases of the moment conditions (6.27).

6.7 In each of the following regressions, y_t is the dependent variable, x_t and z_t are explanatory variables, and α, β, and γ are unknown parameters.

(a) $y_t = \alpha + \beta x_t + \gamma/x_t + u_t$
(b) $y_t = \alpha + \beta x_t + x_t/\gamma + u_t$
(c) $y_t = \alpha + \beta x_t + z_t/\gamma + u_t$
(d) $y_t = \alpha + \beta x_t + z_t/\beta + u_t$
(e) $y_t = \alpha + \beta x_t z_t + u_t$
(f) $y_t = \alpha + \beta\gamma x_t z_t + \gamma z_t + u_t$
(g) $y_t = \alpha + \beta\gamma x_t + \gamma z_t + u_t$
(h) $y_t = \alpha + \beta x_t + \beta x_t^2 + u_t$
(i) $y_t = \alpha + \beta x_t + \gamma x_t^2 + u_t$
(j) $y_t = \alpha + \beta\gamma x_t^3 + u_t$
(k) $y_t = \alpha + \beta x_t + (1 - \beta) z_t + u_t$
(l) $y_t = \alpha + \beta x_t + (\gamma - \beta) z_t + u_t$

For each of these regressions, is it possible to obtain a least-squares estimator of the parameters? In other words, is each of these models identified? If not, explain why not. If so, can the estimator be obtained by ordinary (that is, linear) least squares? If it can, write down the regressand and regressors for the linear regression to be used.

★6.8 Show that a Taylor expansion to second order of an NLS residual gives

$$\hat{u}_t = u_t - \boldsymbol{X}_t(\boldsymbol{\beta}_0)(\hat{\boldsymbol{\beta}} - \boldsymbol{\beta}_0) - \tfrac{1}{2}(\hat{\boldsymbol{\beta}} - \boldsymbol{\beta}_0)^\top \bar{\boldsymbol{H}}_t(\hat{\boldsymbol{\beta}} - \boldsymbol{\beta}_0), \tag{6.93}$$

where $\boldsymbol{\beta}_0$ is the parameter vector of the DGP, and the $k \times k$ matrix $\bar{\boldsymbol{H}}_t \equiv \boldsymbol{H}_t(\bar{\boldsymbol{\beta}})$ is the matrix of second derivatives with respect to $\boldsymbol{\beta}$ of the regression function $x_t(\boldsymbol{\beta})$, evaluated at some $\bar{\boldsymbol{\beta}}$ that satisfies (6.19).

Define $\boldsymbol{b} \equiv n^{1/2}(\hat{\boldsymbol{\beta}} - \boldsymbol{\beta}_0)$. As $n \to \infty$, $\boldsymbol{b}$ tends to the normal random variable $\text{plim}(n^{-1}\boldsymbol{X}_0^\top\boldsymbol{X}_0)^{-1} n^{-1/2}\boldsymbol{X}_0^\top\boldsymbol{u}$. By expressing equation (6.93) in terms of $\boldsymbol{b}$, show that the difference between $\hat{\boldsymbol{u}}^\top\hat{\boldsymbol{u}}$ and $\boldsymbol{u}^\top\boldsymbol{M}_{\boldsymbol{X}_0}\boldsymbol{u}$ tends to 0 as $n \to \infty$. Here $\boldsymbol{M}_{\boldsymbol{X}_0} \equiv \mathbf{I} - \boldsymbol{P}_{\boldsymbol{X}_0}$ is the orthogonal projection on to $\mathcal{S}^\perp(\boldsymbol{X}_0)$.

6.9 Using the result (6.40) on NLS residuals, show that the F statistic computed using the sums of squared residuals from the two GNRs (6.80) and (6.81) is asymptotically equivalent to the F statistic computed using the sums of squared residuals from the nonlinear regressions (6.68) and (6.69).

6.10 Consider a linear regression with AR(2) errors. This can be written as

$$y_t = \boldsymbol{X}_t\boldsymbol{\beta} + u_t, \quad u_t = \rho_1 u_{t-1} + \rho_2 u_{t-2} + \varepsilon_t, \quad \varepsilon_t \sim \text{IID}(0, \sigma^2).$$

Explain how to test the null hypothesis that $\rho_1 = \rho_2 = 0$ by means of a GNR.

6.11 Consider again the ADL model (3.71) of Exercise 3.23, which is reproduced here with a minor notational change:

$$c_t = \alpha + \beta c_{t-1} + \gamma_0 y_t + \gamma_1 y_{t-1} + \varepsilon_t. \tag{6.94}$$

Recall that c_t and y_t are the logarithms of consumption and income, respectively. Show that this model contains as a special case the following linear model with AR(1) errors:

$$c_t = \delta_0 + \delta_1 y_t + u_t, \quad \text{with} \quad u_t = \rho u_{t-1} + \varepsilon_t, \tag{6.95}$$

where ε_t is IID. Write down the relation between the parameters δ_0, δ_1, and ρ of this model and the parameters α, β, γ_0, and γ_1 of (6.94). How many and what restrictions are imposed on the latter set of parameters by the model (6.95)?

6.12 Using the data in the file **consumption.data**, estimate the nonlinear model defined implicitly by (6.95) for the period 1953:1 to 1996:4 by nonlinear least squares. Since pre-sample data are available, you should use all 176 observations for the estimation. Do not use a specialized procedure for AR(1) estimation. For starting values, use the estimates of δ_0, δ_1, and ρ implied by the OLS estimates of equation (6.94). Finding them requires the solution to the previous exercise.

Repeat this exercise, using 0 as the starting value for all three parameters. Does the algorithm converge as rapidly as it did before? Do you obtain the same estimates? If not, which ones are actually the NLS estimates?

Test the restrictions that the nonlinear model imposes on the model (6.94) by means of an asymptotic F test.

6.13 Using the estimates of the model (6.95) from the previous question, generate a single set of simulated data c_t^* for the period 1953:1 to 1996:4. The simulation should be conditional on the pre-sample value (that is, the value for 1952:4) of log consumption. Do this in two different ways. First, generate error terms u_t^* that follow an AR(1) process, and then generate the c_t^* in terms of these u_t^*. Next, perform the simulation directly in terms of the innovations ε_t^*, using the nonlinear model obtained by imposing the appropriate restrictions on (6.94). Show that, if you use the same realizations for the ε_t^*, the simulated values c_t^* are identical. Estimate the model (6.95) using your simulated data.

6.14 The nonlinear model obtained from (6.95) has just three parameters: δ_0, δ_1, and ρ. It can therefore be estimated by the method of moments using three exogenous or predetermined variables. Estimate the model using the constant and the three possible choices of two variables from the set of nonconstant explanatory variables in (6.94).

6.15 Formulate a GNR, based on estimates under the null hypothesis, that allows you to use a t test to test the restriction imposed on the model (6.94) by the model (6.95). Compare the P value for this (asymptotic) t test with the one for the F test of Exercise 6.12.

6.16 Starting from the unconstrained estimates provided by (6.94), obtain one-step efficient estimates of the parameters of (6.95) using the GNR associated with that model. Use the GNR iteratively so as to approach the true NLS estimates more closely, until such time as the sum of squared residuals from the GNR is within 10^{-8} of the one obtained by NLS estimation. Compare the number of iterations of this GNR-based procedure with the number used by the NLS algorithm of your software package.

6.17 Formulate a GNR, based on estimates under the alternative hypothesis, to test the restriction imposed on the model (6.94) by the model (6.95). Your test procedure should just require two OLS regressions.

6.18 Using 199 bootstrap samples, compute a parametric bootstrap P value for the test statistic obtained in Exercise 6.17. Assume that the error terms are normally distributed.

6.19 Test the hypothesis that $\gamma_0 + \gamma_1 = 0$ in (6.94). Do this in three different ways, two of which are valid in the presence of heteroskedasticity of unknown form.

6.20 For the nonlinear regression model defined implicitly by (6.95) and estimated using the data in the file **consumption.data**, perform three different tests of the hypothesis that all the coefficients are the same for the two subsamples 1953:1 to 1970:4 and 1971:1 to 1996:4. Firstly, use an asymptotic F test based on nonlinear estimation of both the restricted and unrestricted models. Secondly, use an asymptotic F test based on a GNR which requires nonlinear estimation only under the null. Finally, use a test that is robust to heteroskedasticity of unknown form. **Hint:** See regressions (6.91) and (6.92).

6.21 The original HRGNR proposed by Davidson and MacKinnon (1985a) is

$$\boldsymbol{\iota} = \acute{\boldsymbol{U}} \boldsymbol{M}_{\acute{\boldsymbol{X}}_1} \acute{\boldsymbol{X}}_2 \boldsymbol{b}_2 + \text{residuals}, \tag{6.96}$$

where $\acute{\boldsymbol{U}}$, $\acute{\boldsymbol{X}}_1$, and $\acute{\boldsymbol{X}}_2$ are as defined in Section 6.8, $\boldsymbol{b}_2$ is a k_2–vector, and $\boldsymbol{M}_{\acute{\boldsymbol{X}}_1}$ is the matrix that projects orthogonally on to $\mathcal{S}^{\perp}(\acute{\boldsymbol{X}}_1)$. The test statistic for the null hypothesis that $\boldsymbol{\beta}_2 = \mathbf{0}$ is n minus the SSR from regression (6.96).

Use regression (6.96), where all the matrices are evaluated at restricted NLS estimates, to retest the hypothesis of the previous question. Comment on the relationship between the test statistic you obtain and the heteroskedasticity-robust test statistic of the previous question that was based on regressions (6.91) and (6.92).

6.22 Suppose that $\boldsymbol{P}$ is a projection matrix with rank r. Without loss of generality, we can assume that $\boldsymbol{P}$ projects on to the span of the columns of an $n \times r$ matrix $\boldsymbol{Z}$. Suppose further that the n–vector $\boldsymbol{z}$ is distributed as $\text{IID}(\mathbf{0}, \sigma^2 \mathbf{I})$. Show that the quadratic form $\boldsymbol{z}^\top \boldsymbol{P} \boldsymbol{z}$ follows the $\chi^2(r)$ distribution asymptotically as $n \to \infty$. (**Hint:** See the proof of Theorem 4.1.)

Chapter 7

Generalized Least Squares and Related Topics

7.1 Introduction

If the parameters of a regression model are to be estimated efficiently by least squares, the error terms must be uncorrelated and have the same variance. These assumptions are needed to prove the Gauss-Markov Theorem and to show that the nonlinear least squares estimator is asymptotically efficient; see Sections 3.5 and 6.3. Moreover, the usual estimators of the covariance matrices of the OLS and NLS estimators are not valid when these assumptions do not hold, although alternative "sandwich" covariance matrix estimators that are asymptotically valid may be available (see Sections 5.5, 6.5, and 6.8). Thus it is clear that we need new estimation methods to handle regression models with error terms that are heteroskedastic, serially correlated, or both. We develop some of these methods in this chapter.

Since heteroskedasticity and serial correlation affect both linear and nonlinear regression models in the same way, there is no harm in limiting our attention to the simpler, linear case. We will be concerned with the model

$$\boldsymbol{y} = \boldsymbol{X\beta} + \boldsymbol{u}, \quad \mathrm{E}(\boldsymbol{u}\boldsymbol{u}^\top) = \boldsymbol{\Omega}, \tag{7.01}$$

where $\boldsymbol{\Omega}$, the covariance matrix of the error terms, is a positive definite $n \times n$ matrix. If $\boldsymbol{\Omega}$ is equal to $\sigma^2\mathbf{I}$, then (7.01) is just the linear regression model (3.03), with error terms that are uncorrelated and homoskedastic. If $\boldsymbol{\Omega}$ is diagonal with nonconstant diagonal elements, then the error terms are still uncorrelated, but they are heteroskedastic. If $\boldsymbol{\Omega}$ is not diagonal, then u_i and u_j are correlated whenever Ω_{ij}, the ij^{th} element of $\boldsymbol{\Omega}$, is nonzero. In econometrics, covariance matrices that are not diagonal are most commonly encountered with time-series data, and the correlations are usually highest for observations that are close in time.

In the next section, we obtain an efficient estimator for the vector $\boldsymbol{\beta}$ in the model (7.01) by transforming the regression so that it satisfies the conditions of the Gauss-Markov theorem. This efficient estimator is called the **generalized least squares**, or **GLS**, estimator. Although it is easy to write down the GLS estimator, it is not always easy to compute it. In Section 7.3, we therefore discuss ways of computing GLS estimates, including the particularly simple case of weighted least squares. In the following section, we relax the often implausible assumption that the matrix $\boldsymbol{\Omega}$ is completely known. Section 7.5 discusses some aspects of heteroskedasticity. Sections 7.6 through 7.9 deal with various aspects of serial correlation, including autoregressive and moving-average processes, testing for serial correlation, GLS and NLS estimation of models with serially correlated errors, and specification tests for models with serially correlated errors. Finally, Section 7.10 discusses error-components models for panel data.

7.2 The GLS Estimator

In order to obtain an efficient estimator of the parameter vector $\boldsymbol{\beta}$ of the linear regression model (7.01), we transform the model so that the transformed model satisfies the conditions of the Gauss-Markov theorem. Estimating the transformed model by OLS therefore yields efficient estimates. The transformation is expressed in terms of an $n \times n$ matrix $\boldsymbol{\Psi}$, which is usually triangular, that satisfies the equation

$$\boldsymbol{\Omega}^{-1} = \boldsymbol{\Psi}\boldsymbol{\Psi}^{\top}. \tag{7.02}$$

As we discussed in Section 3.4, such a matrix can always be found, often by using Crout's algorithm. Premultiplying (7.01) by $\boldsymbol{\Psi}^{\top}$ gives

$$\boldsymbol{\Psi}^{\top}\boldsymbol{y} = \boldsymbol{\Psi}^{\top}\boldsymbol{X}\boldsymbol{\beta} + \boldsymbol{\Psi}^{\top}\boldsymbol{u}. \tag{7.03}$$

Because the covariance matrix $\boldsymbol{\Omega}$ is nonsingular, the matrix $\boldsymbol{\Psi}$ must be as well, and so the transformed regression model (7.03) is perfectly equivalent to the original model (7.01). The OLS estimator of $\boldsymbol{\beta}$ from regression (7.03) is

$$\hat{\boldsymbol{\beta}}_{\mathrm{GLS}} = (\boldsymbol{X}^{\top}\boldsymbol{\Psi}\boldsymbol{\Psi}^{\top}\boldsymbol{X})^{-1}\boldsymbol{X}^{\top}\boldsymbol{\Psi}\boldsymbol{\Psi}^{\top}\boldsymbol{y} = (\boldsymbol{X}^{\top}\boldsymbol{\Omega}^{-1}\boldsymbol{X})^{-1}\boldsymbol{X}^{\top}\boldsymbol{\Omega}^{-1}\boldsymbol{y}. \tag{7.04}$$

This estimator is called the **generalized least squares**, or **GLS**, estimator of $\boldsymbol{\beta}$. It is not difficult to show that the covariance matrix of the transformed error vector $\boldsymbol{\Psi}^{\top}\boldsymbol{u}$ is simply the identity matrix:

$$\begin{aligned}\mathrm{E}(\boldsymbol{\Psi}^{\top}\boldsymbol{u}\boldsymbol{u}^{\top}\boldsymbol{\Psi}) &= \boldsymbol{\Psi}^{\top}\mathrm{E}(\boldsymbol{u}\boldsymbol{u}^{\top})\boldsymbol{\Psi} = \boldsymbol{\Psi}^{\top}\boldsymbol{\Omega}\boldsymbol{\Psi}\\ &= \boldsymbol{\Psi}^{\top}(\boldsymbol{\Psi}\boldsymbol{\Psi}^{\top})^{-1}\boldsymbol{\Psi} = \boldsymbol{\Psi}^{\top}(\boldsymbol{\Psi}^{\top})^{-1}\boldsymbol{\Psi}^{-1}\boldsymbol{\Psi} = \mathbf{I}.\end{aligned}$$

The second equality in the second line here uses a result about the inverse of a product of square matrices that was proved in Exercise 1.17.

Since $\hat{\boldsymbol{\beta}}_{\mathrm{GLS}}$ is just the OLS estimator from (7.03), its covariance matrix can be found directly from the standard formula for the OLS covariance matrix, expression (3.28), if we replace $\boldsymbol{X}$ by $\boldsymbol{\Psi}^{\top}\boldsymbol{X}$ and σ_0^2 by 1:

$$\mathrm{Var}(\hat{\boldsymbol{\beta}}_{\mathrm{GLS}}) = (\boldsymbol{X}^{\top}\boldsymbol{\Psi}\boldsymbol{\Psi}^{\top}\boldsymbol{X})^{-1} = (\boldsymbol{X}^{\top}\boldsymbol{\Omega}^{-1}\boldsymbol{X})^{-1}. \tag{7.05}$$

In order for (7.05) to be valid, the conditions of the Gauss-Markov theorem must be satisfied. Here, this means that $\boldsymbol{\Omega}$ must be the covariance matrix of $\boldsymbol{u}$ *conditional* on the explanatory variables $\boldsymbol{X}$. It is thus permissible for $\boldsymbol{\Omega}$ to depend on $\boldsymbol{X}$, or indeed on any other exogenous variables.

The generalized least squares estimator $\hat{\boldsymbol{\beta}}_{\rm GLS}$ can also be obtained by minimizing the **GLS criterion function**

$$(\boldsymbol{y} - \boldsymbol{X\beta})^{\top}\boldsymbol{\Omega}^{-1}(\boldsymbol{y} - \boldsymbol{X\beta}), \tag{7.06}$$

which is just the sum of squared residuals from the transformed regression (7.03). This criterion function can be thought of as a generalization of the SSR function in which the squares and cross products of the residuals from the original regression (7.01) are weighted by the inverse of the matrix $\boldsymbol{\Omega}$. The effect of such a weighting scheme is clearest when $\boldsymbol{\Omega}$ is a diagonal matrix: In that case, each observation is simply given a weight proportional to the inverse of the variance of its error term.

Efficiency of the GLS Estimator

The GLS estimator $\hat{\boldsymbol{\beta}}_{\rm GLS}$ defined in (7.04) is also the solution of the set of moment conditions

$$\boldsymbol{X}^{\top}\boldsymbol{\Omega}^{-1}(\boldsymbol{y} - \boldsymbol{X}\hat{\boldsymbol{\beta}}_{\rm GLS}) = \boldsymbol{0}. \tag{7.07}$$

These moment conditions are equivalent to the first-order conditions for the minimization of the GLS criterion function (7.06).

Since the GLS estimator is a method-of-moments estimator, it is interesting to compare it with other MM estimators. A general MM estimator for the linear regression model (7.01) is defined in terms of an $n \times k$ matrix of exogenous variables $\boldsymbol{W}$, where k is the dimension of $\boldsymbol{\beta}$, by the equations

$$\boldsymbol{W}^{\top}(\boldsymbol{y} - \boldsymbol{X\beta}) = \boldsymbol{0}. \tag{7.08}$$

These equations are a special case of the moment conditions (6.10) for the nonlinear regression model. Since there are k equations and k unknowns, we can solve (7.08) to obtain the MM estimator

$$\hat{\boldsymbol{\beta}}_{\boldsymbol{W}} \equiv (\boldsymbol{W}^{\top}\boldsymbol{X})^{-1}\boldsymbol{W}^{\top}\boldsymbol{y}. \tag{7.09}$$

The GLS estimator (7.04) is evidently a special case of this MM estimator, with $\boldsymbol{W} = \boldsymbol{\Omega}^{-1}\boldsymbol{X}$.

Under certain assumptions, the MM estimator (7.09) is unbiased for the model (7.01). Suppose that the DGP is a special case of that model, with parameter vector $\boldsymbol{\beta}_0$ and known covariance matrix $\boldsymbol{\Omega}$. We assume that $\boldsymbol{X}$ and $\boldsymbol{W}$ are exogenous, which implies that $\mathrm{E}(\boldsymbol{u} \,|\, \boldsymbol{X}, \boldsymbol{W}) = \boldsymbol{0}$. This rather strong assumption, which is analogous to the assumption (3.08), is necessary for the unbiasedness of $\hat{\boldsymbol{\beta}}_{\boldsymbol{W}}$ and makes it unnecessary to resort to asymptotic analysis. If we merely wanted to prove that $\hat{\boldsymbol{\beta}}_{\boldsymbol{W}}$ is consistent, we could, as in Section 6.2, get away with the much weaker assumption that $\mathrm{E}(u_t \mid \boldsymbol{W}_t) = 0$.

Substituting $\boldsymbol{X}\boldsymbol{\beta}_0 + \boldsymbol{u}$ for $\boldsymbol{y}$ in (7.09), we see that

$$\hat{\boldsymbol{\beta}}_{\boldsymbol{W}} = \boldsymbol{\beta}_0 + (\boldsymbol{W}^\top\boldsymbol{X})^{-1}\boldsymbol{W}^\top\boldsymbol{u}.$$

Therefore, the covariance matrix of $\hat{\boldsymbol{\beta}}_{\boldsymbol{W}}$ is

$$\begin{aligned}\mathrm{Var}(\hat{\boldsymbol{\beta}}_{\boldsymbol{W}}) &= \mathrm{E}\big((\hat{\boldsymbol{\beta}}_{\boldsymbol{W}} - \boldsymbol{\beta}_0)(\hat{\boldsymbol{\beta}}_{\boldsymbol{W}} - \boldsymbol{\beta}_0)^\top\big)\\ &= \mathrm{E}\big((\boldsymbol{W}^\top\boldsymbol{X})^{-1}\boldsymbol{W}^\top\boldsymbol{u}\boldsymbol{u}^\top\boldsymbol{W}(\boldsymbol{X}^\top\boldsymbol{W})^{-1}\big) \qquad (7.10)\\ &= (\boldsymbol{W}^\top\boldsymbol{X})^{-1}\boldsymbol{W}^\top\boldsymbol{\Omega}\boldsymbol{W}(\boldsymbol{X}^\top\boldsymbol{W})^{-1}.\end{aligned}$$

As we would expect, this is a sandwich covariance matrix. When $\boldsymbol{W} = \boldsymbol{X}$, we have the OLS estimator, and $\mathrm{Var}(\hat{\boldsymbol{\beta}}_{\boldsymbol{W}})$ reduces to expression (5.32).

The efficiency of the GLS estimator can be verified by showing that the difference between (7.10), the covariance matrix for the MM estimator $\hat{\boldsymbol{\beta}}_{\boldsymbol{W}}$ defined in (7.09), and (7.05), the covariance matrix for the GLS estimator, is a positive semidefinite matrix. As was shown in Exercise 3.8, this difference is positive semidefinite if and only if the difference between the inverse of (7.05) and the inverse of (7.10), that is, the matrix

$$\boldsymbol{X}^\top\boldsymbol{\Omega}^{-1}\boldsymbol{X} - \boldsymbol{X}^\top\boldsymbol{W}(\boldsymbol{W}^\top\boldsymbol{\Omega}\boldsymbol{W})^{-1}\boldsymbol{W}^\top\boldsymbol{X}, \qquad (7.11)$$

is positive semidefinite. In exercise 7.2, readers are invited to show that this is indeed the case.

The GLS estimator $\hat{\boldsymbol{\beta}}_{\mathrm{GLS}}$ is typically more efficient than the more general MM estimator $\hat{\boldsymbol{\beta}}_{\boldsymbol{W}}$ for all elements of $\boldsymbol{\beta}$, because it is only in very special cases that the matrix (7.11) has any zero diagonal elements. Because the OLS estimator $\hat{\boldsymbol{\beta}}$ is just $\hat{\boldsymbol{\beta}}_{\boldsymbol{W}}$ when $\boldsymbol{W} = \boldsymbol{X}$, we conclude that the GLS estimator $\hat{\boldsymbol{\beta}}_{\mathrm{GLS}}$ in most cases is more efficient, and is never less efficient, than the OLS estimator $\hat{\boldsymbol{\beta}}$.

7.3 Computing GLS Estimates

At first glance, the formula (7.04) for the GLS estimator seems quite simple. To calculate $\hat{\boldsymbol{\beta}}_{\mathrm{GLS}}$ when $\boldsymbol{\Omega}$ is known, we apparently just have to invert $\boldsymbol{\Omega}$, form the matrix $\boldsymbol{X}^\top\boldsymbol{\Omega}^{-1}\boldsymbol{X}$ and invert it, then form the vector $\boldsymbol{X}^\top\boldsymbol{\Omega}^{-1}\boldsymbol{y}$, and, finally, postmultiply the inverse of $\boldsymbol{X}^\top\boldsymbol{\Omega}^{-1}\boldsymbol{X}$ by $\boldsymbol{X}^\top\boldsymbol{\Omega}^{-1}\boldsymbol{y}$. However, GLS estimation is not nearly as easy as it looks. The procedure just described may work acceptably when the sample size n is small, but it rapidly becomes computationally infeasible as n becomes large. The problem is that $\boldsymbol{\Omega}$ is an $n \times n$ matrix. When $n = 1000$, simply storing $\boldsymbol{\Omega}$ and its inverse typically requires 16 MB of memory; when $n = 10{,}000$, storing both these matrices requires 1600 MB. Even if enough memory were available, computing GLS estimates in this naive way would be enormously expensive.

Practical procedures for GLS estimation require us to know quite a lot about the structure of the covariance matrix $\boldsymbol{\Omega}$ and its inverse. GLS estimation is easy to do if the matrix $\boldsymbol{\Psi}$, defined in (7.02), is known and has a form that allows us to calculate $\boldsymbol{\Psi}^\top\boldsymbol{x}$, for any vector $\boldsymbol{x}$, without having to store $\boldsymbol{\Psi}$ itself in memory. If so, we can easily formulate the transformed model (7.03) and estimate it by OLS.

There is one important difference between (7.03) and the usual linear regression model. For the latter, the variance of the error terms is unknown, while for the former, it is known to be 1. Since we can obtain OLS estimates without knowing the variance of the error terms, this suggests that we should not need to know everything about $\boldsymbol{\Omega}$ in order to obtain GLS estimates. Suppose that $\boldsymbol{\Omega} = \sigma^2\boldsymbol{\Delta}$, where the $n \times n$ matrix $\boldsymbol{\Delta}$ is known to the investigator, but the positive scalar σ^2 is unknown. Then if we replace $\boldsymbol{\Omega}$ by $\boldsymbol{\Delta}$ in the definition (7.02) of $\boldsymbol{\Psi}$, we can still run regression (7.03), but the error terms now have variance σ^2 instead of variance 1. When we run this modified regression, we obtain the estimate

$$(\boldsymbol{X}^\top\boldsymbol{\Delta}^{-1}\boldsymbol{X})^{-1}\boldsymbol{X}^\top\boldsymbol{\Delta}^{-1}\boldsymbol{y} = (\boldsymbol{X}^\top\boldsymbol{\Omega}^{-1}\boldsymbol{X})^{-1}\boldsymbol{X}^\top\boldsymbol{\Omega}^{-1}\boldsymbol{y} = \hat{\boldsymbol{\beta}}_{\text{GLS}},$$

where the equality follows immediately from the fact that $\sigma^2/\sigma^2 = 1$. Thus the GLS estimates are the same whether we use $\boldsymbol{\Omega}$ or $\boldsymbol{\Delta}$, that is, whether or not we know σ^2. However, if σ^2 is known, we can use the true covariance matrix (7.05). Otherwise, we must fall back on the estimated covariance matrix

$$\widehat{\text{Var}}(\hat{\boldsymbol{\beta}}_{\text{GLS}}) = s^2(\boldsymbol{X}^\top\boldsymbol{\Delta}^{-1}\boldsymbol{X})^{-1},$$

where s^2 is the usual OLS estimate (3.49) of the error variance from the transformed regression.

Weighted Least Squares

It is particularly easy to obtain GLS estimates when the error terms are heteroskedastic but uncorrelated. This implies that the matrix $\boldsymbol{\Omega}$ is diagonal. Let ω_t^2 denote the tth diagonal element of $\boldsymbol{\Omega}$. Then $\boldsymbol{\Omega}^{-1}$ is a diagonal matrix with t^{th} diagonal element ω_t^{-2}, and $\boldsymbol{\Psi}$ can be chosen as the diagonal matrix with t^{th} diagonal element ω_t^{-1}. Thus we see that, for a typical observation, regression (7.03) can be written as

$$\omega_t^{-1}y_t = \omega_t^{-1}\boldsymbol{X}_t\boldsymbol{\beta} + \omega_t^{-1}u_t. \tag{7.12}$$

This regression is to be estimated by OLS. The regressand and regressors are simply the dependent and independent variables multiplied by ω_t^{-1}, and the variance of the error term is clearly 1.

For obvious reasons, this special case of GLS estimation is often called **weighted least squares**, or **WLS**. The weight given to each observation when we run regression (7.12) is ω_t^{-1}. Observations for which the variance of the error term is large are given low weights, and observations for which it is small are given high weights. In practice, if $\boldsymbol{\Omega} = \sigma^2\boldsymbol{\Delta}$, with $\boldsymbol{\Delta}$ known but σ^2 unknown, regression (7.12) remains valid, provided we reinterpret ω_t^2 as the tth diagonal element of $\boldsymbol{\Delta}$ and recognize that the variance of the error terms is now σ^2 instead of 1.

There are various ways of determining the weights to be used in weighted least squares estimation. In the simplest case, either theory or preliminary testing may suggest that $\mathrm{E}(u_t^2)$ is proportional to z_t^2, where z_t is some variable that we observe. For instance, z_t might be a variable like population or national income. In this case, z_t plays the role of ω_t in equation (7.12), because we want to weight the tth observation by z_t^{-1}. Another possibility is that the data we actually observe were obtained by grouping data on different numbers of individual units. For example, suppose that the error terms for the ungrouped data have constant variance, but that observation t is the average of N_t individual observations, where N_t varies. Special cases of standard results on the variance of a sample mean, which were discussed in Section 3.4, imply that the variance of u_t must then be proportional to $1/N_t$. Thus, in this case, $N_t^{1/2}$ plays the role of ω_t^{-1} in equation (7.12). If the grouped data were sums instead of averages, the variance of u_t would be proportional to N_t, and $N_t^{-1/2}$ would play the role of ω_t^{-1}.

Weighted least squares estimation can easily be performed using any program for OLS estimation. When one is using such a procedure, it is important to remember that all the variables in the regression, including the constant term, must be multiplied by the same weights. Thus if, for example, the original regression is

$$y_t = \beta_1 + \beta_2 x_t + u_t,$$

the weighted regression is

$$y_t/\omega_t = \beta_1(1/\omega_t) + \beta_2(x_t/\omega_t) + u_t/\omega_t.$$

Here the regressand is y_t/ω_t, the regressor that corresponds to the constant term is $1/\omega_t$, and the regressor that corresponds to x_t is x_t/ω_t.

It is possible to report summary statistics like R^2, ESS, and SSR either in terms of the dependent variable y_t or in terms of the transformed regressand y_t/ω_t. However, it really only makes sense to report R^2 in terms of the transformed regressand. As we saw in Section 2.5, R^2 is valid as a measure of goodness of fit only when the residuals are orthogonal to the fitted values. This is true for the residuals and fitted values from OLS estimation of the weighted regression (7.12), but it is not true if those residuals and fitted values are subsequently multiplied by the ω_t in order to make them comparable with the original dependent variable.

Generalized Nonlinear Least Squares

Although, for simplicity, we have focused on the linear regression model, GLS is also applicable to nonlinear regression models. If the vector of regression functions were $\boldsymbol{x}(\boldsymbol{\beta})$ instead of $\boldsymbol{X\beta}$, we could obtain **generalized nonlinear least squares**, or **GNLS**, estimates by minimizing the criterion function

$$\big(\boldsymbol{y} - \boldsymbol{x}(\boldsymbol{\beta})\big)^{\top}\boldsymbol{\Omega}^{-1}\big(\boldsymbol{y} - \boldsymbol{x}(\boldsymbol{\beta})\big), \tag{7.13}$$

which looks just like the GLS criterion function (7.06) for the linear regression model, except that $\boldsymbol{x}(\boldsymbol{\beta})$ replaces $\boldsymbol{X\beta}$. If we differentiate (7.13) with respect to $\boldsymbol{\beta}$ and divide the result by -2, we obtain the moment conditions

$$\boldsymbol{X}^{\top}(\boldsymbol{\beta})\boldsymbol{\Omega}^{-1}\big(\boldsymbol{y} - \boldsymbol{x}(\boldsymbol{\beta})\big) = \mathbf{0}, \tag{7.14}$$

where, as in Chapter 6, $\boldsymbol{X}(\boldsymbol{\beta})$ is the matrix of derivatives of $\boldsymbol{x}(\boldsymbol{\beta})$ with respect to $\boldsymbol{\beta}$. These moment conditions generalize conditions (6.27) for nonlinear least squares in the obvious way, and they are evidently equivalent to the moment conditions (7.07) for the linear case.

Finding estimates that solve equations (7.14) requires some sort of nonlinear minimization procedure; see Section 6.4. For this purpose, and several others, the GNR

$$\boldsymbol{\Psi}^{\top}\big(\boldsymbol{y} - \boldsymbol{x}(\boldsymbol{\beta})\big) = \boldsymbol{\Psi}^{\top}\boldsymbol{X}(\boldsymbol{\beta})\boldsymbol{b} + \text{residuals}. \tag{7.15}$$

is often useful. Equation (7.15) is just the ordinary GNR introduced in equation (6.52), with the regressand and regressors premultiplied by the matrix $\boldsymbol{\Psi}^{\top}$ implicitly defined in equation (7.02). It is the GNR associated with the nonlinear regression model

$$\boldsymbol{\Psi}^{\top}\boldsymbol{y} = \boldsymbol{\Psi}^{\top}\boldsymbol{x}(\boldsymbol{\beta}) + \boldsymbol{\Psi}^{\top}\boldsymbol{u}, \tag{7.16}$$

which is analogous to (7.03). The error terms of (7.16) have covariance matrix proportional to the identity matrix.

Let us denote the tth column of the matrix $\boldsymbol{\Psi}$ by $\boldsymbol{\psi}_t$. Then the asymptotic theory of Chapter 6 for the nonlinear regression model and the ordinary GNR applies also to the transformed regression model (7.16) and its associated GNR (7.15), provided that the *transformed* regression functions $\boldsymbol{\psi}_t^{\top}\boldsymbol{x}(\boldsymbol{\beta})$ are predetermined with respect to the *transformed* error terms $\boldsymbol{\psi}_t^{\top}\boldsymbol{u}$:

$$\mathrm{E}\big(\boldsymbol{\psi}_t^{\top}\boldsymbol{u} \,|\, \boldsymbol{\psi}_t^{\top}\boldsymbol{x}(\boldsymbol{\beta})\big) = 0. \tag{7.17}$$

If $\boldsymbol{\Psi}$ is not a diagonal matrix, this condition is different from the condition that the regression functions $x_t(\boldsymbol{\beta})$ should be predetermined with respect to the u_t. Later in this chapter, we will see that this fact has serious repercussions in models with serial correlation.

7.4 Feasible Generalized Least Squares

In practice, the covariance matrix $\boldsymbol{\Omega}$ is often not known even up to a scalar factor. This makes it impossible to compute GLS estimates. However, in many cases it is reasonable to suppose that $\boldsymbol{\Omega}$, or $\boldsymbol{\Delta}$, depends in a known way on a vector of unknown parameters γ. If so, it may be possible to estimate γ consistently, so as to obtain $\boldsymbol{\Omega}(\hat{\gamma})$, say. Then $\boldsymbol{\Psi}(\hat{\gamma})$ can be defined as in (7.02), and GLS estimates computed conditional on $\boldsymbol{\Psi}(\hat{\gamma})$. This type of procedure is called **feasible generalized least squares**, or **feasible GLS**, because it is feasible in many cases when ordinary GLS is not.

As a simple example, suppose we want to obtain feasible GLS estimates of the linear regression model

$$y_t = \boldsymbol{X}_t\boldsymbol{\beta} + u_t, \quad \mathrm{E}(u_t^2) = \exp(\boldsymbol{Z}_t\gamma), \tag{7.18}$$

where $\boldsymbol{\beta}$ and γ are, respectively, a k-vector and an l-vector of unknown parameters, and $\boldsymbol{X}_t$ and $\boldsymbol{Z}_t$ are conformably dimensioned row vectors of observations on exogenous or predetermined variables that belong to the information set on which we are conditioning. Some or all of the elements of $\boldsymbol{Z}_t$ may well belong to $\boldsymbol{X}_t$. The function $\exp(\boldsymbol{Z}_t\gamma)$ is an example of a **skedastic function**. In the same way that a regression function determines the conditional mean of a random variable, a skedastic function determines its conditional variance. The skedastic function $\exp(\boldsymbol{Z}_t\gamma)$ has the property that it is positive for any vector γ. This is a desirable property for any skedastic function to have, since negative estimated variances would be highly inconvenient.

In order to obtain consistent estimates of γ, usually we must first obtain consistent estimates of the error terms in (7.18). The obvious way to do so is to start by computing OLS estimates $\hat{\boldsymbol{\beta}}$. This allows us to calculate a vector of OLS residuals with typical element $\hat{u}_t$. We can then run the auxiliary linear regression

$$\log \hat{u}_t^2 = \boldsymbol{Z}_t\gamma + v_t, \tag{7.19}$$

over observations $t = 1, \ldots, n$ to find the OLS estimates $\hat{\gamma}$. These estimates are then used to compute

$$\hat{\omega}_t = \big(\exp(\boldsymbol{Z}_t\hat{\gamma})\big)^{1/2}$$

for all t. Finally, feasible GLS estimates of $\boldsymbol{\beta}$ are obtained by using ordinary least squares to estimate regression (7.12), with the estimates $\hat{\omega}_t$ replacing the unknown ω_t. This is an example of **feasible weighted least squares**.

Why Feasible GLS Works

Under suitable regularity conditions, it can be shown that this type of procedure yields a feasible GLS estimator $\hat{\boldsymbol{\beta}}_{\mathrm{F}}$ that is consistent and asymptotically equivalent to the GLS estimator $\hat{\boldsymbol{\beta}}_{\mathrm{GLS}}$. We will not attempt to provide a rigorous proof of this proposition; for that, see Amemiya (1973a). However, we will try to provide an intuitive explanation of why it is true.

If we substitute $\boldsymbol{X\beta}_0+\boldsymbol{u}$ for $\boldsymbol{y}$ into expression (7.04), the formula for the GLS estimator, we find that

$$\hat{\boldsymbol{\beta}}_{\text{GLS}} = \boldsymbol{\beta}_0 + (\boldsymbol{X}^\top\boldsymbol{\Omega}^{-1}\boldsymbol{X})^{-1}\boldsymbol{X}^\top\boldsymbol{\Omega}^{-1}\boldsymbol{u}.$$

Taking $\boldsymbol{\beta}_0$ over to the left-hand side, multiplying each factor by an appropriate power of n, and taking probability limits, we see that

$$n^{1/2}(\hat{\boldsymbol{\beta}}_{\text{GLS}} - \boldsymbol{\beta}_0) \stackrel{a}{=} \Big(\operatorname*{plim}_{n\to\infty} \frac{1}{n}\boldsymbol{X}^\top\boldsymbol{\Omega}^{-1}\boldsymbol{X}\Big)^{-1}\Big(\operatorname*{plim}_{n\to\infty} n^{-1/2}\boldsymbol{X}^\top\boldsymbol{\Omega}^{-1}\boldsymbol{u}\Big). \tag{7.20}$$

Under standard assumptions, the first matrix on the right-hand side is a nonstochastic $k\times k$ matrix with full rank, while the vector that postmultiplies it is a stochastic vector which follows the multivariate normal distribution.

For the feasible GLS estimator, the analog of equation (7.20) is

$$n^{1/2}(\hat{\boldsymbol{\beta}}_{\text{F}} - \boldsymbol{\beta}_0) \stackrel{a}{=} \Big(\operatorname*{plim}_{n\to\infty} \frac{1}{n}\boldsymbol{X}^\top\boldsymbol{\Omega}^{-1}(\hat{\gamma})\boldsymbol{X}\Big)^{-1}\Big(\operatorname*{plim}_{n\to\infty} n^{-1/2}\boldsymbol{X}^\top\boldsymbol{\Omega}^{-1}(\hat{\gamma})\boldsymbol{u}\Big). \tag{7.21}$$

The right-hand sides of expressions (7.21) and (7.20) look very similar, and it is clear that the latter must be asymptotically equivalent to the former if

$$\operatorname*{plim}_{n\to\infty} \frac{1}{n}\boldsymbol{X}^\top\boldsymbol{\Omega}^{-1}(\hat{\gamma})\boldsymbol{X} = \operatorname*{plim}_{n\to\infty} \frac{1}{n}\boldsymbol{X}^\top\boldsymbol{\Omega}^{-1}\boldsymbol{X} \tag{7.22}$$

and

$$\operatorname*{plim}_{n\to\infty} n^{-1/2}\boldsymbol{X}^\top\boldsymbol{\Omega}^{-1}(\hat{\gamma})\boldsymbol{u} = \operatorname*{plim}_{n\to\infty} n^{-1/2}\boldsymbol{X}^\top\boldsymbol{\Omega}^{-1}\boldsymbol{u}. \tag{7.23}$$

A rigorous statement and proof of the conditions under which equations (7.22) and (7.23) hold is beyond the scope of this book. If they are to hold, it is desirable that $\hat{\gamma}$ should be a consistent estimator of γ, and this requires that the OLS estimator $\hat{\boldsymbol{\beta}}$ should be consistent. For example, it can be shown that the estimator obtained by running regression (7.19) would be consistent if the regressand depended on u_t rather than $\hat{u}_t$. Since the regressand is actually $\hat{u}_t$, it is necessary that the residuals $\hat{u}_t$ should consistently estimate the error terms u_t. This in turn requires that $\hat{\boldsymbol{\beta}}$ should be consistent for $\boldsymbol{\beta}_0$. Thus, in general, we cannot expect $\hat{\gamma}$ to be consistent if we do not start with a consistent estimator of $\boldsymbol{\beta}$.

Unfortunately, as we will see later, if $\boldsymbol{\Omega}(\gamma)$ is not diagonal, then the OLS estimator $\hat{\boldsymbol{\beta}}$ is, in general, not consistent whenever any element of $\boldsymbol{X}_t$ is a lagged dependent variable. A lagged dependent variable is predetermined with respect to error terms that are innovations, but not with respect to error terms that are serially correlated. With GLS or feasible GLS estimation, the problem does not arise, because, if the model is correctly specified, the transformed explanatory variables are predetermined with respect to the transformed error terms, as in (7.17). When the OLS estimator is inconsistent, we must obtain a consistent estimator of γ in some other way.

Whether or not feasible GLS is a desirable estimation method in practice depends on how good an estimate of $\boldsymbol{\Omega}$ can be obtained. If $\boldsymbol{\Omega}(\hat{\gamma})$ is a very good estimate, then feasible GLS has essentially the same properties as GLS itself, and inferences based on the GLS covariance matrix (7.05), with $\boldsymbol{\Omega}(\hat{\gamma})$ replacing $\boldsymbol{\Omega}$, should be reasonably reliable, even though they are not exact in finite samples. Note that condition (7.22), in addition to being necessary for the validity of feasible GLS, guarantees that the feasible GLS covariance matrix estimator converges as $n \to \infty$ to the true GLS covariance matrix. On the other hand, if $\boldsymbol{\Omega}(\hat{\gamma})$ is a poor estimate, feasible GLS estimates may have quite different properties from real GLS estimates, and inferences may be quite misleading.

It is entirely possible to iterate a feasible GLS procedure. The estimator $\hat{\boldsymbol{\beta}}_{\mathrm{F}}$ can be used to compute new set of residuals, which can then be used to obtain a second-round estimate of γ, which can be used to calculate second-round feasible GLS estimates, and so on. This procedure can either be stopped after a predetermined number of rounds or continued until convergence is achieved (if it ever is achieved). Iteration does not change the asymptotic distribution of the feasible GLS estimator, but it does change its finite-sample distribution.

Another way to estimate models in which the covariance matrix of the error terms depends on one or more unknown parameters is to use the method of maximum likelihood. This estimation method, in which $\boldsymbol{\beta}$ and γ are estimated jointly, will be discussed in Chapter 10. In many cases, an iterated feasible GLS estimator is the same as a maximum likelihood estimator based on the assumption of normally distributed errors.

7.5 Heteroskedasticity

There are two situations in which the error terms are heteroskedastic but serially uncorrelated. In the first, the form of the heteroskedasticity is completely unknown, while, in the second, the skedastic function is known except for the values of some parameters that can be estimated consistently. Concerning the case of heteroskedasticity of unknown form, we saw in Sections 5.5 and 6.5 how to compute asymptotically valid covariance matrix estimates for OLS and NLS parameter estimates. The fact that these HCCMEs are sandwich covariance matrices makes it clear that, although they are consistent under standard regularity conditions, neither OLS nor NLS is efficient when the error terms are heteroskedastic.

If the variances of all the error terms are known, at least up to a scalar factor, then efficient estimates can be obtained by weighted least squares, which we discussed in Section 7.3. For a linear model, we need to multiply all of the variables by ω_t^{-1}, the inverse of the standard error of u_t, and then use ordinary least squares. The usual OLS covariance matrix is perfectly valid, although it is desirable to replace s^2 by 1 if the variances are completely known, since in that case $s^2 \to 1$ as $n \to \infty$. For a nonlinear model, we need to multiply the dependent variable and the entire regression function by ω_t^{-1} and then use NLS. Once again, the usual NLS covariance matrix is asymptotically valid.

If the form of the heteroskedasticity is known, but the skedastic function depends on unknown parameters, then we can use feasible weighted least squares and still achieve asymptotic efficiency. An example of such a procedure was discussed in the previous section. As we have seen, it makes no difference asymptotically whether the ω_t are known or merely estimated consistently, although it can certainly make a substantial difference in finite samples. Asymptotically, at least, the usual OLS or NLS covariance matrix is just as valid with feasible WLS as with WLS.

Testing for Heteroskedasticity

In some cases, it may be clear from the specification of the model that the error terms must exhibit a particular pattern of heteroskedasticity. In many cases, however, we may hope that the error terms are homoskedastic but be prepared to admit the possibility that they are not. In such cases, if we have no information on the form of the skedastic function, it may be prudent to employ an HCCME, especially if the sample size is large. In a number of simulation experiments, Andrews (1991) has shown that, when the error terms are homoskedastic, use of an HCCME, rather than the usual OLS covariance matrix, frequently has little cost. However, as we saw in Exercise 5.15, this is not always true. In finite samples, tests and confidence intervals based on HCCMEs are somewhat less reliable than ones based on the usual OLS covariance matrix when the latter is appropriate.

If we have information on the form of the skedastic function, we might well wish to use weighted least squares. Before doing so, it is advisable to perform a **specification test** of the null hypothesis that the error terms are homoskedastic against whatever heteroskedastic alternatives may seem reasonable. There are many ways to perform this type of specification test. The simplest approach that is widely applicable, and the only one that we will discuss, involves running an artificial regression in which the regressand is the vector of squared residuals from the model under test.

A reasonably general model of conditional heteroskedasticity is

$$\mathrm{E}(u_t^2 \mid \Omega_t) = h(\delta + \boldsymbol{Z}_t\boldsymbol{\gamma}), \tag{7.24}$$

where the skedastic function $h(\cdot)$ is a nonlinear function that can take on only positive values, $\boldsymbol{Z}_t$ is a $1 \times r$ vector of observations on exogenous or predetermined variables that belong to the information set Ω_t, δ is a scalar parameter, and γ is an r-vector of parameters. Under the null hypothesis that $\gamma = \mathbf{0}$, the function $h(\delta + \boldsymbol{Z}_t\gamma)$ collapses to $h(\delta)$, a constant. One plausible specification of the skedastic function is

$$h(\delta + \boldsymbol{Z}_t\gamma) = \exp(\delta + \boldsymbol{Z}_t\gamma) = \exp(\delta)\exp(\boldsymbol{Z}_t\gamma).$$

Under this specification, the variance of u_t reduces to the constant $\sigma^2 \equiv \exp(\delta)$ when $\gamma = \mathbf{0}$. Since, as we will see, one of the advantages of tests based on artificial regressions is that they do not depend on the functional form of $h(\cdot)$, there is no need for us to consider specifications less general than (7.24).

If we define v_t as the difference between u_t^2 and its conditional expectation, we can rewrite equation (7.24) as

$$u_t^2 = h(\delta + \boldsymbol{Z}_t\gamma) + v_t, \tag{7.25}$$

which has the form of a regression model. While we would not expect the error term v_t to be as well behaved as the error terms in most regression models, since the distribution of u_t^2 is almost always be skewed to the right, it does have mean zero by definition, and we will assume that it has a finite, and constant, variance. This assumption would probably be excessively strong if γ were nonzero, but it seems perfectly reasonable to assume that the variance of v_t is constant under the null hypothesis that $\gamma = \mathbf{0}$.

Suppose, to begin with, that we actually observe the u_t. Since (7.25) has the form of a regression model, we can then test the null hypothesis that $\gamma = \mathbf{0}$ by using a Gauss-Newton regression. Suppose the sample mean of the u_t^2 is $\tilde{\sigma}^2$. Then the obvious estimate of δ under the null hypothesis is just $\tilde{\delta} \equiv h^{-1}(\tilde{\sigma}^2)$. The GNR corresponding to (7.25) is

$$u_t^2 - h(\delta + \boldsymbol{Z}_t\gamma) = h'(\delta + \boldsymbol{Z}_t\gamma)b_\delta + h'(\delta + \boldsymbol{Z}_t\gamma)\boldsymbol{Z}_t\boldsymbol{b}_\gamma + \text{residual},$$

where $h'(\cdot)$ denotes the first derivative of $h(\cdot)$, b_δ is the coefficient that corresponds to δ, and $\boldsymbol{b}_\gamma$ is the r-vector of coefficients that corresponds to γ. When it is evaluated at $\delta = \tilde{\delta}$ and $\gamma = \mathbf{0}$, this GNR simplifies to

$$u_t^2 - \tilde{\sigma}^2 = h'(\tilde{\delta})b_\delta + h'(\tilde{\delta})\boldsymbol{Z}_t\boldsymbol{b}_\gamma + \text{residual}. \tag{7.26}$$

Since $h'(\tilde{\delta})$ is just a constant, its presence has no effect on the explanatory power of the regression. Moreover, since regression (7.26) includes a constant term, both the SSR and the centered R^2 are unchanged if we do not bother to subtract $\tilde{\sigma}^2$ from the left-hand side. Thus, for the purpose of testing the null hypothesis that $\gamma = \mathbf{0}$, regression (7.26) is equivalent to the regression

$$u_t^2 = b_\delta + \boldsymbol{Z}_t\boldsymbol{b}_\gamma + \text{residual}, \tag{7.27}$$

with a suitable redefinition of the artificial parameters b_δ and $\boldsymbol{b}_\gamma$. Observe that regression (7.27) does not depend on the functional form of $h(\cdot)$. Standard results for tests based on the GNR imply that the ordinary F statistic for $\boldsymbol{b}_\gamma = \mathbf{0}$ in this regression, which is printed by most regression packages, must be asymptotically distributed as $F(r, \infty)$ under the null hypothesis; see Section 6.7. Another valid test statistic is n times the centered R^2 from this regression, which is asymptotically distributed as $\chi^2(r)$.

In practice, of course, we do not actually observe the u_t. However, as we noted in Sections 3.6 and 6.3, least squares residuals converge asymptotically to the corresponding error terms when the model is correctly specified. Thus it seems plausible that the test should still be asymptotically valid if we replace u_t^2 in regression (7.27) by $\hat{u}_t^2$, the tth squared residual from least squares estimation of the model under test. The test regression then becomes

$$\hat{u}_t^2 = b_\delta + \boldsymbol{Z}_t \boldsymbol{b}_\gamma + \text{residual}. \tag{7.28}$$

It can be shown that replacing u_t^2 by $\hat{u}_t^2$ does not change the asymptotic distribution of the F and nR^2 statistics for testing the hypothesis $\boldsymbol{b}_\gamma = \mathbf{0}$; see Davidson and MacKinnon (1993, Section 11.5). Of course, since the finite-sample distributions of these test statistics may differ substantially from their asymptotic ones, it is a very good idea to bootstrap them when the sample size is small or moderate. This will be discussed further in Section 7.7.

Tests based on regression (7.28) require us to choose $\boldsymbol{Z}_t$, and there are many ways to do so. One approach is to include functions of some of the original regressors. As we saw in Section 5.5, there are circumstances in which the usual OLS covariance matrix is valid even when there is heteroskedasticity. White (1980) showed that, in a linear regression model, if $\mathrm{E}(u_t^2)$ is constant conditional on the squares and cross-products of all the regressors, then there is no need to use an HCCME. He therefore suggested that $\boldsymbol{Z}_t$ should consist of the squares and cross-products of all the regressors, because, asymptotically, such a test rejects the null whenever heteroskedasticity causes the usual OLS covariance matrix to be invalid. However, unless the number of regressors is very small, this suggestion results in r, the dimension of $\boldsymbol{Z}_t$, being very large. As a consequence, the test is likely to have poor finite-sample properties and low power, unless the sample size is quite large.

If economic theory does not tell us how to choose $\boldsymbol{Z}_t$, there is no simple, mechanical rule for choosing it. The more variables that are included in $\boldsymbol{Z}_t$, the greater is likely to be their ability to explain any observed pattern of heteroskedasticity, but the larger is the number of degrees of freedom for the test statistic. Adding a variable that helps substantially to explain the u_t^2 must surely increase the power of the test. However, adding variables with little explanatory power may simply dilute test power by increasing the number of degrees of freedom without increasing the noncentrality parameter; recall the discussion in Section 4.7. This is most easily seen in the context of χ^2 tests, where the critical values increase monotonically with the number of degrees of freedom. For a test with, say, $r + 1$ degrees of freedom to have as much power as a test with r degrees of freedom, the noncentrality parameter for the former test must be a certain amount larger than the noncentrality parameter for the latter.

7.6 Autoregressive and Moving-Average Processes

The error terms for nearby observations may be correlated, or may appear to be correlated, in any sort of regression model, but this phenomenon is most commonly encountered in models estimated with time-series data, where it is known as **serial correlation** or **autocorrelation**. In practice, what appears to be serial correlation may instead be evidence of a misspecified model, as we discuss in Section 7.9. In some circumstances, though, it is natural to model the serial correlation by assuming that the error terms follow some sort of **stochastic process**. Such a process defines a sequence of random variables. Some of the stochastic processes that are commonly used to model serial correlation will be discussed in this section.

If there is reason to believe that serial correlation may be present, the first step is usually to test the null hypothesis that the errors are serially uncorrelated against a plausible alternative that involves serial correlation. Several ways of doing this will be discussed in the next section. The second step, if evidence of serial correlation is found, is to estimate a model that accounts for it. Estimation methods based on NLS and GLS will be discussed in Section 7.8. The final step, which is extremely important but is often omitted, is to verify that the model which accounts for serial correlation is compatible with the data. Some techniques for doing so will be discussed in Section 7.9.

The AR(1) Process

One of the simplest and most commonly used stochastic processes is the **first-order autoregressive process**, or **AR(1) process**. We have already encountered regression models with error terms that follow such a process in Sections 6.1 and 6.6. Recall from (6.04) that the AR(1) process can be written as

$$u_t = \rho u_{t-1} + \varepsilon_t, \quad \varepsilon_t \sim \text{IID}(0, \sigma_\varepsilon^2), \quad |\rho| < 1. \tag{7.29}$$

The error at time t is equal to some fraction ρ of the error at time $t-1$, with the sign changed if $\rho < 0$, plus the innovation ε_t. Since it is assumed that ε_t is independent of ε_s for all $s \neq t$, ε_t evidently is an innovation, according to the definition of that term in Section 4.5.

The condition in equation (7.29) that $|\rho| < 1$ is called a **stationarity condition**, because it is necessary for the AR(1) process to be **stationary**. There are several definitions of stationarity in time series analysis. According to the one that interests us here, a series with typical element u_t is stationary if the unconditional expectation $\text{E}(u_t)$ and the unconditional variance $\text{Var}(u_t)$ exist and are independent of t, and if the covariance $\text{Cov}(u_t, u_{t-j})$ is also, for any given j, independent of t. This particular definition is sometimes referred to as **covariance stationarity**, or **wide sense stationarity**.

Suppose that, although we begin to observe the series only once $t = 1$, the series has been in existence for an infinite time. We can then compute the variance of u_t by substituting successively for u_{t-1}, u_{t-2}, u_{t-3}, and so on in (7.29). We see that

$$u_t = \varepsilon_t + \rho\varepsilon_{t-1} + \rho^2\varepsilon_{t-2} + \rho^3\varepsilon_{t-3} + \cdots. \tag{7.30}$$

Using the fact that the innovations ε_t, $\varepsilon_{t-1}, \ldots$ are independent, and therefore uncorrelated, the variance of u_t is seen to be

$$\sigma_u^2 \equiv \mathrm{Var}(u_t) = \sigma_\varepsilon^2 + \rho^2\sigma_\varepsilon^2 + \rho^4\sigma_\varepsilon^2 + \rho^6\sigma_\varepsilon^2 + \cdots = \frac{\sigma_\varepsilon^2}{1-\rho^2}. \tag{7.31}$$

The last expression here is indeed independent of t, as required for a stationary process, but the last equality can be true only if the stationarity condition $|\rho| < 1$ holds, since that condition is necessary for the infinite series $1 + \rho^2 + \rho^4 + \rho^6 + \cdots$ to converge. In addition, if $|\rho| > 1$, the last expression in (7.31) is negative, and so cannot be a variance. In most econometric applications, where u_t is the error term appended to a regression model, the stationarity condition is a very reasonable condition to impose, since, without it, the variance of the error terms would increase without limit as the sample size was increased.

It is not necessary to make the rather strange assumption that u_t exists for negative values of t all the way to $-\infty$. If we suppose that the expectation and variance of u_1 are respectively 0 and $\sigma_\varepsilon^2/(1-\rho^2)$, then we see at once that $\mathrm{E}(u_2) = \mathrm{E}(\rho u_1) + \mathrm{E}(\varepsilon_2) = 0$, and that

$$\mathrm{Var}(u_2) = \mathrm{Var}(\rho u_1 + \varepsilon_2) = \sigma_\varepsilon^2\left(\frac{\rho^2}{1-\rho^2} + 1\right) = \frac{\sigma_\varepsilon^2}{1-\rho^2} = \mathrm{Var}(u_1),$$

where the second equality uses the fact that ε_2, because it is an innovation, is uncorrelated with u_1. A simple recursive argument then shows that $\mathrm{Var}(u_t) = \sigma_\varepsilon^2/(1-\rho^2)$ for all t.

The argument in (7.31) shows that $\sigma_u^2 \equiv \sigma_\varepsilon^2/(1-\rho^2)$ is the only admissible value for $\mathrm{Var}(u_t)$ if the series is stationary. Consequently, if the variance of u_1 is *not* equal to σ_u^2, then the series cannot be stationary. However, if the stationarity condition is satisfied, $\mathrm{Var}(u_t)$ must tend to σ_u^2 as t becomes large. This can be seen by repeating the calculation in (7.31), but recognizing that the series has only a finite number of terms. As t grows, the number of terms becomes large, and the value of the finite sum tends to the value of the infinite series, which is the stationary variance σ_u^2.

It is not difficult to see that, for the AR(1) process (7.29), the covariance of u_t and u_{t-1} is independent of t if $\mathrm{Var}(u_t) = \sigma_u^2$ for all t.

$$\mathrm{Cov}(u_t, u_{t-1}) = \mathrm{E}(u_t u_{t-1}) = \mathrm{E}\big((\rho u_{t-1} + \varepsilon_t)u_{t-1}\big) = \rho\sigma_u^2.$$

In order to compute the correlation of u_t and u_{t-1}, we divide $\text{Cov}(u_t, u_{t-1})$ by the square root of the product of the variances of u_t and u_{t-1}, that is, by σ_u^2. We then find that the correlation of u_t and u_{t-1} is just ρ.

The jth order **autocovariance** of the AR(1) process is both the covariance of u_t and u_{t-j} and the covariance of u_t and u_{t+j}. As readers are asked to demonstrate in Exercise 7.4, under the assumption that $\text{Var}(u_1) = \sigma_u^2$, this autocovariance is equal to $\rho^j \sigma_u^2$, independently of t. It follows that the AR(1) process (7.29) is indeed covariance stationary if $\text{Var}(u_1) = \sigma_u^2$. The correlation between u_t and u_{t-j} is of course just ρ^j. Since ρ^j tends to zero quite rapidly as j increases, except when $|\rho|$ is very close to 1, this result implies that an AR(1) process generally exhibits small correlations between observations that are far removed in time, but it may exhibit large correlations between observations that are close in time. Since this is precisely the pattern that is frequently observed in the residuals of regression models estimated using time-series data, it is not surprising that the AR(1) process is often used to account for serial correlation in such models.

If we combine the result (7.31) with the result proved in Exercise 7.4, we see that, if the AR(1) process (7.29) is stationary, the covariance matrix of the vector $\boldsymbol{u}$, which is called the **autocovariance matrix** of the AR(1) process, can be written as

$$\boldsymbol{\Omega}(\rho) = \frac{\sigma_\varepsilon^2}{1-\rho^2} \begin{bmatrix} 1 & \rho & \rho^2 & \cdots & \rho^{n-1} \\ \rho & 1 & \rho & \cdots & \rho^{n-2} \\ \vdots & \vdots & \vdots & & \vdots \\ \rho^{n-1} & \rho^{n-2} & \rho^{n-3} & \cdots & 1 \end{bmatrix}. \tag{7.32}$$

All the u_t have the same variance, σ_u^2, which by (7.31) is the first factor on the right-hand side of (7.32). It follows that the second factor is the matrix of correlations of the error terms, or **autocorrelation matrix**, which we denote $\boldsymbol{\Delta}(\rho)$. We will need to make use of (7.32) in Section 7.8 when we discuss GLS estimation of regression models with AR(1) errors.

Higher-Order Autoregressive Processes

Although the AR(1) process is very useful, it is quite restrictive. A much more general stochastic process is the $\boldsymbol{p}^{\text{th}}$ **order autoregressive process**, or **AR($\boldsymbol{p}$) process**,

$$u_t = \rho_1 u_{t-1} + \rho_2 u_{t-2} + \ldots + \rho_p u_{t-p} + \varepsilon_t, \quad \varepsilon_t \sim \text{IID}(0, \sigma_\varepsilon^2). \tag{7.33}$$

For such a process, u_t depends on up to p lagged values of itself, as well as on ε_t. The AR(p) process (7.33) can also be expressed as

$$(1 - \rho_1 \text{L} - \rho_2 \text{L}^2 - \cdots - \rho_p \text{L}^p) u_t = \varepsilon_t, \quad \varepsilon_t \sim \text{IID}(0, \sigma_\varepsilon^2), \tag{7.34}$$

where L denotes the **lag operator**. The lag operator L has the property that when L multiplies anything with a time subscript, this subscript is lagged one period. Thus $\mathrm{L}u_t = u_{t-1}$, $\mathrm{L}^2 u_t = u_{t-2}$, $\mathrm{L}^3 u_t = u_{t-3}$, and so on. The expression in parentheses in (7.34) is a polynomial in the lag operator L, with coefficients 1 and $-\rho_1, \ldots, -\rho_p$. If we make the definition

$$\rho(z) \equiv \rho_1 z + \rho_2 z^2 + \cdots + \rho_p z^p \tag{7.35}$$

for arbitrary z, we can write the AR(p) process (7.34) very compactly as

$$\big(1 - \rho(\mathrm{L})\big) u_t = \varepsilon_t, \quad \varepsilon_t \sim \mathrm{IID}(0, \sigma_\varepsilon^2).$$

This compact notation is useful, but it does have two disadvantages: The order of the process, p, is not apparent, and there is no way of expressing any restrictions on the ρ_i.

The stationarity condition for an AR(p) process may be expressed in several ways. One of them, based on the definition (7.35), is that all the roots of the polynomial equation

$$1 - \rho(z) = 0 \tag{7.36}$$

must lie **outside the unit circle**. This simply means that all of the (possibly complex) roots of equation (7.36) must be greater than 1 in absolute value.[1] This condition can lead to quite complicated restrictions on the ρ_i for general AR(p) processes. The stationarity condition that $|\rho_1| < 1$ for an AR(1) process is evidently a consequence of this condition. In that case, (7.36) reduces to the equation $1 - \rho_1 z = 0$, the unique root of which is $z = 1/\rho_1$, and this root is greater than 1 in absolute value if and only if $|\rho_1| < 1$. As with the AR(1) process, the stationarity condition for an AR(p) process is necessary but not sufficient. Stationarity requires in addition that the variances and covariances of $u_1, \ldots, u_p$ should be equal to their stationary values. If not, it remains true that $\mathrm{Var}(u_t)$ and $\mathrm{Cov}(u_t, u_{t-j})$ tend to their stationary values for large t if the stationarity condition is satisfied.

In practice, when an AR(p) process is used to model the error terms of a regression model, p is usually chosen to be quite small. By far the most popular choice is the AR(1) process, but AR(2) and AR(4) processes are also encountered reasonably frequently. AR(4) processes are particularly attractive for quarterly data, because seasonality may cause correlation between error terms that are four periods apart.

Moving-Average Processes

Autoregressive processes are not the only way to model stationary time series. Another type of stochastic process is the **moving-average**, or **MA**, process. The simplest of these is the **first-order moving-average**, or **MA(1)**, process

$$u_t = \varepsilon_t + \alpha_1 \varepsilon_{t-1}, \quad \varepsilon_t \sim \mathrm{IID}(0, \sigma_\varepsilon^2), \tag{7.37}$$

[1] For a complex number $a + bi$, a and b real, the absolute value is $(a^2 + b^2)^{1/2}$.

in which the error term u_t is a weighted average of two successive innovations, ε_t and ε_{t-1}.

It is not difficult to calculate the autocovariance matrix for an MA(1) process. From (7.37), we see that the variance of u_t is

$$\sigma_u^2 \equiv \mathrm{E}\big((\varepsilon_t + \alpha_1\varepsilon_{t-1})^2\big) = \sigma_\varepsilon^2 + \alpha_1^2\sigma_\varepsilon^2 = (1+\alpha_1^2)\sigma_\varepsilon^2,$$

the covariance of u_t and u_{t-1} is

$$\mathrm{E}\big((\varepsilon_t + \alpha_1\varepsilon_{t-1})(\varepsilon_{t-1} + \alpha_1\varepsilon_{t-2})\big) = \alpha_1\sigma_\varepsilon^2,$$

and the covariance of u_t and u_{t-j} for $j > 1$ is 0. Therefore, the covariance matrix of the entire vector $\boldsymbol{u}$ is

$$\sigma_\varepsilon^2\boldsymbol{\Delta}(\alpha_1) \equiv \sigma_\varepsilon^2 \begin{bmatrix} 1+\alpha_1^2 & \alpha_1 & 0 & \cdots & 0 & 0 \\ \alpha_1 & 1+\alpha_1^2 & \alpha_1 & \cdots & 0 & 0 \\ \vdots & \vdots & \vdots & & \vdots & \vdots \\ 0 & 0 & 0 & \cdots & \alpha_1 & 1+\alpha_1^2 \end{bmatrix}. \tag{7.38}$$

The autocorrelation matrix is the matrix (7.38) divided by $\sigma_\varepsilon^2(1+\alpha_1^2)$. It is evident that there is no correlation between error terms which are more than one period apart. Moreover, the correlation between successive error terms varies only between -0.5 and 0.5, the smallest and largest possible values of $\alpha_1/(1+\alpha_1^2)$, which are achieved when $\alpha_1 = -1$ and $\alpha_1 = 1$, respectively. Therefore, an MA(1) process cannot be appropriate when the observed correlation between successive residuals is large in absolute value, or when residuals that are not adjacent are correlated.

Just as AR(p) processes generalize the AR(1) process, higher-order moving-average processes generalize the MA(1) process. The **q^{th} order moving-average process**, or **MA(q) process**, may be written as

$$u_t = \varepsilon_t + \alpha_1\varepsilon_{t-1} + \alpha_2\varepsilon_{t-2} + \cdots + \alpha_q\varepsilon_{t-q}, \quad \varepsilon_t \sim \mathrm{IID}(0, \sigma_\varepsilon^2). \tag{7.39}$$

Using lag-operator notation, the process (7.39) can also be written as

$$u_t = (1 + \alpha_1\mathrm{L} + \cdots + \alpha_q\mathrm{L}^q)\varepsilon_t \equiv \big(1 + \alpha(\mathrm{L})\big)\varepsilon_t, \quad \varepsilon_t \sim \mathrm{IID}(0, \sigma_\varepsilon^2),$$

where $\alpha(\mathrm{L})$ is a polynomial in the lag operator.

Autoregressive processes, moving-average processes, and other related stochastic processes have many important applications in both econometrics and macroeconomics. These processes will be discussed further in Chapter 13. Their properties have been studied extensively in the literature on **time-series methods**. A classic reference is Box and Jenkins (1976), which has been updated as Box, Jenkins, and Reinsel (1994). Books that are specifically aimed at economists include Granger and Newbold (1986), Harvey (1989), Hamilton (1994), and Hayashi (2000).

7.7 Testing for Serial Correlation

Over the decades, an enormous amount of research has been devoted to the subject of specification tests for serial correlation in regression models. Even though a great many different tests have been proposed, many of them no longer of much interest, the subject is not really very complicated. As we show in this section, it is perfectly easy to test the null hypothesis that the error terms of a regression model are serially uncorrelated against the alternative that they follow an autoregressive process of any specified order. Most of the tests that we will discuss are straightforward applications of testing procedures which were introduced in Chapters 4 and 6.

As we saw in Section 6.1, the linear regression model

$$y_t = \boldsymbol{X}_t\boldsymbol{\beta} + u_t, \quad u_t = \rho u_{t-1} + \varepsilon_t, \quad \varepsilon_t \sim \mathrm{IID}(0, \sigma_\varepsilon^2), \tag{7.40}$$

in which the error terms follow an AR(1) process, can, if we ignore the first observation, be rewritten as the nonlinear regression model

$$y_t = \rho y_{t-1} + \boldsymbol{X}_t\boldsymbol{\beta} - \rho\boldsymbol{X}_{t-1}\boldsymbol{\beta} + \varepsilon_t, \quad \varepsilon_t \sim \mathrm{IID}(0, \sigma_\varepsilon^2). \tag{7.41}$$

The null hypothesis that $\rho = 0$ can then be tested using any procedure that is appropriate for testing hypotheses about the parameters of nonlinear regression models; see Section 6.7.

One approach is just to estimate the model (7.41) by NLS and calculate the ordinary t statistic for $\rho = 0$. Because the model is nonlinear, and because it includes a lagged dependent variable, this t statistic does not follow the Student's t distribution in finite samples, even if the error terms happen to be normally distributed. However, under the null hypothesis, it must follow the standard normal distribution asymptotically. The F statistic computed using the unrestricted SSR from (7.41) and the restricted SSR from an OLS regression of $\boldsymbol{y}$ on $\boldsymbol{X}$ for the period $t = 2$ to n is also asymptotically valid. Since the model (7.41) is nonlinear, this F statistic is not numerically equal to the square of the t statistic in this case, although the two are asymptotically equal under the null hypothesis.

Tests Based on the GNR

We can avoid having to estimate the nonlinear model (7.41) by using tests based on the Gauss-Newton regression. Let $\tilde{\boldsymbol{\beta}}$ denote the vector of OLS estimates obtained from the restricted model

$$\boldsymbol{y} = \boldsymbol{X}\boldsymbol{\beta} + \boldsymbol{u}, \tag{7.42}$$

and let $\tilde{\boldsymbol{u}}$ denote the vector of OLS residuals from this regression. Then, as we saw in Section 6.7, the GNR for testing the null hypothesis that $\rho = 0$ is

$$\tilde{\boldsymbol{u}} = \boldsymbol{X}\boldsymbol{b} + b_\rho\tilde{\boldsymbol{u}}_1 + \text{residuals}, \tag{7.43}$$

where $\tilde{\boldsymbol{u}}_1$ is a vector with typical element $\tilde{u}_{t-1}$; recall (6.84). The ordinary t statistic for $b_\rho = 0$ in this regression is asymptotically distributed as $\mathrm{N}(0, 1)$ under the null hypothesis.

It is worth noting that the t statistic for $b_\rho = 0$ in the GNR (7.43) is identical to the t statistic for $b_\rho = 0$ in the regression

$$\boldsymbol{y} = \boldsymbol{X\beta} + b_\rho \tilde{\boldsymbol{u}}_1 + \text{residuals}. \tag{7.44}$$

Regression (7.44) is just the original regression model (7.42) with the lagged OLS residuals from that model added as an additional regressor. By use of the FWL Theorem, it can readily be seen that (7.44) has the same SSR and the same estimate of b_ρ as the GNR (7.43). Therefore, a GNR-based test for serial correlation is formally the same as a test for omitted variables, where the omitted variables are lagged residuals from the model under test.

Although regressions (7.43) and (7.44) look perfectly simple, it is not quite clear how they should be implemented. Both the original regression (7.42) and the test regression (7.43) or (7.44) may be estimated either over the entire sample period or over the shorter period from $t = 2$ to n. If one of them is run over the full sample period and the other is run over the shorter period, then $\tilde{\boldsymbol{u}}$ is not orthogonal to $\boldsymbol{X}$. This does not affect the asymptotic distribution of the t statistic, but it may affect its finite-sample distribution. The easiest approach is probably to estimate both equations over the entire sample period. If this is done, the unobserved value of $\tilde{u}_0$ must be replaced by 0 before the test regression is run. As Exercise 7.14 demonstrates, running the GNR (7.43) in different ways results in test statistics that are numerically different, even though they all follow the same asymptotic distribution under the null hypothesis.

Tests based on the GNR have several attractive features in addition to ease of computation. Unlike some other tests that will be discussed shortly, they are asymptotically valid under the relatively weak assumption that $\mathrm{E}(u_t \mid \boldsymbol{X}_t) = 0$, which allows $\boldsymbol{X}_t$ to include lagged dependent variables. Moreover, they are easily generalized to deal with nonlinear regression models. If the original model is nonlinear, we simply need to replace $\boldsymbol{X}_t$ in the test regression (7.43) by $\boldsymbol{X}_t(\tilde{\boldsymbol{\beta}})$, where, as usual, the ith element of $\boldsymbol{X}_t(\tilde{\boldsymbol{\beta}})$ is the derivative of the regression function with respect to the ith parameter, evaluated at the NLS estimates $\tilde{\boldsymbol{\beta}}$ of the model being tested; see Exercise 7.5.

Another very attractive feature of GNR-based tests is that they can readily be used to test against higher-order autoregressive processes and even moving-average processes. For example, in order to test against an AR(p) process, we simply need to run the test regression

$$\tilde{u}_t = \boldsymbol{X}_t \boldsymbol{b} + b_{\rho_1} \tilde{u}_{t-1} + \ldots + b_{\rho_p} \tilde{u}_{t-p} + \text{residual} \tag{7.45}$$

and use an asymptotic F test of the null hypothesis that the coefficients on all the lagged residuals are zero; see Exercise 7.6. Of course, in order to run regression (7.45), we either need to drop the first p observations or replace the unobserved lagged values of $\tilde{u}_t$ with zeros.

If we wish to test against an MA(q) process, it turns out that we can proceed exactly as if we were testing against an AR(q) process. The reason is that an autoregressive process of any order is **locally equivalent** to a moving-average process of the same order. Intuitively, this means that, for large samples, an AR(q) process and an MA(q) process look the same in the neighborhood of the null hypothesis of no serial correlation. Since tests based on the GNR use information on first derivatives only, it should not be surprising that the GNRs used for testing against both alternatives turn out to be identical; see Exercise 7.7.

The use of the GNR (7.43) for testing against AR(1) errors was first suggested by Durbin (1970). Breusch (1978) and Godfrey (1978a, 1978b) subsequently showed how to use GNRs to test against AR(p) and MA(q) errors. For a more detailed treatment of these and related procedures, see Godfrey (1988).

Older, Less Widely Applicable, Tests

Readers should be warned at once that the tests we are about to discuss are not recommended for general use. However, they still appear often enough in current literature and in current econometrics software for it to be necessary that practicing econometricians be familiar with them. Besides, studying them reveals some interesting aspects of models with serially correlated errors.

To begin with, consider the simple regression

$$\tilde{u}_t = b_\rho \tilde{u}_{t-1} + \text{residual}, \quad t = 1, \ldots, n, \tag{7.46}$$

where, as above, the $\tilde{u}_t$ are the residuals from regression (7.42). In order to be able to keep the first observation, we assume that $\tilde{u}_0 = 0$. This regression yields an estimate of b_ρ, which we will call $\tilde{\rho}$ because it is an estimate of ρ based on the residuals under the null. Explicitly, we have

$$\tilde{\rho} = \frac{n^{-1} \sum_{t=1}^{n} \tilde{u}_t \tilde{u}_{t-1}}{n^{-1} \sum_{t=1}^{n} \tilde{u}_{t-1}^2}, \tag{7.47}$$

where we have divided numerator and denominator by n for the purposes of the asymptotic analysis to follow. It turns out that, if the explanatory variables $\boldsymbol{X}$ in (7.42) are all exogenous, then $\tilde{\rho}$ is a consistent estimator of the parameter ρ in model (7.40), or, equivalently, (7.41), where it is not assumed that $\rho = 0$. This slightly surprising result depends crucially on the assumption of exogenous regressors. If one of the variables in $\boldsymbol{X}$ is a lagged dependent variable, the result no longer holds.

Asymptotically, it makes no difference if we replace the sum in the denominator by $n^{-1} \sum_{t=1}^{n} \tilde{u}_t^2$, because we are effectively including just one more term, namely, $\tilde{u}_n^2$. Then we can write the denominator of (7.47) as $n^{-1}\boldsymbol{u}^\top \boldsymbol{M_X u}$, where, as usual, the orthogonal projection matrix $\boldsymbol{M_X}$ projects on to $\mathcal{S}^\perp(\boldsymbol{X})$. If the vector $\boldsymbol{u}$ is generated by a stationary AR(1) process, it can be shown that a law of large numbers can be applied to both the numerator and the denominator of (7.47). Thus, asymptotically, both numerator and denominator can be replaced by their expectations. For a stationary AR(1) process, the covariance matrix $\boldsymbol{\Omega}$ of $\boldsymbol{u}$ is given by (7.32), and so we can compute the expectation of the denominator as follows, making use of the invariance under cyclic permutations of the trace of a matrix product that was first employed in Section 2.6:

$$\begin{aligned} \mathrm{E}\big(n^{-1}\boldsymbol{u}^\top\boldsymbol{M_X}\boldsymbol{u}\big) &= \mathrm{E}\big(n^{-1}\mathrm{Tr}(\boldsymbol{M_X}\boldsymbol{u}\boldsymbol{u}^\top)\big)\\ &= n^{-1}\mathrm{Tr}\big(\boldsymbol{M_X}\mathrm{E}(\boldsymbol{u}\boldsymbol{u}^\top)\big)\\ &= n^{-1}\mathrm{Tr}(\boldsymbol{M_X}\boldsymbol{\Omega})\\ &= n^{-1}\mathrm{Tr}(\boldsymbol{\Omega}) - n^{-1}\mathrm{Tr}(\boldsymbol{P_X}\boldsymbol{\Omega}). \end{aligned} \tag{7.48}$$

Note that, in the passage to the second line, we made use of the exogeneity of $\boldsymbol{X}$, and hence of $\boldsymbol{M_X}$. From (7.32), we see that $n^{-1}\mathrm{Tr}(\boldsymbol{\Omega}) = \sigma_\varepsilon^2/(1-\rho^2)$. For the second term in (7.48), we have that

$$\mathrm{Tr}(\boldsymbol{P_X}\boldsymbol{\Omega}) = \mathrm{Tr}\big(\boldsymbol{X}(\boldsymbol{X}^\top\boldsymbol{X})^{-1}\boldsymbol{X}^\top\boldsymbol{\Omega}\big) = \mathrm{Tr}\big((n^{-1}\boldsymbol{X}^\top\boldsymbol{X})^{-1}n^{-1}\boldsymbol{X}^\top\boldsymbol{\Omega}\boldsymbol{X}\big),$$

where again we have made use of the invariance of the trace under cyclic permutations. Our usual regularity conditions tell us that both $n^{-1}\boldsymbol{X}^\top\boldsymbol{X}$ and $n^{-1}\boldsymbol{X}^\top\boldsymbol{\Omega}\boldsymbol{X}$ tend to finite limits as $n \to \infty$. Thus, on account of the extra factor of n^{-1} in front of the second term in (7.48), that term vanishes asymptotically. It follows that the limit of the denominator of (7.47) is $\sigma_\varepsilon^2/(1-\rho^2)$.

The expectation of the numerator can be handled similarly. It is convenient to introduce an $n \times n$ matrix $\mathbf{L}$ that can be thought of as the matrix expression of the lag operator L. All the elements of $\mathbf{L}$ are zero except those on the diagonal just beneath the principal diagonal, which are all equal to 1:

$$\mathbf{L} = \begin{bmatrix} 0 & 0 & 0 & \cdots & 0 & 0 & 0\\ 1 & 0 & 0 & \cdots & 0 & 0 & 0\\ 0 & 1 & 0 & \cdots & 0 & 0 & 0\\ \vdots & \vdots & \vdots & & \vdots & \vdots & \vdots\\ 0 & 0 & 0 & \cdots & 1 & 0 & 0\\ 0 & 0 & 0 & \cdots & 0 & 1 & 0 \end{bmatrix}. \tag{7.49}$$

It is easy to see that $(\mathbf{L}\boldsymbol{u})_t = u_{t-1}$ for $t = 2,\ldots,n$, and $(\mathbf{L}\boldsymbol{u})_1 = 0$. With this definition, the numerator of (7.47) becomes $n^{-1}\tilde{\boldsymbol{u}}^\top\mathbf{L}\tilde{\boldsymbol{u}} = n^{-1}\boldsymbol{u}^\top\boldsymbol{M_X}\mathbf{L}\boldsymbol{M_X}\boldsymbol{u}$, of which the expectation, by a similar argument to that used above, is

$$n^{-1}\mathrm{E}\big(\mathrm{Tr}(\boldsymbol{M_X}\mathbf{L}\boldsymbol{M_X}\boldsymbol{u}\boldsymbol{u}^\top)\big) = n^{-1}\mathrm{Tr}(\boldsymbol{M_X}\mathbf{L}\boldsymbol{M_X}\boldsymbol{\Omega}). \tag{7.50}$$

When $\boldsymbol{M_X}$ is expressed as $\mathbf{I} - \boldsymbol{P_X}$, the leading term in this expression is just $\text{Tr}(\mathbf{L}\boldsymbol{\Omega})$. By arguments similar to those used above, which readers are invited to make explicit in Exercise 7.8, the other terms, which contain at least one factor of $\boldsymbol{P_X}$, all vanish asymptotically.

It can be seen from (7.49) that premultiplying $\boldsymbol{\Omega}$ by $\mathbf{L}$ pushes all the rows of $\boldsymbol{\Omega}$ down by one row, leaving the first row with nothing but zeros, and with the last row of $\boldsymbol{\Omega}$ falling off the end and being lost. The trace of $\mathbf{L}\boldsymbol{\Omega}$ is thus just the sum of the elements of the first diagonal of $\boldsymbol{\Omega}$ above the principal diagonal. From (7.32), this sum is equal to $n^{-1}(n-1)\sigma_\varepsilon^2\rho/(1-\rho^2)$, which is asymptotically equivalent to $\rho\sigma_\varepsilon^2/(1-\rho^2)$. Combining this result with the earlier one for the denominator, we see that the limit of $\tilde{\rho}$ as $n \to \infty$ is just ρ. This proves our result.

Besides providing a consistent estimator of ρ, regression (7.46) also yields a t statistic for the hypothesis that $b_\rho = 0$. This t statistic provides what is probably the simplest imaginable test for first-order serial correlation, and it is asymptotically valid if the explanatory variables $\boldsymbol{X}$ are exogenous. The easiest way to see this is to show that the t statistic from (7.46) is asymptotically equivalent to the t statistic for $b_\rho = 0$ in the GNR (7.43). If $\tilde{\boldsymbol{u}}_1 \equiv \mathbf{L}\tilde{\boldsymbol{u}}$, the t statistic from the GNR (7.43) may be written as

$$t_{\text{GNR}} = \frac{n^{-1/2}\tilde{\boldsymbol{u}}^\top\boldsymbol{M_X}\tilde{\boldsymbol{u}}_1}{s(n^{-1}\tilde{\boldsymbol{u}}_1^\top\boldsymbol{M_X}\tilde{\boldsymbol{u}}_1)^{1/2}}, \tag{7.51}$$

and the t statistic from the simple regression (7.46) may be written as

$$t_{\text{SR}} = \frac{n^{-1/2}\tilde{\boldsymbol{u}}^\top\tilde{\boldsymbol{u}}_1}{\acute{s}(n^{-1}\tilde{\boldsymbol{u}}_1^\top\tilde{\boldsymbol{u}}_1)^{1/2}}, \tag{7.52}$$

where s and $\acute{s}$ are the square roots of the estimated error variances for (7.43) and (7.46), respectively. Of course, the factors of n in the numerators and denominators of (7.51) and (7.52) cancel out and may be ignored for any purpose except asymptotic analysis.

Since $\tilde{\boldsymbol{u}} = \boldsymbol{M_X}\tilde{\boldsymbol{u}}$, it is clear that both statistics have the same numerator. Moreover, s and $\acute{s}$ are asymptotically equal under the null hypothesis that $\rho = 0$, because (7.43) and (7.46) have the same regressand, and all the parameters tend to zero as $n \to \infty$ for both regressions. Therefore, the residuals, and so also the SSRs for the two regressions, tend to the same limits. Under the assumption that $\boldsymbol{X}$ is exogenous, the second factors in the denominators can be shown to be asymptotically equal by the same sort of reasoning used above: Both have limits of σ_u. Thus we conclude that, when the null hypothesis is true, the test statistics t_{GNR} and t_{SR} are asymptotically equal.

It is probably useful at this point to reissue a warning about the test based on the simple regression (7.46). It is valid *only* if $\boldsymbol{X}$ is exogenous. If $\boldsymbol{X}$ contains variables that are merely predetermined rather than exogenous, such as lagged dependent variables, then the test based on the simple regression is not valid, although the test based on the GNR remains so. The presence of the projection matrix $\boldsymbol{M_X}$ in the second factor in the denominator of (7.51) means that this factor is always smaller than the corresponding factor in the denominator of (7.52). If $\boldsymbol{X}$ is exogenous, this does not matter asymptotically, as we have just seen. However, when $\boldsymbol{X}$ contains lagged dependent variables, it turns out that the limits as $n \to \infty$ of t_{GNR} and t_{SR}, under the null that $\rho = 0$, are the same random variable, except for a deterministic factor that is strictly greater for t_{GNR} than for t_{SR}. Consequently, at least in large samples, t_{SR} rejects the null too infrequently. Readers are asked to investigate this matter for a special case in Exercise 7.13.

The Durbin-Watson Statistic

The best-known test statistic for serial correlation is the ***d* statistic** proposed by Durbin and Watson (1950, 1951) and commonly referred to as the **DW statistic**. Like the estimate $\tilde{\rho}$ defined in (7.47), the DW statistic is completely determined by the least squares residuals of the model under test:

$$\begin{aligned} d &= \frac{\sum_{t=2}^{n}(\tilde{u}_t - \tilde{u}_{t-1})^2}{\sum_{t=1}^{n}\tilde{u}_t^2} \\ &= \frac{n^{-1}\tilde{\boldsymbol{u}}^{\top}\tilde{\boldsymbol{u}} + n^{-1}\tilde{\boldsymbol{u}}_1^{\top}\tilde{\boldsymbol{u}}_1}{n^{-1}\tilde{\boldsymbol{u}}^{\top}\tilde{\boldsymbol{u}}} - \frac{n^{-1}\tilde{u}_1^2 + 2n^{-1}\tilde{\boldsymbol{u}}^{\top}\tilde{\boldsymbol{u}}_1}{n^{-1}\tilde{\boldsymbol{u}}^{\top}\tilde{\boldsymbol{u}}}. \end{aligned} \tag{7.53}$$

If we ignore the difference between $n^{-1}\tilde{\boldsymbol{u}}^{\top}\tilde{\boldsymbol{u}}$ and $n^{-1}\tilde{\boldsymbol{u}}_1^{\top}\tilde{\boldsymbol{u}}_1$, and the term $n^{-1}\tilde{u}_1^2$, both of which clearly tend to zero as $n \to \infty$, it can be seen that the first term in the second line of (7.53) tends to 2 and the second term tends to $-2\tilde{\rho}$. Therefore, d is asymptotically equal to $2 - 2\tilde{\rho}$. Thus, in samples of reasonable size, a value of $d \cong 2$ corresponds to the absence of serial correlation in the residuals, while values of d less than 2 correspond to $\tilde{\rho} > 0$, and values greater than 2 correspond to $\tilde{\rho} < 0$. Just like the t statistic t_{SR} based on the simple regression (7.46), and for essentially the same reason, the DW statistic is not valid when there are lagged dependent variables among the regressors.

In Section 3.6, we saw that, for a correctly specified linear regression model, the residual vector $\tilde{\boldsymbol{u}}$ is equal to $\boldsymbol{M_X u}$. Therefore, even if the error terms are serially independent, the residuals generally display a certain amount of serial correlation. This implies that the finite-sample distributions of all the test statistics we have discussed, including that of the DW statistic, depend on $\boldsymbol{X}$. In practice, applied workers generally make use of the fact that the critical values for d are known to fall between two bounding values, d_L and d_U, which depend only on the sample size, n, the number of regressors, k, and whether or not there is a constant term. These bounding critical values have been tabulated for many values of n and k; see Savin and White (1977).

The standard tables, which are deliberately not printed in this book, contain bounds for one-tailed DW tests of the null hypothesis that $\rho \leq 0$ against the alternative that $\rho > 0$. An investigator should reject the null hypothesis if $d < d_L$, fail to reject if $d > d_U$, and come to no conclusion if $d_L < d < d_U$. For example, for a test at the .05 level when $n = 100$ and $k = 8$, including the constant term, the bounding critical values are $d_L = 1.528$ and $d_U = 1.826$. Therefore, one would reject the null hypothesis if $d < 1.528$ and not reject it if $d > 1.826$. Notice that, even for this not particularly small sample size, the indeterminate region between 1.528 and 1.826 is quite large.

It should by now be evident that the Durbin-Watson statistic, despite its popularity, is not very satisfactory. Using it with standard tables is relatively cumbersome and often yields inconclusive results. Moreover, the standard tables only allow us to perform one-tailed tests against the alternative that $\rho > 0$. Since the alternative that $\rho < 0$ is often of interest as well, the inability to perform a two-tailed test, or a one-tailed test against this alternative, using standard tables is a serious limitation. Although exact P values for both one-tailed and two-tailed tests, which depend on the $\boldsymbol{X}$ matrix, can be obtained by using appropriate software, many computer programs do not offer this capability. In addition, the DW statistic is not valid when the regressors include lagged dependent variables, and it cannot easily be generalized to test for higher-order processes. Happily, the development of simulation-based tests has made the DW statistic obsolete.

Monte Carlo Tests for Serial Correlation

We discussed simulation-based tests, including Monte Carlo tests and bootstrap tests, at some length in Section 4.6. The techniques discussed there can readily be applied to the problem of testing for serial correlation in linear and nonlinear regression models.

All the test statistics we have discussed, namely, $t_{\rm GNR}$, $t_{\rm SR}$, and d, are pivotal under the null hypothesis that $\rho = 0$ when the assumptions of the classical normal linear model are satisfied. This makes it possible to perform Monte Carlo tests that are exact in finite samples. Pivotalness follows from two properties that are shared by all these statistics. The first property is that they depend only on the residuals $\tilde{u}_t$ obtained by estimation under the null hypothesis. The distribution of the residuals depends on the exogenous explanatory variables $\boldsymbol{X}$, but these are given and the same for all DGPs in a classical normal linear model. The distribution does not depend on the parameter vector $\boldsymbol{\beta}$ of the regression function, because, if $\boldsymbol{y} = \boldsymbol{X\beta} + \boldsymbol{u}$, then $\boldsymbol{M_X y} = \boldsymbol{M_X u}$ whatever the value of the vector $\boldsymbol{\beta}$.

The second property that all the statistics we have considered share is **scale invariance**. By this, we mean that multiplying the dependent variable by an arbitrary scalar λ leaves the statistic unchanged. In a linear regression model, multiplying the dependent variable by λ causes the residuals to be multiplied by λ. But the statistics defined in (7.51), (7.52), and (7.53) are clearly unchanged if all the residuals are multiplied by the same constant, and so these statistics are scale invariant. Since the residuals $\tilde{\boldsymbol{u}}$ are equal to $\boldsymbol{M_X u}$, it follows that multiplying σ by an arbitrary λ multiplies the residuals by λ. Consequently, the distributions of the statistics are independent of σ^2 as well as of $\boldsymbol{\beta}$. This implies that, for the classical normal linear model, all three statistics are pivotal.

We now outline how to perform Monte Carlo tests for serial correlation in the context of the classical normal linear model. Let us call the test statistic we are using τ and its realized value $\hat{\tau}$. If we want to test for AR(1) errors, the best choice for the statistic τ is the t statistic t_{GNR} from the GNR (7.43), but it could also be the DW statistic, the t statistic t_{SR} from the simple regression (7.46), or even $\tilde{\rho}$ itself. If we want to test for AR(p) errors, the best choice for τ would be the F statistic from the GNR (7.45), but it could also be the F statistic from a regression of $\tilde{u}_t$ on $\tilde{u}_{t-1}$ through $\tilde{u}_{t-p}$.

The first step, evidently, is to compute $\hat{\tau}$. The next step is to generate B sets of simulated residuals and use each of them to compute a simulated test statistic, say τ_j^*, for $j = 1, \ldots, B$. Because the parameters do not matter, we can simply draw B vectors $\boldsymbol{u}_j^*$ from the $\mathrm{N}(\mathbf{0}, \mathbf{I})$ distribution and regress each of them on $\boldsymbol{X}$ to generate the simulated residuals $\boldsymbol{M_X u}_j^*$, which are then used to compute τ_j^*. This can be done very inexpensively. The final step is to calculate an estimated P value. For a one-tailed test that rejects in the upper tail, this can be done by using equation (4.62). For a two-tailed test, however, there is more than one way to proceed.

The simplest approach, which makes sense if the test statistic is symmetrically distributed around 0, is to calculate the proportion of the τ_j^* that exceed $\hat{\tau}$ in absolute value, which is

$$\hat{p}^*(\hat{\tau}) = \frac{1}{B}\sum_{j=1}^{B} I\big(|\tau_j^*| > |\hat{\tau}|\big). \tag{7.54}$$

For the t_{GNR} statistic, this is equivalent to using an F statistic for $b_\rho = 0$ in equation (7.44) and calculating a one-tailed bootstrap P value. We reject the null hypothesis at level α if $\hat{p}^*(\hat{\tau}) < \alpha$. As we saw in Section 4.6, such a test is exact whenever B is chosen so that $\alpha(B+1)$ is an integer.

In many cases, test statistics for serial correlation are not distributed symmetrically around 0. If examination of the τ_j^* suggests that the symmetry assumption is false, then, as we saw in Section 5.3, we should use

$$\hat{p}^*(\hat{\tau}) = \frac{2}{B}\min\bigg(\sum_{j=1}^{B} I(\tau_j^* > \hat{\tau}), \sum_{j=1}^{B} I(\tau_j^* \le \hat{\tau})\bigg). \tag{7.55}$$

Once again, we reject the null hypothesis at level α if $\hat{p}^*(\hat{\tau}) < \alpha$. This test is exact whenever B is chosen so that $\frac{1}{2}\alpha(B+1)$ is an integer. When the symmetry assumption is not satisfied, the test based on (7.55) should be more powerful than the one based on (7.54).

Bootstrap Tests for Serial Correlation

Whenever the regression function is nonlinear or contains lagged dependent variables, or whenever the distribution of the error terms is unknown, none of the standard test statistics for serial correlation is pivotal. Nevertheless, it is still possible to obtain very accurate inferences, even in quite small samples, by using bootstrap tests. The procedure is essentially the one described in the previous subsection. We still generate B simulated test statistics and use them to compute a P value according to whichever of equations (4.62), (7.54), or (7.55) is appropriate. For best results, the test statistic used should be asymptotically valid for the model that is being tested. In particular, we should avoid d and t_{SR} whenever there are lagged dependent variables.

It is extremely important to generate the bootstrap samples in such a way that they are compatible with the model under test. Ways of generating bootstrap samples for regression models were discussed in Section 4.6. If the model is nonlinear or includes lagged dependent variables, we need to generate $\boldsymbol{y}_j^*$ rather than just $\boldsymbol{u}_j^*$. For this, we need estimates of the parameters of the regression function. If the model includes lagged dependent variables, we must generate the bootstrap samples recursively, as in (4.67). Unless we are going to assume that the error terms are normally distributed, we should draw the bootstrap error terms from the EDF of the residuals for the model under test, after they have been appropriately rescaled. Recall that there is more than one way to do this. The simplest approach is just to multiply each residual by $(n/(n-k))^{1/2}$, as in expression (4.69).

We strongly recommend the use of simulation-based tests for serial correlation, rather than asymptotic tests. Monte Carlo tests are appropriate only in the context of the classical normal linear model, but bootstrap tests are appropriate under much weaker assumptions. It is generally a good idea to test for both AR(1) errors and higher-order autoregressive errors, at least fourth-order in the case of quarterly data, and at least twelfth-order in the case of monthly data.

Heteroskedasticity-Robust Tests

The tests for serial correlation that we have discussed are based on the assumption that the error terms are homoskedastic. When this crucial assumption is violated, the asymptotic distributions of all the test statistics differ from whatever distributions they are supposed to follow asymptotically. However, as we saw in Section 6.8, it is not difficult to modify GNR-based tests to make them robust to heteroskedasticity of unknown form.

Suppose we wish to test the linear regression model (7.42), in which the error terms are serially uncorrelated, against the alternative that the error terms follow an AR(p) process. Under the assumption of homoskedasticity, we could simply run the GNR (7.45) and use an asymptotic F test. If we let $\boldsymbol{Z}$ denote an $n \times p$ matrix with typical element $Z_{ti} = \tilde{u}_{t-i}$, where any missing lagged residuals are replaced by zeros, this GNR can be written as

$$\tilde{\boldsymbol{u}} = \boldsymbol{X}\boldsymbol{b} + \boldsymbol{Z}\boldsymbol{c} + \text{residuals}. \tag{7.56}$$

The ordinary F test for $\boldsymbol{c} = \boldsymbol{0}$ in (7.56) is not robust to heteroskedasticity, but a heteroskedasticity-robust test can easily be computed using the procedure described in Section 6.8. This procedure works as follows:

1. Create the matrices $\tilde{\boldsymbol{U}}\boldsymbol{X}$ and $\tilde{\boldsymbol{U}}\boldsymbol{Z}$ by multiplying the tth row of $\boldsymbol{X}$ and the tth row of $\boldsymbol{Z}$ by $\tilde{u}_t$ for all t.
2. Create the matrices $\tilde{\boldsymbol{U}}^{-1}\boldsymbol{X}$ and $\tilde{\boldsymbol{U}}^{-1}\boldsymbol{Z}$ by dividing the tth row of $\boldsymbol{X}$ and the tth row of $\boldsymbol{Z}$ by $\tilde{u}_t$ for all t.
3. Regress each of the columns of $\tilde{\boldsymbol{U}}^{-1}\boldsymbol{X}$ and $\tilde{\boldsymbol{U}}^{-1}\boldsymbol{Z}$ on $\tilde{\boldsymbol{U}}\boldsymbol{X}$ and $\tilde{\boldsymbol{U}}\boldsymbol{Z}$ jointly. Save the resulting matrices of fitted values and call them $\bar{\boldsymbol{X}}$ and $\bar{\boldsymbol{Z}}$, respectively.
4. Regress $\boldsymbol{\iota}$, a vector of 1s, on $\bar{\boldsymbol{X}}$. Retain the sum of squared residuals from this regression, and call it RSSR. Then regress $\boldsymbol{\iota}$ on $\bar{\boldsymbol{X}}$ and $\bar{\boldsymbol{Z}}$ jointly, retain the sum of squared residuals, and call it USSR.
5. Compute the test statistic RSSR − USSR, which is asymptotically distributed as $\chi^2(p)$ under the null hypothesis.

Although this heteroskedasticity-robust test is asymptotically valid, it is not exact in finite samples. In principle, we should be able to obtain more reliable results by using bootstrap P values instead of asymptotic ones. However, none of the methods of generating bootstrap samples for regression models that we have discussed so far (see Section 4.6) is appropriate for a model with heteroskedastic error terms. Several methods exist, but they are beyond the scope of this book, and there currently exists no method that we can recommend with complete confidence; see Davison and Hinkley (1997), Horowitz (2001), and MacKinnon (2002).

Other Tests Based on OLS Residuals

The tests for serial correlation that we have discussed in this section are by no means the only scale-invariant tests based on least squares residuals that are regularly encountered in econometrics. Many tests for heteroskedasticity, skewness, kurtosis, and other deviations from the NID assumption also have these properties. For example, consider tests for heteroskedasticity based on regression (7.28). Nothing in that regression depends on $\boldsymbol{y}$ except for the squared residuals that constitute the regressand. Further, it is clear that both the F statistic for the hypothesis that $\boldsymbol{b}_\gamma = \boldsymbol{0}$ and n times the centered R^2 are scale invariant. Therefore, for a classical normal linear model with $\boldsymbol{X}$ and $\boldsymbol{Z}$ fixed, these statistics are pivotal. Consequently, Monte Carlo tests based on them, in which we draw the error terms from the N(0, 1) distribution, are exact in finite samples.

When the normality assumption is not appropriate, we have two options. If some other distribution that is known up to a scale parameter is thought to be appropriate, we can draw the error terms from it instead of from the $\mathrm{N}(0,1)$ distribution. Then, if the assumed distribution really is the true one, we obtain an exact test. Alternatively, we can perform a bootstrap test in which the error terms are obtained by resampling the rescaled residuals. This is also appropriate when there are lagged dependent variables among the regressors. The bootstrap test is not exact, but it should still perform well in finite samples no matter how the error terms actually happen to be distributed.

7.8 Estimating Models with Autoregressive Errors

If we decide that the error terms of a regression model are serially correlated, either on the basis of theoretical considerations or as a result of specification testing, and we are confident that the regression function itself is not misspecified, the next step is to estimate a modified model which takes account of the serial correlation. The simplest such model is (7.40), which is the original regression model modified by having the error terms follow an AR(1) process. For ease of reference, we rewrite (7.40) here:

$$y_t = \boldsymbol{X}_t\boldsymbol{\beta} + u_t, \quad u_t = \rho u_{t-1} + \varepsilon_t, \quad \varepsilon_t \sim \mathrm{IID}(0, \sigma_\varepsilon^2). \tag{7.57}$$

In many cases, as we will discuss in the next section, the best approach may actually be to specify a more complicated, dynamic, model for which the error terms are not serially correlated. In this section, however, we ignore this important issue and simply discuss how to estimate the model (7.57) under various assumptions.

Estimation by Feasible GLS

We have seen that, if the u_t follow a stationary AR(1) process, that is, if $|\rho| < 1$ and $\mathrm{Var}(u_1) = \sigma_u^2 = \sigma_\varepsilon^2/(1-\rho^2)$, then the covariance matrix of the entire vector $\boldsymbol{u}$ is the $n \times n$ matrix $\boldsymbol{\Omega}(\rho)$ given in equation (7.32). In order to compute GLS estimates, we need to find a matrix $\boldsymbol{\Psi}$ with the property that $\boldsymbol{\Psi}\boldsymbol{\Psi}^\top$ is proportional to $\boldsymbol{\Omega}^{-1}$. This property is satisfied whenever the covariance matrix of the vector $\boldsymbol{\Psi}^\top\boldsymbol{u}$ is proportional to the identity matrix, which it must be if we choose $\boldsymbol{\Psi}$ in such a way that $\boldsymbol{\Psi}^\top\boldsymbol{u} = \boldsymbol{\varepsilon}$.

For $t = 2, \ldots, n$, we know from (7.29) that

$$\varepsilon_t = u_t - \rho u_{t-1}, \tag{7.58}$$

and this allows us to construct the rows of $\boldsymbol{\Psi}^\top$ except for the first row. The tth row must have 1 in the tth position, $-\rho$ in the $(t-1)^{\text{st}}$ position, and 0s everywhere else.

For the first row of $\boldsymbol{\Psi}^\top$, however, we need to be a little more careful. Under the hypothesis of stationarity of $\boldsymbol{u}$, the variance of u_1 is σ_u^2. Further, since the ε_t are innovations, u_1 is uncorrelated with the ε_t for $t = 2, \ldots, n$. Thus, if we define ε_1 by the formula

$$\varepsilon_1 = (\sigma_\varepsilon/\sigma_u)u_1 = (1-\rho^2)^{1/2}u_1, \tag{7.59}$$

it can be seen that the n–vector $\boldsymbol{\varepsilon}$, with the first component ε_1 defined by (7.59) and the remaining components ε_t defined by (7.58), has a covariance matrix equal to $\sigma_\varepsilon^2 \mathbf{I}$.

Putting together (7.58) and (7.59), we conclude that $\boldsymbol{\Psi}^\top$ should be defined as an $n \times n$ matrix with all diagonal elements equal to 1 except for the first, which is equal to $(1-\rho^2)^{1/2}$, and all other elements equal to 0 except for the ones on the diagonal immediately below the principal diagonal, which are equal to $-\rho$. In terms of $\boldsymbol{\Psi}$ rather than of $\boldsymbol{\Psi}^\top$, we have:

$$\boldsymbol{\Psi}(\rho) = \begin{bmatrix} (1-\rho^2)^{1/2} & -\rho & 0 & \cdots & 0 & 0 \\ 0 & 1 & -\rho & \cdots & 0 & 0 \\ \vdots & \vdots & \vdots & & \vdots & \vdots \\ 0 & 0 & 0 & \cdots & 1 & -\rho \\ 0 & 0 & 0 & \cdots & 0 & 1 \end{bmatrix}, \tag{7.60}$$

where the notation $\boldsymbol{\Psi}(\rho)$ emphasizes that the matrix depends on the usually unknown parameter ρ. The matrix $\boldsymbol{\Psi}\boldsymbol{\Psi}^\top$ is proportional to the inverse of the autocovariance matrix that appears in equation (7.32). The calculations needed to show that this is so are outlined in Exercises 7.9 and 7.10.

It is essential that the AR(1) parameter ρ either be known or be consistently estimable. If we know ρ, we can obtain GLS estimates. If we do not know it but can estimate it consistently, we can obtain feasible GLS estimates. For the case in which the explanatory variables are all exogenous, the simplest way to estimate ρ consistently is to use the estimator $\tilde{\rho}$ from regression (7.46), defined in (7.47). Whatever estimate of ρ is used must satisfy the stationarity condition that $|\rho| < 1$, without which the process would not be stationary, and the transformation for the first observation would involve taking the square root of a negative number. Unfortunately, the estimator $\tilde{\rho}$ is not guaranteed to satisfy the stationarity condition, although, in practice, it is very likely to do so when the model is correctly specified, even if the true value of ρ is quite large in absolute value.

Whether ρ is known or estimated, the next step in GLS estimation is to form the vector $\boldsymbol{\Psi}^\top\boldsymbol{y}$ and the matrix $\boldsymbol{\Psi}^\top\boldsymbol{X}$. It is easy to do this without having to store the $n \times n$ matrix $\boldsymbol{\Psi}$ in computer memory. The first element of $\boldsymbol{\Psi}^\top\boldsymbol{y}$ is $(1-\rho^2)^{1/2}y_1$, and the remaining elements have the form $y_t - \rho y_{t-1}$. Each column of $\boldsymbol{\Psi}^\top\boldsymbol{X}$ has precisely the same form as $\boldsymbol{\Psi}^\top\boldsymbol{y}$ and can be calculated in precisely the same way.

The final step is to run an OLS regression of $\boldsymbol{\Psi}^\top \boldsymbol{y}$ on $\boldsymbol{\Psi}^\top \boldsymbol{X}$. This regression yields the (feasible) GLS estimates

$$\hat{\boldsymbol{\beta}}_{\text{GLS}} = (\boldsymbol{X}^\top \boldsymbol{\Psi} \boldsymbol{\Psi}^\top \boldsymbol{X})^{-1} \boldsymbol{X}^\top \boldsymbol{\Psi} \boldsymbol{\Psi}^\top \boldsymbol{y} \tag{7.61}$$

along with the estimated covariance matrix

$$\widehat{\text{Var}}(\hat{\boldsymbol{\beta}}_{\text{GLS}}) = s^2 (\boldsymbol{X}^\top \boldsymbol{\Psi} \boldsymbol{\Psi}^\top \boldsymbol{X})^{-1}, \tag{7.62}$$

where s^2 is the usual OLS estimate of the variance of the error terms. Of course, the estimator (7.61) is formally identical to (7.04), since (7.61) is valid for any $\boldsymbol{\Psi}$ matrix.

Estimation by Nonlinear Least Squares

If we ignore the first observation, then (7.57), the linear regression model with AR(1) errors, can be written as the nonlinear regression model (7.41). Since the model (7.41) is written in such a way that the error terms are innovations, NLS estimation is consistent whether the explanatory variables are exogenous or merely predetermined. NLS estimates can be obtained by any standard nonlinear minimization algorithm of the type that was discussed in Section 6.4, where the function to be minimized is $\text{SSR}(\boldsymbol{\beta}, \rho)$, the sum of squared residuals for observations 2 through n. Such procedures generally work well, and they can also be used for models with higher-order autoregressive errors; see Exercise 7.17. However, some care must be taken to ensure that the algorithm does not terminate at a local minimum which is not also the global minimum. There is a serious risk of this, especially for models with lagged dependent variables among the regressors.[2]

Whether or not there are lagged dependent variables in $\boldsymbol{X}_t$, a valid estimated covariance matrix can always be obtained by running the GNR (6.67), which corresponds to the model (7.41), with all variables evaluated at the NLS estimates $\hat{\boldsymbol{\beta}}$ and $\hat{\rho}$. This GNR is

$$\begin{aligned} & y_t - \hat{\rho} y_{t-1} - \boldsymbol{X}_t \hat{\boldsymbol{\beta}} + \hat{\rho} \boldsymbol{X}_{t-1} \hat{\boldsymbol{\beta}} \\ & \qquad = (\boldsymbol{X}_t - \hat{\rho} \boldsymbol{X}_{t-1}) \boldsymbol{b} + b_\rho (y_{t-1} - \boldsymbol{X}_{t-1} \hat{\boldsymbol{\beta}}) + \text{residual}. \end{aligned} \tag{7.63}$$

Since the OLS estimates of $\boldsymbol{b}$ and b_ρ must be equal to zero, the sum of squared residuals from regression (7.63) is simply $\text{SSR}(\hat{\boldsymbol{\beta}}, \hat{\rho})$. Therefore, the estimated covariance matrix $\widehat{\text{Var}}(\hat{\boldsymbol{\beta}}, \hat{\rho})$ is

$$\frac{\text{SSR}(\hat{\boldsymbol{\beta}}, \hat{\rho})}{n-k-2} \begin{bmatrix} (\boldsymbol{X} - \hat{\rho} \boldsymbol{X}_1)^\top (\boldsymbol{X} - \hat{\rho} \boldsymbol{X}_1) & (\boldsymbol{X} - \hat{\rho} \boldsymbol{X}_1)^\top \hat{\boldsymbol{u}}_1 \\ \hat{\boldsymbol{u}}_1^\top (\boldsymbol{X} - \hat{\rho} \boldsymbol{X}_1) & \hat{\boldsymbol{u}}_1^\top \hat{\boldsymbol{u}}_1 \end{bmatrix}^{-1}, \tag{7.64}$$

[2] See Dufour, Gaudry, and Liem (1980) and Betancourt and Kelejian (1981).

where the $n \times k$ matrix $\boldsymbol{X}_1$ has typical row $\boldsymbol{X}_{t-1}$, and the vector $\hat{\boldsymbol{u}}_1$ has typical element $y_{t-1} - \boldsymbol{X}_{t-1}\hat{\boldsymbol{\beta}}$. This is the estimated covariance matrix that a good nonlinear regression package should print. The first factor in (7.64) is just the NLS estimate of σ_ε^2. The SSR is divided by $n - k - 2$ because there are $k+1$ parameters in the regression function, one of which is ρ, and we estimate using only $n - 1$ observations.

It is instructive to compute the limit in probability of the matrix (7.64) when $n \to \infty$ for the case in which all the explanatory variables in $\boldsymbol{X}_t$ are exogenous. The parameters are all estimated consistently by NLS, and so the estimates converge to the true parameter values $\boldsymbol{\beta}_0$, ρ_0, and σ_ε^2 as $n \to \infty$. In computing the limit of the denominator of the simple estimator $\tilde{\rho}$ given by (7.47), we saw that $n^{-1}\hat{\boldsymbol{u}}_1^\top\hat{\boldsymbol{u}}_1$ tends to $\sigma_\varepsilon^2/(1-\rho_0^2)$. The limit of $n^{-1}(\boldsymbol{X} - \hat{\rho}\boldsymbol{X}_1)^\top\hat{\boldsymbol{u}}_1$ is the same as that of $n^{-1}(\boldsymbol{X} - \rho_0\boldsymbol{X}_1)^\top\hat{\boldsymbol{u}}_1$ by the consistency of $\hat{\rho}$. In addition, given the exogeneity of $\boldsymbol{X}$, and thus also of $\boldsymbol{X}_1$, it follows at once from a law of large numbers that $n^{-1}(\boldsymbol{X} - \rho_0\boldsymbol{X}_1)^\top\hat{\boldsymbol{u}}_1$ tends to zero. Thus, in this special case, the $(k+1) \times (k+1)$ asymptotic covariance matrix of the vector $n^{1/2}(\hat{\boldsymbol{\beta}} - \boldsymbol{\beta}_0)$ and the scalar $n^{1/2}(\hat{\rho} - \rho_0)$ is

$$\sigma_\varepsilon^2\begin{bmatrix} \operatorname{plim}\frac{1}{n}(\boldsymbol{X} - \rho_0\boldsymbol{X}_1)^\top(\boldsymbol{X} - \rho_0\boldsymbol{X}_1) & \mathbf{0} \\ \mathbf{0}^\top & \sigma_\varepsilon^2/(1-\rho_0^2) \end{bmatrix}^{-1}. \tag{7.65}$$

Because the two off-diagonal blocks are zero, this matrix is said to be **block-diagonal**. As can be verified immediately, the inverse of such a matrix is itself a block-diagonal matrix, of which each block is the inverse of the corresponding block of the original matrix. Thus the asymptotic covariance matrix (7.65) is the limit as $n \to \infty$ of

$$\begin{bmatrix} n\sigma_\varepsilon^2\big((\boldsymbol{X} - \rho_0\boldsymbol{X}_1)^\top(\boldsymbol{X} - \rho_0\boldsymbol{X}_1)\big)^{-1} & \mathbf{0} \\ \mathbf{0}^\top & 1-\rho_0^2 \end{bmatrix}. \tag{7.66}$$

The block-diagonality of the matrix (7.66), which holds only if every one of the regressors in $\boldsymbol{X}_t$ is exogenous, implies that the covariance matrix of $\hat{\boldsymbol{\beta}}$ can be estimated using the GNR (7.63) without the regressor corresponding to ρ. The estimated covariance matrix is just (7.64) without its last row and column. It is easy to see that n times this matrix tends to the top left-hand block of (7.66) as $n \to \infty$.

The lower right-hand element of the matrix (7.66) tells us that, when all the regressors are exogenous, the asymptotic variance of $n^{1/2}(\hat{\rho} - \rho_0)$ is $1 - \rho_0^2$. A sensible estimate of the variance is therefore $\widehat{\operatorname{Var}}(\hat{\rho}) = n^{-1}(1 - \hat{\rho}^2)$. It may seem surprising that the variance of $\hat{\rho}$ does not depend on σ_ε^2. However, we saw earlier that, with exogenous regressors, the consistent estimator $\tilde{\rho}$ of (7.47) is scale invariant. The same is true, asymptotically, of the NLS estimator $\hat{\rho}$, and so its asymptotic variance is independent of σ_ε^2.

Comparison of GLS and NLS

The most obvious difference between estimation by GLS and estimation by NLS is the treatment of the first observation: GLS takes it into account, and NLS does not. This difference reflects the fact that the two procedures are estimating slightly different models. With NLS, all that is required is the stationarity condition that $|\rho| < 1$. With GLS, on the other hand, the error process must actually be stationary. Recall that the stationarity condition is necessary but not sufficient for stationarity of the process. A sufficient condition requires, in addition, that $\text{Var}(u_1) = \sigma_u^2 = \sigma_\varepsilon^2/(1-\rho^2)$, the stationary value of the variance. Thus, if we suspect that $\text{Var}(u_1) \neq \sigma_u^2$, GLS estimation is not appropriate, because the matrix (7.32) is not the covariance matrix of the error terms.

The second major difference between estimation by GLS and estimation by NLS is that the former method estimates $\boldsymbol{\beta}$ conditional on ρ, while the latter method estimates $\boldsymbol{\beta}$ and ρ jointly. Except in the unlikely case in which the value of ρ is known, the first step in GLS is to estimate ρ consistently. If the explanatory variables in the matrix $\boldsymbol{X}$ are all exogenous, there are several procedures that can deliver a consistent estimate of ρ. The weak point is that the estimate is not unique, and in general it is not optimal. One possible solution to this difficulty is to iterate the feasible GLS procedure, as suggested at the end of Section 7.4, and we will consider this solution below.

A more fundamental weakness of GLS arises whenever one or more of the explanatory variables are lagged dependent variables, or, more generally, predetermined but not exogenous variables. Even with a consistent estimator of ρ, one of the conditions for the applicability of feasible GLS, condition (7.23), does not hold when any elements of $\boldsymbol{X}_t$ are not exogenous. It is not simple to see directly just why this is so, but, in the next paragraph, we will obtain indirect evidence by showing that feasible GLS gives an invalid estimator of the covariance matrix. Fortunately, there is not much temptation to use GLS if the non-exogenous explanatory variables are lagged variables, because lagged variables are not observed for the first observation. In all events, the conclusion is simple: We should avoid GLS if the explanatory variables are not all exogenous.

The GLS covariance matrix estimator is (7.62), which is obtained by regressing $\boldsymbol{\Psi}^\top(\hat{\rho})\boldsymbol{y}$ on $\boldsymbol{\Psi}^\top(\hat{\rho})\boldsymbol{X}$ for some consistent estimate $\hat{\rho}$. Since $\boldsymbol{\Psi}^\top(\rho)\boldsymbol{u} = \boldsymbol{\varepsilon}$ by construction, s^2 is an estimator of σ_ε^2. Moreover, the first observation has no impact asymptotically. Therefore, the limit as $n \to \infty$ of n times (7.62) is the matrix

$$\sigma_\varepsilon^2 \operatorname*{plim}_{n\to\infty} \Big(\frac{1}{n}(\boldsymbol{X} - \rho\boldsymbol{X}_1)^\top(\boldsymbol{X} - \rho\boldsymbol{X}_1)\Big)^{-1}. \tag{7.67}$$

In contrast, the NLS covariance matrix estimator is (7.64). With exogenous regressors, n times (7.64) tends to the same limit as (7.66), of which the top left block is just (7.67). But when the regressors are not all exogenous, the argument that the off-diagonal blocks of n times (7.64) tend to zero no longer works, and, in fact, the limits of these blocks are in general nonzero. When a matrix that is not block-diagonal is inverted, the top left block of the inverse is not the same as the inverse of the top left block of the original matrix; see Exercise 7.11. In fact, as readers are asked to show in Exercise 7.12, the top left block of the inverse is greater by a positive semidefinite matrix than the inverse of the top left block. Consequently, the GLS covariance matrix estimator underestimates the true covariance matrix asymptotically.

NLS has only one major weak point, which is that it does not take account of the first observation. Of course, this is really an advantage if the error process satisfies the stationarity condition without actually being stationary, or if some of the explanatory variables are not exogenous. But with a stationary error process and exogenous regressors, we wish to retain the information in the first observation, because it appears that retaining the first observation can sometimes lead to a noticeable efficiency gain in finite samples. The reason is that the transformation for observation 1 is quite different from the transformation for all the other observations. In consequence, the transformed first observation may well be a high leverage point; see Section 2.6. This is particularly likely to happen if one or more of the regressors is strongly trending. If so, dropping the first observation can mean throwing away a lot of information. See Davidson and MacKinnon (1993, Section 10.6) for a much fuller discussion and references.

Efficient Estimation by GLS or NLS

When the error process is stationary and all the regressors are exogenous, it is possible to obtain an estimator with the best features of GLS and NLS by modifying NLS so that it makes use of the information in the first observation and therefore yields an efficient estimator. The first-order conditions (7.07) for GLS estimation of the model (7.57) can be written as

$$\boldsymbol{X}^\top\boldsymbol{\Psi}\boldsymbol{\Psi}^\top(\boldsymbol{y}-\boldsymbol{X\beta})=\boldsymbol{0}.$$

Using (7.60) for $\boldsymbol{\Psi}$, we see that these conditions are

$$\begin{aligned}\sum_{t=2}^{n}(\boldsymbol{X}_t-\rho\boldsymbol{X}_{t-1})^\top\big(y_t-\boldsymbol{X}_t\boldsymbol{\beta}-\rho(y_{t-1}-\boldsymbol{X}_{t-1}\boldsymbol{\beta})\big)&\\ +(1-\rho^2)\boldsymbol{X}_1^\top(y_1-\boldsymbol{X}_1\boldsymbol{\beta})&=\boldsymbol{0}.\end{aligned}\tag{7.68}$$

With NLS estimation, the first-order conditions that define the NLS estimator are the conditions that the regressors in the GNR (7.63) should be orthogonal to the regressand:

$$\begin{aligned}&\sum_{t=2}^{n}(\boldsymbol{X}_t-\rho\boldsymbol{X}_{t-1})^\top\big(y_t-\boldsymbol{X}_t\boldsymbol{\beta}-\rho(y_{t-1}-\boldsymbol{X}_{t-1}\boldsymbol{\beta})\big)=\boldsymbol{0},\ \text{and}\\ &\sum_{t=2}^{n}(y_{t-1}-\boldsymbol{X}_{t-1}\boldsymbol{\beta})\big(y_t-\boldsymbol{X}_t\boldsymbol{\beta}-\rho(y_{t-1}-\boldsymbol{X}_{t-1}\boldsymbol{\beta})\big)=0.\end{aligned}\tag{7.69}$$

For given $\boldsymbol{\beta}$, the second of the NLS conditions can be solved for ρ. If we write $\boldsymbol{u}(\boldsymbol{\beta}) = \boldsymbol{y} - \boldsymbol{X}\boldsymbol{\beta}$, and $\boldsymbol{u}_1(\boldsymbol{\beta}) = \mathbf{L}\boldsymbol{u}(\boldsymbol{\beta})$, where $\mathbf{L}$ is the matrix lag operator defined in (7.49), we see that

$$\rho(\boldsymbol{\beta}) = \frac{\boldsymbol{u}^\top(\boldsymbol{\beta})\boldsymbol{u}_1(\boldsymbol{\beta})}{\boldsymbol{u}_1^\top(\boldsymbol{\beta})\boldsymbol{u}_1(\boldsymbol{\beta})}. \tag{7.70}$$

This formula is similar to the estimator (7.47), except that $\boldsymbol{\beta}$ may take on any value instead of just $\tilde{\boldsymbol{\beta}}$.

In Section 7.4, we mentioned the possibility of using an **iterated feasible GLS** procedure. We can now see precisely how such a procedure would work for this model. In the first step, we obtain the OLS parameter vector $\tilde{\boldsymbol{\beta}}$. In the second step, the formula (7.70) is evaluated at $\boldsymbol{\beta} = \tilde{\boldsymbol{\beta}}$ to obtain $\tilde{\rho}$, a consistent estimate of ρ. In the third step, we use (7.61) to obtain the feasible GLS estimate $\hat{\boldsymbol{\beta}}_{\rm F}$, thus solving the first-order conditions (7.68). At this point, we go back to the second step and insert $\hat{\boldsymbol{\beta}}_{\rm F}$ into (7.70) for an updated estimate of ρ, which we subsequently use in (7.61) for the next estimate of $\boldsymbol{\beta}$. The iterative procedure may then be continued until convergence, assuming that it does converge. If so, then the final estimates, which we will call $\hat{\boldsymbol{\beta}}$ and $\hat{\rho}$, must satisfy the two equations

$$\begin{aligned} &\sum_{t=2}^{n}(\boldsymbol{X}_t - \hat{\rho}\boldsymbol{X}_{t-1})^\top\big(y_t - \boldsymbol{X}_t\hat{\boldsymbol{\beta}} - \hat{\rho}(y_{t-1} - \boldsymbol{X}_{t-1}\hat{\boldsymbol{\beta}})\big) \\ &\qquad\qquad\qquad + (1-\hat{\rho}^2)\boldsymbol{X}_1^\top(y_1 - \boldsymbol{X}_1\hat{\boldsymbol{\beta}}) = \boldsymbol{0}, \text{ and} \\ &\sum_{t=2}^{n}(y_{t-1} - \boldsymbol{X}_{t-1}\hat{\boldsymbol{\beta}})\big(y_t - \boldsymbol{X}_t\hat{\boldsymbol{\beta}} - \hat{\rho}(y_{t-1} - \boldsymbol{X}_{t-1}\hat{\boldsymbol{\beta}})\big) = 0. \end{aligned} \tag{7.71}$$

These conditions are identical to conditions (7.69), except for the term in the first condition coming from the first observation. Thus we see that iterated feasible GLS, *without* the first observation, is identical to NLS. If the first observation is retained, then iterated feasible GLS improves on NLS by taking account of the first observation.

We can also modify NLS to take account of the first observation. To do this, we extend the GNR (6.67), which is given by (7.63) when evaluated at $\hat{\boldsymbol{\beta}}$ and $\hat{\rho}$, by giving it a first observation. For this observation, the regressand is $(1-\rho^2)^{1/2}(y_1 - \boldsymbol{X}_1\boldsymbol{\beta})$, the regressors corresponding to $\boldsymbol{\beta}$ are given by the row vector $(1-\rho^2)^{1/2}\boldsymbol{X}_1$, and the regressor corresponding to ρ is zero. The conditions that the extended regressand should be orthogonal to the extended regressors are exactly the conditions (7.71).

Two asymptotically equivalent procedures can be based on this extended GNR. Both begin by obtaining the NLS estimates of $\boldsymbol{\beta}$ and ρ without the first observation and evaluating the extended GNR at those preliminary NLS estimates. The OLS estimates from the extended GNR can be thought of as a vector of corrections to the initial estimates. For the first procedure, the final estimator is a one-step estimator, defined as in (6.59) by adding the corrections to the preliminary estimates. For the second procedure, this process is iterated. The variables of the extended GNR are evaluated at the one-step estimates, another set of corrections is obtained, these are added to the previous estimates, and iteration continues until the corrections are negligible. If this happens, the iterated estimates once more satisfy the conditions (7.71), and so they are equal to the iterated GLS estimates.

Although the iterated feasible GLS estimator generally performs well, it does have one weakness: There is no way to ensure that $|\hat{\rho}| < 1$. In the unlikely but not impossible event that $|\hat{\rho}| \geq 1$, the estimated covariance matrix (7.62) is not valid, the second term in (7.68) must be negative, and the first observation therefore tends to have a perverse effect on the estimates of $\boldsymbol{\beta}$. In Chapter 10, we will see that maximum likelihood estimation shares the good properties of iterated feasible GLS while also ensuring that the estimate of ρ satisfies the stationarity condition.

The iterated feasible GLS procedure considered above has much in common with a very old, but still widely-used, algorithm for estimating models with stationary AR(1) errors. This algorithm, which is called **iterated Cochrane-Orcutt**, was originally proposed in a classic paper by Cochrane and Orcutt (1949). It works in exactly the same way as iterated feasible GLS, except that it omits the first observation. The properties of this algorithm are explored in Exercises 7.18-19.

7.9 Specification Testing and Serial Correlation

Models estimated using time-series data frequently appear to have error terms which are serially correlated. However, as we will see, many types of misspecification can create the *appearance* of serial correlation. Therefore, finding evidence of serial correlation does not mean that it is necessarily appropriate to model the error terms as following some sort of autoregressive or moving-average process. If the regression function of the original model is misspecified in any way, then a model like (7.41), which has been modified to incorporate AR(1) errors, is probably also misspecified. It is therefore extremely important to test the specification of any regression model that has been "corrected" for serial correlation.

The Appearance of Serial Correlation

There are several types of misspecification of the regression function that can incorrectly create the appearance of serial correlation. For instance, it may be that the true regression function is nonlinear in one or more of the regressors while the estimated one is linear. In that case, depending on how the data are ordered, the residuals from a linear regression model may well appear to be serially correlated. All that is needed is for the independent variables on which the dependent variable depends nonlinearly to be correlated with time.

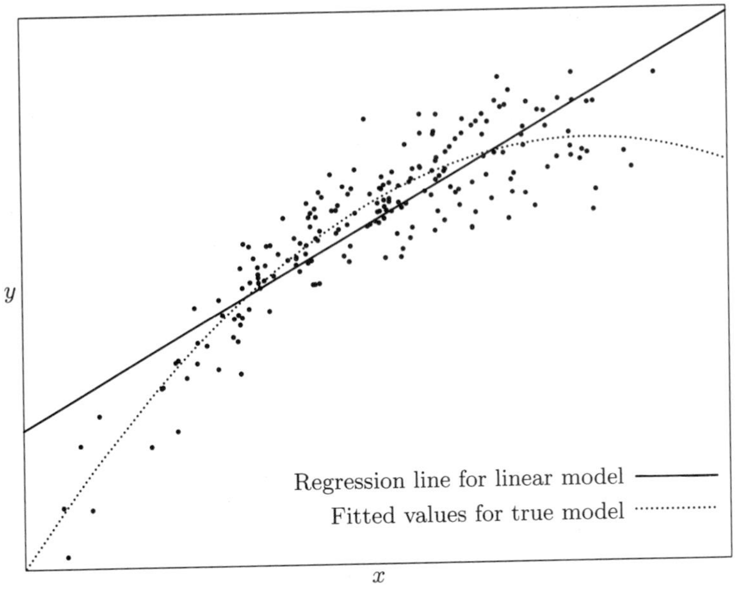

Figure 7.1 The appearance of serial correlation

As a concrete example, consider Figure 7.1, which shows 200 hypothetical observations on a regressor x and a regressand y, together with an OLS regression line and the fitted values from the true, nonlinear model. For the linear model, the residuals are always negative for the smallest and largest values of x, and they tend to be positive for the intermediate values. As a consequence, they appear to be serially correlated: If the observations are ordered according to the value of x, the estimate $\tilde{\rho}$ obtained by regressing the OLS residuals on themselves lagged once is 0.298, and the t statistic for $\rho = 0$ is 4.462. Thus, if the data are ordered in this way, there appears to be strong evidence of serial correlation. But this evidence is misleading. Either plotting the residuals against x or including x^2 as an additional regressor quickly reveals the true nature of the misspecification.

The true regression function in this example contains a term in x^2. Since the linear model omits this term, it is underspecified, in the sense discussed in Section 3.7. Any sort of underspecification has the potential to create the appearance of serial correlation if the incorrectly omitted variables are themselves serially correlated. Therefore, whenever we find evidence of serial correlation, our first reaction should be to think carefully about the specification of the regression function. Perhaps one or more additional independent variables should be included among the regressors. Perhaps powers, cross-products, or lags of some of the existing independent variables need to be included. Or perhaps the regression function should be made dynamic by including one or more lags of the dependent variable.

Common Factor Restrictions

It is extremely common for linear regression models to suffer from **dynamic misspecification**. The simplest example is failing to include a lagged dependent variable among the regressors. More generally, there is dynamic misspecification whenever the regression function incorrectly omits lags of the dependent variable or of one or more independent variables. A somewhat mechanical, but often very effective, way to detect dynamic misspecification in models with autoregressive errors is to test the **common factor restrictions** that are implicit in such models. The idea of testing these restrictions was initially proposed by Sargan (1964). It was further developed by Hendry and Mizon (1978), Mizon and Hendry (1980), Sargan (1980), and others. Hendry (1995) provides a detailed treatment of dynamic specification in linear regression models.

The easiest way to understand what common factor restrictions are, and how they got their name, is to consider a linear regression model with errors that apparently follow an AR(1) process. In this case, there are really three nested models. The first of these is the original linear regression model with error terms that are assumed to be serially independent:

$$H_0\colon \; y_t = \boldsymbol{X}_t\boldsymbol{\beta} + u_t, \quad u_t \sim \text{IID}(0, \sigma^2). \tag{7.72}$$

The second is the nonlinear model (7.41) that is obtained when the error terms in (7.72) follow the AR(1) process (7.29). Although we have already discussed this model extensively, we rewrite it here for convenience:

$$H_1\colon \; y_t = \rho y_{t-1} + \boldsymbol{X}_t\boldsymbol{\beta} - \rho\boldsymbol{X}_{t-1}\boldsymbol{\beta} + \varepsilon_t, \quad \varepsilon_t \sim \text{IID}(0, \sigma_\varepsilon^2). \tag{7.73}$$

The third is the linear model that can be obtained by relaxing the nonlinear restrictions which are implicit in (7.73). This model is

$$H_2\colon \; y_t = \rho y_{t-1} + \boldsymbol{X}_t\boldsymbol{\beta} + \boldsymbol{X}_{t-1}\boldsymbol{\gamma} + \varepsilon_t, \quad \varepsilon_t \sim \text{IID}(0, \sigma_\varepsilon^2), \tag{7.74}$$

where $\boldsymbol{\gamma}$, like $\boldsymbol{\beta}$, is a k–vector. When all three of these models are estimated over the same sample period, the original model, H_0, is a special case of the nonlinear model H_1, which in turn is a special case of the unrestricted linear model H_2. Of course, in order to estimate H_1 and H_2, we need to drop the first observation.

The nonlinear model H_1 imposes on H_2 the restrictions that $\boldsymbol{\gamma} = -\rho\boldsymbol{\beta}$. The reason for calling these restrictions "common factor" restrictions can easily be seen if we rewrite both models using lag operator notation (see Section 7.6). When we do this, the H_1 model becomes

$$(1 - \rho\mathrm{L})y_t = (1 - \rho\mathrm{L})\boldsymbol{X}_t\boldsymbol{\beta} + \varepsilon_t, \tag{7.75}$$

and the H_2 model becomes

$$(1 - \rho\mathrm{L})y_t = \boldsymbol{X}_t\boldsymbol{\beta} + \mathrm{L}\boldsymbol{X}_t\boldsymbol{\gamma} + \varepsilon_t. \tag{7.76}$$

It is evident that in equation (7.75), but not in equation (7.76), the common factor $1 - \rho \mathrm{L}$ appears on both sides of the equation. This is where the term "common factor restrictions" comes from.

How Many Common Factor Restrictions Are There?

There is one feature of common factor restrictions that can be tricky: It is often not obvious just how many restrictions there are. For the case of testing H_1 against H_2, there appear to be k restrictions. The null hypothesis, H_1, has $k+1$ parameters (the k-vector $\boldsymbol{\beta}$ and the scalar ρ), and the alternative hypothesis, H_2, seems to have $2k+1$ parameters (the k-vectors $\boldsymbol{\beta}$ and $\boldsymbol{\gamma}$, and the scalar ρ). Therefore, the number of restrictions appears to be the difference between $2k+1$ and $k+1$, which is k. In fact, however, the number of restrictions is almost always less than k, because, except in rare cases, the number of identifiable parameters in H_2 is less than $2k+1$. We now show why this is the case.

Let us consider a simple example. Suppose the regression function for the original model H_0 is

$$\beta_1 + \beta_2 z_t + \beta_3 t + \beta_4 z_{t-1} + \beta_5 y_{t-1}, \tag{7.77}$$

where z_t is the tth observation on some independent variable, and t is the tth observation on a linear time trend. The regression function for the unrestricted model H_2 that corresponds to (7.77) is

$$\begin{aligned} &\beta_1 + \beta_2 z_t + \beta_3 t + \beta_4 z_{t-1} + \beta_5 y_{t-1} + \rho y_{t-1} \\ &\quad + \gamma_1 + \gamma_2 z_{t-1} + \gamma_3 (t-1) + \gamma_4 z_{t-2} + \gamma_5 y_{t-2}. \end{aligned} \tag{7.78}$$

At first glance, this regression function appears to have 11 parameters. However, it really has only 7, because 4 of them are unidentifiable. We cannot estimate both β_1 and γ_1, because there cannot be two constant terms. Likewise, we cannot estimate both β_4 and γ_2, because there cannot be two coefficients of z_{t-1}, and we cannot estimate both β_5 and ρ, because there cannot be two coefficients of y_{t-1}. We also cannot estimate γ_3 along with β_3 and the constant, because t, $t-1$, and the constant term are perfectly collinear, since $t - (t-1) = 1$. The version of H_2 that can actually be estimated has regression function

$$\delta_1 + \beta_2 z_t + \delta_2 t + \delta_3 z_{t-1} + \delta_4 y_{t-1} + \gamma_4 z_{t-2} + \gamma_5 y_{t-2}, \tag{7.79}$$

where

$$\delta_1 = \beta_1 + \gamma_1 - \gamma_3, \quad \delta_2 = \beta_3 + \gamma_3, \quad \delta_3 = \beta_4 + \gamma_2, \text{ and } \delta_4 = \rho + \beta_5.$$

We see that (7.79) has only 7 identifiable parameters: β_2, γ_4, γ_5, δ_1, δ_2, δ_3, and δ_4, instead of the 11 parameters, many of them not identifiable, of expression (7.78). In contrast, the regression function for the restricted model, H_1, has 6 parameters: β_1 through β_5, and ρ. Therefore, in this example, H_1 imposes just one restriction on H_2.

The phenomenon illustrated in this example arises, to a greater or lesser extent, for almost every model with common factor restrictions. Constant terms, many types of dummy variables (notably, seasonal dummies and time trends), lagged dependent variables, and independent variables that appear with more than one time subscript always lead to an unrestricted model H_2 with some parameters that cannot be identified. Therefore, the number of identifiable parameters is almost always less than $2k+1$, and, in consequence, the number of restrictions is almost always less than k.

Testing Common Factor Restrictions

Any of the techniques discussed in Sections 6.7 and 6.8 can be used to test common factor restrictions. In practice, if the error terms are believed to be homoskedastic, the easiest approach is probably to use an asymptotic F test. For the example of equations (7.73) and (7.74), the restricted sum of squared residuals, RSSR, is obtained from NLS estimation of H_1, and the unrestricted one, USSR, is obtained from OLS estimation of H_2. Then the test statistic is

$$\frac{(\text{RSSR} - \text{USSR})/r}{\text{USSR}/(n-k-r-2)} \overset{a}{\sim} F(r, n-k-r-2), \tag{7.80}$$

where r is the number of restrictions. The number of degrees of freedom in the denominator reflects the fact that the unrestricted model has $k+r+1$ parameters and is estimated using the $n-1$ observations for $t = 2, \ldots, n$.

Of course, since both the null and alternative models involve lagged dependent variables, the test statistic (7.80) does not actually follow the $F(r, n-k-r-2)$ distribution in finite samples. Therefore, when the sample size is not large, it is a good idea to bootstrap the test. As Davidson and MacKinnon (1999a) have shown, highly reliable P values may be obtained in this way, even for very small sample sizes. The bootstrap samples are generated recursively from the restricted model, H_1, using the NLS estimates of that model. As with bootstrap tests for serial correlation, the bootstrap error terms may either be drawn from the normal distribution or obtained by resampling the rescaled NLS residuals; see the discussion in Sections 4.6 and 7.7.

Although this bootstrap procedure is conceptually simple, it may be quite expensive to compute, because the nonlinear model (7.73) must be estimated for every bootstrap sample. It may therefore be more attractive to follow the idea in Exercises 6.17 and 6.18 by bootstrapping a GNR-based test statistic that requires no nonlinear estimation at all. For the H_1 model (7.73), the corresponding GNR is (7.63), but now we wish to evaluate it, not at the NLS estimates from (7.73), but at the estimates $\acute{\boldsymbol{\beta}}$ and $\acute{\rho}$ obtained by estimating the linear H_2 model (7.74). These estimates are root-n consistent under H_2, and so also under H_1, which is contained in H_2 as a special case. Thus the GNR for H_1, which was introduced in Section 6.6, is

$$\begin{aligned} y_t - \acute{\rho} y_{t-1} - \boldsymbol{X}_t \acute{\boldsymbol{\beta}} + \acute{\rho} \boldsymbol{X}_{t-1} \acute{\boldsymbol{\beta}} \\ = (\boldsymbol{X}_t - \acute{\rho} \boldsymbol{X}_{t-1}) \boldsymbol{b} + b_\rho (y_{t-1} - \boldsymbol{X}_{t-1} \acute{\boldsymbol{\beta}}) + \text{residual}. \end{aligned} \tag{7.81}$$

Since H_2 is a linear model, the regressors of the GNR that corresponds to it are just the regressors in (7.74), and the regressand is the same as in (7.81); recall Section 6.5. However, in order to construct the GNR-based F statistic, which has exactly the same form as (7.80), it is not necessary to run the GNR for model H_2 at all. Since the regressand of (7.81) is just the dependent variable of (7.74) plus a linear combination of the independent variables, the residuals from (7.74) are the same as those from its GNR. Consequently, we can evaluate (7.80) with USSR from (7.74) and RSSR from (7.81).

In Section 6.6, we gave the impression that $\acute{\boldsymbol{\beta}}$ and $\acute{\rho}$ are simply the OLS estimates of $\boldsymbol{\beta}$ and ρ from (7.74). When $\boldsymbol{X}$ contains neither lagged dependent variables nor multiple lags of any independent variable, this is true. However, when these conditions are not satisfied, the parameters of (7.74) do not correspond directly to those of (7.73), and this makes it a little more complicated to obtain consistent estimates of these parameters. Just how to do so was discussed in Section 10.3 of Davidson and MacKinnon (1993) and will be illustrated in Exercise 7.16.

Tests of Nested Hypotheses

The models H_0, H_1, and H_2 defined in (7.72) through (7.74) form a **sequence of nested hypotheses**. Such sequences occur quite frequently in many branches of econometrics, and they have an interesting property. Asymptotically, the F statistic for testing H_0 against H_1 is independent of the F statistic for testing H_1 against H_2. This is true whether we actually estimate H_1 or merely use a GNR, and it is also true for other test statistics that are asymptotically equivalent to F statistics. In fact, the result is true for any sequence of nested hypotheses where the test statistics follow χ^2 distributions asymptotically; see Davidson and MacKinnon (1993, Supplement) and Exercise 7.21.

The independence property of tests in a nested sequence has a useful implication. Suppose that τ_{ij} denotes the statistic for testing H_i, which has k_i parameters, against H_j, which has $k_j > k_i$ parameters, where $i = 0, 1$ and $j = 1, 2$, with $j > i$. Then, if each of the test statistics is asymptotically distributed as $\chi^2(k_j - k_i)$,

$$\tau_{02} \overset{a}{=} \tau_{01} + \tau_{12}. \tag{7.82}$$

This result implies that, at least asymptotically, each of the component test statistics is bounded above by the test statistic for H_0 against H_2.

The result (7.82) is not particularly useful in the case of (7.72), (7.73), and (7.74), where all of the test statistics are quite easy to compute. However, it can sometimes come in handy. Suppose, for example, that it is easy to test H_0 against H_2 but hard to test H_0 against H_1. Then, if τ_{02} is small enough that it would not cause us to reject H_0 against H_1 when compared with the appropriate critical value for the $\chi^2(k_1 - k_0)$ distribution, we do not need to bother calculating τ_{01}, because it must be even smaller.

7.10 Models for Panel Data

Many data sets are measured across two dimensions. One dimension is time, and the other is usually called the cross-section dimension. For example, we may have 40 annual observations on 25 countries, or 100 quarterly observations on 50 states, or 6 annual observations on 3100 individuals. Data of this type are often referred to as **panel data**. The error terms for a model using panel data are likely to display certain types of dependence, which should be taken into account when we estimate such a model.

For simplicity, we restrict our attention to the linear regression model

$$y_{it} = \boldsymbol{X}_{it}\boldsymbol{\beta} + u_{it}, \quad i = 1, \ldots, m, \;\; t = 1, \ldots, T, \tag{7.83}$$

where $\boldsymbol{X}_{it}$ is a $1 \times k$ vector of observations on explanatory variables. There are assumed to be m cross-sectional units and T time periods, for a total of $n = mT$ observations. If each u_{it} has expectation zero conditional on its corresponding $\boldsymbol{X}_{it}$, we can estimate equation (7.83) by ordinary least squares. But the OLS estimator is not efficient if the u_{it} are not IID, and the IID assumption is rarely realistic with panel data.

If certain shocks affect the same cross-sectional unit at all points in time, the error terms u_{it} and u_{is} must be correlated for all $t \neq s$. Similarly, if certain shocks affect all cross-sectional units at the same point in time, the error terms u_{it} and u_{jt} must be correlated for all $i \neq j$. In consequence, if we use OLS, not only do we obtain inefficient parameter estimates, but we also obtain an inconsistent estimate of their covariance matrix; recall the discussion of Section 5.5. If the expectation of u_{it} conditional on $\boldsymbol{X}_{it}$ is *not* zero, then, for reasons mentioned in Section 7.4, OLS actually yields inconsistent parameter estimates. This happens, for example, when $\boldsymbol{X}_{it}$ contains lagged dependent variables and the u_{it} are serially correlated.

Error-Components Models

The two most popular approaches for dealing with panel data are both based on what are called **error-components models**. The idea is to specify the error term u_{it} in (7.83) as consisting of two or three separate shocks, each of which is assumed to be independent of the others. A fairly general specification is

$$u_{it} = e_t + v_i + \varepsilon_{it}. \tag{7.84}$$

Here e_t affects all observations for time period t, v_i affects all observations for cross-sectional unit i, and ε_{it} affects only observation it. It is generally assumed that the e_t are independent across t, the v_i are independent across i, and the ε_{it} are independent across all i and t. Classic papers on error-components models include Balestra and Nerlove (1966), Fuller and Battese (1974), and Mundlak (1978).

In order to estimate an error-components model, the e_t and v_i can be regarded as being either fixed or random, in a sense that we will explain. If the e_t and v_i are thought of as **fixed effects**, then they are treated as parameters to be estimated. It turns out that they can then be estimated by OLS using dummy variables. If they are thought of as **random effects**, then we must figure out the covariance matrix of the u_{it} as functions of the variances of the e_t, v_i, and ε_{it}, and use feasible GLS. Each of these approaches can be appropriate in some circumstances but may be inappropriate in others.

In what follows, we simplify the error-components specification (7.84) by eliminating the e_t. Thus we assume that there are shocks specific to each cross-sectional unit, or group, but no time-specific shocks. This assumption is often made in empirical work, and it considerably simplifies the algebra. In addition, we assume that the $\boldsymbol{X}_{it}$ are exogenous. The presence of lagged dependent variables in panel data models raises a number of issues that we do not wish to discuss here; see Arellano and Bond (1991) and Arellano and Bover (1995).

Fixed-Effects Estimation

The model that underlies fixed-effects estimation, based on equation (7.83) and the simplified version of equation (7.84), can be written as follows:

$$\boldsymbol{y} = \boldsymbol{X\beta} + \boldsymbol{D\eta} + \boldsymbol{\varepsilon}, \quad E(\boldsymbol{\varepsilon\varepsilon}^\top) = \sigma_\varepsilon^2 \mathbf{I}_n, \tag{7.85}$$

where $\boldsymbol{y}$ and $\boldsymbol{\varepsilon}$ are n−vectors with typical elements y_{it} and ε_{it}, respectively, and $\boldsymbol{D}$ is an $n \times m$ matrix of dummy variables, constructed in such a way that the element in the row corresponding to observation it, for $i = 1, \ldots, m$ and $t = 1, \ldots, T$, and column j, for $j = 1, \ldots, m$, is equal to 1 if $i = j$ and equal to 0 otherwise.[3] The m−vector $\boldsymbol{\eta}$ has typical element v_i, and so it follows that the n−vector $\boldsymbol{D\eta}$ has element v_i in the row corresponding to observation it. Note that there is exactly one element of $\boldsymbol{D}$ equal to 1 in each row, which implies that the n−vector $\boldsymbol{\iota}$ with each element equal to 1 is a linear combination of the columns of $\boldsymbol{D}$. Consequently, in order to avoid collinear regressors, the matrix $\boldsymbol{X}$ should not contain a constant.

The vector $\boldsymbol{\eta}$ plays the role of a parameter vector, and it is in this sense that the v_i are called *fixed* effects. They could in fact be random; the essential thing

[3] If the data are ordered so that all the observations in the first group appear first, followed by all the observations in the second group, and so on, the row corresponding to observation it is row $T(i-1)+t$.

is that they must be independent of the error terms ε_{it}. They may, however, be correlated with the explanatory variables in the matrix $\boldsymbol{X}$. Whether or not this is the case, the model (7.85), interpreted conditionally on $\boldsymbol{\eta}$, implies that the moment conditions

$$\mathrm{E}\big(\boldsymbol{X}_{it}^{\top}(y_{it} - \boldsymbol{X}_{it}\boldsymbol{\beta} - v_i)\big) = \mathbf{0} \quad \text{and} \quad \mathrm{E}(y_{it} - \boldsymbol{X}_{it}\boldsymbol{\beta} - v_i) = 0$$

are satisfied. The **fixed-effects estimator**, which is the OLS estimator of $\boldsymbol{\beta}$ in equation (7.85), is based on these moment conditions. Because of the way it is computed, this estimator is sometimes called the **least squares dummy variables**, or **LSDV**, estimator.

Let $\boldsymbol{M_D}$ denote the projection matrix $\mathbf{I} - \boldsymbol{D}(\boldsymbol{D}^{\top}\boldsymbol{D})^{-1}\boldsymbol{D}^{\top}$. Then, by the FWL Theorem, we know that the OLS estimator of $\boldsymbol{\beta}$ in (7.85) can be obtained by regressing $\boldsymbol{M_D y}$, the residuals from a regression of $\boldsymbol{y}$ on $\boldsymbol{D}$, on $\boldsymbol{M_D X}$, the matrix of residuals from regressing each of the columns of $\boldsymbol{X}$ on $\boldsymbol{D}$. The fixed-effects estimator is therefore

$$\hat{\boldsymbol{\beta}}_{\mathrm{FE}} = (\boldsymbol{X}^{\top}\boldsymbol{M_D X})^{-1}\boldsymbol{X}^{\top}\boldsymbol{M_D y}. \tag{7.86}$$

For any n–vector $\boldsymbol{x}$, let $\bar{x}_i$ denote the **group mean** $T^{-1}\sum_{t=1}^{T} x_{it}$. Then it is easy to check that element it of the vector $\boldsymbol{M_D x}$ is equal to $x_{it} - \bar{x}_i$, the deviation from the group mean. Since all the variables in (7.86) are premultiplied by $\boldsymbol{M_D}$, it follows that this estimator makes use only of the information in the variation around the mean for each of the m groups. For this reason, it is often called the **within-groups estimator**. Because $\boldsymbol{X}$ and $\boldsymbol{D}$ are exogenous, this estimator is unbiased. Moreover, since the conditions of the Gauss-Markov theorem are satisfied, we can conclude that the fixed-effects estimator is BLUE.

The fixed-effects estimator (7.86) has advantages and disadvantages. It is easy to compute, even when m is very large, because it is never necessary to make direct use of the $n \times n$ matrix $\boldsymbol{M_D}$. All that is needed is to compute the m group means for each variable. In addition, the estimates $\hat{\boldsymbol{\eta}}$ of the fixed effects may well be of interest in their own right. However, the estimator cannot be used with an explanatory variable that takes on the same value for all the observations in each group, because such a column would be collinear with the columns of $\boldsymbol{D}$. More generally, if the explanatory variables in the matrix $\boldsymbol{X}$ are well explained by the dummy variables in $\boldsymbol{D}$, the parameter vector $\boldsymbol{\beta}$ is not estimated at all precisely. It is of course possible to estimate a constant, simply by taking the mean of the estimates $\hat{\boldsymbol{\eta}}$.

Random-Effects Estimation

It is possible to improve on the efficiency of the fixed-effects estimator if one is willing to impose restrictions on the model (7.85). For that model, all we require is that the matrix $\boldsymbol{X}$ of explanatory variables and the cross-sectional errors v_i should both be independent of the ε_{it}, but this does not rule out the possibility of a correlation between them. The restrictions imposed for random-effects estimation require that the v_i should be independent of $\boldsymbol{X}$.

This independence assumption is by no means always plausible. For example, in a panel of observations on individual workers, an observed variable like the hourly wage rate may well be correlated with an unobserved variable like ability, which implicitly enters into the individual-specific error term v_i. However, if the assumption is satisfied, it follows that

$$\mathrm{E}(u_{it} \,|\, \boldsymbol{X}) = \mathrm{E}(v_i + \varepsilon_{it} \,|\, \boldsymbol{X}) = 0, \tag{7.87}$$

since v_i and ε_{it} are then both independent of $\boldsymbol{X}$. Condition (7.87) is precisely the condition which ensures that OLS estimation of the model (7.83), rather than the model (7.85), yields unbiased estimates.

However, OLS estimation of equation (7.83) is not in general efficient, because the u_{it} are not IID. We can calculate the covariance matrix of the u_{it} if we assume that the v_i are IID random variables with mean zero and variance σ_v^2. This assumption accounts for the term "random" effects. From (7.84), setting $e_t = 0$ and using the assumption that the shocks are independent, it is easy to see that

$$\begin{aligned} \mathrm{Var}(u_{it}) &= \sigma_v^2 + \sigma_\varepsilon^2, \\ \mathrm{Cov}(u_{it}u_{is}) &= \sigma_v^2, \text{ and} \\ \mathrm{Cov}(u_{it}u_{js}) &= 0 \text{ for all } i \neq j. \end{aligned}$$

These define the elements of the $n \times n$ covariance matrix $\boldsymbol{\Omega}$, which we need for GLS estimation. If the data are ordered by the cross-sectional units in m blocks of T observations each, this matrix has the form

$$\boldsymbol{\Omega} = \begin{bmatrix} \boldsymbol{\Sigma} & \mathbf{0} & \cdots & \mathbf{0} \\ \mathbf{0} & \boldsymbol{\Sigma} & \cdots & \mathbf{0} \\ \vdots & \vdots & & \vdots \\ \mathbf{0} & \mathbf{0} & \cdots & \boldsymbol{\Sigma} \end{bmatrix},$$

where

$$\boldsymbol{\Sigma} \equiv \sigma_\varepsilon^2 \mathbf{I}_T + \sigma_v^2 \boldsymbol{\iota}\boldsymbol{\iota}^\top \tag{7.88}$$

is the $T \times T$ matrix with $\sigma_v^2 + \sigma_\varepsilon^2$ in every position on the principal diagonal and σ_v^2 everywhere else. Here $\boldsymbol{\iota}$ is a T–vector of 1s.

To obtain GLS estimates of $\boldsymbol{\beta}$, we would need to know the values of σ_ε^2 and σ_v^2, or, at least, the value of their ratio, since, as we saw in Section 7.3, GLS estimation requires only that $\boldsymbol{\Omega}$ should be specified up to a factor. To obtain feasible GLS estimates, we need a consistent estimate of that ratio. However, the reader may have noticed that we have made no use in this section so far of asymptotic concepts, such as that of a consistent estimate. This is because, in order to obtain definite results, we must specify what happens to both m and T when $n = mT$ tends to infinity.

Consider the fixed-effects model (7.85). If m remains fixed as $T \to \infty$, then the number of regressors also remains fixed as $n \to \infty$, and standard asymptotic theory applies. But if T remains fixed as $m \to \infty$, then the number of parameters to be estimated tends to infinity, and the m–vector $\hat{\boldsymbol{\eta}}$ of estimates of the fixed effects is not consistent, because each estimated effect depends only on T observations. It is nevertheless possible to show that, even in this case, $\hat{\boldsymbol{\beta}}$ remains consistent; see Exercise 7.23.

It is always possible to find a consistent estimate of σ_ε^2 by estimating the model (7.85), because, no matter how m and T may behave as $n \to \infty$, there are n residuals. Thus, if we divide the SSR from (7.85) by $n - m - k$, we obtain an unbiased and consistent estimate of σ_ε^2, since the error terms for this model are just the ε_{it}. But the natural estimator of σ_v^2, namely, the sample variance of the m elements of $\hat{\boldsymbol{\eta}}$, is not consistent unless $m \to \infty$. In practice, therefore, it is probably undesirable to use the random-effects estimator when m is small.

There is another way to estimate σ_v^2 consistently if $m \to \infty$ as $n \to \infty$. One starts by running the regression

$$\boldsymbol{P_D y} = \boldsymbol{P_D X\beta} + \text{residuals}, \tag{7.89}$$

where $\boldsymbol{P_D} \equiv \mathbf{I} - \boldsymbol{M_D}$, so as to obtain the **between-groups estimator**

$$\hat{\beta}_{\text{BG}} = (\boldsymbol{X}^\top \boldsymbol{P_D X})^{-1} \boldsymbol{X}^\top \boldsymbol{P_D y}. \tag{7.90}$$

Although regression (7.89) appears to have $n = mT$ observations, it really has only m, because the regressand and all the regressors are the same for every observation in each group. The estimator bears the name "between-groups" because it uses only the variation among the group means. If $m < k$, note that the estimator (7.90) does not even exist, since the matrix $\boldsymbol{X}^\top \boldsymbol{P_D X}$ can have rank at most m.

If the restrictions of the random-effects model are not satisfied, the estimator $\hat{\beta}_{\text{BG}}$, if it exists, is in general biased and inconsistent. To see this, observe that unbiasedness and consistency require that the moment conditions

$$\text{E}\big((\boldsymbol{P_D X})_{it}^\top (y_{it} - \boldsymbol{X}_{it}\boldsymbol{\beta})\big) = \mathbf{0} \tag{7.91}$$

should hold, where $(\boldsymbol{P_D X})_{it}$ is the row labelled it of the $n \times k$ matrix $\boldsymbol{P_D X}$. Since $y_{it} - \boldsymbol{X}_{it}\boldsymbol{\beta} = v_i + \varepsilon_{it}$, and since ε_{it} is independent of everything else in condition (7.91), this condition is equivalent to the absence of correlation between the v_i and the elements of the matrix $\boldsymbol{X}$.

As readers are asked to show in Exercise 7.24, the variance of the error terms in regression (7.89) is $\sigma_v^2 + \sigma_\varepsilon^2/T$. Therefore, if we run it as a regression with m observations, divide the SSR by $m - k$, and then subtract $1/T$ times our estimate of σ_ε^2, we obtain a consistent, but not necessarily positive, estimate of σ_v^2. If the estimate turns out to be negative, we probably should not be estimating an error-components model.

As we will see in the next paragraph, both the OLS estimator of model (7.83) and the feasible GLS estimator of the random-effects model are matrix-weighted averages of the within-groups, or fixed-effects, estimator (7.86) and the between-groups estimator (7.90). For the former to be consistent, we need only the assumptions of the fixed-effects model, but for the latter we need in addition the restrictions of the random-effects model. Thus both the OLS estimator of (7.83) and the feasible GLS estimator are consistent only if the between-groups estimator is consistent.

For the OLS estimator of (7.83),

$$\begin{aligned}\hat{\boldsymbol{\beta}} &= (\boldsymbol{X}^\top\boldsymbol{X})^{-1}\boldsymbol{X}^\top\boldsymbol{y} \\ &= (\boldsymbol{X}^\top\boldsymbol{X})^{-1}(\boldsymbol{X}^\top\boldsymbol{M_D}\boldsymbol{y} + \boldsymbol{X}^\top\boldsymbol{P_D}\boldsymbol{y}) \\ &= (\boldsymbol{X}^\top\boldsymbol{X})^{-1}\boldsymbol{X}^\top\boldsymbol{M_D}\boldsymbol{X}\hat{\boldsymbol{\beta}}_{\text{FE}} + (\boldsymbol{X}^\top\boldsymbol{X})^{-1}\boldsymbol{X}^\top\boldsymbol{P_D}\boldsymbol{X}\hat{\boldsymbol{\beta}}_{\text{BG}},\end{aligned}$$

which shows that the estimator is indeed a matrix-weighted average of $\hat{\boldsymbol{\beta}}_{\text{FE}}$ and $\hat{\boldsymbol{\beta}}_{\text{BG}}$. As readers are asked to show in Exercise 7.25, the GLS estimator of the random-effects model can be obtained by running the OLS regression

$$(\mathbf{I} - \lambda\boldsymbol{P_D})\boldsymbol{y} = (\mathbf{I} - \lambda\boldsymbol{P_D})\boldsymbol{X}\boldsymbol{\beta} + \text{residuals}, \tag{7.92}$$

where the scalar λ is defined by

$$\lambda \equiv 1 - \left(\frac{T\sigma_v^2}{\sigma_\varepsilon^2} + 1\right)^{-1/2}. \tag{7.93}$$

For feasible GLS, we need to replace σ_ε^2 and σ_v^2 by the consistent estimators that were discussed earlier in this subsection.

Equation (7.92) implies that the random-effects GLS estimator is a matrix-weighted average of the OLS estimator for equation (7.83) and the between-groups estimator, and thus also of $\hat{\boldsymbol{\beta}}_{\text{FE}}$ and $\hat{\boldsymbol{\beta}}_{\text{BG}}$. The GLS estimator is identical to the OLS estimator when $\lambda = 0$, which happens when $\sigma_v^2 = 0$, and equal to the within-groups, or fixed-effects, estimator when $\lambda = 1$, which happens when $\sigma_\varepsilon^2 = 0$. Except in these two special cases, the GLS estimator is more efficient, in the context of the random-effects model, than either the OLS estimator or the fixed-effects estimator. But equation (7.92) also implies that the random-effects estimator is inconsistent whenever the between-groups estimator is inconsistent.

Unbalanced Panels

Up to this point, we have assumed that we are dealing with a **balanced panel**, that is, a data set for which there are precisely T observations for each cross-sectional unit. However, it is quite common to encounter **unbalanced panels**, for which the number of observations is not the same for every cross-sectional unit. The fixed-effects estimator can be used with unbalanced panels without any real change. It is still based on regression (7.85), and the only change is that the matrix of dummy variables $\boldsymbol{D}$ no longer has the same number of 1s in each column. The random-effects estimator can also be used with unbalanced panels, but it needs to be modified slightly.

Let us assume that the data are grouped by cross-sectional units. Let T_i denote the number of observations associated with unit i, and partition $\boldsymbol{y}$ and $\boldsymbol{X}$ as follows:

$$\boldsymbol{y} = [\boldsymbol{y}_1 \vdots \boldsymbol{y}_2 \vdots \cdots \vdots \boldsymbol{y}_m], \quad \boldsymbol{X} = [\boldsymbol{X}_1 \vdots \boldsymbol{X}_2 \vdots \cdots \vdots \boldsymbol{X}_m],$$

where $\boldsymbol{y}_i$ and $\boldsymbol{X}_i$ denote the T_i rows of $\boldsymbol{y}$ and $\boldsymbol{X}$ that correspond to the ith unit. By analogy with (7.93), make the definition

$$\lambda_i \equiv 1 - \left(\frac{T_i \sigma_v^2}{\sigma_\varepsilon^2} + 1\right)^{-1/2}.$$

Let $\bar{\boldsymbol{y}}_i$ denote a T_i–vector, each element of which is the mean of the elements of $\boldsymbol{y}_i$. Similarly, let $\bar{\boldsymbol{X}}_i$ denote a $T_i \times k$ matrix, each element of which is the mean of the corresponding column of $\boldsymbol{X}_i$. Then the random-effects estimator can be computed by running the linear regression

$$\begin{bmatrix} \boldsymbol{y}_1 - \lambda_1 \bar{\boldsymbol{y}}_1 \\ \boldsymbol{y}_2 - \lambda_2 \bar{\boldsymbol{y}}_2 \\ \vdots \\ \boldsymbol{y}_m - \lambda_m \bar{\boldsymbol{y}}_m \end{bmatrix} = \begin{bmatrix} \boldsymbol{X}_1 - \lambda_1 \bar{\boldsymbol{X}}_1 \\ \boldsymbol{X}_2 - \lambda_2 \bar{\boldsymbol{X}}_2 \\ \vdots \\ \boldsymbol{X}_m - \lambda_m \bar{\boldsymbol{X}}_m \end{bmatrix} \boldsymbol{\beta} + \text{residuals}. \tag{7.94}$$

Note that $\boldsymbol{P_D y}$ is just $[\bar{\boldsymbol{y}}_1 \vdots \bar{\boldsymbol{y}}_2 \vdots \cdots \vdots \bar{\boldsymbol{y}}_m]$, and similarly for $\boldsymbol{P_D X}$. Therefore, since all the λ_i are equal to λ when the panel is balanced, regression (7.94) reduces to regression (7.92) in that special case.

Group Effects and Individual Data

Error-components models are also relevant for regressions on cross-section data with no time dimension, but where the observations naturally belong to groups. For example, each observation might correspond to a household living in a certain state, and each group would then consist of all the households living in a particular state. In such cases, it is plausible that the error terms for individuals within the same group are correlated. An error-components model that combines a group-specific error v_i, with variance σ_v^2, and an individual-specific error ε_{it}, with variance σ_ε^2, is a natural way to model this sort of correlation. Such a model implies that the correlation between the error terms for observations in the same group is $\rho \equiv \sigma_v^2/(\sigma_v^2 + \sigma_\varepsilon^2)$ and the correlation between the error terms for observations in different groups is zero.

A fixed-effects model is often unsatisfactory for dealing with group effects. In many cases, some explanatory variables are observed only at the group level, so that they have no within-group variation. Such variables are perfectly collinear with the group dummies used in estimating a fixed-effects model, making it impossible to identify the parameters associated with them. On the other hand, they are identified by a random-effects model for an unbalanced panel, because this model takes account of between-group variation. This can be seen from equation (7.94): Collinearity of the transformed group-level variables on the right-hand side occurs only if the explanatory variables are collinear to begin with. The estimates of σ_ε^2 and σ_v^2 needed to compute the λ_i may be obtained in various ways, some of which were discussed in the subsection on random-effects estimation. As we remarked there, these work well only if the number of groups m is not too small.

If it is thought that the within-group correlation ρ is small, it may be tempting to ignore it and use OLS estimation, with the usual OLS covariance matrix. This can be a serious mistake unless ρ is actually zero, since the OLS standard errors can be drastic underestimates even with small values of ρ, as Kloek (1981) and Moulton (1986, 1990) have pointed out. The problem is particularly severe when the number of observations per group is large, as readers are asked to show in Exercise 7.26. The correlation of the error terms within groups means that the effective sample size is much smaller than the actual sample size when there are many observations per group.

In this section, we have presented just a few of the most basic ideas concerning estimation with panel data. Of course, GLS is not the only method that can be used to estimate models for data of this type. The generalized method of moments (Chapter 9) and the method of maximum likelihood (Chapter 10) are also commonly used. For more detailed treatments of various models for panel data, see, among others, Chamberlain (1984), Hsiao (1986, 2001), Ruud (2000, Chapter 24), Baltagi (2001), Arellano and Honoré (2001), Greene (2002, Chapter 14), and Wooldridge (2002).

7.11 Final Remarks

Several important concepts were introduced in the first four sections of this chapter, which dealt with the basic theory of generalized least squares estimation. The concept of an efficient MM estimator, which we introduced in Section 7.2, will be encountered again in the context of generalized instrumental variables estimation (Chapter 8) and generalized method-of-moments estimation (Chapter 9). The key idea of feasible GLS estimation, namely, that an unknown covariance matrix may in some circumstances be replaced by a consistent estimate of that matrix without changing the asymptotic properties of the resulting estimator, will also be encountered again in Chapter 9.

The remainder of the chapter dealt with the treatment of heteroskedasticity and serial correlation in linear regression models, and with error-components models for panel data. Although this material is of considerable practical importance, most of the techniques we discussed, although sometimes complicated in detail, are conceptually straightforward applications of feasible GLS estimation, NLS estimation, and methods for testing hypotheses that were introduced in Chapters 4 and 6.

7.12 Exercises

7.1 Using the fact that $\mathrm{E}(\boldsymbol{u}\boldsymbol{u}^\top \,|\, \boldsymbol{X}) = \boldsymbol{\Omega}$ for regression (7.01), show directly, without appeal to standard OLS results, that the covariance matrix of the GLS estimator $\hat{\boldsymbol{\beta}}_{\rm GLS}$ is given by the rightmost expression of (7.05).

7.2 Show that the matrix (7.11), reproduced here for easy reference,

$$\boldsymbol{X}^\top\boldsymbol{\Omega}^{-1}\boldsymbol{X} - \boldsymbol{X}^\top\boldsymbol{W}(\boldsymbol{W}^\top\boldsymbol{\Omega}\boldsymbol{W})^{-1}\boldsymbol{W}^\top\boldsymbol{X},$$

is positive semidefinite. As in Section 6.2, this may be done by showing that this matrix can be expressed in the form $\boldsymbol{Z}^\top\boldsymbol{M}\boldsymbol{Z}$, for some $n \times k$ matrix $\boldsymbol{Z}$ and some $n \times n$ orthogonal projection matrix $\boldsymbol{M}$. It is helpful to express $\boldsymbol{\Omega}^{-1}$ as $\boldsymbol{\Psi}\boldsymbol{\Psi}^\top$, as in equation (7.02).

7.3 Using the data in the file **earnings.data**, run the regression

$$y_t = \beta_1 d_{1t} + \beta_2 d_{2t} + \beta_3 d_{3t} + u_t,$$

which was previously estimated in Exercise 5.3. Recall that the d_{it} are dummy variables. Then test the null hypothesis that $\mathrm{E}(u_t^2) = \sigma^2$ against the alternative that

$$\mathrm{E}(u_t^2) = \gamma_1 d_{1t} + \gamma_2 d_{2t} + \gamma_3 d_{3t}.$$

Report P values for F and nR^2 tests.

7.4 If u_t follows the stationary AR(1) process

$$u_t = \rho u_{t-1} + \varepsilon_t, \quad \varepsilon_t \sim \mathrm{IID}(0, \sigma_\varepsilon^2), \quad |\rho| < 1,$$

show that $\mathrm{Cov}(u_t u_{t-j}) = \mathrm{Cov}(u_t u_{t+j}) = \rho^j \sigma_\varepsilon^2/(1-\rho^2)$. Then use this result to show that the correlation between u_t and u_{t-j} is just ρ^j.

7.5 Consider the nonlinear regression model $y_t = x_t(\boldsymbol{\beta}) + u_t$. Derive the GNR for testing the null hypothesis that the u_t are serially uncorrelated against the alternative that they follow an AR(1) process.

7.6 Show how to test the null hypothesis that the error terms of the linear regression model $\boldsymbol{y} = \boldsymbol{X\beta} + \boldsymbol{u}$ are serially uncorrelated against the alternative that they follow an AR(4) process by means of a GNR. Derive the test GNR from first principles.

7.7 Consider the following three models, where u_t is assumed to be $\text{IID}(0, \sigma^2)$:

$$\begin{aligned} H_0\colon &\quad y_t = \beta + u_t \\ H_1\colon &\quad y_t = \beta + \rho(y_{t-1} - \beta) + u_t \\ H_2\colon &\quad y_t = \beta + u_t + \alpha u_{t-1} \end{aligned}$$

Explain how to test H_0 against H_1 by using a GNR. Then show that exactly the same test statistic is also appropriate for testing H_0 against H_2.

7.8 Write the trace in the right-hand side of equation (7.50) explicitly in terms of $\boldsymbol{P_X}$ rather than $\boldsymbol{M_X}$, and show that the terms containing one or more factors of $\boldsymbol{P_X}$ all vanish asymptotically.

7.9 By direct matrix multiplication, show that, if $\boldsymbol{\Psi}$ is given by (7.60), then $\boldsymbol{\Psi\Psi}^\top$ is equal to the matrix

$$\begin{bmatrix} 1 & -\rho & 0 & \cdots & 0 & 0 \\ -\rho & 1+\rho^2 & -\rho & \cdots & 0 & 0 \\ \vdots & \vdots & \vdots & & \vdots & \vdots \\ 0 & 0 & 0 & \cdots & 1+\rho^2 & -\rho \\ 0 & 0 & 0 & \cdots & -\rho & 1 \end{bmatrix}.$$

Show further, by direct calculation, that this matrix is proportional to the inverse of the matrix $\boldsymbol{\Omega}$ given in equation (7.32).

7.10 Show that equation (7.30), relating $\boldsymbol{u}$ to $\boldsymbol{\varepsilon}$, can be modified to take account of the definition (7.59) of ε_1, with the result that

$$u_t = \varepsilon_t + \rho\varepsilon_{t-1} + \rho^2\varepsilon_{t-2} + \cdots + \frac{\rho^{t-1}}{(1-\rho^2)^{1/2}}\varepsilon_1. \tag{7.95}$$

The relation $\boldsymbol{\Psi}^\top\boldsymbol{u} = \boldsymbol{\varepsilon}$ implies that $\boldsymbol{u} = (\boldsymbol{\Psi}^\top)^{-1}\boldsymbol{\varepsilon}$. Use the result (7.95) to show that $\boldsymbol{\Psi}^{-1}$ can be written as

$$\begin{bmatrix} \theta & \rho\theta & \rho^2\theta & \cdots & \rho^{n-1}\theta \\ 0 & 1 & \rho & \cdots & \rho^{n-2} \\ 0 & 0 & 1 & \cdots & \rho^{n-3} \\ \vdots & \vdots & \vdots & & \vdots \\ 0 & 0 & 0 & \cdots & 1 \end{bmatrix},$$

where $\theta \equiv (1-\rho^2)^{-1/2}$. Verify by direct calculation that this matrix is the inverse of the $\boldsymbol{\Psi}$ given by (7.60).

7.11 Consider a square, symmetric, nonsingular matrix partitioned as follows

$$\boldsymbol{H} \equiv \begin{bmatrix} \boldsymbol{A} & \boldsymbol{C}^\top \\ \boldsymbol{C} & \boldsymbol{B} \end{bmatrix}, \tag{7.96}$$

where $\boldsymbol{A}$ and $\boldsymbol{B}$ are also square symmetric nonsingular matrices. By using the rules for multiplying partitioned matrices (see Section 1.4), show that $\boldsymbol{H}^{-1}$ can be expressed in partitioned form as

$$\boldsymbol{H}^{-1} = \begin{bmatrix} \boldsymbol{D} & \boldsymbol{E}^{\top} \\ \boldsymbol{E} & \boldsymbol{F} \end{bmatrix},$$

where

$$\begin{aligned} &\boldsymbol{D} = (\boldsymbol{A} - \boldsymbol{C}^{\top}\boldsymbol{B}^{-1}\boldsymbol{C})^{-1}, \\ &\boldsymbol{E} = -\boldsymbol{B}^{-1}\boldsymbol{C}(\boldsymbol{A} - \boldsymbol{C}^{\top}\boldsymbol{B}^{-1}\boldsymbol{C})^{-1} = -(\boldsymbol{B} - \boldsymbol{C}\boldsymbol{A}^{-1}\boldsymbol{C}^{\top})^{-1}\boldsymbol{C}\boldsymbol{A}^{-1}, \text{ and} \\ &\boldsymbol{F} = (\boldsymbol{B} - \boldsymbol{C}\boldsymbol{A}^{-1}\boldsymbol{C}^{\top})^{-1}. \end{aligned}$$

7.12 Suppose that the matrix $\boldsymbol{H}$ of the previous question is positive definite. It therefore follows (see Section 3.4) that there exists a square matrix $\boldsymbol{X}$ such that $\boldsymbol{H} = \boldsymbol{X}^{\top}\boldsymbol{X}$. Partition $\boldsymbol{X}$ as $[\boldsymbol{X}_1 \;\; \boldsymbol{X}_2]$, so that

$$\boldsymbol{X}^{\top}\boldsymbol{X} = \begin{bmatrix} \boldsymbol{X}_1^{\top}\boldsymbol{X}_1 & \boldsymbol{X}_1^{\top}\boldsymbol{X}_2 \\ \boldsymbol{X}_2^{\top}\boldsymbol{X}_1 & \boldsymbol{X}_2^{\top}\boldsymbol{X}_2 \end{bmatrix},$$

where the blocks of the matrix on the right-hand side are the same as the blocks in (7.96). Show that the top left block $\boldsymbol{D}$ of $\boldsymbol{H}^{-1}$ can be expressed as $(\boldsymbol{X}_1^{\top}\boldsymbol{M}_2\boldsymbol{X}_1)^{-1}$, where $\boldsymbol{M}_2 \equiv \mathbf{I} - \boldsymbol{X}_2(\boldsymbol{X}_2^{\top}\boldsymbol{X}_2)^{-1}\boldsymbol{X}_2^{\top}$. Use this result to show that $\boldsymbol{D} - \boldsymbol{A}^{-1} = (\boldsymbol{X}_1^{\top}\boldsymbol{M}_2\boldsymbol{X}_1)^{-1} - (\boldsymbol{X}_1^{\top}\boldsymbol{X}_1)^{-1}$ is a positive semidefinite matrix.

★7.13 Consider testing for first-order serial correlation of the error terms in the regression model

$$\boldsymbol{y} = \beta\boldsymbol{y}_1 + \boldsymbol{u}, \quad |\beta| < 1, \tag{7.97}$$

where $\boldsymbol{y}_1$ is the vector with typical element y_{t-1}, by use of the statistics t_{GNR} and t_{SR} defined in (7.51) and (7.52), respectively. Show first that the vector denoted as $\boldsymbol{M_X}\tilde{\boldsymbol{u}}_1$ in (7.51) and (7.52) is equal to $-\tilde{\beta}\boldsymbol{M_X}\boldsymbol{y}_2$, where $\boldsymbol{y}_2$ is the vector with typical element y_{t-2}, and $\tilde{\beta}$ is the OLS estimate of β from (7.97). Then show that, as $n \to \infty$, t_{GNR} tends to the random variable $\tau \equiv \sigma_u^{-2} \operatorname{plim} n^{-1/2}(\beta\boldsymbol{y}_1 - \boldsymbol{y}_2)^{\top}\boldsymbol{u}$, whereas t_{SR} tends to the same random variable times β. Show finally that t_{GNR}, but not t_{SR}, provides an asymptotically correct test, by showing that the random variable τ is asymptotically distributed as $\text{N}(0, 1)$.

7.14 The file **money.data** contains seasonally adjusted quarterly data for the logarithm of the real money supply, m_t, real GDP, y_t, and the 3-month Treasury Bill rate, r_t, for Canada for the period 1967:1 to 1998:4. A conventional demand for money function is

$$m_t = \beta_1 + \beta_2 r_t + \beta_3 y_t + \beta_4 m_{t-1} + u_t. \tag{7.98}$$

Estimate this model over the period 1968:1 to 1998:4, and then test it for AR(1) errors using two different GNRs that differ in their treatment of the first observation.

7.15 Use nonlinear least squares to estimate, over the period 1968:1 to 1998:4, the model that results if u_t in (7.98) follows an AR(1) process. Then test the common factor restrictions that are implicit in this model. Calculate an asymptotic P value for the test.

7.16 Test the common factor restrictions of Exercise 7.15 again using a GNR. Calculate both an asymptotic P value and a bootstrap P value based on at least $B = 99$ bootstrap samples. **Hint:** To obtain a consistent estimate of ρ for the GNR, use the fact that the coefficient of r_{t-1} in the unrestricted model (7.74) is equal to $-\rho$ times the coefficient of r_t.

7.17 Use nonlinear least squares to estimate, over the period 1968:1 to 1998:4, the model that results if u_t in (7.98) follows an AR(2) process. Is there any evidence that an AR(2) process is needed here?

★7.18 The algorithm called **iterated Cochrane-Orcutt**, alluded to in Section 7.8, is just iterated feasible GLS without the first observation. This algorithm is begun by running the regression $\boldsymbol{y} = \boldsymbol{X\beta} + \boldsymbol{u}$ by OLS, preferably omitting observation 1, in order to obtain the first estimate of $\boldsymbol{\beta}$. The residuals from this equation are then used to estimate ρ according to equation (7.70). What is the next step in this procedure? Complete the description of iterated Cochrane-Orcutt as iterated feasible GLS, showing how each step of the procedure can be carried out using an OLS regression.

Show that, when the algorithm converges, conditions (7.69) for NLS estimation are satisfied. Also show that, unlike iterated feasible GLS including observation 1, this algorithm *must* eventually converge, although perhaps only to a local, rather than the global, minimum of $\text{SSR}(\boldsymbol{\beta}, \rho)$.

7.19 Consider once more the model that you estimated in Exercise 7.15. Estimate this model using the iterated Cochrane-Orcutt algorithm, using a sequence of OLS regressions, and see how many iterations are needed to achieve the same estimates as those achieved by NLS. Compare this number with the number of iterations used by NLS itself.

Repeat the exercise with a starting value of 0.5 for ρ instead of the value of 0 that is conventionally used.

7.20 Test the hypothesis that the error terms of the linear regression model (7.98) are serially uncorrelated against the alternatives that they follow the simple AR(4) process $u_t = \rho_4 u_{t-1} + \varepsilon_t$ and that they follow a general AR(4) process.

Test the hypothesis that the error terms of the nonlinear regression model you estimated in Exercise 7.15 are serially uncorrelated against the same two alternative hypotheses. Use Gauss-Newton regressions.

7.21 Consider the linear regression model

$$\boldsymbol{y} = \boldsymbol{X}_0\boldsymbol{\beta}_0 + \boldsymbol{X}_1\boldsymbol{\beta}_1 + \boldsymbol{X}_2\boldsymbol{\beta}_2 + \boldsymbol{u}, \quad \boldsymbol{u} \sim \text{IID}(\boldsymbol{0}, \sigma^2\mathbf{I}), \tag{7.99}$$

where there are n observations, and k_0, k_1, and k_2 denote the numbers of parameters in $\boldsymbol{\beta}_0$, $\boldsymbol{\beta}_1$, and $\boldsymbol{\beta}_2$, respectively. Let H_0 denote the hypothesis that $\boldsymbol{\beta}_1 = \boldsymbol{0}$ and $\boldsymbol{\beta}_2 = \boldsymbol{0}$, H_1 denote the hypothesis that $\boldsymbol{\beta}_2 = \boldsymbol{0}$, and H_2 denote the model (7.99) with no restrictions.

Show that the F statistics for testing H_0 against H_1 and for testing H_1 against H_2 are asymptotically independent of each other.

7.22 This question uses data on daily returns for the period 1989–1998 for shares of Mobil Corporation from the file **daily-crsp.data**. These data are made available by courtesy of the Center for Research in Security Prices (CRSP); see the comments at the bottom of the file. Regress these returns on a constant and themselves lagged once, twice, three, and four times, dropping the first four observations. Then test the null hypothesis that all coefficients except the constant term are equal to zero, as they should be if market prices fully reflect all available information. Also perform a heteroskedasticity-robust test by running two HRGNRs. Be sure to report P values for both tests.

7.23 Consider the fixed-effects model (7.85). Show that, under mild regularity conditions, which you should specify, the OLS estimator $\hat{\boldsymbol{\beta}}_{\rm FE}$ tends in probability to the true parameter vector $\boldsymbol{\beta}_0$ as m, the number of cross-sectional units, tends to infinity, while T, the number of time periods, remains fixed.

7.24 Suppose that

$$\boldsymbol{y} = \boldsymbol{X\beta} + \boldsymbol{v} + \boldsymbol{\varepsilon}, \tag{7.100}$$

where there are $n = mT$ observations, $\boldsymbol{y}$ is an n–vector with typical element y_{it}, $\boldsymbol{X}$ is an $n \times k$ matrix with typical row $\boldsymbol{X}_{it}$, $\boldsymbol{\varepsilon}$ is an n–vector with typical element ε_{it}, and $\boldsymbol{v}$ is an n–vector with v_i repeated in the positions that correspond to y_{i1} through y_{iT}. Let the v_i have variance σ_v^2 and the ε_{it} have variance σ_ε^2. Given these assumptions, show that the variance of the error terms in regression (7.89) is $\sigma_v^2 + \sigma_\varepsilon^2/T$.

⋆7.25 Show that, for $\boldsymbol{\Sigma}$ defined in (7.88),

$$\boldsymbol{\Sigma}^{-1/2} = \frac{1}{\sigma_\varepsilon}(\mathbf{I}_T - \lambda \boldsymbol{P}_{\iota}),$$

where $\boldsymbol{P}_{\iota} \equiv \boldsymbol{\iota}(\boldsymbol{\iota}^\top\boldsymbol{\iota})^{-1}\boldsymbol{\iota}^\top = (1/T)\boldsymbol{\iota}\boldsymbol{\iota}^\top$, and

$$\lambda = 1 - \left(\frac{T\sigma_v^2}{\sigma_\varepsilon^2} + 1\right)^{-1/2}.$$

Then use this result to show that the GLS estimates of $\boldsymbol{\beta}$ may be obtained by running regression (7.92). What is the covariance matrix of the GLS estimator?

⋆7.26 Suppose that, in the error-components model (7.100), none of the columns of $\boldsymbol{X}$ displays any within-group variation. Recall that, for this model, the data are balanced, with m groups and T observations per group. Show that the OLS and GLS estimators are identical in this special case. Then write down the true covariance matrix of both these estimators. How is this covariance matrix related to the usual one for OLS that would be computed by a regression package under classical assumptions? What happens to this relationship as T and ρ, the correlation of the error terms within groups, change?

Chapter 8

Instrumental Variables Estimation

8.1 Introduction

In Section 3.3, the ordinary least-squares estimator $\hat{\boldsymbol{\beta}}$ was shown to be consistent under condition (3.10), according to which the expectation of the error term u_t associated with observation t is zero conditional on the regressors $\boldsymbol{X}_t$ for that same observation. As we saw in Section 4.5, this condition can also be expressed either by saying that the regressors $\boldsymbol{X}_t$ are predetermined or by saying that the error terms u_t are innovations. When condition (3.10) does not hold, the consistency proof of Section 3.3 is not applicable, and the OLS estimator is in general both biased and inconsistent.

It is not always reasonable to assume that the error terms are innovations. In fact, as we will see in the next section, there are commonly encountered situations in which the error terms are necessarily correlated with some of the regressors for the same observation. Even in these circumstances, however, it is usually possible, although not always easy, to define an information set Ω_t for each observation such that

$$\mathrm{E}(u_t \,|\, \Omega_t) = 0. \tag{8.01}$$

Any regressor of which the value in period t is correlated with u_t cannot belong to Ω_t.

In Section 6.2, method-of-moments (MM) estimators were discussed for both linear and nonlinear regression models. Such estimators are defined by the moment conditions (6.10) in terms of a matrix $\boldsymbol{W}$ of variables, with one row for each observation. They were shown to be consistent provided that the tth row $\boldsymbol{W}_t$ of $\boldsymbol{W}$ belongs to Ω_t, and provided that an asymptotic identification condition is satisfied. In econometrics, these MM estimators are usually called **instrumental variables estimators**, or **IV estimators**. Instrumental variables estimation is introduced in Section 8.3, and a number of important results are discussed. Then finite-sample properties are discussed in Section 8.4, hypothesis testing in Section 8.5, and overidentifying restrictions in Section 8.6. Next, Section 8.7 introduces a procedure for testing whether it is actually necessary to use IV estimation. Bootstrap testing is discussed in Section 8.8. Finally, in Section 8.9, IV estimation of nonlinear regression models is dealt with briefly. A more general class of MM estimators, of which both OLS and IV are special cases, will be the subject of Chapter 9.

8.2 Correlation Between Error Terms and Regressors

We now briefly discuss two common situations in which the error terms are correlated with the regressors and therefore do not have mean zero conditional on them. The first one, usually referred to by the name **errors in variables**, occurs whenever the independent variables in a regression model are measured with error. The second situation, often simply referred to as **simultaneity**, occurs whenever two or more endogenous variables are jointly determined by a system of simultaneous equations.

Errors in Variables

For a variety of reasons, many economic variables are measured with error. For example, macroeconomic time series are often based, in large part, on surveys, and they must therefore suffer from sampling variability. Whenever there are measurement errors, the values economists observe inevitably differ, to a greater or lesser extent, from the true values that economic agents presumably act upon. As we will see, measurement errors in the dependent variable of a regression model are generally of no great consequence, unless they are very large. However, measurement errors in the independent variables cause the error terms to be correlated with the regressors that are measured with error, and this causes OLS to be inconsistent.

The problems caused by errors in variables can be seen quite clearly in the context of the simple linear regression model. Consider the model

$$y_t^\circ = \beta_1 + \beta_2 x_t^\circ + u_t^\circ, \quad u_t^\circ \sim \text{IID}(0, \sigma^2), \tag{8.02}$$

where the variables x_t° and y_t° are not actually observed. Instead, we observe

$$\begin{aligned} x_t &\equiv x_t^\circ + v_{1t}, \text{ and} \\ y_t &\equiv y_t^\circ + v_{2t}. \end{aligned} \tag{8.03}$$

Here v_{1t} and v_{2t} are measurement errors which are assumed, perhaps not realistically in some cases, to be IID with variances ω_1^2 and ω_2^2, respectively, and to be independent of x_t°, y_t°, and u_t°.

If we suppose that the true DGP is a special case of (8.02) along with (8.03), we see from (8.03) that $x_t^\circ = x_t - v_{1t}$ and $y_t^\circ = y_t - v_{2t}$. If we substitute these into (8.02), we find that

$$\begin{aligned} y_t &= \beta_1 + \beta_2(x_t - v_{1t}) + u_t^\circ + v_{2t} \\ &= \beta_1 + \beta_2 x_t + u_t^\circ + v_{2t} - \beta_2 v_{1t} \\ &= \beta_1 + \beta_2 x_t + u_t, \end{aligned} \tag{8.04}$$

where $u_t \equiv u_t^\circ + v_{2t} - \beta_2 v_{1t}$. Thus $\mathrm{Var}(u_t)$ is equal to $\sigma^2 + \omega_2^2 + \beta_2^2\omega_1^2$. The effect of the measurement error in the dependent variable is simply to increase the variance of the error terms. Unless the increase is substantial, this is generally not a serious problem.

The measurement error in the independent variable also increases the variance of the error terms, but it has another, much more severe, consequence as well. Because $x_t = x_t^\circ + v_{1t}$, and u_t depends on v_{1t}, u_t must be correlated with x_t whenever $\beta_2 \neq 0$. In fact, since the random part of x_t is v_{1t}, we see that

$$\mathrm{E}(u_t \,|\, x_t) = \mathrm{E}(u_t \,|\, v_{1t}) = -\beta_2 v_{1t}, \tag{8.05}$$

because we assume that v_{1t} is independent of u_t° and v_{2t}. From (8.05), we can see, using the fact that $\mathrm{E}(u_t) = 0$ unconditionally, that

$$\begin{aligned}\mathrm{Cov}(x_t, u_t) &= \mathrm{E}(x_t u_t) = \mathrm{E}\big(x_t \mathrm{E}(u_t \,|\, x_t)\big)\\ &= -\mathrm{E}\big((x_t^\circ + v_{1t})\beta_2 v_{1t}\big) = -\beta_2\omega_1^2.\end{aligned}$$

This covariance is negative if $\beta_2 > 0$ and positive if $\beta_2 < 0$, and, since it does not depend on the sample size n, it does not go away as n becomes large. An exactly similar argument shows that the assumption that $\mathrm{E}(u_t \,|\, \boldsymbol{X}_t) = 0$ is false whenever any element of $\boldsymbol{X}_t$ is measured with error. In consequence, the OLS estimator is biased and inconsistent.

Errors in variables are a potential problem whenever we try to estimate a consumption function, especially if we are using cross-section data. Many economic theories (for example, Friedman, 1957) suggest that household consumption depends on "permanent" income or "life-cycle" income, but surveys of household behavior almost never measure this. Instead, they typically provide somewhat inaccurate estimates of current income. If we think of y_t as measured consumption, x_t° as permanent income, and x_t as estimated current income, then the above analysis applies directly to the consumption function. The marginal propensity to consume is β_2, which must be positive, causing the correlation between u_t and x_t to be negative. As readers are asked to show in Exercise 8.1, the probability limit of $\hat\beta_2$ is less than the true value β_{20}. In consequence, the OLS estimator $\hat\beta_2$ is biased downward, even asymptotically.

Of course, if our objective is simply to estimate the relationship between the observed dependent variable y_t and the observed independent variable x_t, there is nothing wrong with using ordinary least squares to estimate equation (8.04). In that case, u_t would simply be *defined* as the difference between y_t and its expectation conditional on x_t. But our analysis shows that the OLS estimators of β_1 and β_2 in equation (8.04) are not consistent for the corresponding parameters of equation (8.02). In most cases, it is parameters like these that we want to estimate on the basis of economic theory.

There is an extensive literature on ways to avoid the inconsistency caused by errors in variables. See, among many others, Hausman and Watson (1985),

Leamer (1987), and Dagenais and Dagenais (1997). The simplest and most widely-used approach is just to use an instrumental variables estimator.

Simultaneous Equations

Economic theory often suggests that two or more endogenous variables are determined simultaneously. In this situation, as we will see shortly, all of the endogenous variables must necessarily be correlated with the error terms in all of the equations. This means that none of them may validly appear in the regression functions of models that are to be estimated by least squares.

A classic example, which well illustrates the econometric problems caused by simultaneity, is the determination of price and quantity for a commodity at the partial equilibrium of a competitive market. Suppose that q_t is quantity and p_t is price, both of which would often be in logarithms. A linear (or loglinear) model of demand and supply is

$$q_t = \gamma_d \, p_t + \boldsymbol{X}_t^d \boldsymbol{\beta}_d + u_t^d \tag{8.06}$$

$$q_t = \gamma_s \, p_t + \boldsymbol{X}_t^s \boldsymbol{\beta}_s + u_t^s, \tag{8.07}$$

where equation (8.06) is the demand function and equation (8.07) is the supply function. Here $\boldsymbol{X}_t^d$ and $\boldsymbol{X}_t^s$ are row vectors of observations on exogenous or predetermined variables that appear, respectively, in the demand and supply functions, $\boldsymbol{\beta}_d$ and $\boldsymbol{\beta}_s$ are corresponding vectors of parameters, γ_d and γ_s are scalar parameters, and u_t^d and u_t^s are the error terms in the demand and supply functions. Economic theory predicts that, in most cases, $\gamma_d < 0$ and $\gamma_s > 0$, which is equivalent to saying that the demand curve slopes downward and the supply curve slopes upward.

Equations (8.06) and (8.07) are a pair of linear simultaneous equations for the two unknowns p_t and q_t. For that reason, these equations constitute what is called a **linear simultaneous equations model**. In this case, there are two dependent variables, quantity and price. For estimation purposes, the key feature of the model is that quantity depends on price in both equations.

Since there are two equations and two unknowns, it is straightforward to solve equations (8.06) and (8.07) for p_t and q_t. This is most easily done by rewriting them in matrix notation as

$$\begin{bmatrix} 1 & -\gamma_d \\ 1 & -\gamma_s \end{bmatrix} \begin{bmatrix} q_t \\ p_t \end{bmatrix} = \begin{bmatrix} \boldsymbol{X}_t^d \boldsymbol{\beta}_d \\ \boldsymbol{X}_t^s \boldsymbol{\beta}_s \end{bmatrix} + \begin{bmatrix} u_t^d \\ u_t^s \end{bmatrix}. \tag{8.08}$$

The solution to (8.08), which exists whenever $\gamma_d \neq \gamma_s$, so that the matrix on the left-hand side of (8.08) is nonsingular, is

$$\begin{bmatrix} q_t \\ p_t \end{bmatrix} = \begin{bmatrix} 1 & -\gamma_d \\ 1 & -\gamma_s \end{bmatrix}^{-1} \left(\begin{bmatrix} \boldsymbol{X}_t^d \boldsymbol{\beta}_d \\ \boldsymbol{X}_t^s \boldsymbol{\beta}_s \end{bmatrix} + \begin{bmatrix} u_t^d \\ u_t^s \end{bmatrix} \right). \tag{8.09}$$

It can be seen from this solution that p_t and q_t depend on both u_t^d and u_t^s, and on every exogenous and predetermined variable that appears in either the demand function, the supply function, or both. Therefore, p_t, which appears on the right-hand side of equations (8.06) and (8.07), must be correlated with the error terms in both of those equations. If we rewrote one or both equations so that p_t was on the left-hand side and q_t was on the right-hand side, the problem would not go away, because q_t is also correlated with the error terms in both equations.

It is easy to see that, whenever we have a linear simultaneous equations model, there must be correlation between all of the error terms and all of the endogenous variables. If there are g endogenous variables and g equations, the solution looks very much like (8.09), with the inverse of a $g \times g$ matrix premultiplying the sum of a g-vector of linear combinations of the exogenous and predetermined variables and a g-vector of error terms. If we want to estimate the full system of equations, there are many options, some of which will be discussed in Chapter 12. If we simply want to estimate one equation out of such a system, the most popular approach is to use instrumental variables.

We have discussed two important situations in which the error terms are necessarily correlated with some of the regressors, and the OLS estimator must consequently be inconsistent. This provides a strong motivation to employ estimators that do not suffer from this type of inconsistency. In the remainder of this chapter, we therefore discuss the method of instrumental variables. This method can be used whenever the error terms are correlated with one or more of the explanatory variables, regardless of how that correlation may have arisen.

8.3 Instrumental Variables Estimation

For most of this chapter, we will focus on the linear regression model

$$\boldsymbol{y} = \boldsymbol{X\beta} + \boldsymbol{u}, \quad \mathrm{E}(\boldsymbol{u}\boldsymbol{u}^\top) = \sigma^2\mathbf{I}, \tag{8.10}$$

where at least one of the explanatory variables in the $n \times k$ matrix $\boldsymbol{X}$ is assumed not to be predetermined with respect to the error terms. Suppose that, for each $t = 1, \ldots, n$, condition (8.01) is satisfied for some suitable information set Ω_t, and that we can form an $n \times k$ matrix $\boldsymbol{W}$ with typical row $\boldsymbol{W}_t$ such that all its elements belong to Ω_t. The k variables given by the k columns of $\boldsymbol{W}$ are called **instrumental variables**, or simply **instruments**. Later, we will allow for the possibility that the number of instruments may exceed the number of regressors.

Instrumental variables may be either exogenous or predetermined, and, for a reason that will be explained later, they should always include any columns of $\boldsymbol{X}$ that are exogenous or predetermined. Finding suitable instruments may be quite easy in some cases, but it can be extremely difficult in others. Many empirical controversies in economics are essentially disputes about whether or not certain variables constitute valid instruments.

The Simple IV Estimator

For the linear model (8.10), the moment conditions (6.10) simplify to

$$\boldsymbol{W}^\top(\boldsymbol{y} - \boldsymbol{X\beta}) = \boldsymbol{0}. \tag{8.11}$$

Since there are k equations and k unknowns, we can solve equations (8.11) directly to obtain the **simple IV estimator**

$$\hat{\boldsymbol{\beta}}_{\text{IV}} \equiv (\boldsymbol{W}^\top\boldsymbol{X})^{-1}\boldsymbol{W}^\top\boldsymbol{y}. \tag{8.12}$$

This well-known estimator has a long history (see Morgan, 1990). Whenever $\boldsymbol{W}_t \in \Omega_t$,

$$\text{E}(u_t \mid \boldsymbol{W}_t) = 0, \tag{8.13}$$

and $\boldsymbol{W}_t$ is seen to be predetermined with respect to the error term. Given (8.13), it was shown in Section 6.2 that $\hat{\boldsymbol{\beta}}_{\text{IV}}$ is consistent and asymptotically normal under an identification condition. For asymptotic identification, this condition can be written as

$$\boldsymbol{S}_{\boldsymbol{W}^\top\boldsymbol{X}} \equiv \operatorname*{plim}_{n\to\infty} \frac{1}{n}\boldsymbol{W}^\top\boldsymbol{X} \text{ is deterministic and nonsingular.} \tag{8.14}$$

For identification by any given sample, the condition is just that $\boldsymbol{W}^\top\boldsymbol{X}$ should be nonsingular. If this condition were not satisfied, equations (8.11) would have no unique solution.

It is easy to see directly that the simple IV estimator (8.12) is consistent, and, in so doing, to see that condition (8.13) can be weakened slightly. If the model (8.10) is correctly specified, with true parameter vector $\boldsymbol{\beta}_0$, then it follows that

$$\begin{aligned} \hat{\boldsymbol{\beta}}_{\text{IV}} &= (\boldsymbol{W}^\top\boldsymbol{X})^{-1}\boldsymbol{W}^\top\boldsymbol{X}\boldsymbol{\beta}_0 + (\boldsymbol{W}^\top\boldsymbol{X})^{-1}\boldsymbol{W}^\top\boldsymbol{u} \\ &= \boldsymbol{\beta}_0 + (n^{-1}\boldsymbol{W}^\top\boldsymbol{X})^{-1}n^{-1}\boldsymbol{W}^\top\boldsymbol{u}. \end{aligned} \tag{8.15}$$

Given the assumption (8.14) of asymptotic identification, it is clear that $\hat{\boldsymbol{\beta}}_{\text{IV}}$ is consistent if and only if

$$\operatorname*{plim}_{n\to\infty} \frac{1}{n}\boldsymbol{W}^\top\boldsymbol{u} = \boldsymbol{0}, \tag{8.16}$$

which is precisely the condition (6.16) that was used in the consistency proof in Section 6.2. We usually refer to this condition by saying that the error terms are **asymptotically uncorrelated** with the instruments. Condition (8.16) follows from condition (8.13) by the law of large numbers, but it may hold even if condition (8.13) does not. The weaker condition (8.16) is what is required for the consistency of the IV estimator.

Efficiency Considerations

If the model (8.10) is correctly specified with true parameter vector $\boldsymbol{\beta}_0$ and true error variance σ_0^2, the results of Section 6.2 show that the asymptotic covariance matrix of $n^{1/2}(\hat{\boldsymbol{\beta}}_{\rm IV} - \boldsymbol{\beta}_0)$ is given by (6.25) or (6.26):

$$\begin{aligned} \mathrm{Var}\big(\operatorname*{plim}_{n\to\infty} n^{1/2}(\hat{\boldsymbol{\beta}}_{\rm IV} - \boldsymbol{\beta}_0)\big) &= \sigma_0^2(\boldsymbol{S}_{\boldsymbol{W}^\top\boldsymbol{X}})^{-1}\boldsymbol{S}_{\boldsymbol{W}^\top\boldsymbol{W}}(\boldsymbol{S}_{\boldsymbol{W}^\top\boldsymbol{X}}^\top)^{-1} \\ &= \sigma_0^2 \operatorname*{plim}_{n\to\infty}(n^{-1}\boldsymbol{X}^\top\boldsymbol{P}_{\boldsymbol{W}}\boldsymbol{X})^{-1}, \end{aligned} \tag{8.17}$$

where $\boldsymbol{S}_{\boldsymbol{W}^\top\boldsymbol{W}} \equiv \operatorname{plim} n^{-1}\boldsymbol{W}^\top\boldsymbol{W}$. If we have some choice over what instruments to use in the matrix $\boldsymbol{W}$, it makes sense to choose them so as to minimize the above asymptotic covariance matrix.

First of all, notice that, since (8.17) depends on $\boldsymbol{W}$ only through the orthogonal projection matrix $\boldsymbol{P}_{\boldsymbol{W}}$, all that matters is the space $\mathcal{S}(\boldsymbol{W})$ spanned by the instrumental variables. In fact, as readers are asked to show in Exercise 8.2, the estimator $\hat{\boldsymbol{\beta}}_{\rm IV}$ itself depends on $\boldsymbol{W}$ only through $\boldsymbol{P}_{\boldsymbol{W}}$. This fact is closely related to the result that, for ordinary least squares, fitted values and residuals depend only on the space $\mathcal{S}(\boldsymbol{X})$ spanned by the regressors.

Suppose first that we are at liberty to choose for instruments any variables at all that satisfy the predeterminedness condition (8.13). Then, under reasonable and plausible conditions, we can characterize the **optimal instruments** for IV estimation of the model (8.10). By this, we mean the instruments that minimize the asymptotic covariance matrix (8.17), in the usual sense that any other choice of instruments leads to an asymptotic covariance matrix that differs from the optimal one by a positive semidefinite matrix.

In order to determine the optimal instruments, we must know the data-generating process. In the context of a simultaneous equations model, a single equation like (8.10), even if we know the values of the parameters, cannot be a complete description of the DGP, because at least some of the variables in the matrix $\boldsymbol{X}$ are endogenous. For the DGP to be fully specified, we must know how all the endogenous variables are generated. For the demand-supply model given by equations (8.06) and (8.07), both of those equations are needed to specify the DGP. For a more complicated simultaneous equations model with g endogenous variables, we would need g equations. For the simple errors-in-variables model discussed in Section 8.2, we need equations (8.03) as well as equation (8.02) in order to specify the DGP fully.

Quite generally, we can suppose that the explanatory variables in the regression model (8.10) satisfy the relation

$$\boldsymbol{X} = \bar{\boldsymbol{X}} + \boldsymbol{V}, \qquad \mathrm{E}(\boldsymbol{V}_t \,|\, \Omega_t) = \boldsymbol{0}, \tag{8.18}$$

where the $t^{\rm th}$ row of $\bar{\boldsymbol{X}}$ is $\bar{\boldsymbol{X}}_t = \mathrm{E}(\boldsymbol{X}_t \,|\, \Omega_t)$, and $\boldsymbol{X}_t$ is the $t^{\rm th}$ row of $\boldsymbol{X}$. Thus equation (8.18) can be interpreted as saying that $\bar{\boldsymbol{X}}_t$ is the expectation of $\boldsymbol{X}_t$

conditional on the information set Ω_t. It turns out that the $n \times k$ matrix $\bar{\boldsymbol{X}}$ provides the optimal instruments for (8.10). Of course, in practice, $\bar{\boldsymbol{X}}$ is never observed, and it should be replaced by something that estimates it consistently.

To see that $\bar{\boldsymbol{X}}$ provides the optimal matrix of instruments, it is, as usual, easier to reason in terms of precision matrices rather than covariance matrices. For any valid choice of instruments, the precision matrix corresponding to (8.17) is $1/\sigma_0^2$ times

$$\operatorname*{plim}_{n\to\infty} \frac{1}{n}\boldsymbol{X}^\top \boldsymbol{P_W X} = \operatorname*{plim}_{n\to\infty} \big(n^{-1}\boldsymbol{X}^\top \boldsymbol{W}(n^{-1}\boldsymbol{W}^\top \boldsymbol{W})^{-1} n^{-1}\boldsymbol{W}^\top \boldsymbol{X}\big). \tag{8.19}$$

Using (8.18) and a law of large numbers, we see that

$$\begin{aligned}\operatorname*{plim}_{n\to\infty} \frac{1}{n}\boldsymbol{X}^\top \boldsymbol{W} &= \lim_{n\to\infty} \frac{1}{n}\mathrm{E}(\boldsymbol{X}^\top \boldsymbol{W}) \\ &= \lim_{n\to\infty} \frac{1}{n}\mathrm{E}(\bar{\boldsymbol{X}}^\top \boldsymbol{W}) = \operatorname*{plim}_{n\to\infty} \frac{1}{n}\bar{\boldsymbol{X}}^\top \boldsymbol{W}.\end{aligned} \tag{8.20}$$

The second equality holds because $\mathrm{E}(\boldsymbol{V}^\top \boldsymbol{W}) = \mathbf{O}$, since, by the construction in (8.18), $\boldsymbol{V}_t$ has mean zero conditional on $\boldsymbol{W}_t$. The last equality is just a LLN in reverse. Similarly, we find that $\operatorname{plim} n^{-1}\boldsymbol{W}^\top \boldsymbol{X} = \operatorname{plim} n^{-1}\boldsymbol{W}^\top \bar{\boldsymbol{X}}$. Thus equation (8.19) becomes

$$\operatorname*{plim}_{n\to\infty} \frac{1}{n}\bar{\boldsymbol{X}}^\top \boldsymbol{P_W}\bar{\boldsymbol{X}}. \tag{8.21}$$

If we make the choice $\boldsymbol{W} = \bar{\boldsymbol{X}}$, then (8.21) reduces to $\operatorname{plim} n^{-1}\bar{\boldsymbol{X}}^\top \bar{\boldsymbol{X}}$. The difference between this and (8.21) itself is just $\operatorname{plim} n^{-1}\bar{\boldsymbol{X}}^\top \boldsymbol{M_W}\bar{\boldsymbol{X}}$, which is a positive semidefinite matrix. This shows that $\bar{\boldsymbol{X}}$ is indeed the optimal choice of instrumental variables by the criterion of asymptotic variance.

We mentioned earlier that all the explanatory variables in (8.10) that are exogenous or predetermined should be included in the matrix $\boldsymbol{W}$ of instrumental variables. It is now clear why this is so. If we denote by $\boldsymbol{Z}$ the submatrix of $\boldsymbol{X}$ containing the exogenous or predetermined variables, then $\bar{\boldsymbol{Z}} = \boldsymbol{Z}$, because the row $\boldsymbol{Z}_t$ is already contained in Ω_t. Thus $\boldsymbol{Z}$ is a submatrix of the matrix $\bar{\boldsymbol{X}}$ of optimal instruments. As such, it should always be a submatrix of the matrix of instruments $\boldsymbol{W}$ used for estimation, even if $\boldsymbol{W}$ is not actually equal to $\bar{\boldsymbol{X}}$.

The Generalized IV Estimator

In practice, the information set Ω_t is very frequently specified by providing a list of l instrumental variables that suggest themselves for various reasons. Therefore, we now drop the assumption that the number of instruments is equal to the number of parameters and let $\boldsymbol{W}$ denote an $n \times l$ matrix of instruments. Often, l is greater than k, the number of regressors in the model (8.10). In this case, the model is said to be **overidentified**, because, in general, there is more than one way to formulate moment conditions like (8.11) using the available instruments. If $l = k$, the model (8.10) is said to be **just identified** or **exactly identified**, because there is only one way to formulate the moment conditions. If $l < k$, it is said to be **underidentified**, because there are fewer moment conditions than parameters to be estimated, and equations (8.11) therefore have no unique solution.

If any instruments at all are available, it is normally possible to generate an arbitrarily large collection of them, because *any* deterministic function of the l components of the tth row $\boldsymbol{W}_t$ of $\boldsymbol{W}$ can be used as the tth component of a new instrument.[1] If (8.10) is underidentified, some such procedure is necessary if we wish to obtain consistent estimates of all the elements of $\boldsymbol{\beta}$. Alternatively, we would have to impose at least $k - l$ restrictions on $\boldsymbol{\beta}$ so as to reduce the number of independent parameters that must be estimated to no more than the number of instruments.

For models that are just identified or overidentified, it is often desirable to limit the set of potential instruments to deterministic *linear* functions of the instruments in $\boldsymbol{W}$, rather than allowing arbitrary deterministic functions. We will see shortly that this is not only reasonable but optimal for linear simultaneous equation models. This means that the IV estimator is unique for a just identified model, because there is only one k–dimensional linear space $\mathcal{S}(\boldsymbol{W})$ that can be spanned by the $k = l$ instruments, and, as we saw earlier, the IV estimator for a given model depends only on the space spanned by the instruments.

We can always treat an overidentified model as if it were just identified by choosing exactly k linear combinations of the l columns of $\boldsymbol{W}$. The challenge is to choose these linear combinations optimally. Formally, we seek an $l \times k$ matrix $\boldsymbol{J}$ such that the $n \times k$ matrix $\boldsymbol{WJ}$ is a valid instrument matrix and such that the use of $\boldsymbol{J}$ minimizes the asymptotic covariance matrix of the estimator in the class of IV estimators obtained using an $n \times k$ instrument matrix of the form $\boldsymbol{WJ}^*$ with arbitrary $l \times k$ matrix $\boldsymbol{J}^*$.

There are three requirements that the matrix $\boldsymbol{J}$ must satisfy. The first of these is that it should have full column rank of k. Otherwise, the space spanned by the columns of $\boldsymbol{WJ}$ would have rank less than k, and the model would be underidentified. The second requirement is that $\boldsymbol{J}$ should be at least asymptotically deterministic. If not, it is possible that condition (8.16) applied to $\boldsymbol{WJ}$ could fail to hold. The last requirement is that $\boldsymbol{J}$ be chosen to minimize the asymptotic covariance matrix of the resulting IV estimator, and we now explain how this may be achieved.

If the explanatory variables $\boldsymbol{X}$ satisfy (8.18), then it follows from (8.17) and (8.20) that the asymptotic covariance matrix of the IV estimator computed

[1] This procedure would not work if, for example, all of the original instruments were binary variables.

using $\boldsymbol{WJ}$ as instrument matrix is

$$\sigma_0^2 \operatorname*{plim}_{n\to\infty}(n^{-1}\bar{\boldsymbol{X}}^\top \boldsymbol{P}_{\boldsymbol{WJ}}\bar{\boldsymbol{X}})^{-1}. \tag{8.22}$$

The tth row $\bar{\boldsymbol{X}}_t$ of $\bar{\boldsymbol{X}}$ belongs to Ω_t by construction, and so each element of $\bar{\boldsymbol{X}}_t$ is a deterministic function of the elements of $\boldsymbol{W}_t$. However, the deterministic functions are not necessarily linear with respect to $\boldsymbol{W}_t$. Thus, in general, it is impossible to find a matrix $\boldsymbol{J}$ such that $\bar{\boldsymbol{X}} = \boldsymbol{WJ}$, as would be needed for $\boldsymbol{WJ}$ to constitute a set of truly optimal instruments. A natural second-best solution is to project $\bar{\boldsymbol{X}}$ orthogonally on to the space $\mathcal{S}(\boldsymbol{W})$. This yields the matrix of instruments

$$\boldsymbol{WJ} = \boldsymbol{P_W}\bar{\boldsymbol{X}} = \boldsymbol{W}(\boldsymbol{W}^\top\boldsymbol{W})^{-1}\boldsymbol{W}^\top\bar{\boldsymbol{X}}, \tag{8.23}$$

which implies that

$$\boldsymbol{J} = (\boldsymbol{W}^\top\boldsymbol{W})^{-1}\boldsymbol{W}^\top\bar{\boldsymbol{X}}. \tag{8.24}$$

We now show that these instruments are indeed optimal under the constraint that the instruments should be linear in $\boldsymbol{W}_t$.

By substituting $\boldsymbol{P_W}\bar{\boldsymbol{X}}$ for $\boldsymbol{WJ}$ in (8.22), the asymptotic covariance matrix becomes

$$\sigma_0^2 \operatorname*{plim}_{n\to\infty}(n^{-1}\bar{\boldsymbol{X}}^\top \boldsymbol{P}_{\boldsymbol{P_W}\bar{\boldsymbol{X}}}\bar{\boldsymbol{X}})^{-1}.$$

If we write out the projection matrix $\boldsymbol{P}_{\boldsymbol{P_W}\bar{\boldsymbol{X}}}$ explicitly, we find that

$$\bar{\boldsymbol{X}}^\top\boldsymbol{P}_{\boldsymbol{P_W}\bar{\boldsymbol{X}}}\bar{\boldsymbol{X}} = \bar{\boldsymbol{X}}^\top\boldsymbol{P_W}\bar{\boldsymbol{X}}(\bar{\boldsymbol{X}}^\top\boldsymbol{P_W}\bar{\boldsymbol{X}})^{-1}\bar{\boldsymbol{X}}^\top\boldsymbol{P_W}\bar{\boldsymbol{X}} = \bar{\boldsymbol{X}}^\top\boldsymbol{P_W}\bar{\boldsymbol{X}}. \tag{8.25}$$

Thus, the precision matrix for the estimator that uses instruments $\boldsymbol{P_W}\bar{\boldsymbol{X}}$ is proportional to $\bar{\boldsymbol{X}}^\top\boldsymbol{P_W}\bar{\boldsymbol{X}}$. For the estimator with $\boldsymbol{WJ}$ as instruments, the precision matrix is proportional to $\bar{\boldsymbol{X}}^\top\boldsymbol{P_{WJ}}\bar{\boldsymbol{X}}$. The difference between the two precision matrices is therefore proportional to

$$\bar{\boldsymbol{X}}^\top(\boldsymbol{P_W} - \boldsymbol{P_{WJ}})\bar{\boldsymbol{X}}. \tag{8.26}$$

The k–dimensional subspace $\mathcal{S}(\boldsymbol{WJ})$, which is the image of the orthogonal projection $\boldsymbol{P_{WJ}}$, is a subspace of the l–dimensional space $\mathcal{S}(\boldsymbol{W})$, which is the image of $\boldsymbol{P_W}$. Thus, by the result in Exercise 2.18, the difference $\boldsymbol{P_W} - \boldsymbol{P_{WJ}}$ is itself an orthogonal projection matrix. This implies that the difference (8.26) is a positive semidefinite matrix, and so we can conclude that (8.23) is indeed the optimal choice of instruments of the form $\boldsymbol{WJ}$.

At this point, we come up against the same difficulty as that encountered at the end of Section 6.2, namely, that the optimal instrument choice is infeasible, because we do not know $\bar{\boldsymbol{X}}$. But notice that, from the definition (8.24) of the matrix $\boldsymbol{J}$, we have that

$$\begin{aligned}\operatorname*{plim}_{n\to\infty}\boldsymbol{J} &= \operatorname*{plim}_{n\to\infty}(n^{-1}\boldsymbol{W}^\top\boldsymbol{W})^{-1}n^{-1}\boldsymbol{W}^\top\bar{\boldsymbol{X}}\\ &= \operatorname*{plim}_{n\to\infty}(n^{-1}\boldsymbol{W}^\top\boldsymbol{W})^{-1}n^{-1}\boldsymbol{W}^\top\boldsymbol{X},\end{aligned} \tag{8.27}$$

by (8.20). This suggests, correctly, that we can use $\boldsymbol{P_W X}$ instead of $\boldsymbol{P_W \bar{X}}$ without changing the asymptotic properties of the estimator.

If we use $\boldsymbol{P_W X}$ as the matrix of instrumental variables, the moment conditions (8.11) that define the estimator become

$$\boldsymbol{X}^\top \boldsymbol{P_W}(\boldsymbol{y} - \boldsymbol{X\beta}) = \boldsymbol{0}, \tag{8.28}$$

which can be solved to yield the **generalized IV estimator**, or **GIV estimator**,

$$\hat{\boldsymbol{\beta}}_{\text{IV}} = (\boldsymbol{X}^\top \boldsymbol{P_W X})^{-1} \boldsymbol{X}^\top \boldsymbol{P_W y}, \tag{8.29}$$

which is sometimes just abbreviated as **GIVE**. The estimator (8.29) is indeed a generalization of the simple estimator (8.12), as readers are asked to verify in Exercise 8.3. For this reason, we will usually refer to the IV estimator without distinguishing the simple from the generalized case.

The generalized IV estimator (8.29) can also be obtained by minimizing the **IV criterion function**, which has many properties in common with the sum of squared residuals for models estimated by least squares. This function is defined as follows:

$$Q(\boldsymbol{\beta}, \boldsymbol{y}) = (\boldsymbol{y} - \boldsymbol{X\beta})^\top \boldsymbol{P_W}(\boldsymbol{y} - \boldsymbol{X\beta}). \tag{8.30}$$

Minimizing $Q(\boldsymbol{\beta}, \boldsymbol{y})$ with respect to $\boldsymbol{\beta}$ yields the estimator (8.29), as readers are asked to show in Exercise 8.4.

Identifiability and Consistency of the IV Estimator

In Section 6.2, we defined in (6.12) a k–vector $\boldsymbol{\alpha}(\boldsymbol{\beta})$ of deterministic functions as the probability limits of the functions used in the moment conditions that define an estimator, and we saw that the parameter vector $\boldsymbol{\beta}$ is asymptotically identified if two **asymptotic identification conditions** are satisfied. The first condition is that $\boldsymbol{\alpha}(\boldsymbol{\beta}_0) = \boldsymbol{0}$, and the second is that $\boldsymbol{\alpha}(\boldsymbol{\beta}) \neq \boldsymbol{0}$ for all $\boldsymbol{\beta} \neq \boldsymbol{\beta}_0$.

The analogous vector of functions for the IV estimator is

$$\begin{aligned} \boldsymbol{\alpha}(\boldsymbol{\beta}) &= \operatorname*{plim}_{n\to\infty} \frac{1}{n} \boldsymbol{X}^\top \boldsymbol{P_W}(\boldsymbol{y} - \boldsymbol{X\beta}) \\ &= \boldsymbol{S}_{\boldsymbol{X}^\top\boldsymbol{W}} (\boldsymbol{S}_{\boldsymbol{W}^\top\boldsymbol{W}})^{-1} \operatorname*{plim}_{n\to\infty} \frac{1}{n} \boldsymbol{W}^\top(\boldsymbol{y} - \boldsymbol{X\beta}), \end{aligned} \tag{8.31}$$

where $\boldsymbol{S}_{\boldsymbol{X}^\top\boldsymbol{W}} \equiv \boldsymbol{S}_{\boldsymbol{W}^\top\boldsymbol{X}}^\top$, which was defined in (8.14), and $\boldsymbol{S}_{\boldsymbol{W}^\top\boldsymbol{W}}$ was defined just after (8.17). For asymptotic identification, we assume that both these matrices exist and have full rank. This assumption is analogous to the assumption that $1/n$ times the matrix $\boldsymbol{X}^\top\boldsymbol{X}$ has probability limit $\boldsymbol{S}_{\boldsymbol{X}^\top\boldsymbol{X}}$, a matrix with full rank, which we originally made in Section 3.3 when we proved that the OLS estimator is consistent. If $\boldsymbol{S}_{\boldsymbol{W}^\top\boldsymbol{W}}$ does not have full rank, then at least one of the instruments is perfectly collinear with the others, asymptotically, and should therefore be dropped. If $\boldsymbol{S}_{\boldsymbol{W}^\top\boldsymbol{X}}$ does not have full rank, then the asymptotic version of the moment conditions (8.28) has fewer than k linearly independent equations, and these conditions therefore have no unique solution.

If β_0 is the true parameter vector, then $\boldsymbol{y}-\boldsymbol{X}\boldsymbol{\beta}_0=\boldsymbol{u}$, and the right-hand side of (8.31) vanishes under the assumption (8.16) used to show the consistency of the simple IV estimator. Thus $\boldsymbol{\alpha}(\boldsymbol{\beta}_0)=\mathbf{0}$, and the first condition for asymptotic identification is satisfied.

The second condition requires that $\boldsymbol{\alpha}(\boldsymbol{\beta})\neq\mathbf{0}$ for all $\boldsymbol{\beta}\neq\boldsymbol{\beta}_0$. It is easy to see from (8.31) that

$$\boldsymbol{\alpha}(\boldsymbol{\beta})=\boldsymbol{S}_{\boldsymbol{X}^\top\boldsymbol{W}}(\boldsymbol{S}_{\boldsymbol{W}^\top\boldsymbol{W}})^{-1}\boldsymbol{S}_{\boldsymbol{W}^\top\boldsymbol{X}}(\boldsymbol{\beta}_0-\boldsymbol{\beta}).$$

For this to be nonzero for all nonzero $\boldsymbol{\beta}_0-\boldsymbol{\beta}$, it is necessary and sufficient that the matrix $\boldsymbol{S}_{\boldsymbol{X}^\top\boldsymbol{W}}(\boldsymbol{S}_{\boldsymbol{W}^\top\boldsymbol{W}})^{-1}\boldsymbol{S}_{\boldsymbol{W}^\top\boldsymbol{X}}$ should have full rank k. This must be the case if the matrices $\boldsymbol{S}_{\boldsymbol{W}^\top\boldsymbol{W}}$ and $\boldsymbol{S}_{\boldsymbol{W}^\top\boldsymbol{X}}$ both have full rank, as we have assumed. If $l=k$, the conditions on the two matrices $\boldsymbol{S}_{\boldsymbol{W}^\top\boldsymbol{W}}$ and $\boldsymbol{S}_{\boldsymbol{W}^\top\boldsymbol{X}}$ simplify, as we saw when considering the simple IV estimator, to the single condition (8.14). The condition that $\boldsymbol{S}_{\boldsymbol{X}^\top\boldsymbol{W}}(\boldsymbol{S}_{\boldsymbol{W}^\top\boldsymbol{W}})^{-1}\boldsymbol{S}_{\boldsymbol{W}^\top\boldsymbol{X}}$ has full rank can also be used to show that the probability limit of $1/n$ times the IV criterion function (8.30) has a unique global minimum at $\boldsymbol{\beta}=\boldsymbol{\beta}_0$, as readers are asked to show in Exercise 8.5.

The two asymptotic identification conditions are sufficient for consistency. Because we are dealing here with linear models, there is no need for a sophisticated proof of this fact; see Exercise 8.6. The key assumption is, of course, (8.16). If this assumption did not hold, because any of the instruments was asymptotically correlated with the error terms, the first of the asymptotic identification conditions would not hold either, and the IV estimator would not be consistent.

Asymptotic Distribution of the IV Estimator

Like every estimator that we have studied, the IV estimator is asymptotically normally distributed with an asymptotic covariance matrix that can be estimated consistently. The asymptotic covariance matrix for the simple IV estimator, expression (8.17), turns out to be valid for the generalized IV estimator as well. To see this, we replace $\boldsymbol{W}$ in (8.17) by the asymptotically optimal instruments $\boldsymbol{P_W X}$. As in (8.25), we find that

$$\boldsymbol{X}^\top\boldsymbol{P}_{\boldsymbol{P_W X}}\boldsymbol{X}=\boldsymbol{X}^\top\boldsymbol{P_W X}(\boldsymbol{X}^\top\boldsymbol{P_W X})^{-1}\boldsymbol{X}^\top\boldsymbol{P_W X}=\boldsymbol{X}^\top\boldsymbol{P_W X},$$

from which it follows that (8.17) is unchanged if $\boldsymbol{W}$ is replaced by $\boldsymbol{P_W X}$.

It can also be shown directly that (8.17) is the asymptotic covariance matrix of the generalized IV estimator. From (8.29), it follows that

$$n^{1/2}(\hat{\boldsymbol{\beta}}_{\text{IV}}-\boldsymbol{\beta}_0)=(n^{-1}\boldsymbol{X}^\top\boldsymbol{P_W X})^{-1}n^{-1/2}\boldsymbol{X}^\top\boldsymbol{P_W u}. \tag{8.32}$$

Under reasonable assumptions, a central limit theorem can be applied to the expression $n^{-1/2}\boldsymbol{W}^\top\boldsymbol{u}$, which allows us to conclude that the asymptotic distribution of this expression is multivariate normal, with mean zero and covariance matrix

$$\lim_{n\to\infty}\frac{1}{n}\boldsymbol{W}^\top\mathrm{E}(\boldsymbol{u}\boldsymbol{u}^\top)\boldsymbol{W}=\sigma_0^2\boldsymbol{S}_{\boldsymbol{W}^\top\boldsymbol{W}}, \tag{8.33}$$

since we assume that $\mathrm{E}(\boldsymbol{u}\boldsymbol{u}^\top)=\sigma_0^2\mathbf{I}$. With this result, it can be shown quite simply that (8.17) is the asymptotic covariance matrix of $\hat{\boldsymbol{\beta}}_{\rm IV}$; see Exercise 8.7. In practice, since σ_0^2 is unknown, we use

$$\widehat{\mathrm{Var}}(\hat{\boldsymbol{\beta}}_{\rm IV})=\hat{\sigma}^2(\boldsymbol{X}^\top\boldsymbol{P_W}\boldsymbol{X})^{-1} \tag{8.34}$$

to estimate the covariance matrix of $\hat{\boldsymbol{\beta}}_{\rm IV}$. Here $\hat{\sigma}^2$ is $1/n$ times the sum of the squares of the components of the residual vector $\boldsymbol{y}-\boldsymbol{X}\hat{\boldsymbol{\beta}}$. In contrast to the OLS case, there is no good reason to divide by anything other than n when estimating σ^2. Because IV estimation minimizes the IV criterion function and not the sum of squared residuals, IV residuals are not necessarily too small. Nevertheless, many regression packages divide by $n-k$ instead of by n.

The choice of instruments usually affects the asymptotic covariance matrix of the IV estimator. If some or all of the columns of $\bar{\boldsymbol{X}}$ are not contained in the span $\mathcal{S}(\boldsymbol{W})$ of the instruments, an efficiency gain is potentially available if that span is made larger. Readers are asked in Exercise 8.8 to demonstrate formally that adding an extra instrument by appending a new column to $\boldsymbol{W}$ must, in general, reduce the asymptotic covariance matrix. Of course, it cannot be made smaller than the lower bound $\sigma_0^2(\bar{\boldsymbol{X}}^\top\bar{\boldsymbol{X}})^{-1}$, which is attained if the optimal instruments $\bar{\boldsymbol{X}}$ are available.

When all the regressors can validly be used as instruments, we have $\bar{\boldsymbol{X}}=\boldsymbol{X}$, and the efficient IV estimator coincides with the OLS estimator, as the Gauss-Markov Theorem predicts.

Two-Stage Least Squares

The IV estimator (8.29) is commonly known as the **two-stage least-squares**, or **2SLS**, estimator, because, before the days of good econometrics software packages, it was often calculated in two stages using OLS regressions. In the first stage, each column $\boldsymbol{x}_i$, $i=1,\ldots,k$, of $\boldsymbol{X}$ is regressed on $\boldsymbol{W}$, if necessary. If a regressor $\boldsymbol{x}_i$ is a valid instrument, it is already (or should be) one of the columns of $\boldsymbol{W}$. In that case, since $\boldsymbol{P_W}\boldsymbol{x}_i=\boldsymbol{x}_i$, no first-stage regression is needed, and we say that such a regressor serves as its own instrument.

The fitted values from the first-stage regressions, plus the actual values of any regressors that serve as their own instruments, are collected to form the matrix $\boldsymbol{P_W}\boldsymbol{X}$. Then the second-stage regression,

$$\boldsymbol{y}=\boldsymbol{P_W}\boldsymbol{X}\boldsymbol{\beta}+\text{residuals}, \tag{8.35}$$

is used to obtain the 2SLS estimates. Because $\boldsymbol{P_W}$ is an idempotent matrix, the OLS estimate of $\boldsymbol{\beta}$ from this second-stage regression is

$$\hat{\boldsymbol{\beta}}_{2\text{sls}} = (\boldsymbol{X}^\top \boldsymbol{P_W X})^{-1}\boldsymbol{X}^\top \boldsymbol{P_W y},$$

which is identical to (8.29), the generalized IV estimator $\hat{\boldsymbol{\beta}}_{\text{IV}}$.

If this two-stage procedure is used, some care must be taken when estimating the standard error of the regression and the covariance matrix of the parameter estimates. The OLS estimate of σ^2 from regression (8.35) is

$$s^2 = \frac{\|\boldsymbol{y} - \boldsymbol{P_W X}\hat{\boldsymbol{\beta}}_{\text{IV}}\|^2}{n-k}. \tag{8.36}$$

In contrast, the estimate that was used in the estimated IV covariance matrix (8.34) is

$$\hat{\sigma}^2 = \frac{\|\boldsymbol{y} - \boldsymbol{X}\hat{\boldsymbol{\beta}}_{\text{IV}}\|^2}{n}. \tag{8.37}$$

These two estimates of σ^2 are not asymptotically equivalent, and s^2 is not consistent. The reason is that the residuals from regression (8.35) do not tend to the corresponding error terms as $n \to \infty$, because the regressors in (8.35) are not the true explanatory variables. Therefore, $1/(n-k)$ times the sum of squared residuals is not a consistent estimator of σ^2. Of course, no regression package providing IV or 2SLS estimation would ever use (8.36) to estimate σ^2. Instead, it would use (8.37), or at least something that is asymptotically equivalent to it.

Two-stage least squares was invented by Theil (1953) and Basmann (1957) at a time when computers were very primitive. Consequently, despite the classic papers of Durbin (1954) and Sargan (1958) on instrumental variables estimation, the term "two-stage least squares" came to be very widely used in econometrics, even when the estimator is not actually computed in two stages. We prefer to think of two-stage least squares as simply a particular way to compute the generalized IV estimator, and we will use $\hat{\boldsymbol{\beta}}_{\text{IV}}$ rather than $\hat{\boldsymbol{\beta}}_{2\text{sls}}$ to denote that estimator.

8.4 Finite-Sample Properties of IV Estimators

Unfortunately, the finite-sample distributions of IV estimators are much more complicated than the asymptotic ones. Indeed, except in very special cases, these distributions are unknowable in practice. Although it is consistent, the IV estimator for just identified models has a distribution with such thick tails that its expectation does not even exist. With overidentified models, the expectation of the estimator exists, but it is in general different from the true parameter value, so that the estimator is biased, often very substantially so. In consequence, investigators can easily make serious errors of inference when interpreting IV estimates.

The biases in the OLS estimates of a model like (8.10) arise because the error terms are correlated with some of the regressors. The IV estimator solves this problem asymptotically, because the projections of the regressors on to $\mathcal{S}(\boldsymbol{W})$ are asymptotically uncorrelated with the error terms. However, there must always still be some correlation in finite samples, and this causes the IV estimator to be biased.

Systems of Equations

In order to understand the finite-sample properties of the IV estimator, we need to consider the model (8.10) as part of a system of equations. We therefore change notation somewhat and rewrite (8.10) as

$$\boldsymbol{y} = \boldsymbol{Z\beta}_1 + \boldsymbol{Y\beta}_2 + \boldsymbol{u}, \quad \mathrm{E}(\boldsymbol{uu}^\top) = \sigma^2\mathbf{I}, \tag{8.38}$$

where the matrix of regressors $\boldsymbol{X}$ has been partitioned into two parts, namely, an $n \times k_1$ matrix of exogenous and predetermined variables, $\boldsymbol{Z}$, and an $n \times k_2$ matrix of endogenous variables, $\boldsymbol{Y}$, and the vector $\boldsymbol{\beta}$ has been partitioned conformably into two subvectors $\boldsymbol{\beta}_1$ and $\boldsymbol{\beta}_2$. There are assumed to be $l \geq k$ instruments, of which k_1 are the columns of the matrix $\boldsymbol{Z}$.

The model (8.38) is not fully specified, because it says nothing about how the matrix $\boldsymbol{Y}$ is generated. For each observation t, $t = 1, \ldots, n$, the value y_t of the dependent variable and the values $\boldsymbol{Y}_t$ of the other endogenous variables are assumed to be determined by a set of linear simultaneous equations. The variables in the matrix $\boldsymbol{Y}$ are called **current endogenous variables**, because they are determined simultaneously, row by row, along with $\boldsymbol{y}$. Suppose that all the exogenous and predetermined explanatory variables in the full set of simultaneous equations are included in the $n \times l$ instrument matrix $\boldsymbol{W}$, of which the first k_1 columns are those of $\boldsymbol{Z}$. Then, as can easily be seen by analogy with the explicit result (8.09) for the demand-supply model, we have for each endogenous variable $\boldsymbol{y}_i$, $i = 0, 1, \ldots, k_2$, that

$$\boldsymbol{y}_i = \boldsymbol{W\pi}_i + \boldsymbol{v}_i, \quad \mathrm{E}(\boldsymbol{v}_i \,|\, \boldsymbol{W}) = \mathbf{0}. \tag{8.39}$$

Here $\boldsymbol{y}_0 \equiv \boldsymbol{y}$, and the $\boldsymbol{y}_i$, for $i = 1, \ldots, k_2$, are the columns of $\boldsymbol{Y}$. The $\boldsymbol{\pi}_i$ are l–vectors of unknown coefficients, and the $\boldsymbol{v}_i$ are n–vectors of error terms that are innovations with respect to the instruments.

Equations like (8.39), which have only exogenous and predetermined variables on the right-hand side, are called **reduced form equations**, in contrast with equations like (8.38), which are called **structural equations**. Writing a model as a set of reduced form equations emphasizes the fact that all the endogenous variables are generated by similar mechanisms. In general, the error terms for the various reduced form equations display **contemporaneous correlation**: If v_{ti} denotes a typical element of the vector $\boldsymbol{v}_i$, then, for observation t, the reduced form error terms v_{ti} are generally correlated among themselves and correlated with the error term u_t of the structural equation.

A Simple Example

In order to gain additional intuition about the properties of the IV estimator in finite samples, we consider the very simplest nontrivial example, in which the dependent variable $\boldsymbol{y}$ is explained by only one variable, which we denote by $\boldsymbol{x}$. The regressor $\boldsymbol{x}$ is endogenous, and there is available exactly one exogenous instrument, $\boldsymbol{w}$. In order to keep the example reasonably simple, we suppose that all the error terms, for both $\boldsymbol{y}$ and $\boldsymbol{x}$, are normally distributed. Thus the DGP that simultaneously determines $\boldsymbol{x}$ and $\boldsymbol{y}$ can be written as

$$\begin{aligned} \boldsymbol{y} &= \boldsymbol{x}\beta_0 + \sigma_u \boldsymbol{u}, \\ \boldsymbol{x} &= \boldsymbol{w}\pi_0 + \sigma_v \boldsymbol{v}, \end{aligned} \tag{8.40}$$

where the second equation is analogous to (8.39). By explicitly writing σ_u and σ_v as the standard deviations of the error terms, we can define the vectors $\boldsymbol{u}$ and $\boldsymbol{v}$ to be multivariate standard normal, that is, distributed as $\mathrm{N}(\mathbf{0}, \mathbf{I})$. There is contemporaneous correlation of $\boldsymbol{u}$ and $\boldsymbol{v}$. Therefore, $\mathrm{E}(u_t v_t) = \rho$ for some correlation coefficient ρ such that $-1 < \rho < 1$. The result of Exercise 4.4 shows that the expectation of u_t conditional on v_t is ρv_t, and so we can write $\boldsymbol{u} = \rho\boldsymbol{v} + \boldsymbol{u}_1$, where $\boldsymbol{u}_1$ has mean zero conditional on $\boldsymbol{v}$.

In this simple, just identified, setup, the IV estimator of the parameter β is

$$\hat{\beta}_{\mathrm{IV}} = (\boldsymbol{w}^{\top}\boldsymbol{x})^{-1}\boldsymbol{w}^{\top}\boldsymbol{y} = \beta_0 + \sigma_u(\boldsymbol{w}^{\top}\boldsymbol{x})^{-1}\boldsymbol{w}^{\top}\boldsymbol{u}. \tag{8.41}$$

This expression is clearly unchanged if the instrument $\boldsymbol{w}$ is multiplied by an arbitrary scalar, and so we can, without loss of generality, rescale $\boldsymbol{w}$ so that $\boldsymbol{w}^{\top}\boldsymbol{w} = 1$. Then, using the second equation in (8.40), we find that

$$\hat{\beta}_{\mathrm{IV}} - \beta_0 = \frac{\sigma_u \boldsymbol{w}^{\top}\boldsymbol{u}}{\pi_0 + \sigma_v \boldsymbol{w}^{\top}\boldsymbol{v}} = \frac{\sigma_u \boldsymbol{w}^{\top}(\rho\boldsymbol{v} + \boldsymbol{u}_1)}{\pi_0 + \sigma_v \boldsymbol{w}^{\top}\boldsymbol{v}}.$$

Let us now compute the expectation of this expression conditional on $\boldsymbol{v}$. Since, by construction, $\mathrm{E}(\boldsymbol{u}_1 \,|\, \boldsymbol{v}) = \mathbf{0}$, we obtain

$$\mathrm{E}(\hat{\beta}_{\mathrm{IV}} - \beta_0 \,|\, \boldsymbol{v}) = \frac{\rho\sigma_u}{\sigma_v}\frac{z}{a + z}, \tag{8.42}$$

where we have made the definitions $a \equiv \pi_0/\sigma_v$, and $z \equiv \boldsymbol{w}^{\top}\boldsymbol{v}$. Given our rescaling of $\boldsymbol{w}$, it is easy to see that $z \sim \mathrm{N}(0, 1)$.

If $\rho = 0$, the right-hand side of equation (8.42) vanishes, and so the unconditional expectation of $\hat{\beta}_{\mathrm{IV}} - \beta_0$ vanishes as well. Therefore, in this special case, $\hat{\beta}_{\mathrm{IV}}$ is unbiased. This is as expected, since, if $\rho = 0$, the regressor $\boldsymbol{x}$ is uncorrelated with the error vector $\boldsymbol{u}$. If $\rho \neq 0$, however, the right-hand side of (8.42) is equal to a nonzero factor times the random variable $z/(a + z)$. Unless $a = 0$, this random variable has no expectation. To see this, we can try to calculate it. If the expectation existed, it would be

$$\mathrm{E}\Big(\frac{z}{a+z}\Big) = \int_{-\infty}^{\infty} \frac{x}{a+x}\,\phi(x)\,dx, \tag{8.43}$$

where, as usual, $\phi(\cdot)$ is the density of the standard normal distribution. It is a fairly simple calculus exercise to show that the integral in (8.43) diverges in the neighborhood of $x = -a$.

If $\pi_0 = 0$, then $a = 0$. In this rather odd case, $\boldsymbol{x} = \sigma_v \boldsymbol{v}$ is just noise, as though it were an error term. Therefore, since $z/(a+z)$ reduces to 1, the expectation exists, but it is not zero, and $\hat\beta_{\rm IV}$ is therefore biased.

When $a \neq 0$, which is the usual case, the IV estimator (8.41) is neither biased nor unbiased, because it has no expectation for any finite sample size n. This may seem to contradict the result according to which $\hat\beta_{\rm IV}$ is asymptotically normal, since all the moments of the normal distribution exist. However, the fact that a sequence of random variables converges to a limiting random variable does not necessarily imply that the *moments* of the variables in the sequence converge to those of the limiting variable; see Davidson and MacKinnon (1993, Section 4.5). The estimator (8.41) is a case in point. Fortunately, this possible failure to converge of the moments does not extend to the CDFs of the random variables, which do indeed converge to that of the limit. Consequently, P values and the upper and lower limits of confidence intervals computed with the asymptotic distribution are legitimate approximations, in the sense that they become more and more accurate as the sample size increases.

A less simple calculation can be used to show that, in the overidentified case, the first $l - k$ moments of $\hat{\boldsymbol{\beta}}_{\rm IV}$ exist; see Kinal (1980). This is consistent with the result we have just obtained for an exactly identified model, where $l - k = 0$, and the IV estimator has no moments at all. When the mean of $\hat{\boldsymbol{\beta}}_{\rm IV}$ exists, it is almost never equal to $\boldsymbol{\beta}_0$. Readers will have a much clearer idea of the impact of the existence or nonexistence of moments, and of the bias of the IV estimator, if they work carefully through Exercises 8.10 to 8.13, in which they are asked to generate by simulation the EDFs of the estimator in different situations.

The General Case

We now return to the general case, in which the structural equation (8.38) is being estimated, and the other endogenous variables are generated by the reduced form equations (8.39) for $i = 1, \ldots, k_2$, which correspond to the first-stage regressions for 2SLS. We can group the vectors of fitted values from these regressions into an $n \times k_2$ matrix $\boldsymbol{P_W Y}$. The generalized IV estimator is then equivalent to a simple IV estimator that uses the instruments $\boldsymbol{P_W X} = [\boldsymbol{Z}\ \boldsymbol{P_W Y}]$. By grouping the l–vectors $\boldsymbol{\pi}_i$, $i = 1, \ldots, k_2$ into an

$l \times k_2$ matrix $\boldsymbol{\Pi}_2$ and the vectors of error terms $\boldsymbol{v}_i$ into an $n \times k_2$ matrix $\boldsymbol{V}_2$, we see that

$$\begin{aligned} \boldsymbol{P_W X} &= [\boldsymbol{Z} \;\; \boldsymbol{P_W Y}] = [\boldsymbol{Z} \;\; \boldsymbol{P_W}(\boldsymbol{W\Pi}_2 + \boldsymbol{V}_2)] \\ &= [\boldsymbol{Z} \;\; \boldsymbol{W\Pi}_2 + \boldsymbol{P_W V}_2] = \boldsymbol{W\Pi} + \boldsymbol{P_W V}. \end{aligned} \tag{8.44}$$

Here $\boldsymbol{V}$ is an $n \times k$ matrix of the form $[\mathbf{O} \;\; \boldsymbol{V}_2]$, where the zero block has dimension $n \times k_1$, and $\boldsymbol{\Pi}$ is an $l \times k$ matrix, which can be written as $\boldsymbol{\Pi} = [\boldsymbol{\Pi}_1 \;\; \boldsymbol{\Pi}_2]$, where the $l \times k_1$ matrix $\boldsymbol{\Pi}_1$ is a $k_1 \times k_1$ identity matrix sitting on top of an $(l - k_1) \times k_1$ zero matrix. It is easily checked that these definitions make the last equality in (8.44) correct. Thus $\boldsymbol{P_W X}$ has two components: $\boldsymbol{W\Pi}$, which by assumption is uncorrelated with $\boldsymbol{u}$, and $\boldsymbol{P_W V}$, which is almost always correlated with $\boldsymbol{u}$.

If we substitute the rightmost expression of (8.44) into (8.32), eliminating the factors of powers of n, which are unnecessary in the finite-sample context, we find that

$$\begin{aligned} \hat{\boldsymbol{\beta}}_{\rm IV} - \boldsymbol{\beta}_0 = &\left(\boldsymbol{\Pi}^\top \boldsymbol{W}^\top \boldsymbol{W\Pi} + \boldsymbol{\Pi}^\top \boldsymbol{W}^\top \boldsymbol{V} + \boldsymbol{V}^\top \boldsymbol{W\Pi} + \boldsymbol{V}^\top \boldsymbol{P_W V}\right)^{-1} \\ &\times \left(\boldsymbol{\Pi}^\top \boldsymbol{W}^\top \boldsymbol{u} + \boldsymbol{V}^\top \boldsymbol{P_W u}\right). \end{aligned} \tag{8.45}$$

To make sense of this rather messy expression, first set $\boldsymbol{V} = \mathbf{O}$. The result is

$$\hat{\boldsymbol{\beta}}_{\rm IV} - \boldsymbol{\beta}_0 = (\boldsymbol{\Pi}^\top \boldsymbol{W}^\top \boldsymbol{W\Pi})^{-1} \boldsymbol{\Pi}^\top \boldsymbol{W}^\top \boldsymbol{u}. \tag{8.46}$$

If $\boldsymbol{V} = \mathbf{O}$, the supposedly endogenous variables $\boldsymbol{Y}$ are in fact exogenous or predetermined, and it can be checked (see Exercise 8.14) that, in this case, $\hat{\boldsymbol{\beta}}_{\rm IV}$ is just the OLS estimator for model (8.10).

If $\boldsymbol{V}$ is not zero, but is independent of $\boldsymbol{u}$, then we see immediately that the expectation of (8.45) conditional on $\boldsymbol{V}$ is zero. This case is the analog of the case with $\rho = 0$ in (8.42). Note that we require the full independence of $\boldsymbol{V}$ and $\boldsymbol{u}$ for this to hold. If instead $\boldsymbol{V}$ were just predetermined with respect to $\boldsymbol{u}$, the IV estimator would still have a finite-sample bias, for exactly the same reasons as those leading to finite-sample bias of the OLS estimator with predetermined but not exogenous explanatory variables.

When $\boldsymbol{V}$ and $\boldsymbol{u}$ are contemporaneously correlated, it can be shown that all the terms in (8.45) which involve $\boldsymbol{V}$ do not contribute asymptotically; see Exercise 8.15. Thus we can see that any discrepancy between the finite-sample and asymptotic distributions of $\hat{\boldsymbol{\beta}}_{\rm IV} - \boldsymbol{\beta}_0$ must arise from the terms in (8.45) that involve $\boldsymbol{V}$. In fact, in the absence of other features of the model that could give rise to finite-sample bias, such as lagged dependent variables, the poor finite-sample properties of the IV estimator arise solely from the contemporaneous correlation between $\boldsymbol{P_W V}$ and $\boldsymbol{u}$. In particular, the second term in the second factor of (8.45) generally has a nonzero mean, and this term can be a major source of bias when the correlation between $\boldsymbol{u}$ and some of the columns of $\boldsymbol{V}$ is high.

If the terms involving $\boldsymbol{V}$ in (8.45) are relatively small, the finite-sample distribution of the IV estimator is likely to be well approximated by its asymptotic distribution. However, if these terms are not small, the asymptotic approximation may be poor. Thus our analysis suggests that there are three situations in which the IV estimator is likely to have poor finite-sample properties:

- When l, the number of instruments, is large, $\boldsymbol{W}$ is able to explain much of the variation in $\boldsymbol{V}$; recall from Section 3.8 that adding additional regressors can never reduce the R^2 of a regression. With large l, consequently, $\boldsymbol{P_W V}$ must be relatively large. When the number of instruments is extremely large relative to the sample size, the first-stage regressions may fit so well that $\boldsymbol{P_W Y}$ is very similar to $\boldsymbol{Y}$. In this situation, the IV estimates may be almost as biased as the OLS ones.
- When at least some of the reduced-form regressions (8.39) fit poorly, in the sense that the R^2 is small or the F statistic for all the slope coefficients to be zero is insignificant, the model is said to suffer from **weak instruments**. In this situation, even if $\boldsymbol{P_W V}$ is no larger than usual, it may nevertheless be large relative to $\boldsymbol{W\Pi}$. When the instruments are very weak, the finite-sample distribution of the IV estimator may be very far from its asymptotic distribution even in samples with many thousands of observations. An example of this is furnished by the case in which $a = 0$ in (8.42) in our simple example with one regressor and one instrument. As we saw, the distribution of the estimator is quite different when $a = 0$ from what it is when $a \neq 0$; the distribution when $a \cong 0$ may well be similar to the distribution when $a = 0$.
- When the correlation between $\boldsymbol{u}$ and some of the columns of $\boldsymbol{V}$ is very high, $\boldsymbol{V}^\top \boldsymbol{P_W u}$ tends to be relatively large. Whether it is large enough to cause serious problems for inference depends on the sample size, the number of instruments, and how well the instruments explain the endogenous variables.

It may seem that adding additional instruments must always increase the finite-sample bias of the IV estimator, and Exercise 8.13 illustrates a case in which it does. In that case, the additional instruments do not really belong in the reduced-form regressions. However, if the instruments truly belong in the reduced-form regressions, adding them alleviates the weak instruments problem, and that can actually cause the bias to diminish.

Finite-sample inference in models estimated by instrumental variables is a subject of active research in econometrics. Relatively recent papers on this topic include Nelson and Startz (1990a, 1990b), Buse (1992), Bekker (1994), Bound, Jaeger, and Baker (1995), Dufour (1997), Staiger and Stock (1997), Wang and Zivot (1998), Zivot, Startz, and Nelson (1998), Angrist, Imbens, and Krueger (1999), Blomquist and Dahlberg (1999), Donald and Newey (2001), Hahn and Hausman (2002), Kleibergen (2002), and Stock, Wright, and Yogo (2002). There remain many unsolved problems.

8.5 Hypothesis Testing

Because the finite-sample distributions of IV estimators are almost never known, exact tests of hypotheses based on such estimators are almost never available. However, large-sample tests can be performed in a variety of ways. Since many of the methods of performing these tests are very similar to methods that we have already discussed in Chapters 4 and 6, there is no need to discuss them in detail.

Asymptotic t and Wald Statistics

When there is just one restriction, the easiest approach is simply to compute an asymptotic t test. For example, if we wish to test the hypothesis that $\beta_i = \beta_{0i}$, where β_i is one of the regression parameters, then a suitable test statistic is

$$t_{\beta_i} = \frac{\hat{\beta}_i - \beta_{i0}}{\big(\widehat{\mathrm{Var}}(\hat{\beta}_i)\big)^{1/2}}, \tag{8.47}$$

where $\hat{\beta}_i$ is the IV estimate of β_i, and $\widehat{\mathrm{Var}}(\hat{\beta}_i)$ is the ith diagonal element of the estimated covariance matrix, (8.34). This test statistic does not follow the Student's t distribution in finite samples, but it is asymptotically distributed as $\mathrm{N}(0,1)$ under the null hypothesis.

For testing restrictions on two or more parameters, the natural analog of (8.47) is a Wald statistic. Suppose that $\boldsymbol{\beta}$ is partitioned as $[\boldsymbol{\beta}_1 \;\; \boldsymbol{\beta}_2]$, and we wish to test the hypothesis that $\boldsymbol{\beta}_2 = \boldsymbol{\beta}_{20}$. Then, as in (6.71), the appropriate Wald statistic is

$$W_{\boldsymbol{\beta}_2} = (\hat{\boldsymbol{\beta}}_2 - \boldsymbol{\beta}_{20})^{\top}\big(\widehat{\mathrm{Var}}(\hat{\boldsymbol{\beta}}_2)\big)^{-1}(\hat{\boldsymbol{\beta}}_2 - \boldsymbol{\beta}_{20}), \tag{8.48}$$

where $\widehat{\mathrm{Var}}(\hat{\boldsymbol{\beta}}_2)$ is the submatrix of (8.34) that corresponds to the vector $\boldsymbol{\beta}_2$. This Wald statistic can be thought of as a generalization of the asymptotic t statistic: When $\boldsymbol{\beta}_2$ is a scalar, the square root of (8.48) is (8.47).

The IV Variant of the GNR

In many circumstances, the easiest way to obtain asymptotically valid test statistics for models estimated using instrumental variables is to use a variant of the Gauss-Newton regression. For the model (8.10), this variant, called the **IVGNR**, takes the form

$$\boldsymbol{y} - \boldsymbol{X\beta} = \boldsymbol{P_W X b} + \text{residuals}. \tag{8.49}$$

As with the usual GNR, the variables of the IVGNR must be evaluated at some prespecified value of $\boldsymbol{\beta}$ before the regression can be run, in the usual way, using ordinary least squares.

The IVGNR has the same properties relative to model (8.10) as the ordinary GNR has relative to linear and nonlinear regression models estimated by least squares. The first property is that, if (8.49) is evaluated at $\boldsymbol{\beta} = \hat{\boldsymbol{\beta}}_{\rm IV}$, then the regressors $\boldsymbol{P_W X}$ are orthogonal to the regressand, because the orthogonality conditions, namely,

$$\boldsymbol{X}^\top \boldsymbol{P_W}(\boldsymbol{y} - \boldsymbol{X}\hat{\boldsymbol{\beta}}_{\rm IV}) = \mathbf{0},$$

are just the moment conditions (8.28) that define $\hat{\boldsymbol{\beta}}_{\rm IV}$.

The second property is that, if (8.49) is again evaluated at $\boldsymbol{\beta} = \hat{\boldsymbol{\beta}}_{\rm IV}$, the estimated OLS covariance matrix is asymptotically valid. This matrix is

$$s^2(\boldsymbol{X}^\top \boldsymbol{P_W X})^{-1}. \tag{8.50}$$

Here s^2 is the sum of squared residuals from (8.49), divided by $n - k$. Since $\hat{\boldsymbol{b}} = \mathbf{0}$ because of the orthogonality of the regressand and the regressors, those residuals are the components of the vector $\boldsymbol{y} - \boldsymbol{X}\hat{\boldsymbol{\beta}}_{\rm IV}$, that is, the IV residuals from (8.10). It follows that (8.50), which has exactly the same form as (8.34), is a consistent estimator of the covariance matrix of $\hat{\boldsymbol{\beta}}_{\rm IV}$, where "consistent estimator" is used in the sense of (5.22). As with the ordinary GNR, the estimator $\acute{s}^2$ obtained by running (8.49) with $\boldsymbol{\beta} = \acute{\boldsymbol{\beta}}$ is consistent for the error variance σ^2 if $\acute{\boldsymbol{\beta}}$ is root-n consistent; see Exercise 8.16.

The third property is that, like the ordinary GNR, the IVGNR permits one-step efficient estimation. For linear models, this is true if *any* value of $\boldsymbol{\beta}$ is used in (8.49). If we set $\boldsymbol{\beta} = \acute{\boldsymbol{\beta}}$, then running (8.49) gives the artificial parameter estimates

$$\acute{\boldsymbol{b}} = (\boldsymbol{X}^\top \boldsymbol{P_W X})^{-1}\boldsymbol{X}^\top \boldsymbol{P_W}(\boldsymbol{y} - \boldsymbol{X}\acute{\boldsymbol{\beta}}) = \hat{\boldsymbol{\beta}}_{\rm IV} - \acute{\boldsymbol{\beta}},$$

from which it follows that $\acute{\boldsymbol{\beta}} + \acute{\boldsymbol{b}} = \hat{\boldsymbol{\beta}}_{\rm IV}$ for all $\acute{\boldsymbol{\beta}}$. In the context of nonlinear IV estimation (see Section 8.9), this result, like the one above for $\acute{\sigma}^2$, becomes an approximation that is asymptotically valid only if $\acute{\boldsymbol{\beta}}$ is a root-n consistent estimator of the true $\boldsymbol{\beta}_0$.

Tests Based on the IVGNR

If the restrictions to be tested are all linear restrictions, there is no further loss of generality if we suppose that they are all zero restrictions. Thus the null and alternative hypotheses can be written as

$$H_0\colon\ \boldsymbol{y} = \boldsymbol{X}_1\boldsymbol{\beta}_1 + \boldsymbol{u}, \text{ and} \tag{8.51}$$

$$H_1\colon\ \boldsymbol{y} = \boldsymbol{X}_1\boldsymbol{\beta}_1 + \boldsymbol{X}_2\boldsymbol{\beta}_2 + \boldsymbol{u}, \tag{8.52}$$

where the matrices $\boldsymbol{X}_1$ and $\boldsymbol{X}_2$ are, respectively, $n \times k_1$ and $n \times k_2$, $\boldsymbol{\beta}_1$ is a k_1–vector, and $\boldsymbol{\beta}_2$ is a k_2–vector. As elsewhere in this chapter, it is assumed that $\mathrm{E}(\boldsymbol{uu}^\top) = \sigma^2\mathbf{I}$. Any or all of the columns of $\boldsymbol{X} = [\boldsymbol{X}_1\ \boldsymbol{X}_2]$ may be correlated with the error terms. It is assumed that there exists an $n \times l$ matrix $\boldsymbol{W}$ of instruments, which are asymptotically uncorrelated with the error terms, and that $l \geq k = k_1 + k_2$.

The same matrix of instruments is assumed to be used for the estimation of both H_0 and H_1. While this assumption is natural if we start by estimating H_1 and then impose restrictions on it, it may not be so natural if we start by estimating H_0 and then estimate a less restricted model. A matrix of instruments that would be entirely appropriate for estimating H_0 may be inappropriate for estimating H_1, either because it omits some columns of $\boldsymbol{X}_2$ that are known to be uncorrelated with the errors, or because the number of instruments is greater than k_1 but less than $k_1 + k_2$. It is essential that the $\boldsymbol{W}$ matrix used should be appropriate for estimating H_1 as well as H_0.

Exactly the same reasoning as that used in Section 6.7, based on the three properties of the IVGNR established in the previous subsection, shows that an asymptotically valid test of H_0 against the alternative H_1 is provided by the artificial F statistic obtained from running the following two IVGNRs, which correspond to H_0 and H_1, respectively:

$$\text{IVGNR}_0\colon\ \boldsymbol{y} - \boldsymbol{X}_1\acute{\boldsymbol{\beta}}_1 = \boldsymbol{P_W X}_1\boldsymbol{b}_1 + \text{residuals, and} \tag{8.53}$$

$$\text{IVGNR}_1\colon\ \boldsymbol{y} - \boldsymbol{X}_1\acute{\boldsymbol{\beta}}_1 = \boldsymbol{P_W X}_1\boldsymbol{b}_1 + \boldsymbol{P_W X}_2\boldsymbol{b}_2 + \text{residuals.} \tag{8.54}$$

As in Section 6.7, it is necessary to evaluate both IVGNRs at the same parameter values. Since these values must satisfy the null hypothesis, $\acute{\boldsymbol{\beta}}_2 = \boldsymbol{0}$. This is why the regressand, which is the same for both IVGNRs, does not depend on $\boldsymbol{X}_2$. The artificial F statistic is

$$F = \frac{(\text{SSR}_0 - \text{SSR}_1)/k_2}{\text{SSR}_1/(n-k)}, \tag{8.55}$$

where SSR_0 and SSR_1 denote the sums of squared residuals from (8.53) and (8.54), respectively.

Because both H_0 and H_1 are linear models, the value of $\acute{\boldsymbol{\beta}}$ used to evaluate the regressands of (8.53) and (8.54) has no effect on the difference between the SSRs of the two regressions, which, when divided by k_2, is the numerator of the artificial F statistic. To see this, we need to write the SSRs from the two IVGNRs as quadratic forms in the vector $\boldsymbol{y} - \boldsymbol{X}_1\acute{\boldsymbol{\beta}}_1$ and the projection matrices $\boldsymbol{M}_{\boldsymbol{P_W X}_1}$ and $\boldsymbol{M}_{\boldsymbol{P_W X}}$, respectively. Thus

$$\begin{aligned}\text{SSR}_0 - \text{SSR}_1 &= (\boldsymbol{y} - \boldsymbol{X}_1\acute{\boldsymbol{\beta}}_1)^\top(\boldsymbol{M}_{\boldsymbol{P_W X}_1} - \boldsymbol{M}_{\boldsymbol{P_W X}})(\boldsymbol{y} - \boldsymbol{X}_1\acute{\boldsymbol{\beta}}_1)\\ &= (\boldsymbol{y} - \boldsymbol{X}_1\acute{\boldsymbol{\beta}}_1)^\top(\boldsymbol{P}_{\boldsymbol{P_W X}} - \boldsymbol{P}_{\boldsymbol{P_W X}_1})(\boldsymbol{y} - \boldsymbol{X}_1\acute{\boldsymbol{\beta}}_1),\end{aligned} \tag{8.56}$$

where $\boldsymbol{P}_{\boldsymbol{P_W X}_1}$ and $\boldsymbol{P}_{\boldsymbol{P_W X}}$ project orthogonally on to $\mathcal{S}(\boldsymbol{P_W X}_1)$ and $\mathcal{S}(\boldsymbol{P_W X})$, respectively, and $\boldsymbol{M}_{\boldsymbol{P_W X}_1}$ and $\boldsymbol{M}_{\boldsymbol{P_W X}}$ are the complementary projections. In Exercise 8.17, readers are asked to show that expression (8.56) is equal to the much simpler expression

$$\boldsymbol{y}^\top(\boldsymbol{P}_{\boldsymbol{P_W X}} - \boldsymbol{P}_{\boldsymbol{P_W X}_1})\boldsymbol{y}, \tag{8.57}$$

which does not depend in any way on $\acute{\boldsymbol{\beta}}$.

It is important to note that, although the *difference* between the SSRs of (8.53) and (8.54) does not depend on $\acute{\boldsymbol{\beta}}$, the same is not true of the individual SSRs. Thus, if different values of $\acute{\boldsymbol{\beta}}$ were used for (8.53) and (8.54), we would get a wrong answer. Similarly, it is essential that the same instrument matrix $\boldsymbol{W}$ should be used in both regressions, since otherwise none of the above analysis would go through. It is essential that $\acute{\boldsymbol{\beta}}$ be a consistent estimator under the null hypothesis. Otherwise, the denominator of the test statistic (8.55) would not estimate σ^2 consistently, and (8.55) would not follow the $F(k_2, n-k)$ distribution asymptotically. If (8.53) and (8.54) are correctly formulated, with the same $\acute{\boldsymbol{\beta}}$ and the same instrument matrix $\boldsymbol{W}$, it can be shown that k_2 times the artificial F statistic (8.55) is equal to the Wald statistic (8.48) with $\boldsymbol{\beta}_{20} = \boldsymbol{0}$, except for the estimate of the error variance in the denominator; see Exercise 8.18.

Although the theory presented in Section 6.7 is enough to justify the test based on the IVGNR that we have developed above, it is instructive to check that k_2 times the F statistic is indeed asymptotically distributed as $\chi^2(k_2)$ under the null hypothesis H_0. Because the numerator expression (8.56) does not depend on $\acute{\boldsymbol{\beta}}$, it is perfectly valid to evaluate it with $\acute{\boldsymbol{\beta}}$ equal to the true parameter vector $\boldsymbol{\beta}_0$. Since $\boldsymbol{y} - \boldsymbol{X}\boldsymbol{\beta}_0$ is equal to $\boldsymbol{u}$, the vector of error terms, expression (8.56) becomes

$$\boldsymbol{u}^{\top}(\boldsymbol{P}_{\boldsymbol{P}_{\boldsymbol{W}}\boldsymbol{X}} - \boldsymbol{P}_{\boldsymbol{P}_{\boldsymbol{W}}\boldsymbol{X}_1})\boldsymbol{u}. \tag{8.58}$$

This is a quadratic form in the vector $\boldsymbol{u}$ and the difference of two projection matrices, one of which projects on to a subspace of the image of the other. Using the result of Exercise 2.18, we see that the difference is itself an orthogonal projection matrix, projecting on to a space of dimension $k - k_1 = k_2$. If the vector $\boldsymbol{u}$ were assumed to be normally distributed, and $\boldsymbol{X}$ and $\boldsymbol{W}$ were fixed, we could use Theorem 4.1 to show that $1/\sigma_0^2$ times (8.58) is distributed as $\chi^2(k_2)$. In Exercise 8.19, readers are invited to show that, when the error terms are asymptotically uncorrelated with the instruments, (8.58) is asymptotically distributed as σ_0^2 times a variable that follows the $\chi^2(k_2)$ distribution. Since the denominator of the F statistic (8.55) is a consistent estimator of σ_0^2, we see that k_2 times the F statistic is indeed asymptotically distributed as $\chi^2(k_2)$.

Tests Based on Criterion Functions

It may appear strange to advocate using the IVGNR to compute an artificial F statistic when one can more easily compute a real F statistic from the SSRs obtained by IV estimation of (8.51) and (8.52). However, such a "real" F statistic is not valid, even asymptotically. This can be seen by evaluating the IVGNRs (8.53) and (8.54) at the restricted estimates $\tilde{\boldsymbol{\beta}}$, where $\tilde{\boldsymbol{\beta}}$ is a k–vector with the first k_1 components equal to the IV estimates $\tilde{\boldsymbol{\beta}}_1$ from (8.51) and the last k_2 components zero. The residuals from the IVGNR (8.53) are then exactly the same as those from IV estimation of (8.51). For (8.54), we can use the result of Exercise 8.16 to see that the residuals can be written as

$$\boldsymbol{y} - \boldsymbol{X}\hat{\boldsymbol{\beta}} + \boldsymbol{M_W X}(\hat{\boldsymbol{\beta}} - \tilde{\boldsymbol{\beta}}), \tag{8.59}$$

where $\hat{\boldsymbol{\beta}}$ is the unrestricted IV estimator for (8.52). If all the regressors could serve as their own instruments, we would have $\boldsymbol{M_W X} = \mathbf{O}$, and the last term in expression (8.59) would vanish, leaving just $\boldsymbol{y} - \boldsymbol{X}\hat{\boldsymbol{\beta}}$, the residuals from (8.52). But, when some of the regressors are not used as instruments, the two vectors of residuals are not the same. The analysis of the previous subsection shows clearly that the correct residuals to use for testing purposes are the ones from the two IVGNRs.

The heart of the problem is that IV estimates are not obtained by minimizing the SSR, but rather the IV criterion function (8.30). The proper IV analog for the F statistic is a statistic based on the difference between the values of this criterion function evaluated at the restricted and unrestricted estimates. At the unrestricted estimates $\hat{\boldsymbol{\beta}}$, we obtain

$$Q(\hat{\boldsymbol{\beta}}, \boldsymbol{y}) = (\boldsymbol{y} - \boldsymbol{X}\hat{\boldsymbol{\beta}})^\top \boldsymbol{P_W}(\boldsymbol{y} - \boldsymbol{X}\hat{\boldsymbol{\beta}}). \tag{8.60}$$

Using the explicit expression (8.29) for the IV estimator, we see that (8.60) is equal to

$$\begin{aligned} &\boldsymbol{y}^\top(\mathbf{I} - \boldsymbol{P_W X}(\boldsymbol{X}^\top \boldsymbol{P_W X})^{-1}\boldsymbol{X}^\top)\boldsymbol{P_W}(\mathbf{I} - \boldsymbol{X}(\boldsymbol{X}^\top \boldsymbol{P_W X})^{-1}\boldsymbol{X}^\top \boldsymbol{P_W})\boldsymbol{y} \\ &\quad = \boldsymbol{y}^\top(\boldsymbol{P_W} - \boldsymbol{P_W X}(\boldsymbol{X}^\top \boldsymbol{P_W X})^{-1}\boldsymbol{X}^\top \boldsymbol{P_W})\boldsymbol{y} \\ &\quad = \boldsymbol{y}^\top(\boldsymbol{P_W} - \boldsymbol{P}_{\boldsymbol{P_W X}})\boldsymbol{y}. \end{aligned} \tag{8.61}$$

If Q is now evaluated at the restricted estimates $\tilde{\boldsymbol{\beta}}$, an exactly similar calculation shows that

$$Q(\tilde{\boldsymbol{\beta}}, \boldsymbol{y}) = \boldsymbol{y}^\top(\boldsymbol{P_W} - \boldsymbol{P}_{\boldsymbol{P_W X_1}})\boldsymbol{y}. \tag{8.62}$$

The difference between (8.62) and (8.61) is thus

$$Q(\tilde{\boldsymbol{\beta}}, \boldsymbol{y}) - Q(\hat{\boldsymbol{\beta}}, \boldsymbol{y}) = \boldsymbol{y}^\top(\boldsymbol{P}_{\boldsymbol{P_W X}} - \boldsymbol{P}_{\boldsymbol{P_W X_1}})\boldsymbol{y}. \tag{8.63}$$

This is precisely the difference (8.57) between the SSRs of the two IVGNRs (8.53) and (8.54). Thus we can obtain an asymptotically correct test statistic by dividing (8.63) by any consistent estimate of the error variance σ^2.

The only practical difficulty in computing (8.63) is that some regression packages do not report the minimized value of the IV criterion function. However, this value is very easy to compute, since for any IV regression, restricted or unrestricted, it is equal to the explained sum of squares from a regression of the vector of IV residuals on the instruments $\boldsymbol{W}$, as can be seen at once from equation (8.60).

Heteroskedasticity-Robust Tests

The test statistics discussed so far are valid only under the assumptions that the error terms are serially uncorrelated and homoskedastic. The second of these assumptions can be relaxed if we are prepared to use an HCCME. If $\mathrm{E}(\boldsymbol{u}\boldsymbol{u}^\top) = \boldsymbol{\Omega}$, where $\boldsymbol{\Omega}$ is a diagonal, $n \times n$ matrix, then it can readily be seen from equation (8.32) that the asymptotic covariance matrix of the vector $n^{1/2}(\hat{\boldsymbol{\beta}}_{\mathrm{IV}} - \boldsymbol{\beta}_0)$ has the sandwich form

$$\Big(\operatorname*{plim}_{n\to\infty} \frac{1}{n}\boldsymbol{X}^\top\boldsymbol{P_W X}\Big)^{-1}\Big(\operatorname*{plim}_{n\to\infty} \frac{1}{n}\boldsymbol{X}^\top\boldsymbol{P_W}\boldsymbol{\Omega}\boldsymbol{P_W X}\Big)\Big(\operatorname*{plim}_{n\to\infty} \frac{1}{n}\boldsymbol{X}^\top\boldsymbol{P_W X}\Big)^{-1}. \tag{8.64}$$

Not surprisingly, this looks very much like expression (5.33) for OLS estimation, except that $\boldsymbol{P_W X}$ replaces $\boldsymbol{X}$, and (8.64) involves probability limits rather than ordinary limits because the matrices $\boldsymbol{X}$, and possibly also $\boldsymbol{W}$, are now assumed to be stochastic.

It is not difficult to estimate the asymptotic covariance matrix (8.64). The outside factors, which are of course identical, can be estimated consistently in the obvious way, by using the matrix

$$\Big(\frac{1}{n}\boldsymbol{X}^\top\boldsymbol{P_W X}\Big)^{-1},$$

and the middle factor can be estimated consistently by using the matrix

$$\frac{1}{n}\boldsymbol{X}^\top\boldsymbol{P_W}\hat{\boldsymbol{\Omega}}\boldsymbol{P_W X},$$

where $\hat{\boldsymbol{\Omega}}$ is an $n \times n$ diagonal matrix, the tth diagonal element of which is equal to $\hat{u}_t^2$, the square of the tth IV residual. In practice, since the factors of n are needed only for asymptotic analysis, we use the matrix

$$\widehat{\mathrm{Var}}_{\mathrm{h}}(\hat{\boldsymbol{\beta}}_{\mathrm{IV}}) \equiv (\boldsymbol{X}^\top\boldsymbol{P_W X})^{-1}\boldsymbol{X}^\top\boldsymbol{P_W}\hat{\boldsymbol{\Omega}}\boldsymbol{P_W X}(\boldsymbol{X}^\top\boldsymbol{P_W X})^{-1} \tag{8.65}$$

to estimate the covariance matrix of $\hat{\boldsymbol{\beta}}_{\mathrm{IV}}$. This sandwich covariance matrix estimator has exactly the same form as the HCCME (5.39) for the OLS case. The only difference is that $\boldsymbol{P_W X}$ replaces $\boldsymbol{X}$.

Once the matrix (8.65) has been calculated, we can compute Wald tests that are robust to heteroskedasticity of unknown form. We simply use (8.47) for a test of a single linear restriction, or (8.48) for a test of two or more restrictions, with the HCCME (8.65) replacing the ordinary covariance matrix estimator. Alternatively, we can use the IV variant of the HRGNR introduced in Section 6.8. To obtain this variant, all we need do is to use $\boldsymbol{P_W X}$ in place of $\acute{\boldsymbol{X}}$ in equation (6.90); see Exercise 8.20. Of course, it must be remembered that all these tests are based on asymptotic theory, and there is good reason to believe that this theory may often provide a poor guide to their performance in finite samples.

8.6 Testing Overidentifying Restrictions

The **degree of overidentification** of an overidentified linear regression model is defined to be $l - k$, where, as usual, l is the number of instruments, and k is the number of regressors. Such a model implicitly incorporates $l - k$ **overidentifying restrictions**. These arise because the generalized IV estimator implicitly uses only k **effective instruments**, namely, the k columns of $\boldsymbol{P_W X}$. It does this because it is not possible, in general, to solve the l moment conditions (8.11) for only k unknowns.

In order for a set of instruments to be valid, a sufficient condition is (8.13), according to which the error term u_t has mean zero conditional on $\boldsymbol{W}_t$, the l-vector of current instruments. When this condition is not satisfied, the IV estimator risks being inconsistent. But, if we use for estimation only the k effective instruments in the matrix $\boldsymbol{P_W X}$, it is only those k instruments that need to satisfy condition (8.13). Let $\boldsymbol{W}^*$ be an $n \times (l - k)$ matrix of **extra instruments** such that $\mathcal{S}(\boldsymbol{W}) = \mathcal{S}(\boldsymbol{P_W X}, \boldsymbol{W}^*)$. This means that the l-dimensional span of the full set of instruments is generated by linear combinations of the effective instruments, $\boldsymbol{P_W X}$, and the extra instruments, $\boldsymbol{W}^*$. The overidentifying restrictions require that the extra instruments should also satisfy (8.13). Unlike the conditions for the effective instruments, the overidentifying restrictions can, and always should, be tested.

The matrix $\boldsymbol{W}^*$ is not uniquely determined, but we will see in a moment that this does not matter. For any specific choice of $\boldsymbol{W}^*$, what we wish to test is the set of conditions

$$\mathrm{E}(\boldsymbol{W}_t^{*\top} u_t) = \mathbf{0}. \tag{8.66}$$

Although we do not observe the u_t, we can estimate the vector $\boldsymbol{u}$ by the vector of IV residuals $\hat{\boldsymbol{u}}$. Thus, in order to make our test operational, we form the sample analog of condition (8.66), which is

$$\frac{1}{n}(\boldsymbol{W}^*)^{\top}\hat{\boldsymbol{u}}, \tag{8.67}$$

and check whether this quantity is significantly different from zero.

The model we wish to test is

$$\boldsymbol{y} = \boldsymbol{X\beta} + \boldsymbol{u}, \quad \boldsymbol{u} \sim \mathrm{IID}(\mathbf{0}, \sigma^2\mathbf{I}), \quad \mathrm{E}(\boldsymbol{W}^{\top}\boldsymbol{u}) = \mathbf{0}. \tag{8.68}$$

Testing the overidentifying restrictions implicit in this model is equivalent to testing it against the alternative model

$$\boldsymbol{y} = \boldsymbol{X\beta} + \boldsymbol{W}^*\boldsymbol{\gamma} + \boldsymbol{u}, \quad \boldsymbol{u} \sim \mathrm{IID}(\mathbf{0}, \sigma^2\mathbf{I}), \quad \mathrm{E}(\boldsymbol{W}^{\top}\boldsymbol{u}) = \mathbf{0}. \tag{8.69}$$

This alternative model is constructed in such a way that it is just identified: There are precisely l coefficients to estimate, namely, the k elements of $\boldsymbol{\beta}$ and the $l - k$ elements of $\boldsymbol{\gamma}$, and there are precisely l instruments.

To see why testing (8.68) against (8.69) also tests whether the quantity (8.67) is significantly different from zero, consider the numerator of the artificial IVGNR F test for (8.68) against (8.69). Under the null hypothesis, the generic form of this numerator is given by expression (8.58). For present purposes, the matrix $\boldsymbol{X}_1$ of regressors in the restricted regression becomes $\boldsymbol{X}$, and the matrix $\boldsymbol{X}$ in (8.58) is replaced by $[\boldsymbol{X}\ \ \boldsymbol{W}^*]$, the regressor matrix for (8.69). Since $\boldsymbol{P_W}[\boldsymbol{X}\ \ \boldsymbol{W}^*] = [\boldsymbol{P_W X}\ \ \boldsymbol{W}^*]$, and the span of the columns of this matrix is just $\mathcal{S}(\boldsymbol{W})$, it follows that the first of the two projection matrices in (8.58) becomes simply $\boldsymbol{P_W}$. The second projection matrix is $\boldsymbol{P}_{\boldsymbol{P_W X}}$. One possible choice for $\boldsymbol{W}^*$ would be a matrix the columns of which were all orthogonal to those of $\boldsymbol{P_W X}$. Such a matrix could be constructed from an arbitrary $\boldsymbol{W}^*$ by multiplying it by $\boldsymbol{M}_{\boldsymbol{P_W X}}$. With such a choice, the orthogonality of $\boldsymbol{P_W X}$ and $\boldsymbol{W}^*$ means that, by the result in Exercise 2.18,

$$\boldsymbol{P_W} - \boldsymbol{P}_{\boldsymbol{P_W X}} = \boldsymbol{P}_{\boldsymbol{W}^*}.$$

Therefore, under the null, the numerator of the F statistic is just

$$\boldsymbol{u}^\top \boldsymbol{P}_{\boldsymbol{W}^*}\boldsymbol{u} = \boldsymbol{u}^\top \boldsymbol{W}^*\big((\boldsymbol{W}^*)^\top \boldsymbol{W}^*\big)^{-1}(\boldsymbol{W}^*)^\top \boldsymbol{u}.$$

Since the middle matrix on the right-hand side of this equation is positive definite by construction, it can be seen that the F test is testing whether the vector (8.67) is significantly different from zero.

As we claimed above, implementing a test of the overidentifying restrictions does not require a specific choice of the matrix $\boldsymbol{W}^*$, and in fact it does not require us to construct $\boldsymbol{W}^*$ explicitly at all. To see why, consider the two IVGNRs for the test, evaluated at $\hat{\boldsymbol{\beta}}_{\rm IV}$. They are

$$\hat{\boldsymbol{u}} = \boldsymbol{P_W X b}_1 + \text{residuals, and} \tag{8.70}$$

$$\hat{\boldsymbol{u}} = \boldsymbol{P_W X b}_1 + \boldsymbol{W}^*\boldsymbol{b}_2 + \text{residuals.} \tag{8.71}$$

The numerator of the F statistic is the difference of the two SSRs, which is equal to minus the difference of the two explained sums of squares. The explained sum of squares from regression (8.70) is zero, because the regressand is orthogonal to the regressors. The explained sum of squares from (8.71) is the same as that from the regression

$$\hat{\boldsymbol{u}} = \boldsymbol{W b} + \text{residuals,} \tag{8.72}$$

because, however $\boldsymbol{W}^*$ is chosen, we always have $\mathcal{S}(\boldsymbol{P_W X}, \boldsymbol{W}^*) = \mathcal{S}(\boldsymbol{W})$. The test statistic is therefore equal to the explained sum of squares from (8.72) divided by a consistent estimate of the error variance. One such estimate is $n^{-1}\hat{\boldsymbol{u}}^\top\hat{\boldsymbol{u}}$. Thus one way to compute the test statistic is to regress the residuals $\hat{\boldsymbol{u}}$ from IV estimation of the original model (8.68) on the full set of instruments, and use n times the uncentered R^2 from this regression as the test statistic. If the model (8.68) is correctly specified, the asymptotic distribution of the statistic is $\chi^2(l-k)$.

Another very easy way to test the overidentifying restrictions is to use a test statistic based on the IV criterion function. Since the alternative model (8.69) is just identified, the minimized IV criterion function for it is exactly zero. To see this, note that, for any just identified model, the IV residuals are orthogonal to the full set of instruments by the moment conditions (8.11) used with just identified models. Therefore, when the criterion function (8.30) is evaluated at the IV estimates $\hat{\boldsymbol{\beta}}_{\mathrm{IV}}$, it becomes $\hat{\boldsymbol{u}}^\top \boldsymbol{P_W} \hat{\boldsymbol{u}}$, which is zero because of the orthogonality of $\boldsymbol{W}$ and $\hat{\boldsymbol{u}}$. Thus an appropriate test statistic is just the criterion function $Q(\hat{\boldsymbol{\beta}}_{\mathrm{IV}}, \boldsymbol{y})$ for the original model (8.68), divided by the estimate of the error variance from this same model. A test based on this statistic is often called a **Sargan test**, after Sargan (1958). The test statistic is numerically identical to the one based on regression (8.72), as readers are asked to show in Exercise 8.21.

Although (8.69) is a simple enough model, it actually represents two conceptually different alternatives, because there are two situations in which the "true" parameter vector $\boldsymbol{\gamma}$ in (8.69) could be nonzero. One possibility is that the model (8.68) is correctly specified, but some of the instruments are asymptotically correlated with the error terms and are therefore not valid instruments. The other possibility is that (8.68) is not correctly specified, and some of the instruments (or, possibly, other variables that are correlated with them) have incorrectly been omitted from the regression function. In either case, the overidentification test statistic leads us to reject the null hypothesis whenever the sample size is large enough.

Even if we do not know quite how to interpret a significant value of the overidentification test statistic, it is always a good idea to compute it. If it is significantly larger than it should be by chance under the null hypothesis, one should be extremely cautious in interpreting the estimates, because it is quite likely either that the model is specified incorrectly or that some of the instruments are invalid.

8.7 Durbin-Wu-Hausman Tests

In many cases, we do not know whether we actually need to use instrumental variables. For example, we may suspect that some variables are measured with error, but we may not know whether the errors are large enough to cause enough inconsistency for us to worry about. Or we may suspect that certain explanatory variables are endogenous, but we may not be at all sure of our suspicions, and we may not know how much inconsistency would result if they were justified. In such a case, it may or may not be perfectly reasonable to employ OLS estimation.

If the regressors are valid instruments, then, as we saw in Section 8.3, they are also the optimal instruments. Consequently, the OLS estimator, which is consistent in this case, is preferable to an IV estimator computed with some other valid instrument matrix $\boldsymbol{W}$. In view of this, it would evidently be very useful to be able to test the null hypothesis that the error terms are uncorrelated with all the regressors against the alternative that they are correlated with some of the regressors, although not with the instruments $\boldsymbol{W}$. In this section, we discuss a simple procedure that can be used to perform such a test. This procedure dates back to a famous paper by Durbin (1954), and it was subsequently extended by Wu (1973) and Hausman (1978). We will therefore refer to all tests of this general type as **Durbin-Wu-Hausman tests**, or **DWH tests**.

The null and alternative hypotheses for the DWH test can be expressed as

$$H_0:\ \boldsymbol{y} = \boldsymbol{X\beta} + \boldsymbol{u}, \quad \boldsymbol{u} \sim \mathrm{IID}(\boldsymbol{0}, \sigma^2\mathbf{I}), \quad \mathrm{E}(\boldsymbol{X}^\top\boldsymbol{u}) = \boldsymbol{0}, \text{ and} \tag{8.73}$$

$$H_1:\ \boldsymbol{y} = \boldsymbol{X\beta} + \boldsymbol{u}, \quad \boldsymbol{u} \sim \mathrm{IID}(\boldsymbol{0}, \sigma^2\mathbf{I}), \quad \mathrm{E}(\boldsymbol{W}^\top\boldsymbol{u}) = \boldsymbol{0}. \tag{8.74}$$

Under H_1, the IV estimator $\hat{\boldsymbol{\beta}}_{\mathrm{IV}}$ is consistent, but the OLS estimator $\hat{\boldsymbol{\beta}}_{\mathrm{OLS}}$ is not. Under H_0, both are consistent. Thus, $\operatorname{plim}(\hat{\boldsymbol{\beta}}_{\mathrm{IV}} - \hat{\boldsymbol{\beta}}_{\mathrm{OLS}})$ is zero under the null and nonzero under the alternative. The idea of the DWH test is to check whether the difference $\hat{\boldsymbol{\beta}}_{\mathrm{IV}} - \hat{\boldsymbol{\beta}}_{\mathrm{OLS}}$ is significantly different from zero in the available sample. This difference, which is sometimes called the **vector of contrasts**, can be written as

$$\hat{\boldsymbol{\beta}}_{\mathrm{IV}} - \hat{\boldsymbol{\beta}}_{\mathrm{OLS}} = (\boldsymbol{X}^\top\boldsymbol{P_W X})^{-1}\boldsymbol{X}^\top\boldsymbol{P_W y} - (\boldsymbol{X}^\top\boldsymbol{X})^{-1}\boldsymbol{X}^\top\boldsymbol{y}. \tag{8.75}$$

Expression (8.75) is not very useful as it stands, but it can be converted into a much more useful expression by means of a trick that is often useful in econometrics. We pretend that the first factor of $\hat{\boldsymbol{\beta}}_{\mathrm{IV}}$ is common to both estimators, and take it out as a common factor. This gives

$$\hat{\boldsymbol{\beta}}_{\mathrm{IV}} - \hat{\boldsymbol{\beta}}_{\mathrm{OLS}} = (\boldsymbol{X}^\top\boldsymbol{P_W X})^{-1}\big(\boldsymbol{X}^\top\boldsymbol{P_W y} - \boldsymbol{X}^\top\boldsymbol{P_W X}(\boldsymbol{X}^\top\boldsymbol{X})^{-1}\boldsymbol{X}^\top\boldsymbol{y}\big).$$

Now we can find some genuinely common factors in the two terms of the rightmost factor of this expression. Taking them out yields

$$\begin{aligned}\hat{\boldsymbol{\beta}}_{\mathrm{IV}} - \hat{\boldsymbol{\beta}}_{\mathrm{OLS}} &= (\boldsymbol{X}^\top\boldsymbol{P_W X})^{-1}\boldsymbol{X}^\top\boldsymbol{P_W}\big(\mathbf{I} - \boldsymbol{X}(\boldsymbol{X}^\top\boldsymbol{X})^{-1}\boldsymbol{X}^\top\big)\boldsymbol{y} \\ &= (\boldsymbol{X}^\top\boldsymbol{P_W X})^{-1}\boldsymbol{X}^\top\boldsymbol{P_W M_X y}.\end{aligned} \tag{8.76}$$

The first factor in expression (8.76) is a positive definite matrix, by the identification condition. Therefore, testing whether $\hat{\boldsymbol{\beta}}_{\mathrm{IV}} - \hat{\boldsymbol{\beta}}_{\mathrm{OLS}}$ is significantly different from zero is equivalent to testing whether the vector $\boldsymbol{X}^\top\boldsymbol{P_W M_X y}$ is significantly different from zero.

Under H_0, the preferred estimation technique is OLS, and the OLS residuals are given by the vector $\boldsymbol{M_X y}$. Therefore, we wish to test whether the

k columns of the matrix $\boldsymbol{P_W X}$ are orthogonal to this vector of residuals. Let us partition the matrix of regressors $\boldsymbol{X}$ as in (8.38), so that $\boldsymbol{X} = [\boldsymbol{Z}\ \boldsymbol{Y}]$, where the k_1 columns of $\boldsymbol{Z}$ are included in the matrix of instruments $\boldsymbol{W}$, and the $k_2 = k - k_1$ columns of $\boldsymbol{Y}$ are treated as potentially endogenous. By construction, OLS residuals are orthogonal to all the columns of $\boldsymbol{X}$, in particular to those of $\boldsymbol{Z}$. For these regressors, there is therefore nothing to test: The relation

$$\boldsymbol{Z}^\top \boldsymbol{P_W M_X y} = \boldsymbol{Z}^\top \boldsymbol{M_X y} = \boldsymbol{0}$$

holds identically, because $\boldsymbol{P_W Z} = \boldsymbol{Z}$ and $\boldsymbol{M_X Z} = \mathbf{O}$. The test is thus concerned only with the k_2 elements of $\boldsymbol{Y}^\top \boldsymbol{P_W M_X y}$, which are not in general identically zero, but should not differ from it significantly under H_0.

The easiest way to test whether $\boldsymbol{Y}^\top \boldsymbol{P_W M_X y}$ is significantly different from zero is to use an F test for the k_2 restrictions $\boldsymbol{\delta} = \boldsymbol{0}$ in the OLS regression

$$\boldsymbol{y} = \boldsymbol{X\beta} + \boldsymbol{P_W Y\delta} + \boldsymbol{u}. \tag{8.77}$$

The OLS estimates of $\boldsymbol{\delta}$ from (8.77) are, by the FWL Theorem, the same as those from the FWL regression of $\boldsymbol{M_X y}$ on $\boldsymbol{M_X P_W Y}$, that is,

$$\hat{\boldsymbol{\delta}} = (\boldsymbol{Y}^\top \boldsymbol{P_W M_X P_W Y})^{-1} \boldsymbol{Y}^\top \boldsymbol{P_W M_X y}.$$

Since the inverted matrix is positive definite, we see that testing whether $\boldsymbol{\delta} = \boldsymbol{0}$ is equivalent to testing whether $\boldsymbol{Y}^\top \boldsymbol{P_W M_X y} = \boldsymbol{0}$, as desired. This conclusion could have been foreseen by considering the threefold orthogonal decomposition that is implicitly performed by an F test; recall Section 4.4. The DWH test can also be implemented by means of another F test, which yields exactly the same test statistic; see Exercise 8.22 for details.

The F test based on (8.77) has k_2 and $n - k - k_2$ degrees of freedom. Under H_0, if we assume that $\boldsymbol{X}$ and $\boldsymbol{W}$ are not merely predetermined but also exogenous, and that the error terms $\boldsymbol{u}$ are multivariate normal, the F statistic does indeed have the $F(k_2, n-k-k_2)$ distribution. Under H_0 as it is expressed in (8.73), its asymptotic distribution is $F(k_2, \infty)$, and k_2 times the statistic is asymptotically distributed as $\chi^2(k_2)$.

If the null hypothesis (8.73) is rejected, we are faced with the same sort of ambiguity of interpretation as for the test of overidentifying restrictions. One possibility is that at least some columns of $\boldsymbol{Y}$ are indeed endogenous, but in such a way that the alternative model (8.74) is correctly specified. But we can equally well take (8.77) literally as a model with exogenous or predetermined regressors. In that case, the nature of the misspecification of (8.73) is not that $\boldsymbol{Y}$ is endogenous, but rather that the linear combinations of the instruments given by the columns of $\boldsymbol{P_W Y}$ have explanatory power for the dependent variable $\boldsymbol{y}$ over and above that of $\boldsymbol{X}$. Without further investigation, there is no way to choose between these alternative interpretations.

Tests Based on Vectors of Contrasts

DWH tests are much more widely applicable than we have indicated so far. They can be used whenever there are two estimators, one of which, like $\hat{\beta}_{IV}$, is inefficient but consistent under relatively weak conditions, while the other, like $\hat{\beta}_{OLS}$, is efficient, but only if the stronger conditions required for it to be consistent are satisfied. For example, for the panel data case discussed in Section 7.10, a DWH test can be used to see whether it is valid to employ the random-effects estimator rather than the less efficient fixed-effects estimator; see Hausman (1978) and Hausman and Taylor (1981) for details.

In this case, and many others, it is convenient to base a test directly on the vector of contrasts, that is, the difference between the two vectors of estimates. Suppose we are trying to estimate a k-vector $\boldsymbol{\theta}$ of which the true value is $\boldsymbol{\theta}_0$. Let $\hat{\boldsymbol{\theta}}_{\rm E}$ denote an efficient estimator, and let $\hat{\boldsymbol{\theta}}_{\rm I}$ denote an inefficient estimator that is consistent under weaker conditions. Under mild regularity conditions, an inefficient estimator is always asymptotically equal to an efficient estimator plus a random vector that is uncorrelated with the efficient estimator. We saw an example of this in Section 3.5 when we discussed the Gauss-Markov Theorem; see also Exercise 8.23. Thus, in a broad range of cases, we can write

$$n^{1/2}(\hat{\boldsymbol{\theta}}_{\rm I} - \boldsymbol{\theta}_0) \stackrel{a}{=} n^{1/2}(\hat{\boldsymbol{\theta}}_{\rm E} - \boldsymbol{\theta}_0) + \boldsymbol{v}, \tag{8.78}$$

where $\boldsymbol{v}$ is a random k-vector that is uncorrelated with $n^{1/2}(\hat{\boldsymbol{\theta}}_{\rm E} - \boldsymbol{\theta}_0)$. This vector is asymptotically equal to $n^{1/2}$ times the vector of contrasts, which is just $\hat{\boldsymbol{\theta}}_{\rm I} - \hat{\boldsymbol{\theta}}_{\rm E}$.

In this situation, a DWH test may be based on a quadratic form in the vector of contrasts and the inverse of an estimate of its covariance matrix. From (8.78) and the fact that $\boldsymbol{v}$ is uncorrelated with $n^{1/2}(\hat{\boldsymbol{\theta}}_{\rm E} - \boldsymbol{\theta}_0)$, we see that

$$\mathrm{Var}(\boldsymbol{v}) \stackrel{a}{=} \mathrm{Var}\big(n^{1/2}(\hat{\boldsymbol{\theta}}_{\rm I} - \boldsymbol{\theta}_0)\big) - \mathrm{Var}\big(n^{1/2}(\hat{\boldsymbol{\theta}}_{\rm E} - \boldsymbol{\theta}_0)\big).$$

Whenever standard asymptotic results apply, the vector $n^{1/2}(\hat{\boldsymbol{\theta}}_{\rm I} - \hat{\boldsymbol{\theta}}_{\rm E})$ must be asymptotically normally distributed. Therefore, by Theorem 4.1, a suitable test statistic is

$$(\hat{\boldsymbol{\theta}}_{\rm I} - \hat{\boldsymbol{\theta}}_{\rm E})^{\top}\big(\widehat{\mathrm{Var}}(\hat{\boldsymbol{\theta}}_{\rm I}) - \widehat{\mathrm{Var}}(\hat{\boldsymbol{\theta}}_{\rm E})\big)^{-1}(\hat{\boldsymbol{\theta}}_{\rm I} - \hat{\boldsymbol{\theta}}_{\rm E}), \tag{8.79}$$

where $\widehat{\mathrm{Var}}(\hat{\boldsymbol{\theta}}_{\rm I})$ and $\widehat{\mathrm{Var}}(\hat{\boldsymbol{\theta}}_{\rm E})$ are consistent estimates of the covariance matrices of the two estimators. Tests based on quadratic forms like (8.79) are often called **Hausman tests**.

A problem arises as to the degrees of freedom for the test statistic (8.79). As we have already seen, the DWH test based on regression (8.77) has k_2 degrees of freedom, where k_2 is the number of possibly endogenous variables on the right-hand side of equation (8.73). This is smaller than k, the dimension of the vector $\boldsymbol{\beta}$. A similar phenomenon occurs whenever the covariance matrix $\mathrm{Var}(\boldsymbol{v})$ does not have full rank. It may be hard to check for such a phenomenon, since the rank of the difference between the estimates $\widehat{\mathrm{Var}}(\hat{\boldsymbol{\theta}}_{\mathrm{I}})$ and $\widehat{\mathrm{Var}}(\hat{\boldsymbol{\theta}}_{\mathrm{E}})$ usually has full rank even if $\mathrm{Var}(\boldsymbol{v})$ does not. Worse, this difference may or may not be guaranteed to be a positive definite matrix, in which case the statistic (8.79) cannot be used without modification.

In some such cases, a test statistic can be based on a subvector of the vector of contrasts. This is what would have to be done if $\hat{\boldsymbol{\theta}}_{\mathrm{I}}$ were an IV estimator and $\hat{\boldsymbol{\theta}}_{\mathrm{E}}$ were an OLS estimator. Then a DWH statistic of the form (8.79) would have to be based solely on the coefficients of the possibly endogenous variables. This would yield a Hausman test asymptotically equivalent to the F test based on regression (8.77) that we have already discussed.

8.8 Bootstrap Tests

The difficulty with using the bootstrap for models estimated by IV is that there is more than one endogenous variable. The bootstrap DGP must therefore be formulated in such a way as to generate samples containing bootstrap realizations of both the main dependent variable $\boldsymbol{y}$ and the endogenous explanatory variables, which we denote by $\boldsymbol{Y}$ in the notation of (8.38).

As we saw in Section 8.4, the single equation (8.38) is not a complete specification of a model. We can complete it in various ways, of which the easiest is to use equations (8.39) for $i = 1, \ldots, k_2$. This introduces k_2 vectors $\boldsymbol{\pi}_i$, each containing l parameters. In addition, we must specify the *joint* distribution of the error terms $\boldsymbol{u}$ in the equation for $\boldsymbol{y}$ and the $\boldsymbol{v}_i$ in the equations for $\boldsymbol{Y}$. If we use the notation of (8.44), we can write the reduced form equations for the endogenous explanatory variables in matrix form as

$$\boldsymbol{Y} = \boldsymbol{W\Pi}_2 + \boldsymbol{V}_2, \tag{8.80}$$

where $\boldsymbol{\Pi}_2$ is an $l \times k_2$ matrix, the columns of which are the $\boldsymbol{\pi}_i$ of (8.39), and $\boldsymbol{V}_2$ is an $n \times k_2$ matrix of error terms, the columns of which are the $\boldsymbol{v}_i$ of (8.39). It is convenient to group all the error terms together into one matrix, and so we define the $n \times (k_2 + 1)$ matrix $\boldsymbol{V}$ as $[\boldsymbol{u} \;\; \boldsymbol{V}_2]$. Note that this matrix $\boldsymbol{V}$ is not the same as the one used in Section 8.4. If $\boldsymbol{V}_t$ denotes a typical row of $\boldsymbol{V}$, then we will assume that

$$\mathrm{E}(\boldsymbol{V}_t \boldsymbol{V}_t^{\top}) = \boldsymbol{\Sigma}, \tag{8.81}$$

where $\boldsymbol{\Sigma}$ is a $(k_2+1) \times (k_2+1)$ covariance matrix, the upper left-hand element of which is σ^2, the variance of the error terms in $\boldsymbol{u}$. Together, (8.38), (8.80), and (8.81) constitute a model that, although not quite fully specified (because the distribution of the error terms is not stated), can serve as a basis for various bootstrap procedures.

Suppose that we wish to develop bootstrap versions of the tests considered in Section 8.5, where the null and alternative hypotheses are given by (8.51) and (8.52), respectively. For concreteness, we consider the test implemented by use of the IVGNRs (8.53) and (8.54), although the same principles apply to other forms of test, such as the asymptotic t and Wald tests (8.47) and (8.48), or tests based on the IV criterion function. Note that we now have two different partitions of the matrix $\boldsymbol{X}$ of explanatory variables. First, there is the partition $\boldsymbol{X} = [\boldsymbol{Z} \;\; \boldsymbol{Y}]$, in which $\boldsymbol{Z}$ contains the exogenous or predetermined variables, and $\boldsymbol{Y}$ contains the endogenous ones that are modeled explicitly by (8.80). Then there is the partition $\boldsymbol{X} = [\boldsymbol{X}_1 \;\; \boldsymbol{X}_2]$, in which we separate the variables $\boldsymbol{X}_1$ included under the null from the variables $\boldsymbol{X}_2$ that appear only under the alternative. In general, these two partitions are not related. We can expect that, in most cases, some columns of $\boldsymbol{Y}$ are contained in $\boldsymbol{X}_1$ and some in $\boldsymbol{X}_2$, and similarly for $\boldsymbol{Z}$.

The first step, as usual, is the estimation by IV of the model (8.51) that represents the null hypothesis. From this we obtain the constrained parameter estimates $\tilde{\boldsymbol{\beta}}_1$ and residuals $\tilde{\boldsymbol{u}}$. Next, we formulate and run the two IVGNRs (8.53) and (8.54), evaluated at $\boldsymbol{\beta}_1 = \tilde{\boldsymbol{\beta}}_1$, and compute the F statistic. Then, in order to estimate all the other parameters of the extended model, we run the k_2 reduced form regressions represented by (8.80), obtaining OLS estimates and residuals that we denote respectively by $\hat{\boldsymbol{\Pi}}_2$ and $\hat{\boldsymbol{V}}_2$. We will write $\hat{\boldsymbol{V}}$ to denote $[\tilde{\boldsymbol{u}} \;\; \hat{\boldsymbol{V}}_2]$.

For the bootstrap DGP, suppose first that all the instruments are exogenous. In that case, they are used unchanged in the bootstrap DGP. At this point, we must choose between a parametric and a semiparametric bootstrap. Since the latter is slightly easier, we discuss it first. In most cases, both $\boldsymbol{X}$ and $\boldsymbol{W}$ include a constant, and the residuals $\tilde{\boldsymbol{u}}$ and $\hat{\boldsymbol{V}}$ are centered. If not, as we discussed in Section 4.6, they must be centered before proceeding further. Because we wish the bootstrap DGP to retain the contemporaneous covariance structure of $\boldsymbol{V}$, the bootstrap error terms are drawn as complete rows $\boldsymbol{V}_t^*$ by resampling entire rows of $\hat{\boldsymbol{V}}$. In this way, we draw our bootstrap error terms from the joint empirical distribution of the $\hat{\boldsymbol{V}}_t$. With models estimated by least squares, it is desirable to rescale residuals before they are resampled; again see Section 4.6. Since the columns of $\hat{\boldsymbol{V}}_2$ are least squares residuals, it is probably desirable to rescale them. However, there is no justification for rescaling the vector $\tilde{\boldsymbol{u}}$.

For the parametric bootstrap, we must actually estimate $\boldsymbol{\Sigma}$. The easiest way to do so is to form the matrix

$$\hat{\boldsymbol{\Sigma}} = \frac{1}{n}\hat{\boldsymbol{V}}^\top\hat{\boldsymbol{V}}.$$

Since $\tilde{\boldsymbol{\beta}}_1$ and $\hat{\boldsymbol{\Pi}}_2$ are consistent estimators, it follows that $\hat{\boldsymbol{V}}$ is also consistent for $\boldsymbol{V}$. We can then apply a law of large numbers to each element of $\hat{\boldsymbol{\Sigma}}$ in order to show that it converges as $n \to \infty$ to the corresponding element of the true $\boldsymbol{\Sigma}$. The row vectors of parametric bootstrap error terms $\boldsymbol{V}_t^*$ are then independent drawings from the multivariate normal distribution with mean zero and covariance matrix $\hat{\boldsymbol{\Sigma}}$. In order to make these drawings, the easiest method is to form a $(k_2+1) \times (k_2+1)$ matrix $\hat{\boldsymbol{A}}$ such that $\hat{\boldsymbol{A}}\hat{\boldsymbol{A}}^\top = \hat{\boldsymbol{\Sigma}}$. Usually, $\hat{\boldsymbol{A}}$ is chosen to be upper or lower triangular; recall the discussion of the multivariate normal distribution in Section 4.3. Then, if a random number generator is used to draw (k_2+1)–vectors $\boldsymbol{v}^*$ from $\mathrm{N}(\mathbf{0}, \mathbf{I})$, we see that $\hat{\boldsymbol{A}}\boldsymbol{v}^*$ is a drawing from $\mathrm{N}(\mathbf{0}, \hat{\boldsymbol{\Sigma}})$, as desired.

The rest of the implementation is the same for both the parametric and the semiparametric bootstrap. For each bootstrap replication, the endogenous explanatory variables are first generated by the bootstrap reduced form

$$\boldsymbol{Y}^* = \boldsymbol{W}\hat{\boldsymbol{\Pi}}_2 + \boldsymbol{V}_2^*, \tag{8.82}$$

where $\hat{\boldsymbol{\Pi}}_2$ and $\boldsymbol{V}_2^*$ are just the matrices $\hat{\boldsymbol{\Pi}}$ and $\boldsymbol{V}^*$ without their first columns. Then the main dependent variable is generated so as to satisfy the null hypothesis:

$$\boldsymbol{y}^* = \boldsymbol{X}_1^*\tilde{\boldsymbol{\beta}}_1 + \boldsymbol{u}^*.$$

Here the star on $\boldsymbol{X}_1^*$ indicates that some of the regressors in $\boldsymbol{X}_1$ may be endogenous, and so must have been simulated using (8.82). The bootstrap error terms $\boldsymbol{u}^*$ are just the first column of $\boldsymbol{V}^*$. For each bootstrap sample, the two IVGNRs are estimated, and a bootstrap F statistic is computed. Then, as usual, the bootstrap P value is the proportion of bootstrap F statistics greater than the F statistic computed from the original data.

Bootstrapping tests of overidentifying restrictions follows the same lines. Since the null hypothesis for such a test is just the model being estimated, the only extra work needed is the estimation of the reduced form model (8.80) for the endogenous explanatory variables. Bootstrap error terms are generated by a parametric or semiparametric bootstrap, and the residuals from the IV estimation using the bootstrap data are regressed on the full set of instruments. The simplest test statistic is just the nR^2 from this regression.

It is particularly easy to bootstrap DWH tests, because for them the null hypothesis is that none of the explanatory variables is endogenous. It is therefore quite unnecessary to model them by (8.80), and bootstrap data are generated as for any other model to be estimated by least squares. Note that, if we are prepared to make the strong assumptions of the classical normal linear model under the null, the bootstrap is quite unnecessary, because, as we saw in the previous section, the test statistic has a known finite-sample distribution.

If some of the non-endogenous explanatory variables are lagged dependent variables, or lags of the endogenous explanatory variables, bootstrap samples must be generated recursively, as for the case of the ordinary regression model with a lagged dependent variable, for which the recursive bootstrap DGP was (4.67). Especially if lags of endogenous explanatory variables are involved, this may become quite complicated.

It is worth issuing a warning that, for a number of reasons well beyond the scope of this chapter, the bootstrap method outlined above cannot be expected to work as well as the bootstrap methods for regression models discussed in earlier chapters. Some reasons for this are discussed in Dufour (1997). Bootstrapping of simultaneous equations models is still an active topic of research, and new methods are constantly being developed.

8.9 IV Estimation of Nonlinear Models

In this section, we extend the results of this chapter beyond the linear model (8.10) dealt with up to this point by very briefly discussing instrumental variables estimation of the nonlinear regression model

$$\boldsymbol{y} = \boldsymbol{x}(\boldsymbol{\beta}) + \boldsymbol{u}, \quad \mathrm{E}(\boldsymbol{u}\boldsymbol{u}^\top) = \sigma^2\mathbf{I}, \tag{8.83}$$

where the notation is that of Chapter 6. Some of the results that we will obtain are formally the same as ones previously obtained in Section 6.2 in the context of MM estimation. However, in contrast to what we assumed there, we now assume that at least some of the variables on which the regression functions $x_t(\boldsymbol{\beta})$ depend are not contained in whatever information sets, Ω_t, with respect to which the error terms are innovations. This leads the error terms to be correlated with the regression functions and at least some of their derivatives. In consequence, for essentially the same reasons as in the linear case, the NLS parameter estimates are inconsistent.

If the vector $\boldsymbol{\beta}$ in (8.83) is k-dimensional, consistent MM estimates based on an $n \times k$ matrix of exogenous or predetermined instruments, $\boldsymbol{W}$, can be obtained by solving the moment conditions (6.10):

$$\boldsymbol{W}^\top\big(\boldsymbol{y} - \boldsymbol{x}(\boldsymbol{\beta})\big) = \mathbf{0}.$$

By using arguments similar to those employed in Sections 6.3 and 8.3, it can be shown that the optimal instruments, by the criterion of the asymptotic variance, are given by $\bar{\boldsymbol{X}}_0 \equiv \bar{\boldsymbol{X}}(\boldsymbol{\beta}_0)$. Here, $\boldsymbol{\beta}_0$ denotes the true parameter vector, and the $n \times k$ matrix $\boldsymbol{X}(\boldsymbol{\beta})$, is defined, as in Section 6.2, to be the matrix of partial derivatives of the nonlinear regression functions with respect to the parameters. As in (8.18), the bar signifies expectations conditional on the relevant information sets: The tth row of $\bar{\boldsymbol{X}}_0$ is $\mathrm{E}\big(\boldsymbol{X}_t(\boldsymbol{\beta}_0)\,|\,\Omega_t\big)$, while the tth row of $\boldsymbol{X}_0$ is just $\boldsymbol{X}_t(\boldsymbol{\beta}_0)$.

If we restrict our attention to instruments that can be expressed as linear combinations of the l columns of a given instrument matrix $\boldsymbol{W}$, with $l \geq k$, the analog of the result that the optimal instruments in this class are given by (8.23) is that they are given by $\boldsymbol{P_W}\bar{\boldsymbol{X}}_0$. Since $\boldsymbol{\beta}_0$ is not known, it is convenient to use the same trick as that used for nonlinear least squares by solving the set of moment conditions

$$\boldsymbol{X}^\top(\boldsymbol{\beta})\boldsymbol{P_W}\big(\boldsymbol{y} - \boldsymbol{x}(\boldsymbol{\beta})\big) = \mathbf{0}. \tag{8.84}$$

These moment conditions are the analog in the IV context of conditions (6.27) for the least-squares case. If it exists, the solution to equations (8.84) is the **nonlinear instrumental variables estimator**, or **NLIV estimator**.

The NLIV estimates also minimize the nonlinear IV criterion function

$$Q(\boldsymbol{\beta}, \boldsymbol{y}) = \big(\boldsymbol{y} - \boldsymbol{x}(\boldsymbol{\beta})\big)^{\top} \boldsymbol{P_W} \big(\boldsymbol{y} - \boldsymbol{x}(\boldsymbol{\beta})\big), \tag{8.85}$$

which generalizes the ordinary IV criterion function (8.30) in the obvious way. As usual, the first-order conditions for minimizing (8.85) are equivalent to the moment conditions (8.84), but it is usually easier to minimize $Q(\boldsymbol{\beta}, \boldsymbol{y})$ than it is to solve the moment conditions directly. In contrast to the situation with linear models, minimizing the criterion function (8.85) is, in general, *not* equivalent to replacing the current endogenous regressors $\boldsymbol{Y}$ by $\boldsymbol{P_W Y}$ and then minimizing the sum of squared residuals. The two procedures are equivalent only if $\boldsymbol{x}(\boldsymbol{\beta})$ is a linear function of $\boldsymbol{Y}$. Thus, even though it is quite common to refer to NLIV estimation as **nonlinear two-stage least squares**, it is incorrect and misleading to do so, because NLIV estimates are never actually computed in two stages.

The strong asymptotic identification condition for the NLIV estimator is that the matrix $\boldsymbol{S}_{\boldsymbol{X}_0^{\top}\boldsymbol{W}}(\boldsymbol{S}_{\boldsymbol{W}^{\top}\boldsymbol{W}})^{-1}\boldsymbol{S}_{\boldsymbol{W}^{\top}\boldsymbol{X}_0}$ is positive definite, where $\boldsymbol{S}_{\boldsymbol{X}_0^{\top}\boldsymbol{W}}$ and $\boldsymbol{S}_{\boldsymbol{W}^{\top}\boldsymbol{X}_0}$ are defined, analogously to $\boldsymbol{S}_{\boldsymbol{X}^{\top}\boldsymbol{W}}$ and $\boldsymbol{S}_{\boldsymbol{W}^{\top}\boldsymbol{X}}$, as $\operatorname{plim} n^{-1}\boldsymbol{X}_0^{\top}\boldsymbol{W}$ and $\operatorname{plim} n^{-1}\boldsymbol{W}^{\top}\boldsymbol{X}_0$, respectively. As with nonlinear models estimated by least squares, the strong asymptotic identification condition is sufficient, but not necessary, for ordinary asymptotic identification; see Section 6.2.

If the strong asymptotic identification condition is satisfied, the NLIV estimator can be shown to be consistent by the usual sort of reasoning. It is also asymptotically normal, and it satisfies the equation

$$n^{1/2}(\hat{\boldsymbol{\beta}}_{\text{NLIV}} - \boldsymbol{\beta}_0) \overset{a}{=} (n^{-1}\boldsymbol{X}_0^{\top}\boldsymbol{P_W}\boldsymbol{X}_0)^{-1} n^{-1/2}\boldsymbol{X}_0^{\top}\boldsymbol{P_W}\boldsymbol{u}, \tag{8.86}$$

from which it follows that the asymptotic covariance matrix is

$$\operatorname{Var}\big(\operatorname*{plim}_{n\to\infty} n^{1/2}(\hat{\boldsymbol{\beta}}_{\text{NLIV}} - \boldsymbol{\beta}_0)\big) = \operatorname*{plim}_{n\to\infty} \sigma_0^2\,(n^{-1}\boldsymbol{X}_0^{\top}\boldsymbol{P_W}\boldsymbol{X}_0)^{-1}, \tag{8.87}$$

where σ_0^2 is the true error variance. We previously obtained this result in (6.26) under stronger assumptions about the error terms. Based on (8.87), a suitable estimator of the actual covariance matrix is

$$\widehat{\operatorname{Var}}(\hat{\boldsymbol{\beta}}_{\text{NLIV}}) = \hat{\sigma}^2(\hat{\boldsymbol{X}}^{\top}\boldsymbol{P_W}\hat{\boldsymbol{X}})^{-1}, \tag{8.88}$$

where $\hat{\boldsymbol{X}} \equiv \boldsymbol{X}(\hat{\boldsymbol{\beta}}_{\text{NLIV}})$, and $\hat{\sigma}^2$ is $1/n$ times the SSR from IV estimation of regression (8.83). Readers may find it instructive to compare (8.88) with expression (8.34), the covariance matrix of the generalized IV estimator for a linear regression model.

The nonlinear version of the IVGNR is a simple extension of the linear version given in equation (8.49). It can be written as

$$\boldsymbol{y} - \boldsymbol{x}(\boldsymbol{\beta}) = \boldsymbol{P_W X}(\boldsymbol{\beta})\boldsymbol{b} + \text{residuals.} \tag{8.89}$$

In Exercise 8.24, readers are invited to show that this artificial regression has the properties necessary for its use in hypothesis testing, and to develop a heteroskedasticity-robust version of it. Hypothesis testing can also be carried out on the basis of the nonlinear IV criterion function (8.85), in precisely the same way as for linear models.

Tests of overidentifying restrictions and DWH tests for nonlinear models are likewise simple and obvious extensions of those for linear models. The minimized value of (8.85), when divided by any consistent estimate of σ^2, is asymptotically distributed as $\chi^2(l-k)$ and may be used to test the overidentifying restrictions. Although bootstrapping of nonlinear models estimated by NLIV can be carried out just as in Section 8.8, with the endogenous explanatory variables generated by the set of linear equations (8.80), the requirement that these equations should be linear may often be uncomfortably strong. In such cases, it would be unwise in the present state of the art to make any specific recommendations.

8.10 Final Remarks

Although it is formally very similar to other MM estimators that we have studied, the IV estimator does involve several important new concepts. These include the idea of an instrumental variable, the notion of forming a set of instruments optimally as weighted combinations of a larger number of instruments when that number exceeds the number of parameters, and the concept of overidentifying restrictions.

The optimality of the generalized IV estimator depends critically on the fairly strong assumption that the error terms are homoskedastic and serially uncorrelated. When this assumption is relaxed, it may be possible to obtain MM estimators that are more efficient than the GIV estimator. These "generalized method-of-moments" estimators will be the topic of the next chapter.

8.11 Exercises

8.1 Consider a very simple consumption function, of the form

$$c_i = \beta_1 + \beta_2 y_i^* + u_i^*, \quad u_i^* \sim \text{IID}(0, \sigma^2),$$

where c_i is the logarithm of consumption by household i, and y_i^* is the permanent income of household i, which is not observed. Instead, we observe current income y_i, which is equal to $y_i^* + v_i$, where $v_i \sim \text{IID}(0, \omega^2)$ is assumed to be uncorrelated with y_i^* and u_i. Therefore, we run the regression

$$c_i = \beta_1 + \beta_2 y_i + u_i.$$

Under the plausible assumption that the true value β_{20} is positive, show that y_i is negatively correlated with u_i. Using this result, evaluate the plim of the OLS estimator $\hat{\beta}_2$, and show that this plim is less than β_{20}.

8.2 Consider the simple IV estimator (8.12), computed first with an $n \times k$ matrix $\boldsymbol{W}$ of instrumental variables, and then with another $n \times k$ matrix $\boldsymbol{WJ}$, where $\boldsymbol{J}$ is a $k \times k$ nonsingular matrix. Show that the two estimators coincide. Why does this fact show that (8.12) depends on $\boldsymbol{W}$ only through the orthogonal projection matrix $\boldsymbol{P_W}$?

8.3 Show that, if the matrix of instrumental variables $\boldsymbol{W}$ is $n \times k$, with the same dimensions as the matrix $\boldsymbol{X}$ of explanatory variables, then the generalized IV estimator (8.29) is identical to the simple IV estimator (8.12).

8.4 Show that minimizing the criterion function (8.30) with respect to $\boldsymbol{\beta}$ yields the generalized IV estimator (8.29).

★8.5 Under the usual assumptions of this chapter, including (8.16), show that the plim of

$$\frac{1}{n}Q(\boldsymbol{\beta}_0, \boldsymbol{y}) = \frac{1}{n}(\boldsymbol{y} - \boldsymbol{X\beta}_0)^\top \boldsymbol{P_W}(\boldsymbol{y} - \boldsymbol{X\beta}_0)$$

is zero if $\boldsymbol{y} = \boldsymbol{X\beta}_0 + \boldsymbol{u}$. Under the same assumptions, along with the asymptotic identification condition that $\boldsymbol{S}_{\boldsymbol{X}^\top\boldsymbol{W}}(\boldsymbol{S}_{\boldsymbol{W}^\top\boldsymbol{W}})^{-1}\boldsymbol{S}_{\boldsymbol{W}^\top\boldsymbol{X}}$ has full rank, show further that $\operatorname{plim} n^{-1}Q(\boldsymbol{\beta}, \boldsymbol{y})$ is strictly positive for $\boldsymbol{\beta} \neq \boldsymbol{\beta}_0$.

8.6 Under assumption (8.16) and the asymptotic identification condition that $\boldsymbol{S}_{\boldsymbol{X}^\top\boldsymbol{W}}(\boldsymbol{S}_{\boldsymbol{W}^\top\boldsymbol{W}})^{-1}\boldsymbol{S}_{\boldsymbol{W}^\top\boldsymbol{X}}$ has full rank, show that the GIV estimator $\hat{\boldsymbol{\beta}}_{\rm IV}$ is consistent by explicitly computing the probability limit of the estimator for a DGP such that $\boldsymbol{y} = \boldsymbol{X\beta}_0 + \boldsymbol{u}$.

8.7 Suppose that you can apply a central limit theorem to the vector $n^{-1/2}\boldsymbol{W}^\top\boldsymbol{u}$, with the result that it is asymptotically multivariate normal, with mean $\boldsymbol{0}$ and covariance matrix (8.33). Use equation (8.32) to demonstrate explicitly that, if $\boldsymbol{y} = \boldsymbol{X\beta}_0 + \boldsymbol{u}$, then $n^{1/2}(\hat{\boldsymbol{\beta}}_{\rm IV} - \boldsymbol{\beta}_0)$ is asymptotically normal with mean $\boldsymbol{0}$ and covariance matrix (8.17).

8.8 Suppose that $\boldsymbol{W}_1$ and $\boldsymbol{W}_2$ are, respectively, $n \times l_1$ and $n \times l_2$ matrices of instruments, and that $\boldsymbol{W}_2$ consists of $\boldsymbol{W}_1$ plus $l_2 - l_1$ additional columns. Prove that the generalized IV estimator using $\boldsymbol{W}_2$ is asymptotically more efficient than the generalized IV estimator using $\boldsymbol{W}_1$. To do this, you need to show that the matrix $(\boldsymbol{X}^\top\boldsymbol{P}_{\boldsymbol{W}_1}\boldsymbol{X})^{-1} - (\boldsymbol{X}^\top\boldsymbol{P}_{\boldsymbol{W}_2}\boldsymbol{X})^{-1}$ is positive semidefinite. **Hint:** see Exercise 3.8.

8.9 Show that the simple IV estimator defined in (8.41) is unbiased when the data are generated by (8.40) with $\sigma_v = 0$. Interpret this result.

8.10 Use the DGP (8.40) to generate at least 1000 sets of simulated data for $\boldsymbol{x}$ and $\boldsymbol{y}$ with sample size $n = 10$, using normally distributed error terms and parameter values $\sigma_u = \sigma_v = 1$, $\pi_0 = 1$, $\beta_0 = 0$, and $\rho = 0.5$. For the exogenous instrument $\boldsymbol{w}$, use independent drawings from the standard normal distribution, and then rescale $\boldsymbol{w}$ so that $\boldsymbol{w}^\top\boldsymbol{w}$ is equal to n, rather than 1 as in Section 8.4.

For each simulated data set, compute the IV estimator (8.41). Then draw the empirical distribution of the realizations of the estimator on the same plot as the CDF of the normal distribution with mean zero and variance $\sigma_u^2/n\pi_0^2$. Explain why this is an appropriate way to compare the finite-sample and asymptotic distributions of the estimator.

In addition, for each simulated data set, compute the OLS estimator, and plot the EDF of the realizations of this estimator on the same axes as the EDF of the realizations of the IV estimator.

8.11 Redo Exercise 8.10 for a sample size of $n = 100$. If you have enough computer time available, redo it yet again for $n = 1000$, in order to see how quickly or slowly the finite-sample distribution tends to the asymptotic distribution.

8.12 Redo the simulations of Exercise 8.10, for $n = 10$, generating the exogenous instrument $\boldsymbol{w}$ as follows. For the first experiment, use independent drawings from the uniform distribution on $[-1, 1]$. For the second, use drawings from the AR(1) process $w_t = \alpha w_{t-1} + \varepsilon_t$, where $w_0 = 0$, $\alpha = 0.8$, and the ε_t are independent drawings from $\mathrm{N}(0, 1)$. In all cases, rescale $\boldsymbol{w}$ so that $\boldsymbol{w}^\top\boldsymbol{w} = n$. To what extent does the empirical distribution of $\hat{\beta}_{\mathrm{IV}}$ appear to depend on the properties of $\boldsymbol{w}$? What theoretical explanation can you think of for your results?

8.13 Include one more instrument in the simulations of Exercise 8.10. Continue to use the same DGP for $\boldsymbol{y}$ and $\boldsymbol{x}$, but replace the simple IV estimator by the generalized one, based on two instruments $\boldsymbol{w}$ and $\boldsymbol{z}$, where $\boldsymbol{z}$ is generated independently of everything else in the simulation. See if you can verify the theoretical prediction that the overidentified estimator computed with two instruments is more biased, but has thinner tails, than the just identified estimator.

Repeat the simulations twice more, first with two additional instruments and then with four. What happens to the distribution of the estimator as the number of instruments increases?

8.14 Verify that $\hat{\beta}_{\mathrm{IV}}$ is the OLS estimator for model (8.10) when the regressor matrix is $\boldsymbol{X} = [\boldsymbol{Z}\ \ \boldsymbol{Y}] = \boldsymbol{W\Pi}$, with the matrix $\boldsymbol{V}$ in (8.44) equal to $\mathbf{O}$. Is this estimator consistent? Explain.

★8.15 Verify, by use of the assumption that the instruments in the matrix $\boldsymbol{W}$ are exogenous or predetermined, and by use of a suitable law of large numbers, that all the terms in (8.45) that involve $\boldsymbol{V}$ do not contribute to the probability limit of (8.45) as the sample size tends to infinity.

8.16 Show that the vector of residuals obtained by running the IVGNR (8.49) with $\boldsymbol{\beta} = \acute{\boldsymbol{\beta}}$ is equal to $\boldsymbol{y} - \boldsymbol{X}\hat{\boldsymbol{\beta}}_{\mathrm{IV}} + \boldsymbol{M_W X}(\hat{\boldsymbol{\beta}}_{\mathrm{IV}} - \acute{\boldsymbol{\beta}})$. Use this result to show that $\acute{\sigma}^2$, the estimate of the error variance given by the IVGNR, is consistent for the error variance of the underlying model (8.10) if $\acute{\boldsymbol{\beta}}$ is root-n consistent.

8.17 Prove that expression (8.56) is equal to expression (8.57). **Hint:** Use the facts that $\boldsymbol{P}_{\boldsymbol{P_W X}_1}\boldsymbol{X}_1 = \boldsymbol{P_W X}_1$ and $\boldsymbol{P}_{\boldsymbol{P_W X}}\boldsymbol{P}_{\boldsymbol{P_W X}_1} = \boldsymbol{P}_{\boldsymbol{P_W X}_1}$.

★8.18 Show that k_2 times the artificial F statistic from the pair of IVGNRs (8.53) and (8.54) is asymptotically equal to the Wald statistic (8.48), using reasoning similar to that employed in Section 6.7. Why are these two statistics not numerically identical? Show that the asymptotic equality does not hold if different matrices of instruments are used in the two IVGNRs.

8.19 Sketch a proof of the result that the scalar

$$\frac{1}{\sigma_0^2}\boldsymbol{u}^\top(\boldsymbol{P}_{\boldsymbol{P_W X}} - \boldsymbol{P}_{\boldsymbol{P_W X_1}})\boldsymbol{u},$$

which is expression (8.58) divided by σ_0^2, is asymptotically distributed as $\chi^2(k_2)$ whenever the random vector $\boldsymbol{u}$ is $\text{IID}(\mathbf{0}, \sigma_0^2\mathbf{I})$ and is asymptotically uncorrelated with the instruments $\boldsymbol{W}$. Here $\boldsymbol{X}$ has k columns, $\boldsymbol{X}_1$ has k_1 columns, and $k_2 = k - k_1$.

⋆8.20 The IV variant of the HRGNR (6.90), evaluated at $\boldsymbol{\beta} = \acute{\boldsymbol{\beta}}$, can be written as

$$\boldsymbol{\iota} = \boldsymbol{P}_{\acute{\boldsymbol{U}}\boldsymbol{P_W X}}\acute{\boldsymbol{U}}^{-1}\boldsymbol{P_W X b} + \text{residuals}, \tag{8.90}$$

where $\boldsymbol{\iota}$ is an n-vector of which every component equals 1, and $\acute{\boldsymbol{U}}$ is an $n \times n$ diagonal matrix with t^{th} diagonal element equal to the tth element of the vector $\boldsymbol{y} - \boldsymbol{X}\acute{\boldsymbol{\beta}}$.

Verify that this artificial regression possesses all the requisite properties for hypothesis testing, namely, that

- The regressand in (8.90) is orthogonal to the regressors when $\acute{\boldsymbol{\beta}} = \hat{\boldsymbol{\beta}}_{\text{IV}}$;
- The estimated OLS covariance matrix from (8.90) evaluated at $\acute{\boldsymbol{\beta}} = \hat{\boldsymbol{\beta}}_{\text{IV}}$ is equal to $n/(n-k)$ times the HCCME $\widehat{\text{Var}}_{\text{h}}(\hat{\boldsymbol{\beta}}_{\text{IV}})$ given by (8.65);
- The HRGNR (8.90) allows one-step estimation: The OLS parameter estimates $\acute{\boldsymbol{b}}$ from (8.90) are such that $\hat{\boldsymbol{\beta}}_{\text{IV}} = \acute{\boldsymbol{\beta}} + \acute{\boldsymbol{b}}$.

8.21 Show that nR^2 from the modified IVGNR (8.72) is equal to the Sargan test statistic, that is, the minimized IV criterion function for model (8.68) divided by the IV estimate of the error variance for that model.

8.22 Consider the following OLS regression, where the variables have the same interpretation as in Section 8.7 on DWH tests:

$$\boldsymbol{y} = \boldsymbol{X\beta} + \boldsymbol{M_W Y\zeta} + \boldsymbol{u}. \tag{8.91}$$

Show that an F test of the restrictions $\boldsymbol{\zeta} = \mathbf{0}$ in (8.91) is numerically identical to the F test for $\boldsymbol{\delta} = \mathbf{0}$ in (8.77). Show further that the OLS estimator of $\boldsymbol{\beta}$ from (8.91) is identical to the estimator $\hat{\boldsymbol{\beta}}_{\text{IV}}$ obtained by estimating (8.74) by instrumental variables.

8.23 Show that the difference between the generalized IV estimator $\hat{\boldsymbol{\beta}}_{\text{IV}}$ and the OLS estimator $\hat{\boldsymbol{\beta}}_{\text{OLS}}$, for which an explicit expression is given in equation (8.76), has zero covariance with $\hat{\boldsymbol{\beta}}_{\text{OLS}}$ itself. For simplicity, you may treat the matrix $\boldsymbol{X}$ as fixed.

⋆8.24 Using the same methods as those in Sections 6.5 and 6.6, show that the nonlinear version (8.89) of the IVGNR satisfies the three conditions, analogous to those set out in Exercise 8.20, which are necessary for the use of the IVGNR in hypothesis testing. What is the nonlinear version of the IV variant of the HRGNR? Show that it, too, satisfies the three conditions under the assumption of possibly heteroskedastic error terms.

8.25 The data in the file **money.data** are described in Exercise 7.14. Using these data, estimate the model

$$m_t = \beta_1 + \beta_2 r_t + \beta_3 y_t + \beta_4 m_{t-1} + \beta_5 m_{t-2} + u_t \tag{8.92}$$

by OLS for the period 1968:1 to 1998:4. Then perform a DWH test for the hypothesis that the interest rate, r_t, can be treated as exogenous, using r_{t-1} and r_{t-2} as additional instruments.

8.26 Estimate equation (8.92) by generalized instrumental variables, treating r_t as endogenous and using r_{t-1} and r_{t-2} as additional instruments. Are the estimates much different from the OLS ones? Verify that the IV estimates may also be obtained by OLS estimation of equation (8.91). Are the reported standard errors the same? Explain why or why not.

8.27 Perform a Sargan test of the overidentifying restrictions for the IV estimation you performed in Exercise 8.26. How do you interpret the results of this test?

8.28 The file **demand-supply.data** contains 120 artificial observations on a demand-supply model similar to equations (8.06)–(8.07). The demand equation is

$$q_t = \beta_1 + \beta_2 x_{t2} + \beta_3 x_{t3} + \gamma p_t + u_t, \tag{8.93}$$

where q_t is the log of quantity, p_t is the log of price, x_{t2} is the log of income, and x_{t3} is a dummy variable that accounts for regular demand shifts.

Estimate equation (8.93) by OLS and 2SLS, using the variables x_{t4} and x_{t5} as additional instruments. Does OLS estimation appear to be valid here? Does 2SLS estimation appear to be valid here? Perform whatever tests are appropriate to answer these questions.

Reverse the roles of q_t and p_t in equation (8.93) and estimate the new equation by OLS and 2SLS. How are the two estimates of the coefficient of q_t in the new equation related to the corresponding estimates of γ from the original equation? What do these results suggest about the validity of the OLS and 2SLS estimates?

Chapter 9

The Generalized Method of Moments

9.1 Introduction

The models we have considered in earlier chapters have all been regression models of one sort or another. In this chapter and the next, we introduce more general types of models, along with a general method for performing estimation and inference on them. This technique is called the **generalized method of moments**, or **GMM**, and it includes as special cases all the methods we have so far developed for regression models.

As we explained in Section 3.1, a model is represented by a set of DGPs. Each DGP in the model is characterized by a parameter vector, which we will normally denote by $\boldsymbol{\beta}$ in the case of regression functions and by $\boldsymbol{\theta}$ in the general case. The starting point for GMM estimation is to specify functions, which, for any DGP in the model, depend both on the data generated by that DGP and on the model parameters. When these functions are evaluated at the parameters that correspond to the DGP that generated the data, their expectation must be zero.

As a simple example, consider the linear regression model $y_t = \boldsymbol{X}_t\boldsymbol{\beta} + u_t$. An important part of the model specification is that the error terms have mean zero. These error terms are unobservable, because the parameters $\boldsymbol{\beta}$ of the regression function are unknown. But we can define the residuals $u_t(\boldsymbol{\beta}) \equiv y_t - \boldsymbol{X}_t\boldsymbol{\beta}$ as functions of the observed data and the unknown model parameters, and these functions provide what we need for GMM estimation. If the residuals are evaluated at the parameter vector $\boldsymbol{\beta}_0$ associated with the true DGP, they have mean zero under that DGP, but if they are evaluated at some $\boldsymbol{\beta} \neq \boldsymbol{\beta}_0$, they do not have mean zero. In Chapter 1, we used this fact to develop a method-of-moments (MM) estimator for the parameter vector $\boldsymbol{\beta}$ of the regression function. As we will see in the next section, the various GMM estimators of $\boldsymbol{\beta}$ include as a special case the MM (or OLS) estimator developed in Chapter 1.

In Chapter 6, when we dealt with nonlinear regression models, and again in Chapter 8, we used instrumental variables along with residuals in order to develop MM estimators. The use of instrumental variables is also an essential aspect of GMM, and in this chapter we will once again make use of the various kinds of optimal instruments that were useful in Chapters 6 and 8 in order to develop a wide variety of estimators that are asymptotically efficient for a wide variety of models.

We begin by considering, in the next section, a linear regression model with endogenous explanatory variables and an error covariance matrix that is not proportional to the identity matrix. Such a model requires us to combine the insights of both Chapters 7 and 8 in order to obtain asymptotically efficient estimates. In the process of doing so, we will see how GMM estimation works more generally, and we will be led to develop ways to estimate models with both heteroskedasticity and serial correlation of unknown form. In Section 9.3, we study in some detail the **heteroskedasticity and autocorrelation consistent**, or **HAC**, covariance matrix estimators that we briefly mentioned in Section 5.5. Then, in Section 9.4, we introduce a set of tests, based on **GMM criterion functions**, that are widely used for inference in conjunction with GMM estimation. In Section 9.5, we move beyond regression models to give a more formal and advanced presentation of GMM, and we postpone to this section most of the proofs of consistency, asymptotic normality, and asymptotic efficiency for GMM estimators. In Section 9.6, which depends heavily on the more advanced treatment of the preceding section, we consider the **Method of Simulated Moments**, or **MSM**. This method allows us to obtain GMM estimates by simulation even when we cannot analytically evaluate the functions that play the same role as residuals for a regression model.

9.2 GMM Estimators for Linear Regression Models

Consider the linear regression model

$$\boldsymbol{y} = \boldsymbol{X\beta} + \boldsymbol{u}, \quad \mathrm{E}(\boldsymbol{u}\boldsymbol{u}^\top) = \boldsymbol{\Omega}, \tag{9.01}$$

where there are n observations, and $\boldsymbol{\Omega}$ is an $n \times n$ covariance matrix. As in the previous chapter, some of the explanatory variables that form the $n \times k$ matrix $\boldsymbol{X}$ may not be predetermined with respect to the error terms $\boldsymbol{u}$. However, there is assumed to exist an $n \times l$ matrix of predetermined instrumental variables, $\boldsymbol{W}$, with $n > l$ and $l \geq k$, satisfying the condition $\mathrm{E}(u_t \mid \boldsymbol{W}_t) = 0$ for each row $\boldsymbol{W}_t$ of $\boldsymbol{W}$, $t = 1, \ldots, n$. Any column of $\boldsymbol{X}$ that is predetermined must also be a column of $\boldsymbol{W}$. In addition, we assume that, for all $t, s = 1, \ldots, n$, $\mathrm{E}(u_t u_s \mid \boldsymbol{W}_t, \boldsymbol{W}_s) = \omega_{ts}$, where ω_{ts} is the ts^{th} element of $\boldsymbol{\Omega}$. We will need this assumption later, because it allows us to see that

$$\begin{aligned}
\mathrm{Var}(n^{-1/2}\boldsymbol{W}^\top\boldsymbol{u}) = \tfrac{1}{n}\mathrm{E}(\boldsymbol{W}^\top\boldsymbol{u}\boldsymbol{u}^\top\boldsymbol{W}) &= \tfrac{1}{n}\sum_{t=1}^{n}\sum_{s=1}^{n}\mathrm{E}(u_t u_s \boldsymbol{W}_t^\top\boldsymbol{W}_s) \\
&= \tfrac{1}{n}\sum_{t=1}^{n}\sum_{s=1}^{n}\mathrm{E}\big(\mathrm{E}(u_t u_s \boldsymbol{W}_t^\top\boldsymbol{W}_s \mid \boldsymbol{W}_t, \boldsymbol{W}_s)\big)
\end{aligned}$$

$$= \frac{1}{n}\sum_{t=1}^{n}\sum_{s=1}^{n} \mathrm{E}(\omega_{ts}\boldsymbol{W}_t^{\top}\boldsymbol{W}_s) = \frac{1}{n}\mathrm{E}(\boldsymbol{W}^{\top}\boldsymbol{\Omega}\boldsymbol{W}). \tag{9.02}$$

The assumption that $\mathrm{E}(u_t \,|\, \boldsymbol{W}_t) = 0$ implies that, for all $t = 1, \ldots, n$,

$$\mathrm{E}\big(\boldsymbol{W}_t^{\top}(y_t - \boldsymbol{X}_t\boldsymbol{\beta})\big) = \mathbf{0}. \tag{9.03}$$

These equations form a set of what we may call **theoretical moment conditions**. They were used in Chapter 8 as the starting point for MM estimation of the regression model (9.01). Each theoretical moment condition corresponds to a sample moment, or **empirical moment**, of the form

$$\frac{1}{n}\sum_{t=1}^{n} w_{ti}^{\top}(y_t - \boldsymbol{X}_t\boldsymbol{\beta}) = \frac{1}{n}\boldsymbol{w}_i^{\top}(\boldsymbol{y} - \boldsymbol{X}\boldsymbol{\beta}), \tag{9.04}$$

where $\boldsymbol{w}_i$, $i = 1, \ldots, l$, is the ith column of $\boldsymbol{W}$, and w_{ti} is the ti^{th} element. When $l = k$, we can set these sample moments equal to zero and solve the resulting k equations to obtain the simple IV estimator (8.12). When $l > k$, we must do as we did in Chapter 8 and select k independent linear combinations of the sample moments (9.04) in order to obtain an estimator.

Now let $\boldsymbol{J}$ be an $l \times k$ matrix with full column rank k, and consider the MM estimator obtained by using the k columns of $\boldsymbol{WJ}$ as instruments. This estimator solves the k equations

$$\boldsymbol{J}^{\top}\boldsymbol{W}^{\top}(\boldsymbol{y} - \boldsymbol{X}\boldsymbol{\beta}) = \mathbf{0}, \tag{9.05}$$

which are referred to as **sample moment conditions**, or just **moment conditions** when there is no ambiguity. They are also sometimes called **orthogonality conditions**, since they require that the vector of residuals should be orthogonal to the columns of $\boldsymbol{WJ}$. Let us assume that the data are generated by a DGP which belongs to the model (9.01), with coefficient vector $\boldsymbol{\beta}_0$ and covariance matrix $\boldsymbol{\Omega}_0$. Under this assumption, we have the following explicit expression, suitable for asymptotic analysis, for the estimator $\hat{\boldsymbol{\beta}}$ that solves (9.05):

$$n^{1/2}(\hat{\boldsymbol{\beta}} - \boldsymbol{\beta}_0) = \big(n^{-1}\boldsymbol{J}^{\top}\boldsymbol{W}^{\top}\boldsymbol{X}\big)^{-1} n^{-1/2}\boldsymbol{J}^{\top}\boldsymbol{W}^{\top}\boldsymbol{u}. \tag{9.06}$$

From this, recalling (9.02), we find that the asymptotic covariance matrix of $\hat{\boldsymbol{\beta}}$, that is, the covariance matrix of the plim of $n^{1/2}(\hat{\boldsymbol{\beta}} - \boldsymbol{\beta}_0)$, is

$$\Big(\operatorname*{plim}_{n\to\infty}\frac{1}{n}\boldsymbol{J}^{\top}\boldsymbol{W}^{\top}\boldsymbol{X}\Big)^{-1}\Big(\operatorname*{plim}_{n\to\infty}\frac{1}{n}\boldsymbol{J}^{\top}\boldsymbol{W}^{\top}\boldsymbol{\Omega}_0\boldsymbol{W}\boldsymbol{J}\Big)\Big(\operatorname*{plim}_{n\to\infty}\frac{1}{n}\boldsymbol{X}^{\top}\boldsymbol{W}\boldsymbol{J}\Big)^{-1}. \tag{9.07}$$

This matrix has the familiar sandwich form that we expect to see when an estimator is not asymptotically efficient.

The next step, as in Section 8.3, is to choose $\boldsymbol{J}$ so as to minimize the covariance matrix (9.07). We may reasonably expect that, with such a choice of $\boldsymbol{J}$, the covariance matrix would no longer have the form of a sandwich. The simplest choice of $\boldsymbol{J}$ that eliminates the sandwich in (9.07) is

$$\boldsymbol{J} = (\boldsymbol{W}^\top \boldsymbol{\Omega}_0 \boldsymbol{W})^{-1} \boldsymbol{W}^\top \boldsymbol{X}; \tag{9.08}$$

notice that, in the special case in which $\boldsymbol{\Omega}_0$ is proportional to $\mathbf{I}$, this expression reduces to the result (8.24) that we found in Section 8.3 as the solution for that special case. We can see, therefore, that (9.08) is the appropriate generalization of (8.24) when $\boldsymbol{\Omega}$ is not proportional to an identity matrix. With $\boldsymbol{J}$ defined by (9.08), the covariance matrix (9.07) becomes

$$\operatorname*{plim}_{n\to\infty} \Big(\frac{1}{n} \boldsymbol{X}^\top \boldsymbol{W} (\boldsymbol{W}^\top \boldsymbol{\Omega}_0 \boldsymbol{W})^{-1} \boldsymbol{W}^\top \boldsymbol{X}\Big)^{-1}, \tag{9.09}$$

and the **efficient GMM estimator** is

$$\hat{\beta}_{\rm GMM} = \big(\boldsymbol{X}^\top \boldsymbol{W} (\boldsymbol{W}^\top \boldsymbol{\Omega}_0 \boldsymbol{W})^{-1} \boldsymbol{W}^\top \boldsymbol{X}\big)^{-1} \boldsymbol{X}^\top \boldsymbol{W} (\boldsymbol{W}^\top \boldsymbol{\Omega}_0 \boldsymbol{W})^{-1} \boldsymbol{W}^\top \boldsymbol{y}. \tag{9.10}$$

When $\boldsymbol{\Omega}_0 = \sigma^2 \mathbf{I}$, this estimator reduces to the generalized IV estimator (8.29). In Exercise 9.1, readers are invited to show that the difference between the covariance matrices (9.07) and (9.09) is a positive semidefinite matrix, thereby confirming (9.08) as the optimal choice for $\boldsymbol{J}$.

The GMM Criterion Function

With both GLS and IV estimation, we showed that the efficient estimators could also be derived by minimizing an appropriate criterion function; this function was (7.06) for GLS and (8.30) for IV. Similarly, the efficient GMM estimator (9.10) minimizes the **GMM criterion function**

$$Q(\boldsymbol{\beta}, \boldsymbol{y}) \equiv (\boldsymbol{y} - \boldsymbol{X}\boldsymbol{\beta})^\top \boldsymbol{W} (\boldsymbol{W}^\top \boldsymbol{\Omega}_0 \boldsymbol{W})^{-1} \boldsymbol{W}^\top (\boldsymbol{y} - \boldsymbol{X}\boldsymbol{\beta}), \tag{9.11}$$

as can be seen at once by noting that the first-order conditions for minimizing (9.11) are

$$\boldsymbol{X}^\top \boldsymbol{W} (\boldsymbol{W}^\top \boldsymbol{\Omega}_0 \boldsymbol{W})^{-1} \boldsymbol{W}^\top (\boldsymbol{y} - \boldsymbol{X}\boldsymbol{\beta}) = \mathbf{0}.$$

If $\boldsymbol{\Omega}_0 = \sigma_0^2 \mathbf{I}$, (9.11) reduces to the IV criterion function (8.30), divided by σ_0^2. In Section 8.6, we saw that the minimized value of the IV criterion function, divided by an estimate of σ^2, serves as the statistic for the Sargan test for overidentification. We will see in Section 9.4 that the GMM criterion function (9.11), with the usually unknown matrix $\boldsymbol{\Omega}_0$ replaced by a suitable estimate, can also be used as a test statistic for overidentification.

The criterion function (9.11) is a quadratic form in the vector $\boldsymbol{W}^\top(\boldsymbol{y} - \boldsymbol{X}\boldsymbol{\beta})$ of sample moments and the inverse of the matrix $\boldsymbol{W}^\top \boldsymbol{\Omega}_0 \boldsymbol{W}$. Equivalently, it is a quadratic form in $n^{-1/2} \boldsymbol{W}^\top (\boldsymbol{y} - \boldsymbol{X}\boldsymbol{\beta})$ and the inverse of $n^{-1} \boldsymbol{W}^\top \boldsymbol{\Omega}_0 \boldsymbol{W}$, since the powers of n cancel. Under the sort of regularity conditions we have used in earlier chapters, $n^{-1/2}\boldsymbol{W}^\top(\boldsymbol{y}-\boldsymbol{X\beta}_0)$ satisfies a central limit theorem, and so tends, as $n\to\infty$, to a normal random variable, with mean vector $\mathbf{0}$ and covariance matrix the limit of $n^{-1}\boldsymbol{W}^\top\boldsymbol{\Omega}_0\boldsymbol{W}$. It follows that (9.11) evaluated using the true $\boldsymbol{\beta}_0$ and the true $\boldsymbol{\Omega}_0$ is asymptotically distributed as χ^2 with l degrees of freedom; recall Theorem 4.1, and see Exercise 9.2.

This property of the GMM criterion function is simply a consequence of its structure as a quadratic form in the sample moments used for estimation and the inverse of the asymptotic covariance matrix of these moments evaluated at the true parameters. As we will see in Section 9.4, this property is what makes the GMM criterion function useful for testing. The argument leading to (9.10) shows that this same property of the GMM criterion function leads to the asymptotic efficiency of the estimator that minimizes it.

Provided the instruments are predetermined, so that they satisfy the condition that $\mathrm{E}(u_t\,|\,\boldsymbol{W}_t)=0$, we still obtain a consistent estimator, even when the matrix $\boldsymbol{J}$ used to select linear combinations of the instruments is different from (9.08). Such a consistent, but in general inefficient, estimator can also be obtained by minimizing a quadratic criterion function of the form

$$(\boldsymbol{y}-\boldsymbol{X\beta})^\top\boldsymbol{W\Lambda W}^\top(\boldsymbol{y}-\boldsymbol{X\beta}), \tag{9.12}$$

where the **weighting matrix** $\boldsymbol{\Lambda}$ is $l\times l$, positive definite, and must be at least asymptotically nonrandom. Without loss of generality, $\boldsymbol{\Lambda}$ can be taken to be symmetric; see Exercise 9.3. The inefficient GMM estimator is

$$\hat{\boldsymbol{\beta}}=(\boldsymbol{X}^\top\boldsymbol{W\Lambda W}^\top\boldsymbol{X})^{-1}\boldsymbol{X}^\top\boldsymbol{W\Lambda W}^\top\boldsymbol{y}, \tag{9.13}$$

from which it can be seen that the use of the weighting matrix $\boldsymbol{\Lambda}$ corresponds to the implicit choice $\boldsymbol{J}=\boldsymbol{\Lambda W}^\top\boldsymbol{X}$. For a given choice of $\boldsymbol{J}$, there are various possible choices of $\boldsymbol{\Lambda}$ that give rise to the same estimator; see Exercise 9.4.

When $l=k$, the model is exactly identified, and $\boldsymbol{J}$ is a nonsingular square matrix which has no effect on the estimator. This is most easily seen by looking at the moment conditions (9.05), which are equivalent, when $l=k$, to those obtained by premultiplying them by $(\boldsymbol{J}^\top)^{-1}$. Similarly, if the estimator is defined by minimizing a quadratic form, it does not depend on the choice of $\boldsymbol{\Lambda}$ whenever $l=k$. To see this, consider the first-order conditions for minimizing (9.12), which, up to a scalar factor, are

$$\boldsymbol{X}^\top\boldsymbol{W\Lambda W}^\top(\boldsymbol{y}-\boldsymbol{X\beta})=\mathbf{0}.$$

If $l=k$, $\boldsymbol{X}^\top\boldsymbol{W}$ is a square matrix, and the first-order conditions can be premultiplied by $\boldsymbol{\Lambda}^{-1}(\boldsymbol{X}^\top\boldsymbol{W})^{-1}$. Therefore, the estimator is the solution to the equations $\boldsymbol{W}^\top(\boldsymbol{y}-\boldsymbol{X\beta})=\mathbf{0}$, independently of $\boldsymbol{\Lambda}$. This solution is just the simple IV estimator defined in (8.12).

When $l > k$, the model is overidentified, and the estimator (9.13) depends on the choice of $\boldsymbol{J}$ or $\boldsymbol{\Lambda}$. The efficient GMM estimator, for a given set of instruments, is defined in terms of the true covariance matrix $\boldsymbol{\Omega}_0$, which is usually unknown. If $\boldsymbol{\Omega}_0$ is known up to a scalar multiplicative factor, so that $\boldsymbol{\Omega}_0 = \sigma^2\boldsymbol{\Delta}_0$, with σ^2 unknown and $\boldsymbol{\Delta}_0$ known, then $\boldsymbol{\Delta}_0$ can be used in place of $\boldsymbol{\Omega}_0$ in either (9.10) or (9.11). This is true because multiplying $\boldsymbol{\Omega}_0$ by a scalar leaves (9.10) invariant, and it also leaves invariant the $\boldsymbol{\beta}$ that minimizes (9.11).

GMM Estimation with Heteroskedasticity of Unknown Form

The assumption that $\boldsymbol{\Omega}_0$ is known, even up to a scalar factor, is often too strong. What makes GMM estimation practical more generally is that, in both (9.10) and (9.11), $\boldsymbol{\Omega}_0$ appears only through the $l \times l$ matrix product $\boldsymbol{W}^\top\boldsymbol{\Omega}_0\boldsymbol{W}$. As we saw first in Section 5.5, in the context of heteroskedasticity consistent covariance matrix estimation, n^{-1} times such a matrix can be estimated consistently if $\boldsymbol{\Omega}_0$ is a diagonal matrix. What is needed is a preliminary consistent estimate of the parameter vector $\boldsymbol{\beta}$, which furnishes residuals that are consistent estimates of the error terms.

The preliminary estimates of $\boldsymbol{\beta}$ must be consistent, but they need not be asymptotically efficient, and so we can obtain them by using any convenient choice of $\boldsymbol{J}$ or $\boldsymbol{\Lambda}$. One choice that is often convenient is $\boldsymbol{\Lambda} = (\boldsymbol{W}^\top\boldsymbol{W})^{-1}$, in which case the preliminary estimator is the generalized IV estimator (8.29). We then use the preliminary estimates $\hat{\boldsymbol{\beta}}$ to calculate the residuals $\hat{u}_t \equiv y_t - \boldsymbol{X}\hat{\boldsymbol{\beta}}$. A typical element of the matrix $n^{-1}\boldsymbol{W}^\top\boldsymbol{\Omega}_0\boldsymbol{W}$ can then be estimated by

$$\frac{1}{n}\sum_{t=1}^{n}\hat{u}_t^2 w_{ti} w_{tj}. \tag{9.14}$$

This estimator is very similar to (5.36), and the estimator (9.14) can be proved to be consistent by using arguments just like those employed in Section 5.5.

The matrix with typical element (9.14) can be written as $n^{-1}\boldsymbol{W}^\top\hat{\boldsymbol{\Omega}}\boldsymbol{W}$, where $\hat{\boldsymbol{\Omega}}$ is an $n \times n$ diagonal matrix with typical diagonal element $\hat{u}_t^2$. Then the **feasible efficient GMM estimator** is

$$\hat{\boldsymbol{\beta}}_{\text{FGMM}} = \big(\boldsymbol{X}^\top\boldsymbol{W}(\boldsymbol{W}^\top\hat{\boldsymbol{\Omega}}\boldsymbol{W})^{-1}\boldsymbol{W}^\top\boldsymbol{X}\big)^{-1}\boldsymbol{X}^\top\boldsymbol{W}(\boldsymbol{W}^\top\hat{\boldsymbol{\Omega}}\boldsymbol{W})^{-1}\boldsymbol{W}^\top\boldsymbol{y}, \tag{9.15}$$

which is just (9.10) with $\boldsymbol{\Omega}_0$ replaced by $\hat{\boldsymbol{\Omega}}$. Since $n^{-1}\boldsymbol{W}^\top\hat{\boldsymbol{\Omega}}\boldsymbol{W}$ consistently estimates $n^{-1}\boldsymbol{W}^\top\boldsymbol{\Omega}_0\boldsymbol{W}$, it follows that $\hat{\boldsymbol{\beta}}_{\text{FGMM}}$ is asymptotically equivalent to (9.10). It should be noted that, in calling (9.15) efficient, we mean that it is asymptotically efficient within the class of estimators that use the given instrument set $\boldsymbol{W}$.

Like other procedures that start from a preliminary estimate, this one can be iterated. The GMM residuals $y_t - \boldsymbol{X}\hat{\boldsymbol{\beta}}_{\text{FGMM}}$ can be used to calculate a new estimate of $\boldsymbol{\Omega}$, which can then be used to obtain second-round GMM estimates, which can then be used to calculate yet another estimate of $\boldsymbol{\Omega}$, and so on. This iterative procedure was investigated by Hansen, Heaton, and Yaron (1996), who called it **continuously updated GMM**. Whether we stop after one round or continue until the procedure converges, the estimates have the same asymptotic distribution if the model is correctly specified. However, there is evidence that performing more iterations improves finite-sample performance. In practice, the covariance matrix is estimated by

$$\widehat{\operatorname{Var}}(\hat{\boldsymbol{\beta}}_{\mathrm{FGMM}}) = \big(\boldsymbol{X}^\top\boldsymbol{W}(\boldsymbol{W}^\top\hat{\boldsymbol{\Omega}}\boldsymbol{W})^{-1}\boldsymbol{W}^\top\boldsymbol{X}\big)^{-1}. \tag{9.16}$$

It is not hard to see that n times the estimator (9.16) tends to the asymptotic covariance matrix (9.09) as $n \to \infty$.

Fully Efficient GMM Estimation

In choosing to use a particular matrix of instrumental variables $\boldsymbol{W}$, we are choosing a particular representation of the information sets Ω_t appropriate for each observation in the sample. It is required that $\boldsymbol{W}_t \in \Omega_t$ for all t, and it follows from this that any deterministic function, linear or nonlinear, of the elements of $\boldsymbol{W}_t$ also belongs to Ω_t. It is quite clearly impossible to use all such deterministic functions as actual instrumental variables, and so the econometrician must make a choice. What we have established so far is that, once the choice of $\boldsymbol{W}$ is made, (9.08) gives the optimal set of linear combinations of the columns of $\boldsymbol{W}$ to use for estimation. What remains to be seen is how best to choose $\boldsymbol{W}$ out of all the possible valid instruments, given the information sets Ω_t.

In Section 8.3, we saw that, for the model (9.01) with $\boldsymbol{\Omega} = \sigma^2\mathbf{I}$, the best choice, by the criterion of the asymptotic covariance matrix, is the matrix $\bar{\boldsymbol{X}}$ given in (8.18) by the defining condition that $\mathrm{E}(\boldsymbol{X}_t \,|\, \Omega_t) = \bar{\boldsymbol{X}}_t$, where $\boldsymbol{X}_t$ and $\bar{\boldsymbol{X}}_t$ are the tth rows of $\boldsymbol{X}$ and $\bar{\boldsymbol{X}}$, respectively. However, it is easy to see that this result does not hold unmodified when $\boldsymbol{\Omega}$ is not proportional to an identity matrix. Consider the GMM estimator (9.10), of which (9.15) is the feasible version, in the special case of exogenous explanatory variables, for which the obvious choice of instruments is $\boldsymbol{W} = \boldsymbol{X}$. If, for notational ease, we write $\boldsymbol{\Omega}$ for the true covariance matrix $\boldsymbol{\Omega}_0$, (9.10) becomes

$$\begin{aligned}
\hat{\boldsymbol{\beta}}_{\mathrm{GMM}} &= \big(\boldsymbol{X}^\top\boldsymbol{X}(\boldsymbol{X}^\top\boldsymbol{\Omega}\boldsymbol{X})^{-1}\boldsymbol{X}^\top\boldsymbol{X}\big)^{-1}\boldsymbol{X}^\top\boldsymbol{X}(\boldsymbol{X}^\top\boldsymbol{\Omega}\boldsymbol{X})^{-1}\boldsymbol{X}^\top\boldsymbol{y} \\
&= (\boldsymbol{X}^\top\boldsymbol{X})^{-1}\boldsymbol{X}^\top\boldsymbol{\Omega}\boldsymbol{X}(\boldsymbol{X}^\top\boldsymbol{X})^{-1}\boldsymbol{X}^\top\boldsymbol{X}(\boldsymbol{X}^\top\boldsymbol{\Omega}\boldsymbol{X})^{-1}\boldsymbol{X}^\top\boldsymbol{y} \\
&= (\boldsymbol{X}^\top\boldsymbol{X})^{-1}\boldsymbol{X}^\top\boldsymbol{\Omega}\boldsymbol{X}(\boldsymbol{X}^\top\boldsymbol{\Omega}\boldsymbol{X})^{-1}\boldsymbol{X}^\top\boldsymbol{y} \\
&= (\boldsymbol{X}^\top\boldsymbol{X})^{-1}\boldsymbol{X}^\top\boldsymbol{y} = \hat{\boldsymbol{\beta}}_{\mathrm{OLS}}.
\end{aligned}$$

However, we know from the results of Section 7.2 that the efficient estimator is actually the GLS estimator

$$\hat{\boldsymbol{\beta}}_{\mathrm{GLS}} = (\boldsymbol{X}^\top\boldsymbol{\Omega}^{-1}\boldsymbol{X})^{-1}\boldsymbol{X}^\top\boldsymbol{\Omega}^{-1}\boldsymbol{y}, \tag{9.17}$$

which, except in special cases, is different from $\hat{\boldsymbol{\beta}}_{\mathrm{OLS}}$.

The GLS estimator (9.17) can be interpreted as an IV estimator, in which the instruments are the columns of $\boldsymbol{\Omega}^{-1}\boldsymbol{X}$. Thus it appears that, when $\boldsymbol{\Omega}$ is not a multiple of the identity matrix, the optimal instruments are no longer the explanatory variables $\boldsymbol{X}$, but rather the columns of $\boldsymbol{\Omega}^{-1}\boldsymbol{X}$. This suggests that, when at least some of the explanatory variables in the matrix $\boldsymbol{X}$ are not predetermined, the optimal choice of instruments is given by $\boldsymbol{\Omega}^{-1}\bar{\boldsymbol{X}}$. This choice combines the result of Chapter 7 about the optimality of the GLS estimator with that of Chapter 8 about the best instruments to use in place of explanatory variables that are not predetermined. It leads to the theoretical moment conditions

$$\mathrm{E}\big(\bar{\boldsymbol{X}}^\top\boldsymbol{\Omega}^{-1}(\boldsymbol{y}-\boldsymbol{X}\boldsymbol{\beta})\big) = \boldsymbol{0}. \tag{9.18}$$

Unfortunately, this solution to the optimal instruments problem does not always work, because the moment conditions in (9.18) may not be correct. To see why not, suppose that the error terms are serially correlated, and that $\boldsymbol{\Omega}$ is consequently not a diagonal matrix. The ith element of the matrix product in (9.18) can be expanded as

$$\sum_{t=1}^{n}\sum_{s=1}^{n}\bar{X}_{ti}\,\omega^{ts}(y_s - \boldsymbol{X}_s\boldsymbol{\beta}), \tag{9.19}$$

where ω^{ts} is the ts^{th} element of $\boldsymbol{\Omega}^{-1}$. If we evaluate at the true parameter vector $\boldsymbol{\beta}_0$, we find that $y_s - \boldsymbol{X}_s\boldsymbol{\beta}_0 = u_s$. But, unless the columns of the matrix $\bar{\boldsymbol{X}}$ are exogenous, it is not in general the case that $\mathrm{E}(u_s \,|\, \bar{\boldsymbol{X}}_t) = 0$ for $s \neq t$, and, if this condition is not satisfied, the expectation of (9.19) is not zero in general. This issue was discussed at the end of Section 7.3, and in more detail in Section 7.8, in connection with the use of GLS when one of the explanatory variables is a lagged dependent variable.

Choosing Valid Instruments

As in Section 7.2, we can construct an $n \times n$ matrix $\boldsymbol{\Psi}$, usually triangular, that satisfies the equation $\boldsymbol{\Omega}^{-1} = \boldsymbol{\Psi}\boldsymbol{\Psi}^\top$. As in equation (7.03) of Section 7.2, we can premultiply regression (9.01) by $\boldsymbol{\Psi}^\top$ to get

$$\boldsymbol{\Psi}^\top\boldsymbol{y} = \boldsymbol{\Psi}^\top\boldsymbol{X}\boldsymbol{\beta} + \boldsymbol{\Psi}^\top\boldsymbol{u}, \tag{9.20}$$

with the result that the covariance matrix of the transformed error vector, $\boldsymbol{\Psi}^\top\boldsymbol{u}$, is just the identity matrix. Suppose that we propose to use a matrix $\boldsymbol{Z}$ of instruments in order to estimate the transformed model, so that we are led to consider the theoretical moment conditions

$$\mathrm{E}\big(\boldsymbol{Z}^\top\boldsymbol{\Psi}^\top(\boldsymbol{y}-\boldsymbol{X}\boldsymbol{\beta})\big) = \boldsymbol{0}. \tag{9.21}$$

If these conditions are to be correct, then what we need is that, for each t, $\mathrm{E}\big((\boldsymbol{\Psi}^\top\boldsymbol{u})_t \,|\, \boldsymbol{Z}_t\big) = 0$, where the subscript t is used to select the tth row of the corresponding vector or matrix.

If $\boldsymbol{X}$ is exogenous, the optimal instruments are given by the matrix $\boldsymbol{\Omega}^{-1}\boldsymbol{X}$, and the moment conditions for efficient estimation are $\mathrm{E}\big(\boldsymbol{X}^\top\boldsymbol{\Omega}^{-1}(\boldsymbol{y}-\boldsymbol{X\beta})\big)=\boldsymbol{0}$, which can also be written as

$$\mathrm{E}\big(\boldsymbol{X}^\top\boldsymbol{\Psi}\boldsymbol{\Psi}^\top(\boldsymbol{y}-\boldsymbol{X\beta})\big)=\boldsymbol{0}. \tag{9.22}$$

Comparison with (9.21) shows that the optimal choice of $\boldsymbol{Z}$ is $\boldsymbol{\Psi}^\top\boldsymbol{X}$. Even if $\boldsymbol{X}$ is not exogenous, (9.22) is a correct set of moment conditions if

$$\mathrm{E}\big((\boldsymbol{\Psi}^\top\boldsymbol{u})_t \,|\, (\boldsymbol{\Psi}^\top\boldsymbol{X})_t\big)=0. \tag{9.23}$$

But this is not true in general when $\boldsymbol{X}$ is not exogenous. Consequently, we seek a new definition for $\bar{\boldsymbol{X}}$, such that (9.23) becomes true when $\boldsymbol{X}$ is replaced by $\bar{\boldsymbol{X}}$.

In most cases, it is possible to choose $\boldsymbol{\Psi}$ so that $(\boldsymbol{\Psi}^\top\boldsymbol{u})_t$ is an innovation in the sense of Section 4.5, that is, so that $\mathrm{E}\big((\boldsymbol{\Psi}^\top\boldsymbol{u})_t \,|\, \Omega_t\big)=0$. As an example, see the analysis of models with AR(1) errors in Section 7.8, especially the discussion surrounding (7.58). What is then required for condition (9.23) is that $(\boldsymbol{\Psi}^\top\bar{\boldsymbol{X}})_t$ should be predetermined in period t. If $\boldsymbol{\Omega}$ is diagonal, and so also $\boldsymbol{\Psi}$, the old definition of $\bar{\boldsymbol{X}}$ works, because $(\boldsymbol{\Psi}^\top\bar{\boldsymbol{X}})_t=\Psi_{tt}\bar{\boldsymbol{X}}_t$, where Ψ_{tt} is the tth diagonal element of $\boldsymbol{\Psi}$, and this belongs to Ω_t by construction. If $\boldsymbol{\Omega}$ contains off-diagonal elements, however, the old definition of $\bar{\boldsymbol{X}}$ no longer works in general. Since what we need is that $(\boldsymbol{\Psi}^\top\bar{\boldsymbol{X}})_t$ should belong to Ω_t, we instead define $\bar{\boldsymbol{X}}$ implicitly by the equation

$$\mathrm{E}\big((\boldsymbol{\Psi}^\top\boldsymbol{X})_t \,|\, \Omega_t\big)=(\boldsymbol{\Psi}^\top\bar{\boldsymbol{X}})_t. \tag{9.24}$$

This implicit definition must be implemented on a case-by-case basis. One example is given in Exercise 9.5.

By setting $\boldsymbol{Z}=\boldsymbol{\Psi}^\top\bar{\boldsymbol{X}}$, we find that the moment conditions (9.21) become

$$\mathrm{E}\big(\bar{\boldsymbol{X}}^\top\boldsymbol{\Psi}\boldsymbol{\Psi}^\top(\boldsymbol{y}-\boldsymbol{X\beta})\big)=\mathrm{E}\big(\bar{\boldsymbol{X}}^\top\boldsymbol{\Omega}^{-1}(\boldsymbol{y}-\boldsymbol{X\beta})\big)=\boldsymbol{0}. \tag{9.25}$$

These conditions do indeed use $\boldsymbol{\Omega}^{-1}\bar{\boldsymbol{X}}$ as instruments, albeit with a possibly redefined $\bar{\boldsymbol{X}}$. The estimator based on (9.25) is

$$\hat{\beta}_{\text{EGMM}}\equiv(\bar{\boldsymbol{X}}^\top\boldsymbol{\Omega}^{-1}\bar{\boldsymbol{X}})^{-1}\bar{\boldsymbol{X}}^\top\boldsymbol{\Omega}^{-1}\boldsymbol{y}, \tag{9.26}$$

where EGMM denotes "efficient GMM." The asymptotic covariance matrix of (9.26) can be computed using (9.09), in which, on the basis of (9.25), we see that $\boldsymbol{W}$ is to be replaced by $\boldsymbol{\Psi}^\top\bar{\boldsymbol{X}}$, $\boldsymbol{X}$ by $\boldsymbol{\Psi}^\top\boldsymbol{X}$, and $\boldsymbol{\Omega}$ by $\mathbf{I}$. We cannot apply (9.09) directly with instruments $\boldsymbol{\Omega}^{-1}\bar{\boldsymbol{X}}$, because there is no reason to suppose that the result (9.02) holds for the untransformed error terms $\boldsymbol{u}$ and the instruments $\boldsymbol{\Omega}^{-1}\bar{\boldsymbol{X}}$. The result is

$$\operatorname*{plim}_{n\to\infty}\left(\frac{1}{n}\boldsymbol{X}^\top\boldsymbol{\Omega}^{-1}\bar{\boldsymbol{X}}\left(\frac{1}{n}\bar{\boldsymbol{X}}^\top\boldsymbol{\Omega}^{-1}\bar{\boldsymbol{X}}\right)^{-1}\frac{1}{n}\bar{\boldsymbol{X}}^\top\boldsymbol{\Omega}^{-1}\boldsymbol{X}\right)^{-1}. \tag{9.27}$$

By exactly the same argument as that used in (8.20), we find that, for any matrix $\boldsymbol{Z}$ that satisfies $\boldsymbol{Z}_t \in \Omega_t$,

$$\operatorname*{plim}_{n\to\infty} \frac{1}{n} \boldsymbol{Z}^\top \boldsymbol{\Psi}^\top \boldsymbol{X} = \operatorname*{plim}_{n\to\infty} \frac{1}{n} \boldsymbol{Z}^\top \boldsymbol{\Psi}^\top \bar{\boldsymbol{X}}. \tag{9.28}$$

Since $(\boldsymbol{\Psi}^\top \boldsymbol{X})_t \in \Omega_t$, this implies that

$$\begin{aligned} \operatorname*{plim}_{n\to\infty} \frac{1}{n} \bar{\boldsymbol{X}}^\top \boldsymbol{\Omega}^{-1} \boldsymbol{X} &= \operatorname*{plim}_{n\to\infty} \frac{1}{n} \bar{\boldsymbol{X}}^\top \boldsymbol{\Psi}\boldsymbol{\Psi}^\top \boldsymbol{X} \\ &= \operatorname*{plim}_{n\to\infty} \frac{1}{n} \bar{\boldsymbol{X}}^\top \boldsymbol{\Psi}\boldsymbol{\Psi}^\top \bar{\boldsymbol{X}} = \operatorname*{plim}_{n\to\infty} \frac{1}{n} \bar{\boldsymbol{X}}^\top \boldsymbol{\Omega}^{-1} \bar{\boldsymbol{X}}. \end{aligned}$$

Therefore, the asymptotic covariance matrix (9.27) simplifies to

$$\operatorname*{plim}_{n\to\infty} \Big(\frac{1}{n} \bar{\boldsymbol{X}}^\top \boldsymbol{\Omega}^{-1} \bar{\boldsymbol{X}}\Big)^{-1}. \tag{9.29}$$

Although the matrix (9.09) is less of a sandwich than (9.07), the matrix (9.29) is still less of one than (9.09). This is a clear indication of the fact that the instruments $\boldsymbol{\Omega}^{-1}\bar{\boldsymbol{X}}$, which yield the estimator $\hat{\boldsymbol{\beta}}_{\mathrm{EGMM}}$, are indeed optimal. Readers are asked to check this formally in Exercise 9.7.

In most cases, $\bar{\boldsymbol{X}}$ is not observed, but it can often be estimated consistently. The usual state of affairs is that we have an $n \times l$ matrix $\boldsymbol{W}$ of instruments, such that $\mathcal{S}(\bar{\boldsymbol{X}}) \subseteq \mathcal{S}(\boldsymbol{W})$ and

$$(\boldsymbol{\Psi}^\top \boldsymbol{W})_t \in \Omega_t. \tag{9.30}$$

This last condition is the form taken by the **predeterminedness condition** when $\boldsymbol{\Omega}$ is not proportional to the identity matrix. The theoretical moment conditions used for (overidentified) estimation are then

$$\mathrm{E}\big(\boldsymbol{W}^\top \boldsymbol{\Omega}^{-1}(\boldsymbol{y} - \boldsymbol{X\beta})\big) = \mathrm{E}\big(\boldsymbol{W}^\top \boldsymbol{\Psi}\boldsymbol{\Psi}^\top(\boldsymbol{y} - \boldsymbol{X\beta})\big) = \mathbf{0}, \tag{9.31}$$

from which it can be seen that what we are in fact doing is estimating the transformed model (9.20) using the transformed instruments $\boldsymbol{\Psi}^\top \boldsymbol{W}$. The result of Exercise 9.8 shows that, if indeed $\mathcal{S}(\bar{\boldsymbol{X}}) \subseteq \mathcal{S}(\boldsymbol{W})$, the asymptotic covariance matrix of the resulting estimator is still (9.29). Exercise 9.9 investigates what happens if this condition is not satisfied.

The main obstacle to the use of the efficient estimator $\hat{\boldsymbol{\beta}}_{\mathrm{EGMM}}$ is thus not the difficulty of estimating $\bar{\boldsymbol{X}}$, but rather the fact that $\boldsymbol{\Omega}$ is usually not known. As with the GLS estimators we studied in Chapter 7, $\hat{\boldsymbol{\beta}}_{\mathrm{EGMM}}$ cannot be calculated unless we either know $\boldsymbol{\Omega}$ or can estimate it consistently, usually by knowing the form of $\boldsymbol{\Omega}$ as a function of parameters that can be estimated consistently. But whenever there is heteroskedasticity or serial correlation of unknown form, this is impossible. The best we can then do, asymptotically, is to use the feasible efficient GMM estimator (9.15). Therefore, when we later refer to GMM estimators without further qualification, we will normally mean feasible efficient ones.

9.3 HAC Covariance Matrix Estimation

Up to this point, we have seen how to obtain feasible efficient GMM estimates only when the matrix $\boldsymbol{\Omega}$ is known to be diagonal, in which case we can use the estimator (9.15). In this section, we also allow for the possibility of serial correlation of unknown form, which causes $\boldsymbol{\Omega}$ to have nonzero off-diagonal elements. When the pattern of the serial correlation is unknown, we can still, under fairly weak regularity conditions, estimate the covariance matrix of the sample moments by using a **heteroskedasticity and autocorrelation consistent**, or **HAC**, estimator of the matrix $n^{-1}\boldsymbol{W}^\top\boldsymbol{\Omega}\boldsymbol{W}$. This estimator, multiplied by n, can then be used in place of $\boldsymbol{W}^\top\hat{\boldsymbol{\Omega}}\boldsymbol{W}$ in the feasible efficient GMM estimator (9.15).

The asymptotic covariance matrix of the vector $n^{-1/2}\boldsymbol{W}^\top(\boldsymbol{y}-\boldsymbol{X}\boldsymbol{\beta})$ of sample moments, evaluated at $\boldsymbol{\beta}=\boldsymbol{\beta}_0$, is defined as follows:

$$\boldsymbol{\Sigma} \equiv \operatorname*{plim}_{n\to\infty} \frac{1}{n}\boldsymbol{W}^\top(\boldsymbol{y}-\boldsymbol{X}\boldsymbol{\beta}_0)(\boldsymbol{y}-\boldsymbol{X}\boldsymbol{\beta}_0)^\top\boldsymbol{W} = \operatorname*{plim}_{n\to\infty}\frac{1}{n}\boldsymbol{W}^\top\boldsymbol{\Omega}\boldsymbol{W}. \tag{9.32}$$

A HAC estimator of $\boldsymbol{\Sigma}$ is a matrix $\hat{\boldsymbol{\Sigma}}$ constructed so that $\hat{\boldsymbol{\Sigma}}$ consistently estimates $\boldsymbol{\Sigma}$ when the error terms u_t display any pattern of heteroskedasticity and/or autocorrelation that satisfies certain, generally quite weak, conditions. In order to derive such an estimator, we begin by rewriting the definition of $\boldsymbol{\Sigma}$ in an alternative way:

$$\boldsymbol{\Sigma} = \lim_{n\to\infty}\frac{1}{n}\sum_{t=1}^{n}\sum_{s=1}^{n}\mathrm{E}\big(u_t u_s \boldsymbol{W}_t^{\top}\boldsymbol{W}_s\big), \tag{9.33}$$

in which we assume that a law of large numbers can be used to justify replacing the probability limit in (9.32) by the expectations in (9.33).

For regression models with heteroskedasticity but no autocorrelation, only the terms with $t=s$ contribute to (9.33). Therefore, for such models, we can estimate $\boldsymbol{\Sigma}$ consistently by simply ignoring the expectation operator and replacing the error terms u_t by least-squares residuals $\hat{u}_t$, possibly with a modification designed to offset the tendency for such residuals to be too small. The obvious way to estimate (9.33) when there may be serial correlation is again simply to drop the expectations operator and replace $u_t u_s$ by $\hat{u}_t\hat{u}_s$, where $\hat{u}_t$ denotes the tth residual from some consistent but inefficient estimation procedure, such as generalized IV. Unfortunately, this approach does not work. To see why not, we need to rewrite (9.33) in yet another way. Let us define the **autocovariance matrices** of the $\boldsymbol{W}_t^{\top}u_t$ as follows:

$$\boldsymbol{\Gamma}(j) \equiv \begin{cases} \dfrac{1}{n}\displaystyle\sum_{t=j+1}^{n}\mathrm{E}(u_t u_{t-j}\boldsymbol{W}_t^{\top}\boldsymbol{W}_{t-j}) & \text{for } j \ge 0, \\[2ex] \dfrac{1}{n}\displaystyle\sum_{t=-j+1}^{n}\mathrm{E}(u_{t+j}u_t\boldsymbol{W}_{t+j}^{\top}\boldsymbol{W}_t) & \text{for } j < 0. \end{cases} \tag{9.34}$$

Because there are l moment conditions, these are $l \times l$ matrices. It is easy to check that $\boldsymbol{\Gamma}(j) = \boldsymbol{\Gamma}^\top(-j)$. Then, in terms of the matrices $\boldsymbol{\Gamma}(j)$, expression (9.33) becomes

$$\boldsymbol{\Sigma} = \lim_{n\to\infty} \sum_{j=-n+1}^{n-1} \boldsymbol{\Gamma}(j) = \lim_{n\to\infty} \Big(\boldsymbol{\Gamma}(0) + \sum_{j=1}^{n-1} \big(\boldsymbol{\Gamma}(j) + \boldsymbol{\Gamma}^\top(j)\big)\Big). \tag{9.35}$$

Therefore, in order to estimate $\boldsymbol{\Sigma}$, we apparently need to estimate all of the autocovariance matrices for $j = 0, \ldots, n-1$.

If $\hat{u}_t$ denotes a typical residual from some preliminary estimator, the **sample autocovariance matrix** of order j, $\hat{\boldsymbol{\Gamma}}(j)$, is just the appropriate expression in (9.34), without the expectation operator, and with the random variables u_t and u_{t-j} replaced by $\hat{u}_t$ and $\hat{u}_{t-j}$, respectively. For any $j \geq 0$, this is

$$\hat{\boldsymbol{\Gamma}}(j) = \frac{1}{n} \sum_{t=j+1}^{n} \hat{u}_t \hat{u}_{t-j} \boldsymbol{W}_t^{\top} \boldsymbol{W}_{t-j}. \tag{9.36}$$

Unfortunately, the sample autocovariance matrix $\hat{\boldsymbol{\Gamma}}(j)$ of order j is not a consistent estimator of the true autocovariance matrix for arbitrary j. Suppose, for instance, that $j = n-2$. Then, from (9.36), we see that $\hat{\boldsymbol{\Gamma}}(j)$ has only two terms, and no conceivable law of large numbers can apply to only two terms. In fact, $\hat{\boldsymbol{\Gamma}}(n-2)$ must tend to zero as $n \to \infty$ because of the factor of n^{-1} in its definition.

The solution to this problem is to restrict our attention to models for which the actual autocovariances mimic the behavior of the sample autocovariances, and for which therefore the actual autocovariance of order j tends to zero as $j \to \infty$. A great many stochastic processes generate error terms for which the $\boldsymbol{\Gamma}(j)$ do have this property. In such cases, we can drop most of the sample autocovariance matrices that appear in the sample analog of (9.35) by eliminating ones for which $|j|$ is greater than some chosen threshold, say p. This yields the following estimator for $\boldsymbol{\Sigma}$:

$$\hat{\boldsymbol{\Sigma}}_{\text{HW}} = \hat{\boldsymbol{\Gamma}}(0) + \sum_{j=1}^{p} \big(\hat{\boldsymbol{\Gamma}}(j) + \hat{\boldsymbol{\Gamma}}^\top(j)\big), \tag{9.37}$$

We refer to this estimator as the **Hansen-White estimator**, because it was originally proposed by Hansen (1982) and White and Domowitz (1984); see also White (2000).

For the purposes of asymptotic theory, it is necessary to let the parameter p, which is called the **lag truncation parameter**, go to infinity in (9.37) at some suitable rate as the sample size goes to infinity. A typical rate would be $n^{1/4}$. This ensures that, for large enough n, all the nonzero $\boldsymbol{\Gamma}(j)$ are estimated consistently. Unfortunately, this type of result does not say how large p should be in practice. In most cases, we have a given, finite, sample size, and we need to choose a specific value of p.

The Hansen-White estimator (9.37) suffers from one very serious deficiency: In finite samples, it need not be positive definite or even positive semidefinite. If one happens to encounter a data set that yields a nondefinite $\hat{\boldsymbol{\Sigma}}_{\rm HW}$, then, since the weighting matrix for GMM must be positive definite, (9.37) is unusable. Luckily, there are numerous ways out of this difficulty. The one that is most widely used was suggested by Newey and West (1987). The **Newey-West estimator** they propose is

$$\hat{\boldsymbol{\Sigma}}_{\rm NW} = \hat{\boldsymbol{\Gamma}}(0) + \sum_{j=1}^{p}\left(1 - \frac{j}{p+1}\right)\left(\hat{\boldsymbol{\Gamma}}(j) + \hat{\boldsymbol{\Gamma}}^{\top}(j)\right), \tag{9.38}$$

in which each sample autocovariance matrix $\hat{\boldsymbol{\Gamma}}(j)$ is multiplied by a weight $1 - j/(p+1)$ that decreases linearly as j increases. The weight is $p/(p+1)$ for $j = 1$, and it then decreases by steps of $1/(p+1)$ down to a value of $1/(p+1)$ for $j = p$. This estimator evidently tends to underestimate the autocovariance matrices, especially for larger values of j. Therefore, p should almost certainly be larger for (9.38) than for (9.37). As with the Hansen-White estimator, p must increase as n does, and the appropriate rate is $n^{1/3}$. A procedure for selecting p automatically was proposed by Newey and West (1994), but it is too complicated to discuss here.

Both the Hansen-White and the Newey-West HAC estimators of $\boldsymbol{\Sigma}$ can be written in the form

$$\hat{\boldsymbol{\Sigma}} = \frac{1}{n}\boldsymbol{W}^{\top}\hat{\boldsymbol{\Omega}}\boldsymbol{W} \tag{9.39}$$

for an appropriate choice of $\hat{\boldsymbol{\Omega}}$. This fact, which we will exploit in the next section, follows from the observation that there exist $n \times n$ matrices $\boldsymbol{U}(j)$ such that the $\hat{\boldsymbol{\Gamma}}(j)$ can be expressed in the form $n^{-1}\boldsymbol{W}^{\top}\boldsymbol{U}(j)\boldsymbol{W}$, as readers are asked to check in Exercise 9.10.

The Newey-West estimator is by no means the only HAC estimator that is guaranteed to be positive definite. Andrews (1991) provides a detailed treatment of HAC estimation, suggests some alternatives to the Newey-West estimator, and shows that, in some circumstances, they may perform better than it does in finite samples. A different approach to HAC estimation is suggested by Andrews and Monahan (1992). Since this material is relatively advanced and specialized, we will not pursue it further here. Interested readers may wish to consult Hamilton (1994, Chapter 10) as well as the references already given.

Feasible Efficient GMM Estimation

In practice, efficient GMM estimation in the presence of heteroskedasticity and serial correlation of unknown form works as follows. As in the case with only heteroskedasticity that was discussed in Section 9.2, we first obtain consistent but inefficient estimates, probably by using generalized IV. These estimates yield residuals $\hat{u}_t$, from which we next calculate a matrix $\hat{\boldsymbol{\Sigma}}$ that estimates $\boldsymbol{\Sigma}$ consistently, using (9.37), (9.38), or some other HAC estimator. The feasible efficient GMM estimator, which generalizes (9.15), is then

$$\hat{\beta}_{\text{FGMM}} = (\boldsymbol{X}^\top \boldsymbol{W} \hat{\boldsymbol{\Sigma}}^{-1} \boldsymbol{W}^\top \boldsymbol{X})^{-1} \boldsymbol{X}^\top \boldsymbol{W} \hat{\boldsymbol{\Sigma}}^{-1} \boldsymbol{W}^\top \boldsymbol{y}. \tag{9.40}$$

As before, this procedure may be iterated. The first-round GMM residuals may be used to obtain a new estimate of $\boldsymbol{\Sigma}$, which may be used to obtain second-round GMM estimates, and so on. For a correctly specified model, iteration should not affect the asymptotic properties of the estimates.

We can estimate the covariance matrix of (9.40) by

$$\widehat{\text{Var}}(\hat{\boldsymbol{\beta}}_{\text{FGMM}}) = n(\boldsymbol{X}^\top \boldsymbol{W} \hat{\boldsymbol{\Sigma}}^{-1} \boldsymbol{W}^\top \boldsymbol{X})^{-1}, \tag{9.41}$$

which is the analog of (9.16). The factor of n here is needed to offset the factor of n^{-1} in the definition of $\hat{\boldsymbol{\Sigma}}$. We do not need to include such a factor in (9.40), because the two factors of n^{-1} cancel out. As usual, the covariance matrix estimator (9.41) can be used to construct pseudo-t tests and other Wald tests, and asymptotic confidence intervals and confidence regions may also be based on it. The GMM criterion function that corresponds to (9.40) is

$$\frac{1}{n}(\boldsymbol{y} - \boldsymbol{X\beta})^\top \boldsymbol{W} \hat{\boldsymbol{\Sigma}}^{-1} \boldsymbol{W}^\top (\boldsymbol{y} - \boldsymbol{X\beta}). \tag{9.42}$$

Once again, we need a factor of n^{-1} here to offset the one in $\hat{\boldsymbol{\Sigma}}$.

The feasible efficient GMM estimator (9.40) can be used even when all the columns of $\boldsymbol{X}$ are valid instruments and OLS would be the estimator of choice if the error terms were not heteroskedastic and/or serially correlated. In this case, $\boldsymbol{W}$ typically consists of $\boldsymbol{X}$ augmented by a number of functions of the columns of $\boldsymbol{X}$, such as squares and cross-products, and $\hat{\boldsymbol{\Omega}}$ has squared OLS residuals on the diagonal. This estimator, which was proposed by Cragg (1983) for models with heteroskedastic error terms, is asymptotically more efficient than OLS whenever $\boldsymbol{\Omega}$ is not proportional to an identity matrix.

9.4 Tests Based on the GMM Criterion Function

For models estimated by instrumental variables, we saw in Section 8.5 that any set of r equality restrictions can be tested by taking the difference between the minimized values of the IV criterion function for the restricted and unrestricted models, and then dividing it by a consistent estimate of the error variance. The resulting test statistic is asymptotically distributed as $\chi^2(r)$. For models estimated by (feasible) efficient GMM, a very similar testing procedure is available. In this case, as we will see, the difference between the constrained and unconstrained minima of the GMM criterion function is asymptotically distributed as $\chi^2(r)$. There is no need to divide by an estimate of σ^2, because the GMM criterion function already takes account of the covariance matrix of the error terms.

Tests of Overidentifying Restrictions

Whenever $l > k$, a model estimated by GMM involves $l - k$ overidentifying restrictions. As in the IV case, tests of these restrictions are even easier to perform than tests of other restrictions, because the minimized value of the optimal GMM criterion function (9.11), with $n^{-1}\boldsymbol{W}^\top\boldsymbol{\Omega}_0\boldsymbol{W}$ replaced by a HAC estimate, provides an asymptotically valid test statistic. When the HAC estimate $\hat{\boldsymbol{\Sigma}}$ is expressed as in (9.39), the GMM criterion function (9.42) can be written as

$$Q(\boldsymbol{\beta}, \boldsymbol{y}) \equiv (\boldsymbol{y} - \boldsymbol{X}\boldsymbol{\beta})^\top\boldsymbol{W}(\boldsymbol{W}^\top\hat{\boldsymbol{\Omega}}\boldsymbol{W})^{-1}\boldsymbol{W}^\top(\boldsymbol{y} - \boldsymbol{X}\boldsymbol{\beta}). \tag{9.43}$$

Since HAC estimators are consistent, the asymptotic distribution of (9.43), for given $\boldsymbol{\beta}$, is the same whether we use the unknown true $\boldsymbol{\Omega}_0$ or a matrix $\hat{\boldsymbol{\Omega}}$ that provides a HAC estimate. For simplicity, we therefore use the true $\boldsymbol{\Omega}_0$, omitting the subscript 0 for ease of notation. The asymptotic equivalence of the $\hat{\boldsymbol{\beta}}_{\text{FGMM}}$ of (9.15) or (9.40) and the $\hat{\boldsymbol{\beta}}_{\text{GMM}}$ of (9.10) further implies that what we will prove for the criterion function (9.43) evaluated at $\hat{\boldsymbol{\beta}}_{\text{GMM}}$, with $\hat{\boldsymbol{\Omega}}$ replaced by $\boldsymbol{\Omega}$, is equally true for (9.43) evaluated at $\hat{\boldsymbol{\beta}}_{\text{FGMM}}$.

We remarked in Section 9.2 that $Q(\boldsymbol{\beta}_0, \boldsymbol{y})$, where $\boldsymbol{\beta}_0$ is the true parameter vector, is asymptotically distributed as $\chi^2(l)$. In contrast, the minimized criterion function $Q(\hat{\boldsymbol{\beta}}_{\text{GMM}}, \boldsymbol{y})$ is distributed as $\chi^2(l - k)$, because we lose k degrees of freedom as a consequence of having estimated k parameters. In order to demonstrate this result, we first express (9.43) in terms of an orthogonal projection matrix. This allows us to reuse many of the calculations performed in Chapter 8.

As in Section 9.2, we make use of a possibly triangular matrix $\boldsymbol{\Psi}$ that satisfies the equation $\boldsymbol{\Omega}^{-1} = \boldsymbol{\Psi}\boldsymbol{\Psi}^\top$, or, equivalently,

$$\boldsymbol{\Omega} = (\boldsymbol{\Psi}^\top)^{-1}\boldsymbol{\Psi}^{-1}. \tag{9.44}$$

If the $n \times l$ matrix $\boldsymbol{A}$ is defined as $\boldsymbol{\Psi}^{-1}\boldsymbol{W}$, and $\boldsymbol{P_A} \equiv \boldsymbol{A}(\boldsymbol{A}^\top\boldsymbol{A})^{-1}\boldsymbol{A}^\top$, then

$$\begin{aligned} Q(\boldsymbol{\beta}, \boldsymbol{y}) &= (\boldsymbol{y} - \boldsymbol{X}\boldsymbol{\beta})^\top\boldsymbol{\Psi}\boldsymbol{\Psi}^{-1}\boldsymbol{W}\big(\boldsymbol{W}^\top(\boldsymbol{\Psi}^\top)^{-1}\boldsymbol{\Psi}^{-1}\boldsymbol{W}\big)^{-1}\boldsymbol{W}^\top(\boldsymbol{\Psi}^\top)^{-1}\boldsymbol{\Psi}^\top(\boldsymbol{y} - \boldsymbol{X}\boldsymbol{\beta}) \\ &= (\boldsymbol{y} - \boldsymbol{X}\boldsymbol{\beta})^\top\boldsymbol{\Psi}\boldsymbol{P_A}\boldsymbol{\Psi}^\top(\boldsymbol{y} - \boldsymbol{X}\boldsymbol{\beta}). \end{aligned} \tag{9.45}$$

Since $\hat{\boldsymbol{\beta}}_{\text{GMM}}$ minimizes (9.45), we see that one way to write it is

$$\hat{\boldsymbol{\beta}}_{\text{GMM}} = (\boldsymbol{X}^\top\boldsymbol{\Psi}\boldsymbol{P_A}\boldsymbol{\Psi}^\top\boldsymbol{X})^{-1}\boldsymbol{X}^\top\boldsymbol{\Psi}\boldsymbol{P_A}\boldsymbol{\Psi}^\top\boldsymbol{y}; \tag{9.46}$$

compare (9.10). Expression (9.46) makes it clear that $\hat{\beta}_{\text{GMM}}$ can be thought of as a GIV estimator for the regression of $\boldsymbol{\Psi}^\top \boldsymbol{y}$ on $\boldsymbol{\Psi}^\top \boldsymbol{X}$ using instruments $\boldsymbol{A} \equiv \boldsymbol{\Psi}^{-1}\boldsymbol{W}$. As in (8.61), it can be shown that

$$\boldsymbol{P_A \Psi}^\top(\boldsymbol{y} - \boldsymbol{X}\hat{\beta}_{\text{GMM}}) = \boldsymbol{P_A}(\mathbf{I} - \boldsymbol{P}_{\boldsymbol{P_A\Psi}^\top\boldsymbol{X}})\boldsymbol{\Psi}^\top\boldsymbol{y},$$

where $\boldsymbol{P}_{\boldsymbol{P_A\Psi}^\top\boldsymbol{X}}$ is the orthogonal projection on to the subspace $\mathcal{S}(\boldsymbol{P_A\Psi}^\top\boldsymbol{X})$. It follows that

$$Q(\hat{\beta}_{\text{GMM}}, \boldsymbol{y}) = \boldsymbol{y}^\top\boldsymbol{\Psi}(\boldsymbol{P_A} - \boldsymbol{P}_{\boldsymbol{P_A\Psi}^\top\boldsymbol{X}})\boldsymbol{\Psi}^\top\boldsymbol{y}, \tag{9.47}$$

which is the analog for GMM estimation of expression (8.61) for generalized IV estimation.

Now notice that

$$\begin{aligned}
&(\boldsymbol{P_A} - \boldsymbol{P}_{\boldsymbol{P_A\Psi}^\top\boldsymbol{X}})\boldsymbol{\Psi}^\top\boldsymbol{X} \\
&\quad = \boldsymbol{P_A\Psi}^\top\boldsymbol{X} - \boldsymbol{P_A\Psi}^\top\boldsymbol{X}(\boldsymbol{X}^\top\boldsymbol{\Psi P_A\Psi}^\top\boldsymbol{X})^{-1}\boldsymbol{X}^\top\boldsymbol{\Psi P_A \Psi}^\top\boldsymbol{X} \\
&\quad = \boldsymbol{P_A\Psi}^\top\boldsymbol{X} - \boldsymbol{P_A\Psi}^\top\boldsymbol{X} = \mathbf{O}.
\end{aligned}$$

Since $\boldsymbol{y} = \boldsymbol{X}\beta_0 + \boldsymbol{u}$ if the model we are estimating is correctly specified, this implies that (9.47) is equal to

$$Q(\hat{\beta}_{\text{GMM}}, \boldsymbol{y}) = \boldsymbol{u}^\top\boldsymbol{\Psi}(\boldsymbol{P_A} - \boldsymbol{P}_{\boldsymbol{P_A\Psi}^\top\boldsymbol{X}})\boldsymbol{\Psi}^\top\boldsymbol{u}. \tag{9.48}$$

This expression can be compared with the value of the criterion function evaluated at β_0, which can be obtained directly from (9.45):

$$Q(\beta_0, \boldsymbol{y}) = \boldsymbol{u}^\top\boldsymbol{\Psi P_A \Psi}^\top\boldsymbol{u}. \tag{9.49}$$

The two expressions (9.48) and (9.49) show clearly where the k degrees of freedom are lost when we estimate β. We know that $\text{E}(\boldsymbol{\Psi}^\top\boldsymbol{u}) = \mathbf{0}$ and that $\text{E}(\boldsymbol{\Psi}^\top\boldsymbol{uu}^\top\boldsymbol{\Psi}) = \boldsymbol{\Psi}^\top\boldsymbol{\Omega\Psi} = \mathbf{I}$, by (9.44). The dimension of the space $\mathcal{S}(\boldsymbol{A})$ is equal to l. Therefore, the extension of Theorem 4.1 treated in Exercise 9.2 allows us to conclude that (9.49) is asymptotically distributed as $\chi^2(l)$. Since $\mathcal{S}(\boldsymbol{P_A\Psi}^\top\boldsymbol{X})$ is a k-dimensional subspace of $\mathcal{S}(\boldsymbol{A})$, it follows (see Exercise 2.18) that $\boldsymbol{P_A} - \boldsymbol{P}_{\boldsymbol{P_A\Psi}^\top\boldsymbol{X}}$ is an orthogonal projection on to a space of dimension $l-k$, from which we see that (9.48) is asymptotically distributed as $\chi^2(l-k)$. Replacing β_0 by $\hat{\beta}_{\text{GMM}}$ in (9.48) thus leads to the loss of the k dimensions of the space $\mathcal{S}(\boldsymbol{P_A\Psi}^\top\boldsymbol{X})$, which are "used up" when we obtain $\hat{\beta}_{\text{GMM}}$.

The statistic $Q(\hat{\beta}_{\text{GMM}}, \boldsymbol{y})$ is the analog, for efficient GMM estimation, of the Sargan test statistic that was discussed in Section 8.6. This statistic was suggested by Hansen (1982) in the famous paper that first proposed GMM estimation under that name. It is often called **Hansen's overidentification statistic** or **Hansen's J statistic**. However, we prefer to call it the **Hansen-Sargan**

statistic to stress its close relationship with the Sargan test of overidentifying restrictions in the context of generalized IV estimation.

As in the case of IV estimation, a Hansen-Sargan test may reject the null hypothesis for more than one reason. Perhaps the model is misspecified, either because one or more of the instruments should have been included among the regressors, or for some other reason. Perhaps one or more of the instruments is invalid because it is correlated with the error terms. Or perhaps the finite-sample distribution of the test statistic just happens to differ substantially from its asymptotic distribution. In the case of feasible GMM estimation, especially involving HAC covariance matrices, this last possibility should not be discounted. See, among others, Hansen, Heaton, and Yaron (1996) and West and Wilcox (1996).

Tests of Linear Restrictions

Just as in the case of generalized IV, both linear and nonlinear restrictions on regression models can be tested by using the difference between the constrained and unconstrained minima of the GMM criterion function as a test statistic. Under weak conditions, this test statistic is asymptotically distributed as χ^2 with as many degrees of freedom as there are restrictions to be tested. For simplicity, we restrict our attention to zero restrictions on the linear regression model (9.01). This model can be rewritten as

$$\boldsymbol{y} = \boldsymbol{X}_1\boldsymbol{\beta}_1 + \boldsymbol{X}_2\boldsymbol{\beta}_2 + \boldsymbol{u}, \quad \mathrm{E}(\boldsymbol{u}\boldsymbol{u}^\top) = \boldsymbol{\Omega}, \tag{9.50}$$

where $\boldsymbol{\beta}_1$ is a k_1-vector and $\boldsymbol{\beta}_2$ is a k_2-vector, with $k = k_1 + k_2$. We wish to test the restrictions $\boldsymbol{\beta}_2 = \boldsymbol{0}$.

If we estimate (9.50) by feasible efficient GMM using $\boldsymbol{W}$ as the matrix of instruments, subject to the restriction that $\boldsymbol{\beta}_2 = \boldsymbol{0}$, we obtain the restricted estimates $\tilde{\boldsymbol{\beta}}_{\mathrm{FGMM}} = [\tilde{\boldsymbol{\beta}}_1 \vdots \boldsymbol{0}]$. By the reasoning that leads to (9.48), we see that, if indeed $\boldsymbol{\beta}_2 = \boldsymbol{0}$, the constrained minimum of the criterion function is

$$\begin{aligned} Q(\tilde{\boldsymbol{\beta}}_{\mathrm{FGMM}}, \boldsymbol{y}) &= (\boldsymbol{y} - \boldsymbol{X}_1\tilde{\boldsymbol{\beta}}_1)^\top \boldsymbol{W}(\boldsymbol{W}^\top\hat{\boldsymbol{\Omega}}\boldsymbol{W})^{-1}\boldsymbol{W}^\top(\boldsymbol{y} - \boldsymbol{X}_1\tilde{\boldsymbol{\beta}}_1) \\ &= \boldsymbol{u}^\top\boldsymbol{\Psi}(\boldsymbol{P_A} - \boldsymbol{P}_{\boldsymbol{P_A}\boldsymbol{\Psi}^\top\boldsymbol{X}_1})\boldsymbol{\Psi}^\top\boldsymbol{u}. \end{aligned} \tag{9.51}$$

If we subtract (9.48) from (9.51), we find that the difference between the constrained and unconstrained minima of the criterion function is

$$Q(\tilde{\boldsymbol{\beta}}_{\mathrm{FGMM}}, \boldsymbol{y}) - Q(\hat{\boldsymbol{\beta}}_{\mathrm{FGMM}}, \boldsymbol{y}) = \boldsymbol{u}^\top\boldsymbol{\Psi}(\boldsymbol{P}_{\boldsymbol{P_A}\boldsymbol{\Psi}^\top\boldsymbol{X}} - \boldsymbol{P}_{\boldsymbol{P_A}\boldsymbol{\Psi}^\top\boldsymbol{X}_1})\boldsymbol{\Psi}^\top\boldsymbol{u}. \tag{9.52}$$

Since $\mathcal{S}(\boldsymbol{P_A}\boldsymbol{\Psi}^\top\boldsymbol{X}_1) \subseteq \mathcal{S}(\boldsymbol{P_A}\boldsymbol{\Psi}^\top\boldsymbol{X})$, we see that $\boldsymbol{P}_{\boldsymbol{P_A}\boldsymbol{\Psi}^\top\boldsymbol{X}} - \boldsymbol{P}_{\boldsymbol{P_A}\boldsymbol{\Psi}^\top\boldsymbol{X}_1}$ is an orthogonal projection matrix of which the image is of dimension $k - k_1 = k_2$. Once again, the result of Exercise 9.2 shows that the test statistic (9.52) is asymptotically distributed as $\chi^2(k_2)$ if the null hypothesis that $\boldsymbol{\beta}_2 = \boldsymbol{0}$ is true. This result continues to hold if the restrictions are nonlinear, as we will see in Section 9.5.

The result that the statistic $Q(\tilde{\beta}_{\text{FGMM}}, \boldsymbol{y}) - Q(\hat{\beta}_{\text{FGMM}}, \boldsymbol{y})$ is asymptotically distributed as $\chi^2(k_2)$ depends on two critical features of the construction of the statistic. The first is that the same matrix of instruments $\boldsymbol{W}$ is used for estimating both the restricted and unrestricted models. This was also required in Section 8.5, when we discussed testing restrictions on linear regression models estimated by generalized IV. The second essential feature is that the same weighting matrix $(\boldsymbol{W}^\top \hat{\boldsymbol{\Omega}} \boldsymbol{W})^{-1}$ is used when estimating both models. If, as is usually the case, this matrix has to be estimated, it is important that the *same* estimate be used in both criterion functions. If different instruments or different weighting matrices are used for the two models, (9.52) is no longer in general asymptotically distributed as $\chi^2(k_2)$.

One interesting consequence of the form of (9.52) is that we do not always need to bother estimating the unrestricted model. The test statistic (9.52) must always be less than the constrained minimum $Q(\tilde{\beta}_{\text{FGMM}}, \boldsymbol{y})$. Therefore, if $Q(\tilde{\beta}_{\text{FGMM}}, \boldsymbol{y})$ is less than the critical value for the $\chi^2(k_2)$ distribution at our chosen significance level, we can be sure that the actual test statistic is even smaller and would not lead us to reject the null.

The result that tests of restrictions may be based on the difference between the constrained and unconstrained minima of the GMM criterion function holds only for efficient GMM estimation. It is not true for nonoptimal criterion functions like (9.12), which do not use an estimate of the inverse of the covariance matrix of the sample moments as a weighting matrix. When the GMM estimates minimize a nonoptimal criterion function, the easiest way to test restrictions is probably to use a Wald test; see Sections 6.7 and 8.5. However, we do not recommend performing inference on the basis of nonoptimal GMM estimation.

9.5 GMM Estimators for Nonlinear Models

The principles underlying GMM estimation of nonlinear models are the same as those we have developed for GMM estimation of linear regression models. For every result that we have discussed in the previous three sections, there is an analogous result for nonlinear models. In order to develop these results, we will take a somewhat more general and abstract approach than we have done up to this point. This approach, which is based on the theory of **estimating functions**, was originally developed by Godambe (1960); see also Godambe and Thompson (1978).

The method of estimating functions employs the concept of an **elementary zero function**. Such a function plays the same role as a residual in the estimation of a regression model. It depends on observed variables, at least one of which must be endogenous, and on a k-vector of parameters, $\boldsymbol{\theta}$. As with a residual, the expectation of an elementary zero function must vanish if it is evaluated at the true value of $\boldsymbol{\theta}$, but not in general otherwise.

We let $f_t(\boldsymbol{\theta}, y_t)$ denote an elementary zero function for observation t. It is called "elementary" because it applies to a single observation. In the linear regression case that we have been studying up to this point, $\boldsymbol{\theta}$ would be replaced by $\boldsymbol{\beta}$ and we would have $f_t(\boldsymbol{\beta}, y_t) \equiv y_t - \boldsymbol{X}_t\boldsymbol{\beta}$. In general, we may well have more than one elementary zero function for each observation.

We consider a model $\mathbb{M}$, which, as usual, is to be thought of as a set of DGPs. To each DGP in $\mathbb{M}$, there corresponds a unique value of $\boldsymbol{\theta}$, which is what we often call the "true" value of $\boldsymbol{\theta}$ for that DGP. It is important to note that the uniqueness goes just one way here: A given parameter vector $\boldsymbol{\theta}$ may correspond to many DGPs, perhaps even to an infinite number of them, but each DGP corresponds to just one parameter vector. In order to express the key property of elementary zero functions, we must introduce a symbol for the DGPs of the model $\mathbb{M}$. It is conventional to use the Greek letter μ for this purpose, but then it is necessary to avoid confusion with the conventional use of μ to denote a population mean. It is usually not difficult to distinguish the two uses of the symbol.

The key property of elementary zero functions can now be written as

$$\mathrm{E}_\mu\big(f_t(\boldsymbol{\theta}_\mu, y_t)\big) = 0, \tag{9.53}$$

where $\mathrm{E}_\mu(\cdot)$ denotes the expectation under the DGP μ, and $\boldsymbol{\theta}_\mu$ is the (unique) parameter vector associated with μ. It is assumed that property (9.53) holds for all t and for all $\mu \in \mathbb{M}$.

If estimation based on elementary zero functions is to be possible, these functions must satisfy a number of conditions in addition to condition (9.53). Most importantly, we need to ensure that the model is asymptotically identified. We therefore assume that, for some observations, at least,

$$\mathrm{E}_\mu\big(f_t(\boldsymbol{\theta}, y_t)\big) \neq 0 \quad \text{for all } \boldsymbol{\theta} \neq \boldsymbol{\theta}_\mu. \tag{9.54}$$

This just says that, if we evaluate f_t at a $\boldsymbol{\theta}$ that is different from the $\boldsymbol{\theta}_\mu$ that corresponds to the DGP under which we take expectations, then the expectation of $f_t(\boldsymbol{\theta}, y_t)$ must be nonzero. Condition (9.54) does not have to hold for every observation, but it must hold for a fraction of the observations that does not tend to zero as $n \to \infty$.

In the case of the linear regression model, if we write $\boldsymbol{\beta}_0$ for the true parameter vector, condition (9.54) is satisfied for observation t if, for all $\boldsymbol{\beta} \neq \boldsymbol{\beta}_0$,

$$\mathrm{E}(y_t - \boldsymbol{X}_t\boldsymbol{\beta}) = \mathrm{E}\big(\boldsymbol{X}_t(\boldsymbol{\beta}_0 - \boldsymbol{\beta}) + u_t\big) = \mathrm{E}\big(\boldsymbol{X}_t(\boldsymbol{\beta}_0 - \boldsymbol{\beta})\big) \neq 0. \tag{9.55}$$

It is clear from (9.55) that condition (9.54) must be satisfied whenever the fitted values actually depend on all the components of the vector $\boldsymbol{\beta}$ for at least some fraction of the observations. This is equivalent to the more familiar condition that

$$\boldsymbol{S}_{\boldsymbol{X}^\top\boldsymbol{X}} \equiv \operatorname*{plim}_{n\to\infty} \frac{1}{n}\boldsymbol{X}^\top\boldsymbol{X}$$

is a positive definite matrix; see Section 6.2 for a discussion of similar asymptotic identification conditions.

We also need to make some assumption about the variances and covariances of the elementary zero functions. If there is just one elementary zero function per observation, we let $\boldsymbol{f}(\boldsymbol{\theta}, \boldsymbol{y})$ denote the n-vector with typical element $f_t(\boldsymbol{\theta}, y_t)$. If there are $m > 1$ elementary zero functions per observation, then we can group all of them into a vector $\boldsymbol{f}(\boldsymbol{\theta}, \boldsymbol{y})$ with nm elements. In either event, we then assume that

$$\mathrm{E}\big(\boldsymbol{f}(\boldsymbol{\theta}, \boldsymbol{y})\boldsymbol{f}^{\top}(\boldsymbol{\theta}, \boldsymbol{y})\big) = \boldsymbol{\Omega}, \tag{9.56}$$

where $\boldsymbol{\Omega}$, which implicitly depends on μ, is a finite, positive definite matrix. Thus we are assuming that, under every DGP $\mu \in \mathbb{M}$, each of the f_t has a finite variance and a finite covariance with every f_s for $s \neq t$.

Estimating Functions and Estimating Equations

Like every procedure that is based on the method of moments, the method of estimating functions replaces relationships like (9.53) that hold in expectation with their empirical, or sample, counterparts. Because $\boldsymbol{\theta}$ is a k-vector, we need k **estimating functions** in order to estimate it. In general, these are weighted averages of the elementary zero functions. Equating the estimating functions to zero yields k **estimating equations**, which must be solved in order to obtain the GMM estimator.

As for the linear regression model, the estimating equations are, in fact, just sample moment conditions which, in most cases, are based on instrumental variables. There are generally more instruments than parameters, and so we need to form linear combinations of the instruments in order to construct precisely k estimating equations. Let $\boldsymbol{W}$ be an $n \times l$ matrix of instruments, which are assumed to be predetermined. Usually, one column of $\boldsymbol{W}$ is a vector of 1s. Now define $\boldsymbol{Z} \equiv \boldsymbol{W}\boldsymbol{J}$, where $\boldsymbol{J}$ is an $l \times k$ matrix with full column rank k. Later, we will discuss how $\boldsymbol{J}$, and hence $\boldsymbol{Z}$, should optimally be chosen, but, for the moment, we take $\boldsymbol{Z}$ as given.

If $\boldsymbol{\theta}_\mu$ is the parameter vector for the DGP μ under which we take expectations, the theoretical moment conditions are

$$\mathrm{E}\big(\boldsymbol{Z}_t^{\top} f_t(\boldsymbol{\theta}_\mu, y_t)\big) = \boldsymbol{0}, \tag{9.57}$$

where $\boldsymbol{Z}_t$ is the tth row of $\boldsymbol{Z}$. Later on, when we take explicit account of the covariance matrix $\boldsymbol{\Omega}$ in formulating the estimating equations, we will need to modify these conditions so that they take the form of conditions (9.31), but (9.57) is all that is required at this stage. In fact, even (9.57) is stronger than we really need. It is sufficient to assume that $\boldsymbol{Z}_t$ and $f_t(\boldsymbol{\theta})$ are asymptotically uncorrelated, which, together with some regularity conditions, implies that

$$\operatorname*{plim}_{n\to\infty} \frac{1}{n}\sum_{t=1}^{n} \boldsymbol{Z}_t^{\top} f_t(\boldsymbol{\theta}_\mu, y_t) = \boldsymbol{0}. \tag{9.58}$$

The vector of estimating functions that corresponds to (9.57) or (9.58) is the k–vector $n^{-1}\boldsymbol{Z}^\top\boldsymbol{f}(\boldsymbol{\theta},\boldsymbol{y})$. Equating this vector to zero yields the system of estimating equations

$$\frac{1}{n}\boldsymbol{Z}^\top\boldsymbol{f}(\boldsymbol{\theta},\boldsymbol{y}) = \mathbf{0}, \tag{9.59}$$

and solving this system yields $\hat{\boldsymbol{\theta}}$, the **nonlinear GMM estimator**.

Consistency

If we are to prove that the nonlinear GMM estimator is consistent, we must assume that a law of large numbers applies to the vector $n^{-1}\boldsymbol{Z}^\top\boldsymbol{f}(\boldsymbol{\theta},\boldsymbol{y})$. This allows us to define the k–vector of **limiting estimating functions**,

$$\boldsymbol{\alpha}(\boldsymbol{\theta};\mu) \equiv \operatorname*{plim}_{n\to\infty}{}_{\mu}\,\frac{1}{n}\boldsymbol{Z}^\top\boldsymbol{f}(\boldsymbol{\theta},\boldsymbol{y}). \tag{9.60}$$

In words, $\boldsymbol{\alpha}(\boldsymbol{\theta};\mu)$ is the probability limit, under the DGP μ, of the vector of estimating functions. Setting $\boldsymbol{\alpha}(\boldsymbol{\theta};\mu)$ to $\mathbf{0}$ yields a set of **limiting estimating equations**.

Either (9.57) or the weaker condition (9.58) implies that $\boldsymbol{\alpha}(\boldsymbol{\theta}_\mu;\mu) = \mathbf{0}$ for all $\mu \in \mathbb{M}$. We then need an asymptotic identification condition strong enough to ensure that $\boldsymbol{\alpha}(\boldsymbol{\theta};\mu) \neq \mathbf{0}$ for all $\boldsymbol{\theta} \neq \boldsymbol{\theta}_\mu$. In other words, we require that the vector $\boldsymbol{\theta}_\mu$ must be the unique solution to the system of limiting estimating equations. If we assume that such a condition holds, it is straightforward to prove consistency in the nonrigorous way we used in Sections 6.2 and 8.3. Evaluating equations (9.59) at their solution $\hat{\boldsymbol{\theta}}$, we find that

$$\frac{1}{n}\boldsymbol{Z}^\top\boldsymbol{f}(\hat{\boldsymbol{\theta}},\boldsymbol{y}) = \mathbf{0}. \tag{9.61}$$

As $n \to \infty$, the left-hand side of this system of equations tends under μ to the vector $\boldsymbol{\alpha}(\operatorname{plim}_\mu \hat{\boldsymbol{\theta}};\mu)$, and the right-hand side remains a zero vector. Given the asymptotic identification condition, the equality in (9.61) can hold asymptotically only if

$$\operatorname*{plim}_{n\to\infty}{}_{\mu}\,\hat{\boldsymbol{\theta}} = \boldsymbol{\theta}_\mu.$$

Therefore, we conclude that the nonlinear GMM estimator $\hat{\boldsymbol{\theta}}$, which solves the system of estimating equations (9.59), consistently estimates the parameter vector $\boldsymbol{\theta}_\mu$, for all $\mu \in \mathbb{M}$, provided the asymptotic identification condition is satisfied.

Asymptotic Normality

For ease of notation, we now fix the DGP $\mu \in \mathbb{M}$ and write $\boldsymbol{\theta}_\mu = \boldsymbol{\theta}_0$. Thus $\boldsymbol{\theta}_0$ has its usual interpretation as the "true" parameter vector. In addition, we suppress the explicit mention of the data vector $\boldsymbol{y}$. As usual, the proof that $n^{1/2}(\hat{\boldsymbol{\theta}} - \boldsymbol{\theta}_0)$ is asymptotically normally distributed is based on a Taylor series approximation, a law of large numbers, and a central limit theorem. For the purposes of the first of these, we need to assume that the zero functions f_t are continuously differentiable in the neighborhood of $\boldsymbol{\theta}_0$. If we perform a first-order Taylor expansion of $n^{1/2}$ times (9.59) around $\boldsymbol{\theta}_0$ and introduce some appropriate factors of powers of n, we obtain the result that

$$n^{-1/2}\boldsymbol{Z}^{\top}\boldsymbol{f}(\boldsymbol{\theta}_0) + n^{-1}\boldsymbol{Z}^{\top}\boldsymbol{F}(\bar{\boldsymbol{\theta}})n^{1/2}(\hat{\boldsymbol{\theta}} - \boldsymbol{\theta}_0) = \mathbf{0}, \tag{9.62}$$

where the $n \times k$ matrix $\boldsymbol{F}(\boldsymbol{\theta})$ has typical element

$$F_{ti}(\boldsymbol{\theta}) \equiv \frac{\partial f_t(\boldsymbol{\theta})}{\partial \theta_i}, \tag{9.63}$$

where θ_i is the ith element of $\boldsymbol{\theta}$. This matrix, like $\boldsymbol{f}(\boldsymbol{\theta})$ itself, depends implicitly on the vector $\boldsymbol{y}$ and is therefore stochastic. The notation $\boldsymbol{F}(\bar{\boldsymbol{\theta}})$ in (9.62) is the convenient shorthand we introduced in Section 6.2: Row t of the matrix is the corresponding row of $\boldsymbol{F}(\boldsymbol{\theta})$ evaluated at $\boldsymbol{\theta} = \bar{\boldsymbol{\theta}}_t$, where the $\bar{\boldsymbol{\theta}}_t$ all satisfy the inequality

$$\big\|\bar{\boldsymbol{\theta}}_t - \boldsymbol{\theta}_0\big\| \leq \big\|\hat{\boldsymbol{\theta}}_t - \boldsymbol{\theta}_0\big\|.$$

The consistency of $\hat{\boldsymbol{\theta}}$ then implies that the $\bar{\boldsymbol{\theta}}_t$ also tend to $\boldsymbol{\theta}_0$ as $n \to \infty$. The consistency of the $\bar{\boldsymbol{\theta}}_t$ implies that

$$\operatorname*{plim}_{n\to\infty} \frac{1}{n}\boldsymbol{Z}^{\top}\boldsymbol{F}(\bar{\boldsymbol{\theta}}) = \operatorname*{plim}_{n\to\infty} \frac{1}{n}\boldsymbol{Z}^{\top}\boldsymbol{F}(\boldsymbol{\theta}_0). \tag{9.64}$$

Under reasonable regularity conditions, we can apply a law of large numbers to the right-hand side of (9.64), and the probability limit is then deterministic. For asymptotic normality, we also require that it should be nonsingular. This is a condition of **strong asymptotic identification**, of the sort used in Section 6.2. By a first-order Taylor expansion of $\boldsymbol{\alpha}(\boldsymbol{\theta};\mu)$ around $\boldsymbol{\theta}_0$, where it is equal to $\mathbf{0}$, we see from the definition (9.60) that

$$\boldsymbol{\alpha}(\boldsymbol{\theta};\mu) \overset{a}{=} \operatorname*{plim}_{n\to\infty} \frac{1}{n}\boldsymbol{Z}^{\top}\boldsymbol{F}(\boldsymbol{\theta}_0)(\boldsymbol{\theta} - \boldsymbol{\theta}_0). \tag{9.65}$$

Therefore, the condition that the right-hand side of (9.64) is nonsingular is a strengthening of the condition that $\boldsymbol{\theta}$ is asymptotically identified. Because it is nonsingular, the system of equations

$$\operatorname*{plim}_{n\to\infty} \frac{1}{n}\boldsymbol{Z}^{\top}\boldsymbol{F}(\boldsymbol{\theta}_0)(\boldsymbol{\theta} - \boldsymbol{\theta}_0) = \mathbf{0}$$

has no solution other than $\boldsymbol{\theta} = \boldsymbol{\theta}_0$. By (9.65), this implies that $\boldsymbol{\alpha}(\boldsymbol{\theta};\mu) \neq \mathbf{0}$ for all $\boldsymbol{\theta} \neq \boldsymbol{\theta}_0$, which is the asymptotic identification condition.

Applying the results just discussed to equation (9.62), we find that

$$n^{1/2}(\hat{\boldsymbol{\theta}} - \boldsymbol{\theta}_0) \overset{a}{=} -\Big(\operatorname*{plim}_{n\to\infty} \frac{1}{n}\boldsymbol{Z}^{\top}\boldsymbol{F}(\boldsymbol{\theta}_0)\Big)^{-1} n^{-1/2}\boldsymbol{Z}^{\top}\boldsymbol{f}(\boldsymbol{\theta}_0). \tag{9.66}$$

Next, we apply a central limit theorem to the second factor on the right-hand side of (9.66). Doing so demonstrates that $n^{1/2}(\hat{\boldsymbol{\theta}} - \boldsymbol{\theta}_0)$ is asymptotically normally distributed. By (9.57), the vector $n^{-1/2}\boldsymbol{Z}^\top\boldsymbol{f}(\boldsymbol{\theta}_0)$ must have mean $\mathbf{0}$, and, by (9.56), its covariance matrix is $\operatorname{plim} n^{-1}\boldsymbol{Z}^\top\boldsymbol{\Omega}\boldsymbol{Z}$. In stating this result, we assume that (9.02) holds with the $\boldsymbol{f}(\boldsymbol{\theta}_0)$ in place of the error terms. Then (9.66) implies that the vector $n^{1/2}(\hat{\boldsymbol{\theta}} - \boldsymbol{\theta}_0)$ is asymptotically normally distributed with mean vector $\mathbf{0}$ and covariance matrix

$$\Big(\operatorname*{plim}_{n\to\infty} \frac{1}{n}\boldsymbol{Z}^\top\boldsymbol{F}(\boldsymbol{\theta}_0)\Big)^{-1}\Big(\operatorname*{plim}_{n\to\infty} \frac{1}{n}\boldsymbol{Z}^\top\boldsymbol{\Omega}\boldsymbol{Z}\Big)\Big(\operatorname*{plim}_{n\to\infty} \frac{1}{n}\boldsymbol{F}^\top(\boldsymbol{\theta}_0)\boldsymbol{Z}\Big)^{-1}. \tag{9.67}$$

Since this is a sandwich covariance matrix, it is evident that the nonlinear GMM estimator $\hat{\boldsymbol{\theta}}$ is not, in general, an asymptotically efficient estimator.

Asymptotically Efficient Estimation

In order to obtain an asymptotically efficient nonlinear GMM estimator, we need to choose the estimating functions $n^{-1}\boldsymbol{Z}^\top\boldsymbol{f}(\boldsymbol{\theta})$ optimally. This is equivalent to choosing $\boldsymbol{Z}$ optimally. How we should do this depends on what assumptions we make about $\boldsymbol{F}(\boldsymbol{\theta})$ and $\boldsymbol{\Omega}$, the covariance matrix of $\boldsymbol{f}(\boldsymbol{\theta})$. Not surprisingly, we will obtain results very similar to the results for linear GMM estimation obtained in Section 9.2.

We begin with the simplest possible case, in which $\boldsymbol{\Omega} = \sigma^2\mathbf{I}$, and $\boldsymbol{F}(\boldsymbol{\theta}_0)$ is predetermined in the sense that

$$\mathrm{E}\big(\boldsymbol{F}_t(\boldsymbol{\theta}_0)f_t(\boldsymbol{\theta}_0)\big) = \mathbf{0}, \tag{9.68}$$

where $\boldsymbol{F}_t(\boldsymbol{\theta}_0)$ is the tth row of $\boldsymbol{F}(\boldsymbol{\theta}_0)$. If we ignore the probability limits and the factors of n^{-1}, the sandwich covariance matrix (9.67) is in this case proportional to

$$(\boldsymbol{Z}^\top\boldsymbol{F}_0)^{-1}\boldsymbol{Z}^\top\boldsymbol{Z}(\boldsymbol{F}_0^\top\boldsymbol{Z})^{-1}, \tag{9.69}$$

where, for ease of notation, $\boldsymbol{F}_0 \equiv \boldsymbol{F}(\boldsymbol{\theta}_0)$. The inverse of (9.69), which is proportional to the asymptotic precision matrix of the estimator, is

$$\boldsymbol{F}_0^\top\boldsymbol{Z}(\boldsymbol{Z}^\top\boldsymbol{Z})^{-1}\boldsymbol{Z}^\top\boldsymbol{F}_0 = \boldsymbol{F}_0^\top\boldsymbol{P}_{\boldsymbol{Z}}\boldsymbol{F}_0. \tag{9.70}$$

If we set $\boldsymbol{Z} = \boldsymbol{F}_0$, (9.69) is no longer a sandwich, and (9.70) simplifies to $\boldsymbol{F}_0^\top\boldsymbol{F}_0$. The difference between $\boldsymbol{F}_0^\top\boldsymbol{F}_0$ and the general expression (9.70) is

$$\boldsymbol{F}_0^\top\boldsymbol{F}_0 - \boldsymbol{F}_0^\top\boldsymbol{P}_{\boldsymbol{Z}}\boldsymbol{F}_0 = \boldsymbol{F}_0^\top\boldsymbol{M}_{\boldsymbol{Z}}\boldsymbol{F}_0,$$

which is a positive semidefinite matrix because $\boldsymbol{M}_{\boldsymbol{Z}} \equiv \mathbf{I} - \boldsymbol{P}_{\boldsymbol{Z}}$ is an orthogonal projection matrix. Thus, in this simple case, the optimal instrument matrix is just $\boldsymbol{F}_0$.

Since we do not know $\boldsymbol{\theta}_0$, it is not feasible to use $\boldsymbol{F}_0$ directly as the matrix of instruments. Instead, we use the trick that leads to the moment conditions

(6.27) which define the NLS estimator. This leads us to solve the estimating equations

$$\frac{1}{n}\boldsymbol{F}^{\top}(\boldsymbol{\theta})\boldsymbol{f}(\boldsymbol{\theta}) = \mathbf{0}. \tag{9.71}$$

If $\boldsymbol{\Omega} = \sigma^2\mathbf{I}$, and $\boldsymbol{F}(\boldsymbol{\theta}_0)$ is predetermined, solving these equations yields an asymptotically efficient GMM estimator.

It is not valid to use the columns of $\boldsymbol{F}(\boldsymbol{\theta})$ as instruments if condition (9.68) is not satisfied. In that event, the analysis of Section 8.3, taken up again in Section 9.2, suggests that we should replace the rows of $\boldsymbol{F}_0$ by their expectations conditional on the information sets Ω_t generated by variables that are exogenous or predetermined for observation t. Let us define an $n \times k$ matrix $\bar{\boldsymbol{F}}$, in terms of its typical row $\bar{\boldsymbol{F}}_t$, and another $n \times k$ matrix $\boldsymbol{V}$, as follows:

$$\bar{\boldsymbol{F}}_t \equiv \mathrm{E}\big(\boldsymbol{F}_t(\boldsymbol{\theta}_0)\,|\,\Omega_t\big) \quad \text{and} \quad \boldsymbol{V} \equiv \boldsymbol{F}_0 - \bar{\boldsymbol{F}}. \tag{9.72}$$

The matrices $\bar{\boldsymbol{F}}$ and $\boldsymbol{V}$ are entirely analogous to the matrices $\bar{\boldsymbol{X}}$ and $\boldsymbol{V}$ used in Section 8.3. The definitions (9.72) imply that

$$\operatorname*{plim}_{n\to\infty}\frac{1}{n}\bar{\boldsymbol{F}}^{\top}\boldsymbol{F}_0 = \operatorname*{plim}_{n\to\infty}\frac{1}{n}\bar{\boldsymbol{F}}^{\top}(\bar{\boldsymbol{F}} + \boldsymbol{V}) = \operatorname*{plim}_{n\to\infty}\frac{1}{n}\bar{\boldsymbol{F}}^{\top}\bar{\boldsymbol{F}}. \tag{9.73}$$

The term $\operatorname{plim} n^{-1}\bar{\boldsymbol{F}}^{\top}\boldsymbol{V}$ equals $\mathbf{O}$ because (9.72) implies that $\mathrm{E}(\boldsymbol{V}_t\,|\,\Omega_t) = \mathbf{0}$, and the conditional expectation $\bar{\boldsymbol{F}}_t$ belongs to the information set Ω_t.

To find the asymptotic covariance matrix of $n^{1/2}(\hat{\boldsymbol{\theta}} - \boldsymbol{\theta}_0)$ when $\bar{\boldsymbol{F}}$ is used in place of $\boldsymbol{Z}$ and the covariance matrix of $\boldsymbol{f}(\boldsymbol{\theta})$ is $\sigma^2\mathbf{I}$, we start from expression (9.67). Using (9.73), we obtain

$$\begin{aligned}
&\sigma^2\Big(\operatorname*{plim}_{n\to\infty}\frac{1}{n}\bar{\boldsymbol{F}}^{\top}\boldsymbol{F}_0\Big)^{-1}\Big(\operatorname*{plim}_{n\to\infty}\frac{1}{n}\bar{\boldsymbol{F}}^{\top}\bar{\boldsymbol{F}}\Big)\Big(\operatorname*{plim}_{n\to\infty}\frac{1}{n}\boldsymbol{F}_0^{\top}\bar{\boldsymbol{F}}\Big)^{-1}\\
&= \sigma^2\Big(\operatorname*{plim}_{n\to\infty}\frac{1}{n}\bar{\boldsymbol{F}}^{\top}\bar{\boldsymbol{F}}\Big)^{-1}.
\end{aligned} \tag{9.74}$$

For any other choice of instrument matrix $\boldsymbol{Z}$, the argument giving (9.73) shows that $\operatorname{plim} n^{-1}\boldsymbol{Z}^{\top}\boldsymbol{F}_0 = \operatorname{plim} n^{-1}\boldsymbol{Z}^{\top}\bar{\boldsymbol{F}}$, and so the covariance matrix (9.67) becomes

$$\sigma^2\Big(\operatorname*{plim}_{n\to\infty}\frac{1}{n}\boldsymbol{Z}^{\top}\bar{\boldsymbol{F}}\Big)^{-1}\Big(\operatorname*{plim}_{n\to\infty}\frac{1}{n}\boldsymbol{Z}^{\top}\boldsymbol{Z}\Big)\Big(\operatorname*{plim}_{n\to\infty}\frac{1}{n}\bar{\boldsymbol{F}}^{\top}\boldsymbol{Z}\Big)^{-1}. \tag{9.75}$$

The inverse of (9.75) is $1/\sigma^2$ times the probability limit of

$$\frac{1}{n}\bar{\boldsymbol{F}}^{\top}\boldsymbol{Z}(\boldsymbol{Z}^{\top}\boldsymbol{Z})^{-1}\boldsymbol{Z}^{\top}\bar{\boldsymbol{F}} = \frac{1}{n}\bar{\boldsymbol{F}}^{\top}\boldsymbol{P}_{\boldsymbol{Z}}\bar{\boldsymbol{F}}. \tag{9.76}$$

This expression is analogous to expression (8.21) for the asymptotic precision of the IV estimator for linear regression models with endogenous explanatory variables. Since the difference between $n^{-1}\bar{\boldsymbol{F}}^{\top}\bar{\boldsymbol{F}}$ and (9.76) is the positive semidefinite matrix $n^{-1}\bar{\boldsymbol{F}}^{\top}\boldsymbol{M}_{\boldsymbol{Z}}\bar{\boldsymbol{F}}$, we conclude that (9.74) is indeed the asymptotic covariance matrix that corresponds to the optimal choice of $\boldsymbol{Z}$. Therefore, when $\boldsymbol{F}_t(\boldsymbol{\theta})$ is not predetermined, we should use its expectation conditional on Ω_t in the matrix of instruments.

In practice, of course, the matrix $\bar{\boldsymbol{F}}$ is rarely observed. We therefore need to estimate it. The natural way to do so is to regress $\boldsymbol{F}(\boldsymbol{\theta})$ on an $n \times l$ matrix of instruments $\boldsymbol{W}$, where $l \geq k$, with the inequality holding strictly in most cases. This yields fitted values $\boldsymbol{P_W F}(\boldsymbol{\theta})$. If we estimate $\bar{\boldsymbol{F}}$ in this way, the optimal estimating equations become

$$\frac{1}{n}\boldsymbol{F}^{\top}(\boldsymbol{\theta})\boldsymbol{P_W f}(\boldsymbol{\theta}) = \mathbf{0}. \tag{9.77}$$

By reasoning like that which led to (8.27) and (9.73), it can be seen that these estimating equations are asymptotically equivalent to the same equations with $\bar{\boldsymbol{F}}$ in place of $\boldsymbol{F}(\boldsymbol{\theta})$. In particular, if $\mathcal{S}(\bar{\boldsymbol{F}}) \subseteq \mathcal{S}(\boldsymbol{W})$, the estimator obtained by solving (9.77) is asymptotically equivalent to the one obtained using the optimal instruments $\bar{\boldsymbol{F}}$.

The estimating equations (9.77) generalize the first-order conditions (8.28) for linear IV estimation and the moment conditions (8.84) for nonlinear IV estimation. As readers are asked to show in Exercise 9.14, the solution to (9.77) in the case of the linear regression model is simply the generalized IV estimator (8.29). As can be seen from (9.67), the asymptotic covariance matrix of the estimator $\hat{\boldsymbol{\theta}}$ defined by (9.77) can be estimated by

$$\hat{\sigma}^2(\hat{\boldsymbol{F}}^{\top}\boldsymbol{P_W}\hat{\boldsymbol{F}})^{-1},$$

where $\hat{\boldsymbol{F}} \equiv \boldsymbol{F}(\hat{\boldsymbol{\theta}})$, and $\hat{\sigma}^2 \equiv n^{-1}\sum_{t=1}^{n} f_t^2(\hat{\boldsymbol{\theta}})$, the average of the squares of the elementary zero functions evaluated at $\hat{\boldsymbol{\theta}}$, is a natural estimator of σ^2.

Efficient Estimation with an Unknown Covariance Matrix

When the covariance matrix $\boldsymbol{\Omega}$ is unknown, the GMM estimators defined by the estimating equations (9.71) or (9.77), according to whether or not $\boldsymbol{F}(\boldsymbol{\theta})$ is predetermined, are no longer asymptotically efficient in general. But, just as we did in Section 9.3 with regression models, we can obtain estimates that are efficient for a given set of instruments by using a heteroskedasticity-consistent or a HAC estimator.

Suppose there are $l > k$ instruments which form an $n \times l$ matrix $\boldsymbol{W}$. As in Section 9.2, we can construct estimating equations with instruments $\boldsymbol{Z} = \boldsymbol{WJ}$, using a full-rank $l \times k$ matrix $\boldsymbol{J}$ to select k linear combinations of the full set of instruments. The asymptotic covariance matrix of the estimator obtained by solving these equations is then, by (9.67),

$$\Big(\operatorname*{plim}_{n\to\infty}\frac{1}{n}\boldsymbol{J}^{\top}\boldsymbol{W}^{\top}\boldsymbol{F}_0\Big)^{-1}\Big(\operatorname*{plim}_{n\to\infty}\frac{1}{n}\boldsymbol{J}^{\top}\boldsymbol{W}^{\top}\boldsymbol{\Omega}\boldsymbol{W}\boldsymbol{J}\Big)\Big(\operatorname*{plim}_{n\to\infty}\frac{1}{n}\boldsymbol{F}_0^{\top}\boldsymbol{W}\boldsymbol{J}\Big)^{-1}. \tag{9.78}$$

This looks just like (9.07) with $\boldsymbol{F}_0$ in place of the regressor matrix $\boldsymbol{X}$. The optimal choice of $\boldsymbol{J}$ is therefore just (9.08) with $\boldsymbol{F}_0$ in place of $\boldsymbol{X}$. Since (9.08) depends on the unknown true $\boldsymbol{\Omega}$, we replace $n^{-1}\boldsymbol{W}^\top\boldsymbol{\Omega}\boldsymbol{W}$ by an estimator $\hat{\boldsymbol{\Sigma}}$, which could be either a heteroskedasticity-consistent or a HAC estimator. This yields the estimating equations

$$\boldsymbol{F}^\top(\boldsymbol{\theta})\boldsymbol{W}\hat{\boldsymbol{\Sigma}}^{-1}\boldsymbol{W}^\top\boldsymbol{f}(\boldsymbol{\theta}) = \mathbf{0}, \tag{9.79}$$

and the asymptotic covariance matrix (9.78) simplifies to

$$\Big(\operatorname*{plim}_{n\to\infty} n^{-2}\boldsymbol{F}_0^\top\boldsymbol{W}\hat{\boldsymbol{\Sigma}}^{-1}\boldsymbol{W}^\top\boldsymbol{F}_0\Big)^{-1}, \tag{9.80}$$

in which, if $\boldsymbol{F}(\boldsymbol{\theta})$ is not predetermined, we may write $\bar{\boldsymbol{F}}$ instead of $\boldsymbol{F}_0$ without changing the limit. In practice, we can use

$$\widehat{\operatorname{Var}}(\hat{\boldsymbol{\theta}}) = n(\hat{\boldsymbol{F}}^\top\boldsymbol{W}\hat{\boldsymbol{\Sigma}}^{-1}\boldsymbol{W}^\top\hat{\boldsymbol{F}})^{-1}, \tag{9.81}$$

where $\hat{\boldsymbol{F}} \equiv \boldsymbol{F}(\hat{\boldsymbol{\theta}})$, to estimate the covariance matrix of $\hat{\boldsymbol{\theta}}$. As with the estimator (9.41) for the linear regression case, the factor of n is needed to offset the factor of n^{-1} in $\hat{\boldsymbol{\Sigma}}$. The matrix (9.81) can be used to construct Wald tests and asymptotic confidence intervals in the usual way.

Efficient Estimation with a Known Covariance Matrix

When the covariance matrix $\boldsymbol{\Omega}$ is known, we can obtain a fully efficient GMM estimator. As before, we let $\boldsymbol{\Psi}$ denote an $n \times n$ matrix which satisfies the equation $\boldsymbol{\Omega}^{-1} = \boldsymbol{\Psi}\boldsymbol{\Psi}^\top$. The variance of the vector $\boldsymbol{\Psi}^\top\boldsymbol{f}(\boldsymbol{\theta}_0)$, where $\boldsymbol{\theta}_0$ is the true parameter vector for the DGP that generates the data, is then

$$\mathrm{E}\big(\boldsymbol{\Psi}^\top\boldsymbol{f}(\boldsymbol{\theta}_0)\boldsymbol{f}^\top(\boldsymbol{\theta}_0)\boldsymbol{\Psi}\big) = \boldsymbol{\Psi}^\top\boldsymbol{\Omega}\boldsymbol{\Psi} = \mathbf{I}.$$

Thus the components of the vector $\boldsymbol{\Psi}^\top\boldsymbol{f}(\boldsymbol{\theta})$ form a set of zero functions that are homoskedastic and serially uncorrelated. As we mentioned in Section 9.2, it is often possible to choose $\boldsymbol{\Psi}$ in such a way that these components can be thought of as innovations in the sense of Section 4.5, and in this case $\boldsymbol{\Psi}$ is usually upper triangular.

The matrix $\boldsymbol{\Psi}$ does not depend on the parameters $\boldsymbol{\theta}$. Therefore, the matrix of derivatives of the transformed zero functions in the vector $\boldsymbol{\Psi}^\top\boldsymbol{f}(\boldsymbol{\theta})$ is just $\boldsymbol{\Psi}^\top\boldsymbol{F}(\boldsymbol{\theta})$. Consequently, if the tth row of $\boldsymbol{\Psi}^\top\boldsymbol{F}(\boldsymbol{\theta})$ is predetermined with respect to the tth component of $\boldsymbol{\Psi}^\top\boldsymbol{f}(\boldsymbol{\theta})$, the optimal estimating equations are constructed using the columns of $\boldsymbol{\Psi}^\top\boldsymbol{F}(\boldsymbol{\theta}_0)$ as instruments. Because $\boldsymbol{\theta}_0$ is not known, the optimal instruments are estimated along with the parameters by using the estimating equations

$$\frac{1}{n}\boldsymbol{F}^\top(\boldsymbol{\theta})\boldsymbol{\Psi}\boldsymbol{\Psi}^\top\boldsymbol{f}(\boldsymbol{\theta}) = \frac{1}{n}\boldsymbol{F}^\top(\boldsymbol{\theta})\boldsymbol{\Omega}^{-1}\boldsymbol{f}(\boldsymbol{\theta}) = \mathbf{0}, \tag{9.82}$$

as in (9.71). The asymptotic covariance matrix of the resulting estimator is

$$\operatorname{Var}\big(\operatorname*{plim}_{n\to\infty} n^{1/2}(\hat{\boldsymbol{\theta}} - \boldsymbol{\theta}_0)\big) = \operatorname*{plim}_{n\to\infty}\Big(\frac{1}{n}\boldsymbol{F}_0^{\top}\boldsymbol{\Omega}^{-1}\boldsymbol{F}_0\Big)^{-1}, \tag{9.83}$$

where, as usual, $\boldsymbol{F}_0 \equiv \boldsymbol{F}(\boldsymbol{\theta}_0)$. The derivation of (9.83) from (9.67) is quite straightforward; see Exercise 9.15. In practice, the covariance matrix of $\hat{\boldsymbol{\theta}}$ is normally estimated by

$$\widehat{\operatorname{Var}}(\hat{\boldsymbol{\theta}}) = (\hat{\boldsymbol{F}}^{\top}\boldsymbol{\Omega}^{-1}\hat{\boldsymbol{F}})^{-1}. \tag{9.84}$$

If the tth row of $\boldsymbol{\Psi}^{\top}\boldsymbol{F}(\boldsymbol{\theta})$ is not predetermined with respect to the tth component of $\boldsymbol{\Psi}^{\top}\boldsymbol{f}(\boldsymbol{\theta})$, and if this component is an innovation, then we can determine the optimal instruments just as we did in Section 9.2. By analogy with (9.24), we define the matrix $\bar{\boldsymbol{F}}(\boldsymbol{\theta})$ implicitly by the equation

$$\operatorname{E}\big((\boldsymbol{\Psi}^{\top}\boldsymbol{F}(\boldsymbol{\theta}))_t \,|\, \Omega_t\big) = (\boldsymbol{\Psi}^{\top}\bar{\boldsymbol{F}}(\boldsymbol{\theta}))_t. \tag{9.85}$$

As in Section 9.2, making this definition explicit depends on the details of the particular model under study. The moment conditions for fully efficient estimation are then given by (9.82) with $\boldsymbol{F}(\boldsymbol{\theta})$ replaced by $\bar{\boldsymbol{F}}(\boldsymbol{\theta})$. The asymptotic covariance matrix is (9.83) with $\boldsymbol{F}_0$ replaced by $\bar{\boldsymbol{F}}_0$, and the covariance matrix of $\hat{\boldsymbol{\theta}}$ can be estimated by (9.84) with $\hat{\boldsymbol{F}}$ replaced by $\bar{\boldsymbol{F}}(\hat{\boldsymbol{\theta}})$. All of these claims are proved in the same way as were the corresponding ones for linear regressions in Section 9.2.

When the matrix $\bar{\boldsymbol{F}}(\boldsymbol{\theta})$ is not observable, as is frequently the case, we can often find an $n \times l$ matrix of instruments $\boldsymbol{W}$, where usually $l > k$, such that $\boldsymbol{W}$ satisfies the predeterminedness condition in its form (9.30), and such that $\mathcal{S}(\boldsymbol{F}(\boldsymbol{\theta}_0)) \subseteq \mathcal{S}(\boldsymbol{W})$. In such cases, overidentified estimation that makes use of the transformed zero functions $\boldsymbol{\Psi}^{\top}\boldsymbol{f}(\boldsymbol{\theta})$ and the transformed instruments $\boldsymbol{\Psi}^{\top}\boldsymbol{W}$ yields asymptotically efficient estimates. The results of Exercises 9.8 and 9.9 can also be readily extended to the present nonlinear case.

Minimizing Criterion Functions

The nonlinear GMM estimators we have discussed in this section can all, like the ones for linear regression models, be obtained by minimizing appropriately chosen quadratic forms. We restrict our attention to cases in which $\operatorname{plim} n^{-1}\boldsymbol{F}^{\top}(\boldsymbol{\theta})\boldsymbol{f}(\boldsymbol{\theta}) \neq \mathbf{0}$, and we employ an $n \times l$ matrix of instruments, $\boldsymbol{W}$. When the covariance matrix $\boldsymbol{\Omega}$ of the elementary zero functions is unknown, but a heteroskedasticity-consistent or HAC estimator $\hat{\boldsymbol{\Sigma}}$ is available, the appropriate GMM criterion function is

$$\frac{1}{n}\boldsymbol{f}^{\top}(\boldsymbol{\theta})\boldsymbol{W}\hat{\boldsymbol{\Sigma}}^{-1}\boldsymbol{W}^{\top}\boldsymbol{f}(\boldsymbol{\theta}). \tag{9.86}$$

Minimizing this function with respect to $\boldsymbol{\theta}$ is equivalent to solving the estimating equations (9.79).

In the case in which the matrix $\boldsymbol{\Omega}$ is known, or can be estimated consistently, the fully efficient estimators of the previous subsection can be obtained by minimizing the quadratic form

$$\boldsymbol{f}^\top(\boldsymbol{\theta})\boldsymbol{\Psi}\boldsymbol{P}_{\boldsymbol{\Psi}^\top\boldsymbol{W}}\boldsymbol{\Psi}^\top\boldsymbol{f}(\boldsymbol{\theta}), \tag{9.87}$$

where $\boldsymbol{\Psi}\boldsymbol{\Psi}^\top = \boldsymbol{\Omega}^{-1}$, the components of $\boldsymbol{\Psi}^\top\boldsymbol{f}(\boldsymbol{\theta}_0)$ are innovations, and the matrix $\boldsymbol{W}$ satisfies the predeterminedness condition in the form (9.30). For full efficiency, the span $\mathcal{S}(\boldsymbol{W})$ of the instruments must (asymptotically) include as a subspace the span of the $\bar{\boldsymbol{F}}(\boldsymbol{\theta}_0)$, as defined in (9.85). In Exercise 9.16, readers are asked to check that minimizing (9.87) is asymptotically equivalent to solving the optimal estimating equations.

Fortunately, we need not treat (9.86) and (9.87) separately. As in Section 9.4, expression (9.86) is asymptotically unchanged if we replace $\hat{\boldsymbol{\Sigma}}$ by $n^{-1}\boldsymbol{W}^\top\boldsymbol{\Omega}\boldsymbol{W}$, where $\boldsymbol{\Omega}$ is the true covariance matrix of the zero functions. Making this replacement, we see that both (9.86) and (9.87) can be written as

$$Q(\boldsymbol{\theta}, \boldsymbol{y}) \equiv \boldsymbol{f}^\top(\boldsymbol{\theta})\boldsymbol{\Psi}\boldsymbol{P}_{\boldsymbol{A}}\boldsymbol{\Psi}^\top\boldsymbol{f}(\boldsymbol{\theta}), \tag{9.88}$$

where $\boldsymbol{A} = \boldsymbol{\Psi}^{-1}\boldsymbol{W}$ and $\boldsymbol{A} = \boldsymbol{\Psi}^\top\boldsymbol{W}$ for the criterion functions (9.86) and (9.87), respectively. Note how closely (9.88) resembles expression (9.45) for the linear regression case.

It is often more convenient to compute GMM estimators by minimizing a criterion function than by directly solving a set of estimating equations. One advantage is that algorithms for minimizing functions tend to be more stable numerically than algorithms for solving sets of nonlinear equations. Another advantage is that the criterion function may have more than one stationary point. In this event, the estimating equations are satisfied at each of these stationary points, although the criterion function may have a unique global minimum, which then corresponds to the solution of interest.

However, the main advantage of working with criterion functions is that the minimized value of a GMM criterion function can be used for testing, as we have already discussed for the linear regression case in Section 9.4. Notice that the factor of n^{-1} in (9.86), which does not matter for estimation, is essential when the criterion function is being used for testing. Its role is to offset the factor of n^{-1} in the definition of $\hat{\boldsymbol{\Sigma}}$.

Tests Based on the GMM Criterion Function

The Hansen-Sargan overidentification test statistic is $Q(\hat{\boldsymbol{\theta}}, \boldsymbol{y})$, the minimized value of the GMM criterion function. Up to an irrelevant scalar factor, the first-order conditions for the minimization of (9.88) are

$$\boldsymbol{F}^\top(\hat{\boldsymbol{\theta}})\boldsymbol{\Psi}\boldsymbol{P}_{\boldsymbol{A}}\boldsymbol{\Psi}^\top\boldsymbol{f}(\hat{\boldsymbol{\theta}}) = \boldsymbol{0}, \tag{9.89}$$

and it follows from this, either by a Taylor expansion or directly by using the result (9.66), that

$$n^{1/2}(\hat{\boldsymbol{\theta}} - \boldsymbol{\theta}_0) \overset{a}{=} -\Big(\frac{1}{n}\boldsymbol{F}_0^\top\boldsymbol{\Psi}\boldsymbol{P_A}\boldsymbol{\Psi}^\top\boldsymbol{F}_0\Big)^{-1} n^{-1/2}\boldsymbol{F}_0^\top\boldsymbol{\Psi}\boldsymbol{P_A}\boldsymbol{\Psi}^\top\boldsymbol{f}_0,$$

where, as usual, $\boldsymbol{F}_0$ and $\boldsymbol{f}_0$ denote $\boldsymbol{F}(\boldsymbol{\theta}_0)$ and $\boldsymbol{f}(\boldsymbol{\theta}_0)$, respectively. We now follow quite closely the calculations of Section 9.4 in order to show that the minimized quadratic form $Q(\hat{\boldsymbol{\theta}}, \boldsymbol{y})$ is asymptotically distributed as $\chi^2(l-k)$. By a short Taylor expansion, we see that

$$\begin{aligned}\boldsymbol{P_A}\boldsymbol{\Psi}^\top\boldsymbol{f}(\hat{\boldsymbol{\theta}}) &\overset{a}{=} \boldsymbol{P_A}\boldsymbol{\Psi}^\top\boldsymbol{f}_0 + n^{-1/2}\boldsymbol{P_A}\boldsymbol{\Psi}^\top\boldsymbol{F}_0\, n^{1/2}(\hat{\boldsymbol{\theta}} - \boldsymbol{\theta}_0)\\ &\overset{a}{=} \boldsymbol{P_A}\boldsymbol{\Psi}^\top\boldsymbol{f}_0 - n^{-1/2}\boldsymbol{P_A}\boldsymbol{\Psi}^\top\boldsymbol{F}_0\big(\tfrac{1}{n}\boldsymbol{F}_0^\top\boldsymbol{\Psi}\boldsymbol{P_A}\boldsymbol{\Psi}^\top\boldsymbol{F}_0\big)^{-1} n^{-1/2}\boldsymbol{F}_0^\top\boldsymbol{\Psi}\boldsymbol{P_A}\boldsymbol{\Psi}^\top\boldsymbol{f}_0\\ &= (\mathbf{I} - \boldsymbol{P}_{\boldsymbol{P_A}\boldsymbol{\Psi}^\top\boldsymbol{F}_0})\boldsymbol{P_A}\boldsymbol{\Psi}^\top\boldsymbol{f}_0,\end{aligned}$$

where $\boldsymbol{P}_{\boldsymbol{P_A}\boldsymbol{\Psi}^\top\boldsymbol{F}_0}$ projects orthogonally on to $\mathcal{S}(\boldsymbol{P_A}\boldsymbol{\Psi}^\top\boldsymbol{F}_0)$. Thus $Q(\hat{\boldsymbol{\theta}}, \boldsymbol{y})$, the minimized value of the criterion function (9.88), is

$$\begin{aligned}\boldsymbol{f}^\top(\hat{\boldsymbol{\theta}})\boldsymbol{\Psi}\boldsymbol{P_A}\boldsymbol{\Psi}^\top\boldsymbol{f}(\hat{\boldsymbol{\theta}}) &\overset{a}{=} \boldsymbol{f}_0^\top\boldsymbol{\Psi}\boldsymbol{P_A}(\mathbf{I} - \boldsymbol{P}_{\boldsymbol{P_A}\boldsymbol{\Psi}^\top\boldsymbol{F}_0})\boldsymbol{P_A}\boldsymbol{\Psi}^\top\boldsymbol{f}_0\\ &= \boldsymbol{f}_0^\top\boldsymbol{\Psi}(\boldsymbol{P_A} - \boldsymbol{P}_{\boldsymbol{P_A}\boldsymbol{\Psi}^\top\boldsymbol{F}_0})\boldsymbol{\Psi}^\top\boldsymbol{f}_0.\end{aligned} \tag{9.90}$$

Because $\mathcal{S}(\boldsymbol{P_A}\boldsymbol{\Psi}^\top\boldsymbol{F}_0) \subseteq \mathcal{S}(\boldsymbol{A})$, the difference of projection matrices in the last expression above is itself an orthogonal projection matrix, of which the image is of dimension $l-k$. As with (9.48), we see that estimating $\boldsymbol{\theta}$ uses up k degrees of freedom. By essentially the same argument as was used for (9.48), it can be shown that (9.90) is asymptotically distributed as $\chi^2(l-k)$. Thus, as expected, $Q(\hat{\boldsymbol{\theta}}, \boldsymbol{y})$ is the Hansen-Sargan test statistic for nonlinear GMM estimation.

As in the case of linear regression models, the difference between the GMM criterion function (9.88) evaluated at restricted estimates and evaluated at unrestricted estimates is asymptotically distributed as $\chi^2(r)$ when there are r equality restrictions. We will not prove this result, which was proved for the linear case in Section 9.3. However, we will present a very simple argument which provides an intuitive explanation.

Let $\tilde{\boldsymbol{\theta}}$ and $\hat{\boldsymbol{\theta}}$ denote, respectively, the vectors of restricted and unrestricted (feasible) efficient GMM estimates. From the result for the Hansen-Sargan test that was just proved, we know that $Q(\tilde{\boldsymbol{\theta}}, \boldsymbol{y})$ and $Q(\hat{\boldsymbol{\theta}}, \boldsymbol{y})$ are asymptotically distributed as $\chi^2(l-k+r)$ and $\chi^2(l-k)$, respectively. Therefore, since a random variable that follows the $\chi^2(m)$ distribution is equal to the sum of m independent $\chi^2(1)$ variables,

$$Q(\tilde{\boldsymbol{\theta}}, \boldsymbol{y}) \overset{a}{=} \sum_{i=1}^{l-k+r} x_i^2 \quad\text{and}\quad Q(\hat{\boldsymbol{\theta}}, \boldsymbol{y}) \overset{a}{=} \sum_{i=1}^{l-k} y_i^2, \tag{9.91}$$

where the x_i and y_i are independent, standard normal random variables. Now suppose that the first $l-k$ of the x_i are equal to the corresponding y_i. If so, (9.91) implies that

$$Q(\tilde{\boldsymbol{\theta}}, \boldsymbol{y}) - Q(\hat{\boldsymbol{\theta}}, \boldsymbol{y}) \overset{a}{=} \sum_{i=1}^{l-k+r} x_i^2 - \sum_{i=1}^{l-k} x_i^2 = \sum_{i=l-k+1}^{l-k+r} x_i^2. \tag{9.92}$$

Since the leftmost expression here is the test statistic we are interested in and the rightmost expression is evidently distributed as $\chi^2(r)$, we have apparently proved the result. The proof is not complete, of course, because we have not shown that the first $l-k$ of the x_i are, in fact, equal to the corresponding y_i. To prove this, we would need to show that, asymptotically, $Q(\tilde{\boldsymbol{\theta}}, \boldsymbol{y})$ is equal to $Q(\hat{\boldsymbol{\theta}}, \boldsymbol{y})$ plus another random variable independent of $Q(\hat{\boldsymbol{\theta}}, \boldsymbol{y})$. This other random variable would then be equal to the rightmost expression in (9.92).

Nonlinear GMM Estimators: Overview

We have discussed a large number of nonlinear GMM estimators, and it can be confusing to keep track of them all. We therefore conclude this section with a brief summary of the principal cases that are likely to be encountered in applied econometric work.

Case 1. Scalar covariance matrix: $\boldsymbol{\Omega} = \sigma^2\mathbf{I}$.

When $\operatorname{plim} n^{-1}\boldsymbol{F}^\top(\boldsymbol{\theta})\boldsymbol{f}(\boldsymbol{\theta}) = \mathbf{0}$, we solve the estimating equations (9.71) to obtain an efficient estimator. This is equivalent to minimizing $\boldsymbol{f}^\top(\boldsymbol{\theta})\boldsymbol{f}(\boldsymbol{\theta})$. The estimated covariance matrix of $\hat{\boldsymbol{\theta}}$ is

$$\widehat{\operatorname{Var}}(\hat{\boldsymbol{\theta}}) = \hat{\sigma}^2(\hat{\boldsymbol{F}}^\top\hat{\boldsymbol{F}})^{-1},$$

where $\hat{\sigma}^2$ consistently estimates σ^2. If the model is a nonlinear regression model, then $\hat{\boldsymbol{\theta}}$ is really the nonlinear least-squares estimator discussed in Section 6.3.

When $\operatorname{plim} n^{-1}\boldsymbol{F}^\top(\boldsymbol{\theta})\boldsymbol{f}(\boldsymbol{\theta}) \neq \mathbf{0}$, we must replace $\boldsymbol{F}(\boldsymbol{\theta})$ by an estimate of its conditional expectation. This means that we solve the estimating equations (9.77), which is equivalent to minimizing $\boldsymbol{f}^\top(\boldsymbol{\theta})\boldsymbol{P_W}\boldsymbol{f}(\boldsymbol{\theta})$. The estimated covariance matrix of $\hat{\boldsymbol{\theta}}$ is

$$\widehat{\operatorname{Var}}(\hat{\boldsymbol{\theta}}) = \hat{\sigma}^2(\hat{\boldsymbol{F}}^\top\boldsymbol{P_W}\hat{\boldsymbol{F}})^{-1}.$$

If the model is a nonlinear regression model, then $\hat{\boldsymbol{\theta}}$ is really the nonlinear instrumental variables estimator discussed in Section 8.9.

Case 2. Covariance matrix known up to a scalar factor: $\boldsymbol{\Omega} = \sigma^2\boldsymbol{\Delta}$.

When $\operatorname{plim} n^{-1}\boldsymbol{F}^\top(\boldsymbol{\theta})\boldsymbol{f}(\boldsymbol{\theta}) = \mathbf{0}$, we solve the estimating equations (9.82), with $\boldsymbol{\Omega}$ replaced by $\boldsymbol{\Delta}$, to obtain an efficient estimator. This is equivalent to minimizing $\boldsymbol{f}^\top(\boldsymbol{\theta})\boldsymbol{\Delta}^{-1}\boldsymbol{f}(\boldsymbol{\theta})$. The estimated covariance matrix is

$$\widehat{\operatorname{Var}}(\hat{\boldsymbol{\theta}}) = \hat{\sigma}^2(\hat{\boldsymbol{F}}^\top\boldsymbol{\Delta}^{-1}\hat{\boldsymbol{F}})^{-1},$$

where $\hat{\sigma}^2$ consistently estimates σ^2. If the underlying model is a nonlinear regression model, then $\hat{\boldsymbol{\theta}}$ is really the nonlinear GLS estimator discussed in Section 7.3.

When $\operatorname{plim} n^{-1}\boldsymbol{F}^\top(\boldsymbol{\theta})\boldsymbol{f}(\boldsymbol{\theta}) \neq \mathbf{0}$, we again must replace $\boldsymbol{F}(\boldsymbol{\theta})$ by an estimate of its conditional expectation. This means that we should solve the estimating equations (9.89) with $\boldsymbol{A} = \boldsymbol{\Psi}^\top\boldsymbol{W}$, where $\boldsymbol{\Psi}$ satisfies $\boldsymbol{\Delta}^{-1} = \boldsymbol{\Psi}\boldsymbol{\Psi}^\top$. This is equivalent to minimizing (9.88) with the same definition of $\boldsymbol{A}$. The estimated covariance matrix is

$$\hat{\sigma}^2(\hat{\boldsymbol{F}}^\top\boldsymbol{\Psi}\boldsymbol{P}_{\boldsymbol{\Psi}^\top\boldsymbol{W}}\boldsymbol{\Psi}^\top\hat{\boldsymbol{F}})^{-1}.$$

If the model is a linear regression model, then $\hat{\boldsymbol{\theta}}$ is the fully efficient GMM estimator (9.26) whenever the span of the instruments $\boldsymbol{W}$ includes the span of the optimal instruments $\bar{\boldsymbol{X}}$.

When the matrix $\boldsymbol{\Delta}$ is unknown but depends on a fixed number of parameters that can be estimated consistently, we can replace $\boldsymbol{\Delta}$ by a consistent estimator $\hat{\boldsymbol{\Delta}}$ and proceed as if it were known, as in feasible GLS estimation.

Case 3. Unknown diagonal or general covariance matrix.

This is the most commonly encountered case in which GMM estimation is explicitly used. Fully efficient estimation is no longer possible, but we can still obtain estimates that are efficient for a given set of instruments by using a consistent estimator $\hat{\boldsymbol{\Sigma}}$ of the matrix $\boldsymbol{\Sigma}$ defined in (9.33). This estimator is heteroskedasticity-consistent if $\boldsymbol{\Omega}$ is assumed to be diagonal and some sort of HAC estimator otherwise. Whether or not $\operatorname{plim} n^{-1}\boldsymbol{F}^\top(\boldsymbol{\theta})\boldsymbol{f}(\boldsymbol{\theta}) = \mathbf{0}$, we solve the estimating equations (9.79), which is equivalent to minimizing (9.86). The estimated covariance matrix is (9.81). If there is to be any gain in efficiency relative to NLS or nonlinear IV, it is essential that l, the number of columns of $\boldsymbol{W}$, be greater than k, the number of parameters to be estimated.

The consistent estimator $\hat{\boldsymbol{\Sigma}}$ is usually obtained from initial estimates that are consistent but inefficient. These may be NLS estimates, nonlinear IV estimates, or GMM estimates that do not use the optimal weighting matrix. The efficient GMM estimates are usually obtained by minimizing the criterion function (9.86), and the minimized value of this criterion function then serves as a Hansen-Sargan test statistic.

The first-round estimates $\hat{\boldsymbol{\theta}}$ can be used to obtain a new estimate of $\boldsymbol{\Sigma}$, which can then be used to obtain a second-round estimate of $\boldsymbol{\theta}$, which can be used to obtain yet another estimate of $\boldsymbol{\Sigma}$, and so on, until the process converges or the investigator loses patience. For a correctly specified model, all of these estimators have the same asymptotic distribution. However, performing more than one iteration often improves the finite-sample properties of the estimator. Thus, if computing cost is not a problem, it may well be best to use the continuously updated estimator that has been iterated to convergence.

For a more thorough treatment of the asymptotic theory of GMM estimation, see Newey and McFadden (1994).

9.6 The Method of Simulated Moments

It is often possible to use GMM even when the elementary zero functions cannot be evaluated analytically. Suppose they take the form

$$f_t(y_t, \boldsymbol{\theta}) = h_t(y_t) - m_t(\boldsymbol{\theta}), \quad t = 1, \ldots, n, \tag{9.93}$$

where the function $h_t(y_t)$ depends only on y_t and, possibly, on exogenous or predetermined variables. The function $m_t(\boldsymbol{\theta})$ depends only on exogenous or predetermined variables and on the parameters. Like a regression function, it is the expectation of $h_t(y_t)$, conditional on the information set Ω_t, under a DGP characterized by the parameter vector $\boldsymbol{\theta}$. Estimating such a model by GMM presents no special difficulty if the form of $m_t(\boldsymbol{\theta})$ is known analytically, but this need not be the case.

There are numerous situations in which $m_t(\boldsymbol{\theta})$ may not be known analytically. In particular, it may well occur in models which involve **latent variables**, that is, variables which are not observable by an econometrician. The variables that actually are observed are related to the latent variables in such a way that knowing the former does not permit the values of the latter to be fully recovered. One example, which was discussed in Section 8.2, is economic variables that are observed with measurement error. Another example is variables that are **censored**, in the sense that they are observed only to a limited extent, for instance when only the sign of the variable is observed, or when all negative values are replaced by zeros. Even if the distributions of the latent variables are tractable, those of the observed variables may not be. In particular, it may not be possible to obtain analytic expressions for their expectations, or for the expectations of functions of them.

Even when analytic expressions are not available, it is often possible to obtain simulation-based estimates of the distributions of the observed variables. For example, suppose that an observed variable is equal to a latent variable plus a measurement error of some known distribution, possibly dependent on the parameter vector $\boldsymbol{\theta}$. Suppose further that, for a DGP characterized by $\boldsymbol{\theta}$, we can readily generate simulated values of the latent variable. Simulated values of the observed variable can then be generated by adding simulated measurement errors, drawn from their known distribution, to the simulated values of the latent variable. The mean of these drawings then provides an estimate of the expectation of the observed variable.

In general, an **unbiased simulator** for the unknown expectation $m_t(\boldsymbol{\theta})$ is any function $m_t^*(u_t^*, \boldsymbol{\theta})$ of the model parameters, variables in Ω_t, and a random variable u_t^*, which either has a known distribution or can be simulated, such that, for all $\boldsymbol{\theta}$ in the parameter space, $\mathrm{E}\big(m_t^*(u_t^*, \boldsymbol{\theta})\big) = m_t(\boldsymbol{\theta})$. To simplify notation, we write u_t^* as a scalar random variable, but it may well be a vector of random variables in practical situations of interest.

The conceptually simplest unbiased simulator can be implemented as follows. For given $\boldsymbol{\theta}$, we obtain S simulated values y_{ts}^* of the observed variable under the DGP characterized by $\boldsymbol{\theta}$, making use of S random numbers u^*_{ts}. Then we let $m^*(u^*_{ts}, \boldsymbol{\theta}) = h_t(y^*_{ts})$. If (9.93) is indeed a zero function, then $h_t(y^*_{ts})$ must have expectation $m_t(\boldsymbol{\theta})$, and it is obvious that the sample mean of the simulated values $h(y^*_{ts})$ is a simulation-based estimate of that expectation. This simple simulator, which is applicable whether or not the model involves any latent variables, is not the only possible simulator, and it may not be the most desirable one for some purposes. However, we will not consider more complicated simulators in this book.

If an unbiased simulator is available, the elementary zero functions (9.93) can be replaced by the functions

$$f^*_t(y_t, \boldsymbol{\theta}) = h_t(y_t) - \frac{1}{S}\sum_{s=1}^{S} m^*_t(u^*_{ts}, \boldsymbol{\theta}), \tag{9.94}$$

where the u^*_{ts}, $t = 1, \ldots, n$, $s = 1, \ldots, S$, are mutually independent draws. Since these draws are computer generated, they are evidently independent of the y_t. The functions (9.94) are legitimate elementary zero functions, even in the trivial case in which $S = 1$. If the true DGP is characterized by $\boldsymbol{\theta}_0$, then $\mathrm{E}\big(h_t(y_t)\big) = m_t(\boldsymbol{\theta}_0)$ by definition, and $\mathrm{E}\big(m^*_t(u^*_{ts}, \boldsymbol{\theta}_0)\big) = m_t(\boldsymbol{\theta}_0)$ for all s by construction. It follows that the expectation (9.94) is zero for $\boldsymbol{\theta} = \boldsymbol{\theta}_0$, but not in general for other values of $\boldsymbol{\theta}$.

The application of GMM to the zero functions (9.94) is called the **method of simulated moments**, or **MSM**. We can use an $n \times l$ matrix $\boldsymbol{W}$ of appropriate instruments, with $l \geq k$, in order to form the empirical moments

$$\boldsymbol{W}^\top \boldsymbol{f}^*(\boldsymbol{\theta}), \tag{9.95}$$

in which the n–vector of functions $\boldsymbol{f}^*(\boldsymbol{\theta})$ has typical element $f^*_t(y_t, \boldsymbol{\theta})$. A GMM estimator that is efficient relative to this set of empirical moments may be obtained by minimizing the quadratic form

$$Q(\boldsymbol{\theta}, \boldsymbol{y}) \equiv \frac{1}{n}\boldsymbol{f}^{*\top}(\boldsymbol{\theta})\boldsymbol{W}\hat{\boldsymbol{\Sigma}}^{-1}\boldsymbol{W}^\top \boldsymbol{f}^*(\boldsymbol{\theta}) \tag{9.96}$$

with respect to $\boldsymbol{\theta}$, where $\hat{\boldsymbol{\Sigma}}$ consistently estimates the covariance matrix of $n^{-1/2}\boldsymbol{W}^\top \boldsymbol{f}^*(\boldsymbol{\theta})$.

Minimizing the criterion function (9.96) with respect to $\boldsymbol{\theta}$ proceeds in the usual way, with one important proviso. Each evaluation of $\boldsymbol{f}^*(\boldsymbol{\theta})$ requires a large number of pseudo-random numbers (generally, at least nS of them). It is absolutely essential that the *same* set of random numbers be used every time $\boldsymbol{f}^*(\boldsymbol{\theta})$ is evaluated for a new value of the parameter vector $\boldsymbol{\theta}$. Otherwise, (9.96) would change not only as a result of changes in $\boldsymbol{\theta}$ but also as a result of changes in the random numbers used for the simulation. Therefore, if the algorithm happened to evaluate the criterion function twice at the same parameter vector, it would obtain two different values of $Q(\boldsymbol{\theta}, \boldsymbol{y})$, and it could not possibly tell where the minimum was located.

The details of the simulations, of course, differ from case to case. An important point is that, since we require a fully specified DGP in order to generate the simulated data, it is generally necessary to make stronger distributional assumptions for the purposes of MSM estimation than for the purposes of GMM estimation.

The Asymptotic Distribution of the MSM Estimator

Because the criterion function (9.96) is based on genuine zero functions, the estimator $\hat{\boldsymbol{\theta}}_{\text{MSM}}$ obtained by minimizing it is consistent whenever the parameters are identified. However, as we will see in a moment, using simulated quantities does affect the asymptotic covariance matrix of the estimator, although the effect is generally very small if S is a reasonably large number.

The first-order conditions for minimizing (9.96), ignoring a factor of $2/n$, are

$$\boldsymbol{F}^{*\top}(\boldsymbol{\theta})\boldsymbol{W}\hat{\boldsymbol{\Sigma}}^{-1}\boldsymbol{W}^{\top}\boldsymbol{f}^{*}(\boldsymbol{\theta}) = \mathbf{0}, \tag{9.97}$$

where $\boldsymbol{F}^{*}(\boldsymbol{\theta})$ is the $n \times k$ matrix of which the ti^{th} element is $\partial f_t^{*}(y_t, \boldsymbol{\theta})/\partial\theta_i$. The solution to these equations is $\hat{\boldsymbol{\theta}}_{\text{MSM}}$. Although conditions (9.97) look very similar to conditions (9.79), the covariance matrix is, in general, a good deal more complicated.

From (9.97), it can be seen that the instruments effectively used by the MSM estimator are $\boldsymbol{W}\hat{\boldsymbol{\Sigma}}^{-1}(n^{-1}\boldsymbol{W}^{\top}\boldsymbol{F}_0^{*})$, where $\boldsymbol{F}_0^{*} \equiv \boldsymbol{F}^{*}(\boldsymbol{\theta}_0)$, and a factor of n^{-1} has been used to keep the expression of order unity as $n \to \infty$. If we think of the effective instruments as $\boldsymbol{Z} = \boldsymbol{W}\boldsymbol{J}$, then $\boldsymbol{J} = \hat{\boldsymbol{\Sigma}}^{-1}(n^{-1}\boldsymbol{W}^{\top}\boldsymbol{F}_0^{*})$.

The asymptotic covariance matrix of $n^{1/2}(\hat{\boldsymbol{\theta}}_{\text{MSM}} - \boldsymbol{\theta}_0)$ can now be found by using the general formula (9.78) for the asymptotic covariance matrix of an efficient GMM estimator with unknown covariance matrix. This is a sandwich estimator of the form $\boldsymbol{A}^{-1}\boldsymbol{B}\boldsymbol{A}^{-1}$, and we find that

$$\begin{aligned}\boldsymbol{A} &= \operatorname*{plim}_{n\to\infty}(n^{-1}\boldsymbol{F}_0^{*\top}\boldsymbol{W})\hat{\boldsymbol{\Sigma}}^{-1}(n^{-1}\boldsymbol{W}^{\top}\boldsymbol{F}_0^{*}), \text{ and}\\ \boldsymbol{B} &= \operatorname*{plim}_{n\to\infty}(n^{-1}\boldsymbol{F}_0^{*\top}\boldsymbol{W})\hat{\boldsymbol{\Sigma}}^{-1}(n^{-1}\boldsymbol{W}^{\top}\boldsymbol{\Omega}\boldsymbol{W})\hat{\boldsymbol{\Sigma}}^{-1}(n^{-1}\boldsymbol{W}^{\top}\boldsymbol{F}_0^{*}),\end{aligned} \tag{9.98}$$

where $\boldsymbol{\Omega}$ is the $n \times n$ covariance matrix of $\boldsymbol{f}^{*}(\boldsymbol{\theta}_0)$.

The ti^{th} element of $\boldsymbol{F}^{*}(\boldsymbol{\theta})$ is, from (9.94),

$$F_{ti}^{*}(\boldsymbol{\theta}) = -\frac{1}{S}\sum_{s=1}^{S}\frac{\partial m_t^{*}(u_{ts}^{*}, \boldsymbol{\theta})}{\partial\theta_i}.$$

If m_t^{*} is differentiable with respect to $\boldsymbol{\theta}$ in a neighborhood of $\boldsymbol{\theta}$, then we can differentiate the relation $\mathrm{E}\big(m_t^*(u_t^*,\boldsymbol{\theta})\big) = m_t(\boldsymbol{\theta})$ to find that

$$\mathrm{E}\Big(\frac{\partial m_t^*(u_t^*,\boldsymbol{\theta})}{\partial\theta_i}\Big) = \frac{\partial m_t(\boldsymbol{\theta})}{\partial\theta_i}.$$

We denote by $\boldsymbol{M}(\boldsymbol{\theta})$ the $n\times k$ matrix with typical element $\partial m_t/\partial\theta_i(\boldsymbol{\theta})$. By a law of large numbers, we then see that $\operatorname{plim} n^{-1}\boldsymbol{W}^\top\boldsymbol{F}_0^* = \operatorname{plim} n^{-1}\boldsymbol{W}^\top\boldsymbol{M}_0$, where $\boldsymbol{M}_0 \equiv \boldsymbol{M}(\boldsymbol{\theta}_0)$.

Consider next the covariance matrix $\boldsymbol{\Omega}$ of $\boldsymbol{f}^*(\boldsymbol{\theta}_0)$. The original data y_t are of course completely independent of the simulated u_{ts}^*, and the simulated data are independent across simulations. Thus, from (9.94), we see that

$$\boldsymbol{\Omega} = \mathrm{Var}\big(\boldsymbol{h}(\boldsymbol{y})\big) + \frac{1}{S}\mathrm{Var}\big(\boldsymbol{m}^*(\boldsymbol{\theta}_0)\big), \tag{9.99}$$

where $\boldsymbol{h}(\boldsymbol{y})$ and $\boldsymbol{m}^*(\boldsymbol{\theta})$ are the n–vectors with typical elements $h_t(y_t)$ and $m_t^*(u_t^*,\boldsymbol{\theta})$, respectively. We see that the covariance matrix $\boldsymbol{\Omega}$ has two components, one due to the randomness of the data and the other due to the randomness of the simulations. If the simulator $m_t^*(\cdot)$ is the simple one suggested above, then the simulated data $h_t(y_t^*)$ are generated from the DGP characterized by $\boldsymbol{\theta}$, which is also supposed to have generated the real data. Therefore, it is clear that $\mathrm{Var}\big(\boldsymbol{h}(\boldsymbol{y})\big) = \mathrm{Var}\big(\boldsymbol{m}^*(\boldsymbol{\theta}_0)\big)$, and we conclude that $\boldsymbol{\Omega} = (1+1/S)\mathrm{Var}\big(\boldsymbol{h}(\boldsymbol{y})\big)$.

In general, the $n\times n$ matrix $\boldsymbol{\Omega}$ cannot be estimated consistently, but an HCCME or HAC estimator can be used to provide a consistent estimate of $\boldsymbol{\Sigma}$, the covariance matrix of $n^{-1/2}\boldsymbol{W}^\top\boldsymbol{f}^*(\boldsymbol{\theta}_0)$. For the simple simulator we have been discussing, $\hat{\boldsymbol{\Sigma}}$ is just $1+1/S$ times whatever HAC estimator or HCCME would be appropriate if there were no simulation involved. For other simulators, it may be a little harder to estimate (9.99). In any case, once $\hat{\boldsymbol{\Sigma}}$ is available, we use it to replace $n^{-1}\boldsymbol{W}^\top\boldsymbol{\Omega}\boldsymbol{W}$ in (9.98). We also replace $\operatorname{plim} n^{-1}\boldsymbol{W}^\top\boldsymbol{F}_0^*$ by $\operatorname{plim} n^{-1}\boldsymbol{W}^\top\boldsymbol{M}_0$. The sandwich estimator for the asymptotic covariance matrix then simplifies greatly, and we find that the asymptotic covariance matrix is just

$$\operatorname*{plim}_{n\to\infty}\Big((n^{-1}\boldsymbol{M}_0^\top\boldsymbol{W})\hat{\boldsymbol{\Sigma}}^{-1}(n^{-1}\boldsymbol{W}^\top\boldsymbol{M}_0)\Big)^{-1}.$$

In practice, $\boldsymbol{M}_0$ can be estimated using either analytical or numerical derivatives of $(1/S)\sum_{s=1}^S m_t^*(u_{ts}^*,\hat{\boldsymbol{\theta}})$, evaluated at $\hat{\boldsymbol{\theta}}_{\mathrm{MSM}}$. However, for this to be a reliable estimator, it is necessary for S to be reasonably large. If we let $\hat{\boldsymbol{M}}$ denote the estimate of $\boldsymbol{M}_0$, then in practice we use

$$\widehat{\mathrm{Var}}(\hat{\boldsymbol{\theta}}_{\mathrm{MSM}}) = n(\hat{\boldsymbol{M}}^\top\boldsymbol{W}\hat{\boldsymbol{\Sigma}}^{-1}\boldsymbol{W}^\top\hat{\boldsymbol{M}})^{-1}. \tag{9.100}$$

Notice that (9.100) has essentially the same form as (9.41) and (9.81), the estimated covariance matrices for the feasible efficient GMM estimators of linear regression and general nonlinear models, respectively. The most important new feature of (9.100) is the factor of $1+1/S$, which is buried in $\hat{\boldsymbol{\Sigma}}$.

The Lognormal Distribution: An Example

Since the implementation of MSM estimation typically involves several steps and can be rather tricky, we now work through a simple example in detail. The example is in fact sufficiently simple that there is no need for simulation at all; we can work out the "right answer" directly. This provides a benchmark with which to compare the various other estimators that we consider. In order to motivate these other estimators, we demonstrate how GMM can be used to **match moments** of distributions. Moment matching can be done quite easily when the moments to be matched can be expressed analytically as functions of the parameters to be estimated, and no simulation is needed in such cases. If analytic expressions are not available, moment matching can still be done whenever we can simulate the random variables of which the expectations are the moments to be matched.

A random variable is said to follow the **lognormal distribution** if its logarithm is normally distributed. The lognormal distribution for a scalar random variable y thus depends on just two parameters, the expectation and the variance of $\log y$. Formally, if $z \sim \mathrm{N}(\mu, \sigma^2)$, then the variable $y \equiv \exp(z)$ is lognormally distributed, with a distribution characterized by μ and σ^2.

Suppose we have an n–vector $\boldsymbol{y}$, of which the components y_t are IID, each lognormally distributed with unknown parameters μ and σ^2. The "right" way to estimate these unknown parameters is to take logs of each component of $\boldsymbol{y}$, thus obtaining an n–vector $\boldsymbol{z}$ with typical element z_t, and then to estimate μ and σ^2 by the sample mean and sample variance of the z_t. This can be done by regressing $\boldsymbol{z}$ on a constant.

The above estimation method implicitly **matches** the first and second moments of the log of y_t in order to estimate the parameters. It yields the parameter values that give theoretical moments equal to the corresponding moments in the sample. Since we have two parameters to estimate, we need at least two moments. But other sets of two moments could also be used in order to obtain MM estimators of μ and σ^2. So could sets of more than two moments, although the match could not be perfect, because there would implicitly be overidentifying restrictions.

We now consider precisely how we might estimate μ and σ^2 by matching the first moment of the y_t along with the first moment of the z_t. With this choice, it is once more possible to obtain an analytical answer, because, as the result of Exercise 9.19 shows, the expectation of y_t is $\exp(\mu + \frac{1}{2}\sigma^2)$. Thus, as before, we estimate μ by using $\bar{z}$, the sample mean of the z_t, and then estimate σ^2 by solving the equation

$$\log \bar{y} = \bar{z} + \tfrac{1}{2}\hat{\sigma}^2$$

for $\hat{\sigma}^2$, where $\bar{y}$ is the sample mean of the y_t. The estimate is

$$\hat{\sigma}^2 = 2(\log \bar{y} - \bar{z}). \tag{9.101}$$

This estimate is not, except by random accident, numerically equal to the estimate obtained by regressing $\boldsymbol{z}$ on a constant, and in fact it has a higher variance; see Exercises 9.20 and 9.21.

Let us formalize the estimation procedure described above in terms of zero functions and GMM. The moments used are the first moments of the y_t and the z_t, for $t = 1, \ldots, n$. For each observation, then, there are two elementary zero functions, which serve to express the expectations of the y_t and the z_t in terms of the parameters μ and σ^2. We write these elementary zero functions as follows:

$$f_{t1}(z_t, \mu, \sigma^2) = z_t - \mu; \quad f_{t2}(y_t, \mu, \sigma^2) = y_t - \exp(\mu + \tfrac{1}{2}\sigma^2). \tag{9.102}$$

The derivatives of these functions with respect to the parameters are

$$\frac{\partial f_{t1}}{\partial \mu} = -1; \quad \frac{\partial f_{t1}}{\partial \sigma^2} = 0; \quad \frac{\partial f_{t2}}{\partial \mu} = -e^{\mu+\sigma^2/2}; \quad \frac{\partial f_{t2}}{\partial \sigma^2} = -\frac{1}{2}e^{\mu+\sigma^2/2}. \tag{9.103}$$

These derivatives, which are all deterministic, allow us to find the optimal instruments for the estimation of μ and σ^2 on the basis of the zero functions (9.102), provided that we can also obtain the covariance matrix $\boldsymbol{\Omega}$ of the zero functions.

Notice that, in contrast to many GMM estimation procedures, this one involves two elementary zero functions and no instruments. Nevertheless, we can set the problem up so that it looks like a standard one. Let $\boldsymbol{f}_1(\mu, \sigma^2)$ and $\boldsymbol{f}_2(\mu, \sigma^2)$ be two n−vectors with typical components $f_{t1}(z_t, \mu, \sigma^2)$ and $f_{t2}(y_t, \mu, \sigma^2)$, respectively. For notational simplicity, we suppress the explicit dependence of these vectors on the y_t and the z_t. The $2n$−vector $\boldsymbol{f}(\mu, \sigma^2)$ of the full set of elementary zero functions, and the $2n \times 2$ matrix $\boldsymbol{F}(\mu, \sigma^2)$ of the derivatives with respect to the parameters, can thus be written as

$$\boldsymbol{f}(\mu, \sigma^2) = \begin{bmatrix} \boldsymbol{f}_1(\mu, \sigma^2) \\ \boldsymbol{f}_2(\mu, \sigma^2) \end{bmatrix} \quad \text{and} \quad \boldsymbol{F}(\mu, \sigma^2) = -\begin{bmatrix} \boldsymbol{\iota} & \mathbf{0} \\ a\boldsymbol{\iota} & \frac{1}{2}a\boldsymbol{\iota} \end{bmatrix}, \tag{9.104}$$

where $a \equiv \exp(\mu + {}^1\!/_2\sigma^2)$. The constant vectors $\boldsymbol{\iota}$ in $\boldsymbol{F}(\mu, \sigma^2)$ arise because none of the derivatives in (9.103) depends on t, which is a consequence of the assumption that the data are IID.

Because $\boldsymbol{f}(\mu, \sigma^2)$ is a $2n$−vector, the covariance matrix $\boldsymbol{\Omega}$ is $2n \times 2n$. This matrix can be written as

$$\boldsymbol{\Omega} = E\left(\begin{bmatrix} \boldsymbol{f}_{10} \\ \boldsymbol{f}_{20} \end{bmatrix} [\boldsymbol{f}_{10}^\top \;\; \boldsymbol{f}_{20}^\top]\right),$$

where $\boldsymbol{f}_{i0}$, $i = 1, 2$, is $\boldsymbol{f}_i$ evaluated at the true values μ_0 and σ_0^2. Since the data are IID, $\boldsymbol{\Omega}$ can be partitioned as follows into four $n \times n$ blocks, each of which is proportional to an identity matrix. The result is

$$\boldsymbol{\Omega} = \begin{bmatrix} \sigma_z^2\mathbf{I} & \sigma_{zy}\mathbf{I} \\ \sigma_{yz}\mathbf{I} & \sigma_y^2\mathbf{I} \end{bmatrix}, \tag{9.105}$$

where the coefficients of the identity matrices are the variances and covariances $\sigma_y^2 \equiv \mathrm{Var}(y_t)$, $\sigma_z^2 \equiv \mathrm{Var}(z_t)$, and $\sigma_{yz} = \sigma_{zy} \equiv \mathrm{Cov}(y_t, z_t)$.

We now have everything we need to set up the efficient estimating equations (9.82), which, ignoring the factor of n^{-1}, become

$$\boldsymbol{F}^\top(\mu, \sigma^2)\boldsymbol{\Omega}^{-1}\boldsymbol{f}(\mu, \sigma^2) = \mathbf{0}, \tag{9.106}$$

where $\boldsymbol{f}(\cdot)$ and $\boldsymbol{F}(\cdot)$ are given by (9.104), and $\boldsymbol{\Omega}$ is given by (9.105). By explicitly performing the multiplications of partitioned matrices in (9.106), inverting $\boldsymbol{\Omega}$, and ignoring irrelevant scalar factors, we obtain

$$\begin{bmatrix} \sigma_y^2 - a\sigma_{yz} & a\sigma_z^2 - \sigma_{yz} \\ -\frac{1}{2}a\sigma_{yz} & \frac{1}{2}a\sigma_z^2 \end{bmatrix} \begin{bmatrix} \boldsymbol{\iota}^\top & \mathbf{0} \\ \mathbf{0} & \boldsymbol{\iota}^\top \end{bmatrix} \begin{bmatrix} \boldsymbol{f}_1(\mu, \sigma^2) \\ \boldsymbol{f}_2(\mu, \sigma^2) \end{bmatrix} = \mathbf{0}.$$

Since the leftmost factor above is a 2×2 nonsingular matrix, we see that these estimating equations are equivalent to

$$\boldsymbol{\iota}^\top \boldsymbol{f}_1(\mu, \sigma^2) = \mathbf{0} \quad \text{and} \quad \boldsymbol{\iota}^\top \boldsymbol{f}_2(\mu, \sigma^2) = \mathbf{0}. \tag{9.107}$$

The solution to these two equations is $\hat{\mu} = \bar{z}$ and $\hat{\sigma}^2$ given by (9.101). Curiously, it appears that the explicit expressions for $\boldsymbol{F}(\cdot)$ and $\boldsymbol{\Omega}$ are not needed in order to formulate the estimator. They are needed, however, for the evaluation of expression (9.67) for its asymptotic covariance matrix. This is left as an exercise for the reader; in particular, the same expression for the variance of $\hat{\sigma}^2$ should be found as in the answer to Exercise 9.21.

As we mentioned above, it is possible to use more than two moments. Suppose that, in addition to matching the first moments of the z_t and the y_t, we also wish to match the second moment of the y_t, or, equivalently, the first moment of the y_t^2. Since the log of y_t^2 is just $2z_t$, which is distributed as $\mathrm{N}(2\mu, 4\sigma^2)$, the expectation of y_t^2 is $\exp\bigl(2(\mu + \sigma^2)\bigr)$. We now have three elementary zero functions for each observation, the two given in (9.102) and

$$f_{t3}(y_t, \mu, \sigma^2) = y_t^2 - \exp\bigl(2(\mu + \sigma^2)\bigr).$$

The vector $\boldsymbol{f}(\cdot)$ and the matrix $\boldsymbol{F}(\cdot)$, originally defined in (9.104), now both have $3n$ rows. The latter still has two columns, both of which can be partitioned into three n-vectors, each proportional to $\boldsymbol{\iota}$. Further, the matrix $\boldsymbol{\Omega}$ of (9.105) grows to become a $3n \times 3n$ matrix. It is then a matter of taste whether to set up a just identified estimation problem using as optimal instruments the two columns of $\boldsymbol{\Omega}^{-1}\boldsymbol{F}(\mu, \sigma^2)$, or to use three instruments, which are the columns of the matrix

$$\boldsymbol{W} \equiv \begin{bmatrix} \boldsymbol{\iota} & \mathbf{0} & \mathbf{0} \\ \mathbf{0} & \boldsymbol{\iota} & \mathbf{0} \\ \mathbf{0} & \mathbf{0} & \boldsymbol{\iota} \end{bmatrix}, \tag{9.108}$$

and to construct an optimal weighting matrix. Whichever choice is made, it is necessary to estimate $\boldsymbol{\Omega}$ in order to construct the optimal instruments for the first method, or the optimal weighting matrix for the second.

The procedures we have just described depend on the fact that we know the analytic forms of $\mathrm{E}(z_t)$, $\mathrm{E}(y_t)$, and $\mathrm{E}(y_t^2)$. In more complicated applications, comparable analytic expressions for the moments to be matched might not be available; see Exercise 9.24 for an example. In such cases, simulators can be used to replace such analytic expressions. We illustrate the method for the case of the lognormal distribution, matching the first moments of z_t and y_t, pretending that we do not know the analytic expressions for their expectations.

For any given values of μ and σ^2, we can draw from the lognormal distribution characterized by these values by first using a random number generator to give a drawing u^* from $\mathrm{N}(0,1)$ and then computing $y^* = \exp(\mu + \sigma u^*)$. Thus unbiased simulators for the expectations of $z \equiv \log y$ and of y itself are

$$m_1^*(u^*, \mu, \sigma^2) \equiv \mu + \sigma u^* \quad \text{and} \quad m_2^*(u^*, \mu, \sigma^2) \equiv \exp(\mu + \sigma u^*).$$

If we perform S simulations, the zero functions for MSM estimation can be written as

$$f_{t1}^*(z_t, \mu, \sigma^2) = z_t - \frac{1}{S}\sum_{s=1}^{S} m_1^*(u_{ts}^*, \mu, \sigma^2) \quad \text{and}$$
$$f_{t2}^*(y_t, \mu, \sigma^2) = y_t - \frac{1}{S}\sum_{s=1}^{S} m_2^*(u_{ts}^*, \mu, \sigma^2),$$

where the u_{ts}^* are IID standard normal. Comparison with (9.102) shows clearly how we replace analytic expressions for the moments, assumed to be unknown, by simulation-based estimates.

Since the data are IID, it might appear tempting to use just one set of random numbers, u_s^*, $s = 1, \ldots, S$, for all t. However, doing this would introduce dependence among the zero functions, greatly complicating the computation of their covariance matrix. As S becomes large, of course, the law of large numbers ensures that this effect becomes less and less important. Using just one set of random numbers would in any case not affect the consistency of the MSM estimator, merely that of the covariance matrix estimate.

By analogy with (9.107), we can see that the MSM estimating equations are

$$\boldsymbol{\iota}^{\top}\boldsymbol{f}_1^*(\hat{\mu}, \hat{\sigma}^2) = \mathbf{0} \quad \text{and} \quad \boldsymbol{\iota}^{\top}\boldsymbol{f}_2^*(\hat{\mu}, \hat{\sigma}^2) = \mathbf{0}. \tag{9.109}$$

Here we have again grouped the elementary zero functions into two n-vectors $\boldsymbol{f}_1^*(\cdot)$ and $\boldsymbol{f}_2^*(\cdot)$. Recalling that the random numbers u_{ts}^* are drawn *only once* for the entire procedure, let us make the definitions

$$
\begin{aligned}
m_{t1}(\mu,\sigma^2) &\equiv \frac{1}{S}\sum_{s=1}^{S} m_1^*(u_{ts}^*,\mu,\sigma^2) = \mu + \sigma\frac{1}{S}\sum_{s=1}^{S} u_{ts}^*, \quad\text{and}\\
m_{t2}(\mu,\sigma^2) &\equiv \frac{1}{S}\sum_{s=1}^{S} m_2^*(u_{ts}^*,\mu,\sigma^2) = \frac{1}{S}\sum_{s=1}^{S} \exp(\mu + \sigma u_{ts}^*).
\end{aligned}
\tag{9.110}
$$

It is clear that, as $S \to \infty$, these functions tend for all t to the limits of the expectations of z and y, respectively. It is also not hard to see that these limits are μ and $\exp(\mu + \frac{1}{2}\sigma^2)$.

On dividing by the sample size n and rearranging, the estimating equations (9.109) can be written as

$$
\bar{m}_1(\mu,\sigma^2) = \bar{z} \quad\text{and}\quad \bar{m}_2(\mu,\sigma^2) = \bar{y},
\tag{9.111}
$$

where $\bar{z}$ and $\bar{y}$ are the sample averages of the z_t and the y_t, respectively, and

$$
\bar{m}_i(\mu,\sigma^2) \equiv \frac{1}{n}\sum_{t=1}^{n} m_{ti}(\mu,\sigma^2), \quad i = 1,2.
$$

Equations (9.111) can be solved in various ways. One approach is to turn the problem of solving them into a minimization problem. Let

$$
\boldsymbol{W} \equiv \begin{bmatrix} \boldsymbol{\iota} & \mathbf{0} \\ \mathbf{0} & \boldsymbol{\iota} \end{bmatrix}.
\tag{9.112}
$$

Then it is not difficult to see that minimizing the quadratic form

$$
\begin{bmatrix} \boldsymbol{z} - \boldsymbol{m}_1(\mu,\sigma^2) \\ \boldsymbol{y} - \boldsymbol{m}_2(\mu,\sigma^2) \end{bmatrix}^{\top} \boldsymbol{W}\boldsymbol{W}^{\top} \begin{bmatrix} \boldsymbol{z} - \boldsymbol{m}_1(\mu,\sigma^2) \\ \boldsymbol{y} - \boldsymbol{m}_2(\mu,\sigma^2) \end{bmatrix}
\tag{9.113}
$$

also solves equations (9.111); see Exercise 9.23. Here the n–vectors $\boldsymbol{m}_1(\cdot)$ and $\boldsymbol{m}_2(\cdot)$ have typical elements $m_{t1}(\cdot)$ and $m_{t2}(\cdot)$, respectively.

Alternatively, we can use Newton's Method directly. We discussed this procedure in Section 6.4, in connection with minimizing a nonlinear function, but it can also be applied to sets of equations like (9.111). Suppose that we wish to solve a set of k equations of the form $\boldsymbol{g}(\boldsymbol{\theta}) = \mathbf{0}$ for a k–vector of unknowns $\boldsymbol{\theta}$, where $\boldsymbol{g}(\cdot)$ is also a k–vector. The iterative step analogous to (6.43) is

$$
\boldsymbol{\theta}_{(j+1)} = \boldsymbol{\theta}_{(j)} - \boldsymbol{G}^{-1}(\boldsymbol{\theta}_{(j)})\boldsymbol{g}(\boldsymbol{\theta}_{(j)}),
\tag{9.114}
$$

where $\boldsymbol{G}(\boldsymbol{\theta})$ is the **Jacobian matrix** associated with $\boldsymbol{g}(\boldsymbol{\theta})$. This $k \times k$ matrix contains the derivatives of the components of $\boldsymbol{g}(\boldsymbol{\theta})$ with respect to the elements of $\boldsymbol{\theta}$. For the estimating equations (9.111), the iterative step (9.114) becomes

$$\begin{bmatrix} \mu_{(j+1)} \\ \sigma^2_{(j+1)} \end{bmatrix} = \begin{bmatrix} \mu_{(j)} \\ \sigma^2_{(j)} \end{bmatrix} - \begin{bmatrix} \dfrac{\partial \bar{m}_1}{\partial \mu} & \dfrac{\partial \bar{m}_1}{\partial \sigma^2} \\ \dfrac{\partial \bar{m}_2}{\partial \mu} & \dfrac{\partial \bar{m}_2}{\partial \sigma^2} \end{bmatrix} \begin{bmatrix} \bar{m}_1(\mu_{(j)}, \sigma^2_{(j)}) - \bar{z} \\ \bar{m}_2(\mu_{(j)}, \sigma^2_{(j)}) - \bar{y} \end{bmatrix},$$

where all the partial derivatives are evaluated at $(\mu_{(j)}, \sigma^2_{(j)})$. It should be noted that these partial derivatives *are* known analytically, as they can be calculated directly from (9.110).

To estimate the asymptotic covariance matrix of the MSM estimates, we can use any suitable estimator of (9.81), provided we remember to multiply the result by $1 + 1/S$ in order to account for the simulation randomness. The instrument matrix $\boldsymbol{W}$ of (9.81) is just the matrix $\boldsymbol{W}$ of (9.112). We are pretending that we do not know the analytic form of the matrix $\boldsymbol{F}(\mu, \sigma^2)$ given in (9.104), and so instead we use the matrix of partial derivatives of $\boldsymbol{m}_1$ and $\boldsymbol{m}_2$, evaluated at $\hat{\mu}$ and $\hat{\sigma}^2$. This matrix is

$$\hat{\boldsymbol{F}} \equiv \begin{bmatrix} \dfrac{\partial \boldsymbol{m}_1}{\partial \mu}(\hat{\mu}, \hat{\sigma}^2) & \dfrac{\partial \boldsymbol{m}_1}{\partial \sigma^2}(\hat{\mu}, \hat{\sigma}^2) \\ \dfrac{\partial \boldsymbol{m}_2}{\partial \mu}(\hat{\mu}, \hat{\sigma}^2) & \dfrac{\partial \boldsymbol{m}_2}{\partial \sigma^2}(\hat{\mu}, \hat{\sigma}^2) \end{bmatrix}; \tag{9.115}$$

note that each block in $\hat{\boldsymbol{F}}$ is an n-vector. If we use Newton's Method for the estimation, then all the partial derivatives in this matrix have already been computed. Finally, the covariance matrix $\boldsymbol{\Omega}$ of the elementary zero functions can be estimated using (9.105), by replacing the unknown quantities σ_z^2, σ_y^2, and σ_{zy} with their sample analogs. If we denote the result of this by $\hat{\boldsymbol{\Omega}}$, then our estimate of the covariance matrix of $\hat{\mu}$ and $\hat{\sigma}^2$ is

$$\widehat{\text{Var}} \begin{bmatrix} \hat{\mu} \\ \hat{\sigma}^2 \end{bmatrix} = (\boldsymbol{W}^\top \hat{\boldsymbol{F}})^{-1} \boldsymbol{W}^\top \hat{\boldsymbol{\Omega}} \boldsymbol{W} (\hat{\boldsymbol{F}}^\top \boldsymbol{W})^{-1}, \tag{9.116}$$

with $\boldsymbol{W}$ given by (9.112) and $\hat{\boldsymbol{F}}$ given by (9.115).

MSM Estimation: Conclusion

Although it is very special, the example of the previous subsection illustrates most of the key features of MSM estimation. The example shows how to estimate two parameters by using two or more elementary zero functions, even when there are no genuine instruments. In econometric applications, it is more common for there to be as many elementary zero functions as there are dependent variables, just one in the case of univariate models, and for there to be more instruments than parameters. Also, in many applications, the data are not IID, but this complication generally does not require substantial changes to the methods illustrated above.

Inference in models estimated by MSM is almost always based on asymptotic theory, and it may therefore be quite unreliable in finite samples. Since MSM estimation makes sense only when a model is too intractable for less computationally demanding methods to be applicable, the cost of estimating such a model a large number of times, as would be needed to employ bootstrap methods, is likely to be prohibitive.

Not surprisingly, the literature on MSM is relatively recent. The two classic papers are McFadden (1989), who seems to have coined the name, and Pakes and Pollard (1989). Other important early papers include Lee and Ingram (1991), Keane (1994), McFadden and Ruud (1994), and Gallant and Tauchen (1996). An interesting early application of the method is Duffie and Singleton (1993). Useful references include Hajivassiliou and Ruud (1994), Gouriéroux and Monfort (1996), and van Dijk, Monfort, and Brown (1995), which is a collection of papers, both theoretical and applied.

9.7 Final Remarks

As its name implies, the generalized method of moments is a very general estimation method indeed, and numerous other methods can be thought of as special cases. These include all of the ones we have discussed so far: MM, OLS, NLS, GLS, and IV. Thus the number of techniques that can legitimately be given the label "GMM" is bewilderingly large. To avoid bewilderment, it is best not to attempt to enumerate all the possibilities, but simply to list some of the ways in which various GMM estimators differ:

- Methods for which the explanatory variables are exogenous or predetermined (including OLS, NLS, and GLS), and for which no extra instruments are required, versus methods that do require additional exogenous or predetermined instruments (including linear and nonlinear IV).
- Methods for linear models (including OLS, GLS, linear IV, and the GMM techniques discussed in Section 9.2) versus methods for nonlinear models (including NLS, GNLS, nonlinear IV, and the GMM techniques discussed in Section 9.5).
- Methods that are inefficient for a given set of moment conditions, which have sandwich covariance matrices, versus methods that are efficient for the same set of moment conditions, which do not.
- Methods that are fully efficient, because they are based on optimal instruments, versus methods that are not fully efficient.
- Methods based on a covariance matrix that is known, at least up to a finite number of parameters which can be estimated consistently, versus methods that require an HCCME or a HAC estimator. The latter can never be fully efficient.

- Methods that involve simulation, such as MSM, versus methods where the criterion function can be evaluated analytically.
- Univariate models versus multivariate models. We have not yet discussed any methods for estimating the latter, but we will do so in Chapter 12.

9.8 Exercises

9.1 Show that the difference between the matrix

$$(\boldsymbol{J}^\top\boldsymbol{W}^\top\boldsymbol{X})^{-1}\boldsymbol{J}^\top\boldsymbol{W}^\top\boldsymbol{\Omega}\boldsymbol{W}\boldsymbol{J}(\boldsymbol{X}^\top\boldsymbol{W}\boldsymbol{J})^{-1}$$

and the matrix

$$(\boldsymbol{X}^\top\boldsymbol{W}(\boldsymbol{W}^\top\boldsymbol{\Omega}\boldsymbol{W})^{-1}\boldsymbol{W}^\top\boldsymbol{X})^{-1}$$

is a positive semidefinite matrix. **Hints:** Recall Exercise 3.8. Express the second of the two matrices in terms of the projection matrix $\boldsymbol{P}_{\boldsymbol{\Omega}^{1/2}\boldsymbol{W}}$, and then find a similar projection matrix for the first of them.

9.2 Let the n–vector $\boldsymbol{u}$ be such that $\mathrm{E}(\boldsymbol{u}) = \mathbf{0}$ and $\mathrm{E}(\boldsymbol{u}\boldsymbol{u}^\top) = \mathbf{I}$, and let the $n \times l$ matrix $\boldsymbol{W}$ be such that $\mathrm{E}(\boldsymbol{W}_t u_t) = \mathbf{0}$ and that $\mathrm{E}(u_t u_s \,|\, \boldsymbol{W}_t, \boldsymbol{W}_s) = \delta_{ts}$, where δ_{ts} is the Kronecker delta introduced in Section 1.4. Assume that $\boldsymbol{S}_{\boldsymbol{W}^\top\boldsymbol{W}} \equiv \operatorname{plim} n^{-1}\boldsymbol{W}^\top\boldsymbol{W}$ is finite, deterministic, and positive definite. Explain why the quadratic form $\boldsymbol{u}^\top\boldsymbol{P}_{\boldsymbol{W}}\boldsymbol{u}$ must be asymptotically distributed as $\chi^2(l)$.

9.3 Consider the quadratic form $\boldsymbol{x}^\top\boldsymbol{A}\boldsymbol{x}$, where $\boldsymbol{x}$ is a $p \times 1$ vector and $\boldsymbol{A}$ is a $p \times p$ matrix, which may or may not be symmetric. Show that there exists a symmetric $p \times p$ matrix $\boldsymbol{B}$ such that $\boldsymbol{x}^\top\boldsymbol{B}\boldsymbol{x} = \boldsymbol{x}^\top\boldsymbol{A}\boldsymbol{x}$ for all $p \times 1$ vectors $\boldsymbol{x}$, and give the explicit form of a suitable $\boldsymbol{B}$.

⋆9.4 For the model (9.01) and a specific choice of the $l \times k$ matrix $\boldsymbol{J}$, show that minimizing the quadratic form (9.12) with weighting matrix $\boldsymbol{\Lambda} = \boldsymbol{J}\boldsymbol{J}^\top$ gives the same estimator as solving the moment conditions (9.05) with the given $\boldsymbol{J}$. Assuming that these moment conditions have a unique solution for $\boldsymbol{\beta}$, show that the matrix $\boldsymbol{J}\boldsymbol{J}^\top$ is of rank k, and hence positive semidefinite without being positive definite.

Construct a symmetric, positive definite, $l \times l$ weighting matrix $\boldsymbol{\Lambda}$ such that minimizing (9.12) with this $\boldsymbol{\Lambda}$ leads once more to the same estimator as that given by solving conditions (9.05). It is convenient to take $\boldsymbol{\Lambda}$ in the form $\boldsymbol{J}\boldsymbol{J}^\top + \boldsymbol{N}\boldsymbol{N}^\top$. In the construction of $\boldsymbol{N}$, it may be useful to partition $\boldsymbol{W}$ as $[\boldsymbol{W}_1 \;\; \boldsymbol{W}_2]$, where the $n \times k$ matrix $\boldsymbol{W}_1$ is such that $\boldsymbol{W}_1^\top\boldsymbol{X}$ is nonsingular.

⋆9.5 Consider the linear regression model with serially correlated errors,

$$y_t = \beta_1 + \beta_2 x_t + u_t, \quad u_t = \rho u_{t-1} + \varepsilon_t, \tag{9.117}$$

where the ε_t are IID, and the autoregressive parameter ρ is assumed either to be known or to be estimated consistently. The explanatory variable x_t is assumed to be contemporaneously correlated with ε_t (see Section 8.4 for the definition of contemporaneous correlation).

Recall from Chapter 7 that the covariance matrix $\boldsymbol{\Omega}$ of the vector $\boldsymbol{u}$ with typical element u_t is given by (7.32), and that $\boldsymbol{\Omega}^{-1}$ can be expressed as $\boldsymbol{\Psi}\boldsymbol{\Psi}^\top$, where $\boldsymbol{\Psi}$ is defined in (7.60). Express the model (9.117) in the form (9.20), without taking account of the first observation.

Let Ω_t be the information set for observation t with $\mathrm{E}(\varepsilon_t \,|\, \Omega_t) = 0$. Suppose that there exists a matrix $\boldsymbol{Z}$ of instrumental variables, with $\boldsymbol{Z}_t \in \Omega_t$, such that the explanatory vector $\boldsymbol{x}$ with typical element x_t is related to the instruments by the equation

$$\boldsymbol{x} = \boldsymbol{Z}\boldsymbol{\pi} + \boldsymbol{v}, \tag{9.118}$$

where $\mathrm{E}(v_t \,|\, \Omega_t) = 0$. Derive the explicit form of the expression $(\boldsymbol{\Psi}^\top \bar{\boldsymbol{X}})_t$ defined implicitly by equation (9.24) for the model (9.117). Find a matrix $\boldsymbol{W}$ of instruments that satisfy the predeterminedness condition in the form (9.30) and that lead to asymptotically efficient estimates of the parameters β_1 and β_2 computed on the basis of the theoretical moment conditions (9.31) with your choice of $\boldsymbol{W}$.

★9.6 Consider the model (9.20), where the matrix $\boldsymbol{\Psi}$ is chosen in such a way that the transformed error terms, the $(\boldsymbol{\Psi}^\top \boldsymbol{u})_t$, are innovations with respect to the information sets Ω_t. In other words, $\mathrm{E}((\boldsymbol{\Psi}^\top \boldsymbol{u})_t \,|\, \Omega_t) = 0$. Suppose that the $n \times l$ matrix of instruments $\boldsymbol{W}$ is predetermined in the usual sense that $\boldsymbol{W}_t \in \Omega_t$. Show that these assumptions, along with the assumption that $\mathrm{E}((\boldsymbol{\Psi}^\top \boldsymbol{u})_t^2 \,|\, \Omega_t) = \mathrm{E}((\boldsymbol{\Psi}^\top \boldsymbol{u})_t^2) = 1$ for $t = 1, \ldots, n$, are enough to prove the analog of (9.02), that is, that

$$\mathrm{Var}(n^{-1/2} \boldsymbol{W}^\top \boldsymbol{\Psi}^\top \boldsymbol{u}) = n^{-1} \mathrm{E}(\boldsymbol{W}^\top \boldsymbol{W}).$$

In order to perform just-identified estimation, let the $n \times k$ matrix $\boldsymbol{Z} = \boldsymbol{W}\boldsymbol{J}$, for an $l \times k$ matrix $\boldsymbol{J}$ of full column rank. Compute the asymptotic covariance matrix of the estimator obtained by solving the moment conditions

$$\boldsymbol{Z}^\top \boldsymbol{\Psi}^\top (\boldsymbol{y} - \boldsymbol{X}\boldsymbol{\beta}) = \boldsymbol{J}^\top \boldsymbol{W}^\top \boldsymbol{\Psi}^\top (\boldsymbol{y} - \boldsymbol{X}\boldsymbol{\beta}) = \boldsymbol{0}. \tag{9.119}$$

The covariance matrix you have found should be a sandwich. Find the choice of $\boldsymbol{J}$ that eliminates the sandwich, and show that this choice leads to an asymptotic covariance matrix that is smaller, in the usual sense, than the asymptotic covariance matrix for any other choice of $\boldsymbol{J}$.

Compute the GMM criterion function for model (9.20) with instruments $\boldsymbol{W}$, and show that the estimator found by minimizing this criterion function is just the estimator obtained using the optimal choice of $\boldsymbol{J}$.

9.7 Compare the asymptotic covariance matrix found in the preceding question for the estimator of the parameters of model (9.20), obtained by minimizing the GMM criterion function for the $n \times l$ matrix of predetermined instruments $\boldsymbol{W}$, with the covariance matrix (9.29) that corresponds to estimation with instruments $\boldsymbol{\Psi}^\top \bar{\boldsymbol{X}}$. In particular, show that the difference between the two is a positive semidefinite matrix.

9.8 Consider overidentified estimation based on the moment conditions

$$\mathrm{E}(\boldsymbol{W}^\top \boldsymbol{\Omega}^{-1}(\boldsymbol{y} - \boldsymbol{X}\boldsymbol{\beta})) = \boldsymbol{0},$$

which were given in (9.31), where the $n \times l$ matrix of instruments $\boldsymbol{W}$ satisfies the predeterminedness condition (9.30). Derive the GMM criterion function for these theoretical moment conditions, and show that the estimating equations that result from the minimization of this criterion function are

$$\boldsymbol{X}^\top\boldsymbol{\Omega}^{-1}\boldsymbol{W}(\boldsymbol{W}^\top\boldsymbol{\Omega}^{-1}\boldsymbol{W})^{-1}\boldsymbol{W}^\top\boldsymbol{\Omega}^{-1}(\boldsymbol{y}-\boldsymbol{X\beta}) = \mathbf{0}. \tag{9.120}$$

Suppose that $\mathcal{S}(\bar{\boldsymbol{X}})$, the span of the $n \times k$ matrix $\bar{\boldsymbol{X}}$ of optimal instruments defined by (9.24), is a linear subspace of $\mathcal{S}(\boldsymbol{W})$, the span of the transformed instruments. Show that, in this case, the estimating equations (9.120) are asymptotically equivalent to

$$\bar{\boldsymbol{X}}^\top\boldsymbol{\Omega}^{-1}(\boldsymbol{y}-\boldsymbol{X\beta}) = \mathbf{0},$$

of which the solution is the efficient estimator $\hat{\boldsymbol{\beta}}_{\rm EGMM}$ defined in (9.26).

9.9 Show that the asymptotic covariance matrix of the estimator obtained by solving the estimating equations (9.120) is

$$\operatorname*{plim}_{n\to\infty}\Big(\frac{1}{n}\bar{\boldsymbol{X}}^\top\boldsymbol{\Omega}^{-1}\boldsymbol{W}(\boldsymbol{W}^\top\boldsymbol{\Omega}^{-1}\boldsymbol{W})^{-1}\boldsymbol{W}^\top\boldsymbol{\Omega}^{-1}\bar{\boldsymbol{X}}\Big)^{-1}. \tag{9.121}$$

By expressing this asymptotic covariance matrix in terms of a matrix $\boldsymbol{\Psi}$ that satisfies the equation $\boldsymbol{\Omega}^{-1} = \boldsymbol{\Psi\Psi}^\top$, show that the difference between it and the asymptotic covariance matrix of the efficient estimator $\hat{\boldsymbol{\beta}}_{\rm EGMM}$ of (9.26) is a positive semidefinite matrix.

★9.10 Give the explicit form of the $n \times n$ matrix $\boldsymbol{U}(j)$ for which $\hat{\boldsymbol{\Gamma}}(j)$, defined in (9.36), takes the form $n^{-1}\boldsymbol{W}^\top\boldsymbol{U}(j)\boldsymbol{W}$.

9.11 This question uses data on daily returns for the period 1989–1998 from the file **daily-crsp.data**. These data are made available by courtesy of the Center for Research in Security Prices (CRSP); see the comments at the bottom of the file. Let r_t denote the daily return on shares of Mobil Corporation, and let v_t denote the daily return for the CRSP value-weighted index. Using all but the first four observations (to allow for lags), run the regression

$$r_t = \beta_1 + \beta_2 v_t + u_t$$

by OLS. Report three different sets of standard errors: the usual OLS ones, ones based on the simplest HCCME, and ones based on a more advanced HCCME that corrects for the downward bias in the squared OLS residuals; see Section 5.5. Do the OLS standard errors appear to be reliable?

Assuming that the u_t are heteroskedastic but serially uncorrelated, obtain estimates of the β_i that are more efficient than the OLS ones. For this purpose, use r_{t-1}^2, v_t^2, v_{t-1}^2, and v_{t-2}^2 as additional instruments. Do these estimates appear to be more efficient than the OLS ones?

9.12 Using the data for consumption (C_t) and disposable income (Y_t) contained in the file **consumption.data**, construct the variables $c_t = \log C_t$, $\Delta c_t = c_t - c_{t-1}$, $y_t = \log Y_t$, and $\Delta y_t = y_t - y_{t-1}$. Then, for the period 1953:1 to 1996:4, run the regression

$$\Delta c_t = \beta_1 + \beta_2\Delta y_t + \beta_3\Delta y_{t-1} + u_t \tag{9.122}$$

by OLS, and test the hypothesis that the u_t are serially uncorrelated against the alternative that they follow an AR(1) process.

Calculate eight sets of HAC estimates of the standard errors of the OLS parameter estimates from regression (9.122), using the Newey-West estimator with the lag truncation parameter set to the values $p = 1, 2, 3, 4, 5, 6, 7, 8$.

9.13 Using the squares of Δy_t, Δy_{t-1}, and Δc_{t-1} as additional instruments, obtain feasible efficient GMM estimates of the parameters of (9.122) by minimizing the criterion function (9.42), with $\hat{\boldsymbol{\Sigma}}$ given by the HAC estimators computed in the previous exercise. For $p = 6$, carry out the iterative procedure described in Section 9.3 by which new parameter estimates are used to update the HAC estimator, which is then used to update the parameter estimates. **Warning:** It may be necessary to rescale the instruments so as to avoid numerical problems.

9.14 Suppose that $f_t = y_t - \boldsymbol{X}_t\boldsymbol{\beta}$. Show that, in this special case, the estimating equations (9.77) yield the generalized IV estimator.

9.15 Starting from the asymptotic covariance matrix (9.67), show that, when $\boldsymbol{\Omega}^{-1}\boldsymbol{F}_0$ is used in place of $\boldsymbol{Z}$, the covariance matrix of the resulting estimator is given by (9.83). Then show that, for the linear regression model $\boldsymbol{y} = \boldsymbol{X}\boldsymbol{\beta} + \boldsymbol{u}$ with exogenous explanatory variables $\boldsymbol{X}$, this estimator is the GLS estimator.

★9.16 The minimization of the GMM criterion function (9.87) yields the estimating equations (9.89) with $\boldsymbol{A} = \boldsymbol{\Psi}^\top\boldsymbol{W}$. Assuming that the $n \times l$ instrument matrix $\boldsymbol{W}$ satisfies the predeterminedness condition in the form (9.30), show that these estimating equations are asymptotically equivalent to the equations

$$\bar{\boldsymbol{F}}_0^\top\boldsymbol{\Psi}\boldsymbol{P}_{\boldsymbol{\Psi}^\top\boldsymbol{W}}\boldsymbol{\Psi}^\top\boldsymbol{f}(\hat{\boldsymbol{\theta}}) = \mathbf{0}, \tag{9.123}$$

where, as usual, $\bar{\boldsymbol{F}}_0 \equiv \bar{\boldsymbol{F}}(\boldsymbol{\theta}_0)$, with $\boldsymbol{\theta}_0$ the true parameter vector. Next, derive the asymptotic covariance matrix of the estimator defined by these equations.

Show that the equations (9.123) are the optimal estimating equations for overidentified estimation based on the transformed zero functions $\boldsymbol{\Psi}^\top\boldsymbol{f}(\boldsymbol{\theta})$ and the transformed instruments $\boldsymbol{\Psi}^\top\boldsymbol{W}$. Show further that, if the condition $\mathcal{S}(\bar{\boldsymbol{F}}) \subseteq \mathcal{S}(\boldsymbol{W})$ is satisfied, the asymptotic covariance matrix of the estimator obtained by solving equations (9.123) coincides with the optimal asymptotic covariance matrix (9.83).

★9.17 Suppose the n-vector $\boldsymbol{f}(\boldsymbol{\theta})$ of elementary zero functions has a covariance matrix $\sigma^2\mathbf{I}$. Show that, if the instrumental variables used for GMM estimation are the columns of the $n \times l$ matrix $\boldsymbol{W}$, the GMM criterion function is

$$\frac{1}{\sigma^2}\boldsymbol{f}^\top(\boldsymbol{\theta})\boldsymbol{P}_{\boldsymbol{W}}\boldsymbol{f}(\boldsymbol{\theta}). \tag{9.124}$$

Next, show that, whenever the instruments are predetermined, the artificial regression

$$\boldsymbol{f}(\boldsymbol{\theta}) = -\boldsymbol{P}_{\boldsymbol{W}}\boldsymbol{F}(\boldsymbol{\theta})\boldsymbol{b} + \text{residuals}, \tag{9.125}$$

where $\boldsymbol{F}(\boldsymbol{\theta})$ is defined as usual by (9.63), satisfies all the requisite properties for hypothesis testing. These properties, which are spelled out in detail in Exercise 8.20 in the context of the IVGNR, are that the regressand should be orthogonal to the regressors when they are evaluated at the GMM estimator obtained by minimizing (9.124); that the OLS covariance matrix from (9.125) should be a consistent estimate of the asymptotic variance of that estimator; and that (9.125) should admit one-step estimation.

★9.18 Derive a heteroskedasticity robust version of the artificial regression (9.125), assuming that the covariance matrix of the vector $\boldsymbol{f}(\boldsymbol{\theta})$ of zero functions is diagonal, but otherwise arbitrary.

★9.19 If the scalar random variable z is distributed according to the $\mathrm{N}(\mu, \sigma^2)$ distribution, show that

$$\mathrm{E}(e^z) = \exp(\mu + \tfrac{1}{2}\sigma^2).$$

★9.20 Let the components z_t of the n–vector $\boldsymbol{z}$ be IID drawings from the $\mathrm{N}(\mu, \sigma^2)$ distribution, and let s^2 be the OLS estimate of the error variance from the regression of $\boldsymbol{z}$ on the constant vector $\boldsymbol{\iota}$. Show that the variance of s^2 is $2\sigma^4/(n-1)$.

Would this result still hold if the normality assumption were dropped? Without this assumption, what would you need to know about the distribution of the z_t in order to find the variance of s^2?

★9.21 Using the delta method, obtain an expression for the asymptotic variance of the estimator defined by (9.101) for the variance of the normal distribution underlying a lognormal distribution. Show that this asymptotic variance is greater than that of the sample variance of the normal variables themselves.

★9.22 Describe the two procedures by which the parameters μ and σ^2 of the lognormal distribution can be estimated by the method of simulated moments, matching the first and second moments of the lognormal variable itself, and the first moment of its log. The first procedure should use optimal instruments and be just identified; the second should use the simple instruments of (9.108) and be overidentified.

9.23 Show that minimizing the criterion function (9.113), when $\boldsymbol{W}$ is defined in (9.112), is equivalent to solving equations (9.111). Then show that it is also equivalent to minimizing the criterion function

$$\begin{bmatrix} \boldsymbol{z} - \boldsymbol{m}_1(\mu, \sigma^2) \\ \boldsymbol{y} - \boldsymbol{m}_2(\mu, \sigma^2) \end{bmatrix}^{\top} \boldsymbol{W}(\boldsymbol{W}^{\top}\boldsymbol{W})^{-1}\boldsymbol{W}^{\top} \begin{bmatrix} \boldsymbol{z} - \boldsymbol{m}_1(\mu, \sigma^2) \\ \boldsymbol{y} - \boldsymbol{m}_2(\mu, \sigma^2) \end{bmatrix}, \tag{9.126}$$

which is the criterion function for nonlinear IV estimation.

★9.24 The **Singh-Maddala** distribution is a three-parameter distribution which has been shown to give an acceptable account, up to scale, of the distributions of household income in many countries. It is characterized by the following CDF:

$$F(y) = 1 - \frac{1}{(1 + ay^b)^c}, \quad y > 0,\ a > 0,\ b > 0,\ c > 0. \tag{9.127}$$

Suppose that you have at your disposal the values of the incomes of a random sample of households from a given population. Describe in detail how to use this sample in order to estimate the parameters a, b, and c of (9.127) by the method of simulated moments, basing the estimates on the expectations of y, $\log y$, and $y \log y$. Describe how to construct a consistent estimate of the asymptotic covariance matrix of your estimator.

Chapter 10

The Method of Maximum Likelihood

10.1 Introduction

The method of moments is not the only fundamental principle of estimation, even though the estimation methods for regression models discussed up to this point (ordinary, nonlinear, and generalized least squares, instrumental variables, and GMM) can all be derived from it. In this chapter, we introduce another fundamental method of estimation, namely, the method of **maximum likelihood**. For regression models, if we make the assumption that the error terms are normally distributed, the maximum likelihood, or **ML**, estimators coincide with the various least-squares estimators with which we are already familiar. But maximum likelihood can also be applied to an extremely wide variety of models other than regression models, and it generally yields estimators with excellent asymptotic properties. The major disadvantage of ML estimation is that it requires stronger distributional assumptions than does the method of moments.

In the next section, we introduce the basic ideas of maximum likelihood estimation and discuss a few simple examples. Then, in Section 10.3, we explore the asymptotic properties of ML estimators. Ways of estimating the covariance matrix of an ML estimator will be discussed in Section 10.4. Some methods of hypothesis testing that are available for models estimated by ML will be introduced in Section 10.5 and discussed more formally in Section 10.6. The remainder of the chapter discusses some useful applications of maximum likelihood estimation. Section 10.7 deals with regression models with autoregressive errors, and Section 10.8 deals with models that involve transformations of the dependent variable.

10.2 Basic Concepts of Maximum Likelihood Estimation

Models that are estimated by maximum likelihood must be **fully specified parametric models**, in the sense of Section 1.3. For such a model, once the parameter values are known, all necessary information is available to simulate the dependent variable(s). In Section 1.2, we introduced the concept of the probability density function, or PDF, of a scalar random variable and of the joint density function, or joint PDF, of a set of random variables. If we can simulate the dependent variable, this means that its PDF must be known, both for each observation as a scalar r.v., and for the full sample as a vector r.v.

As usual, we denote the dependent variable by the n–vector $\boldsymbol{y}$. For a given k–vector $\boldsymbol{\theta}$ of parameters, let the joint PDF of $\boldsymbol{y}$ be written as $f(\boldsymbol{y}, \boldsymbol{\theta})$. This joint PDF constitutes the specification of the model. Since a PDF provides an unambiguous recipe for simulation, it suffices to specify the vector $\boldsymbol{\theta}$ in order to give a full characterization of a DGP in the model. Thus there is a one to one correspondence between the DGPs of the model and the admissible parameter vectors.

Maximum likelihood estimation is based on the specification of the model through the joint PDF $f(\boldsymbol{y}, \boldsymbol{\theta})$. When $\boldsymbol{\theta}$ is fixed, the function $f(\cdot, \boldsymbol{\theta})$ of $\boldsymbol{y}$ is interpreted as the PDF of $\boldsymbol{y}$. But if instead $f(\boldsymbol{y}, \boldsymbol{\theta})$ is evaluated at the n–vector $\boldsymbol{y}$ found in a given data set, then the function $f(\boldsymbol{y}, \cdot)$ of the model parameters can no longer be interpreted as a PDF. Instead, it is referred to as the **likelihood function** of the model for the given data set. ML estimation then amounts to maximizing the likelihood function with respect to the parameters. A parameter vector $\hat{\boldsymbol{\theta}}$ at which the likelihood takes on its maximum value is called a **maximum likelihood estimate**, or **MLE**, of the parameters.

In many cases, the successive observations in a sample are assumed to be statistically independent. In that case, the joint density of the entire sample is just the product of the densities of the individual observations. Let $f(y_t, \boldsymbol{\theta})$ denote the PDF of a typical observation, y_t. Then the joint density of the entire sample $\boldsymbol{y}$ is

$$f(\boldsymbol{y}, \boldsymbol{\theta}) = \prod_{t=1}^{n} f(y_t, \boldsymbol{\theta}). \tag{10.01}$$

Because (10.01) is a product, it is often a very large or very small number, perhaps so large or so small that it cannot easily be represented in a computer. For this and a number of other reasons, it is customary to work instead with the **loglikelihood function**

$$\ell(\boldsymbol{y}, \boldsymbol{\theta}) \equiv \log f(\boldsymbol{y}, \boldsymbol{\theta}) = \sum_{t=1}^{n} \ell_t(y_t, \boldsymbol{\theta}), \tag{10.02}$$

where $\ell_t(y_t, \boldsymbol{\theta})$, the **contribution** to the loglikelihood function made by observation t, is equal to $\log f_t(y_t, \boldsymbol{\theta})$. The t subscripts on f_t and ℓ_t have been added to allow for the possibility that the density of y_t may vary from observation to observation, perhaps because there are exogenous variables in the model. Whatever value of $\boldsymbol{\theta}$ maximizes the loglikelihood function (10.02) must also maximize the likelihood function (10.01), because $\ell(\boldsymbol{y}, \boldsymbol{\theta})$ is just a monotonic transformation of $f(\boldsymbol{y}, \boldsymbol{\theta})$.

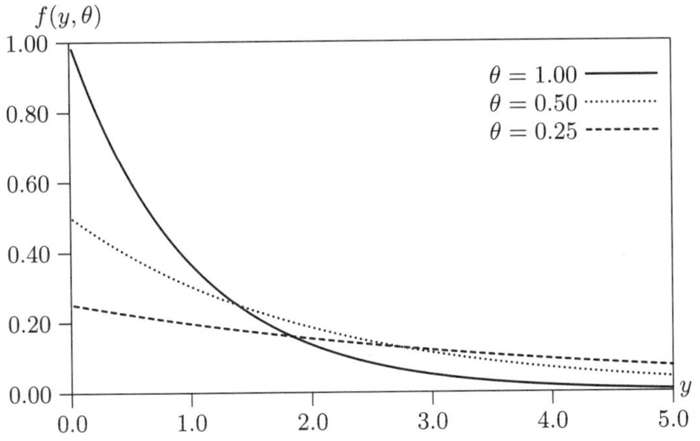

Figure 10.1 The exponential distribution

The Exponential Distribution

As a simple example of ML estimation, suppose that each observation y_t is generated by the density

$$f(y_t, \theta) = \theta e^{-\theta y_t}, \quad y_t > 0, \;\; \theta > 0. \tag{10.03}$$

This is the PDF of what is called the **exponential distribution**.[1] This density is shown in Figure 10.1 for three values of the parameter θ, which is what we wish to estimate. There are assumed to be n independent observations from which to calculate the loglikelihood function.

Taking the logarithm of the density (10.03), we find that the contribution to the loglikelihood from observation t is $\ell_t(y_t, \theta) = \log\theta - \theta y_t$. Therefore,

$$\ell(\boldsymbol{y}, \theta) = \sum_{t=1}^{n} (\log\theta - \theta y_t) = n\log\theta - \theta\sum_{t=1}^{n} y_t. \tag{10.04}$$

To maximize this loglikelihood function with respect to the single unknown parameter θ, we differentiate it with respect to θ and set the derivative equal to 0. The result is

$$\frac{n}{\theta} - \sum_{t=1}^{n} y_t = 0, \tag{10.05}$$

which can easily be solved to yield

$$\hat{\theta} = \frac{n}{\sum_{t=1}^{n} y_t}. \tag{10.06}$$

[1] The exponential distribution is useful for analyzing dependent variables which must be positive, such as waiting times or the duration of unemployment. Models for duration data will be discussed in Section 11.8.

This solution is clearly unique, because the second derivative of (10.04), which is the first derivative of the left-hand side of (10.05), is always negative, which implies that the first derivative can vanish at most once. Since it is unique, the estimator $\hat{\theta}$ defined in (10.06) can be called *the* maximum likelihood estimator that corresponds to the loglikelihood function (10.04).

In this case, interestingly, the ML estimator $\hat{\theta}$ is exactly the same as an MM estimator. As we now show, the expected value of y_t is $1/\theta$. By definition, this expectation is

$$\mathrm{E}(y_t) = \int_0^\infty y_t\,\theta\,e^{-\theta y_t}\,dy_t.$$

Since $-\theta e^{-\theta y_t}$ is the derivative of $e^{-\theta y_t}$ with respect to y_t, we may integrate by parts to obtain

$$\int_0^\infty y_t\,\theta\,e^{-\theta y_t}\,dy_t = -\Big[y_t e^{-\theta y_t}\Big]_0^\infty + \int_0^\infty e^{-\theta y_t}\,dy_t = \Big[-\theta^{-1}e^{-\theta y_t}\Big]_0^\infty = \theta^{-1}.$$

The most natural MM estimator of θ is the one that matches θ^{-1} to the empirical analog of $\mathrm{E}(y_t)$, which is $\bar{y}$, the sample mean. This estimator of θ is therefore $1/\bar{y}$, which is identical to the ML estimator (10.06).

It is not uncommon for an ML estimator to coincide with an MM estimator, as happens in this case. This may suggest that maximum likelihood is not a very useful addition to the econometrician's toolkit, but such an inference would be unwarranted. Even in this simple case, the ML estimator was considerably easier to obtain than the MM estimator, because we did not need to calculate an expectation. In more complicated cases, this advantage of ML estimation is often much more substantial. Moreover, as we will see in the next three sections, the fact that an estimator is an MLE generally ensures that it has a number of desirable asymptotic properties and makes it easy to calculate standard errors and test statistics.[2]

Regression Models with Normal Errors

It is interesting to see what happens when we apply the method of maximum likelihood to the classical normal linear model

$$\boldsymbol{y} = \boldsymbol{X\beta} + \boldsymbol{u}, \quad \boldsymbol{u} \sim \mathrm{N}(\mathbf{0}, \sigma^2\mathbf{I}), \tag{10.07}$$

which was introduced in Section 3.1. For this model, the explanatory variables in the matrix $\boldsymbol{X}$ are assumed to be exogenous. Consequently, in constructing the likelihood function, we may use the density of $\boldsymbol{y}$ conditional on $\boldsymbol{X}$. The

[2] Notice that the abbreviation "MLE" here means "maximum likelihood estimator" rather than "maximum likelihood estimate." We will use "MLE" to mean either of these. Which of them it refers to in any given situation should generally be obvious from the context; see Section 1.5.

elements u_t of the vector $\boldsymbol{u}$ are independently distributed as $\mathrm{N}(0, \sigma^2)$, and so y_t is distributed, conditionally on $\boldsymbol{X}$, as $\mathrm{N}(\boldsymbol{X}_t\boldsymbol{\beta}, \sigma^2)$. Thus the PDF of y_t is, from (4.10),

$$f_t(y_t, \boldsymbol{\beta}, \sigma) = \frac{1}{\sigma\sqrt{2\pi}} \exp\left(-\frac{(y_t - \boldsymbol{X}_t\boldsymbol{\beta})^2}{2\sigma^2}\right). \tag{10.08}$$

The contribution to the loglikelihood function made by the tth observation is the logarithm of (10.08). Since $\log\sigma = \frac{1}{2}\log\sigma^2$, this can be written as

$$\ell_t(y_t, \boldsymbol{\beta}, \sigma) = -\tfrac{1}{2}\log 2\pi - \tfrac{1}{2}\log\sigma^2 - \frac{1}{2\sigma^2}(y_t - \boldsymbol{X}_t\boldsymbol{\beta})^2. \tag{10.09}$$

Since the observations are assumed to be independent, the loglikelihood function is just the sum of these contributions over all t, or

$$\begin{aligned} \ell(\boldsymbol{y}, \boldsymbol{\beta}, \sigma) &= -\tfrac{n}{2}\log 2\pi - \tfrac{n}{2}\log\sigma^2 - \frac{1}{2\sigma^2}\sum_{t=1}^{n}(y_t - \boldsymbol{X}_t\boldsymbol{\beta})^2 \\ &= -\tfrac{n}{2}\log 2\pi - \tfrac{n}{2}\log\sigma^2 - \frac{1}{2\sigma^2}(\boldsymbol{y} - \boldsymbol{X}\boldsymbol{\beta})^{\top}(\boldsymbol{y} - \boldsymbol{X}\boldsymbol{\beta}). \end{aligned} \tag{10.10}$$

In the second line, we rewrite the sum of squared residuals as the inner product of the residual vector with itself. To find the ML estimator, we need to maximize (10.10) with respect to the unknown parameters $\boldsymbol{\beta}$ and σ.

The first step in maximizing $\ell(\boldsymbol{y}, \boldsymbol{\beta}, \sigma)$ is to **concentrate** it with respect to the parameter σ. This means differentiating (10.10) with respect to σ, solving the resulting first-order condition for σ as a function of the data and the remaining parameters, and then substituting the result back into (10.10). This yields the **concentrated loglikelihood function**. The second step is to maximize this function with respect to $\boldsymbol{\beta}$. For models that involve variance parameters, it is very often convenient to concentrate the loglikelihood function in this way.

Differentiating the second line of (10.10) with respect to σ and equating the derivative to zero yields the first-order condition

$$\frac{\partial\ell(\boldsymbol{y}, \boldsymbol{\beta}, \sigma)}{\partial\sigma} = -\frac{n}{\sigma} + \frac{1}{\sigma^3}(\boldsymbol{y} - \boldsymbol{X}\boldsymbol{\beta})^{\top}(\boldsymbol{y} - \boldsymbol{X}\boldsymbol{\beta}) = 0,$$

and solving this yields the result that

$$\hat{\sigma}^2(\boldsymbol{\beta}) = \tfrac{1}{n}(\boldsymbol{y} - \boldsymbol{X}\boldsymbol{\beta})^{\top}(\boldsymbol{y} - \boldsymbol{X}\boldsymbol{\beta}).$$

Here the notation $\hat{\sigma}^2(\boldsymbol{\beta})$ indicates that the value of σ^2 that maximizes (10.10) depends on $\boldsymbol{\beta}$.

Substituting $\hat{\sigma}^2(\boldsymbol{\beta})$ into the second line of (10.10) yields the concentrated loglikelihood function

$$\ell^c(\boldsymbol{y}, \boldsymbol{\beta}) = -\tfrac{n}{2}\log 2\pi - \tfrac{n}{2}\log\Big(\tfrac{1}{n}(\boldsymbol{y} - \boldsymbol{X}\boldsymbol{\beta})^{\top}(\boldsymbol{y} - \boldsymbol{X}\boldsymbol{\beta})\Big) - \tfrac{n}{2}. \tag{10.11}$$

The middle term here is minus $n/2$ times the logarithm of the sum of squared residuals, and the other two terms do not depend on $\boldsymbol{\beta}$. Thus we see that *maximizing* the concentrated loglikelihood function (10.11) is equivalent to *minimizing* the sum of squared residuals as a function of $\boldsymbol{\beta}$. Therefore, the ML estimator $\hat{\boldsymbol{\beta}}$ must be identical to the OLS estimator.

Once $\hat{\boldsymbol{\beta}}$ has been found, the ML estimate $\hat{\sigma}^2$ of σ^2 is $\hat{\sigma}^2(\hat{\boldsymbol{\beta}})$, and the MLE of σ is the positive square root of $\hat{\sigma}^2$. Thus, as we saw in Section 3.6, the MLE $\hat{\sigma}^2$ is biased downward.[3] The actual maximized value of the loglikelihood function can then be written in terms of the sum-of-squared residuals function SSR evaluated at $\hat{\boldsymbol{\beta}}$. From (10.11) we have

$$\ell(\boldsymbol{y}, \hat{\boldsymbol{\beta}}, \hat{\sigma}) = -\frac{n}{2}(1 + \log 2\pi - \log n) - \frac{n}{2}\log \mathrm{SSR}(\hat{\boldsymbol{\beta}}), \tag{10.12}$$

where $\mathrm{SSR}(\hat{\boldsymbol{\beta}})$ denotes the minimized sum of squared residuals.

Although it is convenient to concentrate (10.10) with respect to σ, as we have done, this is not the only way to proceed. In Exercise 10.1, readers are asked to show that the ML estimators of $\boldsymbol{\beta}$ and σ can be obtained equally well by concentrating the loglikelihood with respect to $\boldsymbol{\beta}$ rather than σ.

The fact that the ML and OLS estimators of $\boldsymbol{\beta}$ are identical depends critically on the assumption that the error terms in (10.07) are normally distributed. If we had started with a different assumption about their distribution, we would have obtained a different ML estimator. The asymptotic efficiency result to be discussed in Section 10.4 would then imply that the least-squares estimator is asymptotically less efficient than the ML estimator whenever the two do not coincide.

The Uniform Distribution

As a final example of ML estimation, we consider a somewhat pathological, but rather interesting, example. Suppose that the y_t are generated as independent realizations from the uniform distribution with parameters β_1 and β_2, which can be written as a vector $\boldsymbol{\beta}$; a special case of this distribution was introduced in Section 1.2. The density function for y_t, which is graphed in Figure 10.2, is

$$\begin{aligned} f(y_t, \boldsymbol{\beta}) &= 0 \text{ if } y_t < \beta_1, \\ f(y_t, \boldsymbol{\beta}) &= \frac{1}{\beta_2 - \beta_1} \text{ if } \beta_1 \le y_t \le \beta_2, \\ f(y_t, \boldsymbol{\beta}) &= 0 \text{ if } y_t > \beta_2. \end{aligned}$$

[3] The bias arises because we evaluate $\mathrm{SSR}(\boldsymbol{\beta})$ at $\hat{\boldsymbol{\beta}}$ instead of at the true value $\boldsymbol{\beta}_0$. However, if one thinks of $\hat{\sigma}$ as an estimator of σ, rather than of $\hat{\sigma}^2$ as an estimator of σ^2, then it can be shown that both the OLS and the ML estimators are biased downward.

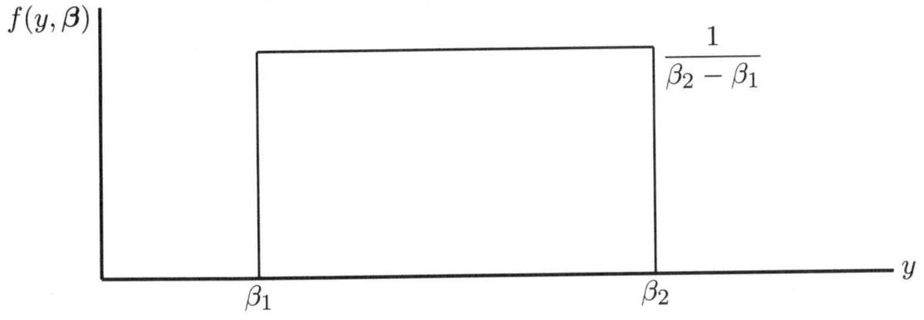

Figure 10.2 The uniform distribution

Provided that $\beta_1 < y_t < \beta_2$ for all observations, the likelihood function is equal to $1/(\beta_2 - \beta_1)^n$, and the loglikelihood function is therefore

$$\ell(\boldsymbol{y}, \boldsymbol{\beta}) = -n \log(\beta_2 - \beta_1).$$

It is easy to verify that this function cannot be maximized by differentiating it with respect to the parameters and setting the partial derivatives to zero. Instead, the way to maximize $\ell(\boldsymbol{y}, \boldsymbol{\beta})$ is to make $\beta_2 - \beta_1$ as small as possible. But we clearly cannot make β_1 larger than the smallest observed y_t, and we cannot make β_2 smaller than the largest observed y_t. Otherwise, the likelihood function would be equal to 0. It follows that the ML estimators are

$$\hat{\beta}_1 = \min(y_t) \quad \text{and} \quad \hat{\beta}_2 = \max(y_t). \tag{10.13}$$

These estimators are rather unusual. For one thing, they always lie on one side of the true value. Because all the y_t must lie between β_1 and β_2, it must be the case that $\hat{\beta}_1 \geq \beta_{10}$ and $\hat{\beta}_2 \leq \beta_{20}$, where β_{10} and β_{20} denote the true parameter values. However, despite this, these estimators turn out to be consistent. Intuitively, this is because, as the sample size gets large, the observed values of y_t fill up the entire space between β_{10} and β_{20}.

The ML estimators defined in (10.13) are **super-consistent**, which means that they approach the true values of the parameters they are estimating at a rate faster than the usual rate of $n^{-1/2}$. Formally, $n^{1/2}(\hat{\beta}_1 - \beta_{10})$ tends to zero as $n \to \infty$, while $n(\hat{\beta}_1 - \beta_{10})$ tends to a limiting random variable; see Exercise 10.2 for more details. Now consider the parameter $\gamma \equiv \frac{1}{2}(\beta_1 + \beta_2)$. One way to estimate it is to use the ML estimator

$$\hat{\gamma} = \frac{1}{2}(\hat{\beta}_1 + \hat{\beta}_2).$$

Another approach would simply be to use the sample mean, say $\bar{\gamma}$, which is a least-squares estimator. But the ML estimator $\hat{\gamma}$ is super-consistent, while $\bar{\gamma}$ is only root-n consistent. This implies that, except perhaps for very small sample sizes, the ML estimator is very much more efficient than the least-squares estimator. In Exercise 10.3, readers are asked to perform a simulation experiment to illustrate this result.

Although economists rarely need to estimate the parameters of a uniform distribution directly, ML estimators with properties similar to those of (10.13) do occur from time to time. In particular, certain econometric models of auctions lead to super-consistent ML estimators; see Donald and Paarsch (1993, 1996). However, because these estimators violate standard regularity conditions, such as those given in Theorems 8.2 and 8.3 of Davidson and MacKinnon (1993), we will not consider them further.

Two Types of ML Estimator

There are two different ways of defining the ML estimator, although most MLEs actually satisfy both definitions. A **Type 1 ML estimator** maximizes the loglikelihood function over the set Θ, where Θ denotes the **parameter space** in which the parameter vector $\boldsymbol{\theta}$ lies, which is generally assumed to be a subset of $\mathbb{R}^k$. This is the natural meaning of an MLE, and all three of the ML estimators just discussed are Type 1 estimators.

If the loglikelihood function is differentiable and attains an *interior* maximum in the parameter space, then the MLE must satisfy the first-order conditions for a maximum. A **Type 2 ML estimator** is defined as a solution to the **likelihood equations**, which are just the following first-order conditions:

$$\boldsymbol{g}(\boldsymbol{y}, \hat{\boldsymbol{\theta}}) = \mathbf{0}, \tag{10.14}$$

where $\boldsymbol{g}(\boldsymbol{y}, \boldsymbol{\theta})$ is the **gradient vector**, or **score vector**, which has typical element

$$g_i(\boldsymbol{y}, \boldsymbol{\theta}) \equiv \frac{\partial \ell(\boldsymbol{y}, \boldsymbol{\theta})}{\partial \theta_i} = \sum_{t=1}^{n} \frac{\partial \ell_t(y_t, \boldsymbol{\theta})}{\partial \theta_i}. \tag{10.15}$$

Because there may be more than one value of $\boldsymbol{\theta}$ that satisfies the likelihood equations (10.14), the definition further requires that the Type 2 estimator $\hat{\boldsymbol{\theta}}$ be associated with a local maximum of $\ell(\boldsymbol{y}, \boldsymbol{\theta})$ and that, as $n \to \infty$, the value of the loglikelihood function associated with $\hat{\boldsymbol{\theta}}$ be higher than the value associated with any other root of the likelihood equations.

The ML estimator (10.06) for the parameter of the exponential distribution and the OLS estimators of $\boldsymbol{\beta}$ and σ^2 in the regression model with normal errors, like most ML estimators, are both Type 1 and Type 2 MLEs. However, the MLEs for the parameters of the uniform distribution defined in (10.13) are Type 1 but not Type 2 MLEs, because they are not the solutions to any set of likelihood equations. In rare circumstances, there also exist MLEs that are Type 2 but not Type 1; see Kiefer (1978) for an example.

Computing ML Estimates

Maximum likelihood estimates are often quite easy to compute. Indeed, for the three examples considered above, we were able to obtain explicit expressions. When no such expressions are available, as is often the case, it is necessary to use some sort of nonlinear maximization procedure. Many such procedures are readily available.

The discussion of Newton's Method and quasi-Newton methods in Section 6.4 applies with very minor changes to ML estimation. Instead of minimizing the sum of squared residuals function $Q(\boldsymbol{\beta})$, we maximize the loglikelihood function $\ell(\boldsymbol{\theta})$. Since the maximization is done with respect to $\boldsymbol{\theta}$ for a given sample $\boldsymbol{y}$, we suppress the explicit dependence of ℓ on $\boldsymbol{y}$. As in the NLS case, Newton's Method makes use of the **Hessian**, which is now a $k \times k$ matrix $\boldsymbol{H}(\boldsymbol{\theta})$ with typical element $\partial^2 \ell(\boldsymbol{\theta})/\partial\theta_i \partial\theta_j$. The Hessian is the matrix of second derivatives of the loglikelihood function, and thus also the matrix of first derivatives of the gradient.

Let $\boldsymbol{\theta}_{(j)}$ denote the value of the vector of estimates at step j of the algorithm, and let $\boldsymbol{g}_{(j)}$ and $\boldsymbol{H}_{(j)}$ denote, respectively, the gradient and the Hessian evaluated at $\boldsymbol{\theta}_{(j)}$. Then the fundamental equation for Newton's Method is

$$\boldsymbol{\theta}_{(j+1)} = \boldsymbol{\theta}_{(j)} - \boldsymbol{H}_{(j)}^{-1} \boldsymbol{g}_{(j)}. \tag{10.16}$$

This may be obtained in exactly the same way as equation (6.42). Because the loglikelihood function is to be maximized, the Hessian should be negative definite, at least when $\boldsymbol{\theta}_{(j)}$ is sufficiently near $\hat{\boldsymbol{\theta}}$. This ensures that the step defined by (10.16) is in an uphill direction.

For the reasons discussed in Section 6.4, Newton's Method usually does not work well, and often does not work at all, when the Hessian is not negative definite. In such cases, one popular way to obtain the MLE is to use some sort of quasi-Newton method, in which (10.16) is replaced by the formula

$$\boldsymbol{\theta}_{(j+1)} = \boldsymbol{\theta}_{(j)} + \alpha_{(j)} \boldsymbol{D}_{(j)}^{-1} \boldsymbol{g}_{(j)},$$

where $\alpha_{(j)}$ is a scalar which is determined at each step, and $\boldsymbol{D}_{(j)}$ is a matrix which approximates $-\boldsymbol{H}_{(j)}$ near the maximum but is constructed so that it is always positive definite. Sometimes, as in the case of NLS estimation, an artificial regression can be used to compute the vector $\boldsymbol{D}_{(j)}^{-1} \boldsymbol{g}_{(j)}$. We will encounter one such artificial regression in Section 10.4, and another, more specialized, one in Section 11.3.

When the loglikelihood function is globally concave and not too flat, maximizing it is usually quite easy. At the other extreme, when the loglikelihood function has several local maxima, doing so can be very difficult. See the discussion in Section 6.4 following Figure 6.3. Everything that is said there about dealing with multiple minima in NLS estimation applies, with certain obvious modifications, to the problem of dealing with multiple maxima in ML estimation.

10.3 Asymptotic Properties of ML Estimators

One of the attractive features of maximum likelihood estimation is that ML estimators are consistent under quite weak regularity conditions and asymptotically normally distributed under somewhat stronger conditions. Therefore, if an estimator is an ML estimator and the regularity conditions are satisfied, it is not necessary to show that it is consistent or derive its asymptotic distribution. In this section, we sketch derivations of the principal asymptotic properties of ML estimators. A rigorous discussion is beyond the scope of this book; interested readers may consult, among other references, Davidson and MacKinnon (1993, Chapter 8) and Newey and McFadden (1994).

Consistency of the MLE

Since almost all maximum likelihood estimators are of Type 1, we will discuss consistency only for this type of MLE. We first show that the expectation of the loglikelihood function is greater when it is evaluated at the true values of the parameters than when it is evaluated at any other values. For consistency, we also need both a finite-sample identification condition and an asymptotic identification condition. The former requires that the loglikelihood be different for different sets of parameter values. If, contrary to this assumption, there were two distinct parameter vectors, $\boldsymbol{\theta}_1$ and $\boldsymbol{\theta}_2$, such that $\ell(\boldsymbol{y}, \boldsymbol{\theta}_1) = \ell(\boldsymbol{y}, \boldsymbol{\theta}_2)$ for all $\boldsymbol{y}$, then it would obviously be impossible to distinguish between $\boldsymbol{\theta}_1$ and $\boldsymbol{\theta}_2$. Thus a finite-sample identification condition is necessary for the model to make sense. The role of the asymptotic identification condition will be discussed below.

Let $L(\boldsymbol{\theta}) = \exp\big(\ell(\boldsymbol{\theta})\big)$ denote the likelihood function, where the dependence on $\boldsymbol{y}$ of both L and ℓ has been suppressed for notational simplicity. We wish to apply a result known as **Jensen's Inequality** to the ratio $L(\boldsymbol{\theta}^*)/L(\boldsymbol{\theta}_0)$, where $\boldsymbol{\theta}_0$ is the true parameter vector and $\boldsymbol{\theta}^*$ is any other vector in the parameter space of the model. Jensen's Inequality tells us that, if X is a real-valued random variable, then $\mathrm{E}\big(h(X)\big) \leq h\big(\mathrm{E}(X)\big)$ whenever $h(\cdot)$ is a concave function. The inequality is strict whenever h is strictly concave over at least part of the **support** of the random variable X, that is, the set of real numbers for which the density of X is nonzero, and the support contains more than one point. See Exercise 10.4 for the proof of a restricted version of Jensen's Inequality.

Since the logarithm is a strictly concave function over the nonnegative real line, and since likelihood functions are nonnegative, we can conclude from Jensen's Inequality that

$$\mathrm{E}_0 \log\left(\frac{L(\boldsymbol{\theta}^*)}{L(\boldsymbol{\theta}_0)}\right) < \log \mathrm{E}_0\left(\frac{L(\boldsymbol{\theta}^*)}{L(\boldsymbol{\theta}_0)}\right), \tag{10.17}$$

with strict inequality for all $\boldsymbol{\theta}^* \neq \boldsymbol{\theta}_0$, on account of the finite-sample identification condition. Here the notation E_0 means the expectation taken under the DGP characterized by the true parameter vector $\boldsymbol{\theta}_0$. Since the joint density of the sample is simply the likelihood function evaluated at $\boldsymbol{\theta}_0$, the expectation on the right-hand side of (10.17) can be expressed as an integral over the support of the vector random variable $\boldsymbol{y}$. We have

$$\mathrm{E}_0\left(\frac{L(\boldsymbol{\theta}^*)}{L(\boldsymbol{\theta}_0)}\right) = \int \frac{L(\boldsymbol{\theta}^*)}{L(\boldsymbol{\theta}_0)} L(\boldsymbol{\theta}_0)\,d\boldsymbol{y} = \int L(\boldsymbol{\theta}^*)\,d\boldsymbol{y} = 1,$$

where the last equality here holds because every density must integrate to 1. Therefore, because $\log 1 = 0$, the inequality (10.17) implies that

$$\mathrm{E}_0 \log\left(\frac{L(\boldsymbol{\theta}^*)}{L(\boldsymbol{\theta}_0)}\right) = \mathrm{E}_0\,\ell(\boldsymbol{\theta}^*) - \mathrm{E}_0\,\ell(\boldsymbol{\theta}_0) < 0. \tag{10.18}$$

In words, (10.18) says that the expectation of the loglikelihood function when evaluated at the true parameter vector, $\boldsymbol{\theta}_0$, is strictly greater than its expectation when evaluated at any other parameter vector, $\boldsymbol{\theta}^*$.

If we can apply a law of large numbers to the contributions to the loglikelihood function, then we can assert that $\operatorname{plim} n^{-1}\ell(\boldsymbol{\theta}) = \lim n^{-1}\mathrm{E}_0\,\ell(\boldsymbol{\theta})$. Then (10.18) implies that

$$\operatorname*{plim}_{n\to\infty} \frac{1}{n}\ell(\boldsymbol{\theta}^*) \le \operatorname*{plim}_{n\to\infty} \frac{1}{n}\ell(\boldsymbol{\theta}_0), \tag{10.19}$$

for all $\boldsymbol{\theta}^* \neq \boldsymbol{\theta}_0$, where the inequality is not necessarily strict, because we have taken a limit. Since the MLE $\hat{\boldsymbol{\theta}}$ maximizes $\ell(\boldsymbol{\theta})$, it must be the case that

$$\operatorname*{plim}_{n\to\infty} \frac{1}{n}\ell(\hat{\boldsymbol{\theta}}) \ge \operatorname*{plim}_{n\to\infty} \frac{1}{n}\ell(\boldsymbol{\theta}_0). \tag{10.20}$$

The only way that (10.19) and (10.20) can both be true is if

$$\operatorname*{plim}_{n\to\infty} \frac{1}{n}\ell(\hat{\boldsymbol{\theta}}) = \operatorname*{plim}_{n\to\infty} \frac{1}{n}\ell(\boldsymbol{\theta}_0). \tag{10.21}$$

In words, (10.21) says that the plim of $1/n$ times the loglikelihood function must be the same when it is evaluated at the MLE $\hat{\boldsymbol{\theta}}$ as when it is evaluated at the true parameter vector $\boldsymbol{\theta}_0$.

By itself, the result (10.21) does not prove that $\hat{\boldsymbol{\theta}}$ is consistent, because the weak inequality does not rule out the possibility that there may be many values $\boldsymbol{\theta}^*$ for which $\operatorname{plim} n^{-1}\ell(\boldsymbol{\theta}^*) = \operatorname{plim} n^{-1}\ell(\boldsymbol{\theta}_0)$. We must therefore explicitly assume that $\operatorname{plim} n^{-1}\ell(\boldsymbol{\theta}^*) \neq \operatorname{plim} n^{-1}\ell(\boldsymbol{\theta}_0)$ for all $\boldsymbol{\theta}^* \neq \boldsymbol{\theta}_0$. This is a form of **asymptotic identification condition**; see Section 6.2. More primitive regularity conditions on the model and the DGP can be invoked to ensure that the MLE is asymptotically identified. For example, we need to rule out pathological cases like (3.20), in which each new observation adds less and less information about one or more of the parameters.

Dependent Observations

Before we can discuss the asymptotic normality of the MLE, we need to introduce some notation and terminology, and we need to establish a few preliminary results. First, we consider the structure of the likelihood and loglikelihood functions for models in which the successive observations are not independent, as is the case, for instance, when a regression function involves lags of the dependent variable.

Recall the definition (1.15) of the density of one random variable conditional on another. This definition can be rewritten so as to take the form of a factorization of the joint density:

$$f(y_1, y_2) = f(y_1)f(y_2 \,|\, y_1), \tag{10.22}$$

where we use y_1 and y_2 in place of the variables x_2 and x_1, respectively, that appear in (1.15). It is permissible to apply (10.22) to situations in which y_1 and y_2 are really vectors of random variables. Accordingly, consider the joint density of three random variables, and group the first two together. Analogously to (10.22), we have

$$f(y_1, y_2, y_3) = f(y_1, y_2)f(y_3 \,|\, y_1, y_2). \tag{10.23}$$

Substituting (10.22) into (10.23) yields the following factorization of the joint density:

$$f(y_1, y_2, y_3) = f(y_1)f(y_2 \,|\, y_1)f(y_3 \,|\, y_1, y_2).$$

For a sample of size n, it is easy to see that this last result generalizes to

$$f(y_1, \ldots, y_n) = f(y_1)f(y_2 \,|\, y_1) \cdots f(y_n \,|\, y_1, \ldots, y_{n-1}).$$

This result can be written using a somewhat more convenient notation as follows:

$$f(\boldsymbol{y}^n) = \prod_{t=1}^{n} f(y_t \,|\, \boldsymbol{y}^{t-1}),$$

where the vector $\boldsymbol{y}^t$ is a t-vector with components $y_1, y_2, \ldots, y_t$. One can think of $\boldsymbol{y}^t$ as the subsample consisting of the first t observations of the full sample. For a model that is to be estimated by maximum likelihood, the density $f(\boldsymbol{y}^n)$ depends on a k-vector of parameters $\boldsymbol{\theta}$, and we can then write

$$f(\boldsymbol{y}^n, \boldsymbol{\theta}) = \prod_{t=1}^{n} f(y_t \,|\, \boldsymbol{y}^{t-1}; \boldsymbol{\theta}). \tag{10.24}$$

The structure of (10.24) is a straightforward generalization of that of (10.01), where the marginal densities of the successive observations are replaced by densities conditional on the preceding observations.

The loglikelihood function corresponding to (10.24) has an additive structure:

$$\ell(\boldsymbol{y}, \boldsymbol{\theta}) = \sum_{t=1}^{n} \ell_t(\boldsymbol{y}^t, \boldsymbol{\theta}), \tag{10.25}$$

where we omit the superscript n from $\boldsymbol{y}$ for the full sample. In addition, in the contributions $\ell_t(\cdot)$ to the loglikelihood, we do not distinguish between the current variable y_t and the lagged variables in the vector $\boldsymbol{y}^{t-1}$. In this way, (10.25) has exactly the same structure as (10.02).

The Gradient

The gradient, or score, vector $\boldsymbol{g}(\boldsymbol{y}, \boldsymbol{\theta})$ is a k–vector that was defined in (10.15). As that equation makes clear, each component of the gradient vector is itself a sum of n contributions, and this remains true when the observations are dependent; the partial derivative of ℓ_t with respect to θ_i now depends on $\boldsymbol{y}^t$ rather than just y_t. It is convenient to group these partial derivatives into a matrix. We define the $n \times k$ matrix $\boldsymbol{G}(\boldsymbol{y}, \boldsymbol{\theta})$ so as to have typical element

$$G_{ti}(\boldsymbol{y}^t, \boldsymbol{\theta}) \equiv \frac{\partial \ell_t(\boldsymbol{y}^t, \boldsymbol{\theta})}{\partial \theta_i}. \tag{10.26}$$

This matrix is called the **matrix of contributions to the gradient**, because

$$g_i(\boldsymbol{y}, \boldsymbol{\theta}) = \sum_{t=1}^{n} G_{ti}(\boldsymbol{y}^t, \boldsymbol{\theta}). \tag{10.27}$$

Thus each element of the gradient vector is the sum of the elements of one of the columns of the matrix $\boldsymbol{G}(\boldsymbol{y}, \boldsymbol{\theta})$.

A crucial property of the matrix $\boldsymbol{G}(\boldsymbol{y}, \boldsymbol{\theta})$ is that, if $\boldsymbol{y}$ is generated by the DGP characterized by $\boldsymbol{\theta}$, then the expectations of all the elements of the matrix, evaluated at $\boldsymbol{\theta}$, are zero. This result is a consequence of the fact that all densities integrate to 1. Since ℓ_t is the log of the density f_t of y_t conditional on $\boldsymbol{y}^{t-1}$, we see that, for all t and for all $\boldsymbol{\theta}$,

$$\int \exp\bigl(\ell_t(\boldsymbol{y}^t, \boldsymbol{\theta})\bigr)\, dy_t = \int f_t(\boldsymbol{y}^t, \boldsymbol{\theta})\, dy_t = 1,$$

where the integral is over the support of y_t. Since this relation holds *identically* in $\boldsymbol{\theta}$, we can differentiate it with respect to the components of $\boldsymbol{\theta}$ and obtain a further set of identities. Under weak regularity conditions, it can be shown that the derivatives of the integral on the left-hand side are the integrals of the derivatives of the integrand. Thus, since the derivative of the constant 1 is 0, we have, identically in $\boldsymbol{\theta}$ and for $i = 1, \ldots, k$,

$$\int \exp\bigl(\ell_t(\boldsymbol{y}^t, \boldsymbol{\theta})\bigr) \frac{\partial \ell_t(\boldsymbol{y}^t, \boldsymbol{\theta})}{\partial \theta_i}\, dy_t = 0. \tag{10.28}$$

Since $\exp(\ell_t(\boldsymbol{y}^t, \boldsymbol{\theta}))$ is, for the DGP characterized by $\boldsymbol{\theta}$, the density of y_t conditional on $\boldsymbol{y}^{t-1}$, this last equation, along with the definition (10.26), gives

$$\mathrm{E}_{\boldsymbol{\theta}}\big(G_{ti}(\boldsymbol{y}^t, \boldsymbol{\theta}) \,|\, \boldsymbol{y}^{t-1}\big) = 0 \tag{10.29}$$

for all $t = 1, \ldots, n$ and $i = 1, \ldots, k$. The notation "$\mathrm{E}_{\boldsymbol{\theta}}$" here means that the expectation is being taken under the DGP characterized by $\boldsymbol{\theta}$. Taking unconditional expectations of (10.29) yields the desired result. Summing (10.29) over $t = 1, \ldots, n$ shows that $\mathrm{E}_{\boldsymbol{\theta}}(g_i(\boldsymbol{y}, \boldsymbol{\theta})) = 0$ for $i = 1, \ldots, k$, or, equivalently, that $\mathrm{E}_{\boldsymbol{\theta}}(\boldsymbol{g}(\boldsymbol{y}, \boldsymbol{\theta})) = \mathbf{0}$.

In addition to the conditional expectations of the elements of the matrix $\boldsymbol{G}(\boldsymbol{y}, \boldsymbol{\theta})$, we can compute the covariances of these elements. Let $t \neq s$, and suppose, without loss of generality, that $t < s$. Then the covariance under the DGP characterized by $\boldsymbol{\theta}$ of the ti^{th} and sj^{th} elements of $\boldsymbol{G}(\boldsymbol{y}, \boldsymbol{\theta})$ is

$$\begin{aligned}\mathrm{E}_{\boldsymbol{\theta}}\big(G_{ti}(\boldsymbol{y}^t, \boldsymbol{\theta})G_{sj}(\boldsymbol{y}^s, \boldsymbol{\theta})\big) &= \mathrm{E}_{\boldsymbol{\theta}}\Big(\mathrm{E}_{\boldsymbol{\theta}}\big(G_{ti}(\boldsymbol{y}^t, \boldsymbol{\theta})G_{sj}(\boldsymbol{y}^s, \boldsymbol{\theta})\big) \,|\, \boldsymbol{y}^t\Big)\\ &= \mathrm{E}_{\boldsymbol{\theta}}\Big(G_{ti}(\boldsymbol{y}^t, \boldsymbol{\theta})\mathrm{E}_{\boldsymbol{\theta}}\big(G_{sj}(\boldsymbol{y}^s, \boldsymbol{\theta}) \,|\, \boldsymbol{y}^t\big)\Big) = 0.\end{aligned} \tag{10.30}$$

The step leading to the second line above follows because $G_{ti}(\cdot)$ is a deterministic function of $\boldsymbol{y}^t$, and the last step follows because the expectation of $G_{sj}(\cdot)$ is zero conditional on $\boldsymbol{y}^{s-1}$, by (10.29), and so also conditional on the subvector $\boldsymbol{y}^t$ of $\boldsymbol{y}^{s-1}$. The above proof shows that the covariance of the two matrix elements is also zero conditional on $\boldsymbol{y}^t$.

The Information Matrix and the Hessian

The covariance matrix of the elements of the tth row $\boldsymbol{G}_t(\boldsymbol{y}^t, \boldsymbol{\theta})$ of $\boldsymbol{G}(\boldsymbol{y}, \boldsymbol{\theta})$ is the $k \times k$ matrix $\boldsymbol{I}_t(\boldsymbol{\theta})$, of which the ij^{th} element is $\mathrm{E}_{\boldsymbol{\theta}}(G_{ti}(\boldsymbol{y}^t, \boldsymbol{\theta})G_{tj}(\boldsymbol{y}^t, \boldsymbol{\theta}))$. As a covariance matrix, $\boldsymbol{I}_t(\boldsymbol{\theta})$ is normally positive definite. The sum of the matrices $\boldsymbol{I}_t(\boldsymbol{\theta})$ over all t is the $k \times k$ matrix

$$\boldsymbol{I}(\boldsymbol{\theta}) \equiv \sum_{t=1}^{n} \boldsymbol{I}_t(\boldsymbol{\theta}) = \sum_{t=1}^{n} \mathrm{E}_{\boldsymbol{\theta}}\big(\boldsymbol{G}_t^{\top}(\boldsymbol{y}, \boldsymbol{\theta})\boldsymbol{G}_t(\boldsymbol{y}, \boldsymbol{\theta})\big), \tag{10.31}$$

which is called the **information matrix**. The matrices $\boldsymbol{I}_t(\boldsymbol{\theta})$ are the **contributions** to the information matrix made by the successive observations.

An equivalent definition of the information matrix, as readers are invited to show in Exercise 10.5, is $\boldsymbol{I}(\boldsymbol{\theta}) \equiv \mathrm{E}_{\boldsymbol{\theta}}(\boldsymbol{g}(\boldsymbol{y}, \boldsymbol{\theta})\boldsymbol{g}^{\top}(\boldsymbol{y}, \boldsymbol{\theta}))$. In this second form, the information matrix is the expectation of the **outer product of the gradient** with itself; see Section 1.4 for the definition of the outer product of two vectors. Less exotically, it is just the covariance matrix of the score vector. As the name suggests, and as we will see shortly, the information matrix is a measure of the total amount of information about the parameters in the sample. The requirement that it should be positive definite is a condition for **strong asymptotic identification** of those parameters, in the same sense as the strong asymptotic identification condition introduced in Section 6.2 for nonlinear regression models.

Closely related to (10.31) is the **asymptotic information matrix**

$$\mathfrak{I}(\boldsymbol{\theta}) \equiv \underset{n\to\infty}{\operatorname{plim}_{\boldsymbol{\theta}}} \frac{1}{n}\boldsymbol{I}(\boldsymbol{\theta}), \tag{10.32}$$

which measures the average amount of information about the parameters that is contained in the observations of the sample. As with the notation $\mathrm{E}_{\boldsymbol{\theta}}$, we use $\operatorname{plim}_{\boldsymbol{\theta}}$ to denote the plim under the DGP characterized by $\boldsymbol{\theta}$.

We have already defined the Hessian $\boldsymbol{H}(\boldsymbol{y}, \boldsymbol{\theta})$. For asymptotic analysis, we are generally more interested in the **asymptotic Hessian**,

$$\mathcal{H}(\boldsymbol{\theta}) \equiv \underset{n\to\infty}{\operatorname{plim}_{\boldsymbol{\theta}}} \frac{1}{n}\boldsymbol{H}(\boldsymbol{y}, \boldsymbol{\theta}), \tag{10.33}$$

than in $\boldsymbol{H}(\boldsymbol{y}, \boldsymbol{\theta})$ itself. The asymptotic Hessian is related to the ordinary Hessian in exactly the same way as the asymptotic information matrix is related to the ordinary information matrix; compare (10.32) and (10.33).

There is a very important relationship between the asymptotic information matrix and the asymptotic Hessian. One version of this relationship, which is called the **information matrix equality**, is

$$\mathfrak{I}(\boldsymbol{\theta}) = -\mathcal{H}(\boldsymbol{\theta}). \tag{10.34}$$

Both the Hessian and the information matrix measure the amount of curvature in the loglikelihood function. Although they are both measuring the same thing, the Hessian is negative definite, at least in the neighborhood of $\hat{\boldsymbol{\theta}}$, while the information matrix is always positive definite; that is why there is a minus sign in (10.34). The proof of (10.34) is the subject of Exercises 10.6 and 10.7. It depends critically on the assumption that the DGP is a special case of the model being estimated.

Asymptotic Normality of the MLE

In order for it to be asymptotically normally distributed, a maximum likelihood estimator must be a Type 2 MLE. In addition, it must satisfy certain regularity conditions, which are discussed in Davidson and MacKinnon (1993, Section 8.5). The Type 2 requirement arises because the proof of asymptotic normality is based on the likelihood equations (10.14), which apply only to Type 2 estimators.

The first step in the proof is to perform a Taylor expansion of the likelihood equations (10.14) around $\boldsymbol{\theta}_0$. This expansion yields

$$\boldsymbol{g}(\hat{\boldsymbol{\theta}}) = \boldsymbol{g}(\boldsymbol{\theta}_0) + \boldsymbol{H}(\bar{\boldsymbol{\theta}})(\hat{\boldsymbol{\theta}} - \boldsymbol{\theta}_0) = \mathbf{0}, \tag{10.35}$$

where we suppress the dependence on $\boldsymbol{y}$ for notational simplicity. The notation $\bar{\boldsymbol{\theta}}$ is our usual shorthand notation for Taylor expansions of vector expressions; see (6.20) and the subsequent discussion. We may therefore write

$$\|\bar{\boldsymbol{\theta}} - \boldsymbol{\theta}_0\| \leq \|\hat{\boldsymbol{\theta}} - \boldsymbol{\theta}_0\|.$$

The fact that the ML estimator $\hat{\boldsymbol{\theta}}$ is consistent then implies that $\bar{\boldsymbol{\theta}}$ is also consistent.

If we solve (10.35) and insert the factors of powers of n that are needed for asymptotic analysis, we obtain the result that

$$n^{1/2}(\hat{\boldsymbol{\theta}} - \boldsymbol{\theta}_0) = -\big(n^{-1}\boldsymbol{H}(\bar{\boldsymbol{\theta}})\big)^{-1}\big(n^{-1/2}\boldsymbol{g}(\boldsymbol{\theta}_0)\big). \tag{10.36}$$

Because $\bar{\boldsymbol{\theta}}$ is consistent, the matrix $n^{-1}\boldsymbol{H}(\bar{\boldsymbol{\theta}})$ which appears in (10.36) must tend to the same nonstochastic limiting matrix as $n^{-1}\boldsymbol{H}(\boldsymbol{\theta}_0)$, namely, $\mathcal{H}(\boldsymbol{\theta}_0)$. Therefore, equation (10.36) implies that

$$n^{1/2}(\hat{\boldsymbol{\theta}} - \boldsymbol{\theta}_0) \stackrel{a}{=} -\mathcal{H}^{-1}(\boldsymbol{\theta}_0)n^{-1/2}\boldsymbol{g}(\boldsymbol{\theta}_0). \tag{10.37}$$

If the information matrix equality, equation (10.34), holds, then this result can equivalently be written as

$$n^{1/2}(\hat{\boldsymbol{\theta}} - \boldsymbol{\theta}_0) \stackrel{a}{=} \mathcal{I}^{-1}(\boldsymbol{\theta}_0)n^{-1/2}\boldsymbol{g}(\boldsymbol{\theta}_0). \tag{10.38}$$

Since the information matrix equality holds only if the model is correctly specified, (10.38) is not in general valid for misspecified models.

The asymptotic normality of the Type 2 MLE follows immediately from the asymptotic equalities (10.37) or (10.38) if it can be shown that the vector $n^{-1/2}\boldsymbol{g}(\boldsymbol{\theta}_0)$ is asymptotically distributed as multivariate normal. As can be seen from (10.27), each element $n^{-1/2}g_i(\boldsymbol{\theta}_0)$ of this vector is $n^{-1/2}$ times a sum of n random variables, each of which has mean 0, by (10.29). Under standard regularity conditions, with which we will not concern ourselves, a multivariate central limit theorem can therefore be applied to this vector. For finite n, the covariance matrix of the score vector is, by definition, the information matrix $\boldsymbol{I}(\boldsymbol{\theta}_0)$. Thus the covariance matrix of the vector $n^{-1/2}\boldsymbol{g}(\boldsymbol{\theta}_0)$ is $n^{-1}\boldsymbol{I}(\boldsymbol{\theta}_0)$, of which, by (10.32), the limit as $n \to \infty$ is the asymptotic information matrix $\mathcal{I}(\boldsymbol{\theta}_0)$. It follows that

$$\operatorname*{plim}_{n\to\infty}\big(n^{-1/2}\boldsymbol{g}(\boldsymbol{\theta}_0)\big) \stackrel{a}{\sim} \mathrm{N}\big(\mathbf{0}, \mathcal{I}(\boldsymbol{\theta}_0)\big). \tag{10.39}$$

This result, when combined with (10.37) or (10.38), implies that the Type 2 MLE is asymptotically normally distributed.

10.4 The Covariance Matrix of the ML Estimator

For Type 2 ML estimators, we can obtain the asymptotic distribution of the estimator by combining the result (10.39) for the asymptotic distribution of $n^{-1/2}\boldsymbol{g}(\boldsymbol{\theta}_0)$ with the result (10.37). The asymptotic distribution of the estimator is the distribution of the random variable $\operatorname{plim} n^{1/2}(\hat{\boldsymbol{\theta}} - \boldsymbol{\theta}_0)$. This distribution is normal, with mean vector zero and covariance matrix

$$\operatorname{Var}\big(\operatorname*{plim}_{n\to\infty} n^{1/2}(\hat{\boldsymbol{\theta}} - \boldsymbol{\theta}_0)\big) = \mathcal{H}^{-1}(\boldsymbol{\theta}_0)\mathcal{I}(\boldsymbol{\theta}_0)\mathcal{H}^{-1}(\boldsymbol{\theta}_0), \tag{10.40}$$

which has the form of a sandwich covariance matrix. When the information matrix equality, equation (10.34), holds, the sandwich simplifies to

$$\operatorname{Var}\big(\operatorname*{plim}_{n\to\infty} n^{1/2}(\hat{\boldsymbol{\theta}} - \boldsymbol{\theta}_0)\big) = \mathcal{I}^{-1}(\boldsymbol{\theta}_0). \tag{10.41}$$

Thus the asymptotic information matrix is seen to be the asymptotic precision matrix of a Type 2 ML estimator. This shows why the matrices $\boldsymbol{I}$ and $\mathcal{I}$ are called *information* matrices of various sorts.

Clearly, any method that allows us to estimate $\mathcal{I}(\boldsymbol{\theta}_0)$ consistently can be used to estimate the covariance matrix of the ML estimates. In fact, several different methods are widely used, because each has advantages in certain situations.

The first method is just to use minus the inverse of the Hessian, evaluated at the vector of ML estimates. Because these estimates are consistent, it is valid to evaluate the Hessian at $\hat{\boldsymbol{\theta}}$ rather than at $\boldsymbol{\theta}_0$. This yields the estimator

$$\widehat{\operatorname{Var}}_{\mathrm{H}}(\hat{\boldsymbol{\theta}}) = -\boldsymbol{H}^{-1}(\hat{\boldsymbol{\theta}}), \tag{10.42}$$

which is referred to as the **empirical Hessian** estimator. Notice that, since it is the covariance matrix of $\hat{\boldsymbol{\theta}}$ in which we are interested, the factor of $n^{1/2}$ is no longer present. This estimator is easy to obtain whenever Newton's Method, or some sort of quasi-Newton method that uses second derivatives, is used to maximize the loglikelihood function. In the case of quasi-Newton methods, $\boldsymbol{H}(\hat{\boldsymbol{\theta}})$ may sometimes be replaced by another matrix that approximates it. Provided that n^{-1} times the approximating matrix converges to $\mathcal{H}(\boldsymbol{\theta})$, this sort of replacement is asymptotically valid.

Although the empirical Hessian estimator often works well, it does not use all the information we have about the model. Especially for simpler models, we may actually be able to find an analytic expression for $\boldsymbol{I}(\boldsymbol{\theta})$. If so, we can use the inverse of $\boldsymbol{I}(\boldsymbol{\theta})$, evaluated at the ML estimates. This yields the **information matrix**, or **IM**, estimator

$$\widehat{\operatorname{Var}}_{\mathrm{IM}}(\hat{\boldsymbol{\theta}}) = \boldsymbol{I}^{-1}(\hat{\boldsymbol{\theta}}). \tag{10.43}$$

The advantage of this estimator is that it normally involves fewer random terms than does the empirical Hessian, and it may therefore be somewhat more efficient. In the case of the classical normal linear model, to be discussed below, it is not at all difficult to obtain $\boldsymbol{I}(\boldsymbol{\theta})$, and the information matrix estimator is therefore the one that is normally used.

The third method is based on (10.31), from which we see that

$$\boldsymbol{I}(\boldsymbol{\theta}_0) = \mathrm{E}\big(\boldsymbol{G}^\top(\boldsymbol{\theta}_0)\boldsymbol{G}(\boldsymbol{\theta}_0)\big).$$

We can therefore estimate $n^{-1}\boldsymbol{I}(\boldsymbol{\theta}_0)$ consistently by $n^{-1}\boldsymbol{G}^\top(\hat{\boldsymbol{\theta}})\boldsymbol{G}(\hat{\boldsymbol{\theta}})$. The corresponding estimator of the covariance matrix, which is usually called the **outer-product-of-the-gradient**, or **OPG**, estimator, is

$$\widehat{\mathrm{Var}}_{\mathrm{OPG}}(\hat{\boldsymbol{\theta}}) = \big(\boldsymbol{G}^\top(\hat{\boldsymbol{\theta}})\boldsymbol{G}(\hat{\boldsymbol{\theta}})\big)^{-1}. \tag{10.44}$$

The OPG estimator has the advantage of being very easy to calculate. Unlike the empirical Hessian, it depends solely on first derivatives. Unlike the IM estimator, it requires no theoretical calculations. However, it tends to be less reliable in finite samples than either of the other two. The OPG estimator is sometimes called the **BHHH** estimator, because it was advocated by Berndt, Hall, Hall, and Hausman (1974) in a very well-known paper.

In practice, the estimators (10.42), (10.43), and (10.44) are all commonly used to estimate the covariance matrix of ML estimates, but many other estimators are available for particular models. Often, it may be difficult to obtain $\boldsymbol{I}(\boldsymbol{\theta})$, but not difficult to obtain another matrix that approximates it asymptotically, by starting either from the matrix $-\boldsymbol{H}(\boldsymbol{\theta})$ or from the matrix $\boldsymbol{G}^\top(\boldsymbol{\theta})\boldsymbol{G}(\boldsymbol{\theta})$ and taking expectations of some elements.

A fourth covariance matrix estimator, which follows directly from (10.40), is the **sandwich estimator**

$$\widehat{\mathrm{Var}}_{\mathrm{S}}(\hat{\boldsymbol{\theta}}) = \boldsymbol{H}^{-1}(\hat{\boldsymbol{\theta}})\boldsymbol{G}^\top(\hat{\boldsymbol{\theta}})\boldsymbol{G}(\hat{\boldsymbol{\theta}})\boldsymbol{H}^{-1}(\hat{\boldsymbol{\theta}}). \tag{10.45}$$

In normal circumstances, this estimator has little to recommend it. It is harder to compute than the OPG estimator and can be just as unreliable in finite samples. However, unlike the other three estimators, it is valid even when the information matrix equality does not hold. Since this equality generally fails to hold when the model is misspecified, it may be desirable to compute (10.45) and compare it with the other estimators.

When an ML estimator is applied to a model which is misspecified in ways that do not affect the consistency of the estimator, it is said to be a **quasi-ML estimator**, or **QMLE**; see White (1982) and Gouriéroux, Monfort, and Trognon (1984). In general, the sandwich covariance matrix estimator (10.45) is valid for QML estimators, but the other covariance matrix estimators, which depend on the information matrix equality, are not valid. At least, they are not valid for all the parameters. We have seen that the ML estimator for a regression model with normal errors is just the OLS estimator. But we know that the latter is consistent under conditions which do not require normality. If the error terms are not normal, therefore, the ML estimator is a QMLE. One consequence of this fact is explored in Exercise 10.8.

The Classical Normal Linear Model

It should help to make the theoretical results just discussed clearer if we apply them to the classical normal linear model. We will therefore discuss various ways of estimating the covariance matrix of the ML estimates $\hat{\boldsymbol{\beta}}$ and $\hat{\sigma}$ jointly. Of course, we saw in Section 3.4 how to estimate the covariance matrix of $\hat{\boldsymbol{\beta}}$ by itself, but we have not yet discussed how to estimate the variance of $\hat{\sigma}$.

For the classical normal linear model, the contribution to the loglikelihood function made by the tth observation is given by expression (10.09). There are $k+1$ parameters. The first k of them are the elements of the vector $\boldsymbol{\beta}$, and the last one is σ. A typical element of any of the first k columns of the matrix $\boldsymbol{G}$, indexed by i, is

$$G_{ti}(\boldsymbol{\beta},\sigma) = \frac{\partial \ell_t}{\partial \beta_i} = \frac{1}{\sigma^2}(y_t - \boldsymbol{X}_t\boldsymbol{\beta})x_{ti}, \quad i = 1,\ldots,k, \tag{10.46}$$

and a typical element of the last column is

$$G_{t,k+1}(\boldsymbol{\beta},\sigma) = \frac{\partial \ell_t}{\partial \sigma} = -\frac{1}{\sigma} + \frac{1}{\sigma^3}(y_t - \boldsymbol{X}_t\boldsymbol{\beta})^2. \tag{10.47}$$

These two equations give us everything we need to calculate the information matrix.

For $i,j = 1,\ldots,k$, the ij^{th} element of $\boldsymbol{G}^\top\boldsymbol{G}$ is

$$\sum_{t=1}^{n} \frac{1}{\sigma^4}(y_t - \boldsymbol{X}_t\boldsymbol{\beta})^2 x_{ti}x_{tj}. \tag{10.48}$$

This is just the sum over all t of $G_{ti}(\boldsymbol{\beta},\sigma)$ times $G_{tj}(\boldsymbol{\beta},\sigma)$ as defined in (10.46). When we evaluate at the true values of $\boldsymbol{\beta}$ and σ, we have that $y_t - \boldsymbol{X}_t\boldsymbol{\beta} = u_t$ and $\mathrm{E}(u_t^2) = \sigma^2$, and so the expectation of this matrix element is easily seen to be

$$\sum_{t=1}^{n} \frac{1}{\sigma^2} x_{ti}x_{tj}. \tag{10.49}$$

In matrix notation, the whole $\boldsymbol{\beta}$-$\boldsymbol{\beta}$ block of $\boldsymbol{G}^\top\boldsymbol{G}$ has expectation $\boldsymbol{X}^\top\boldsymbol{X}/\sigma^2$. The $(i,k+1)^{\text{th}}$ element of $\boldsymbol{G}^\top\boldsymbol{G}$ is

$$\begin{aligned}&\sum_{t=1}^{n}\left(-\frac{1}{\sigma} + \frac{1}{\sigma^3}(y_t - \boldsymbol{X}_t\boldsymbol{\beta})^2\right)\left(\frac{1}{\sigma^2}(y_t - \boldsymbol{X}_t\boldsymbol{\beta})x_{ti}\right)\\ &= -\sum_{t=1}^{n}\frac{1}{\sigma^3}(y_t - \boldsymbol{X}_t\boldsymbol{\beta})x_{ti} + \sum_{t=1}^{n}\frac{1}{\sigma^5}(y_t - \boldsymbol{X}_t\boldsymbol{\beta})^3 x_{ti}.\end{aligned} \tag{10.50}$$

This is the sum over all t of the product of expressions (10.46) and (10.47). We know that $\mathrm{E}(u_t) = 0$, and, if the error terms u_t are normal, we also know that $\mathrm{E}(u_t^3) = 0$. Consequently, the expectation of this sum is 0. This result depends critically on the assumption, following from normality, that the distribution of the error terms is symmetric around zero. For a skewed distribution, the third moment would be nonzero, and (10.50) would therefore not have mean 0.

Finally, the $(k+1), (k+1)^{\text{th}}$ element of $\boldsymbol{G}^\top\boldsymbol{G}$ is

$$\begin{aligned}&\sum_{t=1}^{n}\Big(-\frac{1}{\sigma}+\frac{1}{\sigma^3}(y_t-\boldsymbol{X}_t\boldsymbol{\beta})^2\Big)^2\\&=\frac{n}{\sigma^2}-\sum_{t=1}^{n}\frac{2}{\sigma^4}(y_t-\boldsymbol{X}_t\boldsymbol{\beta})^2+\sum_{t=1}^{n}\frac{1}{\sigma^6}(y_t-\boldsymbol{X}_t\boldsymbol{\beta})^4.\end{aligned} \tag{10.51}$$

This is the sum over all t of the square of expression (10.47). To compute its expectation, we replace $y_t - \boldsymbol{X}_t\boldsymbol{\beta}$ by u_t and use the result that $\mathrm{E}(u_t^4) = 3\sigma^4$; see Exercise 4.2. It is then not hard to see that expression (10.51) has expectation $2n/\sigma^2$. Once more, this result depends crucially on the normality assumption. If the kurtosis of the error terms were greater (or less) than that of the normal distribution, the expectation of expression (10.51) would be larger (or smaller) than $2n/\sigma^2$.

Putting the results (10.49), (10.50), and (10.51) together, the asymptotic information matrix for $\boldsymbol{\beta}$ and σ jointly is seen to be

$$\mathfrak{I}(\boldsymbol{\beta},\sigma) = \operatorname*{plim}_{n\to\infty}\begin{bmatrix} n^{-1}\boldsymbol{X}^\top\boldsymbol{X}/\sigma^2 & \mathbf{0} \\ \mathbf{0}^\top & 2/\sigma^2\end{bmatrix}. \tag{10.52}$$

Inverting this matrix, multiplying the inverse by n^{-1}, and replacing σ by $\hat\sigma$, we find that the IM estimator of the covariance matrix of all the parameter estimates is

$$\widehat{\mathrm{Var}}_{\mathrm{IM}}(\hat{\boldsymbol{\beta}},\hat\sigma) = \begin{bmatrix} \hat\sigma^2(\boldsymbol{X}^\top\boldsymbol{X})^{-1} & \mathbf{0} \\ \mathbf{0}^\top & \hat\sigma^2/2n\end{bmatrix}. \tag{10.53}$$

The upper left-hand block of this matrix would be the familiar OLS covariance matrix if we had used s instead of $\hat\sigma$ to estimate σ. The lower right-hand element is the approximate variance of $\hat\sigma$ under the assumption of normally distributed error terms. If we had treated σ^2 instead of σ as a parameter, the lower right-hand element would have been different; see Exercise 10.10.

It is noteworthy that the information matrix (10.52), and therefore also the estimated covariance matrix (10.53), are block-diagonal. This implies that there is no covariance between $\hat{\boldsymbol{\beta}}$ and $\hat\sigma$. This is a property of all regression models, nonlinear as well as linear, and it is responsible for much of the simplicity of these models. The block-diagonality of the information matrix means that we can make inferences about $\boldsymbol{\beta}$ without taking account of the fact that σ has also been estimated, and we can make inferences about σ without taking account of the fact that $\boldsymbol{\beta}$ has also been estimated. If the information matrix were not block-diagonal, which in most other cases it is not, it would have been necessary to invert the entire matrix in order to obtain any block of the inverse.

Asymptotic Efficiency of the ML Estimator

A Type 2 ML estimator must be at least as asymptotically efficient as any other root-n consistent estimator that is asymptotically unbiased.[4] Therefore, at least in large samples, maximum likelihood estimation possesses an optimality property that is generally not shared by other estimation methods. We will not attempt to prove this result here; see Davidson and MacKinnon (1993, Section 8.8). However, we will discuss it briefly.

Consider any other root-n consistent and asymptotically unbiased estimator, say $\tilde{\boldsymbol{\theta}}$. It can be shown that

$$\operatorname*{plim}_{n\to\infty} n^{1/2}(\tilde{\boldsymbol{\theta}} - \boldsymbol{\theta}_0) = \operatorname*{plim}_{n\to\infty} n^{1/2}(\hat{\boldsymbol{\theta}} - \boldsymbol{\theta}_0) + \boldsymbol{v}, \tag{10.54}$$

where $\boldsymbol{v}$ is a random k-vector that has mean zero and is uncorrelated with the vector $\operatorname{plim} n^{1/2}(\hat{\boldsymbol{\theta}} - \boldsymbol{\theta}_0)$. This means that, from (10.54), we have

$$\operatorname{Var}\bigl(\operatorname*{plim}_{n\to\infty} n^{1/2}(\tilde{\boldsymbol{\theta}} - \boldsymbol{\theta}_0)\bigr) = \operatorname{Var}\bigl(\operatorname*{plim}_{n\to\infty} n^{1/2}(\hat{\boldsymbol{\theta}} - \boldsymbol{\theta}_0)\bigr) + \operatorname{Var}(\boldsymbol{v}). \tag{10.55}$$

Since $\operatorname{Var}(\boldsymbol{v})$ must be a positive semidefinite matrix, we conclude that the asymptotic covariance matrix of the estimator $\tilde{\boldsymbol{\theta}}$ must be larger than that of $\hat{\boldsymbol{\theta}}$, in the usual sense.

The asymptotic equality (10.54) bears a strong, and by no means coincidental, resemblance to a result that we used in Section 3.5 when proving the Gauss-Markov Theorem. This result says that, in the context of the linear regression model, any unbiased linear estimator can be written as the sum of the OLS estimator and a random component which has mean zero and is uncorrelated with the OLS estimator. Asymptotically, equation (10.54) says essentially the same thing in the context of a very much broader class of models. The key property of (10.54) is that $\boldsymbol{v}$ is uncorrelated with $\operatorname{plim} n^{1/2}(\hat{\boldsymbol{\theta}} - \boldsymbol{\theta}_0)$. Therefore, the random vector $\boldsymbol{v}$ simply adds additional noise to the ML estimator.

The asymptotic efficiency result (10.55) is really an asymptotic version of the **Cramér-Rao lower bound**,[5] which actually applies to any unbiased estimator, regardless of sample size. It states that the covariance matrix of such an

[4] All of the root-n consistent estimators that we have discussed are also asymptotically unbiased. However, as is discussed in Davidson and MacKinnon (1993, Section 4.5), it is possible for such an estimator to be asymptotically biased, and we must therefore rule out this possibility explicitly.

[5] This bound was originally suggested by Fisher (1925) and later stated in its modern form by Cramér (1946) and Rao (1945).

estimator can never be smaller than $\boldsymbol{I}^{-1}$, which, as we have seen, is asymptotically equal to the covariance matrix of the ML estimator. Readers are guided through the proof of this classical result in Exercise 10.12. However, since ML estimators are not in general unbiased, it is only the asymptotic version of the bound that is of interest in the context of ML estimation.

The fact that ML estimators attain the Cramér-Rao lower bound asymptotically is one of their many attractive features. However, like the Gauss-Markov Theorem, this result must be interpreted with caution. First of all, it is only true asymptotically. ML estimators may or may not perform well in samples of moderate size. Secondly, there may well exist an asymptotically biased estimator that is more efficient, in the sense of finite-sample mean squared error, than any given ML estimator. For example, the estimator obtained by imposing a restriction that is false, but not grossly incompatible with the data, may well be more efficient than the unrestricted ML estimator. The former cannot be more efficient asymptotically, because the variance of both estimators tends to zero as the sample size tends to infinity and the bias of the biased estimator does not, but it can be more efficient in finite samples.

10.5 Hypothesis Testing

Maximum likelihood estimation offers three different procedures for performing hypothesis tests, two of which usually have several different variants. These three procedures, which are collectively referred to as the **three classical tests**, are the **likelihood ratio**, **Wald**, and **Lagrange multiplier** tests. All three tests are asymptotically equivalent, in the sense that all the test statistics tend to the same random variable (under the null hypothesis, and for DGPs that are "close" to the null hypothesis) as the sample size tends to infinity. If the number of equality restrictions is r, this limiting random variable is distributed as $\chi^2(r)$. We have already discussed Wald tests in Sections 6.7 and 8.5, but we have not yet encountered the other two classical tests, at least not under their usual names.

As we remarked in Section 4.6, a hypothesis in econometrics corresponds to a model. We let the model that corresponds to the alternative hypothesis be characterized by the loglikelihood function $\ell(\boldsymbol{\theta})$. Then the null hypothesis imposes r restrictions, which are in general nonlinear, on $\boldsymbol{\theta}$. We write these as $\boldsymbol{r}(\boldsymbol{\theta}) = \boldsymbol{0}$, where $\boldsymbol{r}(\boldsymbol{\theta})$ is an r-vector of smooth functions of the parameters. Thus the null hypothesis is represented by the model with loglikelihood $\ell(\boldsymbol{\theta})$, where the parameter space is restricted to those values of $\boldsymbol{\theta}$ that satisfy the restrictions $\boldsymbol{r}(\boldsymbol{\theta}) = \boldsymbol{0}$.

Likelihood Ratio Tests

The **likelihood ratio**, or **LR**, test is the simplest of the three classical tests. The test statistic is just twice the difference between the unconstrained maximum value of the loglikelihood function and the maximum subject to the restrictions. Thus the likelihood ratio statistic is just

$$\mathrm{LR} = 2\big(\ell(\hat{\boldsymbol{\theta}}) - \ell(\tilde{\boldsymbol{\theta}})\big), \tag{10.56}$$

where $\tilde{\boldsymbol{\theta}}$ and $\hat{\boldsymbol{\theta}}$ denote, respectively, the restricted and unrestricted maximum likelihood estimates of $\boldsymbol{\theta}$. The LR statistic gets its name from the fact that the right-hand side of equation (10.56) is equal to

$$2\log\left(\frac{L(\hat{\boldsymbol{\theta}})}{L(\tilde{\boldsymbol{\theta}})}\right),$$

or twice the logarithm of the ratio of the likelihood functions. One of its most attractive features is that the LR statistic is trivially easy to compute when both the restricted and unrestricted estimates are available. Whenever we impose, or relax, some restrictions on a model, twice the change in the value of the loglikelihood function provides immediate feedback on whether the restrictions are compatible with the data.

Precisely why the LR statistic is asymptotically distributed as $\chi^2(r)$ is not entirely obvious, and we will not attempt to explain it now. The asymptotic theory of the three classical tests will be discussed in detail in the next section. Some intuition can be gained by looking at the LR test for linear restrictions on the classical normal linear model. The LR statistic turns out to be closely related to the familiar F statistic, which can be written as

$$F = \frac{\big(\mathrm{SSR}(\tilde{\boldsymbol{\beta}}) - \mathrm{SSR}(\hat{\boldsymbol{\beta}})\big)/r}{\mathrm{SSR}(\hat{\boldsymbol{\beta}})/(n-k)}, \tag{10.57}$$

where $\hat{\boldsymbol{\beta}}$ and $\tilde{\boldsymbol{\beta}}$ are the unrestricted and restricted OLS (and hence also ML) estimates, respectively. The LR statistic can also be expressed in terms of the two sums of squared residuals, by use of the formula (10.12), which gives the maximized loglikelihood in terms of the minimized SSR. The statistic is

$$\begin{aligned} 2\big(\ell(\hat{\boldsymbol{\theta}}) - \ell(\tilde{\boldsymbol{\theta}})\big) &= 2\Big(\tfrac{n}{2}\log \mathrm{SSR}(\tilde{\boldsymbol{\beta}}) - \tfrac{n}{2}\log \mathrm{SSR}(\hat{\boldsymbol{\beta}})\Big) \\ &= n\log\left(\frac{\mathrm{SSR}(\tilde{\boldsymbol{\beta}})}{\mathrm{SSR}(\hat{\boldsymbol{\beta}})}\right). \end{aligned} \tag{10.58}$$

We can rewrite the last expression here as

$$n\log\left(1 + \frac{\mathrm{SSR}(\tilde{\boldsymbol{\beta}}) - \mathrm{SSR}(\hat{\boldsymbol{\beta}})}{\mathrm{SSR}(\hat{\boldsymbol{\beta}})}\right) = n\log\left(1 + \frac{r}{n-k}F\right) \cong rF.$$

The approximate equality above follows from the facts that $n/(n-k) \overset{a}{=} 1$ and that $\log(1+a) \cong a$ whenever a is small. Under the null hypothesis, $\mathrm{SSR}(\tilde{\boldsymbol{\beta}})$

should not be much larger than $\mathrm{SSR}(\hat{\boldsymbol{\beta}})$, or, equivalently, $F/(n-k)$ should be a small quantity. Thus this approximation should generally be a good one. In fact, under the null hypothesis, the LR statistic (10.58) is asymptotically equal to r times the F statistic. Whether or not the null is true, the LR statistic is a deterministic, strictly increasing, function of the F statistic. As we will see later, this fact has important consequences if the statistics are bootstrapped. Without bootstrapping, it makes little sense to use an LR test rather than an F test in the context of the classical normal linear model, because the latter, but not the former, is exact in finite samples.

Wald Tests

Unlike LR tests, Wald tests depend only on the estimates of the unrestricted model. There is no real difference between Wald tests in models estimated by maximum likelihood and those in models estimated by other methods; see Sections 6.7 and 8.5. As with the LR test, we wish to test the r restrictions $\boldsymbol{r}(\boldsymbol{\theta}) = \mathbf{0}$. The Wald test statistic is just a quadratic form in the vector $\boldsymbol{r}(\hat{\boldsymbol{\theta}})$ and the inverse of a matrix that estimates its covariance matrix.

By using the delta method (Section 5.6), we find that

$$\mathrm{Var}\big(\boldsymbol{r}(\hat{\boldsymbol{\theta}})\big) \overset{a}{=} \boldsymbol{R}(\boldsymbol{\theta}_0)\mathrm{Var}(\hat{\boldsymbol{\theta}})\boldsymbol{R}^{\top}(\boldsymbol{\theta}_0), \tag{10.59}$$

where $\boldsymbol{R}(\boldsymbol{\theta})$ is an $r \times k$ matrix with typical element $\partial r_i(\boldsymbol{\theta})/\partial\theta_j$. In the last section, we saw that $\mathrm{Var}(\hat{\boldsymbol{\theta}})$ can be estimated in several ways. Substituting any of these estimators, denoted $\widehat{\mathrm{Var}}(\hat{\boldsymbol{\theta}})$, for $\mathrm{Var}(\hat{\boldsymbol{\theta}})$ in (10.59), and replacing the unknown $\boldsymbol{\theta}_0$ by $\hat{\boldsymbol{\theta}}$, we find that the Wald statistic is

$$\mathrm{W} = \boldsymbol{r}^{\top}(\hat{\boldsymbol{\theta}})\big(\boldsymbol{R}(\hat{\boldsymbol{\theta}})\widehat{\mathrm{Var}}(\hat{\boldsymbol{\theta}})\boldsymbol{R}^{\top}(\hat{\boldsymbol{\theta}})\big)^{-1}\boldsymbol{r}(\hat{\boldsymbol{\theta}}). \tag{10.60}$$

This is a quadratic form in the r–vector $\boldsymbol{r}(\hat{\boldsymbol{\theta}})$, which is asymptotically multivariate normal, and the inverse of an estimate of its covariance matrix. It is easy to see, using the first part of Theorem 4.1, that (10.60) is asymptotically distributed as $\chi^2(r)$ under the null hypothesis. As readers are asked to show in Exercise 10.13, the Wald statistic (6.71) is just a special case of the one defined in (10.60). In the case of linear regression models subject to linear restrictions on the parameters, the Wald statistic is, like the LR statistic, a deterministic, strictly increasing, function of the F statistic if the information matrix estimator (10.43) of the covariance matrix of the parameters is used to construct the Wald statistic.

Wald tests are very widely used, in part because the square of every t statistic is really a Wald statistic. Nevertheless, they should be used with caution. Although Wald tests do not necessarily have poor finite-sample properties, and they do not necessarily perform less well in finite samples than the other classical tests, there is a good deal of evidence that they quite often do so. One reason for this is that Wald statistics are not invariant to reformulations of the restrictions. Some formulations may lead to Wald tests that are well-behaved, but others may lead to tests that severely overreject, or (much less commonly) underreject, in samples of moderate size.

As an example, consider the linear regression model

$$y_t = \beta_0 + \beta_1 x_{t1} + \beta_2 x_{t2} + u_t, \tag{10.61}$$

where we wish to test the hypothesis that the product of β_1 and β_2 is 1. To compute a Wald statistic, we need to estimate the covariance matrix of $\hat{\beta}_1$ and $\hat{\beta}_2$. If $\boldsymbol{X}$ denotes the $n \times 2$ matrix with typical element x_{ti}, and $\boldsymbol{M}_\iota$ is the matrix that takes deviations from the mean, then the IM estimator of this covariance matrix is

$$\widehat{\mathrm{Var}}(\hat{\beta}_1, \hat{\beta}_2) = \hat{\sigma}^2(\boldsymbol{X}^\top \boldsymbol{M}_\iota \boldsymbol{X})^{-1}; \tag{10.62}$$

we could of course use s^2 instead of $\hat{\sigma}^2$. For notational convenience, we let V_{11}, V_{12} $(= V_{21})$, and V_{22} denote the three distinct elements of this matrix.

There are many ways to write the single restriction on (10.61) that we wish to test. Three formulations that seem particularly natural are

$$\begin{aligned} r_1(\beta_1, \beta_2) &\equiv \beta_1 - 1/\beta_2 = 0, \\ r_2(\beta_1, \beta_2) &\equiv \beta_2 - 1/\beta_1 = 0, \ \text{ and} \\ r_3(\beta_1, \beta_2) &\equiv \beta_1\beta_2 - 1 = 0. \end{aligned}$$

Each of these ways of writing the restriction leads to a different Wald statistic. If the restriction is written in the form of r_1, then $\boldsymbol{R}(\beta_1, \beta_2) = [1 \quad 1/\beta_2^2]$. Combining this with (10.62), we find after a little algebra that the Wald statistic is

$$\mathrm{W}_1 = \frac{(\hat{\beta}_1 - 1/\hat{\beta}_2)^2}{V_{11} + 2V_{12}/\hat{\beta}_2^2 + V_{22}/\hat{\beta}_2^4}.$$

If instead the restriction is written in the form of r_2, then $\boldsymbol{R}(\beta_1, \beta_2) = [1/\beta_1^2 \quad 1]$, and the Wald statistic is

$$\mathrm{W}_2 = \frac{(\hat{\beta}_2 - 1/\hat{\beta}_1)^2}{V_{11}/\hat{\beta}_1^4 + 2V_{12}/\hat{\beta}_1^2 + V_{22}}.$$

Finally, if the restriction is written in the form of r_3, then $\boldsymbol{R}(\beta_1, \beta_2) = [\beta_2 \quad \beta_1]$, and the Wald statistic is

$$\mathrm{W}_3 = \frac{(\hat{\beta}_1\hat{\beta}_2 - 1)^2}{\hat{\beta}_2^2 V_{11} + 2\hat{\beta}_1\hat{\beta}_2 V_{12} + \hat{\beta}_1^2 V_{22}}.$$

In finite samples, these three Wald statistics can be quite different. Depending on the values of β_1 and β_2, any one of them may perform better or worse than the other two, and they can sometimes overreject severely. The performance of alternative Wald tests in models like (10.61) has been investigated by Gregory and Veall (1985, 1987). Other cases in which Wald tests perform very badly are discussed by Lafontaine and White (1986).

Because of their dubious finite-sample properties and their sensitivity to the way in which the restrictions are written, we recommend against using Wald tests when the outcome of a test is important, except when it would be very costly or inconvenient to estimate the restricted model. Asymptotic t statistics should also be used with great caution, since, as we saw in Section 6.7, every asymptotic t statistic is simply the signed square root of a Wald statistic. Because conventional confidence intervals are based on inverting asymptotic t statistics, they too should be used with caution.

Lagrange Multiplier Tests

The **Lagrange multiplier**, or **LM**, test is the third of the three classical tests. The name suggests that it is based on the vector of Lagrange multipliers from a constrained maximization problem. That can indeed be the case. In practice, however, LM tests are very rarely computed in this way. Instead, they are usually based on the gradient vector, or score vector, of the unrestricted loglikelihood function, evaluated at the restricted estimates. LM tests are very often computed by means of artificial regressions. In fact, as we will see, some of the GNR-based tests that we encountered in Sections 6.7 and 7.7 are essentially Lagrange multiplier tests.

For simplicity, we begin our discussion of LM tests by considering the case in which the restrictions to be tested are zero restrictions, that is, restrictions according to which some of the model parameters are zero. In such cases, the r restrictions can be written as $\boldsymbol{\theta}_2 = \mathbf{0}$, where the parameter vector $\boldsymbol{\theta}$ is partitioned as $\boldsymbol{\theta} = [\boldsymbol{\theta}_1 \vdots \boldsymbol{\theta}_2]$, possibly after some reordering of the elements. The vector $\tilde{\boldsymbol{\theta}}$ of restricted estimates can then be expressed as $\tilde{\boldsymbol{\theta}} = [\tilde{\boldsymbol{\theta}}_1 \vdots \mathbf{0}]$. The vector $\tilde{\boldsymbol{\theta}}_1$ maximizes the restricted loglikelihood function $\ell(\boldsymbol{\theta}_1, \mathbf{0})$, and so it satisfies the restricted likelihood equations

$$\boldsymbol{g}_1(\tilde{\boldsymbol{\theta}}_1, \mathbf{0}) = \mathbf{0}, \tag{10.63}$$

where $\boldsymbol{g}_1(\cdot)$ is the vector whose components are the $k - r$ partial derivatives of $\ell(\cdot)$ with respect to the elements of $\boldsymbol{\theta}_1$.

The formula (10.38), which gives the asymptotic form of an MLE, can be applied to the estimator $\tilde{\boldsymbol{\theta}}$. If we partition the true parameter vector $\boldsymbol{\theta}_0$ as $[\boldsymbol{\theta}_1^0 \vdots \mathbf{0}]$, we find that

$$n^{1/2}(\tilde{\boldsymbol{\theta}}_1 - \boldsymbol{\theta}_1^0) \overset{a}{=} (\mathcal{I}_{11})^{-1}(\boldsymbol{\theta}_0) n^{-1/2} \boldsymbol{g}_1(\boldsymbol{\theta}_0), \tag{10.64}$$

where $\mathcal{I}_{11}(\cdot)$ is the $(k-r) \times (k-r)$ top left block of the asymptotic information matrix $\mathcal{I}(\cdot)$ of the full unrestricted model. This block is, of course, just the asymptotic information matrix for the restricted model.

When the gradient vector of the unrestricted loglikelihood function is evaluated at the restricted estimates $\tilde{\boldsymbol{\theta}}$, the first $k-r$ elements, which are the elements of the vector $\boldsymbol{g}_1(\tilde{\boldsymbol{\theta}})$, are zero, by equation (10.63). However, the r–vector $\boldsymbol{g}_2(\tilde{\boldsymbol{\theta}})$, which contains the remaining r elements, is in general nonzero. In fact, a Taylor expansion gives

$$n^{-1/2}\boldsymbol{g}_2(\tilde{\boldsymbol{\theta}}) = n^{-1/2}\boldsymbol{g}_2(\boldsymbol{\theta}_0) + n^{-1}\boldsymbol{H}_{21}(\bar{\boldsymbol{\theta}})\, n^{1/2}(\tilde{\boldsymbol{\theta}}_1 - \boldsymbol{\theta}_1^0), \tag{10.65}$$

where our usual shorthand notation $\bar{\boldsymbol{\theta}}$ is used for a vector that tends to $\boldsymbol{\theta}_0$ as $n \to \infty$, and $\boldsymbol{H}_{21}(\cdot)$ is the lower left block of the Hessian of the loglikelihood. The information matrix equality (10.34) shows that the limit of (10.65) for a correctly specified model is

$$\begin{aligned}
\operatorname*{plim}_{n\to\infty} n^{-1/2}\boldsymbol{g}_2(\tilde{\boldsymbol{\theta}}) &= \operatorname*{plim}_{n\to\infty} n^{-1/2}\boldsymbol{g}_2(\boldsymbol{\theta}_0) - \mathfrak{I}_{21}^0 \operatorname*{plim}_{n\to\infty} n^{1/2}(\tilde{\boldsymbol{\theta}}_1 - \boldsymbol{\theta}_1^0)\\
&= \operatorname*{plim}_{n\to\infty}\big(n^{-1/2}\boldsymbol{g}_2(\boldsymbol{\theta}_0) - \mathfrak{I}_{21}^0(\mathfrak{I}_{11}^0)^{-1} n^{-1/2}\boldsymbol{g}_1(\boldsymbol{\theta}_0)\big) \qquad (10.66)\\
&= \big[-\mathfrak{I}_{21}^0(\mathfrak{I}_{11}^0)^{-1} \quad \mathbf{I}\big] \operatorname*{plim}_{n\to\infty} \begin{bmatrix} n^{-1/2}\boldsymbol{g}_1(\boldsymbol{\theta}_0)\\ n^{-1/2}\boldsymbol{g}_2(\boldsymbol{\theta}_0)\end{bmatrix},
\end{aligned}$$

where $\mathfrak{I}^0 \equiv \mathfrak{I}(\boldsymbol{\theta}_0)$, $\mathbf{I}$ is an $r \times r$ identify matrix, and the second line follows from (10.64).

Since the variance of the full gradient vector, $\operatorname{plim} n^{-1/2}\boldsymbol{g}(\boldsymbol{\theta})$, is just $\mathfrak{I}_0$, the variance of the last expression in (10.66) is

$$\begin{aligned}
\operatorname{Var}\big(\operatorname*{plim}_{n\to\infty} n^{-1/2}\boldsymbol{g}_2(\tilde{\boldsymbol{\theta}})\big) &= \big[-\mathfrak{I}_{21}^0(\mathfrak{I}_{11}^0)^{-1} \quad \mathbf{I}\big] \begin{bmatrix} \mathfrak{I}_{11}^0 & \mathfrak{I}_{12}^0\\ \mathfrak{I}_{21}^0 & \mathfrak{I}_{22}^0\end{bmatrix} \begin{bmatrix} -(\mathfrak{I}_{11}^0)^{-1}\mathfrak{I}_{12}^0\\ \mathbf{I}\end{bmatrix}\\
&= \mathfrak{I}_{22}^0 - \mathfrak{I}_{21}^0(\mathfrak{I}_{11}^0)^{-1}\mathfrak{I}_{12}^0. \qquad (10.67)
\end{aligned}$$

In Exercise 7.11, expressions were developed for the blocks of the inverses of partitioned matrices. It is easy to see from those expressions that the inverse of (10.67) is the 22 block of $\mathfrak{I}^{-1}(\boldsymbol{\theta}_0)$. Thus, in order to obtain a statistic in asymptotically χ^2 form based on $\boldsymbol{g}_2(\tilde{\boldsymbol{\theta}})$, we can construct the quadratic form

$$\mathrm{LM} = n^{-1/2}\boldsymbol{g}_2^\top(\tilde{\boldsymbol{\theta}})(\tilde{\mathfrak{I}}^{-1})_{22}\, n^{-1/2}\boldsymbol{g}_2(\tilde{\boldsymbol{\theta}}) = \boldsymbol{g}_2^\top(\tilde{\boldsymbol{\theta}})(\tilde{\boldsymbol{I}}^{-1})_{22}\, \boldsymbol{g}_2(\tilde{\boldsymbol{\theta}}), \tag{10.68}$$

in which $\tilde{\mathfrak{I}} = n^{-1}\boldsymbol{I}(\tilde{\boldsymbol{\theta}})$, and the notations $(\tilde{\mathfrak{I}}^{-1})_{22}$ and $(\tilde{\boldsymbol{I}}^{-1})_{22}$ signify the 22 blocks of the inverses of $\tilde{\mathfrak{I}}$ and $\boldsymbol{I}(\tilde{\boldsymbol{\theta}})$, respectively.

Since the statistic (10.68) is a quadratic form in an r–vector, which is asymptotically normally distributed with mean $\mathbf{0}$, and the inverse of an $r \times r$ matrix that consistently estimates the covariance matrix of that vector, it is clear that the LM statistic is asymptotically distributed as $\chi^2(r)$ under the null. However, expression (10.68) is notationally awkward. Because the first-order conditions (10.63) imply that $\boldsymbol{g}_1(\tilde{\boldsymbol{\theta}}) = \mathbf{0}$, we can rewrite it as what appears to be a quadratic form with k rather than r degrees of freedom. We obtain

$$\mathrm{LM} = \boldsymbol{g}^\top(\tilde{\boldsymbol{\theta}})\tilde{\boldsymbol{I}}^{-1}\boldsymbol{g}(\tilde{\boldsymbol{\theta}}), \tag{10.69}$$

where the notational awkwardness has disappeared. In addition, since (10.69) no longer depends on the partitioning of $\boldsymbol{\theta}$ that we used to express the zero restrictions, it is applicable quite generally, whether or not the restrictions are zero restrictions. This follows from the **invariance** of the LM test under reparametrizations of the model; see Exercise 10.15.

Expression (10.69) is the statistic associated with the **score form** of the LM test, often simply called the **score test**, since it it defined in terms of the score vector $\boldsymbol{g}(\boldsymbol{\theta})$ evaluated at the restricted estimates $\tilde{\boldsymbol{\theta}}$. It must, of course, be kept in mind that, despite its appearance, expression (10.69) has only r, and not k, degrees of freedom. This "using up" of $k - r$ degrees of freedom is due to the fact that the $k - r$ elements of $\boldsymbol{\theta}_1$ are estimated. It is entirely analogous to a similar phenomenon discussed in Sections 9.4 and 9.5, in connection with Hansen-Sargan tests.

One way to maximize the loglikelihood function $\ell(\boldsymbol{\theta})$ subject to the restrictions $\boldsymbol{r}(\boldsymbol{\theta}) = \mathbf{0}$ is simultaneously to maximize the Lagrangian

$$\ell(\boldsymbol{\theta}) - \boldsymbol{r}^\top(\boldsymbol{\theta})\boldsymbol{\lambda}$$

with respect to $\boldsymbol{\theta}$ and minimize it with respect to the r–vector of Lagrange multipliers $\boldsymbol{\lambda}$. The first-order conditions that characterize the solution to this problem are the $k + r$ equations

$$\begin{aligned} \boldsymbol{g}(\tilde{\boldsymbol{\theta}}) - \boldsymbol{R}^\top(\tilde{\boldsymbol{\theta}})\tilde{\boldsymbol{\lambda}} &= \mathbf{0} \\ \boldsymbol{r}(\tilde{\boldsymbol{\theta}}) &= \mathbf{0}. \end{aligned}$$

The first set of these equations allows us to rewrite the LM statistic (10.69) in terms of the Lagrange multipliers $\boldsymbol{\lambda}$, thereby obtaining the **LM form** of the test, which is

$$\mathrm{LM} = \tilde{\boldsymbol{\lambda}}^\top\tilde{\boldsymbol{R}}\tilde{\boldsymbol{I}}^{-1}\tilde{\boldsymbol{R}}^\top\tilde{\boldsymbol{\lambda}}, \tag{10.70}$$

where $\tilde{\boldsymbol{R}} \equiv \boldsymbol{R}(\tilde{\boldsymbol{\theta}})$. The score form (10.69) is used much more often than the LM form (10.70), because $\boldsymbol{g}(\tilde{\boldsymbol{\theta}})$ is almost always available, no matter how the restricted estimates are obtained, whereas the vector $\tilde{\boldsymbol{\lambda}}$ is available only if they are obtained by using a Lagrangian.

LM Tests and Artificial Regressions

We have so far assumed that the information matrix estimator used to construct the LM statistic is $\tilde{\boldsymbol{I}} \equiv \boldsymbol{I}(\tilde{\boldsymbol{\theta}})$. Because this estimator is usually more efficient than other estimators of the information matrix, $\tilde{\boldsymbol{I}}$ is often referred to as the **efficient score** estimator of the information matrix. However, there are as many different ways to compute any given LM statistic as there are asymptotically valid ways to estimate the information matrix. In practice, $\tilde{\boldsymbol{I}}$ is often replaced by some other estimator, such as minus the empirical Hessian or the OPG estimator. For example, if the OPG estimator is used in (10.69), the statistic becomes

$$\tilde{\boldsymbol{g}}^\top(\tilde{\boldsymbol{G}}^\top\tilde{\boldsymbol{G}})^{-1}\tilde{\boldsymbol{g}}, \tag{10.71}$$

where $\tilde{\boldsymbol{g}} \equiv \boldsymbol{g}(\tilde{\boldsymbol{\theta}})$ and $\tilde{\boldsymbol{G}} \equiv \boldsymbol{G}(\tilde{\boldsymbol{\theta}})$. This **OPG variant** of the statistic is asymptotically, but not numerically, equivalent to the **efficient score variant** computed using $\tilde{\boldsymbol{I}}$. In contrast, the score and LM forms of the test are numerically equivalent provided both are computed using the same information matrix estimator.

The statistic (10.71) can readily be computed by use of an artificial regression called the **OPG regression**, which has the general form

$$\boldsymbol{\iota} = \boldsymbol{G}(\boldsymbol{\theta})\boldsymbol{c} + \text{residuals}, \tag{10.72}$$

where $\boldsymbol{\iota}$ is an n–vector of 1s. This regression can be constructed for any model for which the loglikelihood function can be written as the sum of n contributions. If we evaluate (10.72) at the vector of restricted estimates $\tilde{\boldsymbol{\theta}}$, it becomes

$$\boldsymbol{\iota} = \tilde{\boldsymbol{G}}\boldsymbol{c} + \text{residuals}, \tag{10.73}$$

and the explained sum of squares is

$$\boldsymbol{\iota}^\top\tilde{\boldsymbol{G}}(\tilde{\boldsymbol{G}}^\top\tilde{\boldsymbol{G}})^{-1}\tilde{\boldsymbol{G}}^\top\boldsymbol{\iota} = \tilde{\boldsymbol{g}}^\top(\tilde{\boldsymbol{G}}^\top\tilde{\boldsymbol{G}})^{-1}\tilde{\boldsymbol{g}},$$

by (10.27). The right-hand side above is equal to expression (10.71), and so the ESS from regression (10.73) is numerically equal to the OPG variant of the LM statistic.

In the case of regression (10.72), the total sum of squares is just n, the squared length of the vector $\boldsymbol{\iota}$. Therefore, ESS $= n -$ SSR. This result gives us a particularly easy way to calculate the LM test statistic, and it also puts an upper bound on it: The OPG variant of the LM statistic can never exceed the number of observations in the OPG regression.

Although the OPG variant of the LM statistic is easy to calculate for a very wide variety of models, it does not have particularly good finite-sample properties. In fact, there is a great deal of evidence to suggest that tests based on this form of the statistic are much more likely to overreject than tests based on any other form and that they can overreject very severely in some cases. Therefore, unless it is bootstrapped, the OPG form of the LM statistic should be used with great caution. See Davidson and MacKinnon (1993, Chapter 13) for references. Fortunately, in many circumstances, other artificial regressions with much better finite-sample properties can be used to compute LM statistics; see Davidson and MacKinnon (2001).

LM Tests and the GNR

Consider again the case of linear restrictions on the parameters of the classical normal linear model. By summing the contributions (10.46) to the gradient, we see that the gradient of the loglikelihood for this model with respect to $\boldsymbol{\beta}$ can be written as

$$\boldsymbol{g}(\boldsymbol{\beta}, \sigma) = \frac{1}{\sigma^2} \boldsymbol{X}^\top (\boldsymbol{y} - \boldsymbol{X\beta}).$$

Since the information matrix (10.52) is block-diagonal, we need not bother with the gradient with respect to σ in order to compute the LM statistic (10.69). From (10.49), we know that the $\boldsymbol{\beta}$-$\boldsymbol{\beta}$ block of the information matrix is $\sigma^{-2}\boldsymbol{X}^\top\boldsymbol{X}$. Thus, if we write the restricted estimates of the parameters as $\tilde{\boldsymbol{\beta}}$ and $\tilde{\sigma}$, the statistic (10.69), computed with the efficient score estimator of the information matrix, takes the form

$$\frac{1}{\tilde{\sigma}^2} (\boldsymbol{y} - \boldsymbol{X}\tilde{\boldsymbol{\beta}})^\top \boldsymbol{X} (\boldsymbol{X}^\top \boldsymbol{X})^{-1} \boldsymbol{X}^\top (\boldsymbol{y} - \boldsymbol{X}\tilde{\boldsymbol{\beta}}). \tag{10.74}$$

This variant of the LM statistic is, like the LR and some variants of the Wald statistic, a deterministic, strictly increasing, function of the F statistic (10.57); see Exercise 10.18.

More generally, for a nonlinear regression model subject to possibly nonlinear restrictions on the parameters, we see that, by analogy with (10.74), the LM statistic can be written as

$$\frac{1}{\tilde{\sigma}^2} (\boldsymbol{y} - \tilde{\boldsymbol{x}})^\top \tilde{\boldsymbol{X}} (\tilde{\boldsymbol{X}}^\top \tilde{\boldsymbol{X}})^{-1} \tilde{\boldsymbol{X}}^\top (\boldsymbol{y} - \tilde{\boldsymbol{x}}), \tag{10.75}$$

where $\tilde{\boldsymbol{x}} \equiv \boldsymbol{x}(\tilde{\boldsymbol{\beta}})$ is the n–vector of nonlinear regression functions evaluated at the restricted ML estimates $\tilde{\boldsymbol{\beta}}$, and $\tilde{\boldsymbol{X}} \equiv \boldsymbol{X}(\tilde{\boldsymbol{\beta}})$ is the $n \times k$ matrix of derivatives of the regression functions with respect to the components of $\boldsymbol{\beta}$. It is easy to show that (10.75) is just n times the uncentered R^2 from the GNR

$$\boldsymbol{y} - \tilde{\boldsymbol{x}} = \tilde{\boldsymbol{X}}\boldsymbol{b} + \text{residuals},$$

which corresponds to the unrestricted nonlinear regression, evaluated at the restricted estimates. As we saw in Section 6.7, this is one of the valid statistics that can be computed using a GNR.

Bootstrapping the Classical Tests

When two or more of the classical test statistics differ substantially in magnitude, or when we have any other reason to believe that asymptotic tests based on them may not be reliable, bootstrap tests provide an attractive alternative to asymptotic ones. Since maximum likelihood requires a fully specified model, it is generally appropriate to use a parametric bootstrap, rather than resampling. For any given parameter vector $\boldsymbol{\theta}$, the likelihood function is the

PDF of the dependent variable. Therefore, parametric bootstrap samples $\boldsymbol{y}^*$ are simply realizations of vector random variables from the distribution characterized by that PDF, evaluated at consistent estimates of the model parameters. These estimates must, of course, satisfy the restrictions to be tested, and so the natural choice, and usually the best one, is the vector of restricted ML estimates.

The procedure we recommend for bootstrapping any of the classical tests is very similar to the procedure for bootstrapping F tests that was discussed in Section 4.6. The model is estimated under the null to obtain the vector of restricted estimates $\tilde{\boldsymbol{\theta}}$, and the desired test statistic, $\hat{\tau}$, is computed. This step may, of course, entail the estimation of the unrestricted model. One then generates B bootstrap samples using the DGP characterized by $\tilde{\boldsymbol{\theta}}$. For each of them, a bootstrap statistic τ_j^*, $j = 1, \ldots, B$, is computed in the same way as was $\hat{\tau}$. A bootstrap P value can then be obtained in the usual way as the proportion of bootstrap statistics more extreme than $\hat{\tau}$ itself; see (4.62).

We strongly recommend use of the bootstrap whenever there is any reason to believe that classical tests based on asymptotic theory may not be reliable, unless calculating a moderate number of τ_j^* is computationally infeasible. When this calculation is expensive, methods that do not use a fixed value of B may be attractive; see Davidson and MacKinnon (2000).

It is important to note that, as we saw earlier in this section for some tests in linear regression models, certain classical test statistics may be deterministic, strictly increasing, functions of other statistics. The bootstrap P values must be identical for statistics related in this way, since a bootstrap P value depends only on the ordering of the statistic $\hat{\tau}$ and the bootstrap statistics τ_j^*, and this ordering is invariant under a deterministic, strictly increasing, function. If we can readily compute a number of test statistics that are not deterministically related, it is desirable to bootstrap all of them at once. This is usually much cheaper than bootstrapping them separately. In general, we would expect the bootstrap P values from the various tests to be fairly similar, at least if the null hypothesis is true.

10.6 The Asymptotic Theory of the Three Classical Tests

In this section, much of which is fairly advanced, we show that the three classical test statistics tend asymptotically to the same random variable. This is true both under the null hypothesis and under alternatives that are close to the null in a sense to be made precise later. The proof, which is limited to the former case, involves obtaining expressions for the probability limits of all three statistics in terms of the asymptotic information matrix $\mathfrak{I} \equiv \mathfrak{I}(\boldsymbol{\theta}_0)$ and the **asymptotic score vector** $\boldsymbol{s} \equiv \operatorname{plim} n^{-1/2}\boldsymbol{g}(\boldsymbol{\theta}_0)$. To avoid cluttering the notation, we omit zero subscripts. The results will be developed explicitly only for restrictions of the form $\boldsymbol{\theta}_2 = \boldsymbol{0}$, but they apply quite generally.

By a second-order Taylor expansion of $\ell(\tilde{\boldsymbol{\theta}})$ around $\hat{\boldsymbol{\theta}}$, we obtain

$$\ell(\tilde{\boldsymbol{\theta}}) = \ell(\hat{\boldsymbol{\theta}}) + \frac{1}{2}(\tilde{\boldsymbol{\theta}} - \hat{\boldsymbol{\theta}})^\top \boldsymbol{H}(\bar{\boldsymbol{\theta}})(\tilde{\boldsymbol{\theta}} - \hat{\boldsymbol{\theta}}),$$

where $\bar{\boldsymbol{\theta}}$ is defined as usual in such an expansion. The first-order term vanishes because of the likelihood equations $\boldsymbol{g}(\hat{\boldsymbol{\theta}}) = \mathbf{0}$. It follows that

$$\text{LR} = 2\big(\ell(\hat{\boldsymbol{\theta}}) - \ell(\tilde{\boldsymbol{\theta}})\big) = -(\tilde{\boldsymbol{\theta}} - \hat{\boldsymbol{\theta}})^\top \boldsymbol{H}(\bar{\boldsymbol{\theta}})(\tilde{\boldsymbol{\theta}} - \hat{\boldsymbol{\theta}}).$$

The information matrix equality and the consistency of $\hat{\boldsymbol{\theta}}$, which implies the consistency of $\bar{\boldsymbol{\theta}}$, then yield the result that

$$\text{LR} \stackrel{a}{=} n(\tilde{\boldsymbol{\theta}} - \hat{\boldsymbol{\theta}})^\top \mathfrak{I}\,(\tilde{\boldsymbol{\theta}} - \hat{\boldsymbol{\theta}}). \tag{10.76}$$

When we take the limit of (10.76), we can use the asymptotic equalities (10.38) and (10.64) to eliminate the estimators that appear in (10.76), replacing them by expressions that involve only the asymptotic information matrix and asymptotic score vector, as follows:

$$\begin{aligned}\operatorname*{plim}_{n\to\infty} n^{1/2}(\hat{\boldsymbol{\theta}} - \tilde{\boldsymbol{\theta}}) &= \operatorname*{plim}_{n\to\infty} n^{1/2}(\hat{\boldsymbol{\theta}} - \boldsymbol{\theta}_0) - \operatorname*{plim}_{n\to\infty} n^{1/2}(\tilde{\boldsymbol{\theta}} - \boldsymbol{\theta}_0)\\ &= \mathfrak{I}^{-1}\boldsymbol{s} - \begin{bmatrix}\mathfrak{I}_{11}^{-1}\boldsymbol{s}_1\\ \mathbf{0}\end{bmatrix}.\end{aligned} \tag{10.77}$$

Here $\mathfrak{I}_{11}$ and $\boldsymbol{s}_1$ denote, respectively, the $(k-r)\times(k-r)$ block of $\mathfrak{I}$ and the subvector of $\boldsymbol{s}$ that correspond to $\boldsymbol{\theta}_1$. We rewrite the last expression in (10.77) as $\boldsymbol{J}\boldsymbol{s}$, where the $k \times k$ symmetric matrix $\boldsymbol{J}$ is defined as

$$\boldsymbol{J} \equiv \mathfrak{I}^{-1} - \begin{bmatrix}\mathfrak{I}_{11}^{-1} & \mathbf{O}\\ \mathbf{O} & \mathbf{O}\end{bmatrix}. \tag{10.78}$$

Using (10.78), the probability limit of (10.76) is seen to be

$$\operatorname*{plim}_{n\to\infty} \text{LR} = \boldsymbol{s}^\top \boldsymbol{J}\,\mathfrak{I}\boldsymbol{J}\boldsymbol{s}. \tag{10.79}$$

Moreover, from (10.78), we have that

$$\mathfrak{I}\boldsymbol{J} = \mathbf{I}_k - \begin{bmatrix}\mathfrak{I}_{11} & \mathfrak{I}_{12}\\ \mathfrak{I}_{21} & \mathfrak{I}_{22}\end{bmatrix}\begin{bmatrix}\mathfrak{I}_{11}^{-1} & \mathbf{O}\\ \mathbf{O} & \mathbf{O}\end{bmatrix} = \begin{bmatrix}\mathbf{O} & \mathbf{O}\\ -\mathfrak{I}_{21}\mathfrak{I}_{11}^{-1} & \mathbf{I}_{k_2}\end{bmatrix}, \tag{10.80}$$

where the suffixes on the two identity matrices above indicate their dimensions. If we denote the last $k \times k$ matrix in (10.80) by $\boldsymbol{Q}$, (10.80) can be written simply as $\mathfrak{I}\boldsymbol{J} = \boldsymbol{Q}$. This in turn implies that $\mathfrak{I}^{-1}\boldsymbol{Q} = \boldsymbol{J}$, and, since

$$\begin{bmatrix}\mathfrak{I}_{11}^{-1} & \mathbf{O}\\ \mathbf{O} & \mathbf{O}\end{bmatrix}\begin{bmatrix}\mathbf{O} & \mathbf{O}\\ -\mathfrak{I}_{21}\mathfrak{I}_{11}^{-1} & \mathbf{I}_{k_2}\end{bmatrix} = \mathbf{O},$$

it follows from (10.78) that $\boldsymbol{J}\boldsymbol{Q} = \boldsymbol{J}$. This implies that $\boldsymbol{J}\mathcal{I}\boldsymbol{J} = \boldsymbol{J}$, from which we conclude that (10.79) can be written as

$$\operatorname*{plim}_{n\to\infty} \mathrm{LR} = \boldsymbol{s}^\top \boldsymbol{J}\boldsymbol{s}. \tag{10.81}$$

This expression, together with the definition (10.78) of the matrix $\boldsymbol{J}$, shows clearly how $k - r$ of the k degrees of freedom of $\boldsymbol{s}^\top \mathcal{I}^{-1}\boldsymbol{s}$ are used up by the process of estimating $\boldsymbol{\theta}_1$ under the null hypothesis.

We now go through a similar exercise for the LM statistic, all variants of which are asymptotically equal to the statistic in (10.69). Consider the last line of (10.66). If we stack the restricted likelihood equations, $\boldsymbol{g}_1(\tilde{\boldsymbol{\theta}}) = \boldsymbol{0}$, on top of this, and use the definitions of $\boldsymbol{Q}$ and $\boldsymbol{s}$, we find that (10.66) can be written as

$$\operatorname*{plim}_{n\to\infty} n^{1/2}\boldsymbol{g}(\tilde{\boldsymbol{\theta}}) = \boldsymbol{Q}\boldsymbol{s}.$$

We then see from (10.69) that

$$\operatorname*{plim}_{n\to\infty} \mathrm{LM} = \boldsymbol{s}^\top\boldsymbol{Q}^\top\mathcal{I}^{-1}\boldsymbol{Q}\boldsymbol{s} = \boldsymbol{s}^\top\boldsymbol{J}\mathcal{I}\boldsymbol{J}\boldsymbol{s} = \boldsymbol{s}^\top\boldsymbol{J}\boldsymbol{s}, \tag{10.82}$$

since $\mathcal{I}^{-1}\boldsymbol{Q} = \boldsymbol{J}$ and $\boldsymbol{J}\mathcal{I}\boldsymbol{J} = \boldsymbol{J}$ by our earlier results. The asymptotic equivalence of the LR and LM statistics follows from (10.81) and (10.82).

The Wald statistic (10.60), for the case of zero restrictions, can be written as

$$\mathrm{W} = \hat{\boldsymbol{\theta}}_2^\top\big((\hat{\boldsymbol{I}}^{-1})_{22}\big)^{-1}\hat{\boldsymbol{\theta}}_2,$$

and the limit of the statistic can therefore be expressed as

$$\operatorname*{plim}_{n\to\infty} \mathrm{W} = \operatorname*{plim}_{n\to\infty} n^{1/2}\hat{\boldsymbol{\theta}}_2^\top\big((\mathcal{I}^{-1})_{22}\big)^{-1}\operatorname*{plim}_{n\to\infty} n^{1/2}\hat{\boldsymbol{\theta}}_2. \tag{10.83}$$

When we were developing the LM statistic in the previous section, we saw that the inverse of the 22 block of $\mathcal{I}^{-1}$ was equal to the last expression in (10.67). From the middle expression in (10.67), we then obtain

$$\begin{aligned}\begin{bmatrix}\mathbf{O} & \mathbf{O}\\ \mathbf{O} & \big((\mathcal{I}^{-1})_{22}\big)^{-1}\end{bmatrix} &= \begin{bmatrix}\mathbf{O} & \mathbf{O}\\ -\mathcal{I}_{21}(\mathcal{I}_{11})^{-1} & \mathbf{I}\end{bmatrix}\begin{bmatrix}\mathcal{I}_{11} & \mathcal{I}_{12}\\ \mathcal{I}_{21} & \mathcal{I}_{22}\end{bmatrix}\begin{bmatrix}\mathbf{O} & -(\mathcal{I}_{11})^{-1}\mathcal{I}_{12}\\ \mathbf{O} & \mathbf{I}\end{bmatrix}\\ &= \boldsymbol{Q}\mathcal{I}\boldsymbol{Q}^\top.\end{aligned}$$

Thus (10.83) becomes, by use of (10.38),

$$\begin{aligned}\operatorname*{plim}_{n\to\infty} \mathrm{W} &= \operatorname*{plim}_{n\to\infty} n^{1/2}(\hat{\boldsymbol{\theta}} - \boldsymbol{\theta}_0)^\top\boldsymbol{Q}\mathcal{I}\boldsymbol{Q}^\top\operatorname*{plim}_{n\to\infty} n^{1/2}(\hat{\boldsymbol{\theta}} - \boldsymbol{\theta}_0)\\ &= \boldsymbol{s}^\top\mathcal{I}^{-1}\boldsymbol{Q}\mathcal{I}\boldsymbol{Q}^\top\mathcal{I}^{-1}\boldsymbol{s} = \boldsymbol{s}^\top\boldsymbol{J}\mathcal{I}\boldsymbol{J}\boldsymbol{s} = \boldsymbol{s}^\top\boldsymbol{J}\boldsymbol{s},\end{aligned} \tag{10.84}$$

where we have made use of the relations among $\mathcal{I}$, $\boldsymbol{J}$, and $\boldsymbol{Q}$ that have previously been established. This result shows that all three classical test statistics tend to the same limiting random variable, namely, $\boldsymbol{s}^\top\boldsymbol{J}\boldsymbol{s}$.

Quadratic Approximations and Classical Test Statistics

The asymptotic equivalence of the three classical test statistics can be understood by a geometric argument based on quadratic approximations to the loglikelihood function. Consider first the case of a classical normal linear model with known error variance. Then it can be seen directly from equation (10.10) that the loglikelihood function is a quadratic function of the parameter vector $\boldsymbol{\beta}$. Therefore, if σ^2 is known, the loglikelihood function is quadratic with respect to all the parameters that have to be estimated.

For simplicity, consider the special case in which there is just one regressor, in the form of a vector $\boldsymbol{x}$, and a single parameter, β. Then the loglikelihood function (10.10) can be written as

$$\ell(\beta) = a + b\beta - \tfrac{1}{2}h\beta^2, \tag{10.85}$$

where a is a numerical constant minus $\boldsymbol{y}^\top\boldsymbol{y}/2$, b is $\boldsymbol{x}^\top\boldsymbol{y}$, and h is $\boldsymbol{x}^\top\boldsymbol{x}$, independent of $\boldsymbol{y}$. We wish to test the restriction that $\beta = 0$.

The gradient of the loglikelihood function (10.85) is

$$g(\beta) \equiv \frac{\partial \ell(\beta)}{\partial \beta} = b - h\beta.$$

Setting this equal to 0, we find that the ML estimate is $\hat{\beta} = b/h$. Therefore, the LR statistic is

$$\mathrm{LR} = 2\big(\ell(\hat{\beta}) - \ell(0)\big) = 2a + 2b\hat{\beta} - h\hat{\beta}^2 - 2a = 2b^2/h - b^2/h = b^2/h.$$

For the loglikelihood function (10.85), $g(0) = b$. The Hessian, which in this simple case is the scalar $-h$, is independent both of $\boldsymbol{y}$ and β, and so the information matrix $I(\beta)$ is the scalar quantity h for all β. It follows that the LM statistic is

$$\mathrm{LM} = g^\top(0) I^{-1}(0) g(0) = b^2/h.$$

Finally, for the Wald statistic, we use the fact that the inverse of the information matrix, h^{-1}, is the asymptotic variance of $\hat{\beta}$. Consequently,

$$\mathrm{W} = \hat{\beta}^2/V(\hat{\beta}) = h(b/h)^2 = b^2/h.$$

Thus we see that, in the special case of the quadratic loglikelihood function (10.85), the three classical test statistics are numerically equal. We would, of course, have obtained the same result if the null hypothesis had been that $\beta = \beta_0$ instead of $\beta = 0$.

In general, the loglikelihood function is not exactly quadratic. However, if we were to take a quadratic approximation to it, we could compute an LR statistic based on that approximation. Provided the approximation is made at a

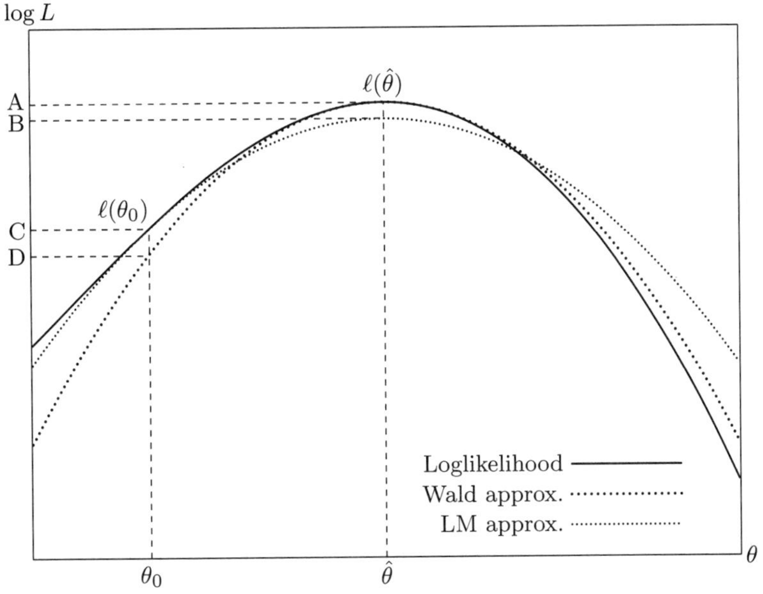

Figure 10.3 LR, LM, and Wald Tests

point that converges to the true parameter value under the null, the approximate LR statistic must have the same asymptotic distribution as the actual statistic. Thus the LM and Wald statistics can be thought of as approximate LR statistics that are computed using different quadratic approximations to the loglikelihood function.

This is illustrated in Figure 10.3 for the case in which there is a single parameter θ and the null hypothesis is that $\theta = \theta_0$. The solid line is the loglikelihood function. The dotted lines are two different quadratic approximations. One of these approximations, which is taken at θ_0, is the basis of the LM statistic. The other, which is taken at $\hat{\theta}$, is the basis of the Wald statistic. The LR statistic is twice the vertical distance CA in the figure. The LM statistic is twice the vertical distance CB, and the Wald statistic is twice the vertical distance DA.

The Three Classical Tests When the Null Is False

The asymptotic equivalence result established in equations (10.79), (10.82), and (10.84) depends on the assumption that the DGP belongs to the null hypothesis. However, the three classical tests yield asymptotically equivalent inferences only if the equivalence holds more generally than just under the null hypothesis.

A test is said to be **consistent** against a DGP that does not belong to the null hypothesis if, under that DGP, the power of the test tends to 1 as the sample size tends to infinity. We saw in Section 4.7 that, if the null and alternative hypotheses are classical normal linear models, power is determined by a noncentrality parameter that must tend to infinity for power to tend to 1. The three classical tests have a property similar to that of the exact tests of the classical normal linear model: Under DGPs in the alternative but not in the null, the classical test statistics tend to random variables that are distributed as noncentral chi-squared with r degrees of freedom, where the noncentrality parameters tend to infinity with the sample size.

If all three classical tests can be shown to be consistent against a given DGP, then they are asymptotically equivalent under this DGP in the sense that, as $n \to \infty$, power tends to 1. But this does not rule out the possibility that, in finite samples, one of the tests may be much more powerful than the others. In order to investigate such a possibility, we want to develop a version of asymptotic theory in which the powers of different tests tend to different limits as $n \to \infty$ if they have very different powers in finite samples.

The simplest case we can study is that of the t statistic for the restriction $\beta_2 = 0$ in the linear regression model

$$\boldsymbol{y} = \boldsymbol{X}_1\boldsymbol{\beta}_1 + \boldsymbol{x}_2\beta_2 + \boldsymbol{u}.$$

The noncentrality parameter λ of the t statistic, in finite samples, is given as a function of β_2 and the error variance σ^2 in equation (4.73), which we repeat here for convenience:

$$\lambda = \frac{1}{\sigma}(\boldsymbol{x}_2^{\top}\boldsymbol{M}_1\boldsymbol{x}_2)^{1/2}\beta_2.$$

For fixed β_2 and σ, λ tends to infinity as $n \to \infty$, since, under the regularity conditions for the classical normal linear model, $n^{-1}\boldsymbol{x}_2^{\top}\boldsymbol{M}_1\boldsymbol{x}_2$ tends to a finite limit, which we denote by $S_{\boldsymbol{x}_2^{\top}\boldsymbol{M}_1\boldsymbol{x}_2}$. It follows that $n^{-1/2}\lambda$, rather than λ itself, tends to a finite limit. But if, instead of keeping β_2 fixed, we subject it to what is called a **Pitman drift**, we can obtain a different result. Let δ be a fixed parameter, and, for each sample size n, let $\beta_2 = n^{-1/2}\delta$. Then

$$\lambda = n^{-1/2}\frac{1}{\sigma}(\boldsymbol{x}_2^{\top}\boldsymbol{M}_1\boldsymbol{x}_2)^{1/2}\delta = \frac{1}{\sigma}(n^{-1}\boldsymbol{x}_2^{\top}\boldsymbol{M}_1\boldsymbol{x}_2)^{1/2}\delta \to \frac{\delta}{\sigma}S_{\boldsymbol{x}_2^{\top}\boldsymbol{M}_1\boldsymbol{x}_2}.$$

Since the limit of λ is no longer infinite, we can compare the possibly different limits obtained for different test statistics. A DGP for which the parameters depend explicitly on the sample size is called a **drifting DGP**.

If the model that corresponds to the alternative hypothesis is characterized by the loglikelihood function $\ell(\boldsymbol{\theta}_1, \boldsymbol{\theta}_2)$, and the null hypothesis is the set of r zero restrictions $\boldsymbol{\theta}_2 = \boldsymbol{0}$, an appropriate drifting DGP for studying power is one for which $\boldsymbol{\theta}_1$ is fixed and $\boldsymbol{\theta}_2$ is given by $n^{-1/2}\boldsymbol{\delta}$ for a fixed r–vector $\boldsymbol{\delta}$. It can then be shown that, under this drifting DGP, just as under the null, the LR, LM, and Wald statistics tend as $n \to \infty$ to the same random variable, which follows a noncentral $\chi^2(r)$ distribution; see Exercise 10.19 for a very simple example. More generally, as discussed by Davidson and MacKinnon (1987), we can allow for drifting DGPs that do not lie within the alternative hypothesis, but that drift toward some fixed DGP in the null hypothesis. It then turns out that, for drifting DGPs that are, in an appropriate sense, equally distant from the null, the noncentrality parameter is maximized by those DGPs that do lie within the alternative hypothesis. This result justifies the intuition that, for a given number of degrees of freedom, tests against an alternative which happens to be true should have more power than tests against other alternatives.

10.7 ML Estimation of Models with Autoregressive Errors

In Section 7.8, we discussed several methods based on generalized or nonlinear least squares for estimating linear regression models with error terms that follow an autoregressive process. An alternative approach is to use maximum likelihood. If it is assumed that the innovations are normally distributed, ML estimation is quite straightforward. With the normality assumption, the model (7.40) considered in Sections 7.7 and 7.8 can be written as

$$y_t = \boldsymbol{X}_t\boldsymbol{\beta} + u_t, \quad u_t = \rho u_{t-1} + \varepsilon_t, \quad \varepsilon_t \sim \text{NID}(0, \sigma_\varepsilon^2), \tag{10.86}$$

in which the error terms follow an AR(1) process with parameter ρ that is assumed to be less than 1 in absolute value. If we omit the first observation, this model can be rewritten as in equation (7.41). The result is just a nonlinear regression model, and so, as we saw in Section 10.2, the ML estimates of $\boldsymbol{\beta}$ and ρ must coincide with the NLS ones.

Maximum likelihood estimation of (10.86) is more interesting if we do not omit the first observation, because, in that case, the ML estimates no longer coincide with either the NLS or the GLS estimates. For observations 2 through n, the contributions to the loglikelihood can be written as in (10.09):

$$\begin{aligned}\ell_t(\boldsymbol{y}^t, \boldsymbol{\beta}, \rho, \sigma_\varepsilon) &= \\ -\frac{1}{2}\log 2\pi - \log\sigma_\varepsilon &- \frac{1}{2\sigma_\varepsilon^2}(y_t - \rho y_{t-1} - \boldsymbol{X}_t\boldsymbol{\beta} + \rho\boldsymbol{X}_{t-1}\boldsymbol{\beta})^2.\end{aligned} \tag{10.87}$$

As required by (10.24), this expression is the log of the density of y_t conditional on the lagged dependent variable y_{t-1}.

For the first observation, the only information we have is that

$$y_1 = \boldsymbol{X}_1\boldsymbol{\beta} + u_1,$$

since the lagged dependent variable y_0 is not observed. However, with the normality assumption, we know from Section 7.8 that $u_1 \sim \mathrm{N}\big(0, \sigma_\varepsilon^2/(1-\rho^2)\big)$. Thus the loglikelihood contribution from the first observation is the log of the density of that distribution, namely,

$$\ell_1(y_1, \boldsymbol{\beta}, \rho, \sigma_\varepsilon) = \\ -\tfrac{1}{2}\log 2\pi - \log\sigma_\varepsilon + \tfrac{1}{2}\log(1-\rho^2) - \frac{1-\rho^2}{2\sigma_\varepsilon^2}(y_1 - \boldsymbol{X}_1\boldsymbol{\beta})^2. \tag{10.88}$$

The loglikelihood function for the model (10.86) based on the entire sample is obtained by adding the contribution (10.88) to the sum of the contributions (10.87), for $t = 2, \ldots, n$. The result is

$$\ell(\boldsymbol{y}, \boldsymbol{\beta}, \rho, \sigma_\varepsilon) = -\tfrac{n}{2}\log 2\pi - n\log\sigma_\varepsilon + \tfrac{1}{2}\log(1-\rho^2) \tag{10.89}$$
$$-\frac{1}{2\sigma_\varepsilon^2}\Big((1-\rho^2)(y_1 - \boldsymbol{X}_1\boldsymbol{\beta})^2 + \sum_{t=2}^{n}(y_t - \rho y_{t-1} - \boldsymbol{X}_t\boldsymbol{\beta} + \rho\boldsymbol{X}_{t-1}\boldsymbol{\beta})^2\Big).$$

The term $\frac{1}{2}\log(1-\rho^2)$ that appears in (10.89) plays an extremely important role in ML estimation. Because it tends to minus infinity as ρ tends to ± 1, its presence in the loglikelihood function ensures that there must be a maximum within the **stationarity region** defined by $|\rho| < 1$. Therefore, maximum likelihood estimation using the full sample is guaranteed to yield an estimate of ρ for which the AR(1) process is stationary. This is not the case for any of the estimation techniques discussed in Section 7.8.

Let us define $u_t(\boldsymbol{\beta})$ as $y_t - \boldsymbol{X}_t\boldsymbol{\beta}$ for $t = 1, \ldots, n$, and let $\hat{u}_t = u_t(\hat{\boldsymbol{\beta}})$. Then, from the first-order conditions for the maximization of (10.89), it can be seen that the ML estimators $\hat{\boldsymbol{\beta}}$, $\hat{\rho}$, and $\hat{\sigma}_\varepsilon^2$ satisfy the following equations:

$$(1-\hat{\rho}^2)\boldsymbol{X}_1^{\top}\hat{u}_1 + \sum_{t=2}^{n}(\boldsymbol{X}_t - \hat{\rho}\boldsymbol{X}_{t-1})^{\top}(\hat{u}_t - \hat{\rho}\hat{u}_{t-1}) = \boldsymbol{0},$$
$$\hat{\rho}\hat{u}_1^2 - \frac{\hat{\rho}\hat{\sigma}_\varepsilon^2}{1-\hat{\rho}^2} + \sum_{t=2}^{n}\hat{u}_{t-1}(\hat{u}_t - \hat{\rho}\hat{u}_{t-1}) = 0, \text{ and} \tag{10.90}$$
$$\hat{\sigma}_\varepsilon^2 = \frac{1}{n}\Big((1-\hat{\rho}^2)\hat{u}_1^2 + \sum_{t=2}^{n}(\hat{u}_t - \hat{\rho}\hat{u}_{t-1})^2\Big).$$

The first two of these equations are similar, but not identical, to the estimating equations (7.71) developed in Section 7.8 for iterated feasible GLS or NLS with account taken of the first observation. In Exercise 10.21, an artificial regression is developed which makes it quite easy to solve equations (10.90). This approach is simpler than the better-known algorithm for finding ML estimates that was proposed by Beach and MacKinnon (1978).

10.8 Transformations of the Dependent Variable

Whenever we specify a regression model, one of the choices we implicitly have to make is whether, and how, to transform the dependent variable. For example, if y_t, a typical observation on the dependent variable, is always positive, it would be perfectly valid to use $\log y_t$, or $y_t^{1/2}$, or one of many other monotonically increasing nonlinear transformations, instead of y_t itself as the regressand.

For concreteness, let us suppose that there are just two alternative models, which we will refer to as Model 1 and Model 2:

$$\begin{aligned} y_t &= \boldsymbol{X}_{t1}\boldsymbol{\beta}_1 + u_t, \quad u_t \sim \text{NID}(0, \sigma_1^2), \text{ and} \\ \log y_t &= \boldsymbol{X}_{t2}\boldsymbol{\beta}_2 + v_t, \quad v_t \sim \text{NID}(0, \sigma_2^2). \end{aligned}$$

Precisely how the regressors of the two competing models are related need not concern us here. In many cases, some of the regressors for one model are transformations of some of the regressors for the other model. For example, $\boldsymbol{X}_{t1}$ might consist of a constant and z_t, and $\boldsymbol{X}_{t2}$ might consist of a constant and $\log z_t$. Model 2 is often called a **loglinear regression** model.

Although we may be able to specify plausible-looking regression models for a number of different transformations of the dependent variable, using any model except the correct one implies that, in general, the error terms are neither normally nor identically distributed. For example, suppose that we estimate Model 1 when the data were actually generated by Model 2 with parameters $\boldsymbol{\beta}_{20}$ and σ_{20}^2. It follows that

$$\begin{aligned} y_t &= \exp(\boldsymbol{X}_{t2}\boldsymbol{\beta}_{20} + v_t) \\ &= \exp(\boldsymbol{X}_{t2}\boldsymbol{\beta}_{20})\exp(v_t) \qquad (10.91) \\ &= \exp(\boldsymbol{X}_{t2}\boldsymbol{\beta}_{20})\exp(\tfrac{1}{2}\sigma_{20}^2) + \exp(\boldsymbol{X}_{t2}\boldsymbol{\beta}_{20})\big(\exp(v_t) - \exp(\tfrac{1}{2}\sigma_{20}^2)\big). \end{aligned}$$

The last line here uses the fact that $\exp(v_t)$ is a lognormal variable, of which the expectation is $\exp(\sigma_{20}^2/2)$; recall Exercise 9.19. Thus the first term in the last line is the conditional mean of y_t, and so the second term, which is y_t minus this conditional mean, is the error term for Model 1.

Even if it should turn out that $\boldsymbol{X}_{t1}\boldsymbol{\beta}_1$, the regression function for Model 1, can provide a reasonably good approximation to the conditional mean in the last line of (10.91), the error terms for that model cannot possibly have the properties we generally assume them to have. If the error terms in Model 2 are normally and identically distributed, then the error terms in Model 1 must be skewed to the right and heteroskedastic. Their skewness is a consequence of the fact that lognormal variables are always skewed to the right (see Exercise 10.20). Because their variance is proportional to the square of $\exp(\boldsymbol{X}_{t2}\boldsymbol{\beta}_{20})$, they are heteroskedastic.

As this example demonstrates, even when the errors in the DGP are normally, identically, and independently distributed, using the wrong transformation of the dependent variable as the regressand yields, in general, a regression with error terms that are neither homoskedastic nor symmetric. Thus, when we encounter heteroskedasticity and skewness in the residuals of a regression, one possible way to eliminate them is to estimate a different regression model in which the dependent variable has been subjected to some sort of nonlinear transformation.

Comparing Alternative Models

It is perfectly easy to subject the dependent variable to various nonlinear transformations and estimate one or more regression models for each of them. However, least-squares estimation does not provide any way to compare the fits of competing models that involve different transformations. But maximum likelihood estimation under the assumption that the error terms are normally distributed does provide a straightforward way to do so. The idea is to compare the loglikelihoods of the alternative models considered as models for the same dependent variable.

For Model 1, in which y_t is the regressand, the concentrated loglikelihood function is simply

$$-\frac{n}{2}\log 2\pi - \frac{n}{2} - \frac{n}{2}\log\biggl(\sum_{t=1}^{n}(y_t - \boldsymbol{X}_{t1}\boldsymbol{\beta}_1)^2\biggr). \tag{10.92}$$

Expression (10.92) is just expression (10.11) specialized to Model 1. Most regression packages report the value of (10.92) evaluated at the OLS estimates as the maximized value of the loglikelihood function.

In order to construct the loglikelihood function for the loglinear Model 2, interpreted as a model for y_t rather than for $\log y_t$, we need the density of y_t as a function of the model parameters. This requires us to use a standard result about **transformations of variables**. Suppose that we wish to know the CDF of a random variable X, but that what we actually know is the CDF of a random variable Z defined as $Z = h(X)$, where $h(\cdot)$ is a strictly increasing deterministic function. Denote this known CDF by F_Z. Then we can obtain the CDF F_X of X as follows.

$$\begin{aligned} F_X(x) &= \Pr(X \le x) = \Pr\bigl(h(X) \le h(x)\bigr) \\ &= \Pr\bigl(Z \le h(x)\bigr) = F_Z\bigl(h(x)\bigr). \end{aligned} \tag{10.93}$$

The second equality above follows because $h(\cdot)$ is strictly increasing. The relation between the densities, or PDFs, of the variables X and Z is obtained by differentiating the leftmost and rightmost quantities in (10.93) with respect to x. Denoting the PDFs by $f_X(\cdot)$ and $f_Z(\cdot)$, we obtain

$$f_X(x) = F'_X(x) = F'_Z\bigl(h(x)\bigr)h'(x) = f_Z\bigl(h(x)\bigr)h'(x).$$

If h is strictly decreasing, the above result must be modified so as to use the absolute value of the derivative. As readers are asked to show in Exercise 10.23, the result then becomes

$$f_X(x) = f_Z\big(h(x)\big)|h'(x)|. \tag{10.94}$$

It is not difficult to see that (10.94) is a perfectly general result which holds for any strictly monotonic function h.

The factor by which $f_Z(z)$ is multiplied in order to produce $f_X(x)$ is the absolute value of what is called the **Jacobian** of the transformation. For Model 2, X is replaced by y_t, and the transformation h is the logarithm, so that Z becomes $\log y_t$. The density of y_t is then given by (10.94) in terms of that of $\log y_t$:

$$f(y_t) = f(\log y_t)\left|\frac{d\log y_t}{dy_t}\right| = \frac{f(\log y_t)}{y_t}, \tag{10.95}$$

where we drop subscripts and denote the PDFs of y_t and $\log y_t$ by $f(y_t)$ and $f(\log y_t)$, respectively.

We can now compute the loglikelihood for Model 2 thought of as a model for the y_t. The concentrated loglikelihood for the $\log y_t$ is given by (10.11):

$$-\frac{n}{2}\log 2\pi - \frac{n}{2} - \frac{n}{2}\log\bigg(\sum_{t=1}^{n}(\log y_t - \boldsymbol{X}_{t2}\boldsymbol{\beta}_2)^2\bigg). \tag{10.96}$$

This expression is the log of the product of the densities of the $\log y_t$. Since the density of y_t, by (10.95), is equal to $1/y_t$ times the density of $\log y_t$, the loglikelihood function we are seeking is

$$-\frac{n}{2}\log 2\pi - \frac{n}{2} - \frac{n}{2}\log\bigg(\sum_{t=1}^{n}(\log y_t - \boldsymbol{X}_{t2}\boldsymbol{\beta}_2)^2\bigg) - \sum_{t=1}^{n}\log y_t. \tag{10.97}$$

The last term here is a **Jacobian term**. It is the sum over all t of the logarithm of the **Jacobian factor** $1/y_t$ in the density of y_t. This Jacobian term is absolutely critical. If it were omitted, Model 2 would be a model for $\log y_t$, and it would make no sense to compare the value of the loglikelihood for (10.96) with the value for Model 1, which is a model for y_t. But when the Jacobian term is included, the loglikelihoods for both models are expressed in terms of y_t, and it is perfectly valid to compare their values. We can say with confidence that the model corresponding to whichever of (10.92) and (10.97) has the largest value is the model that better fits the data.

Most regression packages evaluate expression (10.96) at the OLS estimates for the loglinear model and report that as the maximized value of the loglikelihood function. In order to compute the loglikelihood (10.97), which is what we need if we are to compare the fits of the linear and loglinear models, we have to add the Jacobian term to the value reported by the package.

Of course, the logarithmic transformation is by no means the only one that we might employ in practice. For example, when the y_t are sharply skewed to the right, a transformation like $\sqrt{y_t}$ might make sense; see Exercise 10.28.

Weighted least squares also involves transforming the dependent variable. If we believe that the error variance is proportional to w_t^2, the use of feasible GLS leads us to divide y_t and all the regressors by w_t. When this is done, the Jacobian of the transformation is just $1/w_t$, and the Jacobian term in the loglikelihood function is

$$-\sum_{t=1}^{n} \log w_t. \tag{10.98}$$

In order to compare a model that has y_t as the regressand with another model that has y_t/w_t as the regressand, we need to add (10.98) to the value of the loglikelihood reported for the second model. Doing this makes the loglikelihoods from the two models comparable. If it really is appropriate to use weighted least squares, then the loglikelihood function for the weighted model should be higher than the loglikelihood function for the original model.

The most common nonlinear transformation in econometrics is the logarithmic transformation. Very often, we may find ourselves estimating a number of models, some of which have y_t as the regressand and some of which have $\log y_t$ as the regressand. If we simply want to decide which model fits best, we already know how to do so. We just have to compute the loglikelihood function for each of the models, including the Jacobian term $-\sum_{t=1}^{n} \log y_t$ for models in which the regressand is $\log y_t$, and pick the model with the highest loglikelihood. But if we want to perform a formal statistical test, and perhaps reject one or more of the competing models as incompatible with the data, we must go beyond simply comparing loglikelihood values.

The Box-Cox Regression Model

Most procedures for testing linear and loglinear models make use of the **Box-Cox transformation**,

$$B(x, \lambda) = \begin{cases} \dfrac{x^\lambda - 1}{\lambda} & \text{when } \lambda \neq 0; \\ \log x & \text{when } \lambda = 0, \end{cases}$$

where λ is a parameter, which may be of either sign, and x, the argument of the transformation, must be positive. By l'Hôpital's Rule, $\log x$ is the limit of $(x^\lambda - 1)/\lambda$ as $\lambda \to 0$. Figure 10.4 shows the Box-Cox transformation for various values of λ. In practice, λ generally ranges from somewhat below 0 to somewhat above 1. It can be shown that $B(x, \lambda') \geq B(x, \lambda'')$ for $\lambda' \geq \lambda''$, and this inequality is evident in the figure. Thus the amount of curvature induced by the Box-Cox transformation increases as λ gets farther from 1 in either direction.

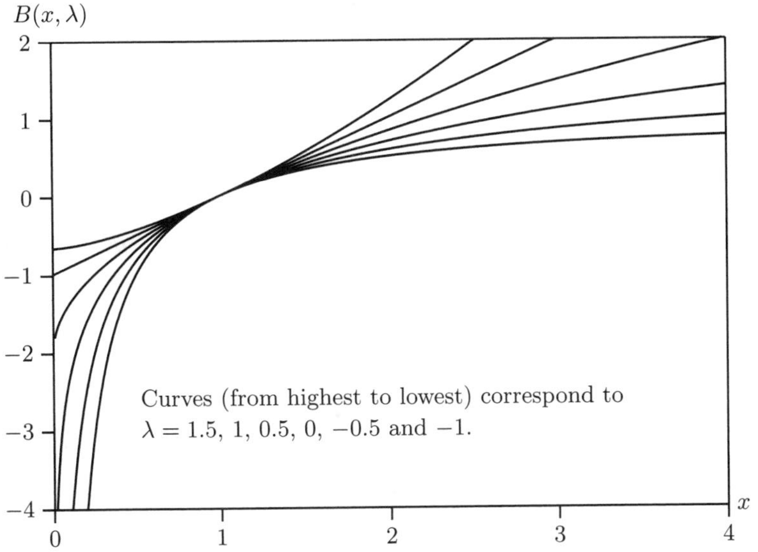

Figure 10.4 Box-Cox transformations for various values of λ

For the purposes of this section, the important thing about the Box-Cox transformation is that it allows us to formulate models which include both linear and loglinear regression models as special cases. In particular, consider the **Box-Cox regression model**

$$B(y_t, \lambda) = \sum_{i=1}^{k_1} \beta_i z_{ti} + \sum_{i=k_1+1}^{k} \beta_i B(x_{ti}, \lambda) + u_t, \quad u_t \sim \text{NID}(0, \sigma^2), \tag{10.99}$$

in which there are k_1 regressors z_{ti} that are not subject to transformation and $k_2 = k - k_1$ nonconstant regressors x_{ti} that are always positive and are subject to transformation. The z_{ti} would include the constant term, if any, in addition to dummy variables and any other regressors that can take on nonpositive values. When $\lambda = 1$, this model reduces to the linear regression model

$$y_t - 1 = \sum_{i=1}^{k_1} \beta_i z_{ti} + \sum_{i=k_1+1}^{k} \beta_i (x_{ti} - 1) + u_t, \quad u_t \sim \text{NID}(0, \sigma^2).$$

Provided there is a constant term, or the equivalent of a constant term, among the z_{ti} regressors, this is equivalent to

$$y_t = \sum_{i=1}^{k_1} \beta_i z_{ti} + \sum_{i=k_1+1}^{k} \beta_i x_{ti} + u_t, \quad u_t \sim \text{NID}(0, \sigma^2), \tag{10.100}$$

with the β_i corresponding to the constant term redefined in the obvious way. When $\lambda = 0$, on the other hand, the Box-Cox model (10.99) reduces to the loglinear regression model

$$\log y_t = \sum_{i=1}^{k_1} \beta_i z_{ti} + \sum_{i=k_1+1}^{k} \beta_i \log x_{ti} + u_t, \quad u_t \sim \text{NID}(0, \sigma^2). \tag{10.101}$$

Thus it is clear that the linear regression model (10.100) and the loglinear regression model (10.101) can both be obtained as special cases of the Box-Cox regression model (10.99).

Testing Linear and Loglinear Regression Models

There are many ways in which we can test (10.100) and (10.101) against (10.99). Conceptually, the simplest is just to estimate all three models and perform two likelihood ratio tests. Let $\ell(\hat{\lambda})$ denote the maximum of the loglikelihood function for the unrestricted Box-Cox model (10.99), which readers are asked to derive in Exercise 10.29. Similarly, let $\ell(1)$ and $\ell(0)$ denote the maxima of the loglikelihood functions for the linear and loglinear models, respectively. Then the statistics for testing the linear and loglinear models against the Box-Cox regression model are

$$2\big(\ell(\hat{\lambda}) - \ell(1)\big) \quad \text{and} \quad 2\big(\ell(\hat{\lambda}) - \ell(0)\big),$$

respectively. If either of these statistics exceeds $\chi^2_{1-\alpha}(1)$, the $1 - \alpha$ quantile of the $\chi^2(1)$ distribution, we may reject the model being tested at level α. In practice, this test tends to be quite powerful in samples of even moderate size, since it does not require a very large test statistic in order to reject the null hypothesis; the two most widely-used critical values are $\chi^2_{0.95}(1) = 3.84$ and $\chi^2_{0.99}(1) = 6.63$.

This procedure is conceptually very simple, but it requires us to estimate λ, which is a bit more work than simply running a linear regression. In some cases, however, we can avoid estimating λ. We know that $\ell(\hat{\lambda})$ must be larger than whichever of $\ell(1)$ and $\ell(0)$ is larger. Therefore, if

$$2\big(\ell(0) - \ell(1)\big) > \chi^2_{1-\alpha}(1), \tag{10.102}$$

we can certainly reject the linear model, even though we have not actually estimated the Box-Cox model or computed the LR test statistic. Similarly, if

$$2\big(\ell(1) - \ell(0)\big) > \chi^2_{1-\alpha}(1), \tag{10.103}$$

we can certainly reject the loglinear model. The quantities (10.102) and (10.103) provide lower bounds for the actual LR statistics. In practice, these lower bounds can often allow us to rule out models that are clearly incompatible with the data.

The fact that one can sometimes put a lower bound on the LR test statistic without actually estimating the unrestricted model is often very convenient. It was noted by Sargan (1964) in the context of choosing between linear and loglinear models, is widely used by applied workers, and has been proposed as a general basis for model selection by Pollak and Wales (1991). The procedure works in only one direction, of course. If, for example, (10.102) allows us to reject the linear model, then it tells us nothing about whether the loglinear model is acceptable to the data.

Lagrange Multiplier Tests

Since it is very easy to estimate linear and loglinear regression models, but somewhat harder to estimate the Box-Cox regression model, it is natural to use LM tests in this context. The first tests of this type were proposed by Godfrey and Wickens (1981). They are based on the OPG regression (10.72). However, as is often the case with tests based on the OPG regression, these tests tend to overreject quite severely in finite samples. Therefore, Davidson and MacKinnon (1985b) proposed Lagrange multiplier tests based on the **double-length artificial regression**, or **DLR**, that they had previously developed in Davidson and MacKinnon (1984a). This artificial regression is called "double-length" because it has $2n$ "observations," two for each of the actual observations in the sample.

For reasons of space, we will not write down the OPG or DLR test regressions here. Readers are asked to derive a special case of the former in Exercise 10.29. The latter, which are somewhat more complicated, are discussed in detail in Davidson and MacKinnon (1993, Chapter 14). If an LM test is to be used, we recommend use of the DLR rather than the OPG variant. There is a good deal of evidence that the DLR variant is much more reliable in finite samples; see Davidson and MacKinnon (1984b) and Godfrey, McAleer, and McKenzie (1988), among others. Of course, either variant of the test may easily be bootstrapped, as discussed in Section 10.6, and the OPG variant should perform acceptably when that is done. Because it is never necessary to estimate the unrestricted model, bootstrapping either of the LM tests is considerably less expensive than bootstrapping the LR test.

10.9 Final Remarks

Maximum likelihood estimation is widely used in many areas of econometrics, and we will encounter a number of important applications in the next four chapters. Readers seeking a more advanced treatment of the theory than we were able to give in this chapter may wish to consult Davidson and MacKinnon (1993), Cox and Hinkley (1974), or Stuart, Ord, and Arnold (1998).

As we have seen, ML estimation has many good properties, although these may be more apparent asymptotically than in finite samples. Its biggest limitation is the need for a fully specified parametric model. However, even if the dependent variable does not follow its assumed distribution, quasi-maximum likelihood estimators may still be consistent, even though they are not asymptotically efficient.

10.10 Exercises

10.1 Show that the ML estimator of the parameters $\boldsymbol{\beta}$ and σ of the classical normal linear model can be obtained by first concentrating the loglikelihood with respect to $\boldsymbol{\beta}$ and then maximizing the concentrated loglikelihood thereby obtained with respect to σ.

★10.2 Let the n–vector $\boldsymbol{y}$ be a vector of mutually independent realizations from the uniform distribution on the interval $[\beta_1, \beta_2]$, usually denoted by $\mathrm{U}(\beta_1, \beta_2)$. Thus, $y_t \sim \mathrm{U}(\beta_1, \beta_2)$ for $t = 1, \ldots, n$. Let $\hat{\beta}_1$ be the ML estimator of β_1 given in (10.13), and suppose that the true values of the parameters are $\beta_1 = 0$ and $\beta_2 = 1$. Show that the CDF of $\hat{\beta}_1$ is

$$F(\beta) \equiv \Pr(\hat{\beta}_1 \leq \beta) = 1 - (1 - \beta)^n.$$

Use this result to show that $n(\hat{\beta}_1 - \beta_{10})$, which in this case is just $n\hat{\beta}_1$, is asymptotically exponentially distributed with $\theta = 1$. Note that the PDF of the exponential distribution was given in (10.03). (**Hint:** The limit as $n \to \infty$ of $(1 + x/n)^n$, for arbitrary real x, is e^x.)

Show that, for arbitrary given β_{10} and β_{20}, with $\beta_{20} > \beta_{10}$, the asymptotic distribution of $n(\hat{\beta}_1 - \beta_{10})$ is characterized by the density (10.03) with $\theta = (\beta_{20} - \beta_{10})^{-1}$.

10.3 Generate 10,000 random samples of sizes 20, 100, and 500 from the uniform $\mathrm{U}(0, 1)$ distribution. For each sample, compute $\bar{\gamma}$, the sample mean, and $\hat{\gamma}$, the average of the largest and smallest observations. Calculate the root mean squared error of each of these estimators for each of the three sample sizes. Do the results accord with what theory predicts?

10.4 Suppose that $h(\cdot)$ is a strictly concave, twice continuously differentiable, function on a possibly infinite interval of the real line. Let X be a random variable of which the support is contained in that interval. Suppose further that the first two moments of X exist. Prove Jensen's Inequality for the random variable X and the strictly concave function h by performing a Taylor expansion of h about $\mathrm{E}(X)$.

10.5 Prove that the definition (10.31) of the information matrix is equivalent to the definition

$$\boldsymbol{I}(\boldsymbol{\theta}) = \mathrm{E}_{\boldsymbol{\theta}}(\boldsymbol{g}(\boldsymbol{y}, \boldsymbol{\theta})\boldsymbol{g}^\top(\boldsymbol{y}, \boldsymbol{\theta})).$$

Hint: Use the result (10.30).

10.6 By differentiating the identity (10.28) with respect to θ_j, show that

$$\mathrm{E}_{\boldsymbol{\theta}}(G_{ti}(\boldsymbol{y}^t, \boldsymbol{\theta})G_{tj}(\boldsymbol{y}^t, \boldsymbol{\theta}) + (\boldsymbol{H}_t)_{ij}(\boldsymbol{y}^t, \boldsymbol{\theta})) = 0, \tag{10.104}$$

where the $k \times k$ matrix $\boldsymbol{H}_t(\boldsymbol{y}^t, \boldsymbol{\theta})$ is the Hessian of the contribution $\ell_t(\boldsymbol{y}^t, \boldsymbol{\theta})$ to the loglikelihood. The simplest way to proceed is to show first that (10.104) also holds if the left-hand side is the expectation conditional on $\boldsymbol{y}^{t-1}$.

10.7 Use the result (10.104) of the preceding exercise to prove the asymptotic information matrix equality (10.34).

10.8 Consider the linear regression model with exogenous explanatory variables,

$$\boldsymbol{y} = \boldsymbol{X\beta} + \boldsymbol{u},$$

where the only assumptions made regarding the error terms are that they are uncorrelated and have mean zero and finite variances that are, in general, different for each observation. The OLS estimator, which is consistent for this model, is equal to the ML estimator of the model under the assumption of homoskedastic normal error terms. The ML estimator is therefore a QMLE for this model. Show that the $k \times k$ block of the sandwich covariance matrix estimator (10.45) that corresponds to $\hat{\boldsymbol{\beta}}$ is a version of the HCCME for the linear regression model.

10.9 Write out explicitly the empirical Hessian estimator of the covariance matrix of $\hat{\boldsymbol{\beta}}$ and $\hat{\sigma}$ for the classical normal linear model. How is it related to the IM estimator (10.53)?

How would your answer change if $\boldsymbol{X\beta}$ in the classical normal linear model were replaced by $\boldsymbol{x}(\boldsymbol{\beta})$, a vector of nonlinear regression functions that implicitly depend on exogenous variables?

10.10 Suppose you treat σ^2 instead of σ as a parameter. Use arguments similar to the ones that led to equation (10.53) to derive the information matrix estimator of the covariance matrix of $\hat{\boldsymbol{\beta}}$ and $\hat{\sigma}^2$. Then show that the same estimator can also be obtained by using the delta method.

⋆10.11 Explain how to compute two different 95% confidence intervals for σ^2. One should be based on the covariance matrix estimator obtained in Exercise 10.10, and the other should be based on the original estimator (10.53). Are both of the intervals symmetric? Which seems more reasonable?

⋆10.12 Let $\tilde{\boldsymbol{\theta}}$ denote any unbiased estimator of the k parameters of a parametric model fully specified by the loglikelihood function $\ell(\boldsymbol{\theta})$. The unbiasedness property can be expressed as the following identity:

$$\int L(\boldsymbol{y}, \boldsymbol{\theta})\,\tilde{\boldsymbol{\theta}}\,d\boldsymbol{y} = \boldsymbol{\theta}. \tag{10.105}$$

By using the relationship between $L(\boldsymbol{y}, \boldsymbol{\theta})$ and $\ell(\boldsymbol{y}, \boldsymbol{\theta})$ and differentiating this identity with respect to the components of $\boldsymbol{\theta}$, show that

$$\mathrm{Cov}_{\boldsymbol{\theta}}\big(\boldsymbol{g}(\boldsymbol{\theta}), (\tilde{\boldsymbol{\theta}} - \boldsymbol{\theta})\big) = \mathbf{I},$$

where $\mathbf{I}$ is a $k \times k$ identity matrix, and the notation $\mathrm{Cov}_{\boldsymbol{\theta}}$ indicates that the covariance is to be calculated under the DGP characterized by $\boldsymbol{\theta}$.

Let $\boldsymbol{V}$ denote the $2k \times 2k$ covariance matrix of the $2k$-vector obtained by stacking the k components of $\boldsymbol{g}(\boldsymbol{\theta})$ above the k components of $\tilde{\boldsymbol{\theta}} - \boldsymbol{\theta}$. Partition this matrix into 4 $k \times k$ blocks as follows:

$$\boldsymbol{V} = \begin{bmatrix} \boldsymbol{V}_1 & \boldsymbol{C} \\ \boldsymbol{C}^\top & \boldsymbol{V}_2 \end{bmatrix},$$

where $\boldsymbol{V}_1$ and $\boldsymbol{V}_2$ are, respectively, the covariance matrices of the vectors $\boldsymbol{g}(\boldsymbol{\theta})$ and $\tilde{\boldsymbol{\theta}} - \boldsymbol{\theta}$ under the DGP characterized by $\boldsymbol{\theta}$. Then use the fact that $\boldsymbol{V}$ is positive semidefinite to show that the difference between $\boldsymbol{V}_2$ and $\boldsymbol{I}^{-1}(\boldsymbol{\theta})$, where $\boldsymbol{I}(\boldsymbol{\theta})$ is the (finite-sample) information matrix for the model, is a positive semidefinite matrix. **Hint:** Use the result of Exercise 7.11.

★10.13 Consider the linear regression model

$$\boldsymbol{y} = \boldsymbol{X}_1\boldsymbol{\beta}_1 + \boldsymbol{X}_2\boldsymbol{\beta}_2 + \boldsymbol{u}, \quad \boldsymbol{u} \sim \mathrm{N}(\boldsymbol{0}, \sigma^2\mathbf{I}). \tag{10.106}$$

Derive the Wald statistic for the hypothesis that $\boldsymbol{\beta}_2 = \boldsymbol{0}$, as a function of the data, from the general formula (10.60). Show that it would be numerically identical to the Wald statistic (6.71) if the same estimate of σ^2 were used.

Show that, if the estimate of σ^2 is either the OLS or the ML estimator based on the unrestricted model (10.106), the Wald statistic is a deterministic, strictly increasing, function of the conventional F statistic. Give the explicit form of this deterministic function. Why can one reasonably expect that this result holds for tests of arbitrary linear restrictions on the parameters, and not only for zero restrictions of the type considered in this exercise?

★10.14 Consider the Wald statistic W, the likelihood ratio statistic LR, and the Lagrange multiplier statistic LM for testing the hypothesis that $\boldsymbol{\beta}_2 = \boldsymbol{0}$ in the linear regression model (10.106). Since these are asymptotic tests, all the estimates of σ^2 are computed using the sample size n in the denominator. Express these three statistics as functions of the squared norms of the three components of the threefold decomposition (4.37) of the dependent variable $\boldsymbol{y}$. By use of the inequalities

$$x > \log(1+x) > \frac{x}{1+x}, \qquad x > 0,$$

show that W > LR > LM.

★10.15 The model specified by the loglikelihood function $\ell(\boldsymbol{\theta})$ is said to be reparametrized if the parameter vector $\boldsymbol{\theta}$ is replaced by another parameter vector $\boldsymbol{\phi}$ related to $\boldsymbol{\theta}$ by a one to one relationship $\boldsymbol{\theta} = \boldsymbol{\Theta}(\boldsymbol{\phi})$ with inverse $\boldsymbol{\phi} = \boldsymbol{\Theta}^{-1}(\boldsymbol{\theta})$. The loglikelihood function for the reparametrized model is then defined as $\ell'(\boldsymbol{\phi}) \equiv \ell(\boldsymbol{\Theta}(\boldsymbol{\phi}))$. Explain why this definition makes sense.

Show that the maximum likelihood estimates $\hat{\boldsymbol{\phi}}$ of the reparametrized model are related to the estimates $\hat{\boldsymbol{\theta}}$ of the original model by the relation $\hat{\boldsymbol{\theta}} = \boldsymbol{\Theta}(\hat{\boldsymbol{\phi}})$. Specify the relationship between the gradients and information matrices of the two models in terms of the derivatives of the components of $\boldsymbol{\phi}$ with respect to those of $\boldsymbol{\theta}$.

Suppose that it is wished to test a set of r restrictions written as $\boldsymbol{r}(\boldsymbol{\theta}) = \boldsymbol{0}$. These restrictions can be applied to the reparametrized model in the form $\boldsymbol{r}'(\boldsymbol{\phi}) \equiv \boldsymbol{r}(\boldsymbol{\Theta}(\boldsymbol{\phi})) = \boldsymbol{0}$. Show that the LR statistic is invariant to whether the restrictions are tested for the original or the reparametrized model. Show that the same is true for the LM statistic (10.69).

★10.16 Show that the artificial OPG regression (10.73) possesses all the properties needed for hypothesis testing in the context of a model estimated by maximum likelihood. Specifically, show that

- the regressand $\boldsymbol{\iota}$ is orthogonal to the regressors $\boldsymbol{G}(\boldsymbol{\theta})$ when the latter are evaluated at the MLE $\hat{\boldsymbol{\theta}}$;
- the estimated OLS covariance matrix from (10.73) evaluated at $\hat{\boldsymbol{\theta}}$, when multiplied by n, consistently estimates the inverse of the asymptotic information matrix;
- the OPG regression (10.73) allows one-step estimation: If the OLS parameter estimates $\acute{\boldsymbol{c}}$ from (10.73) are evaluated at $\boldsymbol{\theta} = \acute{\boldsymbol{\theta}}$, where $\acute{\boldsymbol{\theta}}$ is any root-n consistent estimator of $\boldsymbol{\theta}$, then the one-step estimator $\grave{\boldsymbol{\theta}} \equiv \acute{\boldsymbol{\theta}} + \acute{\boldsymbol{c}}$ is asymptotically equivalent to $\hat{\boldsymbol{\theta}}$, in the sense that $n^{1/2}(\grave{\boldsymbol{\theta}} - \boldsymbol{\theta}_0)$ and $n^{1/2}(\hat{\boldsymbol{\theta}} - \boldsymbol{\theta}_0)$ tend to the same random variable as $n \to \infty$.

10.17 Show that the explained sum of squares from the artificial OPG regression (10.73) is equal to n times the uncentered R^2 from the same regression. Relate this fact to the use of test statistics that take the form of n times the R^2 of a GNR (Section 6.7) or of an IVGNR (Section 8.6 and Exercise 8.21).

10.18 Express the LM statistic (10.74) as a deterministic, strictly increasing, function of the F statistic (10.57).

★10.19 Let the loglikelihood function $\ell(\theta)$ depend on one scalar parameter θ. For this special case, consider the distribution of the LM statistic (10.69) under the drifting DGP characterized by the parameter $\theta = n^{-1/2}\delta$ for a fixed δ. This DGP drifts toward the fixed DGP with $\theta = 0$, which we think of as representing the null hypothesis. Show first that $n^{-1}\boldsymbol{I}(n^{-1/2}\delta) \to \mathcal{I}(0)$ as $n \to \infty$. Here the asymptotic information matrix $\mathcal{I}(\theta)$ is just a scalar, since there is only one parameter.

Next, show that $n^{-1/2}$ times the gradient, evaluated at $\theta = 0$, which we may write as $n^{-1/2}g(0)$, is asymptotically normally distributed with mean $\delta\,\mathcal{I}(0)$ and variance $\mathcal{I}(0)$. Finally, show that the LM statistic is asymptotically distributed as $\chi^2(1)$ with a finite noncentrality parameter, and give the value of that noncentrality parameter.

10.20 Let $z \sim \mathrm{N}(\mu, \sigma^2)$, and consider the lognormal random variable $x \equiv e^z$. Using the result that

$$\mathrm{E}(e^z) = \exp(\mu + \tfrac{1}{2}\sigma^2), \tag{10.107}$$

compute the second, third, and fourth central moments of x. Show that x is skewed to the right and has positive excess kurtosis.

Note: The **excess kurtosis** of a random variable is formally defined as the ratio of the fourth central moment to the square of the variance, minus 3.

★10.21 The GNR proposed in Section 7.8 for NLS estimation of the model (10.86) can be written schematically as

$$\begin{bmatrix} (1-\rho^2)^{1/2}u_1(\boldsymbol{\beta}) \\ u_t(\boldsymbol{\beta}) - \rho u_{t-1}(\boldsymbol{\beta}) \end{bmatrix} = \begin{bmatrix} (1-\rho^2)^{1/2}\boldsymbol{X}_1 & 0 \\ \boldsymbol{X}_t - \rho\boldsymbol{X}_{t-1} & u_{t-1}(\boldsymbol{\beta}) \end{bmatrix} \begin{bmatrix} \boldsymbol{b} \\ b_\rho \end{bmatrix} + \text{residuals},$$

where $u_t(\boldsymbol{\beta}) \equiv y_t - \boldsymbol{X}_t\boldsymbol{\beta}$ for $t = 1, \ldots, n$, and the last $n-1$ rows of the artificial variables are indicated by their typical elements. Append one extra artificial observation to this artificial regression. For this observation, the regressand is $((1-\rho^2)u_1^2(\boldsymbol{\beta})/\sigma_\varepsilon - \sigma_\varepsilon)/\sqrt{2}$, the regressor in the column corresponding to ρ is $\rho\sigma_\varepsilon\sqrt{2}/(1-\rho^2)$, and the regressors in the columns corresponding to the elements of $\boldsymbol{\beta}$ are all 0. Show that, if at each iteration σ_ε^2 is updated by the formula

$$\sigma_\varepsilon^2 = \frac{1}{n}\Big((1-\rho^2)u_1^2(\boldsymbol{\beta}) + \sum_{t=2}^{n}\big(u_t(\boldsymbol{\beta}) - \rho u_{t-1}(\boldsymbol{\beta})\big)^2\Big),$$

then, if the iterations defined by the augmented artificial regression converge, the resulting parameter estimates satisfy the estimating equations (10.90) that define the ML estimator.

The odd-looking factors of $\sqrt{2}$ in the extra observation are there for a reason: Show that, when the artificial regression has converged, σ_ε^{-2} times the matrix of cross-products of the regressors is equivalent to the block of the information matrix that corresponds to $\boldsymbol{\beta}$ and ρ evaluated at the ML estimates. Explain why this means that we can use the OLS covariance matrix from the artificial regression to estimate the covariance matrix of $\hat{\boldsymbol{\beta}}$ and $\hat{\rho}$.

10.22 Using the artificial data in the file **ar1.data**, estimate the model

$$y_t = \beta_1 + \beta_2 x_t + u_t, \quad u_t = \rho u_{t-1} + \varepsilon_t, \quad t = 1, \ldots, 100,$$

which is correctly specified, in two different ways: ML omitting the first observation, and ML using all 100 observations. The second method should yield more efficient estimates of β_1 and β_2. For each of these two parameters, how large a sample of observations similar to the last 99 observations would be needed to obtain estimates as efficient as those obtained by using all 100 observations? Explain why your answer is greater than 100 in both cases.

10.23 Let the two random variables X and Z be related by the deterministic equation $Z = h(X)$, where h is strictly decreasing. Show that the PDFs of the two variables satisfy the equation

$$f_X(x) = -f_Z\big(h(x)\big)h'(x).$$

Then show that (10.94) holds whenever h is a strictly monotonic function.

Let $X = Z^2$. Express the density of X in terms of that of Z, taking account of the possibility that the support of Z may include negative as well as positive numbers.

10.24 Suppose that a dependent variable y follows the exponential distribution given in (10.03), and let $x = y^2$. What is the density of x? Find the ML estimator of the parameter θ based on a sample of n observations x_t which are assumed to follow the distribution of which you have just obtained the density.

10.25 For a sample of n observations y_t generated from the exponential distribution, the loglikelihood function is (10.04), and the ML estimator is (10.06). Derive the asymptotic information matrix $\mathfrak{I}(\theta)$, which is actually a scalar in this case, and use it to show how $n^{1/2}(\hat{\theta} - \theta_0)$ is distributed asymptotically. What is the empirical Hessian estimator of the variance of $\hat{\theta}$? What is the IM estimator?

There is an alternative parametrization of the exponential distribution, in which the parameter is $\phi \equiv 1/\theta$. Write down the loglikelihood function in terms of ϕ and obtain the asymptotic distribution of $n^{1/2}(\hat{\phi} - \phi_0)$. What is the empirical Hessian estimator of the variance of $\hat{\phi}$? What is the IM estimator?

⋆10.26 Consider the ML estimator $\hat{\theta}$ from the previous exercise. Explain how you could obtain an asymptotic confidence interval for θ in three different ways. The first should be based on inverting a Wald test in the θ parametrization, the second should be based on inverting a Wald test in the ϕ parametrization, and the third should be based on inverting an LR test.

Generate 100 observations from the exponential distribution with $\theta = 0.5$, find the ML estimate based on these artificial data, and calculate 95% confidence intervals for θ using the three methods just proposed. **Hint:** To generate the data, use uniformly distributed random numbers and the inverse of the exponential CDF.

10.27 Use the result (10.94) to derive the PDF of the $\mathrm{N}(\mu, \sigma^2)$ distribution from the PDF of the standard normal distribution.

In the classical normal linear model as specified in (10.07), it is the distribution of the error terms $\boldsymbol{u}$ that is specified rather than that of the dependent variable $\boldsymbol{y}$. Reconstruct the loglikelihood function (10.10) starting from the densities of the error terms u_t and using the Jacobians of the transformations that express the y_t in terms of the u_t.

10.28 Consider the model

$$y_t^{1/2} = \boldsymbol{X}_t\boldsymbol{\beta} + u_t, \quad u_t \sim \mathrm{NID}(0, \sigma^2),$$

in which it is assumed that all observations y_t on the dependent variable are positive. Write down the loglikelihood function for this model.

⋆10.29 Derive the loglikelihood function for the Box-Cox regression model (10.99). Then consider the following special case:

$$B(y_t, \lambda) = \beta_1 + \beta_2 B(x_t, \lambda) + u_t, \quad u_t \sim \mathrm{NID}(0, \sigma^2).$$

Derive the OPG regression for this model and explain precisely how to use it to test the hypotheses that the DGP is linear ($\lambda = 1$) and loglinear ($\lambda = 0$).

10.30 Consider the model (9.122) of the Canadian consumption function, with data from the file **consumption.data**, for the period 1953:1 to 1996:4. Compute the value of the maximized loglikelihood for this model regarded as a model for the *level* (not the log) of current consumption.

Formulate a model with the same algebraic form as (9.122), but in levels of the income and consumption variables. Compute the maximized loglikelihood of this second model, and compare it with the value you obtained for the model in logs. Can you draw any conclusion about whether either model is misspecified?

Formulate a third model, using the variables in levels, but dividing them all by current income Y_t in order to account for heteroskedasticity. The result is a weighted least-squares model. Compute the maximized loglikelihood for this model as a model for the level of current consumption. Are there any more conclusions you can draw on the basis of your results?

10.31 Formulate a Box-Cox regression model which includes the first and second models of the previous exercise as special cases. Use the OPG regression to perform an LM test of the hypothesis that the Box-Cox parameter $\lambda = 0$, that is, that the loglinear model is correctly specified. Obtain both asymptotic and bootstrap P values.

10.32 The model (9.122) that was estimated in Exercise 10.30 can be written as

$$\Delta c_t = \beta_1 + \beta_2 \Delta y_t + \beta_3 \Delta y_{t-1} + \sigma\varepsilon_t,$$

where $\varepsilon_t \sim \text{NID}(0, 1)$. Suppose now that the ε_t, instead of being standard normal, follow the Cauchy distribution, with density $f(\varepsilon_t) = (\pi(1 + \varepsilon_t^2))^{-1}$. Estimate the resulting model by maximum likelihood, and compare the maximized value of the loglikelihood with the one obtained in Exercise 9.12.

10.33 Suppose that the dependent variable y_t is a proportion, so that $0 < y_t < 1$, $t = 1, \ldots, n$. An appropriate model for such a dependent variable is

$$\log\left(\frac{y_t}{1 - y_t}\right) = \boldsymbol{X}_t \boldsymbol{\beta} + u_t,$$

where $\boldsymbol{X}_t$ is a $k \times 1$ vector of exogenous variables, and $\boldsymbol{\beta}$ is a k–vector. Write down the loglikelihood function for this model under the assumption that $u_t \sim \text{NID}(0, \sigma^2)$. How would you maximize this loglikelihood function?

Chapter 11

Discrete and Limited Dependent Variables

11.1 Introduction

Although regression models are useful for modeling many types of data, they are not suitable for modeling every type. In particular, they should not be used when the dependent variable is discrete and can therefore take on only a countable number of values, or when it is continuous but is limited in the range of values it can take on. Since variables of these two types arise quite often, it is important to be able to deal with them, and a large number of models has been proposed for doing so. In this chapter, we discuss some of the simplest and most commonly used models for discrete and limited dependent variables.

The most commonly encountered type of dependent variable that cannot be handled properly using a regression model is a **binary dependent variable**. Such a variable can take on only two values, which for practical reasons are almost always coded as 0 and 1. For example, a person may be in or out of the labor force, a commuter may drive to work or take public transit, a household may own or rent the home it resides in, and so on. In each case, the economic agent chooses between two alternatives, one of which is coded as 0 and one of which is coded as 1. A **binary response model** then tries to explain the probability that the agent chooses alternative 1 as a function of some observed explanatory variables. We discuss binary response models at some length in Sections 11.2 and 11.3

A binary dependent variable is a special case of a **discrete dependent variable**. In Section 11.4, we briefly discuss several models for dealing with discrete dependent variables that can take on a fixed number of values. We consider two different cases, one in which the values have a natural ordering, and one in which they do not. Then, in Section 11.5, we discuss models for **count data**, in which the dependent variable can, in principle, take on any nonnegative, integer value.

Sometimes, a dependent variable is continuous but can take on only a limited range of values. For example, most types of consumer spending can be zero or positive but cannot be negative. If we have a sample that includes some zero observations, we need to use a model that explicitly allows for this. By the same token, if the zero observations are excluded from the sample, we need to take account of this omission. Both types of model are discussed in Section 11.6. The related problem of **sample selectivity**, in which certain observations are omitted from the sample in a nonrandom way, is dealt with in Section 11.7. Finally, in Section 11.8, we discuss **duration models**, which attempt to explain how much time elapses before some event occurs or some state changes.

11.2 Binary Response Models: Estimation

In a binary response model, the value of the dependent variable y_t can take on only two values, 0 and 1. Let P_t denote the probability that $y_t = 1$ conditional on the information set Ω_t, which consists of exogenous and predetermined variables. A binary response model serves to model this conditional probability. Since the values are 0 or 1, it is clear that P_t is also the expectation of y_t conditional on Ω_t:

$$P_t \equiv \Pr(y_t = 1 \,|\, \Omega_t) = \mathrm{E}(y_t \,|\, \Omega_t),$$

Thus a binary response model can also be thought of as modeling a conditional expectation.

For many types of dependent variable, we can use a regression model to model conditional expectations, but that is not a sensible thing to do in this case. Suppose that $\boldsymbol{X}_t$ denotes a row vector of length k of variables that belong to the information set Ω_t, almost always including a constant term or the equivalent. Then a linear regression model would specify $\mathrm{E}(y_t \,|\, \Omega_t)$ as $\boldsymbol{X}_t\boldsymbol{\beta}$. But such a model fails to impose the condition that $0 \leq \mathrm{E}(y_t \,|\, \Omega_t) \leq 1$, which must hold because $\mathrm{E}(y_t \,|\, \Omega_t)$ is a probability. Even if this condition happened to hold for all observations in a particular sample, it would always be easy to find values of $\boldsymbol{X}_t$ for which the estimated probability $\boldsymbol{X}_t\hat{\boldsymbol{\beta}}$ would be less than 0 or greater than 1.

Since it makes no sense to have estimated probabilities that are negative or greater than 1, simply regressing y_t on $\boldsymbol{X}_t$ is not an acceptable way to model the conditional expectation of a binary variable. However, as we will see in the next section, such a regression can provide some useful information, and it is therefore not a completely useless thing to do in the early stages of an empirical investigation.

Any reasonable binary response model must ensure that $\mathrm{E}(y_t \,|\, \Omega_t)$ lies in the 0-1 interval. In principle, there are many ways to do this. In practice, however, two very similar models are widely used. Both of these models ensure that $0 < P_t < 1$ by specifying that

$$P_t \equiv \mathrm{E}(y_t \,|\, \Omega_t) = F(\boldsymbol{X}_t\boldsymbol{\beta}). \tag{11.01}$$

Here $\boldsymbol{X}_t\boldsymbol{\beta}$ is an **index function**, which maps from the vector $\boldsymbol{X}_t$ of explanatory variables and the vector $\boldsymbol{\beta}$ of parameters to a scalar index, and $F(x)$ is a **transformation function**, which has the properties that

$$F(-\infty) = 0, \quad F(\infty) = 1, \quad \text{and} \quad f(x) \equiv \frac{dF(x)}{dx} > 0. \tag{11.02}$$

These properties are, in fact, just the defining properties of the CDF of a probability distribution; recall Section 1.2. They ensure that, although the index function $\boldsymbol{X}_t\boldsymbol{\beta}$ can take any value on the real line, the value of $F(\boldsymbol{X}_t\boldsymbol{\beta})$ must lie between 0 and 1.

The properties (11.02) also ensure that $F(x)$ is a nonlinear function. Consequently, changes in the values of the x_{ti}, which are the elements of $\boldsymbol{X}_t$, necessarily affect $\mathrm{E}(y_t \,|\, \Omega_t)$ in a nonlinear fashion. Specifically, when P_t is given by (11.01), its derivative with respect to x_{ti} is

$$\frac{\partial P_t}{\partial x_{ti}} = \frac{\partial F(\boldsymbol{X}_t\boldsymbol{\beta})}{\partial x_{ti}} = f(\boldsymbol{X}_t\boldsymbol{\beta})\beta_i, \tag{11.03}$$

where β_i is the ith element of $\boldsymbol{\beta}$. Therefore, the magnitude of the derivative is proportional to $f(\boldsymbol{X}_t\boldsymbol{\beta})$. For the transformation functions that are almost always employed, $f(\boldsymbol{X}_t\boldsymbol{\beta})$ achieves a maximum at $\boldsymbol{X}_t\boldsymbol{\beta} = 0$ and then falls as $|\boldsymbol{X}_t\boldsymbol{\beta}|$ increases; see the CDFs plotted in Figure 11.1 on page 457. Thus we see from (11.03) that the effect on P_t of a change in one of the independent variables is greatest when $P_t = .5$ and very small when P_t is close to 0 or 1.

The Probit Model

The first of the two widely-used choices for $F(x)$ is the cumulative standard normal distribution function,

$$\Phi(x) \equiv \frac{1}{\sqrt{2\pi}} \int_{-\infty}^{x} \exp\!\left(-\tfrac{1}{2}X^2\right) dX.$$

When $F(\boldsymbol{X}_t\boldsymbol{\beta}) = \Phi(\boldsymbol{X}_t\boldsymbol{\beta})$, (11.01) is called the **probit model**. Although there exists no closed-form expression for $\Phi(x)$, it is easily evaluated numerically, and its first derivative is, of course, simply the standard normal density function, $\phi(x)$, which was defined in expression (1.06).

One reason for the popularity of the probit model is that it can be derived from a model involving an unobserved, or **latent**, variable y_t°. Suppose that

$$y_t^\circ = \boldsymbol{X}_t\boldsymbol{\beta} + u_t, \quad u_t \sim \mathrm{NID}(0, 1). \tag{11.04}$$

We observe only the sign of y_t°, which determines the value of the observed binary variable y_t according to the relationship

$$y_t = 1 \text{ if } y_t^\circ > 0; \;\; y_t = 0 \text{ if } y_t^\circ \le 0. \tag{11.05}$$

Together, equations (11.04) and (11.05) define what is called a **latent variable model**. One way to think of y_t° is as an index of the net utility associated with some action. If the action yields positive net utility, it is undertaken; otherwise, it is not undertaken. Because we observe only the sign of y_t°, we can normalize the variance of u_t to be unity. If the variance of u_t were some other value, say σ^2, we could divide $\boldsymbol{\beta}$, y_t°, and u_t by σ. Then u_t/σ would have variance 1, but the value of y_t would be unchanged. Another way to express this property is to say that the variance of u_t is not *identified* by the binary response model.

We can now compute P_t, the probability that $y_t = 1$. It is

$$\begin{aligned}\Pr(y_t = 1) &= \Pr(y_t^\circ > 0) = \Pr(\boldsymbol{X}_t\boldsymbol{\beta} + u_t > 0)\\ &= \Pr(u_t > -\boldsymbol{X}_t\boldsymbol{\beta}) = \Pr(u_t \le \boldsymbol{X}_t\boldsymbol{\beta}) = \Phi(\boldsymbol{X}_t\boldsymbol{\beta}).\end{aligned} \tag{11.06}$$

The second-last equality in (11.06) makes use of the fact that the standard normal density function is symmetric around zero. The final result is just what we would get by letting $\Phi(\boldsymbol{X}_t\boldsymbol{\beta})$ play the role of the transformation function $F(\boldsymbol{X}_t\boldsymbol{\beta})$ in (11.01). Thus we have derived the probit model from the latent variable model that consists of (11.04) and (11.05).

The Logit Model

The logit model is very similar to the probit model. The only difference is that the function $F(x)$ is now the **logistic function**

$$\Lambda(x) \equiv \frac{1}{1+e^{-x}} = \frac{e^x}{1+e^x}, \tag{11.07}$$

which has first derivative

$$\lambda(x) \equiv \frac{e^x}{(1+e^x)^2} = \Lambda(x)\Lambda(-x). \tag{11.08}$$

This first derivative is evidently symmetric around zero, which implies that $\Lambda(-x) = 1 - \Lambda(x)$. A graph of the logistic function, as well as of the standard normal distribution function, is shown in Figure 11.1 on page 457.

The logit model is most easily derived by assuming that

$$\log\left(\frac{P_t}{1-P_t}\right) = \boldsymbol{X}_t\boldsymbol{\beta},$$

which says that the logarithm of the **odds** (that is, the ratio of the two probabilities) is equal to $\boldsymbol{X}_t\boldsymbol{\beta}$. Solving for P_t, we find that

$$P_t = \frac{\exp(\boldsymbol{X}_t\boldsymbol{\beta})}{1+\exp(\boldsymbol{X}_t\boldsymbol{\beta})} = \frac{1}{1+\exp(-\boldsymbol{X}_t\boldsymbol{\beta})} = \Lambda(\boldsymbol{X}_t\boldsymbol{\beta}).$$

This result is what we would get by letting $\Lambda(\boldsymbol{X}_t\boldsymbol{\beta})$ play the role of the transformation function $F(\boldsymbol{X}_t\boldsymbol{\beta})$ in (11.01).

Maximum Likelihood Estimation of Binary Response Models

By far the most common way to estimate binary response models is to use the method of maximum likelihood. Because the dependent variable is discrete, the likelihood function cannot be defined as a joint density function, as it was in Chapter 10 for models with a continuously distributed dependent variable. When the dependent variable can take on discrete values, the likelihood function for those values should be defined as the probability that the value is realized, rather than as the probability density at that value. With this redefinition, the *sum* of the possible values of the likelihood is equal to 1, just as the *integral* of the possible values of a likelihood based on a continuous distribution is equal to 1.

If, for observation t, the realized value of the dependent variable is y_t, then the likelihood for that observation if $y_t = 1$ is just the probability that $y_t = 1$, and if $y_t = 0$, it is the probability that $y_t = 0$. The logarithm of the appropriate probability is then the contribution to the loglikelihood made by observation t. Since the probability that $y_t = 1$ is $F(\boldsymbol{X}_t\boldsymbol{\beta})$, the contribution to the loglikelihood function for observation t when $y_t = 1$ is $\log F(\boldsymbol{X}_t\boldsymbol{\beta})$. Similarly, the contribution to the loglikelihood function for observation t when $y_t = 0$ is $\log\bigl(1 - F(\boldsymbol{X}_t\boldsymbol{\beta})\bigr)$. Therefore, if $\boldsymbol{y}$ is an n–vector with typical element y_t, the loglikelihood function for $\boldsymbol{y}$ can be written as

$$\ell(\boldsymbol{y}, \boldsymbol{\beta}) = \sum_{t=1}^{n} \Bigl(y_t \log F(\boldsymbol{X}_t\boldsymbol{\beta}) + (1 - y_t)\log\bigl(1 - F(\boldsymbol{X}_t\boldsymbol{\beta})\bigr)\Bigr). \tag{11.09}$$

For each observation, one of the terms inside the large parentheses is always 0, and the other is always negative. The first term is 0 whenever $y_t = 0$, and the second term is 0 whenever $y_t = 1$. When either term is nonzero, it must be negative, because it is equal to the logarithm of a probability, and this probability must be less than 1 whenever $\boldsymbol{X}_t\boldsymbol{\beta}$ is finite. For the model to fit perfectly, $F(\boldsymbol{X}_t\boldsymbol{\beta})$ would have to equal 1 when $y_t = 1$ and 0 when $y_t = 0$, and the entire expression inside the parentheses would then equal 0. This could happen only if $\boldsymbol{X}_t\boldsymbol{\beta} = \infty$ whenever $y_t = 1$, and $\boldsymbol{X}_t\boldsymbol{\beta} = -\infty$ whenever $y_t = 0$. Therefore, we see that (11.09) is bounded above by 0.

Maximizing the loglikelihood function (11.09) is quite easy to do. For the logit and probit models, this function is globally concave with respect to $\boldsymbol{\beta}$ (see Pratt, 1981, and Exercise 11.1). This implies that the first-order conditions, or likelihood equations, uniquely define the ML estimator $\hat{\boldsymbol{\beta}}$, except for one special case we consider in the next subsection but one. These likelihood equations can be written as

$$\sum_{t=1}^{n} \frac{\bigl(y_t - F(\boldsymbol{X}_t\boldsymbol{\beta})\bigr) f(\boldsymbol{X}_t\boldsymbol{\beta}) x_{ti}}{F(\boldsymbol{X}_t\boldsymbol{\beta})\bigl(1 - F(\boldsymbol{X}_t\boldsymbol{\beta})\bigr)} = 0, \quad i = 1, \ldots, k. \tag{11.10}$$

There are many ways to find $\hat{\boldsymbol{\beta}}$ in practice. Because of the global concavity of the loglikelihood function, Newton's Method generally works very well. Another approach, based on an artificial regression, will be discussed in the next section.

Conditions (11.10) look just like the first-order conditions for weighted least-squares estimation of the nonlinear regression model

$$y_t = F(\boldsymbol{X}_t\boldsymbol{\beta}) + v_t, \tag{11.11}$$

where the weight for observation t is

$$\Big(F(\boldsymbol{X}_t\boldsymbol{\beta})\big(1 - F(\boldsymbol{X}_t\boldsymbol{\beta})\big)\Big)^{-1/2}. \tag{11.12}$$

This weight is one over the square root of the variance of $v_t \equiv y_t - F(\boldsymbol{X}_t\boldsymbol{\beta})$, which is a binary random variable. By construction, v_t has mean 0, and its variance is

$$\begin{aligned} \mathrm{E}(v_t^2) &= \mathrm{E}\big(y_t - F(\boldsymbol{X}_t\boldsymbol{\beta})\big)^2 \\ &= F(\boldsymbol{X}_t\boldsymbol{\beta})\big(1 - F(\boldsymbol{X}_t\boldsymbol{\beta})\big)^2 + \big(1 - F(\boldsymbol{X}_t\boldsymbol{\beta})\big)\big(F(\boldsymbol{X}_t\boldsymbol{\beta})\big)^2 \\ &= F(\boldsymbol{X}_t\boldsymbol{\beta})\big(1 - F(\boldsymbol{X}_t\boldsymbol{\beta})\big). \end{aligned} \tag{11.13}$$

Notice how easy it is to take expectations in the case of a binary random variable. There are just two possible outcomes, and the probability of each of them is specified by the model.

Because the variance of v_t in regression (11.11) is not constant, applying nonlinear least squares to that regression would yield an inefficient estimator of the parameter vector $\boldsymbol{\beta}$. ML estimates could be obtained by applying iteratively reweighted nonlinear least squares. However, Newton's method, or a method based on the artificial regression to be discussed in the next section, is more direct and usually much faster.

Since the ML estimator is equivalent to weighted NLS, we can obtain it as an efficient GMM estimator. It is quite easy to construct elementary zero functions for a binary response model. The obvious function for observation t is $y_t - F(\boldsymbol{X}_t\boldsymbol{\beta})$. The covariance matrix of the n-vector of these zero functions is the diagonal matrix with typical element (11.13), and the row vector of derivatives of the zero function for observation t is $-f(\boldsymbol{X}_t\boldsymbol{\beta})\boldsymbol{X}_t$. With this information, we can set up the efficient estimating equations (9.82). As readers are asked to show in Exercise 11.3, these equations are equivalent to the likelihood equations (11.10).

Intuitively, efficient GMM and maximum likelihood give the same estimator because, once it is understood that the y_t are binary variables, the elementary zero functions serve to specify the probabilities $\Pr(y_t = 1)$, and they thus constitute a full specification of the model.

Comparing Probit and Logit Models

In practice, the probit and logit models generally yield very similar predicted probabilities, and the maximized values of the loglikelihood function (11.09) for the two models therefore tend to be very close. A formal comparison of these two values is possible. If twice the difference between them is greater than 3.84, the .05 critical value for the $\chi^2(1)$ distribution, then we can reject whichever model fits less well at the .05 level.[1] Such a procedure was discussed in Section 10.8 in the context of linear and loglinear models. In practice, however, experience shows that this sort of comparison rarely rejects either model unless the sample size is quite large.

In most cases, the only real difference between the probit and logit models is the way in which the elements of $\boldsymbol{\beta}$ are scaled. This difference in scaling occurs because the variance of the distribution for which the logistic function is the CDF can be shown to be $\pi^2/3$, while that of the standard normal distribution is, of course, unity. The logit estimates therefore all tend to be larger in absolute value than the probit estimates, although usually by a factor that is somewhat less than $\pi/\sqrt{3}$. Figure 11.1 plots the standard normal CDF, the logistic function, and the logistic function rescaled to have variance unity.

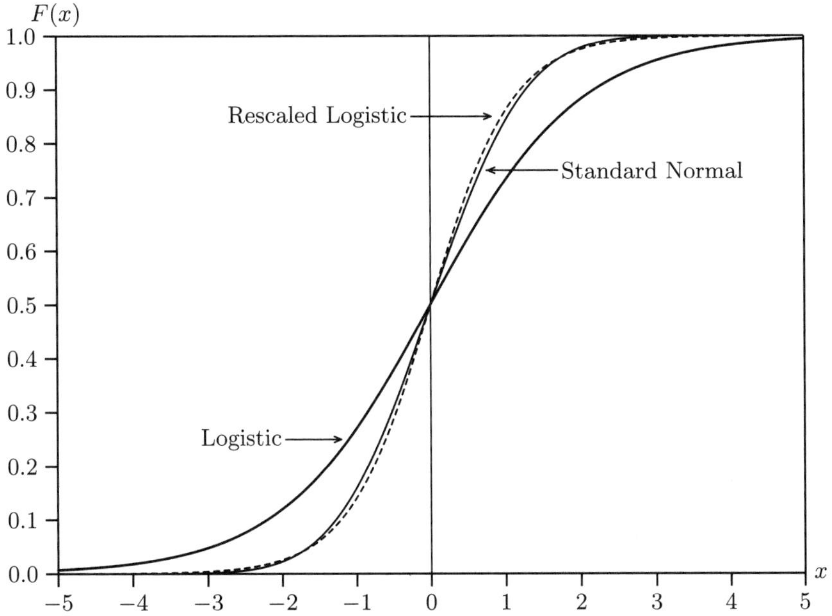

Figure 11.1 Alternative choices for $F(x)$

[1] This assumes that there exists a comprehensive model, with a single additional parameter, which includes the probit and logit models as special cases. It is not difficult to formulate such a model; see Exercise 11.4.

The resemblance between the standard normal CDF and the rescaled logistic function is striking. The main difference is that the rescaled logistic function puts more weight in the extreme tails.

The Perfect Classifier Problem

We have seen that the loglikelihood function (11.09) is bounded above by 0, and that it achieves this bound if $\boldsymbol{X}_t\boldsymbol{\beta} = -\infty$ whenever $y_t = 0$ and $\boldsymbol{X}_t\boldsymbol{\beta} = \infty$ whenever $y_t = 1$. Suppose there is some linear combination of the independent variables, say $\boldsymbol{X}_t\boldsymbol{\beta}^\bullet$, such that

$$\begin{aligned} y_t &= 0 \text{ whenever } \boldsymbol{X}_t\boldsymbol{\beta}^\bullet < 0, \text{ and} \\ y_t &= 1 \text{ whenever } \boldsymbol{X}_t\boldsymbol{\beta}^\bullet > 0. \end{aligned} \tag{11.14}$$

When this happens, there is said to be **complete separation** of the data. In this case, it is possible to make the value of $\ell(\boldsymbol{y}, \boldsymbol{\beta})$ arbitrarily close to 0 by setting $\boldsymbol{\beta} = \gamma\boldsymbol{\beta}^\bullet$ and letting $\gamma \to \infty$. This is precisely what any nonlinear maximization algorithm attempts to do if there exists a vector $\boldsymbol{\beta}^\bullet$ for which conditions (11.14) are satisfied. Because of the limitations of computer arithmetic, the algorithm must eventually terminate with some sort of numerical error at a value of the loglikelihood function that is slightly less than 0. If conditions (11.14) are satisfied, $\boldsymbol{X}_t\boldsymbol{\beta}^\bullet$ is said to be a **perfect classifier**, since it allows us to predict y_t with perfect accuracy for every observation.

The problem of perfect classifiers has a geometrical interpretation. In the k-dimensional space spanned by the columns of the matrix $\boldsymbol{X}$ formed from the row vectors $\boldsymbol{X}_t$, the vector $\boldsymbol{\beta}^\bullet$ defines a hyperplane that passes through the origin and that separates the observations for which $y_t = 1$ from those for which $y_t = 0$. Whenever one column of $\boldsymbol{X}$ is a constant, then the separating hyperplane can be represented in the $(k-1)$-dimensional space of the other explanatory variables. If we write

$$\boldsymbol{X}_t\boldsymbol{\beta}^\bullet = \alpha^\bullet + \boldsymbol{X}_{t2}\boldsymbol{\beta}_2^\bullet,$$

with $\boldsymbol{X}_{t2}$ a $1 \times (k-1)$ vector, then $\boldsymbol{X}_t\boldsymbol{\beta}^\bullet = 0$ is equivalent to $\boldsymbol{X}_{t2}\boldsymbol{\beta}_2^\bullet = -\alpha^\bullet$, which is the equation of a hyperplane in the space of the $\boldsymbol{X}_{t2}$ that in general does not pass through the origin. This is illustrated in Figure 11.2 for the case $k = 3$. The asterisks, which all lie to the northeast of the separating line for which $\boldsymbol{X}_t\boldsymbol{\beta}^\bullet = 0$, represent the $\boldsymbol{X}_{t2}$ for the observations with $y_t = 1$, and the circles to the southwest of the separating line represent them for the observations with $y_t = 0$.

It is clear from Figure 11.2 that, when a perfect classifier occurs, the separating hyperplane is not, in general, unique. One could move the intercept of the separating line in the figure up or down a little while maintaining the separating property. Likewise, one could swivel the line a little about the point of intersection with the vertical axis. Even if the separating hyperplane were

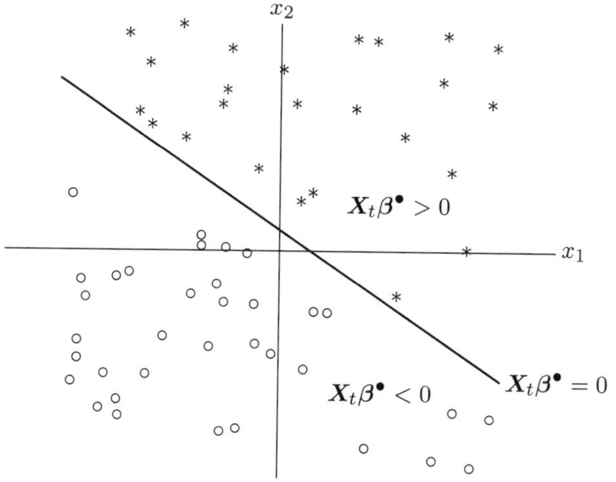

Figure 11.2 A perfect classifier yields a separating hyperplane

unique, we could not identify all the components of $\boldsymbol{\beta}$. This follows from the fact that the equation $\boldsymbol{X}_t\boldsymbol{\beta}^\bullet = 0$ is equivalent to the equation $\boldsymbol{X}_t(c\boldsymbol{\beta}^\bullet) = 0$ for any nonzero scalar c. The separating hyperplane is therefore defined equally well by any multiple of $\boldsymbol{\beta}^\bullet$. Although this suggests that we might be able to estimate $\boldsymbol{\beta}^\bullet$ up to a scalar factor by imposing a normalization on it, there is no question of estimating $\boldsymbol{\beta}^\bullet$ in the usual sense, and inference on it would require methods beyond the scope of this book.

Even when no parameter vector exists that satisfies the inequalities (11.14), there may exist a $\boldsymbol{\beta}^\bullet$ that satisfies the corresponding nonstrict inequalities. There must then be at least one observation with $y_t = 0$ and $\boldsymbol{X}_t\boldsymbol{\beta}^\bullet = 0$, and at least one other observation with $y_t = 1$ and $\boldsymbol{X}_t\boldsymbol{\beta}^\bullet = 0$. In such a case, we speak of **quasi-complete separation** of the data. The separating hyperplane is then unique, and the upper bound of the loglikelihood is no longer zero, as readers are invited to verify in Exercise 11.6.

When there is either complete or quasi-complete separation, no finite ML estimator exists. This is likely to occur in practice when the sample is very small, when almost all of the y_t are equal to 0 or almost all of them are equal to 1, or when the model fits extremely well. Exercise 11.5 is designed to give readers a feel for the circumstances in which ML estimation is likely to fail because there is a perfect classifier.

If a perfect classifier exists, the loglikelihood should be close to its upper bound (which may be 0 or a small negative number) when the maximization algorithm quits. Thus, if the model seems to fit extremely well, or if the algorithm terminates in an unusual way, one should always check to see whether the parameter values imply the existence of a perfect classifier. For a detailed discussion of the perfect classifier problem, see Albert and Anderson (1984).

11.3 Binary Response Models: Inference

Inference about the parameters of binary response models is usually based on the standard results for ML estimation that were discussed in Chapter 10. It can be shown that

$$\operatorname{Var}\big(\operatorname*{plim}_{n\to\infty} n^{1/2}(\hat{\boldsymbol\beta}-\boldsymbol\beta_0)\big) = \operatorname*{plim}_{n\to\infty}\Big(\frac{1}{n}\boldsymbol X^\top \boldsymbol\Upsilon(\boldsymbol\beta_0)\boldsymbol X\Big)^{-1}, \tag{11.15}$$

where $\boldsymbol X$ is an $n\times k$ matrix with typical row $\boldsymbol X_t$, $\boldsymbol\beta_0$ is the true value of $\boldsymbol\beta$, and $\boldsymbol\Upsilon(\boldsymbol\beta)$ is an $n\times n$ diagonal matrix with typical diagonal element

$$\Upsilon_t(\boldsymbol\beta) \equiv \frac{f^2(\boldsymbol X_t\boldsymbol\beta)}{F(\boldsymbol X_t\boldsymbol\beta)\big(1-F(\boldsymbol X_t\boldsymbol\beta)\big)}. \tag{11.16}$$

Not surprisingly, the right-hand side of expression (11.15) looks like the asymptotic covariance matrix for weighted least-squares estimation, with weights (11.12), of the GNR that corresponds to regression (11.11). This GNR is

$$y_t - F(\boldsymbol X_t\boldsymbol\beta) = f(\boldsymbol X_t\boldsymbol\beta)\boldsymbol X_t\boldsymbol b + \text{residual}. \tag{11.17}$$

The factor of $f(\boldsymbol X_t\boldsymbol\beta)$ that multiplies all the regressors of the GNR accounts for the numerator of (11.16). Its denominator is simply the variance of the error term in regression (11.11). Two ways to obtain the asymptotic covariance matrix (11.15) using general results for ML estimation are explored in Exercises 11.7 and 11.8.

In practice, the asymptotic result (11.15) is used to justify the covariance matrix estimator

$$\widehat{\operatorname{Var}}(\hat{\boldsymbol\beta}) = \big(\boldsymbol X^\top\boldsymbol\Upsilon(\hat{\boldsymbol\beta})\boldsymbol X\big)^{-1}, \tag{11.18}$$

in which the unknown $\boldsymbol\beta_0$ is replaced by $\hat{\boldsymbol\beta}$, and the factor of n^{-1}, which is needed only for asymptotic analysis, is omitted. This approximation may be used to obtain standard errors, t statistics, Wald statistics, and confidence intervals that are asymptotically valid. However, none of these is exact in finite samples.

It is clear from equations (11.15) and (11.18) that the ML estimator for the binary response model gives some observations more weight than others. In fact, the weight given to observation t is proportional to the square root of expression (11.16) evaluated at $\boldsymbol\beta=\hat{\boldsymbol\beta}$. It can be shown that, for both the logit and probit models, the maximum weight is given to observations for which $\boldsymbol X_t\boldsymbol\beta = 0$, which implies that $P_t = .5$, while relatively little weight is given to observations for which P_t is close to 0 or 1; see Exercise 11.9. This makes sense, since when P_t is close to 0 or 1, a given change in $\boldsymbol X_t\boldsymbol\beta$ can have little effect on P_t, while when P_t is close to .5, such a change has a much larger effect. Thus we see that ML estimation, quite sensibly, gives more weight to observations that provide more information about the parameter values.

Likelihood Ratio Tests

It is straightforward to test restrictions on binary response models using LR tests. We simply estimate both the restricted and the unrestricted model and calculate twice the difference between the two maximized values of the loglikelihood function. As usual, the LR test statistic is asymptotically distributed as $\chi^2(r)$, where r is the number of restrictions.

One especially simple application of this procedure can be used to test whether the regressors in a binary response model have any explanatory power at all. The null hypothesis is that $\mathrm{E}(y_t \mid \Omega_t)$ is a constant, and the ML estimate of this constant is just $\bar{y}$, the unconditional sample mean of the dependent variable. It is not difficult to show that, under the null hypothesis, the loglikelihood function (11.09) reduces to

$$n\,\bar{y}\log(\bar{y}) + n(1-\bar{y})\log(1-\bar{y}), \tag{11.19}$$

which is very easy to calculate. Twice the difference between the unrestricted maximum of the loglikelihood function and the restricted maximum (11.19) is asymptotically distributed as $\chi^2(k-1)$. This statistic is analogous to the usual F test for all the slope coefficients in a linear regression model to equal zero, and many computer programs routinely compute it.

An Artificial Regression for Binary Choice Models

There is a convenient artificial regression for binary response models.[2] Like the Gauss-Newton regression, to which it is closely related, the **binary response model regression**, or **BRMR**, can be used for a variety of purposes, including parameter estimation, covariance matrix estimation, and hypothesis testing.

The most intuitive way to think of the BRMR is as a modified version of the GNR. The ordinary GNR for the nonlinear regression model (11.11) is (11.17). However, it is inappropriate to use this GNR, because the error terms are heteroskedastic, with variance given by (11.13). We need to divide the regressand and regressors of (11.17) by the square root of (11.13) in order to obtain an artificial regression that has homoskedastic errors. The result is the BRMR,

$$V_t^{-1/2}(\boldsymbol{\beta})\big(y_t - F(\boldsymbol{X}_t\boldsymbol{\beta})\big) = V_t^{-1/2}(\boldsymbol{\beta})f(\boldsymbol{X}_t\boldsymbol{\beta})\boldsymbol{X}_t\boldsymbol{b} + \text{residual}, \tag{11.20}$$

where $V_t(\boldsymbol{\beta}) \equiv F(\boldsymbol{X}_t\boldsymbol{\beta})\big(1 - F(\boldsymbol{X}_t\boldsymbol{\beta})\big)$.

If the BRMR is evaluated at the vector of ML estimates $\hat{\boldsymbol{\beta}}$, it yields the covariance matrix

$$s^2\big(\boldsymbol{X}^\top\boldsymbol{\Upsilon}(\hat{\boldsymbol{\beta}})\boldsymbol{X}\big)^{-1}, \tag{11.21}$$

[2] This regression was originally proposed, independently in somewhat different forms, by Engle (1984) and Davidson and MacKinnon (1984b).

where s is the standard error of the artificial regression. Since (11.20) is a GLS regression, s tends to 1 asymptotically, and expression (11.21) is therefore a valid way to estimate $\text{Var}(\hat{\boldsymbol{\beta}})$. However, because there is no advantage to multiplying by a random variable that tends to 1, it is better simply to use (11.18), which may readily be obtained by dividing (11.21) by s^2.

Like other artificial regressions, the BRMR can be used as part of a numerical maximization algorithm, similar to the ones described in Section 6.4. The formula that determines $\boldsymbol{\beta}_{(j+1)}$, the value of $\boldsymbol{\beta}$ at step $j+1$, is

$$\boldsymbol{\beta}_{(j+1)} = \boldsymbol{\beta}_{(j)} + \alpha_{(j)}\boldsymbol{b}_{(j)},$$

where $\boldsymbol{b}_{(j)}$ is the vector of OLS estimates from the BRMR evaluated at $\boldsymbol{\beta}_{(j)}$, and $\alpha_{(j)}$ may be chosen in several ways. This procedure generally works very well, but a modified Newton procedure is usually even faster.

The BRMR is particularly useful for hypothesis testing. Suppose that $\boldsymbol{\beta}$ is partitioned as $[\boldsymbol{\beta}_1 \vdots \boldsymbol{\beta}_2]$, where $\boldsymbol{\beta}_1$ is a $(k-r)$–vector and $\boldsymbol{\beta}_2$ is an r–vector. If $\tilde{\boldsymbol{\beta}}$ denotes the vector of ML estimates subject to the restriction that $\boldsymbol{\beta}_2 = \mathbf{0}$, we can test that restriction by running the BRMR

$$\tilde{V}_t^{-1/2}(y_t - \tilde{F}_t) = \tilde{V}_t^{-1/2}\tilde{f}_t \boldsymbol{X}_{t1}\boldsymbol{b}_1 + \tilde{V}_t^{-1/2}\tilde{f}_t \boldsymbol{X}_{t2}\boldsymbol{b}_2 + \text{residual}, \tag{11.22}$$

where $\tilde{F}_t \equiv F(\boldsymbol{X}_t\tilde{\boldsymbol{\beta}})$, $\tilde{f}_t \equiv f(\boldsymbol{X}_t\tilde{\boldsymbol{\beta}})$, and $\tilde{V}_t \equiv V_t(\tilde{\boldsymbol{\beta}})$. Here $\boldsymbol{X}_t$ has been partitioned into two vectors, $\boldsymbol{X}_{t1}$ and $\boldsymbol{X}_{t2}$, corresponding to the partitioning of $\boldsymbol{\beta}$. The regressors that correspond to $\boldsymbol{\beta}_1$ are orthogonal to the regressand, while those that correspond to $\boldsymbol{\beta}_2$ are not. All the usual test statistics for $\boldsymbol{b}_2 = \mathbf{0}$ are valid. The best test statistic to use in finite samples is probably the explained sum of squares from regression (11.22). It is asymptotically distributed as $\chi^2(r)$ under the null hypothesis. An F statistic is also asymptotically valid, but since its denominator of s^2 is random, and there is no need to estimate the variance of (11.22), the explained sum of squares is preferable.

In the special case of the null hypothesis that all the slope coefficients are zero, regression (11.22) simplifies dramatically. In this case, $\boldsymbol{X}_{t1}$ is just unity, and $\tilde{V}_t$, $\tilde{F}_t$, and $\tilde{f}_t$ are all constants that do not depend on t. Since neither subtracting a constant from the regressand nor multiplying the regressand and regressors by a constant has any effect on the F statistic for $\boldsymbol{b}_2 = \mathbf{0}$, regression (11.22) is equivalent to the much simpler regression

$$\boldsymbol{y} = c_1 + \boldsymbol{X}_2\boldsymbol{c}_2 + \text{residuals}. \tag{11.23}$$

The ordinary F statistic for $\boldsymbol{c}_2 = \mathbf{0}$ in regression (11.23) is an asymptotically valid test statistic for the hypothesis that $\boldsymbol{\beta}_2 = \mathbf{0}$. The fact that (11.23) is just an OLS regression of $\boldsymbol{y}$ on the constant and explanatory variables accounts for the claim we made in Section 11.2 that such a regression is not always completely useless!

Bootstrap Inference

Because binary response models are fully parametric, it is straightforward to bootstrap them using procedures similar to those discussed in Sections 4.6 and 5.3. For the model specified by (11.01), the bootstrap DGP is required to generate binary variables y_t^*, $t = 1, \ldots, n$, in such a way that

$$P_t^* \equiv \mathrm{E}(y_t^* \mid \boldsymbol{X}_t) = F(\boldsymbol{X}_t\hat{\boldsymbol{\beta}}),$$

where $\hat{\boldsymbol{\beta}}$ is a vector of ML estimates. For a bootstrap test, this vector would be subject to whatever restrictions are being tested. In order to generate y_t^*, the easiest way to proceed is to draw u_t^* from the uniform distribution $\mathrm{U}(0,1)$ and set $y_t^* = I(u_t^* \le P_t^*)$, where, as usual, $I(\cdot)$ is an indicator function. Alternatively, in the case of the probit model, we can generate bootstrap samples by using (11.04) to generate latent variables and (11.05) to convert these to the binary dependent variables we actually need.

Bootstrap methods for binary response models may or may not yield more accurate inferences than asymptotic ones. In the case of test statistics, where the bootstrap samples must be generated under the null hypothesis, there seems to be evidence that bootstrap P values are generally more accurate than asymptotic ones. The value of bootstrapping appears to be particularly great when the number of restrictions is large and the sample size is moderate. However, in the case of confidence intervals, the evidence is rather mixed.

The bootstrap can also be used to reduce the bias of the ML estimates. As we saw in Section 3.6, regression models tend to fit too well in finite samples, in the sense that the residuals tend to be smaller than the true error terms. Binary response models also tend to fit too well, in the sense that the fitted probabilities, the $F(\boldsymbol{X}_t\hat{\boldsymbol{\beta}})$, tend to be closer to 0 and 1 than the true probabilities, the $F(\boldsymbol{X}_t\boldsymbol{\beta}_0)$. This overfitting causes the elements of $\hat{\boldsymbol{\beta}}$ to be biased away from zero.

If we generate B bootstrap samples using the parameter vector $\hat{\boldsymbol{\beta}}$, we can estimate the bias using

$$\mathrm{Bias}^*(\hat{\boldsymbol{\beta}}) = \frac{1}{B}\sum_{j=1}^{B}\hat{\boldsymbol{\beta}}_j^* - \hat{\boldsymbol{\beta}},$$

where $\hat{\boldsymbol{\beta}}_j^*$ is the estimate of $\boldsymbol{\beta}$ using the jth bootstrap sample. Therefore, a bias-corrected estimate is

$$\hat{\boldsymbol{\beta}}_{\text{bc}} \equiv \hat{\boldsymbol{\beta}} - \mathrm{Bias}^*(\hat{\boldsymbol{\beta}}) = 2\hat{\boldsymbol{\beta}} - \frac{1}{B}\sum_{j=1}^{B}\hat{\boldsymbol{\beta}}_j^*.$$

Simulation results in MacKinnon and Smith (1998), which are by no means definitive, suggest that this estimator is less biased and has smaller mean squared error than the usual ML estimator.

The finite-sample bias of the ML estimator in binary response models can cause an important practical problem for the bootstrap. Since the probabilities associated with $\hat{\boldsymbol{\beta}}$ tend to be more extreme than the true ones, samples generated using $\hat{\boldsymbol{\beta}}$ are more prone to having a perfect classifier. Therefore, even though there is no perfect classifier for the original data, there may well be perfect classifiers for some of the bootstrap samples. The simplest way to deal with this problem is just to throw away any bootstrap samples for which a perfect classifier exists. However, if there is more than a handful of such samples, the bootstrap results must then be viewed with skepticism.

Specification Tests

Maximum likelihood estimation of binary response models almost always yields inconsistent estimates if the form of the transformation function, that is, $F(\boldsymbol{X}_t\boldsymbol{\beta})$, is misspecified. It is therefore very important to test whether this function has been specified correctly.

In Section 11.2, we derived the probit model by starting with the latent variable model (11.04), which has normally distributed, homoskedastic errors. A more general specification for a latent variable model, which allows for the error terms to be heteroskedastic, is

$$y_t^\circ = \boldsymbol{X}_t\boldsymbol{\beta} + u_t, \quad u_t \sim \mathrm{N}\big(0, \exp(2\boldsymbol{Z}_t\boldsymbol{\gamma})\big), \tag{11.24}$$

where $\boldsymbol{Z}_t$ is a row vector of length r of observations on variables that belong to the information set Ω_t, and $\boldsymbol{\gamma}$ is an r–vector of parameters to be estimated along with $\boldsymbol{\beta}$. To ensure that both $\boldsymbol{\beta}$ and $\boldsymbol{\gamma}$ are identifiable, $\boldsymbol{Z}_t$ must not include a constant term or the equivalent. With this precaution, the model (11.04) is obtained by setting $\boldsymbol{\gamma} = \mathbf{0}$. Combining (11.24) with (11.05) yields the model

$$P_t \equiv \mathrm{E}(y_t \,|\, \Omega_t) = \Phi\bigg(\frac{\boldsymbol{X}_t\boldsymbol{\beta}}{\exp(\boldsymbol{Z}_t\boldsymbol{\gamma})}\bigg),$$

in which P_t depends on both the regression function $\boldsymbol{X}_t\boldsymbol{\beta}$ and the skedastic function $\exp(2\boldsymbol{Z}_t\boldsymbol{\gamma})$. Thus it is clear that heteroskedasticity of the u_t in a latent variable model affects the form of the transformation function.

Even when the binary response model being used is not the probit model, it still seems quite reasonable to consider the alternative hypothesis

$$P_t = F\bigg(\frac{\boldsymbol{X}_t\boldsymbol{\beta}}{\exp(\boldsymbol{Z}_t\boldsymbol{\gamma})}\bigg). \tag{11.25}$$

We can test against this alternative by using a BRMR to test the hypothesis that $\boldsymbol{\gamma} = \mathbf{0}$. The appropriate BRMR is

$$\tilde{V}_t^{-1/2}(y_t - \tilde{F}_t) = \tilde{V}_t^{-1/2}\tilde{f}_t\boldsymbol{X}_t\boldsymbol{b} - \tilde{V}_t^{-1/2}\boldsymbol{X}_t\tilde{\boldsymbol{\beta}}\tilde{f}_t\boldsymbol{Z}_t\boldsymbol{c} + \text{residual}, \tag{11.26}$$

where $\tilde{F}_t$, $\tilde{f}_t$, and $\tilde{V}_t$ are evaluated at the ML estimates $\tilde{\boldsymbol{\beta}}$ computed under the null hypothesis that $\boldsymbol{\gamma} = \mathbf{0}$ in (11.25). These are just the ordinary estimates for the binary response model defined by $P_t = F(\boldsymbol{X}_t\boldsymbol{\beta})$; they are usually probit or logit estimates. The explained sum of squares from (11.26) is asymptotically distributed as $\chi^2(r)$ under the null hypothesis.

Heteroskedasticity is not the only phenomenon that may lead the transformation function $F(\boldsymbol{X}_t\boldsymbol{\beta})$ to be specified incorrectly. Consider the family of models for which

$$P_t \equiv \mathrm{E}(y_t \mid \Omega_t) = F\left(\frac{\tau(\delta \boldsymbol{X}_t\boldsymbol{\beta})}{\delta}\right), \tag{11.27}$$

where δ is a scalar parameter, and $\tau(\cdot)$ may be any scalar function that is monotonically increasing in its argument and satisfies the conditions

$$\tau(0) = 0, \quad \tau'(0) = 1, \quad \text{and } \tau''(0) \neq 0, \tag{11.28}$$

where $\tau'(0)$ and $\tau''(0)$ are the first and second derivatives of $\tau(x)$, evaluated at $x = 0$. The family of models (11.27) allows for a wide range of transformation functions. It was considered by MacKinnon and Magee (1990), who showed, by using l'Hôpital's Rule, that

$$\lim_{\delta \to 0}\left(\frac{\tau(\delta x)}{\delta}\right) = x \quad \text{and} \quad \lim_{\delta \to 0}\left(\frac{\partial\big(\tau(\delta x)/\delta\big)}{\partial \delta}\right) = \tfrac{1}{2}x^2\tau''(0). \tag{11.29}$$

Hence the BRMR for testing the null hypothesis that $\delta = 0$ is

$$\tilde{V}_t^{-1/2}(y_t - \tilde{F}_t) = \tilde{V}_t^{-1/2}\tilde{f}_t \boldsymbol{X}_t\boldsymbol{b} + \tilde{V}_t^{-1/2}(\boldsymbol{X}_t\tilde{\boldsymbol{\beta}})^2\tilde{f}_t d + \text{residual}, \tag{11.30}$$

where everything is evaluated at the ML estimates $\tilde{\boldsymbol{\beta}}$ of the ordinary binary response model that (11.27) reduces to when $\delta = 0$. The constant factor $\tau''(0)/2$ that arises from (11.29) is irrelevant for testing and has been omitted. Thus regression (11.30) simply treats the squared values of the index function evaluated at $\tilde{\boldsymbol{\beta}}$ as if they were observations on a possibly omitted regressor, and the ordinary t statistic for $d = 0$ provides an asymptotically valid test.[3]

Tests based on the BRMRs (11.26) and (11.30) are valid only asymptotically. It is extremely likely that their finite-sample performance could be improved by using bootstrap P values instead of asymptotic ones. Since, in both cases, the null hypothesis is just an ordinary binary response model, computing bootstrap P values by using the procedures discussed in the previous subsection is quite straightforward.

[3] There is a strong resemblance between regression (11.30) and the test regression for the RESET test (Ramsey, 1969), in which squared fitted values are added to an OLS regression as a test for functional form. As MacKinnon and Magee (1990) showed, this resemblance is not coincidental.

11.4 Models for More Than Two Discrete Responses

Discrete dependent variables that can take on three or more different values are by no means uncommon in economics, and a large number of models has been devised to deal with such cases. These are sometimes referred to as **qualitative response models** and sometimes as **discrete choice models**. The binary response models we have already studied are special cases.

Discrete choice models can be divided into two types: ones designed to deal with **ordered responses**, and ones designed to deal with **unordered responses**. Surveys often produce ordered response data. For example, respondents might be asked whether they strongly agree, agree, neither agree nor disagree, disagree, or strongly disagree with some statement. Here there are five possible responses, which evidently can be ordered in a natural way. In many other cases, however, there is no natural way to order the various choices. A classic example is the choice of transportation mode. For intercity travel, people often have a choice among flying, driving, taking the train, and taking the bus. There is no natural way to order these four choices.

The Ordered Probit Model

The most widely-used model for ordered response data is the **ordered probit model**. This model can easily be derived from a latent variable model. The model for the latent variable is

$$y_t^\circ = \boldsymbol{X}_t\boldsymbol{\beta} + u_t, \quad u_t \sim \text{NID}(0, 1), \tag{11.31}$$

which is identical to the latent variable model (11.04) that led to the ordinary probit model. As in the case of the latter, what we actually observe is a discrete variable y_t that can take on a limited, known, number of values. For simplicity, we assume that the number of values is just 3. It should be obvious how to extend the model to cases in which y_t can take on any known number of values.

The relation between the observed variable y_t and the latent variable y_t° is assumed to be given by

$$\begin{aligned} y_t &= 0 \text{ if } y_t^\circ < \gamma_1; \\ y_t &= 1 \text{ if } \gamma_1 \le y_t^\circ < \gamma_2; \\ y_t &= 2 \text{ if } y_t^\circ \ge \gamma_2. \end{aligned} \tag{11.32}$$

Thus $y_t = 0$ for small values of y_t°, $y_t = 1$ for intermediate values, and $y_t = 2$ for large values. The boundaries between the three cases are determined by the parameters γ_1 and γ_2. These **threshold parameters**, which usually must be estimated, determine how the values of y_t° get translated into the three possible values of y_t. It is essential that $\gamma_2 > \gamma_1$. Otherwise, the first and last lines of (11.32) would be incompatible, and we could never observe $y_t = 1$.

If $\boldsymbol{X}_t$ contains a constant term, it is impossible to identify the constant along with γ_1 and γ_2. To see this, suppose that the constant is equal to α. Then it is easy to check that y_t is unchanged if we replace the constant by $\alpha + \delta$ and replace γ_i by $\gamma_i + \delta$ for $i = 1, 2$. The easiest, but not the only, solution to this identification problem is just to set $\alpha = 0$. We adopt this solution here. In general, with no constant, the ordered probit model has as many threshold parameters as choices, less one. When there are just two choices, the single threshold parameter is equivalent to a constant, and the ordered probit model reduces to the ordinary probit model, with a constant.

In order to work out the loglikelihood function for this model, we need the probabilities of the three events $y_t = 0$, $y_t = 1$, and $y_t = 2$. The probability that $y_t = 0$ is

$$\begin{aligned}\Pr(y_t = 0) &= \Pr(y_t^\circ < \gamma_1) = \Pr(\boldsymbol{X}_t\boldsymbol{\beta} + u_t < \gamma_1)\\ &= \Pr(u_t < \gamma_1 - \boldsymbol{X}_t\boldsymbol{\beta}) = \Phi(\gamma_1 - \boldsymbol{X}_t\boldsymbol{\beta}).\end{aligned}$$

Similarly, the probability that $y_t = 2$ is

$$\begin{aligned}\Pr(y_t = 2) &= \Pr(y_t^\circ \geq \gamma_2) = \Pr(\boldsymbol{X}_t\boldsymbol{\beta} + u_t \geq \gamma_2)\\ &= \Pr(u_t \geq \gamma_2 - \boldsymbol{X}_t\boldsymbol{\beta}) = \Phi(\boldsymbol{X}_t\boldsymbol{\beta} - \gamma_2).\end{aligned}$$

Finally, the probability that $y_t = 1$ is

$$\begin{aligned}\Pr(y_t = 1) &= 1 - \Pr(y_t = 0) - \Pr(y_t = 2)\\ &= 1 - \Phi(\gamma_1 - \boldsymbol{X}_t\boldsymbol{\beta}) - \Phi(\boldsymbol{X}_t\boldsymbol{\beta} - \gamma_2)\\ &= \Phi(\gamma_2 - \boldsymbol{X}_t\boldsymbol{\beta}) - \Phi(\gamma_1 - \boldsymbol{X}_t\boldsymbol{\beta}).\end{aligned}$$

These probabilities depend solely on the value of the index function, $\boldsymbol{X}_t\boldsymbol{\beta}$, and on the two threshold parameters.

The loglikelihood function for the ordered probit model derived from (11.31) and (11.32) is

$$\begin{aligned}\ell(\boldsymbol{\beta}, \gamma_1, \gamma_2) = &\sum_{y_t=0} \log\big(\Phi(\gamma_1 - \boldsymbol{X}_t\boldsymbol{\beta})\big) + \sum_{y_t=2} \log\big(\Phi(\boldsymbol{X}_t\boldsymbol{\beta} - \gamma_2)\big)\\ &+ \sum_{y_t=1} \log\big(\Phi(\gamma_2 - \boldsymbol{X}_t\boldsymbol{\beta}) - \Phi(\gamma_1 - \boldsymbol{X}_t\boldsymbol{\beta})\big).\end{aligned} \tag{11.33}$$

Maximizing (11.33) numerically is generally not difficult to do, although steps may have to be taken to ensure that γ_2 is always greater than γ_1. Note that the function Φ in (11.33) may be replaced by any function F that satisfies the conditions (11.02), although it may then be harder to derive the probabilities from a latent variable model. Thus the ordered probit model is by no means the only qualitative response model for ordered data.

The ordered probit model is widely used in applied econometric work. A simple, graphical exposition of this model is provided by Becker and Kennedy (1992). Like the ordinary probit model, the ordered probit model can be generalized in a number of ways; see, for example, Terza (1985). An interesting application of a generalized version, which allows for heteroskedasticity, is Hausman, Lo, and MacKinlay (1992). They apply the model to price changes on the New York Stock Exchange at the level of individual trades. Because the price change from one trade to the next almost always takes on one of a small number of possible values, an ordered probit model is an appropriate way to model these changes.

The Multinomial Logit Model

The key feature of ordered qualitative response models like the ordered probit model is that all the choices depend on a single index function. This makes sense only when the responses have a natural ordering. A different sort of model is evidently necessary to deal with unordered responses. The most popular of these is the **multinomial logit model**, sometimes called the **multiple logit model**, which has been widely used in applied work.

The multinomial logit model is designed to handle $J+1$ responses, for $J \geq 1$. According to this model, the probability that any one of them is observed is

$$\Pr(y_t = l) = \frac{\exp(\boldsymbol{W}_{tl}\boldsymbol{\beta}^l)}{\sum_{j=0}^{J}\exp(\boldsymbol{W}_{tj}\boldsymbol{\beta}^j)} \quad \text{for } l = 0, \ldots, J. \tag{11.34}$$

Here $\boldsymbol{W}_{tj}$ is a row vector of length k_j of observations on variables that belong to the information set of interest, and $\boldsymbol{\beta}^j$ is a k_j-vector of parameters, usually different for each $j = 0, \ldots, J$.

Estimation of the multinomial logit model is reasonably straightforward. The loglikelihood function can be written as

$$\sum_{t=1}^{n}\bigg(\sum_{j=0}^{J} I(y_t = j)\boldsymbol{W}_{tj}\boldsymbol{\beta}^j - \log\Big(\sum_{j=0}^{J}\exp(\boldsymbol{W}_{tj}\boldsymbol{\beta}^j)\Big)\bigg), \tag{11.35}$$

where $I(\cdot)$ is the indicator function. Thus each observation contributes two terms to the loglikelihood function. The first is $\boldsymbol{W}_{tj}\boldsymbol{\beta}^j$, where $y_t = j$, and the second is minus the logarithm of the denominator that appears in (11.34). It is generally not difficult to maximize (11.35) by using some sort of modified Newton method, provided there are no perfect classifiers, since the loglikelihood function (11.35) is globally concave with respect to the entire vector of parameters, $[\boldsymbol{\beta}^0 \vdots \ldots \vdots \boldsymbol{\beta}^J]$; see Exercise 11.16.

Some special cases of the multinomial logit model are of interest. One of these arises when the explanatory variables $\boldsymbol{W}_{tj}$ are the same for each choice j. If a model is intended to explain which of an unordered set of outcomes applies to the different individuals in a sample, then the probabilities of all of these outcomes can be expected to depend on the same set of characteristics for each individual. For instance, a student wondering how to spend Saturday night may be able to choose among studying, partying, visiting parents, or going to the movies. In choosing, the student takes into account things like grades on the previous midterm, the length of time since the last visit home, the interest of what is being shown at the local movie theater, and so on. All these variables affect the probability of each possible outcome.

For models of this sort, it is not possible to identity $J+1$ parameter vectors $\boldsymbol{\beta}^j$, $j = 0, \ldots, J$. To see this, let $\boldsymbol{X}_t$ denote the common set of explanatory variables for observation t, and define $\boldsymbol{\gamma}^j \equiv \boldsymbol{\beta}^j - \boldsymbol{\beta}^0$ for $j = 1, \ldots, J$. On replacing the $\boldsymbol{W}_{tj}$ by $\boldsymbol{X}_t$ for all j, the probabilities defined in (11.34) become, for $l = 1, \ldots, J$,

$$\Pr(y_t = l) = \frac{\exp(\boldsymbol{X}_t\boldsymbol{\beta}^l)}{\sum_{j=0}^{J}\exp(\boldsymbol{X}_t\boldsymbol{\beta}^j)} = \frac{\exp(\boldsymbol{X}_t\boldsymbol{\gamma}^l)}{1+\sum_{j=1}^{J}\exp(\boldsymbol{X}_t\boldsymbol{\gamma}^j)},$$

where the second equality is obtained by dividing both the numerator and the denominator by $\exp(\boldsymbol{X}_t\boldsymbol{\beta}^0)$. For outcome 0, the probability is just

$$\Pr(y_t = 0) = \frac{1}{1+\sum_{j=1}^{J}\exp(\boldsymbol{X}_t\boldsymbol{\gamma}^j)}.$$

It follows that all $J+1$ probabilities can be expressed in terms of the parameters $\boldsymbol{\gamma}^j$, $j = 1, \ldots, J$, independently of $\boldsymbol{\beta}^0$. In practice, it is easiest to impose the restriction that $\boldsymbol{\beta}^0 = \mathbf{0}$, which is then enough to identify the parameters $\boldsymbol{\beta}^j$, $j = 1, \ldots, J$. When $J = 1$, it is easy to see that this model reduces to the ordinary logit model with a single index function $\boldsymbol{X}_t\boldsymbol{\beta}^1$.

In certain cases, some but not all of the explanatory variables are common to all outcomes. In that event, for the common variables, a separate parameter cannot be identified for each outcome, for the same reason as above. In order to set up a model for which all the parameters are identified, it is necessary to set to zero those components of $\boldsymbol{\beta}^0$ that correspond to the common variables. Thus, for instance, at most J of the $\boldsymbol{W}_{tj}$ vectors can include a constant.

Another special case of interest is the so-called **conditional logit model**. For this model, the probability that agent t makes choice l is

$$\Pr(y_t = l) = \frac{\exp(\boldsymbol{W}_{tl}\boldsymbol{\beta})}{\sum_{j=0}^{J}\exp(\boldsymbol{W}_{tj}\boldsymbol{\beta})}. \tag{11.36}$$

where $\boldsymbol{W}_{tj}$ is a row vector with k components for each $j = 0, \ldots, J$, and $\boldsymbol{\beta}$ is a k-vector of parameters, the same for each j. This model has been extensively used to model the choice among competing modes of transportation. The usual interpretation is that the elements of $\boldsymbol{W}_{tj}$ are the characteristics of choice j for agent t, and agents make their choice by considering the weighted sums $\boldsymbol{W}_{tj}\boldsymbol{\beta}$ of these characteristics.

It is necessary that none of the explanatory variables in the $\boldsymbol{W}_{tj}$ vectors should be the same for all $J+1$ choices. In other words, no single variable should appear in each and every $\boldsymbol{W}_{tj}$. It is easy to see from (11.36) that, if there were such a variable, say w_{ti}, for some $i = 1, \ldots, k$, then this variable would be multiplied by the *same* parameter β_i for each choice. In consequence, the factor $\exp(w_{ti}\beta_i)$ would appear in the numerator and in every term of the denominator of (11.36) and could be cancelled out. This implies, in particular, that none of the explanatory variables can be constant for all $t = 1, \ldots, n$ and all $j = 0, \ldots, J$.

An important property of the general multinomial logit model defined by the set of probabilities (11.34) is that

$$\frac{\Pr(y_t = l)}{\Pr(y_t = j)} = \frac{\exp(\boldsymbol{W}_{tl}\boldsymbol{\beta}^l)}{\exp(\boldsymbol{W}_{tj}\boldsymbol{\beta}^j)}.$$

for any two responses l and j. Therefore, the ratio of the probabilities of any two responses depends solely on the explanatory variables $\boldsymbol{W}_{tl}$ and $\boldsymbol{W}_{tj}$ and the parameters $\boldsymbol{\beta}^l$ and $\boldsymbol{\beta}^j$ associated with those two responses. It does not depend on the explanatory variables or parameter vectors specific to any of the other responses. This property of the model is called the **independence of irrelevant alternatives**, or **IIA**, property.

The IIA property is often quite implausible. For example, suppose there are three modes of public transportation between a pair of cities: the bus, which is slow but cheap, the airplane, which is fast but expensive, and the train, which is a little faster than the bus and a lot cheaper than the airplane. Now consider what the model says would happen if the rail line were upgraded, causing the train to become much faster but considerably more expensive. Intuitively, we might expect a lot of people who previously flew to take the train instead, but relatively few to switch from the bus to the train. However, this is not what the model says. Instead, the IIA property implies that the ratio of travelers who fly to travelers who take the bus is the same whatever the characteristics of the train.

Although the IIA property is often not a plausible one, it can easily be tested; see Hausman and McFadden (1984), McFadden (1987), and Exercise 11.22. The simplicity of the multinomial logit model, despite the IIA property, makes this model very attractive for cases in which it does not appear to be incompatible with the data.

The Nested Logit Model

A discrete choice model that does not possess the IIA property is the **nested logit model**. For this model, the set of possible choices is decomposed into subsets. Let the set of outcomes $\{0, 1, \ldots, J\}$ be partitioned into m disjoint subsets A_i, $i = 1, \ldots, m$. The model then supposes that, conditional on choosing an outcome in subset A_i, the choice among the members of A_i is governed by a standard multinomial logit model. We have, for $j \in A_i$, that

$$\Pr(y_t = j \mid y_t \in A_i) = \frac{\exp(\boldsymbol{W}_{tj}\boldsymbol{\beta}^j/\theta_i)}{\sum_{l\in A_i}\exp(\boldsymbol{W}_{tl}\boldsymbol{\beta}^l/\theta_i)}. \tag{11.37}$$

It is clear that the parameter θ_i, which can be thought of as a scale parameter for the parameter vectors $\boldsymbol{\beta}^j$, $j \in A_i$, is not identifiable on the basis of choice within the elements of subset A_i. However, it is what determines the probability of choosing some element in A_i. Specifically, we assume that

$$\Pr(y_t \in A_i) = \frac{\exp(\theta_i h_{ti})}{\sum_{k=1}^m \exp(\theta_k h_{tk})}, \tag{11.38}$$

where we have defined the **inclusive value** of subset A_i as:

$$h_{ti} = \log\Big(\sum_{j\in A_i}\exp(\boldsymbol{W}_{tj}\boldsymbol{\beta}^j/\theta_i)\Big). \tag{11.39}$$

Since it follows at once from (11.38) that $\sum_{i=1}^m \Pr(y_t \in A_i) = 1$, we can see that y_t must belong to one of the disjoint sets A_i.

By putting together (11.37) and (11.38), we obtain the $J + 1$ probabilities for the different outcomes. For each $j = 0, \ldots, J$, let $i(j)$ be the subset containing j. In other words, $j \in A_{i(j)}$. Then we have that

$$\begin{aligned}\Pr(y_t = j) &= \Pr(y_t = j \mid y_t \in A_{i(j)})\Pr(y_t \in A_{i(j)})\\ &= \frac{\exp(\boldsymbol{W}_{tj}\boldsymbol{\beta}^j/\theta_{i(j)})}{\sum_{l\in A_{i(j)}}\exp(\boldsymbol{W}_{tl}\boldsymbol{\beta}^l/\theta_{i(j)})}\,\frac{\exp(\theta_{i(j)}h_{ti(j)})}{\sum_{k=1}^m\exp(\theta_k h_{tk})}.\end{aligned} \tag{11.40}$$

It is not hard to check that, if $\theta_i = 1$ for all $i = 1, \ldots, m$, the probabilities (11.40) reduce to the probabilities (11.34) of the usual multinomial logit model; see Exercise 11.17. Thus the multinomial logit model is contained within the nested logit model as a special case. It follows, therefore, that testing the multinomial logit model against the alternative of the nested logit model, for some appropriate choice of the subsets A_i, is one way to test whether the IIA property is compatible with the data.

An Artificial Regression for Discrete Choice Models

In order to perform the test of the IIA property mentioned just above, and to perform inference generally in the context of discrete choice models, it is convenient to be able to make use of an artificial regression. The simplest such artificial regression was proposed by McFadden (1987) for multinomial logit models. In this section, we present a generalized version that can be applied to any discrete choice model. We call this the **discrete choice artificial regression**, or **DCAR**.

As usual, we assume that there are $J+1$ possible outcomes, numbered from $j=0$ to $j=J$. Let the probability of choosing outcome j for observation t be given by the function $\Pi_{tj}(\boldsymbol{\theta})$, where $\boldsymbol{\theta}$ is a k-vector of parameters. For the multinomial logit model, $\boldsymbol{\theta}$ would include all of the independent parameters in the set of parameter vectors $\boldsymbol{\beta}^j$, $j=0,\ldots,J$. The function $\Pi_{tj}(\cdot)$ usually also depends on exogenous or predetermined explanatory variables that are not made explicit in the notation. We require that $\sum_{j=0}^{J}\Pi_{tj}(\boldsymbol{\theta})=1$ for all $t=1,\ldots,n$ and for all admissible parameter vectors $\boldsymbol{\theta}$, in order that the set of $J+1$ outcomes should be exhaustive.

For each observation t, $t=1,\ldots,n$, define the $J+1$ indicator variables d_{tj} as $d_{tj}=I(y_t=j)$. Then the loglikelihood function of the discrete choice model is given by

$$\ell(\boldsymbol{y},\boldsymbol{\theta})=\sum_{t=1}^{n}\sum_{j=0}^{J}d_{tj}\log\Pi_{tj}(\boldsymbol{\theta}). \tag{11.41}$$

Just as for the loglikelihood functions (11.09) and (11.35), the contribution made by observation t is the logarithm of the probability that y_t should have taken on its observed value.

The DCAR has $n(J+1)$ "observations," $J+1$ for each real observation. For observation t, the $J+1$ components of the regressand, evaluated at $\boldsymbol{\theta}$, are given by $\Pi_{tj}^{-1/2}(\boldsymbol{\theta})\big(d_{tj}-\Pi_{tj}(\boldsymbol{\theta})\big)$, $j=0,\ldots,J$. The components of the regressor corresponding to parameter θ_i, $i=1,\ldots,k$, are given by $\Pi_{tj}^{-1/2}(\boldsymbol{\theta})\partial\Pi_{tj}(\boldsymbol{\theta})/\partial\theta_i$. Thus the DCAR may be written as

$$\Pi_{tj}^{-1/2}(\boldsymbol{\theta})\big(d_{tj}-\Pi_{tj}(\boldsymbol{\theta})\big)=\Pi_{tj}^{-1/2}(\boldsymbol{\theta})\boldsymbol{T}_{tj}(\boldsymbol{\theta})\boldsymbol{b}+\text{residual}, \tag{11.42}$$

for $t=1,\ldots,n$ and $j=0,\ldots,J$. Here $\boldsymbol{T}_{tj}(\boldsymbol{\theta})$ denotes the $1\times k$ vector of the partial derivatives of $\Pi_{tj}(\boldsymbol{\theta})$ with respect to the components of $\boldsymbol{\theta}$, and, as usual, $\boldsymbol{b}$ is a k-vector of artificial parameters. It is easy to see that the scalar product of the regressand and the regressor corresponding to θ_i is

$$\sum_{t=1}^{n}\sum_{j=0}^{J}\frac{\big(d_{tj}-\Pi_{tj}(\boldsymbol{\theta})\big)\partial\Pi_{tj}(\boldsymbol{\theta})/\partial\theta_i}{\Pi_{tj}(\boldsymbol{\theta})}. \tag{11.43}$$

The derivative of the loglikelihood function (11.41) with respect to θ_i is

$$\frac{\partial\ell(\boldsymbol{\theta})}{\partial\theta_i}=\sum_{t=1}^{n}\sum_{j=0}^{J}d_{tj}\frac{\partial\Pi_{tj}(\boldsymbol{\theta})/\partial\theta_i}{\Pi_{tj}(\boldsymbol{\theta})},$$

and we can see that this is equal to (11.43), because differentiating the identity $\sum_{j=0}^{J}\Pi_{tj}(\boldsymbol{\theta})=1$ with respect to θ_i shows that $\sum_{j=0}^{J}\partial\Pi_{tj}(\boldsymbol{\theta})/\partial\theta_i=0$.

It follows that the regressand is orthogonal to all the regressors when all the artificial variables are evaluated at the maximum likelihood estimates $\hat{\boldsymbol{\theta}}$.

In Exercises 11.18 and 11.19, readers are asked to show that regression (11.42), the DCAR, satisfies the other requirements for an artificial regression used for hypothesis testing, as set out in Exercise 8.20. See also Exercise 11.22, in which readers are asked to implement by artificial regression the test of the IIA property discussed at the end of the previous subsection.

As with binary response models, it is easy to bootstrap discrete choice models, because they are fully parametrically specified. For the model characterized by the loglikelihood function (11.41), an easy way to implement the bootstrap DGP is, first, to construct the cumulative probabilities $P_{tj}(\hat{\boldsymbol{\theta}}) \equiv \sum_{i=0}^{j} \Pi_{ti}(\hat{\boldsymbol{\theta}})$, for $j = 0, \ldots, J-1$, and then to draw a random number, u_t^* say for observation t, from the uniform distribution U(0, 1). The bootstrap dependent variable y_t^* is then set equal to

$$y_t^* = \sum_{j=0}^{J-1} I\big(u_t^* \geq P_{tj}(\hat{\boldsymbol{\theta}})\big).$$

All of the indicator functions in the above sum are zero if $u_t^* < P_{t0}(\hat{\boldsymbol{\theta}}) = \Pi_{t0}(\hat{\boldsymbol{\theta}})$, an event which occurs with probability $\Pi_{t0}(\hat{\boldsymbol{\theta}})$, as desired. Similarly, $y_t^* = j$ for $j = 1, \ldots, J$ if and only if $P_{t(j-1)}(\hat{\boldsymbol{\theta}}) \leq u_t^* < P_{tj}(\hat{\boldsymbol{\theta}})$, an event that occurs with probability $\Pi_{tj}(\hat{\boldsymbol{\theta}}) = P_{tj}(\hat{\boldsymbol{\theta}}) - P_{t(j-1)}(\hat{\boldsymbol{\theta}})$.

The Multinomial Probit Model

Another discrete choice model that can sometimes be used when the IIA property is unacceptable is the **multinomial probit model**. This model is theoretically attractive but computationally burdensome. The $J+1$ possible outcomes are generated by the latent variable model

$$y_{tj}^{\circ} = \boldsymbol{W}_{tj}\boldsymbol{\beta}^j + u_{tj}, \qquad \boldsymbol{u}_t \sim \mathrm{N}(\mathbf{0}, \boldsymbol{\Omega}), \tag{11.44}$$

where the y_{tj}° are not observed, and $\boldsymbol{u}_t$ is a $1 \times (J+1)$ vector with typical element u_{tj}. What we observe are the binary variables y_{tj}, which are assumed to be determined as follows:

$$\begin{aligned} y_{tj} &= 1 \text{ if } y_{tj}^{\circ} - y_{ti}^{\circ} \geq 0 \text{ for all } i = 0, \ldots, J, \\ y_{tj} &= 0 \text{ otherwise.} \end{aligned} \tag{11.45}$$

As with the multinomial logit model, separate coefficients cannot be identified for all $J+1$ outcomes if an explanatory variable is common to all of the index functions $\boldsymbol{W}_{tj}\boldsymbol{\beta}^j$. The solution to this problem is the same as before: We set the components of $\boldsymbol{\beta}^0$ equal to 0 for all such variables.

It is clear from (11.45) that the observed y_{tj} depend only on the differences $y^\circ_{tj} - y^\circ_{t0}$, $j = 1, \ldots, J$. Let z°_{tj} be equal to this difference. Then

$$\begin{aligned} y_{tj} &= 1 \text{ if } z^\circ_{tj} \geq z^\circ_{ti} \text{ for all } i = 1, \ldots, J, \text{ and } z^\circ_{tj} \geq 0, \\ y_{tj} &= 0 \text{ otherwise.} \end{aligned} \tag{11.46}$$

Thus the probabilities $\Pr(y_{tj} = 1)$ are completely determined by the joint distribution of the z°_{tj}. We write the covariance matrix of this distribution as $\boldsymbol{\Sigma}$, where $\boldsymbol{\Sigma}$ is a $J \times J$ symmetric positive definite matrix, uniquely determined by the $(J+1) \times (J+1)$ matrix $\boldsymbol{\Omega}$ of (11.44), although $\boldsymbol{\Omega}$ is not uniquely determined by $\boldsymbol{\Sigma}$. It follows that the matrix $\boldsymbol{\Omega}$ cannot be identified on the basis of the observed variables y_t alone.

In fact, even $\boldsymbol{\Sigma}$ is identified only up to scale. This can be seen by observing that, if all the z°_{tj} in (11.46) are multiplied by the same positive constant, the values of the y_{tj} remain unchanged. In practice, it is customary to set the first diagonal element of $\boldsymbol{\Sigma}$ equal to 1 in order to set the scale of $\boldsymbol{\Sigma}$. Once the scale is fixed, then the only other restriction on $\boldsymbol{\Sigma}$ is that it must be symmetric and positive definite. In particular, it may well have nonzero off-diagonal elements, and these give the multinomial probit model a flexibility that is not shared by the multinomial logit model. In consequence, the multinomial probit model does not have the IIA property.

The latent variable model (11.44) can be interpreted as a model determining the utility levels yielded by the different outcomes. Then the correlation between z°_{tj} and z°_{ti}, for $i \neq j$, might measure the extent to which a preference for flying over driving, say, is correlated with a preference for taking the train over driving. In this example of transportation mode choice, we are assuming that driving is outcome 0. It seems fair to say that, although these correlations are what provides multinomial probit with greater flexibility than multinomial logit, they are a little difficult to interpret directly.

Unfortunately, the multinomial probit model is not at all easy to estimate. The event $y_{tj} = 1$ is observed if and only if

$$y^\circ_{tj} - y^\circ_{ti} \geq 0 \text{ for all } i = 1, \ldots, J+1,$$

and the probability of this event is given by a J–dimensional integral. Therefore, in order to evaluate the loglikelihood function just once, the integral corresponding to whatever event occurred must be computed for every observation in the sample. This must generally be done a large number of times during the course of whatever nonlinear optimization procedure is used. Evaluating high-dimensional integrals of the normal distribution is analytically intractable. Consequently, except when J is very small, the multinomial probit model is usually estimated by simulation-based methods, including the method of simulated moments, which was discussed in Section 9.6. See Hajivassiliou and Ruud (1994) and Gouriéroux and Monfort (1996) for discussions of some of the methods that have been proposed.

The treatment of qualitative response models in this section has necessarily been incomplete. Detailed surveys of the older literature include Amemiya (1985, Chapter 9) and McFadden (1984). For a more up-to-date survey, but one that is relatively superficial, see Maddala and Flores-Lagunes (2001).

11.5 Models for Count Data

Many economic variables are nonnegative integers. Examples include the number of patents granted to a firm and the number of visits to the hospital by an individual, where each is measured over some period of time. Data of this type are called **event count data** or, simply, **count data**. In many cases, the count is 0 for a substantial fraction of the observations.

One might think of using an ordered discrete choice model like the ordered probit model to handle data of this type. However, this is usually not appropriate, because such a model requires the number of possible outcomes to be fixed and known. Instead, we need a model for which any nonnegative integer value is a valid, although perhaps very unlikely, value. One way to obtain such a model is to start from a distribution which has this property. The most popular distribution of this type is the **Poisson distribution**. If a discrete random variable Y follows the Poisson distribution, then

$$\Pr(Y = y) = \frac{e^{-\lambda}\lambda^y}{y!}, \quad y = 0, 1, 2, \ldots. \tag{11.47}$$

This distribution is characterized by a single parameter, λ. It can be shown that the probabilities (11.47) sum to 1 over $y = 0, 1, 2, \ldots$, and that the mean and the variance of a Poisson random variable are both equal to λ, which must therefore take on only positive values; see Exercise 11.23.

The Poisson Regression Model

The simplest model for count data is the **Poisson regression model**, which is obtained by replacing the parameter λ in (11.47) by a nonnegative function of regressors and parameters. The most popular choice for this function is the **exponential mean function**

$$\lambda_t(\boldsymbol{\beta}) \equiv \exp(\boldsymbol{X}_t\boldsymbol{\beta}), \tag{11.48}$$

which makes use of the linear index function $\boldsymbol{X}_t\boldsymbol{\beta}$. Other specifications for the index function, possibly nonlinear, can also be used. Because the linear index function in (11.48) is the argument of an exponential, the model specified by (11.48) is sometimes called **loglinear**, since the log of $\lambda_t(\boldsymbol{\beta})$ is linear in $\boldsymbol{\beta}$. For any valid choice of $\lambda_t(\boldsymbol{\beta})$, we obtain the Poisson regression model

$$\Pr(Y_t = y) = \frac{\exp\big(-\lambda_t(\boldsymbol{\beta})\big)\big(\lambda_t(\boldsymbol{\beta})\big)^y}{y!}, \quad y = 0, 1, 2, \ldots. \tag{11.49}$$

If the observed count value for observation t is y_t, then the contribution to the loglikelihood function is the logarithm of the right-hand side of (11.49), evaluated at $y = y_t$. Therefore, the entire loglikelihood function is

$$\ell(\boldsymbol{y}, \boldsymbol{\beta}) = \sum_{t=1}^{n} \big(-\exp(\boldsymbol{X}_t\boldsymbol{\beta}) + y_t\boldsymbol{X}_t\boldsymbol{\beta} - \log y_t!\big) \tag{11.50}$$

under the exponential mean specification (11.48).

Maximizing the function (11.50) is not difficult. The likelihood equations are

$$\frac{\partial \ell(\boldsymbol{y}, \boldsymbol{\beta})}{\partial \boldsymbol{\beta}} = \sum_{t=1}^{n} \big(y_t - \exp(\boldsymbol{X}_t\boldsymbol{\beta})\big)\boldsymbol{X}_t = \mathbf{0}, \tag{11.51}$$

and the Hessian matrix is

$$\boldsymbol{H}(\boldsymbol{\beta}) = -\sum_{t=1}^{n} \exp(\boldsymbol{X}_t\boldsymbol{\beta})\boldsymbol{X}_t^{\top}\boldsymbol{X}_t = -\boldsymbol{X}^{\top}\boldsymbol{\Upsilon}(\boldsymbol{\beta})\boldsymbol{X}, \tag{11.52}$$

where $\boldsymbol{\Upsilon}(\boldsymbol{\beta})$ is an $n \times n$ diagonal matrix with typical diagonal element equal to $\Upsilon_t(\boldsymbol{\beta}) \equiv \exp(\boldsymbol{X}_t\boldsymbol{\beta})$. Since $\boldsymbol{H}(\boldsymbol{\beta})$ is negative definite, optimization techniques based on Newton's Method generally work very well. Inferences may be based on the standard asymptotic result (10.41) that the asymptotic covariance matrix is equal to the inverse of the information matrix. This leads to the estimator

$$\widehat{\mathrm{Var}}(\hat{\boldsymbol{\beta}}) = (\boldsymbol{X}^{\top}\hat{\boldsymbol{\Upsilon}}\boldsymbol{X})^{-1}, \tag{11.53}$$

where $\hat{\boldsymbol{\Upsilon}} \equiv \boldsymbol{\Upsilon}(\hat{\boldsymbol{\beta}})$. This estimated covariance matrix looks very much like the one for weighted least-squares estimation. In fact, if we were to run the nonlinear regression

$$y_t = \exp(\boldsymbol{X}_t\boldsymbol{\beta}) + u_t \tag{11.54}$$

by weighted least squares, using weights $\Upsilon_t^{-1/2}(\boldsymbol{\beta}) = \exp(-\frac{1}{2}\boldsymbol{X}_t\boldsymbol{\beta})$, the first-order conditions, treating the weights as fixed, would be equations (11.51). Regression (11.54) is the analog for the Poisson regression model of regression (11.11) for the binary response model. Thus ML estimation of the Poisson regression model specified by (11.49), where $\lambda_t(\boldsymbol{\beta})$ is given by an exponential mean function, is seen to be equivalent to weighted NLS estimation of the nonlinear regression model (11.54).

The weighted NLS interpretation suggests that an artificial regression must be available. This is indeed the case. Just as the BRMR (11.20) is the GNR that corresponds to the weighted version of (11.11), the artificial regression for the Poisson regression model is the GNR that corresponds to the weighted version of (11.54), namely,

$$\exp(-\tfrac{1}{2}\boldsymbol{X}_t\boldsymbol{\beta})\big(y_t - \exp(\boldsymbol{X}_t\boldsymbol{\beta})\big) = \exp(\tfrac{1}{2}\boldsymbol{X}_t\boldsymbol{\beta})\boldsymbol{X}_t\boldsymbol{b} + \text{residual}. \tag{11.55}$$

Like the GNR and the BRMR, this regression may be used for a number of purposes, including estimating the covariance matrix of $\hat{\boldsymbol{\beta}}$. It is particularly useful for testing restrictions on $\boldsymbol{\beta}$ without having to estimate the model more than once; see Exercise 11.25.

Testing for Overdispersion in the Poisson Regression Model

Although its simplicity makes it attractive, the Poisson regression model is rarely entirely satisfactory. In practice, even though it may predict the mean event count accurately, it frequently tends to underpredict the frequency of zeros and large counts, because the variance of the actual data is larger than the variance predicted by the Poisson model. This failure of the model is called **overdispersion**. Before accepting a Poisson regression model, even tentatively, it is highly advisable to test it for overdispersion.

Several tests for overdispersion have been proposed. The simplest of these are based on the artificial OPG regression that we introduced in Section 10.5 for models estimated by maximum likelihood. The regressand of the OPG regression is equal to 1 for each observation, and the regressors are the partial derivatives of the loglikelihood contribution with respect to the parameters. Thus observation t of the OPG regression based on the loglikelihood function (11.50) can be written as

$$1 = \big(y_t - \exp(\boldsymbol{X}_t\boldsymbol{\beta})\big)\boldsymbol{X}_t\boldsymbol{b} + \text{residual}. \tag{11.56}$$

When the regressors in (11.56) are evaluated at the ML estimates $\hat{\boldsymbol{\beta}}$, they are orthogonal to the regressand.

If the variance of y_t is indeed equal to $\exp(\boldsymbol{X}_t\boldsymbol{\beta})$, its mean according to the loglinear Poisson regression model, then the quantity

$$z_t(\boldsymbol{\beta}) \equiv \big(y_t - \exp(\boldsymbol{X}_t\boldsymbol{\beta})\big)^2 - y_t \tag{11.57}$$

has expectation 0.[4] We can test whether the expectation is really zero by running the OPG regression (11.56), adding an extra regressor with typical element $z_t(\hat{\boldsymbol{\beta}})$. Both n minus the sum of squared residuals from this augmented OPG regression and the t statistic associated with the extra regressor provide asymptotically valid test statistics; the former is asymptotically distributed as $\chi^2(1)$ under the null hypothesis, while the latter is asymptotically distributed as $\mathrm{N}(0,1)$.

Testing can be made a little simpler if we note that the extra regressor (11.57) is uncorrelated with the regressors in (11.56) under the null. This is a simple

[4] The quantity $\big(y_t - \exp(\boldsymbol{X}_t\boldsymbol{\beta})\big)^2 - \exp(\boldsymbol{X}_t\boldsymbol{\beta})$ also has expectation 0 and could be used in place of (11.57) in an OPG test regression. However, the simplifications that are discussed below would not be possible if the test regressor were redefined in this way.

consequence of the fact, which readers are asked to demonstrate in Exercise 11.24, that the third central moment of the Poisson distribution with parameter λ is equal to λ. We may write the testing OPG regression as

$$\boldsymbol{\iota} = \hat{\boldsymbol{G}}\boldsymbol{b} + c\hat{\boldsymbol{z}} + \text{residuals}, \tag{11.58}$$

where $\boldsymbol{\iota}$ is an n-vector of 1s, the matrix $\hat{\boldsymbol{G}} \equiv \boldsymbol{G}(\hat{\boldsymbol{\beta}})$ contains the regressors of (11.56) evaluated at $\hat{\boldsymbol{\beta}}$, and $\hat{\boldsymbol{z}} \equiv \boldsymbol{z}(\hat{\boldsymbol{\beta}})$ is the extra regressor, with typical element $z_t(\hat{\boldsymbol{\beta}})$. By the FWL Theorem, a test of the hypothesis that $c = 0$ can equally well be performed by running the FWL regression

$$\hat{\boldsymbol{M}}_{\boldsymbol{G}}\boldsymbol{\iota} = c\hat{\boldsymbol{M}}_{\boldsymbol{G}}\hat{\boldsymbol{z}} + \text{residuals}, \tag{11.59}$$

where $\hat{\boldsymbol{M}}_{\boldsymbol{G}}$ is the orthogonal projection matrix that projects on to the orthogonal complement of the span of the columns of $\hat{\boldsymbol{G}}$. But, since those columns are orthogonal to $\boldsymbol{\iota}$, the regressand of (11.59) is just $\boldsymbol{\iota}$. In addition, because $\boldsymbol{z}(\boldsymbol{\beta})$ is uncorrelated with the columns of $\boldsymbol{G}(\boldsymbol{\beta})$, the regressor is asymptotically equal to $\hat{\boldsymbol{z}}$. Therefore, regressions (11.58) and (11.59) are asymptotically equivalent to a regression of $\boldsymbol{\iota}$ on $\hat{\boldsymbol{z}}$. Once again, either the explained sum of squares or the t statistic for $c = 0$ yields an asymptotically valid test.

In Exercise 4.9, we saw that every t statistic is proportional to the cotangent of a certain angle, namely, the angle between the regressand and the regressor of the FWL regression that can be used to compute the statistic. Since this angle does not depend on which vector is the regressor and which vector is the regressand, this result implies that the t statistic from regressing $\boldsymbol{\iota}$ on $\hat{\boldsymbol{z}}$ is identical to the t statistic from regressing $\hat{\boldsymbol{z}}$ on $\boldsymbol{\iota}$. If we run the regression in this direction, however, we do not obtain the same ESS. Nevertheless, the ESS can be used as a valid statistic if the variables are scaled by estimates of the standard deviations of the elements of $\boldsymbol{z}(\boldsymbol{\beta})$. This rescaling yields the artificial regression that is most commonly used to test for overdispersion in the Poisson regression model.

Observe that, if Y is a random variable which follows the Poisson distribution with parameter λ, then

$$\begin{aligned}
\mathrm{E}\Big(\big((Y-\lambda)^2 - Y\big)^2\Big) &= \mathrm{E}\Big(\big((Y-\lambda)^2 - (Y-\lambda) - \lambda\big)^2\Big) \\
&= \mathrm{E}\big((Y-\lambda)^4\big) + \mathrm{E}\big((Y-\lambda)^2\big) + \lambda^2 \\
&\quad - 2\mathrm{E}\big((Y-\lambda)^3\big) - 2\lambda\mathrm{E}\big((Y-\lambda)^2\big) - 2\lambda\mathrm{E}(Y-\lambda) \\
&= \lambda + 3\lambda^2 + \lambda + \lambda^2 - 2\lambda - 2\lambda^2 = 2\lambda^2,
\end{aligned}$$

where we have used the result of Exercise 11.24 for both the third and fourth central moments of the Poisson distribution. A suitable testing regression with scaled variables can therefore be written as

$$\frac{1}{\sqrt{2}}\exp(-\boldsymbol{X}_t\hat{\boldsymbol{\beta}})z_t(\hat{\boldsymbol{\beta}}) = \frac{1}{\sqrt{2}}\exp(-\boldsymbol{X}_t\hat{\boldsymbol{\beta}})c + \text{residual}, \tag{11.60}$$

and both the t statistic and the explained sum of squares provide asymptotically valid test statistics.

The tests based on regression (11.60) were originally proposed by Cameron and Trivedi (1990). They also suggest tests based on regressions like (11.60), but with the regressor of (11.60) multiplied by various functions of the fitted values $\exp(\boldsymbol{X}_t\hat{\boldsymbol{\beta}})$. Common choices are the fitted values themselves or their squares. Cameron and Trivedi show that a test in which the regressor is multiplied by the function $g(\exp(\boldsymbol{X}_t\hat{\boldsymbol{\beta}}))$ of the fitted value has greatest power against DGPs for which the true variance of y_t is of the form $\exp(\boldsymbol{X}_t\boldsymbol{\beta}) + \alpha g(\exp(\boldsymbol{X}_t\boldsymbol{\beta}))$ for some scalar α. Tests with more than one degree of freedom can be performed by using several regressors constructed in this way. In all cases, an appropriate test statistic is the ESS. It is asymptotically distributed under the null as $\chi^2(r)$, where r is the number of regressors.

Other tests for overdispersion have been proposed by Cameron and Trivedi (1986), Lee (1986), and Mullahy (1997). Note that the finite-sample distributions of all these test statistics may differ substantially from their asymptotic ones. Better results may well be obtained by using bootstrap P values. A parametric bootstrap DGP is appropriate. It can easily be implemented by using a procedure for obtaining drawings from the Poisson distribution similar to the one we discussed for discrete choice models in the previous section.

Consequences of Overdispersion in the Poisson Regression Model

Finding evidence of overdispersion does not necessarily mean that we must abandon the Poisson regression model. Since the model is equivalent to weighted NLS, and weighted NLS is consistent even when the weights are incorrect, the ML estimator $\hat{\boldsymbol{\beta}}$ must be consistent whenever the exponential mean function $\lambda_t(\boldsymbol{\beta})$ is correctly specified. In this situation, $\hat{\boldsymbol{\beta}}$ is actually a quasi-ML estimator, or QMLE; see Section 10.4. However, as is generally the case for quasi-ML estimators, the covariance matrix estimator (11.53) is not valid if the entire model is not specified correctly.

To find the asymptotic covariance matrix of $\hat{\boldsymbol{\beta}}$ when the model is not correctly specified, we may use the result (10.40), which is true for every quasi-ML estimator. If we replace the generic parameter vector $\boldsymbol{\theta}$ of that equation by $\boldsymbol{\beta}$, we obtain

$$\operatorname{Var}\big(\operatorname*{plim}_{n\to\infty} n^{1/2}(\hat{\boldsymbol{\beta}} - \boldsymbol{\beta}_0)\big) = \mathcal{H}^{-1}(\boldsymbol{\beta}_0)\mathcal{I}(\boldsymbol{\beta}_0)\mathcal{H}^{-1}(\boldsymbol{\beta}_0). \tag{11.61}$$

For the Poisson regression model, we see from (11.52) that

$$\mathcal{H}(\boldsymbol{\beta}_0) = -\operatorname*{plim}_{n\to\infty}\frac{1}{n}\sum_{t=1}^{n}\exp(\boldsymbol{X}_t\boldsymbol{\beta}_0)\boldsymbol{X}_t^{\top}\boldsymbol{X}_t = -\operatorname*{plim}_{n\to\infty}\frac{1}{n}\boldsymbol{X}^{\top}\boldsymbol{\Upsilon}(\boldsymbol{\beta}_0)\boldsymbol{X}. \tag{11.62}$$

From the definitions (10.31) and (10.32), and from the expression given in (11.51) for the gradient of the loglikelihood, it follows that the asymptotic information matrix is

$$\mathcal{I}(\boldsymbol{\beta}_0) = \operatorname*{plim}_{n\to\infty} \frac{1}{n}\sum_{t=1}^{n} \omega_t^2(\boldsymbol{\beta}_0)\boldsymbol{X}_t^\top \boldsymbol{X}_t = \operatorname*{plim}_{n\to\infty} \frac{1}{n}\boldsymbol{X}^\top \boldsymbol{\Omega}(\boldsymbol{\beta}_0)\boldsymbol{X}, \tag{11.63}$$

where $\omega_t^2(\boldsymbol{\beta}_0) \equiv \mathrm{E}\big(y_t - \exp(\boldsymbol{X}_t\boldsymbol{\beta}_0)\big)^2$ is the conditional variance of y_t, and $\boldsymbol{\Omega}(\boldsymbol{\beta}_0)$ is the diagonal matrix with typical diagonal element $\omega_t^2(\boldsymbol{\beta}_0)$.

When the model is correctly specified, the conditional variance ω_t^2 is equal to the conditional mean $\exp(\boldsymbol{X}_t\boldsymbol{\beta}_0)$, and the asymptotic covariance matrix (11.61) simplifies to $\mathcal{I}^{-1}(\boldsymbol{\beta}_0) = -\mathcal{H}^{-1}(\boldsymbol{\beta}_0)$. When the model is not correctly specified, however, this simplification does not occur.

One quite plausible specification for the conditional variance of y_t is

$$\omega_t^2(\boldsymbol{\beta}) = \gamma^2\exp(\boldsymbol{X}_t\boldsymbol{\beta}), \tag{11.64}$$

in which the conditional variance is proportional to the conditional mean. Under this specification, the asymptotic covariance matrix (11.61) simplifies to γ^2 times $-\mathcal{H}^{-1}(\boldsymbol{\beta}_0)$. Since this is not a sandwich covariance matrix, it is clear that $\hat{\boldsymbol{\beta}}$ remains asymptotically efficient in this special case. An easy way to estimate this covariance matrix is simply to run the artificial regression (11.55), with $\boldsymbol{\beta} = \hat{\boldsymbol{\beta}}$. Because s^2 provides a consistent estimator of γ^2, the OLS covariance matrix from this regression is asymptotically valid; see Exercise 11.26.

Even if we do not specify the conditional variance of y_t, we can obtain an asymptotically valid covariance matrix whenever the matrices (11.62) and (11.63) can be estimated consistently. To do this, we need to use a sandwich estimator similar to the HCCME discussed in Section 5.5. We can estimate (11.62) consistently if we replace $\boldsymbol{\beta}_0$ by $\hat{\boldsymbol{\beta}}$. In order to estimate (11.63) consistently, we replace the conditional variance $\omega_t^2(\boldsymbol{\beta}_0)$ by the squared residual $(y_t - \exp(\boldsymbol{X}_t\hat{\boldsymbol{\beta}}))^2$. Thus a valid estimator of $\mathrm{Var}(\hat{\boldsymbol{\beta}})$ when only the conditional mean part of the Poisson regression model is correctly specified is

$$\widehat{\mathrm{Var}}_{\mathrm{h}}(\hat{\boldsymbol{\beta}}) = (\boldsymbol{X}^\top\hat{\boldsymbol{\Upsilon}}\boldsymbol{X})^{-1}\boldsymbol{X}^\top\hat{\boldsymbol{\Omega}}\boldsymbol{X}(\boldsymbol{X}^\top\hat{\boldsymbol{\Upsilon}}\boldsymbol{X})^{-1}, \tag{11.65}$$

where $\hat{\boldsymbol{\Omega}}$ is the $n \times n$ diagonal matrix with diagonal element t given by $(y_t - \exp(\boldsymbol{X}_t\hat{\boldsymbol{\beta}}))^2$. As in Section 5.5, the "h" subscript indicates that the matrix (11.65) is valid in the presence of heteroskedasticity of unknown form. Given the substantial risk of misspecification, it is strongly recommended to use the sandwich estimator (11.65) rather than (11.53) in practical applications. Notice that the sandwich estimator is very easy to calculate without any special software. If we run the artificial regression (11.55) and ask the regression package to compute an HCCME, it gives us either (11.65) or something that is asymptotically equal to (11.65); see Exercise 11.27.

Of course, except in the special case of (11.64), the ML estimator $\hat{\boldsymbol{\beta}}$ is not asymptotically efficient when the Poisson regression model is not correctly specified. The fact that the covariance matrix has the sandwich form makes this clear. Moreover, $\hat{\boldsymbol{\beta}}$ is not even consistent if the conditional mean function $\exp(\boldsymbol{X}_t\boldsymbol{\beta})$ is not correctly specified. Many other models for count data have been suggested, and one or more of them may well fit better than the Poisson regression model does. Wooldridge (1999) and Cameron and Trivedi (2001) provide more advanced introductions to the topic of count data, and Cameron and Trivedi (1998) provides a detailed treatment of a large number of different models for data of this type.

11.6 Models for Censored and Truncated Data

Continuous dependent variables can sometimes take only a limited range of values. This may happen because they have been censored or truncated in some way. These two terms are easily confused. A sample is said to be **truncated** if some observations have been systematically excluded from the sample. For example, a sample of households with incomes under \$200,000 explicitly excludes households with incomes over that level. It is not a random sample of all households. If the dependent variable is income, or something correlated with income, results using the truncated sample could potentially be quite misleading.

On the other hand, a sample has been **censored** if no observations have been systematically excluded, but some of the information contained in them has been suppressed. Think of a "censor" who reads people's mail and blacks out certain parts of it. The recipients still get their mail, but parts of it are unreadable. To continue the previous example, suppose that households with all income levels are included in the sample, but for those with incomes in excess of \$200,000, the amount reported is always exactly \$200,000. This sort of censoring is often done in practice, presumably to protect the privacy of high-income respondents. In this case, the censored sample is still a random sample of all households, but the values reported for high-income households are not the true values.

Any dependent variable that has been either censored or truncated is said to be a **limited dependent variable**. Special methods are needed to deal with such variables because, if we simply use least squares, the consequences of truncation and censoring can be severe. Consider the regression model

$$y_t^\circ = \beta_1 + \beta_2 x_t + u_t, \quad u_t \sim \text{NID}(0, \sigma^2), \tag{11.66}$$

where y_t° is a latent variable. We actually observe y_t, which differs from y_t° because it is either truncated or censored. For simplicity, suppose that censorship or truncation occurs whenever y_t° is less than 0. Clearly, the larger is the error term u_t, the larger is y_t°, and thus the greater must be the probability that $y_t^\circ \geq 0$. This probability must also depend on x_t. Thus, for the sample

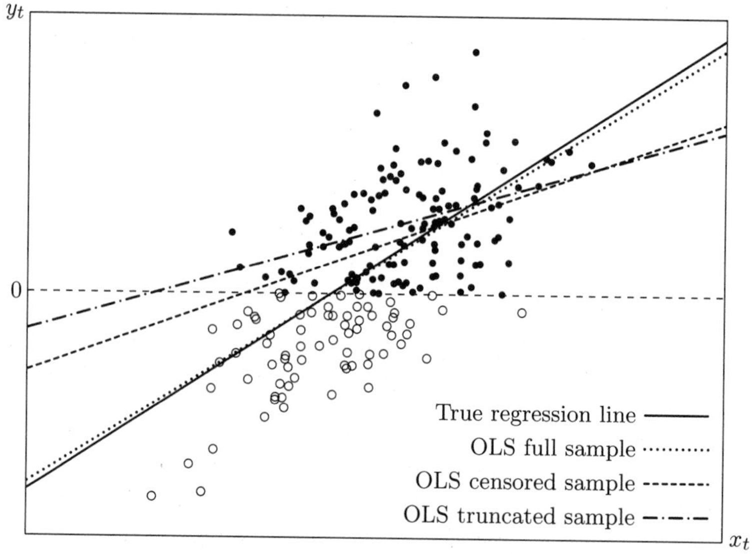

Figure 11.3 Effects of censoring and truncation

we actually observe, u_t does not have conditional mean 0 and is not uncorrelated with x_t. Since the error terms no longer satisfy these key assumptions, it is not surprising that OLS estimation using truncated or censored samples yields estimators that are biased and inconsistent.

The consequences of censoring and truncation are illustrated in Figure 11.3. The figure shows 200 (x_t, y_t°) pairs generated from the model (11.66). The 71 observations with $y_t^\circ < 0$ are shown as circles, and the 129 observations with $y_t = y_t^\circ \geq 0$ are shown as black dots. The solid line is the true regression function, and the nearby dotted line is the regression function obtained by OLS estimation using all the observations. When the data are truncated, the observations with $y_t^\circ < 0$ are discarded. OLS estimation using this truncated sample yields the regression line shown in dots and dashes. When the data are censored, these 71 observations are retained, but y_t is set equal to 0 for all of them. OLS estimation using this censored sample yields the dashed regression line. Neither of these regression lines is at all close to the true one.

In this example, the consequences of either censoring or truncation are quite severe. Just how severe they are in any particular case depends on σ^2, the variance of the error terms in the model (11.66), and on the extent of the censoring or truncation. If σ^2 is very small relative to the variation in the fitted values, so is the bias induced by limiting the dependent variable. This bias is also small if few observations are censored or truncated. Conversely, when σ^2 is large and many observations are censored or truncated, the bias can be extremely large.

Truncated Regression Models

It is quite simple to estimate a truncated regression model by maximum likelihood if the distribution of the error terms in the latent variable model is assumed to be known. By far the most common assumption is that the error terms are normally, independently, and identically distributed, as in (11.66). We restrict our attention to this special case.

If the regression function for the latent variable model is $\boldsymbol{X}_t\boldsymbol{\beta}$, the probability that y_t° is included in the sample is

$$\begin{aligned}\Pr(y_t^\circ \geq 0) &= \Pr(\boldsymbol{X}_t\boldsymbol{\beta} + u_t \geq 0)\\ &= 1 - \Pr(u_t < -\boldsymbol{X}_t\boldsymbol{\beta}) = 1 - \Pr(u_t/\sigma < -\boldsymbol{X}_t\boldsymbol{\beta}/\sigma)\\ &= 1 - \Phi(-\boldsymbol{X}_t\boldsymbol{\beta}/\sigma) = \Phi(\boldsymbol{X}_t\boldsymbol{\beta}/\sigma).\end{aligned}$$

When $y_t^\circ \geq 0$ and y_t is observed, the density of y_t is proportional to the density of y_t°. Otherwise, the density of y_t is 0. The factor of proportionality, which is needed to ensure that the density of y_t integrates to unity, is the inverse of the probability that $y_t^\circ \geq 0$. Therefore, the density of y_t can be written as

$$\frac{\sigma^{-1}\phi\big((y_t - \boldsymbol{X}_t\boldsymbol{\beta})/\sigma\big)}{\Phi(\boldsymbol{X}_t\boldsymbol{\beta}/\sigma)}.$$

This implies that the loglikelihood function, which is the sum over all t of the log of the density of y_t, is

$$\begin{aligned}\ell(\boldsymbol{y}, \boldsymbol{\beta}, \sigma) = &-\tfrac{n}{2}\log(2\pi) - n\log(\sigma) - \frac{1}{2\sigma^2}\sum_{t=1}^{n}(y_t - \boldsymbol{X}_t\boldsymbol{\beta})^2\\ &-\sum_{t=1}^{n}\log\Phi(\boldsymbol{X}_t\boldsymbol{\beta}/\sigma).\end{aligned} \tag{11.67}$$

Maximization of expression (11.67) is generally not difficult. Even though the loglikelihood function is not globally concave, there is a unique MLE; see Orme and Ruud (2002).

The first three terms in expression (11.67) comprise the loglikelihood function that corresponds to OLS regression; see equation (10.10). The last term is minus the summation over all t of the logarithms of the probabilities that an observation with regression function $\boldsymbol{X}_t\boldsymbol{\beta}$ belongs to the sample. Since these probabilities must be less than 1, this term must always be positive. It can be made larger by making the probabilities smaller. Thus the maximization algorithm chooses the parameters in such a way that these probabilities are smaller than they would be for the OLS estimates. The presence of this fourth term therefore causes the ML estimates of $\boldsymbol{\beta}$ and σ to differ, often substantially, from their least-squares counterparts, and it ensures that the ML estimates are consistent.

It is not difficult to modify this model to allow for other forms of truncation. The sample can be truncated from above, from below, or from both above and below. The truncation points must be known, but they can be fixed or they can vary across observations. See Exercises 11.29 and 11.30.

Censored Regression Models

The most popular model for censored data is the **tobit model**, which was first suggested in Tobin (1958), which is quite a famous paper. The simplest version of the tobit model is

$$\begin{aligned} y_t^\circ &= \boldsymbol{X}_t\boldsymbol{\beta} + u_t, \quad u_t \sim \text{NID}(0, \sigma^2), \\ y_t &= y_t^\circ \text{ if } y_t^\circ > 0; \quad y_t = 0 \text{ otherwise.} \end{aligned}$$

Here y_t° is a latent variable that is observed whenever it is positive. However, when the latent variable is negative, the observation is censored, and we simply observe $y_t = 0$. The tobit model can readily be modified to allow for censoring from above instead of from below or for censoring from both above and below. It can also be modified to allow the point at which the censoring occurs to vary across observations in a deterministic way; see Exercise 11.31.

The loglikelihood function for the tobit model is a little unusual, but it is not difficult to derive. First, it is easy to see that

$$\begin{aligned} \Pr(y_t = 0) &= \Pr(y_t^\circ \le 0) = \Pr(\boldsymbol{X}_t\boldsymbol{\beta} + u_t \le 0) \\ &= \Pr\Big(\frac{u_t}{\sigma} \le \frac{-\boldsymbol{X}_t\boldsymbol{\beta}}{\sigma}\Big) = \Phi(-\boldsymbol{X}_t\boldsymbol{\beta}/\sigma). \end{aligned}$$

Therefore, since there is a positive probability that $y_t = 0$, the contribution to the loglikelihood function made by observations with $y_t = 0$ is not the log of the density, but the log of that positive probability, namely,

$$\ell_t(y_t, \boldsymbol{\beta}, \sigma) = \log \Phi(-\boldsymbol{X}_t\boldsymbol{\beta}/\sigma). \tag{11.68}$$

If y_t is positive, the density of y_t exists, and the contribution to the loglikelihood is its logarithm,

$$\log\Big(\frac{1}{\sigma}\phi\big((y_t - \boldsymbol{X}_t\boldsymbol{\beta})/\sigma\big)\Big), \tag{11.69}$$

which is the contribution to the loglikelihood function for an observation in a classical normal linear regression model without any censoring.

Combining expression (11.68), the contribution for the censored observations, with expression (11.69), the contribution for the uncensored ones, we find that the loglikelihood function for the tobit model is

$$\sum_{y_t=0} \log \Phi(-\boldsymbol{X}_t\boldsymbol{\beta}/\sigma) + \sum_{y_t>0} \log\Big(\frac{1}{\sigma}\phi\big((y_t - \boldsymbol{X}_t\boldsymbol{\beta})/\sigma\big)\Big). \tag{11.70}$$

This loglikelihood function is rather curious. The first term is the sum of the logs of probabilities, for the censored observations, while the second is the sum of the logs of densities, for the uncensored observations. This reflects the fact that the dependent variable in a tobit model has a distribution that is a mixture of discrete and continuous random variables. This fact does not, however, prevent the ML estimator for the tobit model from having the usual properties of consistency and asymptotic normality, as was shown explicitly by Amemiya (1973c).

It is generally somewhat easier to maximize the loglikelihood function (11.70) if the tobit model is reparametrized. The new parameters are $\gamma \equiv \boldsymbol{\beta}/\sigma$ and $h \equiv 1/\sigma$. Since the loglikelihood function can be shown to be globally concave in the latter parametrization (Olsen, 1978), there must be a unique maximum no matter which parametrization is used. Even without any reparametrization, it is generally not at all difficult to maximize (11.70) by using a quasi-Newton algorithm.

The $(k+1) \times (k+1)$ covariance matrix of the ML estimates may, as usual, be estimated in several ways. Analytic expressions for the information matrix exist (Amemiya, 1973c), and at least two artificial regressions are available. One of these is the OPG regression that we discussed in Section 10.5, and the other is a double-length regression proposed by Orme (1995). The latter is substantially more complicated than the former, but it seems to work very much better. Since the tobit model is fully specified, it is straightforward to employ the parametric bootstrap. Simulation results in Davidson and MacKinnon (1999a) suggest that inferences based on it can be much more reliable than ones based only on asymptotic theory.

Testing the Tobit Model

There is an interesting relationship among the tobit, truncated regression, and probit models. If we both add and subtract the term $\sum_{y_t>0} \log\big(\Phi(\boldsymbol{X}_t\boldsymbol{\beta}/\sigma)\big)$ from the tobit loglikelihood function (11.70), the latter becomes

$$\begin{aligned}&\sum_{y_t>0} \log\Big(\frac{1}{\sigma}\phi\big((y_t - \boldsymbol{X}_t\boldsymbol{\beta})/\sigma\big)\Big) - \sum_{y_t>0} \log \Phi(\boldsymbol{X}_t\boldsymbol{\beta}/\sigma)\\ &+ \sum_{y_t=0} \log \Phi(-\boldsymbol{X}_t\boldsymbol{\beta}/\sigma) + \sum_{y_t>0} \log \Phi(\boldsymbol{X}_t\boldsymbol{\beta}/\sigma).\end{aligned} \tag{11.71}$$

The first line of (11.71) is the loglikelihood function for a truncated regression model estimated over all the observations for which $y_t > 0$; compare (11.67). The second line is the loglikelihood function for a probit model with index function $\boldsymbol{X}_t\boldsymbol{\beta}/\sigma$; compare (11.09). Of course, if all we had was the second line here, we could not identify $\boldsymbol{\beta}$ and σ separately, but since we also have the first line, that is not a problem.

Writing the tobit loglikelihood function in the form of (11.71) makes it clear that this model is really a probit model combined with a truncated regression model, with the coefficient vectors in the two models restricted to be proportional to each other. This restriction can easily be tested by means of an LR test with k degrees of freedom. If this test leads to a rejection of the null hypothesis, then we probably should not be using a tobit model.

Of course, like all econometric models, the tobit model can and should be tested for a variety of types of possible misspecification. A large number of tests can be based on the OPG regression and on the double-length regression of Orme (1995). Tests based on the OPG regression are discussed by Pagan and Vella (1989) and Smith (1989). See also Chesher and Irish (1987).

11.7 Sample Selectivity

In the previous section, we considered samples truncated on the basis of the value of the dependent variable. Many samples are truncated on the basis of another variable that is correlated with the dependent variable. For example, people may choose to enter the labor force if their market wage exceeds their reservation wage and choose to stay out of it otherwise. Then a sample of people who are in the labor force must exclude those whose reservation wage exceeds their market wage. If the dependent variable, whatever it may be, is correlated with the difference between reservation and market wages, least squares yields inconsistent estimates. In this case, the sample is said to have been **selected** on the basis of this difference. The consequences of this type of sample selection are often said to be due to **sample selectivity**.

Let us consider a simple model that involves sample selectivity. Suppose that y_t° and z_t° are two latent variables, generated by the bivariate process

$$\begin{bmatrix} y_t^\circ \\ z_t^\circ \end{bmatrix} = \begin{bmatrix} \boldsymbol{X}_t\boldsymbol{\beta} \\ \boldsymbol{W}_t\boldsymbol{\gamma} \end{bmatrix} + \begin{bmatrix} u_t \\ v_t \end{bmatrix}, \quad \begin{bmatrix} u_t \\ v_t \end{bmatrix} \sim \text{NID}\left(\boldsymbol{0}, \begin{bmatrix} \sigma^2 & \rho\sigma \\ \rho\sigma & 1 \end{bmatrix}\right), \tag{11.72}$$

where $\boldsymbol{X}_t$ and $\boldsymbol{W}_t$ are vectors of observations on exogenous or predetermined variables, $\boldsymbol{\beta}$ and $\boldsymbol{\gamma}$ are unknown parameter vectors, σ is the standard deviation of u_t, and ρ is the correlation between u_t and v_t. The restriction that the variance of v_t is equal to 1 is imposed because only the sign of z_t° is observed. In fact, the variables that are actually observed are y_t and z_t, and they are related to y_t° and z_t° as follows:

$$\begin{aligned} &y_t = y_t^\circ \;\text{ if }\; z_t^\circ > 0; \;\; y_t \;\text{ unobserved otherwise;} \\ &z_t = 1 \;\text{ if }\; z_t^\circ > 0; \;\; z_t = 0 \;\text{ otherwise.} \end{aligned} \tag{11.73}$$

Thus there are two types of observations, those for which we observe $y_t = y_t^\circ$ and $z_t = 1$, along with both $\boldsymbol{X}_t$ and $\boldsymbol{W}_t$, and those for which we observe only $z_t = 0$ and $\boldsymbol{W}_t$.

Each observation contributes a factor to the likelihood function for this model that can be written as

$$I(z_t = 0)\Pr(z_t = 0) + I(z_t = 1)\Pr(z_t = 1) f(y_t^\circ \,|\, z_t = 1),$$

where $f(y_t^\circ \,|\, z_t = 1)$ denotes the density of y_t° conditional on $z_t = 1$. This is the appropriate way to specify the likelihood because, if we integrate with respect to y_t° and sum over the two possible values of z_t, the result is 1. Note also that the value of y_t° is needed only if it is observed, that is, if $z_t = 1$. The loglikelihood function is

$$\sum_{z_t=0} \log \Pr(z_t = 0) + \sum_{z_t=1} \log\bigl(\Pr(z_t = 1) f(y_t^\circ \,|\, z_t = 1)\bigr). \tag{11.74}$$

The first term of (11.74), which comes from the observations with $z_t = 0$, is exactly the same as the corresponding term in a probit model. The second term comes from the observations with $z_t = 1$. By using the fact that we can factor a joint density any way we please, it can also be written as

$$\sum_{z_t=1} \log\bigl(\Pr(z_t = 1 \,|\, y_t^\circ) f(y_t^\circ)\bigr),$$

where $f(y_t^\circ)$ is the density of y_t° conditional on predetermined or exogenous variables, which is just a normal density with mean $\boldsymbol{X}_t\boldsymbol{\beta}$ and variance σ^2.

In order to write out the loglikelihood function (11.74) explicitly, we must calculate $\Pr(z_t = 1 \,|\, y_t^\circ)$. Since u_t and v_t are bivariate normal, we can write $v_t = \rho u_t/\sigma + \varepsilon_t$, where ε_t is a normally distributed random variable with mean 0 and variance $1 - \rho^2$. Thus

$$z_t^\circ = \boldsymbol{W}_t\boldsymbol{\gamma} + \rho(y_t^\circ - \boldsymbol{X}_t\boldsymbol{\beta})/\sigma + \varepsilon_t, \quad \varepsilon_t \sim \mathrm{NID}(0, 1 - \rho^2).$$

Because $y_t = y_t^\circ$ when $z_t = 1$, it follows that

$$\Pr(z_t = 1 \,|\, y_t^\circ) = \Phi\biggl(\frac{\boldsymbol{W}_t\boldsymbol{\gamma} + \rho(y_t - \boldsymbol{X}_t\boldsymbol{\beta})/\sigma}{(1 - \rho^2)^{1/2}}\biggr).$$

Thus the loglikelihood function (11.74) becomes

$$\begin{aligned} &\sum_{z_t=0} \log \Phi(-\boldsymbol{W}_t\boldsymbol{\gamma}) + \sum_{z_t=1} \log\Bigl(\frac{1}{\sigma}\phi\bigl((y_t - \boldsymbol{X}_t\boldsymbol{\beta})/\sigma\bigr)\Bigr) \\ &+ \sum_{z_t=1} \log \Phi\biggl(\frac{\boldsymbol{W}_t\boldsymbol{\gamma} + \rho(y_t - \boldsymbol{X}_t\boldsymbol{\beta})/\sigma}{(1 - \rho^2)^{1/2}}\biggr). \end{aligned} \tag{11.75}$$

The first term looks like the corresponding term for a standard probit model in which z_t is explained by $\boldsymbol{W}_t$, the second term looks like the loglikelihood function for a linear regression of y_t on $\boldsymbol{X}_t$, with normal errors, and the third term is one that we have not seen before. If $\rho = 0$, this term would collapse to the term corresponding to observations with $z_t = 1$ in the probit model for z_t, and we could estimate the probit model and the regression model separately. In general, however, this term forces us to estimate both equations together by making the probability that $z_t = 1$ depend on $y_t - \boldsymbol{X}_t\boldsymbol{\beta}$.

Heckman's Two-Step Method

From the point of view of asymptotic efficiency, the best way to estimate the model characterized by (11.72) and (11.73) is simply to maximize the loglikelihood function (11.75). With modern computing equipment and appropriate software, this is not unreasonably difficult to do, although numerical problems can be encountered when ρ approaches ± 1. Instead of ML estimation, however, it is popular to use a computationally simpler technique, which is known as **Heckman's two-step method**; see Heckman (1976, 1979). Although we do not recommend that practitioners rely solely on this method, it can be useful for preliminary work, and it yields insights into the nature of sample selectivity. In addition, it provides a good starting point for the nonlinear algorithm used to obtain the MLE.

Heckman's two-step method is based on the fact that the first equation of (11.72), for observations where y_t is observed, can be rewritten as

$$y_t = \boldsymbol{X}_t\boldsymbol{\beta} + \rho\sigma v_t + e_t. \tag{11.76}$$

Here the error term u_t is divided into two parts, one perfectly correlated with v_t, the error term in the equation for the latent variable z_t°, and one independent of v_t. The idea is to replace the unobserved error term v_t in (11.76) by its mean conditional on $z_t = 1$ and on the explanatory variables $\boldsymbol{W}_t$. This conditional mean is

$$\mathrm{E}(v_t \,|\, z_t = 1, \boldsymbol{W}_t) = \mathrm{E}(v_t \,|\, v_t > -\boldsymbol{W}_t\boldsymbol{\gamma}, \boldsymbol{W}_t) = \frac{\phi(\boldsymbol{W}_t\boldsymbol{\gamma})}{\Phi(\boldsymbol{W}_t\boldsymbol{\gamma})}, \tag{11.77}$$

where readers are asked to prove the last equality in Exercise 11.32. The quantity $\phi(x)/\Phi(x)$ is known as the **inverse Mills ratio**; see Johnson, Kotz, and Balakrishnan (1994). In the first step of Heckman's two-step method, an ordinary probit model is used to obtain consistent estimates $\hat{\boldsymbol{\gamma}}$ of the parameters of the selection equation. In the second step, the unobserved v_t in regression (11.76) is replaced by the **selectivity regressor** $\phi(\boldsymbol{W}_t\hat{\boldsymbol{\gamma}})/\Phi(\boldsymbol{W}_t\hat{\boldsymbol{\gamma}})$, and regression (11.76) becomes

$$y_t = \boldsymbol{X}_t\boldsymbol{\beta} + \rho\sigma\frac{\phi(\boldsymbol{W}_t\hat{\boldsymbol{\gamma}})}{\Phi(\boldsymbol{W}_t\hat{\boldsymbol{\gamma}})} + \text{residual}. \tag{11.78}$$

This **Heckman regression**, as it is often called, is easy to estimate by OLS and yields consistent estimates of $\boldsymbol{\beta}$.

Regression (11.78) provides a test for sample selectivity as well as an estimation technique. The coefficient of the selectivity regressor is $\rho\sigma$. Since $\sigma \neq 0$, the ordinary t statistic for this coefficient to be zero can be used to test the hypothesis that $\rho = 0$, and it is asymptotically distributed as $\mathrm{N}(0, 1)$ under the null hypothesis. If this coefficient is not significantly different from zero, the investigator may reasonably decide that selectivity is not a problem and proceed to use least squares as usual.

Although the Heckman regression (11.78) yields consistent estimates of $\boldsymbol{\beta}$, the OLS covariance matrix is valid only when $\rho = 0$. The problem is that the selectivity regressor is being treated like any other regressor, when it is in fact part of the error term. It is possible to obtain a valid covariance matrix estimate to go along with the two-step estimates of $\boldsymbol{\beta}$ from (11.78), but the calculation is quite cumbersome, and the estimated covariance matrix is not always positive definite. See Greene (1981) and Lee (1982) for details.

It should be stressed that the consistency of this two-step estimator, like that of the ML estimator, depends critically on the assumption of bivariate normality. This can be seen from the specification of the selectivity regressor as the inverse Mills ratio (11.77). When the elements of $\boldsymbol{W}_t$ are the same as the elements of $\boldsymbol{X}_t$, as is often the case in practice, it is only the nonlinearity of the inverse Mills ratio as a function of $\boldsymbol{W}_t\boldsymbol{\gamma}$ that makes the parameters of the second-step regression identifiable. The form of the nonlinear relationship would be different if the error terms did not follow the normal distribution.

11.8 Duration Models

Economists are sometimes interested in how much time elapses before some event occurs. For example, they may be interested in the length of labor disputes (that is, strike duration), the age of first marriage for men and women (that is, the duration of the state of being single), the duration of unemployment spells, the duration between trades on a stock exchange, or the length of time people wait before trading in a car. In this section, we will discuss some simple econometric models for duration data of this type.

In many cases, each observation in the sample consists of a measured duration, denoted t_i, and a $1 \times k$ vector of exogenous variables, denoted $\boldsymbol{X}_i$. In adopting this formulation, we have implicitly ruled out the possibility, which more complicated models can allow for, that the exogenous variables may change as time passes. To avoid notational confusion, we use i to index observations. In theory, duration is a nonnegative, continuous random variable. In practice, however, t_i is often reported as an integer number of weeks or months. When it is always a small integer, a count data model like the ones discussed in Section 11.5 may be appropriate. However, when t_i can take on a large number of integer values, it is conventional to model duration as being continuous. Almost all of the literature deals with the continuous case.

Survivor Functions and Hazard Functions

In practice, interest often centers not so much on how t_i is related to $\boldsymbol{X}_i$ but rather on how the probability that a state will endure varies over the duration of the state. For example, we may be interested in seeing how the probability that someone finds a job changes as the length of time they have been unemployed increases. Before we can answer this sort of question, we need to discuss a few fundamental concepts.

Suppose that how long a state endures is measured by T, a nonnegative, continuous random variable with PDF $f(t)$ and CDF $F(t)$, where t is a realization of T. Then the **survivor function** is defined as

$$S(t) \equiv 1 - F(t).$$

This is the probability that a state which started at time $t = 0$ is still going on at time t. The probability that it ends in any short period of time, say the period from time t to time $t + \Delta t$, is

$$\Pr(t < T \le t + \Delta t) = F(t + \Delta t) - F(t). \tag{11.79}$$

This probability is unconditional. For many purposes, we may be interested in the probability that a state ends between time t and time $t + \Delta t$, conditional on having reached time t in the first place. This probability is

$$\Pr(t < T \le t + \Delta t \,|\, T \ge t) = \frac{F(t + \Delta t) - F(t)}{S(t)}. \tag{11.80}$$

Since we are dealing with continuous time, it is natural to divide (11.79) and (11.80) by Δt and consider what happens as $\Delta t \to 0$. The limit of $1/\Delta t$ times (11.79) as $\Delta t \to 0$ is simply the PDF $f(t)$, and the limit of $1/\Delta t$ times the right-hand side of equation (11.80) is

$$h(t) \equiv \frac{f(t)}{S(t)} = \frac{f(t)}{1 - F(t)}. \tag{11.81}$$

The function $h(t)$ defined in (11.81) is called the **hazard function**. For many purposes, it is more interesting to model the hazard function than to model the survivor function directly.

Functional Forms

For a parametric model of duration, we need to specify a functional form for one of the functions $F(t)$, $S(t)$, $f(t)$, or $h(t)$, which then implies functional forms for the others. One of the simplest possible choices is the exponential distribution, which was discussed in Section 10.2. For this distribution,

$$f(t, \theta) = \theta e^{-\theta t}, \quad \text{and} \quad F(t, \theta) = 1 - e^{-\theta t}, \quad \theta > 0.$$

Therefore, the hazard function is

$$h(t) = \frac{f(t)}{S(t)} = \frac{\theta e^{-\theta t}}{e^{-\theta t}} = \theta.$$

Thus, if duration follows an exponential distribution, the hazard function is simply a constant.

Since the restriction that the hazard function is a constant is a very strong one, the exponential distribution is rarely used in applied work. A much more flexible functional form is provided by the **Weibull distribution**, which has two parameters, θ and α. For this distribution,

$$F(t, \theta, \alpha) = 1 - \exp\big(-(\theta t)^{\alpha}\big). \tag{11.82}$$

As readers are asked to show in Exercise 11.33, the survivor, density, and hazard functions for the Weibull distribution are as follows:

$$\begin{aligned} S(t) &= \exp\big(-(\theta t)^{\alpha}\big); \\ f(t) &= \alpha\theta^{\alpha}t^{\alpha-1}\exp\big(-(\theta t)^{\alpha}\big); \\ h(t) &= \alpha\theta^{\alpha}t^{\alpha-1}. \end{aligned} \tag{11.83}$$

When $\alpha = 1$, it is easy to see that the Weibull distribution collapses to the exponential, and the hazard is just a constant. For $\alpha < 1$, the hazard is decreasing over time, and for $\alpha > 1$, the hazard is increasing. Hazard functions of the former type are said to exhibit **negative duration dependence**, while those of the latter type are said to exhibit **positive duration dependence**. In the same way, a constant hazard is said to be **duration independent**.

Although the Weibull distribution is not nearly as restrictive as the exponential, it does not allow for the possibility that the hazard may first increase and then decrease over time, which is something that is frequently observed in practice. Various other distributions do allow for this type of behavior. A particularly simple one is the **lognormal distribution**, which was discussed in Section 9.6. Suppose that $\log t$ is distributed as $\mathrm{N}(\mu, \sigma^2)$. Then we have

$$\begin{aligned} F(t) &= \Phi\Big(\frac{1}{\sigma}(\log t - \mu)\Big), \\ S(t) &= 1 - \Phi\Big(\frac{1}{\sigma}(\log t - \mu)\Big) = \Phi\Big(-\frac{1}{\sigma}(\log t - \mu)\Big), \\ f(t) &= \frac{1}{\sigma t}\phi\Big(\frac{1}{\sigma}(\log t - \mu)\Big), \text{ and} \\ h(t) &= \frac{1}{\sigma t}\frac{\phi\big((\log t - \mu)/\sigma\big)}{\Phi\big(-(\log t - \mu)/\sigma\big)}. \end{aligned}$$

For this distribution, the hazard rises quite rapidly and then falls rather slowly. This behavior can be observed in Figure 11.4, which shows several hazard functions based on the exponential, Weibull, and lognormal distributions.

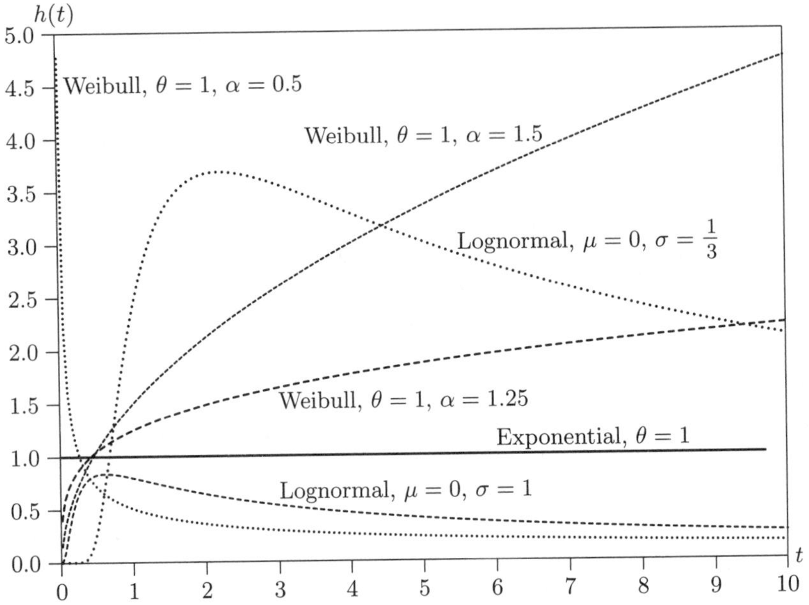

Figure 11.4 Various hazard functions

Maximum Likelihood Estimation

It is reasonably straightforward to estimate many duration models by maximum likelihood. In the simplest case, the data consist of n observations t_i on observed durations, each with an associated regressor vector $\boldsymbol{X}_i$. Then the loglikelihood function for $\boldsymbol{t}$, the entire vector of observations, is just

$$\ell(\boldsymbol{t}, \boldsymbol{\theta}) = \sum_{i=1}^{n} \log f(t_i \,|\, \boldsymbol{X}_i, \boldsymbol{\theta}), \tag{11.84}$$

where $f(t_i \,|\, \boldsymbol{X}_i, \boldsymbol{\theta})$ denotes the density of t_i conditional on the data vector $\boldsymbol{X}_i$ for the parameter vector $\boldsymbol{\theta}$. In many cases, it may be easier to write the loglikelihood function as

$$\ell(\boldsymbol{t}, \boldsymbol{\theta}) = \sum_{i=1}^{n} \log h(t_i \,|\, \boldsymbol{X}_i, \boldsymbol{\theta}) + \sum_{i=1}^{n} \log S(t_i \,|\, \boldsymbol{X}_i, \boldsymbol{\theta}), \tag{11.85}$$

where $h(t_i \,|\, \boldsymbol{X}_i, \boldsymbol{\theta})$ is the hazard function and $S(t_i \,|\, \boldsymbol{X}_i, \boldsymbol{\theta})$ is the survivor function. The equivalence of (11.84) and (11.85) is ensured by (11.81), in which the hazard function was defined.

As with other models we have looked at in this chapter, it is convenient to let the loglikelihood depend on explanatory variables through an index function. As an example, suppose that duration follows a Weibull distribution, with a parameter θ_i for observation i that has the form of the exponential mean function (11.48), so that $\theta_i = \exp(\boldsymbol{X}_i\boldsymbol{\beta}) > 0$. From (11.83) we see that the hazard and survivor functions for observation i are

$$\alpha \exp(\alpha \boldsymbol{X}_i\boldsymbol{\beta})t^{\alpha-1} \quad \text{and} \quad \exp\bigl(-t^{\alpha}\exp(\alpha\boldsymbol{X}_i\boldsymbol{\beta})\bigr),$$

respectively. In practice, it is simpler to absorb the factor of α into the parameter vector $\boldsymbol{\beta}$, so as to yield an exponent of just $\boldsymbol{X}_i\boldsymbol{\beta}$ in these expressions. Then the loglikelihood function (11.85) becomes

$$\ell(\boldsymbol{t},\boldsymbol{\beta},\alpha) = n\log\alpha + \sum_{t=1}^{n}\boldsymbol{X}_i\boldsymbol{\beta} + (\alpha-1)\sum_{t=1}^{n}t_i - \sum_{t=1}^{n}t_i^{\alpha}\exp(\boldsymbol{X}_i\boldsymbol{\beta}),$$

and ML estimates of the parameters α and $\boldsymbol{\beta}$ are obtained by maximizing this function in the usual way.

In practice, many data sets contain observations for which t_i is not actually observed. For example, if we have a sample of people who entered unemployment at various points in time, it is extremely likely that some people in the sample were still unemployed when data collection ended. If we omit such observations, we are effectively using a truncated data set, and we therefore obtain inconsistent estimates. However, if we include them but treat the observed t_i as if they were the lengths of completed spells of unemployment, we also obtain inconsistent estimates. In both cases, the inconsistency occurs for essentially the same reasons as it does when we apply OLS to a sample that has been truncated or censored; see Section 11.6.

If we are using ML estimation, it is easy enough to deal with duration data that have been censored in this way, provided we know that censorship has occurred. For ordinary, uncensored observations, the contribution to the loglikelihood function is a contribution like those in (11.84) or (11.85). For censored observations, where the observed t_i is the duration of an **incomplete spell**, it is the logarithm of the probability of censoring, which is the probability that the duration exceeds t_i, that is, the log of the survivor function. Therefore, if U denotes the set of uncensored observations, the loglikelihood function for the entire sample can be written as

$$\ell(\boldsymbol{t},\boldsymbol{\theta}) = \sum_{i\in U}\log h(t_i \,|\, \boldsymbol{X}_i,\boldsymbol{\theta}) + \sum_{i=1}^{n}\log S(t_i \,|\, \boldsymbol{X}_i,\boldsymbol{\theta}). \tag{11.86}$$

Notice that uncensored observations contribute to both terms in equation (11.86), while censored observations contribute only to the second term. When there is no censoring, the same observations contribute to both terms, and the loglikelihood function (11.86) reduces to (11.85).

Proportional Hazard Models

One class of models that is quite widely used is the class of **proportional hazard models**, originally proposed by Cox (1972), in which the hazard function for the ith economic agent is given by

$$h(\boldsymbol{X}_i, t) = g_1(\boldsymbol{X}_i)\, g_2(t), \tag{11.87}$$

for various specifications of the functions $g_1(\boldsymbol{X}_i)$ and $g_2(t)$. The latter is called the **baseline hazard function**. An implication of (11.87) is that the ratio of the hazards for any two agents, say the ones indexed by i and j, depends on the regressors but does not depend on t. This ratio is

$$\frac{h(\boldsymbol{X}_i, t)}{h(\boldsymbol{X}_j, t)} = \frac{g_1(\boldsymbol{X}_i)\, g_2(t)}{g_1(\boldsymbol{X}_j)\, g_2(t)} = \frac{g_1(\boldsymbol{X}_i)}{g_1(\boldsymbol{X}_j)}.$$

Thus the ratio of the conditional probability that agent i exits the state to the probability that agent j does so is constrained to be the same for all t. This makes proportional hazard models econometrically convenient, but they do impose fairly strong restrictions on behavior.

Both the exponential and Weibull distributions lead to proportional hazard models. As we have already seen, a natural specification of $g_1(\boldsymbol{X}_i)$ for these models is $\exp(\boldsymbol{X}_i\boldsymbol{\beta})$. For the exponential distribution, the baseline hazard function is just 1, and for the Weibull distribution it is $\alpha t^{\alpha-1}$.

One attractive feature of proportional hazards models is that it is possible to obtain consistent estimates of the parameters of the function $g_1(\boldsymbol{X}_i)$, without estimating those of $g_2(t)$ at all, by using a method called **partial likelihood** which we will not attempt to describe; see Cox and Oakes (1984) or Lancaster (1990). The baseline hazard function $g_2(t)$ can then be estimated in various ways, some of which do not require us to specify its functional form.

Complications

The class of duration models that we have discussed is quite limited. It does not allow the exogenous variables to change over time, and it does not allow for any **individual heterogeneity**, that is, variation in the hazard function across agents. The latter has serious implications for econometric inference. Suppose, for simplicity, that there are two types of agent, each with a constant hazard, which is twice as high for agents of type H as for those of type L. If we estimate a duration model for all agents together, we must observe negative duration dependence, because the type H agents exit the state more rapidly than the type L agents, and the ratio of type H to type L agents declines as duration increases.

There has been a great deal of work on duration models during the past two decades, and there are now numerous models that allow for time-varying explanatory variables and/or individual heterogeneity. Classic references are

Heckman and Singer (1984), Kiefer (1988), and Lancaster (1990). More recent work is discussed in Neumann (1999), Gouriéroux and Jasiak (2001), and van den Berg (2001).

11.9 Final Remarks

This chapter has dealt with a large number of types of dependent variable for which ordinary regression models are not appropriate: binary dependent variables (Sections 11.2 and 11.3); discrete dependent variables that can take on more than two values, which may or may not be ordered (Section 11.4); count data (Section 11.5); limited dependent variables, which may be either censored or truncated (Section 11.6); dependent variables where the observations included in the sample have been determined endogenously (Section 11.7); and duration data (Section 11.8). In most cases, we have made strong distributional assumptions and relied on maximum likelihood estimation. This is generally the easiest way to proceed, but it can lead to seriously misleading results if the assumptions are false. It is therefore important that the specification of these models be tested carefully.

11.10 Exercises

⋆11.1 Consider the contribution made by observation t to the loglikelihood function (11.09) for a binary response model. Show that this contribution is globally concave with respect to $\boldsymbol{\beta}$ if the function F is such that $F(-x) = 1-F(x)$, and if it, its derivative f, and its second derivative f' satisfy the condition

$$f'(x)F(x) - f^2(x) < 0 \tag{11.88}$$

for all real finite x.

Show that condition (11.88) is satisfied by both the logistic function $\Lambda(\cdot)$, defined in (11.07), and the standard normal CDF $\Phi(\cdot)$.

11.2 Prove that, for the logit model, the likelihood equations (11.10) reduce to

$$\sum_{t=1}^{n} x_{ti}(y_t - \Lambda(\boldsymbol{X}_t\boldsymbol{\beta})) = 0, \quad i = 1, \ldots, k.$$

11.3 Show that the efficient GMM estimating equations (9.82), when applied to the binary response model specified by (11.01), are equivalent to the likelihood equations (11.10).

11.4 If $F_1(\cdot)$ and $F_2(\cdot)$ are two CDFs defined on the real line, show that any convex combination $(1-\alpha)F_1(\cdot) + \alpha F_2(\cdot)$ of them is also a properly defined CDF. Use this fact to construct a model that nests the logit model for which $\Pr(y_t = 1) = \Lambda(\boldsymbol{X}_t\boldsymbol{\beta})$ and the probit model for which $\Pr(y_t = 1) = \Phi(\boldsymbol{X}_t\boldsymbol{\beta})$ with just one additional parameter.

★11.5 Consider the latent variable model

$$y_t^\circ = \beta_1 + \beta_2 x_t + u_t, \quad u_t \sim \mathrm{N}(0,1),$$

$$y_t = 1 \text{ if } y_t^\circ > 0, \;\; y_t = 0 \text{ if } y_t^\circ \leq 0.$$

Suppose that $x_t \sim \mathrm{N}(0,1)$. Generate 500 samples of 20 observations on (x_t, y_t) pairs, 100 assuming that $\beta_1 = 0$ and $\beta_2 = 1$, 100 assuming that $\beta_1 = 1$ and $\beta_2 = 1$, 100 assuming that $\beta_1 = -1$ and $\beta_2 = 1$, 100 assuming that $\beta_1 = 0$ and $\beta_1 = 2$, 100 assuming that $\beta_1 = 0$ and $\beta_1 = -2$, and 100 assuming that $\beta_1 = 0$ and $\beta_2 = 3$. For each of the 500 samples, attempt to estimate a probit model. In each of the five cases, what proportion of the time does the estimation fail because of perfect classifiers? Explain why there were more failures in some cases than in others.

Repeat this exercise for five sets of 100 samples of size 40, with the same parameter values. What do you conclude about the effect of sample size on the perfect classifier problem?

11.6 Suppose that there is quasi-complete separation of the data used to estimate the binary response model (11.01), with a transformation function F such that $F(-x) = 1 - F(x)$ for all real x, and a separating hyperplane defined by the parameter vector $\boldsymbol{\beta}^\bullet$. Show that the upper bound of the loglikelihood function (11.09) is equal to $-n_b \log 2$, where n_b is the number of observations for which $\boldsymbol{X}_t\boldsymbol{\beta}^\bullet = 0$.

11.7 The contribution to the loglikelihood function (11.09) made by observation t is $y_t \log F(\boldsymbol{X}_t\boldsymbol{\beta}) + (1 - y_t)\log(1 - F(\boldsymbol{X}_t\boldsymbol{\beta}))$. First, find G_{ti}, the derivative of this contribution with respect to β_i. Next, show that the expectation of G_{ti} is zero when it is evaluated at the true $\boldsymbol{\beta}$. Then obtain a typical element of the asymptotic information matrix by using the fact that it is equal to $\lim_{n\to\infty} n^{-1}\sum_{t=1}^{n} \mathrm{E}(G_{ti}G_{tj})$. Finally, show that the asymptotic covariance matrix (11.15) is equal to the inverse of this asymptotic information matrix.

11.8 Calculate the Hessian matrix corresponding to the loglikelihood function (11.09). Then use the fact that minus the expectation of the asymptotic Hessian is equal to the asymptotic information matrix to obtain the same result for the latter that you obtained in the previous exercise.

★11.9 Plot $\Upsilon_t(\boldsymbol{\beta})$, which is defined in equation (11.16), as a function of $\boldsymbol{X}_t\boldsymbol{\beta}$ for both the logit and probit models. For the logit model only, prove that $\Upsilon_t(\boldsymbol{\beta})$ achieves its maximum value when $\boldsymbol{X}_t\boldsymbol{\beta} = 0$ and declines monotonically as $|\boldsymbol{X}_t\boldsymbol{\beta}|$ increases.

11.10 The file **participation.data**, which is taken from Gerfin (1996), contains data for 872 Swiss women who may or may not participate in the labor force. The variables in the file are:

y_t	Labor force participation variable (0 or 1).
I_t	Log of nonlabor income.
A_t	Age in decades (years divided by 10).
E_t	Education in years.
nu_t	Number of children under 7 years of age.
no_t	Number of children over 7 years of age.
F_t	Citizenship dummy variable (1 if not Swiss).

The dependent variable is y_t. For the standard specification, the regressors are all of the other variables, plus A_t^2. Estimate the standard specification as both a probit and a logit model. Is there any reason to prefer one of these two models?

11.11 For the probit model estimated in Exercise 11.10, obtain at least three sensible sets of standard error estimates. If possible, these should include ones based on the Hessian, ones based on the OPG estimator (10.44), and ones based on the information matrix estimator (11.18). You may make use of the BRMR, regression (11.20), and/or the OPG regression (10.72), if appropriate.

11.12 Test the hypothesis that the probit model estimated in Exercise 11.10 should include two additional regressors, namely, the squares of nu_t and no_t. Do this in three different ways, by calculating an LR statistic and two LM statistics based on the OPG and BRMR regressions.

11.13 Use the BRMR (11.30) to test the specification of the probit model estimated in Exercise 11.10. Then use the BRMR (11.26) to test for heteroskedasticity, where $\boldsymbol{Z}_t$ consists of all the regressors except the constant term.

⋆11.14 Show, by use of l'Hôpital's Rule or otherwise, that the two results in (11.29) hold for all functions $\tau(\cdot)$ which satisfy conditions (11.28).

11.15 For the probit model estimated in Exercise 11.10, the estimated probability that $y_t = 1$ for observation t is $\Phi(\boldsymbol{X}_t\hat{\boldsymbol{\beta}})$. Compute this estimated probability for every observation, and also compute two confidence intervals at the .95 level for the actual probabilities. Both confidence intervals should be based on the covariance matrix estimator (11.18). One of them should use the delta method (Section 5.6), and the other should be obtained by transforming the end points of a confidence interval for the index function. Compare the two intervals for the observations numbered 2, 63, and 311 in the sample. Are both intervals symmetric about the estimated probability? Which of them provides more reasonable answers?

⋆11.16 Consider the expression

$$-\log\Bigg(\sum_{j=0}^{J}\exp(\boldsymbol{W}_{tj}\boldsymbol{\beta}^j)\Bigg), \tag{11.89}$$

which appears in the loglikelihood function (11.35) of the multinomial logit model. Let the vector $\boldsymbol{\beta}^j$ have k_j components, let $k \equiv k_0 + \ldots + k_J$, and let $\boldsymbol{\beta} \equiv [\boldsymbol{\beta}^0 \;\vdots\; \ldots \;\vdots\; \boldsymbol{\beta}^J]$. The $k \times k$ Hessian matrix $\boldsymbol{H}$ of (11.89) with respect to $\boldsymbol{\beta}$ can be partitioned into blocks of dimension $k_i \times k_j$, $i = 0, \ldots, J$, $j = 0, \ldots, J$, containing the second-order partial derivatives of (11.89) with respect to an element of $\boldsymbol{\beta}^i$ and an element of $\boldsymbol{\beta}^j$. Show that, for $i \neq j$, the (i, j) block can be written as

$$p_i p_j \boldsymbol{W}_{ti}^{\top}\boldsymbol{W}_{tj},$$

where $p_i \equiv \exp(\boldsymbol{W}_{ti}\boldsymbol{\beta}^i)/(\sum_{j=0}^{J}\exp(\boldsymbol{W}_{tj}\boldsymbol{\beta}^j))$ is the probability ascribed to choice i by the multinomial logit model. Then show that the diagonal (i, i) block can be written as

$$-p_i(1 - p_i)\boldsymbol{W}_{ti}^{\top}\boldsymbol{W}_{ti}.$$

Let the k–vector $\boldsymbol{a}$ be partitioned conformably with the above partitioning of the Hessian $\boldsymbol{H}$, so that we can write $\boldsymbol{a} = [\boldsymbol{a}_0 \,\vdots\, \ldots \,\vdots\, \boldsymbol{a}_J]$, where each of the vectors $\boldsymbol{a}_j$ has k_j components for $j = 0, \ldots, J$. Show that the quadratic form $\boldsymbol{a}^\top \boldsymbol{H}\boldsymbol{a}$ is equal to

$$\Big(\sum_{j=0}^{J} p_j w_j\Big)^2 - \sum_{j=0}^{J} p_j w_j^2, \tag{11.90}$$

where the scalar product w_j is defined as $\boldsymbol{W}_{tj}\boldsymbol{a}_j$.

Show that expression (11.90) is nonpositive, and explain why this result shows that the multinomial logit loglikelihood function (11.35) is globally concave.

11.17 Show that the nested logit model reduces to the multinomial logit model if $\theta_i = 1$ for all $i = 1, \ldots, m$. Then show that it also does so if all the subsets A_i used to define the former model are singletons.

⋆11.18 Show that the expectation of the Hessian of the loglikelihood function (11.41), evaluated at the parameter vector $\boldsymbol{\theta}$, is equal to the negative of the $k \times k$ matrix

$$\boldsymbol{I}(\boldsymbol{\theta}) \equiv \sum_{t=1}^{n} \sum_{j=0}^{J} \frac{1}{\Pi_{tj}(\boldsymbol{\theta})} \boldsymbol{T}_{tj}^\top(\boldsymbol{\theta}) \boldsymbol{T}_{tj}(\boldsymbol{\theta}), \tag{11.91}$$

where $\boldsymbol{T}_{tj}(\boldsymbol{\theta})$ is the $1 \times k$ vector of partial derivatives of $\Pi_{tj}(\boldsymbol{\theta})$ with respect to the components of $\boldsymbol{\theta}$. Demonstrate that (11.91) can also be computed using the outer product of the gradient definition of the information matrix.

Use the above result to show that the matrix of sums of squares and cross-products of the regressors of the DCAR, regression (11.42), evaluated at $\boldsymbol{\theta}$, is $\boldsymbol{I}(\boldsymbol{\theta})$. Show further that $1/s^2$ times the estimated OLS covariance matrix from (11.42) is an asymptotically valid estimate of the covariance matrix of the MLE $\hat{\boldsymbol{\theta}}$ if the artificial variables are evaluated at $\hat{\boldsymbol{\theta}}$.

⋆11.19 Let the one-step estimator $\grave{\boldsymbol{\theta}}$ be defined as usual for the discrete choice artificial regression (11.42) evaluated at a root-n consistent estimator $\acute{\boldsymbol{\theta}}$ as $\grave{\boldsymbol{\theta}} = \acute{\boldsymbol{\theta}} + \acute{\boldsymbol{b}}$, where $\acute{\boldsymbol{b}}$ is the vector of OLS parameter estimates from (11.42). Show that $\grave{\boldsymbol{\theta}}$ is asymptotically equivalent to the MLE $\hat{\boldsymbol{\theta}}$.

11.20 Consider the binary choice model characterized by the probabilities (11.01). Both the BRMR (11.20) and the DCAR (11.42) with $J = 1$ apply to this model, but the two artificial regressions are obviously different, since the BRMR has n artificial observations when the sample size is n, while the DCAR has $2n$. Show that the two artificial regressions are nevertheless equivalent, in the sense that all scalar products of corresponding pairs of artificial variables, regressand or regressor, are identical for the two regressions.

⋆11.21 In terms of the notation of the DCAR, regression (11.42), the probability Π_{tj} that $y_t = j$, $j = 0, \ldots, J$, for the nested logit model is given by expression (11.40). Show that, if the index $i(j)$ is such that $j \in A_{i(j)}$, the partial derivative of Π_{tj} with respect to θ_i, evaluated at $\theta_k = 1$ for $k = 1, \ldots, m$, where m is the number of subsets A_k, is

$$\frac{\partial \Pi_{tj}}{\partial \theta_i} = \Pi_{tj}\big(\delta_{i(j)i} v_{tj} - \sum_{l \in A_i} \Pi_{tl} v_{tl}\big).$$

Here $v_{tj} \equiv -\boldsymbol{W}_{tj}\boldsymbol{\beta}^j + h_{ti(j)}$, where h_{ti} denotes the inclusive value (11.39) of subset A_i, and δ_{ij} is the Kronecker delta.

When $\theta_k = 1$, $k = 1, \ldots, m$, the nested logit probabilities reduce to the multinomial logit probabilities (11.34). Show that, if the Π_{tj} are given by (11.34), then the vector of partial derivatives of Π_{tj} with respect to the components of $\boldsymbol{\beta}^l$ is $\Pi_{tj}\boldsymbol{W}_{tl}(\delta_{jl} - \Pi_{tl})$.

⋆11.22 Explain how to use the DCAR (11.42) to test the IIA assumption for the conditional logit model (11.36). This involves testing it against the nested logit model (11.40) with the $\boldsymbol{\beta}^j$ constrained to be the same. Do this for the special case in which $J = 2$, $A_1 = \{0, 1\}$, $A_2 = \{2\}$. **Hint:** Use the results proved in the preceding exercise.

11.23 Using the fact that the infinite series expansion of the exponential function, convergent for all real z, is

$$\exp z = \sum_{n=0}^{\infty} \frac{z^n}{n!},$$

where by convention we define $0! = 1$, show that $\sum_{y=0}^{\infty} e^{-\lambda}\lambda^y/y! = 1$, and that therefore the Poisson distribution defined by (11.58) is well defined on the nonnegative integers. Then show that the expectation and variance of a random variable Y that follows the Poisson distribution are both equal to λ.

11.24 Let the nth uncentered moment of the Poisson distribution with parameter λ be denoted by $M_n(\lambda)$. Show that these moments can be generated by the recurrence $M_{n+1}(\lambda) = \lambda(M_n(\lambda) + M_n'(\lambda))$, where $M_n'(\lambda)$ is the derivative of $M_n(\lambda)$. Using this result, show that the third and fourth *central* moments of the Poisson distribution are λ and $\lambda + 3\lambda^2$, respectively.

11.25 Explain precisely how you would use the artificial regression (11.55) to test the hypothesis that $\boldsymbol{\beta}_2 = \boldsymbol{0}$ in the Poisson regression model for which $\lambda_t(\boldsymbol{\beta}) = \exp(\boldsymbol{X}_{t1}\boldsymbol{\beta}_1 + \boldsymbol{X}_{t2}\boldsymbol{\beta}_2)$. Here $\boldsymbol{\beta}_1$ is a k_1–vector and $\boldsymbol{\beta}_2$ is a k_2–vector, with $k = k_1 + k_2$. Consider two cases, one in which the model is estimated subject to the restriction and one in which it is estimated unrestrictedly.

⋆11.26 Suppose that y_t is a count variable, with conditional mean $\mathrm{E}(y_t) = \exp(\boldsymbol{X}_t\boldsymbol{\beta})$ and conditional variance $\mathrm{E}(y_t - \exp(\boldsymbol{X}_t\boldsymbol{\beta}))^2 = \gamma^2\exp(\boldsymbol{X}_t\boldsymbol{\beta})$. Show that ML estimates of $\boldsymbol{\beta}$ under the incorrect assumption that y_t is generated by a Poisson regression model with mean $\exp(\boldsymbol{X}_t\boldsymbol{\beta})$ are asymptotically efficient in this case. Also show that the OLS covariance matrix from the artificial regression (11.55) is asymptotically valid.

11.27 Suppose that y_t is a count variable with conditional mean $\mathrm{E}(y_t) = \exp(\boldsymbol{X}_t\boldsymbol{\beta})$ and unknown conditional variance. Show that, if the artificial regression (11.55) is evaluated at the ML estimates for a Poisson regression model which specifies the conditional mean correctly, the HCCME HC_0 for that artificial regression is numerically equal to expression (11.65), which is an asymptotically valid covariance matrix estimator in this case.

11.28 The file **count.data**, which is taken from Gurmu (1997), contains data for 485 household heads who may or may not have visited a doctor during a certain period of time. The variables in the file are:

y_t Number of doctor visits (a nonnegative integer).
C_t Number of children in the household.
A_t A measure of access to health care.
H_t A measure of health status.

Using these data, obtain ML estimates of a Poisson regression model to explain the variable y_t, where

$$\lambda_t(\boldsymbol{\beta}) = \exp(\beta_1 + \beta_2 C_t + \beta_3 A_t + \beta_4 H_t).$$

In addition to the estimates of the parameters, report three different standard errors. One of these should be based on the inverse of the information matrix, which is valid only when the model is correctly specified. The other two should be computed using the artificial regression (11.55). One of them should be valid under the assumption that the conditional variance is proportional to $\lambda_t(\boldsymbol{\beta})$, and the other should be valid whenever the conditional mean is specified correctly. Can you explain the differences among the three sets of standard errors?

Test the model for overdispersion in two different ways. One test should be based on the OPG regression, and the other should be based on the testing regression (11.60). Note that this model is *not* the one actually estimated in Gurmu (1997).

11.29 Consider the latent variable model

$$y_t^\circ = \boldsymbol{X}_t\boldsymbol{\beta} + u_t, \quad u_t \sim \text{NID}(0, \sigma^2), \tag{11.92}$$

where $y_t = y_t^\circ$ whenever $y_t^\circ \leq y^{\max}$ and is not observed otherwise. Write down the loglikelihood function for a sample of n observations on y_t.

11.30 As in the previous question, suppose that y_t° is given by (11.92). Assume that $y_t = y_t^\circ$ whenever $y^{\min} \leq y_t^\circ \leq y^{\max}$ and is not observed otherwise. Write down the loglikelihood function for a sample of n observations on y_t.

11.31 Suppose that $y_t^\circ = \boldsymbol{X}_t\boldsymbol{\beta} + u_t$ with $u_t \sim \text{NID}(0, \sigma^2)$. Suppose further that $y_t = y_t^\circ$ if $y_t < y_t^c$, and $y_t = y_t^c$ otherwise, where y_t^c is the known value at which censoring occurs for observation t. Write down the loglikelihood function for this model.

⋆11.32 Let z be distributed as N(0, 1). Show that $\text{E}(z \,|\, z < x) = -\phi(x)/\Phi(x)$, where Φ and ϕ are, respectively, the CDF and PDF of the standard normal distribution. Then show that $\text{E}(z \,|\, z > x) = \phi(x)/\Phi(-x) = \phi(-x)/\Phi(-x)$. The second result explains why the inverse Mills ratio appears in (11.77).

11.33 Starting from expression (11.82) for the CDF of the Weibull distribution, show that the survivor function, the PDF, and the hazard function are as given in (11.83).

Chapter 12

Multivariate Models

12.1 Introduction

Up to this point, almost all the models we have discussed have involved just one equation. In most cases, there has been only one equation because there has been only one dependent variable. Even in the few cases in which there were several dependent variables, interest centered on just one of them. For example, in the case of the simultaneous equations model that was discussed in Chapter 8, we chose to estimate just one structural equation at a time.

In this chapter, we discuss models which jointly determine the values of two or more dependent variables using two or more equations. Such models are called **multivariate** because they attempt to explain multiple dependent variables. As we will see, the class of multivariate models is considerably larger than the class of simultaneous equations models. Every simultaneous equations model is a multivariate model, but many interesting multivariate models are not simultaneous equations models.

In the next section, which is quite long, we provide a detailed discussion of GLS, feasible GLS, and ML estimation of systems of linear regressions. Then, in Section 12.3, we discuss the estimation of systems of nonlinear equations which may involve cross-equation restrictions but do not involve simultaneity. Next, in Section 12.4, we provide a much more detailed treatment of the linear simultaneous equations model than we did in Chapter 8. We approach it from the point of view of GMM estimation, which leads to the well-known 3SLS estimator. In Section 12.5, we discuss the application of maximum likelihood to this model. Finally, in Section 12.6, we briefly discuss some of the methods for estimating nonlinear simultaneous equations models.

12.2 Seemingly Unrelated Linear Regressions

The **multivariate linear regression model** was investigated by Zellner (1962), who called it the **seemingly unrelated regressions model**. An **SUR system**, as such a model is often called, involves n observations on each of g dependent variables. In principle, these could be any set of variables measured at the same points in time or for the same cross-section. In practice, however, the dependent variables are often quite similar to each other. For example, in the time-series context, each of them might be the output of a different industry or the inflation rate for a different country. In view of this, it might seem more appropriate to speak of "seemingly related regressions," but the terminology is too well-established to change.

We suppose that there are g dependent variables indexed by i. Let $\boldsymbol{y}_i$ denote the n–vector of observations on the ith dependent variable, $\boldsymbol{X}_i$ denote the $n \times k_i$ matrix of regressors for the ith equation, $\boldsymbol{\beta}_i$ denote the k_i–vector of parameters, and $\boldsymbol{u}_i$ denote the n–vector of error terms. Then the ith equation of a multivariate linear regression model may be written as

$$\boldsymbol{y}_i = \boldsymbol{X}_i\boldsymbol{\beta}_i + \boldsymbol{u}_i, \quad \mathrm{E}(\boldsymbol{u}_i\boldsymbol{u}_i^{\top}) = \sigma_{ii}\mathbf{I}_n, \tag{12.01}$$

where $\mathbf{I}_n$ is the $n \times n$ identity matrix. The reason we use σ_{ii} to denote the variance of the error terms will become apparent shortly. In most cases, some columns are common to two or more of the matrices $\boldsymbol{X}_i$. For instance, if every equation has a constant term, each of the $\boldsymbol{X}_i$ must contain a column of 1s.

Since equation (12.01) is just a linear regression model with IID errors, we can perfectly well estimate it by ordinary least squares if we assume that all the columns of $\boldsymbol{X}_i$ are either exogenous or predetermined. If we do this, however, we ignore the possibility that the error terms may be correlated across the equations of the system. In many cases, it is plausible that u_{ti}, the error term for observation t of equation i, should be correlated with u_{tj}, the error term for observation t of equation j. For example, we might expect that a macroeconomic shock which affects the inflation rate in one country would simultaneously affect the inflation rate in other countries as well.

To allow for this possibility, the assumption that is usually made about the error terms in the model (12.01) is

$$\mathrm{E}(u_{ti}u_{tj}) = \sigma_{ij} \text{ for all } t, \quad \mathrm{E}(u_{ti}u_{sj}) = 0 \text{ for all } t \neq s, \tag{12.02}$$

where σ_{ij} is the ij^{th} element of the $g \times g$ positive definite matrix $\boldsymbol{\Sigma}$. This assumption allows all the u_{ti} for a given t to be correlated, but it specifies that they are homoskedastic and independent across t. The matrix $\boldsymbol{\Sigma}$ is called the **contemporaneous covariance matrix**, a term inspired by the time-series context. The error terms u_{ti} may be arranged into an $n \times g$ matrix $\boldsymbol{U}$, of which a typical row is the $1 \times g$ vector $\boldsymbol{U}_t$. It then follows from (12.02) that

$$\mathrm{E}(\boldsymbol{U}_t^{\top}\boldsymbol{U}_t) = \frac{1}{n}\mathrm{E}(\boldsymbol{U}^{\top}\boldsymbol{U}) = \boldsymbol{\Sigma}. \tag{12.03}$$

If we combine equations (12.01), for $i = 1, \ldots, g$, with assumption (12.02), we obtain the classical SUR model.

We have not yet made any sort of exogeneity or predeterminedness assumption. A rather strong assumption is that $\mathrm{E}(\boldsymbol{U} \,|\, \boldsymbol{X}) = \mathbf{O}$, where $\boldsymbol{X}$ is an $n \times l$ matrix with full rank, the set of columns of which is the union of all the linearly independent columns of all the matrices $\boldsymbol{X}_i$. Thus l is the total number of variables that appear in any of the $\boldsymbol{X}_i$ matrices. This exogeneity assumption, which is the analog of assumption (3.08) for univariate regression models, is undoubtedly too strong in many cases. A considerably weaker assumption is that $\mathrm{E}(\boldsymbol{U}_t \,|\, \boldsymbol{X}_t) = \mathbf{0}$, where $\boldsymbol{X}_t$ is the tth row of $\boldsymbol{X}$. This is the analog of the predeterminedness assumption (3.10) for univariate regression models. The results that we will state are valid under either of these assumptions.

Precisely how we want to estimate a linear SUR system depends on what further assumptions we make about the matrix $\boldsymbol{\Sigma}$ and the distribution of the error terms. In the simplest case, $\boldsymbol{\Sigma}$ is assumed to be known, at least up to a scalar factor, and the distribution of the error terms is unspecified. The appropriate estimation method is then generalized least squares. If we relax the assumption that $\boldsymbol{\Sigma}$ is known, then we need to use feasible GLS. If we continue to assume that $\boldsymbol{\Sigma}$ is unknown but impose the assumption that the error terms are normally distributed, then we may want to use maximum likelihood, which is generally consistent even when the normality assumption is false. In practice, both feasible GLS and ML are widely used.

GLS Estimation with a Known Covariance Matrix

Even though it is rarely a realistic assumption, we begin by assuming that the contemporaneous covariance matrix $\boldsymbol{\Sigma}$ of a linear SUR system is known, and we consider how to estimate the model by GLS. Once we have seen how to do so, it will be easy to see how to estimate such a model by other methods. The trick is to convert a system of g linear equations and n observations into what looks like a single equation with gn observations and a known $gn \times gn$ covariance matrix that depends on $\boldsymbol{\Sigma}$.

By making appropriate definitions, we can write the entire SUR system of which a typical equation is (12.01) as

$$\boldsymbol{y}_\bullet = \boldsymbol{X}_\bullet \boldsymbol{\beta}_\bullet + \boldsymbol{u}_\bullet. \tag{12.04}$$

Here $\boldsymbol{y}_\bullet$ is a gn–vector consisting of the n–vectors $\boldsymbol{y}_1$ through $\boldsymbol{y}_g$ stacked vertically, and $\boldsymbol{u}_\bullet$ is similarly the vector of $\boldsymbol{u}_1$ through $\boldsymbol{u}_g$ stacked vertically. The matrix $\boldsymbol{X}_\bullet$ is a $gn \times k$ block-diagonal matrix, where k is equal to $\sum_{i=1}^{g} k_i$. The diagonal blocks are the matrices $\boldsymbol{X}_1$ through $\boldsymbol{X}_g$. Thus we have

$$\boldsymbol{X}_\bullet \equiv \begin{bmatrix} \boldsymbol{X}_1 & \mathbf{O} & \cdots & \mathbf{O} \\ \mathbf{O} & \boldsymbol{X}_2 & \cdots & \mathbf{O} \\ \vdots & \vdots & \vdots & \vdots \\ \mathbf{O} & \mathbf{O} & \cdots & \boldsymbol{X}_g \end{bmatrix}, \tag{12.05}$$

where each of the $\mathbf{O}$ blocks has n rows and as many columns as the $\boldsymbol{X}_i$ block that it shares those columns with. To be conformable with $\boldsymbol{X}_\bullet$, the vector $\boldsymbol{\beta}_\bullet$ is a k–vector consisting of the vectors $\boldsymbol{\beta}_1$ through $\boldsymbol{\beta}_g$ stacked vertically.

From the above definitions and the rules for matrix multiplication, it is not difficult to see that

$$\begin{bmatrix} \boldsymbol{y}_1 \\ \vdots \\ \boldsymbol{y}_g \end{bmatrix} \equiv \boldsymbol{y}_\bullet = \boldsymbol{X}_\bullet \boldsymbol{\beta}_\bullet + \boldsymbol{u}_\bullet = \begin{bmatrix} \boldsymbol{X}_1\boldsymbol{\beta}_1 \\ \vdots \\ \boldsymbol{X}_g\boldsymbol{\beta}_g \end{bmatrix} + \begin{bmatrix} \boldsymbol{u}_1 \\ \vdots \\ \boldsymbol{u}_g \end{bmatrix}.$$

Thus it is apparent that the single equation (12.04) is precisely what we obtain by stacking the equations (12.01) vertically, for $i = 1, \ldots, g$. Using the notation of (12.04), we can write the OLS estimator for the entire system very compactly as

$$\hat{\boldsymbol{\beta}}_\bullet^{\rm OLS} = (\boldsymbol{X}_\bullet^\top \boldsymbol{X}_\bullet)^{-1} \boldsymbol{X}_\bullet^\top \boldsymbol{y}_\bullet, \tag{12.06}$$

as readers are asked to verify in Exercise 12.4. But the assumptions we have made about $\boldsymbol{u}_\bullet$ imply that this estimator is not efficient.

The next step is to figure out the covariance matrix of the vector $\boldsymbol{u}_\bullet$. Since the error terms are assumed to have mean zero, this matrix is just the expectation of the matrix $\boldsymbol{u}_\bullet \boldsymbol{u}_\bullet^\top$. Under assumption (12.02), we find that

$$\begin{aligned} {\rm E}(\boldsymbol{u}_\bullet \boldsymbol{u}_\bullet^\top) &= \begin{bmatrix} {\rm E}(\boldsymbol{u}_1\boldsymbol{u}_1^\top) & \cdots & {\rm E}(\boldsymbol{u}_1\boldsymbol{u}_g^\top) \\ \vdots & \vdots & \vdots \\ {\rm E}(\boldsymbol{u}_g\boldsymbol{u}_1^\top) & \cdots & {\rm E}(\boldsymbol{u}_g\boldsymbol{u}_g^\top) \end{bmatrix} \\ &= \begin{bmatrix} \sigma_{11}\mathbf{I}_n & \cdots & \sigma_{1g}\mathbf{I}_n \\ \vdots & \vdots & \vdots \\ \sigma_{g1}\mathbf{I}_n & \cdots & \sigma_{gg}\mathbf{I}_n \end{bmatrix} \equiv \boldsymbol{\Sigma}_\bullet. \end{aligned} \tag{12.07}$$

Here, $\boldsymbol{\Sigma}_\bullet$ is a symmetric $gn \times gn$ covariance matrix. In Exercise 12.1, readers are asked to show that $\boldsymbol{\Sigma}_\bullet$ is positive definite whenever $\boldsymbol{\Sigma}$ is.

The matrix $\boldsymbol{\Sigma}_\bullet$ can be written more compactly as $\boldsymbol{\Sigma}_\bullet \equiv \boldsymbol{\Sigma} \otimes \mathbf{I}_n$ if we use the **Kronecker product** symbol $\otimes$. The Kronecker product $\boldsymbol{A} \otimes \boldsymbol{B}$ of a $p \times q$ matrix $\boldsymbol{A}$ and an $r \times s$ matrix $\boldsymbol{B}$ is a $pr \times qs$ matrix consisting of pq blocks, laid out in the pattern of the elements of $\boldsymbol{A}$. For $i = 1, \ldots, p$ and $j = 1, \ldots, q$, the $ij^{\rm th}$ block of the Kronecker product is the $r \times s$ matrix $a_{ij}\boldsymbol{B}$, where a_{ij} is the $ij^{\rm th}$ element of $\boldsymbol{A}$. As can be seen from (12.07), that is exactly how the blocks of $\boldsymbol{\Sigma}_\bullet$ are defined in terms of $\mathbf{I}_n$ and the elements of $\boldsymbol{\Sigma}$.

Kronecker products have a number of useful properties. In particular, if $\boldsymbol{A}$, $\boldsymbol{B}$, $\boldsymbol{C}$, and $\boldsymbol{D}$ are conformable matrices, then the following relationships hold:

$$\begin{aligned} (\boldsymbol{A} \otimes \boldsymbol{B})^\top &= \boldsymbol{A}^\top \otimes \boldsymbol{B}^\top, \\ (\boldsymbol{A} \otimes \boldsymbol{B})(\boldsymbol{C} \otimes \boldsymbol{D}) &= (\boldsymbol{AC}) \otimes (\boldsymbol{BD}), \text{ and} \\ (\boldsymbol{A} \otimes \boldsymbol{B})^{-1} &= \boldsymbol{A}^{-1} \otimes \boldsymbol{B}^{-1}. \end{aligned} \tag{12.08}$$

Of course, the last line of (12.08) can be true only for nonsingular, square matrices $\boldsymbol{A}$ and $\boldsymbol{B}$. The Kronecker product is not commutative, by which we mean that $\boldsymbol{A} \otimes \boldsymbol{B}$ and $\boldsymbol{B} \otimes \boldsymbol{A}$ are different matrices. However, the elements of these two products are the same; they are just laid out differently. In fact, it can be shown that $\boldsymbol{B} \otimes \boldsymbol{A}$ can be obtained from $\boldsymbol{A} \otimes \boldsymbol{B}$ by a sequence of interchanges of rows and columns. Exercise 12.2 asks readers to prove these properties of Kronecker products. For an exceedingly detailed discussion of the properties of Kronecker products, see Magnus and Neudecker (1988).

As we have seen, the system of equations defined by (12.01) and (12.02) is equivalent to the single equation (12.04), with gn observations and error terms that have covariance matrix $\boldsymbol{\Sigma}_\bullet$. Therefore, when the matrix $\boldsymbol{\Sigma}$ is known, we can obtain consistent and efficient estimates of the $\boldsymbol{\beta}_i$, or equivalently of $\boldsymbol{\beta}_\bullet$, simply by using the classical GLS estimator (7.04). We find that

$$\begin{aligned}\hat{\boldsymbol{\beta}}_\bullet^{\text{GLS}} &= (\boldsymbol{X}_\bullet^\top \boldsymbol{\Sigma}_\bullet^{-1} \boldsymbol{X}_\bullet)^{-1} \boldsymbol{X}_\bullet^\top \boldsymbol{\Sigma}_\bullet^{-1} \boldsymbol{y}_\bullet \\ &= \big(\boldsymbol{X}_\bullet^\top (\boldsymbol{\Sigma}^{-1} \otimes \mathbf{I}_n) \boldsymbol{X}_\bullet\big)^{-1} \boldsymbol{X}_\bullet^\top (\boldsymbol{\Sigma}^{-1} \otimes \mathbf{I}_n) \boldsymbol{y}_\bullet, \end{aligned} \tag{12.09}$$

where, to obtain the second line, we have used the last of equations (12.08). This GLS estimator is sometimes called the **SUR estimator**. From the result (7.05) for GLS estimation, its covariance matrix is

$$\operatorname{Var}(\hat{\boldsymbol{\beta}}_\bullet^{\text{GLS}}) = \big(\boldsymbol{X}_\bullet^\top (\boldsymbol{\Sigma}^{-1} \otimes \mathbf{I}_n) \boldsymbol{X}_\bullet\big)^{-1}. \tag{12.10}$$

Since $\boldsymbol{\Sigma}$ is assumed to be known, we can use this covariance matrix directly, because there are no variance parameters to estimate.

As in the univariate case, there is a criterion function associated with the GLS estimator (7.04). This criterion function is simply expression (7.06) adapted to the model (12.04), namely,

$$(\boldsymbol{y}_\bullet - \boldsymbol{X}_\bullet \boldsymbol{\beta}_\bullet)^\top (\boldsymbol{\Sigma}^{-1} \otimes \mathbf{I}_n)(\boldsymbol{y}_\bullet - \boldsymbol{X}_\bullet \boldsymbol{\beta}_\bullet). \tag{12.11}$$

The first-order conditions for the minimization of (12.11) with respect to $\boldsymbol{\beta}_\bullet$ can be written as

$$\boldsymbol{X}_\bullet^\top (\boldsymbol{\Sigma}^{-1} \otimes \mathbf{I}_n)(\boldsymbol{y}_\bullet - \boldsymbol{X}_\bullet \hat{\boldsymbol{\beta}}_\bullet) = \mathbf{0}. \tag{12.12}$$

These moment conditions, which are analogous to conditions (7.07) for the case of univariate GLS estimation, can be interpreted as a set of estimating equations that define the GLS estimator (12.09).

In the slightly less unrealistic situation in which $\boldsymbol{\Sigma}$ is assumed to be known only up to a scalar factor, so that $\boldsymbol{\Sigma} = \sigma^2 \boldsymbol{\Delta}$, the form of (12.09) would be unchanged, but with $\boldsymbol{\Delta}$ replacing $\boldsymbol{\Sigma}$, and the covariance matrix (12.10) would become

$$\operatorname{Var}(\hat{\boldsymbol{\beta}}_\bullet^{\text{GLS}}) = \sigma^2 \big(\boldsymbol{X}_\bullet^\top (\boldsymbol{\Delta}^{-1} \otimes \mathbf{I}_n) \boldsymbol{X}_\bullet\big)^{-1}.$$

In practice, to estimate $\operatorname{Var}(\hat{\boldsymbol{\beta}}_\bullet^{\rm GLS})$, we replace σ^2 by something that estimates it consistently. Two natural estimators are

$$\hat{\sigma}^2 \equiv \frac{1}{gn}\hat{\boldsymbol{u}}_\bullet^\top(\boldsymbol{\Delta}^{-1}\otimes \mathbf{I}_n)\hat{\boldsymbol{u}}_\bullet, \quad \text{and}$$

$$s^2 \equiv \frac{1}{(gn-k)}\hat{\boldsymbol{u}}_\bullet^\top(\boldsymbol{\Delta}^{-1}\otimes \mathbf{I}_n)\hat{\boldsymbol{u}}_\bullet,$$

where $\hat{\boldsymbol{u}}_\bullet$ denotes the vector of error terms from GLS estimation of (12.04). The first estimator is analogous to the ML estimator of σ^2 in the linear regression model, and the second one is analogous to the OLS estimator.

At this point, a word of warning is in order. Although the GLS estimator (12.09) has quite a simple form, it can be expensive to compute when gn is large. In consequence, no sensible regression package would actually use this formula. We can proceed more efficiently by working directly with the estimating equations (12.12). Writing them out explicitly, we obtain

$$\begin{aligned}
&\boldsymbol{X}_\bullet^\top(\boldsymbol{\Sigma}^{-1}\otimes \mathbf{I}_n)(\boldsymbol{y}_\bullet - \boldsymbol{X}_\bullet\hat{\boldsymbol{\beta}}_\bullet)\\
&= \begin{bmatrix} \boldsymbol{X}_1^\top & \cdots & \mathbf{O}\\ \vdots & \ddots & \vdots\\ \mathbf{O} & \cdots & \boldsymbol{X}_g^\top \end{bmatrix}
\begin{bmatrix} \sigma^{11}\mathbf{I}_n & \cdots & \sigma^{1g}\mathbf{I}_n\\ \vdots & \ddots & \vdots\\ \sigma^{g1}\mathbf{I}_n & \cdots & \sigma^{gg}\mathbf{I}_n \end{bmatrix}
\begin{bmatrix} \boldsymbol{y}_1 - \boldsymbol{X}_1\hat{\boldsymbol{\beta}}_1^{\rm GLS}\\ \vdots\\ \boldsymbol{y}_g - \boldsymbol{X}_g\hat{\boldsymbol{\beta}}_g^{\rm GLS} \end{bmatrix}\\
&= \begin{bmatrix} \sigma^{11}\boldsymbol{X}_1^\top & \cdots & \sigma^{1g}\boldsymbol{X}_1^\top\\ \vdots & \ddots & \vdots\\ \sigma^{g1}\boldsymbol{X}_g^\top & \cdots & \sigma^{gg}\boldsymbol{X}_g^\top \end{bmatrix}
\begin{bmatrix} \boldsymbol{y}_1 - \boldsymbol{X}_1\hat{\boldsymbol{\beta}}_1^{\rm GLS}\\ \vdots\\ \boldsymbol{y}_g - \boldsymbol{X}_g\hat{\boldsymbol{\beta}}_g^{\rm GLS} \end{bmatrix} = \mathbf{0},
\end{aligned}\tag{12.13}$$

where σ^{ij} denotes the $ij^{\rm th}$ element of the matrix $\boldsymbol{\Sigma}^{-1}$. By solving the k equations (12.13) for the $\hat{\boldsymbol{\beta}}_i$, we find easily enough (see Exercise 12.5) that

$$\hat{\boldsymbol{\beta}}_\bullet^{\rm GLS} = \begin{bmatrix} \sigma^{11}\boldsymbol{X}_1^\top\boldsymbol{X}_1 & \cdots & \sigma^{1g}\boldsymbol{X}_1^\top\boldsymbol{X}_g\\ \vdots & \ddots & \vdots\\ \sigma^{g1}\boldsymbol{X}_g^\top\boldsymbol{X}_1 & \cdots & \sigma^{gg}\boldsymbol{X}_g^\top\boldsymbol{X}_g \end{bmatrix}^{-1}
\begin{bmatrix} \sum_{j=1}^g \sigma^{1j}\boldsymbol{X}_1^\top\boldsymbol{y}_j\\ \vdots\\ \sum_{j=1}^g \sigma^{gj}\boldsymbol{X}_g^\top\boldsymbol{y}_j \end{bmatrix}. \tag{12.14}$$

Although this expression may look more complicated than (12.09), it is much less costly to compute. Recall that we grouped all the linearly independent explanatory variables of the entire SUR system into the $n\times l$ matrix $\boldsymbol{X}$. By computing the matrix product $\boldsymbol{X}^\top\boldsymbol{X}$, we may obtain all the blocks of the form $\boldsymbol{X}_i^\top\boldsymbol{X}_j$ merely by selecting the appropriate rows and corresponding columns of this product. Similarly, if we form the $n\times g$ matrix $\boldsymbol{Y}$ by stacking the g dependent variables horizontally rather than vertically, so that

$$\boldsymbol{Y} \equiv [\,\boldsymbol{y}_1 \quad \cdots \quad \boldsymbol{y}_g\,],$$

then all the vectors of the form $\boldsymbol{X}_i^\top \boldsymbol{y}_j$ needed on the right-hand side of (12.14) can be extracted as a selection of the elements of the jth column of the product $\boldsymbol{X}^\top \boldsymbol{Y}$.

The covariance matrix (12.10) can also be expressed in a form more suitable for computation. By a calculation just like the one that gave us (12.13), we see that (12.10) can be expressed as

$$\operatorname{Var}(\hat{\boldsymbol{\beta}}_\bullet^{\text{GLS}}) = \begin{bmatrix} \sigma^{11}\boldsymbol{X}_1^\top \boldsymbol{X}_1 & \cdots & \sigma^{1g}\boldsymbol{X}_1^\top \boldsymbol{X}_g \\ \vdots & \ddots & \vdots \\ \sigma^{g1}\boldsymbol{X}_g^\top \boldsymbol{X}_1 & \cdots & \sigma^{gg}\boldsymbol{X}_g^\top \boldsymbol{X}_g \end{bmatrix}^{-1}. \tag{12.15}$$

Again, all the blocks here are selections of rows and columns of $\boldsymbol{X}^\top \boldsymbol{X}$.

For the purposes of further analysis, the estimating equations (12.13) can be expressed more concisely by writing out the ith row as follows:

$$\sum_{j=1}^{g} \sigma^{ij} \boldsymbol{X}_i^\top (\boldsymbol{y}_j - \boldsymbol{X}_j \hat{\boldsymbol{\beta}}_j^{\text{GLS}}) = \mathbf{0}. \tag{12.16}$$

The matrix equation (12.13) is clearly equivalent to the set of equations (12.16) for $i = 1, \ldots, g$.

Feasible GLS Estimation

In practice, the contemporaneous covariance matrix $\boldsymbol{\Sigma}$ is very rarely known. When it is not, the easiest approach is simply to replace $\boldsymbol{\Sigma}$ in (12.09) by a matrix that estimates it consistently. In principle, there are many ways to do so, but the most natural approach is to base the estimate on OLS residuals. This leads to the following feasible GLS procedure, which is probably the most commonly-used procedure for estimating linear SUR systems.

The first step is to estimate each of the equations by OLS. This yields consistent, but inefficient, estimates of the $\boldsymbol{\beta}_i$, along with g vectors of least-squares residuals $\hat{\boldsymbol{u}}_i$. The natural estimator of $\boldsymbol{\Sigma}$ is then

$$\hat{\boldsymbol{\Sigma}} \equiv \frac{1}{n} \hat{\boldsymbol{U}}^\top \hat{\boldsymbol{U}}, \tag{12.17}$$

where $\hat{\boldsymbol{U}}$ is an $n \times g$ matrix with i^{th} column $\hat{\boldsymbol{u}}_i$. By construction, the matrix $\hat{\boldsymbol{\Sigma}}$ is symmetric, and it is positive definite whenever the columns of $\hat{\boldsymbol{U}}$ are not linearly dependent. The feasible GLS estimator is given by

$$\hat{\boldsymbol{\beta}}_\bullet^{\text{F}} = \big(\boldsymbol{X}_\bullet^\top (\hat{\boldsymbol{\Sigma}}^{-1} \otimes \mathbf{I}_n) \boldsymbol{X}_\bullet\big)^{-1} \boldsymbol{X}_\bullet^\top (\hat{\boldsymbol{\Sigma}}^{-1} \otimes \mathbf{I}_n) \boldsymbol{y}_\bullet, \tag{12.18}$$

and the natural way to estimate its covariance matrix is

$$\widehat{\operatorname{Var}}(\hat{\boldsymbol{\beta}}_\bullet^{\text{F}}) = \big(\boldsymbol{X}_\bullet^\top (\hat{\boldsymbol{\Sigma}}^{-1} \otimes \mathbf{I}_n) \boldsymbol{X}_\bullet\big)^{-1}. \tag{12.19}$$

As expected, the feasible GLS estimator (12.18) and the estimated covariance matrix (12.19) have precisely the same forms as their full GLS counterparts, which are (12.09) and (12.10), respectively.

Because we divided by n in (12.17), $\hat{\boldsymbol{\Sigma}}$ must be a biased estimator of $\boldsymbol{\Sigma}$. If k_i is the same for all i, then it would seem natural to divide by $n - k_i$ instead, and this would at least produce unbiased estimates of the diagonal elements. But we cannot do that when k_i is not the same in all equations. If we were to divide different elements of $\hat{\boldsymbol{U}}^\top\hat{\boldsymbol{U}}$ by different quantities, the resulting estimate of $\boldsymbol{\Sigma}$ would not necessarily be positive definite.

Replacing $\boldsymbol{\Sigma}$ with an estimator $\hat{\boldsymbol{\Sigma}}$ based on OLS estimates, or indeed any other estimator, inevitably degrades the finite-sample properties of the GLS estimator. In general, we would expect the performance of the feasible GLS estimator, relative to that of the GLS estimator, to be especially poor when the sample size is small and the number of equations is large. Under the strong assumption that all the regressors are exogenous, exact inference based on the normal and χ^2 distributions is possible whenever the error terms are normally distributed and $\boldsymbol{\Sigma}$ is known, but this is not the case when $\boldsymbol{\Sigma}$ has to be estimated. Not surprisingly, there is evidence that bootstrapping can yield more reliable inferences than using asymptotic theory for SUR models; see, among others, Rilstone and Veall (1996) and Fiebig and Kim (2000).

Cases in Which OLS Estimation Is Efficient

The SUR estimator (12.09) is efficient under the assumptions we have made, because it is just a special case of the GLS estimator (7.04), the efficiency of which was proved in Section 7.2. In contrast, the OLS estimator (12.06) is, in general, inefficient. The reason is that, unless the matrix $\boldsymbol{\Sigma}$ is proportional to an identity matrix, the error terms of equation (12.04) are not IID. Nevertheless, there are two important special cases in which the OLS estimator is numerically identical to the SUR estimator, and therefore just as efficient.

In the first case, the matrix $\boldsymbol{\Sigma}$ is diagonal, although the diagonal elements need not be the same. This implies that the error terms of equation (12.04) are heteroskedastic but serially independent. It might seem that this heteroskedasticity would cause inefficiency, but that turns out not to be the case. If $\boldsymbol{\Sigma}$ is diagonal, then so is $\boldsymbol{\Sigma}^{-1}$, which means that $\sigma^{ij} = 0$ for $i \neq j$. In that case, the estimating equations (12.16) simplify to

$$\sigma^{ii}\boldsymbol{X}_i^\top(\boldsymbol{y}_i - \boldsymbol{X}_i\hat{\boldsymbol{\beta}}_i^{\rm GLS}) = \boldsymbol{0}, \quad i = 1, \ldots, g.$$

The factors σ^{ii}, which must be nonzero, have no influence on the solutions to the above equations, which are therefore the same as the solutions to the g independent sets of equations $\boldsymbol{X}_i^\top(\boldsymbol{y}_i - \boldsymbol{X}_i\hat{\boldsymbol{\beta}}_i) = \boldsymbol{0}$ which define the equation-by-equation OLS estimator (12.06). Thus, if the error terms are uncorrelated across equations, the GLS and OLS estimators are numerically identical. The "seemingly" unrelated equations are indeed unrelated in this case.

In the second case, the matrix $\boldsymbol{\Sigma}$ is not diagonal, but all the regressor matrices $\boldsymbol{X}_1$ through $\boldsymbol{X}_g$ are the same, and are thus all equal to the matrix $\boldsymbol{X}$ that contains all the explanatory variables. Thus the estimating equations (12.16) become

$$\sum_{j=1}^{g} \sigma^{ij} \boldsymbol{X}^{\top}(\boldsymbol{y}_j - \boldsymbol{X}\hat{\boldsymbol{\beta}}_j^{\mathrm{GLS}}) = \boldsymbol{0}, \quad i = 1, \ldots, g.$$

If we multiply these equations by σ_{mi}, for any m between 1 and g, and sum over i from 1 to g, we obtain

$$\sum_{i=1}^{g} \sum_{j=1}^{g} \sigma_{mi} \sigma^{ij} \boldsymbol{X}^{\top}(\boldsymbol{y}_j - \boldsymbol{X}\hat{\boldsymbol{\beta}}_j^{\mathrm{GLS}}) = \boldsymbol{0}. \tag{12.20}$$

Since the σ_{mi} are elements of $\boldsymbol{\Sigma}$ and the σ^{ij} are elements of its inverse, it follows that the sum $\sum_{i=1}^{g} \sigma_{mi}\sigma^{ij}$ is equal to δ_{mj}, the Kronecker delta, which is equal to 1 if $m = j$ and to 0 otherwise. Thus, for each $m = 1, \ldots, g$, there is just one nonzero term on the left-hand side of (12.20) after the sum over i is performed, namely, that for which $j = m$. In consequence, equations (12.20) collapse to

$$\boldsymbol{X}^{\top}(\boldsymbol{y}_m - \boldsymbol{X}\hat{\boldsymbol{\beta}}_m^{\mathrm{GLS}}) = \boldsymbol{0}.$$

Since these are the estimating equations that define the OLS estimator of the mth equation, we conclude that $\hat{\boldsymbol{\beta}}_m^{\mathrm{GLS}} = \hat{\boldsymbol{\beta}}_m^{\mathrm{OLS}}$ for all m.

A GMM Interpretation

The above proof is straightforward enough, but it is not particularly intuitive. A much more intuitive way to see why the SUR estimator is identical to the OLS estimator in this special case is to interpret all of the estimators we have been studying as GMM estimators. This interpretation also provides a number of other insights and suggests a simple way of testing the overidentifying restrictions that are implicitly present whenever the SUR and OLS estimators are not identical.

Consider the gl theoretical moment conditions

$$\mathrm{E}\big(\boldsymbol{X}^{\top}(\boldsymbol{y}_i - \boldsymbol{X}_i\boldsymbol{\beta}_i)\big) = \boldsymbol{0}, \ \text{ for } i = 1, \ldots, g, \tag{12.21}$$

which state that every regressor, whether or not it appears in a particular equation, must be uncorrelated with the error terms for every equation. In the general case, these moment conditions are used to estimate k parameters, where $k = \sum_{i=1}^{g} k_i$. Since, in general, $k < gl$, we have more moment conditions than parameters, and we can choose a set of linear combinations of the conditions that minimizes the covariance matrix of the estimator. As is clear from the estimating equations (12.12), that is precisely what the SUR estimator (12.09) does. Although these estimating equations were derived from the principles of GLS, they are evidently the empirical counterpart of the optimal moment conditions (9.18) given in Section 9.2 in the context of GMM for the case of a known covariance matrix and exogenous regressors. Therefore, the SUR estimator is, in general, an efficient GMM estimator.

In the special case in which every equation has the same regressors, the number of parameters is also equal to gl. Therefore, we have just as many parameters as moment conditions, and the empirical counterpart of (12.21) collapses to

$$\boldsymbol{X}^{\top}(\boldsymbol{y}_i - \boldsymbol{X}\boldsymbol{\beta}_i) = \mathbf{0}, \quad \text{for } i = 1, \ldots, g,$$

which are just the moment conditions that define the equation-by-equation OLS estimator. Each of these g sets of equations can be solved for the l parameters in $\boldsymbol{\beta}_i$, and the unique solution is $\hat{\boldsymbol{\beta}}_i^{\text{OLS}}$.

We can now see that the two cases in which OLS is efficient arise for two quite different reasons. Clearly, no efficiency gain relative to OLS is possible unless there are more moment conditions than the OLS estimator utilizes. In other words, there can be no efficiency gain unless $gl > k$. In the second case, OLS is efficient because $gl = k$. In the first case, there are in general additional moment conditions, but, because there is no contemporaneous correlation, they are not informative about the model parameters.

We now derive the efficient GMM estimator from first principles and show that it is identical to the SUR estimator. We start from the set of gl sample moments

$$(\mathbf{I}_g \otimes \boldsymbol{X})^{\top}(\boldsymbol{\Sigma}^{-1} \otimes \mathbf{I}_n)(\boldsymbol{y}_\bullet - \boldsymbol{X}_\bullet\boldsymbol{\beta}_\bullet). \tag{12.22}$$

These provide the sample analog, for the linear SUR model, of the left-hand side of the theoretical moment conditions (9.18). The matrix in the middle is the inverse of the covariance matrix of the stacked vector of error terms. Using the second result in (12.08), expression (12.22) can be rewritten as

$$(\boldsymbol{\Sigma}^{-1} \otimes \boldsymbol{X}^{\top})(\boldsymbol{y}_\bullet - \boldsymbol{X}_\bullet\boldsymbol{\beta}_\bullet). \tag{12.23}$$

The covariance matrix of this gl–vector is

$$(\boldsymbol{\Sigma}^{-1} \otimes \boldsymbol{X}^{\top})(\boldsymbol{\Sigma} \otimes \mathbf{I}_n)(\boldsymbol{\Sigma}^{-1} \otimes \boldsymbol{X}) = \boldsymbol{\Sigma}^{-1} \otimes \boldsymbol{X}^{\top}\boldsymbol{X}, \tag{12.24}$$

where we have made repeated use of the second result in (12.08). Combining (12.23) and (12.24) to construct the appropriate quadratic form, we find that the criterion function for fully efficient GMM estimation is

$$\begin{aligned}&(\boldsymbol{y}_\bullet - \boldsymbol{X}_\bullet\boldsymbol{\beta}_\bullet)^{\top}(\boldsymbol{\Sigma}^{-1} \otimes \boldsymbol{X})\big(\boldsymbol{\Sigma} \otimes (\boldsymbol{X}^{\top}\boldsymbol{X})^{-1}\big)(\boldsymbol{\Sigma}^{-1} \otimes \boldsymbol{X}^{\top})(\boldsymbol{y}_\bullet - \boldsymbol{X}_\bullet\boldsymbol{\beta}_\bullet)\\ &\quad = (\boldsymbol{y}_\bullet - \boldsymbol{X}_\bullet\boldsymbol{\beta}_\bullet)^{\top}(\boldsymbol{\Sigma}^{-1} \otimes \boldsymbol{P}_{\boldsymbol{X}})(\boldsymbol{y}_\bullet - \boldsymbol{X}_\bullet\boldsymbol{\beta}_\bullet),\end{aligned} \tag{12.25}$$

where, as usual, $\boldsymbol{P}_{\boldsymbol{X}}$ is the hat matrix, which projects orthogonally on to the subspace spanned by the columns of $\boldsymbol{X}$.

It is not hard to see that the vector $\hat{\beta}_\bullet^{\rm GMM}$ which minimizes expression (12.25) must be identical to $\hat{\beta}_\bullet^{\rm GLS}$. The first-order conditions may be written as

$$\sum_{j=1}^{g} \sigma^{ij} X_i^\top P_X (y_j - X_j \hat{\beta}_j^{\rm GMM}) = \mathbf{0}. \tag{12.26}$$

But since each of the matrices X_i lies in $\mathcal{S}(X)$, it must be the case that $P_X X_i = X_i$, and so conditions (12.26) are actually identical to conditions (12.16), which define the GLS estimator.

Since the GLS, and equally the feasible GLS, estimator can be interpreted as efficient GMM estimators, it is natural to test the overidentifying restrictions that these estimators depend on. These are the restrictions that certain columns of X do not appear in certain equations. The usual Hansen-Sargan statistic, which is just the minimized value of the criterion function (12.25), is asymptotically distributed as $\chi^2(gl - k)$ under the null hypothesis. As usual, the degrees of freedom for the test is equal to the number of moment conditions minus the number of estimated parameters. Investigators should always report the Hansen-Sargan statistic whenever they estimate a multivariate regression model using feasible GLS.

Since feasible GLS is really a feasible efficient GMM estimator, we might prefer to use the continuously updated GMM estimator, which was introduced in Section 9.2. Although the latter estimator is asymptotically equivalent to the one-step feasible GMM estimator, it may have better properties in finite samples. In this case, the continuously updated estimator is simply iterated feasible GLS, and it works as follows. After obtaining the feasible GLS estimator (12.18), we use it to recompute the residuals. These are then used in the formula (12.17) to obtain an updated estimate of the contemporaneous covariance matrix Σ, which is then plugged back into the formula (12.18) to obtain an updated estimate of $\beta_\bullet$. This procedure may be repeated as many times as desired. If the procedure converges, then, as we will see shortly, the estimator that results is equal to the ML estimator computed under the assumption of normal error terms.

Determinants of Square Matrices

The most popular alternative to feasible GLS estimation is maximum likelihood estimation under the assumption that the error terms are normally distributed. We will discuss this estimation method in the next subsection. However, in order to develop the theory of ML estimation for systems of equations, we must first say a few words about **determinants**.

A $p \times p$ square matrix A defines a mapping from Euclidean p-dimensional space, E^p, into itself, by which a vector $x \in E^p$ is mapped into the p-vector Ax. The determinant of A is a scalar quantity which measures the extent to which this mapping expands or contracts p-dimensional volumes in E^p.

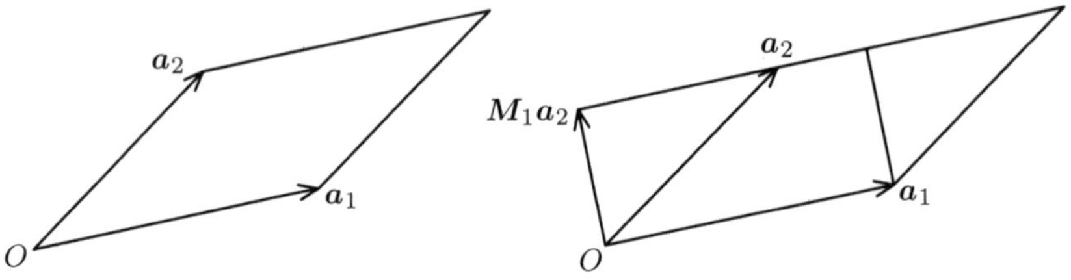

(a) The parallelogram defined by a_1 and a_2

(b) Rectangle of equal area formed with a_1 and M_1a_2

Figure 12.1 Determinants in two dimensions

Consider a simple example in E^2. Volume in 2–dimensional space is just area. The simplest area to consider is the unit square, which can be defined as the parallelogram defined by the two unit basis vectors $\boldsymbol{e}_1$ and $\boldsymbol{e}_2$, where $\boldsymbol{e}_i$ has only one nonzero component, in position i. The area of the unit square is, by definition, 1. The image of the unit square under the mapping defined by a 2×2 matrix $\boldsymbol{A}$ is the parallelogram defined by the two columns of the matrix

$$\boldsymbol{A}[\,\boldsymbol{e}_1 \quad \boldsymbol{e}_2\,] = \boldsymbol{A}\mathbf{I} = \boldsymbol{A} \equiv [\,\boldsymbol{a}_1 \quad \boldsymbol{a}_2\,],$$

where $\boldsymbol{a}_1$ and $\boldsymbol{a}_2$ are the two columns of $\boldsymbol{A}$. The area of a parallelogram in Euclidean geometry is given by base times height, where the length of either one of the two defining vectors can be taken as the base, and the height is then the perpendicular distance between the two parallel sides that correspond to this choice of base. This is illustrated in Figure 12.1.

If we choose $\boldsymbol{a}_1$ as the base, then, as we can see from the figure, the height is the length of the vector $\boldsymbol{M}_1\boldsymbol{a}_2$, where $\boldsymbol{M}_1$ is the orthogonal projection on to the orthogonal complement of $\boldsymbol{a}_1$. Thus the area of the parallelogram defined by $\boldsymbol{a}_1$ and $\boldsymbol{a}_2$ is $\|\boldsymbol{a}_1\|\,\|\boldsymbol{M}_1\boldsymbol{a}_2\|$. By use of Pythagoras' Theorem and a little algebra (see Exercise 12.6), it can be seen that

$$\|\boldsymbol{a}_1\|\,\|\boldsymbol{M}_1\boldsymbol{a}_2\| = |a_{11}a_{22} - a_{12}a_{21}|, \tag{12.27}$$

where a_{ij} is the ij^{th} element of $\boldsymbol{A}$. This quantity is the absolute value of the determinant of $\boldsymbol{A}$, which we write as $|\det \boldsymbol{A}|$. The determinant itself, which is defined as $a_{11}a_{22} - a_{12}a_{21}$, can be of either sign. Its signed value can be written as "$\det \boldsymbol{A}$", but it is more commonly, and perhaps somewhat confusingly, written as $|\boldsymbol{A}|$.

Algebraic expressions for determinants of square matrices of dimension higher than 2 can be found easily enough, but we will have no need of them. We will, however, need to make use of some of the properties of determinants. The principal properties that will matter to us are as follows:

- The determinant of the transpose of a matrix is equal to the determinant of the matrix itself. That is, $|\boldsymbol{A}^\top| = |\boldsymbol{A}|$.

- The determinant of a triangular matrix is the product of its diagonal elements.
- Since a diagonal matrix can be regarded as a special triangular matrix, its determinant is also the product of its diagonal elements.
- Since an identity matrix is a diagonal matrix with all diagonal elements equal to unity, the determinant of an identity matrix is 1.
- If a matrix can be partitioned so as to be block-diagonal, then its determinant is the product of the determinants of the diagonal blocks.
- Interchanging two rows, or two columns, of a matrix leaves the absolute value of the determinant unchanged but changes its sign.
- The determinant of the product of two square matrices of the same dimensions is the product of their determinants, from which it follows that the determinant of $\boldsymbol{A}^{-1}$ is the reciprocal of the determinant of $\boldsymbol{A}$.
- If a matrix can be inverted, its determinant must be nonzero. Conversely, if a matrix is singular, its determinant is 0.
- The derivative of $\log|\boldsymbol{A}|$ with respect to the ij^{th} element a_{ij} of $\boldsymbol{A}$ is the ji^{th} element of $\boldsymbol{A}^{-1}$.

Maximum Likelihood Estimation

If we assume that the error terms of an SUR system are normally distributed, the system can be estimated by maximum likelihood. The model to be estimated can be written as

$$\boldsymbol{y}_\bullet = \boldsymbol{X}_\bullet \boldsymbol{\beta}_\bullet + \boldsymbol{u}_\bullet, \quad \boldsymbol{u}_\bullet \sim \mathrm{N}(\mathbf{0}, \boldsymbol{\Sigma} \otimes \mathbf{I}_n). \tag{12.28}$$

The loglikelihood function for this model is the logarithm of the joint density of the components of the vector $\boldsymbol{y}_\bullet$. In order to derive that density, we must start with the density of the vector $\boldsymbol{u}_\bullet$.

Up to this point, we have not actually written down the density of a random vector that follows the multivariate normal distribution. We will do so in a moment. But first, we state a more fundamental result, which extends the result (10.94) that was proved in Section 10.8 for univariate densities of transformations of variables to the case of multivariate densities.

Let $\boldsymbol{z}$ be a random m–vector with known density $f_{\boldsymbol{z}}(\boldsymbol{z})$, and let $\boldsymbol{x}$ be another random m–vector such that $\boldsymbol{z} = \boldsymbol{h}(\boldsymbol{x})$, where the deterministic function $\boldsymbol{h}(\cdot)$ is a one to one mapping of the support of the random vector $\boldsymbol{x}$, which is a subset of $\mathbb{R}^m$, into the support of $\boldsymbol{z}$. Then the multivariate analog of the result (10.94) is

$$f_{\boldsymbol{x}}(\boldsymbol{x}) = f_{\boldsymbol{z}}\big(\boldsymbol{h}(\boldsymbol{x})\big)\big|\det \boldsymbol{J}(\boldsymbol{x})\big|, \tag{12.29}$$

where $\boldsymbol{J}(\boldsymbol{x}) \equiv \partial \boldsymbol{h}(\boldsymbol{x})/\partial \boldsymbol{x}$ is the Jacobian matrix of the transformation, that is, the $m \times m$ matrix containing the derivatives of the components of $\boldsymbol{h}(\boldsymbol{x})$ with respect to those of $\boldsymbol{x}$, and we have written $|\det \boldsymbol{J}(\boldsymbol{x})|$ to signify the absolute value of the determinant.

Using (12.29), it is not difficult to show that, if the $m \times 1$ vector $\boldsymbol{z}$ follows the multivariate normal distribution with mean vector $\mathbf{0}$ and covariance matrix $\boldsymbol{\Omega}$, then its density is equal to

$$(2\pi)^{-m/2}|\boldsymbol{\Omega}|^{-1/2}\exp\big(-\tfrac{1}{2}\boldsymbol{z}^\top\boldsymbol{\Omega}^{-1}\boldsymbol{z}\big). \tag{12.30}$$

Readers are asked to prove a slightly more general result in Exercise 12.8.

For the system (12.28), the function $\boldsymbol{h}(\cdot)$ that gives $\boldsymbol{u}_\bullet$ as a function of $\boldsymbol{y}_\bullet$ is the right-hand side of the equation

$$\boldsymbol{u}_\bullet = \boldsymbol{y}_\bullet - \boldsymbol{X}_\bullet\boldsymbol{\beta}_\bullet. \tag{12.31}$$

Thus we see that, if there are no lagged dependent variables in the matrix $\boldsymbol{X}_\bullet$, then the Jacobian of the transformation is just the identity matrix, of which the determinant is 1.

The Jacobian is, in general, much more complicated if there are lagged dependent variables, because the elements of $\boldsymbol{X}_\bullet$ depend on the elements of $\boldsymbol{y}_\bullet$. However, as readers are invited to check in Exercise 12.10, even though the Jacobian is not equal to the identity matrix in such a case, its determinant is still 1. Therefore, we can ignore the Jacobian when we compute the density of $\boldsymbol{y}_\bullet$. When we substitute (12.31) into (12.30), as the result (12.29) tells us to do, we find that the density of $\boldsymbol{y}_\bullet$ is $(2\pi)^{-gn/2}$ times

$$|\boldsymbol{\Sigma}\otimes\mathbf{I}_n|^{-1/2}\exp\big(-\tfrac{1}{2}(\boldsymbol{y}_\bullet - \boldsymbol{X}_\bullet\boldsymbol{\beta}_\bullet)^\top(\boldsymbol{\Sigma}^{-1}\otimes\mathbf{I}_n)(\boldsymbol{y}_\bullet - \boldsymbol{X}_\bullet\boldsymbol{\beta}_\bullet)\big). \tag{12.32}$$

Jointly maximizing the logarithm of this function with respect to $\boldsymbol{\beta}_\bullet$ and the elements of $\boldsymbol{\Sigma}$ gives the ML estimator of the SUR system.

The argument of the exponential function in (12.32) plays the same role for a multivariate linear regression model as the sum of squares term plays in the loglikelihood function (10.10) for a linear regression model with IID normal errors. In fact, it is clear from (12.32) that maximizing the loglikelihood with respect to $\boldsymbol{\beta}_\bullet$ for a given $\boldsymbol{\Sigma}$ is equivalent to minimizing the function

$$(\boldsymbol{y}_\bullet - \boldsymbol{X}_\bullet\boldsymbol{\beta}_\bullet)^\top(\boldsymbol{\Sigma}^{-1}\otimes\mathbf{I}_n)(\boldsymbol{y}_\bullet - \boldsymbol{X}_\bullet\boldsymbol{\beta}_\bullet)$$

with respect to $\boldsymbol{\beta}_\bullet$. This expression is just the criterion function (12.11) that is minimized in order to obtain the GLS estimator (12.09). Therefore, the ML estimator $\hat{\boldsymbol{\beta}}_\bullet^{\rm ML}$ must have exactly the same form as (12.09), with the matrix $\boldsymbol{\Sigma}$ replaced by its ML estimator $\hat{\boldsymbol{\Sigma}}_{\rm ML}$, which we will derive shortly.

It follows from (12.32) that the loglikelihood function $\ell(\boldsymbol{\Sigma}, \boldsymbol{\beta}_\bullet)$ for the model (12.28) can be written as

$$-\frac{gn}{2}\log 2\pi - \frac{1}{2}\log|\boldsymbol{\Sigma}\otimes\mathbf{I}_n| - \frac{1}{2}(\boldsymbol{y}_\bullet - \boldsymbol{X}_\bullet\boldsymbol{\beta}_\bullet)^\top(\boldsymbol{\Sigma}^{-1}\otimes\mathbf{I}_n)(\boldsymbol{y}_\bullet - \boldsymbol{X}_\bullet\boldsymbol{\beta}_\bullet).$$

The properties of determinants set out in the previous subsection can be used to show that the determinant of $\boldsymbol{\Sigma} \otimes \mathbf{I}_n$ is $|\boldsymbol{\Sigma}|^n$; see Exercise 12.11. Thus this loglikelihood function simplifies to

$$-\frac{gn}{2}\log 2\pi - \frac{n}{2}\log|\boldsymbol{\Sigma}| - \frac{1}{2}(\boldsymbol{y}_\bullet - \boldsymbol{X}_\bullet\boldsymbol{\beta}_\bullet)^\top(\boldsymbol{\Sigma}^{-1} \otimes \mathbf{I}_n)(\boldsymbol{y}_\bullet - \boldsymbol{X}_\bullet\boldsymbol{\beta}_\bullet). \quad (12.33)$$

We have already seen how to maximize the function (12.33) with respect to $\boldsymbol{\beta}_\bullet$ conditional on $\boldsymbol{\Sigma}$. Now we want to maximize it with respect to $\boldsymbol{\Sigma}$.

Maximizing $\ell(\boldsymbol{\Sigma}, \boldsymbol{\beta}_\bullet)$ with respect to $\boldsymbol{\Sigma}$ is of course equivalent to maximizing it with respect to $\boldsymbol{\Sigma}^{-1}$, and it turns out to be technically simpler to differentiate with respect to the elements of the latter matrix. Note first that, since the determinant of the inverse of a matrix is the reciprocal of the determinant of the matrix itself, we have $-\log|\boldsymbol{\Sigma}| = \log|\boldsymbol{\Sigma}^{-1}|$, so that we can readily express all of (12.33) in terms of $\boldsymbol{\Sigma}^{-1}$ rather than $\boldsymbol{\Sigma}$.

It is obvious that the derivative of any $p \times q$ matrix $\boldsymbol{A}$ with respect to its ij^{th} element is the $p \times q$ matrix $\boldsymbol{E}_{ij}$, all the elements of which are 0, except for the ij^{th}, which is 1. Recall that we write the ij^{th} element of $\boldsymbol{\Sigma}^{-1}$ as σ^{ij}. We therefore find that

$$\frac{\partial \boldsymbol{\Sigma}^{-1}}{\partial \sigma^{ij}} = \boldsymbol{E}_{ij}, \quad (12.34)$$

where in this case $\boldsymbol{E}_{ij}$ is a $g \times g$ matrix. We remarked in our earlier discussion of determinants that the derivative of $\log|\boldsymbol{A}|$ with respect to a_{ij} is the ji^{th} element of $\boldsymbol{A}^{-1}$. Armed with this result and (12.34), we see that the derivative of the loglikelihood function $\ell(\boldsymbol{\Sigma}, \boldsymbol{\beta}_\bullet)$ with respect to the element σ^{ij} is

$$\frac{\partial \ell(\boldsymbol{\Sigma}, \boldsymbol{\beta}_\bullet)}{\partial \sigma^{ij}} = \frac{n}{2}\sigma_{ij} - \frac{1}{2}(\boldsymbol{y}_\bullet - \boldsymbol{X}_\bullet\boldsymbol{\beta}_\bullet)^\top(\boldsymbol{E}_{ij} \otimes \mathbf{I}_n)(\boldsymbol{y}_\bullet - \boldsymbol{X}_\bullet\boldsymbol{\beta}_\bullet). \quad (12.35)$$

The Kronecker product $\boldsymbol{E}_{ij} \otimes \mathbf{I}_n$ has only one nonzero block containing $\mathbf{I}_n$. It is easy to conclude from this that

$$(\boldsymbol{y}_\bullet - \boldsymbol{X}_\bullet\boldsymbol{\beta}_\bullet)^\top(\boldsymbol{E}_{ij} \otimes \mathbf{I}_n)(\boldsymbol{y}_\bullet - \boldsymbol{X}_\bullet\boldsymbol{\beta}_\bullet) = (\boldsymbol{y}_i - \boldsymbol{X}_i\boldsymbol{\beta}_i)^\top(\boldsymbol{y}_j - \boldsymbol{X}_j\boldsymbol{\beta}_j).$$

By equating the partial derivative (12.35) to zero, we find that the ML estimator $\hat{\sigma}_{ij}^{\text{ML}}$ is

$$\hat{\sigma}_{ij}^{\text{ML}} = \frac{1}{n}(\boldsymbol{y}_i - \boldsymbol{X}_i\hat{\boldsymbol{\beta}}_i^{\text{ML}})^\top(\boldsymbol{y}_j - \boldsymbol{X}_j\hat{\boldsymbol{\beta}}_j^{\text{ML}}).$$

If we define the $n \times g$ matrix $\boldsymbol{U}(\boldsymbol{\beta}_\bullet)$ to have i^{th} column $\boldsymbol{y}_i - \boldsymbol{X}_i\boldsymbol{\beta}_i$, then we can conveniently write the ML estimator of $\boldsymbol{\Sigma}$ as follows:

$$\hat{\boldsymbol{\Sigma}}_{\text{ML}} = \frac{1}{n}\boldsymbol{U}^\top(\hat{\boldsymbol{\beta}}_\bullet^{\text{ML}})\boldsymbol{U}(\hat{\boldsymbol{\beta}}_\bullet^{\text{ML}}). \quad (12.36)$$

This looks like equation (12.17), which defines the covariance matrix used in feasible GLS estimation. Equations (12.36) and (12.17) have exactly the same form, but they are based on different matrices of residuals. Equation (12.36) and equation (12.09) evaluated at $\hat{\boldsymbol{\Sigma}}^{\rm ML}$, that is

$$\hat{\boldsymbol{\beta}}_\bullet^{\rm ML} = \big(\boldsymbol{X}_\bullet^\top(\hat{\boldsymbol{\Sigma}}_{\rm ML}^{-1} \otimes \mathbf{I}_n)\boldsymbol{X}_\bullet\big)^{-1}\boldsymbol{X}_\bullet^\top(\hat{\boldsymbol{\Sigma}}_{\rm ML}^{-1} \otimes \mathbf{I}_n)\boldsymbol{y}_\bullet, \tag{12.37}$$

together define the ML estimator for the model (12.28).

Equations (12.36) and (12.37) are exactly the ones that are used by the continuously updated GMM estimator to update the estimates of $\boldsymbol{\Sigma}$ and $\boldsymbol{\beta}_\bullet$, respectively. It follows that, if the continuous updating procedure converges, it converges to the ML estimator. Consequently, we can estimate the covariance matrix of $\hat{\boldsymbol{\beta}}_\bullet^{\rm ML}$ in the same way as for the GLS or GMM estimator, by the formula

$$\widehat{\rm Var}(\hat{\boldsymbol{\beta}}_\bullet^{\rm ML}) = \big(\boldsymbol{X}_\bullet^\top(\hat{\boldsymbol{\Sigma}}_{\rm ML}^{-1} \otimes \mathbf{I}_n)\boldsymbol{X}_\bullet\big)^{-1}. \tag{12.38}$$

It is also possible to estimate the covariance matrix of the estimated contemporaneous covariance matrix, $\hat{\boldsymbol{\Sigma}}^{\rm ML}$, although this is rarely done. If the elements of $\boldsymbol{\Sigma}$ are stacked in a vector of length g^2, a suitable estimator is

$$\widehat{\rm Var}\big(\boldsymbol{\Sigma}(\hat{\boldsymbol{\beta}}_\bullet^{\rm ML})\big) = \frac{2}{n}\,\boldsymbol{\Sigma}(\hat{\boldsymbol{\beta}}_\bullet^{\rm ML}) \otimes \boldsymbol{\Sigma}(\hat{\boldsymbol{\beta}}_\bullet^{\rm ML}). \tag{12.39}$$

Notice that the estimated variance of any diagonal element of $\boldsymbol{\Sigma}$ is just twice the square of that element, divided by n. This is precisely what is obtained for the univariate case in Exercise 10.10. As with that result, the asymptotic validity of (12.39) depends critically on the assumption that the error terms are multivariate normal.

As we saw in Chapter 10, ML estimators are consistent and asymptotically efficient *if* the underlying model is correctly specified. It may therefore seem that the asymptotic efficiency of the ML estimator (12.37) depends critically on the multivariate normality assumption. However, the fact that the ML estimator is identical to the continuously updated efficient GMM estimator means that it is in fact efficient in the same sense as the latter. When the errors are not normal, the estimator is more properly termed a QMLE (see Section 10.4). As such, it is consistent, but not necessarily efficient, under assumptions about the error terms that are no stronger than those needed for feasible GLS to be consistent. Moreover, if the stronger assumptions made in (12.02) hold, even without normality, then the estimator (12.38) of $\mathrm{Var}(\hat{\boldsymbol{\beta}}_\bullet^{\rm ML})$ is asymptotically valid. If the error terms are not normal, it would be necessary to have information about their actual distribution in order to derive an estimator with a smaller asymptotic variance than (12.37).

It is of considerable theoretical interest to concentrate the loglikelihood function (12.33) with respect to $\boldsymbol{\Sigma}$. In order to do so, we use the first-order conditions that led to (12.36) to define $\boldsymbol{\Sigma}(\boldsymbol{\beta}_\bullet)$ as the matrix that maximizes (12.33) for given $\boldsymbol{\beta}_\bullet$. We find that

$$\boldsymbol{\Sigma}(\boldsymbol{\beta}_\bullet) \equiv \frac{1}{n}\boldsymbol{U}^\top(\boldsymbol{\beta}_\bullet)\boldsymbol{U}(\boldsymbol{\beta}_\bullet).$$

A calculation of a type that should now be familiar then shows that

$$\begin{aligned}(\boldsymbol{y}_\bullet - \boldsymbol{X}_\bullet\boldsymbol{\beta}_\bullet)^\top(\boldsymbol{\Sigma}^{-1}\otimes\mathbf{I}_n)(\boldsymbol{y}_\bullet - \boldsymbol{X}_\bullet\boldsymbol{\beta}_\bullet)\\ = \sum_{i=1}^{g}\sum_{j=1}^{g}\sigma^{ij}(\boldsymbol{y}_i - \boldsymbol{X}_i\boldsymbol{\beta}_i)^\top(\boldsymbol{y}_j - \boldsymbol{X}_j\boldsymbol{\beta}_j).\end{aligned} \tag{12.40}$$

When $\sigma^{ij} = \sigma^{ij}(\boldsymbol{\beta}_\bullet)$, which denotes the ij^{th} element of $\boldsymbol{\Sigma}^{-1}(\boldsymbol{\beta}_\bullet)$, the right-hand side of equation (12.40) is

$$\begin{aligned}\sum_{i=1}^{g}\sum_{j=1}^{g}\sigma^{ij}(\boldsymbol{\beta}_\bullet)\big(\boldsymbol{U}^\top(\boldsymbol{\beta}_\bullet)\boldsymbol{U}(\boldsymbol{\beta}_\bullet)\big)_{ij} &= n\sum_{i=1}^{g}\sum_{j=1}^{g}\sigma^{ij}(\boldsymbol{\beta}_\bullet)\sigma_{ij}(\boldsymbol{\beta}_\bullet)\\ &= n\sum_{i=1}^{g}(\mathbf{I}_g)_{ii} = n\,\mathrm{Tr}(\mathbf{I}_g) = gn,\end{aligned}$$

where we have made use of the trace operator, which sums the diagonal elements of a square matrix; see Section 2.6. By substituting this result into expression (12.33), we see that the concentrated loglikelihood function can be written as

$$-\frac{gn}{2}(\log 2\pi + 1) - \frac{n}{2}\log\Big|\frac{1}{n}\boldsymbol{U}^\top(\boldsymbol{\beta}_\bullet)\boldsymbol{U}(\boldsymbol{\beta}_\bullet)\Big|. \tag{12.41}$$

This expression depends on the data only through the determinant of the covariance matrix of the residuals. It is the multivariate generalization of the concentrated loglikelihood function (10.11) that we obtained in Section 10.2 in the univariate case. We saw there that the concentrated function depends on the data only through the sum of squared residuals.

It is quite possible to minimize the determinant in (12.41) with respect to $\boldsymbol{\beta}_\bullet$ directly. It may or may not be numerically simpler to do so than to solve the coupled equations (12.37) and (12.36).

We saw in Section 3.6 that the squared residuals of a univariate regression model tend to be smaller than the squared error terms, because least-squares estimates make the sum of squared residuals as small as possible. For a similar reason, the residuals from ML estimation of a multivariate regression model tend to be too small and too highly correlated with each other. We observe both effects, because the determinant of $\boldsymbol{\Sigma}$ can be made smaller either by reducing the sums of squared residuals associated with the individual equations or by increasing the correlations among the residuals. This is likely to be most noticeable when g and/or the k_i are large relative to n.

Although feasible GLS and ML with the assumption of normally distributed errors are by far the most commonly used methods of estimating linear SUR systems, they are by no means the only ones that have been proposed. For fuller treatments, a classic reference on linear SUR systems is Srivastava and Giles (1987), and a useful recent survey paper is Fiebig (2001).

12.3 Systems of Nonlinear Regressions

Many multivariate regression models are nonlinear. For example, economists routinely estimate **demand systems**, in which the shares of consumer expenditure on various classes of goods and services are explained by incomes, prices, and perhaps other explanatory variables. Demand systems may be estimated using aggregate time-series data, cross-section data, or mixed time-series/cross-section (panel) data on households.[1]

The **multivariate nonlinear regression model** is a system of nonlinear regressions which can be written as

$$y_{ti} = x_{ti}(\boldsymbol{\beta}) + u_{ti}, \quad t = 1, \ldots, n, \;\; i = 1, \ldots, g. \tag{12.42}$$

Here y_{ti} is the tth observation on the ith dependent variable, $x_{ti}(\boldsymbol{\beta})$ is the tth observation on the regression function which determines the conditional mean of that dependent variable, $\boldsymbol{\beta}$ is a k–vector of parameters to be estimated, and u_{ti} is an error term which is assumed to have mean zero conditional on all the explanatory variables that implicitly appear in all the regression functions $x_{tj}(\boldsymbol{\beta})$, $j = 1, \ldots, g$. In the demand system case, y_{ti} would be the share of expenditure on commodity i for observation t, and the explanatory variables would include prices and income. We assume that the error terms in (12.42), like those in (12.01), satisfy assumption (12.02). They are serially uncorrelated, homoskedastic within each equation, and have contemporaneous covariance matrix $\boldsymbol{\Sigma}$ with typical element σ_{ij}.

The equations of the system (12.42) can also be written using essentially the same notation as we used for univariate nonlinear regression models in Chapter 6. If, for each $i = 1, \ldots, g$, the n–vectors $\boldsymbol{y}_i$, $\boldsymbol{x}_i(\boldsymbol{\beta})$, and $\boldsymbol{u}_i$ are defined to have typical elements y_{ti}, u_{ti}, and $x_{ti}(\boldsymbol{\beta})$, respectively, then the entire system can be expressed as

$$\boldsymbol{y}_i = \boldsymbol{x}_i(\boldsymbol{\beta}) + \boldsymbol{u}_i, \quad \mathrm{E}(\boldsymbol{u}_i\boldsymbol{u}_j^{\top}) = \sigma_{ij}\mathbf{I}_n, \quad i, j = 1, \ldots, g. \tag{12.43}$$

We have written (12.42) and (12.43) in such a way that there is just a single vector of parameters, denoted $\boldsymbol{\beta}$. Every individual parameter may, at least in principle, appear in every equation, although that is rare in practice. In the demand systems case, however, some but not all of the parameters typically do appear in every equation of the system. Thus systems of nonlinear regressions very often involve **cross-equation restrictions**.

Multivariate nonlinear regression models can be estimated in essentially the same way as the multivariate linear regression model (12.01). Feasible GLS

[1] The literature on demand systems is vast; see, among many others, Christensen, Jorgenson, and Lau (1975), Barten (1977), Deaton and Muellbauer (1980), Pollak and Wales (1981, 1987), Browning and Meghir (1991), Lewbel (1991), and Blundell, Browning, and Meghir (1994).

and maximum likelihood are both commonly used. The results we obtained in the previous section still apply, provided they are modified to allow for the nonlinearity of the regression functions and for cross-equation restrictions. Our discussion will therefore be quite brief.

Estimation

We saw in Section 7.3 that nonlinear GLS estimates can be obtained either by minimizing the criterion function (7.13) or, equivalently, by solving the set of first-order conditions (7.14). For the multivariate nonlinear regression model (12.42), the criterion function can be written so that it looks very much like expression (12.11). Let $\boldsymbol{y}_\bullet$ once again denote a gn–vector of the $\boldsymbol{y}_i$ stacked vertically, and let $\boldsymbol{x}_\bullet(\boldsymbol{\beta})$ denote a gn–vector of the $\boldsymbol{x}_i(\boldsymbol{\beta})$ stacked in the same way. The criterion function (7.13) then becomes

$$\big(\boldsymbol{y}_\bullet - \boldsymbol{x}_\bullet(\boldsymbol{\beta})\big)^{\top}(\boldsymbol{\Sigma}^{-1} \otimes \mathbf{I}_n)\big(\boldsymbol{y}_\bullet - \boldsymbol{x}_\bullet(\boldsymbol{\beta})\big). \tag{12.44}$$

Minimizing (12.44) with respect to $\boldsymbol{\beta}$ yields nonlinear GLS estimates which, by the results of Section 7.2, are consistent and asymptotically efficient under standard regularity conditions.

The first-order conditions for the minimization of (12.44) give rise to the following moment conditions, which have a very similar form to the moment conditions (12.12) that we found for the linear case:

$$\boldsymbol{X}_\bullet^{\top}(\boldsymbol{\beta})(\boldsymbol{\Sigma}^{-1} \otimes \mathbf{I}_n)\big(\boldsymbol{y}_\bullet - \boldsymbol{x}_\bullet(\boldsymbol{\beta})\big) = \mathbf{0}. \tag{12.45}$$

Here, the $gn \times k$ matrix $\boldsymbol{X}_\bullet(\boldsymbol{\beta})$ is a matrix of partial derivatives of the $x_{ti}(\boldsymbol{\beta})$. If the $n \times k$ matrices $\boldsymbol{X}_i(\boldsymbol{\beta})$ are defined, just as in the univariate case, so that the tj^{th} element of $\boldsymbol{X}_i(\boldsymbol{\beta})$ is $\partial x_{ti}(\boldsymbol{\beta})/\partial \beta_j$, for $t = 1, \ldots, n$, $j = 1, \ldots, k$, then $\boldsymbol{X}_\bullet(\boldsymbol{\beta})$ is the matrix formed by stacking the $\boldsymbol{X}_i(\boldsymbol{\beta})$ vertically. Except in the special case in which each parameter appears in only one equation of the system, $\boldsymbol{X}_\bullet(\boldsymbol{\beta})$ does not have the block-diagonal structure of $\boldsymbol{X}_\bullet$ in (12.05).

Despite this fact, it is not hard to show that the moment conditions (12.45) can be expressed in a compact form like (12.16), but with a double sum. As readers are asked to check in Exercise 12.12, we obtain estimating equations of the form

$$\sum_{i=1}^{g}\sum_{j=1}^{g} \sigma^{ij} \boldsymbol{X}_i^{\top}(\boldsymbol{\beta})\big(\boldsymbol{y}_j - \boldsymbol{x}_j(\boldsymbol{\beta})\big) = \mathbf{0}. \tag{12.46}$$

The vector $\hat{\boldsymbol{\beta}}^{\text{GLS}}$ that solves these equations is the nonlinear GLS estimator.

Adapting expression (7.05) to the model (12.43) gives the standard estimate of the covariance matrix of the nonlinear GLS estimator, namely,

$$\widehat{\operatorname{Var}}(\hat{\boldsymbol{\beta}}^{\text{GLS}}) = \big(\boldsymbol{X}_\bullet^{\top}(\hat{\boldsymbol{\beta}}^{\text{GLS}})(\boldsymbol{\Sigma}^{-1} \otimes \mathbf{I}_n)\boldsymbol{X}_\bullet(\hat{\boldsymbol{\beta}}^{\text{GLS}})\big)^{-1}. \tag{12.47}$$

This can also be written (see Exercise 12.12 again) as

$$\widehat{\operatorname{Var}}(\hat{\boldsymbol{\beta}}^{\mathrm{GLS}}) = \Big(\sum_{i=1}^{g}\sum_{j=1}^{g}\sigma^{ij}\boldsymbol{X}_i^{\top}(\hat{\boldsymbol{\beta}}^{\mathrm{GLS}})\boldsymbol{X}_j(\hat{\boldsymbol{\beta}}^{\mathrm{GLS}})\Big)^{-1}. \tag{12.48}$$

Feasible GLS estimation works in essentially the same way for nonlinear multivariate regression models as it does for linear ones. The individual equations of the system are first estimated separately by either ordinary or nonlinear least squares, as appropriate. The residuals are then grouped into an $n \times g$ matrix $\hat{\boldsymbol{U}}$, and equation (12.17) is used to obtain the estimate $\hat{\boldsymbol{\Sigma}}$. We can then replace $\boldsymbol{\Sigma}$ by $\hat{\boldsymbol{\Sigma}}$ in the GLS criterion function (12.44) or in the moment conditions (12.45) to obtain the feasible GLS estimator $\hat{\boldsymbol{\beta}}^{\mathrm{F}}$. We may also use a continuously updated estimator, alternately updating our estimates of $\boldsymbol{\beta}$ and $\boldsymbol{\Sigma}$. If this iterated feasible GLS procedure converges, then we have obtained ML estimates, although there may well be more computationally attractive ways to do so.

Maximum likelihood estimation under the assumption of normality is very popular for multivariate nonlinear regression models. For the system (12.42), the loglikelihood function can be written as

$$-\frac{gn}{2}\log 2\pi - \frac{n}{2}\log|\boldsymbol{\Sigma}| - \frac{1}{2}\big(\boldsymbol{y}_\bullet - \boldsymbol{x}_\bullet(\boldsymbol{\beta})\big)^{\top}(\boldsymbol{\Sigma}^{-1}\otimes \mathbf{I}_n)\big(\boldsymbol{y}_\bullet - \boldsymbol{x}_\bullet(\boldsymbol{\beta})\big). \tag{12.49}$$

This is the analog of the loglikelihood function (12.33) for the linear case. Maximizing (12.49) with respect to $\boldsymbol{\beta}$ for given $\boldsymbol{\Sigma}$ is equivalent to minimizing the criterion function (12.44) with respect to $\boldsymbol{\beta}$, and so the first-order conditions are equations (12.45). Maximizing (12.49) with respect to $\boldsymbol{\Sigma}$ for given $\boldsymbol{\beta}$ leads to first-order conditions that can be written as

$$\boldsymbol{\Sigma}(\boldsymbol{\beta}) = \frac{1}{n}\boldsymbol{U}^{\top}(\boldsymbol{\beta})\boldsymbol{U}(\boldsymbol{\beta}),$$

in exactly the same way as the maximization of (12.33) with respect to $\boldsymbol{\Sigma}$ led to equation (12.36). Here the $n \times g$ matrix $\boldsymbol{U}(\boldsymbol{\beta})$ is defined so that its ith column is $\boldsymbol{y}_i - \boldsymbol{x}_i(\boldsymbol{\beta})$.

Thus the estimating equations that define the ML estimator are

$$\begin{aligned} &\boldsymbol{X}_\bullet^{\top}(\hat{\boldsymbol{\beta}}^{\mathrm{ML}})(\hat{\boldsymbol{\Sigma}}_{\mathrm{ML}}^{-1}\otimes \mathbf{I}_n)\big(\boldsymbol{y}_\bullet - \boldsymbol{x}_\bullet(\hat{\boldsymbol{\beta}}^{\mathrm{ML}})\big) = \mathbf{0}, \quad \text{and} \\ &\hat{\boldsymbol{\Sigma}}_{\mathrm{ML}} = \frac{1}{n}\boldsymbol{U}^{\top}(\hat{\boldsymbol{\beta}}^{\mathrm{ML}})\boldsymbol{U}(\hat{\boldsymbol{\beta}}^{\mathrm{ML}}). \end{aligned} \tag{12.50}$$

As in the linear case, these are also the estimating equations for the continuously updated GMM estimator. The covariance matrix of $\hat{\boldsymbol{\beta}}^{\mathrm{ML}}$ is, of course, given by either of the formulas (12.47) or (12.48) evaluated at $\hat{\boldsymbol{\beta}}^{\mathrm{ML}}$ and $\hat{\boldsymbol{\Sigma}}_{\mathrm{ML}}$. The loglikelihood function concentrated with respect to $\boldsymbol{\Sigma}$ can be written, just like expression (12.41), as

$$-\frac{gn}{2}(\log 2\pi + 1) - \frac{n}{2}\log\left|\frac{1}{n}\boldsymbol{U}^\top(\boldsymbol{\beta})\boldsymbol{U}(\boldsymbol{\beta})\right|. \tag{12.51}$$

As in the linear case, it may or may not be numerically easier to maximize the concentrated function directly than to solve the estimating equations (12.50).

The Gauss-Newton Regression

The Gauss-Newton regression can be very useful in the context of multivariate regression models, both linear and nonlinear. The starting point for setting up the GNR for both types of multivariate model is equation (7.15), the GNR for the standard univariate model $\boldsymbol{y} = \boldsymbol{x}(\boldsymbol{\beta}) + \boldsymbol{u}$, with $\mathrm{Var}(\boldsymbol{u}) = \boldsymbol{\Omega}$. This GNR takes the form

$$\boldsymbol{\Psi}^\top\big(\boldsymbol{y} - \boldsymbol{x}(\boldsymbol{\beta})\big) = \boldsymbol{\Psi}^\top\boldsymbol{X}(\boldsymbol{\beta})\boldsymbol{b} + \text{residuals},$$

where, as usual, $\boldsymbol{X}(\boldsymbol{\beta})$ is the matrix of partial derivatives of the regression functions, and $\boldsymbol{\Psi}$ is such that $\boldsymbol{\Psi}\boldsymbol{\Psi}^\top = \boldsymbol{\Omega}^{-1}$.

Expressed as a univariate regression, the multivariate model (12.43) becomes

$$\boldsymbol{y}_\bullet = \boldsymbol{x}_\bullet(\boldsymbol{\beta}) + \boldsymbol{u}_\bullet, \quad \mathrm{Var}(\boldsymbol{u}_\bullet) = \boldsymbol{\Sigma} \otimes \mathbf{I}_n. \tag{12.52}$$

If we now define the $g \times g$ matrix $\boldsymbol{\Psi}$ such that $\boldsymbol{\Psi}\boldsymbol{\Psi}^\top = \boldsymbol{\Sigma}^{-1}$, it is clear that

$$(\boldsymbol{\Psi} \otimes \mathbf{I}_n)(\boldsymbol{\Psi} \otimes \mathbf{I}_n)^\top = (\boldsymbol{\Psi} \otimes \mathbf{I}_n)(\boldsymbol{\Psi}^\top \otimes \mathbf{I}_n) = (\boldsymbol{\Psi}\boldsymbol{\Psi}^\top \otimes \mathbf{I}_n) = \boldsymbol{\Sigma}^{-1} \otimes \mathbf{I}_n,$$

where the last expression is the inverse of the covariance matrix of $\boldsymbol{u}_\bullet$. From (7.15), the GNR corresponding to (12.52) is therefore

$$(\boldsymbol{\Psi}^\top \otimes \mathbf{I}_n)\big(\boldsymbol{y}_\bullet - \boldsymbol{x}_\bullet(\boldsymbol{\beta})\big) = (\boldsymbol{\Psi}^\top \otimes \mathbf{I}_n)\boldsymbol{X}_\bullet(\boldsymbol{\beta})\boldsymbol{b} + \text{residuals}. \tag{12.53}$$

The $gn \times k$ matrix $\boldsymbol{X}_\bullet(\boldsymbol{\beta})$ is the matrix of partial derivatives that we already defined for use in the moment conditions (12.45). Observe that, as required for a properly defined artificial regression, the inner product of the regressand with the matrix of regressors yields the left-hand side of the moment conditions (12.45), and the inverse of the inner product of the regressor matrix with itself has the same form as the covariance matrix (12.47).

The Gauss-Newton regression (12.53) can be useful in a number of contexts. It provides a convenient way to solve the estimating equations (12.45) in order to obtain an estimate of $\boldsymbol{\beta}$ for given $\boldsymbol{\Sigma}$, and it automatically computes the covariance matrix estimate (12.47) as well. Because feasible GLS and ML estimation are algebraically identical as regards the estimation of the parameter vector $\boldsymbol{\beta}$, the GNR is useful in both contexts. In practice, it is frequently used to calculate test statistics for restrictions on $\boldsymbol{\beta}$; see Section 6.7. Another important use is to impose cross-equation restrictions after equation-by-equation estimation. For this purpose, the multivariate GNR is just as useful for linear systems as for nonlinear ones; see Exercise 12.13.

12.4 Linear Simultaneous Equations Models

In Chapter 8, we dealt with instrumental variables estimation of a single equation in which some of the explanatory variables are endogenous. As we noted there, it is necessary to have information about the data-generating process for all of the endogenous variables in order to determine the optimal instruments. However, we actually dealt with only one equation, or at least only one equation at a time. The model that we consider in this section and the next, namely, the **linear simultaneous equations model**, extends what we did in Chapter 8 to a model in which all of the endogenous variables have the same status. Our objective is to obtain efficient estimates of the full set of parameters that appear in all of the simultaneous equations.

The Model

The ith equation of a linear simultaneous system can be written as

$$\boldsymbol{y}_i = \boldsymbol{X}_i\boldsymbol{\beta}_i + \boldsymbol{u}_i = \boldsymbol{Z}_i\boldsymbol{\beta}_{1i} + \boldsymbol{Y}_i\boldsymbol{\beta}_{2i} + \boldsymbol{u}_i, \tag{12.54}$$

where $\boldsymbol{X}_i$ is an $n \times k_i$ matrix of explanatory variables that can be partitioned as $\boldsymbol{X}_i = [\,\boldsymbol{Z}_i \quad \boldsymbol{Y}_i\,]$. Here $\boldsymbol{Z}_i$ is an $n \times k_{1i}$ matrix of variables that are assumed to be exogenous or predetermined, and $\boldsymbol{Y}_i$ is an $n \times k_{2i}$ matrix of endogenous variables, with $k_{1i} + k_{2i} = k_i$. The k_i–vector $\boldsymbol{\beta}_i$ of parameters can be partitioned as $[\boldsymbol{\beta}_{1i} \,\vdots\, \boldsymbol{\beta}_{2i}]$ to conform with the partitioning of $\boldsymbol{X}$. The g endogenous variables $\boldsymbol{y}_1$ through $\boldsymbol{y}_g$ are assumed to be jointly generated by g equations of the form (12.54). The number of exogenous or predetermined variables that appear anywhere in the system is l. This implies that $k_{1i} \leq l$ for all i.[2]

We make the standard assumption (12.02) about the error terms. Thus we allow for contemporaneous correlation, but not for heteroskedasticity or serial correlation. It is, of course, quite possible to allow for these extra complications, but they are not admitted in the context of the model currently under discussion, which thus has a distinctly classical flavor, as befits a model that has inspired a long and distinguished literature.

Except for the explicit distinction between endogenous and predetermined explanatory variables, equation (12.54) looks very much like the typical equation (12.01) of an SUR system. However, there is one important difference, which is concealed by the notation. It is that, as with the simple demand-supply model of Section 8.2, the dependent variables $\boldsymbol{y}_i$ are not necessarily distinct.

[2] Readers should be warned that the notation we have introduced in equation (12.54) is not universal. In particular, some authors reverse the definitions of $\boldsymbol{X}_i$ and $\boldsymbol{Z}_i$ and then define $\boldsymbol{X}$ to be the $n \times l$ matrix of all the exogenous and predetermined variables, which we will denote below by $\boldsymbol{W}$. Our notation emphasizes the similarities between the linear simultaneous equations model (12.54) and the linear SUR system (12.01), as well as making it clear that $\boldsymbol{W}$ plays the role of a matrix of instruments.

Since equations (12.54) form a simultaneous system, it is arbitrary which one of the endogenous variables is put on the left-hand side with a coefficient of 1, at least in any equation in which more than one endogenous variable appears. It is a matter of simple algebra to select one of the variables in the matrix $\boldsymbol{Y}_i$, take it over to the left-hand side while taking $\boldsymbol{y}_i$ over to the right, and then rescale the coefficients so that the selected variable has a coefficient of 1. This point can be important in practice.

Just as we did with the linear SUR model, we can convert the system of equations (12.54) to a single equation by stacking them vertically. As before, the gn–vectors $\boldsymbol{y}_\bullet$ and $\boldsymbol{u}_\bullet$ consist of the $\boldsymbol{y}_i$ and the $\boldsymbol{u}_i$, respectively, stacked vertically. The $gn \times k$ matrix $\boldsymbol{X}_\bullet$, where $k = k_1 + \ldots + k_g$, is defined to be a block-diagonal matrix with diagonal blocks $\boldsymbol{X}_i$, just as in equation (12.05). The full system can then be written as

$$\boldsymbol{y}_\bullet = \boldsymbol{X}_\bullet \boldsymbol{\beta}_\bullet + \boldsymbol{u}_\bullet, \quad \mathrm{E}(\boldsymbol{u}_\bullet \boldsymbol{u}_\bullet^\top) = \boldsymbol{\Sigma} \otimes \mathbf{I}_n, \tag{12.55}$$

where the k–vector $\boldsymbol{\beta}_\bullet$ is formed by stacking the $\boldsymbol{\beta}_i$ vertically. As before, the $g \times g$ matrix $\boldsymbol{\Sigma}$ is the contemporaneous covariance matrix of the error terms. The true value of $\boldsymbol{\beta}_\bullet$ will be denoted $\boldsymbol{\beta}_\bullet^0$.

Efficient GMM Estimation

One of the main reasons for estimating a full system of equations is to obtain an efficiency gain relative to single-equation estimation. In Section 9.2, we saw how to obtain the most efficient possible estimator for a single equation in the context of efficient GMM estimation. The theoretical moment conditions that lead to such an estimator are given in equation (9.18), which we rewrite here for easy reference:

$$\mathrm{E}\big(\bar{\boldsymbol{X}}^\top \boldsymbol{\Omega}^{-1}(\boldsymbol{y} - \boldsymbol{X}\boldsymbol{\beta})\big) = \mathbf{0}. \tag{9.18}$$

Because we are assuming that there is no serial correlation, these moment conditions are also valid for the linear simultaneous equations model (12.54). We simply need to reinterpret them in terms of that model.

In reinterpreting the moment conditions (9.18), it is clear that $\boldsymbol{y}_\bullet$ replaces the vector $\boldsymbol{y}$, $\boldsymbol{X}_\bullet \boldsymbol{\beta}_\bullet$ replaces the vector $\boldsymbol{X}\boldsymbol{\beta}$, and $\boldsymbol{\Sigma}^{-1} \otimes \mathbf{I}_n$ replaces the matrix $\boldsymbol{\Omega}^{-1}$. What is not quite so clear is what replaces the matrix $\bar{\boldsymbol{X}}$. Recall that $\bar{\boldsymbol{X}}$ in (9.18) is the matrix defined row by row so as to contain the expectations of the explanatory variables for each observation conditional on the information that is predetermined for that observation. We need to obtain the matrix that corresponds to $\bar{\boldsymbol{X}}$ in equation (9.18) for the model (12.55).

Let $\boldsymbol{W}$ denote an $n \times l$ matrix of exogenous and predetermined variables, the columns of which are all of the linearly independent columns of the $\boldsymbol{Z}_i$. For these variables, the expectations conditional on predetermined information are just the variables themselves. Thus we only need worry about the endogenous explanatory variables. Because their joint DGP is given by the system of linear equations (12.54), it must be possible to solve these equations for the endogenous variables as functions of the predetermined variables and the error terms. Since these equations are linear and have the same form for all observations, the solution must have the form

$$\boldsymbol{y}_i = \boldsymbol{W}\boldsymbol{\pi}_i + \text{error terms}, \tag{12.56}$$

where $\boldsymbol{\pi}_i$ is an l-vector of parameters that are, in general, nonlinear functions of the parameters $\boldsymbol{\beta}_\bullet$. As the notation indicates, the variables contained in the matrix $\boldsymbol{W}$ serve as instrumental variables for the estimation of the model parameters. Later, we will investigate more fully the nature of the $\boldsymbol{\pi}_i$. We pay little attention to the error terms, because our objective is to compute the conditional expectations of the elements of the $\boldsymbol{y}_i$, and we know that each of the error terms must have expectation 0 conditional on all the exogenous and predetermined variables.

The vector of conditional expectations of the elements of $\boldsymbol{y}_i$ is just $\boldsymbol{W}\boldsymbol{\pi}_i$. Since equations (12.56) take the form of linear regressions with exogenous and predetermined explanatory variables, OLS estimates of the $\boldsymbol{\pi}_i$ are consistent. As we saw in Section 12.2, they are also efficient, even though the error terms generally display contemporaneous correlation, because the same regressors appear in every equation. Thus we can replace the unknown $\boldsymbol{\pi}_i$ by their OLS estimates based on equations (12.56). This means that the conditional expectations of the vectors $\boldsymbol{y}_i$ are estimated by the OLS fitted values, that is, the vectors $\boldsymbol{W}\hat{\boldsymbol{\pi}}_i = \boldsymbol{P_W}\boldsymbol{y}_i$. When this is done, the matrices that contain the estimates of the conditional expectations of the elements of the $\boldsymbol{X}_i$ can be written as

$$\hat{\boldsymbol{X}}_i \equiv [\,\boldsymbol{Z}_i \quad \boldsymbol{P_W}\boldsymbol{Y}_i\,] = \boldsymbol{P_W}\,[\,\boldsymbol{Z}_i \quad \boldsymbol{Y}_i\,] = \boldsymbol{P_W}\boldsymbol{X}_i. \tag{12.57}$$

We write $\hat{\boldsymbol{X}}_i$ rather than $\bar{\boldsymbol{X}}_i$ because the unknown conditional expectations are estimated. The step from the second to the third expression in (12.57) is possible because all the columns of all the $\boldsymbol{Z}_i$ are, by construction, contained in the span of the columns of $\boldsymbol{W}$.

We are now ready to construct the matrix to be used in place of $\bar{\boldsymbol{X}}$ in (9.18). It is the block-diagonal $gn \times k$ matrix $\hat{\boldsymbol{X}}_\bullet$, with diagonal blocks the $\hat{\boldsymbol{X}}_i$. This allows us to write the estimating equations for efficient GMM estimation as

$$\hat{\boldsymbol{X}}_\bullet^\top(\boldsymbol{\Sigma}^{-1} \otimes \mathbf{I}_n)(\boldsymbol{y}_\bullet - \boldsymbol{X}_\bullet\boldsymbol{\beta}_\bullet) = \mathbf{0}. \tag{12.58}$$

These equations, which are the empirical versions of the theoretical moment conditions (9.18), can be rewritten in several other ways. In particular, they can be written in the form

$$\begin{bmatrix} \sigma^{11}\boldsymbol{X}_1^\top\boldsymbol{P_W} & \cdots & \sigma^{1g}\boldsymbol{X}_1^\top\boldsymbol{P_W} \\ \vdots & \ddots & \vdots \\ \sigma^{g1}\boldsymbol{X}_g^\top\boldsymbol{P_W} & \cdots & \sigma^{gg}\boldsymbol{X}_g^\top\boldsymbol{P_W} \end{bmatrix} \begin{bmatrix} \boldsymbol{y}_1 - \boldsymbol{X}_1\boldsymbol{\beta}_1 \\ \vdots \\ \boldsymbol{y}_g - \boldsymbol{X}_g\boldsymbol{\beta}_g \end{bmatrix} = \mathbf{0},$$

by analogy with equation (12.13), and in the form

$$\sum_{j=1}^{g} \sigma^{ij} \boldsymbol{X}_i^\top \boldsymbol{P_W}(\boldsymbol{y}_j - \boldsymbol{X}_j\boldsymbol{\beta}_j) = \mathbf{0}, \quad i = 1, \ldots, g, \tag{12.59}$$

by analogy with equation (12.16). It is also straightforward to check (see Exercise 12.14) that they can be written as

$$\boldsymbol{X}_\bullet^\top(\boldsymbol{\Sigma}^{-1} \otimes \boldsymbol{P_W})(\boldsymbol{y}_\bullet - \boldsymbol{X}_\bullet\boldsymbol{\beta}_\bullet) = \mathbf{0}, \tag{12.60}$$

from which it follows immediately that equations (12.58) are equivalent to the first-order conditions for the minimization of the criterion function

$$(\boldsymbol{y}_\bullet - \boldsymbol{X}_\bullet\boldsymbol{\beta}_\bullet)^\top(\boldsymbol{\Sigma}^{-1} \otimes \boldsymbol{P_W})(\boldsymbol{y}_\bullet - \boldsymbol{X}_\bullet\boldsymbol{\beta}_\bullet). \tag{12.61}$$

The efficient GMM estimator $\hat{\boldsymbol{\beta}}_\bullet^{\rm GMM}$ defined by (12.60) is the analog for a linear simultaneous equations system of the GLS estimator (12.09) for an SUR system.

The asymptotic covariance matrix of $\hat{\boldsymbol{\beta}}_\bullet^{\rm GMM}$ can readily be obtained from expression (9.29). In the notation of (12.58), we find that

$$\operatorname{Var}\bigl(\operatorname*{plim}_{n\to\infty} n^{1/2}(\hat{\boldsymbol{\beta}}_\bullet^{\rm GMM} - \boldsymbol{\beta}_\bullet^0)\bigr) = \operatorname*{plim}_{n\to\infty}\Bigl(\frac{1}{n}\hat{\boldsymbol{X}}_\bullet^\top(\boldsymbol{\Sigma}^{-1} \otimes \mathbf{I}_n)\hat{\boldsymbol{X}}_\bullet\Bigr)^{-1}. \tag{12.62}$$

This covariance matrix can also be written, in the notation of (12.60), as

$$\operatorname*{plim}_{n\to\infty}\Bigl(\frac{1}{n}\boldsymbol{X}_\bullet^\top(\boldsymbol{\Sigma}^{-1} \otimes \boldsymbol{P_W})\boldsymbol{X}_\bullet\Bigr)^{-1}. \tag{12.63}$$

Of course, the estimator $\hat{\boldsymbol{\beta}}_\bullet^{\rm GMM}$ is not feasible if, as is almost always the case, the matrix $\boldsymbol{\Sigma}$ is unknown. However, it is obvious that we can deal with this problem by using a procedure analogous to feasible GLS estimation of an SUR system. We will return to this issue at the end of this section.

Two Special Cases

If the matrix $\boldsymbol{\Sigma}$ is diagonal, then equations (12.59) simplify to

$$\sigma^{ii} \boldsymbol{X}_i^\top \boldsymbol{P_W}(\boldsymbol{y}_i - \boldsymbol{X}_i\boldsymbol{\beta}_i) = \mathbf{0}, \quad i = 1, \ldots, g. \tag{12.64}$$

The factors of σ^{ii} have no influence on the solutions to these equations, which are therefore just the generalized IV, or 2SLS, estimators for each of the equations of the system treated individually, with a common matrix $\boldsymbol{W}$ of instrumental variables. This result is the analog of what we found for an SUR system with diagonal $\boldsymbol{\Sigma}$. Here it is the equation-by-equation IV estimator that takes the place of the equation-by-equation OLS estimator.

Just as single-equation OLS estimation is consistent but in general inefficient for an SUR system, so is single-equation IV estimation consistent but in general inefficient for the linear simultaneous equations model. As readers are asked to verify in Exercise 12.15, the estimating equations (12.64), without the factors of σ^{ii}, can be rewritten for the entire system as

$$\boldsymbol{X}_\bullet^\top(\mathbf{I}_g \otimes \boldsymbol{P_W})(\boldsymbol{y}_\bullet - \boldsymbol{X}_\bullet\boldsymbol{\beta}_\bullet) = \mathbf{0}. \tag{12.65}$$

In general, solving equations (12.65) yields an inefficient estimator unless the true contemporaneous covariance matrix $\boldsymbol{\Sigma}$ is diagonal.

There is, however, another case in which the estimating equations (12.65) yield an asymptotically efficient estimator. This case is analogous to the case of an SUR system with the same explanatory variables in each equation, but it takes a rather different form in this context. What we require is that each of the equations in the system should be just identified.

When we say that a single equation is just identified by an IV estimator, part of what we mean is that the number of instruments is equal to the number of explanatory variables, or, equivalently for a linear regression, to the number of parameters. If equation i is just identified, therefore, the two matrices $\boldsymbol{W}$ and $\boldsymbol{P_W X}_i$ have the same dimensions. In fact, they span the same linear subspace provided that $\boldsymbol{P_W X}_i$ is of full column rank. Consequently, there exists an $l \times l$ matrix $\boldsymbol{J}_i$ such that $\boldsymbol{P_W X}_i \boldsymbol{J}_i = \boldsymbol{W}$. Premultiplying the ith equation of (12.59) by $\boldsymbol{J}_i^\top$ thus gives

$$\sum_{j=1}^{g} \sigma^{ij} \boldsymbol{W}^\top(\boldsymbol{y}_j - \boldsymbol{X}_j\boldsymbol{\beta}_j) = \mathbf{0}.$$

If all the equations of a simultaneous equations system are just identified, then the above relation holds for each $i = 1, \ldots, g$. We can then multiply equation i by σ_{mi} and sum over i, as in equation (12.20). This yields the decoupled estimating equations

$$\boldsymbol{W}^\top(\boldsymbol{y}_m - \boldsymbol{X}_m\boldsymbol{\beta}_m) = \mathbf{0}, \quad m = 1, \ldots, g,$$

which define the single-equation (simple) IV estimators in the just-identified case. Therefore, as with the SUR model, there is no advantage to system estimation rather than equation-by-equation estimation when every equation is just identified, because the estimating equations use up all of the available moment conditions.

Identification

In order to be able to solve the estimating equations (12.60) for $\boldsymbol{\beta}_\bullet$, it must be possible to invert the matrix

$$\boldsymbol{X}_\bullet^\top(\boldsymbol{\Sigma}^{-1} \otimes \boldsymbol{P_W})\boldsymbol{X}_\bullet. \tag{12.66}$$

Thus, in finite samples, the parameters of the model (12.55) are identified if this matrix is nonsingular. Although this statement is accurate, it is neither complete nor transparent. In particular, even if the matrix (12.66) is singular, it may still be possible to identify some of the parameters.

Whenever the contemporaneous covariance matrix $\boldsymbol{\Sigma}$ is nonsingular, it can be shown, as spelled out in Exercise 12.16, that the matrix (12.66) is singular if and only if at least one of the matrices $\boldsymbol{P_W X}_i$ does not have full column rank. In other words, the system of equations is unidentified if and only if at least one of its component equations is unidentified. The result of the exercise also shows that the parameters of those equations for which $\boldsymbol{P_W X}_i$ does have full column rank can be identified uniquely by the estimating equations (12.60). In consequence, provided that $\boldsymbol{\Sigma}$ is nonsingular, we can study identification equation by equation without loss of generality.

A necessary condition for $\boldsymbol{P_W X}_i$ to have full column rank is that l, the number of instruments contained in the matrix $\boldsymbol{W}$, should be no less than k_i, the number of explanatory variables contained in $\boldsymbol{X}_i$. This condition is called the **order condition** for identification of equation i. It is an accounting condition, and, as such, can be expressed in more than one way. Recall that we defined k_{1i} as the number of exogenous or predetermined explanatory variables in $\boldsymbol{X}_i$, that is, the dimension of the matrix $\boldsymbol{Z}_i$. Since the total number of exogenous or predetermined variables in the full system is l, the number of such variables *excluded* from equation i is $l - k_{1i}$. The number of endogenous explanatory variables *included* in equation i is, by definition k_{2i}, which is the dimension of the matrix $\boldsymbol{Y}_i$. Therefore, the inequality $l \geq k_i$ is equivalent to

$$l \geq k_{1i} + k_{2i} \quad \text{or} \quad l - k_{1i} \geq k_{2i}. \tag{12.67}$$

The second inequality here says that the number of predetermined variables excluded from an equation must be at least as great as the number of endogenous explanatory variables in that equation.

The necessary and sufficient condition for the identification of the parameters of equation i is that $\boldsymbol{P_W X}_i$ should have full column rank of k_i. This condition, which is, not surprisingly, called the **rank condition** for identification, holds whenever the $k_i \times k_i$ matrix $\boldsymbol{X}_i^\top \boldsymbol{P_W X}_i$ is nonsingular. It is easy to check whether the rank condition holds for any given data set. However, it is not so easy to check whether it holds asymptotically. The problem is that, because some of the columns of $\boldsymbol{X}_i$ are endogenous, $\operatorname{plim} n^{-1}\boldsymbol{X}_i^\top \boldsymbol{P_W X}_i$ depends on the parameters of the DGP. This point is important, and we will discuss it at some length below.

Structural and Reduced Forms

When the equations of a linear simultaneous equations model are written in the form (12.54), it is normally the case that each equation has a direct economic interpretation. In the model of Section 8.2, for instance, the two equations are intended to correspond to demand and supply functions. It is for this reason that these are called **structural equations**. The full system of equations constitutes what is called the **structural form** of the model.

It is convenient for our subsequent analysis to stack the equations (12.54) horizontally, instead of vertically as in the system (12.55). We thus define the $n \times g$ matrix $\boldsymbol{Y}$ as $[\boldsymbol{y}_1 \quad \boldsymbol{y}_2 \quad \cdots \quad \boldsymbol{y}_g]$. Similarly, the vectors $\boldsymbol{u}_i$ of error terms can be stacked side by side to form the $n \times g$ matrix $\boldsymbol{U}$. In this notation, the entire set of equations (12.54) can be represented as

$$\boldsymbol{Y\Gamma} = \boldsymbol{WB} + \boldsymbol{U}, \tag{12.68}$$

where the $g \times g$ matrix $\boldsymbol{\Gamma}$ and the $l \times g$ matrix $\boldsymbol{B}$ are defined in such a way as to make (12.68) equivalent to (12.54). Each equation of the system (12.54) contributes one column to (12.68). This can be seen by writing equation i of (12.54) in the form

$$[\boldsymbol{y}_i \quad \boldsymbol{Y}_i]\begin{bmatrix} 1 \\ -\boldsymbol{\beta}_{2i} \end{bmatrix} = \boldsymbol{Z}_i\boldsymbol{\beta}_{1i} + \boldsymbol{u}_i. \tag{12.69}$$

All of the columns of $\boldsymbol{Y}_i$ are also columns of $\boldsymbol{Y}$, as is $\boldsymbol{y}_i$ itself, and so column i of the matrix $\boldsymbol{\Gamma}$ has 1 for element i, and the elements of the vector $-\boldsymbol{\beta}_{2i}$ for the other nonzero elements. The endogenous variables that are excluded from equation i contribute zero elements to the column. Similarly, all the columns of $\boldsymbol{Z}_i$ are also columns of $\boldsymbol{W}$, and so the nonzero elements of column i of $\boldsymbol{B}$ are the elements of $\boldsymbol{\beta}_{1i}$, in appropriate positions. The "structure" of the structural equations is embodied in the structure of the matrices $\boldsymbol{\Gamma}$ and $\boldsymbol{B}$.

If (12.68) is to represent a model by which the g endogenous variables are generated, it is necessary for $\boldsymbol{\Gamma}$ to be nonsingular. We can thus postmultiply both sides of equation (12.68) by $\boldsymbol{\Gamma}^{-1}$ to obtain

$$\boldsymbol{Y} = \boldsymbol{WB\Gamma}^{-1} + \boldsymbol{V}, \tag{12.70}$$

where $\boldsymbol{V} \equiv \boldsymbol{U\Gamma}^{-1}$. The representation (12.70) is called the **reduced form** of the model, and its component equations (the columns of the matrix equation) are the **reduced form equations**. These reduced form equations are regressions, which in general are nonlinear in the parameters. Because they have only exogenous or predetermined regressors, they can be estimated consistently by nonlinear least squares.

Unless all the equations of the system are just identified, (12.70) is in fact what is called the **restricted reduced form** or **RRF**. This is in contrast to the **unrestricted reduced form**, or **URF**, which can be written as

$$\boldsymbol{Y} = \boldsymbol{W\Pi} + \boldsymbol{V}, \tag{12.71}$$

where $\boldsymbol{\Pi}$ is an unrestricted $l \times g$ matrix. Notice that equation (12.56) is simply the ith equation of this system, with $\boldsymbol{y}_i$ the ith column of the matrix $\boldsymbol{Y}$ and $\boldsymbol{\pi}_i$ the ith column of the matrix $\boldsymbol{\Pi}$.

It may at first sight seem odd to refer to (12.70) as the *restricted* reduced form and to (12.71) as the *unrestricted* one. The URF (12.71) has gl regression coefficients, since $\boldsymbol{\Pi}$ is an $l \times g$ matrix, while the RRF (12.70) appears to have $gl + g^2$ parameters, since $\boldsymbol{B}$ is $l \times g$ and $\boldsymbol{\Gamma}$ is $g \times g$. But remember that $\boldsymbol{\Gamma}$ has g elements which are constrained to equal 1, and both $\boldsymbol{\Gamma}$ and $\boldsymbol{B}$ have many zero elements corresponding to excluded endogenous and predetermined explanatory variables, respectively. As readers are invited to show in Exercise 12.18, if all the equations of the system are just identified, so that the order condition (12.67) is satisfied with equality for each $i = 1, \ldots, g$, then there are exactly as many parameters in the RRF as in the URF. When some of the order conditions are inequalities, there are fewer parameters in the RRF than in the URF.

Asymptotic Identification

Whether or not the parameters of a linear simultaneous system are identified by a given data set depends only on the order condition and the properties of the actual data, but this is not true of asymptotic identification. Since the parameters must be asymptotically identified if the parameter estimates are to be consistent, it is worth studying in some detail the conditions for asymptotic identification in such a system.

We assume that the probability limit of $n^{-1}\boldsymbol{W}^\top\boldsymbol{U}$ is a zero matrix and that the $l \times l$ matrix

$$\boldsymbol{S}_{\boldsymbol{W}^\top\boldsymbol{W}} \equiv \operatorname*{plim}_{n\to\infty} \frac{1}{n}\boldsymbol{W}^\top\boldsymbol{W}$$

is positive definite and, consequently, nonsingular. The nonsingularity of the matrix $\boldsymbol{W}^\top\boldsymbol{W}$ is not necessary for identification by a given data set, since, if there are enough instruments, it is quite possible that each of the matrices $\boldsymbol{P_W X}_i$, $i = 1, \ldots, g$, should have full column rank even though some of the instruments are linearly dependent. Similarly, it is not *necessary* that $\boldsymbol{S}_{\boldsymbol{W}^\top\boldsymbol{W}}$ should be nonsingular for asymptotic identification. However, since it is always possible to eliminate linearly dependent instruments, it is convenient to make the nonsingularity assumption. By doing so, we make it clearer how asymptotic identification depends on the actual parameter values.

For simplicity of notation, we focus on the asymptotic identification of the first equation of the system, which can be written as

$$\boldsymbol{y}_1 = \boldsymbol{Z}_1\boldsymbol{\beta}_{11} + \boldsymbol{Y}_1\boldsymbol{\beta}_{21} + \boldsymbol{u}_1. \tag{12.72}$$

Since identification can be treated equation by equation without loss of generality, and since the ordering of the equations is quite arbitrary, our results will be perfectly general. The matrix $\boldsymbol{X}_1$ of explanatory variables for the first equation is $\boldsymbol{X}_1 = [\,\boldsymbol{Z}_1 \quad \boldsymbol{Y}_1\,]$. Recall that the $n \times l$ matrix $\boldsymbol{W}$ contains all the linearly independent columns of the $\boldsymbol{Z}_i$, and in particular those of $\boldsymbol{Z}_1$. Let us order the columns of $\boldsymbol{W}$ so that the k_{11} columns of $\boldsymbol{Z}_1$ come first.

The $n \times k_{21}$ matrix $\boldsymbol{Y}_1$ is given by a selection of the columns of the matrix $\boldsymbol{Y}$. The first column of $\boldsymbol{Y}$, which corresponds to the equation we are studying, is not among these, because $\boldsymbol{y}_1$ appears only on the left-hand side of that equation. However, we can freely reorder the remaining columns of $\boldsymbol{Y}$ so that the k_{21} columns of $\boldsymbol{Y}_1$ are the columns 2 through $k_{21}+1$ of $\boldsymbol{Y}$. This done, we can express the first $k_{21}+1$ columns of the URF (12.71), in partitioned form, as

$$[\,\boldsymbol{y}_1 \quad \boldsymbol{Y}_1\,] = [\,\boldsymbol{Z}_1 \quad \boldsymbol{W}_1\,]\begin{bmatrix} \boldsymbol{\pi}_{11} & \boldsymbol{\Pi}_{11} \\ \boldsymbol{\pi}_{21} & \boldsymbol{\Pi}_{21} \end{bmatrix} + [\,\boldsymbol{v}_1 \quad \boldsymbol{V}_1\,], \tag{12.73}$$

where we have introduced some further convenient notation. First, the $n \times (l - k_{11})$ matrix $\boldsymbol{W}_1$ contains all the columns of $\boldsymbol{W}$ that are not in $\boldsymbol{Z}_1$. Then, for the ordering that we have chosen for the columns of $\boldsymbol{Y}$ and $\boldsymbol{W}$, $\boldsymbol{\pi}_{11}$ is the $k_{11} \times 1$ vector of parameters in the first reduced form equation (that is, the equation that defines $\boldsymbol{y}_1$) associated with the instruments in the matrix $\boldsymbol{Z}_1$, while the $(l - k_{11}) \times 1$ vector $\boldsymbol{\pi}_{21}$ contains the parameters of the first reduced form equation associated with the instruments in $\boldsymbol{W}_1$. Finally, the matrices $\boldsymbol{\Pi}_{11}$ and $\boldsymbol{\Pi}_{21}$ are, respectively, of dimensions $k_{11} \times k_{21}$ and $(l - k_{11}) \times k_{21}$. They contain the parameters of the reduced form equations numbered 2 through $k_{21}+1$ and associated with the instruments in $\boldsymbol{Z}_1$ and $\boldsymbol{W}_1$, respectively. The matrix $[\,\boldsymbol{v}_1 \quad \boldsymbol{V}_1\,]$ of error terms is partitioned in the same way as the left-hand side of (12.73).

We can write the matrix $\boldsymbol{P_W X}_1$ as

$$\boldsymbol{P_W X}_1 = \boldsymbol{P_W}[\,\boldsymbol{Z}_1 \quad \boldsymbol{Y}_1\,] = [\,\boldsymbol{Z}_1 \quad \boldsymbol{P_W Y}_1\,], \tag{12.74}$$

because $\boldsymbol{P_W Z}_1 = \boldsymbol{Z}_1$. With the help of (12.73), the second block of the rightmost expression above becomes

$$\boldsymbol{P_W Y}_1 = [\,\boldsymbol{Z}_1 \quad \boldsymbol{W}_1\,]\begin{bmatrix} \boldsymbol{\Pi}_{11} \\ \boldsymbol{\Pi}_{21} \end{bmatrix} + \boldsymbol{P_W V}_1, \tag{12.75}$$

where we again use the fact that $\boldsymbol{P_W}[\,\boldsymbol{Z}_1 \quad \boldsymbol{W}_1\,] = [\,\boldsymbol{Z}_1 \quad \boldsymbol{W}_1\,]$, and $\boldsymbol{\Pi}_{11}$ and $\boldsymbol{\Pi}_{21}$ contain the true parameter values. Reorganizing equations (12.74) and (12.75) gives

$$\boldsymbol{P_W X}_1 = \boldsymbol{W}\begin{bmatrix} \mathbf{I}_{k_{11}} & \boldsymbol{\Pi}_{11} \\ \mathbf{O} & \boldsymbol{\Pi}_{21} \end{bmatrix} + [\,\mathbf{O} \quad \boldsymbol{P_W V}_1\,]. \tag{12.76}$$

The necessary and sufficient condition for the asymptotic identification of the parameters of the first equation is the nonsingularity of the probability limit as $n \to \infty$ of the matrix $n^{-1}\boldsymbol{X}_1^{\top}\boldsymbol{P_W X}_1$. It is easy to see from (12.76) that this limit is

$$\operatorname*{plim}_{n\to\infty} \frac{1}{n}\boldsymbol{X}_1^{\top}\boldsymbol{P_W X}_1 = \begin{bmatrix} \mathbf{I}_{k_{11}} & \mathbf{O} \\ \boldsymbol{\Pi}_{11}^{\top} & \boldsymbol{\Pi}_{21}^{\top} \end{bmatrix} \boldsymbol{S}_{\boldsymbol{W}^{\top}\boldsymbol{W}} \begin{bmatrix} \mathbf{I}_{k_{11}} & \boldsymbol{\Pi}_{11} \\ \mathbf{O} & \boldsymbol{\Pi}_{21} \end{bmatrix}.$$

In Exercise 12.19, readers are invited to check that everything that depends on the matrix $\boldsymbol{V}$ does indeed tend to zero in the above limit. Since we assumed that $\boldsymbol{S}_{\boldsymbol{W}^\top\boldsymbol{W}}$ is positive definite, it follows that equation (12.72) is asymptotically identified if and only if the matrix

$$\begin{bmatrix} \mathbf{I}_{k_{11}} & \boldsymbol{\Pi}_{11} \\ \mathbf{O} & \boldsymbol{\Pi}_{21} \end{bmatrix} \tag{12.77}$$

is of full column rank $k_1 = k_{11} + k_{21}$. Because this matrix has l rows, this is not possible unless $l > k_1$, that is, unless the order condition is satisfied. However, even if the order condition is satisfied, there can perfectly well exist parameter values for which (12.77) does not have full column rank. The important conclusion of this analysis is that asymptotic identification of an equation in a linear simultaneous system depends not only on the properties of the instrumental variables $\boldsymbol{W}$, but also on the specific parameter values of the DGP.

In Exercise 12.20, readers are asked to show that the matrix (12.77) has full column rank if and only if the $(l - k_{11}) \times k_{21}$ submatrix $\boldsymbol{\Pi}_{21}$ has full column rank. While this is a simple enough condition, it is expressed in terms of the reduced form parameters, which are usually not subject to a simple interpretation. It is therefore desirable to have a characterization of the asymptotic identification condition in terms of the structural parameters. In Exercise 12.21, notation that is suitable for deriving such a characterization is proposed, and readers are asked to develop it in Exercise 12.22.

The numerical condition that the matrix (12.66) be nonsingular is satisfied by almost all data sets, even when the rank condition for asymptotic identification is not satisfied. When this happens, the failure of that condition manifests itself as the phenomenon of **weak instruments** that we discussed in Section 8.4. In such a case, we might be tempted to add additional instruments, such as lags of the instruments themselves or other predetermined variables that may be correlated with them. But doing this cannot lead to asymptotic identification, because it would simply append columns of zeros to the matrix $\boldsymbol{\Pi}$ of reduced form coefficients, and it is obvious that such an operation cannot convert a matrix of deficient rank into one of full rank.

A discussion of asymptotic identification that is more detailed than the present one, but still reasonably compact, is provided by Davidson and MacKinnon (1993, Section 18.3). Much fuller treatments may be found in Fisher (1976) and Hsiao (1983).

Three-Stage Least Squares

The efficient GMM estimator defined by the estimating equations (12.60) is not feasible unless $\boldsymbol{\Sigma}$ is known. However, we can compute a feasible GMM estimator if we can obtain a consistent estimate of $\boldsymbol{\Sigma}$, and this is easy to do. We first estimate the individual equations of the system by generalized IV, or two-stage least squares, to use the traditional terminology. This inefficient equation-by-equation estimator is characterized formally by the estimating equations (12.65). After computing it, we then use the 2SLS residuals to compute the matrix $\hat{\boldsymbol{\Sigma}}_{\rm 2SLS}$, as in (12.17). Using $\hat{\boldsymbol{\Sigma}}_{\rm 2SLS}$ in place of $\boldsymbol{\Sigma}$ in equations (12.60) yields the popular **three-stage least-squares**, or **3SLS**, estimator, which was originally proposed by Zellner and Theil (1962). This estimator can be written as

$$\hat{\boldsymbol{\beta}}_{\bullet}^{\rm 3SLS} = \big(\boldsymbol{X}_{\bullet}^{\top}(\hat{\boldsymbol{\Sigma}}_{\rm 2SLS}^{-1} \otimes \boldsymbol{P}_{\boldsymbol{W}})\boldsymbol{X}_{\bullet}\big)^{-1}\boldsymbol{X}_{\bullet}^{\top}(\hat{\boldsymbol{\Sigma}}_{\rm 2SLS}^{-1} \otimes \boldsymbol{P}_{\boldsymbol{W}})\boldsymbol{y}_{\bullet}. \tag{12.78}$$

The relationship between this 3SLS estimator and the 2SLS estimator for the entire system is essentially the same as the relationship between the feasible GLS estimator (12.18) for an SUR system and the OLS estimator (12.06). As with (12.18), we may wish to compute the continuously updated version of the 3SLS estimator (12.78), in which case we iteratively update the estimates of $\boldsymbol{\beta}_{\bullet}$ and $\boldsymbol{\Sigma}$ by using equations (12.78) and (12.17), respectively.

From the results (12.62) and (12.63), it is clear that we can estimate the covariance matrix of the classical 3SLS estimator (12.78) by

$$\widehat{\rm Var}(\hat{\boldsymbol{\beta}}_{\bullet}^{\rm 3SLS}) = \big(\boldsymbol{X}_{\bullet}^{\top}(\hat{\boldsymbol{\Sigma}}_{\rm 2SLS}^{-1} \otimes \boldsymbol{P}_{\boldsymbol{W}})\boldsymbol{X}_{\bullet}\big)^{-1}, \tag{12.79}$$

which is analogous to (12.19) for the SUR case. Asymptotically valid inferences can then be made in the usual way. As with the SUR estimator, we can perform a Hansen-Sargan test of the overidentifying restrictions by using the fact that, under the null hypothesis, the criterion function (12.61) evaluated at $\hat{\boldsymbol{\beta}}_{\bullet}^{\rm 3SLS}$ and $\hat{\boldsymbol{\Sigma}}_{\rm 2SLS}$ is asymptotically distributed as $\chi^2(gl-k)$. Of course, this is also true if the procedure has been iterated one or more times.

12.5 Maximum Likelihood Estimation

Like the SUR model, the linear simultaneous equations model can be estimated by maximum likelihood under the assumption that the error terms, in addition to satisfying the requirements (12.02), are normally distributed. In contrast to the situation with an SUR system, where the ML estimator is numerically identical to the continuously updated feasible GLS estimator, the ML estimator of a linear simultaneous equations model is, in general, different from the continuously updated 3SLS estimator. The ML and 3SLS estimators are, however, asymptotically equivalent, whether or not the latter is continuously updated.

Because the algebra of ML estimation is quite complicated, we have divided our treatment of the subject between this section and a technical appendix, which appears at the end of the chapter, just prior to the exercises. All of the principal results are stated and discussed in this section, but many of them are derived in the appendix.

Full-Information Maximum Likelihood

The maximum likelihood estimator of a linear simultaneous system is called the **full-information maximum likelihood**, or **FIML**, estimator. It is so called because it uses information about all the equations in the system, unlike the limited-information maximum likelihood estimator (LIML) that will be discussed later in this section.

The loglikelihood function that must be maximized to obtain the FIML estimator can be written in several different ways. In terms of the notation used in equation (12.55), it is

$$\begin{aligned} &-\frac{gn}{2}\log 2\pi - \frac{n}{2}\log|\boldsymbol{\Sigma}| + n\log|\det\boldsymbol{\Gamma}| \\ &\quad -\frac{1}{2}(\boldsymbol{y}_\bullet - \boldsymbol{X}_\bullet\boldsymbol{\beta}_\bullet)^\top(\boldsymbol{\Sigma}^{-1}\otimes\mathbf{I}_n)(\boldsymbol{y}_\bullet - \boldsymbol{X}_\bullet\boldsymbol{\beta}_\bullet). \end{aligned} \tag{12.80}$$

This looks very much like the loglikelihood function (12.49) for a multivariate nonlinear regression model with normally distributed errors. The principal difference is the third term, $n\log|\det\boldsymbol{\Gamma}|$, which is a Jacobian term. This term is the logarithm of the absolute value of the Jacobian of the transformation from $\boldsymbol{u}_\bullet$ to $\boldsymbol{y}_\bullet$. As we will see in the appendix, the loglikelihood function can also be written without an explicit Jacobian term if we start from the restricted reduced form (12.70).

Maximizing the loglikelihood function (12.80) with respect to $\boldsymbol{\Sigma}$ is exactly the same as maximizing the loglikelihood function (12.33) with respect to it. If we had ML estimates of $\boldsymbol{\beta}_\bullet$, or, equivalently, of $\boldsymbol{B}$ and $\boldsymbol{\Gamma}$, the ML estimate of $\boldsymbol{\Sigma}$ would be

$$\hat{\boldsymbol{\Sigma}}_{\text{ML}} = \frac{1}{n}(\boldsymbol{Y}\hat{\boldsymbol{\Gamma}}_{\text{ML}} - \boldsymbol{W}\hat{\boldsymbol{B}}_{\text{ML}})^\top(\boldsymbol{Y}\hat{\boldsymbol{\Gamma}}_{\text{ML}} - \boldsymbol{W}\hat{\boldsymbol{B}}_{\text{ML}}), \tag{12.81}$$

which is just the sample covariance matrix of the structural-form error terms; compare equation (12.36).

Recall from (12.54) that the parameter vector $\boldsymbol{\beta}_i$ of equation i contains both the vector $\boldsymbol{\beta}_{1i}$, which is associated with the predetermined explanatory variables, and the vector $\boldsymbol{\beta}_{2i}$, which is associated with the endogenous explanatory variables. As is clear from equation (12.69), the matrix $\boldsymbol{B}$ is determined by the $\boldsymbol{\beta}_{1i}$ alone, and the matrix $\boldsymbol{\Gamma}$ by the $\boldsymbol{\beta}_{2i}$ alone. We can obtain the first-order conditions for maximizing the loglikelihood function (12.80) with respect to the $\boldsymbol{\beta}_{1i}$ in exactly the same way as we obtained conditions (12.12) from the criterion function (12.11) for an SUR system. The first-order conditions that we seek can be written as

$$\boldsymbol{Z}_\bullet^\top(\boldsymbol{\Sigma}^{-1}\otimes\mathbf{I}_n)(\boldsymbol{y}_\bullet - \boldsymbol{X}_\bullet\boldsymbol{\beta}_\bullet) = \mathbf{0}, \tag{12.82}$$

where the $gn \times \sum_i k_{1i}$ matrix $\boldsymbol{Z}_\bullet$ is defined, similarly to $\boldsymbol{X}_\bullet$, as a matrix with diagonal blocks $\boldsymbol{Z}_i$. The number of equations in (12.82) is $\sum_i k_{1i}$, since there is one equation for each of the $\boldsymbol{\beta}_{1i}$.

Since it is rather complicated to work out the first-order conditions for the maximization of (12.80) with respect to the $\boldsymbol{\beta}_{2i}$, we leave this derivation to the appendix. These conditions can be expressed as

$$\boldsymbol{Y}_{\bullet}^{\top}(\boldsymbol{B},\boldsymbol{\Gamma})(\boldsymbol{\Sigma}^{-1}\otimes\mathbf{I}_n)(\boldsymbol{y}_{\bullet}-\boldsymbol{X}_{\bullet}\boldsymbol{\beta}_{\bullet})=\mathbf{0}, \tag{12.83}$$

where the $gn\times\sum_i k_{2i}$ matrix $\boldsymbol{Y}_{\bullet}(\boldsymbol{B},\boldsymbol{\Gamma})$ is again defined in terms of diagonal blocks. Block i is the $n\times k_{2i}$ matrix $\boldsymbol{Y}_i(\boldsymbol{B},\boldsymbol{\Gamma})$, which is the submatrix of $\boldsymbol{WB\Gamma}^{-1}$ formed by selecting the columns that correspond to the columns of the matrix $\boldsymbol{Y}_i$ of included endogenous explanatory variables in equation i. The conditions (12.82) and (12.83) can be grouped together as

$$\boldsymbol{X}_{\bullet}^{\top}(\boldsymbol{B},\boldsymbol{\Gamma})(\boldsymbol{\Sigma}^{-1}\otimes\mathbf{I}_n)(\boldsymbol{y}_{\bullet}-\boldsymbol{X}_{\bullet}\boldsymbol{\beta}_{\bullet})=\mathbf{0}, \tag{12.84}$$

where the ith diagonal block of $\boldsymbol{X}_{\bullet}(\boldsymbol{B},\boldsymbol{\Gamma})$ is the $n\times k_i$ matrix $[\boldsymbol{Z}_i \quad \boldsymbol{Y}_i(\boldsymbol{B},\boldsymbol{\Gamma})]$. There are $k=\sum_i k_{1i}+\sum_i k_{2i}$ equations in (12.84).

With (12.81) and (12.84), we have assembled all of the first-order conditions that define the FIML estimator. We write them here as a set of estimating equations:

$$\begin{aligned}&\boldsymbol{X}_{\bullet}^{\top}(\hat{\boldsymbol{B}}_{\text{ML}},\hat{\boldsymbol{\Gamma}}_{\text{ML}})(\hat{\boldsymbol{\Sigma}}_{\text{ML}}^{-1}\otimes\mathbf{I}_n)(\boldsymbol{y}_{\bullet}-\boldsymbol{X}_{\bullet}\hat{\boldsymbol{\beta}}_{\bullet}^{\text{ML}})=\mathbf{0}, \text{ and}\\&\hat{\boldsymbol{\Sigma}}_{\text{ML}}=\frac{1}{n}(\boldsymbol{Y}\hat{\boldsymbol{\Gamma}}_{\text{ML}}-\boldsymbol{W}\hat{\boldsymbol{B}}_{\text{ML}})^{\top}(\boldsymbol{Y}\hat{\boldsymbol{\Gamma}}_{\text{ML}}-\boldsymbol{W}\hat{\boldsymbol{B}}_{\text{ML}}).\end{aligned} \tag{12.85}$$

Solving these equations, which must of course be done numerically, yields the FIML estimator.

There are many numerical methods for obtaining FIML estimates. One of them is to make use of the artificial regression

$$(\boldsymbol{\Psi}^{\top}\otimes\mathbf{I}_n)(\boldsymbol{y}_{\bullet}-\boldsymbol{X}_{\bullet}\boldsymbol{\beta}_{\bullet})=(\boldsymbol{\Psi}^{\top}\otimes\mathbf{I}_n)\boldsymbol{X}_{\bullet}(\boldsymbol{B},\boldsymbol{\Gamma})\boldsymbol{b}+\text{residuals}, \tag{12.86}$$

where, as usual, $\boldsymbol{\Psi\Psi}^{\top}=\boldsymbol{\Sigma}^{-1}$. This is analogous to the multivariate GNR (12.53). If we start from initial consistent estimates, this artificial regression can be used to update the estimates of $\boldsymbol{B}$ and $\boldsymbol{\Gamma}$, and equation (12.81) can be used to update the estimate of $\boldsymbol{\Sigma}$. Like other artificial regressions, (12.86) can also be used to compute test statistics and covariance matrices.

Another approach is to concentrate the loglikelihood function with respect to $\boldsymbol{\Sigma}$. As readers are asked to show in Exercise 12.24, the concentrated loglikelihood function can be written as

$$-\frac{gn}{2}(\log 2\pi+1)+n\log|\det\boldsymbol{\Gamma}|-\frac{n}{2}\log\left|\frac{1}{n}(\boldsymbol{Y\Gamma}-\boldsymbol{XB})^{\top}(\boldsymbol{Y\Gamma}-\boldsymbol{XB})\right|, \tag{12.87}$$

which is the analog of (12.41) and (12.51). Expression (12.87) may be maximized directly with respect to $\boldsymbol{B}$ and $\boldsymbol{\Gamma}$ to yield $\hat{\boldsymbol{B}}_{\text{ML}}$ and $\hat{\boldsymbol{\Gamma}}_{\text{ML}}$. This approach may or may not be easier numerically than solving equations (12.85).

The FIML estimator is not defined if the matrix $(\boldsymbol{Y\Gamma} - \boldsymbol{XB})^{\top}(\boldsymbol{Y\Gamma} - \boldsymbol{XB})$ that appears in (12.87) does not have full rank for all admissible values of $\boldsymbol{B}$ and $\boldsymbol{\Gamma}$, and this requires that $n \geq g+k$. This result suggests that n may have to be substantially greater than $g+k$ if FIML is to have good finite-sample properties; see Sargan (1975) and Brown (1981).

Comparison with Three-Stage Least Squares

Even though the FIML and 3SLS estimators are asymptotically equivalent, the FIML estimator is not, in general, equal to the continuously updated 3SLS estimator. In order to study the relationship between the two estimators, we write out explicitly the estimating equations for 3SLS and compare them with the estimating equations (12.85) for FIML. Equations (12.58) and (12.17) imply that the continuously updated version of the 3SLS estimator is defined by the equations

$$\begin{aligned} &\hat{\boldsymbol{X}}_{\bullet}^{\top}(\hat{\boldsymbol{\Sigma}}_{\text{3SLS}}^{-1} \otimes \mathbf{I}_n)(\boldsymbol{y}_{\bullet} - \boldsymbol{X}_{\bullet}\hat{\boldsymbol{\beta}}_{\bullet}^{\text{3SLS}}) = \mathbf{0}, \text{ and} \\ &\hat{\boldsymbol{\Sigma}}_{\text{3SLS}} = \frac{1}{n}(\boldsymbol{Y}\hat{\boldsymbol{\Gamma}}_{\text{3SLS}} - \boldsymbol{W}\hat{\boldsymbol{B}}_{\text{3SLS}})^{\top}(\boldsymbol{Y}\hat{\boldsymbol{\Gamma}}_{\text{3SLS}} - \boldsymbol{W}\hat{\boldsymbol{B}}_{\text{3SLS}}). \end{aligned} \tag{12.88}$$

The second of these equations has exactly the same form as the second equation of (12.85). The first equation is also very similar to the first equation of (12.85), but there is one difference. In (12.85), the leftmost matrix on the left-hand side of the first equation is the transpose of $\boldsymbol{X}_{\bullet}(\hat{\boldsymbol{B}}_{\text{ML}}, \hat{\boldsymbol{\Gamma}}_{\text{ML}})$, of which the typical diagonal block is $[\,\boldsymbol{Z}_i \quad \boldsymbol{Y}_i(\hat{\boldsymbol{B}}_{\text{ML}}, \hat{\boldsymbol{\Gamma}}_{\text{ML}})\,]$. In contrast, the corresponding matrix in the first equation of (12.88) is the transpose of $\hat{\boldsymbol{X}}_{\bullet}$, of which the typical diagonal block is, from (12.57), $[\,\boldsymbol{Z}_i \quad \boldsymbol{P_W Y}_i\,]$.

In both cases, the matrix is an estimate of the matrix of optimal instruments for equation i, that is, the matrix of the expectations of the explanatory variables conditional on all predetermined information. It is clear from the RRF (12.70) that this matrix is $[\,\boldsymbol{Z}_i \quad \boldsymbol{Y}_i(\boldsymbol{B}, \boldsymbol{\Gamma})\,]$, where $\boldsymbol{B}$ and $\boldsymbol{\Gamma}$ are the true parameters of the DGP. FIML uses the FIML estimates of $\boldsymbol{B}$ and $\boldsymbol{\Gamma}$ in place of the true values, while 3SLS estimates $\boldsymbol{Y}_i(\boldsymbol{B}, \boldsymbol{\Gamma})$ by $\boldsymbol{P_W Y}_i$, that is, by the fitted values from estimation of the *unrestricted* reduced form (12.71). The latter is, in general, less efficient than the former.

If the restricted and unrestricted reduced forms are equivalent, as they must be if all the equations of the system are just identified, then the estimating equations (12.88) and (12.85) are also equivalent, and the 3SLS and FIML estimators must coincide. In this case, as we saw in the last section, 3SLS is also the same as 2SLS, that is, equation-by-equation IV estimation. Thus all the estimators we have considered are identical in the just-identified case. When there are overidentifying restrictions, and 3SLS is used without continuous updating, then the 3SLS estimators of $\boldsymbol{B}$ and $\boldsymbol{\Gamma}$ are replaced by the 2SLS ones in the second equation of (12.88). Solving this equation yields the classical 3SLS estimator (12.78), which is evidently much easier to compute than the FIML estimator.

Our treatment of the relationship between 3SLS and FIML has been quite brief. For much fuller treatments, see Hausman (1975) and Hendry (1976).

Inference Based on FIML Estimates

Since the first equation of (12.85) is just an estimating equation for efficient GMM, we can estimate the covariance matrix of $\hat{\boldsymbol{\beta}}_\bullet^{\rm ML}$ by the obvious estimate of n^{-1} times the asymptotic covariance matrix (12.63), namely,

$$\widehat{\rm Var}(\hat{\boldsymbol{\beta}}_\bullet^{\rm ML}) = \big(\boldsymbol{X}_\bullet^\top(\hat{\boldsymbol{B}}_{\rm ML}, \hat{\boldsymbol{\Gamma}}_{\rm ML})(\hat{\boldsymbol{\Sigma}}_{\rm ML}^{-1} \otimes \mathbf{I}_n)\boldsymbol{X}_\bullet(\hat{\boldsymbol{B}}_{\rm ML}, \hat{\boldsymbol{\Gamma}}_{\rm ML})\big)^{-1}. \qquad (12.89)$$

Notice that, if we evaluate the artificial regression (12.86) at the ML estimates, then $1/s^2$ times the OLS covariance matrix is equal to this matrix.

There are two differences between the estimated covariance matrix for FIML given in equation (12.89) and the estimated covariance matrix for the classical 3SLS estimator given in equation (12.79). The first is that they use different estimates of $\boldsymbol{\Sigma}$. The second is that, in (12.89), the endogenous variables in $\boldsymbol{X}_\bullet$ are replaced by their fitted values, based on the FIML estimates, while in (12.79) they are replaced by their projections on to $\mathcal{S}(\boldsymbol{W})$.

If the model (12.54) is correctly specified, and the error terms really do satisfy the assumptions we have made about them, then each row $\boldsymbol{V}_t$ of the matrix of error terms $\boldsymbol{V}$ in the URF (12.71) must have properties like those of the structural error terms $\boldsymbol{U}_t$ in (12.03). This implies that the error terms in every equation of the URF must be homoskedastic and serially independent. This suggests that the first step in testing the statistical assumptions on which FIML estimation is based should *always* be to perform tests for heteroskedasticity and serial correlation on the equations of the unrestricted reduced form; suitable testing procedures were discussed in Sections 7.5 and 7.7. If there is strong evidence that the $\boldsymbol{V}_t$ are not IID, then either at least one of the structural equations is misspecified, or we need to make more complicated assumptions about the error terms.

It is also important to test any overidentifying restrictions. In the case of FIML, it is natural to use a likelihood ratio test rather than a Hansen-Sargan test, as we suggested for 3SLS and SUR estimation. The number of restrictions is, once again, $gl - k$, the difference between the number of coefficients in the URF and the number in the structural model. The restricted value of the loglikelihood function is the maximized value of either the loglikelihood function (12.80) or the concentrated loglikelihood function (12.87), and the unrestricted value is

$$-\frac{gn}{2}(\log 2\pi + 1) - \frac{n}{2}\log\left|\frac{1}{n}(\boldsymbol{Y} - \boldsymbol{W}\hat{\boldsymbol{\Pi}})^\top(\boldsymbol{Y} - \boldsymbol{W}\hat{\boldsymbol{\Pi}})\right|,$$

where $\hat{\boldsymbol{\Pi}}$ denotes the matrix of OLS estimates of the parameters of the URF. Twice the difference between the unrestricted and restricted values of the loglikelihood function is asymptotically distributed as $\chi^2(gl - k)$ if the model is correctly specified and the overidentifying restrictions are satisfied.

Limited-Information Maximum Likelihood

When a system of equations consists of just one structural equation, together with one or more reduced-form equations, the FIML estimator of the structural equation reduces to a single-equation estimator. We can write the single structural equation as

$$\boldsymbol{y} = \boldsymbol{Z}\boldsymbol{\beta}_1 + \boldsymbol{Y}\boldsymbol{\beta}_2 + \boldsymbol{u}, \tag{12.90}$$

where we use a notation similar to that of (12.54), but without indices on the variables and parameters. There are k_1 elements in $\boldsymbol{\beta}_1$ and k_2 in $\boldsymbol{\beta}_2$, with $k = k_1 + k_2$. A complete simultaneous system can be formed by combining (12.90) with the equations of the unrestricted reduced form for the endogenous variables in the matrix $\boldsymbol{Y}$. We write these equations as

$$\boldsymbol{Y} = \boldsymbol{W}\boldsymbol{\Pi} + \boldsymbol{V} = \boldsymbol{Z}\boldsymbol{\Pi}_1 + \boldsymbol{W}_1\boldsymbol{\Pi}_2 + \boldsymbol{V}, \tag{12.91}$$

where the matrix $\boldsymbol{W}_1$ contains all the predetermined instruments that are excluded from the matrix $\boldsymbol{Z}$.

Since the equations of the unrestricted reduced form are just identified by construction, the only equation of the system consisting of (12.90) and (12.91) that can be overidentified is (12.90) itself. If it is also just identified, then, as we have seen, 3SLS and FIML estimation both give exactly the same results as IV estimation of (12.90) by itself. If equation (12.90) is overidentified, then it turns out that 3SLS, without continuous updating, also gives the same estimates of the parameters of (12.90) as IV estimation. Readers are asked to prove this result in Exercise 12.27. However, continuously updated 3SLS and ML give different, and possibly better, estimates in this case.

Maximum likelihood estimation of equation (12.90), implicitly treating it as part of a system with (12.91), is called **limited-information maximum likelihood**, or **LIML**. The terminology "limited-information" refers to the fact that no use is made of any overidentifying or cross-equation restrictions that may apply to the parameters of the matrix $\boldsymbol{\Pi}$ of reduced-form coefficients. Formally, LIML is FIML applied to a system in which only one equation is overidentified. However, as we will see, LIML is in fact a single-equation estimation method, in the same sense that 2SLS applied to (12.90) alone is a single-equation method. The calculations necessary to see this are rather complicated, and so here we will simply state the principal result, which dates back as far as Anderson and Rubin (1949). A derivation of this result may be found in Davidson and MacKinnon (1993, Chapter 18).

The Anderson-Rubin result is that the LIML estimate of $\boldsymbol{\beta}_2$ in equation (12.90) is given by minimizing the ratio

$$\kappa \equiv \frac{(\boldsymbol{y} - \boldsymbol{Y}\boldsymbol{\beta}_2)^\top \boldsymbol{M}_{\boldsymbol{Z}}(\boldsymbol{y} - \boldsymbol{Y}\boldsymbol{\beta}_2)}{(\boldsymbol{y} - \boldsymbol{Y}\boldsymbol{\beta}_2)^\top \boldsymbol{M}_{\boldsymbol{W}}(\boldsymbol{y} - \boldsymbol{Y}\boldsymbol{\beta}_2)}, \tag{12.92}$$

where $\boldsymbol{M}_{\boldsymbol{Z}}$ projects off the predetermined variables included in (12.90), and $\boldsymbol{M}_{\boldsymbol{W}}$ projects off all the instruments, both those in $\boldsymbol{Z}$ and those in $\boldsymbol{W}_1$.

The value $\hat{\kappa}$ that minimizes (12.92) may be found by a non-iterative procedure that is discussed in the appendix. The maximized value of the loglikelihood function is then

$$-\frac{gn}{2}\log(2\pi) - \frac{n}{2}\log(\hat{\kappa}) - \frac{n}{2}\log|\boldsymbol{Y}_*^\top \boldsymbol{M_W} \boldsymbol{Y}_*|, \tag{12.93}$$

where $\boldsymbol{Y}_* \equiv [\boldsymbol{y} \;\; \boldsymbol{Y}]$.

If we write equation (12.90) as $\boldsymbol{y} = \boldsymbol{X\beta} + \boldsymbol{u}$, then the LIML estimator of $\boldsymbol{\beta}$ is defined by the estimating equations

$$\boldsymbol{X}^\top(\mathbf{I} - \hat{\kappa}\boldsymbol{M_W})(\boldsymbol{y} - \boldsymbol{X}\hat{\boldsymbol{\beta}}^{\text{LIML}}) = \mathbf{0}, \tag{12.94}$$

which can be solved explicitly once $\hat{\kappa}$ has been computed. We find that

$$\hat{\boldsymbol{\beta}}^{\text{LIML}} = (\boldsymbol{X}^\top(\mathbf{I} - \hat{\kappa}\boldsymbol{M_W})\boldsymbol{X})^{-1}\boldsymbol{X}^\top(\mathbf{I} - \hat{\kappa}\boldsymbol{M_W})\boldsymbol{y}. \tag{12.95}$$

A suitable estimate of the covariance matrix of the LIML estimator is

$$\widehat{\text{Var}}(\hat{\boldsymbol{\beta}}^{\text{LIML}}) = \hat{\sigma}^2(\boldsymbol{X}^\top(\mathbf{I} - \hat{\kappa}\boldsymbol{M_W})\boldsymbol{X})^{-1}, \tag{12.96}$$

where

$$\hat{\sigma}^2 \equiv \frac{1}{n}(\boldsymbol{y} - \boldsymbol{X}\hat{\boldsymbol{\beta}}^{\text{LIML}})^\top(\boldsymbol{y} - \boldsymbol{X}\hat{\boldsymbol{\beta}}^{\text{LIML}}).$$

Given (12.96), confidence intervals, asymptotic t tests, and Wald tests can readily be computed in the usual way.

Since $\boldsymbol{W} = [\,\boldsymbol{Z} \quad \boldsymbol{W}_1\,]$ is the matrix containing all the instruments, we can decompose $\boldsymbol{M_W}$ as $\boldsymbol{M_Z} - \boldsymbol{P}_{\boldsymbol{M_Z W}_1}$. This makes it clear that $\kappa \geq 1$, since the numerator of (12.92) cannot be smaller than the denominator. If equation (12.90) is just identified, then, by the order condition, $\boldsymbol{Y}$ and $\boldsymbol{W}_1$ have the same number of columns. In this case, it can be shown that the minimized value of κ is actually equal to 1; see Exercise 12.28.

In the context of 2SLS estimation, we saw in Section 8.6 that the Hansen-Sargan test can be used to test overidentifying restrictions. In the case of LIML estimation, it is easier to test these restrictions by a likelihood ratio test. As shown in Exercise 12.28, the maximized loglikelihood of the unconstrained model for which the overidentifying restrictions of (12.90) are relaxed is the same as expression (12.93) for the constrained model, but with $\kappa = 1$. Thus the LR statistic for testing the overidentifying restrictions, which is twice the difference between the unconstrained and constrained maxima, is simply equal to $n\log\hat{\kappa}$. This test statistic was first proposed by Anderson and Rubin (1950). Since there are $l - k$ overidentifying restrictions, the LR statistic is asymptotically distributed as $\chi^2(l - k)$.

K-Class Estimators

In equation (12.94), we have written the LIML estimating equations in the form of the estimating equations for a ***K*-class** estimator, following Theil (1961). The K-class is the set of estimators defined by the estimating equations (12.94) with an arbitrary scalar K replacing $\hat{\kappa}$. The LIML estimator is thus a K-class estimator with $K = \hat{\kappa}$. Similarly, the 2SLS estimator (12.60) is a K-class estimator with $K = 1$, and the OLS estimator is a K-class estimator with $K = 0$.

Numerous other K-class estimators have been proposed. It can be shown that, under standard regularity conditions, these estimators are consistent whenever the plim of K is 1. Thus 2SLS is consistent, and OLS is inconsistent. Since $n \log \hat{\kappa}$ is asymptotically distributed as $\chi^2(l-k)$ when the overidentifying restrictions are satisfied, it must be the case that $\operatorname{plim} \log \hat{\kappa} = 0$, which implies that $\operatorname{plim} \hat{\kappa} = 1$. It follows that LIML is asymptotically equivalent to 2SLS. In finite samples, however, the properties of LIML may be quite different from those of 2SLS. The strangest feature of the LIML estimator is that it has no finite moments. This implies that its density tends to have very thick tails, as readers are asked to illustrate in Exercise 12.32. However, if we measure bias by comparing the median of the estimator with the true value, the LIML estimator is generally much less biased than the 2SLS estimator.

Fuller (1977) has proposed a modified LIML estimator that sets K equal to $\hat{\kappa} - \alpha/(n-k)$, where α is a positive constant that must be chosen by the investigator. One good choice is $\alpha = 1$, since it yields estimates that are approximately unbiased. In contrast to the LIML estimator, which has no finite moments, Fuller's modified estimator has all moments finite provided the sample size is large enough. Mariano (2001) provides a recent summary of the finite-sample properties of LIML, 2SLS, and other K-class estimators.

Invariance of ML Estimators

One important feature of the FIML and LIML estimators is that they are invariant to any reparametrization of the model. This is actually a general property of all ML estimators, which was explored in Exercise 10.15. Since simultaneous equations systems can be parametrized in many different ways, this is a useful property for these estimators to have. It means that two investigators using the same data set must obtain the same estimates even if they employ different parametrizations.

As an example, consider the two-equation demand-supply model that was first discussed in Section 8.2:

$$q_t = \gamma_d\, p_t + \boldsymbol{X}_t^d \boldsymbol{\beta}_d + u_t^d \tag{12.97}$$

$$q_t = \gamma_s\, p_t + \boldsymbol{X}_t^s \boldsymbol{\beta}_s + u_t^s. \tag{12.98}$$

As the notation indicates, equation (12.97) is a demand function, and equation (12.98) is a supply function. In this system, p_t and q_t denote the price and quantity of some commodity in period t, which may well be in logarithms, $\boldsymbol{X}_t^d$ and $\boldsymbol{X}_t^s$ are row vectors of exogenous or predetermined variables, $\boldsymbol{\beta}_d$ and $\boldsymbol{\beta}_s$ are the corresponding vectors of parameters, and γ_d and γ_s are the slopes of the demand and supply functions, which can be interpreted as elasticities if p_t and q_t are in logarithms.

Now suppose that we reparametrize the supply function as

$$p_t = \gamma_s' q_t + \boldsymbol{X}_t^s \boldsymbol{\beta}_s' + u_t'^s, \tag{12.99}$$

where $\gamma_s' = 1/\gamma_s$ and $\boldsymbol{\beta}_s' = -\boldsymbol{\beta}_s/\gamma_s$. The invariance property of maximum likelihood implies that, if we first use FIML to estimate the system consisting of equations (12.97) and (12.98) and then use it to estimate the system consisting of equations (12.97) and (12.99), we obtain exactly the same estimates of the parameters of equation (12.97). Moreover, the estimated parameters of equations (12.98) and (12.99) bear precisely the same relationship as the true parameters. That is,

$$\hat{\gamma}_s' = 1/\hat{\gamma}_s \quad \text{and} \quad \hat{\boldsymbol{\beta}}_s' = -\hat{\boldsymbol{\beta}}_s/\hat{\gamma}_s. \tag{12.100}$$

If we use LIML to estimate equations (12.98) and (12.99), the two sets of LIML estimates likewise satisfy conditions (12.100).

The invariance property of LIML and FIML is not shared by 2SLS, 3SLS, or any other GMM estimator. If, for example, we use 3SLS to estimate the two versions of this system of equations, the two sets of estimates do not satisfy conditions (12.100); see Exercise 12.31.

12.6 Nonlinear Simultaneous Equations Models

As we saw in Section 12.3, it is fairly straightforward to extend the SUR model so as to allow for the possibility of nonlinearity. However, additional complications can arise with nonlinear simultaneous equations models. With an SUR system, the right-hand sides of the several regressions do not depend on current endogenous variables, but this is not true of a simultaneous system. If endogenous variables enter nonlinearly in such a system, then, since it is not always possible to find solutions to nonlinear equations in closed form, it may be infeasible to set up a reduced form in which each endogenous variable is expressed as a function only of predetermined variables and parameters.

Feasible Efficient GMM

The easiest way to take account of all interesting cases is to work in terms of zero functions and treat the nonlinear simultaneous system by the methods we developed in Section 9.5 for nonlinear GMM. The main extension needed for a simultaneous system is just that each elementary zero function depends, in general, on a vector of endogenous variables, rather than on just one.

Suppose that there are g equations that, for each observation, simultaneously determine g endogenous variables, and suppose further that these equations can be written as

$$f_{ti}(\boldsymbol{Y}_t, \boldsymbol{\theta}) = u_{ti}, \quad t = 1, \ldots, n, \quad i = 1, \ldots, g.$$

The functions $f_{ti}(\cdot)$ depend implicitly on predetermined explanatory variables. They are, in general, nonlinear functions of both the $1 \times g$ vector $\boldsymbol{Y}_t$ that contains the endogenous variables for observation t and the k–vector $\boldsymbol{\theta}$ of model parameters. The u_{ti} are error terms with mean zero. In some cases, we may be ready to assume that the u_{ti} satisfy the conditions (12.02) that we have imposed on the other models considered in this chapter.

It is clear that the f_{ti} are elementary zero functions. We may stack them in the way we stacked the dependent variables of an SUR system. First, we define the n–vectors $\boldsymbol{f}_i(\boldsymbol{Y}, \boldsymbol{\theta})$, $i = 1, \ldots, g$, so that the tth element of $\boldsymbol{f}_i(\boldsymbol{Y}, \boldsymbol{\theta})$ is $f_{ti}(\boldsymbol{Y}_t, \boldsymbol{\theta})$, where $\boldsymbol{Y}$ is the $n \times g$ matrix of which the tth row is $\boldsymbol{Y}_t$. Then we stack the $\boldsymbol{f}_i$ vertically to construct the $gn \times 1$ vector $\boldsymbol{f}_\bullet(\boldsymbol{Y}, \boldsymbol{\theta})$. Under assumptions (12.02), the covariance matrix of this stacked vector is $\boldsymbol{\Sigma} \otimes \mathbf{I}_n$.

According to the theory developed in Section 9.5, the optimal instruments for efficient GMM are given in terms of the matrix $\bar{\boldsymbol{F}}(\boldsymbol{\theta})$ defined in equation (9.85). If, as before, we define the $g \times g$ matrix $\boldsymbol{\Psi}$ such that $\boldsymbol{\Psi}\boldsymbol{\Psi}^\top = \boldsymbol{\Sigma}^{-1}$, then the matrix $\boldsymbol{\Psi}$ of (9.85) becomes $\boldsymbol{\Psi} \otimes \mathbf{I}_n$ in the present case. The matrix $\boldsymbol{F}(\boldsymbol{\theta})$ of that equation becomes a $gn \times k$ matrix $\boldsymbol{F}_\bullet(\boldsymbol{Y}, \boldsymbol{\theta})$, of which the ti^{th} element is the derivative of the tth element of $\boldsymbol{f}_\bullet(\boldsymbol{Y}, \boldsymbol{\theta})$ with respect to θ_i, the ith element of $\boldsymbol{\theta}$. Under assumptions (12.02), the matrix $\bar{\boldsymbol{F}}_\bullet$ needed for the optimal estimating equations is just the $gn \times k$ matrix of which the tth row is the expectation of the tth row of $\boldsymbol{F}_\bullet$ conditional on all information predetermined at time t. The estimating equations we need correspond to equations (9.82). However, as discussed in the paragraph following (9.82), we must use $\bar{\boldsymbol{F}}_\bullet(\boldsymbol{\theta})$ instead of $\boldsymbol{F}_\bullet(\boldsymbol{\theta})$ in formulating the optimal instruments. We obtain

$$\bar{\boldsymbol{F}}_\bullet^\top(\boldsymbol{\theta})(\boldsymbol{\Sigma}^{-1} \otimes \mathbf{I}_n)\boldsymbol{f}_\bullet(\boldsymbol{Y}, \boldsymbol{\theta}) = \mathbf{0}. \tag{12.101}$$

Although the notation differs slightly, the only important difference between (9.82) and (12.101) is that the latter equations involve $\bar{\boldsymbol{F}}_\bullet(\boldsymbol{\theta})$ instead of $\boldsymbol{F}_\bullet(\boldsymbol{\theta})$. There is also no factor of n^{-1} in (12.101), an omission that evidently has no effect on the solution.

It is precisely in the construction of the matrix $\bar{\boldsymbol{F}}_\bullet$ that difficulties may arise. Since there may be no analytical expression for some or all of the endogenous variables, there may be no direct way of computing or even estimating $\bar{\boldsymbol{F}}_\bullet$. In that case, we may proceed as in Section 9.5 by selecting a set of $l \geq k$ instruments, that we group into the $n \times l$ matrix $\boldsymbol{W}$. We then replace the estimating equations (12.101) by

$$\boldsymbol{F}_\bullet^\top(\boldsymbol{Y}, \boldsymbol{\theta})(\boldsymbol{\Sigma}^{-1} \otimes \boldsymbol{P}_{\boldsymbol{W}})\boldsymbol{f}_\bullet(\boldsymbol{Y}, \boldsymbol{\theta}) = \mathbf{0}, \tag{12.102}$$

which closely resemble equations (12.60) for the linear case. Equivalently, we may minimize the criterion function

$$\boldsymbol{f}_{\bullet}^{\top}(\boldsymbol{Y},\boldsymbol{\theta})(\boldsymbol{\Sigma}^{-1}\otimes \boldsymbol{P}_W)\boldsymbol{f}_{\bullet}(\boldsymbol{Y},\boldsymbol{\theta}), \tag{12.103}$$

which is comparable to expression (12.61) for the linear case. The first-order conditions for minimizing (12.103) with respect to $\boldsymbol{\theta}$ are equivalent to the estimating equations (12.102).

If, as is usually the case, the matrix $\boldsymbol{\Sigma}$ is not known, then we must first obtain preliminary consistent estimates, say $\acute{\boldsymbol{\theta}}$. We might do this by solving the estimating equations (12.102) or minimizing the criterion function (12.103) with $\boldsymbol{\Sigma}$ replaced by an identity matrix. Alternatively, if cross-equation restrictions are not needed for identification, we might estimate each equation separately by the methods of Section 9.5. We can then use these preliminary estimates to form an estimate of $\boldsymbol{\Sigma}$ by the formula

$$\acute{\boldsymbol{\Sigma}} = \frac{1}{n}\begin{bmatrix} \boldsymbol{f}_1^{\top}(\boldsymbol{Y},\acute{\boldsymbol{\theta}}) \\ \vdots \\ \boldsymbol{f}_g^{\top}(\boldsymbol{Y},\acute{\boldsymbol{\theta}}) \end{bmatrix} \big[\, \boldsymbol{f}_1(\boldsymbol{Y},\acute{\boldsymbol{\theta}}) \quad \cdots \quad \boldsymbol{f}_g(\boldsymbol{Y},\acute{\boldsymbol{\theta}})\,\big].$$

This estimate can then be used in either (12.102) or (12.103) to obtain more efficient estimates. We can either stop after one round or iterate to obtain continuously updated estimates.

The one-round procedure yields a generalization of the **nonlinear instrumental variables**, or **NLIV**, estimator $\hat{\boldsymbol{\theta}}_{\rm NLIV}$, which we first encountered in Section 8.9. It was originally proposed by Jorgenson and Laffont (1974). In Exercise 12.33, readers are asked to write down the first-order conditions that define the estimator $\hat{\boldsymbol{\theta}}_{\rm NLIV}$, along with the usual estimate of its covariance matrix.

The NLIV estimator is sometimes called **nonlinear three-stage least squares**, or **NL3SLS**. We prefer not to do so, because that name is quite misleading. For the reasons discussed in Section 8.9 in connection with nonlinear two-stage least squares, we never actually replace endogenous variables by their fitted values from reduced-form regressions. Moreover, there are really just two stages, the first in which preliminary consistent estimates are obtained, the second in which (12.102) or (12.103) is used with the estimated $\boldsymbol{\Sigma}$.

Nonlinear FIML Estimation

The other full-system estimation method that is widely used is **nonlinear FIML**. In order to derive the loglikelihood function, it is convenient to stack the vectors $\boldsymbol{f}_i(\boldsymbol{Y},\boldsymbol{\theta})$ horizontally. Let $\boldsymbol{h}_t(\boldsymbol{Y}_t,\boldsymbol{\theta})$ be a $1\times g$ row vector containing the elements $f_{t1},\ldots,f_{tg}$. Then the model to be estimated can be written as

$$\boldsymbol{h}_t(\boldsymbol{Y}_t,\boldsymbol{\theta}) = \boldsymbol{U}_t, \quad \boldsymbol{U}_t \sim \text{NID}(\boldsymbol{0},\boldsymbol{\Sigma}). \tag{12.104}$$

The row vector $\boldsymbol{U}_t$ contains the error terms u_{ti}, $i = 1, \ldots, g$, which are now assumed to be multivariate normal. In order to obtain the density of $\boldsymbol{Y}_t$, we start from the density of $\boldsymbol{U}_t$, replace $\boldsymbol{U}_t$ by $\boldsymbol{h}_t(\boldsymbol{Y}_t, \boldsymbol{\theta})$, and multiply by the Jacobian factor $|\det \boldsymbol{J}_t|$, where $\boldsymbol{J}_t \equiv \partial \boldsymbol{h}_t(\boldsymbol{\theta})/\partial \boldsymbol{Y}_t$ is the $g \times g$ matrix of derivatives of $\boldsymbol{h}_t$ with respect to the elements of $\boldsymbol{Y}_t$. The result is

$$(2\pi)^{-g/2}|\det \boldsymbol{J}_t||\boldsymbol{\Sigma}|^{-1/2}\exp\Big(-\frac{1}{2}\boldsymbol{h}_t(\boldsymbol{Y}_t, \boldsymbol{\theta})\boldsymbol{\Sigma}^{-1}\boldsymbol{h}_t^{\top}(\boldsymbol{Y}_t, \boldsymbol{\theta})\Big).$$

Taking the logarithm of this, summing it over all observations, and then concentrating the result with respect to $\boldsymbol{\Sigma}$, yields the concentrated loglikelihood function for the model (12.104):

$$-\frac{gn}{2}(\log 2\pi + 1) + \sum_{t=1}^{n}\log|\det \boldsymbol{J}_t| - \frac{n}{2}\log\Big|\frac{1}{n}\sum_{t=1}^{n}\boldsymbol{h}_t^{\top}(\boldsymbol{Y}_t, \boldsymbol{\theta})\boldsymbol{h}_t(\boldsymbol{Y}_t, \boldsymbol{\theta})\Big|.$$

The main difference between this function and its counterpart for the linear case, expression (12.87), is that the Jacobian matrices $\boldsymbol{J}_t$ are in general different for each observation. Evaluating all these determinants could well be expensive when n is large and g is not very small.

Another difference between the linear and nonlinear cases is that, in the latter, FIML and NLIV are not even asymptotically equivalent in general. In fact, if the error terms are not normally distributed, the FIML estimator may actually be inconsistent; see Phillips (1982). If the errors are indeed normal, then, for the usual reasons, the FIML estimator is more efficient asymptotically than the NLIV estimator, although its efficiency may come at a price in terms of computational complexity. More detailed treatments of nonlinear FIML estimation may be found in Amemiya (1985, Chapter 8) and Gallant (1987, Chapter 6).

12.7 Final Remarks

Notation is a bugbear with multivariate regression models. These models can be written in many equivalent ways, and notation that is well suited to one estimation method may not be convenient for another. Once the notational hurdle has been crossed, we have seen that it is not excessively difficult to estimate multivariate regression models, including simultaneous equations models, using a variety of familiar techniques. All the procedures we have discussed use some combination of (feasible) generalized least squares, instrumental variables, GMM, and maximum likelihood. Except in the case of nonlinear simultaneous equations models, there is always a technique based on feasible GLS and/or instrumental variables that is asymptotically equivalent to maximum likelihood.

12.8 Appendix: Detailed Results on FIML and LIML

This appendix derives several results on FIML and LIML estimation that were too technical to include in the main text.

First-Order Conditions for FIML

For the purpose of obtaining the first-order conditions (12.83), it is convenient to write the loglikelihood function (12.80) in terms of the restricted reduced form (12.70). In the RRF, the $\boldsymbol{y}_i$ are stacked horizontally. However, if we are to use the same approach as for the SUR model, we must stack them vertically. The ith column of (12.70) can be written as

$$\boldsymbol{y}_i = \boldsymbol{W}\boldsymbol{B}\gamma^i + \boldsymbol{v}_i, \tag{12.105}$$

where the g–vector γ^i is the ith column of $\boldsymbol{\Gamma}^{-1}$, and $\boldsymbol{v}_i$ is the ith column of $\boldsymbol{V}$. Then equations (12.105) can be written as

$$\begin{aligned} \boldsymbol{y}_\bullet &= (\mathbf{I}_g \otimes \boldsymbol{W}\boldsymbol{B})\gamma^\bullet + \boldsymbol{v}_\bullet \\ &= (\mathbf{I}_g \otimes \boldsymbol{W})\boldsymbol{\pi}_\bullet + \boldsymbol{v}_\bullet \\ &= \boldsymbol{W}_\bullet\boldsymbol{\pi}_\bullet + \boldsymbol{v}_\bullet. \end{aligned} \tag{12.106}$$

Here the g^2–vector $\gamma^\bullet$ contains the γ^i stacked vertically, the gn–vector $\boldsymbol{v}_\bullet$ contains the $\boldsymbol{v}_i$ stacked vertically, the $gl \times gn$ matrix $\boldsymbol{W}_\bullet$ denotes $\mathbf{I}_g \otimes \boldsymbol{W}$, and the gl–vector $\boldsymbol{\pi}_\bullet$ contains the $\boldsymbol{\pi}_i$ stacked vertically. The $\boldsymbol{\pi}_i$ are the columns of the matrix $\boldsymbol{\Pi}$, defined here as $\boldsymbol{B}\boldsymbol{\Gamma}^{-1}$, as in the restricted reduced form.

By rewriting the last equation in (12.106) so that $\boldsymbol{v}_\bullet$ is a function of $\boldsymbol{y}_\bullet$, we obtain the transformation that gives $\boldsymbol{v}_\bullet$ in terms of $\boldsymbol{y}_\bullet$. Exactly as with the transformation (12.31), the determinant of the Jacobian of this transformation is 1. Thus, in order to obtain the joint density of $\boldsymbol{y}_\bullet$, we simply have to find the density of the vector $\boldsymbol{v}_\bullet$ and then replace $\boldsymbol{v}_\bullet$ by $\boldsymbol{y}_\bullet - \boldsymbol{W}_\bullet\boldsymbol{\pi}_\bullet$.

Since we have assumed that $\boldsymbol{v}_\bullet$ is multivariate normal, and we know that its expectation is a zero vector, the only thing we need to write down its density is its covariance matrix. Recall that $\boldsymbol{V} = \boldsymbol{U}\boldsymbol{\Gamma}^{-1}$, where $\boldsymbol{U}$ is the matrix of structural form errors. Thus

$$\boldsymbol{v}_i = \boldsymbol{U}\gamma^i = \sum_{j=1}^{g} \boldsymbol{u}_j \gamma^{ji}, \quad i = 1, \ldots, g,$$

where γ^{ji} is the ji^{th} element of $\boldsymbol{\Gamma}^{-1}$. By stacking these equations vertically, it is not hard to see that

$$\boldsymbol{v}_\bullet = \big((\boldsymbol{\Gamma}^\top)^{-1} \otimes \mathbf{I}_n\big)\boldsymbol{u}_\bullet.$$

Since the covariance matrix of $\boldsymbol{u}_\bullet$ is assumed to be $\boldsymbol{\Sigma}\otimes\mathbf{I}_n$, it follows that the covariance matrix of $\boldsymbol{v}_\bullet$ can be written as

$$\begin{aligned}\operatorname{Var}(\boldsymbol{v}_\bullet) = \operatorname{E}(\boldsymbol{v}_\bullet\boldsymbol{v}_\bullet^\top) &= \big((\boldsymbol{\Gamma}^\top)^{-1}\otimes\mathbf{I}_n\big)(\boldsymbol{\Sigma}\otimes\mathbf{I}_n)(\boldsymbol{\Gamma}^{-1}\otimes\mathbf{I}_n)\\ &= (\boldsymbol{\Gamma}^\top)^{-1}\boldsymbol{\Sigma}\boldsymbol{\Gamma}^{-1}\otimes\mathbf{I}_n.\end{aligned}$$

For some of the following calculations, it will be convenient to denote the matrix $(\boldsymbol{\Gamma}^\top)^{-1}\boldsymbol{\Sigma}\boldsymbol{\Gamma}^{-1}$ by $\boldsymbol{\Omega}$.

Using this notation, the density of $\boldsymbol{y}_\bullet$ is $(2\pi)^{-gn/2}$ times

$$|\boldsymbol{\Omega}\otimes\mathbf{I}_n|^{-1/2}\exp\big(-\tfrac{1}{2}(\boldsymbol{y}_\bullet-\boldsymbol{W}_\bullet\boldsymbol{\pi}_\bullet)^\top(\boldsymbol{\Omega}^{-1}\otimes\mathbf{I}_n)(\boldsymbol{y}_\bullet-\boldsymbol{W}_\bullet\boldsymbol{\pi}_\bullet)\big).$$

This may be compared with (12.32), the analogous expression for a linear SUR system. It follows that the loglikelihood function for the linear simultaneous equations model can be written as

$$-\frac{gn}{2}\log 2\pi-\frac{n}{2}\log|\boldsymbol{\Omega}|-\tfrac{1}{2}(\boldsymbol{y}_\bullet-\boldsymbol{W}_\bullet\boldsymbol{\pi}_\bullet)^\top(\boldsymbol{\Omega}^{-1}\otimes\mathbf{I}_n)(\boldsymbol{y}_\bullet-\boldsymbol{W}_\bullet\boldsymbol{\pi}_\bullet).\quad(12.107)$$

This expression is deceptively simple, because the vector $\boldsymbol{\pi}_\bullet$ depends in a complicated way on the vector of structural parameters $\boldsymbol{\beta}_\bullet$. However, since (12.107) depends on $\boldsymbol{\Omega}$ in precisely the same way in which expression (12.33), the loglikelihood function for a linear SUR system, depends on $\boldsymbol{\Sigma}$, the ML estimator of $\boldsymbol{\Omega}$ must have exactly the same form as (12.36).

It is of interest to compare the loglikelihood functions (12.107) and (12.80). A little algebra, which is detailed in Exercise 12.23, shows that

$$(\boldsymbol{\Gamma}^\top\otimes\mathbf{I}_n)(\boldsymbol{y}_\bullet-\boldsymbol{W}_\bullet\boldsymbol{\pi}_\bullet)=\boldsymbol{y}_\bullet-\boldsymbol{X}_\bullet\boldsymbol{\beta}_\bullet,\quad(12.108)$$

which is the vector of residuals from the structural form expressed as in (12.55) in stacked form. Thus the quadratic form that appears in (12.107) can also be written as

$$(\boldsymbol{y}_\bullet-\boldsymbol{X}_\bullet\boldsymbol{\beta}_\bullet)^\top(\boldsymbol{\Sigma}^{-1}\otimes\mathbf{I}_n)(\boldsymbol{y}_\bullet-\boldsymbol{X}_\bullet\boldsymbol{\beta}_\bullet).\quad(12.109)$$

Now consider the second term in (12.107). By the definition of $\boldsymbol{\Omega}$ and the properties of determinants, this term is

$$-\frac{n}{2}\log|\boldsymbol{\Omega}|=-\frac{n}{2}\log\big(|\det\boldsymbol{\Gamma}|^{-2}|\boldsymbol{\Sigma}|\big)=n\log|\det\boldsymbol{\Gamma}|-\frac{n}{2}\log|\boldsymbol{\Sigma}|.\quad(12.110)$$

If we start with (12.107) and replace the quadratic form by expression (12.109) and the second term by the rightmost expression in (12.110), we obtain the loglikelihood function (12.80). Thus we see that these two ways of writing the loglikelihood function are indeed equivalent.

In order to write down the ML estimator of $\boldsymbol{\Omega}$, we define the $n\times g$ matrix $\boldsymbol{V}(\boldsymbol{\beta}_\bullet)$ to have i^{th} column $\boldsymbol{y}_i-\boldsymbol{W}\boldsymbol{B}\boldsymbol{\gamma}^i$, which is just the ith block of the vector $\boldsymbol{y}_\bullet - \boldsymbol{W}_\bullet\boldsymbol{\pi}_\bullet$. It follows that $\boldsymbol{V}(\boldsymbol{\beta}_\bullet) = \boldsymbol{Y} - \boldsymbol{W}\boldsymbol{B}\boldsymbol{\Gamma}^{-1}$. When evaluated at the ML estimator $\hat{\boldsymbol{\beta}}_\bullet^{\rm ML}$, this is just the ML estimator of the errors of the RRF (12.70). By analogy with (12.36), we find that

$$\hat{\boldsymbol{\Omega}}_{\rm ML} = \frac{1}{n}\boldsymbol{V}^\top(\hat{\boldsymbol{\beta}}_\bullet^{\rm ML})\boldsymbol{V}(\hat{\boldsymbol{\beta}}_\bullet^{\rm ML}).$$

We are entitled to write $\boldsymbol{V}$ as a function of $\boldsymbol{\beta}_\bullet$ here because, as we saw when defining the RRF, the matrices $\boldsymbol{B}$ and $\boldsymbol{\Gamma}$ on which (12.107) depends through the vector $\boldsymbol{W}_\bullet\boldsymbol{\pi}_\bullet$ are uniquely determined by the structural parameters in the vector $\boldsymbol{\beta}_\bullet$. Conversely, if we obtain ML estimators of the matrices $\boldsymbol{B}$ and $\boldsymbol{\Gamma}$, these uniquely determine the ML estimator of $\boldsymbol{\beta}_\bullet$.

Only the last term of the loglikelihood function (12.107) depends on $\boldsymbol{B}$ and $\boldsymbol{\Gamma}$. Therefore, conditional on $\boldsymbol{\Sigma}$, the maximization of (12.107) reduces as usual to the minimization of a quadratic form, which in this case is

$$(\boldsymbol{y}_\bullet - \boldsymbol{W}_\bullet\boldsymbol{\pi}_\bullet)^\top(\boldsymbol{\Omega}^{-1}\otimes\mathbf{I}_n)(\boldsymbol{y}_\bullet - \boldsymbol{W}_\bullet\boldsymbol{\pi}_\bullet). \tag{12.111}$$

From the definition of $\boldsymbol{\Omega}$ and the properties (12.08) of Kronecker products, we observe that $\boldsymbol{\Omega}^{-1}\otimes\mathbf{I}_n = (\boldsymbol{\Gamma}\otimes\mathbf{I}_n)(\boldsymbol{\Sigma}^{-1}\otimes\mathbf{I}_n)(\boldsymbol{\Gamma}^\top\otimes\mathbf{I}_n)$.

From the first equation in (12.106), we can see that the quadratic form (12.111) can also be written as

$$\big(\boldsymbol{y}_\bullet - (\mathbf{I}_g\otimes\boldsymbol{W}\boldsymbol{B})\boldsymbol{\gamma}^\bullet\big)^\top(\boldsymbol{\Omega}^{-1}\otimes\mathbf{I}_n)\big(\boldsymbol{y}_\bullet - (\mathbf{I}_g\otimes\boldsymbol{W}\boldsymbol{B})\boldsymbol{\gamma}^\bullet\big).$$

From this expression, we see that the partial derivatives of (12.107) with respect to the g^2 elements of $\boldsymbol{\gamma}^\bullet$ are the g^2 elements of the vector

$$(\mathbf{I}_g\otimes\boldsymbol{B}^\top\boldsymbol{W}^\top)(\boldsymbol{\Omega}^{-1}\otimes\mathbf{I}_n)\big(\boldsymbol{y}_\bullet - (\mathbf{I}_g\otimes\boldsymbol{W}\boldsymbol{B})\boldsymbol{\gamma}^\bullet\big). \tag{12.112}$$

The conditions we seek are not given by simply equating the elements of this vector to zero, because many elements of the matrix $\boldsymbol{\Gamma}$ are restricted to be equal to 0 or 1. The restrictions translate into complicated conditions on the elements of $\boldsymbol{\gamma}^\bullet$ which, fortunately, we need not concern ourselves with. Rather, we compute the derivatives of $\boldsymbol{\gamma}^\bullet$ with respect to any element γ_{ij} of $\boldsymbol{\Gamma}$ which is *not* restricted, and then use the chain rule to obtain the derivative of (12.107) with respect to γ_{ij}. We can then quite properly equate the resulting derivative to zero in order to obtain a first-order condition.

The vectors that are stacked in $\boldsymbol{\gamma}^\bullet$ are the columns of $\boldsymbol{\Gamma}^{-1}$, and it is therefore not hard to see that $(\boldsymbol{\Gamma}^\top\otimes\mathbf{I}_g)\boldsymbol{\gamma}^\bullet$ is a vector of g^2 components that are all either 0 or 1, and thus independent of the elements of $\boldsymbol{\Gamma}$. Differentiating this relation with respect to γ_{ij} thus gives

$$(\boldsymbol{E}_{ji}\otimes\mathbf{I}_g)\boldsymbol{\gamma}^\bullet + (\boldsymbol{\Gamma}^\top\otimes\mathbf{I}_g)\frac{\partial\boldsymbol{\gamma}^\bullet}{\partial\gamma_{ij}} = \mathbf{0},$$

where $\boldsymbol{E}_{ji}$ is a $g \times g$ matrix of which the ji^{th} element is 1 and the other elements are 0. Consequently, the derivative of $\boldsymbol{\gamma}^{\bullet}$ with respect to γ_{ij} is the g^2–vector

$$-\big((\boldsymbol{\Gamma}^{\top})^{-1} \otimes \mathbf{I}_g\big)(\boldsymbol{E}_{ji} \otimes \mathbf{I}_g)\boldsymbol{\gamma}^{\bullet}.$$

The derivative of expression (12.107) with respect to γ_{ij} is the scalar product of this vector with the vector (12.112), that is, the negative of

$$\begin{aligned}
&\boldsymbol{\gamma}^{\bullet\top}(\boldsymbol{E}_{ij} \otimes \mathbf{I}_g)(\boldsymbol{\Gamma}^{-1} \otimes \mathbf{I}_g)(\mathbf{I}_g \otimes \boldsymbol{B}^{\top}\boldsymbol{W}^{\top})(\boldsymbol{\Omega}^{-1} \otimes \mathbf{I}_n)(\boldsymbol{y}_{\bullet} - \boldsymbol{W}_{\bullet}\boldsymbol{\pi}_{\bullet})\\
&\quad = \boldsymbol{\gamma}^{\bullet\top}(\boldsymbol{E}_{ij} \otimes \mathbf{I}_g)(\boldsymbol{\Gamma}^{-1} \otimes \boldsymbol{B}^{\top}\boldsymbol{W}^{\top})(\boldsymbol{\Gamma} \otimes \mathbf{I}_n)(\boldsymbol{\Sigma}^{-1} \otimes \mathbf{I}_n)(\boldsymbol{y}_{\bullet} - \boldsymbol{X}_{\bullet}\boldsymbol{\beta}_{\bullet})\\
&\quad = \boldsymbol{\gamma}^{\bullet\top}(\boldsymbol{E}_{ij} \otimes \boldsymbol{B}^{\top}\boldsymbol{W}^{\top})(\boldsymbol{\Sigma}^{-1} \otimes \mathbf{I}_n)(\boldsymbol{y}_{\bullet} - \boldsymbol{X}_{\bullet}\boldsymbol{\beta}_{\bullet}).
\end{aligned} \tag{12.113}$$

The second line above makes use of the expression of $\boldsymbol{\Omega}$ in terms of $\boldsymbol{\Gamma}$ and $\boldsymbol{\Sigma}$, and of the result (12.108). It is straightforward to see that (12.113) is one row of the left-hand side of (12.83), which therefore contains all the first-order conditions with respect to the unrestricted elements of $\boldsymbol{\Gamma}$.

Eigenvalues and Eigenvectors

Before we can discuss LIML estimation, we need to introduce a few more concepts of matrix algebra. A scalar λ is said to be an **eigenvalue** (also called a **characteristic root** or a **latent root**) of a matrix $\boldsymbol{A}$ if there exists a nonzero vector $\boldsymbol{\xi}$ such that

$$\boldsymbol{A}\boldsymbol{\xi} = \lambda\boldsymbol{\xi}. \tag{12.114}$$

Thus the action of $\boldsymbol{A}$ on $\boldsymbol{\xi}$ produces a vector with the same direction as $\boldsymbol{\xi}$, but a different length unless $\lambda = 1$. The vector $\boldsymbol{\xi}$ is called the **eigenvector** that corresponds to the eigenvalue λ. Although these concepts are defined quite generally, we will restrict our attention to the eigenvalues and eigenvectors of real symmetric matrices.

Equation (12.114) implies that

$$(\boldsymbol{A} - \lambda\mathbf{I})\boldsymbol{\xi} = \mathbf{0}, \tag{12.115}$$

from which we conclude that the matrix $\boldsymbol{A} - \lambda\mathbf{I}$ is singular. Its determinant, $|\boldsymbol{A} - \lambda\mathbf{I}|$, is therefore equal to zero. It can be shown that this determinant is a polynomial in λ. The degree of the polynomial is m if $\boldsymbol{A}$ is $m \times m$. The fundamental theorem of algebra tells us that such a polynomial has m complex roots, say $\lambda_1, \ldots, \lambda_m$. To each λ_i there must correspond an eigenvector $\boldsymbol{\xi}_i$. This eigenvector is determined only up to a scale factor, because if $\boldsymbol{\xi}_i$ is an eigenvector corresponding to λ_i, then so is $\alpha\boldsymbol{\xi}_i$ for any nonzero scalar α. The eigenvector $\boldsymbol{\xi}_i$ does not necessarily have real elements if λ_i itself is not real.

If $\boldsymbol{A}$ is a real symmetric matrix, it can be shown that the eigenvalues λ_i are all real and that the eigenvectors can be chosen to be real as well. If $\boldsymbol{A}$ is also a positive definite matrix, then all its eigenvalues are positive. This follows from the facts that $\boldsymbol{\xi}^{\top}\boldsymbol{A}\boldsymbol{\xi} = \lambda\boldsymbol{\xi}^{\top}\boldsymbol{\xi}$ and that both $\boldsymbol{\xi}^{\top}\boldsymbol{\xi}$ and $\boldsymbol{\xi}^{\top}\boldsymbol{A}\boldsymbol{\xi}$ must be positive scalars when $\boldsymbol{A}$ is positive definite.

The eigenvectors of a real symmetric matrix can be chosen to be mutually orthogonal. Consider any two eigenvectors $\boldsymbol{\xi}_i$ and $\boldsymbol{\xi}_j$ that correspond to two distinct eigenvalues λ_i and λ_j. We see that

$$\lambda_i \boldsymbol{\xi}_j^\top \boldsymbol{\xi}_i = \boldsymbol{\xi}_j^\top \boldsymbol{A}\boldsymbol{\xi}_i = (\boldsymbol{A}\boldsymbol{\xi}_j)^\top \boldsymbol{\xi}_i = \lambda_j \boldsymbol{\xi}_j^\top \boldsymbol{\xi}_i. \tag{12.116}$$

But this is impossible unless $\boldsymbol{\xi}_j^\top \boldsymbol{\xi}_i = 0$. Thus we conclude that $\boldsymbol{\xi}_i$ and $\boldsymbol{\xi}_j$ are necessarily orthogonal. If not all the eigenvalues are distinct, then two (or more) eigenvectors may correspond to one and the same eigenvalue. When that happens, these two eigenvectors span a space that is orthogonal to all other eigenvalues by the reasoning just given. Since any linear combination of the two eigenvectors is also an eigenvector corresponding to the one eigenvalue, we may choose an orthogonal set of them. Thus, whether or not all the eigenvalues are distinct, eigenvectors may be chosen to be **orthonormal**, by which we mean that they are mutually orthogonal and each has norm equal to 1. When the eigenvectors of a real symmetric matrix $\boldsymbol{A}$ are chosen in this way, they provide an **orthonormal basis** for $\mathbb{S}(\boldsymbol{A})$.

Let $\boldsymbol{\Xi} \equiv [\,\boldsymbol{\xi}_1 \;\; \cdots \;\; \boldsymbol{\xi}_m\,]$ be a matrix the columns of which are an orthonormal set of eigenvectors of $\boldsymbol{A}$, corresponding to the eigenvalues λ_i, $i = 1, \ldots, m$. Then we can write the eigenvalue relationship (12.114) for all the eigenvalues at once as

$$\boldsymbol{A\Xi} = \boldsymbol{\Xi\Lambda}, \tag{12.117}$$

where $\boldsymbol{\Lambda}$ is a diagonal matrix with λ_i as its ith diagonal element. The ith column of $\boldsymbol{A\Xi}$ is $\boldsymbol{A}\boldsymbol{\xi}_i$, and the ith column of $\boldsymbol{\Xi\Lambda}$ is $\lambda_i \boldsymbol{\xi}_i$. Since the columns of the matrix $\boldsymbol{\Xi}$ are orthonormal, we find that $\boldsymbol{\Xi}^\top\boldsymbol{\Xi} = \mathbf{I}$, which implies that $\boldsymbol{\Xi}^\top = \boldsymbol{\Xi}^{-1}$. A matrix with this property is said to be an **orthogonal matrix**. Postmultiplying (12.117) by $\boldsymbol{\Xi}^\top$ gives

$$\boldsymbol{A} = \boldsymbol{\Xi\Lambda\Xi}^\top. \tag{12.118}$$

Taking determinants of both sides of (12.118), we obtain

$$|\boldsymbol{A}| = |\boldsymbol{\Xi}||\boldsymbol{\Xi}^\top||\boldsymbol{\Lambda}| = |\boldsymbol{\Xi}||\boldsymbol{\Xi}^{-1}||\boldsymbol{\Lambda}| = |\boldsymbol{\Lambda}| = \prod_{i=1}^{m} \lambda_i,$$

from which we may deduce the important result that the determinant of a symmetric matrix is the product of its eigenvalues. In fact, this result holds for nonsymmetric matrices as well.

LIML Estimation

Consider the system of equations consisting of the structural equation (12.90) and the reduced form equations (12.91). The matrix of coefficients of the endogenous variables in this system of equations is

$$\begin{bmatrix} 1 & \mathbf{0} \\ -\boldsymbol{\beta}_2 & \mathbf{I} \end{bmatrix}.$$

Because this matrix is triangular, its determinant is simply the product of the elements on the principal diagonal, which is 1. Therefore, there is no Jacobian term in the loglikelihood function (12.80) for such a system, and the ML estimates may be obtained by minimizing the determinant

$$\big|(\boldsymbol{Y} - \boldsymbol{XB\Gamma}^{-1})^\top(\boldsymbol{Y} - \boldsymbol{XB\Gamma}^{-1})\big| = \big|(\boldsymbol{Y\Gamma} - \boldsymbol{XB})^\top(\boldsymbol{Y\Gamma} - \boldsymbol{XB})\big|.$$

It can, with considerable effort, be shown that minimizing this determinant is equivalent to minimizing the ratio

$$\kappa \equiv \frac{(\boldsymbol{y} - \boldsymbol{Y\beta}_2)^\top \boldsymbol{M_Z}(\boldsymbol{y} - \boldsymbol{Y\beta}_2)}{(\boldsymbol{y} - \boldsymbol{Y\beta}_2)^\top \boldsymbol{M_W}(\boldsymbol{y} - \boldsymbol{Y\beta}_2)} = \frac{\boldsymbol{\gamma}^\top \boldsymbol{Y}_*^\top \boldsymbol{M_Z Y}_* \boldsymbol{\gamma}}{\boldsymbol{\gamma}^\top \boldsymbol{Y}_*^\top \boldsymbol{M_W Y}_* \boldsymbol{\gamma}}, \tag{12.119}$$

where $\boldsymbol{Y}_* \equiv [\boldsymbol{y} \quad \boldsymbol{Y}]$ and $\boldsymbol{\gamma} = [1 \;\vdots\; -\boldsymbol{\beta}_2]$; see Davidson and MacKinnon (1993, Chapter 18).

It is possible to minimize κ without doing any sort of nonlinear optimization. The first-order conditions obtained by differentiating the rightmost expression in (12.119) with respect to $\boldsymbol{\gamma}$ are

$$2\boldsymbol{Y}^{*\top}\boldsymbol{M_Z Y}^*\boldsymbol{\gamma}(\boldsymbol{\gamma}^\top \boldsymbol{Y}^{*\top}\boldsymbol{M_W Y}^*\boldsymbol{\gamma}) - 2\boldsymbol{Y}^{*\top}\boldsymbol{M_W Y}^*\boldsymbol{\gamma}(\boldsymbol{\gamma}^\top \boldsymbol{Y}^{*\top}\boldsymbol{M_Z Y}^*\boldsymbol{\gamma}) = \boldsymbol{0}.$$

If we divide both sides by $2\boldsymbol{\gamma}^\top \boldsymbol{Y}^{*\top}\boldsymbol{M_W Y}^*\boldsymbol{\gamma}$, this becomes

$$\boldsymbol{Y}^{*\top}\boldsymbol{M_Z Y}^*\boldsymbol{\gamma} - \kappa \boldsymbol{Y}^{*\top}\boldsymbol{M_W Y}^*\boldsymbol{\gamma} = \boldsymbol{0}. \tag{12.120}$$

An equivalent set of first-order conditions can be obtained by premultiplying (12.120) by $(\boldsymbol{Y}^{*\top}\boldsymbol{M_W Y}^*)^{-1/2}$ and inserting that factor multiplied by its inverse before $\boldsymbol{\gamma}$. After some rearrangement, this yields

$$\big((\boldsymbol{Y}^{*\top}\boldsymbol{M_W Y}^*)^{-1/2}\boldsymbol{Y}^{*\top}\boldsymbol{M_Z Y}^*(\boldsymbol{Y}^{*\top}\boldsymbol{M_W Y}^*)^{-1/2} - \kappa\mathbf{I}\big)\boldsymbol{\gamma}^* = \boldsymbol{0},$$

where $\boldsymbol{\gamma}^* \equiv (\boldsymbol{Y}^{*\top}\boldsymbol{M_W Y}^*)^{1/2}\boldsymbol{\gamma}$. This set of first-order conditions now has the form of a standard eigenvalue-eigenvector problem for a real symmetric matrix; see equation (12.115). Thus it is clear that $\hat{\kappa}$ is an eigenvalue of the matrix

$$(\boldsymbol{Y}^{*\top}\boldsymbol{M_W Y}^*)^{-1/2}\boldsymbol{Y}^{*\top}\boldsymbol{M_Z Y}^*(\boldsymbol{Y}^{*\top}\boldsymbol{M_W Y}^*)^{-1/2}, \tag{12.121}$$

which depends only on observable data, and not on unknown parameters. In fact, $\hat{\kappa}$ must be the smallest eigenvalue, because it is the smallest possible value of the ratio (12.119). Given $\hat{\kappa}$, we can use equations (12.95) to compute the LIML estimates. It is worthy of note that, if there is only one endogenous variable in the matrix $\boldsymbol{Y}$, then the determinantal equation that determines the eigenvalues of (12.121) is just a quadratic equation, of which the smaller root is $\hat{\kappa}$, which can therefore be expressed in this case as a closed-form function of the data.

12.9 Exercises

★12.1 Show that the $gn \times gn$ covariance matrix $\boldsymbol{\Sigma}_{\bullet}$ defined in equation (12.07) is positive definite if and only if the $g \times g$ matrix $\boldsymbol{\Sigma}$ used to define it is positive definite.

★12.2 Prove the first result of equations (12.08) for an arbitrary $p \times q$ matrix $\boldsymbol{A}$ and an arbitrary $r \times s$ matrix $\boldsymbol{B}$. Prove the second result for $\boldsymbol{A}$ and $\boldsymbol{B}$ as above, and for $\boldsymbol{C}$ and $\boldsymbol{D}$ arbitrary $q \times t$ and $s \times u$ matrices, respectively. Prove the third result in (12.08) for an arbitrary nonsingular $p \times p$ matrix $\boldsymbol{A}$ and nonsingular $r \times r$ matrix $\boldsymbol{B}$.

Give details of the interchanges of rows and columns needed to convert $\boldsymbol{A} \otimes \boldsymbol{B}$ into $\boldsymbol{B} \otimes \boldsymbol{A}$, where $\boldsymbol{A}$ is $p \times q$ and $\boldsymbol{B}$ is $r \times s$.

★12.3 If $\boldsymbol{B}$ is positive definite, show that $\mathbf{I} \otimes \boldsymbol{B}$ is also positive definite, where $\mathbf{I}$ is an identity matrix of arbitrary dimension. What about $\boldsymbol{B} \otimes \mathbf{I}$? If $\boldsymbol{A}$ is another positive definite matrix, is it the case that $\boldsymbol{B} \otimes \boldsymbol{A}$ is positive definite?

12.4 Show explicitly that expression (12.06) provides the OLS estimates of the parameters of all the equations of the SUR system.

12.5 Show explicitly that expression (12.14) for the GLS estimator of the parameters of an SUR system follows from the estimating equations (12.13).

12.6 Show that, for any two vectors $\boldsymbol{a}_1$ and $\boldsymbol{a}_2$ in E^2, the quantity $\|\boldsymbol{a}_1\|^2 \|\boldsymbol{M}_1 \boldsymbol{a}_2\|^2$, where $\boldsymbol{M}_1$ is the orthogonal projection on to the orthogonal complement of $\boldsymbol{a}_1$ in E^2, is equal to the square of $a_{11}a_{22} - a_{12}a_{21}$, where a_{ij} denotes the ith element of $\boldsymbol{a}_j$, for $i, j = 1, 2$.

12.7 Using only the properties of determinants listed at the end of the subsection on determinants in Section 12.2, show that the determinant of a positive definite matrix $\boldsymbol{B}$ is positive. (**Hint:** write $\boldsymbol{B} = \boldsymbol{A}\boldsymbol{A}^{\top}$.) Show further that, if $\boldsymbol{B}$ is positive semidefinite, without being positive definite, then its determinant must be zero.

★12.8 Suppose that m independent random variables, z_i, each of which is distributed as $\mathrm{N}(0, 1)$, are grouped into an m–vector $\boldsymbol{z}$. Let $\boldsymbol{x} = \boldsymbol{\mu} + \boldsymbol{A}\boldsymbol{z}$, where $\boldsymbol{\mu}$ is an m–vector and $\boldsymbol{A}$ is a nonsingular $m \times m$ matrix, and let $\boldsymbol{\Omega} \equiv \boldsymbol{A}\boldsymbol{A}^{\top}$. Show that the mean of the vector $\boldsymbol{x}$ is $\boldsymbol{\mu}$ and its covariance matrix is $\boldsymbol{\Omega}$. Then show that the density of $\boldsymbol{x}$ is

$$(2\pi)^{-m/2}|\boldsymbol{\Omega}|^{-1/2}\exp\bigl(-\tfrac{1}{2}(\boldsymbol{x}-\boldsymbol{\mu})^{\top}\boldsymbol{\Omega}^{-1}(\boldsymbol{x}-\boldsymbol{\mu})\bigr). \tag{12.122}$$

This extends the result of Exercise 4.5 for the bivariate normal density to the multivariate normal density. **Hints:** Remember that the joint density of m independent random variables is equal to the product of their densities, and use the result (12.29).

12.9 Consider a univariate linear regression model in which the regressors may include lags of the dependent variable. Let $\boldsymbol{y}$ and $\boldsymbol{u}$ denote, respectively, the vectors of observations on the dependent variable and the error terms, and assume that $\boldsymbol{u} \sim \mathrm{N}(\mathbf{0}, \sigma^2\mathbf{I}_n)$. Show that, even though the Jacobian matrix of the transformation (12.31) is not an identity matrix, the determinant of the Jacobian is unity. Then write down the loglikelihood function for this model.

For simplicity, assume that any lagged values of the dependent variable prior to the sample period are observed.

★12.10 Consider a multivariate linear regression model of the form (12.28) in which the regressors may include lags of the dependent variables and the error terms are normally distributed. By ordering the data appropriately, show that the determinant of the Jacobian of the transformation (12.31) is equal to unity. Then explain why this implies that the loglikelihood function, conditional on pre-sample observations, can be written as (12.33).

12.11 Let $\boldsymbol{A}$ and $\boldsymbol{B}$ be square matrices, of dimensions $p \times p$ and $q \times q$, respectively. Use the properties of determinants given in Section 12.2 to show that the determinant of $\boldsymbol{A} \otimes \boldsymbol{B}$ is equal to that of $\boldsymbol{B} \otimes \boldsymbol{A}$.

Use this result, along with any other needed properties of determinants given in Section 12.2, to show that the determinant of $\boldsymbol{\Sigma} \otimes \mathbf{I}_n$ is $|\boldsymbol{\Sigma}|^n$.

12.12 Verify that the moment conditions (12.45) and the estimating equations (12.46) are equivalent. Show also that expressions (12.47) and (12.48) for the covariance matrix estimator for the nonlinear SUR model are equivalent. Explain how (12.48) is related to the covariance matrix estimator (12.15) that corresponds to it in the linear case.

★12.13 The **linear expenditure system** is a system of demand equations that can be written as

$$s_i = \frac{\gamma_i p_i}{E} + \alpha_i \bigg(\frac{E - \sum_{j=1}^{m+1} p_j \gamma_j}{E} \bigg). \tag{12.123}$$

Here, s_i, for $i = 1, \ldots, m$, is the share of total expenditure E spent on commodity i conditional on E and the prices p_i, for $i = 1, \ldots, m+1$. The equation indexed by $i = m+1$ is omitted as redundant, because the sum of the expenditure shares spent on all commodities is necessarily equal to 1. The model parameters are the α_i, $i = 1, \ldots, m$, the γ_i, $i = 1, \ldots, m+1$, and the $m \times m$ contemporaneous covariance matrix $\boldsymbol{\Sigma}$.

Express the system (12.123) as a linear SUR system by use of a suitable nonlinear reparametrization. The equations of the resulting system must be subject to a set of cross-equation restrictions. Express these restrictions in terms of the new parameters, and then set up a GNR in the manner of Section 12.3 that allows one to obtain restricted estimates of the α_i and γ_i.

12.14 Show that the estimating equations (12.60) are equivalent to the estimating equations (12.58).

12.15 Show that the estimating equations (12.65) are equivalent to the equations that correspond to the equation-by-equation IV (or 2SLS) estimator for all the equations of the system jointly.

★12.16 The $k \times k$ matrix $\boldsymbol{X}_{\bullet}^{\top}(\boldsymbol{\Sigma}^{-1} \otimes \boldsymbol{P_W})\boldsymbol{X}_{\bullet}$ given in expression (12.66) is positive semidefinite by construction. Show this property explicitly by expressing the matrix in the form $\boldsymbol{A}^{\top}\boldsymbol{A}$, where $\boldsymbol{A}$ is a matrix with k columns and at least k rows that should depend on a $g \times g$ nonsingular matrix $\boldsymbol{\Psi}$ which satisfies the relation $\boldsymbol{\Psi}\boldsymbol{\Psi}^{\top} = \boldsymbol{\Sigma}^{-1}$.

Show that a positive semidefinite matrix expressed in the form $\boldsymbol{A}^{\top}\boldsymbol{A}$ is positive definite if and only if $\boldsymbol{A}$ has full column rank. In the present case, the matrix $\boldsymbol{A}$ fails to have full column rank if and only if there exists a k–vector $\boldsymbol{\beta}$, different from zero, such that $\boldsymbol{A\beta} = \mathbf{0}$. Since $k = \sum_{i=1}^{g} k_i$, we may write the vector $\boldsymbol{\beta}$ as $[\boldsymbol{\beta}_1 \vdots \ldots \vdots \boldsymbol{\beta}_g]$, where $\boldsymbol{\beta}_i$ is a k_i–vector for $i = 1, \ldots, g$. Show that there exists a nonzero $\boldsymbol{\beta}$ such that $\boldsymbol{A\beta} = \mathbf{0}$ if and only if, for at least one i, there is a nonzero $\boldsymbol{\beta}_i$ such that $\boldsymbol{P_W X}_i \boldsymbol{\beta}_i = \mathbf{0}$, that is, if $\boldsymbol{P_W X}_i$ does not have full column rank.

Show that, if $\boldsymbol{P_W X}_i$ has full column rank, then there exists a unique solution of the estimating equations (12.60) for the parameters $\boldsymbol{\beta}_i$ of equation i.

12.17 Consider the linear simultaneous equations model

$$\begin{aligned} y_{t1} &= \beta_{11} + \beta_{21}x_{t2} + \beta_{31}x_{t3} + \gamma_{21}y_{t2} + u_{t1} \\ y_{t2} &= \beta_{12} + \beta_{22}x_{t2} + \beta_{42}x_{t4} + \beta_{52}x_{t5} + \gamma_{21}y_{t1} + u_{t2}. \end{aligned} \tag{12.124}$$

If this model is written in the matrix notation of (12.68), precisely what are the matrices $\boldsymbol{B}$ and $\boldsymbol{\Gamma}$ equal to?

12.18 Demonstrate that, if each equation in the linear simultaneous equations model (12.54) is just identified, in the sense that the order condition for identification is satisfied as an equality, then the number of restrictions on the elements of the matrices $\boldsymbol{\Gamma}$ and $\boldsymbol{B}$ of the restricted reduced form (12.70) is exactly g^2. In other words, demonstrate that the restricted and unrestricted reduced forms have the same number of parameters in this case.

12.19 Show that all terms that depend on the matrix $\boldsymbol{V}$ of error terms in the finite-sample expression for $n^{-1}\boldsymbol{X}_1^{\top}\boldsymbol{P_W X}_1$ obtained from equation (12.76) tend to zero as $n \to \infty$.

12.20 Consider the following $p \times q$ partitioned matrix

$$\boldsymbol{A} = \begin{bmatrix} \mathbf{I}_m & \boldsymbol{A}_{12} \\ \mathbf{O} & \boldsymbol{A}_{22} \end{bmatrix},$$

where $m < \min(p, q)$. Show that $\boldsymbol{A}$ has full column rank if and only if $\boldsymbol{A}_{22}$ has full column rank. **Hint:** In order to do so, one can show that the existence of a nonzero q–vector $\boldsymbol{x}$ such that $\boldsymbol{Ax} = \mathbf{0}$ implies the existence of a nonzero $(q - m)$–vector $\boldsymbol{x}_2$ such that $\boldsymbol{A}_{22}\boldsymbol{x}_2 = \mathbf{0}$, and vice versa.

⋆12.21 Consider equation (12.72), the first structural equation of the linear simultaneous system (12.68), with the variables ordered as described in the discussion of the asymptotic identification of this equation. Let the matrices $\boldsymbol{\Gamma}$ and $\boldsymbol{B}$ of the full system (12.68) be partitioned as follows:

$$\boldsymbol{B} = \begin{bmatrix} \boldsymbol{\beta}_{11} & \boldsymbol{B}_{12} \\ \mathbf{0} & \boldsymbol{B}_{22} \end{bmatrix} \quad \text{and} \quad \boldsymbol{\Gamma} = \begin{bmatrix} 1 & \boldsymbol{\Gamma}_{02} \\ -\boldsymbol{\beta}_{21} & \boldsymbol{\Gamma}_{12} \\ \mathbf{0} & \boldsymbol{\Gamma}_{22} \end{bmatrix},$$

where $\boldsymbol{\beta}_{11}$ is a k_{11}–vector, $\boldsymbol{B}_{12}$ and $\boldsymbol{B}_{22}$ are, respectively, $k_{11} \times (g-1)$ and $(l - k_{11}) \times (g-1)$ matrices, $\boldsymbol{\beta}_{21}$ is a k_{21}–vector, and $\boldsymbol{\Gamma}_{02}$, $\boldsymbol{\Gamma}_{12}$, and $\boldsymbol{\Gamma}_{22}$ are, respectively, $1 \times (g-1)$, $k_{21} \times (g-1)$, and $(g - k_{21} - 1) \times (g-1)$ matrices. Check that the restrictions imposed in this partitioning correspond correctly to the structure of (12.72).

Let $\boldsymbol{\Gamma}^{-1}$ be partitioned as

$$\boldsymbol{\Gamma}^{-1} = \begin{bmatrix} \gamma^{00} & \boldsymbol{\Gamma}^{01} & \boldsymbol{\Gamma}^{02} \\ \gamma^{10} & \boldsymbol{\Gamma}^{11} & \boldsymbol{\Gamma}^{12} \end{bmatrix},$$

where the rows of $\boldsymbol{\Gamma}^{-1}$ are partitioned in the same pattern as the columns of $\boldsymbol{\Gamma}$, and vice versa. Show that $\boldsymbol{\Gamma}_{22}\boldsymbol{\Gamma}^{12}$ is an identity matrix, and that $\boldsymbol{\Gamma}_{22}\boldsymbol{\Gamma}^{11}$ is a zero matrix, and specify the dimensions of these matrices. Show also that the matrix $[\boldsymbol{\Gamma}^{11} \;\; \boldsymbol{\Gamma}^{12}]$ is square and nonsingular.

⋆12.22 It was shown in Section 12.4 that the rank condition for the asymptotic identification of equation (12.72) is that the $(l - k_{11}) \times k_{21}$ matrix $\boldsymbol{\Pi}_{21}$ of the unrestricted reduced form (12.73) should have full column rank. Show that, in terms of the structural parameters, $\boldsymbol{\Pi}_{21}$ is equal to $\boldsymbol{B}_{22}\boldsymbol{\Gamma}^{11}$. Then consider the matrix

$$\begin{bmatrix} \boldsymbol{\Gamma}_{22} \\ \boldsymbol{B}_{22} \end{bmatrix}, \tag{12.125}$$

and show, by postmultiplying it by the nonsingular matrix $[\boldsymbol{\Gamma}^{11} \;\; \boldsymbol{\Gamma}^{12}]$, that it is of full column rank $g - 1$ if and only if $\boldsymbol{B}_{22}\boldsymbol{\Gamma}^{11}$ is of full column rank. Conclude that the rank condition for the asymptotic identification of (12.72) is that (12.125) should have full column rank.

⋆12.23 Consider the expression $(\boldsymbol{\Gamma}^{\top} \otimes \mathbf{I}_n)\boldsymbol{y}_{\bullet}$, in the notation of Section 12.5. Show that it is equal to a gn–vector that can be written as

$$\begin{bmatrix} \boldsymbol{Y}\gamma_1 \\ \vdots \\ \boldsymbol{Y}\gamma_m \end{bmatrix},$$

where γ_i, $i = 1, \ldots, g$, is the ith column of $\boldsymbol{\Gamma}$.

Show similarly that $(\boldsymbol{\Gamma}^{\top} \otimes \mathbf{I}_n)(\mathbf{I}_g \otimes \boldsymbol{W}\boldsymbol{B})\gamma^{\bullet}$ is equal to a gn–vector that can be written as

$$\begin{bmatrix} \boldsymbol{W}\boldsymbol{b}_1 \\ \vdots \\ \boldsymbol{W}\boldsymbol{b}_m \end{bmatrix},$$

where $\boldsymbol{b}_i$ is the ith column of $\boldsymbol{B}$.

Using these results, demonstrate that $(\boldsymbol{\Gamma}^{\top} \otimes \mathbf{I}_n)(\boldsymbol{y}_{\bullet} - (\mathbf{I}_g \otimes \boldsymbol{W}\boldsymbol{B})\gamma^{\bullet})$ is equal to $\boldsymbol{y}_{\bullet} - \boldsymbol{X}_{\bullet}\boldsymbol{\beta}_{\bullet}$. Explain why this proves the result (12.108).

12.24 By expressing the loglikelihood function (12.107) for the linear simultaneous equations model in terms of $\boldsymbol{\Sigma}$ rather than $\boldsymbol{\Omega}$, show that concentrating the resulting function with respect to $\boldsymbol{\Sigma}$ yields the concentrated loglikelihood function (12.87).

12.25 Write down the concentrated loglikelihood function for the restricted reduced form (12.70) as a special case of (12.51). Then show that this concentrated loglikelihood function is identical to expression (12.87).

12.26 In the model (12.124), what is the identification status of each of the two equations? How would your answer change if an additional regressor, x_{t6}, were added to the first equation only, to the second equation only, or to both equations?

⋆12.27 Consider the linear simultaneous system of equations (12.90) and (12.91). Write down the estimating equations for the 3SLS estimator for the system, and show that they define the same estimator of the parameters of (12.90) as the IV estimator applied to that equation alone with instruments $\boldsymbol{W}$.

State and prove the analogous result for an SUR system in which only one equation is overidentified.

⋆12.28 In the just-identified case of LIML estimation, for which, in the notation of (12.91), the number of excluded instruments in the matrix $\boldsymbol{W}_1$ is equal to the number of included endogenous variables in the matrix $\boldsymbol{Y}$, show that the minimized value of the ratio κ given by (12.92) is equal to the global minimum of 1. Show further that the vector of estimates $\hat{\boldsymbol{\beta}}_2$ that attains this minimum is the IV, or 2SLS, estimator of $\boldsymbol{\beta}_2$ for equation (12.90) with instruments $\boldsymbol{W}$.

In the overidentified case of LIML estimation, explicitly formulate a model containing the model consisting of (12.90) and (12.91) as a special case, with the overidentifying restrictions relaxed. Show that the maximized loglikelihood for this unconstrained model is the same function of the data as for the constrained model, but with $\hat{\kappa}$ replaced by 1.

12.29 Consider the demand-supply model

$$\begin{aligned} q_t &= \beta_{11} + \beta_{21}x_{t2} + \beta_{31}x_{t3} + \gamma_{21}p_t + u_{t1} \\ q_t &= \beta_{12} + \beta_{42}x_{t4} + \beta_{52}x_{t5} + \gamma_{22}p_t + u_{t2}, \end{aligned} \tag{12.126}$$

where q_t is the log of quantity, p_t is the log of price, x_{t2} is the log of income, x_{t3} is a dummy variable that accounts for regular demand shifts, and x_{t4} and x_{t5} are the prices of inputs. Thus the first equation of (12.126) is a demand function and the second equation is a supply function.

For this model, precisely what is the vector $\boldsymbol{\beta}_\bullet$ that was introduced in equation (12.55)? What are the matrices $\boldsymbol{B}$ and $\boldsymbol{\Gamma}$ that were introduced in equation (12.68)? How many overidentifying restrictions are there?

12.30 The file **demand-supply.data** contains 120 observations generated by the model (12.126). Estimate this model by 2SLS, LIML, 3SLS, and FIML. In each case, test the overidentifying restrictions, either for each equation individually or for the whole system, as appropriate.

12.31 The second equation of (12.126) can be rewritten as

$$p_t = \beta'_{12} + \beta'_{42}x_{t4} + \beta'_{52}xt5 + \gamma'_{22}q_t + u'_{t2}. \tag{12.127}$$

Estimate the system that consists of the first equation of (12.126) and equation (12.127) by 3SLS and FIML. What is the relationship between the FIML estimates of this system and the FIML estimates of (12.126)? What is the relationship between the two sets of 3SLS estimates?

12.32 Consider the system

$$y_1 = \beta + \gamma y_2 + \boldsymbol{u}, \quad y_2 = \boldsymbol{W}\boldsymbol{\pi}_1 + \boldsymbol{v}, \tag{12.128}$$

in which the first equation is the only structural equation and the first column of $\boldsymbol{W}$ is a vector of 1s. For sample size $n = 25$, and for $l = 2, 4, 6, 8$, generate $l - 1$ additional instrumental variables as independent drawings from $\mathrm{N}(0, 1)$. Generate the endogenous variables $\boldsymbol{y}_1$ and $\boldsymbol{y}_2$ using the DGP given by (12.128) with $\beta = 1$ and $\gamma = 1$, $\boldsymbol{\pi}_1$ an l-vector with every element equal to 1, and the 2×2 contemporaneous covariance matrix $\boldsymbol{\Sigma}$ such that the diagonal elements are equal to 4, and the off-diagonal elements to 2. Estimate the parameters β and γ using both IV (2SLS) and LIML.

Repeat the exercise many times and plot the empirical distributions of the two estimators of γ. How do their properties vary with the degree of overidentification?

12.33 What are the first-order conditions for minimizing expression (12.103), the NLIV criterion function? What is the usual estimate of the covariance matrix of the NLIV estimator?

Chapter 13

Methods for Stationary Time-Series Data

13.1 Introduction

Time-series data have special features that often require the use of specialized econometric techniques. We have already dealt with some of these. For example, we discussed methods for dealing with serial correlation in Sections 7.6 through 7.9 and in Section 10.7, and we discussed heteroskedasticity and autocorrelation consistent (HAC) covariance matrices in Section 9.3. In this chapter and the next, we discuss a variety of techniques that are commonly used to model, and test hypotheses about, economic time series.

A first point concerns notation. In the time-series literature, it is usual to refer to a variable, series, or process by its typical element. For instance, one may speak of a variable y_t or a set of variables $\boldsymbol{Y}_t$, rather than defining a vector $\boldsymbol{y}$ or a matrix $\boldsymbol{Y}$. We will make free use of this convention in our discussion of time series.

The methods we will discuss fall naturally into two groups. Some of them are intended for use with stationary time series, and others are intended for use with nonstationary time series. We defined stationarity in Section 7.6. Recall that a random process for a time series y_t is said to be covariance stationary if the unconditional expectation and variance of y_t, and the unconditional covariance between y_t and y_{t-j}, for any lag j, are the same for all t. In this chapter, we restrict our attention to time series that are covariance stationary. Nonstationary time series and techniques for dealing with them will be discussed in Chapter 14.

Section 13.2 discusses stochastic processes that can be used to model the way in which the conditional mean of a single time series evolves over time. These are based on the autoregressive and moving-average processes that were introduced in Section 7.6. Section 13.3 discusses methods for estimating this sort of univariate time-series model. Section 13.4 then discusses single-equation dynamic regression models, which provide richer ways to model the relationships among time-series variables than do static regression models. Section 13.5 deals with seasonality and seasonal adjustment. Section 13.6 discusses autoregressive conditional heteroskedasticity, which provides a way to model the evolution of the conditional variance of a time series. Finally, Section 13.7 deals with vector autoregressions, which are a particularly simple and commonly used way to model multivariate time series.

13.2 Autoregressive and Moving-Average Processes

In Section 7.6, we introduced the concept of a stochastic process and briefly discussed autoregressive and moving-average processes. Our purpose there was to provide methods for modeling serial dependence in the error terms of a regression model. But these processes can also be used directly to model the dynamic evolution of an economic time series. When they are used for this purpose, it is common to add a constant term, because most economic time series do not have mean zero.

Autoregressive Processes

In Section 7.6, we discussed the pth order autoregressive, or AR(p), process. If we add a constant term, such a process can be written, with slightly different notation, as

$$y_t = \gamma + \rho_1 y_{t-1} + \rho_2 y_{t-2} + \ldots + \rho_p y_{t-p} + \varepsilon_t, \quad \varepsilon_t \sim \text{IID}(0, \sigma_\varepsilon^2). \tag{13.01}$$

According to this specification, the ε_t are homoskedastic and uncorrelated innovations. The process for ε_t is often referred to as **white noise**, by a peculiar mixed metaphor, of long standing, which cheerfully mixes a visual and an auditory image. Throughout this chapter, the notation ε_t refers to a white noise process with variance σ_ε^2.

Note that the constant term γ in equation (13.01) is *not* the unconditional mean of y_t. We assume throughout this chapter that the processes we consider are covariance stationary, in the sense that was given to that term in Section 7.6. This implies that $\mu \equiv \text{E}(y_t)$ does not depend on t. Thus, by equating the expectations of both sides of (13.01), we find that

$$\mu = \gamma + \mu \sum_{i=1}^{p} \rho_i.$$

Solving this equation for μ yields the result that

$$\mu = \frac{\gamma}{1 - \sum_{i=1}^{p} \rho_i}. \tag{13.02}$$

If we define $u_t = y_t - \mu$, it is then easy to see that

$$u_t = \sum_{i=1}^{p} \rho_i u_{t-i} + \varepsilon_t, \tag{13.03}$$

which is exactly the definition (7.33) of an AR(p) process given in Section 7.6. In the lag operator notation we introduced in that section, equation (13.03) can also be written as

$$u_t = \rho(\mathrm{L})u_t + \varepsilon_t, \quad \text{or as} \quad \big(1 - \rho(\mathrm{L})\big)u_t = \varepsilon_t,$$

where the polynomial ρ is defined by equation (7.35), that is, $\rho(z) = \rho_1 z + \rho_2 z^2 + \ldots + \rho_p z^p$. Similarly, the expression for the unconditional mean μ in equation (13.02) can be written as $\gamma/(1 - \rho(1))$.

For u_t an AR(1) process, the **autocovariance matrix** was given in Section 7.6 by equation (7.32). The elements of this matrix are called the **autocovariances** of the AR(1) process. If the matrix is multiplied by a scalar chosen to make the diagonal elements equal to unity, the result is the **autocorrelation matrix**. For an AR(p) process, the autocovariances and the corresponding autocorrelations can be computed by using a set of equations called the **Yule-Walker equations**. We discuss these equations in detail for an AR(2) process; the generalization to the AR(p) case is straightforward but algebraically more complicated.

An AR(2) process without a constant term is defined by the equation

$$u_t = \rho_1 u_{t-1} + \rho_2 u_{t-2} + \varepsilon_t. \tag{13.04}$$

Let v_0 denote the unconditional variance of u_t, and let v_i denote the covariance of u_t and u_{t-i}, for $i = 1, 2, \ldots$. Because the process is stationary, the v_i, which are by definition the autocovariances of the AR(2) process, do not depend on t. Multiplying equation (13.04) by u_t and taking expectations of both sides, we find that

$$v_0 = \rho_1 v_1 + \rho_2 v_2 + \sigma_\varepsilon^2. \tag{13.05}$$

Because u_{t-1} and u_{t-2} are uncorrelated with the innovation ε_t, the last term on the right-hand side here is $\mathrm{E}(u_t\varepsilon_t) = \mathrm{E}(\varepsilon_t^2) = \sigma_\varepsilon^2$. Similarly, multiplying equation (13.04) by u_{t-1} and u_{t-2} and taking expectations, we find that

$$v_1 = \rho_1 v_0 + \rho_2 v_1 \quad \text{and} \quad v_2 = \rho_1 v_1 + \rho_2 v_0. \tag{13.06}$$

Equations (13.05) and (13.06) can be rewritten as a set of three simultaneous linear equations for v_0, v_1, and v_2:

$$\begin{aligned} v_0 - \rho_1 v_1 - \rho_2 v_2 &= \sigma_\varepsilon^2 \\ \rho_1 v_0 + (\rho_2 - 1)v_1 &= 0 \\ \rho_2 v_0 + \rho_1 v_1 - v_2 &= 0. \end{aligned} \tag{13.07}$$

These equations are the first three Yule-Walker equations for the AR(2) process. As readers are asked to show in Exercise 13.1, their solution is

$$v_0 = \frac{\sigma_\varepsilon^2}{D}(1 - \rho_2), \quad v_1 = \frac{\sigma_\varepsilon^2}{D}\rho_1, \quad v_2 = \frac{\sigma_\varepsilon^2}{D}\big(\rho_1^2 + \rho_2(1 - \rho_2)\big), \tag{13.08}$$

where $D \equiv (1 + \rho_2)(1 + \rho_1 - \rho_2)(1 - \rho_1 - \rho_2)$.

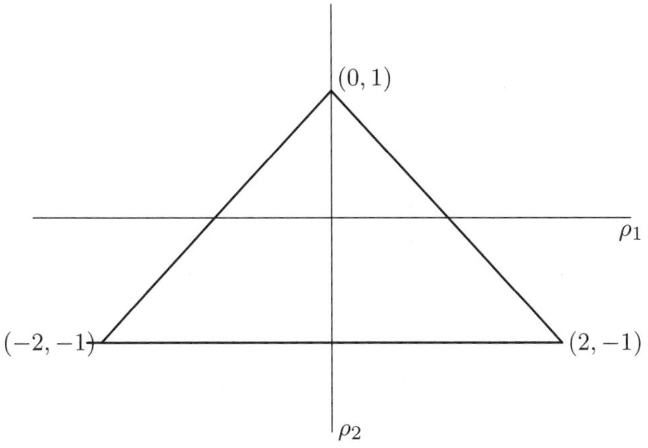

Figure 13.1 The stationarity triangle for an AR(2) process

The result (13.08) makes it clear that ρ_1 and ρ_2 are not the autocorrelations of an AR(2) process. Recall that, for an AR(1) process, the same ρ that appears in the defining equation $u_t = \rho u_{t-1} + \varepsilon_t$ is also the correlation of u_t and u_{t-1}. This simple result does not generalize to higher-order processes. Similarly, the autocovariances and autocorrelations of u_t and u_{t-i} for $i > 2$ have a more complicated form for AR processes of order greater than 1. They can, however, be determined readily enough by using the Yule-Walker equations. Thus, if we multiply both sides of equation (13.04) by u_{t-i} for any $i \geq 2$, and take expectations, we obtain the equation

$$v_i = \rho_1 v_{i-1} + \rho_2 v_{i-2}.$$

Since v_0, v_1, and v_2 are given by equations (13.08), this equation allows us to solve recursively for any v_i with $i > 2$.

Necessary conditions for the stationarity of the AR(2) process follow directly from equations (13.08). The 3×3 covariance matrix

$$\begin{bmatrix} v_0 & v_1 & v_2 \\ v_1 & v_0 & v_1 \\ v_2 & v_1 & v_0 \end{bmatrix} \tag{13.09}$$

of any three consecutive elements of an AR(2) process must be a positive definite matrix. Otherwise, the solution (13.08) to the first three Yule-Walker equations, based on the hypothesis of stationarity, would make no sense. The denominator D evidently must not vanish if this solution is to be finite. In Exercise 12.3, readers are asked to show that the lines along which it vanishes in the plane of ρ_1 and ρ_2 define the edges of a **stationarity triangle** such that the matrix (13.09) is positive definite only in the interior of this triangle. The stationarity triangle is shown in Figure 13.1.

Moving-Average Processes

A qth order moving-average, or MA(q), process with a constant term can be written as

$$y_t = \mu + \alpha_0 \varepsilon_t + \alpha_1 \varepsilon_{t-1} + \ldots + \alpha_q \varepsilon_{t-q}, \tag{13.10}$$

where the ε_t are white noise, and the coefficient α_0 is generally normalized to 1 for purposes of identification. The expectation of the y_t is readily seen to be μ, and so we can write

$$u_t \equiv y_t - \mu = \varepsilon_t + \sum_{j=1}^{q} \alpha_j \varepsilon_{t-j} = \big(1 + \alpha(\mathrm{L})\big)\varepsilon_t,$$

where the polynomial α is defined by $\alpha(z) = \sum_{j=1}^{q} \alpha_j z^j$.

The autocovariances of an MA process are much easier to calculate than those of an AR process. Since the ε_t are white noise, and hence uncorrelated, the variance of the u_t is seen to be

$$\mathrm{Var}(u_t) = \mathrm{E}(u_t^2) = \sigma_\varepsilon^2 \big(1 + \sum_{j=1}^{q} \alpha_j^2\big). \tag{13.11}$$

Similarly, the jth order autocovariance is, for $j > 0$,

$$\mathrm{E}(u_t u_{t-j}) = \begin{cases} \sigma_\varepsilon^2 \big(\alpha_j + \sum_{i=1}^{q-j} \alpha_{j+i}\alpha_i\big) & \text{for } j < q, \\ \sigma_\varepsilon^2 \alpha_j & \text{for } j = q, \text{ and} \\ 0 & \text{for } j > q. \end{cases} \tag{13.12}$$

Using (13.12) and (13.11), we can calculate the autocorrelation $\rho(j)$ between y_t and y_{t-j} for $j > 0$.[1] We find that

$$\rho(j) = \frac{\alpha_j + \sum_{i=1}^{q-j} \alpha_{j+i}\alpha_i}{1 + \sum_{i=1}^{q} \alpha_i^2} \;\text{ for } j \le q, \quad \rho(j) = 0 \text{ otherwise}, \tag{13.13}$$

where it is understood that, for $j = q$, the numerator is just α_j. The fact that all of the autocorrelations are equal to 0 for $j > q$ is sometimes convenient, but it suggests that q may often have to be large if an MA(q) model is to be satisfactory. Expression (13.13) also implies that q must be large if an MA(q) model is to display any autocorrelation coefficients that are big in absolute value. Recall from Section 7.6 that, for an MA(1) model, the largest possible absolute value of $\rho(1)$ is only 0.5.

[1] The notation ρ is unfortunately in common use both for the parameters of an AR process and for the autocorrelations of an AR or MA process. We therefore distinguish between the parameter ρ_i and the autocorrelation $\rho(j)$.

If we want to allow for nonzero autocorrelations at all lags, we have to allow the order of the MA process, q, to be infinite. This means replacing (13.10) by the **infinite-order moving-average process**

$$u_t = \varepsilon_t + \sum_{i=1}^{\infty} \alpha_i \varepsilon_{t-i} = \big(1 + \alpha(\mathrm{L})\big)\varepsilon_t, \tag{13.14}$$

where $\alpha(\mathrm{L})$ is no longer a polynomial, but rather a (formal) infinite power series in the lag operator L. Of course, this **MA(∞) process** is impossible to estimate in practice. Nevertheless, it is of theoretical interest, provided that

$$\mathrm{Var}(u_t) = \sigma_\varepsilon^2 \Big(1 + \sum_{i=1}^{\infty} \alpha_i^2\Big)$$

is a finite quantity. A necessary and sufficient condition for this to be the case is that the coefficients α_j are **square summable**, which means that

$$\lim_{q\to\infty} \sum_{i=1}^{q} \alpha_i^2 < \infty. \tag{13.15}$$

We will implicitly assume that all the MA(∞) processes we encounter satisfy condition (13.15).

Any stationary AR(p) process can be represented as an MA(∞) process. We will not attempt to prove this fundamental result in general; see Fuller (1995), among many others. However, we can easily show how it works in the case of a stationary AR(1) process. Such a process can be written as

$$(1 - \rho_1 \mathrm{L})u_t = \varepsilon_t.$$

The natural way to solve this equation for u_t as a function of ε_t is to multiply both sides by the inverse of $1 - \rho_1\mathrm{L}$. The result is

$$u_t = (1 - \rho_1 \mathrm{L})^{-1}\varepsilon_t. \tag{13.16}$$

Formally, this is the solution we are seeking. But we need to explain what it means to invert $1 - \rho_1\mathrm{L}$.

In general, if $A(\mathrm{L})$ and $B(\mathrm{L})$ are power series in L, each including a constant term independent of L that is not necessarily equal to 1, then $B(\mathrm{L})$ is the inverse of $A(\mathrm{L})$ if $B(\mathrm{L})A(\mathrm{L}) = 1$. Here the product $B(\mathrm{L})A(\mathrm{L})$ is the infinite power series in L obtained by formally multiplying together the power series $B(\mathrm{L})$ and $A(\mathrm{L})$; see Exercise 13.5. The relation $B(\mathrm{L})A(\mathrm{L}) = 1$ then requires that the result of this multiplication should be a series with only one term, the first. Moreover, this term, which corresponds to L^0, must equal 1.

We will not consider general methods for inverting a polynomial in the lag operator; see Hamilton (1994) or Hayashi (2000), among many others. In this particular case, though, the solution turns out to be

$$(1 - \rho_1\mathrm{L})^{-1} = 1 + \rho_1\mathrm{L} + \rho_1^2\mathrm{L}^2 + \dots. \tag{13.17}$$

To see this, note that $\rho_1\mathrm{L}$ times the right-hand side of equation (13.17) is the same series without the first term of 1. Thus, as required,

$$(1 - \rho_1\mathrm{L})^{-1} - \rho_1\mathrm{L}(1 - \rho_1\mathrm{L})^{-1} = (1 - \rho_1\mathrm{L})(1 - \rho_1\mathrm{L})^{-1} = 1.$$

We can now use this result to solve equation (13.16). We find that

$$u_t = \varepsilon_t + \rho_1\varepsilon_{t-1} + \rho_1^2\varepsilon_{t-2} + \dots. \tag{13.18}$$

It is clear that (13.18) is a special case of the MA(∞) process (13.14), with $\alpha_i = \rho_1^i$ for $i = 0, \dots, \infty$. Square summability of the α_i is easy to check provided that $|\rho_1| < 1$.

In general, if we can write a stationary AR(p) process as

$$\big(1 - \rho(\mathrm{L})\big)u_t = \varepsilon_t, \tag{13.19}$$

where $\rho(\mathrm{L})$ is a polynomial of degree p in the lag operator, then there exists an MA(∞) process

$$u_t = \big(1 + \alpha(\mathrm{L})\big)\varepsilon_t, \tag{13.20}$$

where $\alpha(\mathrm{L})$ is an infinite series in L such that $(1 - \rho(\mathrm{L}))(1 + \alpha(\mathrm{L})) = 1$. This result provides an alternative way to the Yule-Walker equations to calculate the variance, autocovariances, and autocorrelations of an AR(p) process by using equations (13.11), (13.12), and (13.13), after we have solved for $\alpha(\mathrm{L})$. However, these methods make use of the theory of functions of a complex variable, and so they are not elementary.

The close relationship between AR and MA processes goes both ways. If (13.20) is an MA(q) process that is **invertible**, then there exists a stationary AR(∞) process of the form (13.19) with

$$\big(1 - \rho(\mathrm{L})\big)\big(1 + \alpha(\mathrm{L})\big) = 1.$$

The condition for a moving-average process to be invertible is formally the same as the condition for an autoregressive process to be stationary; see the discussion around equation (7.36). We require that all the roots of the polynomial equation $1 + \alpha(z) = 0$ must lie outside the unit circle. For an MA(1) process, the invertibility condition is simply that $|\alpha_1| < 1$.

ARMA Processes

If our objective is to model the evolution of a time series as parsimoniously as possible, it may well be desirable to employ a stochastic process that has both autoregressive and moving-average components. This is the **autoregressive moving-average process**, or **ARMA process**. In general, we can write an **ARMA(p,q) process** with nonzero mean as

$$\big(1-\rho(\mathrm{L})\big)y_t = \gamma + \big(1+\alpha(\mathrm{L})\big)\varepsilon_t, \tag{13.21}$$

and a process with zero mean as

$$\big(1-\rho(\mathrm{L})\big)u_t = \big(1+\alpha(\mathrm{L})\big)\varepsilon_t, \tag{13.22}$$

where $\rho(\mathrm{L})$ and $\alpha(\mathrm{L})$ are, respectively, a pth order and a qth order polynomial in the lag operator, neither of which includes a constant term. If the process is stationary, the expectation of y_t given by (13.21) is $\mu \equiv \gamma/\big(1-\rho(1)\big)$, just as for the AR($p$) process (13.01). Provided the autoregressive part is stationary and the moving-average part is invertible, an ARMA(p,q) process can always be represented as either an MA(∞) or an AR(∞) process.

The most commonly encountered ARMA process is the **ARMA(1,1) process**, which, when there is no constant term, has the form

$$u_t = \rho_1 u_{t-1} + \varepsilon_t + \alpha_1\varepsilon_{t-1}. \tag{13.23}$$

This process has one autoregressive and one moving-average parameter.

The Yule-Walker method can be extended to compute the autocovariances of an ARMA process. We illustrate this for the ARMA(1, 1) case and invite readers to generalize the procedure in Exercise 13.6. As before, we denote the ith autocovariance by v_i, and we let $\mathrm{E}(u_t\varepsilon_{t-i}) = w_i$, for $i = 0, 1, \ldots$. Note that $\mathrm{E}(u_t\varepsilon_s) = 0$ for all $s > t$. If we multiply (13.23) by ε_t and take expectations, we see that $w_0 = \sigma_\varepsilon^2$. If we then multiply (13.23) by ε_{t-1} and repeat the process, we find that $w_1 = \rho_1 w_0 + \alpha_1\sigma_\varepsilon^2$, from which we conclude that $w_1 = \sigma_\varepsilon^2(\rho_1+\alpha_1)$. Although we do not need them at present, we note that the w_i for $i > 1$ can be found by multiplying (13.23) by ε_{t-i}, which gives the recursion $w_i = \rho_1 w_{i-1}$, with solution $w_i = \sigma_\varepsilon^2\rho_1^{i-1}(\rho_1+\alpha_1)$.

Next, we imitate the way in which the Yule-Walker equations are set up for an AR process. Multiplying equation (13.23) first by u_t and then by u_{t-1}, and subsequently taking expectations, gives

$$\begin{aligned} v_0 &= \rho_1 v_1 + w_0 + \alpha_1 w_1 = \rho_1 v_1 + \sigma_\varepsilon^2(1+\alpha_1\rho_1+\alpha_1^2), \text{ and} \\ v_1 &= \rho_1 v_0 + \alpha_1 w_0 = \rho_1 v_0 + \alpha_1\sigma_\varepsilon^2, \end{aligned}$$

where we have used the expressions for w_0 and w_1 given in the previous paragraph. When these two equations are solved for v_0 and v_1, they yield

$$v_0 = \sigma_\varepsilon^2 \frac{1 + 2\rho_1\alpha_1 + \alpha_1^2}{1 - \rho_1^2}, \quad \text{and} \quad v_1 = \sigma_\varepsilon^2 \frac{\rho_1 + \rho_1^2\alpha_1 + \rho_1\alpha_1^2 + \alpha_1}{1 - \rho_1^2}. \tag{13.24}$$

Finally, multiplying equation (13.23) by u_{t-i} for $i > 1$ and taking expectations gives $v_i = \rho_1 v_{i-1}$, from which we conclude that

$$v_i = \sigma_\varepsilon^2 \frac{\rho_1^{i-1}(\rho_1 + \rho_1^2\alpha_1 + \rho_1\alpha_1^2 + \alpha_1)}{1 - \rho_1^2}. \tag{13.25}$$

Equation (13.25) provides all the autocovariances of an ARMA(1, 1) process. Using it and the first of equations (13.24), we can derive the autocorrelations.

Autocorrelation Functions

As we have seen, the autocorrelation between u_t and u_{t-j} can be calculated theoretically for any known stationary ARMA process. The **autocorrelation function**, or **ACF**, expresses the autocorrelation as a function of the lag j for $j = 1, 2 \ldots$. If we have a sample y_t, $t = 1, \ldots, n$, from an ARMA process of possibly unknown order, then the jth order autocorrelation $\rho(j)$ can be estimated by using the formula

$$\hat{\rho}(j) = \frac{\widehat{\text{Cov}}(y_t, y_{t-j})}{\widehat{\text{Var}}(y_t)}, \tag{13.26}$$

where

$$\widehat{\text{Cov}}(y_t, y_{t-j}) = \frac{1}{n-1} \sum_{t=j+1}^{n} (y_t - \bar{y})(y_{t-j} - \bar{y}), \tag{13.27}$$

and

$$\widehat{\text{Var}}(y_t) = \frac{1}{n-1} \sum_{t=1}^{n} (y_t - \bar{y})^2. \tag{13.28}$$

In equations (13.27) and (13.28), $\bar{y}$ is the mean of the y_t. Of course, (13.28) is just the special case of (13.27) in which $j = 0$. It may seem odd to divide by $n - 1$ rather than by $n - j - 1$ in (13.27). However, if we did not use the same denominator for every j, the estimated autocorrelation matrix would not necessarily be positive definite. Because the denominator is the same, the factors of $1/(n - 1)$ cancel in the formula (13.26).

The **empirical ACF**, or **sample ACF**, expresses the $\hat{\rho}(j)$, defined in equation (13.26), as a function of the lag j. Graphing the sample ACF provides a convenient way to see what the pattern of serial dependence in any observed time series looks like, and it may help to suggest what sort of stochastic process would provide a good way to model the data. For example, if the data were generated by an MA(1) process, we would expect that $\hat{\rho}(1)$ would be an estimate of α_1 and all the other $\hat{\rho}(j)$ would be approximately equal to zero. If the data were generated by an AR(1) process with $\rho_1 > 0$, we would expect that $\hat{\rho}(1)$ would be an estimate of ρ_1 and would be relatively large, the next few $\hat{\rho}(j)$ would be progressively smaller, and the ones for large j would be approximately equal to zero. A graph of the sample ACF is sometimes called a **correlogram**; see Exercise 13.15.

The **partial autocorrelation function**, or **PACF**, is another way to characterize the relationship between y_t and its lagged values. The partial autocorrelation coefficient of order j is defined as the true value of the coefficient $\rho_j^{(j)}$ in the linear regression

$$y_t = \gamma^{(j)} + \rho_1^{(j)} y_{t-1} + \ldots + \rho_j^{(j)} y_{t-j} + \varepsilon_t, \tag{13.29}$$

or, equivalently, in the minimization problem

$$\min_{\gamma^{(j)},\, \rho_i^{(j)}} \mathrm{E}\Big(y_t - \gamma^{(j)} - \sum_{i=1}^{j} \rho_i^{(j)} y_{t-i}\Big)^2. \tag{13.30}$$

The superscript "(j)" appears on all the coefficients in regression (13.29) to make it plain that all the coefficients, not just the last one, are functions of j, the number of lags. We can calculate the **empirical PACF**, or **sample PACF**, up to order J by running regression (13.29) for $j = 1, \ldots, J$ and retaining only the estimate $\hat{\rho}_j^{(j)}$ for each j. Just as a graph of the sample ACF may help to suggest what sort of stochastic process would provide a good way to model the data, so a graph of the sample PACF, interpreted properly, may do the same. For example, if the data were generated by an AR(2) process, we would expect the first two partial autocorrelations to be relatively large, and all the remaining ones to be insignificantly different from zero.

13.3 Estimating AR, MA, and ARMA Models

All of the time-series models that we have discussed so far are special cases of an ARMA(p, q) model with a constant term, which can be written as

$$y_t = \gamma + \sum_{i=1}^{p} \rho_i y_{t-i} + \varepsilon_t + \sum_{j=1}^{q} \alpha_j \varepsilon_{t-j}, \tag{13.31}$$

where the ε_t are assumed to be white noise. There are $p+q+1$ parameters to estimate in the model (13.31): the ρ_i, for $i = 1, \ldots, p$, the α_j, for $j = 1, \ldots, q$, and γ. Recall that γ is not the unconditional expectation of y_t unless all of the ρ_i are zero.

For our present purposes, it is perfectly convenient to work with models that allow y_t to depend on exogenous explanatory variables and are therefore even more general than (13.31). Such models are sometimes referred to as **ARMAX models**. The 'X' indicates that y_t depends on a row vector $\boldsymbol{X}_t$ of exogenous variables as well as on its own lagged values. An ARMAX(p,q) model takes the form

$$y_t = \boldsymbol{X}_t\boldsymbol{\beta} + u_t, \quad u_t \sim \text{ARMA}(p,q), \quad \text{E}(u_t) = 0, \tag{13.32}$$

where $\boldsymbol{X}_t\boldsymbol{\beta}$ is the mean of y_t conditional on $\boldsymbol{X}_t$ but not conditional on lagged values of y_t. The ARMA model (13.31) can evidently be recast in the form of the ARMAX model (13.32); see Exercise 13.13.

Estimation of AR Models

We have already studied a variety of ways of estimating the model (13.32) when u_t follows an AR(1) process. In Chapter 7, we discussed three estimation methods. The first was estimation by a nonlinear regression, in which the first observation is dropped from the sample. The second was estimation by feasible GLS, possibly iterated, in which the first observation can be taken into account. The third was estimation by the GNR that corresponds to the nonlinear regression with an extra artificial observation corresponding to the first observation. It turned out that estimation by iterated feasible GLS and by this extended artificial regression, both taking the first observation into account, yield the same estimates. Then, in Chapter 10, we discussed estimation by maximum likelihood, and, in Exercise 10.21, we showed how to extend the GNR by yet another artificial observation in such a way that it provides the ML estimates if convergence is achieved.

Similar estimation methods exist for models in which the error terms follow an AR(p) process with $p > 1$. The easiest method is just to drop the first p observations and estimate the nonlinear regression model

$$y_t = \boldsymbol{X}_t\boldsymbol{\beta} + \sum_{i=1}^{p} \rho_i(y_{t-i} - \boldsymbol{X}_{t-i}\boldsymbol{\beta}) + \varepsilon_t$$

by nonlinear least squares. If this is a pure time-series model for which $\boldsymbol{X}_t\boldsymbol{\beta} = \beta$, then this is equivalent to OLS estimation of the model

$$y_t = \gamma + \sum_{i=1}^{p} \rho_i y_{t-i} + \varepsilon_t,$$

where the relationship between γ and β is derived in Exercise 13.13. This approach is the simplest and most widely used for pure autoregressive models. It has the advantage that, although the ρ_i (but not their estimates) must satisfy the necessary condition for stationarity, the error terms u_t need not be stationary. This issue was mentioned in Section 7.8, in the context of the AR(1) model, where it was seen that the variance of the first error term u_1 must satisfy a certain condition for u_t to be stationary.

Maximum Likelihood Estimation

If we are prepared to assume that u_t is indeed stationary, it is desirable not to lose the information in the first p observations. The most convenient way to achieve this goal is to use maximum likelihood under the assumption that the white noise process ε_t is normal. In addition to using more information, maximum likelihood has the advantage that the estimates of the ρ_j are automatically constrained to satisfy the stationarity conditions.

For any ARMA(p, q) process in the error terms u_t, the assumption that the ε_t are normally distributed implies that the u_t are normally distributed, and so also the dependent variable y_t, conditional on the explanatory variables. For an observed sample of size n from the ARMAX model (13.32), let $\boldsymbol{y}$ denote the n-vector of which the elements are $y_1, \ldots, y_n$. The expectation of $\boldsymbol{y}$ conditional on the explanatory variables is $\boldsymbol{X\beta}$, where $\boldsymbol{X}$ is the $n \times k$ matrix with typical row $\boldsymbol{X}_t$. Let $\boldsymbol{\Omega}$ denote the autocovariance matrix of the vector $\boldsymbol{y}$. This matrix can be written as

$$\boldsymbol{\Omega} = \begin{bmatrix} v_0 & v_1 & v_2 & \cdots & v_{n-1} \\ v_1 & v_0 & v_1 & \cdots & v_{n-2} \\ v_2 & v_1 & v_0 & \cdots & v_{n-3} \\ \vdots & \vdots & \vdots & \ddots & \vdots \\ v_{n-1} & v_{n-2} & v_{n-3} & \cdots & v_0 \end{bmatrix}, \tag{13.33}$$

where, as before, v_i is the stationary covariance of u_t and u_{t-i}, and v_0 is the stationary variance of the u_t. Then, using expression (12.122) for the multivariate normal density, we see that the log of the joint density of the observed sample is

$$-\frac{n}{2}\log 2\pi - \frac{1}{2}\log|\boldsymbol{\Omega}| - \frac{1}{2}(\boldsymbol{y} - \boldsymbol{X\beta})^{\top}\boldsymbol{\Omega}^{-1}(\boldsymbol{y} - \boldsymbol{X\beta}). \tag{13.34}$$

In order to construct the loglikelihood function for the ARMAX model (13.32), the v_i must be expressed as functions of the parameters ρ_i and α_j of the ARMA(p, q) process that generates the error terms. Doing this allows us to replace $\boldsymbol{\Omega}$ in the log density (13.34) by a matrix function of these parameters. Unfortunately, a loglikelihood function in the form of (13.34) is difficult to work with, because of the presence of the $n \times n$ matrix $\boldsymbol{\Omega}$. Most of the difficulty disappears if we can find an upper-triangular matrix $\boldsymbol{\Psi}$ such that $\boldsymbol{\Psi\Psi}^{\top} = \boldsymbol{\Omega}^{-1}$, as was necessary when, in Section 7.8, we wished to estimate by feasible GLS a model like (13.32) with AR(1) errors. It then becomes possible to decompose expression (13.34) into a sum of contributions that are easier to work with than (13.34) itself.

If the errors are generated by an AR(p) process, with no MA component, then such a matrix $\boldsymbol{\Psi}$ is relatively easy to find, as we will illustrate in a moment for the AR(2) case. However, if an MA component is present, matters are more difficult. Even for MA(1) errors, the algebra is quite complicated; see Hamilton (1994, Chapter 5) for a convincing demonstration of this fact. For general ARMA(p, q) processes, a technique called the **Kalman filter** can be used to evaluate the successive contributions to the loglikelihood for given parameter values, and can thus serve as the basis of an algorithm for maximizing the loglikelihood. This technique, to which Hamilton (1994, Chapter 13) provides an accessible introduction, is unfortunately beyond the scope of this book. A somewhat simpler approach, which solves for the parameters of $\boldsymbol{\Psi}$ recursively, has been proposed by Galbraith and Zinde-Walsh (1992).

We now turn our attention to the case in which the errors follow an AR(2) process. In Section 7.8, we constructed a matrix $\boldsymbol{\Psi}$ corresponding to the stationary covariance matrix of an AR(1) process by finding n linear combinations of the error terms u_t that were homoskedastic and serially uncorrelated. We perform a similar exercise for AR(2) errors here. This will show how to set about the necessary algebra for more general AR(p) processes.

Errors generated by an AR(2) process satisfy equation (13.04). Therefore, for $t \geq 3$, we can solve for ε_t to obtain

$$\varepsilon_t = u_t - \rho_1 u_{t-1} - \rho_2 u_{t-2}, \quad t = 3, \ldots, n. \tag{13.35}$$

Under the normality assumption, the fact that the ε_t are white noise means that they are mutually independent. Thus observations 3 through n make contributions to the loglikelihood of the form

$$\begin{aligned}&\ell_t(\boldsymbol{y}^t, \boldsymbol{\beta}, \rho_1, \rho_2, \sigma_\varepsilon) = \\ &\quad -\tfrac{1}{2}\log 2\pi - \log \sigma_\varepsilon - \frac{1}{2\sigma_\varepsilon^2}\big(u_t(\boldsymbol{\beta}) - \rho_1 u_{t-1}(\boldsymbol{\beta}) - \rho_2 u_{t-2}(\boldsymbol{\beta})\big)^2,\end{aligned} \tag{13.36}$$

where $\boldsymbol{y}^t$ is the vector that consists of y_1 through y_t, $u_t(\boldsymbol{\beta}) \equiv y_t - \boldsymbol{X}_t\boldsymbol{\beta}$, and σ_ε^2 is as usual the variance of the ε_t. The contribution (13.36) is analogous to the contribution (10.87) for the AR(1) case.

The variance of the first error term, u_1, is just the stationary variance v_0 given by (13.08). We can therefore define ε_1 as $\sigma_\varepsilon u_1/\sqrt{v_0}$, that is,

$$\varepsilon_1 = \Big(\frac{D}{1-\rho_2}\Big)^{1/2} u_1, \tag{13.37}$$

where D was defined just after equations (13.08). By construction, ε_1 has the same variance σ_ε^2 as the ε_t for $t \geq 3$. Since the ε_t are innovations, it follows that, for $t > 1$, ε_t is independent of u_1, and hence of ε_1. For the loglikelihood contribution from observation 1, we therefore take the log density of ε_1, plus a Jacobian term which is the log of the derivative of ε_1 with respect to u_1. The result is readily seen to be

$$\begin{aligned}&\ell_1(y_1, \boldsymbol{\beta}, \rho_1, \rho_2, \sigma_\varepsilon) = \\ &\quad -\tfrac{1}{2}\log 2\pi - \log \sigma_\varepsilon + \tfrac{1}{2}\log \frac{D}{1-\rho_2} - \frac{D}{2\sigma_\varepsilon^2(1-\rho_2)}\, u_1^2(\boldsymbol{\beta}).\end{aligned} \tag{13.38}$$

Finding a suitable expression for ε_2 is a little trickier. What we seek is a linear combination of u_1 and u_2 that has variance σ_ε^2 and is independent of u_1. By construction, any such linear combination is independent of the ε_t for $t > 2$. A little algebra shows that the appropriate linear combination is

$$\sigma_\varepsilon\Big(\frac{v_0}{v_0^2 - v_1^2}\Big)^{1/2}\Big(u_2 - \frac{v_1}{v_0}u_1\Big).$$

Use of the explicit expressions for v_0 and v_1 given in equations (13.08) then shows that

$$\varepsilon_2 = (1-\rho_2^2)^{1/2}\Big(u_2 - \frac{\rho_1}{1-\rho_2}u_1\Big), \tag{13.39}$$

as readers are invited to check in Exercise 13.9. The derivative of ε_2 with respect to u_2 is $(1-\rho_2^2)^{1/2}$, and so the contribution to the loglikelihood from observation 2 can be written as

$$\begin{aligned} \ell_2(\boldsymbol{y}^2, \boldsymbol{\beta}, \rho_1, \rho_2, \sigma_\varepsilon) = &-\tfrac{1}{2}\log 2\pi - \log\sigma_\varepsilon + \tfrac{1}{2}\log(1-\rho_2^2) \\ &- \frac{1-\rho_2^2}{2\sigma_\varepsilon^2}\Big(u_2(\boldsymbol{\beta}) - \frac{\rho_1}{1-\rho_2}u_1(\boldsymbol{\beta})\Big)^2. \end{aligned} \tag{13.40}$$

Summing the contributions (13.36), (13.38), and (13.40) gives the loglikelihood function for the entire sample. It may then be maximized with respect to $\boldsymbol{\beta}$, ρ_1, ρ_2, and σ_ε^2 by standard numerical methods.

Exercise 13.10 asks readers to check that the $n \times n$ matrix $\boldsymbol{\Psi}$ defined implicitly by the relation $\boldsymbol{\Psi}^\top \boldsymbol{u} = \boldsymbol{\varepsilon}$, where the elements of $\boldsymbol{\varepsilon}$ are defined by (13.35), (13.37), and (13.39), is indeed upper triangular and such that $\boldsymbol{\Psi}\boldsymbol{\Psi}^\top$ is equal to $1/\sigma_\varepsilon^2$ times the inverse of the covariance matrix (13.33) for the v_i that correspond to an AR(2) process.

Estimation of MA and ARMA Models

Just why moving-average and ARMA models are more difficult to estimate than pure autoregressive models is apparent if we consider the MA(1) model

$$y_t = \mu + \varepsilon_t - \alpha_1\varepsilon_{t-1}, \tag{13.41}$$

where for simplicity the only explanatory variable is a constant, and we have changed the sign of α_1. For the first three observations, if we substitute recursively for ε_{t-1}, equation (13.41) can be written as

$$\begin{aligned} y_1 &= \mu - \alpha_1\varepsilon_0 + \varepsilon_1, \\ y_2 &= (1+\alpha_1)\mu - \alpha_1 y_1 - \alpha_1^2\varepsilon_0 + \varepsilon_2, \\ y_3 &= (1+\alpha_1+\alpha_1^2)\mu - \alpha_1 y_2 - \alpha_1^2 y_1 - \alpha_1^3\varepsilon_0 + \varepsilon_3. \end{aligned}$$

It is not difficult to see that, for arbitrary t, this becomes

$$y_t = \Big(\sum_{s=0}^{t-1} \alpha_1^s\Big)\mu - \sum_{s=1}^{t-1} \alpha_1^s y_{t-s} - \alpha_1^t \varepsilon_0 + \varepsilon_t. \tag{13.42}$$

Were it not for the presence of the unobserved ε_0, equation (13.42) would be a nonlinear regression model, albeit a rather complicated one in which the form of the regression function depends explicitly on t.

This fact can be used to develop tractable methods for estimating a model where the errors have an MA component without going to the trouble of setting up the complicated loglikelihood. The estimates are not equal to ML estimates, and are in general less efficient, although in some cases they are asymptotically equivalent. The simplest approach, which is sometimes rather misleadingly called **conditional least squares**, is just to assume that any unobserved pre-sample innovations, such as ε_0, are equal to 0, an assumption that is harmless asymptotically. A more sophisticated approach is to "backcast" the pre-sample innovations from initial estimates of the other parameters and then run the nonlinear regression (13.42) conditional on the backcasts, that is, the backward forecasts. Yet another approach is to treat the unobserved innovations as parameters to be estimated jointly by maximum likelihood with the parameters of the MA process and those of the regression function.

Alternative statistical packages use a number of different methods for estimating models with ARMA errors, and they may therefore yield different estimates; see Newbold, Agiakloglou, and Miller (1994) for a more detailed account. Moreover, even if they provide the same estimates, different packages may well provide different standard errors. In the case of ML estimation, for example, these may be based on the empirical Hessian estimator (10.42), the OPG estimator (10.44), or the sandwich estimator (10.45), among others. If the innovations are heteroskedastic, only the sandwich estimator is valid.

A more detailed discussion of standard methods for estimating AR, MA, and ARMA models is beyond the scope of this book. Detailed treatments may be found in Box, Jenkins, and Reinsel (1994, Chapter 7), Hamilton (1994, Chapter 5), and Fuller (1995, Chapter 8), among others.

Indirect Inference

There is another approach to estimating ARMA models, which is unlikely to be used by statistical packages but is worthy of attention if the available sample is not too small. It is an application of the method of **indirect inference**, which was developed by Smith (1993) and Gouriéroux, Monfort, and Renault (1993). The idea is that, when a model is difficult to estimate, there may be an **auxiliary model** that is not too different from the model of interest but is much easier to estimate. For any two such models, there must exist so-called **binding functions** that relate the parameters of the model of interest to those of the auxiliary model. The idea of indirect inference is to estimate the parameters of interest from the parameter estimates of the auxiliary model by using the relationships given by the binding functions.

Because pure AR models are easy to estimate and can be used as auxiliary models, it is natural to use this approach with models that have an MA component. For simplicity, suppose the model of interest is the pure time-series MA(1) model (13.41), and the auxiliary model is the AR(1) model

$$y_t = \gamma + \rho y_{t-1} + u_t, \tag{13.43}$$

which we estimate by OLS to obtain estimates $\hat{\gamma}$ and $\hat{\rho}$. Let us define the elementary zero function $u_t(\gamma, \rho)$ as $y_t - \gamma - \rho y_{t-1}$. Then the estimating equations satisfied by $\hat{\gamma}$ and $\hat{\rho}$ are

$$\sum_{t=2}^{n} u_t(\gamma, \rho) = 0 \quad \text{and} \quad \sum_{t=2}^{n} y_{t-1} u_t(\gamma, \rho) = 0. \tag{13.44}$$

If y_t is indeed generated by (13.41) for particular values of μ and α_1, then we may define the **pseudo-true values** of the parameters γ and ρ of the auxiliary model (13.43) as those values for which the expectations of the left-hand sides of equations (13.44) are zero. These equations can thus be interpreted as correctly specified, albeit inefficient, estimating equations for the pseudo-true values. The theory of Section 9.5 then shows that $\hat{\gamma}$ and $\hat{\rho}$ are consistent for the pseudo-true values and asymptotically normal, with asymptotic covariance matrix given by a version of the sandwich matrix (9.67).

The pseudo-true values can be calculated as follows. Replacing y_t and y_{t-1} in the definition of $u_t(\gamma, \rho)$ by the expressions given by (13.41), we see that

$$u_t(\gamma, \rho) = (1 - \rho)\mu - \gamma + \varepsilon_t - (\alpha_1 + \rho)\varepsilon_{t-1} + \alpha_1 \rho \varepsilon_{t-2}. \tag{13.45}$$

The expectation of the right-hand side of this equation is just $(1 - \rho)\mu - \gamma$. Similarly, the expectation of $y_{t-1} u_t(\gamma, \rho)$ can be seen to be

$$\mu\big((1 - \rho)\mu - \gamma\big) - \sigma_\varepsilon^2(\alpha_1 + \rho) - \sigma_\varepsilon^2 \alpha_1^2 \rho.$$

Equating these expectations to zero shows us that the pseudo-true values are

$$\gamma = \frac{\mu(1 + \alpha_1 + \alpha_1^2)}{1 + \alpha_1^2} \quad \text{and} \quad \rho = \frac{-\alpha_1}{1 + \alpha_1^2} \tag{13.46}$$

in terms of the true parameters μ and α_1.

Equations (13.46) express the binding functions that link the parameters of model (13.41) to those of the auxiliary model (13.43). The indirect estimates $\hat{\mu}$ and $\hat{\alpha}_1$ are obtained by solving these equations with γ and ρ replaced by $\hat{\gamma}$

and $\hat{\rho}$. Note that, since the second equation of (13.46) is a quadratic equation for α_1 in terms of ρ, there are in general two solutions for α_1, which may be complex. See Exercise 13.11 for further elucidation of this point.

In order to estimate the covariance matrix of $\hat{\mu}$ and $\hat{\alpha}_1$, we must first estimate the covariance matrix of $\hat{\gamma}$ and $\hat{\rho}$. Let us define the $n \times 2$ matrix $\boldsymbol{Z}$ as $[\boldsymbol{\iota} \;\; \boldsymbol{y}_{-1}]$, that is, a matrix of which the first column is a vector of 1s and the second the vector of the y_t lagged. Then, since the Jacobian of the zero functions $u_t(\gamma, \rho)$ is just $-\boldsymbol{Z}$, it is easy to see that the covariance matrix (9.67) becomes

$$\operatorname*{plim}_{n\to\infty} \frac{1}{n}(\boldsymbol{Z}^\top\boldsymbol{Z})^{-1}\boldsymbol{Z}^\top\boldsymbol{\Omega}\boldsymbol{Z}(\boldsymbol{Z}^\top\boldsymbol{Z})^{-1}, \tag{13.47}$$

where $\boldsymbol{\Omega}$ is the covariance matrix of the error terms u_t, which are given by the $u_t(\gamma, \rho)$ evaluated at the pseudo-true values. If we drop the probability limit and the factor of n^{-1} in expression (13.47) and replace $\boldsymbol{\Omega}$ by a suitable estimate, we obtain an estimate of the covariance matrix of $\hat{\gamma}$ and $\hat{\rho}$. Instead of estimating $\boldsymbol{\Omega}$ directly, it is convenient to employ a HAC estimator of the middle factor of expression (13.47).[2] Since, as can be seen from equation (13.45), the u_t have nonzero autocovariances only up to order 2, it is natural in this case to use the Hansen-White estimator (9.37) with lag truncation parameter set equal to 2. Finally, an estimate of the covariance matrix of $\hat{\mu}$ and $\hat{\alpha}_1$ can be obtained from the one for $\hat{\gamma}$ and $\hat{\rho}$ by the delta method (Section 5.6) using the relation (13.46) between the true and pseudo-true parameters.

In this example, indirect inference is particularly simple because the auxiliary model (13.43) has just as many parameters as the model of interest (13.41). However, this is rarely the case. We saw in Section 13.2 that a finite-order MA or ARMA process can always be represented by an AR(∞) process. This suggests that, when estimating an MA or ARMA model, we should use as an auxiliary model an AR(p) model with p substantially greater than the number of parameters in the model of interest. See Galbraith and Zinde-Walsh (1994, 1997) for implementations of this approach which solve for the binding functions analytically.

Clearly, indirect inference is impossible if the auxiliary model has fewer parameters than the model of interest. If, as is commonly the case, it has more, then the parameters of the model of interest are overidentified. This means that we cannot just solve for them from the estimates of the auxiliary model. Instead, we need to minimize a suitable criterion function, so as to make the estimates of the auxiliary model as close as possible, in the appropriate sense, to the values implied by the parameter estimates of the model of interest. In the next paragraph, we explain how to do this in a very general setting.

[2] In this special case, an expression for $\boldsymbol{\Omega}$ as a function of α, ρ, and σ_ε^2 can be obtained from equation (13.45), so that we can estimate $\boldsymbol{\Omega}$ as a function of consistent estimates of those parameters. In most cases, however, it is necessary to use a HAC estimator.

Let the estimates of the pseudo-true parameters be an l–vector $\hat{\boldsymbol{\beta}}$, let the parameters of the model of interest be a k–vector $\boldsymbol{\theta}$, and let the binding functions be an l–vector $\boldsymbol{b}(\boldsymbol{\theta})$, with $l > k$. Then the indirect estimator of $\boldsymbol{\theta}$ is obtained by minimizing the quadratic form

$$\big(\hat{\boldsymbol{\beta}} - \boldsymbol{b}(\boldsymbol{\theta})\big)^{\top}\hat{\boldsymbol{\Sigma}}^{-1}\big(\hat{\boldsymbol{\beta}} - \boldsymbol{b}(\boldsymbol{\theta})\big) \tag{13.48}$$

with respect to $\boldsymbol{\theta}$, where $\hat{\boldsymbol{\Sigma}}$ is a consistent estimate of the $l \times l$ covariance matrix of $\hat{\boldsymbol{\beta}}$. Minimizing this quadratic form minimizes the length of the vector $\hat{\boldsymbol{\beta}} - \boldsymbol{b}(\boldsymbol{\theta})$ after that vector has been transformed so that its covariance matrix is approximately the identity matrix.

Expression (13.48) looks very much like a criterion function for efficient GMM estimation. Not surprisingly, it can be shown that, under suitable regularity conditions, the minimized value of this criterion function is asymptotically distributed as $\chi^2(l-k)$. This provides a simple way to test the overidentifying restrictions that must hold if the model of interest actually generated the data. As with efficient GMM estimation, tests of restrictions on the vector $\boldsymbol{\theta}$ can be based on the difference between the restricted and unrestricted values of expression (13.48).

In many applications, including general ARMA processes, it can be difficult or impossible to find tractable analytic expressions for the binding functions. In that case, they may be estimated by simulation. This works well if it is easy to draw simulated samples from DGPs in the model of interest, and also easy to estimate the auxiliary model. Simulations are then carried out as follows. In order to evaluate the criterion function (13.48) at a parameter vector $\boldsymbol{\theta}$, we draw S independent simulated data sets from the DGP characterized by $\boldsymbol{\theta}$, and for each of them we compute the estimate $\boldsymbol{\beta}_s^*(\boldsymbol{\theta})$ of the parameters of the auxiliary model. The binding functions are then estimated by

$$\boldsymbol{b}^*(\boldsymbol{\theta}) = \frac{1}{S}\sum_{s=1}^{S}\boldsymbol{\beta}_s^*(\boldsymbol{\theta}).$$

We then use $\boldsymbol{b}^*(\boldsymbol{\theta})$ in place of $\boldsymbol{b}(\boldsymbol{\theta})$ when we evaluate the criterion function (13.48). As with the method of simulated moments (Section 9.6), the *same* random numbers should be used to compute $\boldsymbol{\beta}_s^*$ for each given s and for all $\boldsymbol{\theta}$. Much more detailed discussions of indirect inference can be found in Smith (1993) and Gouriéroux, Monfort, and Renault (1993).

Simulating ARMA Processes

Simulating data from an MA(q) process is trivially easy. For a sample of size n, one generates white-noise innovations ε_t for $t = -q+1, \ldots, 0, \ldots, n$. These are most commonly generated from the normal distribution, but any continuous distribution with mean 0 and finite variance can be used. Then, for $t = 1, \ldots, n$, the simulated data are given by

$$u_t^* = \varepsilon_t + \sum_{j=1}^{q} \alpha_j \varepsilon_{t-j}.$$

There is no need to worry about missing pre-sample innovations in the context of simulation, because they are simulated along with the other innovations.

Simulating data from an AR(p) process is not quite so easy, because of the initial observations. Recursive simulation can be used for all but the first p observations, using the equation

$$u_t^* = \sum_{i=1}^{p} \rho_i u_{t-i}^* + \varepsilon_t. \tag{13.49}$$

For an AR(1) process, the first simulated observation u_1^* can be drawn from the **stationary distribution** of the process, by which we mean the unconditional distribution of u_t. This distribution has mean zero and variance $\sigma_\varepsilon^2/(1-\rho_1^2)$. The remaining observations are then generated recursively. When $p > 1$, the first p observations must be drawn from the stationary distribution of p consecutive elements of the AR(p) series. This distribution has mean vector zero and covariance matrix $\boldsymbol{\Omega}$ given by expression (13.33) with $n = p$. Once the specific form of this covariance matrix has been determined, perhaps by solving the Yule-Walker equations, and $\boldsymbol{\Omega}$ has been evaluated for the specific values of the ρ_i, a $p \times p$ lower-triangular matrix $\boldsymbol{A}$ can be found such that $\boldsymbol{A}\boldsymbol{A}^\top = \boldsymbol{\Omega}$; see the discussion of the multivariate normal distribution in Section 4.3. We then generate $\boldsymbol{\varepsilon}_p$ as a p–vector of white noise innovations and construct the p–vector $\boldsymbol{u}_p^*$ of the first p observations as $\boldsymbol{u}_p^* = \boldsymbol{A}\boldsymbol{\varepsilon}_p$. The remaining observations are then generated recursively.

Since it may take considerable effort to find $\boldsymbol{\Omega}$, a simpler technique is often used. One starts the recursion (13.49) for a large negative value of t with essentially arbitrary starting values, often zero. By making the starting value of t far enough in the past, the joint distribution of u_1^* through u_p^* can be made arbitrarily close to the stationary distribution. The values of u_t^* for nonpositive t are then discarded.

Starting the recursion far in the past also works with an ARMA(p, q) process. However, at least for simple models, we can exploit the covariances computed by the extension of the Yule-Walker method discussed in Section 13.2. The process (13.22) can be written explicitly as

$$u_t^* = \sum_{i=1}^{p} \rho_i u_{t-i}^* + \varepsilon_t + \sum_{j=1}^{q} \alpha_j \varepsilon_{t-j}. \tag{13.50}$$

In order to be able to compute the u_t^* recursively, we need starting values for $u_1^*, \ldots, u_p^*$ and $\varepsilon_{p-q+1}, \ldots, \varepsilon_p$. Given these, we can compute u_{p+1}^* by drawing the innovation ε_{p+1} and using equation (13.50) for $t = p + 1, \ldots, n$. The starting values can be drawn from the joint stationary distribution characterized by the autocovariances v_i and covariances w_j discussed in the previous section. In Exercise 13.12, readers are asked to find this distribution for the relatively simple ARMA(1, 1) case.

13.4 Single-Equation Dynamic Models

Economists often wish to model the relationship between the current value of a dependent variable y_t, the current and lagged values of one or more independent variables, and, quite possibly, lagged values of y_t itself. This sort of model can be motivated in many ways. Perhaps it takes time for economic agents to perceive that the independent variables have changed, or perhaps it is costly for them to adjust their behavior. In this section, we briefly discuss a number of models of this type. For notational simplicity, we assume that there is only one independent variable, denoted x_t. In practice, of course, there is usually more than one such variable, but it will be obvious how to extend the models we discuss to handle this more general case.

Distributed Lag Models

When a dependent variable depends on current and lagged values of x_t, but not on lagged values of itself, we have what is called a **distributed lag model**. When there is only one independent variable, plus a constant term, such a model can be written as

$$y_t = \delta + \sum_{j=0}^{q} \beta_j x_{t-j} + u_t, \quad u_t \sim \text{IID}(0, \sigma^2), \tag{13.51}$$

in which y_t depends on the current value of x_t and on q lagged values. The constant term δ and the coefficients β_j are to be estimated.

In many cases, x_t is positively correlated with some or all of the lagged values x_{t-j} for $j \geq 1$. In consequence, the OLS estimates of the β_j in equation (13.51) may be quite imprecise. However, this is generally not a problem if we are merely interested in the long-run impact of changes in the independent variable. This long-run impact is

$$\gamma \equiv \sum_{j=0}^{q} \beta_j = \sum_{j=0}^{q} \frac{\partial y_t}{\partial x_{t-j}}. \tag{13.52}$$

We can estimate (13.51) and then calculate the estimate $\hat{\gamma}$ using (13.52), or we can obtain $\hat{\gamma}$ directly by reparametrizing regression (13.51) as

$$y_t = \delta + \gamma x_t + \sum_{j=1}^{q} \beta_j (x_{t-j} - x_t) + u_t. \tag{13.53}$$

The advantage of this reparametrization is that the standard error of $\hat{\gamma}$ is immediately available from the regression output.

In Section 3.4, we derived an expression for the variance of a weighted sum of parameter estimates. Expression (3.33), which can be written in a more intuitive fashion as (3.68), can be applied directly to $\hat{\gamma}$, which is an unweighted sum. If we do so, we find that

$$\mathrm{Var}(\hat{\gamma}) = \boldsymbol{\iota}^\top \mathrm{Var}(\hat{\boldsymbol{\beta}})\boldsymbol{\iota} = \sum_{j=0}^{q} \mathrm{Var}(\hat{\beta}_j) + 2\sum_{j=1}^{q}\sum_{k=0}^{j-1} \mathrm{Cov}(\hat{\beta}_j, \hat{\beta}_k), \tag{13.54}$$

where the smallest value of j in the double summation is 1 rather than 0, because no valid value of k exists for $j = 0$. When x_{t-j} is positively correlated with x_{t-k} for all $j \neq k$, the covariance terms in (13.54) are generally all negative. When the correlations are large, these covariance terms can often be large in absolute value, so much so that $\mathrm{Var}(\hat{\gamma})$ may be smaller than the variance of $\hat{\beta}_j$ for some or all j. If we are interested in the long-run impact of x_t on y_t, it is therefore perfectly sensible just to estimate equation (13.53).

The Partial Adjustment Model

One popular alternative to distributed lag models like (13.51) is the **partial adjustment model**, which dates back at least to Nerlove (1958). Suppose that the desired level of an economic variable y_t is y_t°. This desired level is assumed to depend on a vector of exogenous variables $\boldsymbol{X}_t$ according to

$$y_t^\circ = \boldsymbol{X}_t\boldsymbol{\beta}^\circ + e_t, \quad e_t \sim \mathrm{IID}(0, \sigma_e^2). \tag{13.55}$$

Because of adjustment costs, y_t is not equal to y_t° in every period. Instead, it is assumed to adjust toward y_t° according to the equation

$$y_t - y_{t-1} = (1-\delta)(y_t^\circ - y_{t-1}) + v_t, \quad v_t \sim \mathrm{IID}(0, \sigma_v^2), \tag{13.56}$$

where δ is an adjustment parameter that is assumed to be positive and strictly less than 1. Solving (13.55) and (13.56) for y_t, we find that

$$\begin{aligned} y_t &= y_{t-1} - (1-\delta)y_{t-1} + (1-\delta)\boldsymbol{X}_t\boldsymbol{\beta}^\circ + (1-\delta)e_t + v_t \\ &= \boldsymbol{X}_t\boldsymbol{\beta} + \delta y_{t-1} + u_t, \end{aligned} \tag{13.57}$$

where $\boldsymbol{\beta} \equiv (1-\delta)\boldsymbol{\beta}^\circ$ and $u_t \equiv (1-\delta)e_t + v_t$. Thus the partial adjustment model leads to a linear regression of y_t on $\boldsymbol{X}_t$ and y_{t-1}. The coefficient of y_{t-1} is the adjustment parameter, and estimates of $\boldsymbol{\beta}^\circ$ can be obtained from the OLS estimates of $\boldsymbol{\beta}$ and δ. This model does not make sense if $\delta < 0$ or if $\delta \geq 1$. Moreover, when δ is close to 1, the implied speed of adjustment may be implausibly slow.

Equation (13.57) can be solved for y_t as a function of current and lagged values of $\boldsymbol{X}_t$ and u_t. Under the assumption that $|\delta| < 1$, we find that

$$y_t = \sum_{j=0}^{\infty} \delta^j \boldsymbol{X}_{t-j}\boldsymbol{\beta} + \sum_{j=0}^{\infty} \delta^j u_{t-j}.$$

Thus we see that the partial adjustment model implies a particular form of distributed lag. However, in contrast to the model (13.51), y_t now depends on lagged values of the error terms u_t as well as on lagged values of the exogenous variables $\boldsymbol{X}_t$. This makes sense in many cases. If the regressors affect y_t via a distributed lag, and if the error terms reflect the combined influence of other regressors that have been omitted, then it is surely plausible that the omitted regressors would also affect y_t via a distributed lag. However, the restriction that the same distributed lag coefficients should apply to all the regressors and to the error terms may be excessively strong in many cases.

The partial adjustment model is only one of many economic models that can be used to justify the inclusion of one or more lags of the dependent variables in regression functions. Others are discussed in Dhrymes (1971) and Hendry, Pagan, and Sargan (1984). We now consider a general family of regression models that include lagged dependent and lagged independent variables.

Autoregressive Distributed Lag Models

For simplicity of notation, we will continue to discuss only models with a single independent variable, x_t. In this case, an **autoregressive distributed lag**, or **ADL**, model can be written as

$$y_t = \beta_0 + \sum_{i=1}^{p} \beta_i y_{t-i} + \sum_{j=0}^{q} \gamma_j x_{t-j} + u_t, \quad u_t \sim \text{IID}(0, \sigma^2). \tag{13.58}$$

Because there are p lags on y_t and q lags on x_t, this is sometimes called an **ADL(p, q)** model.

A widely encountered special case of (13.58) is the **ADL(1, 1)** model

$$y_t = \beta_0 + \beta_1 y_{t-1} + \gamma_0 x_t + \gamma_1 x_{t-1} + u_t. \tag{13.59}$$

Because most results that are true for the ADL(1, 1) model are also true, with obvious modifications, for the more general ADL(p, q) model, we will largely confine our discussion to this special case.

Although the ADL(1, 1) model is quite simple, many commonly encountered models are special cases of it. When $\beta_1 = \gamma_1 = 0$, we have a static regression model with IID errors; when $\gamma_0 = \gamma_1 = 0$, we have a univariate AR(1) model; when $\gamma_1 = 0$, we have a partial adjustment model; when $\gamma_1 = -\beta_1\gamma_0$, we have a static regression model with AR(1) errors; and when $\beta_1 = 1$ and $\gamma_1 = -\gamma_0$, we have a model in first differences that can be written as

$$\Delta y_t = \beta_0 + \gamma_0 \Delta x_t + u_t.$$

Before we accept any of these special cases, it makes sense to test them against (13.59). This can be done by means of asymptotic t or F tests, which it may be wise to bootstrap when the sample size is not large.

It is usually desirable to impose the condition that $|\beta_1| < 1$ in (13.59). Strictly speaking, this is not a stationarity condition, since we cannot expect y_t to be stationary without imposing further conditions on the explanatory variable x_t. However, it is easy to see that, if this condition is violated, the dependent variable y_t exhibits explosive behavior. If the condition is satisfied, there may exist a long-run equilibrium relationship between y_t and x_t, which can be used to develop a particularly interesting reparametrization of (13.59).

Suppose there exists an equilibrium value x° to which x_t would converge as $t \to \infty$ in the absence of shocks. Then, in the absence of the error terms u_t, y_t would converge to a steady-state long-run equilibrium value y° such that

$$y^\circ = \beta_0 + \beta_1 y^\circ + (\gamma_0 + \gamma_1)x^\circ.$$

Solving this equation for y° as a function of x° yields

$$\begin{aligned} y^\circ &= \frac{\beta_0}{1-\beta_1} + \frac{\gamma_0 + \gamma_1}{1-\beta_1} x^\circ \\ &= \frac{\beta_0}{1-\beta_1} + \lambda x^\circ, \end{aligned} \tag{13.60}$$

where

$$\lambda \equiv \frac{\gamma_0 + \gamma_1}{1-\beta_1}. \tag{13.61}$$

This is the long-run derivative of y° with respect to x°, and it is an elasticity if both series are in logarithms. An estimate of λ can be computed directly from the estimates of the parameters of (13.59). Note that the result (13.60) and the definition (13.61) make sense only if the condition $|\beta_1| < 1$ is satisfied.

Because it is so general, the ADL(p, q) model is a good place to start when attempting to specify a dynamic regression model. In many cases, setting $p = q = 1$ is sufficiently general, but with quarterly data it may be wise to start with $p = q = 4$. Of course, we very often want to impose restrictions on such a model. Depending on how we write the model, different restrictions may naturally suggest themselves. These can be tested in the usual way by means of asymptotic F and t tests, which may be bootstrapped to improve their finite-sample properties.

Error-Correction Models

It is a straightforward exercise to check that the ADL(1, 1) model of equation (13.59) can be rewritten as

$$\Delta y_t = \beta_0 + (\beta_1 - 1)(y_{t-1} - \lambda x_{t-1}) + \gamma_0 \Delta x_t + u_t, \tag{13.62}$$

where λ was defined in (13.61). Equation (13.62) is called an **error-correction model**. It expresses the ADL(1, 1) model in terms of an **error-correction mechanism**; both the model and mechanism are often abbreviated to **ECM**.[3] Although the model (13.62) appears to be nonlinear, it is really just a reparametrization of the linear model (13.59). If the latter is estimated by OLS, an appropriate GNR can be used to obtain the covariance matrix of the estimates of the parameters of (13.62). Alternatively, any good NLS package should do this for us if we start it at the OLS estimates.

The difference between y_{t-1} and λx_{t-1} in the ECM (13.62) measures the extent to which the long-run equilibrium relationship between x_t and y_t is not satisfied. Consequently, the parameter $\beta_1 - 1$ can be interpreted as the proportion of the resulting disequilibrium that is reflected in the movement of y_t in one period. In this respect, $\beta_1 - 1$ is essentially the same as the parameter $\delta - 1$ of the partial adjustment model. The term $(\beta_1 - 1)(y_{t-1} - \lambda x_{t-1})$ that appears in (13.62) is the **error-correction term**. Of course, many ADL models in addition to the ADL(1, 1) model can be rewritten as error-correction models. An important feature of error-correction models is that they can also be used with nonstationary data, as we will discuss in Chapter 14.

13.5 Seasonality

As we observed in Section 2.5, many economic time series display a regular pattern of seasonal variation over the course of every year. **Seasonality**, as such a pattern is called, may be caused by seasonal variation in the weather or by the timing of statutory holidays, school vacation periods, and so on. Many time series that are observed quarterly, monthly, weekly, or daily display some form of seasonality, and this can have important implications for applied econometric work. Failing to account properly for seasonality can easily cause us to make incorrect inferences, especially in dynamic models.

There are two different ways to deal with seasonality in economic data. One approach is to try to model it explicitly. We might, for example, attempt to explain the seasonal variation in a dependent variable by the seasonal variation in some of the independent variables, perhaps including weather variables or, more commonly, seasonal dummy variables, which were discussed

[3] Error-correction models were first used by Hendry and Anderson (1977) and Davidson, Hendry, Srba, and Yeo (1978). See Banerjee, Dolado, Galbraith, and Hendry (1993) for a detailed treatment.

in Section 2.5. Alternatively, we can model the error terms as following a seasonal ARMA process, or we can explicitly estimate a seasonal ADL model.

The second way to deal with seasonality is usually less satisfactory. It depends on the use of **seasonally adjusted** data, that is, data which have been filtered in such a way that they represent what the series would supposedly have been in the absence of seasonal variation. Indeed, many statistical agencies release only seasonally adjusted data for many time series, and economists often treat these data as if they were genuine. However, as we will see later in this section, using seasonally adjusted data can have unfortunate consequences.

Seasonal ARMA Processes

One way to deal with seasonality is to model the error terms of a regression model as following a **seasonal ARMA process**, that is, an ARMA process with nonzero coefficients only, or principally, at seasonal lags. In practice, purely autoregressive processes, with no moving-average component, are generally used. The simplest and most commonly encountered example is the **simple AR(4) process**

$$u_t = \rho_4 u_{t-4} + \varepsilon_t, \tag{13.63}$$

where ρ_4 is a parameter to be estimated, and, as usual, ε_t is white noise. Of course, this process makes sense only for quarterly data. Another purely seasonal AR process for quarterly data is the restricted AR(8) process

$$u_t = \rho_4 u_{t-4} + \rho_8 u_{t-8} + \varepsilon_t, \tag{13.64}$$

which is analogous to an AR(2) process for nonseasonal data.

In many cases, error terms may exhibit both seasonal and nonseasonal serial correlation. This suggests combining a purely seasonal with a nonseasonal process. Suppose, for example, that we wish to combine an AR(1) process and a simple AR(4) process. The most natural approach is probably to combine them multiplicatively. Using lag-operator notation, we obtain

$$(1 - \rho_1 \mathrm{L})(1 - \rho_4 \mathrm{L}^4)u_t = \varepsilon_t.$$

This can be rewritten as

$$u_t = \rho_1 u_{t-1} + \rho_4 u_{t-4} - \rho_1 \rho_4 u_{t-5} + \varepsilon_t. \tag{13.65}$$

Notice that the coefficient of u_{t-5} in equation (13.65) is equal to the negative of the product of the coefficients of u_{t-1} and u_{t-4}. This restriction can easily be tested. If it does not hold, then we should presumably consider more general ARMA processes with some coefficients at seasonal lags.

If adequate account of seasonality is not taken, there is often evidence of fourth-order serial correlation in a regression model. Thus testing for it often provides a useful diagnostic test. Moreover, seasonal autoregressive processes provide a parsimonious way to model seasonal variation that is not explained by the regressors. The simple AR(4) process (13.63) uses only one extra parameter, and the restricted AR(8) process (13.64) uses only two. However, just as evidence of first-order serial correlation does not mean that the error terms really follow an AR(1) process, evidence of fourth-order serial correlation does not mean that they really follow an AR(4) process.

By themselves, seasonal ARMA processes cannot capture one important feature of seasonality, namely, the fact that different seasons of the year have different characteristics: Summer is not just winter with a different label. However, an ARMA process makes no distinction among the dynamical processes associated with the different seasons. One simple way to alleviate this problem would be to use seasonal dummy variables as well as a seasonal ARMA process. Another potential difficulty is that the seasonal variation of many time series is not stationary, in which case a stationary ARMA process cannot adequately account for it. Trending seasonal variables may help to cope with nonstationary seasonality, as we will discuss shortly in the context of a specific example.

Seasonal ADL Models

Suppose we start with a static regression model in which y_t equals $\boldsymbol{X}_t\boldsymbol{\beta} + u_t$ and then add three quarterly dummy variables, s_{t1} through s_{t3}, assuming that there is a constant among the other explanatory variables. The dummies may be ordinary quarterly dummies, or else the modified dummies, defined in equations (2.49), that sum to zero over each year. We then allow the error term u_t to follow the simple AR(4) process (13.63). Solving for u_{t-4} yields the nonlinear regression model

$$y_t = \rho_4 y_{t-4} + \boldsymbol{X}_t\boldsymbol{\beta} - \rho_4\boldsymbol{X}_{t-4}\boldsymbol{\beta} + \sum_{j=1}^{3}\delta_j s_{tj} + \varepsilon_t. \tag{13.66}$$

There are no lagged seasonal dummies in this model because they would be collinear with the existing regressors.

Equation (13.66) is a special case of the **seasonal ADL model**

$$y_t = \gamma_4 y_{t-4} + \boldsymbol{X}_t\boldsymbol{\beta}_1 + \boldsymbol{X}_{t-4}\boldsymbol{\beta}_4 + \sum_{j=1}^{3}\delta_j s_{tj} + \varepsilon_t, \tag{13.67}$$

which is just a linear regression model in which y_t depends on y_{t-4}, the three seasonal dummies, $\boldsymbol{X}_t$, and $\boldsymbol{X}_{t-4}$. Before accepting the model (13.66), one would always want to test the common factor restrictions that it imposes on (13.67); this can readily be done by using asymptotic F tests, as discussed in Section 7.9. One would almost certainly also want to estimate ADL models both more and less general than (13.67), especially if the common factor restrictions are rejected. For example, it would not be surprising if y_{t-1} and at least some components of $\boldsymbol{X}_{t-1}$ also belonged in the model, but it would also not be surprising if some components of $\boldsymbol{X}_{t-4}$ did not belong.

Seasonally Adjusted Data

Instead of attempting to model seasonality, many economists prefer to avoid dealing with it entirely by using seasonally adjusted data. Although the idea of seasonally adjusting a time series is intuitively appealing, it is very hard to do so in practice without resorting to highly unrealistic assumptions. Seasonal adjustment of a series y_t makes sense if, for all t, we can write $y_t = y_t^\circ + y_t^s$, where y_t° is a time series that contains no seasonal variation at all, and y_t^s is a time series that contains nothing but seasonal variation. However, this is surely an extreme assumption, which would be false in almost any economic model of seasonal variation that could reasonably be imagined.

To make the discussion more concrete, consider Figure 13.2, which shows the logarithm of urban housing starts in Canada, quarterly, for the period 1966 to 2001. The solid line represents the actual data, and the dotted line represents a seasonally adjusted series.[4] It is clear from the figure that housing starts in Canada are highly seasonal, with the first (winter) quarter usually having a much smaller number of starts than the other three quarters. There is also some indication that the magnitude of the seasonal variation may have become smaller in the latter part of the sample, perhaps because of changes in construction technology.

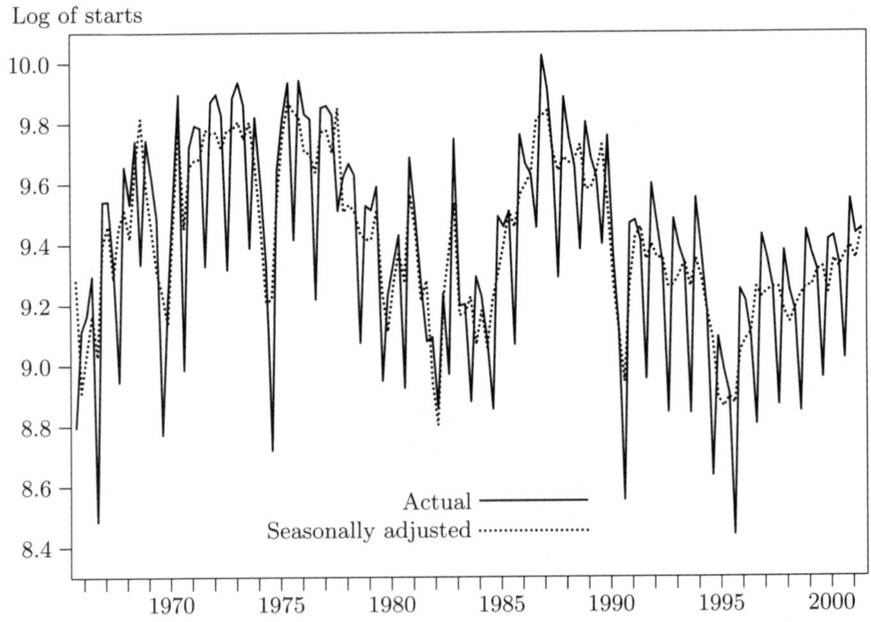

Figure 13.2 Urban housing starts in Canada, 1966–2001

[4] These data come from Statistics Canada. The actual data, which start in 1948, are from CANSIM series J6001, and the adjusted data, which start in 1966, are from CANSIM series J9001.

Seasonal Adjustment by Regression

In Section 2.5, we discussed the use of seasonal dummy variables to construct seasonally adjusted data by regression. Although this approach is easy to implement and easy to analyze, it has a number of disadvantages, some of which we briefly discuss here. Because of these disadvantages, it is almost never used by official statistical agencies.

One problem with the simplest form of seasonal adjustment by regression is that it does not allow the pattern of seasonality to change over time. However, as Figure 13.2 illustrates, seasonal patterns often seem to do precisely that. A natural way to model this is to add additional seasonal dummy variables that have been interacted with powers of a time trend that increases annually. In the case of quarterly data, such a trend would be

$$\boldsymbol{t}_q^\top \equiv [1\ 1\ 1\ 1\ 2\ 2\ 2\ 2\ 3\ 3\ 3\ 3 \cdots]. \tag{13.68}$$

The reason $\boldsymbol{t}_q$ takes this rather odd form is that, when it is multiplied by the seasonal dummies, the resulting trending dummies always sum to zero over each year. If one simply multiplied seasonal dummies by an ordinary time trend, that would not be the case.

Let $\boldsymbol{S}$ denote a matrix of seasonal dummies and seasonal dummies that have been interacted with powers of $\boldsymbol{t}_q$ or, in the case of data at other than quarterly frequencies, whatever annually increasing trend term is appropriate. In the case of quarterly data, $\boldsymbol{S}$ would normally have 3, 6, 9, or maybe 12 columns. In the case of monthly data, it would normally have 11, 22, or 33 columns. In all cases, every one of the variables in $\boldsymbol{S}$ should sum to zero over each year. Then, if $\boldsymbol{y}$ denotes the vector of observations on a series to be seasonally adjusted, we could run the regression

$$\boldsymbol{y} = \beta_0 + \boldsymbol{S\delta} + \boldsymbol{u} \tag{13.69}$$

and estimate the seasonally adjusted series as $\boldsymbol{y}' = \boldsymbol{y} - \boldsymbol{S}\hat{\boldsymbol{\delta}}$. Unfortunately, although equations like (13.69) often provide a reasonable approximation to observed seasonal patterns, they frequently fail to do so, as readers will find when they answer Exercise 13.17.

Another problem with using seasonal dummies is that, as additional observations become available, the estimates from the dummy variable regression do not stay the same. It is inevitable that, as the sample size increases, the estimates of $\boldsymbol{\delta}$ in equation (13.69) change, and so every element of $\boldsymbol{y}'$ must change every time a new observation becomes available. This is clearly a most undesirable feature from the point of view of users of official statistics. Moreover, as the sample size gets larger, the number of trend terms may need to increase if a polynomial is to continue to provide an adequate approximation to changes in the pattern of seasonal variation.

Seasonal Adjustment and Linear Filters

The seasonal adjustment procedures that are actually used by statistical agencies tend to be very complicated. They attempt to deal with a host of practical problems, including changes in seasonal patterns over time, variations in the number of shopping days and the dates of holidays from year to year, and the fact that pre-sample and post-sample observations are not available. We will not attempt to discuss these methods at all.

Although official methods of seasonal adjustment are very complicated, they can often be approximated remarkably well by much simpler procedures based on what are called **linear filters**. Let $\boldsymbol{y}$ be an n–vector of observations (often in logarithms rather than levels) on a series that has not been seasonally adjusted. Then a linear filter consists of an $n \times n$ matrix $\boldsymbol{\Phi}$, with rows that sum to 1, such that the seasonally adjusted series $\boldsymbol{y}'$ is equal to $\boldsymbol{\Phi y}$. Each row of the matrix $\boldsymbol{\Phi}$ consists of a vector of **filter weights**. Thus each element y'_t of the seasonally adjusted series is equal to a weighted average of current, leading, and lagged values of y_t.

Let us consider a simple example for quarterly data. Suppose we first create three-term and eleven-term moving averages

$$\bar{y}_t \equiv \frac{1}{3}(y_{t-4} + y_t + y_{t+4}) \quad \text{and} \quad \tilde{y}_t \equiv \frac{1}{11}\sum_{j=-5}^{5} y_{t+j}.$$

The difference between $\bar{y}_t$ and $\tilde{y}_t$ is a rolling estimate of the amount by which the value of y_t for the current quarter tends to differ from its average value over the year. Thus one way to define a seasonally adjusted series would be

$$\begin{aligned} y_t^* &\equiv y_t - \bar{y}_t + \tilde{y}_t \\ &= .0909\,y_{t-5} - .2424\,y_{t-4} + .0909\,y_{t-3} + .0909\,y_{t-2} \\ &\quad + .0909\,y_{t-1} + .7576\,y_t + .0909\,y_{t+1} + .0909\,y_{t+2} \\ &\quad + .0909\,y_{t+3} - .2424\,y_{t+4} + .0909\,y_{t+5}. \end{aligned} \tag{13.70}$$

This example corresponds to a linear filter in which, for $5 < p < n-5$, the pth row of $\boldsymbol{\Phi}$ would consist first of $p-6$ zeros, followed by the eleven coefficients that appear in (13.70), followed by $n-p-5$ more zeros.

Although this example is very simple, the basic approach that it illustrates may be found, in various modified forms, in almost all official seasonal adjustment procedures. The latter generally do not actually employ linear filters, but they do employ a number of moving averages in a way similar to the example. These moving averages tend to be longer than the ones in the example, and they often give progressively less weight to observations farther from t. An important feature of almost all seasonally adjusted data is that, as in the example, the weight given to y_t is generally well below 1. For more on the relationship between official procedures and ones based on linear filters, see Burridge and Wallis (1984) and Ghysels and Perron (1993).

We have claimed that official seasonal adjustment procedures in most cases have much the same properties as linear filters applied to either the levels or the logarithms of the raw data. This assertion can be checked empirically by regressing a seasonally adjusted series on a number of leads and lags of the corresponding seasonally unadjusted series. If the assertion is accurate, such a regression should fit well, and the coefficients should have a distinctive pattern. The coefficient of the current value of the raw series should be fairly large but less than 1, the coefficients of seasonal lags and leads should be negative, and the coefficients of other lags and leads should be small and positive. In other words, the coefficients should resemble those in equation (13.70). In Exercise 13.17, readers are asked to see whether a linear filter provides a good approximation to the method actually used for seasonally adjusting the housing starts data.

Consequences of Using Seasonally Adjusted Data

The consequences of using seasonally adjusted data depend on how the data were actually generated and the nature of the procedures used for seasonal adjustment. For simplicity, we will suppose that

$$\boldsymbol{y} = \boldsymbol{y}_\circ + \boldsymbol{y}_s \quad \text{and} \quad \boldsymbol{X} = \boldsymbol{X}_\circ + \boldsymbol{X}_s,$$

where $\boldsymbol{y}_s$ and $\boldsymbol{X}_s$ contain all the seasonal variation in $\boldsymbol{y}$ and $\boldsymbol{X}$, respectively, and $\boldsymbol{y}_\circ$ and $\boldsymbol{X}_\circ$ contain all other economically interesting variation. Suppose further that the DGP is

$$\boldsymbol{y}_\circ = \boldsymbol{X}_\circ \boldsymbol{\beta}_0 + \boldsymbol{u}, \quad \boldsymbol{u} \sim \text{IID}(\boldsymbol{0}, \sigma^2 \mathbf{I}). \tag{13.71}$$

Thus the economic relationship in which we are interested involves only the nonseasonal components of the data.

If the same linear filter is applied to every series, the seasonally adjusted data are $\boldsymbol{\Phi y}$ and $\boldsymbol{\Phi X}$, and the OLS estimator using those data is

$$\hat{\boldsymbol{\beta}}_{\text{S}} = (\boldsymbol{X}^\top \boldsymbol{\Phi}^\top \boldsymbol{\Phi X})^{-1} \boldsymbol{X}^\top \boldsymbol{\Phi}^\top \boldsymbol{\Phi y}. \tag{13.72}$$

This looks very much like a GLS estimator, with the matrix $\boldsymbol{\Phi}^\top \boldsymbol{\Phi}$ playing the role of the inverse covariance matrix.

The properties of the estimator $\hat{\boldsymbol{\beta}}_{\text{S}}$ defined in equation (13.72) depend on how the filter weights are chosen. Ideally, the filter would completely eliminate seasonality, so that

$$\boldsymbol{\Phi y} = \boldsymbol{\Phi y}_\circ \quad \text{and} \quad \boldsymbol{\Phi X} = \boldsymbol{\Phi X}_\circ.$$

In this ideal case, we see that

$$\begin{aligned}\hat{\boldsymbol\beta}_{\rm S} &= (\boldsymbol X_\circ^\top \boldsymbol\Phi^\top \boldsymbol\Phi \boldsymbol X_\circ)^{-1} \boldsymbol X_\circ^\top \boldsymbol\Phi^\top \boldsymbol\Phi \boldsymbol y_\circ \\ &= \boldsymbol\beta_0 + (\boldsymbol X_\circ^\top \boldsymbol\Phi^\top \boldsymbol\Phi \boldsymbol X_\circ)^{-1} \boldsymbol X_\circ^\top \boldsymbol\Phi^\top \boldsymbol\Phi \boldsymbol u.\end{aligned} \tag{13.73}$$

If every column of $\boldsymbol X$ is exogenous, and not merely predetermined, it is clear that the second term in the last line here has expectation zero, which implies that $\mathrm{E}(\hat{\boldsymbol\beta}_{\rm S}) = \boldsymbol\beta_0$. Thus we see that, under the exogeneity assumption, the OLS estimator that uses seasonally adjusted data is unbiased. But this is a very strong assumption for time-series data.

Moreover, this estimator is not efficient. If the elements of $\boldsymbol u$ are actually homoskedastic and serially independent, as we assumed in (13.71), then the Gauss-Markov Theorem implies that the efficient estimator would be obtained by an OLS regression of $\boldsymbol y_\circ$ on $\boldsymbol X_\circ$. Instead, $\hat{\boldsymbol\beta}_{\rm S}$ is equivalent to the estimator from a certain GLS regression of $\boldsymbol y_\circ$ on $\boldsymbol X_\circ$. Of course, the efficient estimator is not feasible here, because we do not observe $\boldsymbol y_\circ$ and $\boldsymbol X_\circ$.

In many cases, we can prove consistency under much weaker assumptions than are needed to prove unbiasedness; see Sections 3.2 and 3.3. In particular, for OLS to be consistent, we usually just need the regressors to be predetermined. However, in the case of data that have been seasonally adjusted by means of a linear filter, this assumption is not sufficient. In fact, the exogeneity assumption that is needed in order to prove that $\hat{\boldsymbol\beta}_{\rm S}$ is unbiased is also needed in order to prove that it is consistent. From (13.73) it follows that

$$\operatorname*{plim}_{n\to\infty} \hat{\boldsymbol\beta}_{\rm S} = \boldsymbol\beta_0 + \operatorname*{plim}_{n\to\infty}\Big(\frac{1}{n}\boldsymbol X_\circ^\top \boldsymbol\Phi^\top \boldsymbol\Phi \boldsymbol X_\circ\Big)^{-1} \operatorname*{plim}_{n\to\infty}\Big(\frac{1}{n}\boldsymbol X_\circ^\top \boldsymbol\Phi^\top \boldsymbol\Phi \boldsymbol u\Big),$$

provided we impose sufficient conditions for the probability limits to exist and be nonstochastic. The predeterminedness assumption (3.10) evidently does not allow us to claim that the second probability limit here is a zero vector. On the contrary, any correlation between error terms and regressors at leads and lags that are given nonzero weights by the filter generally causes it to be a nonzero vector. Therefore, the estimator $\hat{\boldsymbol\beta}_{\rm S}$ is inconsistent if the regressors are merely predetermined.

Although the exogeneity assumption is always dubious in the case of time-series data, it is certainly false when the regressors include one or more lags of the dependent variable. There has been some work on the consequences of using seasonally adjusted data in this case; see Jaeger and Kunst (1990), Ghysels (1990), and Ghysels and Perron (1993), among others. It appears that, in models with a single lag of the dependent variable, estimates of the coefficient of the lagged dependent variable can be severely biased when seasonally adjusted data are used. This bias does not vanish as the sample size increases, and its magnitude can be substantial; see Davidson and MacKinnon (1993, Chapter 19) for an illustration.

Seasonally adjusted data are very commonly used in applied econometric work. Indeed, it is difficult to avoid doing so in many cases, either because the actual data are not available or because it is the seasonally adjusted series that are really of interest. However, the results we have just discussed suggest that, especially for dynamic models, the undesirable consequences of using seasonally adjusted data may be quite severe.

13.6 Autoregressive Conditional Heteroskedasticity

With time-series data, it is not uncommon for least-squares residuals to be quite small in absolute value for a number of successive periods of time, then much larger for a while, then smaller again, and so on. This phenomenon of **time-varying volatility** is often encountered in models for stock returns, foreign exchange rates, and other series that are determined in financial markets. Numerous models for dealing with this phenomenon have been proposed. One very popular approach is based on the concept of **autoregressive conditional heteroskedasticity**, or **ARCH**, that was introduced by Engle (1982). The basic idea of ARCH models is that the variance of the error term at time t depends on the realized values of the squared error terms in previous time periods.

If u_t denotes the error term adhering to a regression model, which may be linear or nonlinear, and Ω_{t-1} denotes an information set that consists of data observed through period $t-1$, then what is called an **ARCH(q) process** can be written as

$$u_t = \sigma_t \varepsilon_t; \quad \sigma_t^2 \equiv \mathrm{E}(u_t^2 \,|\, \Omega_{t-1}) = \alpha_0 + \sum_{i=1}^{q} \alpha_i u_{t-i}^2, \tag{13.74}$$

where $\alpha_i > 0$ for $i = 0, 1, \ldots, q$, and ε_t is white noise with variance 1. Here and throughout this section, σ_t is understood to be the positive square root of σ_t^2. The skedastic function for the ARCH(q) process is the rightmost expression in (13.74). Since this function depends on t, the model is, as its name claims, heteroskedastic. The term "conditional" is due to the fact that, unlike the skedastic functions we have so far encountered, the ARCH skedastic function is not exogenous, but merely predetermined. Thus the model prescribes the variance of u_t *conditional* on the past of the process.

Because the conditional variance of u_t is a function of u_{t-1}, it is clear that u_t and u_{t-1} are not independent. They are, however, uncorrelated:

$$\mathrm{E}(u_t u_{t-1}) = \mathrm{E}\big(\mathrm{E}(u_t u_{t-1} \,|\, \Omega_{t-1})\big) = \mathrm{E}\big(u_{t-1}\sigma_t \mathrm{E}(\varepsilon_t \,|\, \Omega_{t-1})\big) = 0,$$

where we have used the facts that $\sigma_t \in \Omega_{t-1}$ and that ε_t is an innovation. Almost identical reasoning shows that $\mathrm{E}(u_t u_s) = 0$ for all $s < t$. Thus the ARCH process involves only heteroskedasticity, not serial correlation.

If an ARCH(q) process is covariance stationary, then σ^2, the unconditional expectation of u_t^2, exists and is independent of t. Under the stationarity assumption, we may take the unconditional expectation of the second equation of (13.74), from which we find that

$$\sigma^2 = \alpha_0 + \sigma^2 \sum_{i=1}^{q} \alpha_i.$$

Therefore,

$$\sigma^2 = \frac{\alpha_0}{1 - \sum_{i=1}^{q} \alpha_i}. \tag{13.75}$$

The condition $\sum_{i=1}^{q} \alpha_i < 1$ is required for σ^2 to be positive, and so it is also a necessary condition for stationarity. It is of course necessary that the conditional variances σ_t^2 should be positive, and that is why we require that $\alpha_i > 0$ for all i. If that requirement were not satisfied, realizations of some of the σ_t^2 could be negative.

Unfortunately, the ARCH(q) process has not proven to be very satisfactory in applied work. Many financial time series display time-varying volatility that is highly persistent, but the correlation between successive values of u_t^2 is not very high; see Pagan (1996). In order to accommodate these two empirical regularities, q must be large. But if q is large, the ARCH(q) process has a lot of parameters to estimate, and the requirement that all the α_i should be positive may not be satisfied if it is not explicitly imposed.

GARCH Models

The **generalized ARCH model**, which was proposed by Bollerslev (1986), is much more widely used than the original ARCH model. We may write a **GARCH(p, q) process** as

$$u_t = \sigma_t \varepsilon_t; \quad \sigma_t^2 \equiv \mathrm{E}(u_t^2 \,|\, \Omega_{t-1}) = \alpha_0 + \sum_{i=1}^{q} \alpha_i u_{t-i}^2 + \sum_{j=1}^{p} \delta_j \sigma_{t-j}^2. \tag{13.76}$$

The conditional variance here can be written more compactly as

$$\sigma_t^2 = \alpha_0 + \alpha(\mathrm{L}) u_t^2 + \delta(\mathrm{L}) \sigma_t^2, \tag{13.77}$$

where $\alpha(\mathrm{L})$ and $\delta(\mathrm{L})$ are polynomials in the lag operator L, neither of which includes a constant term. All of the parameters in the infinite-order autoregressive representation

$$\big(1 - \delta(\mathrm{L})\big)^{-1} \alpha(\mathrm{L})$$

must be nonnegative. Otherwise, as in the case of an ARCH(q) model with one or more of the $\alpha_i < 0$, we could have negative conditional variances.

There is a strong resemblance between the GARCH(p, q) process (13.77) and the ARMA(p, q) process (13.21). In fact, if we let $\delta(\mathrm{L}) = \rho(\mathrm{L})$, $\alpha_0 = \gamma$,

$\sigma_t^2 = y_t$, and $u_t^2 = \varepsilon_t$, we see that the former becomes formally the same as an ARMA(p, q) process in which the coefficient of ε_t equals 0. However, the formal similarity between the two processes masks some important differences. In a GARCH process, the σ_t^2 are not observable, and $\mathrm{E}(u_t^2) = \sigma_t^2 \neq 0$.

The simplest and by far the most popular GARCH model is the **GARCH(1,1) process**, for which the conditional variance can be written as

$$\sigma_t^2 = \alpha_0 + \alpha_1 u_{t-1}^2 + \delta_1 \sigma_{t-1}^2. \tag{13.78}$$

Under the hypothesis of covariance stationarity, the unconditional variance σ^2 can be found by taking the unconditional expectation of equation (13.78). We find that

$$\sigma^2 = \alpha_0 + \alpha_1 \sigma^2 + \delta_1 \sigma^2.$$

Solving this equation yields the result that

$$\sigma^2 = \frac{\alpha_0}{1 - \alpha_1 - \delta_1}. \tag{13.79}$$

For this unconditional variance to exist, it must be the case that $\alpha_1 + \delta_1 < 1$, and for it to be positive, we require that $\alpha_0 > 0$.

The GARCH$(1, 1)$ process generally seems to work quite well in practice. In many cases, it cannot be rejected against any more general GARCH(p, q) process. An interesting empirical regularity is that the estimate $\hat{\alpha}_1$ is often small and positive, with the estimate $\hat{\delta}_1$ much larger, and the sum of the coefficients, $\hat{\alpha}_1 + \hat{\delta}_1$, between 0.9 and 1. These parameter values imply that the time-varying volatility is highly persistent.

Testing for ARCH Errors

It is easy to test a regression model for the presence of ARCH or GARCH errors. Imagine, for the moment, that we actually observe the u_t. Then we can replace σ_t^2 by $u_t^2 - e_t$, where e_t is defined to be the difference between u_t^2 and its conditional expectation. This allows us to rewrite the GARCH(p, q) model (13.76) as

$$u_t^2 = \alpha_0 + \sum_{i=1}^{\max(p,q)} (\alpha_i + \delta_i) u_{t-i}^2 + e_t - \sum_{j=1}^{p} \delta_j e_{t-j}. \tag{13.80}$$

In this equation, we have replaced all of the σ_{t-j}^2 by $u_{t-j}^2 - e_{t-j}$ and then grouped the two summations that involve the u_{t-i}^2. Of course, if $p \neq q$, either some of the α_i or some of the δ_i in the first summation are identically zero. Equation (13.80) can now be interpreted as a regression model with dependent variable u_t^2 and MA(p) errors. If one were actually to estimate (13.80), the MA structure would yield estimates of the δ_j, and the estimated coefficients of the u_{t-i}^2 would then allow the α_i to be estimated.

Rather than estimating (13.80), it is easier to base a test on the Gauss-Newton regression that corresponds to (13.80), evaluated under the null hypothesis that $\alpha_i = 0$ for $i = 1, \ldots, q$ and $\delta_j = 0$ for $j = 1, \ldots, p$. Since equation (13.80) is linear with respect to the α_i and the δ_j, the GNR is easy to derive. It is

$$u_t^2 - \alpha_0 = b_0 + \sum_{i=1}^{\max(p,q)} b_i u_{t-i}^2 + \text{residual}. \tag{13.81}$$

The artificial parameter b_0 here corresponds to the real parameter α_0, and the b_i, for $i = 1, \ldots, \max(p, q)$, correspond to the sums $\alpha_i + \delta_i$, because, under the null, the α_i and δ_i are not separately identifiable. In the regressand, α_0 would normally be the error variance estimated under the null. However, its value is irrelevant if we are using equation (13.81) for testing, because there is a constant term on the right-hand side.

Under the alternative, the GNR should, strictly speaking, incorporate the MA structure of the error terms of (13.80). But, since these error terms are white noise under the null, a valid test can be constructed without taking account of the MA structure. The price to be paid for this simplification is that the α_i and the δ_i remain unidentified as separate parameters, which means that the test is the same for all GARCH(p, q) alternatives with the same value of $\max(p, q)$.

In practice, of course, we do not observe the u_t. But, as for the GNR-based tests against other types of heteroskedasticity that we discussed in Section 7.5, it is asymptotically valid to replace the unobserved u_t by the least-squares residuals $\hat{u}_t$. Thus the test regression is actually

$$\hat{u}_t^2 = b_0 + \sum_{i=1}^{\max(p,q)} b_i\, \hat{u}_{t-i}^2 + \text{residual}, \tag{13.82}$$

where we have arbitrarily set $\alpha_0 = 0$. Because of the lags, this GNR would normally be run over the last $n - \max(p, q)$ observations only. As usual, there are several possible test statistics. The easiest to compute is probably n times the *centered* R^2, which is asymptotically distributed as $\chi^2\big(\max(p, q)\big)$ under the null. It is also asymptotically valid to use the standard F statistic for all of the slope coefficients to be 0, treating it as if it followed the F distribution with $\max(p, q)$ and $n - 2\max(p, q) - 1$ degrees of freedom. These tests can easily be bootstrapped, and it is often wise to do so. We can use either a parametric or a semiparametric bootstrap DGP.

Because it is very easy to compute a test statistic using regression (13.82), these tests are the most commonly used procedures to detect autoregressive conditional heteroskedasticity. However, other procedures may well perform better. In particular, Lee and King (1993) and Demos and Sentana (1998) have proposed various tests which take into account the fact that the alternative hypothesis is one-sided. These one-sided tests have better power than tests based on the Gauss-Newton regression (13.82).

The Stationary Distribution for ARCH and GARCH Processes

In the case of an ARMA process, the stationary, or unconditional, distribution of the u_t is normal whenever the innovations ε_t are normal white noise. However, this is not true for ARCH and GARCH processes, because the mapping from the ε_t to the u_t is nonlinear. As we will see, the stationary distribution is not normal, and it may not even have a fourth moment. For simplicity, we will confine our attention to the fourth moment of the ARCH(1) process. Other moments of this process, and moments of the GARCH(1, 1) process, are treated in the exercises.

For an ARCH(1) process with normal white noise innovations, or indeed any such ARCH or GARCH process, the distribution of u_t is normal *conditional* on Ω_{t-1}. Since the variance of this distribution is σ_t^2, the fourth moment is $3\sigma_t^4$, as we saw in Exercise 4.2. For an ARCH(1) process, $\sigma_t^2 = \alpha_0 + \alpha_1 u_{t-1}^2$. Therefore,

$$\mathrm{E}(u_t^4 \,|\, \Omega_{t-1}) = 3(\alpha_0 + \alpha_1 u_{t-1}^2)^2 = 3\alpha_0^2 + 6\alpha_0\alpha_1 u_{t-1}^2 + 3\alpha_1^2 u_{t-1}^4.$$

If we assume that the unconditional fourth moment exists and denote it by m_4, we can take the unconditional expectation of this relation to obtain

$$m_4 = 3\alpha_0^2 + \frac{6\alpha_0^2\alpha_1}{1-\alpha_1} + 3\alpha_1^2 m_4,$$

where we have used the implication of equation (13.75) that the unconditional second moment is $\alpha_0/(1-\alpha_1)$. Solving this equation for m_4, we find that

$$m_4 = \frac{3\alpha_0^2(1+\alpha_1)}{(1-\alpha_1)(1-3\alpha_1^2)}. \tag{13.83}$$

This result evidently cannot hold unless $3\alpha_1^2 < 1$. In fact, if this condition fails, the fourth moment does not exist. From the result (13.83), we can see that $m_4 > 3\sigma^4 = 3\alpha_0^2/(1-\alpha_1)^2$ whenever $\alpha_1 > 0$. Thus, whatever the stationary distribution of u_t might be, it certainly cannot be normal. At the time of writing there is, as far as the authors are aware, no explicit, analytical characterization of the stationary distribution for general ARCH and GARCH processes.

Estimating ARCH and GARCH Models

Since ARCH and GARCH processes induce heteroskedasticity, it might seem natural to estimate a regression model with ARCH or GARCH errors by using feasible GLS. The first step would be to estimate the underlying regression model by OLS or NLS in order to obtain consistent but inefficient estimates of the regression parameters, along with least-squares residuals $\hat{u}_t$. The second step would be to estimate the parameters of the ARCH or GARCH process by treating the $\hat{u}_t^2$ as if they were actual squared error terms and estimating a model with a specification something like (13.80), again by least squares. The final step would be to estimate the original regression model by feasible weighted least squares, using weights proportional to the inverse square roots of the fitted values from the model for the $\hat{u}_t^2$.

This approach is very rarely used, because it is not asymptotically efficient. The skedastic function, which would, for example, be the right-hand side of equation (13.78) in the case of a GARCH(1, 1) model, depends on the lagged squared residuals, which in turn depend on the estimates of the regression function. Because of this, estimating both functions together yields more efficient estimates than estimating each of them conditional on estimates of the other; see Engle (1982).

The most popular way to estimate models with GARCH errors is to assume that the error terms are normally distributed and use maximum likelihood. We can write a linear regression model with GARCH errors defined in terms of a normal innovation process as

$$\frac{y_t - \boldsymbol{X}_t\boldsymbol{\beta}}{\sigma_t(\boldsymbol{\beta}, \boldsymbol{\theta})} = \varepsilon_t, \quad \varepsilon_t \sim \mathrm{N}(0, 1), \tag{13.84}$$

where y_t is the dependent variable, $\boldsymbol{X}_t$ is a vector of exogenous or predetermined regressors, and $\boldsymbol{\beta}$ is a vector of regression parameters. The skedastic function $\sigma_t^2(\boldsymbol{\beta}, \boldsymbol{\theta})$ is defined for some particular choice of p and q by equation (13.76) with u_t replaced by $y_t - \boldsymbol{X}_t\boldsymbol{\beta}$. It therefore depends on $\boldsymbol{\beta}$ as well as on the α_i and δ_j that appear in (13.76), which we denote collectively by $\boldsymbol{\theta}$. The density of y_t conditional on Ω_{t-1} is then

$$\frac{1}{\sigma_t(\boldsymbol{\beta}, \boldsymbol{\theta})}\,\phi\left(\frac{y_t - \boldsymbol{X}_t\boldsymbol{\beta}}{\sigma_t(\boldsymbol{\beta}, \boldsymbol{\theta})}\right), \tag{13.85}$$

where $\phi(\cdot)$ denotes the standard normal density. The first factor in (13.85) is a Jacobian factor which reflects the fact that the derivative of ε_t with respect to y_t is $\sigma_t^{-1}(\boldsymbol{\beta}, \boldsymbol{\theta})$; see Section 10.8.

By taking the logarithm of expression (13.85), we find that the contribution to the loglikelihood function made by the tth observation is

$$\ell_t(\boldsymbol{\beta}, \boldsymbol{\theta}) = -\tfrac{1}{2}\log 2\pi - \tfrac{1}{2}\log\bigl(\sigma_t^2(\boldsymbol{\beta}, \boldsymbol{\theta})\bigr) - \frac{1}{2}\frac{(y_t - \boldsymbol{X}_t\boldsymbol{\beta})^2}{\sigma_t^2(\boldsymbol{\beta}, \boldsymbol{\theta})}. \tag{13.86}$$

Unfortunately, it is not entirely straightforward to evaluate this expression. The problem is the skedastic function $\sigma_t^2(\boldsymbol{\beta}, \boldsymbol{\theta})$, which is defined implicitly by the recursion (13.77). This recursion does not constitute a complete definition because it does not provide starting values to initialize the recursion. In trying to find suitable starting values, we run into the difficulty, mentioned in the previous subsection, that there exists no closed-form expression for the stationary GARCH density.

If we are dealing with an ARCH(q) model, we can sidestep this problem by conditioning on the first q observations. Since, in this case, the skedastic function $\sigma_t^2(\boldsymbol{\beta}, \boldsymbol{\theta})$ is determined completely by q lags of the squared residuals, there is no missing information for observations $q+1$ through n. We can therefore sum the contributions (13.86) for just those observations, and then maximize the result. This leads to ML estimates *conditional* on the first q observations. But such a procedure works only for models with pure ARCH errors, and these models are very rarely used in practice.

With a GARCH(p, q) model, p starting values of σ_t^2 are needed in addition to $\max(0, q-p)$ starting values of the squared residuals in order to initialize the recursion (13.77). It is therefore necessary to resort to some sort of *ad hoc* procedure to specify the starting values. A not very good idea is just to set all unknown pre-sample values of $\hat{u}_t^2$ and σ_t^2 to zero. A better idea is to replace them by an estimate of their common unconditional expectation. At least two different ways of doing this are in common use. The first is to replace the unconditional expectation by the appropriate function of the $\boldsymbol{\theta}$ parameters, which would be given by the rightmost expression in equations (13.79) for GARCH(1, 1). The second is to use the sum of squared residuals from OLS estimation, divided by n.

Another approach, similar to one we discussed for models with MA errors, is to treat the unknown starting values as extra parameters, and to maximize the loglikelihood with respect to them, $\boldsymbol{\beta}$, and $\boldsymbol{\theta}$ jointly. In all but huge samples, the choice of starting values can have a significant effect on the parameter estimates. Consequently, different programs for GARCH estimation can produce very different results. This unsatisfactory state of affairs, documented convincingly by Brooks, Burke, and Persand (2001), results from doing ML estimation conditional on different things.

For any choice of starting values, maximizing a loglikelihood function obtained by summing the contributions (13.86) is not particularly easy, especially in the case of GARCH models. Numerical difficulties seem to be quite common. It is vital to use analytical, rather than numerical, first derivatives, and for some algorithms it is highly desirable to use analytical second derivatives as well; these may be found in Fiorentini, Calzolari, and Panattoni (1996). Exercise 13.22 proposes an artificial regression, which makes use of first derivatives only. Not all software packages provide reliable estimates and standard errors; see McCullough and Renfro (1999) and Brooks, Burke, and Persand (2001). Therefore, we strongly recommend estimating this type of model more than once using different options and different computer programs.

Although GARCH models have error terms with thicker tails than those of the normal distribution, data from financial markets often have tails even thicker than those implied by a GARCH model with normal ε_t. It is therefore quite common to modify (13.84) by assuming that the ε_t follow a distribution with thicker tails than the standard normal. One possibility is the Student's t distribution with a small number of degrees of freedom, which may be chosen in advance or estimated. Maximum likelihood estimation then proceeds in the usual way.

We can use any of the estimators discussed in Section 10.4 to estimate the covariance matrix of the ML estimates. One of these, the information matrix estimator, can be computed by means of the artificial regression that is introduced in Exercise 13.22. If the error terms are not distributed according to the normal or whatever distribution we have assumed, the ML estimates are still consistent, but they are not asymptotically efficient. In this case, the sandwich covariance matrix estimator (10.45) is consistent, but covariance matrix estimators that rely on the information matrix equality generally are not. A variant of the sandwich estimator specifically adapted to GARCH models was derived by Bollerslev and Wooldridge (1992). These and other possible variants are discussed and compared by Fiorentini, Calzolari, and Panattoni (1996).[5]

Simulating ARCH and GARCH Models

ARCH and GARCH models can be simulated recursively in much the same way as ARMA models. The successive values of the σ_t^2 are computed on the basis of past realizations of the u_t^2 and σ_t^2 series, and the u_t are generated as $\sigma_t \varepsilon_t$ for a white-noise series ε_t, which is often but not always normal. However, the problem of finding suitable starting values for the recursion is much harder for ARCH and GARCH models than for ARMA ones, because we cannot simply draw them from the stationary distribution.

The easiest approach is the one already mentioned in the ARMA context, whereby one starts the recursion for some large negative t and discards the elements of the simulated series for nonpositive t. It is natural to set the initial values of σ_t^2 in this recursion to the unconditional expectation of the u_t^2 or, in the bootstrap case, to an estimate of this unconditional expectation. However, this approach is not entirely satisfactory for bootstrapping, where we wish to condition on the observed data as far as possible. One possibility would be to condition on the first $\max(p, q)$ observations, using the first q squared residuals as the initial values of u_t^2 and the first p squared residuals as the initial values of σ_t^2. However, since much work remains to be done on bootstrapping ARCH and GARCH models, we cannot recommend this or any other approach at the present time.

Our discussion of autoregressive conditional heteroskedasticity has necessarily been quite superficial. There have been many extensions of the basic ARCH

[5] It is stated in this paper and elsewhere in the literature that the information matrix is block-diagonal with respect to $\boldsymbol{\beta}$ and $\boldsymbol{\theta}$. This is misleading, since it is true only if the information matrix is defined using *unconditional* expectations. If the contribution of observation t to the information matrix is computed as an expectation conditional on Ω_{t-1}, as it should be for efficiency, then the information matrix is not block-diagonal.

and GARCH models discussed here, among them the **exponential GARCH** model of Nelson (1991) and the **absolute GARCH** model of Hentschel (1995). These models are intended to explain empirical features of financial time series that the standard GARCH model cannot capture. More detailed treatments may be found in Bollerslev, Chou, and Kroner (1992), Bollerslev, Engle, and Nelson (1994), Hamilton (1994, Chapter 21), and Pagan (1996).

13.7 Vector Autoregressions

The dynamic models discussed in Section 13.4 were single-equation models. But we often want to model the dynamic relationships among several time-series variables. A simple way to do so without making many assumptions is to use what is called a **vector autoregression**, or **VAR**, model, which is the multivariate analog of an autoregressive model for a single time series.

Let the $1 \times g$ vector $\boldsymbol{Y}_t$ denote the tth observation on a set of g variables. Then a vector autoregressive model of order p, sometimes referred to as a **VAR(p) model**, can be written as

$$\boldsymbol{Y}_t = \boldsymbol{\alpha} + \sum_{j=1}^{p} \boldsymbol{Y}_{t-j}\boldsymbol{\Phi}_j + \boldsymbol{U}_t, \quad \boldsymbol{U}_t \sim \text{IID}(\boldsymbol{0}, \boldsymbol{\Sigma}), \tag{13.87}$$

where $\boldsymbol{U}_t$ is a $1 \times g$ vector of error terms, $\boldsymbol{\alpha}$ is a $1 \times g$ vector of constant terms, and the $\boldsymbol{\Phi}_j$, for $j = 1, \ldots, p$, are $g \times g$ matrices of coefficients, all of which are to be estimated. If y_{ti} denotes the ith element of $\boldsymbol{Y}_t$ and $\phi_{j,ki}$ denotes the ki^{th} element of $\boldsymbol{\Phi}_j$, then the ith column of (13.87) can be written as

$$y_{ti} = \alpha_i + \sum_{j=1}^{p}\sum_{k=1}^{m} y_{t-j,k}\,\phi_{j,ki} + u_{ti}.$$

This is just a linear regression, in which y_{ti} depends on a constant term and lags 1 through p of all of the g variables in the system. Thus we see that the VAR (13.87) has the form of a multivariate linear regression model, or SUR model, like the ones we discussed in Section 12.2.

To see this clearly, let us make the definitions

$$\boldsymbol{X}_t \equiv [1 \quad \boldsymbol{Y}_{t-1} \quad \cdots \quad \boldsymbol{Y}_{t-p}] \quad \text{and} \quad \boldsymbol{\Pi} \equiv \begin{bmatrix} \boldsymbol{\alpha} \\ \boldsymbol{\Phi}_1 \\ \vdots \\ \boldsymbol{\Phi}_p \end{bmatrix}.$$

The row vector $\boldsymbol{X}_t$ has $k \equiv gp + 1$ elements, and the matrix $\boldsymbol{\Pi}$ is $k \times g$. With these definitions, the VAR (13.87) becomes

$$\boldsymbol{Y}_t = \boldsymbol{X}_t\boldsymbol{\Pi} + \boldsymbol{U}_t, \quad \boldsymbol{U}_t \sim \text{IID}(\boldsymbol{0}, \boldsymbol{\Sigma}), \tag{13.88}$$

which has the form of a multivariate regression model. In fact, if we stack the rows, it has precisely the same form as (12.71), which is the unrestricted reduced form for a linear simultaneous equations model. Thus a VAR can be thought of as a set of reduced form linear equations relating the endogenous variables in the vector $\boldsymbol{Y}_t$ to the predetermined variables that are collected in the vector $\boldsymbol{X}_t$. Except for the constant term, these predetermined variables are the first p lags of all the endogenous variables themselves.

Estimating a vector autoregression is very easy. As we saw in Section 12.2, it is appropriate to estimate a linear system like (13.88), in which the same regressors appear in every equation, by ordinary least squares. In such a case, OLS is both the efficient GLS estimator and the maximum likelihood estimator under the assumption of multivariate normal errors. If $\hat{\boldsymbol{\Pi}}$ denotes the matrix of OLS estimates, it follows from (12.41) that the maximized value of the loglikelihood function is

$$-\frac{gn}{2}(\log 2\pi + 1) - \frac{n}{2}\log|\hat{\boldsymbol{\Sigma}}|, \tag{13.89}$$

where

$$\hat{\boldsymbol{\Sigma}} \equiv \frac{1}{n}(\boldsymbol{Y} - \boldsymbol{X}\hat{\boldsymbol{\Pi}})^{\top}(\boldsymbol{Y} - \boldsymbol{X}\hat{\boldsymbol{\Pi}}) = \frac{1}{n}\sum_{t=1}^{n}\hat{\boldsymbol{U}}_t^{\top}\hat{\boldsymbol{U}}_t \tag{13.90}$$

is the ML estimate of the covariance matrix $\boldsymbol{\Sigma}$. Here $\boldsymbol{Y}$ is the $n \times g$ matrix with typical row $\boldsymbol{Y}_t$, $\boldsymbol{X}$ is the $n \times k$ matrix with typical row $\boldsymbol{X}_t$, and $\hat{\boldsymbol{U}}_t$ is the row vector of OLS residuals for observation t. The estimate (13.90) is often of considerable interest, because it captures the covariances between the innovations in the various equations.

When specifying a VAR, it is important to determine how many lags need to be included. If one wishes to test the null hypothesis that the longest lag in the system is p against the alternative that it is $p+1$, the easiest way to do so is to compute the LR statistic

$$n\big(\log|\hat{\boldsymbol{\Sigma}}(p)| - \log|\hat{\boldsymbol{\Sigma}}(p+1)|\big), \tag{13.91}$$

where $\hat{\boldsymbol{\Sigma}}(p)$ and $\hat{\boldsymbol{\Sigma}}(p+1)$ denote the ML estimates of $\boldsymbol{\Sigma}$ for systems with p and $p+1$ lags, respectively; both of these may be computed using (13.90). This test statistic is asymptotically distributed as $\chi^2(g^2)$. However, unless the sample size n is large relative to the number of parameters in the system ($g + pg^2$ under the null, and $g + (p+1)g^2$ under the alternative), the finite-sample distribution of the LR statistic (13.91) may differ substantially from its asymptotic one. In consequence, this is a case in which it is often very desirable to compute bootstrap rather than asymptotic P values.

Since there is more than one way to generate bootstrap samples for a VAR, it is worth saying a bit more about this. We suggest using (13.87) to generate the data recursively, with OLS estimates under the null replacing the unknown parameters. The bootstrap error terms are obtained by resampling the row vectors $\tilde{\boldsymbol{U}}_t$, where $\tilde{\boldsymbol{U}}_t$ is equal to $(n/(n-1-gp))^{1/2}$ times the row vector $\hat{\boldsymbol{U}}_t$ of OLS residuals, and actual pre-sample values of $\boldsymbol{Y}_t$ are used to start the recursive process of generating the bootstrap data. Limited simulation evidence suggests that this procedure yields much more accurate P values for tests based on (13.91) than using the $\chi^2(g^2)$ distribution.

If we wish to construct confidence intervals for, or test hypotheses about, individual parameters in a VAR, we can use the OLS standard errors, which are asymptotically valid. Similarly, if we wish to test hypotheses concerning two or more parameters in a single equation, we can compute Wald tests in the usual way based on the OLS covariance matrix for that equation. However, if we wish to test hypotheses concerning coefficients in two or more equations, we need the covariance matrix of the parameter estimates for the entire system.

We saw in Chapter 12 that the estimated covariance matrix for the feasible GLS estimates of a multivariate regression model is given by expression (12.19), and the one for the ML estimates is given by expression (12.38). These two covariance matrices differ only because they use different estimates of $\boldsymbol{\Sigma}$. As in Section 12.2, we let $\boldsymbol{X}_\bullet \equiv \mathbf{I}_g \otimes \boldsymbol{X}$, which is a $gn \times gk$ matrix. Then, if all the parameters are stacked into a vector of length gk, both covariance matrices have the form

$$\big(\boldsymbol{X}_\bullet^\top(\hat{\boldsymbol{\Sigma}}^{-1} \otimes \mathbf{I}_n)\boldsymbol{X}_\bullet\big)^{-1}.$$

Using the rules for manipulating Kronecker products given in equations (12.08), we see that

$$\big(\boldsymbol{X}_\bullet^\top(\hat{\boldsymbol{\Sigma}}^{-1} \otimes \mathbf{I}_n)\boldsymbol{X}_\bullet\big)^{-1} = \big((\mathbf{I}_g \otimes \boldsymbol{X}^\top)(\hat{\boldsymbol{\Sigma}}^{-1} \otimes \mathbf{I}_n)(\mathbf{I}_g \otimes \boldsymbol{X})\big)^{-1} = \hat{\boldsymbol{\Sigma}} \otimes (\boldsymbol{X}^\top\boldsymbol{X})^{-1}.$$

Thus the covariance matrix for all the coefficients of a VAR is easily computed from $\hat{\boldsymbol{\Sigma}}$, which is given in (13.90), and the inverse of the $\boldsymbol{X}^\top\boldsymbol{X}$ matrix.

The idea of using vector autoregressions instead of structural models to model macroeconomic dynamics is often attributed to Sims (1980). Our treatment has been very brief. For a more detailed introductory treatment, with many references, see Lütkepohl (2001). For a review of macroeconomic applications of VARs, see Stock and Watson (2001).

Granger Causality

One common use of vector autoregressions is to test the hypothesis that one or more of the variables in a VAR do not "Granger cause" the others. The concept of **Granger causality** was developed by Granger (1969). Other, closely related, definitions of causality have been suggested, notably by Sims (1972). Suppose we divide the variables in a VAR into two groups, $\boldsymbol{Y}_{t1}$ and $\boldsymbol{Y}_{t2}$, which are row vectors of dimensions g_1 and g_2, respectively. Then we may say that $\boldsymbol{Y}_{t2}$ does not Granger cause $\boldsymbol{Y}_{t1}$ if the distribution of $\boldsymbol{Y}_{t1}$, conditional on past values of both $\boldsymbol{Y}_{t1}$ and $\boldsymbol{Y}_{t2}$, is the same as the distribution of $\boldsymbol{Y}_{t1}$ conditional only on its own past values.

In practice, it would be very difficult to test whether the entire distribution of $\boldsymbol{Y}_{t1}$ depends on past values of $\boldsymbol{Y}_{t2}$. Therefore, we almost always content ourselves with asking whether the conditional mean of $\boldsymbol{Y}_{t1}$ depends on past values of $\boldsymbol{Y}_{t2}$. In terms of the VAR (13.87), this is equivalent to imposing restrictions on the equations that correspond to $\boldsymbol{Y}_{t1}$. We can rewrite the VAR as

$$[\boldsymbol{Y}_{t1}\;\; \boldsymbol{Y}_{t2}] = [\boldsymbol{\alpha}_1\;\; \boldsymbol{\alpha}_2] + \sum_{j=1}^{p} [\boldsymbol{Y}_{t-j,1}\;\; \boldsymbol{Y}_{t-j,2}] \begin{bmatrix} \boldsymbol{\Phi}_{j,11} & \boldsymbol{\Phi}_{j,12} \\ \boldsymbol{\Phi}_{j,21} & \boldsymbol{\Phi}_{j,22} \end{bmatrix} + [\boldsymbol{U}_{t1}\;\; \boldsymbol{U}_{t2}],$$

where the matrices $\boldsymbol{\Phi}_j$ have been partitioned to conform with the partition of $\boldsymbol{Y}_t$ and its lags. If $\boldsymbol{Y}_{t2}$ does not Granger cause $\boldsymbol{Y}_{t1}$, then all of the $\boldsymbol{\Phi}_{j,21}$ must be zero matrices. Similarly, if $\boldsymbol{Y}_{t1}$ does not Granger cause $\boldsymbol{Y}_{t2}$, then all of the $\boldsymbol{\Phi}_{j,12}$ must be zero matrices.

Since the $\boldsymbol{\Phi}_{j,21}$ appear only in the equations for $\boldsymbol{Y}_{t1}$, it is easy to test the hypothesis that they are all zero. We obtain ML estimates of the two systems of equations

$$\boldsymbol{Y}_{t1} = \boldsymbol{\alpha}_1 + \sum_{j=1}^{p} \boldsymbol{Y}_{t-j,1} \boldsymbol{\Phi}_{j,11} + \boldsymbol{U}_{t1}, \text{ and} \tag{13.92}$$

$$\boldsymbol{Y}_{t1} = \boldsymbol{\alpha}_1 + \sum_{j=1}^{p} (\boldsymbol{Y}_{t-j,1} \boldsymbol{\Phi}_{j,11} + \boldsymbol{Y}_{t-j,2} \boldsymbol{\Phi}_{j,21}) + \boldsymbol{U}_{t1}, \tag{13.93}$$

which may be done using OLS for each equation, and then calculate the value of the loglikelihood function for each of the systems. As in (13.89), the loglikelihood depends only on the estimate of $\boldsymbol{\Sigma}_{11}$, the $g_1 \times g_1$ upper left-hand block of $\boldsymbol{\Sigma}$. This may easily be calculated using the OLS residuals, as in (13.90). We obtain the LR statistic

$$n\big(\log|\tilde{\boldsymbol{\Sigma}}_{11}| - \log|\hat{\boldsymbol{\Sigma}}_{11}|\big), \tag{13.94}$$

where $\tilde{\boldsymbol{\Sigma}}_{11}$ denotes the estimate of $\boldsymbol{\Sigma}_{11}$ based on the OLS residuals from equations (13.92), and $\hat{\boldsymbol{\Sigma}}_{11}$ denotes the estimate of $\boldsymbol{\Sigma}_{11}$ based on the OLS residuals from equations (13.93). The statistic (13.94) is asymptotically distributed as $\chi^2(pg_1g_2)$, but more reliable inferences in finite samples can almost certainly be obtained by bootstrapping.

In practice, we are very commonly interested in testing Granger causality for a single dependent variable. In that case, equations (13.92) and (13.93) are univariate regressions. The restricted model, equation (13.92), becomes a regression of y_{t1} on a constant and p of its own lagged values. The unrestricted model, equation (13.93), adds p lagged values of g_2 additional variables to this regression. We can then perform an asymptotic F test of the hypothesis that the pg_2 coefficients of the lags of all the additional variables are jointly equal to zero. For this test to be asymptotically valid, the error terms must be homoskedastic. If this assumption does not seem to be correct, we should instead perform a heteroskedasticity-robust test, as discussed in Section 6.8.

Our discussion of Granger causality has been quite brief. Hamilton (1994, Chapter 11) provides a much more detailed discussion of this topic. That book also discusses a number of other aspects of VAR models in more detail than we have done here.

13.8 Final Remarks

The analysis of time-series data has engaged the interest of a great many statisticians and econometricians and generated a massive literature. This chapter has provided only a superficial introduction to the subject. In particular, we have said nothing at all about frequency domain methods, because they are a bit too specialized for this book. See Brockwell and Davis (1991), Box, Jenkins, and Reinsel (1994, Chapter 2), Hamilton (1994, Chapter 6), and Fuller (1995), among many others.

This chapter has dealt only with stationary time series. A great many economic time series are, or at least appear to be, nonstationary. Therefore, in the next chapter, we turn our attention to methods for dealing with nonstationary time series. Such methods have been a subject of an enormous amount of research in econometrics during the past two decades.

13.9 Exercises

13.1 Show that the solution to the Yule-Walker equations (13.07) for the AR(2) process is given by equations (13.08).

13.2 Demonstrate that the first $p+1$ Yule-Walker equations for the AR(p) process $u_t = \sum_{i=1}^{p} \rho_i u_{t-i} + \varepsilon_t$ are

$$v_0 - \sum_{i=1}^{p} \rho_i v_i = \sigma_\varepsilon^2, \quad \text{and}$$

$$\rho_i v_0 - v_i + \sum_{j=1,\, j\neq i}^{p} \rho_j v_{|i-j|} = 0, \quad i = 1, \ldots, p. \tag{13.95}$$

Then rewrite these equations using matrix notation.

13.3 Consider the AR(2) process

$$u_t = \rho_1 u_{t-1} + \rho_2 u_{t-2} + \varepsilon_t,$$

for which the covariance matrix (13.09) of three consecutive observations has elements specified by equations (13.08). Show that necessary conditions for stationarity are that ρ_1 and ρ_2 lie inside the stationarity triangle which is shown in Figure 13.1 and defined by the inequalities

$$\rho_1 + \rho_2 < 1, \quad \rho_2 - \rho_1 < 1, \text{ and } \rho_2 > -1.$$

This can be done by showing that, outside the stationarity triangle, the matrix (13.09) is not positive definite.

★13.4 Show that, along the edges $\rho_1 + \rho_2 = 1$ and $\rho_1 - \rho_2 = -1$ of the AR(2) stationarity triangle, both roots of the polynomial $1 - \rho_1 z - \rho_2 z^2$ are real, one of them equal to 1 and the other greater than 1 in absolute value. Show further that, along the edge $\rho_2 = -1$, both roots are complex and equal to 1 in absolute value. How are these facts related to the general condition for the stationarity of an AR process?

13.5 Let $A(z)$ and $B(z)$ be two formal infinite power series in z, as follows:

$$A(z) = \sum_{i=0}^{\infty} a_i z^i \quad \text{and} \quad B(z) = \sum_{j=0}^{\infty} b_j z^j.$$

Let the formal product $A(z)B(z)$ be expressed similarly as the infinite series

$$C(z) = \sum_{k=0}^{\infty} c_k z^k.$$

Show that the coefficients c_k are given by the **convolution** of the coefficients a_i and b_j, according to the formula

$$c_k = \sum_{i=0}^{k} a_i b_{k-i}, \quad k = 0, 1, \ldots.$$

★13.6 Show that the method illustrated in Section 13.2 for obtaining the autocovariances of an ARMA(1, 1) process can be extended to the ARMA(p, q) case. Since explicit formulas are hard to obtain for general p and q, it is enough to indicate a recursive method for obtaining the solution.

13.7 Plot the autocorrelation function for the ARMA(2, 1) process

$$u_t = \rho_1 u_{t-1} + \rho_2 u_{t-2} + \varepsilon_t + \alpha_1 \varepsilon_{t-1}$$

for lags $j = 0, 1, \ldots, 20$ and for parameter values $\rho_1 = 0.8$, $\rho_2 = -0.6$, and $\alpha_1 = 0.5$. Repeat the exercise with $\rho_2 = 0$, the other two parameters being unchanged, in order to see how the moving-average component affects the ACF in this case.

13.8 Consider the p Yule-Walker equations (13.95) for an AR(p) process as a set of simultaneous linear equations for the ρ_i, $i = 1, \ldots, p$, given the autocovariances v_i, $i = 0, 1, \ldots, p$. Show that the ρ_i which solve these equations for given v_i are also the solutions to the first-order conditions for the problem (13.30) used to define the partial autocorrelation coefficients for a process characterized by the autocovariances v_i. Use this result to explain why the pth partial autocorrelation coefficient for a given stationary process depends only on the first p (ordinary) autocorrelation coefficients.

13.9 Show that ε_2, as given by expression (13.39), has variance σ_ε^2 and is independent of both ε_1 as given by (13.37) and the ε_t for $t > 2$.

13.10 Define the $n \times n$ matrix $\boldsymbol{\Psi}$ so that $\boldsymbol{\Psi}^\top \boldsymbol{u} = \boldsymbol{\varepsilon}$, where the elements of the n-vector $\boldsymbol{\varepsilon}$ are defined by equations (13.35), (13.37), and (13.39). Show that $\boldsymbol{\Psi}$ is upper triangular, and write down the matrix $\boldsymbol{\Psi}\boldsymbol{\Psi}^\top$. Explain how $\boldsymbol{\Psi}\boldsymbol{\Psi}^\top$ is related to the inverse of the covariance matrix (13.33), where the autocovariances v_i are those of the AR(2) process $u_t = \rho_1 u_{t-1} + \rho_2 u_{t-2} + \varepsilon_t$.

13.11 Show that the second equation in (13.46) has real solutions for α_1 in terms of ρ only if $|\rho| \leq 0.5$. Explain why this makes sense. Show that if $\rho = \pm 0.5$, then $\alpha_1 = \mp 1$. Show finally that, if $|\rho| < 0.5$, exactly one of the solutions for α_1 satisfies the invertibility condition that $|\alpha_1| < 1$.

13.12 The ARMA(1, 1) process

$$u_t = \rho_1 u_{t-1} + \varepsilon_t + \alpha_1 \varepsilon_{t-1}, \quad \varepsilon_t \sim \text{NID}(0, \sigma_\varepsilon^2),$$

can be simulated recursively if we have starting values for u_1 and ε_1, which in turn can be generated from the joint stationary distribution of these two random variables. Characterize this joint distribution.

13.13 Rewrite the ARMA(p, q) model (13.31) in the form of the ARMAX(p, q) model (13.32) with $\boldsymbol{X}_t\boldsymbol{\beta} = \beta$. Show precisely how β is related to γ.

★13.14 Consider the MAX(1) model

$$y_t = \boldsymbol{X}_t\boldsymbol{\beta} + \varepsilon_t - \alpha\varepsilon_{t-1}.$$

Show how to estimate the parameters of this model by indirect inference using as auxiliary model the nonlinear regression corresponding to AR(1) errors,

$$y_t = \boldsymbol{X}_t\boldsymbol{\gamma} + \rho y_{t-1} - \rho\boldsymbol{X}_{t-1}\boldsymbol{\gamma} + u_t.$$

In particular, show that, for true parameter values $\boldsymbol{\beta}$ and α, the pseudo-true values are $\boldsymbol{\gamma} = \boldsymbol{\beta}$ and $\rho = -\alpha/(1+\alpha^2)$.

13.15 This question uses the data in the file **intrates-m.data**, which contains four monthly interest rate series for the United States from 1955 to 2001. Take the first difference of two of these series, the federal funds rate, r_t^s, and the 10-year treasury bond rate, r_t^l. Then graph both the empirical ACF and the empirical PACF of each of the differenced series for $J = 24$ for the period from 1957:1 to 2001:12. Does it seem likely that an AR(1) process would provide a good model for either of these series? What about an MA(1) process?

13.16 For the two series r_t^s and r_t^l used in the previous exercise, estimate AR(1), AR(2), MA(1), ARMA(1, 1), ARMA(2, 1), and ARMA(2, 2) models with constant terms by maximum likelihood and record the values of the loglikelihood functions. In each case, which is the most parsimonious model that seems to be compatible with the data?

13.17 The file **hstarts.data** contains the housing starts data graphed in Figure 13.2. For the period 1966:1 to 2001:4, regress the unadjusted series h_t on a constant, h_{t-1}, the three seasonal dummies defined in (2.49), those dummies interacted with the elements of the trend vector $\boldsymbol{T}$ defined in (13.68), and those dummies interacted with the squares of the elements of $\boldsymbol{t}_q$. Then test the null hypothesis that the error terms for this regression are serially independent against the alternative that they follow the simple AR(4) process (13.63).

For the period 1966:1 to 1999:4, regress the adjusted series h'_t on the unadjusted series h_t, a constant, and the nine seasonal dummy variables used in the previous regression.

For the period 1966:1 to 1999:4, run the regression

$$h'_t = \beta_0 + \sum_{j=-8}^{8} \delta_j h_t + u_t.$$

Compare the performance of this regression with that of the dummy variable regression you just estimated. Which of them provides a better approximation to the way in which the seasonally adjusted data were actually generated?

⋆13.18 Consider the GARCH(1, 1) model with conditional variance given by equation (13.78). Calculate the unconditional fourth moment of the stationary distribution of the series u_t generated as $u_t = \sigma_t \varepsilon_t$ with $\varepsilon_t \sim \text{NID}(0, 1)$. It may be advisable to begin by calculating the unconditional fourth moment of the stationary distribution of σ_t. What is the necessary condition for the existence of these fourth moments? Show that, when the parameter δ_1 is zero, this condition becomes $3\alpha_1^2 < 1$, as for an ARCH(1) process.

13.19 This exercise is an extension of Exercise 4.2. By considering the derivative of the function $z^{2r+1}\phi(z)$, where $\phi(\cdot)$ is the standard normal density, and using an inductive argument, show that the $(2r)^{\text{th}}$ moment of the N(0, 1) distribution is equal to $\prod_{j=1}^{r}(2j-1)$.

⋆13.20 Use the result of the previous exercise to show that a necessary condition for the existence of the $2r^{\text{th}}$ moment of the ARCH(1) process

$$u_t = \sigma_t \varepsilon_t; \quad \sigma_t^2 = \alpha_0 + \alpha_1 u_{t-1}^2; \quad \varepsilon_t \sim \text{NID}(0, 1)$$

is that $\alpha_1^r \prod_{j=1}^{r}(2j-1) < 1$.

⋆13.21 Consider the regression model $\boldsymbol{y} = \boldsymbol{X\beta} + \boldsymbol{u}$, where $\boldsymbol{X}$ is an $n \times k$ matrix, in which the errors follow a GARCH(1, 1) process with conditional variance given by equation (13.78). Show that the skedastic function $\sigma_t^2(\boldsymbol{\beta}, \boldsymbol{\theta})$ used in the loglikelihood contribution $\ell_t(\boldsymbol{\beta}, \boldsymbol{\theta})$ given in (13.86) can be written explicitly as

$$\sigma_t^2(\boldsymbol{\beta}, \boldsymbol{\theta}) = \frac{\alpha_0(1-\delta_1^{t-1})}{1-\delta_1} + \alpha_1 \sum_{s=1}^{t-1} \delta_1^{s-1} u_{t-s}^2 + \frac{\alpha_0 \delta_1^{t-1}}{1-\alpha_1-\delta_1}, \tag{13.96}$$

where u_t stands for the residual $y_t - \boldsymbol{X}_t\boldsymbol{\beta}$, and all unavailable instances of both u_t^2 and σ_t^2 are replaced by the unconditional expectation $\alpha_0/(1-\alpha_1-\delta_1)$.

Then show that the first-order partial derivatives of $\ell_t(\boldsymbol{\beta}, \boldsymbol{\theta})$ can be written as follows:

$$\frac{\partial \ell_t}{\partial \boldsymbol{\beta}} = \frac{\partial \ell_t}{\partial u_t}\frac{\partial u_t}{\partial \boldsymbol{\beta}} + \frac{\partial \ell_t}{\partial \sigma_t^2}\frac{\partial \sigma_t^2}{\partial \boldsymbol{\beta}} = \frac{\boldsymbol{X}_t u_t}{\sigma_t^2} - \frac{\alpha_1(u_t^2 - \sigma_t^2)}{\sigma_t^4}\sum_{s=1}^{t-1}\delta_1^{s-1}\boldsymbol{X}_{t-s}u_{t-s}$$

$$\frac{\partial \ell_t}{\partial \alpha_0} = \frac{\partial \ell_t}{\partial \sigma_t^2}\frac{\partial \sigma_t^2}{\partial \alpha_0} = \frac{u_t^2 - \sigma_t^2}{2\sigma_t^4}\Big(\frac{1-\delta_1^{t-1}}{1-\delta_1} + \frac{\delta_1^{t-1}}{1-\alpha_1-\delta_1}\Big), \tag{13.97}$$

$$\frac{\partial \ell_t}{\partial \alpha_1} = \frac{\partial \ell_t}{\partial \sigma_t^2}\frac{\partial \sigma_t^2}{\partial \alpha_1} = \frac{u_t^2 - \sigma_t^2}{2\sigma_t^4}\bigg(\sum_{s=1}^{t-1}\delta_1^{s-1}u_{t-s}^2 + \frac{\alpha_0\delta_1^{t-1}}{(1-\alpha_1-\delta_1)^2}\bigg),$$

$$\frac{\partial \ell_t}{\partial \delta_1} = \frac{\partial \ell_t}{\partial \sigma_t^2}\frac{\partial \sigma_t^2}{\partial \delta_1} = \frac{u_t^2 - \sigma_t^2}{2\sigma_t^4}\bigg(-\frac{\alpha_0(t-1)\delta_1^{t-2}}{1-\delta_1} + \frac{\alpha_0(1-\delta_1^{t-1})}{(1-\delta_1)^2}$$
$$+ \alpha_1\sum_{s=1}^{t-1}(s-1)\delta_1^{s-2}u_{t-s}^2 + \frac{\alpha_0(t-1)\delta_1^{t-2}}{1-\alpha_1-\delta_1} + \frac{\alpha_0\delta_1^{t-1}}{(1-\alpha_1-\delta_1)^2}\bigg).$$

⋆13.22 Consider the following artificial regression in connection with the model with GARCH(1, 1) errors considered in the preceding exercise. Each real observation corresponds to two artificial observations. For observation t, the two corresponding elements of the regressand are

$$u_t/\sigma_t \quad \text{and} \quad (u_t^2 - \sigma_t^2)/(\sigma_t^2\sqrt{2}).$$

The elements of the regressors that correspond to the elements of $\boldsymbol{\beta}$ are the elements of

$$\frac{\boldsymbol{X}_t}{\sigma_t} \quad \text{and} \quad -\frac{\alpha_1\sqrt{2}}{\sigma_t^2}\sum_{s=1}^{t-1}\delta_1^{s-1}\boldsymbol{X}_{t-s}u_{t-s}.$$

Similarly, the elements of the regressor that corresponds to α_0 are 0 and

$$\frac{1}{\sigma_t^2\sqrt{2}}\Big(\frac{1-\delta_1^{t-1}}{1-\delta_1} + \frac{\delta_1^{t-1}}{1-\alpha_1-\delta_1}\Big),$$

and those of the regressor that corresponds to α_1 are 0 and

$$\frac{1}{\sigma_t^2\sqrt{2}}\bigg(\sum_{s=1}^{t-1}\delta_1^{s-1}u_{t-s}^2 + \frac{\alpha_0\delta_1^{t-1}}{(1-\alpha_1-\delta_1)^2}\bigg).$$

Finally, the elements of the regressor that corresponds to δ_1 are 0 and

$$\frac{1}{\sigma_t^2\sqrt{2}}\bigg(-\frac{\alpha_0(t-1)\delta_1^{t-2}}{1-\delta_1} + \frac{\alpha_0(1-\delta_1^{t-1})}{(1-\delta_1)^2}$$
$$+ \alpha_1\sum_{s=1}^{t-1}(s-1)\delta_1^{s-2}u_{t-s}^2 + \frac{\alpha_0(t-1)\delta_1^{t-2}}{1-\alpha_1-\delta_1} + \frac{\alpha_0\delta_1^{t-1}}{(1-\alpha_1-\delta_1)^2}\bigg).$$

Show that, when the regressand is orthogonal to the regressors, the sums over all the observations of the contributions (13.97) to the gradient of the loglikelihood are zero.

Let $\boldsymbol{R}(\beta, \boldsymbol{\theta})$ denote the $2n \times (k+3)$ matrix of the regressors, and let $\hat{\beta}$ and $\hat{\boldsymbol{\theta}}$ denote the ML estimates. Then show that $\boldsymbol{R}^\top(\hat{\beta}, \hat{\boldsymbol{\theta}})\boldsymbol{R}(\hat{\beta}, \hat{\boldsymbol{\theta}})$ is the information matrix, where the contribution from observation t is computed as an expectation conditional on the information set Ω_t.

13.23 This question uses data on monthly returns for the period 1969–1998 for shares of General Electric Corporation from the file **monthly-crsp.data**. These data are made available by courtesy of the Center for Research in Security Prices (CRSP); see the comments at the bottom of the file. Let R_t denote the return on GE shares in month t. For the entire sample period, regress R_t on a constant and d_t, where d_t is a dummy variable that is equal to 1 in November, December, January, and February, and equal to 0 in all other months. Then test the hypothesis that the error terms are IID against the alternative that they follow a GARCH(1, 1) process.

13.24 Using the data from the previous question, estimate the GARCH(1, 1) model

$$R_t = \beta_1 + \beta_2 d_t + u_t, \quad \sigma_t^2 \equiv \mathrm{E}(u_t^2) = \alpha_0 + \alpha_1 u_{t-1}^2 + \delta_1 \sigma_{t-1}^2. \tag{13.98}$$

Estimate this model by maximum likelihood, and perform an asymptotic Wald test of the hypothesis that $\alpha_1 + \delta_1 = 1$. Then calculate the unconditional variance σ^2 given by (13.79) and construct a .95 confidence interval for it. Compare this with the estimate of the unconditional variance from the linear regression model estimated in the previous question.

13.25 Using the ML estimates of the model (13.98) from the previous question, plot both $\hat{u}_t^2$ and the estimated conditional variance $\hat{\sigma}_t^2$ against time. Put both series on the same axes. Comment on the relationship between the two series.

13.26 Define the rescaled residuals from the model (13.98) as $\hat{\varepsilon}_t = \hat{u}_t/\hat{\sigma}_t$. Plot the EDF of the rescaled residuals on the same axes as the CDF of the standard normal distribution. Does there appear to be any evidence that the rescaled residuals are not normally distributed?

13.27 The file **intrates-q.data** contains quarterly data for 1955 to 2001 on four US interest rate series. Take first differences of these four series and, using data for the period 1957:1 to 2001:4, estimate a vector autoregression with two lags. Then estimate a VAR with three lags and test the hypothesis that p, the maximum lag, is equal to 2 at the .05 level.

13.28 Using the same first-differenced data as in the previous question, and using models with two lags, test the hypothesis that the federal funds rate does not Granger cause the 10-year bond rate. Then test the hypothesis that the 10-year bond rate does not Granger cause the federal funds rate. Perform both tests in two different ways, one of which assumes that the error variance is constant and one of which allows for heteroskedasticity of unknown form.

Chapter 14

Unit Roots and Cointegration

14.1 Introduction

In this chapter, we turn our attention to models for a particular type of nonstationary time series. For present purposes, the usual definition of covariance stationarity is too strict. We consider instead an asymptotic version, which requires only that, as $t \to \infty$, the first and second moments tend to fixed stationary values, and the covariances of the elements y_t and y_s tend to stationary values that depend only on $|t-s|$. Such a series is said to be integrated to order zero, or **I(0)**, for a reason that will be clear in a moment.

A nonstationary time series is said to be integrated to order one, or **I(1)**,[1] if the series of its first differences, $\Delta y_t \equiv y_t - y_{t-1}$, is I(0). More generally, a series is **integrated to order** $\boldsymbol{d}$, or $\mathbf{I}(\boldsymbol{d})$, if it must be differenced d times before an I(0) series results. A series is I(1) if it contains what is called a **unit root**, a concept that we will elucidate in the next section. As we will see there, using standard regression methods with variables that are I(1) can yield highly misleading results. It is therefore important to be able to test the hypothesis that a time series has a unit root. In Sections 14.3 and 14.4, we discuss a number of ways of doing so. Section 14.5 introduces the concept of **cointegration**, a phenomenon whereby two or more series with unit roots may be related, and discusses estimation in this context. Section 14.6 then discusses three ways of testing for the presence of cointegration.

14.2 Random Walks and Unit Roots

The asymptotic results we have developed so far depend on various regularity conditions that are violated if nonstationary time series are included in the set of variables in a model. In such cases, specialized econometric methods must be employed that are strikingly different from those we have studied

[1] In the literature, such series are usually described as being integrated *of* order one, but this usage strikes us as being needlessly ungrammatical.

so far. The fundamental building block for many of these methods is the **standardized random walk process**, which is defined as follows in terms of a unit-variance white-noise process ε_t:

$$w_t = w_{t-1} + \varepsilon_t, \quad w_0 = 0, \quad \varepsilon_t \sim \text{IID}(0, 1). \tag{14.01}$$

Equation (14.01) is a recursion that can easily be solved to give

$$w_t = \sum_{s=1}^{t} \varepsilon_s. \tag{14.02}$$

It follows from (14.02) that the unconditional expectation $\text{E}(w_t) = 0$ for all t. In addition, w_t satisfies the **martingale property** that $\text{E}(w_t \mid \Omega_{t-1}) = w_{t-1}$ for all t, where as usual the information set Ω_{t-1} contains all information that is available at time $t-1$, including in particular w_{t-1}. The martingale property often makes economic sense, especially in the study of financial markets. We use the notation w_t here partly because "w" is the first letter of "walk" and partly because a random walk is the discrete-time analog of a continuous-time stochastic process called a **Wiener process**, which plays a very important role in the asymptotic theory of nonstationary time series.

The clearest way to see that w_t is nonstationary is to compute $\text{Var}(w_t)$. Since ε_t is white noise, we see directly that $\text{Var}(w_t) = t$. Not only does this variance depend on t, thus violating the stationarity condition, but, in addition, it actually tends to infinity as $t \to \infty$, so that w_t cannot be I(0).

Although the standardized random walk process (14.01) is very simple, more realistic models are closely related to it. In practice, for example, an economic time series is unlikely to have variance 1. Thus the very simplest nonstationary time-series process for data that we might actually observe is the **random walk process**

$$y_t = y_{t-1} + e_t, \quad y_0 = 0, \quad e_t \sim \text{IID}(0, \sigma^2), \tag{14.03}$$

where e_t is still white noise, but with arbitrary variance σ^2. This process, which is often simply referred to as a **random walk**, can be based on the process (14.01) using the equation $y_t = \sigma w_t$. If we wish to relax the assumption that $y_0 = 0$, we can subtract y_0 from both sides of the equation so as to obtain the relationship

$$y_t - y_0 = y_{t-1} - y_0 + e_t.$$

The equation $y_t = y_0 + \sigma w_t$ then relates y_t to a series w_t generated by the standardized random walk process (14.01).

The next obvious generalization is to add a constant term. If we do so, we obtain the model

$$y_t = \gamma_1 + y_{t-1} + e_t. \tag{14.04}$$

This model is often called a **random walk with drift**, and the constant term is called a **drift parameter**. To understand this terminology, subtract $y_0 + \gamma_1 t$ from both sides of (14.04). This yields

$$\begin{aligned} y_t - y_0 - \gamma_1 t &= \gamma_1 + y_{t-1} - y_0 - \gamma_1 t + e_t \\ &= y_{t-1} - y_0 - \gamma_1 (t-1) + e_t, \end{aligned}$$

and it follows that y_t can be generated by the equation $y_t = y_0 + \gamma_1 t + \sigma w_t$. The trend term $\gamma_1 t$ is the drift in this process.

It is clear that, if we take first differences of the y_t generated by a process like (14.03) or (14.04), we obtain a time series that is I(0). In the latter case, for example,

$$\Delta y_t \equiv y_t - y_{t-1} = \gamma_1 + e_t.$$

Thus we see that y_t is integrated to order one, or I(1). This property is the result of the fact that y_t has a **unit root**.

The term "unit root" comes from the fact that the random walk process (14.03) can be expressed as

$$(1 - \mathrm{L}) y_t = e_t, \tag{14.05}$$

where L denotes the lag operator. As we saw in Sections 7.6 and 13.2, an autoregressive process u_t always satisfies an equation of the form

$$\big(1 - \rho(\mathrm{L})\big) u_t = e_t, \tag{14.06}$$

where $\rho(\mathrm{L})$ is a polynomial in the lag operator L with no constant term, and e_t is white noise. The process (14.06) is stationary if and only if all the roots of the polynomial equation $1 - \rho(z) = 0$ lie strictly outside the unit circle in the complex plane, that is, are greater than 1 in absolute value. A root that is equal to 1 is called a unit root. Any series that has precisely one such root, with all other roots outside the unit circle, is an I(1) process, as readers are asked to check in Exercise 14.2.

A random walk process like (14.05) is a particularly simple example of an AR process with a unit root. A slightly more complicated example is

$$y_t = (1 + \rho_2) y_{t-1} - \rho_2 y_{t-2} + u_t, \quad |\rho_2| < 1,$$

which is an AR(2) process with only one free parameter. In this case, the polynomial in the lag operator is $1 - (1 + \rho_2)\mathrm{L} + \rho_2 \mathrm{L}^2 = (1 - \mathrm{L})(1 - \rho_2 \mathrm{L})$, and its roots are 1 and $1/\rho_2 > 1$.

Same-Order Notation

Before we can discuss models in which one or more of the variables has a unit root, it is necessary to introduce the concept of the **same-order relation** and its associated notation. Almost all of the quantities that we encounter in econometrics depend on the sample size. In many cases, when we are using asymptotic theory, the only thing about these quantities that concerns us is the rate at which they change as the sample size changes. The same-order relation provides a very convenient way to deal with such cases.

To begin with, let us suppose that $f(n)$ is a real-valued function of the positive integer n, and p is a rational number. Then we say that $f(n)$ is of the same order as n^p if there exists a constant K, independent of n, and a positive integer N such that

$$\left|\frac{f(n)}{n^p}\right| < K \text{ for all } n > N.$$

When $f(n)$ is of the same order as n^p, we can write

$$f(n) = O(n^p).$$

Of course, this equation does not express an equality in the usual sense. But, as we will see in a moment, this "big O" notation is often very convenient.

The definition we have just given is appropriate only if $f(n)$ is a deterministic function. However, in most econometric applications, some or all of the quantities with which we are concerned are stochastic rather than deterministic. To deal with such quantities, we need to make use of the **stochastic same-order relation**. Let $\{a_n\}$ be a sequence of random variables indexed by the positive integer n. Then we say that a_n is of order n^p in probability if, for all $\varepsilon > 0$, there exist a constant K and a positive integer N such that

$$\Pr\left(\left|\frac{a_n}{n^p}\right| > K\right) < \varepsilon \text{ for all } n > N. \tag{14.07}$$

When a_n is of order n^p in probability, we can write

$$a_n = O_p(n^p).$$

In most cases, it is obvious that a quantity is stochastic, and there is no harm in writing $O(n^p)$ when we really mean $O_p(n^p)$. The properties of the same-order relations are the same in the deterministic and stochastic cases.

The same-order relations are useful because we can manipulate them as if they were simply powers of n. Suppose, for example, that we are dealing with two functions, $f(n)$ and $g(n)$, which are $O(n^p)$ and $O(n^q)$, respectively. Then

$$\begin{aligned} f(n)g(n) &= O(n^p)O(n^q) = O(n^{p+q}), \text{ and} \\ f(n) + g(n) &= O(n^p) + O(n^q) = O(n^{\max(p,q)}). \end{aligned} \tag{14.08}$$

In the first line here, we see that the order of the product of the two functions is just n raised to the sum of p and q. In the second line, we see that the order of the sum of the functions is just n raised to the maximum of p and q. Both these properties of the same-order relations are often very useful in asymptotic analysis.

Let us see how the same-order relations can be applied to a linear regression model that satisfies the standard assumptions for consistency and asymptotic normality. We start with the standard result, from equations (3.05), that

$$\hat{\boldsymbol{\beta}} = \boldsymbol{\beta}_0 + (\boldsymbol{X}^\top\boldsymbol{X})^{-1}\boldsymbol{X}^\top\boldsymbol{u}.$$

In Chapters 3 and 4, we made the assumption that $n^{-1}\boldsymbol{X}^\top\boldsymbol{X}$ has a probability limit of $\boldsymbol{S}_{\boldsymbol{X}^\top\boldsymbol{X}}$, which is a finite, positive definite, deterministic matrix; recall equations (3.17) and (4.49). It follows readily from the definition (3.15) of a probability limit that each element of the matrix $n^{-1}\boldsymbol{X}^\top\boldsymbol{X}$ is $O_p(1)$. Similarly, in order to apply a central limit theorem, we supposed that $n^{-1/2}\boldsymbol{X}^\top\boldsymbol{u}$ has a probability limit which is a normally distributed random variable with expectation zero and finite variance; recall equation (4.53). This implies that $n^{-1/2}\boldsymbol{X}^\top\boldsymbol{u} = O_p(1)$.

The definition (14.07) lets us rewrite the above results as

$$\boldsymbol{X}^\top\boldsymbol{X} = O_p(n) \quad \text{and} \quad \boldsymbol{X}^\top\boldsymbol{u} = O_p(n^{1/2}). \tag{14.09}$$

From equations (14.09) and the first of equations (14.08), we see that

$$n^{1/2}(\hat{\boldsymbol{\beta}} - \boldsymbol{\beta}_0) = n^{1/2}(\boldsymbol{X}^\top\boldsymbol{X})^{-1}\boldsymbol{X}^\top\boldsymbol{u} = n^{1/2}O_p(n^{-1})O_p(n^{1/2}) = O_p(1).$$

This result is not at all new; in fact, it follows from equation (6.38) specialized to a linear regression. But it is clear that the O_p notation provides a simple way of seeing why we have to multiply $\hat{\boldsymbol{\beta}} - \boldsymbol{\beta}_0$ by $n^{1/2}$, rather than some other power of n, in order to find its asymptotic distribution.

As this example illustrates, in the asymptotic analysis of econometric models for which all variables satisfy standard regularity conditions, the power p to which n is raised is generally -1, $-\frac{1}{2}$, 0, $\frac{1}{2}$, or 1. For models in which some or all of the variables have a unit root, however, we will encounter several other values of p.

Regressors with a Unit Root

Whenever a variable with a unit root is used as a regressor in a linear regression model, the standard assumptions that we have made for asymptotic analysis are violated. In particular, we have assumed up to now that, for the linear regression model $\boldsymbol{y} = \boldsymbol{X}\boldsymbol{\beta} + \boldsymbol{u}$, the probability limit of the matrix $n^{-1}\boldsymbol{X}^\top\boldsymbol{X}$ is the finite, positive definite matrix $\boldsymbol{S}_{\boldsymbol{X}^\top\boldsymbol{X}}$. But this assumption is false whenever one or more of the regressors have a unit root.

To see this, consider the simplest case. Whenever one of the regressors is the random walk w_t defined in (14.01), one element of $\boldsymbol{X}^\top\boldsymbol{X}$ is $\sum_{t=1}^{n} w_t^2$, which by equation (14.02) is equal to

$$\sum_{t=1}^{n}\Bigl(\sum_{r=1}^{t}\sum_{s=1}^{t}\varepsilon_r\varepsilon_s\Bigr). \tag{14.10}$$

The expectation of $\varepsilon_r\varepsilon_s$ is zero for $r \neq s$. Therefore, only terms with $r = s$ contribute to the expectation of (14.10), which, since $\mathrm{E}(\varepsilon_r^2) = 1$, is

$$\sum_{t=1}^{n}\sum_{r=1}^{t}\mathrm{E}(\varepsilon_r^2) = \sum_{t=1}^{n} t = \tfrac{1}{2}n(n+1). \tag{14.11}$$

Here we have used a result concerning the sum of the first n positive integers that readers are asked to demonstrate in Exercise 14.4. Let $\boldsymbol{w}$ denote the n–vector with typical element w_t. Then the expectation of $n^{-1}\boldsymbol{w}^\top\boldsymbol{w}$ is $(n+1)/2$, which is evidently $O(n)$. It is therefore impossible that $n^{-1}\boldsymbol{w}^\top\boldsymbol{w}$ should have a finite probability limit.

This fact has extremely serious consequences for asymptotic analysis. It implies that none of the results on consistency and asymptotic normality that we have discussed up to now is applicable to models where one or more of the regressors have a unit root. All such results have been based on the assumption that the matrix $n^{-1}\boldsymbol{X}^\top\boldsymbol{X}$, or the analogs of this matrix for nonlinear regression models, models estimated by IV and GMM, and models estimated by maximum likelihood, tends to a finite, positive definite matrix. It is consequently very important to know whether or not an economic variable has a unit root. A few of the many techniques for answering this question will be discussed in the next section. In the next subsection, we investigate some of the phenomena that arise when the usual regularity conditions for linear regression models are not satisfied.

Spurious Regressions

If x_t and y_t are time series that are entirely independent of each other, we might hope that running the simple linear regression

$$y_t = \beta_1 + \beta_2 x_t + v_t \tag{14.12}$$

would usually produce an insignificant estimate of β_2 and an R^2 near 0. However, this is so only under quite restrictive conditions on the nature of the x_t and y_t. In particular, if x_t and y_t are independent random walks, the t statistic for $\beta_2 = 0$ does not follow the Student's t or standard normal distribution, even asymptotically. Instead, its absolute value tends to become larger and larger as the sample size n increases. Ultimately, as $n \to \infty$, it rejects the null hypothesis that $\beta_2 = 0$ with probability 1. Moreover, the R^2 does not

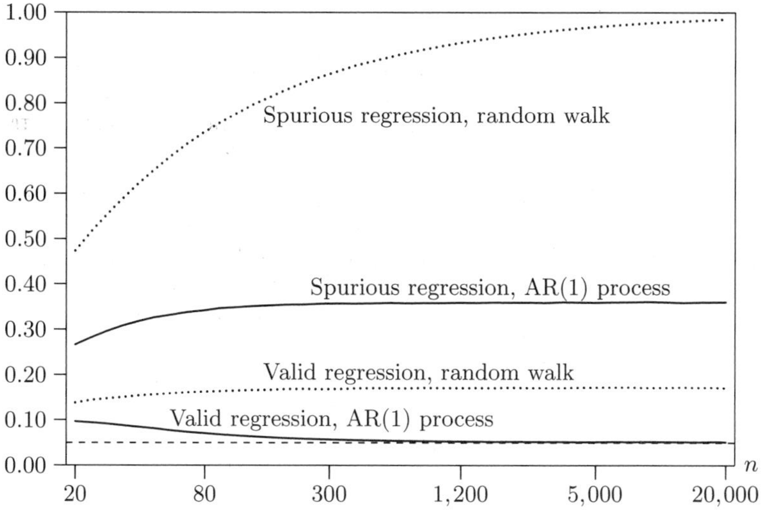

Figure 14.1 Rejection frequencies for spurious and valid regressions

converge to 0 but to a random, positive number that varies from sample to sample. When a regression model like (14.12) appears to find relationships that do not really exist, it is called a **spurious regression**.

We have not as yet developed the theory necessary to understand spurious regression with I(1) series. It is therefore worthwhile to illustrate the phenomenon with some computer simulations. For a large number of sample sizes between 20 and 20, 000, we generated one million series of (x_t, y_t) pairs independently from the random walk model (14.03) and then ran the spurious regression (14.12). The dotted line near the top in Figure 14.1 shows the proportion of the time that the t statistic for $\beta_2 = 0$ rejected the null hypothesis at the .05 level as a function of n. This proportion is very high even for small sample sizes, and it is clearly tending to unity as n increases.

Upon reflection, it is not entirely surprising that tests based on the spurious regression model (14.12) do not yield sensible results. Under the null hypothesis that $\beta_2 = 0$, this model says that y_t is equal to a constant plus an IID error term. But in fact y_t is a random walk generated by the DGP (14.03). Thus the null hypothesis that we are testing is false, and it is very common for a test to reject a false null hypothesis, even when the alternative is also false. We saw an example of this in Section 7.9; for an advanced discussion, see Davidson and MacKinnon (1987).

It might seem that we could obtain sensible results by running the regression

$$y_t = \beta_1 + \beta_2 x_t + \beta_3 y_{t-1} + v_t, \tag{14.13}$$

since, if we set $\beta_1 = 0$, $\beta_2 = 0$, and $\beta_3 = 1$, regression (14.13) reduces to the random walk (14.03), which is in fact the DGP for y_t in our simulations, with $v_t = e_t$ being white noise. Thus it is a valid regression model to estimate. The lower dotted line in Figure 14.1 shows the proportion of the time that the t statistic for $\beta_2 = 0$ in regression (14.13) rejected the null hypothesis at the .05 level. Although this proportion no longer tends to unity as n increases, it clearly tends to a number substantially larger than 0.05. This overrejection is a consequence of running a regression that involves I(1) variables. Both y_t and y_{t-1} are I(1) in this case, and, as we will see in Section 14.5, this implies that the t statistic for $\beta_2 = 0$ does not have its usual asymptotic distribution, as one might suspect given that the $n^{-1}\boldsymbol{X}^\top\boldsymbol{X}$ matrix does not have a finite plim.

The results in Figure 14.1 show clearly that spurious regressions actually involve at least two different phenomena. The first is that they involve testing false null hypotheses, and the second is that standard asymptotic results do not hold whenever at least one of the regressors is I(1), even when a model is correctly specified.

As Granger (2001) has stressed, spurious regression can occur even when all variables are stationary. To illustrate this, Figure 14.1 also shows results of a second set of simulation experiments. These are similar to the original ones, except that x_t and y_t are now generated from independent AR(1) processes with mean zero and autoregressive parameter $\rho_1 = 0.8$. The higher solid line shows that, even for these data, which are stationary as well as independent, running the spurious regression (14.12) results in the null hypothesis being rejected a very substantial proportion of the time. In contrast to the previous results, however, this proportion does not keep increasing with the sample size. Moreover, as we see from the lower solid line, running the valid regression (14.13) leads to approximately correct rejection frequencies, at least for larger sample sizes. Readers are invited to explore these issues further in Exercises 14.6 and 14.7.

It is of interest to see just what gives rise to spurious regression with two independent AR(1) series that are stationary. In this case, the $n^{-1}\boldsymbol{X}^\top\boldsymbol{X}$ matrix does have a finite, deterministic, positive definite plim, and so that regularity condition at least is satisfied. However, because neither the constant nor x_t has any explanatory power for y_t in (14.12), the true error term for observation t is $v_t = y_t$, which is not white noise, but rather an AR(1) process. This suggests that the problem can be made to go away if we do not use the inappropriate OLS covariance matrix estimator, but instead use a HAC estimator that takes suitable account of the serial correlation of the errors. This is true asymptotically, but overrejection remains very significant until the sample size is of the order of several thousand; see Exercise 14.8. The use of HAC estimators is explored further in Exercises 14.9 and 14.10.

As the results in Figure 14.1 illustrate, there is a serious risk of appearing to find relationships between economic time series that are actually independent. This risk can be far from negligible with stationary series that exhibit substantial serial correlation, but it is particularly severe with nonstationary ones. The phenomenon of spurious regressions was brought to the attention of econometricians by Granger and Newbold (1974), who used simulation methods that were very crude by today's standards. Subsequently, Phillips (1986) and Durlauf and Phillips (1988) proved a number of theoretical results about spurious regressions involving nonstationary time series. Granger (2001) provides a brief overview and survey of the literature.

14.3 Unit Root Tests

For a number of reasons, it can be important to know whether or not an economic time series has a unit root. As Figure 14.1 illustrates, the distributions of estimators and test statistics associated with I(1) regressors may well differ sharply from those associated with regressors that are I(0). Moreover, as Nelson and Plosser (1982) were among the first to point out, nonstationarity often has important economic implications. It is therefore very important to be able to detect the presence of unit roots in time series, normally by the use of what are called **unit root tests**. For these tests, the null hypothesis is that the time series has a unit root and the alternative is that it is I(0).

Dickey-Fuller Tests

The simplest and most widely-used tests for unit roots are variants of ones developed by Dickey and Fuller (1979). These tests are therefore referred to as **Dickey-Fuller tests**, or **DF tests**. Consider the simplest imaginable AR(1) model,

$$y_t = \beta y_{t-1} + \sigma\varepsilon_t, \tag{14.14}$$

where ε_t is white noise with variance 1. When $\beta = 1$, this model has a unit root and becomes a random walk process. If we subtract y_{t-1} from both sides and replace $\sigma\varepsilon_t$ by e_t, we obtain

$$\Delta y_t = (\beta - 1)y_{t-1} + e_t. \tag{14.15}$$

Thus, in order to test the null hypothesis of a unit root, we can simply test the hypothesis that the coefficient of y_{t-1} in equation (14.15) is equal to 0 against the alternative that it is negative.

Regression (14.15) is an example of what is sometimes called an **unbalanced regression** because, under the null hypothesis, the regressand is I(0) and the sole regressor is I(1). Under the alternative hypothesis, both variables are I(0), and the regression becomes balanced again.

The obvious way to test the unit root hypothesis is to use the t statistic for the hypothesis $\beta - 1 = 0$ in regression (14.15), testing against the alternative that this quantity is negative. This implies a one-tailed test. In fact, this statistic is referred to, not as a t statistic, but as a **τ statistic**, because, as we will see, its distribution is not the same as that of an ordinary t statistic, even asymptotically. Another possible test statistic is n times the OLS estimate of $\beta-1$ from (14.15). This statistic is called a **z statistic**. Precisely why the z statistic is valid will become clear in the next subsection. Since the z statistic is a little easier to analyze than the τ statistic, we focus on it for the moment.

The z statistic from the test regression (14.15) is

$$z = n\frac{\sum_{t=1}^{n} y_{t-1}\Delta y_t}{\sum_{t=1}^{n} y_{t-1}^2},$$

where, for ease of notation in summations, we suppose that y_0 is observed. Under the null hypothesis, the data are generated by a DGP of the form

$$y_t = y_{t-1} + \sigma\varepsilon_t, \tag{14.16}$$

or, equivalently, $y_t = y_0 + \sigma w_t$, where w_t is a standardized random walk defined in terms of ε_t by (14.01). For such a DGP, a little algebra shows that the z statistic becomes

$$z = n\frac{\sigma^2\sum_{t=1}^{n} w_{t-1}\varepsilon_t + \sigma y_0 w_n}{\sigma^2\sum_{t=1}^{n} w_{t-1}^2 + 2y_0\sigma\sum_{t=1}^{n} w_{t-1} + ny_0^2}. \tag{14.17}$$

Since the right-hand side of this equation depends on y_0 and σ in a nontrivial manner, the z statistic is not pivotal for the model (14.16). However, when $y_0 = 0$, z no longer depends on σ, and it becomes a function of the random walk w_t alone. In this special case, the distribution of z can be calculated, perhaps analytically and certainly by simulation, provided we know the distribution of the ε_t.

In most cases, we do not wish to assume that $y_0 = 0$. Therefore, we must look further for a suitable test statistic. Subtracting y_0 from both y_t and y_{t-1} in equation (14.14) gives

$$\Delta y_t = (1-\beta)y_0 + (\beta-1)y_{t-1} + \sigma\varepsilon_t.$$

Unlike (14.15), this regression has a constant term. This suggests that we should replace (14.15) by the test regression

$$\Delta y_t = \gamma_0 + (\beta-1)y_{t-1} + e_t. \tag{14.18}$$

Since $y_t = y_0 + \sigma w_t$, we may write $\boldsymbol{y} = y_0\boldsymbol{\iota} + \sigma\boldsymbol{w}$, where the notation should be obvious. The z statistic from (14.18) is still $n(\hat\beta - 1)$, and so, by application of the FWL theorem, it can be written under the null as

$$z = n\frac{\sum_{t=1}^{n}(\boldsymbol{M_\iota y})_{t-1}\Delta y_t}{\sum_{t=1}^{n}(\boldsymbol{M_\iota y})_{t-1}^2} = n\frac{\sum_{t=1}^{n}(\boldsymbol{M_\iota y})_{t-1}\sigma\varepsilon_t}{\sum_{t=1}^{n}(\boldsymbol{M_\iota y})_{t-1}^2}, \tag{14.19}$$

where M_ι is the orthogonal projection that replaces a series by its deviations from the mean. Since $M_\iota y = \sigma M_\iota w$, it follows that

$$z = n \frac{\sum_{t=1}^{n} (M_\iota w)_{t-1} \varepsilon_t}{\sum_{t=1}^{n} (M_\iota w)_{t-1}^2}, \tag{14.20}$$

where a factor of σ^2 has been cancelled from the numerator and denominator. Since the w_t are determined by the ε_t, the new statistic depends only on the series ε_t, and so it is pivotal for the model (14.16).

If we wish to test the unit root hypothesis in a model where the random walk has a drift, the appropriate test regression is

$$\Delta y_t = \gamma_0 + \gamma_1 t + (\beta - 1) y_{t-1} + e_t, \tag{14.21}$$

and if we wish to test the unit root hypothesis in a model where the random walk has both a drift and a trend, the appropriate test regression is

$$\Delta y_t = \gamma_0 + \gamma_1 t + \gamma_2 t^2 + (\beta - 1) y_{t-1} + e_t; \tag{14.22}$$

see Exercise 14.11. Notice that regression (14.15) contains no deterministic regressors, (14.18) has one, (14.21) two, and (14.22) three. In the last three cases, the test regression always contains one deterministic regressor that does not appear under the null hypothesis.

Dickey-Fuller tests of the null hypothesis that there is a unit root may be based on any of regressions (14.15), (14.18), (14.21), or (14.22). In practice, regressions (14.18) and (14.21) are the most commonly used. The assumptions required for regression (14.15) to yield a valid test are usually considered to be too strong, while those that lead to regression (14.22) are often considered to be unnecessarily weak.

The z and τ statistics based on the testing regression (14.15) are denoted as z_{nc} and τ_{nc}, respectively. The subscript "nc" indicates that (14.15) has *no* *c*onstant term. Similarly, z statistics based on regressions (14.18), (14.21), and (14.22) are written as z_c, z_{ct}, and z_{ctt}, respectively, because these test regressions contain a *c*onstant, a *c*onstant and a *t*rend, or a *c*onstant and two *t*rends, respectively. A similar notation is used for the τ statistics. It is important to note that all eight of these statistics have different distributions, both in finite samples and asymptotically, even under their corresponding null hypotheses.

The standard test statistics for $\gamma_1 = 0$ in regression (14.21) and for $\gamma_2 = 0$ or $\gamma_1 = \gamma_2 = 0$ in regression (14.22) do not have their usual asymptotic distributions under the null hypothesis of a unit root; see Dickey and Fuller (1981). Therefore, instead of formally testing whether the coefficients of t and t^2 are equal to 0, many authors simply report the results of more than one unit root test.

Asymptotic Distributions of Dickey-Fuller Statistics

The eight Dickey-Fuller test statistics that we have discussed have distributions that tend to eight different asymptotic distributions as the sample size tends to infinity. These asymptotic distributions are referred to as **nonstandard distributions** or as **Dickey-Fuller distributions**.

We will analyze only the simplest case, that of the z_{nc} statistic, which is applicable only for the model (14.16) with $y_0 = 0$. For DGPs in that model, the test statistic (14.17) simplifies to

$$z_{nc} = n\frac{\sum_{t=2}^{n} w_{t-1}\varepsilon_t}{\sum_{t=1}^{n-1} w_t^2}. \tag{14.23}$$

We begin by considering the numerator of this expression. By (14.02), we have that

$$\sum_{t=2}^{n} w_{t-1}\varepsilon_t = \sum_{t=2}^{n}\Big(\varepsilon_t\sum_{s=1}^{t-1}\varepsilon_s\Big). \tag{14.24}$$

Since $\mathrm{E}(\varepsilon_t\varepsilon_s) = 0$ for $s < t$, it is clear that the expectation of this quantity is zero. The right-hand side of (14.24) has $\sum_{t=2}^{n}(t-1) = n(n-1)/2$ terms; recall the result used in (14.11). It is easy to see that the covariance of any two different terms of the double sum is zero, while the variance of each term is just 1. Consequently, the variance of (14.24) is $n(n-1)/2$. The variance of n^{-1} times (14.24) is therefore $(1-n^{-1})/2$, which tends to one half as $n \to \infty$. We conclude that n^{-1} times (14.24) is $O_p(1)$ as $n \to \infty$.

We saw in the last section, in equation (14.11), that the expectation of $\sum_{t=1}^{n} w_t^2$ is $n(n+1)/2$. Thus the expectation of the denominator of (14.23) is $n(n-1)/2$, since the last term of the sum is missing. It can be checked by a somewhat longer calculation (see Exercise 14.12) that the variance of the denominator is $O(n^4)$ as $n \to \infty$, and so both the expectation and variance of the denominator divided by n^2 are $O(1)$. We may therefore write (14.23) as

$$z_{nc} = \frac{n^{-1}\sum_{t=2}^{n} w_{t-1}\varepsilon_t}{n^{-2}\sum_{t=1}^{n-1} w_t^2}, \tag{14.25}$$

where everything is of order unity. This explains why $\hat\beta - 1$ is multiplied by n, rather than by $n^{1/2}$ or some other power of n, to obtain the z statistic.

In order to have convenient expressions for the probability limits of the random variables in the numerator and denominator of expression (14.25), we can make use of a continuous-time stochastic process called the **standardized Wiener process**, or sometimes **Brownian motion**. This process, denoted $W(r)$ for $0 \le r \le 1$, can be interpreted as the limit of the standardized random walk w_t as the length of each interval becomes infinitesimally small. It is defined as

$$W(r) \equiv \operatorname*{plim}_{n\to\infty} n^{-1/2} w_{[rn]} = \operatorname*{plim}_{n\to\infty} n^{-1/2}\sum_{t=1}^{[rn]}\varepsilon_t, \tag{14.26}$$

where $[rn]$ means the integer part of the quantity rn, which is a number between 0 and n. Intuitively, a Wiener process is like a continuous random walk defined on the 0–1 interval. Even though it is continuous, it varies erratically on any subinterval. Since ε_t is white noise, it follows from the central limit theorem that $W(r)$ is normally distributed for each $r \in [0, 1]$. Clearly, $\mathrm{E}(W(r)) = 0$, and, since $\mathrm{Var}(w_t) = t$, it can be seen that $\mathrm{Var}(W(r)) = r$. Thus $W(r)$ follows the $\mathrm{N}(0, r)$ distribution. For further properties of the Wiener process, see Exercise 14.13.

We can now express the limit as $n \to \infty$ of the numerator of the right-hand side of equation (14.25) in terms of the Wiener process $W(r)$. Note first that, since $w_{t+1} - w_t = \varepsilon_{t+1}$,

$$\sum_{t=1}^{n} w_t^2 = \sum_{t=0}^{n-1} \big(w_t + (w_{t+1} - w_t)\big)^2 = \sum_{t=0}^{n-1} w_t^2 + 2\sum_{t=0}^{n-1} w_t\varepsilon_{t+1} + \sum_{t=0}^{n-1} \varepsilon_{t+1}^2.$$

Since $w_0 = 0$, the term on the left-hand side above is the same as the first term of the rightmost expression, except for the term w_n^2. Thus we find that

$$\sum_{t=0}^{n-1} w_t\varepsilon_{t+1} = \sum_{t=1}^{n} w_{t-1}\varepsilon_t = \frac{1}{2}\Big(w_n^2 - \sum_{t=1}^{n} \varepsilon_t^2\Big).$$

Dividing by n and taking the limit as $n \to \infty$ gives

$$\operatorname*{plim}_{n\to\infty} \frac{1}{n}\sum_{t=1}^{n} w_{t-1}\varepsilon_t = \frac{1}{2}\big(W^2(1) - 1\big), \tag{14.27}$$

where we have used the law of large numbers to see that $\operatorname{plim} n^{-1}\sum \varepsilon_t^2 = 1$. Even in finite samples, it makes no difference whether the summation starts at $t = 1$ or $t = 2$ here, because $w_0 = 0$.

For the denominator of the right-hand side of equation (14.25), we see that

$$n^{-2}\sum_{t=1}^{n-1} w_t^2 \overset{a}{=} \frac{1}{n}\sum_{t=1}^{n-1} W^2\Big(\frac{t}{n}\Big).$$

If f is an ordinary nonrandom function defined on $[0, 1]$, the Riemann integral of f on that interval can be defined as the following limit:

$$\int_0^1 f(x)\,dx \equiv \lim_{n\to\infty} \frac{1}{n}\sum_{t=1}^{n} f\Big(\frac{t}{n}\Big). \tag{14.28}$$

It turns out to be possible to extend this definition to random integrands in a natural way. We may therefore write

$$\operatorname*{plim}_{n\to\infty} n^{-2}\sum_{t=1}^{n-1} w_t^2 = \int_0^1 W^2(r)\,dr. \tag{14.29}$$

The results (14.27) and (14.29) allow us to conclude that

$$\operatorname*{plim}_{n\to\infty} z_{nc} = \frac{\frac{1}{2}\big(W^2(1) - 1\big)}{\int_0^1 W^2(r)\,dr}. \tag{14.30}$$

A similar calculation (see Exercise 14.14) shows that

$$\operatorname*{plim}_{n\to\infty} \tau_{nc} = \frac{\frac{1}{2}\big(W^2(1) - 1\big)}{\big(\int_0^1 W^2(r)\,dr\big)^{1/2}}. \tag{14.31}$$

More formal proofs of these results can be found in many places, including Banerjee, Dolado, Galbraith, and Hendry (1993, Chapter 4), Hamilton (1994, Chapter 17), Fuller (1996), Hayashi (2000, Chapter 9), and Bierens (2001).

Results for the other six test statistics are more complicated. For z_c and τ_c, the limiting random variables can be expressed in terms of a centered Wiener process. Similarly, for z_{ct} and τ_{ct}, one needs a Wiener process that has been centered and detrended, and so on. For details, see Phillips and Perron (1988) and Bierens (2001). Exercise 14.15 looks in more detail at the limit of z_c.

Unfortunately, although the quantities (14.30) and (14.31) and their analogs for the other test statistics have well-defined distributions, there are no simple, analytical expressions for them.[2] In practice, therefore, these distributions are always evaluated by simulation methods. Published critical values are based on a very large number of simulations of either the actual test statistics or of quantities, based on simulated random walks, that approximate the expressions to which the statistics converge asymptotically under the null hypothesis. For example, in the case of (14.31), the quantity to which τ_{nc} tends asymptotically, such an approximation is given by

$$\frac{\frac{1}{2}(w_n^2 - 1)}{\big(n^{-1}\sum_{t=1}^{n} w_t^2\big)^{1/2}},$$

where the w_t are generated by the standardized random walk process (14.01).

Various critical values for unit root and related tests have been reported in the literature. Not all of these are particularly accurate. Some authors fail to use a sufficiently large number of replications, and many report results based on a single finite value of n instead of using more sophisticated techniques in order to estimate the asymptotic distributions of interest. See MacKinnon (1991, 1994, 1996). The last of these papers probably gives the most accurate estimates of Dickey-Fuller distributions that have been published. It also provides programs, which are freely available, that make it easy to calculate critical values and P values for all of the test statistics discussed here.

[2] Abadir (1995) does provide an analytical expression for the distribution of τ_{nc}, but it is certainly not simple.

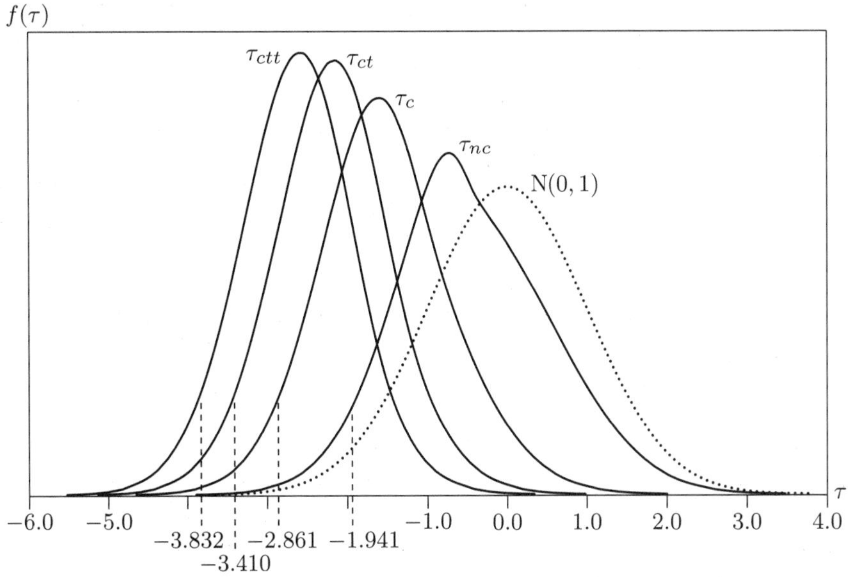

Figure 14.2 Asymptotic densities of Dickey-Fuller τ tests

The asymptotic densities of the τ_{nc}, τ_c, τ_{ct}, and τ_{ctt} statistics are shown in Figure 14.2. For purposes of comparison, the standard normal density is also shown. The differences between it and the four Dickey-Fuller τ distributions are striking. The critical values for one-tail tests at the .05 level based on the Dickey-Fuller distributions are also marked on the figure. These critical values become more negative as the number of deterministic regressors in the test regression increases. For the standard normal distribution, the corresponding critical value would be -1.645.

The asymptotic densities of the z_{nc}, z_c, z_{ct}, and z_{ctt} statistics are shown in Figure 14.3. These are much more spread out than the densities of the corresponding τ statistics, and the critical values are much larger in absolute value. Once again, these critical values become more negative as the number of deterministic regressors in the test regression increases. Since the test statistics are equal to $n(\hat{\beta} - 1)$, it is easy to see how these critical values are related to $\hat{\beta}$ for any given sample size. For example, when $n = 100$, the z_c test rejects the null hypothesis of a unit root whenever $\hat{\beta} < 0.859$, and the z_{ct} test rejects the null whenever $\hat{\beta} < 0.783$. Evidently, these tests have little power if the data are actually generated by a stationary AR(1) process with β reasonably close to unity.

Of course, the finite-sample distributions of Dickey-Fuller test statistics are not the same as their asymptotic distributions, although the latter generally provide reasonable approximations for samples of moderate size. The programs in MacKinnon (1996) actually provide finite-sample critical values and

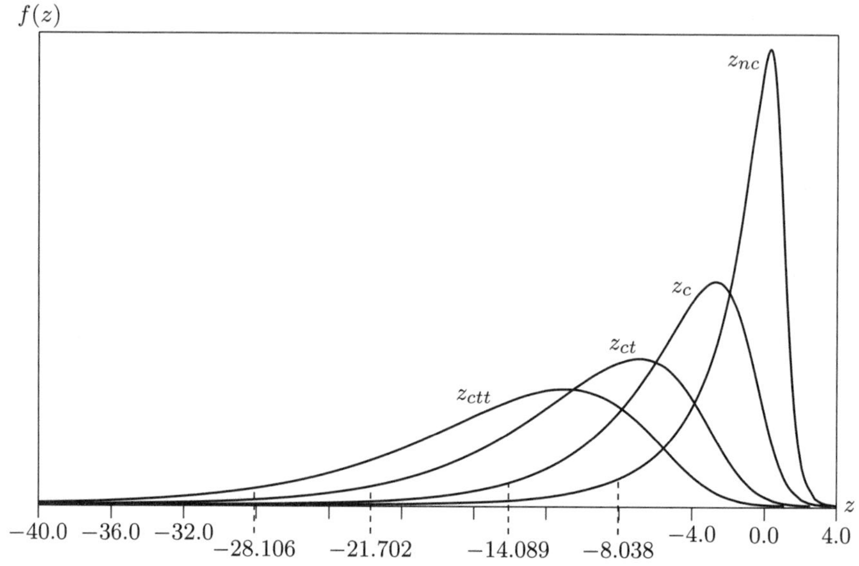

Figure 14.3 Asymptotic densities of Dickey-Fuller z tests

P values as well as asymptotic ones, but only under the strong assumptions that the error terms are normally and identically distributed. Neither of these assumptions is required for the asymptotic distributions to be valid. However, the assumption that the error terms are serially independent, which is often not at all plausible in practice, is required.

14.4 Serial Correlation and Unit Root Tests

Because the unit root test regressions (14.15), (14.18), (14.21), and (14.22) do not include any economic variables beyond y_{t-1}, the error terms u_t may well be serially correlated. This very often seems to be the case in practice. But this means that the Dickey-Fuller tests we have described are no longer asymptotically valid. A good many ways of modifying the tests have been proposed in order to make them valid in the presence of serial correlation of unknown form. The most popular approach is to use what are called **augmented Dickey-Fuller**, or **ADF**, tests. They were proposed originally by Dickey and Fuller (1979) under the assumption that the error terms follow an AR process of known order. Subsequent work by Said and Dickey (1984) and Phillips and Perron (1988) showed that they are asymptotically valid under much less restrictive assumptions.

Consider the test regressions (14.15), (14.18), (14.21), or (14.22). We can write any of these regressions as

$$\Delta y_t = \boldsymbol{X}_t \boldsymbol{\gamma}^{\circ} + (\beta - 1)y_{t-1} + u_t, \tag{14.32}$$

where $\boldsymbol{X}_t$ is a row vector that consists of whatever deterministic regressors are included in the test regression. Now suppose, for simplicity, that the error term u_t in (14.32) follows the stationary AR(1) process $u_t = \rho_1 u_{t-1} + e_t$, where e_t is white noise. Then regression (14.32) would become

$$\begin{aligned}\Delta y_t &= \boldsymbol{X}_t\boldsymbol{\gamma}^\circ - \rho_1\boldsymbol{X}_{t-1}\boldsymbol{\gamma}^\circ + (\rho_1+\beta-1)y_{t-1} - \beta\rho_1 y_{t-2} + e_t\\ &= \boldsymbol{X}_t\boldsymbol{\gamma} + (\rho_1+\beta-1-\beta\rho_1)y_{t-1} + \beta\rho_1(y_{t-1}-y_{t-2}) + e_t\\ &= \boldsymbol{X}_t\boldsymbol{\gamma} + (\beta-1)(1-\rho_1)y_{t-1} + \beta\rho_1\Delta y_{t-1} + e_t\\ &\equiv \boldsymbol{X}_t\boldsymbol{\gamma} + \beta' y_{t-1} + \delta_1\Delta y_{t-1} + e_t. \end{aligned} \tag{14.33}$$

We are able to replace $\boldsymbol{X}_t\boldsymbol{\gamma}^\circ - \rho_1\boldsymbol{X}_{t-1}\boldsymbol{\gamma}^\circ$ by $\boldsymbol{X}_t\boldsymbol{\gamma}$ in the second line here, for some choice of $\boldsymbol{\gamma}$, because every column of $\boldsymbol{X}_{t-1}$ lies in $\mathcal{S}(\boldsymbol{X})$. This is a consequence of the fact that $\boldsymbol{X}_t$ can include only deterministic variables such as a constant, a linear trend, and so on. Each element of $\boldsymbol{\gamma}$ is a linear combination of the elements of $\boldsymbol{\gamma}^\circ$. Expression (14.33) is just the regression function of (14.32), with one additional regressor, namely, Δy_{t-1}. Adding this regressor has caused the serially dependent error term u_t to be replaced by the white-noise error term e_t.

The ADF version of the τ statistic is simply the ordinary t statistic for the coefficient β' on y_{t-1} in (14.33) to be zero. If the serial correlation in the error terms were fully accounted for by an AR(1) process, it turns out that this statistic would have exactly the same asymptotic distribution as the ordinary τ statistic for the same specification of $\boldsymbol{X}_t$. The fact that β' is equal to $(\beta-1)(1-\rho_1)$ rather than $\beta-1$ does not matter. Because it is assumed that $|\rho_1| < 1$, this coefficient can be zero only if $\beta = 1$. Thus a test for $\beta' = 0$ in regression (14.33) is equivalent to a test for $\beta = 1$.

It is very easy to compute ADF τ statistics using regressions like (14.33), but it is not quite so easy to compute the corresponding z statistics. If $\hat{\beta}'$ were multiplied by n, the result would be $n(\hat{\beta}-1)(1-\hat{\rho}_1)$ rather than $n(\hat{\beta}-1)$. The former statistic clearly would not have the same asymptotic distribution as the latter. To avoid this problem, we need to divide by $1-\hat{\rho}_1$. Thus, a valid ADF z statistic based on regression (14.33) is $n\hat{\beta}'/(1-\hat{\rho}_1)$.

In this simple example, we were able to handle serial correlation by adding a single regressor, Δy_{t-1}, to the test regression. It is easy to see that, if u_t followed an AR(p) process, we would have to add p additional regressors, namely, Δy_{t-1}, Δy_{t-2}, and so on up to Δy_{t-p}. But if the error terms followed a moving-average process, or a process with a moving-average component, it might seem that we would have to add an infinite number of lagged values of Δy_t in order to model them. However, we do not have to do anything so extreme. As Said and Dickey (1984) showed, we can validly use ADF tests even when there is a moving-average component in the errors, provided we let the number of lags of Δy_t that are included tend to infinity at an appropriate rate, which turns out to be a rate slower than $n^{1/3}$. See Galbraith and Zinde-Walsh (1999). This is a consequence of the fact that every moving-average and ARMA process has an AR(∞) representation; see Section 13.2.

To summarize, provided the number of lags p is chosen appropriately, we can always base both types of ADF test on the regression

$$\Delta y_t = \boldsymbol{X}_t \gamma + \beta' y_{t-1} + \sum_{j=1}^{p} \delta_j \Delta y_{t-j} + e_t, \tag{14.34}$$

where $\boldsymbol{X}_t$ is a row vector of deterministic regressors, and β' and the δ_j are functions of β and the p coefficients in the AR(p) representation of the process for the error terms. The τ statistic is just the ordinary t statistic for $\beta' = 0$, and the z statistic is

$$z = \frac{n\hat{\beta}'}{(1 - \sum_{j=1}^{p} \hat{\delta}_j)}. \tag{14.35}$$

Under the null hypothesis of a unit root, and for a suitable choice of p (which must increase with n), the asymptotic distributions of both z and τ statistics are the same as those of ordinary Dickey-Fuller statistics for the same set of regressors $\boldsymbol{X}_t$. Because a general proof of this result is cumbersome, it is omitted, but an important part of the proof is treated in Exercise 14.17.

In practice, of course, since n is fixed for any sample, knowing that p should increase at a rate slower than $n^{1/3}$ provides no help in choosing p. Moreover, investigators do not know what process is actually generating the error terms. Thus what is generally done is simply to add as many lags of Δy_t as appear to be necessary to remove any serial correlation in the residuals. Formal procedures for determining just how many lags to add are discussed by Ng and Perron (1995, 2001). As we will discuss in the next section, conventional methods of inference, such as t and F tests, are asymptotically valid for any parameter that can be written as the coefficient of an I(0) variable. Since Δy_t is I(0) under the null hypothesis, this result applies to regression (14.34), and we can use standard methods for determining how many lags to include. If too few lags of Δy_t are added, the ADF test may tend to overreject the null hypothesis when it is true, but adding too many lags tends to reduce the power of the test.

The finite-sample performance of ADF tests is rather mixed. When the serial correlation in the error terms is well approximated by a low-order AR(p) process without any large, negative roots, ADF tests generally perform quite well in samples of moderate size. However, when the error terms seem to follow an MA or ARMA process in which the moving-average polynomial has a large negative root, they tend to overreject severely. For evidence on this point, see Schwert (1989) and Perron and Ng (1996), among others. Standard techniques for bootstrapping ADF tests do not seem to work particularly well in this situation, although they can improve matters somewhat; see Li and

Maddala (1996). The problem is that it is difficult to generate bootstrap error terms with the same time-series properties as the unknown process that actually generated the u_t. Recent work in this area includes Park (2002) and Chang and Park (2003).

Alternatives to ADF Tests

Many alternatives to, and variations of, augmented Dickey-Fuller tests have been proposed. Among the best known are the tests proposed by Phillips and Perron (1988). These **Phillips-Perron**, or **PP**, tests have the same asymptotic distributions as the corresponding ADF z and τ tests, but they are computed quite differently. The test statistics are based on a regression like (14.32), without any modification to allow for serial correlation. A form of HAC estimator is then used when computing the test statistics to ensure that serial correlation does not affect their asymptotic distributions. Because there is now a good deal of evidence that PP tests perform less well in finite samples than ADF tests, we will not discuss them further; see Schwert (1989) and Perron and Ng (1996), among others, for evidence on this point.

A procedure that does have some advantages over the standard ADF test is the **ADF-GLS test** proposed by Elliott, Rothenberg, and Stock (1996). The idea is to obtain higher power by estimating $\boldsymbol{\gamma}$ prior to estimating β'. As can readily be seen from Figures 14.2 and 14.3, the more deterministic regressors we include in $\boldsymbol{X}_t$, the larger (in absolute value) become the critical values for ADF tests based on regression (14.33). Inevitably, this reduces the power of the tests. The ADF-GLS test estimates $\boldsymbol{\gamma}^\circ$ by running the regression

$$y_t - \bar{\rho} y_{t-1} = (\boldsymbol{X}_t - \bar{\rho}\boldsymbol{X}_{t-1})\boldsymbol{\gamma}^\circ + v_t, \tag{14.36}$$

where $\boldsymbol{X}_t$ contains either a constant or a constant and a trend, and the fixed scalar $\bar{\rho}$ is equal to $1 + \bar{c}/n$, with $\bar{c} = -7$ when $\boldsymbol{X}_t$ contains just a constant and $\bar{c} = -13.5$ when it contains both a constant and a trend. Notice that $\bar{\rho}$ tends to unity as $n \to \infty$. Let $\hat{\boldsymbol{\gamma}}^\circ$ denote the estimate of $\boldsymbol{\gamma}^\circ$ obtained from regression (14.36). Then construct the variable $y'_t = y_t - \boldsymbol{X}_t\hat{\boldsymbol{\gamma}}^\circ$ and run the test regression

$$\Delta y'_t = \beta' y'_{t-1} + \sum_{j=1}^{p} \delta_j \Delta y'_{t-j} + e_t,$$

which looks just like regression (14.33) for the case with no constant term. The test statistic is the ordinary t statistic for $\beta' = 0$. When $\boldsymbol{X}_t$ contains only a constant term, this test statistic has exactly the same asymptotic distribution as τ_{nc}. When $\boldsymbol{X}_t$ contains both a constant and a trend, it has an asymptotic distribution that was derived and tabulated by Elliott, Rothenberg, and Stock (1996). This distribution, which depends on $\bar{c}$, is quite close to that of τ_c.

There is a massive literature on unit root tests, most of which we will not attempt to discuss. Hayashi (2000) and Bierens (2001) provide recent treatments that are more detailed than ours.

14.5 Cointegration

Economic theory often suggests that two or more economic variables should be linked more or less closely. Examples include interest rates on assets of different maturities, prices of similar commodities in different countries, disposable income and consumption, government spending and tax revenues, wages and prices, and the money supply and the price level. Although deterministic relationships among the variables in any one of these sets are usually assumed to hold only in the long run, economic forces are expected to act in the direction of eliminating short-run deviations from these long-term relationships.

A great many of the economic variables mentioned above are, or at least appear to be, I(1). As we saw in Section 14.2, random variables which are I(1) tend to diverge as $n \to \infty$, because their unconditional variances are proportional to n. Thus it might seem that two or more such variables could never be expected to obey any sort of long-run relationship. But, as we will see, variables that are all individually I(1), and hence divergent, can in a certain sense diverge together. Formally, it is possible for some linear combinations of a set of I(1) variables to be I(0). If that is the case, the variables are said to be **cointegrated**. When variables are cointegrated, they satisfy one or more long-run relationships, although they may diverge substantially from these relationships in the short run.

VAR Models with Unit Roots

In Chapter 13, we saw that a convenient way to model several time series simultaneously is to use a vector autoregression, or VAR model, of the type introduced in Section 13.7. Just as with univariate AR models, a VAR model can have unit roots and so give rise to nonstationary series. We begin by considering the simplest case, namely, a VAR(1) model with just two variables. We assume, at least for the present, that there are neither constants nor trends. Therefore, we can write the model as

$$\begin{aligned} y_{t1} &= \phi_{11}y_{t-1,1} + \phi_{12}y_{t-1,2} + u_{t1}, \\ y_{t2} &= \phi_{21}y_{t-1,1} + \phi_{22}y_{t-1,2} + u_{t2}, \end{aligned} \qquad \begin{bmatrix} u_{t1} \\ u_{t2} \end{bmatrix} \sim \mathrm{IID}(\mathbf{0}, \boldsymbol{\Omega}). \tag{14.37}$$

Let $\boldsymbol{z}_t$ and $\boldsymbol{u}_t$ be 2-vectors, the former with elements y_{t1} and y_{t2} and the latter with elements u_{t1} and u_{t2}, and let $\boldsymbol{\Phi}$ be the 2×2 matrix with ij^{th} element ϕ_{ij}. Then equations (14.37) can be written as

$$\boldsymbol{z}_t = \boldsymbol{\Phi}\boldsymbol{z}_{t-1} + \boldsymbol{u}_t, \qquad \boldsymbol{u}_t \sim \mathrm{IID}(\mathbf{0}, \boldsymbol{\Omega}). \tag{14.38}$$

In order to keep the analysis as simple as possible, we assume that $\boldsymbol{z}_0 = \mathbf{0}$. This implies that the solution to the recursion (14.38) is

$$\boldsymbol{z}_t = \sum_{s=1}^{t} \boldsymbol{\Phi}^{t-s}\boldsymbol{u}_s. \tag{14.39}$$

A univariate AR model has a unit root if the coefficient on the lagged dependent variable is equal to unity. Analogously, as we now show, the VAR model (14.37) has a unit root if an eigenvalue of the matrix $\boldsymbol{\Phi}$ is equal to 1.

Recall from Section 12.8 that the matrix $\boldsymbol{\Phi}$ has an eigenvalue λ and corresponding eigenvector $\boldsymbol{\xi}$ if $\boldsymbol{\Phi\xi} = \lambda\boldsymbol{\xi}$. For a 2×2 matrix, there are two eigenvalues, λ_1 and λ_2. If $\lambda_1 \neq \lambda_2$, there are two corresponding eigenvectors, $\boldsymbol{\xi}_1$ and $\boldsymbol{\xi}_2$, which are linearly independent; see Exercise 14.18. If $\lambda_1 = \lambda_2$, we assume, with only a slight loss of generality, that there still exist two linearly independent eigenvectors $\boldsymbol{\xi}_1$ and $\boldsymbol{\xi}_2$. Then, as in equation (12.117), we can write

$$\boldsymbol{\Phi\Xi} = \boldsymbol{\Xi\Lambda}, \text{ with } \boldsymbol{\Xi} \equiv [\boldsymbol{\xi}_1 \quad \boldsymbol{\xi}_2] \text{ and } \boldsymbol{\Lambda} = \begin{bmatrix} \lambda_1 & 0 \\ 0 & \lambda_2 \end{bmatrix}.$$

It follows that $\boldsymbol{\Phi}^2\boldsymbol{\Xi} = \boldsymbol{\Phi}(\boldsymbol{\Phi\Xi}) = \boldsymbol{\Phi\Xi\Lambda} = \boldsymbol{\Xi\Lambda}^2$. Performing this operation repeatedly shows that, for any positive integer s, $\boldsymbol{\Phi}^s\boldsymbol{\Xi} = \boldsymbol{\Xi\Lambda}^s$.

The solution (14.39) can be rewritten in terms of the eigenvalues and eigenvectors of $\boldsymbol{\Phi}$ as follows:

$$\boldsymbol{\Xi}^{-1}\boldsymbol{z}_t = \sum_{s=1}^{t} \boldsymbol{\Lambda}^{t-s}\boldsymbol{\Xi}^{-1}\boldsymbol{u}_s. \tag{14.40}$$

The inverse matrix $\boldsymbol{\Xi}^{-1}$ exists because $\boldsymbol{\xi}_1$ and $\boldsymbol{\xi}_2$ are linearly independent. It is then not hard to show that the solution (14.40) can be written as

$$\begin{aligned} y_{t1} &= \xi_{11}\sum_{s=1}^{t}\lambda_1^{t-s}e_{s1} + \xi_{12}\sum_{s=1}^{t}\lambda_2^{t-s}e_{s2}, \\ y_{t2} &= \xi_{21}\sum_{s=1}^{t}\lambda_1^{t-s}e_{s1} + \xi_{22}\sum_{s=1}^{t}\lambda_2^{t-s}e_{s2}, \end{aligned} \tag{14.41}$$

where $\boldsymbol{e}_t \equiv [e_{t1} \,\vdots\, e_{t2}] \sim \text{IID}(\boldsymbol{0}, \boldsymbol{\Sigma})$, $\boldsymbol{\Sigma} \equiv \boldsymbol{\Xi}^{-1}\boldsymbol{\Omega}(\boldsymbol{\Xi}^{\top})^{-1}$, and ξ_{ij} is the ij^{th} element of $\boldsymbol{\Xi}$.

It can be seen from equations (14.41) that the series y_{t1} and y_{t2} are both linear combinations of the two series

$$v_{t1} \equiv \sum_{s=1}^{t}\lambda_1^{t-s}e_{s1} \quad \text{and} \quad v_{t2} \equiv \sum_{s=1}^{t}\lambda_2^{t-s}e_{s2}. \tag{14.42}$$

If both eigenvalues are less than 1 in absolute value, then v_{t1} and v_{t2} are I(0). If both eigenvalues are equal to 1, then the two series are random walks, and consequently y_{t1} and y_{t2} are I(1). If one eigenvalue, say λ_1, is equal to 1 while the other is less than 1 in absolute value, then v_{t1} is a random walk, and v_{t2} is I(0). In general, then, both y_{t1} and y_{t2} are I(1), although there exists a linear combination of them, namely v_{t2}, that is I(0). According to the definition we gave above, y_{t1} and y_{t2} are cointegrated in this case. Each differs from a multiple of the random walk v_{t1} by a process that, being I(0), does not diverge and has a finite variance as $t \to \infty$.

Quite generally, if the series y_{t1} and y_{t2} are cointegrated, then there exists a 2–vector $\boldsymbol{\eta}$ with elements η_1 and η_2 such that

$$\nu_t \equiv \boldsymbol{\eta}^\top \boldsymbol{z}_t = \eta_1 y_{t1} + \eta_2 y_{t2} \tag{14.43}$$

is I(0). The vector $\boldsymbol{\eta}$ is called a **cointegrating vector**. It is clearly not unique, since it could be multiplied by any nonzero scalar without affecting anything except the sign and the scale of ν_t.

Equation (14.43) is an example of a **cointegrating regression**. This particular one is unnecessarily restrictive. In practice, we might expect the relationship between y_{t1} and y_{t2} to change gradually over time. We can allow for this by adding a constant term and, perhaps, one or more trend terms, so as to obtain

$$\boldsymbol{\eta}^\top \boldsymbol{z}_t = \boldsymbol{X}_t \gamma + \nu_t, \tag{14.44}$$

where $\boldsymbol{X}_t$ denotes a deterministic row vector that may or may not have any elements. If it does, the first element is a constant, the second, if it exists, is normally a linear time trend, the third, if it exists, is normally a quadratic time trend, and so on. There could also be seasonal dummy variables in $\boldsymbol{X}_t$. Since $\boldsymbol{z}_t$ could contain more than two variables, equation (14.44) is actually a very general way of writing a cointegrating regression. The error term $\nu_t = \boldsymbol{\eta}^\top \boldsymbol{z}_t - \boldsymbol{X}_t \gamma$ that is implicitly defined in equation (14.44) is called the **equilibrium error**.

Unless each of a set of cointegrated variables is I(1), the cointegrating vector is trivial, since it has only one nonzero element, namely, the one that corresponds to the I(0) variable. Therefore, before estimating equations like (14.43) and (14.44), it is customary to test the null hypothesis that each of the series in $\boldsymbol{z}_t$ has a unit root. If this hypothesis is rejected for any of the series, it is pointless to retain it in the set of possibly cointegrated variables.

When there are more than two variables involved, there may be more than one cointegrating vector. For the remainder of this section, however, we will focus on the case in which there is just one such vector. The more general case, in which there are g variables and up to $g - 1$ cointegrating vectors, will be discussed in the next section.

It is not entirely clear how to specify the deterministic vector $\boldsymbol{X}_t$ in a cointegrating regression like (14.44). Ordinary t and F tests are not valid, partly because the stochastic regressors are not I(0) and any trending regressors do not satisfy the usual conditions for the matrix $n^{-1}\boldsymbol{X}^\top\boldsymbol{X}$ to tend to a positive definite matrix as $n \to \infty$, and partly because the error terms are likely to display serial correlation. As with unit root tests, investigators commonly use several choices for $\boldsymbol{X}_t$ and present several sets of results.

Estimating Cointegrating Vectors

If we have a set of I(1) variables that may be cointegrated, we usually wish to estimate the parameters of the cointegrating vector $\boldsymbol{\eta}$. Logic dictates that, before doing so, we should perform one or more tests to see if the data seem compatible with the existence of a cointegrating vector, but it is easier to discuss estimation before testing. Testing is the topic of the next section.

The simplest way to estimate a cointegrating vector is just to pick one of the I(1) variables and regress it on $\boldsymbol{X}_t$ and the other I(1) variables by OLS. Let $\boldsymbol{Y}_t \equiv [y_t \quad \boldsymbol{Y}_{t2}]$ be a $1 \times g$ row vector containing all the I(1) variables, y_t being the one selected as regressand. The OLS regression can then be written as

$$y_t = \boldsymbol{X}_t \boldsymbol{\gamma} + \boldsymbol{Y}_{t2} \boldsymbol{\eta}_2 + \nu_t, \tag{14.45}$$

where $\boldsymbol{\eta} = [1 \;\vdots\; -\boldsymbol{\eta}_2]$. The nonuniqueness of $\boldsymbol{\eta}$ is resolved here by setting the first element to 1. The OLS estimator $\hat{\boldsymbol{\eta}}_2^{\text{L}}$ is known as the **levels estimator**.

At first sight, this approach seems to ignore all the precepts of good econometric practice. If the y_{ti} are generated by a DGP belonging to a VAR model, such as (14.37) in the case of two variables, then they are all endogenous. Therefore, unless the error terms in every equation of the VAR model happen to be uncorrelated with those in every other equation, the regressors $\boldsymbol{Y}_{t2}$ in equation (14.45) must be correlated with the error term ν_t. In addition, this error term is often serially correlated. As we will see below, for the model (14.37), ν_t depends on the serially correlated series v_{t2} defined in the second of equations (14.42). Nevertheless, the levels estimator of the vector $\boldsymbol{\eta}_2$ is not only consistent but **super-consistent**, in a sense to be made explicit shortly. This result indicates just how different asymptotic theory is when I(1) variables are involved.

Let us suppose that we have two cointegrated series, y_{t1} and y_{t2}, generated by equations (14.41), with $\lambda_1 = 1$ and $|\lambda_2| < 1$. By use of (14.42), we have

$$y_{t1} = \xi_{11} v_{t1} + \xi_{12} v_{t2}, \quad \text{and} \quad y_{t2} = \xi_{21} v_{t1} + \xi_{22} v_{t2}, \tag{14.46}$$

where v_{t1} is a random walk, and v_{t2} is I(0). For simplicity, suppose that $\boldsymbol{X}_t$ is empty in regression (14.45), $y_t = y_{t1}$, and $\boldsymbol{Y}_{t2}$ has the single element y_{t2}. Then the levels estimator is

$$\hat{\eta}_2^{\text{L}} = \frac{\sum_{t=1}^n y_{t2} y_{t1}}{\sum_{t=1}^n y_{t2}^2}, \tag{14.47}$$

where $\hat{\eta}_2^{\text{L}}$ is the OLS estimator of the single element of $\boldsymbol{\eta}_2$.

It follows from equations (14.46) that the denominator of the right-hand side of equation (14.47) is

$$\xi_{21}^2 \sum_{t=1}^n v_{t1}^2 + 2\xi_{21}\xi_{22} \sum_{t=1}^n v_{t1} v_{t2} + \xi_{22}^2 \sum_{t=1}^n v_{t2}^2. \tag{14.48}$$

Since $\text{Var}(e_{t1}) = \sigma_{11}$, the element in the first row and column of the covariance matrix $\boldsymbol{\Sigma}$ of the innovations e_{t1} and e_{t2}, we see that the random walk v_{t1} can be expressed as $\sigma_{11}^{1/2} w_t$, for a standardized random walk w_t. We saw from the argument following expression (14.10) that $\sum_{t=1}^{n} w_t^2 = O(n^2)$ as $n \to \infty$, and so the first term of (14.48) is $O(n^2)$. The series v_{t2} has a stationary variance; in fact $\text{E}(v_{t2}^2)$ tends to $\sigma_{22}/(1 - |\lambda_2|^2)$ as $t \to \infty$. By the law of large numbers, therefore, the last term of (14.48), divided by n, tends to this stationary variance as $n \to \infty$. The term itself is thus $O(n)$. By an argument similar to the one we used to show that the expression (14.24) is $O(n)$, we can show that the middle term in (14.48) is $O(n)$; see Exercise 14.19.

In like manner, we see that the numerator of the right-hand side of (14.47) is

$$\xi_{11}\xi_{21}\sum_{t=1}^{n} v_{t1}^2 + (\xi_{11}\xi_{22} + \xi_{12}\xi_{21})\sum_{t=1}^{n} v_{t1}v_{t2} + \xi_{12}\xi_{22}\sum_{t=1}^{n} v_{t2}^2. \tag{14.49}$$

The first term here is $O(n^2)$, and the other two are $O(n)$. Thus, if we divide both numerator and denominator in (14.47) by n^2, only the first terms in expressions (14.48) and (14.49) contribute nonzero limits as $n \to \infty$. The factors $\xi_{21}\sum v_{t1}^2$ cancel, and the limit of $\hat{\eta}_2^{\text{L}}$ is therefore seen to be ξ_{11}/ξ_{21}. From equations (14.46), it follows that

$$y_{t1} - \frac{\xi_{11}}{\xi_{21}} y_{t2} = \frac{\xi_{12}\xi_{21} - \xi_{11}\xi_{22}}{\xi_{21}} v_{t2}, \tag{14.50}$$

from which, given that v_{t2} is stationary, we conclude that $[1 \;\vdots\; -\xi_{11}/\xi_{21}]$ is indeed the cointegrating vector. It follows that $\hat{\eta}_2^{\text{L}}$ is consistent for the parameter $\eta_2 \equiv \xi_{11}/\xi_{21}$.

If we divide expression (14.48) by $\xi_{21}\sum v_{t1}^2$, which is $O(n^2)$, we obtain the result $\xi_{21} + O(n^{-1})$, since the last two terms of (14.48) are $O(n)$. Similarly, dividing expression (14.49) by the same quantity gives $\xi_{11} + O(n^{-1})$. It follows that $\hat{\eta}_2^{\text{L}} - \eta_2 = O(n^{-1})$. This is the property of **super-consistency** mentioned above. It implies that the estimation error $\hat{\eta}_2^{\text{L}} - \eta_2$ tends to zero like n^{-1} as $n \to \infty$. We may say that $\hat{\eta}_2^{\text{L}}$ is ***n*-consistent**, unlike the root-n consistent estimators of conventional asymptotic theory. Note, however, that instincts based on conventional theory are correct to the extent that $\hat{\eta}_2^{\text{L}}$ is biased in finite samples. This fact can be worrisome in practice, and it is therefore often desirable to find alternative ways of estimating cointegrating vectors.

With a little more work, it can be seen that the super-consistency result applies more generally to cointegrating regressions like (14.44), with deterministic regressors such as a constant and a trend, when one element of $\boldsymbol{Y}_t$ is arbitrarily given a coefficient of unity and the others moved to the right-hand side. For a rigorous discussion of this result, see Stock (1987). Note also that we do not as yet have the means to perform statistical inference on cointegrating vectors, since we have not studied the asymptotic distribution of the order-unity quantity $n(\hat{\boldsymbol{\eta}}_2^{\text{L}} - \boldsymbol{\eta}_2)$, which turns out to be nonstandard. We will discuss this point further later in this section.

Estimation Using an ECM

We mentioned in Section 13.4 that an error correction model can be used even when the data are nonstationary. In order to justify this assertion, we start again from the simplest case, in which the two series y_{t1} and y_{t2} are generated by the two equations (14.46). From the definition (14.42) of the I(0) process v_{t2}, we have

$$\Delta v_{t2} = (\lambda_2 - 1)v_{t-1,2} + e_{t2}. \tag{14.51}$$

We may invert equations (14.46) as follows:

$$v_{t1} = \xi^{11} y_{t1} + \xi^{12} y_{t2}, \quad \text{and} \quad v_{t2} = \xi^{21} y_{t1} + \xi^{22} y_{t2}, \tag{14.52}$$

where ξ^{ij} is the ij^{th} element of the inverse of the eigenvector matrix Ξ with typical element ξ_{ij}. If we use the expression for v_{t2} and its first difference given by equations (14.52), then equation (14.51) becomes

$$\xi^{21}\Delta y_{t1} = -\xi^{22}\Delta y_{t2} + (\lambda_2 - 1)(\xi^{21} y_{t-1,1} + \xi^{22} y_{t-1,2}) + e_{t2}.$$

Dividing by ξ^{21} and noting that the relation between Ξ and Ξ^{-1} implies that $\xi^{21}\xi_{11} + \xi^{22}\xi_{21} = 0$, we obtain the error-correction model

$$\Delta y_{t1} = \eta_2 \Delta y_{t2} + (\lambda_2 - 1)(y_{t-1,1} - \eta_2 y_{t-1,2}) + e'_{t2}, \tag{14.53}$$

where, as above, $\eta_2 = \xi_{11}/\xi_{21}$ is the second component of the cointegrating vector, and $e'_{t2} = e_{t2}/\xi^{21}$. Although the notation is somewhat different from that used in Section 13.3, it is easy enough to see that equation (14.53) is a special case of an ECM like (13.62). Notice that it must be estimated by nonlinear least squares.

In general, equation (14.53) is an unbalanced regression, because it mixes the first differences, which are I(0), with the levels, which are I(1). But the linear combination $y_{t-1,1} - \eta_2 y_{t-1,2}$ is I(0), on account of the cointegration of y_{t1} and y_{t2}. The term $(\lambda_2 - 1)(y_{t-1,1} - \eta_2 y_{t-1,2})$ is precisely the error-correction term of this ECM. Indeed, $y_{t-1,1} - \eta_2 y_{t-1,2}$ is the equilibrium error, and it influences Δy_{t1} through the negative coefficient $\lambda_2 - 1$.

The parameter η_2 appears twice in (14.53), once in the equilibrium error, and once as the coefficient of Δy_{t2}. The implied restriction is a consequence of the very special structure of the DGP (14.46). It is the parameter that appears in the equilibrium error that defines the cointegrating vector, not the coefficient of Δy_{t2}. This follows because it is the equilibrium error that defines the *long-run* relationship linking y_{t1} and y_{t2}, whereas the coefficient of Δy_{t2} is a *short-run* multiplier, determining the immediate impact of a change in y_{t2} on y_{t1}. It is usually thought to be too restrictive to require that the long-run and short-run multipliers should be the same, and so, for the purposes of estimation and testing, equation (14.53) is normally replaced by

$$\Delta y_{t1} = \alpha \Delta y_{t2} + \delta_1 y_{t-1,1} + \delta_2 y_{t-1,2} + e_t, \tag{14.54}$$

where the new parameter α is the short-run multiplier, $\delta_1 = \lambda_2 - 1$, and $\delta_2 = (1 - \lambda_2)\eta_2$. Since (14.54) is just a linear regression, the parameter of interest, which is η_2, can be estimated by $\hat{\eta}_2^{\rm E} \equiv -\hat{\delta}_2/\hat{\delta}_1$, using the OLS estimates of δ_1 and δ_2.

Equation (14.54) is without doubt an unbalanced regression, and so we must expect that the OLS estimates do not have their usual distributions. It turns out that the **ECM estimator** $\hat{\eta}_2^{\rm E}$ is a super-consistent estimator of η_2. In fact, it is usually less biased than the levels estimator $\hat{\eta}_2^{\rm L}$ obtained from the simple regression of y_{t2} on y_{t1}, as readers are invited to check by simulation in Exercise 14.21.

In the general case, with k cointegrated variables, we may estimate the cointegrating vector using the linear regression

$$\Delta y_t = \boldsymbol{X}_t\boldsymbol{\gamma} + \Delta\boldsymbol{Y}_{t2}\boldsymbol{\alpha} + \delta y_{t-1} + \boldsymbol{Y}_{t-1,2}\boldsymbol{\delta}_2 + e_t, \tag{14.55}$$

where, as before, $\boldsymbol{X}_t$ is a vector of deterministic regressors, $\boldsymbol{\gamma}$ is the associated parameter vector, $\boldsymbol{Y}_t = [y_t \quad \boldsymbol{Y}_{t2}]$ is a $1 \times k$ vector, δ is a scalar, and $\boldsymbol{\alpha}$ and $\boldsymbol{\delta}_2$ are both $(k-1)$–vectors. Regression (14.54) is evidently a special case of regression (14.55). The super-consistent ECM estimator of $\boldsymbol{\eta}_2$ is then the ratio of the OLS estimator $\hat{\boldsymbol{\alpha}}$ to the OLS estimator $\hat{\delta}$.

Other Approaches

When we cannot, or do not want to, specify an ECM, at least two other methods are available for estimating a cointegrating vector. One, proposed by Phillips and Hansen (1990), is called **fully modified estimation**. The idea is to modify the OLS estimate of $\boldsymbol{\eta}_2$ in equation (14.45) by subtracting an estimate of the bias. The result turns out to be asymptotically multivariate normal, and it is possible to estimate its asymptotic covariance matrix. To explain just how fully modified estimation works would require more space than we have available. Interested readers should consult the original paper or Banerjee, Dolado, Galbraith, and Hendry (1993, Chapter 7).

A second approach, which is due to Saikkonen (1991), is much simpler to describe and implement. We run the regression

$$y_t = \boldsymbol{X}_t\boldsymbol{\gamma} + \boldsymbol{Y}_{t2}\boldsymbol{\eta}_2 + \sum_{j=-p}^{p} \Delta\boldsymbol{Y}_{t+j,2}\boldsymbol{\delta}_j + \nu_t \tag{14.56}$$

by OLS. Observe that regression (14.56) is just regression (14.45) with the addition of p leads and p lags of the first differences of $\boldsymbol{Y}_{t2}$. As with augmented Dickey-Fuller tests, the idea is to add enough leads and lags so that the error terms appear to be serially independent. Provided that p is allowed to increase at the appropriate rate as $n \to \infty$, this regression yields estimates that are asymptotically efficient.

Inference in Regressions with I(1) Variables

From what we have said so far, it might seem that standard asymptotic results never apply when a regression contains one or more regressors that are I(1). This is true for spurious regressions like (14.12), for unit root test regressions like (14.18), and for error-correction models like (14.54). In all these cases, certain statistics that are computed as ordinary t statistics actually follow nonstandard distributions asymptotically.

However, it is not true that the t statistic on every parameter in a regression that involves I(1) variables follows a nonstandard distribution asymptotically. It is not even true that the t statistic on every coefficient of an I(1) variable follows such a distribution. Instead, as Sims, Stock, and Watson (1990) showed in a famous paper, the t statistic on any parameter that appears only as the coefficient of an I(0) variable, perhaps after the regressors are rearranged, follows the standard normal distribution asymptotically. Similarly, an F statistic for a test of the hypothesis that any set of parameters is zero follows its usual asymptotic distribution if all the parameters can be written as coefficients of I(0) variables *at the same time*. On the other hand, t statistics and F statistics corresponding to parameters that do not satisfy this condition generally follow nonstandard limiting distributions, although there are certain exceptions that we will not discuss here; see West (1988) and Sims, Stock, and Watson (1990).

We will not attempt to prove these results, which are by no means trivial. Proofs may be found in the original paper by Sims *et al.*, and there is a somewhat simpler discussion in Banerjee, Dolado, Galbraith, and Hendry (1993, Chapter 6). Instead, we will consider two examples that should serve to illustrate the nature of the results. First, consider a simple ECM reparametrized as equation (14.54). When y_{t1} and y_{t2} are not cointegrated, it is impossible to arrange things so that δ_1 is the coefficient of an I(0) variable. Therefore, the t statistic for $\delta_1 = 0$ follows a nonstandard distribution asymptotically. However, when y_{t1} and y_{t2} are cointegrated, the quantity $y_{t-1,1} - \eta_2 y_{t-1,2}$ is I(0). In this case, therefore, δ_1 is the coefficient of an I(0) variable, and the t statistic for $\delta_1 = d_1$ is asymptotically distributed as N(0, 1), if the true value of δ_1 is the negative number d_1.

We can rewrite equation (14.54) as

$$\Delta y_{t1} = \alpha \Delta y_{t2} - \delta_2(\eta_1 y_{t-1,1} - y_{t-1,2}) + e_t, \tag{14.57}$$

where $\eta_1 = 1/\eta_2 = -\delta_1/\delta_2$. In equation (14.57), δ_2 is written as the coefficient of a variable that is I(0) if y_{t1} and y_{t2} are cointegrated. It follows that the t statistic for a test that δ_2 is equal to its true (presumably positive) value is asymptotically distributed as N(0, 1).

We have just seen that, when y_{t1} and y_{t2} are cointegrated, equation (14.54) can be rewritten is such a way that either δ_1 or δ_2 is the coefficient of an I(0) variable. Consequently, the t statistic on *every* coefficient in (14.54) is asymptotically normally distributed. Despite this, it is *not* the case that an F statistic for a test concerning both δ_1 and δ_2 follows its usual asymptotic distribution under the null hypothesis. This is because we cannot rewrite (14.54) so that *both* δ_1 and δ_2 are coefficients of I(0) variables at the same time. Indeed, if $\hat{\delta}_1$ and $\hat{\delta}_2$ were jointly asymptotically normal, the ratio $\hat{\eta}_2^{\rm E}$ would also be asymptotically normal, with the same rate of convergence, in contradiction of the result that $\hat{\eta}_2^{\rm E}$ is super-consistent.

It is not obvious how it is possible for both $\hat{\delta}_1$ and $\hat{\delta}_2$ to be asymptotically normal, with the usual root-n rate of convergence, while the ratio $\hat{\eta}_2^{\rm E}$ is super-consistent. The phenomenon is explained by the fact, which we will not attempt to demonstrate in detail here, that the two random variables $n^{1/2}(\hat{\delta}_1 - \delta_1)/\delta_1$ and $n^{1/2}(\hat{\delta}_2 - \delta_2)/\delta_2$ tend as $n \to \infty$ to exactly the same random variable, and so differ only at order $n^{-1/2}$. The two variables are therefore perfectly correlated asymptotically. It is straightforward to show (see Exercise 14.23) that this implies that

$$-\hat{\eta}_2^{\rm E} = \frac{\hat{\delta}_2}{\hat{\delta}_1} = \frac{\delta_2}{\delta_1} + O_p(n^{-1}). \tag{14.58}$$

This result expresses the super-consistency of $\hat{\eta}_2^{\rm E}$.

As a second example, consider the augmented Dickey-Fuller test regression

$$\Delta y_t = \gamma + \beta' y_{t-1} + \delta_1 \Delta y_{t-1} + e_t, \tag{14.59}$$

which is a special case of equation (14.33). This can be rewritten as

$$\begin{aligned} \Delta y_t &= \gamma + \beta' y_{t-1} + \delta_1 y_{t-1} - \delta_1 y_{t-2} + e_t \\ &= \gamma + \beta'(y_{t-1} - y_{t-2}) + \delta_1 y_{t-1} + (\beta' - \delta_1) y_{t-2} + e_t. \end{aligned} \tag{14.60}$$

When y_t is I(1), we cannot write this regression in such a way that β' is the coefficient of an I(0) variable. In the second line of (14.60), it does multiply such a variable, since $y_{t-1} - y_{t-2}$ is I(0), but it also multiplies y_{t-2}, which is I(1). Thus we may expect that the t statistic for $\beta' = 0$ has a nonstandard asymptotic distribution. As we saw in Section 14.3, that is indeed the case, since it follows the Dickey-Fuller τ_c distribution graphed in Figure 14.2.

On the other hand, because Δy_{t-1} is I(0), the t statistic for $\delta_1 = 0$ in equation (14.59) does follow the standard normal distribution asymptotically. Moreover, F tests for the coefficients of more than one lag of Δy_t to be jointly zero also yield statistics that follow the usual asymptotic F distribution. That is why we can validly use standard tests to decide how many lags of Δy_{t-1} to include in the test regression (14.34) that is used to perform augmented Dickey-Fuller tests.

Estimation by a Vector Autoregression

The procedures we have discussed so far for estimating and making inferences about cointegrating vectors are all in essence single-equation methods. A very popular alternative to those methods is to estimate a vector autoregression, or VAR, for all of the possibly cointegrated variables. The best-known such methods were introduced by Johansen (1988, 1991) and initially applied by Johansen and Juselius (1990, 1992), and a similar approach was introduced independently by Ahn and Reinsel (1988, 1990). Johansen (1995) provides a detailed exposition. An advantage of these methods is that they can allow for more than one cointegrating relation among a set of more than two variables.

Consider the VAR

$$\boldsymbol{Y}_t = \boldsymbol{X}_t\boldsymbol{B} + \sum_{i=1}^{p+1} \boldsymbol{Y}_{t-i}\,\boldsymbol{\Phi}_i + \boldsymbol{U}_t, \tag{14.61}$$

where $\boldsymbol{Y}_t$ is a $1 \times g$ vector of observations on the levels of a set of variables, each of which is assumed to be I(1), $\boldsymbol{X}_t$ (which may or may not be present) is a row vector of deterministic variables, such as a constant term and a trend, $\boldsymbol{B}$ is a matrix of coefficients of those deterministic regressors, $\boldsymbol{U}_t$ is a $1 \times g$ vector of error terms, and the $\boldsymbol{\Phi}_i$ are $g \times g$ matrices of coefficients.

The VAR (14.61) is written in levels. It can be reparametrized as

$$\Delta\boldsymbol{Y}_t = \boldsymbol{X}_t\boldsymbol{B} + \boldsymbol{Y}_{t-1}\boldsymbol{\Pi} + \sum_{i=1}^{p} \Delta\boldsymbol{Y}_{t-i}\boldsymbol{\Gamma}_i + \boldsymbol{U}_t, \tag{14.62}$$

where it is not difficult to verify that $\boldsymbol{\Gamma}_p = -\boldsymbol{\Phi}_{p+1}$, $\boldsymbol{\Gamma}_i = \boldsymbol{\Gamma}_{i+1} - \boldsymbol{\Phi}_{i+1}$ for $i = 1, \ldots, p$, and

$$\boldsymbol{\Pi} = \sum_{i=1}^{p+1} \boldsymbol{\Phi}_i - \mathbf{I}_g.$$

Equation (14.62) is the multivariate analog of the augmented Dickey-Fuller test regression (14.34). In that regression, we tested the null hypothesis of a unit root by testing whether the coefficient of y_{t-1} is 0. In very much the same way, we can test whether and to what extent the variables in $\boldsymbol{Y}_t$ are cointegrated by testing hypotheses about the $g \times g$ matrix $\boldsymbol{\Pi}$, which is called the **impact matrix**.

If we assume, as usual, that the differenced variables are I(0), then everything in equation (14.62) except the term $\boldsymbol{Y}_{t-1}\boldsymbol{\Pi}$ is I(0). Therefore, if the equation is to be satisfied, this term must be I(0) as well. It clearly is so if the matrix $\boldsymbol{\Pi}$ is a zero matrix. In this extreme case, there is no cointegration at all. However, it can also be I(0) if $\boldsymbol{\Pi}$ is nonzero but does not have full rank. In fact, the rank of $\boldsymbol{\Pi}$ is the number of cointegrating relations.

To see why this is so, suppose that the matrix $\boldsymbol{\Pi}$ has rank r, with $0 \leq r < g$. In this case, we can always write

$$\boldsymbol{\Pi} = \boldsymbol{\eta}\boldsymbol{\alpha}^\top, \tag{14.63}$$

where $\boldsymbol{\eta}$ and $\boldsymbol{\alpha}$ are both $g \times r$ matrices. Recall that the rank of a matrix is the number of linearly independent columns. Here, any set of r linearly independent columns of $\boldsymbol{\Pi}$ is a set of linear combinations of the r columns of $\boldsymbol{\eta}$. See also Exercise 14.20. When equation (14.63) holds, we see that $\boldsymbol{Y}_{t-1}\boldsymbol{\Pi} = \boldsymbol{Y}_{t-1}\boldsymbol{\eta}\boldsymbol{\alpha}^\top$. This term is I(0) if and only if the r columns of $\boldsymbol{Y}_{t-1}\boldsymbol{\eta}$ are I(0). Thus, for each of the r columns $\boldsymbol{\eta}_i$ of $\boldsymbol{\eta}$, $\boldsymbol{Y}_{t-1}\boldsymbol{\eta}_i$ is I(0). In other words, $\boldsymbol{\eta}_i$ is a cointegrating vector. Since the $\boldsymbol{\eta}_i$ are linearly independent, it follows that there are r independent cointegrating relations.

We can now see just how the number of cointegrating vectors is related to the rank of the matrix $\boldsymbol{\Pi}$. In the extreme case in which $r = 0$, there are no cointegrating vectors at all, and $\boldsymbol{\Pi} = \mathbf{O}$. When $r = 1$, there is a single cointegrating vector, which is proportional to $\boldsymbol{\eta}_1$. When $r = 2$, there is a two-dimensional space of cointegrating vectors, spanned by $\boldsymbol{\eta}_1$ and $\boldsymbol{\eta}_2$. When $r = 3$, there is a three-dimensional space of cointegrating vectors, spanned by $\boldsymbol{\eta}_1$, $\boldsymbol{\eta}_2$, and $\boldsymbol{\eta}_3$, and so on. Our assumptions exclude the case with $r = g$, since we have assumed that all the elements of $\boldsymbol{Y}_t$ are I(1). If $r = g$, every linear combination of these elements would be stationary, which implies that all the elements of $\boldsymbol{Y}_t$ are I(0).

The system (14.62) with the constraint (14.63) imposed can be written as

$$\Delta\boldsymbol{Y}_t = \boldsymbol{X}_t\boldsymbol{B} + \boldsymbol{Y}_{t-1}\boldsymbol{\eta}\boldsymbol{\alpha}^\top + \sum_{i=1}^{p}\Delta\boldsymbol{Y}_{t-i}\boldsymbol{\Gamma}_i + \boldsymbol{U}_t. \tag{14.64}$$

Estimating this system of equations yields estimates of the r cointegrating vectors. However, it can be seen from (14.64) that not all of the elements of $\boldsymbol{\eta}$ and $\boldsymbol{\alpha}$ can be identified, since the factorization (14.63) is not unique for a given $\boldsymbol{\Pi}$. In fact, if $\boldsymbol{\Theta}$ is any nonsingular $r \times r$ matrix,

$$\boldsymbol{\eta}\boldsymbol{\Theta}\boldsymbol{\Theta}^{-1}\boldsymbol{\alpha}^\top = \boldsymbol{\eta}\boldsymbol{\alpha}^\top. \tag{14.65}$$

It is therefore necessary to make some additional assumption in order to convert equation (14.64) into an identified model.

We now consider the simpler case in which $g = 2$, $r = 1$, and $p = 0$. In this case, the VAR (14.62) becomes

$$\begin{aligned}\Delta y_{t1} &= \boldsymbol{X}_t\boldsymbol{b}_1 + \pi_{11}y_{t-1,1} + \pi_{21}y_{t-1,2} + u_{t1},\\ \Delta y_{t2} &= \boldsymbol{X}_t\boldsymbol{b}_2 + \pi_{12}y_{t-1,1} + \pi_{22}y_{t-1,2} + u_{t2},\end{aligned} \tag{14.66}$$

in obvious notation. If one forgets for a moment about the terms $\boldsymbol{X}_t\boldsymbol{b}_i$, this pair of equations can be deduced from the model (14.37), with $\pi_{21} = \phi_{12}$, $\pi_{12} = \phi_{21}$, and $\pi_{ii} = \phi_{ii} - 1$, $i = 1, 2$. We saw in connection with the system (14.37) that, if y_{t1} and y_{t2} are cointegrated, then the matrix $\boldsymbol{\Phi}$ of (14.38) has one unit eigenvalue and the other eigenvalue less than 1 in absolute value. This requirement is identical to requiring the matrix

$$\begin{bmatrix} \pi_{11} & \pi_{21} \\ \pi_{12} & \pi_{22} \end{bmatrix}$$

to have one zero eigenvalue and the other between -2 and 0. Let the zero eigenvalue correspond to the eigenvector $[\eta_2 \;\vdots\; 1]$. Then it follows that

$$\pi_{21} = -\eta_2 \pi_{11} \quad \text{and} \quad \pi_{22} = -\eta_2 \pi_{12}.$$

Thus the pair of equations corresponding in this special case to the set of equations (14.64), incorporating an identifying restriction, is

$$\begin{aligned} \Delta y_{t1} &= \boldsymbol{X}_t \boldsymbol{b}_1 + \pi_{11}(y_{t-1,1} - \eta_2 y_{t-1,2}) + u_{t1}, \\ \Delta y_{t2} &= \boldsymbol{X}_t \boldsymbol{b}_2 + \pi_{12}(y_{t-1,1} - \eta_2 y_{t-1,2}) + u_{t2}, \end{aligned} \tag{14.67}$$

from which it is clear that the cointegrating vector is $[1 \;\vdots\; -\eta_2]$.

Unlike equations (14.66), the restricted equations (14.67) are nonlinear. There are at least two convenient ways to estimate them. One is first to estimate the unrestricted equations (14.66) and then use the GNR (12.53) discussed in Section 12.3, possibly with continuous updating of the estimate of the contemporaneous covariance matrix. Another is to use maximum likelihood, under the assumption that the error terms u_{t1} and u_{t2} are jointly normally distributed. This second method extends straightforwardly to the estimation of the more general restricted VAR (14.64). The normality assumption is not really restrictive, since the ML estimator is a QMLE even when the normality assumption is not satisfied; see Section 10.4.

Maximum likelihood estimation of a system of nonlinear equations was treated in Section 12.3. We saw there that one approach is to minimize the determinant of the matrix of sums of squares and cross-products of the residuals. The hard work can be restricted to the minimization with respect to η_2, since, for fixed η_2, the regression functions in (14.67) are linear with respect to the other parameters. As functions of η_2, then, the residuals can be written as $\boldsymbol{M}_{\boldsymbol{X},\boldsymbol{v}} \Delta \boldsymbol{y}_i$, where the $\boldsymbol{y}_i$, for $i = 1, 2$, are n-vectors with typical elements y_{ti}, and $\boldsymbol{v}$ is an n-vector with typical element $y_{t-1,1} - \eta_2 y_{t-1,2}$, for the given η_2. Here $\boldsymbol{M}_{\boldsymbol{X},\boldsymbol{v}}$ denotes an orthogonal projection on to $\mathcal{S}^\perp([\boldsymbol{X}\;\; \boldsymbol{v}])$.

For simplicity, we suppose for the moment that $\boldsymbol{X}$ is an empty matrix. The general case will be dealt with in more detail in the next section. Then the determinant that we wish to minimize with respect to η_2 is the determinant of the matrix $\Delta \boldsymbol{Y}^\top \boldsymbol{M}_{\boldsymbol{v}} \Delta \boldsymbol{Y}$, where $\Delta \boldsymbol{Y} = [\Delta \boldsymbol{y}_1 \;\; \Delta \boldsymbol{y}_2]$. A certain amount of algebra (see Exercise 14.24) shows that this determinant is equal to the determinant of $\Delta \boldsymbol{Y}^\top \Delta \boldsymbol{Y}$ times the ratio

$$\kappa \equiv \frac{\boldsymbol{v}^\top \boldsymbol{M}_{\Delta \boldsymbol{Y}} \boldsymbol{v}}{\boldsymbol{v}^\top \boldsymbol{v}}. \tag{14.68}$$

Since $\Delta \boldsymbol{Y}^\top \Delta \boldsymbol{Y}$ depends only on the data and not on η_2, it is enough to minimize κ with respect to η_2. The notation κ is intended to be reminiscent of the notation used in Section 12.5 in the context of LIML estimation, since the algebra of LIML is very similar to that used here. In the present simple case, the first-order condition for minimizing κ reduces to a quadratic equation for η_2. Of the two roots of this equation, we select the one for which the value of κ given by equation (14.68) is smaller; see Exercise 14.25 for details.

As with the other methods we have discussed, estimating a cointegrating vector by a VAR yields a super-consistent estimator. In general, except perhaps for quite small sample sizes, the bias of this VAR estimator is less than that of both the levels estimator (14.47) and the ECM estimator obtained by running regression (14.54). For small sample sizes, there appears to be a tendency for the distribution of the VAR estimator to involve a small number of extreme outliers, leading it to have a higher variance than the other two estimators. This phenomenon apparently disappears as the sample size increases, however; see Exercise 14.26.

14.6 Testing for Cointegration

The three methods discussed in the last section for estimating a cointegrating vector can all be extended to provide tests for whether cointegrating relations exist for a set of I(1) variables, and, in the case in which a VAR is used, to determine how many such relations exist. We begin with a method based on the cointegrating regression (14.45).

Engle-Granger Tests

The simplest, and probably still the most popular, way to test for cointegration was proposed by Engle and Granger (1987). The idea is to estimate the cointegrating regression (14.45) by OLS and then subject the resulting estimates of ν_t to a Dickey-Fuller test, which is usually augmented to deal with serial correlation. We saw in the last section that, if the variables $\boldsymbol{Y}_t$ are cointegrated, then the OLS estimator of $\boldsymbol{\eta}_2$ from equation (14.45) is super-consistent. The residuals $\hat{\nu}_t$ are then super-consistent estimators of the particular linear combination of the elements of $\boldsymbol{Y}_t$ that is I(0). If, however, the variables are not cointegrated, there is no such linear combination, and the residuals, being a linear combination of I(1) variables, are themselves I(1). Therefore, they have a unit root. Thus, when we subject the series $\hat{\nu}_t$ to a unit root test, the null hypothesis of the test is that ν_t *does* have a unit root, that is, that the variables in $\boldsymbol{Y}_t$ are *not* cointegrated.

It may seem curious to have a null hypothesis of no cointegration, but this follows inevitably from the nature of any unit root test. Recall from the simple model (14.37) that, when there is no cointegration, the matrix $\boldsymbol{\Phi}$ of (14.38) is restricted so as to have two unit eigenvalues. The alternative hypothesis of cointegration implies that there is just one, the only constraint on the other eigenvalue being that its absolute value should be less than 1. It is therefore natural from this point of view to have a test with a null hypothesis of no cointegration, with the restriction that there are two unit roots, against an alternative of cointegration, with only one. This feature applies to all the tests for cointegration that we consider.

The first step of the Engle-Granger procedure is to obtain the residuals $\hat{\nu}_t$ from regression (14.45). An augmented **Engle-Granger (EG) test** is then performed in almost exactly the same way as an augmented Dickey-Fuller test, by running the regression

$$\Delta\hat{\nu}_t = \boldsymbol{X}_t\gamma + \beta'\hat{\nu}_{t-1} + \sum_{j=1}^{p}\delta_j\Delta\hat{\nu}_{t-j} + e_t, \tag{14.69}$$

where p is chosen to remove any evidence of serial correlation in the residuals. As with the ADF test, the test statistic may be either a τ statistic or a z statistic, although the former is more common. We let $\tau_c(g)$ denote the t statistic for $\beta' = 0$ in (14.69) when $\boldsymbol{X}_t$ contains only a constant term and the vector $\boldsymbol{\eta}_2$ has $g-1$ elements to be estimated. Similarly, $\tau_{nc}(g)$, $\tau_{ct}(g)$, and $\tau_{ctt}(g)$ denote t statistics for the same null hypothesis, where the indicated deterministic terms are included in $\boldsymbol{X}_t$. By the same token, $z_{nc}(g)$, $z_c(g)$, $z_{ct}(g)$, and $z_{ctt}(g)$ denote the corresponding z statistics. As before, these are defined by equation (14.35).

As the above notation suggests, the asymptotic distributions of these test statistics depend on g. When $g = 1$, we have a limiting case, since there is then only one variable, y_t, which is I(1) under the null hypothesis and I(0) under the alternative. Not surprisingly, for $g = 1$, the asymptotic distribution of each of the Engle-Granger statistics is identical to the asymptotic distribution of the corresponding Dickey-Fuller statistic. To see this, note that the residuals $\hat{\nu}_t$ are in this case just y_t itself projected off whatever is in $\boldsymbol{X}_t$. The result then follows from the FWL Theorem, which implies that regressing y_t on $\boldsymbol{X}_t$ and then running regression (14.69) is the same (except for the initial observations) as directly running an ADF testing regression like (14.33). If there is more than one variable, but some or all of the components of the cointegrating vector are known, then the proper value of g is 1 plus the number of parameters to be estimated in order to estimate $\boldsymbol{\eta}_2$. Thus, if all the parameters are known, we have $g = 1$ whatever the number of variables.

Figure 14.4 shows the asymptotic densities of the $\tau_c(g)$ tests for $g = 1, \ldots, 12$. The densities move steadily to the left as g, the number of possibly cointegrated variables, increases. In consequence, the critical values become larger in absolute value, and the power of the test diminishes. The other Engle-Granger tests display similar patterns.

Since a set of g I(1) variables is cointegrated if there is a linear combination of them that is I(0), any g independent linear combinations of the variables

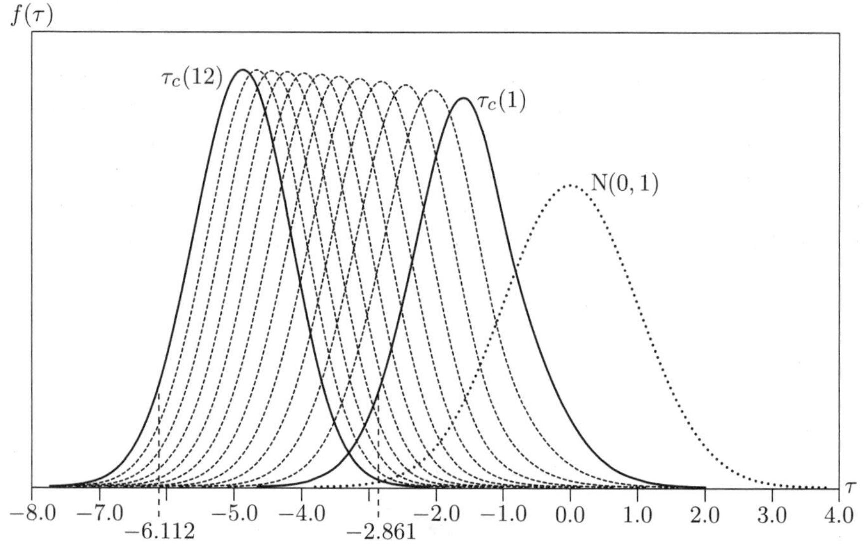

Figure 14.4 Asymptotic densities of Engle-Granger τ_c tests

is also a cointegrated set. In other words, cointegration is a property of the linear space spanned by the variables, not of the particular choice of variables that span the space. A problem with Engle-Granger test statistics is that they depend on the particular choice of $\boldsymbol{Y}_{t2}$ in the first step regression (14.45), or, more precisely, on the linear subspace spanned by the variables in $\boldsymbol{Y}_{t2}$. The asymptotic distribution of the test statistic under the null hypothesis is the same regardless of how $\boldsymbol{Y}_{t2}$ is chosen, but the actual test statistic is not. Consequently, Engle-Granger tests with the same data but different choices of $\boldsymbol{Y}_{t2}$ can, and often do, lead to quite different inferences.

ECM Tests

A second way to test for cointegration involves the estimation of an error-correction model. We can base an **ECM test** for the null hypothesis that the set of variables $\boldsymbol{Y}_t = [y_t \quad \boldsymbol{Y}_{t2}]$ is not cointegrated on equation (14.55). If no linear combination of the variables in $\boldsymbol{Y}_t$ is I(0), then the coefficients δ and $\boldsymbol{\delta}_2$ in that equation must be zero. A suitable test statistic is thus the t statistic for $\delta = 0$. Of course, since the regressor y_{t-1} is I(1), this **ECM statistic** does not follow the N(0, 1) distribution asymptotically. Instead, if $\boldsymbol{Y}_t$ is a $1 \times g$ vector, it follows the distribution that Ericsson and MacKinnon (2002) call the $\kappa_d(g)$ distribution, where d is one of nc, c, ct, or ctt, depending on which deterministic regressors are included in $\boldsymbol{X}_t$.

When $g = 1$, the asymptotic distribution of the ECM statistic is identical to that of the corresponding Dickey-Fuller τ statistic. This follows immediately

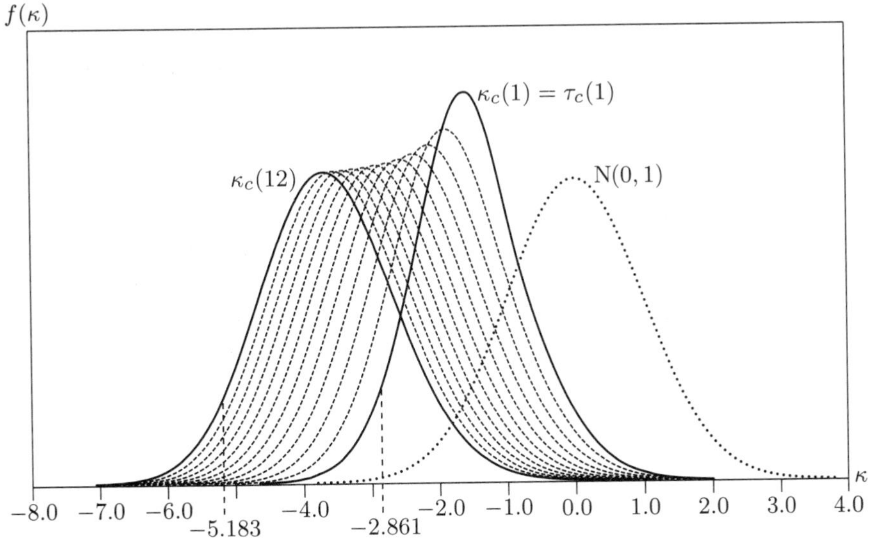

Figure 14.5 Asymptotic densities of ECM κ_c tests

from the fact that, for $g = 1$, equation (14.55) collapses to

$$\Delta y_t = \boldsymbol{X}_t\gamma + \delta y_{t-1} + e_t,$$

which is equivalent to equation (14.32). However, when $g > 1$, the distributions of the various κ statistics are not the same as those of the corresponding Engle-Granger τ statistics.

Equation (14.55) is less likely to suffer from serial correlation than the Engle-Granger test regression (14.69) because the error-correction term often has considerable explanatory power when there really is cointegration. If serial correlation is a problem, one can add lagged values of both Δy_t and $\Delta \boldsymbol{Y}_{t2}$ to equation (14.55) without affecting the asymptotic distributions of the test statistics. Indeed, one can add any stochastic variable that is I(0) and exogenous or predetermined, as well as nontrending deterministic variables. Thus it is possible to perform ECM tests within the context of a well-specified econometric model, of which equation (14.55) is a special case. Indeed, this is probably the best way to perform such a test, and it is one of the things that makes ECM tests attractive.

Figure 14.5 shows the densities of the $\kappa_c(g)$ statistics for $g = 1, \ldots, 12$. This figure is comparable to Figure 14.4. It can be seen that, for $g > 1$, the critical values are somewhat smaller in absolute value than they are for the corresponding EG tests. The distributions of the κ statistics are also more spread out than those of the corresponding τ statistics, with positive values much more likely to occur.

Under the alternative hypothesis of cointegration, an ECM test is more likely to reject the false null than an EG test. Consider equation (14.54). Subtracting $\eta_2 \Delta y_{t2}$ from both sides and rearranging, we obtain

$$\Delta(y_{t1} - \eta_2 y_{t2}) = \delta_1(y_{t-1,1} - \eta_2 y_{t-1,2}) + (\alpha - \eta_2)\Delta y_{t2} + e_t. \qquad (14.70)$$

If we replace η_2 by its estimate (14.47) and omit the term $(\alpha - \eta_2)\Delta y_{t2}$, this is just a version of the Engle-Granger test regression (14.69). We remarked in our discussion of the estimation of η_2 by an ECM that the restriction that $\alpha = \eta_2$ is often too strong for comfort. When this restriction is false, we may expect (14.70) to fit better than (14.69) and to be less likely to suffer from serially correlated errors. Thus we should expect the EG test to have less power than the ECM test in most cases. It must be noted, however, that the ECM test shares with the EG test the disadvantage that it depends on the particular choice of $\boldsymbol{Y}_{t2}$.

For more detailed discussions of ECM tests, see Campos, Ericsson, and Hendry (1996), Banerjee, Dolado, and Mestre (1998), and Ericsson and MacKinnon (2002). The densities graphed in Figure 14.5 are taken from the last of these papers, which provides programs that can be used to compute critical values and P values for these tests.

Tests Based on a Vector Autoregression

A third way to test for cointegration is based on the VAR (14.62). The idea is to estimate this VAR subject to the constraint (14.63) for various values of the rank r of the impact matrix $\boldsymbol{\Pi}$, using ML estimation based on the assumption that the error vector $\boldsymbol{U}_t$ is multivariate normal for each t and independent across observations. Null hypotheses for which there are any number of cointegrating relations from 0 to $g-1$ can then be tested against alternatives with a greater number of relations, up to a maximum of g. Of course, if there really were g cointegrating relations, all the variables would be I(0), and so this case is usually only of theoretical interest. The most convenient test statistics are likelihood ratio (LR) statistics.

We saw in the last section that a convenient way to obtain ML estimates of the restricted VAR (14.64) is to minimize the determinant of the matrix of sums of squares and cross-products of the residuals. We now describe how to do this in general, and how to use the result in order to compute estimates of sets of cointegrating vectors and LR test statistics. We will not enter into a discussion of why the recipes we provide work, since doing so would be rather complicated. But, since the methodology is in very common use in practice, we will give detailed instructions as to how it can be implemented. See Banerjee, Dolado, Galbraith, and Hendry (1993, Chapter 8), Davidson (2000, Chapter 16), and Johansen (1995) for more detailed treatments.

The first step is to concentrate the $\boldsymbol{B}$ and $\boldsymbol{\Gamma}_i$ parameters out of the VAR (14.64). We can do this by regressing both $\Delta\boldsymbol{Y}_t$ and $\boldsymbol{Y}_{t-1}$ on the deterministic variables $\boldsymbol{X}_t$ and the lags $\Delta\boldsymbol{Y}_{t-1}$ through $\Delta\boldsymbol{Y}_{t-p}$. This requires us to run $2g$ OLS regressions, all of which involve the same regressors, and yields two sets of residuals,

$$\begin{aligned}\hat{\boldsymbol{V}}_{t1} &= \Delta\boldsymbol{Y}_t - \Delta\hat{\boldsymbol{Y}}_t, \text{ and}\\ \hat{\boldsymbol{V}}_{t2} &= \boldsymbol{Y}_{t-1} - \hat{\boldsymbol{Y}}_{t-1},\end{aligned} \tag{14.71}$$

where $\hat{\boldsymbol{V}}_{t1}$ and $\hat{\boldsymbol{V}}_{t2}$ are both $1 \times g$ vectors. In equations (14.71), $\Delta\hat{\boldsymbol{Y}}_t$ and $\hat{\boldsymbol{Y}}_{t-1}$ denote the fitted values from the regressions on $\boldsymbol{X}_t$ and $\Delta\boldsymbol{Y}_{t-1}$ through $\Delta\boldsymbol{Y}_{t-p}$.

The next step is to compute the $g \times g$ sample covariance matrices

$$\hat{\boldsymbol{\Sigma}}_{jl} = \frac{1}{n}\sum_{t=1}^{n} \hat{\boldsymbol{V}}_{tj}^{\top}\hat{\boldsymbol{V}}_{tl}, \quad j = 1, 2, \ \ l = 1, 2.$$

Then we must find the solutions λ_i and $\boldsymbol{z}_i$, for $i = 1, \ldots, g$, to the equations

$$(\lambda_i \hat{\boldsymbol{\Sigma}}_{22} - \hat{\boldsymbol{\Sigma}}_{21}\hat{\boldsymbol{\Sigma}}_{11}^{-1}\hat{\boldsymbol{\Sigma}}_{12})\boldsymbol{z}_i = \mathbf{0}, \tag{14.72}$$

which are similar to equations (12.115) for finding the eigenvalues and eigenvectors of a matrix. The eigenvalue-eigenvector problem we actually solve is for the positive definite symmetric matrix

$$\boldsymbol{A} \equiv \hat{\boldsymbol{\Psi}}_{22}^{\top}\hat{\boldsymbol{\Sigma}}_{21}\hat{\boldsymbol{\Sigma}}_{11}^{-1}\hat{\boldsymbol{\Sigma}}_{12}\hat{\boldsymbol{\Psi}}_{22}, \tag{14.73}$$

where $\hat{\boldsymbol{\Psi}}_{22}\hat{\boldsymbol{\Psi}}_{22}^{\top} = \hat{\boldsymbol{\Sigma}}_{22}^{-1}$. The eigenvalues of this matrix turn out to be the λ_i that we seek. We sort these from largest to smallest, so that $\lambda_i > \lambda_j$ for $i < j$. Then we choose the corresponding eigenvectors to be the columns of a $g \times g$ matrix $\boldsymbol{\Xi}$ which is such that $\boldsymbol{\Xi}^{\top}\boldsymbol{\Xi} = \mathbf{I}$. This can be done using the construction that leads to equation (12.117), which allows us to conclude that $\boldsymbol{A\Xi} = \boldsymbol{\Xi\Lambda}$, where the diagonal entries of the diagonal matrix $\boldsymbol{\Lambda}$ are the (ordered) eigenvalues λ_i. It is then easy to show that the columns $\boldsymbol{z}_i$ of the matrix $\boldsymbol{Z} \equiv \hat{\boldsymbol{\Psi}}_{22}\boldsymbol{\Xi}$ solve the equations (14.72) along with the λ_i, and that the matrix $\boldsymbol{Z}$ satisfies the relation

$$\boldsymbol{Z}^{\top}\hat{\boldsymbol{\Sigma}}_{22}\boldsymbol{Z} = \mathbf{I}_g. \tag{14.74}$$

The purpose of solving equations (14.72) in this way is that the first r columns of $\boldsymbol{Z}$ are the ML estimates $\hat{\boldsymbol{\eta}}$ of $\boldsymbol{\eta}$, with equations (14.74) providing the necessary identifying restrictions so that $\boldsymbol{\alpha}$ and $\boldsymbol{\eta}$ are uniquely determined; recall the indeterminacy expressed by equation (14.65). As we remarked in the last section, once $\boldsymbol{\eta}$ is given, the equations (14.64) are linear in the other parameters, which can therefore be estimated by least squares.

It can be shown that the maximized loglikelihood function for the restricted model (14.64) is

$$-\frac{gn}{2}(\log 2\pi + 1) - \frac{n}{2}\sum_{i=1}^{r}\log(1 - \lambda_i). \tag{14.75}$$

Thus we can calculate the maximized loglikelihood function for any value of the number of cointegrating vectors, once we have found the eigenvalues of the matrix (14.73). For given r, (14.75) depends on the r largest eigenvalues. Note that it must be the case that $0 < \lambda_i < 1$ for all i, because the matrix $\boldsymbol{A}$ is positive definite, and because, if $\lambda_i \geq 1$, the loglikelihood function (14.75) would not exist.

As r increases, so does the value of the maximized loglikelihood function given by expression (14.75). This makes sense, since we are imposing fewer restrictions. To test the null hypothesis that $r = r_1$ against the alternative that $r = r_2$, for $r_1 < r_2 \leq g$, we compute the LR statistic

$$-n \sum_{i=r_1+1}^{r_2} \log(1 - \lambda_i). \tag{14.76}$$

This is often called the **trace statistic**, because it can be thought of as the sum of a subset of the elements on the principal diagonal of the diagonal matrix $-n \log(\mathbf{I} - \boldsymbol{\Lambda})$. Because the impact matrix $\boldsymbol{\Pi}$ cannot be written as a matrix of coefficients of I(0) variables (recall the discussion in the last section), the distributions of the trace statistic are nonstandard. These distributions have been tabulated for a number of values of $r_2 - r_1$. Typically, the trace statistic is used to test the null hypothesis that there are r cointegrating vectors against the alternative that there are g of them.

When the null hypothesis is that there are r cointegrating vectors and the alternative is that there are $r + 1$ of them, there is just one term in the sum that appears in expression (14.76). The test statistic is then

$$-n \log(1 - \lambda_{r+1}) = -n \log(1 - \lambda_{\max}), \tag{14.77}$$

where $\lambda_{\max}$ is the largest eigenvalue of those that correspond to eigenvectors which have not been incorporated into $\hat{\boldsymbol{\eta}}$ under the null hypothesis. For obvious reasons, this test statistic is often called the $\boldsymbol{\lambda_{\max}}$ **statistic**. The distributions of this statistic for various values of r have been tabulated.

Like those of unit root tests and single-equation cointegration tests, the asymptotic distributions of the trace and $\lambda_{\max}$ statistics depend on what deterministic regressors are included in $\boldsymbol{X}_t$. To complicate matters, it may well be desirable to impose restrictions on the matrix $\boldsymbol{B}$, and the distributions also depend on what restrictions, if any, are imposed.

A further complication is that some of the I(1) variables may be known not to be cointegrated. In that case, we can divide $\boldsymbol{Y}_t$ into two parts, treating the variables in one part as exogenous and those in the other part as potentially cointegrated. The distributions of the test statistics then depend on how many exogenous variables there are. For details, see Harbo, Johansen, Nielsen, and Rahbek (1998) and Pesaran, Shin, and Smith (2000).

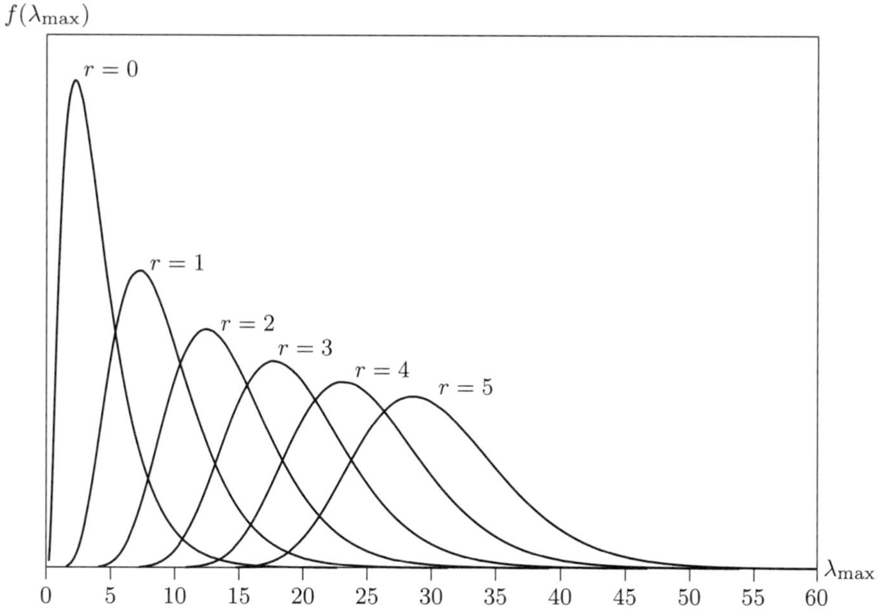

Figure 14.6 Asymptotic densities of some λ_{max} tests

Figure 14.6 shows the densities of the λ_{max} statistics for the null hypotheses that $r = 0, 1, 2, 3, 4, 5$ under one popular assumption about the matrix $\boldsymbol{B}$, namely, that $\boldsymbol{X}_t$ consists only of a constant, and that there are certain restrictions on $\boldsymbol{B}$. This was called "Case II" by Pesaran, Shin, and Smith (2000) and "Case 1*" by Osterwald-Lenum (1992). We see from the figure that the mean and variance of the λ_{max} statistic become larger as r increases, and that its density becomes more symmetrical. The mean and variance of the trace statistic, which coincides with the λ_{max} statistic when $g - r = 1$, increase even more rapidly as $g - r$ increases. Figure 14.6 is based on results from MacKinnon, Haug, and Michelis (1999), which provides programs that can be used to compute asymptotic critical values and P values for the λ_{max} and trace statistics for all the standard cases, including systems with exogenous I(1) variables.

Unlike EG and ECM tests, tests based on the trace or λ_{max} statistics are invariant when the variables $\boldsymbol{Y}_t$ are replaced by independent linear combinations of them. We will not take the time to prove this important property, but it is a reasonably straightforward consequence of the definitions given in this section. Intuitively, it is a consequence of the fact that no particular variable or linear combination of variables is singled out in the specification of the VAR (14.64), in contrast to the specifications of the regressions used to implement EG and ECM tests.

14.7 Final Remarks

This chapter has provided a reasonably brief introduction to the modeling of nonstationary time series, a topic which has engendered a massive literature in a relatively short period of time. A deeper treatment would have required a book instead of a chapter. The asymptotic theory that is applicable when some variables have unit roots is very different from the conventional asymptotic theory that we have encountered in previous chapters. Moreover, the enormous number of different tests, each with its own nonstandard limiting distribution, can be intimidating. However, we have seen that the same fundamental ideas underlie many of the techniques for both estimation and hypothesis testing in models that involve variables which have unit roots.

14.8 Exercises

14.1 Calculate the autocovariance $\mathrm{E}(w_t w_s)$, $s < t$, of the standardized random walk given by (14.01).

14.2 Suppose that $(1 - \rho(\mathrm{L}))u_t = e_t$ is the autoregressive representation of the series u_t, where e_t is white noise, and $\rho(z)$ is a polynomial of degree p with no constant term. If u_t has exactly one unit root, with all other roots outside the unit circle, show that the polynomial $1 - \rho(z)$ can be factorized as

$$1 - \rho(z) = (1 - z)(1 - \rho_0(z)),$$

where $1-\rho_0(z)$ is a polynomial of degree $p-1$ with no constant term and all its roots strictly outside the unit circle. Give the autoregressive representation of the first-differenced series $(1 - \mathrm{L})u_t$, and show that it implies that this series is stationary.

14.3 Generate 220 observations on three simulated standard random walks using the DGP (14.03), with a normal white-noise error process having variance 1, and then three simulated random walks with $y_0 = 5$, $y_0 = 10$, and $y_0 = 20$. Plot all six simulated series on the same graph, showing only the observations after the twentieth. Can you reliably distinguish visually between the random walks that have zero and nonzero starting values?

Perform a similar exercise where the three random walks of the second set are generated with drift, using the DGP (14.04), with $y_0 = 0$ and the drift parameter $\gamma_1 = 0.1$. Is this value of γ_1 large enough to permit visual identification of the random walks with and without drift?

⋆14.4 Establish the three results

$$\sum_{t=1}^{n} t = \tfrac{1}{2}n(n+1), \quad \sum_{t=1}^{n} t^2 = \tfrac{1}{6}n(n+1)(2n+1), \quad \sum_{t=1}^{n} t^3 = \tfrac{1}{4}n^2(n+1)^2$$

by inductive arguments. That is, show directly that the results are true for $n = 1$, and then for each one show that, if the result is true for a given n, it is also true for $n + 1$.

⋆**14.5** Consider the following random walk, in which a second-order polynomial in time is included in the defining equation:

$$y_t = \beta_0 + \beta_1 t + \beta_2 t^2 + y_{t-1} + u_t, \quad u_t \sim \text{IID}(0, \sigma^2).$$

Show that y_t can be generated in terms of a standardized random walk w_t that satisfies (14.01) by the equation

$$y_t = y_0 + \beta_0 t + \beta_1 \tfrac{1}{2} t(t+1) + \beta_2 \tfrac{1}{6} t(t+1)(2t+1) + \sigma w_t.$$

Can you obtain a similar result for the case in which the second-order polynomial is replaced by a polynomial of degree p in time?

14.6 For sample sizes of 50, 100, 200, 400, and 800, generate N pairs of data from the DGP

$$y_t = \rho_1 y_{t-1} + u_{t1}, \quad y_0 = 0, \quad u_{t1} \sim \text{NID}(0, 1),$$
$$x_t = \rho_2 x_{t-1} + u_{t2}, \quad x_0 = 0, \quad u_{t2} \sim \text{NID}(0, 1),$$

for the following values of ρ_1 and ρ_2: -0.7, 0.0, 0.7, and 1. Then run regression (14.12) and record the proportion of the time that the ordinary t test for $\beta_2 = 0$ rejects the null hypothesis at the .05 level. Thus you need to perform 16 experiments for each of 5 sample sizes. Choose a reasonably large value of N, but not so large that you use an unreasonable amount of computer time. The smallest value that would probably make sense is $N = 10{,}000$.

For which values of ρ_1 and ρ_2 does it seem plausible that the t test based on the spurious regression (14.12) rejects the correct proportion of the time asymptotically? For which values is it clear that the test overrejects asymptotically? Are there any values for which it appears that the test underrejects asymptotically?

Was it really necessary to run all 16 experiments? Explain.

14.7 Repeat the previous exercise using regression (14.13) instead of regression (14.12). For which values of ρ_1 and ρ_2 does it seem plausible that the t test based on this regression rejects the correct proportion of the time asymptotically? For which values is it clear that the test overrejects asymptotically? Are there any values for which it appears that the test underrejects asymptotically?

14.8 Perform experiments similar to those of Exercise 14.6 with $\rho_1 = \rho_2 = 0.8$, this time using a HAC covariance matrix estimator instead of the OLS covariance matrix estimator for the computation of the t statistic. A reasonable rule of thumb is to set the lag truncation parameter p equal to three times the fourth root of the sample size, rounded to the nearest integer. Also perform experiments with sample sizes of 1,600, 3,200, and 6,400 in order to see just how slowly the HAC t statistic approaches its asymptotic distribution.

14.9 Repeat Exercise 14.8 with unit root processes in place of stationary AR(1) processes. You should find that the use of a HAC estimator alleviates the extent of spurious regression, in the sense that the probability of rejection tends to 1 more slowly as $n \to \infty$. Intuitively, why should using a HAC estimator work, even if only in very large samples, with stationary AR(1) processes but not with unit root processes?

14.10 The HAC estimators used in the preceding two exercises are estimates of the covariance matrix

$$(\boldsymbol{X}^\top\boldsymbol{X})^{-1}\boldsymbol{X}^\top\boldsymbol{\Omega}\boldsymbol{X}(\boldsymbol{X}^\top\boldsymbol{X})^{-1}, \tag{14.78}$$

where $\boldsymbol{\Omega}$ is the true covariance matrix of the error terms. Perform another set of experiments, for sample sizes of 20, 40, and 80, on the performance of the t statistic for $\beta_2 = 0$ in regression (14.12), with ρ_1 and ρ_2 equal to either 0.8 or 1. This time, use the true $\boldsymbol{\Omega}$ in expression (14.78) rather than using a HAC estimator. You should find that the rejection rate is very close to nominal even for these small samples. **Hint:** The result of Exercise 7.10 with $\theta = 1$ is useful for the construction of the matrix $\boldsymbol{X}^\top\boldsymbol{\Omega}\boldsymbol{X}$.

★**14.11** Consider the model with typical DGP

$$y_t = \sum_{i=0}^{p} \beta_i t^i + y_{t-1} + \sigma\varepsilon_t, \quad \varepsilon_t \sim \text{IID}(0,1). \tag{14.79}$$

Show that the z and τ statistics from the testing regression

$$\Delta y_t = \sum_{i=0}^{p+1} \gamma_i t^i + (\beta - 1)y_{t-1} + e_t$$

are pivotal when the DGP is (14.79) and the distribution of the white-noise process ε_t is known.

★**14.12** Show that

$$\sum_{t=1}^{n} w_t^2 = \sum_{t=1}^{n} (n-t+1)\varepsilon_t^2 + 2\sum_{t=2}^{n}\sum_{s=1}^{t-1}(n-t+1)\varepsilon_t\varepsilon_s,$$

where w_t is the standardized random walk (14.02). Then demonstrate that a typical term from the first summation is uncorrelated with every other term from the first summation and with every term from the second (double) summation. Also demonstrate that every term from the double summation is uncorrelated with every other such term.

Let the fourth moment of the white-noise process ε_t be m_4. Show that the variance of $\sum_{t=1}^{n} w_t^2$ is then equal to

$$\frac{m_4}{6}n(n+1)(2n+1) + \tfrac{1}{3}n^2(n^2-1),$$

which is of order n^4 as $n \to \infty$. **Hint:** Use the results of Exercise 14.4.

14.13 Consider the standardized Wiener process $W(r)$ defined by (14.26). Show that, for $0 \le r_1 < r_2 \le r_3 < r_4 \le 1$, $W(r_2) - W(r_1)$ and $W(r_4) - W(r_3)$ are independent. This property is called the property of **independent increments** of the Wiener process. Show that the covariance of $W(r)$ and $W(s)$ is equal to $\min(r, s)$.

The process $G(r)$, $r \in [0,1]$, defined by $G(r) = W(r) - rW(1)$, where $W(r)$ is a standardized Wiener process, is called a **Brownian bridge**. Show that $G(r) \sim \mathrm{N}(0, r(1-r))$, and that the covariance of $G(r)$ and $G(s)$ is $s(1-r)$ for $r > s$.

★14.14 By using arguments similar to those leading to the result (14.30) for the z_{nc} statistic, demonstrate the result (14.31) for the τ_{nc} statistic.

★14.15 Show that, if w_t is the standardized random walk (14.01), $\sum_{t=1}^{n} w_t$ is of order $n^{3/2}$ as $n \to \infty$. By use of the definition (14.28) of the Riemann integral, show that

$$\operatorname*{plim}_{n\to\infty} n^{-3/2} \sum_{t=1}^{n} w_t = \int_0^1 W(r)\, dr,$$

and demonstrate that this plim is distributed as $\mathrm{N}(0, 1/3)$. **Hint:** Use the results of Exercise 14.4.

Show that the probability limit of the formula (14.20) for the statistic z_c can be written in terms of a standardized Wiener process $W(r)$ as

$$\operatorname*{plim}_{n\to\infty} z_c = \frac{\frac{1}{2}(W^2(1) - 1) - W(1)\int_0^1 W(r)\, dr}{\int_0^1 W^2(r)\, dr - \left(\int_0^1 W(r)\, dr\right)^2}.$$

14.16 The file **intrates-m.data** contains several monthly interest rate series for the United States from 1955 to 2001. Let R_t denote the 10-year government bond rate. Using data for 1957 through 2001, test the hypothesis that this series has a unit root with ADF τ_c, τ_{ct}, τ_{ctt}, z_c, z_{ct}, and z_{ctt} tests, using whatever value(s) of p seem reasonable.

★14.17 Consider the simplest ADF testing regression

$$\Delta y_t = \beta' y_{t-1} + \delta \Delta y_{t-1} + e_t,$$

and suppose the data are generated by the standardized random walk (14.01), with $y_t = w_t$. If $\boldsymbol{M}_1$ is the orthogonal projection matrix that yields residuals from a regression on the lagged dependent variable Δy_{t-1}, and if $\boldsymbol{y}_{-1}$ is the n-vector with typical element y_{t-1}, show that the expressions

$$\frac{1}{n}\sum_{t=1}^{n} (\boldsymbol{M}_1 \boldsymbol{y}_{-1})_t \varepsilon_t \quad \text{and} \quad \frac{1}{n}\sum_{t=1}^{n} y_{t-1}\varepsilon_t$$

have the same probability limit as $n \to \infty$. Then derive the analogous result for the two expressions

$$\frac{1}{n^2}\sum_{t=1}^{n} (\boldsymbol{M}_1 \boldsymbol{y}_{-1})_t^2 \quad \text{and} \quad \frac{1}{n^2}\sum_{t=1}^{n} y_{t-1}^2.$$

★14.18 Let the $p \times p$ matrix $\boldsymbol{A}$ have q distinct eigenvalues $\lambda_1, \ldots, \lambda_q$, where $q \le p$. Let the p-vectors $\boldsymbol{\xi}_i$, $i = 1, \ldots, q$, be corresponding eigenvectors, so that $\boldsymbol{A}\boldsymbol{\xi}_i = \lambda_i \boldsymbol{\xi}_i$. Prove that the $\boldsymbol{\xi}_i$ are linearly independent.

⋆14.19 Consider the expression $n^{-1}\sum_{t=1}^{n} v_{t1}v_{t2}$, where v_{t1} and v_{t2} are given by the equations (14.42), with $\lambda_i \le 1$, $i = 1, 2$, the inequality being strict in at least one case. Show that the expectation and variance of this expression both tend to finite limits as $n \to \infty$. For the variance, the easiest way to proceed is to express the v_{ti} as in (14.42), and to consider only the nonzero contributions to the second moment.

14.20 If the $p \times q$ matrix $\boldsymbol{A}$ has rank r, where $r \le p$ and $r \le q$, show that there exist a $p \times r$ matrix $\boldsymbol{B}$ and a $q \times r$ matrix $\boldsymbol{C}$, both of full column rank r, such that $\boldsymbol{A} = \boldsymbol{B}\boldsymbol{C}^{\top}$. Show further that any matrix of the form $\boldsymbol{B}\boldsymbol{C}^{\top}$, where $\boldsymbol{B}$ is $p \times r$ with $r \le p$ and $\boldsymbol{C}$ is $q \times r$ with $r \le q$, has rank r if both $\boldsymbol{B}$ and $\boldsymbol{C}$ have rank r.

14.21 Generate two I(1) series y_{t1} and y_{t2} using the DGP given by (14.46) with $\xi_{11} = 1$, $\xi_{12} = 0.5$, $\xi_{21} = 0.7$, and $\xi_{22} = 0.3$. The series v_{t1} and v_{t2} should be generated by (14.42), with $\lambda_1 = 1$ and $\lambda_2 = 0.7$, the series e_{t1} and e_{t2} being white noise with a contemporaneous covariance matrix

$$\boldsymbol{\Sigma} = \begin{bmatrix} 1 & 0.7 \\ 0.7 & 1.5 \end{bmatrix}.$$

Perform a set of simulation experiments for sample sizes $n = 25, 50, 100, 200, 400$, and 800 in which the parameter η_2 of the stationary linear combination $y_{t1} - \eta_2 y_{t2}$ is estimated first by $\hat{\eta}_2^{\mathrm{L}}$ defined in equation (14.47) and then by $\hat{\eta}_2^{\mathrm{E}} = -\hat{\delta}_2/\hat{\delta}_1$ from the regression (14.54). The true value of η_2 can be deduced from equation (14.50). You should observe that the first estimator is substantially more biased than the second.

Verify the super-consistency of both estimators by computing the first two moments of $n(\hat{\eta}_2 - \eta_2)$. They should be roughly constant as n varies, at least for larger values of n.

14.22 Generate three independent pairs of cointegrated series using the DGP of the preceding exercise for sample size 100. Plot all six series on one graph. Can you tell by eye which are the cointegrated pairs of series?

14.23 Show that, if

$$\frac{n^{1/2}(\hat{\delta}_i - \delta_i)}{\delta_i} = \theta + O_p(n^{-1/2}),$$

for $i = 1, 2$, then the ratio $\hat{\delta}_2/\hat{\delta}_1$ is super-consistent. In other words, show that equation (14.58) holds.

⋆14.24 Let $\boldsymbol{A} \equiv [\boldsymbol{a}_1 \;\; \boldsymbol{a}_2]$ be an $n \times 2$ matrix, and let θ be the angle between the nonzero vectors $\boldsymbol{a}_1$ and $\boldsymbol{a}_2$. Show that the columns of the matrix

$$\boldsymbol{A}\boldsymbol{B} \equiv \boldsymbol{A} \begin{bmatrix} \|\boldsymbol{a}_1\|^{-1} & -\|\boldsymbol{a}_1\|^{-1}\cot\theta \\ 0 & \|\boldsymbol{a}_2\|^{-1}\operatorname{cosec}\theta \end{bmatrix}$$

are orthonormal. Use this result to show that the determinant of the 2×2 matrix $\boldsymbol{A}^{\top}\boldsymbol{A}$ is equal to $\|\boldsymbol{a}_1\|^2\|\boldsymbol{M}_1\boldsymbol{a}_2\|^2$, where $\boldsymbol{M}_1$ is the orthogonal projection on to $\mathcal{S}^{\perp}(\boldsymbol{a}_1)$.

Let $\boldsymbol{v}$ be an n-vector, and let $\boldsymbol{M}_{\boldsymbol{v}}$ project orthogonally on to $\mathcal{S}^{\perp}(\boldsymbol{v})$. Show that the determinant of the 2×2 matrix $\boldsymbol{A}^{\top}\boldsymbol{M}_{\boldsymbol{v}}\boldsymbol{A}$ is equal to the determinant of $\boldsymbol{A}^\top\boldsymbol{A}$ multiplied by $\boldsymbol{v}^\top\boldsymbol{M_A}\boldsymbol{v}/\boldsymbol{v}^\top\boldsymbol{v}$, where $\boldsymbol{M_A}$ projects orthogonally on to $\mathcal{S}^\perp(\boldsymbol{A})$. **Hint:** Construct a 2×2 matrix $\boldsymbol{C}$ such that the columns of $\boldsymbol{AC}$ are orthonormal, with the first being parallel to $\boldsymbol{P_A}\boldsymbol{v}$.

14.25 Show that the first-order condition for minimizing the κ given in expression (14.68) with respect to η_2, where $\boldsymbol{v} = \boldsymbol{y}_1 - \eta_2\boldsymbol{y}_2$, is equivalent to requiring that η_2 should be a solution to the quadratic equation

$$\begin{aligned}&\eta_2^2(\boldsymbol{y}_2^\top\boldsymbol{y}_2\,\boldsymbol{y}_1^\top\boldsymbol{M}_{\Delta\boldsymbol{Y}}\boldsymbol{y}_2 - \boldsymbol{y}_1^\top\boldsymbol{y}_2\,\boldsymbol{y}_2^\top\boldsymbol{M}_{\Delta\boldsymbol{Y}}\boldsymbol{y}_2)\\&\quad+\eta(\boldsymbol{y}_1^\top\boldsymbol{y}_1\,\boldsymbol{y}_2^\top\boldsymbol{M}_{\Delta\boldsymbol{Y}}\boldsymbol{y}_2 - \boldsymbol{y}_2^\top\boldsymbol{y}_2\,\boldsymbol{y}_1^\top\boldsymbol{M}_{\Delta\boldsymbol{Y}}\boldsymbol{y}_1)\\&\quad+(\boldsymbol{y}_1^\top\boldsymbol{y}_2\,\boldsymbol{y}_1^\top\boldsymbol{M}_{\Delta\boldsymbol{Y}}\boldsymbol{y}_1 - \boldsymbol{y}_1^\top\boldsymbol{y}_1\,\boldsymbol{y}_1^\top\boldsymbol{M}_{\Delta\boldsymbol{Y}}\boldsymbol{y}_2) = 0.\end{aligned} \tag{14.80}$$

14.26 Repeat the simulation experiments of Exercise 14.21 for the VAR estimator of the parameter η_2 of the cointegration relation. The easiest way to proceed is to solve the quadratic equation (14.80), choosing the root for which κ is smallest.

14.27 Let r_t denote the logarithm of the 10-year government bond rate, and let s_t denote the logarithm of the 1-year government bond rate, where monthly data on both rates are available in the file **intrates-m.data**. Using data for 1957 through 2001, use whatever augmented Engle-Granger τ tests seem appropriate to test the null hypothesis that these two series are not cointegrated.

14.28 Consider once again the Canadian consumption data in the file **consumption.data**, for the period 1953:1 to 1996:4. Perform a variety of appropriate tests of the hypotheses that the levels of consumption and income have unit roots. Repeat the exercise for the logs of these variables.

If you fail to reject the hypotheses that the levels or the logs of these variables have unit roots, proceed to test whether they are cointegrated, using two versions of the EG test procedure, one with consumption, the other with income, as the regressand in the cointegrating regression. Similarly, perform two versions of the ECM test. Finally, test the null hypothesis of no cointegration using Johansen's VAR-based procedure.

Chapter 15

Testing the Specification of Econometric Models

15.1 Introduction

As we first saw in Section 3.7, estimating a misspecified regression model generally yields biased and inconsistent parameter estimates. This is true for regression models whenever we incorrectly omit one or more regressors that are correlated with the regressors included in the model. Except in certain special cases, some of which we have discussed, it is also true for more general types of model and more general types of misspecification. This suggests that the specification of every econometric model should be thoroughly tested before we even tentatively accept its results.

We have already discussed a large number of procedures that can be used as specification tests. These include t and F tests for omitted variables and for parameter constancy (Section 4.4), along with similar tests for nonlinear regression models (Section 6.7) and IV regression (Section 8.5), tests for heteroskedasticity (Section 7.5), tests for serial correlation (Section 7.7), tests of common factor restrictions (Section 7.9), DWH tests (Section 8.7), tests of overidentifying restrictions (Sections 8.6, 9.4, 9.5, 12.4, and 12.5), and the three classical tests for models estimated by maximum likelihood, notably LM tests (Section 10.6).

In this chapter, we discuss a number of other procedures that are designed for testing the specification of econometric models. Some of these procedures explicitly involve testing a model against a less restricted alternative. Others do not make the alternative explicit and are intended to have power against a large number of plausible alternatives. In the next section, we discuss a variety of tests that are based on artificial regressions. Then, in Section 15.3, we discuss nonnested hypothesis tests, which are designed to test the specification of a model when alternative models are available. In Section 15.4, we discuss model selection based on information criteria. Finally, in Section 15.5, we introduce the concept of nonparametric estimation. Nonparametric methods avoid specification errors caused by imposing an incorrect functional form, and the validity of parametric models can be checked by comparing them with nonparametric ones.

15.2 Specification Tests Based on Artificial Regressions

In previous chapters, we have encountered numerous examples of **artificial regressions**. These include the Gauss-Newton regression (Section 6.7) and its heteroskedasticity-robust variant (Section 6.8), the OPG regression (Section 10.5), and the binary response model regression (Section 11.3). We can write any of these artificial regressions as

$$\boldsymbol{r}(\boldsymbol{\theta}) = \boldsymbol{R}(\boldsymbol{\theta})\boldsymbol{b} + \text{residuals}, \tag{15.01}$$

where $\boldsymbol{\theta}$ is a parameter vector of length k, $\boldsymbol{r}(\boldsymbol{\theta})$ is a vector, often but by no means always of length equal to the sample size n, and $\boldsymbol{R}(\boldsymbol{\theta})$ is a matrix with as many rows as $\boldsymbol{r}(\boldsymbol{\theta})$ and k columns. For example, in the case of the GNR, $\boldsymbol{r}(\boldsymbol{\theta})$ is a vector of residuals, written as a function of the data and parameters, and $\boldsymbol{R}(\boldsymbol{\theta})$ is a matrix of derivatives of the regression function with respect to the parameters.

In order for (15.01) to be a valid artificial regression, the vector $\boldsymbol{r}(\boldsymbol{\theta})$ and the matrix $\boldsymbol{R}(\boldsymbol{\theta})$ must satisfy certain properties, which all of the artificial regressions we have studied do satisfy. These properties are given in outline in Exercise 8.20, and we restate them more formally here. We use a notation that was introduced in Section 9.5, whereby $\mathbb{M}$ denotes a model, μ denotes a DGP which belongs to that model, and plim_μ means a probability limit taken under the DGP μ. See the discussion in Section 9.5.

An artificial regression of the form (15.01) corresponds to a model $\mathbb{M}$ with parameter vector $\boldsymbol{\theta}$, and to a root-n consistent asymptotically normal estimator $\hat{\boldsymbol{\theta}}$ of that parameter vector, if and only if the following three conditions are satisfied:

- The artificial regressand and the artificial regressors are orthogonal when evaluated at $\hat{\boldsymbol{\theta}}$, that is,
$$\boldsymbol{R}^\top(\hat{\boldsymbol{\theta}})\boldsymbol{r}(\hat{\boldsymbol{\theta}}) = \boldsymbol{0}.$$

- Under any DGP $\mu \in \mathbb{M}$, the asymptotic covariance matrix of $\hat{\boldsymbol{\theta}}$ is given *either* by
$$\operatorname{Var}\big(\operatorname*{plim}_{n\to\infty}{}_\mu\, n^{1/2}(\hat{\boldsymbol{\theta}} - \boldsymbol{\theta}_\mu)\big) = \operatorname*{plim}_{n\to\infty}{}_\mu \big(n^{-1}\boldsymbol{R}^\top(\acute{\boldsymbol{\theta}})\boldsymbol{R}(\acute{\boldsymbol{\theta}})\big)^{-1}, \tag{15.02}$$
where $\boldsymbol{\theta}_\mu$ is the true parameter vector for the DGP μ and n is the sample size, *or* by
$$\operatorname{Var}\big(\operatorname*{plim}_{n\to\infty}{}_\mu\, n^{1/2}(\hat{\boldsymbol{\theta}} - \boldsymbol{\theta}_\mu)\big) = \operatorname*{plim}_{n\to\infty}{}_\mu\, \acute{s}^2\big(n^{-1}\boldsymbol{R}^\top(\acute{\boldsymbol{\theta}})\boldsymbol{R}(\acute{\boldsymbol{\theta}})\big)^{-1}, \tag{15.03}$$
where $\acute{s}^2$ is the OLS estimate of the error variance obtained by running regression (15.01) with $\boldsymbol{\theta} = \acute{\boldsymbol{\theta}}$. Here, $\acute{\boldsymbol{\theta}}$ may be any root-n consistent estimator, not necessarily the same as $\hat{\boldsymbol{\theta}}$.

- The artificial regression allows for one-step estimation, in the sense that, if $\acute{\boldsymbol{b}}$ denotes the vector of OLS parameter estimates obtained by running regression (15.01) with $\boldsymbol{\theta} = \acute{\boldsymbol{\theta}}$, then, under any DGP $\mu \in \mathbb{M}$,

$$\operatorname*{plim}_{n\to\infty}{}_{\mu}\, n^{1/2}(\acute{\boldsymbol{\theta}} + \acute{\boldsymbol{b}} - \boldsymbol{\theta}_{\mu}) = \operatorname*{plim}_{n\to\infty}{}_{\mu}\, n^{1/2}(\hat{\boldsymbol{\theta}} - \boldsymbol{\theta}_{\mu}). \tag{15.04}$$

  Equivalently, making use of the O_p notation introduced in Section 14.2, the property (15.04) may be expressed as $\acute{\boldsymbol{\theta}} + \acute{\boldsymbol{b}} = \hat{\boldsymbol{\theta}} + O_p(n^{-1})$.

The Gauss-Newton regression for a nonlinear regression model, together with the least-squares estimator of the parameters of the model, satisfies the above conditions. For the GNR, the asymptotic covariance matrix is given by equation (15.03). The OPG regression for any model that can be estimated by maximum likelihood, together with the ML estimator of its parameters, also satisfies the above conditions, but the asymptotic covariance matrix is given by equation (15.02). See Davidson and MacKinnon (2001) for a more detailed discussion of artificial regressions.

Now consider the artificial regression

$$\boldsymbol{r}(\acute{\boldsymbol{\theta}}) = \boldsymbol{R}(\acute{\boldsymbol{\theta}})\boldsymbol{b} + \boldsymbol{Z}(\acute{\boldsymbol{\theta}})\boldsymbol{c} + \text{residuals}, \tag{15.05}$$

where $\acute{\boldsymbol{Z}} \equiv \boldsymbol{Z}(\acute{\boldsymbol{\theta}})$ is a matrix with r columns that depends on the same sample data and parameter estimates as $\acute{\boldsymbol{r}} \equiv \boldsymbol{r}(\acute{\boldsymbol{\theta}})$ and $\acute{\boldsymbol{R}} \equiv \boldsymbol{R}(\acute{\boldsymbol{\theta}})$. We have previously encountered instances of regressions like (15.05), where both $\boldsymbol{R}(\boldsymbol{\theta})$ and $\boldsymbol{Z}(\boldsymbol{\theta})$ were matrices of derivatives, with $\boldsymbol{R}(\boldsymbol{\theta})$ corresponding to the parameters of a restricted version of the model and $\boldsymbol{Z}(\boldsymbol{\theta})$ corresponding to additional parameters that appear only in the unrestricted model. In such a case, if the root-n consistent estimator $\acute{\boldsymbol{\theta}}$ satisfies the restrictions, then running an artificial regression like (15.05) and testing the hypothesis that $\boldsymbol{c} = \boldsymbol{0}$ provides a way of testing those restrictions; recall the discussion in Section 6.7 in the context of the GNR. In many cases, $\acute{\boldsymbol{\theta}}$ is conveniently chosen as the vector of estimates from the restricted model.

A great many specification tests may be based on artificial regressions of the form (15.05). The null hypothesis under test is that the model $\mathbb{M}$ to which regression (15.01) corresponds is correctly specified. It is not necessary that the matrix $\acute{\boldsymbol{Z}}$ should explicitly be a matrix of derivatives. In fact, any matrix $\boldsymbol{Z}(\boldsymbol{\theta})$ which satisfies the following three conditions can be used in (15.05) to obtain a valid specification test:

R1. For every DGP $\mu \in \mathbb{M}$,

$$\operatorname*{plim}_{n\to\infty}{}_{\mu}\, n^{-1}\boldsymbol{Z}^{\top}(\boldsymbol{\theta}_{\mu})\boldsymbol{r}(\boldsymbol{\theta}_{\mu}) = \boldsymbol{0}. \tag{15.06}$$

A sufficient condition for (15.06) to hold is that $\mathrm{E}_{\mu}\big(\boldsymbol{Z}_t^{\top}(\boldsymbol{\theta}_{\mu})r_t(\boldsymbol{\theta}_{\mu})\big) = \boldsymbol{0}$ for all $t = 1, \ldots, N$, where N is the number of elements of $\boldsymbol{r}$, and $\boldsymbol{Z}_t$ and

r_t are, respectively, the tth row and t^{th} element of $\boldsymbol{Z}$ and $\boldsymbol{r}$. We require that $N \to \infty$ as $n \to \infty$.

R2. Let $\boldsymbol{r}_\mu$, $\boldsymbol{R}_\mu$, and $\boldsymbol{Z}_\mu$ denote $\boldsymbol{r}(\boldsymbol{\theta}_\mu)$, $\boldsymbol{R}(\boldsymbol{\theta}_\mu)$, and $\boldsymbol{Z}(\boldsymbol{\theta}_\mu)$, respectively. Then, for any $\mu \in \mathbb{M}$, if the asymptotic covariance matrix is given by (15.02), the matrix

$$\operatorname*{plim}_{n\to\infty}{}_\mu \frac{1}{n} \begin{bmatrix} \boldsymbol{R}_\mu{}^\top \boldsymbol{R}_\mu & \boldsymbol{R}_\mu{}^\top \boldsymbol{Z}_\mu \\ \boldsymbol{Z}_\mu{}^\top \boldsymbol{R}_\mu & \boldsymbol{Z}_\mu{}^\top \boldsymbol{Z}_\mu \end{bmatrix} \tag{15.07}$$

is the covariance matrix of the plim of the vector $n^{-1/2}[\boldsymbol{R}_\mu{}^\top \boldsymbol{r}_\mu \; \vdots \; \boldsymbol{Z}_\mu{}^\top \boldsymbol{r}_\mu]$, which is required to be asymptotically multivariate normal. If instead the asymptotic covariance matrix is given by equation (15.03), then the matrix (15.07) must be multiplied by the probability limit of the estimated error variance from the artificial regression.

R3. The Jacobian matrix containing the partial derivatives of the elements of the vector $n^{-1}\boldsymbol{Z}^\top(\boldsymbol{\theta})\boldsymbol{r}(\boldsymbol{\theta})$ with respect to the elements of $\boldsymbol{\theta}$, evaluated at $\boldsymbol{\theta}_\mu$, is asymptotically equal, under the DGP μ, to $-n^{-1}\boldsymbol{Z}_\mu{}^\top \boldsymbol{R}_\mu$. Formally, this Jacobian matrix is equal to $-n^{-1}\boldsymbol{Z}_\mu{}^\top \boldsymbol{R}_\mu + O_p(n^{-1/2})$.

Since a proof of the sufficiency of these conditions requires a good deal of algebra, we relegate it to a technical appendix.

When these conditions are satisfied, we can test the correct specification of the model $\mathbb{M}$ against an alternative in which equation (15.06) does not hold by testing the hypothesis that $\boldsymbol{c} = \boldsymbol{0}$ in regression (15.05). If the asymptotic covariance matrix is given by equation (15.02), then the difference between the explained sum of squares from regression (15.05) and the ESS from regression (15.01), evaluated at $\acute{\boldsymbol{\theta}}$, must be asymptotically distributed as $\chi^2(r)$ under the null hypothesis. This is not true when the asymptotic covariance matrix is given by equation (15.03), in which case we can use an asymptotic t test if $r = 1$ or an asymptotic F test if $r > 1$.

The RESET Test

One of the oldest specification tests for linear regression models, but one that is still widely used, is the **regression specification error test**, or **RESET test**, which was originally proposed by Ramsey (1969). The idea is to test the null hypothesis that

$$y_t = \boldsymbol{X}_t\boldsymbol{\beta} + u_t, \quad u_t \sim \text{IID}(0, \sigma^2), \tag{15.08}$$

where the explanatory variables $\boldsymbol{X}_t$ are predetermined with respect to the error terms u_t, against the rather vaguely specified alternative that $\text{E}(y_t|\boldsymbol{X}_t)$ is a nonlinear function of the elements of $\boldsymbol{X}_t$. The simplest version of RESET involves regressing y_t on $\boldsymbol{X}_t$ to obtain fitted values $\boldsymbol{X}_t\hat{\boldsymbol{\beta}}$ and then running the regression

$$y_t = \boldsymbol{X}_t\boldsymbol{\beta} + \gamma(\boldsymbol{X}_t\hat{\boldsymbol{\beta}})^2 + u_t. \tag{15.09}$$

The test statistic is the ordinary t statistic for $\gamma = 0$.

At first glance, the RESET procedure may not seem to be based on an artificial regression. But it is easy to show (Exercise 15.2) that the t statistic for $\gamma = 0$ in regression (15.09) is identical to the t statistic for $c = 0$ in the GNR

$$\hat{u}_t = \boldsymbol{X}_t \boldsymbol{b} + c(\boldsymbol{X}_t \hat{\boldsymbol{\beta}})^2 + \text{residual}, \tag{15.10}$$

where $\hat{u}_t$ is the tth residual from regression (15.08). The test regression (15.10) is clearly a special case of the artificial regression (15.05), with $\hat{\boldsymbol{\beta}}$ playing the role of $\acute{\boldsymbol{\theta}}$ and $(\boldsymbol{X}_t \hat{\boldsymbol{\beta}})^2$ playing the role of $\acute{\boldsymbol{Z}}$. It is not hard to check that the three conditions for a valid specification test regression are satisfied. First, the predeterminedness of $\boldsymbol{X}_t$ implies that $\mathrm{E}\big((\boldsymbol{X}_t\boldsymbol{\beta}_0)^2(y_t - \boldsymbol{X}_t\boldsymbol{\beta}_0)\big) = 0$, where $\boldsymbol{\beta}_0$ is the true parameter vector, so that condition R1 holds. Condition R2 is equally easy to check. For condition R3, let $\boldsymbol{z}(\boldsymbol{\beta})$ be the n–vector with typical element $(\boldsymbol{X}_t\boldsymbol{\beta})^2$. Then the derivative of $n^{-1}\boldsymbol{z}^\top(\boldsymbol{\beta})(y_t - \boldsymbol{X}_t\boldsymbol{\beta})$ with respect to β_i, for $i = 1, \ldots, k$, evaluated at $\boldsymbol{\beta}_0$, is

$$\frac{2}{n}\sum_{t=1}^{n} \boldsymbol{X}_t\boldsymbol{\beta}_0\, x_{ti}\, u_t - \frac{1}{n}\sum_{t=1}^{n} (\boldsymbol{X}_t\boldsymbol{\beta}_0)^2 x_{ti}.$$

The first term above is $n^{-1/2}$ times an expression which, by a central limit theorem, is asymptotically normal with mean zero and finite variance. It is therefore $O_p(n^{-1/2})$. The second term is an element of the vector $-n^{-1}\boldsymbol{z}^\top(\boldsymbol{\beta}_0)\boldsymbol{X}$. Thus condition R3 holds, and the RESET test, implemented either by either of the regressions (15.09) or (15.10), is seen to be asymptotically valid.

Actually, the RESET test is not merely valid asymptotically. It is exact in finite samples whenever the model that is being tested satisfies the strong assumptions needed for t statistics to have their namesake distribution; see Section 4.4 for a statement of those assumptions. To see why, note that the vector of fitted values $\boldsymbol{X}\hat{\boldsymbol{\beta}}$ is orthogonal to the residual vector $\hat{\boldsymbol{u}}$, so that $\mathrm{E}(\hat{\boldsymbol{\beta}}^\top\boldsymbol{X}^\top\hat{\boldsymbol{u}}) = 0$. Under the assumption of normal errors, it follows that $\boldsymbol{X}\hat{\boldsymbol{\beta}}$ is independent of $\hat{\boldsymbol{u}}$. As Milliken and Graybill (1970) first showed, and as readers are invited to show in Exercise 15.3, this implies that the t statistic for $c = 0$ yields an exact test under classical assumptions.

Like most specification tests, the RESET procedure is designed to have power against a variety of alternatives. However, it can also be derived as a test against a specific alternative. Suppose that

$$y_t = \frac{\tau(\delta \boldsymbol{X}_t\boldsymbol{\beta})}{\delta} + u_t, \tag{15.11}$$

where δ is a scalar parameter, and $\tau(x)$ may be any scalar function that is monotonically increasing in its argument x and satisfies the conditions

$$\tau(0) = 0, \;\; \tau'(0) = 1, \;\; \text{and } \tau''(0) \neq 0,$$

where $\tau'(0)$ and $\tau''(0)$ are the first and second derivatives of $\tau(x)$, evaluated at $x = 0$. A simple example of such a function is

$$\tau(x) = x + x^2.$$

We first encountered the family of functions $\tau(\cdot)$ in Section 11.3, in connection with tests of the functional form of binary response models.

By l'Hôpital's Rule, the nonlinear regression model (15.11) reduces to the linear regression model (15.08) when $\delta = 0$. It is not hard to show, using equations (11.29), that the GNR for testing the null hypothesis that $\delta = 0$ is

$$y_t - \boldsymbol{X}_t\hat{\boldsymbol{\beta}} = \boldsymbol{X}_t\boldsymbol{b} + c(\boldsymbol{X}_t\hat{\boldsymbol{\beta}})^2\,\frac{1}{2}\tau''(0) + \text{residual},$$

which, since $\tau''(0)/2$ is just a constant, is equivalent to regression (15.10). Thus RESET can be derived as a test of $\delta = 0$ in the nonlinear regression model (15.11). For more details, see MacKinnon and Magee (1990), which also discusses some other specification tests that can be used to test (15.08) against nonlinear models involving transformations of the dependent variable.

Some versions of the RESET procedure add the cube, and sometimes also the fourth power, of $\boldsymbol{X}_t\hat{\boldsymbol{\beta}}$ to the test regression (15.09). This makes no sense if the alternative is (15.11), but it may give the test more power against some other alternatives. In general, however, we recommend the simplest version of the test, namely, the t test for $\gamma = 0$ in regression (15.09).

Conditional Moment Tests

If a model $\mathbb{M}$ is correctly specified, many random quantities that are functions of the dependent variable(s) should have expectations of zero. Often, these expectations are taken conditional on some information set. For example, in the linear regression model (15.08), the expectation of the error term u_t, conditional on any variable in the information set Ω_t relative to which the model is supposed to give the conditional mean of y_t, should be equal to zero. For any z_t that belongs to Ω_t, therefore, we have $\mathrm{E}(z_t u_t) = 0$ for all observations t. This sort of requirement, following from the hypothesis that $\mathbb{M}$ is correctly specified, is known as a **moment condition**.

A moment condition is purely theoretical. However, we can often calculate the empirical counterpart of a moment condition and use it as the basis of a **conditional moment test**. For a linear regression, of course, we already know how to perform such a test: We add z_t to regression (15.08) and look at the t statistic for this additional regressor to have a coefficient of 0.

More generally, consider a moment condition of the form

$$\mathrm{E}_{\boldsymbol{\theta}}\big(m_t(y_t, \boldsymbol{\theta})\big) = 0, \quad t = 1, \ldots, n, \tag{15.12}$$

where y_t is the dependent variable, and $\boldsymbol{\theta}$ is the vector of parameters for the model $\mathbb{M}$. As the notation implies, the expectation in (15.12) is computed using a DGP in $\mathbb{M}$ with parameter vector $\boldsymbol{\theta}$. The t subscript on the **moment function** $m_t(y_t, \boldsymbol{\theta})$ indicates that, in general, moment functions also depend on exogenous or predetermined variables. Equation (15.12) implies that the $m_t(y_t, \boldsymbol{\theta})$ are elementary zero functions in the sense of Section 9.5. We cannot test whether condition (15.12) holds for each observation, but we can test whether it holds on average. Since we will be interested in asymptotic tests, it is natural to consider the probability limit of the average. Thus we can replace (15.12) by the somewhat weaker condition

$$\operatorname*{plim}_{n\to\infty}{}_{\mu}\, \frac{1}{n}\sum_{t=1}^{n} m_t(y_t, \boldsymbol{\theta}) = 0. \tag{15.13}$$

The empirical counterpart of the left-hand side of condition (15.13) is

$$m(\boldsymbol{y}, \hat{\boldsymbol{\theta}}) \equiv \frac{1}{n}\sum_{t=1}^{n} m_t(y_t, \hat{\boldsymbol{\theta}}), \tag{15.14}$$

where $\boldsymbol{y}$ denotes the vector with typical element y_t, and $\hat{\boldsymbol{\theta}}$ denotes a vector of estimates of $\boldsymbol{\theta}$ from the model under test. The quantity $m(\boldsymbol{y}, \hat{\boldsymbol{\theta}})$ is referred to as an **empirical moment**. We wish to test whether its value is significantly different from zero.

In order to do so, we need an estimate of the variance of $m(\boldsymbol{y}, \hat{\boldsymbol{\theta}})$. It might seem that, since the empirical moment is just the sample mean of the $m_t(y_t, \hat{\boldsymbol{\theta}})$, this variance could be consistently estimated by the usual sample variance,

$$\frac{1}{n-1}\sum_{t=1}^{n}\big(m_t(y_t, \hat{\boldsymbol{\theta}}) - m(\boldsymbol{y}, \hat{\boldsymbol{\theta}})\big)^2. \tag{15.15}$$

If $\hat{\boldsymbol{\theta}}$ were replaced by the true value $\boldsymbol{\theta}_0$ in expression (15.14), then we could indeed use the sample variance (15.15) with $\hat{\boldsymbol{\theta}}$ replaced by $\boldsymbol{\theta}_0$ to estimate the variance of the empirical moment. But, because the vector $\hat{\boldsymbol{\theta}}$ is random, on account of its dependence on $\boldsymbol{y}$, we have to take this **parameter uncertainty** into account when we estimate the variance of $m(\boldsymbol{y}, \hat{\boldsymbol{\theta}})$.

The easiest way to see the effects of parameter uncertainty is to consider conditional moment tests based on artificial regressions. Suppose there is an artificial regression of the form (15.01) in correspondence with the model $\mathbb{M}$ and the estimator $\hat{\boldsymbol{\theta}}$ which allows us to write the moment function $m_t(y_t, \boldsymbol{\theta})$ as the product $z_t(y_t, \boldsymbol{\theta})r_t(y_t, \boldsymbol{\theta})$ of a factor z_t and the regressand r_t of the artificial regression. If the number N of artificial observations is not equal to the sample size n, some algebraic manipulation may be needed in order to express the moment functions in a convenient form, but we ignore such problems here and suppose that $N = n$.

Now consider the artificial regression of which the typical observation is

$$r_t(y_t, \boldsymbol{\theta}) = \boldsymbol{R}_t(y_t, \boldsymbol{\theta})\boldsymbol{b} + c z_t(y_t, \boldsymbol{\theta}) + \text{residual}. \tag{15.16}$$

If the z_t satisfy conditions R1–R3, then the t statistic for $c = 0$ is a valid test statistic whenever equation (15.16) is evaluated at a root-n consistent estimate of $\boldsymbol{\theta}$, in particular, at $\hat{\boldsymbol{\theta}}$. By applying the FWL Theorem to this equation and taking probability limits, it is not difficult to see that this t statistic is actually testing the hypothesis that

$$\operatorname*{plim}_{n\to\infty} \frac{1}{n} \boldsymbol{z}_0^\top \boldsymbol{M}_{\boldsymbol{R}_0} \boldsymbol{r}_0 = 0, \tag{15.17}$$

where $\boldsymbol{z}_0 \equiv \boldsymbol{z}(\boldsymbol{\theta}_0)$, $\boldsymbol{R}_0 \equiv \boldsymbol{R}(\boldsymbol{\theta}_0)$, and $\boldsymbol{M}_{\boldsymbol{R}_0}$ is the matrix that projects orthogonally on to $\mathcal{S}^\perp(\boldsymbol{R}_0)$. Asymptotically, equation (15.17) is precisely the moment condition that we wish to test, as can be seen from the following argument:

$$\begin{aligned} n^{1/2} m(\hat{\boldsymbol{\theta}}) &= n^{-1/2} \boldsymbol{z}^\top(\hat{\boldsymbol{\theta}}) \boldsymbol{r}(\hat{\boldsymbol{\theta}}) \\ &= n^{-1/2} \boldsymbol{z}_0^\top \boldsymbol{r}_0 + n^{-1} \boldsymbol{z}_0^\top \boldsymbol{R}_0\, n^{1/2}(\hat{\boldsymbol{\theta}} - \boldsymbol{\theta}_0) + O_p(n^{-1/2}) \\ &= n^{-1/2} \boldsymbol{z}_0^\top \boldsymbol{M}_{\boldsymbol{R}_0} \boldsymbol{r}_0 + O_p(n^{-1/2}), \end{aligned} \tag{15.18}$$

where for notational ease we have suppressed the dependence on the dependent variable. The steps leading to (15.18) are very similar to the derivation of a closely related result in the technical appendix, and interested readers are urged to consult the latter. If there were no parameter uncertainty, the second term in the second line above would vanish, and the leading-order term in expression (15.18) would simply be $n^{-1/2}\boldsymbol{z}_0^\top \boldsymbol{r}_0$.

It is clear from expression (15.18) that, as we indicated above, the asymptotic variance of $n^{1/2} m(\hat{\boldsymbol{\theta}})$ is smaller than that of $n^{1/2} m(\boldsymbol{\theta}_0)$, because the projection $\boldsymbol{M}_{\boldsymbol{R}_0}$ appears in the leading-order term for the former empirical moment but not in the leading-order term for the latter one. The reduction in variance caused by the projection is a phenomenon analogous to the loss of degrees of freedom in Hansen-Sargan tests caused by the need to estimate parameters; recall the discussion in Section 9.4. Indeed, since moment functions are zero functions, conditional moment tests can be interpreted as tests of overidentifying restrictions.

Examples of Conditional Moment Tests

Suppose the model under test is the nonlinear regression model (6.01), and the moment functions can be written as

$$m_t(\boldsymbol{\beta}) = z_t(\boldsymbol{\beta}) u_t(\boldsymbol{\beta}), \tag{15.19}$$

where $u_t(\boldsymbol{\beta}) \equiv y_t - x_t(\boldsymbol{\beta})$ is the tth residual, and $z_t(\boldsymbol{\beta})$ is some function of exogenous or predetermined variables and the parameters. We are using $\boldsymbol{\beta}$ instead of $\boldsymbol{\theta}$ to denote the vector of parameter estimates here because the regression function is $x_t(\boldsymbol{\beta})$. In this case, as we now show, a test of the moment condition (15.13) can be based on the following Gauss-Newton regression:

$$u_t(\hat{\boldsymbol{\beta}}) = \boldsymbol{X}_t(\hat{\boldsymbol{\beta}})\boldsymbol{b} + c z_t(\hat{\boldsymbol{\beta}}) + \text{residual}, \tag{15.20}$$

where $\hat{\boldsymbol{\beta}}$ is the vector of NLS estimates of the parameters, and $\boldsymbol{X}_t(\boldsymbol{\beta})$ is the k-vector of derivatives of $x_t(\boldsymbol{\beta})$ with respect to the elements of $\boldsymbol{\beta}$.

Since the NLS estimator $\hat{\boldsymbol{\beta}}$ is root-n consistent and asymptotically normal under the usual regularity conditions for nonlinear regression, all we have to show is that conditions R1–R3 are satisfied by the GNR (15.20). Condition R1 is trivially satisfied, since what it requires is precisely what we wish to test. Condition R2, for the covariance matrix (15.03), follows easily from the fact that $\boldsymbol{X}_t(\boldsymbol{\beta})$ and $z_t(\boldsymbol{\beta})$ depend on the data only through exogenous or predetermined variables.

Condition R3 requires a little more work, however. Let $\boldsymbol{z}(\boldsymbol{\beta})$ and $\boldsymbol{u}(\boldsymbol{\beta})$ be the n-vectors with typical elements $z_t(\boldsymbol{\beta})$ and $u_t(\boldsymbol{\beta})$, respectively. The derivative of $n^{-1}\boldsymbol{z}^\top(\boldsymbol{\beta})\boldsymbol{u}(\boldsymbol{\beta})$ with respect to any component β_i of the vector $\boldsymbol{\beta}$ is

$$\frac{1}{n}\frac{\partial \boldsymbol{z}^\top(\boldsymbol{\beta})}{\partial \beta_i}\boldsymbol{u}(\boldsymbol{\beta}) - \frac{1}{n}\boldsymbol{z}^\top(\boldsymbol{\beta})\frac{\partial \boldsymbol{x}(\boldsymbol{\beta})}{\partial \beta_i}. \tag{15.21}$$

Since the elements of $\boldsymbol{z}(\boldsymbol{\beta})$ are predetermined, so are those of its derivative with respect to β_i, and since $\boldsymbol{u}(\boldsymbol{\beta}_0)$ is just the vector of error terms, it follows from a law of large numbers that the first term of expression (15.21) tends to zero as $n \to \infty$. In fact, by a central limit theorem, this term is $O_p(n^{-1/2})$. The $n \times k$ matrix $\boldsymbol{X}(\boldsymbol{\beta})$ has typical column $\partial \boldsymbol{x}(\boldsymbol{\beta})/\partial \beta_i$. Therefore, the Jacobian matrix of $n^{-1}\boldsymbol{z}^\top(\boldsymbol{\beta})\boldsymbol{u}(\boldsymbol{\beta})$ is asymptotically equal to $-n^{-1}\boldsymbol{z}^\top(\boldsymbol{\beta}_0)\boldsymbol{X}(\boldsymbol{\beta}_0)$, which is condition R3 for the GNR (15.20). Thus we conclude that this GNR can be used to test the moment condition (15.13).

The above reasoning can easily be generalized to allow us to test more than one moment condition at a time. Let $\boldsymbol{Z}(\boldsymbol{\beta})$ denote an $n \times r$ matrix of functions of the data, each column of which is asymptotically orthogonal to the vector $\boldsymbol{u}$ under the null hypothesis that is to be tested, in the sense that $\operatorname{plim} n^{-1}\boldsymbol{Z}^\top(\boldsymbol{\beta}_0)\boldsymbol{u} = \boldsymbol{0}$. Now consider the artificial regression

$$\boldsymbol{u}(\hat{\boldsymbol{\beta}}) = \boldsymbol{X}(\hat{\boldsymbol{\beta}})\boldsymbol{b} + \boldsymbol{Z}(\hat{\boldsymbol{\beta}})\boldsymbol{c} + \text{residuals}. \tag{15.22}$$

As readers are asked to show in Exercise 15.5, n times the uncentered R^2 from this regression is asymptotically distributed as $\chi^2(r)$ under the null hypothesis. An ordinary F test for $\boldsymbol{c} = \boldsymbol{0}$ is also asymptotically valid.

Conditional moment tests based on the GNR are often useful for linear and nonlinear regression models, but they evidently cannot be used when the GNR itself is not applicable. With models estimated by maximum likelihood, tests can be based on the OPG regression that was introduced in Section 10.5. This artificial regression applies whenever there is a Type 2 MLE $\hat{\boldsymbol{\theta}}$ that is root-n consistent and asymptotically normal; see Section 10.3.

The OPG regression was originally given in equation (10.72). It is repeated here for convenience with a minor change of notation:

$$\boldsymbol{\iota} = \boldsymbol{G}(\boldsymbol{\theta})\boldsymbol{b} + \text{residuals}. \tag{15.23}$$

The regressand is an n–vector of 1s, and the regressor matrix is the matrix of contributions to the gradient, with typical element defined by (10.26). The artificial regression corresponds to the model implicitly defined by the matrix $\boldsymbol{G}(\boldsymbol{\theta})$, together with the ML estimator $\hat{\boldsymbol{\theta}}$. Let $\boldsymbol{m}(\boldsymbol{\theta})$ be the n–vector with typical element the moment function $m_t(y_t, \boldsymbol{\theta})$ that is to be tested, where once more the notation hides the dependence on the data. Then the testing regression is simplicity itself: We add $\boldsymbol{m}(\boldsymbol{\theta})$ to regression (15.23) as an extra regressor, obtaining

$$\boldsymbol{\iota} = \boldsymbol{G}(\boldsymbol{\theta})\boldsymbol{b} + c\boldsymbol{m}(\boldsymbol{\theta}) + \text{residuals}. \tag{15.24}$$

The test statistic is the t statistic on the extra regressor. The regressors here can be evaluated at any root-n consistent estimator, but it is most common to use the MLE $\hat{\boldsymbol{\theta}}$.

If several moment conditions are to be tested simultaneously, then we can form the $n \times r$ matrix $\boldsymbol{M}(\boldsymbol{\theta})$, each column of which is a vector of moment functions. The testing regression is then

$$\boldsymbol{\iota} = \boldsymbol{G}(\boldsymbol{\theta}) + \boldsymbol{M}(\boldsymbol{\theta})\boldsymbol{c} + \text{residuals}. \tag{15.25}$$

When the regressors are evaluated at the MLE $\hat{\boldsymbol{\theta}}$, several asymptotically valid test statistics are available, including the explained sum of squares, n times the uncentered R^2, and the F statistic for the artificial hypothesis that $\boldsymbol{c} = \boldsymbol{0}$. The first two of these statistics are distributed asymptotically as $\chi^2(r)$ under the null hypothesis, as is r times the third. If the regressors in equation (15.25) are not evaluated at $\hat{\boldsymbol{\theta}}$, but at some other root-n consistent estimate, then only the F statistic is asymptotically valid.

The artificial regression (15.23) is valid for a very wide variety of models. Condition R2 requires that we be able to apply a central limit theorem to the scalar product $n^{-1/2}\boldsymbol{m}^\top(\boldsymbol{\theta}_0)\boldsymbol{\iota}$, where, as usual, $\boldsymbol{\theta}_0$ is the true parameter vector. If the expectation of each moment function $m_t(\boldsymbol{\theta}_0)$ is zero conditional on an appropriate information set Ω_t, then it is normally a routine matter to find a suitable central limit theorem. Condition R3 is also satisfied under very mild regularity conditions. What it requires is that the derivatives of $n^{-1}\boldsymbol{m}^\top(\boldsymbol{\theta})\boldsymbol{\iota}$ with respect to the elements of $\boldsymbol{\theta}$, evaluated at $\boldsymbol{\theta}_0$, should be given by minus the elements of the vector $n^{-1}\boldsymbol{m}^\top(\boldsymbol{\theta}_0)\boldsymbol{G}(\boldsymbol{\theta}_0)$, up to a term of order $n^{-1/2}$. Formally, we require that

$$\frac{1}{n}\sum_{t=1}^{n} \frac{\partial m_t(\boldsymbol{\theta})}{\partial \boldsymbol{\theta}}\bigg|_{\boldsymbol{\theta}=\boldsymbol{\theta}_0} = -\frac{1}{n}\sum_{t=1}^{n} m_t(\boldsymbol{\theta}_0)\boldsymbol{G}_t(\boldsymbol{\theta}_0) + O_p(n^{-1/2}), \tag{15.26}$$

where $\boldsymbol{G}_t(\boldsymbol{\theta})$ is the tth row of $\boldsymbol{G}(\boldsymbol{\theta})$. Readers are invited in Exercise 15.6 to show that equation (15.26) holds under the usual regularity conditions for ML estimation. This property and its use in conditional moment tests implemented by an OPG regression were first established by Newey (1985). It is straightforward to extend this result to the case in which we have a matrix $\boldsymbol{M}(\boldsymbol{\theta})$ of moment functions.

As we noted in Section 10.5, many tests based on the OPG regression are prone to overreject the null hypothesis, sometimes very severely, in finite samples. It is therefore often a good idea to bootstrap conditional moment tests based on the OPG regression. Since the model under test is estimated by maximum likelihood, a fully parametric bootstrap is appropriate. It is generally quite easy to implement such a bootstrap, unless estimating the original model is unusually difficult or expensive.

Tests for Skewness and Kurtosis

One common application of conditional moment tests is checking the residuals from an econometric model for skewness and excess kurtosis. By "excess" kurtosis, we mean a fourth moment greater than $3\sigma^4$, the value for the normal distribution; see Exercise 4.2. The presence of significant departures from normality may indicate that a model is misspecified, or it may indicate that we should use a different estimation method. For example, although least squares may still perform well in the presence of moderate skewness and excess kurtosis, it cannot be expected to do so when the error terms are extremely skewed or have very thick tails.

Both skewness and excess kurtosis are often encountered in returns data from financial markets, especially when the returns are measured over short periods of time. A good model should eliminate, or at least substantially reduce, the skewness and excess kurtosis that is generally evident in daily, weekly, and, to a lesser extent, monthly returns data. Thus one way to evaluate a model for financial returns, such as the ARCH models that were discussed in Section 13.5, is to test the residuals for skewness and excess kurtosis.

We cannot base tests for skewness and excess kurtosis in regression models on the GNR, because the GNR is designed only for testing against alternatives that involve the conditional mean of the dependent variable. There is no way to define functions $z_t(\boldsymbol{\beta})$ that depend on parameters and exogenous or predetermined variables in such a way that the moment function (15.19) corresponds to the condition we wish to test. Instead, one valid approach is to test the slightly stronger assumption that the error terms are normally distributed by using the OPG regression. We now discuss this approach and show that even simpler tests are available.

The OPG regression that corresponds to the linear regression model

$$\boldsymbol{y} = \boldsymbol{X\beta} + \boldsymbol{u}, \quad \boldsymbol{u} \sim \mathrm{N}(\boldsymbol{0}, \sigma^2\mathbf{I}),$$

where the regressors include a constant or the equivalent, can be written as

$$1 = \frac{1}{\sigma^2}u_t(\boldsymbol{\beta})\boldsymbol{X}_t\boldsymbol{b} + b_\sigma \frac{u_t^2(\boldsymbol{\beta}) - \sigma^2}{\sigma^3} + \text{residual}. \tag{15.27}$$

Here $u_t(\boldsymbol{\beta}) \equiv y_t - \boldsymbol{X}_t\boldsymbol{\beta}$, and the assumption that the error terms are normal implies that they are not skewed and do not suffer from excess kurtosis. To test the assumption that they are not skewed, the appropriate test regressor for observation t is just $u_t^3(\boldsymbol{\beta})$. For testing purposes, all the regressors are to be evaluated at the OLS estimates $\hat{\boldsymbol{\beta}}$ and $\hat{\sigma}^2 \equiv \text{SSR}/n$. Thus an appropriate testing regression is

$$1 = \frac{1}{\hat{\sigma}^2} u_t(\hat{\boldsymbol{\beta}})\boldsymbol{X}_t\boldsymbol{b} + b_\sigma \frac{u_t^2(\hat{\boldsymbol{\beta}}) - \hat{\sigma}^2}{\hat{\sigma}^3} + c u_t^3(\hat{\boldsymbol{\beta}}) + \text{residual}. \tag{15.28}$$

This is just a special case of regression (15.24), and the test statistic is simply the t statistic for $c = 0$.

Regression (15.28) is unnecessarily complicated. First, observe that the test regressor is asymptotically orthogonal under the null to the regressor that corresponds to the parameter σ. To see this, evaluate the regressors at the true $\boldsymbol{\beta}_0$ instead of at $\hat{\boldsymbol{\beta}}$. Then the residuals $u_t(\boldsymbol{\beta}_0)$ are just the error terms u_t, and so we see that

$$\operatorname*{plim}_{n\to\infty} \frac{1}{n} \sum_{t=1}^{n} \frac{u_t^2 - \sigma^2}{\sigma^3} u_t^3 = 0.$$

This result uses a law of large numbers and follows from the facts that $\text{E}(u_t^5) = \text{E}(u_t^3) = 0$ if u_t is normally distributed. Thus the t statistic for $c = 0$ from regression (15.28) is asymptotically unchanged if we simply omit the regressor corresponding to σ.

This t statistic is also unchanged, in finite samples, if we add to $u_t^3(\boldsymbol{\beta})$ any linear combination of the regressors that correspond to $\boldsymbol{\beta}$; recall the discussion in Section 2.4 in connection with the FWL Theorem. Thus, since we assumed that there is a constant term in the regression, the t statistic is unchanged if we replace $u_t^3(\boldsymbol{\beta})$ by $u_t^3(\boldsymbol{\beta}) - 3\sigma^2 u_t(\boldsymbol{\beta})$. Doing so makes the new test regressor asymptotically orthogonal to all the regressors that correspond to $\boldsymbol{\beta}$, as can be seen from the following calculation:

$$\operatorname*{plim}_{n\to\infty} \frac{1}{n} \sum_{t=1}^{n} \boldsymbol{X}_t u_t(u_t^3 - 3\sigma^2 u_t) = \lim_{n\to\infty} \frac{1}{n} \sum_{t=1}^{n} \boldsymbol{X}_t \text{E}(u_t^4 - 3\sigma^2 u_t^2) = \boldsymbol{0}.$$

The second equality uses the fact that, when u_t is normal, $\text{E}(u_t^4) = 3\sigma^4$. Therefore, it makes no difference asymptotically if we omit the regressors that correspond to $\boldsymbol{\beta}$.

The above arguments imply that we can obtain a valid test simply by using the t statistic from the regression

$$1 = c\big(u_t^3(\hat{\boldsymbol{\beta}}) - 3\hat{\sigma}^2 u_t(\hat{\boldsymbol{\beta}})\big) + \text{residual}, \tag{15.29}$$

which is numerically identical to the t statistic for the sample mean of the single regressor here to be 0. Because the plim of the error variance is just 1, since the regressor and regressand are asymptotically orthogonal, both of these t statistics are asymptotically equal to

$$\frac{n^{-1/2}\sum_{t=1}^{n}(\hat{u}_t^3 - 3\hat{\sigma}^2\hat{u}_t)}{\big(n^{-1}\sum_{t=1}^{n}(\hat{u}_t^3 - 3\hat{\sigma}^2\hat{u}_t)^2\big)^{1/2}}, \tag{15.30}$$

where $\hat{u}_t \equiv u_t(\hat{\boldsymbol{\beta}})$. Since the OLS residuals from a regression that includes a constant sum to 0, the numerator of this expression simplifies to $n^{-1/2}\sum \hat{u}_t^3$. The sixth moment of the normal distribution is $15\sigma^6$ (see Exercise 13.19), and so the plim of the denominator is the square root of

$$\mathrm{E}(u_t^6 - 6\sigma^2 u_t^4 + 9\sigma^4 u_t^2) = \sigma^6(15 - 18 + 9) = 6\sigma^6.$$

It follows that expression (15.30) is asymptotically equal to the much simpler test statistic

$$\tau_3 \equiv (6n)^{-1/2}\sum_{t=1}^{n} e_t^3, \tag{15.31}$$

which is expressed in terms of the **normalized residuals** $e_t \equiv \hat{u}_t/\hat{\sigma}$. The asymptotic distribution of the test statistic τ_3 is standard normal under the null hypothesis that the error terms are normally distributed.

It follows from (15.31) that the variance of $n^{-1/2}\sum \hat{u}_t^3$ is $6\sigma^6$. In contrast, the variance of $n^{-1/2}\sum u_t^3$, which is equal to the variance of u_t^3, is $15\sigma^6$; see Exercise 13.19. Thus, in this case, the reduction in variance due to parameter uncertainty is very considerable.

The tth observation of the regressor needed to test for excess kurtosis is $u_t^4 - 3\sigma^4$. It is easy to check that this regressor can be made asymptotically orthogonal to the other regressors in (15.27) without changing the t statistic by subtracting $6\sigma^5$ times the regressor corresponding to σ, so as to yield $u_t^4 - 6\sigma^2 u_t^2 + 3\sigma^4$. Dividing this by σ^4 also has no effect on the t statistic, and so running the test regression

$$1 = c(e_t^4 - 6e_t^2 + 3) + \text{residual}, \tag{15.32}$$

which is defined in terms of the normalized residuals, provides an appropriate test statistic. As readers are invited to check in Exercise 15.8, this statistic is asymptotically equivalent to the simpler statistic

$$\tau_4 \equiv (24n)^{-1/2}\sum_{t=1}^{n}(e_t^4 - 3). \tag{15.33}$$

It is important that the denominator of the normalized residual be the ML estimator $\hat{\sigma}$ rather than the usual least-squares estimator s, as this choice ensures that the sum of the e_t^2 is precisely n. Like τ_3, the statistic τ_4 has an asymptotic $\mathrm{N}(0, 1)$ distribution under the null hypothesis of normality.

The squares of τ_3 and τ_4 are widely used as a test statistics for skewness and excess kurtosis; they are both asymptotically distributed as $\chi^2(1)$. However, we prefer to use the statistics themselves rather than their squares, since the sign is informative. The statistic τ_3 is positive when the residuals are skewed to the right and negative when they are skewed to the left. Similarly, the statistic τ_4 is positive if there is positive excess kurtosis and negative if there is negative excess kurtosis.

It can be shown (see Exercise 15.8 again) that the test statistics (15.31) and (15.33) are asymptotically independent under the null. Therefore, a joint test for skewness and excess kurtosis can be based on the statistic

$$\tau_{3,4} \equiv \tau_3^2 + \tau_4^2, \tag{15.34}$$

which is asymptotically distributed as $\chi^2(2)$ when the error terms are normally distributed. The statistics τ_3, τ_4, and $\tau_{3,4}$ were proposed, in slightly different forms, by Jarque and Bera (1980) and Kiefer and Salmon (1983); see also Bera and Jarque (1982). Many regression packages calculate these statistics as a matter of course.

The statistics τ_3, τ_4, and $\tau_{3,4}$ defined in equations (15.31), (15.33), and (15.34) depend solely on normalized residuals. This implies that, for a linear regression model with fixed regressors, they are pivotal under the null hypothesis of normality. Therefore, if we use the parametric bootstrap in this situation, we can obtain exact tests based on these statistics; see the discussion at the end of Section 7.7. Even for nonlinear regression models or models with lagged dependent variables, parametric bootstrap tests should work very much better than asymptotic tests.

The statistics τ_3, τ_4, and $\tau_{3,4}$ are not valid if the regression model that furnishes the normalized residuals does not contain a constant or the equivalent. However, tests based on the OPG regression are valid quite generally. In many cases, ones based on regressions like (15.29) and (15.32) are also valid; see Bontemps and Meddahi (2004). These techniques can be used to test for skewness and excess kurtosis in models that are not regression models, such as the models with ARCH errors that were discussed in Section 13.6.

Information Matrix Tests

In Section 10.3, we first encountered the **information matrix equality**. This famous result, which is given in equation (10.34), tells us that, for a model estimated by maximum likelihood with parameter vector $\boldsymbol{\theta}$, the asymptotic information matrix, $\mathcal{I}(\boldsymbol{\theta})$, is equal to minus the asymptotic Hessian, $\mathcal{H}(\boldsymbol{\theta})$. The proof of this result, which was given in Exercises 10.6 and 10.7, depends on the DGP being a special case of the model. Therefore, we should expect that, in general, the information matrix equality does not hold when the model we are estimating is misspecified. This suggests that testing this equality is one way to test the specification of a statistical model. This idea was first suggested by White (1982), who called tests based on it **information matrix tests**, or **IM tests**. These tests were later reinterpreted as conditional moment tests by Newey (1985) and White (1987).

Consider a statistical model characterized by the loglikelihood function

$$\ell(\boldsymbol{y},\boldsymbol{\theta}) = \sum_{t=1}^{n} \ell_t(\boldsymbol{y}^t,\boldsymbol{\theta}),$$

in the standard notation of equation (10.25). The null hypothesis for the IM test is that

$$\operatorname*{plim}_{n\to\infty} \frac{1}{n} \sum_{t=1}^{n} \left(\frac{\partial^2 \ell_t(\boldsymbol{\theta})}{\partial\theta_i \partial\theta_j} + \frac{\partial \ell_t(\boldsymbol{\theta})}{\partial\theta_i} \frac{\partial \ell_t(\boldsymbol{\theta})}{\partial\theta_j} \right) = 0, \tag{15.35}$$

for $i = 1, \ldots, k$ and $j = 1, \ldots, i$. Expression (15.35) is a typical element of the information matrix equality. The first term is an element of the asymptotic Hessian, and the second term is the corresponding element of the outer product of the gradient, the expectation of which is the asymptotic information matrix. Since both these matrices are symmetric, there are $\frac{1}{2}k(k+1)$ distinct conditions of the form (15.35).

Equation (15.35) is a conditional moment in the form (15.13). We can therefore calculate IM test statistics by means of the OPG regression, a procedure that was originally suggested by Chesher (1983) and Lancaster (1984). The matrix $\boldsymbol{M}(\boldsymbol{\theta})$ that appears in regression (15.25) is constructed as an $n \times \frac{1}{2}k(k+1)$ matrix with typical element

$$\frac{\partial^2 \ell_t(\boldsymbol{\theta})}{\partial\theta_i \partial\theta_j} + \frac{\partial \ell_t(\boldsymbol{\theta})}{\partial\theta_i} \frac{\partial \ell_t(\boldsymbol{\theta})}{\partial\theta_j}. \tag{15.36}$$

This matrix and the other matrix of regressors $\boldsymbol{G}(\boldsymbol{\theta})$ in (15.25) are usually evaluated at the ML estimates $\hat{\boldsymbol{\theta}}$. The test statistic is then the explained sum of squares, or, equivalently, $n -$ SSR from this regression. If the matrix $[\boldsymbol{G}(\hat{\boldsymbol{\theta}})\;\; \boldsymbol{M}(\hat{\boldsymbol{\theta}})]$ has full rank, this test statistic is asymptotically distributed as $\chi^2\big(\frac{1}{2}k(k+1)\big)$. If it does not have full rank, as is the case for linear regression models with a constant term, one or more columns of $\boldsymbol{M}(\hat{\boldsymbol{\theta}})$ have to be dropped, and the number of degrees of freedom for the test reduced accordingly.

In Exercise 15.11, readers are asked to develop the OPG version of the information matrix test for a particular linear regression model. As the exercise shows, the IM test in this case is sensitive to excess kurtosis, skewness, skewness interacted with the regressors, and any form of heteroskedasticity that the test of White (1980), which we discussed in Section 7.5, would detect; see Hall (1987). This suggests that we might well learn more about what is wrong with a regression model by testing for heteroskedasticity, skewness, and kurtosis separately instead of performing an information matrix test. We should certainly do that if the IM test rejects the null hypothesis.

As we have remarked before, tests based on the OPG regression are extremely prone to overreject in finite samples. This is particularly true for information matrix tests when the number of parameters is not small; see Davidson and MacKinnon (1992, 1998). Fortunately, the OPG variant of the IM test is by no means the only one that can be used. Davidson and MacKinnon (1998) compare the OPG version of the IM test for linear regression models with two other versions. One of these is the efficient score, or ES, variant (see Section 10.5), and the other is based on the double-length regression, or DLR, originally proposed by Davidson and MacKinnon (1984a). They also compare the OPG variant of the IM test for probit models with an efficient score variant that was proposed by Orme (1988). Although the DLR and both ES versions of the IM test are much more reliable than the corresponding OPG versions, their finite-sample properties are far from ideal, and they too should be bootstrapped whenever the sample size is not extremely large.

15.3 Nonnested Hypothesis Tests

Hypothesis testing usually involves nested models, in which the model that represents the null hypothesis is a special case of a more general model that represents the alternative hypothesis. For such a model, we can always test the null hypothesis by testing the restrictions that it imposes on the alternative. But economic theory often suggests models that are **nonnested**. This means that neither model can be written as a special case of the other without imposing restrictions on both models. In such a case, we cannot simply test one of the models against the other, less restricted, one.

There is an extensive literature on **nonnested hypothesis testing**. It provides a number of ways to test the specification of statistical models when one or more nonnested alternatives exists. In this section, we briefly discuss some of the simplest and most widely-used nonnested hypothesis tests, primarily in the context of regression models.

Testing Nonnested Linear Regression Models

Suppose we have two competing economic theories which imply different linear regression models for a dependent variable y_t conditional on some information set. We can write the two models as

$$\begin{aligned} H_1&: \quad \boldsymbol{y} = \boldsymbol{X\beta} + \boldsymbol{u}_1, \quad \text{and} \\ H_2&: \quad \boldsymbol{y} = \boldsymbol{Z\gamma} + \boldsymbol{u}_2. \end{aligned} \tag{15.37}$$

Here $\boldsymbol{y}$ is an n–vector with typical element y_t, and the regressor matrices $\boldsymbol{X}$ and $\boldsymbol{Z}$, which contain exogenous or predetermined variables, are $n \times k_1$ and $n \times k_2$, respectively. For simplicity, we will assume that, if the hypothesis H_i holds, then $\mathrm{E}(\boldsymbol{u}_i\boldsymbol{u}_i^\top) = \sigma_i^2\mathbf{I}$, for $i = 1, 2$. Thus OLS estimation is appropriate for whichever model actually generated the data, and we can base inferences on the usual OLS covariance matrix.

For the models H_1 and H_2 given in equations (15.37) to be nonnested, it must be the case that neither of them is a special case of the other. This implies that $\mathcal{S}(\boldsymbol{X})$ cannot be a subspace of $\mathcal{S}(\boldsymbol{Z})$, and vice versa. In other words, there must be at least one regressor among the columns of $\boldsymbol{X}$ that does not lie in $\mathcal{S}(\boldsymbol{Z})$, and there must be at least one regressor among the columns of $\boldsymbol{Z}$ that does not lie in $\mathcal{S}(\boldsymbol{X})$. We will assume that this is the case.

The simplest and most widely-used nonnested hypothesis tests start from the **artificial comprehensive model**

$$\boldsymbol{y} = (1-\alpha)\boldsymbol{X\beta} + \alpha\boldsymbol{Z\gamma} + \boldsymbol{u}, \tag{15.38}$$

where α is a scalar parameter. When $\alpha = 0$, equation (15.38) reduces to H_1, and when $\alpha = 1$, it reduces to H_2. Thus it might seem that, to test H_1, we could simply estimate this model and test whether $\alpha = 0$. However, this is not possible, because at least one, and usually quite a few, of the parameters of equation (15.38) cannot be identified. There are $k_1 + k_2 + 1$ parameters in the regression function of the artificial model, but the number of parameters that can be identified is the dimension of the subspace $\mathcal{S}(\boldsymbol{X}, \boldsymbol{Z})$. This cannot exceed $k_1 + k_2$ and is usually smaller, because some of the regressors, or linear combinations of them, may appear in both regression functions.

The simplest way to base a test on equation (15.38) is to estimate a restricted version of it that is identified, namely, the **inclusive regression**

$$\boldsymbol{y} = \boldsymbol{X\beta}' + \boldsymbol{Z}'\boldsymbol{\gamma}' + \boldsymbol{u}, \tag{15.39}$$

where the $n \times k_2'$ matrix $\boldsymbol{Z}'$ consists of the k_2' columns of $\boldsymbol{Z}$ that do not lie in $\mathcal{S}(\boldsymbol{X})$. Thus $\mathcal{S}(\boldsymbol{X}, \boldsymbol{Z}) = \mathcal{S}(\boldsymbol{X}, \boldsymbol{Z}')$, and the dimension of this space is $k_1 + k_2'$. We can estimate the model (15.39) by OLS and test the null hypothesis that $\boldsymbol{\gamma}' = \boldsymbol{0}$ by using an ordinary F test with k_2' and $n - k_1 - k_2'$ degrees of freedom. This provides an easy and reliable way to test H_1.

Although the F test for $\boldsymbol{\gamma}' = \boldsymbol{0}$ in the inclusive regression (15.39) has much to recommend it, it is not often thought of as a nonnested hypothesis test, and it does not generalize in a very satisfactory way to the case of nonlinear regression models. Moreover, it is generally less powerful than the nonnested hypothesis tests that we are about to discuss when H_2 actually generated the data. We will have more to say about this test below.

Another way to make equation (15.38) identified is to replace the unknown vector $\boldsymbol{\gamma}$ by a vector of parameter estimates. This idea was first suggested by Davidson and MacKinnon (1981), who proposed that $\boldsymbol{\gamma}$ be replaced by $\hat{\boldsymbol{\gamma}}$, the vector of OLS estimates of the H_2 model. Thus, if $\boldsymbol{\beta}$ is redefined appropriately, equation (15.38) becomes

$$\begin{aligned} \boldsymbol{y} &= \boldsymbol{X\beta} + \alpha\boldsymbol{Z}\hat{\boldsymbol{\gamma}} + \boldsymbol{u} \\ &= \boldsymbol{X\beta} + \alpha\boldsymbol{P}_{Z}\boldsymbol{y} + \boldsymbol{u}, \end{aligned} \tag{15.40}$$

where, as usual, $\boldsymbol{P_Z}$ denotes the matrix $\boldsymbol{Z}(\boldsymbol{Z}^\top\boldsymbol{Z})^{-1}\boldsymbol{Z}^\top$. This leads to the nonnested hypothesis test that Davidson and MacKinnon (1981) called the ***J* test**. It is based on the ordinary t statistic for $\alpha = 0$ in equation (15.40), which is called the ***J* statistic**.[1]

It is not at all obvious that the J statistic is asymptotically distributed as $\mathrm{N}(0,1)$ under the null hypothesis that the data were generated by H_1. After all, as can be seen from the second equation of (15.40), the test regressor depends on the regressand. Thus one might expect the regressand to be positively correlated with the test regressor, even when the null hypothesis is true. This is generally the case, but only in finite samples. The proof that the J statistic is asymptotically valid depends on the fact that, under the null hypothesis, the numerator of the test statistic is

$$\boldsymbol{y}^\top\boldsymbol{M_X}\boldsymbol{P_Z}\boldsymbol{y} = \boldsymbol{u}^\top\boldsymbol{M_X}\boldsymbol{P_Z}\boldsymbol{X}\boldsymbol{\beta}_0 + \boldsymbol{u}^\top\boldsymbol{M_X}\boldsymbol{P_Z}\boldsymbol{u}, \tag{15.41}$$

where $\boldsymbol{\beta}_0$ is the true parameter vector. The left-hand side of this equation can easily be obtained by applying the FWL Theorem to the second line of equation (15.40). The right-hand side follows when we replace $\boldsymbol{y}$ by $\boldsymbol{X}\boldsymbol{\beta}_0 + \boldsymbol{u}$. There are only two terms on the right-hand side of the equation, because $\boldsymbol{\beta}_0^\top\boldsymbol{X}^\top\boldsymbol{M_X} = \boldsymbol{0}$.

The first term on the right-hand side of equation (15.41) is a weighted average of the elements of the vector $\boldsymbol{u}$. Under standard regularity conditions, we may apply a central limit theorem to it, with the result that this term is $O_p(n^{1/2})$. In contrast, the second term is $O_p(1)$, as can be seen from the following:

$$\begin{aligned}\boldsymbol{u}^\top\boldsymbol{M_X}\boldsymbol{P_Z}\boldsymbol{u} &= \boldsymbol{u}^\top\boldsymbol{P_Z}\boldsymbol{u} - \boldsymbol{u}^\top\boldsymbol{P_X}\boldsymbol{P_Z}\boldsymbol{u}\\ &= n^{-1/2}\boldsymbol{u}^\top\boldsymbol{Z}(n^{-1}\boldsymbol{Z}^\top\boldsymbol{Z})^{-1}n^{-1/2}\boldsymbol{Z}^\top\boldsymbol{u}\\ &\quad - n^{-1/2}\boldsymbol{u}^\top\boldsymbol{X}(n^{-1}\boldsymbol{X}^\top\boldsymbol{X})^{-1}n^{-1}\boldsymbol{X}^\top\boldsymbol{Z}(n^{-1}\boldsymbol{Z}^\top\boldsymbol{Z})^{-1}n^{-1/2}\boldsymbol{Z}^\top\boldsymbol{u}.\end{aligned}$$

Since the error terms from the H_1 model are uncorrelated with the regressors of the H_2 model when the former is true, we can apply a central limit theorem to both $n^{-1/2}\boldsymbol{X}^\top\boldsymbol{u}$ and $n^{-1/2}\boldsymbol{Z}^\top\boldsymbol{u}$, so that these expressions are both $O_p(1)$. So too, under standard regularity conditions, are the cross-product matrices of the form $n^{-1}\boldsymbol{W}^\top\boldsymbol{W}$, where $\boldsymbol{W}$ stands for either $\boldsymbol{X}$ or $\boldsymbol{Z}$. It follows that $n^{-1/2}$ times the numerator of the J statistic has the same asymptotic distribution as $n^{-1/2}$ times the first term in (15.41). This distribution is

$$\mathrm{N}(0, n^{-1}\sigma_1^2\,\boldsymbol{\beta}_0^\top\boldsymbol{X}^\top\boldsymbol{P_Z}\boldsymbol{M_X}\boldsymbol{P_Z}\boldsymbol{X}\boldsymbol{\beta}_0). \tag{15.42}$$

It can be shown that n^{-1} times the square of the denominator of the test

[1] This J statistic should not be confused with the Hansen-Sargan statistic discussed in Section 9.4, which some authors refer to as the J statistic.

statistic consistently estimates the variance that appears in expression (15.42); see Exercise 15.12. The J statistic itself is therefore asymptotically distributed as N(0, 1) under the null hypothesis.

Although the J test is asymptotically valid, it generally is not exact in finite samples, although there is an exception in one very special case, which is treated in Exercise 15.13. In fact, because the second term on the right-hand side of equation (15.41) usually has a positive expectation under the null, the numerator of the J statistic generally has a positive mean, and so does the test statistic itself. In consequence, the J test tends to overreject, often quite severely, in finite samples. Theoretical results in Davidson and MacKinnon (2002a), which are consistent with the results of simulation experiments reported in a number of papers, suggest that the overrejection tends to be particularly severe when at least one of the following conditions holds:

- The sample size is small;
- The model under test does not fit very well;
- The number of regressors in H_2 that do not appear in H_1 is large.

Bootstrapping the J test dramatically improves its finite-sample performance. The bootstrap data may be generated under H_1 using either a fully parametric or a semiparametric bootstrap DGP, as discussed in Section 4.6. If the latter is used, it is very important to rescale the residuals before they are resampled. In most cases, the bootstrap J test is quite reliable, even in very small samples; see Godfrey (1998) and Davidson and MacKinnon (2002a). An even more reliable test may be obtained by using a more sophisticated bootstrapping procedure proposed by Davidson and MacKinnon (2002b).

Another way to obtain a nonnested test that is more reliable than the asymptotic J test in finite samples is to replace $\hat{\gamma}$ in the first line of equation (15.40) by another estimate of γ, namely,

$$\tilde{\gamma} \equiv (\boldsymbol{Z}^\top \boldsymbol{Z})^{-1} \boldsymbol{Z}^\top \boldsymbol{P_X y}. \tag{15.43}$$

This estimate may be obtained by regressing $\boldsymbol{P_X y}$ on $\boldsymbol{Z}$. It is an estimate of the expectation of $\hat{\gamma}$ when H_1 actually generates the data. The test regression is then

$$\begin{aligned} \boldsymbol{y} &= \boldsymbol{X\beta} + \alpha \boldsymbol{Z}\tilde{\gamma} + \boldsymbol{u} \\ &= \boldsymbol{X\beta} + \alpha \boldsymbol{P_Z P_X y} + \boldsymbol{u}, \end{aligned} \tag{15.44}$$

and the test statistic is, once again, the t statistic for $\alpha = 0$. This test statistic, which was originally proposed by Fisher and McAleer (1981), is called the **J_A statistic**. The resulting J_A test has much better finite-sample properties under the null hypothesis than the ordinary J test. In fact, the test is exact whenever both the H_1 and H_2 models satisfy all the assumptions of the classical normal linear model, for exactly the same reason that the RESET test is exact in a similar situation; see Godfrey (1983) and Exercise 15.3.

Unfortunately, the excellent performance of the J_A test under the null is not accompanied by equally good performance under the alternative. As can be seen from the second of equations (15.44), the vector $\boldsymbol{y}$ is projected onto $\boldsymbol{X}$ before $\boldsymbol{\gamma}$ is estimated. In consequence, $\tilde{\boldsymbol{\gamma}}$ may differ greatly from $\hat{\boldsymbol{\gamma}}$ when H_1 is false, and evidence that the H_1 model is incorrect may therefore be suppressed. Simulation experiments have shown that the J_A test can be very much less powerful than the J test; see, for example, Davidson and MacKinnon (1982). A rejection by the J_A test should be taken very seriously, but a failure to reject provides little information. In contrast, the J test, when bootstrapped, appears to be both reliable and powerful in samples of reasonable size.

The J and J_A tests are by no means the only nonnested tests that have been proposed for linear regression models. In particular, several tests have been based on the pioneering work of Cox (1961, 1962), which we will discuss further below. The most notable of these were proposed by Pesaran (1974) and Godfrey and Pesaran (1983). However, since these tests are asymptotically equivalent to the J test, have finite-sample properties that are either dreadful (for the first test) or mediocre (for the second one), and are more complicated to compute than the J test, especially in the case of the second one, there appears to be no reason to employ them in practice.

Testing Nonnested Nonlinear Regression Models

The J test can readily be extended to nonlinear regression models. Suppose the two models are

$$\begin{aligned} H_1\colon &\quad \boldsymbol{y} = \boldsymbol{x}(\boldsymbol{\beta}) + \boldsymbol{u}_1, \text{ and} \\ H_2\colon &\quad \boldsymbol{y} = \boldsymbol{z}(\boldsymbol{\gamma}) + \boldsymbol{u}_2. \end{aligned} \tag{15.45}$$

When we say that these two models are nonnested, we mean that there are values of $\boldsymbol{\beta}$, usually infinitely many of them, for which there is no admissible $\boldsymbol{\gamma}$ for which $\boldsymbol{x}(\boldsymbol{\beta}) = \boldsymbol{z}(\boldsymbol{\gamma})$, and, similarly, values of $\boldsymbol{\gamma}$ for which there is no admissible $\boldsymbol{\beta}$ such that $\boldsymbol{z}(\boldsymbol{\gamma}) = \boldsymbol{x}(\boldsymbol{\beta})$. In other words, neither model is a special case of the other unless we impose restrictions on both models. The artificial comprehensive model analogous to equation (15.38) is

$$\boldsymbol{y} = (1-\alpha)\boldsymbol{x}(\boldsymbol{\beta}) + \alpha\boldsymbol{z}(\boldsymbol{\gamma}) + \boldsymbol{u},$$

and the J statistic is the t statistic for $\alpha = 0$ in the nonlinear regression

$$\boldsymbol{y} = (1-\alpha)\boldsymbol{x}(\boldsymbol{\beta}) + \alpha\hat{\boldsymbol{z}} + \text{residuals}, \tag{15.46}$$

where $\hat{\boldsymbol{z}} \equiv \boldsymbol{z}(\hat{\boldsymbol{\gamma}})$, $\hat{\boldsymbol{\gamma}}$ being the vector of NLS estimates of the regression model H_2. It can be shown that, under suitable regularity conditions, this test statistic is asymptotically distributed as $\mathrm{N}(0,1)$ under H_1; see Davidson and MacKinnon (1981).

Because some of the parameters of the nonlinear regression (15.46) may not be well identified, the J statistic can be difficult to compute. This difficulty can be avoided in the usual way, that is, by running the GNR which corresponds to equation (15.46), evaluated at $\alpha = 0$ and $\boldsymbol{\beta} = \hat{\boldsymbol{\beta}}$. This GNR is

$$\boldsymbol{y} - \hat{\boldsymbol{x}} = \hat{\boldsymbol{X}}\boldsymbol{b} + a(\hat{\boldsymbol{z}} - \hat{\boldsymbol{x}}) + \text{residuals}, \tag{15.47}$$

where $\hat{\boldsymbol{x}} \equiv \boldsymbol{x}(\hat{\boldsymbol{\beta}})$, and $\hat{\boldsymbol{X}} \equiv \boldsymbol{X}(\hat{\boldsymbol{\beta}})$ is the matrix of derivatives of $\boldsymbol{x}(\boldsymbol{\beta})$ with respect to $\boldsymbol{\beta}$, evaluated at the NLS estimates $\hat{\boldsymbol{\beta}}$. The ordinary t statistic for $a = 0$ in regression (15.47) is called the ***P* statistic**. Under the null hypothesis, it is asymptotically equal to the corresponding J statistic. The P test is much more commonly used than the J test when the H_1 model is nonlinear.

Numerous other nonnested tests are available for nonlinear regression models. These include the P_A test, which is related to the P test in precisely the same way as the J_A test is related to the J test in the case of linear models. Because H_1 is nonlinear, the P_A test may not be particularly reliable in finite samples, and, like the J_A test, it can suffer from a serious lack of power. In contrast, a bootstrap version of the P test should be reasonably reliable and quite powerful. We therefore recommend using it rather than the P_A test if computer time is not a constraint.

The J and P tests can both be made robust to heteroskedasticity of unknown form either by using heteroskedasticity-robust standard errors (Section 5.5) or by using the HRGNR (Section 6.8). Like ordinary J and P tests, these tests should be bootstrapped. However, bootstrapping heteroskedasticity-robust tests requires procedures different from those used to bootstrap ordinary t and F tests, because the bootstrap DGP has to preserve the relationship between the regressors and the variances of the error terms. This means that we cannot use IID errors or resampled residuals. For introductory discussions of bootstrap methods for regression models with heteroskedastic errors, see Horowitz (2001) and MacKinnon (2002).

It is straightforward to extend the J and P tests to handle more than two nonnested alternatives. For concreteness, suppose there are three competing models. Then a J test of H_1 could be based on an F statistic for the joint significance of the fitted values from H_2 and H_3 when they are added to the regression for H_1. Similarly, a P test of H_1 could be based on an F statistic for the joint significance of the difference between the fitted values from H_2 and H_1, and the difference between the fitted values from H_3 and H_1, when they are both added to the GNR for H_1 evaluated at the least-squares estimates of that model.

The P test can also be extended to linear and nonlinear multivariate regression models; see Davidson and MacKinnon (1983). One starts by formulating an artificial comprehensive model analogous to (15.38), with just one additional parameter, replaces the parameters of the H_2 model by suitable estimates, and then obtains a P test based on the multivariate GNR (12.53) for the model under test. Because there is more than one plausible way to specify the artificial comprehensive model, more than one such test can be computed.

Interpreting Nonnested Tests

All of the nonnested hypothesis tests that we have discussed are really just specification tests of the H_1 model from either equations (15.37) or (15.45). If we reject the null hypothesis, there is no implication that the H_2 model is true. To say anything about the validity of the H_2 model, we need to test it. This can be done by interchanging the roles of the two models. For example, the J test of H_2 in the linear case would be based on the regression

$$\begin{aligned} \boldsymbol{y} &= \boldsymbol{Z\gamma} + \alpha' \boldsymbol{X}\hat{\boldsymbol{\beta}} + \boldsymbol{u} \\ &= \boldsymbol{Z\gamma} + \alpha' \boldsymbol{P_X y} + \boldsymbol{u}, \end{aligned} \tag{15.48}$$

where $\alpha' = 1 - \alpha$. The J statistic would then be the ordinary t statistic for $\alpha' = 0$ in regression (15.48).

When we perform a pair of nonnested tests, testing each of H_1 and H_2 against the other, there are four possible outcomes:

- Reject H_1 but do not reject H_2;
- Reject H_2 but do not reject H_1;
- Reject both models;
- Do not reject either model.

Since the first two outcomes lead us to prefer one of the models, it is tempting to see them as natural and desirable. However, the last two outcomes, which are by no means uncommon in practice, can also be very informative. If both models are rejected, then we need to find some other model that fits better. If neither model is rejected, then we have learned that the data appear to be compatible with both hypotheses.

Because nonnested hypothesis tests are designed as specification tests, rather than as procedures for choosing among competing models, it is not at all surprising that they sometimes do not lead us to choose one model over the other. If we simply want to choose the "best" model out of some set of competing models, whether or not any of them is satisfactory, then we should use a completely different approach, based on what are called **information criteria**. This approach will be discussed in the next section.

Encompassing Tests

If the true DGP belongs to model H_1, then it should be possible to derive the properties of parameter estimates from model H_2 in terms of the properties of model H_1. This is the idea behind what are called **encompassing tests**. It is very similar to the idea behind indirect inference, a topic we briefly discussed in Section 13.3. **Binding functions**, as defined in the context of indirect inference, specify the plim of the parameter estimates from model H_2 in terms of the parameters of the true DGP, which is assumed to be in H_1. Thus a test of H_1 can be based on a comparison of the actual H_2 parameter estimates and estimates of the values of the binding functions under the assumption that H_1 generated the data.

As a concrete example, consider the linear case in which the two models are given by equations (15.37). If the DGP is a special case of H_1 with parameters β_0, the binding functions evaluated at β_0 give the plim of the vector $\hat{\gamma}$ obtained by estimating H_2. Since the columns of Z are assumed to be exogenous or predetermined, we see that

$$\operatorname*{plim}_{n\to\infty} \hat{\gamma} = \Big(\operatorname*{plim}_{n\to\infty} \frac{1}{n} \boldsymbol{Z}^\top \boldsymbol{Z}\Big)^{-1} \Big(\operatorname*{plim}_{n\to\infty} \frac{1}{n} \boldsymbol{Z}^\top \boldsymbol{X}\boldsymbol{\beta}_0\Big).$$

We can estimate this probability limit by dropping the plims on the right-hand side and replacing $\boldsymbol{\beta}_0$ by $\hat{\boldsymbol{\beta}}$. Doing so yields the estimator $\tilde{\gamma}$ defined in equation (15.43). An encompassing test can therefore be based on the vector of contrasts between $\hat{\gamma}$ and $\tilde{\gamma}$. This vector is

$$(\boldsymbol{Z}^\top\boldsymbol{Z})^{-1}\boldsymbol{Z}^\top\boldsymbol{y} - (\boldsymbol{Z}^\top\boldsymbol{Z})^{-1}\boldsymbol{Z}^\top\boldsymbol{P_X}\boldsymbol{y} = (\boldsymbol{Z}^\top\boldsymbol{Z})^{-1}\boldsymbol{Z}^\top\boldsymbol{M_X}\boldsymbol{y}. \tag{15.49}$$

The leading factor $(\boldsymbol{Z}^\top\boldsymbol{Z})^{-1}$ has no effect on the test, because it is just a square matrix of full rank. Since some columns of $\boldsymbol{Z}$ generally lie in $\mathcal{S}(\boldsymbol{X})$, some of the columns of the matrix $\boldsymbol{Z}^\top\boldsymbol{M_X}$ usually are identically zero. Thus, as before, we let $\boldsymbol{Z}'$ denote the remaining columns of $\boldsymbol{Z}$. Then what we really want to test is whether the plim of the vector $n^{-1}\boldsymbol{Z}'^\top\boldsymbol{M_X}\boldsymbol{y}$ is zero. This calls for a conditional moment test. Since the model H_1 is linear, such a test can be implemented without an explicit GNR simply by using the columns of $\boldsymbol{Z}'$ as test regressors, that is, by using the inclusive regression (15.39) as a test regression. The test statistic is just the F statistic for $\gamma' = \boldsymbol{0}$ in (15.39), which we have already discussed.

The parallels between this sort of encompassing test and the DWH test discussed in Section 8.6 are illuminating. Both tests can be implemented as F tests—in the case of the DWH test, an F test based on regression (8.77). In both cases, the F test almost always has fewer degrees of freedom in the numerator than the number of parameters. The interested reader may find it worthwhile to show explicitly that a DWH test can be set up as a conditional moment test.

For a detailed discussion of the concept of encompassing and various tests that are based on it, see Hendry (1995, Chapter 14). Encompassing tests are available for a variety of nonlinear models; see Mizon and Richard (1986). However, there can be practical difficulties with these tests. These difficulties are similar to the ones that can arise with Hausman tests which are based directly on a vector of contrasts; see Section 8.6. The basic problem is that it can be difficult to ascertain the dimension of the space analogous to $\mathcal{S}(\boldsymbol{X}, \boldsymbol{Z})$, and, in consequence, it can be difficult to determine the appropriate number of degrees of freedom for the test.

Cox Tests

Nonnested hypothesis tests are available for a large number of models that are not regression models. Most of these tests are based on one of two approaches. The first approach, which previously led to the J and P tests, involves forming an artificial comprehensive model and then replacing the parameters of the H_2 model by estimates that are asymptotically nonstochastic. As an example of this approach, Exercise 15.19 asks readers to derive a test similar to the P test for binary response models. The second approach, which we briefly discuss in this subsection, is based on two classic papers by Cox (1961, 1962). It leads to what are generally called **Cox tests**.

Suppose the two nonnested models are each to be estimated by maximum likelihood, and that their loglikelihood functions are

$$\ell_1(\boldsymbol{\theta}_1) = \sum_{t=1}^{n} \ell_{1t}(\boldsymbol{\theta}_1) \quad \text{and} \quad \ell_2(\boldsymbol{\theta}_2) = \sum_{t=1}^{n} \ell_{2t}(\boldsymbol{\theta}_2), \tag{15.50}$$

for models H_1 and H_2, respectively. The notation, which is similar to that used in Chapter 10, omits the dependence on the data for clarity. Cox's idea was to extend the idea of a likelihood ratio test, and so he considered what would be the LR statistic if H_1 were nested in H_2, namely, $2\big(\ell_2(\hat{\boldsymbol{\theta}}_2) - \ell_1(\hat{\boldsymbol{\theta}}_1)\big)$, where $\hat{\boldsymbol{\theta}}_1$ and $\hat{\boldsymbol{\theta}}_2$ are the ML estimates of the two models.

The statistical properties of the LR statistic are quite different when H_1 and H_2 are nonnested rather than nested. In particular, it is necessary to divide the statistic by $n^{1/2}$ in order to obtain a random variable with a well-defined asymptotic distribution. It is then convenient to center this variable by subtracting its expectation. Since, according to equations (15.50), both $\ell_1(\boldsymbol{\theta}_1)$ and $\ell_2(\boldsymbol{\theta}_2)$ are sums of contributions, it is reasonable to suppose that the expression

$$2n^{-1/2}\big(\ell_2(\hat{\boldsymbol{\theta}}_2) - \ell_1(\hat{\boldsymbol{\theta}}_1)\big) - 2n^{-1/2}\mathrm{E}_{\boldsymbol{\theta}_1}\big(\ell_2(\hat{\boldsymbol{\theta}}_2) - \ell_1(\hat{\boldsymbol{\theta}}_1)\big) \tag{15.51}$$

is asymptotically normal, where the notation $\mathrm{E}_{\boldsymbol{\theta}_1}$ denotes an expectation taken under the DGP in the H_1 model with parameter vector $\boldsymbol{\theta}_1$.

Since the parameter vector $\boldsymbol{\theta}_1$ is not known, the expectation in (15.51) cannot be calculated. It is natural to estimate it by replacing the true $\boldsymbol{\theta}_1$ by the ML estimate $\hat{\boldsymbol{\theta}}_1$, but then we face the problem of parameter uncertainty if we wish to estimate the variance of the result. Cox solved this problem by showing that, under H_1, the statistic

$$T_1 \equiv 2n^{-1/2}\big(\ell_2(\hat{\boldsymbol{\theta}}_2) - \ell_1(\hat{\boldsymbol{\theta}}_1)\big) - 2n^{-1/2}\mathrm{E}_{\hat{\boldsymbol{\theta}}_1}\big(\ell_2(\hat{\boldsymbol{\theta}}_2) - \ell_1(\hat{\boldsymbol{\theta}}_1)\big) \tag{15.52}$$

is indeed asymptotically normally distributed, with mean 0 and a variance that can be estimated consistently using a formula given in his 1962 paper.

In some commonly encountered cases, the statistic T_1 defined in (15.52) is unnecessarily complicated. One such case is considered in Exercise 15.20. In these cases, T_1 is asymptotically equivalent to the simpler statistic

$$T_1' \equiv 2n^{-1/2}\Big(\ell_2(\hat{\boldsymbol{\theta}}_2) - \mathrm{E}_{\hat{\boldsymbol{\theta}}_1}\big(\ell_2(\hat{\boldsymbol{\theta}}_2)\big)\Big), \tag{15.53}$$

in which the difference between $\ell_1(\hat{\boldsymbol{\theta}}_1)$ and its expectation has been omitted. When the statistic (15.53) is applicable, it can be seen that the Cox test is a type of encompassing test. The test compares the maximized loglikelihood function for model H_2 with its expectation under the DGP in model H_1 with parameter vector $\hat{\boldsymbol{\theta}}_1$. The expectation $\mathrm{E}_{\hat{\boldsymbol{\theta}}_1}\big(\ell_2(\hat{\boldsymbol{\theta}}_2)\big)$ can be interpreted naturally as the binding function for $\ell_2(\hat{\boldsymbol{\theta}}_2)$.

The Cox test can also be interpreted as a conditional moment test. The single moment condition can be written as

$$\operatorname*{plim}_{\boldsymbol{\theta}_1} \frac{1}{n}\sum_{t=1}^{n}\Big(\ell_{2t}(\hat{\boldsymbol{\theta}}_2) - \ell_{1t}(\hat{\boldsymbol{\theta}}_1) - \mathrm{E}_{\boldsymbol{\theta}_1}\big(\ell_{2t}(\hat{\boldsymbol{\theta}}_2) - \ell_{1t}(\hat{\boldsymbol{\theta}}_1)\big)\Big) = 0,$$

and the corresponding empirical moment as

$$\frac{1}{n}\sum_{t=1}^{n}\Big(\ell_{2t}(\hat{\boldsymbol{\theta}}_2) - \ell_{1t}(\hat{\boldsymbol{\theta}}_1) - \mathrm{E}_{\hat{\boldsymbol{\theta}}_1}\big(\ell_{2t}(\hat{\boldsymbol{\theta}}_2) - \ell_{1t}(\hat{\boldsymbol{\theta}}_1)\big)\Big).$$

This conditional moment interpretation leads naturally to an implementation of the Cox test by artificial regression. The easiest one to set up is, as usual, the OPG regression. Since there is only one test regressor, it takes the form of regression (15.24). The matrix $\hat{\boldsymbol{G}}$ in the test regression is the matrix of contributions to the gradient for the H_1 model, evaluated at $\hat{\boldsymbol{\theta}}_1$. The test regressor has typical element

$$\ell_{2t}(\hat{\boldsymbol{\theta}}_2) - \ell_{1t}(\hat{\boldsymbol{\theta}}_1) - \mathrm{E}_{\hat{\boldsymbol{\theta}}_1}\big(\ell_{2t}(\hat{\boldsymbol{\theta}}_2) - \ell_{1t}(\hat{\boldsymbol{\theta}}_1)\big). \tag{15.54}$$

It can be shown that this test regressor satisfies conditions R1–R3. Notice that we need to compute n expectations, rather than the single expectation needed for the more conventional Cox test based on the statistic T_1 defined in equation (15.52).

For regression models, there is a close relationship between Cox tests and tests based on artificial comprehensive models. Cox tests for linear and nonlinear regression models were derived by Pesaran (1974) and Pesaran and Deaton (1978), respectively. These tests were shown to be asymptotically equivalent to the corresponding J and P tests by Davidson and MacKinnon (1981).[2]

[2] The negative of the Cox statistic, as formulated in these papers, is asymptotically equal to the corresponding J or P test. Note that Cox statistics as we have defined them are opposite in sign to most of the ones in the literature.

The main difficulty involved in calculating a Cox test is obtaining either the expectation under H_1 of $\ell_2(\hat{\boldsymbol{\theta}}_2) - \ell_1(\hat{\boldsymbol{\theta}}_1)$ or the expectations under H_1 of the $\ell_{2t}(\hat{\boldsymbol{\theta}}_2) - \ell_{1t}(\hat{\boldsymbol{\theta}}_1)$. Since the test is valid only asymptotically, it is legitimate to replace the expectation in (15.52) by a probability limit, which may be simpler to evaluate analytically than the expectation. In cases in which no analytic expression is available, we may evaluate the expectations by simulation. After estimating the H_1 model, we generate S sets of simulated data from the DGP with parameter vector $\hat{\boldsymbol{\theta}}_1$, estimate both models using the simulated data, and then estimate the expectation of $\ell_{2t}(\hat{\boldsymbol{\theta}}_2) - \ell_{1t}(\hat{\boldsymbol{\theta}}_1)$ as

$$\frac{1}{S}\sum_{s=1}^{S}\big(\ell_{2t}(\hat{\boldsymbol{\theta}}^*_{2s}) - \ell_{1t}(\hat{\boldsymbol{\theta}}^*_{1s})\big), \tag{15.55}$$

where $\hat{\boldsymbol{\theta}}^*_{is}$, for $i = 1, 2$, denotes the estimate of $\boldsymbol{\theta}_i$ based on the sth set of simulated data. The expectation of $\ell_2(\hat{\boldsymbol{\theta}}_2) - \ell_1(\hat{\boldsymbol{\theta}}_1)$ may then be obtained by summing expression (15.55) over all t.

As we have remarked before, the OPG regression does not have very good finite-sample properties. This suggests that it is generally wise to bootstrap any test based on it. When the expectation under H_1 of $\ell_2(\hat{\boldsymbol{\theta}}_2) - \ell_1(\hat{\boldsymbol{\theta}}_1)$ can be calculated without simulation, this should generally pose no serious difficulty. However, if we have to use simulation, bootstrapping involves estimating the H_2 model $S + 1$ times for each of B bootstrap samples, and this may be computationally demanding.

Our discussion of nonnested hypothesis testing has necessarily omitted many topics. Survey articles on this subject include Gouriéroux and Monfort (1994), McAleer (1995), and Pesaran and Weeks (2001). In general, nonnested tests based on asymptotic theory have poor finite-sample properties. It is therefore desirable to bootstrap them in many, if not most, cases. However, except for tests of linear regression models (Davidson and MacKinnon, 2002a), not much is known about the finite-sample properties of bootstrapped nonnested hypothesis tests.

15.4 Model Selection Based on Information Criteria

As we remarked in the previous section, testing each of two nonnested models against the other may or may not allow us to choose one model over the other. More generally, if we have m models and perform $m(m - 1)$ pairwise tests, we cannot reasonably expect to find that one and only one of the models is never rejected. Thus, if our objective is to choose the best model out of the m competing models, and we do not care whether even the best model is false, we should not use nonnested hypothesis tests. Instead, we should use a procedure explicitly designed for **model selection**. Such a procedure generally involves calculating some sort of criterion function for each of the models and picking the model for which that function is maximized or minimized.

For concreteness, suppose that, for the same dependent variable or variables, we have m competing models that are estimated by maximum likelihood, ordinary least squares, or nonlinear least squares. Let $\boldsymbol{\theta}_i$ be the k_i–vector of parameters for the ith model, and let $\ell_i(\hat{\boldsymbol{\theta}}_i)$ denote the maximized value of the loglikelihood function for that model, which we may take to be $-\frac{1}{2}n\log \text{SSR}$ in the case of models estimated by least squares. It might seem natural to pick the model with the largest value of $\ell_i(\hat{\boldsymbol{\theta}}_i)$. However, if the models are nested, this simply leads us to pick the model with the greatest number of parameters, even when other models fit almost as well. This violates the principle that, when each one of a set of nested models is correctly specified, we should prefer the one that has fewest parameters to estimate. This model is called the most **parsimonious** model of the set. With nonnested models, it is not necessarily the case that the least parsimonious of them yields the greatest value of the loglikelihood function, but, whenever $k_i > k_j$, model i plainly has an advantage over model j and therefore tends to be chosen too often when parsimony is a concern.

To avoid this problem, we evidently need to penalize models with a large number of parameters. This idea leads to various criterion functions that can be used to rank competing models. The most widely used of these is probably the **Akaike information criterion**, or **AIC** (Akaike, 1973). There is more than one version of the AIC. For model i, the simplest version is

$$\text{AIC}_i = \ell_i(\hat{\boldsymbol{\theta}}_i) - k_i. \tag{15.56}$$

Thus we reduce the loglikelihood function of each model by 1 for every estimated parameter, and we then choose the model that maximizes AIC_i. The original form of the AIC is equivalent to (15.56) but a bit more complicated, and it is supposed to be minimized instead of maximized. Users of black-box software packages should make sure that they understand precisely what is being printed if a package prints what it calls the AIC.

The AIC does not always respect the need for parsimony any more than the maximized loglikelihood function. Consider two nested models, H_1 and H_2, with k and $k+1$ parameters, respectively. Asymptotically, twice the difference between the two loglikelihood functions is distributed as $\chi^2(1)$ if H_1 is correctly specified. Therefore, the probability that AIC_2 is greater than AIC_1 tends in large samples to the probability mass in the right-hand tail of the $\chi^2(1)$ distribution beyond 2, which is 0.1573. Thus, even with an infinitely large sample, we choose the less parsimonious model nearly 16% of the time. This example illustrates a general problem. Whenever two or more models are nested, the AIC may fail to choose the most parsimonious of those that are correctly specified. If all the models are nonnested, and only one is well specified, the AIC chooses that one asymptotically, but so does simply picking the model with the largest value of the loglikelihood function.

A popular alternative to the AIC, which avoids the problem discussed in the preceding paragraph, is the **Bayesian information criterion**, or **BIC**, which was proposed by Schwarz (1978). For model i, the BIC is

$$\mathrm{BIC}_i = \ell_i(\hat{\boldsymbol{\theta}}_i) - \frac{1}{2}k_i \log n. \tag{15.57}$$

The factor of $\log n$ in the penalty term ensures that, as $n \to \infty$, the penalty for having an additional parameter becomes very large. Thus, asymptotically, there is no danger of choosing an insufficiently parsimonious model. If we compare a false but parsimonious model H_2 with a correctly-specified model H_1 that may have more parameters, the BIC chooses H_1 asymptotically, since, as readers are asked to check in Exercise 15.23, the difference $\mathrm{BIC}_1 - \mathrm{BIC}_2$ tends to infinity with the sample size.

It is possible to extend the Akaike and Bayesian information criteria to models that are not estimated by maximum likelihood or least squares. See Andrews and Lu (2001) for a detailed discussion in the context of GMM estimation. The penalty terms depend on the number of overidentifying restrictions rather than on the number of parameters only. These penalty terms are twice as large as the ones that appear in equations (15.56) and (15.57), because likelihood ratio tests (Section 10.5) involve a factor of two, while tests based on GMM criterion functions (Section 9.4) do not involve such a factor.

15.5 Nonparametric Estimation

Estimation by nonparametric methods has become an area of major interest in both statistics and econometrics over the past twenty-five years. The term "nonparametric" can have more than one meaning. We use it here rather loosely to refer to a variety of estimation techniques that do not explicitly involve estimating parameters. We first discuss nonparametric density estimation and then move on to discuss nonparametric regression. Nonparametric methods can be used to provide alternatives against which to test parametric models, and we briefly discuss this sort of test at the end of the section.

We have already encountered a few nonparametric estimators. In particular, the HAC estimators that were introduced in Section 9.3 are explicitly nonparametric. Another example is the empirical distribution function, or EDF, which was introduced in Section 4.5. As we saw there, if a sample is drawn from some univariate distribution, then the EDF consistently estimates the cumulative distribution function, or CDF. Since resampling from residuals is equivalent to drawing values randomly from the EDF, as we saw in Section 4.6, many bootstrap methods implicitly make use of nonparametric estimates.

The probability density function (PDF) associated with a given distribution is the derivative of the CDF, if the derivative exists. Since an EDF is, by construction, a discontinuous function, its derivative does not exist at the points of discontinuity. Elsewhere, an EDF is locally constant, and so, at those points where the derivative exists, it is zero. Thus, if we wish to estimate a density, we clearly cannot do so by differentiating the EDF.

Estimation of Density Functions

One traditional way of estimating a PDF is to form a **histogram**. Given a sample x_t, $t = 1, \ldots, n$, of independent realizations of a random variable X, the interval containing the x_t is partitioned into a set of subintervals by a set of points z_i, $i = 1, \ldots, m$, with $z_i < z_j$ for $i < j$, where m is typically much smaller than n. Like the EDF, the histogram is a locally constant function with discontinuities. Unlike the EDF, the histogram is discontinuous at the z_i, not the x_t. For arbitrary argument x, let i be such that $z_i \leq x < z_{i+1}$. Then the histogram is defined as

$$\hat{f}(x) = \frac{1}{n}\sum_{t=1}^{n} \frac{I(z_i \leq x_t < z_{i+1})}{z_{i+1} - z_i}, \tag{15.58}$$

where, as usual, $I(\cdot)$ denotes an indicator function, and the notation $\hat{f}(x)$ is motivated by the fact that the histogram is an estimate of a density function. Thus the value of the histogram at x is the proportion of the sample points contained in the same **bin** as x, divided by the length of the bin, that is, the length of the segment $[z_i, z_{i+1}]$. It is thus quite precisely the density of sample points in that segment.

The histogram (15.58) is entirely dependent on the choice of the partitioning points z_i. If there were only one segment, $[z_1, z_2]$, covering the whole range of the sample, then the histogram would be constant over that range, and the estimated density would therefore correspond to a uniform distribution. If the partition were exceedingly fine, with a value of m much greater than the sample size, then most bins would be empty, and the histogram would be equal to 0 for values of x in those bins. For the bins that contained one or more points, the value of the histogram would be very large, since the denominator $z_{i+1} - z_i$ would tend to zero as the partition became finer.

In the limit with just one bin, the histogram is completely smooth, being constant over the sample range. In the other limit of an infinite number of bins, the histogram is completely unsmooth, its values alternating between zero and infinity. Neither limit is at all useful. What we seek is some intermediate degree of smoothness. More sophisticated methods of density estimation, which we introduce in the next subsection, must, like the histogram, make a choice of how smooth the estimated density should be. The choice depends on what is called the **bandwidth**, or **window width**, which corresponds to the width of a typical segment for a histogram.

Kernel Estimation

The empirical distribution function, or EDF, of a sample was first defined in Section 4.5. The definition, which is repeated here for convenience, is

$$\hat{F}(x) \equiv \frac{1}{n}\sum_{t=1}^{n} I(x_t \leq x). \tag{15.59}$$

The discontinuous indicator function $I(x_t \leq x)$, or equivalently $I(x \geq x_t)$, can be interpreted as the CDF of a degenerate random variable which puts all its probability mass on x_t, and the EDF can then be thought of as the unweighted average of these CDFs. As is clear from Figure 4.6, such a discontinuous EDF can, when graphed, provide the appearance of a smooth approximation to a CDF when the sample size is moderately large. But the interpretation of the indicator functions as CDFs suggests that we can obtain a genuinely smooth estimate of the CDF by replacing the discontinuous function $I(x \geq x_t)$ by a continuous CDF, with support in an interval containing x_t.

Let $K(z)$ be any continuous CDF corresponding to a distribution with mean 0. This function is called a **cumulative kernel**. It usually corresponds to a distribution that is symmetric around the origin, such as the standard normal. Then a smooth estimate of the CDF could be obtained by replacing the indicator function $I(x_t \leq x)$ in equation (15.59) by $K(x - x_t)$. It is convenient to be able to control the degree of smoothness of the estimate. Accordingly, we set the variance of the distribution characterized by $K(z)$ equal to 1 and introduce the bandwidth parameter h as a scaling parameter for the actual smoothing distribution. This gives the **kernel CDF estimator**

$$\hat{F}_h(x) = \frac{1}{n}\sum_{t=1}^{n} K\Big(\frac{x - x_t}{h}\Big). \tag{15.60}$$

Evidently, this estimator depends on the choice of the cumulative kernel and on the bandwidth. As h tends to zero, it is easy to see that a typical term of the summation on the right-hand side tends to $I(x \geq x_t)$, and so $\hat{F}_h(x)$ tends to the EDF $\hat{F}(x)$ as $h \to 0$. At the other extreme, as h becomes large, a typical term of the summation tends to the constant value $K(0)$, which makes the kernel estimator $\hat{F}_h(x)$ very much too smooth. In the usual case in which $K(z)$ is symmetric, $\hat{F}_h(x)$ tends to 0.5 as $h \to \infty$.

Kernel methods can also be used for density estimation. In fact, they are much more commonly used to estimate PDFs than to estimate CDFs. For density estimation, we choose a function $K(z)$ that is not only continuous but also differentiable and define the **kernel function** $k(z)$, often simply called the **kernel**, as $K'(z)$. Then, if we differentiate equation (15.60) with respect to x, we obtain the **kernel density estimator**

$$\hat{f}_h(x) = \frac{1}{nh}\sum_{t=1}^{n} k\Big(\frac{x - x_t}{h}\Big). \tag{15.61}$$

Like the kernel CDF estimator (15.60), the kernel density estimator depends on both the choice of kernel k and the bandwidth h. It turns out that the choice of kernel is much less critical than the choice of bandwidth. One very popular choice for k is the **Gaussian kernel**, which is just the standard normal density ϕ. It gives a positive (although perhaps very small) weight to every point in the sample. Another commonly used kernel, which has certain optimality properties, is the **Epanechnikov kernel**,

$$k(z) = \frac{3(1 - z^2/5)}{4\sqrt{5}} \quad \text{for } |z| < \sqrt{5}, \quad 0 \text{ otherwise.}$$

This kernel gives a positive weight only to points for which $|(x_t - x)|/h < \sqrt{5}$. In practice, the Gaussian and Epanechnikov kernels generally give very similar estimates if they are based on similar values of h.

Choosing the Bandwidth

The kernel density estimator (15.61) is very sensitive to the value of the bandwidth parameter h, and there is an extremely large and highly technical literature on how best to choose it. See Silverman (1986), Härdle (1990), Wand and Jones (1995), or Pagan and Ullah (1999) for introductions to this literature. The estimator $\hat{f}_h(x)$ is biased, unless the density is genuinely constant, which is almost never the case, and too large a value of h gives rise to **oversmoothing**. This suggests that, to make bias small, h should be small. However, when h is too small, the estimator suffers from **undersmoothing**, which implies that the variance of $\hat{f}_h(x)$ is large. Thus any choice of h inevitably involves a tradeoff between the bias and the variance. This suggests that we should choose h to minimize the expectation of the squared error, defined as

$$\mathrm{E}\big(\hat{f}_h(x) - f(x)\big)^2 = \big(\mathrm{E}\hat{f}_h(x) - f(x)\big)^2 + \mathrm{Var}\big(\hat{f}_h(x)\big), \tag{15.62}$$

that is, the square of the bias of $\hat{f}_h(x)$ plus its variance. If we are interested in the entire density rather than just the density at a single point, which is often but not always the case, then we would like to minimize the integral over all x of either side of equation (15.62).

Under fairly general regularity conditions, it can be shown that any h that minimizes the expectation (15.62) or its integral must be proportional to $n^{-1/5}$; see Exercise 15.25. The factor of proportionality depends on the true distribution of the data. Two popular choices for h are

$$h = 1.059\,s n^{-1/5}, \text{ and} \tag{15.63}$$

$$h = 0.785(\hat{q}_{.75} - \hat{q}_{.25})n^{-1/5}, \tag{15.64}$$

where s is the standard deviation of the x_t, and $\hat{q}_{.75} - \hat{q}_{.25}$ is the difference between the estimated .75 and .25 quantiles of the data, which is known as the **interquartile range**, or **IQR**. When the data are approximately normally distributed, it makes sense to use s to measure the spread of the data. In fact, the value of h given in equation (15.63) is optimal for data that are normally distributed when using a Gaussian kernel. The factor of 1.059 is really $(4/3)^{1/5}$, a quantity that appears in the proof of optimality. When the data have thick tails, s tends to overestimate the spread, and it is better to use the interquartile range. Note that the factor of 0.785 in equation (15.64) is 1.059 divided by 1.349, which is the interquartile range for the standard normal distribution. Thus, if the data were normally distributed, both s and $\mathrm{IQR}/1.349$ would be estimates of σ.

Although the values given in equations (15.63) and (15.64) should work quite well in many cases, they may tend to oversmooth a bit when the data are strongly skewed or bimodal. Therefore, as a rule of thumb, Silverman (1986) suggests using

$$h = 0.9 \min(s, \mathrm{IQR}/1.349) n^{-1/5}. \tag{15.65}$$

This is the minimum of the values defined in equation (15.63) and (15.64), but with the factor of 1.059 replaced by 0.9 in order to reduce the risk of oversmoothing.

It should be noted that the bandwidths appropriate for kernel estimation of densities are *not* appropriate for kernel estimation of CDFs. Under the same (extremely strong) assumptions that led to the value $h = 1.059 s n^{-1/5}$ for density estimation, it can be shown that $h = 1.587 s n^{-1/3}$ is optimal for CDF estimation. However, $h = 1.3 s n^{-1/3}$ may be a better choice if interest centers on tail quantiles. See Azzalini (1981) or Wand and Jones (1995).

An Illustration of Kernel Density Estimation

Figure 15.1 shows an estimated density for daily percentage returns on IBM common stock. It is based on 9939 observations from July, 1962 to December, 2001. A Gaussian kernel with h given by equation (15.64) was used. We

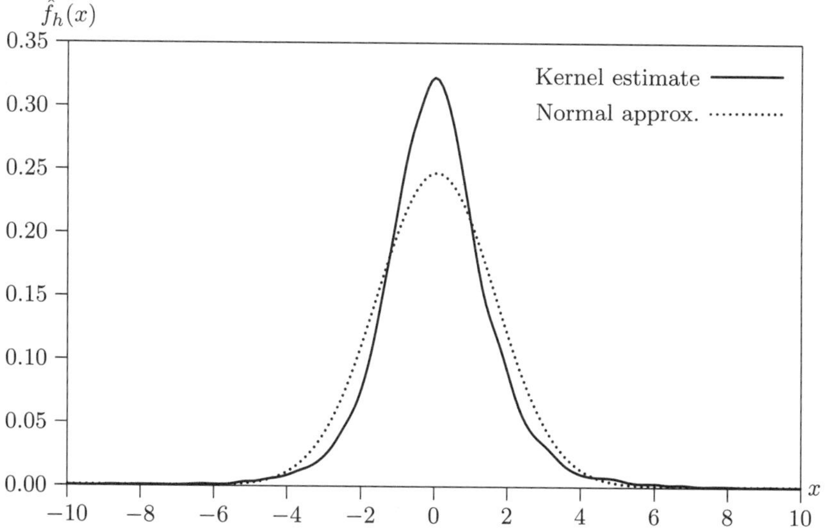

Figure 15.1 Estimates of the density of IBM stock returns

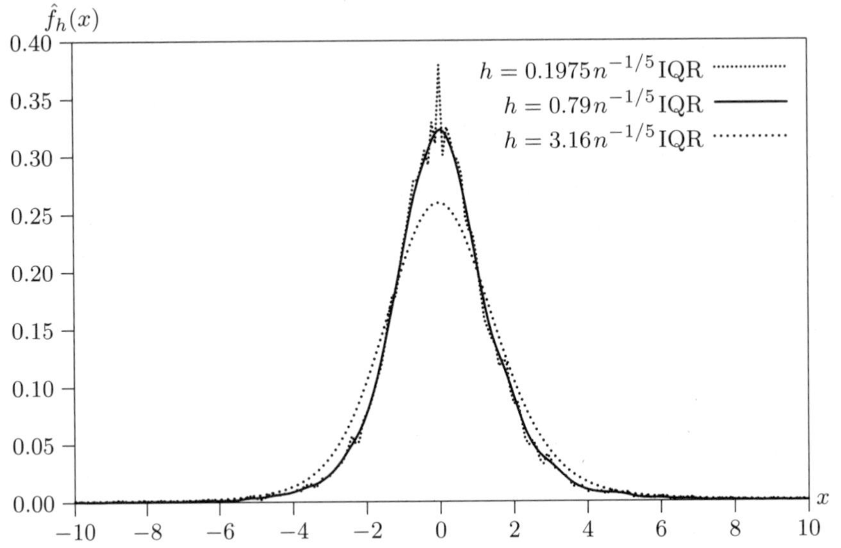

Figure 15.2 Effect of h on kernel density estimates

also tried using the somewhat larger value of h given by equation (15.63), the somewhat smaller value (Silverman's rule of thumb) given by equation (15.65), and an Epanechnikov instead of a Gaussian kernel. The alternative density estimates were so close to the one shown in the figure that it is not worth plotting them, although the peak was very slightly higher when we used Silverman's rule of thumb. Note that we did not estimate $\hat{f}_h(x)$ for every point in the sample, but only for 201 evenly-spaced points between −10 and 10. It makes sense to do something like this when the objective is simply to plot an estimated density and the sample size is large.

Figure 15.1 also shows a normal density with the same mean and variance as the data. This normal density looks very different from the kernel estimate. As we noted in Section 15.2, returns data from financial markets commonly display excess kurtosis. The kernel density estimates strongly suggest that this empirical regularity holds for the IBM stock returns, since the density appears to be much more peaked and to have thicker tails than the normal. The thicker tails are hard to see in the figure, but they are evident if one looks closely at $\hat{f}_h(x)$ for larger absolute values of x. For example, $\hat{f}_h(8) = 0.0006051$ and $\hat{f}_h(-8) = 0.0005470$, while the corresponding values for the normal density are just 0.0000014 and 0.0000010.

Figure 15.2 shows the same estimated density as Figure 15.1, plus two others. Both of the new estimates used a Gaussian kernel, but with h either four times larger or four times smaller than the value given in equation (15.64). When h is too large, the estimated density is very smooth, but it is much less peaked than the one based on a sensible choice of h. Thus it is evident that, for many values of x, these oversmoothed estimates are severely biased. In contrast, when h is too small, the estimated density has roughly the same shape as before, but it is extremely jagged. Thus it is evident that the variance of these undersmoothed estimates is quite high.

The example in Figures 15.1 and 15.2 involves 9939 observations, which is a rather large number. Kernel density estimation cannot be expected to work nearly as well when the sample size is small, because there are not enough observations in the vicinity of many values of x to obtain good estimates of $f(x)$ for those values.

Nonparametric Regression

The fitted values from a regression model are estimates of the expectation of the dependent variable conditional on the values of the explanatory variables for each observation. The linear regression model (1.01) is perhaps the simplest such model, since it makes use of only one explanatory variable, x_t, and the expectation of the dependent variable y_t conditional on x_t is assumed to be an affine function of x_t. This very strong assumption can of course be relaxed by using powers or other nonlinear transformations of x_t as additional regressors. An alternative approach is to use a **nonparametric regression**, which estimates $\mathrm{E}(y_t \,|\, x_t)$ directly, without making any assumptions about functional form.

The simplest approach to nonparametric regression is **kernel regression**, a technique similar to kernel density estimation. We suppose that two random variables Y and X are jointly distributed, and we wish to estimate the conditional expectation $\mu(x) \equiv \mathrm{E}(Y \,|\, x)$ as a function of x, using a sample of paired observations (y_t, x_t) for $t = 1, \ldots, n$. For given x, consider the function $G(x)$ defined as

$$G(x) = \mathrm{E}\big(Y \cdot I(X \le x)\big) = \int_{-\infty}^{x} \int_{-\infty}^{\infty} y\, f(y, z)\, dy\, dz,$$

where $f(y, x)$ is the joint density of Y and X. Let $g(x) \equiv G'(x)$ denote the first derivative of $G(X)$. Then

$$g(x) = \int_{-\infty}^{\infty} y f(y, x) dy = f(x) \int_{-\infty}^{\infty} y f(y \,|\, x) dy = f(x) \mathrm{E}(Y \,|\, x),$$

where $f(x)$ is the marginal density of X, and $f(y \,|\, x)$ is the density of Y conditional on $X = x$.

A natural unbiased estimator of $G(x)$ is $n^{-1} \sum_{t=1}^{n} y_t I(x_t \le x)$, but this, like the EDF, is discontinuous and cannot be differentiated. As with the kernel CDF estimator (15.60), therefore, we replace this estimator by the biased but smooth estimator

$$\hat{G}_h(x) = \frac{1}{n} \sum_{t=1}^{n} y_t K\Big(\frac{x - x_t}{h}\Big), \tag{15.66}$$

where K is a cumulative kernel (that is, the CDF of a distribution with mean 0 and variance 1), and h is a bandwidth parameter. Defining $\hat{g}_h(x)$ as the derivative of (15.66) and using the kernel estimator (15.61) to estimate the marginal density of X leads to the following estimator of $\mu(x)$:

$$\hat{\mu}_h(x) = \frac{\hat{g}_h(x)}{\hat{f}_h(x)}.$$

This is called the **Nadaraya-Watson estimator**, and it simplifies to

$$\hat{\mu}_h(x) = \frac{\sum_{t=1}^n y_t k_t}{\sum_{t=1}^n k_t}, \quad k_t \equiv k\Big(\frac{x - x_t}{h}\Big), \tag{15.67}$$

where $k \equiv K'$ is a kernel function.

The Nadaraya-Watson estimator is the solution to the estimating equation

$$\sum_{t=1}^n k_t \big(y_t - \hat{\mu}_h(x)\big) = 0.$$

This can be thought of as the empirical counterpart of a weighted average of the elementary zero functions $y_t - \mu(x)$. But these elementary zero functions do not have mean 0, because the conditional expectation of y_t is not $\mu(x)$ but $\mu(x_t)$. This is evidently a source of bias. The correct, but infeasible, zero function would instead be $y_t - \mu(x_t)$.

A better approximation to the correct zero function is given by the two-term Taylor expansion $\mu(x) + \mu'(x)(x_t - x)$, in which both $\mu(x)$ and $\mu'(x)$ are unknown. Both of these unknowns can be estimated simultaneously by solving the two estimating equations

$$\begin{aligned} \sum_{t=1}^n k_t \big(y_t - \mu(x) - \mu'(x)(x_t - x)\big) = 0 \quad \text{and} \\ \sum_{t=1}^n k_t (x_t - x)\big(y_t - \mu(x) - \mu'(x)(x_t - x)\big) = 0. \end{aligned} \tag{15.68}$$

These estimating equations are at least approximately correct, because the random variable $Y - \mathrm{E}(Y \,|\, X)$, of which the $y_t - \mu(x) - \mu'(x)(x_t - x)$ are approximate realizations, is uncorrelated with $X - x$. The simplest way to solve equations (15.68) is to run the linear regression

$$k_t^{1/2} y_t = \mu(x) k_t^{1/2} + \mu'(x) k_t^{1/2}(x_t - x) + \text{residual}, \tag{15.69}$$

so as to obtain the **locally linear estimator** of $\mu(x)$, which is just the first estimated coefficient. Regression (15.69) is to be run for every value of x for which we wish to estimate $\mathrm{E}(Y \mid x)$. Taylor expansions with more terms can be handled simply by adding additional regressors of the form $k_t^{1/2}(x_t - x)^i$ to (15.69), with i an integer greater than 1. See Fan and Gijbels (1996) for a detailed discussion of the numerous other methods of kernel regression.

Up to this point, we have assumed that there is just one regressor. Although kernel regression can be used when there are several regressors, its performance tends to become much worse as the number of regressors k increases. Intuitively, the reason for which it suffers from this **curse of dimensionality** is that the fraction of sample points that are close to any point at which we wish to evaluate the conditional expectation declines rapidly as k increases. In consequence, when k is greater than 1 or 2, we generally need a very large sample for estimates to be at all precise.

As an example, suppose that the regressors follow independent $\mathrm{N}(0,1)$ distributions, the point $\boldsymbol{x}$ is the origin, and we define "close" to mean that the Euclidean distance between $\boldsymbol{x}_t$ and the origin is no greater than 0.5. As the notation indicates, $\boldsymbol{x}$ and $\boldsymbol{x}_t$ are now, in general, vectors. When $k = 1$, the fraction of the $\boldsymbol{x}_t$ that are close to the origin in this sense is 0.383; when $k = 2$, it is 0.118; when $k = 3$, it is 0.031; and so on. See Exercise 15.29. This example is typical. In general, the proportion of the sample points for which $\boldsymbol{x}_t$ is close to any specified $\boldsymbol{x}$ decreases rapidly as k increases.

Cross Validation

The optimal choice of h for kernel regression is not, in general, the same as for kernel density estimation. When there are k regressors, h should be proportional to $n^{-1/(k+4)}$. The optimal choice of h depends on a number of things, including the values of x for which we wish to compute $\mathrm{E}(Y \mid x)$, the kernel, and the shape of the true (but unknown) regression function. Consequently, there is no widely-used rule of thumb for choosing h like the ones we discussed for kernel density estimation. Instead, it is customary to choose h by some sort of data-based method. One popular approach is to use a technique called **cross validation**, which we now discuss in the context of kernel regression.[3]

Suppose we choose a bandwidth h and calculate a kernel estimate $\hat{y}_h(x_t)$ for each value of x_t in the sample. This may be a Nadaraya-Watson estimate, a locally linear estimate, or some other type of kernel regression estimate. In order to compute $\hat{y}_h(x_t)$, we make use of the values $k\big((x_t - x_s)/h\big)$ of the kernel function for all $s = 1, \ldots, n$. As $h \to 0$, these values tend to 0 for all s such that $x_s \neq x_t$. If the only such s is t itself, it follows that $\hat{y}_h(x_t)$ tends to y_t as $h \to 0$. In the event of ties, $\hat{y}_h(x_t)$ tends to the average of the y_s for which s is such that $x_s = x_t$. The residual $\hat{y}_h(x_t) - y_t$ thus tends to 0 in

[3] Cross validation can also be used to choose the bandwidth for kernel density estimation; see Silverman (1986).

the former case, and to the deviation of y_t from the mean of the y_s with tied values of x_s in the latter case.

This rules out the sum of the squares of the $\hat{y}_h(x_t) - y_t$ as a useful criterion function for the choice of h, since it tends monotonically to a lower limit as $h \to 0$. Instead, it is common to use what is called a **leave-one-out** estimator. We encountered such estimators in Section 2.6, in connection with leverage. Here, the estimator has the same form as a regular kernel estimator, except that observation t is omitted when we estimate $\mathrm{E}(Y \,|\, x_t)$. Thus there is no tendency for the leave-one-out estimate $\hat{y}_h^{(t)}(x_t)$ to converge to y_t as $h \to 0$. Another problem may arise, however. We saw above that, as $h \to 0$, the values $k\big((x_t - x_s)/h\big)$ of the kernel function used to compute $\hat{y}_h(x_t)$ tend to 0 unless $x_s = x_t$. If we forget about ties, this means that the leave-one-out estimator tends to 0. Otherwise, the leave-one-out estimator has exactly the same properties as the ordinary kernel estimator when x is not one of the sample points.

We define the **cross-validation function** by the formula

$$\mathrm{CV}(h) = \frac{1}{n} \sum_{t=1}^{n} w(x_t)\big(y_t - \hat{y}_h^{(t)}(x_t)\big)^2. \tag{15.70}$$

Here $w(x_t)$ is a weight, which could just be 1 for all observations, but should be set to 0 for all t for which $\hat{y}_h^{(t)}(x_t)$ is 0, or very close to 0, because $k\big((x_t - x_s)/h\big)$ is 0 or very small for all $s \neq t$. When we use cross validation, we evaluate $\mathrm{CV}(h)$ for a number of values of h and pick the value that minimizes it. This makes sense, because, when the weights are chosen appropriately, the cross-validation function (15.70) provides a reasonable way to estimate the average squared error of $\hat{y}_h(x)$ over the range of values of x in which we are interested. It is attractive to use nonconstant weights if we are more interested in obtaining good estimates of $\mathrm{E}(Y \,|\, x)$ for some values of x than for others. The weight might well be 0 for values of x_t that are far from the values of x in which we are interested.

A Numerical Example

It is instructive to see how kernel regression works in practice. For purposes of illustration, we generated 400 observations from an artificial DGP that was linear for x_t below a certain value and quite nonlinear beyond that point. It is obvious that a linear regression model fits these data very badly.

Figure 15.3 shows the data and two sets of Nadaraya-Watson kernel estimates based on an Epanechnikov kernel. The first set, shown as a solid line, used a baseline bandwidth $h = sn^{-1/5}$, which, by analogy with results for kernel density estimation, seems like a reasonable value to start with. Although these estimates look sensible for most values of x_t, they perform poorly for extreme values. In particular, they severely overestimate $\mathrm{E}(Y \,|\, x)$ for the largest values of x. This happens because, when x is large, there are few or no values of x_t

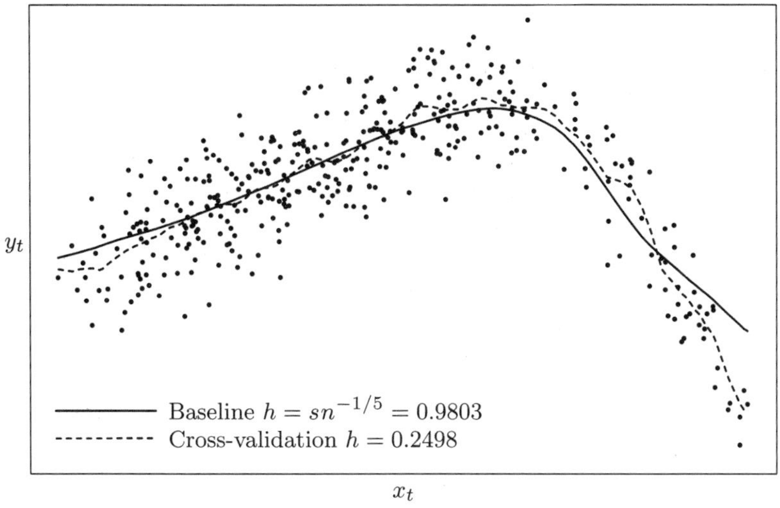

Figure 15.3 Nadaraya-Watson kernel regression using simulated data

greater than x. Consequently, most of the values of y_t of which $\hat{y}_h(x)$ is a weighted average are associated with values of x_t smaller than x.

The second set of estimates shown in Figure 15.3 used a value of h chosen by cross validation. The only way to avoid severely overestimating $\text{E}(Y \mid x)$ for the more extreme values of x is to make the bandwidth quite small, and indeed the value of h given by cross validation is much smaller than the baseline value. But making h small causes $\hat{y}_h(x)$ to wiggle around much more than seems reasonable. Thus neither set of Nadaraya-Watson estimates is at all satisfactory.

Figure 15.4 shows the same data and two sets of locally linear kernel estimates, both also based on an Epanechnikov kernel. These estimates are much more plausible than the previous ones. The h chosen by cross validation is smaller than the baseline value, but it is large enough that $\hat{y}_h(x)$ is generally quite smooth, and there is not much difference between the two sets of estimates. The values of the cross-validation function (15.70) provide further evidence that the locally linear estimates are better than the Nadaraya-Watson ones. For the baseline value of h, these values are 2.4947 and 2.8525, respectively. For the optimal values of h, they are 2.4693 and 2.4960.

The Partially Linear Model

Although it often requires many explanatory variables to give a satisfactory account of a dependent variable y_t, we may be willing to use a parametric specification for all but one of these variables. The **partially linear model** expresses y_t as the sum of an ordinary linear regression function $\boldsymbol{X}_t\boldsymbol{\beta}$ and a function $\mu(z_t)$ that we are unwilling to specify parametrically. Here $\boldsymbol{X}_t$ is a

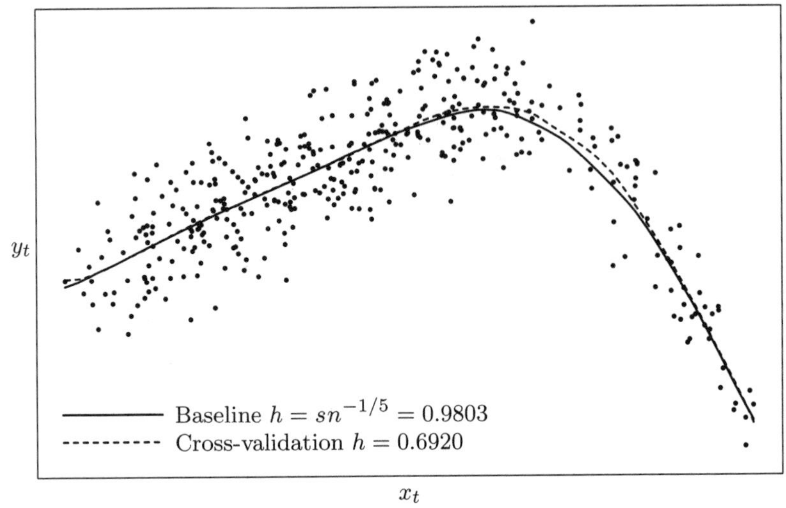

Figure 15.4 Locally linear kernel regression using simulated data

$1 \times k$ vector containing the explanatory variables that contribute linearly to the expectation of y_t, and z_t is an explanatory variable that contributes nonlinearly through the unspecified function μ. A model of this sort circumvents the curse of dimensionality, because there is only one variable, z_t, for which nonparametric estimation is needed. In some applications, it is possible to have more than one such variable, but the curse of dimensionality reappears in such cases.

The partially linear model can be written as

$$y_t = \boldsymbol{X}_t\boldsymbol{\beta} + \mu(z_t) + u_t, \quad u_t \sim \mathrm{IID}(0, \sigma^2), \tag{15.71}$$

where the error terms u_t are assumed to be independent of the explanatory variables $\boldsymbol{X}_t$ and z_t. Suppose that we are chiefly interested in estimating the parameter vector $\boldsymbol{\beta}$. If the function $\mu(z_t)$ were linear, of the form γz_t, then we could use the FWL Theorem to eliminate z_t from the equation (15.71) by use of the projection matrix $\boldsymbol{M_z}$.

A similar device is used with a nonparametrically specified function $\mu(z_t)$. If we take the expectation of both sides of equation (15.71) conditional on z_t, we find that

$$\mathrm{E}(y_t \mid z_t) = \mathrm{E}(\boldsymbol{X}_t \mid z_t)\boldsymbol{\beta} + \mu(z_t). \tag{15.72}$$

Subtracting (15.72) from (15.71) then gives

$$y_t - \mathrm{E}(y_t \mid z_t) = \big(\boldsymbol{X}_t - \mathrm{E}(\boldsymbol{X}_t \mid z_t)\big)\boldsymbol{\beta} + u_t. \tag{15.73}$$

Instead of using a linear orthogonal projection to eliminate z_t, we arrive at equation (15.73) by subtracting the expectation conditional on z_t. The vector of explanatory variables $\boldsymbol{X}_t$ cannot include a variable x_t that is a deterministic function of z_t, since then $x_t - \mathrm{E}(x_t \,|\, z_t) = 0$. In particular, there cannot be a constant among the explanatory variables.

If the conditional expectations were known, equation (15.73) would be a linear regression model with parameter vector $\boldsymbol{\beta}$ and homoskedastic, serially uncorrelated errors, which could therefore be estimated by OLS. Even if they are not known, the conditional expectations in (15.73) can be estimated by a nonparametric regression. If we use a kernel function k and bandwidth parameter h, the Nadaraya-Watson estimate of $\mathrm{E}(y_t \,|\, z_t)$ is

$$\hat{y}_t \equiv \frac{\sum_{s=1}^{n} k_{ts}\, y_s}{\sum_{s=1}^{n} k_{ts}}, \tag{15.74}$$

where $k_{ts} \equiv k(z_t - z_s)/h$, and n is the sample size. The conditional expectations of the components of $\boldsymbol{X}_t$ are estimated in exactly the same way, using exactly the same k_{ts}, a fact that makes for some economy of computation. We denote the vector of estimates as $\hat{\boldsymbol{X}}_t$. The partially linear estimator $\hat{\boldsymbol{\beta}}$ is then the OLS estimator from the linear regression

$$y_t - \hat{y}_t = (\boldsymbol{X}_t - \hat{\boldsymbol{X}}_t)\boldsymbol{\beta} + u_t. \tag{15.75}$$

We have seen that, with a suitable choice of bandwidth, the nonparametric estimate (15.74) is consistent. Thus $y_t - \hat{y}_t \stackrel{a}{=} y_t - \mathrm{E}(y_t \,|\, z_t)$, with a similar result for $\hat{\boldsymbol{X}}_t$. Consequently, we may expect that

$$\begin{aligned} &\frac{1}{n}\sum_{t=1}^{n}(\boldsymbol{X}_t - \hat{\boldsymbol{X}}_t)^{\top}(\boldsymbol{X}_t - \hat{\boldsymbol{X}}_t) \\ &\qquad \stackrel{a}{=} \frac{1}{n}\sum_{t=1}^{n}\big(\boldsymbol{X}_t - \mathrm{E}(\boldsymbol{X}_t \,|\, z_t)\big)^{\top}\big(\boldsymbol{X}_t - \mathrm{E}(\boldsymbol{X}_t \,|\, z_t)\big) \end{aligned} \tag{15.76}$$

under suitable regularity conditions. Similarly, we expect that

$$\begin{aligned} &n^{-1/2}\sum_{t=1}^{n}(\boldsymbol{X}_t - \hat{\boldsymbol{X}}_t)\big(y_t - \hat{y}_t - (\boldsymbol{X}_t - \hat{\boldsymbol{X}}_t)\boldsymbol{\beta}\big) \\ &\qquad \stackrel{a}{=} n^{-1/2}\sum_{t=1}^{n}\big(\boldsymbol{X}_t - \mathrm{E}(\boldsymbol{X}_t \,|\, z_t)\big)u_t. \end{aligned} \tag{15.77}$$

If (15.76) and (15.77) are correct, then it is easy to see that the partially linear estimator $\hat{\boldsymbol{\beta}}$ satisfies the equation

$$\begin{aligned} n^{1/2}(\hat{\boldsymbol{\beta}} - \boldsymbol{\beta}_0) \stackrel{a}{=} \Big(\frac{1}{n}\sum_{t=1}^{n}\big(\boldsymbol{X}_t - \mathrm{E}(\boldsymbol{X}_t \,|\, z_t)\big)^{\top}\big(\boldsymbol{X}_t - \mathrm{E}(\boldsymbol{X}_t \,|\, z_t)\big)\Big)^{-1} \times \\ n^{-1/2}\sum_{t=1}^{n}\big(\boldsymbol{X}_t - \mathrm{E}(\boldsymbol{X}_t \,|\, z_t)\big)u_t, \end{aligned}$$

where $\boldsymbol{\beta}_0$ denotes the true value of $\boldsymbol{\beta}$. This implies that $\hat{\boldsymbol{\beta}}$ is asymptotically normal, and that its asymptotic covariance matrix is consistently estimated by n times the OLS covariance matrix estimator from regression (15.75).

Once $\hat{\boldsymbol{\beta}}$ has been estimated, the nonparametric estimator of the function $\mu(z)$ can readily be computed as

$$\hat{\mu}(z_t) = \hat{y}_t - \hat{\boldsymbol{X}}_t\hat{\boldsymbol{\beta}}.$$

This estimator will have essentially the same properties as the usual Nadaraya-Watson estimator (15.67). Of course, we could use locally linear estimators of $\mathrm{E}(y_t \,|\, z_t)$ and $\mathrm{E}(\boldsymbol{X}_t \,|\, z_t)$ in equation (15.75) instead of Nadaraya-Watson estimators, and doing so might well lead to better results.

Regularity conditions for equations (15.76) and (15.77) to hold are not very restrictive, but, since they involve conditions on all the explanatory variables, the kernel function, and the bandwidth parameter, they are hard to express in a comprehensible manner. The partially linear model in the form we have given here was popularized by Robinson (1988), in which the distinctly gory details of the regularity conditions can be found.

Our treatment of nonparametric estimation has necessarily been superficial. Much more detailed discussions may be found in Härdle (1990), Yatchew (1998), and Pagan and Ullah (1999). There is a vast literature on techniques for nonparametric regression. In addition to the references already cited, see Green and Silverman (1994), Simonoff (1996), Eubank (1999), and Loader (1999), among others.

Assessing the Specification of Parametric Models

Nonparametric methods can be useful even when we are primarily interested in estimating a parametric model. Graphical methods can be especially valuable. Looking at the fitted values from a kernel regression may suggest what sort of parametric nonlinear regression function could be expected to provide a good fit. Graphing the fitted values from a parametric model alongside those from a kernel regression may indicate in what respects, if any, the parametric model needs improvement.

More formal methods exist for testing the validity of a parametric regression model using the evidence provided by a nonparametric one. In fact, many testing procedures have been proposed. Some of these are explicitly based on the J and P tests that were discussed in Section 15.2. Examples include the tests proposed by Wooldridge (1992) and Delgado and Stengos (1994), neither of which uses kernel regression to estimate the nonparametric model. These tests require that the parametric null and nonparametric alternative models should be nonnested. Many other tests do not have this requirement, and so they can be used to test the null hypothesis that $\mathrm{E}(Y \,|\, X)$ has a specific, parametric, functional form. Examples include Zheng (1996), Li and Wang (1998), Ellison and Ellison (2000), and Horowitz and Spokoiny (2001), all of which use some variant of kernel regression. Tests that do not use kernel regression have been proposed by Yatchew (1992) and Hong and White (1995), among others.

Although most of these tests are conceptually simple, and some of them are also simple to compute, their asymptotic validity generally depends on technical assumptions that may be difficult to verify. Moreover, their finite-sample performance, as asymptotic tests, is often not very good. For both these reasons, it is highly desirable to bootstrap them. Even if a test statistic is not asymptotically pivotal, bootstrap P values are almost always asymptotically valid. If a test statistic is asymptotically pivotal, as is the case for the tests proposed in all of the papers cited above when the required conditions hold, then bootstrap P values should be more accurate than asymptotic P values, in the sense that we discussed at the end of Section 4.6.

It is quite easy to bootstrap this sort of test statistic. For example, consider the test statistic

$$\frac{(\boldsymbol{y}-\hat{\boldsymbol{x}})^{\top}(\boldsymbol{y}-\hat{\boldsymbol{x}})-(\boldsymbol{y}-\hat{\boldsymbol{y}})^{\top}(\boldsymbol{y}-\hat{\boldsymbol{y}})}{(\boldsymbol{y}-\hat{\boldsymbol{x}})^{\top}(\boldsymbol{y}-\hat{\boldsymbol{x}})/(n-k)}, \tag{15.78}$$

which is closely related to the statistics proposed by Yatchew (1992) and Hong and White (1995). In expression (15.78), $\boldsymbol{y}$ is the vector of observations on the dependent variable, $\hat{\boldsymbol{x}}$ is the vector of fitted values from the parametric model, $\hat{\boldsymbol{y}}$ is the vector of fitted values from the nonparametric model, and k is the number of parameters. When the nonparametric model involves the same regressors as the parametric one, we would expect this statistic to be positive if the bandwidth for the nonparametric regression has been chosen sensibly. Thus we want to reject the null hypothesis whenever expression (15.78) is positive and sufficiently large.

When the null hypothesis is a static regression model, it is natural to specify the bootstrap DGP as

$$\boldsymbol{y}^* = \hat{\boldsymbol{x}} + \boldsymbol{u}^*,$$

where $\boldsymbol{u}^*$ is an n–vector with typical element u_t^* obtained by resampling the rescaled residuals from the parametric model. When the null hypothesis is a dynamic model, the vector $\boldsymbol{y}^*$ should be generated recursively, as in equation (4.66). For each bootstrap sample, we estimate both the parametric model and the nonparametric one and then use the two sets of estimates to compute the test statistic (15.78). A bootstrap P value is then computed in the usual way as the proportion of the bootstrap statistics that are larger than the actual test statistic; see equation (4.62).

This procedure is conceptually straightforward, but it can be computationally costly. The cost is high whenever the parametric model involves nonlinear estimation and/or the bandwidth for the nonparametric model is chosen by cross validation. In general, we recommend using simpler procedures, such as the

RESET test, F tests for omitted powers and cross-products of the regressors, and nonnested hypothesis tests, prior to explicitly testing a parametric model against one or more nonparametric alternatives. Doing the latter makes sense only if the simpler procedures fail to find conclusive evidence of misspecification.

15.6 Final Remarks

It is difficult to overemphasize the importance of testing the specification of econometric models thoroughly before using them for any purpose. For this reason, several procedures for model specification testing have been discussed in this chapter and elsewhere in the book. Many of these procedures are based on artificial regressions, because they require estimation of the model under test only, and artificial regressions are generally quite easy to set up.

We must use caution when performing more than one specification test on the same model. Even when every one of the tests is exact, which is very rarely true in practice, the probability that at least one test rejects a correctly specified model by chance can be quite large; see Exercise 15.30. As readers are asked to show in that exercise, it is easy to control the overall significance level of several tests taken together if all the test statistics are independent. However, it is not at all easy to do so without sacrificing power when the test statistics are not independent, which they generally are not; see Savin (1980) for an introduction to this topic.

For more detailed treatments of some aspects of model specification testing in econometrics, see Godfrey (1988) and White (1994). The second of these books is very much more advanced than the discussion in this chapter.

15.7 Appendix: Test Regressors in Artificial Regressions

In this appendix, we sketch a proof of why the three conditions R1–R3 given in Section 15.2 make it admissible to base an asymptotic test on the artificial regression (15.05). We assume that the DGP belongs to the model $\mathbb{M}$ and is characterized by the parameter vector $\boldsymbol{\theta}_0$. We deal only with the case in which the asymptotic covariance matrix of the estimator $\hat{\boldsymbol{\theta}}$ is given by equation (15.02). The other case, in which it is given by equation (15.03), is dealt with in Exercise 15.4.

The explained sums of squares from the restricted artificial regression (15.01), evaluated at the root-n consistent estimator $\acute{\boldsymbol{\theta}}$, and the unrestricted artificial regression (15.05) can be written as

$$\acute{\boldsymbol{r}}^\top \boldsymbol{P}_{\acute{R}} \acute{\boldsymbol{r}} \quad \text{and} \quad \acute{\boldsymbol{r}}^\top \boldsymbol{P}_{\acute{R},\acute{Z}} \acute{\boldsymbol{r}},$$

respectively, where $\boldsymbol{P}_{\acute{R}}$ is the orthogonal projection on to the columns of $\acute{\boldsymbol{R}}$, and $\boldsymbol{P}_{\acute{R},\acute{Z}}$ is the orthogonal projection on to the columns of $\acute{\boldsymbol{R}}$ and $\acute{\boldsymbol{Z}}$ jointly.

The difference between the two explained sums of squares is therefore

$$\acute{\boldsymbol{r}}^\top(\boldsymbol{P}_{\acute{R},\acute{Z}} - \boldsymbol{P}_{\acute{R}})\acute{\boldsymbol{r}} = \acute{\boldsymbol{r}}^\top \boldsymbol{P}_{\boldsymbol{M}_{\acute{R}}\acute{Z}}\acute{\boldsymbol{r}} = \acute{\boldsymbol{r}}^\top \boldsymbol{M}_{\acute{R}}\acute{\boldsymbol{Z}}(\acute{\boldsymbol{Z}}^\top \boldsymbol{M}_{\acute{R}}\acute{\boldsymbol{Z}})^{-1}\acute{\boldsymbol{Z}}^\top \boldsymbol{M}_{\acute{R}}\acute{\boldsymbol{r}}, \quad (15.79)$$

where $\boldsymbol{M}_{\acute{R}} \equiv \mathbf{I} - \boldsymbol{P}_{\acute{R}}$. Note that expression (15.79) could also be computed as the difference between the sums of squared residuals from regressions (15.01) and (15.05).

Now consider the r–vector $n^{-1/2}\acute{\boldsymbol{Z}}^\top \boldsymbol{M}_{\acute{R}}\acute{\boldsymbol{r}}$. It is equal to

$$n^{-1/2}\acute{\boldsymbol{Z}}^\top\acute{\boldsymbol{r}} - n^{-1}\acute{\boldsymbol{Z}}^\top\acute{\boldsymbol{R}}\, n^{1/2}(\acute{\boldsymbol{R}}^\top\acute{\boldsymbol{R}})^{-1}\acute{\boldsymbol{R}}^\top\acute{\boldsymbol{r}}. \quad (15.80)$$

A Taylor expansion of the first term in expression (15.80) around the true value $\boldsymbol{\theta}_0$ gives

$$n^{-1/2}\acute{\boldsymbol{Z}}^\top\acute{\boldsymbol{r}} = n^{-1/2}\boldsymbol{Z}_0^\top\boldsymbol{r}_0 - n^{-1}\boldsymbol{Z}_0^\top\boldsymbol{R}_0\, n^{1/2}(\acute{\boldsymbol{\theta}} - \boldsymbol{\theta}_0) + O_p(n^{-1/2}), \quad (15.81)$$

where $\boldsymbol{r}_0 \equiv \boldsymbol{r}(\boldsymbol{\theta}_0)$, $\boldsymbol{R}_0 \equiv \boldsymbol{R}(\boldsymbol{\theta}_0)$, and $\boldsymbol{Z}_0 \equiv \boldsymbol{Z}(\boldsymbol{\theta}_0)$. Here we have used condition R3 in the evaluation of the Jacobian of $\boldsymbol{Z}^\top(\boldsymbol{\theta})\boldsymbol{r}(\boldsymbol{\theta})$. By the requirement that an artificial regression admits one-step estimation, the second term in expression (15.80) is equal to

$$-n^{-1}\acute{\boldsymbol{Z}}^\top\acute{\boldsymbol{R}}\, n^{1/2}(\hat{\boldsymbol{\theta}} - \acute{\boldsymbol{\theta}}) + O_p(n^{-1/2}).$$

Because $\acute{\boldsymbol{\theta}}$ is root-n consistent, we can replace $n^{-1}\acute{\boldsymbol{Z}}^\top\acute{\boldsymbol{R}}$ in this expression by $n^{-1}\boldsymbol{Z}_0^\top\boldsymbol{R}_0 + O_p(n^{-1/2})$, to obtain

$$-n^{-1}\boldsymbol{Z}_0^\top\boldsymbol{R}_0\, n^{1/2}(\hat{\boldsymbol{\theta}} - \boldsymbol{\theta}_0) + n^{-1}\boldsymbol{Z}_0^\top\boldsymbol{R}_0\, n^{1/2}(\acute{\boldsymbol{\theta}} - \boldsymbol{\theta}_0) + O_p(n^{-1/2}). \quad (15.82)$$

When we add expressions (15.81) and (15.82), the terms that involve $\acute{\boldsymbol{\theta}}$ cancel, and so the complete expression (15.80) becomes

$$\begin{aligned}
&n^{-1/2}\boldsymbol{Z}_0^\top\boldsymbol{r}_0 - n^{-1}\boldsymbol{Z}_0^\top\boldsymbol{R}_0\, n^{1/2}(\hat{\boldsymbol{\theta}} - \boldsymbol{\theta}_0) + O_p(n^{-1/2})\\
&= n^{-1/2}\boldsymbol{Z}_0^\top\boldsymbol{r}_0 - n^{-1}\boldsymbol{Z}_0^\top\boldsymbol{R}_0\, n^{1/2}(\boldsymbol{R}_0^\top\boldsymbol{R}_0)^{-1}\boldsymbol{R}_0^\top\boldsymbol{r}_0 + O_p(n^{-1/2})\\
&= n^{-1/2}\boldsymbol{Z}_0^\top\boldsymbol{M}_{\boldsymbol{R}_0}\boldsymbol{r}_0 + O_p(n^{-1/2}).
\end{aligned}$$

In the second line here, we have used the one-step property for $\boldsymbol{\theta}_0$ rather than $\acute{\boldsymbol{\theta}}$, since $\boldsymbol{\theta}_0$ is trivially root-n consistent for itself. Thus we conclude that

$$n^{-1/2}\acute{\boldsymbol{Z}}^\top\acute{\boldsymbol{r}} = n^{-1/2}\boldsymbol{Z}_0^\top\boldsymbol{M}_{\boldsymbol{R}_0}\boldsymbol{r}_0 + O_p(n^{-1/2}) \quad (15.83)$$

for all $\acute{\boldsymbol{\theta}}$ such that $\acute{\boldsymbol{\theta}} - \boldsymbol{\theta}_0 = O_p(n^{-1/2})$.

The asymptotic covariance matrix of the vector $n^{-1/2}\boldsymbol{Z}_0^\top\boldsymbol{M}_{\boldsymbol{R}_0}\boldsymbol{r}_0$ is

$$\mathrm{Var}\big(\operatorname*{plim}_{n\to\infty} n^{-1/2}\boldsymbol{Z}_0^\top\boldsymbol{M}_{\boldsymbol{R}_0}\boldsymbol{r}_0\big) = \operatorname*{plim}_{n\to\infty}\frac{1}{n}\boldsymbol{Z}_0^\top\boldsymbol{M}_{\boldsymbol{R}_0}\boldsymbol{r}_0\boldsymbol{r}_0^\top\boldsymbol{M}_{\boldsymbol{R}_0}\boldsymbol{Z}_0.$$

If we replace $\boldsymbol{M}_{\boldsymbol{R}_0}$ by $\mathbf{I}-\boldsymbol{R}_0(\boldsymbol{R}_0^\top\boldsymbol{R}_0)^{-1}\boldsymbol{R}_0^\top$, the right-hand side of this equation becomes

$$\begin{aligned}
&\operatorname*{plim}_{n\to\infty}\frac{1}{n}\boldsymbol{Z}_0^\top\boldsymbol{r}_0\boldsymbol{r}_0^\top\boldsymbol{Z}_0 - \operatorname*{plim}_{n\to\infty}\frac{1}{n}\boldsymbol{Z}_0^\top\boldsymbol{R}_0(\boldsymbol{R}_0^\top\boldsymbol{R}_0)^{-1}\boldsymbol{R}_0^\top\boldsymbol{r}_0\boldsymbol{r}_0^\top\boldsymbol{Z}_0\\
&\quad - \operatorname*{plim}_{n\to\infty}\frac{1}{n}\boldsymbol{Z}_0^\top\boldsymbol{r}_0\boldsymbol{r}_0^\top\boldsymbol{R}_0(\boldsymbol{R}_0^\top\boldsymbol{R}_0)^{-1}\boldsymbol{R}_0^\top\boldsymbol{Z}_0\\
&\quad + \operatorname*{plim}_{n\to\infty}\frac{1}{n}\boldsymbol{Z}_0^\top\boldsymbol{R}_0(\boldsymbol{R}_0^\top\boldsymbol{R}_0)^{-1}\boldsymbol{R}_0^\top\boldsymbol{r}_0\boldsymbol{r}_0^\top\boldsymbol{R}_0(\boldsymbol{R}_0^\top\boldsymbol{R}_0)^{-1}\boldsymbol{R}_0^\top\boldsymbol{Z}_0.
\end{aligned}$$

By making use of condition R2, we can replace the limits of expressions like $n^{-1}\boldsymbol{R}_0^\top\boldsymbol{r}_0\boldsymbol{r}_0^\top\boldsymbol{R}_0$ by those of expressions like $n^{-1}\boldsymbol{R}_0^\top\boldsymbol{R}_0$. When we do this, the rather lengthy expression above collapses to

$$\begin{aligned}
&\operatorname*{plim}_{n\to\infty}\Big(\frac{1}{n}\boldsymbol{Z}_0^\top\boldsymbol{Z}_0 - \frac{1}{n}\boldsymbol{Z}_0^\top\boldsymbol{R}_0(\boldsymbol{R}_0^\top\boldsymbol{R}_0)^{-1}\boldsymbol{R}_0^\top\boldsymbol{Z}_0\Big)\\
&\qquad = \operatorname*{plim}_{n\to\infty}\frac{1}{n}\boldsymbol{Z}_0^\top\boldsymbol{M}_{\boldsymbol{R}_0}\boldsymbol{Z}_0.
\end{aligned} \tag{15.84}$$

The root-n consistency of $\acute{\boldsymbol{\theta}}$ and the result (15.83) imply that the asymptotic covariance matrix of $n^{-1/2}\acute{\boldsymbol{Z}}^\top\acute{\boldsymbol{r}}$ is equal to the right-hand side of equation (15.84) for all $\acute{\boldsymbol{\theta}}$ such that $\acute{\boldsymbol{\theta}}-\boldsymbol{\theta}_0 = O_p(n^{-1/2})$. Moreover, the consistency of $\acute{\boldsymbol{\theta}}$ also implies that

$$\operatorname*{plim}_{n\to\infty}\frac{1}{n}\acute{\boldsymbol{Z}}^\top\boldsymbol{M}_{\acute{\boldsymbol{R}}}\acute{\boldsymbol{Z}} = \operatorname*{plim}_{n\to\infty}\frac{1}{n}\boldsymbol{Z}_0^\top\boldsymbol{M}_{\boldsymbol{R}_0}\boldsymbol{Z}_0.$$

It follows from this result and the result (15.83) that the test statistic (15.79) is asymptotically equal to

$$(n^{-1/2}\boldsymbol{r}_0^\top\boldsymbol{M}_{\boldsymbol{R}_0}\boldsymbol{Z}_0)(n^{-1}\boldsymbol{Z}_0^\top\boldsymbol{M}_{\boldsymbol{R}_0}\boldsymbol{Z}_0)^{-1}(n^{-1/2}\boldsymbol{Z}_0^\top\boldsymbol{M}_{\boldsymbol{R}_0}\boldsymbol{r}_0). \tag{15.85}$$

This is a quadratic form in the r–vector $n^{-1/2}\boldsymbol{Z}_0^\top\boldsymbol{M}_{\boldsymbol{R}_0}\boldsymbol{r}_0$, which is asymptotically normal by condition R2, and the inverse of its asymptotic covariance matrix. By Theorem 4.1, therefore, the statistic (15.85) is asymptotically distributed as $\chi^2(r)$.

Calculations very similar to those above can be used to show that, when the asymptotic covariance matrix of $\hat{\boldsymbol{\theta}}$ is given by equation (15.03), F statistics computed from the unrestricted artificial regression (15.05) and the restricted one (15.01) evaluated at $\acute{\boldsymbol{\theta}}$ have their namesake distributions asymptotically under the hypothesis that the true DGP is contained in the model $\mathbb{M}$. We leave the proof of this as Exercise 15.4.

15.8 Exercises

15.1 If the linear regression model $\boldsymbol{y} = \boldsymbol{X\beta} + \boldsymbol{u}$, with error terms $u_t \sim \text{IID}(0, \sigma^2)$, is estimated using the $n \times l$ matrix $\boldsymbol{W}$ of instrumental variables, an artificial regression that corresponds to this model and this estimator is the IVGNR

$$\boldsymbol{y} - \boldsymbol{X\beta} = \boldsymbol{P_W X b} + \text{residuals}.$$

Suppose that we wish to test whether the n–vector $\boldsymbol{z}$ is predetermined with respect to the error terms in $\boldsymbol{u}$, that is, whether $\text{plim}\, n^{-1}\boldsymbol{z}^\top\boldsymbol{u} = 0$. Show that the obvious testing regression, namely,

$$\boldsymbol{y} - \boldsymbol{X\beta} = \boldsymbol{P_W X b} + c\boldsymbol{z} + \text{residuals}, \tag{15.86}$$

does *not* satisfy all three of the conditions given in Section 15.2 for a valid testing regression. What other artificial regression could be used to obtain a valid test statistic?

15.2 Show that the t statistic for $\gamma = 0$ in regression (15.09) is numerically identical to the t statistic for $c = 0$ in regression (15.10).

⋆15.3 Suppose the dependent variable $\boldsymbol{y}$ is generated by the DGP

$$\boldsymbol{y} = \boldsymbol{X\beta}_0 + \boldsymbol{u}, \quad \boldsymbol{u} \sim \text{N}(\boldsymbol{0}, \sigma_0^2\mathbf{I}),$$

where the $n \times k$ matrix $\boldsymbol{X}$ is independent of $\boldsymbol{u}$. Let $\boldsymbol{z}$ be a vector that is not necessarily independent of $\boldsymbol{u}$, but is independent of $\boldsymbol{M_X u}$. Show that the t statistic on $\boldsymbol{z}$ in the linear regression $\boldsymbol{y} = \boldsymbol{X\beta} + c\boldsymbol{z} + \boldsymbol{u}$ follows the Student's t distribution with $n - k - 1$ degrees of freedom.

⋆15.4 Let (15.01) be an artificial regression corresponding to a model $\mathbb{M}$ and an asymptotically normal root-n consistent estimator $\hat{\boldsymbol{\theta}}$ of the parameters of $\mathbb{M}$, with the asymptotic covariance matrix of $\hat{\boldsymbol{\theta}}$ given by (15.03). Show that, whenever $\acute{\boldsymbol{\theta}}$ is a root-n consistent estimator, r times the F statistic for the artificial hypothesis that $\boldsymbol{c} = \boldsymbol{0}$ in the artificial regression (15.05) is asymptotically distributed as $\chi^2(r)$ under any DGP in $\mathbb{M}$.

15.5 Suppose the vector $\boldsymbol{y}$ is generated by the nonlinear regression model (6.01), and $\boldsymbol{Z}(\boldsymbol{\beta})$ is an $n \times r$ matrix such that

$$\operatorname*{plim}_{n\to\infty} \frac{1}{n}\boldsymbol{Z}^\top(\boldsymbol{\beta})\boldsymbol{u} = \boldsymbol{0}.$$

Show that n times the uncentered R^2 from regression (15.22) is asymptotically distributed as $\chi^2(r)$.

⋆15.6 Consider a fully parametrized model for which the tth observation is characterized by a conditional density function $f_t(\boldsymbol{y}^t, \boldsymbol{\theta})$, where the vector $\boldsymbol{y}^t$ contains the observations $y_1, \ldots, y_t$ on the dependent variable. The density is that of y_t conditional on $\boldsymbol{y}^{t-1}$. Let the moment function $m_t(\boldsymbol{\theta})$, which implicitly depends on y_t and possibly also on $\boldsymbol{y}^{t-1}$, have expectation zero conditional on $\boldsymbol{y}^{t-1}$ when evaluated at the true parameter vector $\boldsymbol{\theta}_0$. Show that

$$\text{E}\big(m_t(\boldsymbol{\theta}_0)\boldsymbol{G}_t(\boldsymbol{\theta}_0)\big) = -\text{E}\Big(\frac{\partial m_t(\boldsymbol{\theta})}{\partial \boldsymbol{\theta}}\Big)\Big|_{\boldsymbol{\theta}=\boldsymbol{\theta}_0},$$

where $\boldsymbol{G}_t(\boldsymbol{\theta})$ is the row vector of derivatives of $\log f_t(\boldsymbol{y}^t, \boldsymbol{\theta})$, the contribution to the loglikelihood function made by the tth observation, and $\partial m_t/\partial\boldsymbol{\theta}(\boldsymbol{\theta})$ denotes the row vector of derivatives of $m_t(\boldsymbol{\theta})$ with respect to $\boldsymbol{\theta}$. All expectations are taken under the density $f_t(\boldsymbol{y}^t, \boldsymbol{\theta})$. **Hint:** Use the same approach as in Exercise 10.6.

Explain why this result implies equation (15.26) under condition R2 of Section 15.2. **Hint:** Apply a central limit theorem to the appropriate expression.

15.7 Consider the following artificial regression, which was originally proposed by Tauchen (1985):

$$\hat{\boldsymbol{m}} = \hat{\boldsymbol{G}}\boldsymbol{b}' + c'\boldsymbol{\iota} + \text{residuals}.$$

Show that the t statistic for $c' = 0$ from this regression is identical to the t statistic for $c = 0$ from the OPG regression (15.24). **Hint:** See Exercise 4.9.

⋆15.8 Show that the regressor in the testing regression (15.32) is asymptotically orthogonal to the regressors in the OPG regression (15.27), when all regressors are evaluated at root-n consistent estimators $\acute{\boldsymbol{\beta}}$ and $\acute{s}$. Note that two vectors $\boldsymbol{a}$ and $\boldsymbol{b}$ are said to be asymptotically orthogonal if $\operatorname{plim} n^{-1}\boldsymbol{a}^\top\boldsymbol{b} = 0$.

Prove that the t statistic from regression (15.32) is asymptotically equivalent to the statistic τ_4 defined by (15.33).

Show also that the statistics τ_3 and τ_4 are asymptotically independent under the null of normality.

⋆15.9 Suppose you have a sample of n IID observations u_t, $t = 1, \ldots, n$, on a variable that is supposed to follow the standard normal distribution. What is the very simplest way to test the null hypothesis of normality against alternatives allowing the u_t to be skewed, to have excess kurtosis, or both? Are your proposed tests exact or asymptotic?

Suppose now that the variance of the u_t is unknown and must be estimated from the sample. Are all of the tests you just proposed still valid? If not, explain how some or all of them need to be modified. **Hint:** Recall that the regressor corresponding to σ is asymptotically orthogonal to the test regressor in the OPG regression (15.28).

15.10 This question uses data on monthly returns for the period 1969–1998 for shares of General Electric Corporation from the file **monthly-crsp.data**. These data are made available by courtesy of the Center for Research in Security Prices (CRSP); see the comments at the bottom of the file. Let R_t denote the return on GE shares in month t. For the entire sample period, regress R_t on a constant and d_t, where d_t is a dummy variable that is equal to 1 in November, December, January, and February, and equal to 0 in all other months. Then test the residuals for evidence of skewness and excess kurtosis, both individually and jointly. Use asymptotic tests based on normalized residuals and tests based on the OPG regressions (15.29) and (15.32).

⋆15.11 Consider the classical linear regression model

$$y_t = \beta_1 + \beta_2 x_{t2} + \beta_3 x_{t3} + u_t, \quad u_t \sim \text{NID}(0, \sigma^2),$$

where x_{t2} and x_{t3} are exogenous variables, and there are n observations. Write down the contribution to the loglikelihood made by the tth observation.

Then calculate the matrix $\boldsymbol{M}(\hat{\boldsymbol{\theta}})$ of which the typical element is expression (15.36) evaluated at the ML estimates. How many columns does this matrix have? What is a typical element of each of the columns?

Explain how to compute an information matrix test for this model using the OPG regression (15.25). How many regressors does the test regression have? What test statistic would you use, and how many degrees of freedom does it have? What types of misspecification is this test sensitive to?

⋆15.12 Show that the J statistic computed using regression (15.40) is given by

$$J = \frac{(n - k_1 - 1)^{1/2}\boldsymbol{y}^\top \boldsymbol{M_X P_Z y}}{\big(\boldsymbol{y}^\top \boldsymbol{M_X y}\, \boldsymbol{y}^\top \boldsymbol{P_Z M_X P_Z y} - (\boldsymbol{y}^\top \boldsymbol{M_X P_Z y})^2\big)^{1/2}}.$$

Use this expression to show that the probability limit under hypothesis H_1 of n^{-1} times the square of the denominator is

$$\sigma_0^2 \operatorname*{plim}_{n\to\infty} \frac{1}{n} \boldsymbol{\beta}_0^\top \boldsymbol{X}^\top \boldsymbol{P_Z M_X P_Z X \beta}_0,$$

where $\boldsymbol{\beta}_0$ and σ_0^2 are the true parameters.

15.13 Consider the nonnested linear regression models given in equations (15.37). Suppose that just one column of $\boldsymbol{Z}$ does not lie in $\mathcal{S}(\boldsymbol{X})$. In this special case, how is the J statistic for testing H_1 from regression (15.40) related to the F statistic for $\boldsymbol{\gamma}' = \mathbf{0}$ in the inclusive regression (15.39)?

15.14 How is the P statistic from equation (15.47) related to the J statistic from equation (15.46) when the regression function $\boldsymbol{x}(\boldsymbol{\beta})$ for the H_1 model can be written as $\boldsymbol{X\beta}$?

15.15 The P test regression (15.47) can be interpreted as a Gauss-Newton regression for testing a moment condition. Make this moment condition explicit and explain why it makes sense.

15.16 This question uses data from the file **consumption.data**. As in previous exercises that use these data, c_t is the log of consumption, and y_t is the log of disposable income. All models are to be estimated, and all tests calculated, for the 176 observations from 1953:1 to 1996:4.

Using ordinary least squares, estimate the ADL model in levels,

$$c_t = \alpha + \beta c_{t-1} + \gamma_0 y_t + \gamma_1 y_{t-1} + u_t, \tag{15.87}$$

and the ADL model in first differences,

$$\Delta c_t = \alpha' + \beta' \Delta c_{t-1} + \gamma_0' \Delta y_t + \gamma_1' \Delta y_{t-1} + u_t, \tag{15.88}$$

where $\Delta c_t \equiv c_t - c_{t-1}$ and $\Delta y_t \equiv y_t - y_{t-1}$.

Test each of these two models against the other using a J test. Then test both models against a more general model that includes both of them as special cases. Report asymptotically valid P values for all four tests.

15.17 Calculate semiparametric bootstrap P values for the four tests of the previous exercise, using the procedure discussed in Section 4.6. Do the bootstrap tests yield the same inferences as the asymptotic ones? What can you tentatively conclude from these results?

⋆15.18 Consider the two nonnested linear regression models H_1 and H_2 given in equations (15.37). An encompassing test can be based on the estimate of the error variance of model H_2 rather than on the estimates of the parameters $\boldsymbol{\gamma}$. Let $\hat{\sigma}_2^2$ be the usual ML estimator obtained from estimating H_2. Compute the expectation of $\hat{\sigma}_2^2$ under the DGP in model H_1 with parameters $\boldsymbol{\beta}$ and σ_1^2. Explain how to estimate this expectation based on the parameter estimates for model H_1. Let $\tilde{\sigma}_2^2$ denote the consistent estimator you are proposing.

Show that $n^{1/2}(\hat{\sigma}_2^2 - \tilde{\sigma}_2^2)$ is asymptotically equal to a random variable that is proportional to $\boldsymbol{u}^\top \boldsymbol{M_X P_Z X}\boldsymbol{\beta}_0$, in the notation of equation (15.41). What does this result imply about the relationship between the variance encompassing test and the J test?

15.19 Consider the binary response models

$$H_1: \quad \mathrm{E}(y_t \,|\, \Omega_t) = F_1(\boldsymbol{X}_t\boldsymbol{\beta}), \text{ and}$$

$$H_2: \quad \mathrm{E}(y_t \,|\, \Omega_t) = F_2(\boldsymbol{Z}_t\boldsymbol{\gamma}),$$

where $F_1(\cdot)$ and $F_2(\cdot)$ may be any transformation functions that satisfy conditions (11.02). Starting from the artificial comprehensive model

$$\mathrm{E}(y_t \,|\, \Omega_t) = (1-\alpha)F_1(\boldsymbol{X}_t\boldsymbol{\beta}) + \alpha F_2(\boldsymbol{Z}_t\boldsymbol{\gamma}), \tag{15.89}$$

show how to compute a nonnested hypothesis test similar to the P test but based on the BRMR (Section 11.3) instead of the GNR.

⋆15.20 Consider the nonnested linear regression models (15.37) and suppose that the data are generated by a DGP in H_1 with parameters $\boldsymbol{\beta}$ and σ_1^2 and with IID normal errors. Calculate the statistics T_1 and T_1', which were defined in equations (15.52) and (15.53), respectively, and show that they are both asymptotically equal to

$$T_1^{\mathrm{OLS}} = n^{1/2} \log\left(\frac{\hat{\sigma}_1^2 + \hat{\sigma}_a^2}{\hat{\sigma}_2^2}\right), \tag{15.90}$$

where $\hat{\sigma}_i^2$, for $i = 1, 2$, is the ML estimate of the error variance from estimating model H_i, and $\hat{\sigma}_a^2 \equiv n^{-1}\|\boldsymbol{M_Z P_X y}\|^2$.

Show that the statistic T_1^{OLS} is asymptotically proportional to the J statistic for testing H_1 and also, therefore, to the variance encompassing test statistic of Exercise 15.18. Why is it not surprising that the Cox test, which can be interpreted as an encompassing test based on the maximized loglikelihood, should be asymptotically equivalent to the variance encompassing test?

Show that the asymptotic variance of the statistic (15.90) is

$$\frac{4\sigma_1^2}{(\sigma_1^2 + \sigma_a^2)^2} \operatorname*{plim}_{n\to\infty} \frac{1}{n}\|\boldsymbol{M_X P_Z X}\boldsymbol{\beta}\|^2,$$

where $\sigma_a^2 \equiv \operatorname{plim} \hat{\sigma}_a^2$. Use this result to write down a Cox statistic that is asymptotically distributed as $\mathrm{N}(0, 1)$.

★**15.21** Set up the OPG artificial regression for the Cox test of model H_1 against H_2 in (15.37), assuming IID normal errors. In particular, show that, in the notation of Exercise 15.20, the typical element of the test regressor (15.54) takes the form

$$\log\left(\frac{\hat{\sigma}_1^2+\hat{\sigma}_a^2}{\hat{\sigma}_2^2}\right)-\frac{\hat{u}_{2t}^2}{\hat{\sigma}_2^2}+\frac{\hat{\sigma}_1^2+(\boldsymbol{M_Z P_X y})_t^2}{\hat{\sigma}_1^2+\hat{\sigma}_a^2}, \tag{15.91}$$

where $\hat{u}_{2t}$ is a typical element of the vector $\boldsymbol{M_Z y}$.

15.22 The file **nonnested.data** contains 40 observations on the artificial variables $\boldsymbol{x}_1$, $\boldsymbol{x}_2$, $\boldsymbol{z}_2$, $\boldsymbol{z}_3$, and $\boldsymbol{z}_4$. Consider the nonnested linear regression models

$$H_1: \quad \boldsymbol{y}=\alpha_1\boldsymbol{\iota}+\beta_1\boldsymbol{x}_1+\beta_2\boldsymbol{x}_2+\boldsymbol{u}, \text{ and}$$
$$H_2: \quad \boldsymbol{y}=\alpha_2\boldsymbol{\iota}+\gamma_1\boldsymbol{x}_1+\gamma_2\boldsymbol{z}_2+\gamma_3\boldsymbol{z}_3+\gamma_4\boldsymbol{z}_4+\boldsymbol{u}.$$

Perform a simulation experiment where, for each replication, the dependent variable $\boldsymbol{y}$ is generated by the DGP in H_1 with $\alpha_1=0$, $\beta_1=\beta_2=1$, and normally distributed error terms with variance $\sigma_1^2=2.25$. For each simulated data set, compute three statistics for testing H_1: the J statistic, the Cox statistic of Exercise 15.20, and the Cox statistic based on an OPG artificial regression, with test regressor having typical element (15.91). Graphically compare the empirical distribution functions of the simulated statistics with the CDF of the N(0, 1) distribution. Also report the rejection frequencies for one-tailed tests at the .01, .05, and .10 levels.

Perform another experiment using data generated by $\boldsymbol{y}=\boldsymbol{x}_1+\boldsymbol{x}_2+0.5\boldsymbol{z}_3+\boldsymbol{u}$, with $\boldsymbol{u}\sim \text{NID}(0, 2.25)$. Also compute the F test based on the inclusive regression (15.39). Given that three of the four statistics have finite-sample distributions different from their asymptotic distributions, how can one use the results of both experiments to measure the ability of the statistics to discriminate between the DGPs of the two experiments?

15.23 Consider two nonnested models H_1 and H_2 characterized by the loglikelihood functions (15.50). If the true DGP μ belongs to H_1 and not to H_2, show that

$$\operatorname*{plim}_{n\to\infty}{}_{\mu}\, \frac{1}{n}\big(\ell_1(\hat{\boldsymbol{\theta}}_1)-\ell_2(\hat{\boldsymbol{\theta}}_2)\big)>0, \tag{15.92}$$

where $\hat{\boldsymbol{\theta}}_1$ and $\hat{\boldsymbol{\theta}}_2$ are the MLEs of the two models. **Hint:** Use Jensen's inequality for the contribution to the two likelihood functions from each observation.

Let BIC_i denote the Bayesian information criterion (15.57) for model H_i. Use (15.92) to show that $\text{BIC}_1-\text{BIC}_2$ tends to $+\infty$ as $n\to\infty$.

15.24 Show that the kernel density estimator defined in equation (15.61) is nonnegative and integrates to unity.

★**15.25** For a given choice of bandwidth, the expectation of the estimate $\hat{f}_h(x)$ of (15.61) is h^{-1} times the expectation of the random variable $k((x-X)/h)$, where X denotes the random variable of which the x_t are IID realizations. Assume that k is symmetric about the origin. Show that the bias of $\hat{f}_h(x)$ is independent of the sample size n and roughly proportional to h^2 for small h. More formally, this means that the bias is $O(h^2)$ as $h\to 0$.

Show also that the variance of $\hat{f}_h(x)$ is of order $(nh)^{-1}$ as $n \to \infty$ and $h \to 0$. Why do these facts imply that the bandwidth h that minimizes the expectation of the squared error of $\hat{f}_h(x)$ must be of order $n^{-1/5}$ as $n \to \infty$?

15.26 A subsample of the data used for Figures 15.1 and 15.2 can be found in the file **daily-crsp.data**, for the period from January 1989 to December 1998. Estimate the density of the percentage daily returns on IBM stock (the data in the file times 100) employing the bandwidth given by equation (15.64), using both Gaussian and Epanechnikov kernels. Also perform the estimation using the uniform kernel $k(z) = 1/(2\sqrt{3})$ for $|z| < \sqrt{3}$ and $k(z) = 0$ outside this range. Finally, compute a histogram with bin width equal to the bandwidths of the kernel estimators. Graph all four sets of results. What conclusions can you draw from them?

15.27 Regress the IBM daily returns in **daily-crsp.data** on the returns for the CRSP value-weighted index in the same file by nonparametric regression. Multiply both returns by 100 so that they are in percentage terms. Estimate the conditional expectation only for returns on the index, x_t, that are less than 2.5% in absolute value. Compute both the Nadaraya-Watson estimator and the locally linear estimator using an Epanechnikov kernel. For both estimators, use the bandwidth (15.64) computed using the IQR of the index returns.

Compute the cross-validation function (15.70), with weights equal to 1 when $|x_t| \leq 2.5$ and equal to 0 otherwise, for both the Nadaraya-Watson and the locally linear estimators. Calculate this function over a wide range of values between 0.05 and 5 (the bandwidth (15.64) lies within this range), and find an approximately optimal bandwidth for each of the estimators. Compare your results using the "optimal" bandwidth with the ones using the bandwidth (15.64). Also compare them with an OLS regression of the IBM returns on a constant and the index returns.

15.28 The file **partlin.data** contains 400 observations on three artificial variables, $\boldsymbol{z}$, $\boldsymbol{x}^\circ$, and $\boldsymbol{y}^\circ$. The vector $\boldsymbol{z}$ is to be interpreted as a vector of observations on an exogenous explanatory variable, while $\boldsymbol{x}^\circ$ and $\boldsymbol{y}^\circ$ contain nonlinear deterministic functions of $\boldsymbol{z}$. The random vector $\boldsymbol{x}$ is to be generated by the equation

$$\boldsymbol{x} = \boldsymbol{x}^\circ + \boldsymbol{u}_x, \quad \boldsymbol{u}_x \sim \text{IID}(0, \sigma_x^2), \tag{15.93}$$

and the random vector $\boldsymbol{y}$ by

$$\boldsymbol{y} = \boldsymbol{y}^\circ + \beta\boldsymbol{x} + \boldsymbol{u}_y, \quad \boldsymbol{u}_y \sim \text{IID}(0, \sigma_y^2). \tag{15.94}$$

Perform a simulation experiment in which, for each replication, you generate $\boldsymbol{x}$ and $\boldsymbol{y}$ using (15.93) and (15.94), with $\beta = \sigma_x^2 = \sigma_y^2 = 1$, and then compute the partially linear estimator of β in the model

$$y_t = \beta x_t + \mu(z_t) + u_t.$$

Do this using both Nadaraya-Watson and locally linear nonparametric estimates of $\text{E}(y_t \mid z_t)$ and $\text{E}(x_t \mid z_t)$, with bandwidth determined (for simplicity) by equation (15.63). Compare the distributions of the two partially linear estimators. For both estimators, plot the distribution of the t statistic for $\beta = 1$, and compare it with the standard normal distribution.

15.29 Suppose that the k–vector $\boldsymbol{x}_t \sim \mathrm{N}(\mathbf{0}, \mathbf{I})$. What is the probability that the Euclidean distance between $\boldsymbol{x}_t$ and the origin is less than 1 if $k = 1$? What is it if $k = 2$, $k = 3$, and $k = 4$? What are the probabilities that the distance is less than 2 for the same values of k?

15.30 Let τ_1 and τ_2 each be distributed as $\mathrm{N}(0, 1)$, with correlation ρ. For $\rho = -0.9$, -0.5, 0, 0.5, and 0.9, generate at least 10,000 realizations of τ_1 and τ_2. Then calculate the proportion of the time that at least one of the two statistics is greater than the .95 quantile of the standard normal distribution. What does this experiment tell us about the overall significance level when we perform two tests that are not independent?

References

Abadir, K. M. (1995). "The limiting distribution of the t ratio under a unit root," *Econometric Theory*, **11**, 775–93.

Ahn, S. K., and G. C. Reinsel (1988). "Nested reduced rank autoregressive models for multiple time series," *Journal of the American Statistical Association*, **83**, 849–56.

Ahn, S. K., and G. C. Reinsel (1990). "Estimation for partially nonstationary multivariate autoregressive models," *Journal of the American Statistical Association*, **85**, 813–23.

Akaike, H. (1973). "Information theory and an extension of the maximum likelihood principle," in *Second International Symposium on Information Theory*, ed. B. Petrov and F. Csake, Budapest, Akademiai Kiado.

Albert, A., and J. A. Anderson (1984). "On the existence of maximum likelihood estimates in logistic regression models," *Biometrika*, **71**, 1–10.

Amemiya, T. (1973a). "Generalized least squares with an estimated autocovariance matrix," *Econometrica*, **41**, 723–32.

Amemiya, T. (1973b). "Regression analysis when the variance of the dependent variable is proportional to the square of its expectation," *Journal of the American Statistical Association*, **68**, 928–34.

Amemiya, T. (1973c). "Regression analysis when the dependent variable is truncated normal," *Econometrica*, **41**, 997–1016.

Amemiya, T. (1985). *Advanced Econometrics*, Cambridge, Mass., Harvard University Press.

Anderson, T. W., and H. Rubin (1949). "Estimation of the parameters of a single equation in a complete system of stochastic equations," *Annals of Mathematical Statistics*, **20**, 46–63.

Anderson, T. W., and H. Rubin (1950). "The asymptotic properties of estimates of the parameters of a single equation in a complete system of stochastic equations," *Annals of Mathematical Statistics*, **21**, 570–82.

Andrews, D. W. K. (1991). "Heteroskedasticity and autocorrelation consistent covariance matrix estimation," *Econometrica*, **59**, 817–58.

Andrews, D. W. K. (1997). "A stopping rule for the computation of generalized method of moments estimators," *Econometrica*, **65**, 913–31.

Andrews, D. W. K., and B. Lu (2001). "Consistent model and moment selection procedures for GMM estimation with application to dynamic panel data models." *Journal of Econometrics*, **101**, 123–64.

Andrews, D. W. K., and J. C. Monahan (1992). "An improved heteroskedasticity and autocorrelation consistent covariance matrix estimator," *Econometrica*, **60**, 953–66.

Angrist, J. D., G. W. Imbens, and A. B. Krueger (1999). "Jackknife instrumental variables estimation," *Journal of Applied Econometrics*, **14**, 57–67.

Arellano, M., and S. Bond (1991). "Some tests of specification for panel data: Monte Carlo evidence and an application to employment equations," *Review of Economic Studies*, **58**, 277–97.

Arellano, M., and O. Bover (1995). "Another look at instrumental variable estimation of error-components models," *Journal of Econometrics*, **68**, 29–51.

Arellano, M., and B. Honoré (2001). "Panel data models: Some recent developments," Ch. 53 in *Handbook of Econometrics*, Vol. 5, ed. J. J. Heckman and E. E. Leamer, Amsterdam, North-Holland.

Azzalini, A. (1981). "A note on the estimation of a distribution function and quantiles by a kernel method," *Biometrika*, **68**, 326–28.

Balestra, P., and M. Nerlove (1966). "Pooling cross section and time series data in the estimation of a dynamic model: The demand for natural gas," *Econometrica*, **34**, 585–612.

Baltagi, B. (2001). *Econometric Analysis of Panel Data*, second edition, New York, John Wiley & Sons.

Banerjee, A., J. J. Dolado, J. W. Galbraith, and D. F. Hendry (1993). *Co-Integration, Error-Correction, and the Econometric Analysis of Non-Stationary Data*, Oxford, Oxford University Press.

Banerjee, A., J. J. Dolado, and R. Mestre (1998). "Error-correction mechanism tests for cointegration in a single-equation framework," *Journal of Time Series Analysis*, **19**, 267–83.

Bard, Y. (1974). *Nonlinear Parameter Estimation*, New York, Academic Press.

Barten, A. P. (1977). "The system of consumer demand functions approach: A review," *Econometrica*, **45**, 23–51.

Basmann, R. L. (1957). "A generalized classical method of linear estimation of coefficients in a structural equation," *Econometrica*, **25**, 77–83.

Bates, D. M., and D. G. Watts (1988). *Nonlinear Regression Analysis and Its Applications*, New York, John Wiley & Sons.

Beach, C. M., and J. G. MacKinnon (1978). "A maximum likelihood procedure for regression with autocorrelated errors," *Econometrica*, **46**, 51–58.

Becker, W. E., and P. E. Kennedy (1992). "A graphical exposition of the ordered probit," *Econometric Theory*, **8**, 127–31.

Bekker, P. A. (1994). "Alternative approximations to the distributions of instrumental variables estimators," *Econometrica*, **62**, 657–81.

Bera, A. K., and C. M. Jarque (1982). "Model specification tests: A simultaneous approach," *Journal of Econometrics*, **20**, 59–82.

Beran, R. (1988). "Prepivoting test statistics: A bootstrap view of asymptotic refinements," *Journal of the American Statistical Association*, **83**, 687–97.

Berndt, E. R., B. H. Hall, R. E. Hall, and J. A. Hausman (1974). "Estimation and inference in nonlinear structural models," *Annals of Economic and Social Measurement*, **3**, 653–65.

Betancourt, R., and H. Kelejian (1981). "Lagged endogenous variables and the Cochrane-Orcutt procedure," *Econometrica*, **49**, 1073–78.

Bierens, H. J. (2001). "Unit roots," Ch. 29 in *A Companion to Econometric Theory*, ed. B. Baltagi, Oxford, Blackwell Publishers, 610–33.

Billingsley, P. (1979). *Probability and Measure*, New York, John Wiley & Sons.

Blomquist, S., and M. Dahlberg (1999). "Small sample properties of LIML and jackknife IV estimators: Experiments with weak instruments," *Journal of Applied Econometrics*, **14**, 69–88.

Blundell, R., M. Browning, and C. Meghir (1994). "Consumer demand and the life-cycle allocation of household expenditures," *Review of Economic Studies*, **61**, 57–80.

Bollerslev, T. (1986). "Generalized autoregressive conditional heteroskedasticity," *Journal of Econometrics*, **31**, 307–27.

Bollerslev, T., R. Y. Chou, and K. F. Kroner (1992). "ARCH modeling in finance: A review of the theory and empirical evidence," *Journal of Econometrics*, **52**, 5–59.

Bollerslev, T., R. F. Engle, and D. B. Nelson (1994). "ARCH Models," Ch. 49 in *Handbook of Econometrics*, Vol. 4, ed. R. F. Engle and D. L. McFadden, Amsterdam, North-Holland, 2959–3038.

Bollerslev, T., and J. M. Wooldridge (1992). "Quasi-maximum likelihood estimation and inference in dynamic models with time-varying covariances," *Econometric Reviews*, **11**, 143–72.

Bontemps, C., and N. Meddahi (2004). "Testing normality: A GMM approach," *Journal of Econometrics*, forthcoming.

Bound, J., D. A. Jaeger, and R. M. Baker (1995). "Problems with instrumental variables estimation when the correlation between the instruments and the exogenous explanatory variable is weak," *Journal of the American Statistical Association*, **90**, 443–50.

Box, G. E. P., and G. M. Jenkins (1976). *Time Series Analysis, Forecasting and Control*, revised edition, San Francisco, Holden Day.

Box, G. E. P., G. M. Jenkins, and G. C. Reinsel (1994). *Time Series Analysis, Forecasting and Control*, third edition, Englewood Cliffs, N.J., Prentice-Hall.

Breusch, T. S. (1978). "Testing for autocorrelation in dynamic linear models," *Australian Economic Papers*, **17**, 334–55.

Brockwell, P. J., and R. A. Davis (1991). *Time Series: Theory and Methods*, second edition, New York, Springer-Verlag.

Brooks, C., S. P. Burke, and G. Persand (2001). "Benchmarks and the Accuracy of GARCH Model Estimation," *International Journal of Forecasting*, **17**, 45–56.

Brown, B. W. (1981). "Sample size requirements in full information maximum likelihood estimation," *International Economic Review*, **22**, 443–59.

Browning, M., and C. Meghir (1991). "The effects of male and female labor supply on commodity demands," *Econometrica*, **59**, 925–51.

Bryant, P. (1984). "Geometry, statistics, probability: Variations on a common theme," *The American Statistician*, **38**, 38–48.

Burridge, P., and K. F. Wallis (1984). "Unobserved-components models for seasonal adjustment filters," *Journal of Business and Economic Statistics*, **2**, 350–59.

Buse, A. (1992). "The bias of instrumental variable estimators," *Econometrica*, **60**, 173–80.

Cameron, A. C., and P. K. Trivedi (1986). "Econometric models based on count data: Comparisons and applications of some estimators and tests," *Journal of Applied Econometrics*, **1**, 29–53.

Cameron, A. C., and P. K. Trivedi (1990). "Regression-based tests for overdispersion in the Poisson model," *Journal of Econometrics*, **46**, 347–64.

Cameron, A. C., and P. K. Trivedi (1998). *Regression Analysis of Count Data*, Cambridge, Cambridge University Press.

Cameron, A. C., and P. K. Trivedi (2001). "Essentials of count data regression," Ch. 15 in *A Companion to Econometric Theory*, ed. B. Baltagi, Oxford, Blackwell Publishers, 331–48.

Campos, J., N. R. Ericsson, and D. F. Hendry (1996). "Cointegration tests in the presence of structural breaks," *Journal of Econometrics*, **70**, 187–220.

Chamberlain, G. (1984). "Panel data," Ch. 22 in *Handbook of Econometrics*, Vol. 2, ed. Z. Griliches and M. D. Intriligator, Amsterdam, North-Holland, 1247–318.

Chang, Y., and J. Y. Park (2003). "A sieve bootstrap for the test of a unit root," *Journal of Time Series Analysis*, **24**, 379–400.

Chesher, A. (1983). "The information matrix test: Simplified calculation via a score test interpretation," *Economics Letters*, **13**, 45–48.

Chesher, A. (1989). "Hájek inequalities, measures of leverage and the size of heteroskedasticity robust tests," *Econometrica*, **57**, 971–77.

Chesher, A., and G. Austin (1991). "The finite-sample distributions of heteroskedasticity robust Wald statistics," *Journal of Econometrics*, **47**, 153–73.

Chesher, A., and M. Irish (1987). "Residual analysis in the grouped and censored normal linear model," *Journal of Econometrics*, **34**, 33–61.

Chow, G. C. (1960). "Tests of equality between sets of coefficients in two linear regressions," *Econometrica*, **28**, 591–605.

Christensen, L. R., D. W. Jorgenson, and L. J. Lau (1975). "Transcendental logarithmic utility functions," *American Economic Review*, **65**, 367–83.

Cochrane, D., and G. H. Orcutt (1949). "Application of least squares regression to relationships containing autocorrelated error terms," *Journal of the American Statistical Association*, **44**, 32–61.

Cox, D. R. (1961). "Tests of separate families of hypotheses," *Proceedings of the Fourth Berkeley Symposium on Mathematical Statistics and Probability*, **1**, 105–23.

Cox, D. R. (1962). "Further results on tests of separate families of hypotheses," *Journal of the Royal Statistical Society*, Series B, **24**, 406–24.

Cox, D. R. (1972). "Regression models and life tables" (with discussion), *Journal of the Royal Statistical Society*, Series B, **34**, 187–220.

Cox, D. R., and D. V. Hinkley (1974). *Theoretical Statistics*, London, Chapman and Hall.

Cox, D. R., and D. Oakes (1984). *Analysis of Survival Data*, London, Chapman and Hall.

Cragg, J. G. (1983). "More efficient estimation in the presence of heteroskedasticity of unknown form," *Econometrica*, **51**, 751–63.

Cramér, H. (1946). *Mathematical Methods of Statistics*, Princeton, Princeton University Press.

Dagenais, M. G., and D. L. Dagenais (1997). "Higher moment estimators for linear regression models with errors in the variables," *Journal of Econometrics*, **76**, 193–221.

Das Gupta, S., and Perlman, M. D. (1974). "Power of the noncentral F test: Effect of additional variates on Hotelling's T^2 test," *Journal of the American Statistical Association*, **69**, 174–80.

Davidson, J. E. H. (1994). *Stochastic Limit Theory: An Introduction for Econometricians*, Oxford, Oxford University Press.

Davidson, J. E. H. (2000). *Econometric Theory*, Oxford, Blackwell Publishers.

Davidson, J. E. H., D. F. Hendry, F. Srba, and S. Yeo (1978). "Econometric modelling of the aggregate time-series relationship between consumers' expenditure and income in the United Kingdom," *Economic Journal*, **88**, 661–92.

Davidson, R., and J. G. MacKinnon (1981). "Several tests for model specification in the presence of alternative hypotheses," *Econometrica*, **49**, 781–93.

Davidson, R., and J. G. MacKinnon (1982). "Some non-nested hypothesis tests and the relations among them," *Review of Economic Studies*, **49**, 551–65.

Davidson, R., and J. G. MacKinnon (1983). "Testing the specification of multivariate models in the presence of alternative hypotheses," *Journal of Econometrics*, **23**, 301–13.

Davidson, R., and J. G. MacKinnon (1984a). "Model specification tests based on artificial linear regressions," *International Economic Review*, **25**, 485–502.

Davidson, R., and J. G. MacKinnon (1984b). "Convenient specification tests for logit and probit models," *Journal of Econometrics*, **25**, 241–62.

Davidson, R., and J. G. MacKinnon (1985a). "Heteroskedasticity-robust tests in regression directions," *Annales de l'INSEE*, **59/60**, 183–218.

Davidson, R., and J. G. MacKinnon (1985b). "Testing linear and loglinear regressions against Box-Cox alternatives," *Canadian Journal of Economics*, **18**, 499–517.

Davidson, R., and J. G. MacKinnon (1987). "Implicit alternatives and the local power of test statistics," *Econometrica*, **55**, 1305–29.

Davidson, R., and J. G. MacKinnon (1992). "A new form of the information matrix test," *Econometrica*, **60**, 145–57.

Davidson, R., and J. G. MacKinnon (1993). *Estimation and Inference in Econometrics*, New York, Oxford University Press.

Davidson, R., and J. G. MacKinnon (1998). "Graphical methods for investigating the size and power of hypothesis tests," *The Manchester School*, **66**, 1–26.

Davidson, R., and J. G. MacKinnon (1999a). "Bootstrap testing in nonlinear models," *International Economic Review*, **40**, 487–508.

Davidson, R., and J. G. MacKinnon (1999b). "The size distortion of bootstrap tests," *Econometric Theory*, **15**, 361–76.

Davidson, R., and J. G. MacKinnon (2000). "Bootstrap tests: How many bootstraps?" *Econometric Reviews*, **19**, 55–68.

Davidson, R., and J. G. MacKinnon (2001). "Artifical Regressions," Ch. 1 in *A Companion to Econometric Theory*, ed. B. Baltagi, Oxford, Blackwell Publishers, 16–37.

Davidson, R., and J. G. MacKinnon (2002a). "Bootstrap *J* tests of nonnested linear regression models," *Journal of Econometrics*, **109**, 167–93.

Davidson, R., and J. G. MacKinnon (2002b). "Fast double bootstrap tests of nonnested linear regression models," *Econometric Reviews*, **21**, 417–27.

Davison, A. C., and D. V. Hinkley (1997). *Bootstrap Methods and Their Application*, Cambridge, Cambridge University Press.

Deaton, A. S., and J. Muellbauer (1980). *Economics and Consumer Behaviour*, Cambridge, Cambridge University Press.

Delgado, M. A., and T. Stengos (1994). "Semiparametric specification testing of non-nested econometric models," *Review of Economic Studies*, **61**, 291–303.

Demos, A., and E. Sentana (1998). "Testing for GARCH effects: A one-sided approach," *Journal of Econometrics*, **86**, 97–127.

Dhrymes, P. J. (1971). *Distributed Lags: Problems of Estimation and Formulation*, San Francisco, Holden-Day.

DiCiccio, T. J., and B. Efron (1996). "Bootstrap confidence intervals" (with discussion), *Statistical Science*, **11**, 189–228.

Dickey, D. A., and W. A. Fuller (1979). "Distribution of the estimators for autoregressive time series with a unit root," *Journal of the American Statistical Association*, **74**, 427–31.

Dickey, D. A., and W. A. Fuller (1981). "Likelihood ratio statistics for autoregressive time series with a unit root," *Econometrica*, **49**, 1057–72.

Donald, S. G., and W. K. Newey (2001). "Choosing the number of instruments," *Econometrica*, **69**, 1161–91.

Donald, S. G., and H. J. Paarsch (1993). "Piecewise pseudo-maximum likelihood estimation in empirical models of auctions," *International Economic Review*, **34**, 121–48.

Donald, S. G., and H .J. Paarsch (1996). "Identification, estimation, and testing in parametric empirical models of auctions within the independent private values paradigm," *Econometric Theory*, **12**, 517–67.

Dorsey, R. E., and W. J. Mayer (1995). "Genetic algorithms for estimation problems with multiple optima, nondifferentiability, and other irregular features," *Journal of Business and Economic Statistics*, **13**, 53–66.

Duffie, D., and K. J. Singleton (1993). "Simulated moments estimation of Markov models of asset prices," *Econometrica*, **61**, 929–52.

Dufour, J.-M. (1982). "Generalized Chow tests for structural change: A coordinate-free approach," *International Economic Review*, **23**, 565–75.

Dufour, J.-M. (1997). "Some impossibility theorems in econometrics with application to structural and dynamic models," *Econometrica*, **65**, 1365–88.

Dufour, J.-M., M. J. I. Gaudry, and T. C. Liem (1980). "The Cochrane-Orcutt procedure: Numerical examples of multiple admissible minima," *Economics Letters*, **6**, 43–48.

Dufour, J.-M., and L. Khalaf (2001). "Monte Carlo test methods in econometrics," Ch. 23 in *A Companion to Econometric Theory*, ed. B. Baltagi, Oxford, Blackwell Publishers, 494–519.

Durbin, J. (1954). "Errors in variables," *Review of the International Statistical Institute*, **22**, 23–32.

Durbin, J. (1959). "Efficient estimation of parameters in moving-average models," *Biometrika*, **46**, 306–16.

Durbin, J. (1970). "Testing for serial correlation in least-squares regression when some of the regressors are lagged dependent variables," *Econometrica*, **38**, 410–21.

Durbin, J., and G. S. Watson (1950). "Testing for serial correlation in least squares regression I," *Biometrika*, **37**, 409–28.

Durbin, J., and G. S. Watson (1951). "Testing for serial correlation in least squares regression II," *Biometrika*, **38**, 159–78.

Durlauf, S. N., and P. C. B. Phillips (1988). "Trends versus random walks in time series analysis," *Econometrica*, **56**, 1333–54.

Efron, B. (1979). "Bootstrapping methods: Another look at the jackknife," *Annals of Statistics*, **7**, 1–26.

Efron, B., and R. J. Tibshirani (1993). *An Introduction to the Bootstrap*, New York, Chapman and Hall.

Eicker, F. (1963). "Asymptotic normality and consistency of the least squares estimators for families of linear regressions," *Annals of Mathematical Statistics*, **34**, 447–56.

Eicker, F. (1967). "Limit theorems for regressions with unequal and dependent errors," in *Fifth Berkeley Symposium on Mathematical Statistics and Probability*, ed. L. M. Le Cam and J. Neyman, Berkeley, University of California, **1**, 59–82.

Elliott, G., T. J. Rothenberg, and J. H. Stock (1996). "Efficient tests for an autoregressive unit root," *Econometrica*, **64**, 813–36.

Ellison, G., and S. F. Ellison (2000). "A simple framework for nonparametric specification testing," *Journal of Econometrics*, **96**, 1–23.

Engle, R. F. (1982). "Autoregressive conditional heteroskedasticity with estimates of the variance of United Kingdom inflation," *Econometrica*, **50**, 987–1007.

Engle, R. F. (1984). "Wald, likelihood ratio and Lagrange multiplier tests in econometrics," Ch. 13 in *Handbook of Econometrics*, Vol. 2, ed. Z. Griliches and M. D. Intriligator, Amsterdam, North-Holland, 775–826.

Engle, R. F., and C. W. J. Granger (1987). "Co-integration and error correction: Representation, estimation and testing," *Econometrica*, **55**, 251–76.

Ericsson, N. R., and J. G. MacKinnon (2002). "Distributions of error correction tests for cointegration," *Econometrics Journal*, **5**, 285–318.

Eubank, R. L. (1999). *Nonparametric Regression and Spline Smoothing*, second edition, New York, Marcel Dekker.

Fan, J., and I. Gijbels (1996). *Local Polynomial Modelling and Its Applications*, London, Chapman and Hall.

Fiebig, D. G. (2001). "Seemingly unrelated regression," Ch. 5 in *A Companion to Econometric Theory*, ed. B. Baltagi, Oxford, Blackwell Publishers, 101–21.

Fiebig, D. G., and J. H. Kim (2000). "Estimation and inference in SUR models when the number of equations is large," *Econometric Reviews*, **19**, 105–30.

Fisher, F. M. (1970). "Tests of equality between sets of coefficients in two linear regressions: An expository note," *Econometrica*, **38**, 361–66.

Fisher, F. M. (1976). *The Identification Problem in Econometrics*, Huntington, N.Y., Krieger.

Fisher, G. R., and M. McAleer (1981). "Alternative procedures and associated tests of significance for non-nested hypotheses," *Journal of Econometrics*, **16**, 103–19.

Fisher, R. A. (1925). "The theory of statistical estimation," *Proceedings of the Cambridge Philosophical Society*, **22**, 700–25.

Fiorentini, G., G. Calzolari, and L. Panattoni (1996). "Analytic derivatives and the computation of GARCH estimates," *Journal of Applied Econometrics*, **11**, 399–417.

Friedman, M. (1957). *A Theory of the Consumption Function*, Princeton, Princeton University Press.

Frisch, R., and F. V. Waugh (1933). "Partial time regressions as compared with individual trends," *Econometrica*, **1**, 387–401.

Fuller, W. A. (1977). "Some properties of a modification of the limited information estimator," *Econometrica*, **45**, 939–53.

Fuller, W. A. (1996). *Introduction to Statistical Time Series*, second edition, New York, John Wiley & Sons.

Fuller, W. A., and G. E. Battese (1974). "Estimation of linear models with crossed-error structure," *Journal of Econometrics*, **2**, 67–78.

Galbraith, J. W., and V. Zinde-Walsh (1992). "The GLS transformation matrix and a semi-recursive estimator for the linear regression model with ARMA errors," *Econometric Theory*, **8**, 95–111.

Galbraith, J. W., and V. Zinde-Walsh (1994). "A simple noniterative estimator for moving average models," *Biometrika*, **81**, 143–55.

Galbraith, J. W., and V. Zinde-Walsh (1997). "On some simple, autoregression-based estimation and identification techniques for ARMA models," *Biometrika*, **84**, 685–96.

Galbraith, J. W., and V. Zinde-Walsh (1999). "On the distributions of Augmented Dickey-Fuller statistics in processes with moving average components," *Journal of Econometrics*, **93**, 25–47.

Gallant, A. R. (1987). *Nonlinear Statistical Models*, New York, John Wiley & Sons.

Gallant, A. R. (1997). *An Introduction to Econometric Theory: Measure-Theoretic Probability and Statistics with Applications to Economics*, Princeton, Princeton University Press.

Gallant, A. R., and G. E. Tauchen (1996). "Which moments to match?," *Econometric Theory*, **12**, 657–81.

Gentle, J. E. (1998). *Random Number Generation and Monte Carlo Methods*, New York, Springer-Verlag.

Gerfin, M. (1996). "Parametric and semiparametric estimation of the binary response model of labour market participation," *Journal of Applied Econometrics*, **11**, 321–40.

Ghysels, E. (1990). "Unit root tests and the statistical pitfalls of seasonal adjustment: The case of U. S. post war real GNP," *Journal of Business and Economic Statistics*, **8**, 145–52.

Ghysels, E., and D. R. Osborn (2001). *The Econometric Analysis of Seasonal Time Series*, Cambridge, Cambridge University Press.

Ghysels, E., and P. Perron (1993). "The effect of seasonal adjustment filters on tests for a unit root," *Journal of Econometrics*, **55**, 57–98.

Gill, P. E., W. Murray, and M. H. Wright (1981). *Practical Optimization*, New York, Academic Press.

Godambe, V. P. (1960). "An optimum property of regular maximum likelihood estimation," *Annals of Mathematical Statistics* **31**, 1208–11.

Godambe, V. P., and M. E. Thompson (1978). "Some aspects of the theory of estimating equations," *Journal of Statistical Planning and Inference*, **2**, 95–104.

Godfrey, L. G. (1978a). "Testing against general autoregressive and moving average error models when the regressors include lagged dependent variables," *Econometrica*, **46**, 1293–301.

Godfrey, L. G. (1978b). "Testing for higher order serial correlation in regression equations when the regressors include lagged dependent variables," *Econometrica*, **46**, 1303–10.

Godfrey, L. G. (1983). "Testing non-nested models after estimation by instrumental variables or least squares," *Econometrica*, **51**, 355–65.

Godfrey, L. G. (1988). *Misspecification Tests in Econometrics*, Cambridge, Cambridge University Press.

Godfrey, L. G. (1998). "Tests of non-nested regression models: Some results on small sample behaviour and the bootstrap," *Journal of Econometrics*, **84**, 59–74.

Godfrey, L. G., M. McAleer, and C. R. McKenzie (1988). "Variable addition and Lagrange Multiplier tests for linear and logarithmic regression models," *Review of Economics and Statistics*, **70**, 492–503.

Godfrey, L. G., and M. H. Pesaran (1983). "Tests of non-nested regression models: Small sample adjustments and Monte Carlo evidence," *Journal of Econometrics*, **21**, 133–54.

Godfrey, L. G., and M. R. Wickens (1981). "Testing linear and log-linear regressions for functional form," *Review of Economic Studies*, **48**, 487–96.

Goffe, W. L., G. D. Ferrier, and J. Rogers (1994). "Global optimization of statistical functions with simulated annealing," *Journal of Econometrics*, **60**, 65–99.

Gouriéroux, C., and J. Jasiak (2001). "Durations," Ch. 21 in *A Companion to Econometric Theory*, ed. B. Baltagi, Oxford, Blackwell Publishers, 444–65.

Gouriéroux, C., and A. Monfort (1994). "Testing non-nested hypotheses," Ch. 44 in *Handbook of Econometrics*, Vol. 4, ed. R. F. Engle and D. L. McFadden, Amsterdam, North-Holland, 2583–637.

Gouriéroux, C., and A. Monfort (1996). *Simulation Based Econometric Methods*, Oxford, Oxford University Press.

Gouriéroux, C., A. Monfort, and E. Renault (1993). "Indirect inference," *Journal of Applied Econometrics*, **8**, S85–S118.

Gouriéroux, C., A. Monfort, and A. Trognon (1984). "Pseudo-maximum likelihood methods: Theory," *Econometrica*, **52**, 681–700.

Granger, C. W. J. (1969). "Investigating causal relations by econometric models and cross-spectral methods," *Econometrica*, **37**, 424–38.

Granger, C. W. J. (2001). "Spurious regressions in econometrics," Ch. 26 in *A Companion to Econometric Theory*, ed. B. Baltagi, Oxford, Blackwell Publishers, 557–61.

Granger, C. W. J., and P. Newbold (1974). "Spurious regressions in econometrics," *Journal of Econometrics*, **2**, 111–20.

Granger, C. W. J., and P. Newbold (1986). *Forecasting Economic Time Series*, second edition, Orlando, Florida, Academic Press.

Green, P. J., and B. W. Silverman (1994). *Nonparametric Regression and Generalized Linear Models: A Roughness Penalty Approach*, London, Chapman and Hall.

Greene, W. H. (1981). "Sample selection bias as a specification error: Comment," *Econometrica*, **49**, 795–98.

Greene, W. H. (2002). *Econometric Analysis*, fifth edition, New York, Prentice-Hall.

Gregory, A. W., and M. R. Veall (1985). "On formulating Wald tests for nonlinear restrictions," *Econometrica*, **53**, 1465–68.

Gregory, A. W., and M. R. Veall (1987). "Formulating Wald tests of the restrictions implied by the rational expectations hypothesis," *Journal of Applied Econometrics*, **2**, 61–68.

Gurmu, S. (1997). "Semiparametric estimation of hurdle regression models with an application to medicaid utilization," *Journal of Applied Econometrics*, **12**, 225–42.

Hahn, J., and J. A. Hausman (2002). "A new specification test for the validity of instrumental variables," *Econometrica*, **70**, 153–89.

Hajivassiliou, V. A., and P. A. Ruud (1994). "Classical estimation methods for LDV models using simulation," Ch. 40 in *Handbook of Econometrics*, Vol. 4, ed. R. F. Engle and D. L. McFadden, Amsterdam, Elsevier, 2383–441.

Hall, A. (1987). "The information matrix test for the linear model," *Review of Economic Studies*, **54**, 257–63.

Hall, P. (1992). *The Bootstrap and Edgeworth Expansion*, New York, Springer-Verlag.

Hamilton, J. D. (1994). *Time Series Analysis*, Princeton, Princeton University Press.

Hansen, L. P. (1982). "Large sample properties of generalized method of moments estimators," *Econometrica*, **50**, 1029–54.

Hansen, L. P., J. Heaton, and A. Yaron (1996). "Finite-sample properties of some alternative GMM estimators," *Journal of Business and Economic Statistics*, **14** 262–80.

Harbo, I., S. Johansen, B. Nielsen, and A. Rahbek (1998). "Asymptotic inference on cointegrating rank in partial systems," *Journal of Business and Economic Statistics*, **16**, 388–99.

Härdle, W. (1990). *Applied Nonparametric Regression*, Cambridge, Cambridge University Press.

Harvey, A. C. (1989). *Forecasting, Structural Time Series Models and the Kalman Filter*, Cambridge, Cambridge University Press.

Hausman, J. A. (1975). "An instrumental variable approach to full information estimation for linear and certain nonlinear econometric models," *Econometrica*, **43**, 727–38.

Hausman, J. A. (1978). "Specification tests in econometrics," *Econometrica*, **46**, 1251–72.

Hausman, J. A., A. W. Lo, and A. C. MacKinlay (1992). "An ordered probit analysis of transaction stock prices," *Journal of Financial Economics*, **31**, 319–79.

Hausman, J. A., and D. L. McFadden (1984). "A specification test for the multinomial logit model," *Econometrica*, **52**, 1219–40.

Hausman, J. A., and W. E. Taylor (1981). "Panel data and unobservable individual effects," *Econometrica*, **49**, 1377–98.

Hausman, J. A., and M. W. Watson (1985). "Errors-in-variables and seasonal adjustment procedures," *Journal of the American Statistical Association*, **80**, 531–40.

Hayashi, F. (2000). *Econometrics*, Princeton, Princeton University Press.

Heckman, J. J. (1976). "The common structure of statistical models of truncation, sample selection and limited dependent variables and a simple estimator for such models," *Annals of Economic and Social Measurement*, **5**, 475–92.

Heckman, J. J. (1979). "Sample selection bias as a specification error," *Econometrica*, **47**, 153–61.

Heckman, J. J., and B. Singer (1984). "A method for minimizing the impact of distributional assumptions in econometric models for duration data," *Econometrica*, **52**, 271–320.

Hendry, D. F. (1976). "The structure of simultaneous equations estimators," *Journal of Econometrics*, **4**, 51–88.

Hendry, D. F. (1995). *Dynamic Econometrics*, Oxford, Oxford University Press.

Hendry, D. F., and G. J. Anderson (1977). "Testing dynamic specification in small simultaneous models: An application to a model of building society behavior in the United Kingdom," in *Frontiers of Quantitative Economics*, Vol. IIIA, ed. M. D. Intriligator, Amsterdam, North-Holland.

Hendry, D. F., and G. E. Mizon (1978). "Serial correlation as a convenient simplification not a nuisance: A comment on a study of the demand for money by the Bank of England," *Economic Journal*, **88**, 549–63.

Hendry, D. F., A. R. Pagan, and J. D. Sargan (1984). "Dynamic specification," Ch. 18 in *Handbook of Econometrics*, Vol. 2, ed. Z. Griliches and M. D. Intriligator, Amsterdam, North-Holland, 1023–100.

Hentschel, L. (1995). "All in the family: Nesting symmetric and asymmetric GARCH models," *Journal of Financial Economics*, **39**, 71–104.

Herr, D. G. (1980). "On the history of the use of geometry in the general linear model," *The American Statistician*, **34**, 43–47.

Hinkley, D. V. (1977). "Jackknifing in unbalanced situations," *Technometrics*, **19**, 285–92.

Hong, Y., and H. White (1995). "Consistent specification testing via nonparametric series regression," *Econometrica*, **63**, 1133–59.

Horowitz, J. L. (1994). "Bootstrap-based critical values for the information matrix test," *Journal of Econometrics*, **61**, 395–411.

Horowitz, J. L. (2001). "The Bootstrap," Ch. 52 in *Handbook of Econometrics*, Vol. 5, ed. J. J. Heckman and E. E. Leamer, Amsterdam, North-Holland.

Horowitz, J. L., and V. G. Spokoiny (2001). "An adaptive, rate-optimal test of a parametric mean-regression model against a nonparametric alternative," *Econometrica*, **69**, 599–631.

Hsiao, C. (1983). "Identification," Ch. 4 in *Handbook of Econometrics*, Vol. 1, ed. Z. Griliches and M. D. Intriligator, Amsterdam, North-Holland, 223–83.

Hsiao, C. (1986). *Analysis of Panel Data*, Cambridge, Cambridge University Press.

Hsiao, C. (2001). "Panel data models," Ch. 16 in *A Companion to Econometric Theory*, ed. B. Baltagi, Oxford, Blackwell Publishers, 349–65.

Hylleberg, S. (1986). *Seasonality in Regression*, New York, Academic Press.

Hylleberg, S. (1992). *Modelling Seasonality*, Oxford, Oxford University Press.

Jaeger, A., and R. M. Kunst (1990). "Seasonal adjustment and measuring persistence in output," *Journal of Applied Econometrics*, **5**, 47–58.

Jarque, C. M., and A. K. Bera (1980). "Efficient tests for normality, heteroskedasticity and serial independence of regression residuals," *Economics Letters*, **6**, 255–59.

Johansen, S. (1988). "Statistical analysis of cointegrating vectors," *Journal of Economic Dynamics and Control*, **12**, 231–54.

Johansen, S. (1991). "Estimation and hypothesis testing of cointegration in Gaussian vector autoregressive models," *Econometrica*, **59**, 1551–80.

Johansen, S. (1995). *Likelihood-Based Inference in Cointegrated Vector Autoregressive Models*, Oxford, Oxford University Press.

Johansen, S., and K. Juselius (1990). "Maximum likelihood estimation and inference on cointegration — with applications to the demand for money," *Oxford Bulletin of Economics and Statistics*, **52**, 169–210.

Johansen, S., and K. Juselius (1992). "Testing structural hypotheses in a multivariate cointegration analysis of the PPP and the UIP for UK," *Journal of Econometrics*, **53**, 211–44.

Johnson, N. L., S. Kotz, and N. Balakrishnan (1994). *Continuous Univariate Distributions*, Vol. 1, second edition, New York, John Wiley & Sons.

Jorgenson, D. W., and J.-J. Laffont (1974). "Efficient estimation of nonlinear simultaneous equations with additive disturbances," *Annals of Economic and Social Measurement*, **3**, 615–40.

Keane, M. P. (1994). "A computationally practical simulation estimator for panel data," *Econometrica*, **62**, 95–116.

Kiefer, N. M. (1978). "Discrete parameter variation: Efficient estimation of a switching regression model," *Econometrica*, **46**, 427–34.

Kiefer, N. M. (1988). "Economic duration data and hazard functions," *Journal of Economic Literature*, **26**, 646–79.

Kiefer, N. M., and M. Salmon (1983). "Testing normality in econometric models," *Economics Letters*, **11**, 123–27.

Kinal, T. W. (1980). "The existence of moments of k-class estimators," *Econometrica*, **48**, 241–49.

Kiviet, J. F. (1986). "On the rigour of some misspecification tests for modelling dynamic relationships," *Review of Economic Studies*, **53**, 241–61.

Kleibergen, F. (2002). "Pivotal statistics for testing structural parameters in instrumental variables regression," *Econometrica*, **70**, 1781–803.

Kloek, T. (1981). "OLS estimation in a model where a microvariable is explained by aggregates and contemporaneous disturbances are equicorrelated," *Econometrica*, **49**, 205–7.

Knuth, Donald E. (1998). *The Art of Computer Programming*, Vol. 2, *Seminumerical Algorithms*, third edition, Reading, Mass., Addison-Wesley.

Lafontaine, F., and K. J. White (1986). "Obtaining any Wald statistic you want," *Economics Letters*, **21**, 35–40.

Lancaster, T. (1984). "The covariance matrix of the information matrix test," *Econometrica*, **52**, 1051–53.

Lancaster, T. (1990). *The Econometric Analysis of Transition Data*, Cambridge, Cambridge University Press.

Leamer, E. E. (1987). "Errors in variables in linear systems," *Econometrica*, **55**, 893–909.

Lee, B., and B. Ingram (1991). "Simulation estimation of time series models," *Journal of Econometrics*, **47**, 197–205.

Lee, J. H. H., and M. L. King (1993). "A locally most powerful mean based score test for ARCH and GARCH regression disturbances," *Journal of Business and Economic Statistics*, **11**, 17–27.

Lee, L.-F. (1982). "Some approaches to the correction of selectivity bias," *Review of Economic Studies*, **49**, 355–72.

Lee, L.-F. (1986). "Specification test for Poisson regression models," *International Economic Review*, **27**, 689–706.

Lewbel, A. (1991). "The rank of demand systems: Theory and nonparametric estimation," *Econometrica*, **59**, 711–30.

Li, H., and G. S. Maddala (1996). "Bootstrapping time series models" (with discussion), *Econometric Reviews*, **15**, 115–95.

Li, Q., and S. Wang (1998). "A simple consistent bootstrap test for a parametric regression function," *Journal of Econometrics*, **87**, 145–65.

Loader, C. (1999). *Local Regression and Likelihood*, New York, Springer.

Long, J. S., and L. H. Ervin (2000). "Using heteroscedasticity consistent standard errors in the linear regression model," *The American Statistician*, **54**, 217–24.

Lovell, M. C. (1963). "Seasonal adjustment of economic time series," *Journal of the American Statistical Association*, **58**, 993–1010.

Lütkepohl, H. (2001). "Vector autoregressions," Ch. 32 in *A Companion to Econometric Theory*, ed. B. Baltagi, Oxford, Blackwell Publishers, 678–99.

MacKinnon, J. G. (1983). "Model specification tests against non-nested alternatives" (with discussion and reply), *Econometric Reviews*, **2**, 85–157.

MacKinnon, J. G. (1991). "Critical values for cointegration tests," Ch. 13 in *Long-Run Economic Relationships: Readings in Cointegration*, ed. R. F. Engle and C. W. J. Granger, Oxford, Oxford University Press, 267–76.

MacKinnon, J. G. (1994). "Approximate asymptotic distribution functions for unit-root and cointegration tests," *Journal of Business and Economic Statistics*, **12**, 167–76.

MacKinnon, J. G. (1996). "Numerical distribution functions for unit root and cointegration tests," *Journal of Applied Econometrics*, **11**, 601–18.

MacKinnon, J. G. (2002). "Bootstrap inference in econometrics," *Canadian Journal of Economics*, **35**, 615–45.

MacKinnon, J. G., A. A. Haug, and L. Michelis (1999). "Numerical distribution functions of likelihood ratio tests for cointegration," *Journal of Applied Econometrics*, **14**, 563–77.

MacKinnon, J. G., and L. Magee (1990). "Transforming the dependent variable in regression models," *International Economic Review*, **31**, 315–39.

MacKinnon, J. G., and A. A. Smith, Jr. (1998). "Approximate bias correction in econometrics," *Journal of Econometrics*, **85**, 205–30.

MacKinnon, J. G., and H. White (1985). "Some heteroskedasticity consistent covariance matrix estimators with improved finite sample properties," *Journal of Econometrics*, **29**, 305–25.

Maddala, G. S., and A. Flores-Lagunes (2001). "Qualitative response models," Ch. 17 in *A Companion to Econometric Theory*, ed. B. Baltagi, Oxford, Blackwell Publishers, 366–82.

Magnus, J. R., and H. Neudecker (1988). *Matrix Differential Calculus with Applications in Statistics and Econometrics*, New York, John Wiley & Sons.

Mariano, R. S. (2001). "Simultaneous equation model estimators: Statistical properties and practical implications," Ch. 6 in *A Companion to Econometric Theory*, ed. B. Baltagi, Oxford, Blackwell Publishers, 122–43.

McAleer, M. (1995). "The significance of testing empirical non-nested models," *Journal of Econometrics*, **67**, 149–71.

McCullough, B. D. (1999). "Econometric software reliability: EViews, LIMDEP, SHAZAM and TSP," *Journal of Applied Econometrics*, **14**, 191–202.

McCullough, B. D. (2003). "Some details of nonlinear estimation," Ch. 8 in *Numerical Methods in Statistical Computing for the Social Sciences*, ed. M. Altman, J. Gill, and M. P. McDonald, New York, Wiley, 245–67.

McCullough, B. D., and C. G. Renfro (1999). "Benchmarks and software standards: A case study of GARCH procedures," *Journal of Economic and Social Measurement*, **25**, 59–71.

McCullough, B. D., and H. D. Vinod (2003). "Verifying the solution from a nonlinear solver: A case study," *American Economic Review*, **93**, 873–92.

McFadden, D. L. (1984). "Econometric analysis of qualitative response models," Ch. 24 in *Handbook of Econometrics*, Vol. 2, ed. Z. Griliches and M. D. Intriligator, Amsterdam, North-Holland, 1395–457.

McFadden, D. L. (1987). "Regression-based specification tests for the multinomial logit model," *Journal of Econometrics*, **34**, 63–82.

McFadden, D. L. (1989). "A method of simulated moments for estimation of discrete response models without numerical integration," *Econometrica*, **57**, 995–1026.

McFadden, D. L., and P. A. Ruud (1994). "Estimation by simulation," *Review of Economics and Statistics*, **76**, 591–608.

Milliken, G. A., and F. A. Graybill (1970). "Extensions of the general linear hypothesis model," *Journal of the American Statistical Association*, **65**, 797–807.

Mittelhammer, R. (1996). *Mathematical Statistics for Economics and Business*, New York, Springer-Verlag.

Mizon, G. E., and D. F. Hendry (1980). "An empirical and Monte Carlo analysis of tests of dynamic specification," *Review of Economic Studies*, **47**, 21–45.

Mizon, G. E., and J.-F. Richard (1986). "The encompassing principle and its application to testing non-nested hypotheses," *Econometrica*, **54**, 657–78.

Morgan, M. S. (1990). *The History of Econometric Ideas*, Cambridge, Cambridge University Press.

Moulton, B. R. (1986). "Random group effects and the precision of regression estimates," *Journal of Econometrics*, **32**, 385–97.

Moulton, B. R. (1990). "An illustration of a pitfall in estimating the effects of aggregate variables on micro units," *Review of Economics and Statistics*, **72**, 334–38.

Mullahy, J. (1997). "Heterogeneity, excess zeros, and the structure of count data models," *Journal of Applied Econometrics*, **12**, 337–50.

Mundlak, Y. (1978). "On the pooling of time series and cross sectional data," *Econometrica*, **46**, 69–86.

Nelson, C. R., and C. I. Plosser (1982). "Trends and random walks in macroeconomic time series: Some evidence and implications," *Journal of Monetary Economics*, **10**, 139–62.

Nelson, C. R., and R. Startz (1990a). "The distribution of the instrumental variables estimator and its t-ratio when the instrument is a poor one," *Journal of Business*, **63**, S125–40.

Nelson, C. R., and R. Startz (1990b). "Some further results on the exact small sample properties of the instrumental variables estimator," *Econometrica*, **58**, 967–76.

Nelson, D. B. (1991). "Conditional heteroskedasticity in asset returns: A new approach," *Econometrica*, **59**, 347–70.

Nerlove, M. (1958). *The Dynamics of Supply: Estimation of Farmers' Response to Price*, Baltimore, Johns Hopkins Press.

Neumann, G. R. (1999). "Search models and duration data," Ch. 7 in *Handbook of Applied Econometrics*, Vol. II, ed. H. M. Pesaran and P. Schmidt, Oxford, Blackwell.

Newbold, P., C. Agiakloglou, and J. Miller (1994). "Adventures with ARIMA software," *International Journal of Forecasting*, **10**, 573–81.

Newey, W. K. (1985). "Maximum likelihood specification testing and conditional moment tests," *Econometrica*, **53**, 1047–70.

Newey, W. K., and D. L. McFadden (1994). "Large sample estimation and hypothesis testing," Ch. 36 in *Handbook of Econometrics*, Vol. 4, ed. F. F. Engle and D. L. McFadden, Amsterdam, North-Holland, 2111–245.

Newey, W. K., and K. D. West (1987). "A simple, positive semi-definite, heteroskedasticity and autocorrelation consistent covariance matrix," *Econometrica*, **55**, 703–8.

Newey, W. K., and K. D. West (1994). "Automatic lag selection in covariance matrix estimation," *Review of Economic Studies*, **61**, 631–53.

Ng, S., and P. Perron (1995). "Unit root tests in ARMA models with data dependent methods for the selection of the trancation lag," *Journal of the American Statistical Association*, **90**, 268–81.

Ng, S., and P. Perron (2001). "Lag length selection and the construction of unit root tests with good size and power," *Econometrica*, **69**, 1519–54.

Olsen, R. J. (1978). "Note on the uniqueness of the maximum likelihood estimator of the tobit model," *Econometrica*, **46**, 1211–15.

Orme, C. D. (1988). "The calculation of the information matrix test for binary data models," *The Manchester School*, **56**, 370–76.

Orme, C. D. (1995). "On the use of artificial regressions in certain microeconometric models," *Econometric Theory*, **11**, 290–305.

Orme, C. D., and P. A. Ruud (2002). "On the uniqueness of the maximum likelihood estimator," *Economics Letters*, **75**, 209–17.

Osterwald-Lenum, M. (1992). "A note with quantiles of the asymptotic distribution of the maximum likelihood cointegration rank test statistics," *Oxford Bulletin of Economics and Statistics*, **54**, 461–71.

Pagan, A. R. (1996). "The econometrics of financial markets," *Journal of Empirical Finance*, **3**, 15–102.

Pagan, A. R., and A. Ullah (1999). *Nonparametric Econometrics*, Cambridge, Cambridge University Press.

Pagan, A. R., and F. Vella (1989). "Diagnostic tests for models based on individual data: A survey," *Journal of Applied Econometrics*, **4**, S29–59.

Pakes, A., and D. Pollard, (1989). "Simulation and the asymptotics of optimization estimators," *Econometrica*, **57**, 1027–57.

Park, J. Y. (2002). "An invariance principle for sieve bootstrap in time series," *Econometric Theory*, **18**, 469–90.

Perron, P., and S. Ng (1996). "Useful modifications to unit root tests with dependent errors and their local asymptotic properties," *Review of Economic Studies*, **63**, 435–65.

Pesaran, M. H. (1974). "On the general problem of model selection," *Review of Economic Studies*, **41**, 153–71.

Pesaran, M. H., and A. S. Deaton (1978). "Testing non-nested nonlinear regression models," *Econometrica*, **46**, 677–94.

Pesaran, M. H., Y. Shin, and R. J. Smith (2000). "Structural analysis of vector error correction models with exogenous I(1) variables," *Journal of Econometrics*, **97**, 293–343.

Pesaran, M. H., and M. Weeks (2001). "Non-nested hypothesis testing: An overview," Ch. 13 in *A Companion to Econometric Theory*, ed. B. Baltagi, Oxford, Blackwell Publishers, 279–309.

Phillips, P. C. B. (1982). "On the consistency of nonlinear FIML," *Econometrica*, **50**, 1307–24.

Phillips, P. C. B. (1986). "Understanding spurious regressions in econometrics," *Journal of Econometrics*, **33**, 311–40.

Phillips, P. C. B., and B. E. Hansen (1990). "Statistical inference in instrumental variables regression with I(1) processes," *Review of Economic Studies*, **57**, 99–125.

Phillips, P. C. B., and J. Y. Park (1988). "On the formulation of Wald tests of nonlinear restrictions," *Econometrica*, **56**, 1065–83.

Phillips, P. C. B., and P. Perron (1988). "Testing for a unit root in time series regression," *Biometrika*, **75**, 335–46.

Pollak, R. A., and T. J. Wales (1981). "Demographic variables in demand analysis," *Econometrica*, **49**, 1533–51.

Pollak, R. A., and T. J. Wales (1987). "Pooling international consumption data," *Review of Economics and Statistics*, **69**, 90–99.

Pollak, R. A., and T. J. Wales (1991). "The likelihood dominance criterion: A new approach to model selection," *Journal of Econometrics*, **47**, 227–42.

Pratt, J. W. (1981). "Concavity of the loglikelihood," *Journal of the American Statistical Association*, **76**, 103–6.

Press, W. H., S. A. Teukolsky, W. T. Vetterling, and B. P. Flannery (1992a). *Numerical Recipes in C*, second edition, Cambridge, Cambridge University Press.

Press, W. H., S. A. Teukolsky, W. T. Vetterling, and B. P. Flannery (1992b). *Numerical Recipes in Fortran*, second edition, Cambridge, Cambridge University Press.

Quandt, R. E. (1983). "Computational problems and methods," Ch. 12 in *Handbook of Econometrics*, Vol. 1, ed. Z. Griliches and M. D. Intriligator, Amsterdam, North-Holland, 699–771.

Ramsey, J. B. (1969). "Tests for specification errors in classical linear least-squares regression analysis," *Journal of the Royal Statistical Society*, Series B, **31**, 350–71.

Rao, C. R. (1945). "Information and accuracy attainable in estimation of statistical parameters," *Bulletin of the Calcutta Mathematical Society*, **37**, 81–91.

Rilstone, P., and M. R. Veall (1996). "Using bootstrapped confidence intervals for improved inferences with seemingly unrelated regression equations," *Econometric Theory*, **12**, 569–80.

Robinson, P. M. (1988). "Root-N consistent semiparametric regression," *Econometrica*, **56**, 931–54.

Ruud, P. A. (2000). *An Introduction to Classical Econometric Theory*, New York, Oxford University Press.

Said, E. S., and D. A. Dickey (1984). "Testing for unit roots in autoregressive-moving average models of unknown order," *Biometrika*, **71**, 599–607.

Saikkonen, P. (1991). "Asymptotically efficient estimation of cointegration regressions," *Econometric Theory*, **7**, 1–21.

Sargan, J. D. (1958). "The estimation of economic relationships using instrumental variables," *Econometrica*, **26**, 393–415.

Sargan, J. D. (1964). "Wages and prices in the United Kingdom: A study in econometric methodology," in *Econometric Analysis for National Economic Planning*, ed. P. E. Hart, G. Mills, and J. K. Whitaker, London, Butterworths; reprinted in *Quantitative Economics and Econometric Analysis*, ed. K. F. Wallis and D. F. Hendry (1984), Oxford, Basil Blackwell.

Sargan, J. D. (1975). "Asymptotic theory and large models," *International Economic Review*, **16**, 75–91.

Sargan J. D. (1980). "Some tests of dynamic specification for a single equation," *Econometrica*, **48**, 879–97.

Savin, N. E. (1980). "The Bonferroni and the Scheffé multiple comparison procedures," *Review of Economic Studies*, **47**, 255–73.

Savin, N. E., and K. J. White (1977). "The Durbin-Watson test for serial correlation with extreme sample sizes or many regressors," *Econometrica*, **45**, 1989–96.

Schwarz, G. (1978). "Estimating the dimension of a model," *Annals of Statistics*, **6**, 461–64.

Schwert, G. W. (1989). "Testing for unit roots: A Monte Carlo investigation," *Journal of Business and Economic Statistics*, **7**, 147–59.

Seber, G. A. F. (1980). *The Linear Hypothesis: A General Theory*, second edition, London, Charles Griffin.

Seber, G. A. F., and C. J. Wild (1989). *Nonlinear Regression*, New York, John Wiley & Sons.

Silverman, B. W. (1986). *Density Estimation for Statistics and Data Analysis*, London, Chapman and Hall.

Simonoff, J. S. (1996). *Smoothing Methods in Statistics*, New York, Springer-Verlag.

Sims, C. A. (1972). "Money, income and causality," *American Economic Review*, **62**, 540–52.

Sims, C. A. (1980). "Macroeconomics and reality," *Econometrica*, **48**, 1–48.

Sims, C. A., J. H. Stock, and M. W. Watson (1990). "Inference in linear time series models with some unit roots," *Econometrica*, **58**, 113–44.

Smith, A. A., Jr. (1993). "Estimating nonlinear time-series models using simulated vector autoregressions," *Journal of Applied Econometrics*, **8**, S63–S84.

Smith, R. J. (1989). "On the use of distributional mis-specification checks in limited dependent variable models," *Economic Journal*, **99**, 178–92.

Snedecor, G. W. (1934). *Calculation and Interpretation of Analysis of Variance and Covariance*, Ames, Iowa, Collegiate Press.

Srivastava, V. K., and D. E. A. Giles (1987). *Seemingly Unrelated Regression Equations Models*, New York, Marcel Dekker.

Staiger, D., and J. H. Stock (1997). "Instrumental variables regressions with weak instruments," *Econometrica*, **65**, 557–86.

Stock, J. H. (1987). "Asymptotic properties of least squares estimators of cointegrating vectors," *Econometrica*, **55**, 1035–56.

Stock, J. H., and M. W. Watson (2001). "Vector autoregressions," *Journal of Economic Perspectives*, **15**, 101–15.

Stock, J. H., J. H. Wright, and M. Yogo (2002). "A survey of weak instruments and weak identification in generalized method of moments," *Journal of Business and Economic Statistics*, **20**, 518–29.

Stuart, A., J. K. Ord, and S. Arnold (1998). *Kendall's Advanced Theory of Statistics*, Vol. 2A: *Classical Inference and the Linear Model*, sixth edition, London, Edward Arnold.

Tauchen, G. E. (1985). "Diagnostic testing and evaluation of maximum likelihood models," *Journal of Econometrics*, **30**, 415–43.

Terza, J. (1985). "Ordinal probit: A generalization," *Communications in Statistics*, **14**, 1–12.

Theil, H. (1953). "Repeated least squares applied to complete equation systems," The Hague, Central Planning Bureau, mimeo.

Theil, H. (1961). *Economic Forecasts and Policy*, second edition, Amsterdam, North-Holland.

Theil, H. (1963). "On the use of incomplete prior information in regression analysis," *Journal of the American Statistical Association*, **58**, 401–14.

Theil, H., and A. S. Goldberger (1961). "On pure and mixed estimation in economics," *International Economic Review*, **2**, 65–78.

Tobin, J. (1958). "Estimation of relationships for limited dependent variables," *Econometrica*, **26**, 24–36.

van den Berg, G. J. (2001). "Duration models: Specification, identification, and multiple durations," Ch. 55 in *Handbook of Econometrics*, Vol. 5, ed. J. J. Heckman and E. E. Leamer, Amsterdam, North-Holland.

van Dijk, H. K., A. Monfort, and B. W. Brown (ed.) (1995). *Econometric Inference Using Simulation Techniques*, Chichester, John Wiley & Sons.

Veall, M. R. (1990). "Testing for a global maximum in an econometric context," *Econometrica*, **58**, 1459–65.

Wald, A. (1943). "Tests of statistical hypotheses concerning several parameters when the number of observations is large," *Transactions of the American Mathematical Society*, **54**, 426–82.

Wand, M. P., and M. C. Jones (1995). *Kernel Smoothing*, London, Chapman and Hall.

Wang, J., and E. Zivot (1998). "Inference on structural parameters in instrumental variables regression with weak instruments," *Econometrica*, **66**, 1389–404.

West, K. D. (1988). "Asymptotic normality, when regressors have a unit root," *Econometrica*, **56**, 1397–417.

West, K. D., and D. M. Wilcox (1996). "A comparison of alternative instrumental variables estimators of a dynamic linear model," *Journal of Business and Economic Statistics*, **14**, 281–93.

White, H. (1980). "A heteroskedasticity-consistent covariance matrix estimator and a direct test for heteroskedasticity," *Econometrica*, **48**, 817–38.

White, H. (1982). "Maximum likelihood estimation of misspecified models," *Econometrica*, **50**, 1–26.

White, H. (1987). "Specification Testing in Dynamic models," Ch. 1 in *Advances in Econometrics — Fifth World Congress*, Vol. 1, ed. T. Bewley, Cambridge, Cambridge University Press.

White, H. (1994). *Estimation, Inference and Specification Analysis*, Cambridge, Cambridge University Press.

White, H. (2000). *Asymptotic Theory for Econometricians*, revised edition, Orlando, Academic Press.

White, H., and I. Domowitz (1984). "Nonlinear regression with dependent observations," *Econometrica*, **52**, 143–61.

Wooldridge, J. M. (1990). "A unified approach to robust, regression-based specification tests," *Econometric Theory*, **6**, 17–43.

Wooldridge, J. M. (1991). "On the application of robust, regression-based diagnostics to models of conditional means and conditional variances," *Journal of Econometrics*, **47**, 5–46.

Wooldridge, J. M. (1992). "A test for functional form against nonparametric alternatives," *Econometric Theory*, **8**, 452–75.

Wooldridge, J. M. (1999). "Quasi-likelihood methods for count data," Ch. 8 in *Handbook of Applied Econometrics*, Vol. II, ed. H. M. Pesaran and P. Schmidt, Oxford, Blackwell.

Wooldridge, J. M. (2002). *Econometric Analysis of Cross Section and Panel Data*, Cambridge, Mass., MIT Press.

Wu, D.-M. (1973). "Alternative tests of independence between stochastic regressors and disturbances," *Econometrica*, **41**, 733–50.

Yatchew, A. (1992). "Nonparametric regression tests based on least squares," *Econometric Theory*, **8**, 435–51.

Yatchew, A. (1998). "Nonparametric regression techniques in econometrics," *Journal of Economic Literature*, **36**, 669–721.

Zellner, A. (1962). "An efficient method of estimating seemingly unrelated regressions, and tests for aggregation bias," *Journal of the American Statistical Association*, **57**, 348–68.

Zellner, A., and H. Theil (1962). "Three-stage least squares: Simultaneous estimation of simultaneous equations," *Econometrica*, **30**, 54–78.

Zheng, J. X. (1996). "A consistent test of functional form via nonparametric estimation techniques," *Journal of Econometrics*, **75**, 263–89.

Zivot, E., R. Startz, and C. R. Nelson (1998). "Valid confidence intervals and inference in the presence of weak instruments," *International Economic Review*, **39**, 1119–44.

Author Index

Subject Index